American Casebook Series
Hornbook Series and Basic Legal Texts
Black Letter Series and Nutshell Series

of

WEST PUBLISHING COMPANY
P.O. Box 64526
St. Paul, Minnesota 55164–0526

Accounting

FARIS' ACCOUNTING AND LAW IN A NUTSHELL, 377 pages, 1984. Softcover. (Text)

FIFLIS' ACCOUNTING ISSUES FOR LAWYERS, TEACHING MATERIALS, , 706 pages, 1991. Teacher's Manual available. (Casebook)

SIEGEL AND SIEGEL'S ACCOUNTING AND FINANCIAL DISCLOSURE: A GUIDE TO BASIC CONCEPTS, 259 pages, 1983. Softcover. (Text)

Administrative Law

BONFIELD AND ASIMOW'S STATE AND FEDERAL ADMINISTRATIVE LAW, 826 pages, 1989. Teacher's Manual available. (Casebook)

GELLHORN AND LEVIN'S ADMINISTRATIVE LAW AND PROCESS IN A NUTSHELL, Third Edition, 479 pages, 1990. Softcover. (Text)

MASHAW AND MERRILL'S CASES AND MATERIALS ON ADMINISTRATIVE LAW—THE AMERICAN PUBLIC LAW SYSTEM, Second Edition, 976 pages, 1985. (Casebook) 1989 Supplement.

ROBINSON, GELLHORN AND BRUFF'S THE ADMINISTRATIVE PROCESS, Third Edition, 978 pages, 1986. (Casebook)

Admiralty

HEALY AND SHARPE'S CASES AND MATERIALS ON ADMIRALTY, Second Edition, 876 pages, 1986. (Casebook)

MARAIST'S ADMIRALTY IN A NUTSHELL, Second Edition, 379 pages, 1988. Softcover. (Text)

SCHOENBAUM'S HORNBOOK ON ADMIRALTY

AND MARITIME LAW, Student Edition, 692 pages, 1987 with 1989 pocket part. (Text)

Agency—Partnership

DEMOTT'S FIDUCIARY OBLIGATION, AGENCY AND PARTNERSHIP: DUTIES IN ONGOING BUSINESS RELATIONSHIPS, 740 pages, 1991. Teacher's Manual available. (Casebook)

FESSLER'S ALTERNATIVES TO INCORPORATION FOR PERSONS IN QUEST OF PROFIT, Third Edition, 339 pages, 1991. Softcover. (Casebook)

HENN'S CASES AND MATERIALS ON AGENCY, PARTNERSHIP AND OTHER UNINCORPORATED BUSINESS ENTERPRISES, Second Edition, 733 pages, 1985. Teacher's Manual available. (Casebook)

REUSCHLEIN AND GREGORY'S HORNBOOK ON THE LAW OF AGENCY AND PARTNERSHIP, Second Edition, 683 pages, 1990. (Text)

SELECTED CORPORATION AND PARTNERSHIP STATUTES, RULES AND FORMS. Softcover. 937 pages, 1991.

STEFFEN AND KERR'S CASES ON AGENCY-PARTNERSHIP, Fourth Edition, 859 pages, 1980. (Casebook)

STEFFEN'S AGENCY-PARTNERSHIP IN A NUTSHELL, 364 pages, 1977. Softcover. (Text)

Agricultural Law

MEYER, PEDERSEN, THORSON AND DAVIDSON'S AGRICULTURAL LAW: CASES AND MATERIALS, 931 pages, 1985. Teacher's Manual available. (Casebook)

Alternative Dispute Resolution

KANOWITZ' CASES AND MATERIALS ON ALTER-

Alternative Dispute Resolution—Cont'd

NATIVE DISPUTE RESOLUTION, 1024 pages, 1986. Teacher's Manual available. (Casebook) 1990 Supplement.

RISKIN AND WESTBROOK'S DISPUTE RESOLUTION AND LAWYERS, 468 pages, 1987. Teacher's Manual available. (Casebook)

RISKIN AND WESTBROOK'S DISPUTE RESOLUTION AND LAWYERS, Abridged Edition, 223 pages, 1987. Softcover. Teacher's Manual available. (Casebook)

American Indian Law

CANBY'S AMERICAN INDIAN LAW IN A NUTSHELL, Second Edition, 336 pages, 1988. Softcover. (Text)

GETCHES AND WILKINSON'S CASES AND MATERIALS ON FEDERAL INDIAN LAW, Second Edition, 880 pages, 1986. (Casebook)

Antitrust—see also Regulated Industries, Trade Regulation

FOX AND SULLIVAN'S CASES AND MATERIALS ON ANTITRUST, 935 pages, 1989. Teacher's Manual available. (Casebook)

GELLHORN'S ANTITRUST LAW AND ECONOMICS IN A NUTSHELL, Third Edition, 472 pages, 1986. Softcover. (Text)

HOVENKAMP'S BLACK LETTER ON ANTITRUST, 323 pages, 1986. Softcover. (Review)

HOVENKAMP'S HORNBOOK ON ECONOMICS AND FEDERAL ANTITRUST LAW, Student Edition, 414 pages, 1985. (Text)

POSNER AND EASTERBROOK'S CASES AND ECONOMIC NOTES ON ANTITRUST, Second Edition, 1077 pages, 1981. (Casebook) 1984–85 Supplement.

SULLIVAN'S HORNBOOK OF THE LAW OF ANTITRUST, 886 pages, 1977. (Text)

Appellate Advocacy—see Trial and Appellate Advocacy

Architecture and Engineering Law

SWEET'S LEGAL ASPECTS OF ARCHITECTURE, ENGINEERING AND THE CONSTRUCTION PROCESS, Fourth Edition, 889 pages, 1989. Teacher's Manual available. (Casebook)

Art Law

DUBOFF'S ART LAW IN A NUTSHELL, 335 pages, 1984. Softcover. (Text)

Banking Law

BANKING LAW: SELECTED STATUTES AND REGULATIONS. Softcover. 263 pages, 1991.

LOVETT'S BANKING AND FINANCIAL INSTITUTIONS LAW IN A NUTSHELL, Second Edition, 464 pages, 1988. Softcover. (Text)

SYMONS AND WHITE'S BANKING LAW: TEACHING MATERIALS, Third Edition, 818 pages, 1991. Teacher's Manual available. (Casebook)

    Statutory Supplement. *See Banking Law: Selected Statutes*

Business Planning—see also Corporate Finance

PAINTER'S PROBLEMS AND MATERIALS IN BUSINESS PLANNING, Second Edition, 1008 pages, 1984. (Casebook) 1990 Supplement.

    Statutory Supplement. *See Selected Corporation and Partnership*

Civil Procedure—see also Federal Jurisdiction and Procedure

AMERICAN BAR ASSOCIATION SECTION OF LITIGATION—READINGS ON ADVERSARIAL JUSTICE: THE AMERICAN APPROACH TO ADJUDICATION, 217 pages, 1988. Softcover. (Coursebook)

CLERMONT'S BLACK LETTER ON CIVIL PROCEDURE, Second Edition, 332 pages, 1988. Softcover. (Review)

COUND, FRIEDENTHAL, MILLER AND SEXTON'S CASES AND MATERIALS ON CIVIL PROCEDURE, Fifth Edition, 1284 pages, 1989. Teacher's Manual available. (Casebook)

COUND, FRIEDENTHAL, MILLER AND SEXTON'S CIVIL PROCEDURE SUPPLEMENT. 476 pages, 1991. Softcover. (Casebook Supplement)

FEDERAL RULES OF CIVIL PROCEDURE—EDUCATIONAL EDITION. Softcover. 816 pages, 1991.

FRIEDENTHAL, KANE AND MILLER'S HORNBOOK ON CIVIL PROCEDURE, 876 pages, 1985. (Text)

KANE AND LEVINE'S CIVIL PROCEDURE IN CALIFORNIA: STATE AND FEDERAL 543 pages, 1991. Softcover. (Casebook Supplement)

KANE'S CIVIL PROCEDURE IN A NUTSHELL, Third Edition, 303 pages, 1991. Softcover. (Text)

KOFFLER AND REPPY'S HORNBOOK ON COM-

Civil Procedure—Cont'd

MON LAW PLEADING, 663 pages, 1969. (Text)

LEVINE, SLOMANSON AND WINGATE'S CALIFORNIA CIVIL PROCEDURE, CASES AND MATERIALS, . 546 pages, 1991. (Casebook)

MARCUS, REDISH AND SHERMAN'S CIVIL PROCEDURE: A MODERN APPROACH, 1027 pages, 1989. Teacher's Manual available. (Casebook) 1991 Supplement.

MARCUS AND SHERMAN'S COMPLEX LITIGATION–CASES AND MATERIALS ON ADVANCED CIVIL PROCEDURE, 846 pages, 1985. Teacher's Manual available. (Casebook) 1989 Supplement.

PARK AND MCFARLAND'S COMPUTER-AIDED EXERCISES ON CIVIL PROCEDURE, Third Edition, 210 pages, 1991. Softcover. (Coursebook)

SIEGEL'S HORNBOOK ON NEW YORK PRACTICE, Second Edition, Student Edition, 1068 pages, 1991. Softcover. (Text)

Commercial Law

BAILEY AND HAGEDORN'S SECURED TRANSACTIONS IN A NUTSHELL, Third Edition, 390 pages, 1988. Softcover. (Text)

EPSTEIN, MARTIN, HENNING AND NICKLES' BASIC UNIFORM COMMERCIAL CODE TEACHING MATERIALS, Third Edition, 704 pages, 1988. Teacher's Manual available. (Casebook)

HENSON'S HORNBOOK ON SECURED TRANSACTIONS UNDER THE U.C.C., Second Edition, 504 pages, 1979, with 1979 pocket part. (Text)

MURRAY'S COMMERCIAL LAW, PROBLEMS AND MATERIALS, 366 pages, 1975. Teacher's Manual available. Softcover. (Coursebook)

NICKLES' BLACK LETTER ON COMMERCIAL PAPER, 450 pages, 1988. Softcover. (Review)

NICKLES, MATHESON AND DOLAN'S MATERIALS FOR UNDERSTANDING CREDIT AND PAYMENT SYSTEMS, 923 pages, 1987. Teacher's Manual available. (Casebook)

NORDSTROM, MURRAY AND CLOVIS' PROBLEMS AND MATERIALS ON SALES, 515 pages, 1982. (Casebook)

NORDSTROM, MURRAY AND CLOVIS' PROBLEMS AND MATERIALS ON SECURED TRANSACTIONS,

594 pages, 1987. (Casebook)

RUBIN AND COOTER'S THE PAYMENT SYSTEM: CASES, MATERIALS AND ISSUES, 885 pages, 1989. Teacher's Manual Available. (Casebook)

SELECTED COMMERCIAL STATUTES. Softcover. 1851 pages, 1991.

SPEIDEL'S BLACK LETTER ON SALES AND SALES FINANCING, 363 pages, 1984. Softcover. (Review)

SPEIDEL, SUMMERS AND WHITE'S COMMERCIAL LAW: TEACHING MATERIALS, Fourth Edition, 1448 pages, 1987. Teacher's Manual available. (Casebook)

SPEIDEL, SUMMERS AND WHITE'S COMMERCIAL PAPER: TEACHING MATERIALS, Fourth Edition, 578 pages, 1987. Reprint from Speidel et al., Commercial Law, Fourth Edition. Teacher's Manual available. (Casebook)

SPEIDEL, SUMMERS AND WHITE'S SALES: TEACHING MATERIALS, Fourth Edition, 804 pages, 1987. Reprint from Speidel et al., Commercial Law, Fourth Edition. Teacher's Manual available. (Casebook)

SPEIDEL, SUMMERS AND WHITE'S SECURED TRANSACTIONS: TEACHING MATERIALS, Fourth Edition, 485 pages, 1987. Reprint from Speidel et al., Commercial Law, Fourth Edition. Teacher's Manual available. (Casebook)

STOCKTON'S SALES IN A NUTSHELL, Second Edition, 370 pages, 1981. Softcover. (Text)

STONE'S UNIFORM COMMERCIAL CODE IN A NUTSHELL, Third Edition, 580 pages, 1989. Softcover. (Text)

WEBER AND SPEIDEL'S COMMERCIAL PAPER IN A NUTSHELL, Third Edition, 404 pages, 1982. Softcover. (Text)

WHITE AND SUMMERS' HORNBOOK ON THE UNIFORM COMMERCIAL CODE, Third Edition, Student Edition, 1386 pages, 1988. (Text)

Community Property

MENNELL AND BOYKOFF'S COMMUNITY PROPERTY IN A NUTSHELL, Second Edition, 432 pages, 1988. Softcover. (Text)

VERRALL AND BIRD'S CASES AND MATERIALS ON CALIFORNIA COMMUNITY PROPERTY, Fifth

Community Property—Cont'd
Edition, 604 pages, 1988. (Casebook)

Comparative Law

BARTON, GIBBS, LI AND MERRYMAN'S LAW IN RADICALLY DIFFERENT CULTURES, 960 pages, 1983. (Casebook)

GLENDON, GORDON AND OSAKWE'S COMPARATIVE LEGAL TRADITIONS: TEXT, MATERIALS AND CASES ON THE CIVIL LAW, COMMON LAW AND SOCIALIST LAW TRADITIONS, 1091 pages, 1985. (Casebook)

GLENDON, GORDON AND OSAKWE'S COMPARATIVE LEGAL TRADITIONS IN A NUTSHELL. 402 pages, 1982. Softcover. (Text)

Computers and Law

MAGGS, SOMA AND SPROWL'S COMPUTER LAW—CASES, COMMENTS, AND QUESTIONS, Approximately 725 pages, 1992. Teacher's Manual available. (Casebook)

MAGGS AND SPROWL'S COMPUTER APPLICATIONS IN THE LAW, 316 pages, 1987. (Coursebook)

MASON'S USING COMPUTERS IN THE LAW: AN INTRODUCTION AND PRACTICAL GUIDE, Second Edition, 288 pages, 1988. Softcover. (Coursebook)

Conflict of Laws

CRAMTON, CURRIE AND KAY'S CASES–COMMENTS–QUESTIONS ON CONFLICT OF LAWS, Fourth Edition, 876 pages, 1987. (Casebook)

HAY'S BLACK LETTER ON CONFLICT OF LAWS, 330 pages, 1989. Softcover. (Review)

SCOLES AND HAY'S HORNBOOK ON CONFLICT OF LAWS, Student Edition, approximately 1025 pages, 1992. (Text)

SIEGEL'S CONFLICTS IN A NUTSHELL, 470 pages, 1982. Softcover. (Text)

Constitutional Law—Civil Rights—see also First Amendment and Foreign Relations and National Security Law

ABERNATHY'S CIVIL RIGHTS AND CONSTITUTIONAL LITIGATION, CASES AND MATERIALS, Second Edition, approximately 750 pages, 1992. (Casebook)

BARRON AND DIENES' BLACK LETTER ON CONSTITUTIONAL LAW, Third Edition, 440 pages, 1991. Softcover. (Review)

BARRON AND DIENES' CONSTITUTIONAL LAW IN A NUTSHELL, Second Edition, 483 pages, 1991. Softcover. (Text)

ENGDAHL'S CONSTITUTIONAL FEDERALISM IN A NUTSHELL, Second Edition, 411 pages, 1987. Softcover. (Text)

FARBER AND SHERRY'S HISTORY OF THE AMERICAN CONSTITUTION, 458 pages, 1990. Softcover. Teacher's Manual available. (Text)

GARVEY AND ALEINIKOFF'S MODERN CONSTITUTIONAL THEORY: A READER, Second Edition, 559 pages, 1991. Softcover. (Reader)

LOCKHART, KAMISAR, CHOPER AND SHIFFRIN'S CONSTITUTIONAL LAW: CASES–COMMENTS–QUESTIONS, Seventh Edition, 1643 pages, 1991. (Casebook) 1991 Supplement.

LOCKHART, KAMISAR, CHOPER AND SHIFFRIN'S THE AMERICAN CONSTITUTION: CASES AND MATERIALS, Seventh Edition, approximately 1200 pages, 1991. Abridged version of Lockhart, et al., Constitutional Law: Cases–Comments–Questions, Seventh Edition. (Casebook) 1991 Supplement.

LOCKHART, KAMISAR, CHOPER AND SHIFFRIN'S CONSTITUTIONAL RIGHTS AND LIBERTIES: CASES AND MATERIALS, Seventh Edition, approximately 1375 pages, 1991. Reprint from Lockhart, et al., Constitutional Law: Cases–Comments–Questions, Seventh Edition. (Casebook) 1991 Supplement.

MARKS AND COOPER'S STATE CONSTITUTIONAL LAW IN A NUTSHELL, 329 pages, 1988. Softcover. (Text)

NOWAK AND ROTUNDA'S HORNBOOK ON CONSTITUTIONAL LAW, Fourth Edition, 1357 pages, 1991. (Text)

ROTUNDA'S MODERN CONSTITUTIONAL LAW: CASES AND NOTES, Third Edition, 1085 pages, 1989. (Casebook) 1991 Supplement.

VIEIRA'S CONSTITUTIONAL CIVIL RIGHTS IN A NUTSHELL, Second Edition, 322 pages, 1990. Softcover. (Text)

WILLIAMS' CONSTITUTIONAL ANALYSIS IN A NUTSHELL, 388 pages, 1979. Softcover. (Text)

Consumer Law—see also Commercial Law

EPSTEIN AND NICKLES' CONSUMER LAW IN A NUTSHELL, Second Edition, 418 pages, 1981. Softcover. (Text)

Consumer Law—Cont'd

SELECTED COMMERCIAL STATUTES. Softcover. 1851 pages, 1991.

SPANOGLE, ROHNER, PRIDGEN AND RASOR'S CASES AND MATERIALS ON CONSUMER LAW, Second Edition, 916 pages, 1991. Teacher's Manual available. (Casebook)

Contracts

CALAMARI AND PERILLO'S BLACK LETTER ON CONTRACTS, Second Edition, 462 pages, 1990. Softcover. (Review)

CALAMARI AND PERILLO'S HORNBOOK ON CONTRACTS, Third Edition, 1049 pages, 1987. (Text)

CALAMARI, PERILLO AND BENDER'S CASES AND PROBLEMS ON CONTRACTS, Second Edition, 905 pages, 1989. Teacher's Manual Available. (Casebook)

CORBIN'S TEXT ON CONTRACTS, One Volume Student Edition, 1224 pages, 1952. (Text)

FESSLER AND LOISEAUX'S CASES AND MATERIALS ON CONTRACTS—MORALITY, ECONOMICS AND THE MARKET PLACE, 837 pages, 1982. Teacher's Manual available. (Casebook)

FRIEDMAN'S CONTRACT REMEDIES IN A NUTSHELL, 323 pages, 1981. Softcover. (Text)

FULLER AND EISENBERG'S CASES ON BASIC CONTRACT LAW, Fifth Edition, 1037 pages, 1990. (Casebook)

HAMILTON, RAU AND WEINTRAUB'S CASES AND MATERIALS ON CONTRACTS, Second Edition, approximately 850 pages, May, 1992 Pub. (Casebook)

KEYES' GOVERNMENT CONTRACTS IN A NUTSHELL, Second Edition, 557 pages, 1990. Softcover. (Text)

SCHABER AND ROHWER'S CONTRACTS IN A NUTSHELL, Third Edition, 457 pages, 1990. Softcover. (Text)

SUMMERS AND HILLMAN'S CONTRACT AND RELATED OBLIGATION: THEORY, DOCTRINE AND PRACTICE, Second Edition, approximately 1100, March, 1992 Pub. Teacher's Manual available. (Casebook)

Copyright—see Patent and Copyright Law

Corporate Finance—see also Business Planning

HAMILTON'S CASES AND MATERIALS ON COR-

PORATION FINANCE, Second Edition, 1221 pages, 1989. (Casebook)

OESTERLE'S THE LAW OF MERGERS, ACQUISITIONS AND REORGANIZATIONS, 1096 pages, 1991. (Casebook)

Corporations

HAMILTON'S BLACK LETTER ON CORPORATIONS, Second Edition, 513 pages, 1986. Softcover. (Review)

HAMILTON'S CASES AND MATERIALS ON CORPORATIONS—INCLUDING PARTNERSHIPS AND LIMITED PARTNERSHIPS, Fourth Edition, 1248 pages, 1990. Teacher's Manual available. (Casebook) 1990 Statutory Supplement.

HAMILTON'S THE LAW OF CORPORATIONS IN A NUTSHELL, Third Edition, 518 pages, 1991. Softcover. (Text)

HENN'S TEACHING MATERIALS ON THE LAW OF CORPORATIONS, Second Edition, 1204 pages, 1986. Teacher's Manual available. (Casebook)

Statutory Supplement. *See Selected Corporation and Partnership*

HENN AND ALEXANDER'S HORNBOOK ON LAWS OF CORPORATIONS, Third Edition, Student Edition, 1371 pages, 1983, with 1986 pocket part. (Text)

SELECTED CORPORATION AND PARTNERSHIP STATUTES, RULES AND FORMS. Softcover. 937 pages, 1991.

SOLOMON, SCHWARTZ AND BAUMAN'S MATERIALS AND PROBLEMS ON CORPORATIONS: LAW AND POLICY, Second Edition, 1391 pages, 1988. Teacher's Manual available. (Casebook) 1990 Supplement.

Statutory Supplement. *See Selected Corporation and Partnership*

Corrections

KRANTZ' THE LAW OF CORRECTIONS AND PRISONERS' RIGHTS IN A NUTSHELL, Third Edition, 407 pages, 1988. Softcover. (Text)

KRANTZ AND BRANHAM'S CASES AND MATERIALS ON THE LAW OF SENTENCING, CORRECTIONS AND PRISONERS' RIGHTS, Fourth Edition, 619 pages, 1991. Teacher's Manual available. (Casebook)

ROBBINS' CASES AND MATERIALS ON POST-CONVICTION REMEDIES, 506 pages, 1982.

Corrections—Cont'd
(Casebook)

Creditors' Rights

BANKRUPTCY CODE, RULES AND OFFICIAL FORMS, LAW SCHOOL EDITION. 909 pages, 1991. Softcover.

EPSTEIN'S DEBTOR-CREDITOR LAW IN A NUT-SHELL, Fourth Edition, 401 pages, 1991. Softcover. (Text)

EPSTEIN, LANDERS AND NICKLES' CASES AND MATERIALS ON DEBTORS AND CREDITORS, Third Edition, 1059 pages, 1987. Teacher's Manual available. (Casebook)

LOPUCKI'S PLAYER'S MANUAL FOR THE DEBTOR-CREDITOR GAME, 123 pages, 1985. Softcover. (Coursebook)

NICKLES AND EPSTEIN'S BLACK LETTER ON CREDITORS' RIGHTS AND BANKRUPTCY, 576 pages, 1989. (Review)

RIESENFELD'S CASES AND MATERIALS ON CREDITORS' REMEDIES AND DEBTORS' PROTECTION, Fourth Edition, 914 pages, 1987. (Casebook) 1990 Supplement.

WHITE'S CASES AND MATERIALS ON BANK-RUPTCY AND CREDITORS' RIGHTS, 812 pages, 1985. Teacher's Manual available. (Casebook) 1987 Supplement.

Criminal Law and Criminal Procedure—see also Corrections, Juvenile Justice

ABRAMS' FEDERAL CRIMINAL LAW AND ITS ENFORCEMENT, 866 pages, 1986. (Casebook) 1988 Supplement.

AMERICAN CRIMINAL JUSTICE PROCESS: SELECTED RULES, STATUTES AND GUIDELINES. 723 pages, 1989. Softcover.

DIX AND SHARLOT'S CASES AND MATERIALS ON CRIMINAL LAW, Third Edition, 846 pages, 1987. (Casebook)

GRANO'S PROBLEMS IN CRIMINAL PROCEDURE, Second Edition, 176 pages, 1981. Teacher's Manual available. Softcover. (Coursebook)

HEYMANN AND KENETY'S THE MURDER TRIAL OF WILBUR JACKSON: A HOMICIDE IN THE FAMILY, Second Edition, 347 pages, 1985. (Coursebook)

ISRAEL, KAMISAR AND LAFAVE'S CRIMINAL PROCEDURE AND THE CONSTITUTION: LEADING

SUPREME COURT CASES AND INTRODUCTORY TEXT. 767 pages, 1991 Edition. Softcover. (Casebook)

ISRAEL AND LAFAVE'S CRIMINAL PROCEDURE—CONSTITUTIONAL LIMITATIONS IN A NUTSHELL, Fourth Edition, 461 pages, 1988. Softcover. (Text)

JOHNSON'S CASES, MATERIALS AND TEXT ON CRIMINAL LAW, Fourth Edition, 759 pages, 1990. Teacher's Manual available. (Casebook)

JOHNSON'S CASES AND MATERIALS ON CRIMINAL PROCEDURE, 859 pages, 1988. (Casebook) 1991 Supplement.

KAMISAR, LAFAVE AND ISRAEL'S MODERN CRIMINAL PROCEDURE: CASES, COMMENTS AND QUESTIONS, Seventh Edition, 1593 pages, 1990. (Casebook) 1991 Supplement.

KAMISAR, LAFAVE AND ISRAEL'S BASIC CRIMINAL PROCEDURE: CASES, COMMENTS AND QUESTIONS, Seventh Edition, 792 pages, 1990. Softcover reprint from Kamisar, et al., Modern Criminal Procedure: Cases, Comments and Questions, Seventh Edition. (Casebook) 1991 Supplement.

LAFAVE'S MODERN CRIMINAL LAW: CASES, COMMENTS AND QUESTIONS, Second Edition, 903 pages, 1988. (Casebook)

LAFAVE AND ISRAEL'S HORNBOOK ON CRIMINAL PROCEDURE, Second Edition, approximately 1350 pages, 1992. (Text)

LAFAVE AND SCOTT'S HORNBOOK ON CRIMINAL LAW, Second Edition, 918 pages, 1986. (Text)

LOEWY'S CRIMINAL LAW IN A NUTSHELL, Second Edition, 321 pages, 1987. Softcover. (Text)

LOW'S BLACK LETTER ON CRIMINAL LAW, Revised First Edition, 443 pages, 1990. Softcover. (Review)

SALTZBURG AND CAPRA'S CASES AND COMMENTARY ON AMERICAN CRIMINAL PROCEDURE, Fourth Edition, approximately 1300 pages, May, 1992 Pub. Teacher's Manual available. (Casebook)

VORENBERG'S CASES ON CRIMINAL LAW AND PROCEDURE, Second Edition, 1088 pages, 1981. Teacher's Manual available. (Casebook) 1990 Supplement.

Domestic Relations

CLARK'S HORNBOOK ON DOMESTIC RELATIONS, Second Edition, Student Edition, 1050 pages, 1988. (Text)

CLARK AND GLOWINSKY'S CASES AND PROBLEMS ON DOMESTIC RELATIONS, Fourth Edition. 1150 pages, 1990. Teacher's Manual available. (Casebook)

KRAUSE'S BLACK LETTER ON FAMILY LAW, 314 pages, 1988. Softcover. (Review)

KRAUSE'S CASES, COMMENTS AND QUESTIONS ON FAMILY LAW, Third Edition, 1433 pages, 1990. (Casebook)

KRAUSE'S FAMILY LAW IN A NUTSHELL, Second Edition, 444 pages, 1986. Softcover. (Text)

KRAUSKOPF'S CASES ON PROPERTY DIVISION AT MARRIAGE DISSOLUTION, 250 pages, 1984. Softcover. (Casebook)

Economics, Law and—see also Antitrust, Regulated Industries

BARNES AND STOUT'S CASES AND MATERIALS ON LAW AND ECONOMICS, Approximately 550 pages, March, 1992 Pub. (Casebook)

GOETZ' CASES AND MATERIALS ON LAW AND ECONOMICS, 547 pages, 1984. (Casebook)

MALLOY'S LAW AND ECONOMICS: A COMPARATIVE APPROACH TO THEORY AND PRACTICE, 166 pages, 1990. Softcover. (Text)

Education Law

ALEXANDER AND ALEXANDER'S THE LAW OF SCHOOLS, STUDENTS AND TEACHERS IN A NUTSHELL, 409 pages, 1984. Softcover. (Text)

YUDOF, KIRP AND LEVIN'S EDUCATIONAL POLICY AND THE LAW, Third Edition, 860 pages, 1992. (Casebook)

Employment Discrimination—see also Gender Discrimination

ESTREICHER AND HARPER'S CASES AND MATERIALS ON THE LAW GOVERNING THE EMPLOYMENT RELATIONSHIP, 962 pages, 1990. Teacher's Manual available. (Casebook) Statutory Supplement. 1991 Supplement.

JONES, MURPHY AND BELTON'S CASES AND MATERIALS ON DISCRIMINATION IN EMPLOYMENT, (The Labor Law Group). Fifth Edition, 1116 pages, 1987. (Casebook) 1990 Supplement.

PLAYER'S FEDERAL LAW OF EMPLOYMENT DISCRIMINATION IN A NUTSHELL, Third Edition, approximately 270 pages, 1992. Softcover. (Text)

PLAYER'S HORNBOOK ON EMPLOYMENT DISCRIMINATION LAW, Student Edition, 708 pages, 1988. (Text)

PLAYER, SHOBEN AND LIEBERWITZ' CASES AND MATERIALS ON EMPLOYMENT DISCRIMINATION LAW, 827 pages, 1990. Teacher's Manual available. (Casebook)

Energy and Natural Resources Law—see also Oil and Gas

LAITOS' CASES AND MATERIALS ON NATURAL RESOURCES LAW, 938 pages, 1985. Teacher's Manual available. (Casebook)

LAITOS AND TOMAIN'S ENERGY AND NATURAL RESOURCES LAW IN A NUTSHELL, Approximately 525 pages, 1992. Softcover. (Text)

SELECTED ENVIRONMENTAL LAW STATUTES—EDUCATIONAL EDITION. Softcover. 1256 pages, 1991.

Environmental Law—see also Energy and Natural Resources Law; Sea, Law of

BONINE AND MCGARITY'S THE LAW OF ENVIRONMENTAL PROTECTION: CASES—LEGISLATION—POLICIES, Second Edition, approximately 1050 pages, 1992. (Casebook)

FINDLEY AND FARBER'S CASES AND MATERIALS ON ENVIRONMENTAL LAW, Third Edition, 763 pages, 1991. (Casebook)

FINDLEY AND FARBER'S ENVIRONMENTAL LAW IN A NUTSHELL, Third Edition, approximately 375 pages, February, 1992 Pub. Softcover. (Text)

PLATER, ABRAMS AND GOLDFARB'S ENVIRONMENTAL LAW AND POLICY: NATURE, LAW AND SOCIETY, Approximately 950 pages, 1992. Teacher's Manual available. (Casebook)

RODGERS' HORNBOOK ON ENVIRONMENTAL LAW, 956 pages, 1977, with 1984 pocket part. (Text)

SELECTED ENVIRONMENTAL LAW STATUTES—EDUCATIONAL EDITION. Softcover. 1256 pages, 1991.

Equity—see Remedies

Estate Planning—see also Trusts and Estates; Taxation—Estate and Gift

LYNN'S AN INTRODUCTION TO ESTATE PLANNING IN A NUTSHELL, Third Edition, 370 pages, 1983. Softcover. (Text)

Evidence

BROUN AND BLAKEY'S BLACK LETTER ON EVIDENCE, 269 pages, 1984. Softcover. (Review)

BROUN, MEISENHOLDER, STRONG AND MOSTELLER'S PROBLEMS IN EVIDENCE, Third Edition, 238 pages, 1988. Teacher's Manual available. Softcover. (Coursebook)

CLEARY, STRONG, BROUN AND MOSTELLER'S CASES AND MATERIALS ON EVIDENCE, Fourth Edition, 1060 pages, 1988. (Casebook)

FEDERAL RULES OF EVIDENCE FOR UNITED STATES COURTS AND MAGISTRATES. Softcover. 381 pages, 1990.

FRIEDMAN'S THE ELEMENTS OF EVIDENCE, 315 pages, 1991. Teacher's Manual available. (Coursebook)

GRAHAM'S FEDERAL RULES OF EVIDENCE IN A NUTSHELL, Third Edition, approximately 475 pages, 1992. Softcover. (Text)

LEMPERT AND SALTZBURG'S A MODERN APPROACH TO EVIDENCE: TEXT, PROBLEMS, TRANSCRIPTS AND CASES, Second Edition, 1232 pages, 1983. Teacher's Manual available. (Casebook)

LILLY'S AN INTRODUCTION TO THE LAW OF EVIDENCE, Second Edition, 585 pages, 1987. (Text)

McCORMICK, SUTTON AND WELLBORN'S CASES AND MATERIALS ON EVIDENCE, Sixth Edition, 1067 pages, 1987. (Casebook)

McCORMICK'S HORNBOOK ON EVIDENCE, Fourth Edition, Student Edition, approximately 1150 pages, March, 1992 Pub. (Text)

ROTHSTEIN'S EVIDENCE IN A NUTSHELL: STATE AND FEDERAL RULES, Second Edition, 514 pages, 1981. Softcover. (Text)

Federal Jurisdiction and Procedure

CURRIE'S CASES AND MATERIALS ON FEDERAL COURTS, Fourth Edition, 783 pages, 1990. (Casebook)

CURRIE'S FEDERAL JURISDICTION IN A NUTSHELL, Third Edition, 242 pages, 1990.

Softcover. (Text)

FEDERAL RULES OF CIVIL PROCEDURE—EDUCATIONAL EDITION. Softcover. 816 pages, 1991.

REDISH'S BLACK LETTER ON FEDERAL JURISDICTION, Second Edition, 234 pages, 1991. Softcover. (Review)

REDISH'S CASES, COMMENTS AND QUESTIONS ON FEDERAL COURTS, Second Edition, 1122 pages, 1989. (Casebook) 1990 Supplement.

VETRI AND MERRILL'S FEDERAL COURTS PROBLEMS AND MATERIALS, Second Edition, 232 pages, 1984. Softcover. (Coursebook)

WRIGHT'S HORNBOOK ON FEDERAL COURTS, Fourth Edition, Student Edition, 870 pages, 1983. (Text)

First Amendment

SHIFFRIN AND CHOPER'S FIRST AMENDMENT, CASES—COMMENTS—QUESTIONS, 759 pages, 1991. Softcover. (Casebook) 1991 Supplement.

Foreign Relations and National Security Law

FRANCK AND GLENNON'S FOREIGN RELATIONS AND NATIONAL SECURITY LAW, 941 pages, 1987. (Casebook)

Future Interests—see Trusts and Estates

Gender Discrimination—see also Employment Discrimination

KAY'S TEXT, CASES AND MATERIALS ON SEX-BASED DISCRIMINATION, Third Edition, 1001 pages, 1988. (Casebook) 1990 Supplement.

THOMAS' SEX DISCRIMINATION IN A NUTSHELL, Second Edition, 395 pages, 1991. Softcover. (Text)

Health Law—see Medicine, Law and

Human Rights—see International Law

Immigration Law

ALEINIKOFF AND MARTIN'S IMMIGRATION: PROCESS AND POLICY, Second Edition, 1056 pages, 1991. (Casebook)

  Statutory Supplement. *See Immigration and Nationality Laws*

IMMIGRATION AND NATIONALITY LAWS OF THE UNITED STATES: SELECTED STATUTES, REGULATIONS AND FORMS. Softcover. 477 pages,

Immigration Law—Cont'd

1991.

WEISSBRODT'S IMMIGRATION LAW AND PROCE-
DURE IN A NUTSHELL, Second Edition, 438
pages, 1989, Softcover. (Text)

Indian Law—see American Indian Law

Insurance Law

DEVINE AND TERRY'S PROBLEMS IN INSUR-
ANCE LAW, 240 pages, 1989. Softcover.
Teacher's Manual available. (Coursebook)

DOBBYN'S INSURANCE LAW IN A NUTSHELL,
Second Edition, 316 pages, 1989. Softcover. (Text)

KEETON'S CASES ON BASIC INSURANCE LAW,
Second Edition, 1086 pages, 1977. Teacher's Manual available. (Casebook)

KEETON'S COMPUTER-AIDED AND WORKBOOK
EXERCISES ON INSURANCE LAW, 255 pages,
1990. Softcover. (Coursebook)

KEETON AND WIDISS' INSURANCE LAW, Student Edition, 1359 pages, 1988. (Text)

WIDISS AND KEETON'S COURSE SUPPLEMENT
TO KEETON AND WIDISS' INSURANCE LAW,
502 pages, 1988. Softcover. Teacher's
Manual available. (Casebook)

WIDISS' INSURANCE: MATERIALS ON FUNDA-
MENTAL PRINCIPLES, LEGAL DOCTRINES AND
REGULATORY ACTS, 1186 pages, 1989.
Teacher's Manual available. (Casebook)

YORK AND WHELAN'S CASES, MATERIALS AND
PROBLEMS ON GENERAL PRACTICE INSURANCE
LAW, Second Edition, 787 pages, 1988.
Teacher's Manual available. (Casebook)

International Law—see also Sea, Law of

BUERGENTHAL'S INTERNATIONAL HUMAN
RIGHTS IN A NUTSHELL, 283 pages, 1988.
Softcover. (Text)

BUERGENTHAL AND MAIER'S PUBLIC INTERNA-
TIONAL LAW IN A NUTSHELL, Second Edition,
275 pages, 1990. Softcover. (Text)

FOLSOM'S EUROPEAN COMMUNITY LAW IN A
NUTSHELL, Approximately 425 pages,
1992. Softcover. (Text)

FOLSOM, GORDON AND SPANOGLE'S INTERNA-
TIONAL BUSINESS TRANSACTIONS—A PROB-
LEM-ORIENTED COURSEBOOK, Second Edition,
1237 pages, 1991. Teacher's Manual
available. (Casebook) 1991 Documents

Supplement.

FOLSOM, GORDON AND SPANOGLE'S INTERNA-
TIONAL BUSINESS TRANSACTIONS IN A NUT-
SHELL, Third Edition, 509 pages, 1988.
Softcover. (Text)

HENKIN, PUGH, SCHACHTER AND SMIT'S
CASES AND MATERIALS ON INTERNATIONAL
LAW, Second Edition, 1517 pages, 1987.
(Casebook) Documents Supplement.

JACKSON AND DAVEY'S CASES, MATERIALS
AND TEXT ON LEGAL PROBLEMS OF INTERNA-
TIONAL ECONOMIC RELATIONS, Second Edi-
tion, 1269 pages, 1986. (Casebook) 1989
Documents Supplement.

KIRGIS' INTERNATIONAL ORGANIZATIONS IN
THEIR LEGAL SETTING, 1016 pages, 1977.
Teacher's Manual available. (Casebook)
1981 Supplement.

WESTON, FALK AND D'AMATO'S INTERNATION-
AL LAW AND WORLD ORDER—A PROBLEM-
ORIENTED COURSEBOOK, Second Edition,
1335 pages, 1990. Teacher's Manual
available. (Casebook) Documents Supplement.

Interviewing and Counseling

BINDER AND PRICE'S LEGAL INTERVIEWING
AND COUNSELING, 232 pages, 1977.
Softcover. Teacher's Manual available.
(Coursebook)

BINDER, BERGMAN AND PRICE'S LAWYERS AS
COUNSELORS: A CLIENT–CENTERED AP-
PROACH, 427 pages, 1991. Softcover.
(Coursebook)

SHAFFER AND ELKINS' LEGAL INTERVIEWING
AND COUNSELING IN A NUTSHELL, Second
Edition, 487 pages, 1987. Softcover.
(Text)

Introduction to Law—see Legal Method
and Legal System

Introduction to Law Study

HEGLAND'S INTRODUCTION TO THE STUDY AND
PRACTICE OF LAW IN A NUTSHELL, 418 pages,
1983. Softcover. (Text)

KINYON'S INTRODUCTION TO LAW STUDY AND
LAW EXAMINATIONS IN A NUTSHELL, 389
pages, 1971. Softcover. (Text)

Judicial Process—see Legal Method and
Legal System

Jurisprudence

CHRISTIE'S JURISPRUDENCE—TEXT AND READINGS ON THE PHILOSOPHY OF LAW, 1056 pages, 1973. (Casebook)

Juvenile Justice

FOX'S JUVENILE COURTS IN A NUTSHELL, Third Edition, 291 pages, 1984. Softcover. (Text)

Labor and Employment Law—see also Employment Discrimination, Workers' Compensation

FINKIN, GOLDMAN AND SUMMERS' LEGAL PROTECTION OF INDIVIDUAL EMPLOYEES, (The Labor Law Group). 1164 pages, 1989. (Casebook)

GORMAN'S BASIC TEXT ON LABOR LAW—UNIONIZATION AND COLLECTIVE BARGAINING, 914 pages, 1976. (Text)

LESLIE'S LABOR LAW IN A NUTSHELL, Third Edition, approximately 400 pages, 1992. Softcover. (Text)

NOLAN'S LABOR ARBITRATION LAW AND PRACTICE IN A NUTSHELL, 358 pages, 1979. Softcover. (Text)

OBERER, HANSLOWE, ANDERSEN AND HEINSZ' CASES AND MATERIALS ON LABOR LAW—COLLECTIVE BARGAINING IN A FREE SOCIETY, Third Edition, 1163 pages, 1986. Teacher's Manual available. (Casebook) Statutory Supplement. 1991 Case Supplement.

RABIN, SILVERSTEIN AND SCHATZKI'S LABOR AND EMPLOYMENT LAW: PROBLEMS, CASES AND MATERIALS IN THE LAW OF WORK, (The Labor Law Group). 1014 pages, 1988. Teacher's Manual available. (Casebook) 1988 Statutory Supplement.

Land Finance—Property Security—see Real Estate Transactions

Land Use

CALLIES AND FREILICH'S CASES AND MATERIALS ON LAND USE, 1233 pages, 1986. (Casebook) 1991 Supplement.

HAGMAN AND JUERGENSMEYER'S HORNBOOK ON URBAN PLANNING AND LAND DEVELOPMENT CONTROL LAW, Second Edition, Student Edition, 680 pages, 1986. (Text)

WRIGHT AND GITELMAN'S CASES AND MATERIALS ON LAND USE, Fourth Edition, 1255 pages, 1991. Teacher's Manual available.

(Casebook)

WRIGHT AND WRIGHT'S LAND USE IN A NUTSHELL, Second Edition, 356 pages, 1985. Softcover. (Text)

Legal History—see also Legal Method and Legal System

PRESSER AND ZAINALDIN'S CASES AND MATERIALS ON LAW AND JURISPRUDENCE IN AMERICAN HISTORY, Second Edition, 1092 pages, 1989. Teacher's Manual available. (Casebook)

Legal Method and Legal System—see also Legal Research, Legal Writing

ALDISERT'S READINGS, MATERIALS AND CASES IN THE JUDICIAL PROCESS, 948 pages, 1976. (Casebook)

BERCH AND BERCH'S INTRODUCTION TO LEGAL METHOD AND PROCESS, 550 pages, 1985. Teacher's Manual available. (Casebook)

BODENHEIMER, OAKLEY AND LOVE'S READINGS AND CASES ON AN INTRODUCTION TO THE ANGLO-AMERICAN LEGAL SYSTEM, Second Edition, 166 pages, 1988. Softcover. (Casebook)

DAVIES AND LAWRY'S INSTITUTIONS AND METHODS OF THE LAW—INTRODUCTORY TEACHING MATERIALS, 547 pages, 1982. Teacher's Manual available. (Casebook)

DVORKIN, HIMMELSTEIN AND LESNICK'S BECOMING A LAWYER: A HUMANISTIC PERSPECTIVE ON LEGAL EDUCATION AND PROFESSIONALISM, 211 pages, 1981. Softcover. (Text)

KEETON'S JUDGING, 842 pages, 1990. Softcover. (Coursebook)

KELSO AND KELSO'S STUDYING LAW: AN INTRODUCTION, 587 pages, 1984. (Coursebook)

KEMPIN'S HISTORICAL INTRODUCTION TO ANGLO-AMERICAN LAW IN A NUTSHELL, Third Edition, 323 pages, 1990. Softcover. (Text)

MEADOR'S AMERICAN COURTS, 113 pages, 1991. Softcover. (Text)

REYNOLDS' JUDICIAL PROCESS IN A NUTSHELL, Second Edition, 308 pages, 1991. Softcover. (Text)

Legal Research

COHEN'S LEGAL RESEARCH IN A NUTSHELL, Fourth Edition, 452 pages, 1985. Soft-

Legal Research—Cont'd

cover. (Text)

COHEN, BERRING AND OLSON'S HOW TO FIND THE LAW, Ninth Edition, 716 pages, 1989. (Text)

COHEN, BERRING AND OLSON'S FINDING THE LAW, 570 pages, 1989. Softcover reprint from Cohen, Berring and Olson's How to Find the Law, Ninth Edition. (Coursebook)

Legal Research Exercises, 3rd Ed., for use with Cohen, Berring and Olson, 229 pages, 1989. Teacher's Manual available.

ROMBAUER'S LEGAL PROBLEM SOLVING— ANALYSIS, RESEARCH AND WRITING, Fifth Edition, 524 pages, 1991. Softcover. Teacher's Manual with problems available. (Coursebook)

STATSKY'S LEGAL RESEARCH AND WRITING, Third Edition, 257 pages, 1986. Softcover. (Coursebook)

TEPLY'S LEGAL RESEARCH AND CITATION, Third Edition, 472 pages, 1989. Softcover. (Coursebook)

Student Library Exercises, 3rd ed., 391 pages, 1989. Answer Key available.

Legal Writing and Drafting

CHILD'S DRAFTING LEGAL DOCUMENTS: PRINCIPLES AND PRACTICES, Second Edition, approximately 300 pages, April, 1992 Pub. Softcover. Teacher's Manual available. (Coursebook)

DICKERSON'S MATERIALS ON LEGAL DRAFTING, 425 pages, 1981. Teacher's Manual available. (Coursebook)

FELSENFELD AND SIEGEL'S WRITING CONTRACTS IN PLAIN ENGLISH, 290 pages, 1981. Softcover. (Text)

GOPEN'S WRITING FROM A LEGAL PERSPECTIVE, 225 pages, 1981. (Text)

MARTINEAU'S DRAFTING LEGISLATION AND RULES IN PLAIN ENGLISH, 155 pages, 1991. Softcover. Teacher's Manual available. (Text)

MELLINKOFF'S DICTIONARY OF AMERICAN LEGAL USAGE, Approximately 900 pages, March, 1992 Pub. (Text)

MELLINKOFF'S LEGAL WRITING—SENSE AND

NONSENSE, 242 pages, 1982. Softcover. Teacher's Manual available. (Text)

PRATT'S LEGAL WRITING: A SYSTEMATIC APPROACH, 468 pages, 1990. Teacher's Manual available. (Coursebook)

RAY AND COX'S BEYOND THE BASICS: A TEXT FOR ADVANCED LEGAL WRITING, 427 pages, 1991. Softcover. Teacher's Manual available. (Text)

RAY AND RAMSFIELD'S LEGAL WRITING: GETTING IT RIGHT AND GETTING IT WRITTEN, 250 pages, 1987. Softcover. (Text)

SQUIRES AND ROMBAUER'S LEGAL WRITING IN A NUTSHELL, 294 pages, 1982. Softcover. (Text)

STATSKY AND WERNET'S CASE ANALYSIS AND FUNDAMENTALS OF LEGAL WRITING, Third Edition, 424 pages, 1989. Teacher's Manual available. (Text)

TEPLY'S LEGAL WRITING, ANALYSIS AND ORAL ARGUMENT, 576 pages, 1990. Softcover. Teacher's Manual available. (Coursebook)

WEIHOFEN'S LEGAL WRITING STYLE, Second Edition, 332 pages, 1980. (Text)

Legislation—see also **Legal Writing and Drafting**

DAVIES' LEGISLATIVE LAW AND PROCESS IN A NUTSHELL, Second Edition, 346 pages, 1986. Softcover. (Text)

ESKRIDGE AND FRICKEY'S CASES AND MATERIALS ON LEGISLATION: STATUTES AND THE CREATION OF PUBLIC POLICY, 937 pages, 1988. Teacher's Manual available. (Casebook) 1990 Supplement.

NUTTING AND DICKERSON'S CASES AND MATERIALS ON LEGISLATION, Fifth Edition, 744 pages, 1978. (Casebook)

STATSKY'S LEGISLATIVE ANALYSIS AND DRAFTING, Second Edition, 217 pages, 1984. Teacher's Manual available. (Text)

Local Government

FRUG'S CASES AND MATERIALS ON LOCAL GOVERNMENT LAW, 1005 pages, 1988. (Casebook) 1991 Supplement.

MCCARTHY'S LOCAL GOVERNMENT LAW IN A NUTSHELL, Third Edition, 435 pages, 1990. Softcover. (Text)

REYNOLDS' HORNBOOK ON LOCAL GOVERN-

Local Government—Cont'd

MENT LAW, 860 pages, 1982, with 1990 pocket part. (Text)

VALENTE AND MCCARTHY'S CASES AND MATERIALS ON LOCAL GOVERNMENT LAW, Fourth Edition, approximately 1150 pages, 1992. Teacher's Manual available. (Casebook)

Mass Communication Law

GILLMOR, BARRON, SIMON AND TERRY'S CASES AND COMMENT ON MASS COMMUNICATION LAW, Fifth Edition, 947 pages, 1990. (Casebook)

GINSBURG, BOTEIN AND DIRECTOR'S REGULATION OF THE ELECTRONIC MASS MEDIA: LAW AND POLICY FOR RADIO, TELEVISION, CABLE AND THE NEW VIDEO TECHNOLOGIES, Second Edition, 657 pages, 1991. (Casebook) Statutory Supplement.

ZUCKMAN, GAYNES, CARTER AND DEE'S MASS COMMUNICATIONS LAW IN A NUTSHELL, Third Edition, 538 pages, 1988. Softcover. (Text)

Medicine, Law and

FISCINA, BOUMIL, SHARPE AND HEAD'S MEDICAL LIABILITY, 487 pages, 1991. Teacher's Manual available. (Casebook)

FURROW, JOHNSON, JOST AND SCHWARTZ' HEALTH LAW: CASES, MATERIALS AND PROBLEMS, Second Edition, 1236 pages, 1991. Teacher's Manual available. (Casebook)

FURROW, JOHNSON, JOST AND SCHWARTZ' BIOETHICS: HEALTH CARE LAW AND ETHICS, Reprint from Furrow et al., Health Law, Second Edition. Softcover. Teacher's Manual available. (Casebook)

FURROW, JOHNSON, JOST AND SCHWARTZ' THE LAW OF HEALTH CARE ORGANIZATION AND FINANCE, Reprint from Furrow et al., Health Law, Second Edition. Softcover. Teacher's Manual available.

FURROW, JOHNSON, JOST AND SCHWARTZ' LIABILITY AND QUALITY ISSUES IN HEALTH CARE, Reprint from Furrow et al., Health Law, Second Edition. Softcover. Teacher's Manual available. (Casebook)

HALL AND ELLMAN'S HEALTH CARE LAW AND ETHICS IN A NUTSHELL, 401 pages, 1990. Softcover (Text)

JARVIS, CLOSEN, HERMANN AND LEONARD'S AIDS LAW IN A NUTSHELL, 349 pages, 1991. Softcover. (Text)

KING'S THE LAW OF MEDICAL MALPRACTICE IN A NUTSHELL, Second Edition, 342 pages, 1986. Softcover. (Text)

SHAPIRO AND SPECE'S CASES, MATERIALS AND PROBLEMS ON BIOETHICS AND LAW, 892 pages, 1981. (Casebook) 1991 Supplement.

Military Law

SHANOR AND TERRELL'S MILITARY LAW IN A NUTSHELL, 378 pages, 1980. Softcover. (Text)

Mortgages—see Real Estate Transactions

Natural Resources Law—see Energy and Natural Resources Law, Environmental Law

Negotiation

GIFFORD'S LEGAL NEGOTIATION: THEORY AND APPLICATIONS, 225 pages, 1989. Softcover. (Text)

TEPLY'S LEGAL NEGOTIATION IN A NUTSHELL, Approximately 250 pages, 1992. Softcover. (Text)

WILLIAMS' LEGAL NEGOTIATION AND SETTLEMENT, 207 pages, 1983. Softcover. Teacher's Manual available. (Coursebook)

Office Practice—see also Computers and Law, Interviewing and Counseling, Negotiation

HEGLAND'S TRIAL AND PRACTICE SKILLS IN A NUTSHELL, 346 pages, 1978. Softcover (Text)

MUNNEKE'S LAW PRACTICE MANAGEMENT: MATERIALS AND CASES, 634 pages, 1991. Teacher's Manual available. (Casebook)

Oil and Gas—see also Energy and Natural Resources Law

HEMINGWAY'S HORNBOOK ON THE LAW OF OIL AND GAS, Third Edition, Student Edition, approximately 700 pages, 1992. (Text)

KUNTZ, LOWE, ANDERSON AND SMITH'S CASES AND MATERIALS ON OIL AND GAS LAW, 857 pages, 1986. Teacher's Manual available. (Casebook) Forms Manual. Revised.

LOWE'S OIL AND GAS LAW IN A NUTSHELL,

Oil and Gas—Cont'd

Second Edition, 465 pages, 1988. Softcover. (Text)

Partnership—see Agency—Partnership

Patent and Copyright Law

CHOATE, FRANCIS AND COLLINS' CASES AND MATERIALS ON PATENT LAW, INCLUDING TRADE SECRETS, COPYRIGHTS, TRADEMARKS, Third Edition, 1009 pages, 1987. (Casebook)

HALPERN, SHIPLEY AND ABRAMS' CASES AND MATERIALS ON COPYRIGHT, Approximately 700 pages, April, 1992 Pub. (Casebook)

MILLER AND DAVIS' INTELLECTUAL PROPERTY—PATENTS, TRADEMARKS AND COPYRIGHT IN A NUTSHELL, Second Edition, 437 pages, 1990. Softcover. (Text)

NIMMER, MARCUS, MYERS AND NIMMER'S CASES AND MATERIALS ON COPYRIGHT AND OTHER ASPECTS OF ENTERTAINMENT LITIGATION—INCLUDING UNFAIR COMPETITION, DEFAMATION, PRIVACY, ILLUSTRATED, Fourth Edition, 1177 pages, 1991. (Casebook) Statutory Supplement. See *Selected Intellectual Property Statutes*

SELECTED INTELLECTUAL PROPERTY AND UNFAIR COMPETITION STATUTES, REGULATIONS AND TREATIES. Softcover.

Products Liability

FISCHER AND POWERS' CASES AND MATERIALS ON PRODUCTS LIABILITY, 685 pages, 1988. Teacher's Manual available. (Casebook)

PHILLIPS' PRODUCTS LIABILITY IN A NUTSHELL, Third Edition, 307 pages, 1988. Softcover. (Text)

Professional Responsibility

ARONSON, DEVINE AND FISCH'S PROBLEMS, CASES AND MATERIALS IN PROFESSIONAL RESPONSIBILITY, 745 pages, 1985. Teacher's Manual available. (Casebook)

ARONSON AND WECKSTEIN'S PROFESSIONAL RESPONSIBILITY IN A NUTSHELL, Second Edition, 514 pages, 1991. Softcover. (Text)

MELLINKOFF'S THE CONSCIENCE OF A LAWYER, 304 pages, 1973. (Text)

PIRSIG AND KIRWIN'S CASES AND MATERIALS ON PROFESSIONAL RESPONSIBILITY, Fourth Edition, 603 pages, 1984. Teacher's Manual available. (Casebook)

ROTUNDA'S BLACK LETTER ON PROFESSIONAL RESPONSIBILITY, Third Edition, approximately 400 pages, 1992. Softcover. (Review)

SCHWARTZ AND WYDICK'S PROBLEMS IN LEGAL ETHICS, Second Edition, 341 pages, 1988. (Coursebook)

SELECTED STATUTES, RULES AND STANDARDS ON THE LEGAL PROFESSION. Softcover. 844 pages, 1991.

SMITH AND MALLEN'S PREVENTING LEGAL MALPRACTICE, 264 pages, 1989. Reprint from Mallen and Smith's Legal Malpractice, Third Edition. (Text)

SUTTON AND DZIENKOWSKI'S CASES AND MATERIALS ON PROFESSIONAL RESPONSIBILITY FOR LAWYERS, 839 pages, 1989. Teacher's Manual available. (Casebook)

WOLFRAM'S HORNBOOK ON MODERN LEGAL ETHICS, Student Edition, 1120 pages, 1986. (Text)

Property—see also Real Estate Transactions, Land Use, Trusts and Estates

BERNHARDT'S BLACK LETTER ON PROPERTY, Second Edition, 388 pages, 1991. Softcover. (Review)

BERNHARDT'S REAL PROPERTY IN A NUTSHELL, Second Edition, 448 pages, 1981. Softcover. (Text)

BOYER, HOVENKAMP AND KURTZ' THE LAW OF PROPERTY, AN INTRODUCTORY SURVEY, Fourth Edition, 696 pages, 1991. (Text)

BROWDER, CUNNINGHAM, NELSON, STOEBUCK AND WHITMAN'S CASES ON BASIC PROPERTY LAW, Fifth Edition, 1386 pages, 1989. Teacher's Manual available. (Casebook)

BRUCE, ELY AND BOSTICK'S CASES AND MATERIALS ON MODERN PROPERTY LAW, Second Edition, 953 pages, 1989. Teacher's Manual available. (Casebook)

BURKE'S PERSONAL PROPERTY IN A NUTSHELL, 322 pages, 1983. Softcover. (Text)

CUNNINGHAM, STOEBUCK AND WHITMAN'S HORNBOOK ON THE LAW OF PROPERTY, Student Edition, 916 pages, 1984, with 1987 pocket part. (Text)

DONAHUE, KAUPER AND MARTIN'S CASES ON PROPERTY, Second Edition, 1362 pages,

Property—Cont'd

1983. Teacher's Manual available. (Casebook)

HILL'S LANDLORD AND TENANT LAW IN A NUTSHELL, Second Edition, 311 pages, 1986. Softcover. (Text)

JOHNSON, JOST, SALSICH AND SHAFFER'S PROPERTY LAW, CASES, MATERIALS AND PROBLEMS, Approximately 925 pages, April, 1992 Pub. (Casebook)

KURTZ AND HOVENKAMP'S CASES AND MATERIALS ON AMERICAN PROPERTY LAW, 1296 pages, 1987. Teacher's Manual available. (Casebook) 1991 Supplement.

MOYNIHAN'S INTRODUCTION TO REAL PROPERTY, Second Edition, 239 pages, 1988. (Text)

Psychiatry, Law and

REISNER AND SLOBOGIN'S LAW AND THE MENTAL HEALTH SYSTEM, CIVIL AND CRIMINAL ASPECTS, Second Edition, 1117 pages, 1990. (Casebook)

Real Estate Transactions

BRUCE'S REAL ESTATE FINANCE IN A NUTSHELL, Third Edition, 287 pages, 1991. Softcover. (Text)

MAXWELL, RIESENFELD, HETLAND AND WARREN'S CASES ON CALIFORNIA SECURITY TRANSACTIONS IN LAND, Fourth Edition, approximately 775 pages, 1992. (Casebook)

NELSON AND WHITMAN'S BLACK LETTER ON LAND TRANSACTIONS AND FINANCE, Second Edition, 466 pages, 1988. Softcover. (Review)

NELSON AND WHITMAN'S CASES ON REAL ESTATE TRANSFER, FINANCE AND DEVELOPMENT, Third Edition, 1184 pages, 1987. (Casebook)

NELSON AND WHITMAN'S HORNBOOK ON REAL ESTATE FINANCE LAW, Second Edition, 941 pages, 1985 with 1989 pocket part. (Text)

Regulated Industries—see also Mass Communication Law, Banking Law

GELLHORN AND PIERCE'S REGULATED INDUSTRIES IN A NUTSHELL, Second Edition, 389 pages, 1987. Softcover. (Text)

MORGAN, HARRISON AND VERKUIL'S CASES AND MATERIALS ON ECONOMIC REGULATION OF BUSINESS, Second Edition, 666 pages,

1985. (Casebook)

Remedies

DOBBS' HORNBOOK ON REMEDIES, 1067 pages, 1973. (Text)

DOBBS' PROBLEMS IN REMEDIES. 137 pages, 1974. Teacher's Manual available. Softcover. (Coursebook)

DOBBYN'S INJUNCTIONS IN A NUTSHELL, 264 pages, 1974. Softcover. (Text)

FRIEDMAN'S CONTRACT REMEDIES IN A NUTSHELL, 323 pages, 1981. Softcover. (Text)

LEAVELL, LOVE AND NELSON'S CASES AND MATERIALS ON EQUITABLE REMEDIES, RESTITUTION AND DAMAGES, Fourth Edition, 1111 pages, 1986. Teacher's Manual available. (Casebook)

O'CONNELL'S REMEDIES IN A NUTSHELL, Second Edition, 320 pages, 1985. Softcover. (Text)

SCHOENBROD, MACBETH, LEVINE AND JUNG'S CASES AND MATERIALS ON REMEDIES: PUBLIC AND PRIVATE, 848 pages, 1990. Teacher's Manual available. (Casebook)

YORK, BAUMAN AND RENDLEMAN'S CASES AND MATERIALS ON REMEDIES, Fifth Edition, approximately 1275 pages, 1992. (Casebook)

Sea, Law of

SOHN AND GUSTAFSON'S THE LAW OF THE SEA IN A NUTSHELL, 264 pages, 1984. Softcover. (Text)

Securities Regulation

HAZEN'S HORNBOOK ON THE LAW OF SECURITIES REGULATION, Second Edition, Student Edition, 1082 pages, 1990. (Text)

RATNER'S SECURITIES REGULATION IN A NUTSHELL, Third Edition, 316 pages, 1988. Softcover. (Text)

RATNER AND HAZEN'S SECURITIES REGULATION: CASES AND MATERIALS, Fourth Edition, 1062 pages, 1991. Teacher's Manual available. (Casebook) Problems and Sample Documents Supplement.

    Statutory Supplement. *See Securities Regulation, Selected Statutes*

SECURITIES REGULATION, SELECTED STATUTES, RULES, AND FORMS. Softcover. Approximately 1375 pages, 1992.

Sports Law

SCHUBERT, SMITH AND TRENTADUE'S SPORTS LAW, 395 pages, 1986. (Text)

Tax Practice and Procedure

GARBIS, RUBIN AND MORGAN'S CASES AND MATERIALS ON TAX PROCEDURE AND TAX FRAUD, Third Edition, approximately 925 pages, 1992. Teacher's Manual available. (Casebook)

MORGAN'S TAX PROCEDURE AND TAX FRAUD IN A NUTSHELL, 400 pages, 1990. Softcover. (Text)

Taxation—Corporate

KAHN AND GANN'S CORPORATE TAXATION, Third Edition, 980 pages, 1989. Teacher's Manual available. (Casebook) 1991 Supplement.

SCHWARZ AND LATHROPE'S BLACK LETTER ON CORPORATE AND PARTNERSHIP TAXATION, 537 pages, 1991. Softcover. (Review)

WEIDENBRUCH AND BURKE'S FEDERAL INCOME TAXATION OF CORPORATIONS AND STOCKHOLDERS IN A NUTSHELL, Third Edition, 309 pages, 1989. Softcover. (Text)

Taxation—Estate & Gift—see also Estate Planning, Trusts and Estates

MCNULTY'S FEDERAL ESTATE AND GIFT TAXATION IN A NUTSHELL, Fourth Edition, 496 pages, 1989. Softcover. (Text)

PEAT AND WILLBANKS' FEDERAL ESTATE AND GIFT TAXATION: AN ANALYSIS AND CRITIQUE, 265 pages, 1991. Softcover. (Text)

PENNELL'S CASES AND MATERIALS ON INCOME TAXATION OF TRUSTS, ESTATES, GRANTORS AND BENEFICIARIES, 460 pages, 1987. Teacher's Manual available. (Casebook)

Taxation—Individual

DODGE'S THE LOGIC OF TAX, 343 pages, 1989. Softcover. (Text)

GUNN AND WARD'S CASES, TEXT AND PROBLEMS ON FEDERAL INCOME TAXATION, Third Edition, approximately 850 pages, May, 1992 Pub. Teacher's Manual available. (Casebook)

HUDSON AND LIND'S BLACK LETTER ON FEDERAL INCOME TAXATION, Third Edition, 406 pages, 1990. Softcover. (Review)

KRAGEN AND MCNULTY'S CASES AND MATERIALS ON FEDERAL INCOME TAXATION—INDIVIDUALS, CORPORATIONS, PARTNERSHIPS, Fourth Edition, 1287 pages, 1985. (Casebook)

MCNULTY'S FEDERAL INCOME TAXATION OF INDIVIDUALS IN A NUTSHELL, Fourth Edition, 503 pages, 1988. Softcover. (Text)

POSIN'S HORNBOOK ON FEDERAL INCOME TAXATION, Student Edition, 491 pages, 1983, with 1989 pocket part. (Text)

ROSE AND CHOMMIE'S HORNBOOK ON FEDERAL INCOME TAXATION, Third Edition, 923 pages, 1988, with 1991 pocket part. (Text)

SELECTED FEDERAL TAXATION STATUTES AND REGULATIONS. Softcover. 1690 pages, 1992.

Taxation—International

DOERNBERG'S INTERNATIONAL TAXATION IN A NUTSHELL, 325 pages, 1989. Softcover. (Text)

KAPLAN'S FEDERAL TAXATION OF INTERNATIONAL TRANSACTIONS: PRINCIPLES, PLANNING AND POLICY, 635 pages, 1988. (Casebook)

Taxation—Partnership

BERGER AND WIEDENBECK'S CASES AND MATERIALS ON PARTNERSHIP TAXATION, 788 pages, 1989. Teacher's Manual available. (Casebook) 1991 Supplement.

BISHOP AND BROOKS' FEDERAL PARTNERSHIP TAXATION: A GUIDE TO THE LEADING CASES, STATUTES, AND REGULATIONS, 545 pages, 1990. Softcover. (Text)

BURKE'S FEDERAL INCOME TAXATION OF PARTNERSHIPS IN A NUTSHELL, Approximately 400 pages, February, 1992 Pub. Softcover. (Text)

SCHWARZ AND LATHROPE'S BLACK LETTER ON CORPORATE AND PARTNERSHIP TAXATION, 537 pages, 1991. Softcover. (Review)

Taxation—State & Local

GELFAND AND SALSICH'S STATE AND LOCAL TAXATION AND FINANCE IN A NUTSHELL, 309 pages, 1986. Softcover. (Text)

HELLERSTEIN AND HELLERSTEIN'S CASES AND MATERIALS ON STATE AND LOCAL TAXATION, Fifth Edition, 1071 pages, 1988. (Casebook)

Torts—see also Products Liability

CHRISTIE AND MEEKS' CASES AND MATERIALS ON THE LAW OF TORTS, Second Edition, 1264 pages, 1990. (Casebook)

DOBBS' TORTS AND COMPENSATION—PERSONAL ACCOUNTABILITY AND SOCIAL RESPONSIBILITY FOR INJURY, 955 pages, 1985. Teacher's Manual available. (Casebook) 1990 Supplement.

KEETON, KEETON, SARGENTICH AND STEINER'S CASES AND MATERIALS ON TORT AND ACCIDENT LAW, Second Edition, 1318 pages, 1989. (Casebook)

KIONKA'S BLACK LETTER ON TORTS, 339 pages, 1988. Softcover. (Review)

KIONKA'S TORTS IN A NUTSHELL, Second Edition, approximately 500 pages, March, 1992 Pub. Softcover. (Text)

MALONE'S TORTS IN A NUTSHELL: INJURIES TO FAMILY, SOCIAL AND TRADE RELATIONS, 358 pages, 1979. Softcover. (Text)

PROSSER AND KEETON'S HORNBOOK ON TORTS, Fifth Edition, Student Edition, 1286 pages, 1984 with 1988 pocket part. (Text)

ROBERTSON, POWERS AND ANDERSON'S CASES AND MATERIALS ON TORTS, 932 pages, 1989. Teacher's Manual available. (Casebook)

Trade Regulation—see also Antitrust, Regulated Industries

MCMANIS' UNFAIR TRADE PRACTICES IN A NUTSHELL, Second Edition, 464 pages, 1988. Softcover. (Text)

SCHECHTER'S BLACK LETTER ON UNFAIR TRADE PRACTICES, 272 pages, 1986. Softcover. (Review)

WESTON, MAGGS AND SCHECHTER'S UNFAIR TRADE PRACTICES AND CONSUMER PROTECTION, CASES AND COMMENTS, Fifth Edition, approximately 975 pages, 1992. Teacher's Manual available. (Casebook)

Trial and Appellate Advocacy—see also Civil Procedure

APPELLATE ADVOCACY, HANDBOOK OF, Second Edition, 182 pages, 1986. Softcover. (Text)

BERGMAN'S TRIAL ADVOCACY IN A NUTSHELL, Second Edition, 354 pages, 1989. Softcover. (Text)

BINDER AND BERGMAN'S FACT INVESTIGATION:

FROM HYPOTHESIS TO PROOF, 354 pages, 1984. Teacher's Manual available. (Coursebook)

CARLSON'S ADJUDICATION OF CRIMINAL JUSTICE: PROBLEMS AND REFERENCES, 130 pages, 1986. Softcover. (Casebook)

CARLSON AND IMWINKELRIED'S DYNAMICS OF TRIAL PRACTICE: PROBLEMS AND MATERIALS, 414 pages, 1989. Teacher's Manual available. (Coursebook) 1990 Supplement.

DESSEM'S PRETRIAL LITIGATION: LAW, POLICY AND PRACTICE, 608 pages, 1991. Softcover. Teacher's Manual available. (Coursebook)

DEVINE'S NON-JURY CASE FILES FOR TRIAL ADVOCACY, 258 pages, 1991. (Coursebook)

GOLDBERG'S THE FIRST TRIAL (WHERE DO I SIT? WHAT DO I SAY?) IN A NUTSHELL, 396 pages, 1982. Softcover. (Text)

HAYDOCK, HERR, AND STEMPEL'S FUNDAMENTALS OF PRE-TRIAL LITIGATION, Second Edition, approximately 700 pages, 1992. Softcover. Teacher's Manual available. (Coursebook)

HAYDOCK AND SONSTENG'S TRIAL: THEORIES, TACTICS, TECHNIQUES, 711 pages, 1991. Softcover. (Text)

HEGLAND'S TRIAL AND PRACTICE SKILLS IN A NUTSHELL, 346 pages, 1978. Softcover. (Text)

HORNSTEIN'S APPELLATE ADVOCACY IN A NUTSHELL, 325 pages, 1984. Softcover. (Text)

JEANS' HANDBOOK ON TRIAL ADVOCACY, Student Edition, 473 pages, 1975. Softcover. (Text)

LISNEK AND KAUFMAN'S DEPOSITIONS: PROCEDURE, STRATEGY AND TECHNIQUE, Law School and CLE Edition. 250 pages, 1990. Softcover. (Text)

MARTINEAU'S CASES AND MATERIALS ON APPELLATE PRACTICE AND PROCEDURE, 565 pages, 1987. (Casebook)

NOLAN'S CASES AND MATERIALS ON TRIAL PRACTICE, 518 pages, 1981. (Casebook)

SONSTENG, HAYDOCK AND BOYD'S THE TRIALBOOK: A TOTAL SYSTEM FOR PREPARATION AND PRESENTATION OF A CASE, 404 pages, 1984. Softcover. (Coursebook)

WHARTON, HAYDOCK AND SONSTENG'S CALI-

Trial and Appellate Advocacy—Cont'd

FORNIA CIVIL TRIALBOOK, Law School and CLE Edition. 148 pages, 1990. Softcover. (Text)

Trusts and Estates

ATKINSON'S HORNBOOK ON WILLS, Second Edition, 975 pages, 1953. (Text)

AVERILL'S UNIFORM PROBATE CODE IN A NUT-SHELL, Second Edition, 454 pages, 1987. Softcover. (Text)

BOGERT'S HORNBOOK ON TRUSTS, Sixth Edition, Student Edition, 794 pages, 1987. (Text)

CLARK, LUSKY AND MURPHY'S CASES AND MATERIALS ON GRATUITOUS TRANSFERS, Third Edition, 970 pages, 1985. (Casebook)

DODGE'S WILLS, TRUSTS AND ESTATE PLAN-NING–LAW AND TAXATION, CASES AND MATERIALS, 665 pages, 1988. (Casebook)

MCGOVERN'S CASES AND MATERIALS ON WILLS, TRUSTS AND FUTURE INTERESTS: AN INTRODUCTION TO ESTATE PLANNING, 750 pages, 1983. (Casebook)

MCGOVERN, KURTZ AND REIN'S HORNBOOK ON WILLS, TRUSTS AND ESTATES–INCLUDING TAXATION AND FUTURE INTERESTS, 996 pages, 1988. (Text)

MENNELL'S WILLS AND TRUSTS IN A NUT-SHELL, 392 pages, 1979. Softcover. (Text)

SIMES' HORNBOOK ON FUTURE INTERESTS, Second Edition, 355 pages, 1966. (Text)

TURANO AND RADIGAN'S HORNBOOK ON NEW YORK ESTATE ADMINISTRATION, 676 pages, 1986 with 1991 pocket part. (Text)

UNIFORM PROBATE CODE, OFFICIAL TEXT WITH COMMENTS. 839 pages, 1990. Softcover.

WAGGONER'S FUTURE INTERESTS IN A NUT-SHELL, 361 pages, 1981. Softcover. (Text)

WATERBURY'S MATERIALS ON TRUSTS AND ES-TATES, 1039 pages, 1986. Teacher's Manual available. (Casebook)

Water Law—see also Energy and Natural Resources Law, Environmental Law

GETCHES' WATER LAW IN A NUTSHELL, Second Edition, 459 pages, 1990. Softcover. (Text)

SAX, ABRAMS AND THOMPSON'S LEGAL CON-TROL OF WATER RESOURCES: CASES AND MATERIALS, Second Edition, 987 pages, 1991. Teacher's Manual available. (Casebook)

TRELEASE AND GOULD'S CASES AND MATERI-ALS ON WATER LAW, Fourth Edition, 816 pages, 1986. (Casebook)

Wills—see Trusts and Estates

Workers' Compensation

HOOD, HARDY AND LEWIS' WORKERS' COM-PENSATION AND EMPLOYEE PROTECTION LAWS IN A NUTSHELL, Second Edition, 361 pages, 1990. Softcover. (Text)

MALONE, PLANT AND LITTLE'S CASES ON WORKERS' COMPENSATION AND EMPLOYMENT RIGHTS, Second Edition, 951 pages, 1980. Teacher's Manual available. (Casebook)

[xviii]

CASES AND MATERIALS ON
LAW AND ECONOMICS

By

David W. Barnes
Professor of Law, University of Denver

Lynn A. Stout
Professor of Law, Georgetown University

AMERICAN CASEBOOK SERIES ®

WEST PUBLISHING CO.
ST. PAUL, MINN., 1992

COPYRIGHT © 1992 By WEST PUBLISHING CO.
                         610 Opperman Drive
                         P.O. Box 64526
                         St. Paul, MN 55164–0526

Library of Congress Cataloging-in-Publication Data

Barnes, David W.
    Cases and materials on law and economics / David W. Barnes and
  Lynn A. Stout.
       p.   cm. — (American casebook series)
    Includes index.
    ISBN 0–314–00188–3
    1. Law—United States—Cases. 2. Economics. I. Stout, Lynn A.,
  1957– . II. Title. III. Series.
  KF385.A4B37 1992
  349.73—dc20
  [347.3]   91–48360
                                                               CIP

ISBN 0–314–00188–3

For Rose, with great appreciation.
D.W.B.

For Sally.
L.A.S.

*

Preface

During the past three decades, scholars wielding the tools of economics have marched through the curricula of American law schools, applying economic analysis to one substantive area of law after another. Accustomed to formal theoretical models of institutions and human behavior, "law and economics" scholars often examine legal rules in the abstract rather than discussing their application to specific cases. By contrast, conventional law teaching begins with specific cases and abstracts from those cases the general principles governing decisions. This book combines the theory of economics and the pedagogy of law by exploring economic analysis of law primarily through reported judicial opinions and agency decisions. Excerpts from classic writings have been included to give a flavor for the type of discourse in which law and economics scholars engage.

The typical law and economics course applies economic analysis to a number of substantive areas of law. This book accommodates that tradition by providing cases, excerpts, and textual notes and questions in a wide variety of legal areas embracing common law, statutory, and constitutional rules. Chapters 2, 3, and 4 focus on cases drawn from the common law areas of property law, torts, and contracts. Chapter 6's analysis of regulation includes materials raising issues of occupational safety and health, environmental regulation, postal regulation, cable television, and consumer protection, along with tax and antitrust cases. Chapter 7 examines constitutional questions of equal protection, due process, separation of powers, voting rights, the police power, and judicial review, among others.

Chapters 1 and 2 provide the preamble to any selection of subsequent chapters in the book. Chapter 1 introduces the basic economic assumptions of rationality and scarcity and the concepts of utility maximization, wealth maximization, and allocative efficiency. Chapter 2 examines the fundamental economic problem of externalities and, with a discussion of the Coase Theorem, considers the relative advantages of property and liability rules in addressing externalities. Chapters 1 and 2 thus provide the basic intellectual tools necessary to the economic analysis of law. Each subsequent Chapter is independent and may stand alone. Students need not, for example, be familiar with the microeconomic theory discussed in Chapter 6 to understand the materials in any other chapter. Chapters 3 through 7 may be read in any order and any of those Chapters may be omitted.

Chapters 2, 3, and 4 deal with the three areas of law which virtually all law students study in their first year of law school: property, torts (personal injury), and contracts. Because those common law courses provide the foundation for most legal educations, Chapters 2, 3 and 4 allow law students to explore the implications of economic analysis in familiar legal contexts where they are most likely to feel at home.

One surprising result of a detailed survey of common law doctrines is that common law rules appear, in large part, to maximize social wealth. Chapter 5 briefly discusses how the law could have evolved to serve such an economic goal when there is remarkably little evidence that lawmakers and judges are particularly aware of, able to engage in, or favorably disposed towards economic analysis. In presenting an evolutionary theory of common law efficiency, Chapter 5 also provides judicial opinions and materials inviting students to consider the economics of the litigation process and the factors that determine which cases go to trial and which are settled, how cases are decided and why they are appealed.

This book is designed for readers with no prior economic training. Until Chapter 6, the materials require no familiarity with microeconomic theory or the graphic techniques of economics. Chapter 6 introduces the fundamentals of microeconomics necessary to understanding regulatory law and antitrust. The first half of Chapter 6 leads the reader gradually through the theories of supply, demand, and price and quantity equilibrium, and introduces the graphic representation of those concepts. Cases explore the concepts of opportunity cost, normal economic profit, economic rent, and the theory of cost, including total, average, and marginal cost. Those concepts are applied to a variety of issues including the incidence of taxation and tort liability and the efficient level of pollution control. The second half of Chapter 6 applies those microeconomic tools and consumer welfare theory to antitrust law and the regulation of natural monopolies. Instructors preferring a more technical and graphic approach to economic analysis of law may assign Chapter 6 early on in order to acquaint students with those techniques. No other chapter, however, relies extensively on graphic materials.

Chapter 7 is a particularly exciting addition to the law and economics literature. It introduces the emerging field of "public choice" and applies public choice theory to cases involving a wide array of constitutional issues. Chapter 7 examines the economic justifications for a coercive state, the economic and distributional implications of using legislative voting to make collective decisions, and the economic logic of constitutional devices such as separation of powers, an independent judiciary, and special protections for the political and property rights of individuals and oppressed classes.

A case orientation should appeal to those eager to escape the artificial assumptions associated with economics, as well as those eager to explore the ethical and distributional dimensions of law. Analyzing reported decisions requires economics to come to grips with reality. In some circumstances, the assumptions made to facilitate economic analysis seem clearly implausible. Factual contexts also highlight the distributional and ethical implications of economic analysis of law. Rather than gloss over such issues, the materials regularly raise the normative implications of particular legal rules. Chapter 3's discussion of torts, for instance, draws the reader's attention to the distributional implications of alternative measures of damages. Chapter 4 considers contract law's bias in favor of the status quo from which bargaining takes place and the implications of unequal bargaining power. Chapter 7's analysis of constitutional law highlights the distribution of power among society's members and the distributional implications of alternative mechanisms for institutionalizing state coercion. This book is a vehicle for appreciating and critically examining, rather than merely promoting, the economic analysis of law.

Most footnotes and citations contained in reported opinions and other quoted materials have been omitted without any indication. In the rare occasions where such footnotes have been included, they are reproduced with their original numbering. All other omissions from excerpted texts are indicated by asterisks.

DAVID W. BARNES
LYNN A. STOUT

March, 1992

*

Acknowledgments

There is no section of this book that did not benefit from the hard work and close attention of Rosemary McCool, who was as concerned as either of the authors with the quality of this book. As researcher of interesting and provocative cases, as editor, as test audience, as stylistic coordinator, and as critic, Rose is extraordinary. She deserves a great deal of credit for the production of this book. Almost every time she suggests alternative wording of a sentence or paragraph, I preferred her approach to mine. Every time she hints at an ambiguity in a note or question, there is indeed one. Even after graduating from law school and beginning her legal career, she cannot keep from peeking at drafts, looking for both substantive and stylistic errors. Thank you, Rose, for your hours of toil.

Jim Alm is a professor of economics at the University of Colorado and an old friend. He provided many useful comments on the discussion of microeconomic theory in Chapter 6. Critiquing a one chapter introduction to a complex subject to which he devotes many courses, and trying to teach and persuade a particularly stubborn lawyer (even one trained in economics) must have tried his patience. I would love to blame any remaining errors in that Chapter on Jim, since he is such a good friend and was so helpful. However, convention forbids it (and the fault is, of course, our own).

Professor Arthur Best, doomed to occupy the office next to mine at the University of Denver, deserves special recognition for his contributions throughout. His experience in the areas of property and tort law was particularly useful in the early stages of writing. More significantly, Arthur graciously fielded queries on all topics without regard to whether he had any expertise in the area. His great commonsense, intuition, and savvy were invaluable.

Many others deserve special acknowledgment. Professor Linz Audain from the Washington College of Law at American University devoted a great deal of effort to a thorough reading and critique of the first five chapters. Professor Audain made more excellent suggestions for notes and comments than we could include in the book. Those suggestions we could not include will enrich our teaching. Professor Daniel Q. Posin from Tulane University School of Law provided comments that improved the accuracy of our analysis and the stylistic quality of the book. I would also like to thank Walter J. Kendall, John Cirace, Gary Schwartz, George M. Cohen, Kenneth Dau-Schmidt, Jonathan Rose, William P. Kratzke, George Hay and others for sharing their comments and their law and economics course materials.

Among my own colleagues at the University of Denver, Jimmy
Winokur provided useful assistance with the property chapter, Steve
Pepper gave helpful comments on the torts chapter, and Neil Littlefield
assisted with the section on contract remedies and the language of
contract law generally. Tom Crandall, now at the University of Toledo
College of Law, helped my understanding of unconscionability and
duress in the contracts chapter. My secretary for most of this project,
Marjean Rickert, suffered through many of the inevitably tedious tasks
associated with producing this book and deserves special credit for
putting up with my peculiarities. Research assistants Don McCoy and
Hollie Ranucci made valuable contributions to the selection of cases. I
would like to thank all of these colleagues for their contributions.

Lastly, I would like to acknowledge that Lynn A. Stout is a woman
of tremendous patience.

David W. Barnes

Special thanks are due all who contributed to this book, and
especially to my colleagues Dan Ernst, Mike Seidman, Warren
Schwartz, and Si Wasserstrom for their helpfulness and insights. I am
particularly grateful to Bill Eskridge for his invaluable help in navigat-
ing the shoals of social choice theory. Mindy Pittell Hurwitz, John
Lewis, Jr., Kelly McClosky, Susan Pohl, Diane Rohleder, Maurice
Stucke, and Jami Silverman each provided essential research and
editorial assistance.

Lynn A. Stout

Posner, Gratuitous Promises in Economics and Law, 6 J. Legal Studies 411–13 (1977). Copyright © 1977 by the University of Chicago, University of Chicago Press. Reprinted with permission.

Priest, The Common Law Process and the Selection of Efficient Rules, 6 J. Legal Studies 65–73, 81–82 (1977). Copyright © 1977 by the University of Chicago, University of Chicago Press. Reprinted with permission.

J. Rawls, A Theory of Justice 3–4, 11, 12, 13, 14–15, 22, 60–62, 136–37, 140–41, 151–53 (1971). Copyright © 1971 by the President and Fellows of Harvard College, Harvard University Press. Reprinted with permission.

Shavell, Strict Liability Versus Negligence, 9 J. Legal Studies 1–3, 22–23 (1980). Copyright © 1980 by the University of Chicago, University of Chicago Press. Reprinted with permission.

Williamson, Economics As An Antitrust Defense Revisited, 125 U. Pa.L.Rev. 699, 704, 706–708 (1977). Copyright © 1977 by The University of Pennsylvania. Reprinted with permission.

*

Summary of Contents

Table of Contents

*

Table of Cases

The principal cases are in bold type. Cases cited or discussed in the text are roman type. References are to pages. Cases cited in principal cases and within other quoted materials are not included.

*

CASES AND MATERIALS ON
LAW AND ECONOMICS

*

Chapter 1

INTRODUCTION

The law is designed to resolve the conflicting claims that arise when people interact in society. Benefits from the use and ownership of property, from promises based on contracts, and from engaging in activities that present risks to others are accompanied by corresponding burdens: the burden of being excluded from another's property, the obligation to perform one's own promises, and the risk of injury caused by another's activity. Legal rules allocate the benefits and burdens of social interaction, following complex, everchanging, and sometimes unfathomable doctrines.

Economics also is concerned with how to resolve competing claims. While there are economists evaluating law from all political perspectives, many take the traditional or neo-classical perspective that allocates the benefits and burdens of a legal rule according to a single principle, *economic efficiency*. Given the appeal of a single principle on which to base judgments regarding the propriety of legal rules and the fact that both law and economics are concerned fundamentally with the same questions, it is not surprising that lawyers and legal scholars have looked to economics for guidance in evaluating the wisdom and likely effects of legal rules.

This casebook introduces the basic concepts of economics and applies them to legal problems. Economic analysis can shed light on the consequences of the law's murky operations by focusing on the incentives created by the law. Applying economic principles to legal problems brings a better understanding of the implications of legal rules.

A. EFFICIENCY AND UTILITY MAXIMIZATION

Economics studies rational choice in a world of scarcity. The fundamental goal of economic analysis is getting the most from the scarce resources available to satisfy society's needs and wants by allocating them efficiently among competing uses. The meaning of these terms—rational choice, scarcity, and efficiency—are explored in the following cases.

CIDIS v. WHITE

District Court, Nassau County, Fourth District, 1972.
71 Misc.2d 481, 336 N.Y.S.2d 362.

GITELMAN, JUDGE.

In this action, plaintiff, a duly licensed optometrist, was requested by defendant, Carol Ann White, an infant, 19 years of age, to furnish her with contact lenses. She advised plaintiff that she urgently desired them as soon as possible. She agreed to pay $225.00 for the lenses and gave the doctor her personal check for $100.00. Plaintiff, accordingly, after examining infant defendant's eyes immediately ordered the lenses from his laboratory and incurred an indebtedness of $110.00. The examination was held on Thursday evening, the lenses were ordered on Friday, and received by the doctor on Saturday. On Monday morning the infant called and disaffirmed her contract on advice and insistence of her father, and stopped payment on her check. The infant was 19 years of age, working, and although living at home with her parents, paid for her room and board.

The plaintiff established that the contact lenses could be used by no one but the infant and have no market value at all, thus resulting in an absolute loss to the plaintiff of $110.00.

The question presents itself as to whether or not the contact lenses were "necessaries." The term "necessaries" as used in the law relating to the liability of infants therefor is a relative term, somewhat flexible, except when applied to such things as are obviously requisite for the maintenance of existence, and also depends on the social position and situation in life of the infant.

An analogy may be drawn between the instant case and the situation that existed in the case of Vichnes v. Transcontinental & Western Air, Inc. and in Bach v. Long Island Jewish Hospital. In the *Vichnes* case an infant purchased a round trip ticket to California and after using it tried to disaffirm and recover the money he paid. The Appellate Term reversed the Municipal Court and dismissed his claim. In the *Bach* case, an emancipated infant attempted to disaffirm her consent to a cosmetic operation performed on her. The Supreme Court, Nassau County, refused to permit her to do so. In both of these cases, the infant had received full benefit and could not place the defendant in status quo. So also in this case, since the contact lenses are of no value to anyone except the infant defendant, the plaintiff has suffered a loss and cannot be put back in status quo except by payment of a reasonable sum.

The Court has in mind the case of International Text Book Co. v. Connelly, which holds that an infant is not liable for a sum in excess of the fair value of the necessaries furnished even though he has contracted to pay more.

Accordingly, and for the purpose of doing substantial justice between the parties, judgment is granted in favor of the plaintiff and against the defendant, Carol Ann White, in the sum of $150.00. Since the defendant, Carol Ann White, is emancipated, no judgment may be granted against her father, the defendant, Richard A. White, and accordingly the complaint is dismissed as to him. During the trial the father urged that his daughter should not be penalized for obeying her father. The Court suggests that there is nothing to prevent the father from paying the judgment for his daughter, if he is so minded.

Notes and Questions

1. The study of economics begins with assumptions about what motivates people to act. In *Cidis,* both White and Cidis apparently entered the contract voluntarily and deliberately—neither was forced to deal with the other. Given such facts, it seems likely that each entered the contract out of self-interest. Each expected to be happier, better-off, and more satisfied after the exchange.

Economists usually do not bother with why people desire certain things or whether they should desire those things at all. Recognizing and accepting that people find happiness in different ways, economists are more interested in *how* individuals pursue happiness, satisfaction, and fulfillment—what economists refer to as *utility.*

Question: Is it reasonable to suppose that both Cidis and White thought they were improving their own levels of utility when they struck their bargain, even though it is quite unlikely they actually thought of it in those terms?

2. Economists assume that people generally prefer more utility to less utility. Rational individuals therefore attempt to *maximize* their utility and extract the highest possible level of happiness from the limited resources available to them. Rational maximization requires more of people than simply striking bargains that leave them better off. To maximize her utility, Carol Ann White must use her presumably limited monetary resources to buy those items that bring her the *most* utility. It would be irrational for her to spend $225 on contact lenses if another use of the money—say, to purchase a stereo—would bring her even more happiness.

While White may have thought that she would gain the most utility by using her $225 to buy contact lenses, her father obviously had different ideas. Perhaps he thought his daughter's interests would be better served by using the money for school books or college tuition. In making such a decision, White's father implicitly recognized that the world is a place of *scarcity.* Valuable resources—including food, energy, land, time, and labor, not to mention Carol Ann's bankroll—are finite in amount. Allocating resources to one purpose often sacrifices the opportunity to use those resources for something else. Using clean air as a dumping ground for airborne pollutants interferes with using the air for healthy breathing. A government on a balanced budget must choose between spending money on nuclear weapons or social programs.

Economists refer to the opportunities foregone by choosing to use limited resources for another purpose as the *opportunity cost* of using the resources. By spending her $225 on contact lenses, White incurred the opportunity cost of not being able to spend that money on school books or college tuition. From an opportunity cost perspective, she gave up school books and tuition payments for the lenses. She rationally maximized her utility (was a *rational maximizer*) only if she valued the lenses more than the other opportunities she sacrificed.

   Questions: What opportunity cost did Cidis incur when he spent his time providing contact lenses for White? Would Cidis be a rational maximizer if he could have used the same time to sell lenses to someone willing to pay more than White?

   3. Scarcity and rationality provide the basis for understanding the concept of *efficiency*. Scarcity does not mean that every item desired is as hard to find as a flawless diamond. Scarcity in an economic sense means that the item's supply is sufficiently limited that not enough exists to satisfy all desires. The item must be allocated among competing uses. Rationality is more controversial, primarily because it is often misunderstood. Economists do not believe that everyone always acts rationally. People sometimes behave in an apparently self-destructive fashion. People sometimes make mistakes and are sometimes too tired or uninformed to choose wisely among alternatives. Economists do assume, however, that people *generally* attempt to make themselves as well-off as possible. Economists also recognize that sometimes people gain utility by making others better off as well.

   When resources are scarce, rational maximizers want to use their resources to the best possible advantage—to "get the most" out of them. If people seek happiness or utility, allocating scarce resources efficiently means allocating them in a fashion that maximizes the happiness or utility people derive from them.

   The exchange Cidis and White contemplated provides an example of an efficient reallocation that may increase the level of utility derived from scarce resources. No rational maximizer would give up one resource in exchange for another unless she valued the second resource more. If Cidis and White were rational maximizers, then at the time of the contract White valued the lenses more than the $225, and Cidis valued the money more than the lenses and the time needed to fit them. The exchange would not increase the total amount of resources available, but it would increase the total amount of utility those resources provided by making both Cidis and White feel better off. Thus, if Cidis and White were rational maximizers, it would have been efficient to allow them to reallocate their resources through exchange.

   4. As the preceding note suggests, voluntary exchange can be an important means of efficiently redistributing resources so as to maximize utility. In most cases, the law respects and enforces voluntary contractual exchanges. In Cidis v. White, however, the court refused to require White

to perform the terms of her contractual obligation because, under New York State law, she was still a minor. The contracts of minors are generally regarded as voidable or unenforceable against the minor, although an adult who contracts with a minor will be bound. Even if the contract is for necessaries, a minor is liable only if she has actually used the necessaries or is for some other reason unable to return them so as to restore the merchant to the status quo. If Cidis had sought to enforce his contract with White before the lenses had been ordered from the laboratory, the contract would have been unenforceable.

Questions: Does the legal rule that minors lack capacity to enter binding contracts imply that utility maximization is unimportant, at least for minors? Might there be another explanation for the rule?

5. Denying minors the capacity to enter into binding contracts yet holding adult sellers to their promises might discourage adults from providing goods and services to minors. An exception to the incapacity rule is made for the provision of "necessaries," "such things as are obviously requisite for the maintenance of existence."

Question: Is this exception based simply on a desire to provide essential services to minors or on a conclusion that minors are more likely to be rational when it comes to necessities? Keep in mind the limitation on enforcement of a minor's contract that requires return of the "necessaries" or limits the amount the minor must pay to the "fair value" of the goods received.

6. When setting the fair value the minor must pay, the court is substituting its own judgment regarding an item's value for the voluntary bargaining of the parties.

Question: Under what circumstances could a court determination of the exchange price lead to an inefficient allocation of resources?

7. It is difficult for a decisionmaker (other than the parties to an exchange) to estimate how much utility other persons gain or lose as a result of an exchange. Of course, the decisionmaker can always ask the parties involved. But there may be reason to doubt the accuracy of a party's response when he is not required to "put his money where his mouth is." Consider Carol Ann White's incentives had the Court, after ruling that she was not bound by the contract, asked her what the "fair value" of the lenses was.

Because of the difficulty of estimating how much utility someone else derives from a particular good or service, economists prefer whenever possible to rely on the individual's behavior as the best measure of the value she attaches to that good or service. If individuals are rational maximizers, their behavior in choosing how to allocate their resources will be a reliable reflection of their values. If Carol Ann chooses to buy contact lenses rather than school books, that indicates Carol Ann gets more utility from the lenses. The economist's assumption that individuals' actual choices reflect their preferences and values is described as the *theory of revealed preferences.*

B. EFFICIENCY AND WEALTH MAXIMIZATION

Allocative efficiency means using scarce resources to the greatest possible advantage, "getting the most" out of them. Whether a particular use is efficient will depend, by definition, on what exactly one wants to gain or accomplish. One might wish to allocate resources so as to maximize the utility people derive from them in order to achieve the greatest overall level of happiness. While a laudable goal in theory, in practice utility maximization can be difficult to implement. No direct means of measuring utility exists. If Carol Ann White chooses to purchase contact lenses, presumably she derives utility from the lenses. Unfortunately, it is impossible to know how *much* utility she derives. There is no ready way to measure how many "utils" Carol Ann gleans from contact lenses as opposed to textbooks, much less compare the value of one person's utils to another person's.

One can measure, however, the amount of money Carol Ann is willing to pay for her lenses. If Carol Ann decides to spend $225 on contact lenses but would only pay $100 for school books, one can determine not only that Carol Ann values the lenses more than the books, but also that she values the lenses at least $125 more. Individuals' willingness to pay money for particular goods can serve as a rough indicator of the value they attach to those goods. The more money a person is willing to pay for something, the more utility she expects to derive from it and the more she values it. Perhaps it is sensible to pursue a policy of maximizing wealth (the dollar value of scarce resources as measured by individuals' willingness and ability to pay for them) instead of maximizing utility.

ROSS v. WILSON
Court of Appeals of New York, 1955.
308 N.Y. 605, 127 N.E.2d 697.

Van Voorhis, Judge.

The controversy in this proceeding concerns the sale of the school-house which served common school district No. 1 of the Towns of Ellicott and Gerry, in Chautauqua County, before it was superseded by a central school district. This district had been known as the Ross Mills District. In February, 1953, the board of education of the recently formed central school district called a special meeting of the qualified voters of the former common school district to vote upon whether to close the school and sell the school property. Such procedure is required by subdivision 6 of section 1804 of the Education Law, which also provides that if the common school district schoolhouse is sold, the net proceeds be apportioned among the taxpayers of the common school district.

At the special meeting of the common school district called by the board of education in 1953, four propositions were submitted: (1)

Should the school of the former common school district be closed? (2) Should the school property be sold to Ross Mills Church of God for $2,000? (3) Should the property be sold to Ross Grange No. 305 for $3,000? (4) Should the property be sold by public auction to the highest bidder? The notice stated that proposition number 1 would be voted upon, "and as many of the succeeding propositions as is necessary to dispose of the property". At the meeting, the proposal to close the school was carried. A motion was then made but declared out of order that the meeting should next ballot upon whether to sell the school property at public auction to the highest bidder. Then proposition number 2 was presented to the meeting to sell the school property to Ross Mills Church of God for $2,000. It was carried by a vote of 32 to 24. That ended the meeting.

* * * [S]ubdivision 6 of section 1804 of the Education Law, pursuant to which this schoolhouse was sold, does not expressly state that it must be sold to the highest bidder upon the organization of a central school district. * * *

* * *

* * * But if the Legislature does not require a schoolhouse to be sold at public auction, it by no means follows from that circumstance that the Legislature intended to authorize the public officials charged with the administration of school property, or even the majority of qualified electors voting at a school district meeting, to sell the property for a smaller amount than has been offered with due formality by a proper purchaser for a lawful use. * * * Whichever procedure is prescribed by the Legislature for selling this publicly owned property, it was the duty of the board of trustees and of the district meeting to obtain the best price obtainable in their judgment for any lawful use of the premises. In this respect, their powers and duties are similar to those of trustees. * * *

* * *

The amount of money involved is small, but the principle is important; the offer which was rejected was to pay 50% more for this schoolhouse than the one which was accepted. Bogert, writing on Trusts and Trustees, says (§ 745): "Whether the trustee should endeavor to sell by negotiation with possible buyers, or should put the property up at auction, depends upon the circumstances of the individual case. He should use the method which will, considering the place of sale and the type of property for sale, be apt to bring the best price." In the present situation, the Legislature has determined that it was not necessary to sell this property at auction, although that procedure would have been permissible, but the latitude allowed in the method of sale was designed to enable these public fiduciaries to adopt the method which in their judgment would bring the best price, and it was their duty to sell at the best price which it brought, not deliberately to select and to favor a buyer at a lower price than was otherwise obtainable. * * *

* * *

* * * The direct result of what occurred is, in effect, to approve a contribution of $1,000 by the school district to the church. * * *

This contribution by a common school district to a particular church is not made in aid of any educational activity conducted by the church, but operates as an outright gift of public funds to a church for its general church purposes. Even if the facts of the case did not present the special situation of the use of public money for the support of a religious establishment, neither a common school district meeting, nor the district trustees, are empowered to expend the resources of the school district for other than educational objects. * * *

* * *

For the reasons mentioned, we think that there was a total lack of power in the school district to accept an offer of $2,000 from the Church of God of Ross Mills and at the same time to reject an equally bona fide offer of $3,000 from the grange. * * * The order appealed from should be reversed and the determinations of the Commissioner of Education and of the board of education approving the sale to the Church of God of Ross Mills should be annulled, with costs to appellants in this court and in the Appellate Division.

* * *

Notes and Questions

1. The resource to be allocated in *Ross* was a schoolhouse no longer required for educational purposes. Buildings are scarce and the schoolhouse potentially could serve various other needs. Wealth maximizing would require the schoolhouse to be allocated to the group or individual who valued it most highly, as measured by willingness to pay money for it.

Between a willing buyer and seller, it is easily determined who values the schoolhouse more. If the buyer is willing and able to pay enough to induce the seller to part with the building, the buyer must attach a higher dollar value to the building than the seller does. Thus, the school district's sale of the schoolhouse to the Ross Mills Church of God for $2,000 would increase the monetary value of the schoolhouse. In *Ross,* the bargain between the School District and the Church of God did not mean the schoolhouse would go it its *most* valuable use, only that it would go to a *more* valuable use. Another potential buyer may be willing and able to pay even more; in this case, the Grange had offered $3,000. Negotiations among all parties interested in purchasing the schoolhouse—including the Ross Mills Church of God, the Grange, and any other bidders—would reveal who was willing to pay the highest price, and so valued the schoolhouse the most.

Questions: How did the school district's decision to ignore the Grange's offer and sell the schoolhouse to the Church of God for $2,000 interfere with maximizing wealth—i.e., the value of resources as measured by people's willingness to pay for them? Did the school district's decision to sell to the Church of God for $2,000 really amount to a "contribution" to the Church of $1,000? Would the Church of God have been better or worse off if the Grange had only bid $1,999?

2. The notes following *Cidis* examined how voluntary exchange can efficiently redistribute resources in a fashion that increases overall utility. As *Ross* illustrates, voluntary exchange can also increase wealth. Indeed, voluntary negotiations among all interested parties can *maximize* wealth by ensuring that a particular resource is allocated to the highest bidder who, by definition, values the resource the most as measured by willingness to pay.

To appreciate wealth maximization, it may be useful to envision society's wealth as a pie. Other things being equal, a larger pie is preferable to a smaller one because there is more wealth to divide among society's members. Among economists, the Gross Domestic Product (GDP) is a familiar measure of the total value (wealth) of the goods and services produced in the United States during a given time period. It measures the quantity of goods and services produced and the values actually placed upon them, in terms of the prices paid for them. If in a given year the total goods and services produced yields a higher value, then the GDP increases, and society has more wealth.

The GDP may be too narrow a measure of social well-being because many scarce resources allocated by society are not included in the "goods and services" category. Goods such as clean air, privacy, and leisure time are rarely traded in the marketplace but are desirable and scarce commodities that people would be willing to bargain for and exchange if markets existed. A more comprehensive measure of the size of the social "pie" would reflect all the items people value, not just goods and services traded on organized markets. Thus, the goal of wealth maximization should perhaps be the greatest possible "gross domestic valuation" or "GDV." GDV is maximized and society is best off when every resource—tangible and intangible, market and non-market—goes to its highest-valued use.

Ross typifies most cases in which the court exhibits no conscious concern for wealth maximization as a social goal and no explicit recognition of the social implications of arrangements that interfere with the parties' ability to bargain freely over the purchase and sale of scarce resources. Rather, the court seems concerned only with the taxpayers' rights and the apparent unfairness of depriving them of the ability to obtain the best price for their property.

Questions: Suppose that in open bidding the prosperous farmers who belong to the Ross Grange were willing to offer $3,000 for the schoolhouse, while the impoverished members of the Ross Mills Church were only willing to pay $2000. Would that necessarily mean that the Grange's members would derive more utility from the schoolhouse? Would the auction system maximize utility?

3. If some allocations might be wealth maximizing but not utility maximizing (and vice versa), one should be careful in choosing what to maximize. This Chapter has already explored some of the difficulties of adopting utility maximization as a goal. In particular, it is impossible to gauge even one person's level of utility or satisfaction. Even if it were possible, one cannot compare the value of one person's utils to another

person's utils. In addition to the problems of measuring and making interpersonal comparisons of utility, utility maximization also has undesirable distributional implications. Some people may have a greater capacity to enjoy life and derive satisfaction from scarce resources. Following the principle of utility maximization, resources would be allocated to those happy-go-lucky individuals who have a greater capacity for enjoyment while dour and impossible-to-satisfy law or economics professors would go without any resources.

Wealth maximization avoids some of the measurement problems associated with utility maximization. Although one may not trust what people always *say* about how highly they value a particular good or service, one can usually trust their behavior when they express their willingness (and ability) to pay through the actual purchase or sale of resources. Moreover, while the utils of two people are not comparable, one person's dollar is as valuable as another's. Money thus provides a common measuring rod for comparing the relative values that different persons attach to particular resources.

Because wealth is much easier to quantify than utility, economists customarily use individuals' relative willingness and ability to pay money to judge the propriety of a particular reallocation of resources. But defining the value of a resource according to peoples' willingness and ability to pay for it also has distributional implications. Wealth maximizing inevitably requires that a greater share of resources go to wealthier people. Even if the poor congregation of the Ross Mills Church of God coveted the schoolhouse while the prosperous farmers of the Grange only mildly preferred it, the Grange's greater wealth might enable the farmers to outbid the Church.

> *Questions:* If the New York Court of Appeals had upheld the school district's decision to sell the schoolhouse to the Ross Mills Church of God for $2,000, can one be certain that that decision would interfere with wealth maximization, i.e., prevent the schoolhouse from going to its most valuable use? Might a subsequent *reallocation* correct the inefficiency resulting from the school district's decision?

4. In an earlier appeal before the New York Commissioner of Education, the Commissioner had upheld the district's discretion to sell to a lower bidder on the ground that "[t]he type and character of the purchaser * * * is often a matter of vital import to the rural communities of this State. * * * If the sale were mandated to be to the highest bidder, it may well be that a 'saloon', filling station or other enterprise undesirable to a specific community might be forced upon it." 127 N.E.2d at 699.

Suppose that the Grange would derive more utility from the schoolhouse than the Church, and the Grange was willing and able to pay more than the Church. Does this mean that the Grange's use of the schoolhouse is the most valuable use? Others in the community might be affected by the sale of the schoolhouse to the Grange, as they might be affected by the sale to a saloon. Those adversely (or positively) affected by the sale to a particular party might even be willing and able to express their desires by paying to ensure that the schoolhouse went to a particular party.

Question: If the preferences of parties adversely (or positively) affected by a sale are not taken into account, does a decision to sell the schoolhouse to the highest bidder necessarily maximize utility? Wealth?

C. COMPARING UTILITY AND WEALTH MAXIMIZATION: THE PARETO CRITERIA AND THE ROLE OF COMPENSATION

Both utility and wealth maximization share a common feature— judgments as to the desirability of allocations depend on the initial distribution of certain characteristics among society's members. For utility maximization, the characteristic is the capacity to derive happiness, pleasure, or satisfaction; in the case of wealth maximization, the characteristic is wealth. Many find the implications of relying for policy purposes on initial distributions of capacity to derive pleasure or of wealth troubling. A classification scheme designed by Vilfredo Pareto in the early 1900's provides one solution to this problem and also to the analytical difficulties presented by the impossibility of interpersonal utility comparisons. A neutral, nonjudgmental method for identifying desirable allocations and changes in the allocation of goods, Pareto's system still enjoys wide-spread use because of its appealing and generally accepted criteria for judgment.

The first application of the Pareto criteria is to evaluate the desirability of *changes* in the distribution of goods. Pareto's system allows that evaluation without regard to the desirability of the *initial* distribution among individuals of either their abilities to pay or enjoy and without the need for interpersonal utility comparisons. Imagine a society in which all resources have already been allocated to particular individuals. Now imagine a change in allocations that left at least one person better off and no one worse off. Surely that change is desirable from any perspective. Economists refer to such a change in the allocation of resources as a *Pareto superior* change.

The voluntary exchange of goods or services for money or other goods or services is a simple example of a Pareto superior reallocation of rights. The optometrist, Cidis, only agreed to sell the contact lenses to Carol Ann White because he valued the $225 more than the lenses and the labor required to fit them. White agreed to buy the lenses because she thought she would be better off with them than with the $225. At least one party is better off, probably both. If the parties are acting rationally and no one else is adversely affected by the sale, only a misanthrope would prefer the original allocation of resources to the reallocation.

Any reallocation of resources that leaves at least one person worse off is described as *Pareto inferior.* If Cidis is forced to give the lenses to White without charge, then she is better off but he is worse off. From a utility maximizing perspective, one cannot say that her gain in utility is greater than his loss in utility. Because one person is worse off, economists conclude that the change is Pareto inferior to the prior allocation.

Pareto superiority and inferiority are ways of evaluating changes in allocations; a reallocation is Pareto superior if at least one party is made better off and no one is made worse off, but Pareto inferior if at least one party is made worse off. A second common use of Pareto's system is to evaluate allocations themselves rather than changes in allocations. *Pareto optimal* describes a characteristic of an allocation rather than a reallocation.

An allocation of resources is Pareto optimal if there is no possible reallocation that could make at least one person better off without making someone worse off. Suppose that society has allocated its resources so that Cidis has the contact lenses (along with the skill to fit them) and White has $225. If Cidis is willing to fit and sell the lenses for $225 and White is willing and able to pay that price, this original allocation is *not* Pareto optimal because a later exchange (reallocation) could make someone person better off without making anyone worse off. Now suppose that White buys the lenses for $225. Now no reallocation could make anyone better off without making someone worse off. If the contact lenses are with the person who values them most, then no one will be willing and able to pay her enough to make her give them up. That is Pareto optimal; optimal since all resources are going to their highest valued use; "Pareto" optimal because no further Pareto superior reallocations are possible.

Given a limited amount of resources, it is possible for more than one Pareto optimal allocation to exist. Suppose Cidis owns the contact lenses and has the skills required to fit them, while White strongly desires the lenses but does not have $225. The allocation of the lenses to Cidis is Pareto optimal because White cannot be made better off (by giving her the lenses) without making Cidis worse off. Yet, if the lenses are initially allocated to White, that allocation may also be Pareto optimal, since White cannot give Cidis the lenses without making herself worse off and White may be unwilling to sell them to Cidis for any price he would be willing to pay.

Although Pareto's system of evaluating allocations and reallocations of resources is widely accepted, its practical value is limited. The Pareto criteria for evaluating changes in allocations are quite strict: if a million people benefit and one is harmed, the reallocation is still Pareto inferior. If many different allocations of resources pass the test of Pareto optimality, how can one determine which allocation is best? United States v. Causby examines one possible method of expanding the usefulness of Pareto's classifications: compensation for forced reallocations.

UNITED STATES v. CAUSBY

Supreme Court of the United States, 1946.
328 U.S. 256, 66 S.Ct. 1062, 90 L.Ed. 1206.

DOUGLAS, JUSTICE.

* * *

Respondents own 2.8 acres near an airport outside of Greensboro, North Carolina. It has on it a dwelling house, and also various outbuildings which were mainly used for raising chickens. The end of the airport's northwest-southeast runway is 2,220 feet from respondents' barn and 2,275 feet from their house. The path of glide to this runway passes directly over the property—which is 100 feet wide and 1,200 feet long. The 30 to 1 safe glide angle approved by the Civil Aeronautics Authority passes over this property at 83 feet, which is 67 feet above the house, 63 feet above the barn and 18 feet above the highest tree. * * *

* * * Since the United States began operations in May, 1942, its four-motored heavy bombers, other planes of the heavier type, and its fighter planes have frequently passed over respondents' land buildings in considerable numbers and rather close together. They come close enough at times to appear barely to miss the tops of the trees and at times so close to the tops of the trees as to blow the old leaves off. The noise is startling. And at night the glare from the planes brightly lights up the place. As a result of the noise, respondents had to give up their chicken business. As many as six to ten of their chickens were killed in one day by flying into the walls from fright. The total chickens lost in that manner was about 150. Production [of eggs] also fell off. The result was the destruction of the use of the property as a commercial chicken farm. Respondents are frequently deprived of their sleep and the family has become nervous and frightened. Although there have been no airplane accidents on respondents' property, there have been several accidents near the airport and close to respondents' place. These are the essential facts found by the Court of Claims. On the basis of these facts, it found that respondents' property had depreciated in value. It held that the United States had taken an easement over the property on June 1, 1942, and that the value of the property destroyed and the easement taken was $2,000.

* * *

* * * [T]he United States conceded on oral argument that if the flights over respondents' property rendered it uninhabitable, there would be a taking compensable under the Fifth Amendment. It is the owner's loss, not the taker's gain, which is the measure of the value of the property taken. Market value fairly determined is the normal measure of the recovery. And that value may reflect the use to which the land could readily be converted, as well as the existing use. If, by reason of the frequency and altitude of the flights, respondents could not use this land for any purpose, their loss would be complete. It would be as complete as if the United States had entered upon the surface of the land and taken exclusive possession of it.

We agree that in those circumstances there would be a taking. Though it would be only an easement of flight which was taken, that easement, if permanent and not merely temporary, normally would be the equivalent of a fee interest. It would be a definite exercise of complete dominion and control over the surface of the land. The fact that the planes never touched the surface would be as irrelevant as the absence in this day of the feudal livery of seisin on the transfer of real estate. * * * In the supposed case the line of flight is over the land. And the land is appropriated as directly and completely as if it were used for the runways themselves.

There is no material difference between the supposed case and the present one, except that here enjoyment and use of the land are not completely destroyed. But that does not seem to us to be controlling. The path of glide for airplanes might reduce a valuable factory site to grazing land, an orchard to a vegetable patch, a residential section to a wheat field. Some value would remain. But the use of the airspace immediately above the land would limit the utility of the land and cause a diminution in its value. * * *

* * * The airplane is part of the modern environment of life, and the inconveniences which it causes are normally not compensable under the Fifth Amendment. The airspace, apart from the immediate reaches above the land, is part of the public domain. We need not determine at this time what those precise limits are. Flights over private land are not a taking, unless they are so low and so frequent as to be a direct and immediate interference with the enjoyment and use of the land. We need not speculate on that phase of the present case. For the findings of the Court of Claims plainly establish that there was a diminution in value of the property and that the frequent, low-level flights were the direct and immediate cause. We agree with the Court of Claims that a servitude has been imposed upon the land.

Notes and Questions

1. The reallocation of rights in *Causby* seems wealth maximizing since the government probably would have been willing to pay more for the use of the Causbys' airspace than the Causbys would have been willing to pay to keep it. The reallocation may even have been utility maximizing, though an informed guess is harder to make, because there is no easy way to compare (or even talk about) the pleasure or satisfaction lost by the chicken farmers and gained by the government. For a reallocation to be Pareto superior, however, neither party can be left worse off as a result. Without sufficient compensation to return the harmed party to her earlier position, the Pareto criteria for superiority will not be met. Full compensation ensures that the reallocation of airspace rights from the Causbys to the military was Pareto superior.

If a reallocation is Pareto superior, it increases both social utility and wealth. Consider the position of one party (the government in *Causby*) who is entitled to take another's property only after fully compensating the other. In *Causby*, the compensation awarded was $2,000. If that figure was properly calculated, the Causbys would suffer neither decreased utility nor reduced wealth from the taking. If either loss occurred, compensation was not truly "full." At this point, a rational government would only take the Causbys' property if the benefits exceeded $2,000. Should the government proceed with the taking, it must value the airspace more (get more utility from the airspace) than the $2,000. The efficient result is that government has more wealth and utility and the Causbys have no less.

Questions: Is the government more or less likely to take private property if compensation is not required? Are such uncompensated reallocations (takings) utility maximizing? Wealth maximizing?

2. The government in the taking context does not consciously consider the utility and wealth maximizing consequences of a reallocation any more than do private parties to an exchange. It is extremely unlikely that either the optometrist or the contact lens purchaser in *Cidis* actually considered the social implications of their exchange of resources or that the school district in *Ross* considered whether the sale to the Church affected the aggregate level of society's wealth. The beauty of the compensation requirement is that utility and wealth are maximized by people concerned only with their own well-being.

3. While full compensation is sufficient to guarantee that utility and wealth are maximized, it is not always necessary. A reallocation without compensation may also maximize utility and wealth. If a decisionmaker (such as a court or legislature) knows for certain which resource use generates the most utility or is valued most highly then compensation is unnecessary. Thus, in *Causby,* the court could have simply allowed the government to invade the Causby's airspace without paying any compensation.

Without compensation, however, it is difficult to ascertain which allocations are utility and wealth maximizing. The reallocation in *Causby* was almost certainly wealth maximizing. The loss of the Causby's chicken farm was a necessary sacrifice if the runway was to be used for military operations. During World War II, military operations were extremely important and valuable in promoting national interests of the United States. As measured by willingness and ability to pay, the value of the airspace for defense purposes would seem to be much greater than its value to the Causbys for quietly raising chickens. To ensure wealth maximization, it seems unnecessary to put this reallocation to the compensation test.

Because of the difficulties inherent in systematically comparing the Causbys' loss in utility to the nation's gain, however, it is harder to conclude that the reallocation is utility maximizing without compensation. It is easily said that all Americans should be pleased by the liberation of Europe from the Nazis. But one cannot rigorously compare the government's gain from using that runway to the Causby's loss when the government destroyed their livelihood and the peace and quiet of their family farm. The difficulty in comparing utility gains and losses among different people makes the compensation test more necessary to ensure that a reallocation maximizes utility.

4. The analytical difficulties inherent in utility maximization have led many scholars in law and economics to focus on wealth maximization. Since it is easier to measure, some find wealth a useful surrogate for utility. For others, wealth maximization's appeal rests on its own merits. Because maximizing wealth does not always maximize utility, however, several schools of thought in economics have emerged.

Under one school, the Pareto criteria are appropriate for judging whether a reallocation is efficient. This view implies that full compensation must be paid whenever a reallocation of resources would otherwise leave someone worse off. Without compensation, there is no way to be certain that the benefits enjoyed by the winning party outweigh the harm suffered by the loser.

Since many changes in policy involve making some people better off and some worse off, economists Kaldor and Hicks studied alternatives to the compensation requirement. Under the *Kaldor–Hicks* position, compensation need not be paid for a reallocation to be efficient. A reallocation is efficient if there is sufficient gain to create the *potential* for full compensation. As long as the winner gains more than the loser loses, the loser does not actually have to be paid.

Like Pareto's approach, the Kaldor–Hicks approach requires compensation that is "full," that is, enough compensation that the loser would be no worse off after the reallocation. If the winner would be willing and able to pay such "full compensation," then the reallocation meets the Kaldor–Hicks test and the compensation need not actually be paid. From the Kaldor–Hicks perspective, it is not necessary, or even desirable, that the compensation be paid; compensating everyone who suffers as a result of state action is complicated and expensive, and interferes with the government's everyday operation.

In *Causby,* the Paretian perspective would require that full compensation actually be paid in order to be certain that the benefit to the government from using the airspace over the chicken farm outweighed the Causbys' losses. Under the Kaldor–Hicks position, since it was obvious that the value of the airspace to a wartime military was greater than its value to the Causbys in raising chickens, compensation was unnecessary for the taking to be efficient.

A policy designed to ensure that the loser is "no worse off" inevitably requires a measure of the appropriate level of compensation. To be "no worse off," the loser must receive enough compensation to obtain the same level of utility as before the reallocation.

Questions: If the government would be willing and able to pay "full compensation" in *Causby,* does the Kaldor–Hicks approach maximize both utility and wealth? If the potential compensation for a taking is calculated by the property's fair market value, can a policy maker be assured that the Kaldor-Hicks criterion maximizes both utility and wealth?

5. The preceding note focused on the Pareto and Kaldor–Hicks criteria for evaluating reallocations of resources. To test your understanding of the utility and wealth maximization characteristics of these alternative tests, consider the following policy analysis. Suppose that the decisionmaker could establish the maximum each party was willing and able to pay for the airspace and found that the Government was willing and able to pay more. Following the Kaldor–Hicks requirement, the decisionmaker would then award the airspace to the Government, figuring that, since the Government was willing and able to pay more, it could potentially compensate the Causbys.

Questions: Would the decisionmaker's approach guarantee that both utility and wealth were maximized? Does the reallocation from the Causbys to the Government meet the Pareto and Kaldor–Hicks criteria for superior reallocations?

6. In this book, an efficient allocation of resources is one that cannot be improved in either the Paretian or Kaldor–Hicks sense. If an allocation is efficient, a reallocation that benefits one person more than it harms another is impossible and compensation is unavailable. When describing a change in the law as efficient, the Kaldor–Hicks convention is usually followed, although Pareto's approach is not abandoned. Pareto's approach is appealing for reasons unrelated to wealth or utility maximization. While economics typically has little to say about what is fair or just, Pareto's criteria are appealing from a fairness perspective; justice seems to require compensation of people who, like the Causbys, suffer from a governmental policy.

D. EFFICIENCY AND EQUITY

Economists usually resist identifying particular individuals or classes of people as the proper recipients of rights to use or consume certain resources. To seem more scientific and to increase the acceptability of their conclusions among people with diverse social and political perspectives, they work hard to preserve the appearance of neutrality in their analysis. Economic analysis typically focuses on determining which allocation of scarce resources maximizes wealth. Economics is generally concerned with efficiency, not fairness.

Focusing on efficiency rather than fairness does not make economics a neutral and unbiased exercise. Directing resources to their most valuable uses and measuring value according to willingness and ability to pay biases allocations towards those with the greatest ability to pay. Among individuals with equally strong desires to own a certain house, the individual with the greater willingness and ability to express that desire by giving up money or other resources is judged the highest-valuing user; allocating the resource to his use is, by definition, allocatively efficient. Because efficiency analysis proceeds from a preexisting set of endowments of wealth, it does not question whether the initial distribution of "abilities to pay" is proper.

PITSENBERGER v. PITSENBERGER

Court of Appeals of Maryland, 1980.
287 Md. 20, 410 A.2d 1052.

MURPHY, CHIEF JUDGE.

This is the first case in which we consider the constitutionality of Maryland's new legislation on property disposition in divorce and annulment * * *

* * *

John and Mary Pitsenberger were married on June 30, 1962, in Alexandria, Virginia. Five children were born as a result of the marriage. In August of 1978, Mary left the family home in Rockville, Maryland, taking two of the parties' five minor children and $10,000 from the parties' joint savings account. About one month later, the other three children went to live with Mary in a small three bedroom townhouse in Derwood, Maryland. Mary rented the house on a month-to-month lease, but she was informed that the lease would not be renewed after May of 1979. While living with Mary, the children remained enrolled in the neighborhood schools near the family home. Mary drove them to school each day.

On January 2, 1979, Mary filed a bill of complaint for a divorce *a mensa et thoro* on the grounds of constructive desertion in the Circuit Court for Montgomery County. She sought pendente lite custody of the children, child support, alimony and, pursuant to § 3–6A–06(d), an exclusive use and possession order for the family home and family use personal property (furniture, appliances, household furnishings and a 1973 Dodge Dart). On February 9, 1979, John filed his answer and a cross-bill of complaint for divorce *a mensa et thoro* on the grounds of desertion.

On February 16, 1979, a hearing was held before a domestic relations master to determine pendente lite the issues of child custody and support, alimony, and the need of the parties and the children to remain in the family home. Mary testified that she was on welfare and lacked funds to rent another house or apartment. Despite John's yearly salary of approximately $47,000, she said she had received no child support since August, 1978. With respect to alternative living arrangements, Mary explained that her mother's residence, a small three bedroom house in Alexandria, Virginia, provided insufficient living room for her family. The only other alternative was to stay at the three bedroom house of her brother-in-law and his wife and two children. Even if they could reside there on an emergency basis, she would have to drive each day from Bowie, Maryland, to the children's schools.   * * *

The master recommended that Mary be awarded pendente lite custody of the minor children and that John pay $1,000 per month child support, as well as pay the mortgage, taxes and insurance for the family home. The master also recommended that Mary be awarded pendente lite use of the family home, the family personal property located in the home and the Dodge Dart * * *. These recommendations were adopted by the circuit court on May 23, 1979, and its order specified that Mary was awarded the *exclusive* use of the family home.

* * *

John * * * argues that § 3–6A–06 permits the unlawful taking of private property without just compensation in violation of the Fifth and Fourteenth Amendments of the United States Constitution, Article 24 of the Maryland Declaration of Rights, and Article III, section 40 of the Maryland Constitution. John contends that the use and possession order signed by the court on May 23, 1979, effectively takes his property by awarding Mary the exclusive use of the family home and family use personal property. John asserts that he is entitled to compensation in the amount of the fair market value of his possessory interest in the family home and for relocation expenses.

To constitute a taking in the constitutional sense, so that the State must pay compensation, the state action must deprive the owner of all beneficial use of the property * * * [I]t is not enough for the property owner to show that the state action causes substantial loss or hardship. John, as guardian of his minor children, is charged with their support, care and welfare. Because his children have the use of the family home and family use personal property, John is in fact using his property to properly house his children. John therefore has not been deprived of all beneficial use of his property. In sum, the use and possession order does not amount to a "taking" of private property in violation of the federal or state constitutions.

We thus conclude that Mary was properly awarded pendente lite use and possession of the family and family use personal property.

Notes and Questions

1. The Maryland statute applied in *Pitsenberger* required a divorce court to divide a couple's property "fairly and equitably." In *Pitsenberger,* fairness and equity apparently required that Mary keep the family home and car, while John be ordered to leave the home. Three possible approaches to the equity and fairness issue are discussed below.

a. *Just Desserts.* The property should be assigned to the most deserving spouse. This approach requires a definition of "deserving." Perhaps the home and car should be awarded to the person who wants to remain married. If, hypothetically, John wanted to remain married but Mary insisted on a divorce after beginning an adulterous liaison, Mary should get nothing. Alternatively, perhaps the spouse who needs the property most deserves it. In that case, the lion's share should go to unemployed Mary while salaried John gets little or nothing.

b. *Equality of Treatment.* After selling the home and car, the decisionmaker divides the proceeds evenly between the parties. Under this rule, the Pitsenbergers should share the market value of these possessions.

c. *Ratified Consent.* The court should award the property to the individual in whose name the property is held and enforce any reallocation to which the parties consented. Thus, the court should enter an order that the property in John's and Mary's names belonged to John and Mary respectively, but should approve any swaps the two might agree to make.

Questions: Which view of fairness most closely approaches wealth maximization? Which views most closely reflect or offend our sense of fairness or equity?

2. An efficiency perspective on this distributional question might suggest that the property should be awarded to the person willing and able to pay more for it.

Questions: If the court awarded the home and car to the person who valued the property more, to whom would the property probably be awarded? Would this be a wealth maximizing allocation of resources?

3. People's willingness and ability to pay to influence the allocation of resources such as the Pitsenberger's house naturally depends on their wealth. The allocation of John's income between Mary and John is quite likely to influence the value they place on the house. Because the distribution of wealth among people influences the allocations that result from bargaining, changes in the distribution of wealth may change the allocation of resources. Alternative allocations of John's salary will affect who gets the house.

Compare two allocations of John's salary. In the first, Mary is awarded none of his salary and, in the second, Mary is awarded 70% of his salary. Imagine that after these distributions of John's salary are made, the house is allocated to the person willing and able to pay the most for it. Under the first allocation, it is quite probable that John will get the house. Under the second, it is more likely that Mary will get the house.

Question: Do the alternative allocations of John's salary affect the efficiency of the allocation of the house?

4. Returning to the principle of ratified consent, suppose that, after much discussion, the parties agreed that Mary would be allowed to rent the house, car and other property for $200 per month from her welfare check.

Questions: Would enforcing such a solution be wealth maximizing? Would it be utility maximizing? Does the fact that both parties consent to this arrangement make it seem fairer?

Chapter 2

======================================

PROPERTY RIGHTS AND
NUISANCE LAW

The institution of private property is one of the foundations of the common law. A property right is a right to the control of a valuable resource, tangible resources such as land or automobiles as well as intangibles such as labor or a patentable idea. Control includes the right to use or consume a resource or to transfer it to another. The economic analysis of property law examines why and when property rights are created, how to protect such rights, and to whom such rights should be assigned.

A. EXTERNALITIES AND INEFFICIENCY

The law governing real property use is an obvious place to begin the journey into efficiency analysis. The market for the right to *possess* land provides a convenient focus for economists' bargaining orientation. As applied to property, however, the efficiency goal is to allocate each parcel of land to its most valuable *use*. While the familiar market in land sales readily accommodates bargaining to determine which user should possess a particular parcel, no comparably well-developed market exists to facilitate bargaining over which of several conflicting uses of neighboring parcels should prevail. As the following materials reveal, solutions to incompatible uses involve the allocation of property rights as well as common law and regulatory approaches.

1. INTERNALIZING EXTERNALITIES THROUGH DAMAGE AWARDS

ORCHARD VIEW FARMS, INC. v. MARTIN MARIETTA ALUMINUM, INC.

United States District Court Oregon, 1980.
500 F.Supp. 984.

BURNS, CHIEF JUDGE:

This diversity case is before the court on remand from the Ninth Circuit Court of Appeals for a retrial on the issue of punitive damages.

On March 31, 1971, Orchard View Farms, Inc. (Orchard View) filed this trespass action, seeking compensatory and punitive damages for injuries to its orchards between March 31, 1965 and the filing date. These injuries were alleged to have been caused by fluoride emitted from the aluminum reduction plant operated by Martin Marietta Aluminum, Inc. (the company or Martin Marietta). In April and May, 1973, the case was tried to a jury, which awarded Orchard View $103,655 compensatory damages and $250,000 punitive damages.

* * *

In essence, any business is socially obliged to carry on an enterprise that is a net benefit, or at least not a net loss, to society. * * *

In a world where all costs of production were borne by the enterprise, determining whether a firm produced a net benefit, or at least not a net detriment, to society would be as simple as examining the company's balance sheet of income and expenses. In the real world the task is more complex, because enterprises can sometimes shift a portion of their costs of production onto others. In the case of an industrial plant emitting pollution, those harmed by the emissions are, in effect, involuntarily bearing some of the firm's production costs.

Our society has not demanded that such externalized costs of production be completely eliminated. Instead, we tolerate externalities such as pollution as long as the enterprise remains productive: that is, producing greater value than the total of its internalized and externalized costs of production. A business that does not achieve net productivity is harmful to society, detracting from the standard of living it is designed to enhance. Because firms can sometimes impose a portion of their production costs upon others, the mere fact that a company continues to operate at a profit is not in itself conclusive evidence that it produces a net benefit to society.

Our system of law attempts to ensure that businesses are, on balance, socially beneficial by requiring that each enterprise bear its total production costs, as accurately as those costs can be ascertained. A fundamental means to this end is the institution of tort liability, which requires that persons harmed by business or other activity be compensated by the perpetrator of the damage. * * *

* * *

A business enterprise has a societal obligation to determine whether its emissions will result in harm to others. Because the damage from pollution can be difficult to perceive due to its subtle or incremental nature, and because it can be difficult to trace to its cause, the obligation of the enterprise extends not only to observation of property in the surrounding region but also to initiation and completion of unbiased scientific studies designed to detect the potential adverse effects of the substances emitted.

I find that the company failed to fulfill this obligation before or during the 1965–71 claim period by taking less than full cognizance of the damage inflicted upon the orchards and by generally shirking its responsibility to undertake competent scientific inquiry into the adverse effects of its emissions.

Notes and Questions

1. The court characterized the pollution in *Orchard View Farms* as an "externalized cost" of Martin Marietta's aluminum-making activities. A cost is "external to" or "outside of" an economic actor's decisionmaking if he is not required to account for it when maximizing his well-being. If it does not have to pay for the damage to Orchard View Farms, Martin Marietta does not need to consider that damage when deciding how to maximize profits from its aluminum production. Industrial pollution is a classic example of an external cost.

Externalities are costs imposed or benefits conferred on others as a result of an individual's activities that he is not required to (in the case of costs) or able to (in the case of benefits) take into account in his decisionmaking.

Questions: What is an example of an external benefit one landowner might confer on another? How do externalities affect the extent to which people impose costs and confer benefits on others?

2. Using their current technologies, the plaintiff cannot grow trees and the defendant cannot produce aluminum solely within their own parcels' boundaries without affecting their neighbors. The air the farm uses to nourish its trees is the same air Martin Marietta uses to carry away its airborne fluoride particles. Neither party is interested in possessing the other's land, so the allocation of the land is not at issue. The issue involves uses of land and the allocation of a second resource, the stream of air. It is not possible for both parties to use that stream of air compatibly using their current technologies. While the farm may be able to grow its trees under a dome with filtered air or the plant may be able to wash all of the fluoride particles out of its emissions, neither possibility is presented in this case. The issue is who gets the right to use the stream of air.

Questions: The plaintiff was awarded damages to compensate it for the harm to its trees from the fluoride particles. Does that mean that the use of the stream of air was been allocated to the farm? Does it mean that the farm's use of the air was the more highly-valued use?

3. Consider how the court in *Orchard View Farms* viewed its role in the process of achieving allocative efficiency: "Our system of law attempts to ensure that businesses are, on balance, socially beneficial by requiring that each enterprise bear its total production costs."

> *Questions:* Is the court's task finding which use is more valuable? Or does the court merely enable other parties to determine which use is more valuable? Note how this compares to the court's role in United States v. Causby in Chapter 1. Did either court decide which use is the most valuable or did it merely facilitate the determination? If the court did not decide how resources were allocated, who did?

4. Imagine a transaction between a buyer and seller of one ton of aluminum ingot. The seller is willing to sell aluminum for no less than $4 a ton and the buyer is willing and able to pay as much as $4.50 a ton. An exchange appears to be Pareto superior. The difference between the values the buyer and setter attach to the aluminum appears to ensure that the costs of producing a ton of aluminum (the bauxite ore, the electricity, the labor) are outweighed by the benefit the ton provides to the buyer.

From *Orchard View Farms,* however, one of the costs of producing aluminum is damage to the neighboring farm. If forced to pay damages resulting from his pollution, the manufacturer might be unable to sell that ton of ingot at a price high enough to ensure a profit. Once all the costs are considered, the buyer may be unwilling to pay the full cost of a ton of aluminum. Without internalizing costs, an inefficiently large amount of aluminum may be produced.

> *Question:* What damages should be awarded to ensure that the allocatively efficient amount of resources are devoted to aluminum production?

5. The court's main concern in *Orchard View Farm* was that the defendant pay for his external costs. The external costs need not be eliminated; as much pollution as is efficient may continue. An allocatively efficient level of output of aluminum will occur even if the plaintiff is not compensated, as long as the defendant gives up an amount equal to the external costs imposed. The determination of the amount of plaintiff's injury is critical to calculating the optimal level of payment the firm must internalize, however, and it seems only fair that the payment should go to the person who suffers. Damages give plaintiffs an incentive to provide evidence on the magnitude of the external costs.

> *Question:* If the damages were calculated, paid, and then dumped into the ocean (after taking out the attorneys' fee, of course!), would the defendant still take the amount of its liability for damages into account in deciding how much to produce?

6. In some cases, particularly class actions for environmental harms, damages are paid into a fund dedicated to a public use. To create proper incentives for the polluter, however, it must be assured that the polluter does not benefit from such a fund.

> Questions: If, instead of dumping the damages into the ocean or paying them to the plaintiff, the damages were paid into a drug rehabilitation program or the school budget in the town where the factory was

located, would the payment of damages still provide the proper incentives to the polluter?

2. INTERNALIZING EXTERNALITIES THROUGH REGULATION

UNITED STATES v. THE CITY OF NIAGARA FALLS

U.S. District Court, Western District of New York, 1989.
706 F.Supp. 1053.

CURTIN, DISTRICT JUDGE.

* * *

* * * Defendant City of Niagara Falls [City] owns and operates a municipal sewerage system consisting of the WWTP [Niagara Falls Wastewater Treatment Plant] and a related ancillary wastewater and stormwater collection system, which includes the FST [Falls Street Tunnel]. The FST is a large, rock-hewn tunnel under the streets of Niagara Falls, New York, that for many years collected sewage, industrial waste, stormwater and groundwater and sent the combined flow to the WWTP for treatment prior to discharge into the Niagara River. * * *

During the early 1970s, it became evident that the WWTP was discharging an unacceptably high amount of toxic pollutants into the river. On January 9, 1974, pursuant to Section 402(a) of the Clean Water Act, the Regional Administrator of the Environmental Protection Agency [EPA] issued defendant NPDES Permit No. NY0026336, effective January 30, 1975, which established the terms and conditions under which the City may discharge pollutants. Pursuant to that permit, a new system was constructed at the WWTP to allow for chemical-physical treatment of sewage, followed by carbon adsorption. Completed in early 1978 at an approximate cost of $61 million (75% of which was derived from federal grants, and 12.5% from state grants), the carbon treatment system failed in July, 1978. [While that system was being repaired, the City discharged untreated water through the FST directly into the river. After repairs, the City failed to redivert the water back through the Wastewater Treatment Plant. Plaintiffs brought suit for a permanent injunction ordering the City to redivert the water.]

* * *

* * * [T]he discharge is a violation of that part of the Clean Water Act fundamental to furthering the Act's major underlying purpose of "establish[ing] a comprehensive long-range policy for the elimination of water pollution," as well as the stated objectives "to restore and maintain the chemical, physical, and biological integrity of the Nation's waters," and to "preserv[e] ... the environment and ... [protect] ... mankind and wildlife from harmful chemicals." The untreated FST discharge, therefore, continues not merely in derogation of "the integrity of the permit process" * * *, but is a violation which undermines the substantive policies, purposes, and objectives of the Clean Water Act, a violation for which this court has already determined plaintiffs are entitled to relief. The instant case is thus one in which injunctive relief, if warranted on balancing the equities, is proper as a means of furthering those policies, purposes and objectives.

* * *

* * * The essential balance that must be struck is whether the harm to the environment caused by the FST discharge is outweighed by the engineering difficulties which the City would face, and the economic burden which the users of the City's sewer system would bear, should all or part of that discharge be ordered to be re-diverted through the WWTP for treatment.

* * *

* * * I am convinced that injunctive relief is appropriate in this case * * *. Accordingly, I find that the most prudent exercise of discretion under all of the circumstances presented would be to grant plaintiff's request for a permanent injunction ordering immediate re-diversion of the maximum portion of the FST flow that can now be accomplished [to the WWTP].

* * *

Notes and Questions

1. The Clean Water Act addresses the external costs of water pollution by limiting the pollutants that can be added to navigable waters by any source, a regulation comparable to limiting the amount of fluoride Martin Marietta can emit from its aluminum plant. Rather than relying on a liability system to internalize costs and thereby reduce externalities to an allocatively efficient level, the Clean Water Act simply prohibits undesirable pollution. It attempts to control the total by estimating the limitations that must be imposed on each pollution source in order to reach its goal. This solution substitutes the government's judgment for the private parties' in calculating the optimal amount of pollution. Economists usually assume that individuals can determine better than government bureaucrats the value individuals place on resources.

Question: What are the risks of using government directives to control external costs like pollution?

2. The Clean Water Act established a federal system of control over water quality in navigable waters. Without federal regulation of water pollution, states and municipalities could allow or prohibit pollution as they chose. To attract industry and development from neighboring areas, jurisdictions could compete by providing more lenient pollution laws.

Questions: In the context of the Clean Water Act, how does this competition lead to the inefficient allocation of resources? What are the states' incentives without federal intervention and how might they lead to inefficient overpollution?

3. The regulatory approach of the Clean Water Act supplements the common law rights of owners of property on waterways. Sections 850 and 850A of the Restatement (Second) of Torts detail the waterfront property owners' rights. Section 850 states:

> A riparian proprietor is subject to liability for making an unreasonable use of the water or a watercourse or lake that causes harm to another riparian proprietor's reasonable use of water or his land.

Section 850A (h) makes clear that one factor relevant when determining the reasonableness of a use is "the protection of existing values of water uses, land, investments and enterprises." Comment (a) to § 850A concludes that "It is usually unreasonable * * * for a new user to destroy existing values created by a use that was reasonable in its inception."

> *Question:* Translated into its application to waterways, does this Restatement rule lead to an efficient use of the common waterway?

4. Private ownership can encourage the efficient use of a resource when a single owner enjoys all the benefits, and suffers all the costs, of a particular use of that resource. In this situation, no external costs or benefits escape unnoticed. The second major economic advantage of a private property system is that it permits exchange. Bargaining allows resources to be exchanged among users who assign different values and allows rights to be transferred to those who value them most highly. In 1776, Adam Smith lauded this process of exchange in The Wealth of Nations:

> Every individual endeavors to employ his capital so that its produce may be of greatest value. He generally neither intends to promote the public interest, nor knows how much he is promoting it. He intends only his own security, only his own gain. And he is in this led by an invisible hand to promote an end which was no part of his intention. By pursuing his own interest he frequently promotes that of society more effectively than when he really intends to promote it.

The next section explores in greater detail the role of private property and exchange in resolving the externality problems arising from conflicting uses of resources.

3. INTERNALIZING EXTERNALITIES THROUGH PRIVATIZATION

Orchard View Farms and *City of Niagara Falls* provide examples of two different ways the law can reduce the risk of inefficient resource allocation due to externalities. Liability rules such as those applied in *Orchard View Farms* encourage individuals and businesses to consider the impact of their activity on others by making them liable for any external costs they impose. The regulatory scheme in *City of Niagara Falls* employs a judge, bureaucrat or other decisionmaker to evaluate the costs and benefits of using the resource in a particular way and then directly allocate the resource to its most valuable use.

A third potential means of internalizing externalities is *privatization*. If a single person owns a particular resource, he enjoys the benefits of careful management and suffers the costs of abuse—he will use the resource efficiently because both costs and benefits are now "internalized" rather than borne by someone else. Consider how privatization might prevent the "Tragedy of the Commons."

HARDIN, THE TRAGEDY OF THE COMMONS *
162 Science 1243, 1244–45 (December 13, 1968).

The tragedy of the commons develops this way. Picture a pasture open to all. It is to be expected that each herdsman will try to keep as many cattle as possible on the commons. * * * At this point, the inherent logic of the commons remorselessly generate tragedy.

As a rational being, each herdsman seeks to maximize his gains. Explicitly or implicitly, more or less consciously, he asks, "What is the utility to *me* of adding one more animal to my herd?" This utility has one negative and one positive component.

1. The positive component is a function of the increment of one animal. Since the herdsman receives all the proceeds from the sale of the additional animal, the positive utility is nearly +1.

2. The negative component is a function of the additional overgrazing created by one animal. Since, however, the effects of overgrazing are shared by all the herdsmen, the negative utility for any particular decision-making herdsman is only a fraction of –1.

Adding together the component partial utilities, the rational herdsman concludes that the only sensible course for him is to add another animal to his herd. And another; and another.... But this is the conclusion reached by each and every rational herdsman sharing a commons. Therein is the tragedy. Each man is locked into a system that compels him to increase his herd without limit—in a world that is limited. Ruin is the destination toward which all men rush, each pursuing his own best interest in a society that believes in the freedom of the commons. Freedom in a commons brings ruin to all.

* * *

In an approximate way, the logic of the commons has been understood for a long time, perhaps since the discovery of agriculture or the invention of private property * * *.

Notes and Questions

1. The "Tragedy of the Commons" occurs when a decisionmaker's act—adding another animal to the commons—produces a net benefit to the decisionmaker, but imposes such substantial external costs on others that the overall resulting losses outweigh the benefits of the act. Nevertheless, rational herdsmen may continue to add cattle to an overgrazed commons. They know that acting responsibly (not adding cattle) would only allow more self-interested herdsmen to add more. The commons would still be

overgrazed, and the self-sacrificing herdsman would be worse off for behaving responsibly.

2. The following example of cattle grazing in a common field illustrates how overproduction of cattle (or overgrazing of grass) will result from herdsmen's failure to internalize their overgrazing costs. Table 2–1 reflects the benefits from increasing the size of the cattle herd allowed to graze on the common. There is no direct cost to those who allow their cattle to graze. The only cost is to the commons, which loses grass and suffers wear and tear. Column 1 indicates different numbers of grazing cattle. Column 2 indicates how much weight each cow gains as a result of a week of grazing. Column 2 shows that, for some reason, perhaps the cattle's greater contentment, adding a second cow increases the weekly weight gain per cow from 7 to 9 pounds. After the second cow, however, the gain per cow per week declines due to the common's small size and the cows getting in each other's way competing for the best grass. Note that even with eight or nine cattle, they all continue to gain weight. Each of eight or nine people have an incentive to bring a cow to graze. At ten cattle, however, the common is overcrowded, the cattle fight, the field produces less grass, and the cattle lose weight each week. No individual has any incentive to bring a cow to this crowded common so the herd size will level off at nine cows.

Table 2–1

Tragedy of the Commons-Illustrated

(1)	(2)	(3)	(4)
Number of Cattle	Weight Gain per Cow per Week from Grazing	Total Weight Gain per Week	Additional Beef for Society Due to Increasing Herd Size by One Cow
1	7	7	7
2	9	18	11
3	8	24	6
4	7	28	4
5	6	30	2
6	5	30	0
7	4	28	–2
8	3	24	–4
9	1	9	–15
10	–1	–10	–19

An individual deciding whether to put his animal on the common will look at Column 2. That column shows that until there are nine cattle on the common, any person who grazes his cow there will benefit because the cow will gain weight. From a societal viewpoint, however, Columns 3 and 4 rather than Column 2 present the relevant information. Rather than considering individual gains from cattle grazing, the societal perspective considers the number of cattle appropriate to yield the greatest weight of cattle for society as a whole. Column 3 presents the total increase in weight of cattle per week. Column 4 indicates the additional pounds of beef due to increasing the herd size by one cow. Increasing the size from one to two, for instance, increases the total weight gain by seven pounds while increasing the size from three to four increases the total weight gain by four pounds. The total weight gain is greatest at five or six cattle, though adding the sixth cow contributes nothing additional to the weight of beef available to society. Adding cattle beyond six actually diminishes social welfare so the optimum from a social perspective is five or six.

Unlike the individual optimum, which focuses only on column 2, the social optimum accounts for the effect of adding additional cattle on the weight gain by other cattle. The addition of another cow has external effects on the cattle already there. Without recognition of these effects and limitation of the number of cattle, society will tend naturally towards the tragedy of inefficient overuse of the commons. The legal question is how to structure resource use so that the outcome is efficient. One arrangement that may resolve this inefficiency is private property.

> *Questions:* If a single individual owned the commons and was deciding how many cattle to graze, would the private property owner's optimum be the same as the social optimum? If a single individual owned the common and rented it to those who wished to graze cattle on the commons in exchange for a percentage of the weight gain, what number of grazing cattle would generate the greatest profit for the landowner?

3. A second arrangement would be centralizing decisionmaking in a single authority.

> *Question:* If a commune with centralized decisionmaking were to decide how many cattle should graze to gain the most beef, would the communal optimum resemble the private property optimum or the societal optimum?

4. Under a third institutional arrangement, the central authority permits the first cattle raiser to put his cow on the common, but any person who subsequently added an animal would have to pay damages for the decreased beef production of the cattle already there.

> *Question:* Would this damages solution result in the same number of cattle grazing as the private property optimum or the social optimum?

5. Hardin's description of the Tragedy of the Commons as "remorseless" implies that people inevitably will refuse to recognize the obvious and curb their selfish instincts.

> *Question:* If the herdsmen know that too many cattle spoil the commons, why does Hardin assume that they will not voluntarily refrain from pasturing too many animals?

6. The institution of private property can be regarded as a legal response to the problem of external costs. As the previous questions suggest, private property is not the only possible response to the abuse of a common resource. Water and atmospheric pollution by firms like Martin Marietta is as much an inefficient "tragedy" as the overgrazing of a common pasture. Yet the court in *Orchard View Farms* never suggests

that the solution is for Martin Marietta to pollute only the air immediately above its own property; in other words, create a right to "private" air.

The reason should be obvious. It is highly impracticable (if not impossible) to segregate the atmosphere into private "plots" of air at any reasonable expense. When deciding whether to create private rights to a common resource, one must consider whether it is efficient to do so. Creating private property rights—whether to land, water, air, or animals—will only be efficient when the benefits of doing so exceed the costs.

The principal benefit of private rights is the internalization of excessive external costs. Thus, creating a private right will only be beneficial when it cures some inefficiency. For example, dividing a common pasture into private plots might allow a society of herdsmen to increase beef production by 1,000 pounds, because private grazing eliminates overgrazing. If beef sells at $1 a pound, the potential benefit is $1,000.

To ignore the costs of creating property rights, however, would not be sensible. These might include the cost of identifying and/or segregating one owner's property from another's as well as the cost of enforcing the right. Herdsmen deciding to subdivide a common grazing area might have to consider the cost of building fences to identify their land and keep cattle from straying, and of hiring a marshall to settle disputes. If these costs exceed $1,000, common ownership, with all of its externalities, might be more efficient than private ownership.

Harold Demsetz illustrated this point with the history of private property rights among Native Americans. See, Demsetz, Toward a Theory of Property Rights, 57 Am. Econ. Rev. 347 (No. 2, 1967). With the arrival of the French and a commercial fur trade in Labrador, animal pelts became far more valuable. In response to overhunting of furbearing animals such as marten and beaver, the tribes of Labrador quickly developed a system of private rights to land that allowed one individual or family to exclude others from hunting the area.

In contrast, the tribes of the Plains did not develop private rights to land. While overhunting plains buffalo was a problem, to create and enforce a private right to hunt buffalo was costly; buffalo are migratory and ornery beasts, and it was far too expensive to fence them in. In contrast, hunting rights in Labrador could be established by simply blazing trees. Thus, the development of property rights depends as much on its costs as its benefits.

7. The court in *Orchard View Farms* allowed punitive damages to encourage plaintiffs' suits, which force defendants to internalize the costs of pollution. Fearing that the promise of compensation alone was insufficient, the court observed, at 500 F.Supp. 989:

> In the context of pollution, however, the tort system does not always operate smoothly to impose liability for compensatory damages. Among the difficulties encountered are * * * that the harm may be inflicted in small amounts upon a large number of people, none of whom individually suffer sufficient damage to warrant the time and expense of legal action and whose organization into a plaintiff class is

hindered by what has come to be known as the Tragedy of the Commons.

In an accompanying footnote, the court suggested, 500 F.Supp. at 989 n.1:

> Organizing a plaintiff class is hindered by the fact that the benefit of a successful lawsuit against the polluter for compensation is not limited to the plaintiffs. Persons damaged by the pollution but not contributing to the legal action also benefit due to the collateral estoppel effects of the initial lawsuit in subsequent actions and because the first plaintiff or group of plaintiffs has already done the work of organizing some relevant evidence and locating experts willing to testify. Thus, each person damaged by the pollution has an economic incentive to let someone else bring the first lawsuit and then to take a "free ride" or at least a discount excursion to obtaining his own compensation.

The Tragedy of the Commons idea came from a story illustrating that if everyone can benefit from a commonly shared resource without taking into account the costs their activity imposes on others, people have an incentive to overuse that resource. In the context of aluminum production, the manufacturer's failure to take into account its pollution's effect on the common stream of air results in too much pollution and aluminum production relative to the allocatively efficient amount. *Orchard View Farms* prevents the polluter from treating the surrounding air and land as a commons.

The *Orchard View Farm* footnote excerpted above turns the traditional commons illustration on its head. In Hardin's example, people were ignoring external harms and overindulging in grazing. In the footnote, the plaintiffs are ignoring external benefits and underindulging in beneficial lawsuits. Each person to sue a polluter successfully creates an external benefit by assembling evidence of the polluter's activity and halting pollution that may have damaged many. Since no plaintiff producing this benefit is entitled to compensation from others he has benefitted, an underproduction of such suits is likely. Punitive damages increase the incentives.

8. The "commons" approach helps identify which externalities require federal regulation and which are addressed efficiently by state or local regulation. Since efficiency requires the internalization of externalities, the smallest appropriate geographic area over which the regulator must have jurisdiction is the area in which the external effects of the activity in question are felt.

Questions: Based on the regulation of the commons, what is the appropriate level of governmental control, from local to federal, to engage in the following activities: (1) control of water pollution in navigable waters, (2) impose zoning requirements, (3) enforce nuisance law to prevent loud parties or child pornography, (4) reduce acid rain to an efficient level, (5) protect the ozone layer? How is the analysis affected by the desirability of uniformity? Administrability? By the existence of a "national consensus" that everyone should share the same quality of life (e.g., Clean Air Act)?

4. THE PRISONER'S DILEMMA

Imagine the following scenario. You and an accomplice decide to rob a bank. Unfortunately, both of you are arrested just before entering the bank when a sharp-eyed but over-eager bank guard spots the pistols you are both carrying under your coats. You are both put in jail—in separate cells.

The U.S. Attorney offers you the following deal.

"We've got you cold for illegal possession of firearms. That's a two-year sentence right there. But I know you were planning more than just a stroll with a pistol. If I can prove you were attempting to rob that bank, you'll get fifteen years in jail."

You answer, "I never set foot in that bank, and you'll never be able to prove I intended to rob it. Two years is the most you can put me away for."

"Maybe," the U.S. Attorney replies, "and maybe not. But I've got a deal that can get you off scot-free. If you'll agree to testify against your accomplice, I promise to drop the charges against you. You'll spend no time in jail. Of course, your accomplice will get fifteen years."

"That sounds like a good deal," you say. "At least for me. There must be a catch."

"Of course," the U.S. Attorney replies. "I'm making an identical offer to your accomplice. And if you both squeal, you'll both get fifteen years—although I'll recommend five years off for each of you, in light of your cooperation."

Game theorists call this scenario "The Prisoner's Dilemma." The Prisoner's Dilemma illustrates how self-interest can lead rational individuals to pursue a course leading to mutual self-destruction, even when that destruction is perfectly foreseeable.

Consider the plight of the prisoner receiving an offer like the U.S. Attorney's. Whatever the prisoner's accomplice decides, the prisoner is better off testifying. If his accomplice remains silent and the prisoner squeals, the prisoner gets off scot-free; and if the accomplice testifies, the prisoner can still get a fifteen-year sentence reduced to ten by testifying as well.

The accomplice makes the same calculation and reaches the same conclusion. Neither party has an incentive to sacrifice himself by remaining silent. That will only create an opportunity for the other party to get an even greater benefit from squealing. Unless both prisoners can get together somehow to make a deal, they will both testify, to their mutual loss. Their self-destructive actions will be perfectly rational and perfectly foreseeable.

Notes and Questions

1. One obvious connection between the Prisoner's Dilemma and the Tragedy of the Commons is that all individuals are expected to further

their self-interest. Rational individuals will not attempt to control the external costs they impose on others because they recognize that there is nothing to be gained by behaving responsibly. It will not stop others from imposing costs on them. In a world of self-interested individuals, a unilateral attempt to behave responsibly only puts the responsible party at a competitive disadvantage. Thus, rational maximizers cannot be expected to avoid imposing external costs—externalities will not solve themselves. Prisoners seek to minimize their own punishment without regard to their confederate's interests. Herdsmen are expected to maximize their profits without any concern for the welfare of other herdsmen or society.

Question: Assuming that the self-interested model accurately depicts how people make decisions, how can each herdsman's position be analogized to each prisoner's?

2. A second connection among the Prisoner's Dilemma, externalities, and private property is that the Prisoner's Dilemma illustrates the potential gains when parties can find a means to control external costs. If the two prisoners could only get together, they might be able to arrange a deal where each would refuse to testify against the other and both would receive likely sentences of two years rather than ten. Garrett Hardin and others have suggested that one hope of controlling external costs may lie with private property.

Question: How does privatizing the common eliminate the Prisoner's Dilemma for herdsmen?

B. ASSIGNING AND EXCHANGING RIGHTS

1. COMPETING USES AND THE COEXISTENCE OF PROPERTY RIGHTS

Even if it is agreed that assigning private property rights may lead to an efficient allocation of resources, the question remains, to whom should such rights be assigned? Assigning property rights involves more than determining real estate boundaries. Property is not a patch of ground but a collection of rights to the exclusive use of resources. For example, ownership of real property may involve the right to occupy the land; the right to occupy or control the use of the airspace above the land to a particular altitude or even infinitely; the right to receive the sunlight and rain that falls on the land; the right to erect structures on the land that block light and rain from others; the right to clean air passing over the land; and the right to use air passing over the land to carry away smoke and other pollutants. The following cases explore the criteria courts may use in deciding to whom such rights should be assigned.

BRYANT v. LEFEVER
Court of Appeals, 1879.
4 C.P.Div. 172, 48 L.J. 380, C.P.

BRAMWELL, L.J.:

The plaintiff says that he is possessed of a house, that for more than twenty years this house and its occupants have had the wind blow to, over and from it, and that he has, as so possessed, the right that it should continue to do so. That the defendants have interfered with this right and prevented the free access and departure of the wind. He adds that they have committed a nuisance to him as so possessed. He has proved that he is possessed of a house more than twenty years old, that the wind had access to it and passage over it for twenty years without the hindrance recently caused by the defendants; that the defendants have caused a hindrance by putting on the roof of their house (which is as old as the plaintiff's), timber to a considerable height, thereby preventing the wind blowing to and over the plaintiff's house when in some directions, and passing away from it when in others; that this causes his chimneys to smoke as they did not before, to the extent of being a nuisance. The question is if this shews a cause of action. First, what is the right of the occupier of a house in relation to air, independently of length of enjoyment? It is the same as that which land and its owner or occupier have, it is not greater because a house has been built. That puts no greater burthen or disability on adjoining owners. What then is the right of land and its owner or occupier? It is to have all natural incidents and advantages as nature would produce them. There is a right to all the light and heat that would come, to all the rain that would fall, to all the wind that would blow; a right that the rain which would pass over the land should not be stopped and made to fall on it, a right that the heat from the sun should not be stopped and reflected on it, a right that the wind should not be checked, but should be able to escape freely; and if it were possible that these rights were interfered with by one having no right, no doubt an action would lie. But these natural rights are subject to the right of adjoining owners, who for the benefit of the community have and must have rights in relation to that use and enjoyment of their property that qualify and interfere with those of their neighbours; right to use their property in the various ways in which property is commonly and lawfully used. A hedge, a wall, a fruit tree, would each affect the land next to which it was planted or built. They would keep off some light, some air, some heat, some rain when coming from one direction, and prevent the escape of air, of heat, of wind, of rain when coming from the other. But nobody could doubt that in such case no action would lie. Nor will it in the case of a house being built and having such consequences. That is an ordinary and lawful use of property as much so as the building of a wall or planting of a fence, or an orchard. Of course the same reasoning applies to the putting of timber on the top of a house which, if not a common, is a perfectly lawful act, and it would be absurd to suppose that the defendants could lawfully put another storey to their house with the consequences to the plaintiff of which he complains, but cannot put an equal height of timber. These are elementary and obvious considerations, but if borne in mind will assist very materially in the decision of this case.

* * *

But it is said, and the jury have found, that the defendants have done that which has caused a nuisance to the plaintiff's house. We think there is no evidence of this. No doubt there is a nuisance, but it is not of the defendants' causing. They have done nothing in causing the nuisance. Their house and their timber are harmless enough. It is the plaintiff who causes the nuisance by lighting a coal fire in a place the chimney of which is placed so near the defendants' wall that the smoke does not escape, but comes into the house. Let the plaintiff cease to light his fire; let him move his chimney; let him carry it higher, and there would be no nuisance. Who, then, causes it? It would be very clear that the plaintiff did, if he had built the house or chimney after the defendants had put the timber on their roof; and it is really the same though he did so before the timber was there. But (what is in truth the same answer) if the defendants cause the nuisance, they have a right to do so. If the plaintiff has not the right to the passage of air, except subject to the defendants' right to build or put timber on their house, then his right is subject to their right, and though a nuisance follows from the exercise of their right, they are not liable. *Sic utere tuo ut alienum no laedas* is a good maxim. But, in our opinion, the defendants do not infringe it. The plaintiff would, if he succeeded. We are of opinion that judgment should be for the defendants on the cause of action the subject of this appeal.

COASE, THE PROBLEM OF SOCIAL COST *
3 J. L. & Econ. 1, 2, 13 (1960).

This paper is concerned with those actions of business firms which have harmful effects on others. The standard example is that of a factory the smoke from which has harmful effects on those occupying neighbouring properties. The economic analysis of such a situation has usually proceeded in terms of a divergence between the private and social product of the factory * * *. The conclusions to which this kind of analysis seems to have led most economists is that it would be desirable to make the owner of the factory liable for the damage caused to those injured by the smoke, or alternatively, to place a tax on the factory owner varying with the amount of smoke produced and equivalent in money terms to the damage it would cause, or finally, to exclude the factory from residential districts (and presumably from other areas in which the emission of smoke would have harmful effects on others). It is my contention that the suggested courses of action are inappropriate * * *.

* * *

The traditional approach has tended to obscure the nature of the choice that has to be made. The question is commonly thought of as one in which A inflicts harm on B and what has to be decided is: how should we restrain A? But this is wrong. We are dealing with a problem of a reciprocal nature. To avoid the harm to B would inflict harm on A. The real question that has to be decided is: should A be allowed to harm B or should B be allowed to harm A? The problem is to avoid the more serious harm. * * *

* * *

* * * Who caused the smoke nuisance [in Bryant v. LeFever]? The answer seems fairly clear. The smoke nuisance was caused both by the man who built the wall *and* by the man who lit the fires. Given the fires, there would have been no smoke nuisance without the wall; given the wall, there would have been no smoke nuisance without the fires. Eliminate the wall *or* the fires and the smoke nuisance would disappear. [I]t is clear that *both* were responsible and *both* should be forced to include the loss of amenity due to the smoke as a cost in deciding whether to continue the activity which gives rise to the smoke. * * *

The judge's contention that it was the man who lit the fires who alone caused the smoke nuisance is true only if we assume that the wall is the given factor. This is what the judges did by deciding that the man who erected the higher wall had a legal right to do so. The case would have been even more interesting if the smoke from the chimneys had injured the timber. * * * [T]here can be little doubt that the man who lit the fires would have been liable for the ensuing damage to the timber, in spite of the fact that no damage had occurred until the high wall was built by the man who owned the timber.

Notes and Questions

1. In *Bryant,* a pollution case with a novel twist, only the person emitting the smoke suffers the harm. The factual complexity giving rise to the lawsuit is that before the neighbors added another story to their house and piled lumber on top, the wind drew the smoke up the chimney just fine. The argument that the neighbors were the *cause* of the smoke backing up in the chimney is quite appealing. If the neighbors were required to pay damages, then they would have an incentive to internalize the costs of their construction activities.

From Coase's perspective, however, both parties were engaged in activities which, when combined, resulted in damage. If there is no natural or obvious way to determine which party "causes" the harm in an incompatible uses case, the court's decision boils down to which party's use should be protected, the storage of lumber or the drafting of smoke. According to Coase, the problem is to "avoid the more serious harm"; that is, to protect the use with the greater value. Another way to phrase the question is to ask which party should internalize the costs of the activities, that is, be given an incentive to decide whether the activity should continue, cease, or be modified in some way.

Even though both the plaintiff and the defendant could take some action to minimize the cost, one party could avoid the detriment at less cost. Suppose that if the plaintiff must bear the cost of the smoking chimney, his only alternative is building his chimney higher, at a cost of

£60. If the defendant must bear the cost, he might store his timber elsewhere, which would eliminate the plaintiff's harm but result in storage fees of £20 per year. Ignoring the distributional implications, eliminating the harm for £20 is preferred. The same benefit is achieved more inexpensively by making the person who can avoid the injury at the lowest cost liable for the costs.

Realizing that sometimes one party may be better able to avoid the harms of incompatible uses has led law and economics scholars to support rules placing liability on the party who can avoid the injury at the lowest cost, the *best cost avoider*. Ronald Coase's observation that every party to the injury "causes" the injury removes the moral overtones, the aura of blameworthiness, associated with conflicting land uses and allows analysts to focus on maximizing the value of land use. The "best cost avoider" approach supplies a substitute for the "causation" approach.

2. If the plaintiff could avoid the smoke only by building a new chimney for £40 and the defendant could avoid the injury only by renting storage space for £20, the defendant is the best cost avoider. But if the defendant does not have the £20, he will be unable to rent the storage space or pay the £40 for damages. Since neither choice is viable, his only alternative is to cease storing timber. Suppose that storing wood is the defendant's occupation. Putting the defendant out of work may seem to be a harsh result if the plaintiff is wealthy enough to build a higher chimney.

Question: Could such a result possibly be economically efficient?

3. Imagine that the plaintiff could avoid the injury by maintaining a higher chimney at a cost of £60 per year and the defendant could avoid the injury only by building a separate structure to hold his timber, at the cost of £50 per year. The plaintiff's damage, if neither of these precautions is taken, is £40 per year.

Question: If the injury can only be avoided by means that are more expensive than the cost of the accident, is making the best cost avoider liable still allocatively efficient?

STURGES v. BRIDGMAN

Chancery Division, 1879.
XI C.D. 852.

THESIGER, L.J.:

The Defendant in this case is the occupier, for the purpose of his business as a confectioner, of a house in *Wigmore Street*. In the rear of the house is a kitchen, and in that kitchen there are now, and have been for over twenty years, two large mortars in which the meat and other materials of the confectionery are pounded. The Plaintiff, who is a physician, is the occupier of a house in *Wimpole Street*, which until recently had a garden at the rear, the wall of which garden was a party-wall between the Plaintiff's and the Defendant's premises, and formed the back wall of the Defendant's kitchen. The Plaintiff has, however, recently built upon the site of the garden a consulting-room, one of the side walls of which is the wall just described. It has been proved that in the case of the mortars, before and at the time of action brought, a noise was caused which seriously inconveniences the Plaintiff in the use of his consulting-room, and which, unless the Defendant had acquired a right to impose the inconvenience, would constitute an actionable nuisance. The Defendant contends that he had acquired the right * * * by uninterrupted [use] for more than twenty years.

* * * [T]he laws governing the acquisition of easements by [use] stands thus: Consent or acquiescence of the owner of the [affected land] lies at the root of prescription. * * * [A] man cannot, as a general rule, be said to consent to or acquiesce in the acquisition by his neighbour of an easement through an enjoyment of which he has no knowledge, actual or constructive, or which he contests and endeavours to interrupt, or which he temporarily licenses. It is a mere extension of the same notion, or rather it is a principle into which by strict analysis it may be resolved, to hold, that an enjoyment which a man cannot prevent raises no presumption of consent or acquiescence. * * *

It is said that if this principle is applied in cases like the present, and were carried out to its logical consequences, it would result in the most serious practical inconveniences, for a man might go—say into the midst of the tanneries of Bermondsey, or into any other locality devoted to a particular trade or manufacture of a noisy or unsavoury character, and, by building a private residence upon a vacant piece of land, put a stop to such trade or manufacture altogether. The case also is put of a blacksmith's forge built away from all habitations, but to which, in course of time, habitations approach. We do not think that either of these hypothetical cases presents any real difficulty. As regards the first, it may be answered that whether anything is a nuisance or not is a question to be determined, not merely by an abstract consideration of the thing itself, but in reference to its circumstances; what would be a nuisance in Belgrave Square would not necessarily be so in Bermondsey; and where a locality is devoted to a particular trade or manufacture carried on by the traders or manufacturers in a particular and established manner not constituting a public nuisance, Judges and juries would be justified in finding and may be trusted to find, that the trade or manufacture so carried on in that locality is not a private or actionable wrong. As regards the blacksmith's forge, that is really an *idem per item* case with the present. It would be on the one hand in a very high degree unreasonable and undesirable that there should be a right of action for acts which are not in the present condition of the adjoining land, and possibly never will be any annoyance or inconvenience to either its owner or occupier; and it would be on the other hand in an equally degree unjust, and from a public point of view, inexpedient that the use and value of the adjoining land should, for all time and under all circumstances, be restricted and diminished by reason of the continuance of acts incapable of physical interruption, and which the law gives no power to prevent. The smith in the case supposed might protect himself by taking a sufficient curtilage to ensure what he does from being at any time an annoyance to his neighbour, but the neighbour himself would be powerless in the matter. Individual cases of hardship may occur in the strict carrying out of the principle upon which we found our judgment, but the negation of the principle would lead even more to individual hardship, and would at the same time produce a prejudicial effect upon the development of land for residential purposes. The Master of the Rolls in the Court below took substantially the same view of the matter as ourselves and granted the relief which the Plaintiff prayed for, and we are of opinion that his order is right and should be affirmed * * * .

Notes and Questions

1. The confectioner in *Sturges* argued that he had acquired a right to use his noisy mortars because he had used them without uninterruption for more than twenty years (the period traditionally held sufficient to acquire an "easement by prescription" in England). During those years, the plaintiff-doctor had no way to know about the defendant's mortars. Therefore, the doctor was in no position either to have objected or acquiesced to their use. Without the actual or constructive knowledge necessary to challenge the use, the court holds, the presumption of acquiescence (the foundation for an easement by prescription) is untenable and no easement is granted.

Prescriptive easements have a counterpart in the law of adverse possession, which permits a person in possession of another's land to acquire not only the right to use that land but even title to that land. In either case, the use (for an easement) or possession (for title) must be "open and notorious" and the adverse use or possession must continue for a statutory time period. This ensures that the landowner will have an opportunity to detect the use or possession and its adverse character. Easements by prescription and adverse possession serve an efficiency purpose by allocating rights from an owner who is not using his land and who fails to object to another's use or possession of his land to someone using the scarce resource as an owner normally would.

A presumption underlying adverse possession is that the adverse possessor values the land more than someone not using it at all. Under an alternative theory, the person not objecting to a continuously ongoing externality of which he could reasonably have been aware suffers less harm if the adverse use continues than the adverse claimant would suffer if barred from the use or possession after so long.

Questions: Is use always valued more highly than non-use? Do the requirements that the use be open and notorious and continue for a long time period provide any protection for the landowner who values his land in its natural state?

2. Having disposed of the issue of priority in time, Lord Justice Thesiger established that whether an activity is a nuisance depends on all the circumstances, in particular, where the activity is carried out and which party was in the best position to take precautions to avoid harming those whose land uses came later (a blacksmith could, at the time of setting

up his shop, acquire sufficient surrounding land that what he does would be no annoyance to his neighbors).

Question: From the perspective of allocating resources to their most valuable uses, why are these factors relevant to whether a use is a nuisance?

3.   Lord Justice Thesiger was explicitly promoting the development of cities and towns: "From a public point of view, [it would be] inexpedient that the use and value of the adjoining land should, for all time and under all circumstances be restricted and diminished by reason of the continuance of acts incapable of physical interruption." Yet he clearly was concerned with residential development even though the plaintiff in *Sturges* wanted to develop his residence to further his medical practice: "The negation of this principle would * * * produce a prejudicial effect upon the development of land for residential purposes."

From an efficiency perspective, there is no obvious reason to believe that land is generally valued more for residential than industrial or business purposes. The Lord Justice decided that residential use was more valuable but did not indicate what evidence supported his decision. Without evidence as to the value of competing uses, he relied on evidence about the neighborhood's characteristics and, inevitably, on his own values.

Questions: Is there a significant danger that the Lord Justice's closer identification with the doctor, a fellow professional, than with the confectioner, a tradesman, would affect his judgment about the relative value of their activities, about the significance of development of land for residential uses? Could class biases of this sort result in the inefficient allocation of land?

2.   THE COASE THEOREM AND THE EFFICIENT EXCHANGE OF RIGHTS

In a free market with no obstacles to bargaining between the parties, voluntary exchange allocates goods to their most valuable uses. The previous section illustrated courts' attempts to wrestle with cases where the economic issue is the allocation of "costs" rather than goods. In his classic article, The Problem of Social Cost (which may have inspired the law and economics movement), Ronald Coase presented the fundamental insight that voluntary exchange not only allocates goods efficiently, but *costs* as well. Coase proposed that, as long as the parties can bargain freely, they will eventually come to an agreement that minimizes the costs or harms resulting from incompatible property uses. He noted, "It is always possible to modify by transactions in the market the initial legal delimitation of rights. And, of course, if such market transactions are costless, such a rearrangement of rights will always take place if it would lead to an increase in the value of production." That proposition, known as the *Coase Theorem,* is often stated as follows: As long as there are no obstacles to bargaining between the parties involved, resources will be allocated efficiently regardless of how property rights are initially assigned.

Coase's Theorem is a dramatic assertion because it means that, if there are no transaction costs, judges do not affect the allocative efficiency of resource use by assigning rights or liability to one party or the other. As Coase put it, "It is necessary to know whether the damaging business is liable or not for damage caused since without the establishment of this initial delimitation of rights there can be no market transactions to transfer and recombine them. But the ultimate result (which maximizes the value of production) is independent of the legal position if the pricing system is assumed to work without cost. * * * Judges have to decide on legal liability but this should not confuse economists about the nature of the economic problem involved." The excerpted opinions devote much attention to justifying their chosen assignments of rights. Coase's Theorem, however, implies that time could be saved by simply assigning rights randomly. If parties seeking conflicting land uses can bargain about which use should prevail, the party who values his use most highly will always prevail.

Consider the application of Coase's Theorem to *Fontainebleau Hotel*. Does it matter whether the law assigns a property right to cast a shadow to the Fontainebleau, or a right to sunlight to the Eden Roc?

FONTAINEBLEAU HOTEL CORP. v. FORTY–FIVE TWENTY–FIVE, INC.

District Court of Appeals of Florida, 1959.
114 So.2d 357.

PER CURIAM.

This is an interlocutory appeal from an order temporarily enjoining the appellants from continuing with the construction of a fourteen-story addition to the Fontainebleau Hotel, owned and operated by the appellants. Appellee, plaintiff below, owns the Eden Roc Hotel, which was constructed in 1955, about a year after the Fontainebleau, and adjoins the Fontainebleau on the north. Both are luxury hotels, facing the Atlantic Ocean. The proposed addition to Fontainebleau is being constructed twenty feet from its north property line, 130 feet from the mean high water mark of the Atlantic Ocean, and 76 feet 8 inches from the ocean bulkhead line. The 14–story tower will extend 160 feet above grade in height and is 416 feet long from east to west. During the winter months, from around two o'clock in the afternoon for the remainder of the day, the shadow of the addition will extend over the cabana, swimming pool, and sunbathing areas of the Eden Roc, which are located in the southern portion of its property.

* * *

The chancellor heard considerable testimony on the issues made by the complaint and the answer and, as noted, entered a temporary injunction restraining the defendants from continuing with the construction of the addition. His reason for so doing was stated by him, in a memorandum opinion, as follows:

> "In granting the temporary injunction in this case the Court wishes to make several things very clear. * * * It is based solely on the proposition that no one has a right to use his property to the injury of another. In this case it is clear from the evidence that the proposed use by the Fontainebleau will materially damage the Eden Roc. There is evidence indicating that the construction of the proposed annex by the Fontainebleau is malicious or deliberate for the purpose of injuring the Eden Roc, but it is scarcely sufficient, standing alone, to afford a basis for equitable relief."

This is indeed a novel application of the maxim *sic utere tuo ut alienum non laedas*. This maxim does not mean that one must never use his own property in such a way as to do any injury to his neighbor. It means only that one must use his property so as not to injure the lawful *rights* of another. In Reaver v. Martin Theatres, under this maxim, it was stated that "it is well settled that a property owner may put his own property to any reasonable and lawful use, so long as he does not thereby deprive the adjoining landowner of any right of enjoyment of his property *which is recognized and protected by law, and so long as his use is not such a one as the law will pronounce a nuisance.*" [Emphasis supplied by this Court.]

No American decision has been cited, and independent research has revealed none, in which it has been held that—in the absence of some contractual or statutory obligation—a landowner has a legal right to the free flow of light and air across the adjoining land of his neighbor. * * *

There being, then, no legal right to the free flow of light and air from the adjoining land, it is universally held that where a structure serves a useful and beneficial purpose, it does not give rise to a cause of action, either for damages or for an injunction under the maxim *sic utere tuo ut alienum non laedas,* even though it causes injury to another by cutting off the light and air and interfering with the view that would otherwise be available over adjoining land in its natural state, regardless of the fact that the structure may have been erected partly for spite.

We see no reason for departing from this universal rule. * * *

Since it affirmatively appears that the plaintiff has not established a cause of action against the defendants by reason of the structure here in question, the order granting a temporary injunction should be and it is hereby reversed with directions to dismiss the complaint.

Notes and Questions

1. Nowhere in its discussion of the parties' relative rights does the court in *Fontainebleau* consider whether the Eden Roc's sunny swimming pool or the Fontainebleau's 14–story addition was more valuable. Finding no precedent for giving a landowner a legal right to the flow of sunlight

across a neighbor's adjoining land, the Florida Court of Appeals resolved the issue without considering which use was more valuable. A court determined to allocate resources to their most valuable uses would have to acknowledge that sometimes the right to sunlight is valuable, especially to Miami Beach hotels.

The facts of *Fontainebleau* provide an opportunity to illustrate the Coase Theorem that, absent impediments to exchange, the court's initial allocation of the right will not affect the ultimate efficiency of resource use. The mere existence of damage to the Eden Roc does not mean that the addition to the Fontainebleau was not the more valuable use. If the addition added $1,000,000 annually to the Fontainebleau's profits while reducing the Eden Roc's profits by only $500,000 annually, then using the land for the addition increased the value of beachfront property in Miami Beach. If these values are correct, then the court reached an efficient result, without explicitly attempting to do so.

> *Questions:* If the court had come out the other way, had granted an injunction halting the construction, would the Eden Roc have enforced the injunction or would the owners of the Fontainebleau have paid the Eden Roc to allow them to build? How much would the Fontainebleau be willing to pay annually?

> 2. Suppose that the tower would damage the Eden Roc ($750,000 in lost profits annually) more than it would aid the Fontainebleau ($500,000 additional annual profits).

> *Questions:* If the parties could bargain freely, would the Eden Roc's owners be willing and able to pay more to stop the construction than the Fontainebleau would gain by having the construction? Would bargaining lead to an efficient allocation of resources? If the court enjoined construction under these facts, what result would the Fontainebleau's bargaining produce?

> 3. Reexamine Sturges v. Bridgman and Bryant v. Lefever. According to Coase, the possibility of bargaining eliminates the need for the court to find whose land use is more valuable.

> *Question:* Would bargaining have ensured that the most valuable use prevailed in each of those cases regardless of how the court ruled?

PRAH v. MARETTI

Supreme Court of Wisconsin, 1982.
108 Wis.2d 223, 321 N.W.2d 182.

ABRAHAMSON, JUSTICE.

* * *

According to the complaint, the plaintiff is the owner of a residence which was constructed during the years 1978–1979. The complaint alleges that the residence has a solar system which includes collectors on the roof to supply energy for heat and hot water and that after the plaintiff built his solar-heated house, the defendant purchased the lot adjacent to and immediately to the south of the plaintiff's lot and commenced planning construction of a home. The complaint further states that when the plaintiff learned of defendant's plans to build the house he advised the defendant that if the house were built at the proposed location, defendant's house would substantially and adversely affect the integrity of plaintiff's solar system and could cause plaintiff other damage. Nevertheless, the defendant began construction. The complaint further alleges that the plaintiff is entitled to "unrestricted use of the sun and its solar power" and demands judgment for injunctive relief and damages.

* * *

This court's reluctance in the nineteenth and early part of the twentieth century to provide broader protection for a landowner's access to sunlight was premised on three policy considerations. First, the right of landowners to use their property as they wished, as long as they did not cause physical damage to a neighbor, was jealously guarded.

Second, sunlight was valued only for aesthetic enjoyment or as illumination. Since artificial light could be used for illumination, loss of sunlight was at most a personal annoyance which was given little, if any, weight by society.

Third, society had a significant interest in not restricting or impeding land development. This court repeatedly emphasized that in the growth period of the nineteenth and early twentieth centuries change is to be expected and is essential to property and that recognition of a right to sunlight would hinder property development. * * *

Considering these three policies, this court concluded that in the absence of an express agreement granting access to sunlight, a landowner's obstruction of another's access to sunlight was not actionable. These three policies are no longer fully accepted or applicable. They reflect factual circumstances and social priorities that are now obsolete.

First, society has increasingly regulated the use of land by the landowner for the general welfare.

Second, access to sunlight has taken on a new significance in recent years. In this case the plaintiff seeks to protect access to sunlight, not for aesthetic reasons or as a source of illumination but as a source of energy. Access to sunlight as an energy source is of significance both to the landowner who invests in solar collectors and to a society which has an interest in developing alternative sources of energy.

Third, the policy of favoring unhindered private development in an expanding economy is no longer in harmony with the realities of our society. The need for easy and rapid development is not as great today as it once was, while our perception of the value of sunlight as a source of energy has increased significantly.

Courts should not implement obsolete policies that have lost their vigor over the course of the years. The law of private nuisance is better suited to resolve landowners' disputes about property development in the 1980's than is a rigid rule which does not recognize a landowner's interest in access to sunlight. * * *

* * *

* * * Recognition of a nuisance claim for unreasonable obstruction of access to sunlight will not prevent land development or unduly hinder the use of adjoining land. It will promote the reasonable use and enjoyment of land in a manner suitable to the 1980's. That obstruction of access to light might be found to constitute a nuisance in certain circumstances does not mean that it will be or must be found to constitute a nuisance under all circumstances. The result in each case depends on whether the conduct complained of is unreasonable.

Accordingly we hold that the plaintiff in this case has stated a claim under which relief can be granted.

Notes and Questions

1. Assuming that there are no impediments to bargaining between Prah and Maretti, the Coase Theorem states that bargaining will inevitably produce an efficient allocation of sunlight, whether to Maretti's house or to Prah's solar collectors. The failure to halt construction of the hotel addition in *Fontainebleau* meant that the plaintiff would have to take the initiative in bargaining with the defendant. It might appear that the only consequence of the Wisconsin Supreme Court recognizing that blocking sunlight could be a nuisance in *Prah* is that in Wisconsin the defendant would have to take the initiative in bargaining with the plaintiff. Ronald Coase believed that: "[W]ithout the establishment of [an] initial delimitation of rights there can be no market transactions to transfer and recombine them." In other words, the courts' only role is to ensure that rights are clearly assigned to *someone*. If the initial allocation is clear, the parties are in a position to discuss a reallocation.

   Question: Justice Abrahamson apparently believed that recognizing a right to sunlight would promote the development of alternative energy sources. If the Coase Theorem is correct can Justice Abrahamson also be correct?

2. *The Invariance Hypothesis:* According to the Coase Theorem, if building the new home is worth more to the Marettis than the sunlight is worth to Prah, the new home will be built so long as the Marettis have enough funds to bribe Prah into allowing it. If sunlight is more valuable to Prah than the new construction is to the Marettis, the Marettis will not build their home so long as Prah has sufficient funds to bribe them not to. The court's decision is irrelevant to the efficient allocation of resources and what the court does appears to have no effect on the property's ultimate use. In other words, rights will end up with the party willing to pay the most for them, and the court's original allocation of right has no effect on that willingness to pay.

This interpretation of the Coase Theorem is referred to as the "Invariance Hypothesis" or the "Strong Version" of the Coase Theorem. The Invariance Hypothesis posits that as long as no obstacles to transactions exist between affected parties, the allocation of resources will be efficient *and* that efficient allocation of resources will be the same regardless of how property rights are initially assigned.

The Invariance Hypothesis is derived from an example involving a cattle raiser and a neighboring farmer developed by Coase to explain his theory. To simplify Coase's example somewhat, assume that the cattle raiser's cow is worth $5 and can be expected to stray and damage $10 of the farmer's crops. To appreciate the possibility that the allocation of resources does not depend on the rights assignment, consider three allocation questions:

a. Will the rights assignment affect whether the rancher keeps the cow? If the rancher has the right to let her cow trample the farmer's crops, the farmer has an incentive to offer the rancher a payment in return for the rancher getting rid of the cow. The farmer would pay up to $10 to avoid the damage from the cow. This is more than the cow is worth, so a rational rancher is likely to allow herself to be bribed, for some amount between $5 and $10, to get rid of the cow. But if the rancher does not have the right to trample the farmer's crops, the rancher will also get rid of the cow, preferring to get rid of a $5 cow rather than pay $10 for the damage it causes.

b. Will the rights assignment affect whether a fence is built to contain the cow? Perhaps the cow could be prevented from trampling the crops by building a fence between the two properties. Assume that the cost of the fence would be $3. If the rancher has the right to let her cow trample the farmer's crop, the farmer will build the $3 fence—this is cheaper than either suffering $10 in crop damage, or giving the rancher a bribe between $5 and $10 to get rid of the cow. And once again, if the rancher does not have the right to trample the farmer's crops, the rancher will build the fence. A $3 fence is cheaper than either paying $10 in damages or getting rid of a $5 cow. Either way, the fence gets built.

c. Will the rights assignment affect whether the farmer plants crops? Suppose that the cow destroyed crops worth $10, but which cost $8 to grow. If the rancher has the right to let her cow trample the farmer's crops, the farmer will stop growing crops altogether. The farmer is unwilling to pay more than $2—the net value of the destroyed crops—as a bribe to the rancher, and the rancher will not accept such a small amount to get rid of a $5 cow. Similarly, if the rancher does not have the right to trample the farmer's crops, the rancher will pay the farmer a bribe not to plant. After all, if the crops are planted the rancher will either have to pay $10 in damages or get rid of a $5 cow; it is less expensive to pay the farmer a bribe between $2 and $5 not to plant. Once again, whether the right is assigned to the farmer or the rancher, no crops are planted.

Part of the symmetry in outcomes is explained by the fact that the potential for exchange appears to internalize otherwise-external costs completely. For the rancher, the damage done by the cow is a cost whether she has to compensate the farmer for his loss, or simply give up the opportunity to get a payment from the farmer by keeping the cow. Similarly, if the farmer has the right to exclude the cow, excluding it is a cost because he gives up the opportunity to get a payment. If the farmer does not have the right, then excluding the cow costs him the amount of the payment he must make. The assignment of rights determines who receives and who pays bribes, but the allocation of resources to crops, cattle, and fences does not vary.

Coase's version of these hypothetical situations is only slightly more complicated. He assumed that the increased crop damage as the herd got larger was as shown below:

Size of Herd (No. of Cows)	Annual Crop Loss (in dollars)
1	1
2	3
3	6
4	10

If the cattle raiser has the right to trample the farmer's crop, the farmer has an incentive to bargain with her to keep the size of the herd relatively small. The farmer is willing to pay an amount equal to the damage done by a cow to prevent the cattle raiser from increasing her herd size. Thus, the farmer would pay up to one dollar to avoid the damage from the first cow, two dollars (the *additional* damage done) to prevent the herd from increasing from one to two cows, three dollars (the *additional* damage done by adding the third cow) to prevent the herd from expanding from two cows to three, and four dollars (the *additional* damage done by adding the fourth cow) to prevent expansion from three to four. The cattle raiser will decide how large a herd to have depending on the bribe the farmer is willing to pay and how much each cow is worth in the market for beef. If each cow is worth enough, no bribe that the farmer is willing to pay will reduce the herd size, but if each cow is worth $3.50 as beef, then the cattle raiser would rather take a bribe greater than $3.50 not to add the cow to her herd. Since the farmer is willing to pay an amount up to four dollars, the bribe is likely to occur if there are no obstacles to bargaining.

If the cattle raiser has no right to trample the farmer's crops, the cattle raiser has an incentive to bargain with the farmer to allow her cattle to trample. The cattle raiser is willing to pay an amount no greater than the value of each cow to have trampling rights. Once again, if each cow is worth $3.50, the cattle raiser will have a herd of three, because she will not be able to strike a bargain for rights to the fourth, which would add an additional four dollars in crop loss to the farmer, more than that cow is worth to the cattle raiser.

3. Limitations on the Invariance Hypothesis: Those challenging the Invariance Hypothesis generally focus on the conclusion that the allocation of resources is unaffected by the assignment of rights rather than the conclusion that the allocation will be efficient. The most obvious problem with the Invariance Hypothesis involves the parties' relative willingness and ability to buy rights. The initial assignment of rights *does* affect the parties' relative wealth. Since a party's willingness and ability to pay are affected by wealth, the assignment of a right to one party may determine the outcome in terms of the actual uses to which resources are put.

To understand the wealth effects of the rights assignment, consider how a rancher's valuation of her pet dog depends on how rights are assigned. Suppose that the rancher's dog can be expected to stray and kill $10 of a neighboring farmer's chickens. The dog could be restrained with a $3 fence. If the rancher had the right to let her dog roam free, the farmer would be willing to build the $3 fence to avoid the $10 in lost chickens. But if the rancher must pay for the dog's damage, and if the rancher is too poor to build a $3 fence—the dog must go. Implicit in the farmer's willingness to build the fence is the assumption that the rancher was unwilling to accept less than $3 to get rid of the dog. If the rancher must pay for the damage, however, and is poor, the rancher may not be willing and able to pay $3 to build the fence. The result in both cases is efficient. However, the initial allocation of the rights, by affecting the parties' willingness and ability to pay, has changed which outcome is efficient. The rancher valued the dog at more than $3 when assigned the right to let it roam free, so building a $3 fence made economic sense to the farmer. When forced to pay for its damage, the rancher valued the dog at less than $3, so building a $3 fence did not make economic sense to her.

The limitations of the Invariance Hypothesis have led many economists to adopt the version of the Coase Theorem with which this section started: As long as there are no obstacles to transactions between affected parties, the resources will be allocated efficiently regardless of how property rights are initially assigned.

Questions: The discussion of the invariance of the allocative efficiency that would result from bargaining in *Prah* in Question 2 above included two qualifications: "so long as the Marettis have enough funds to bribe Prah" and "so long as Prah has sufficient funds to bribe the Marettis." How is the wealth of Prah and the Marettis affected by the assignment of rights? Might the distribution of wealth affect whether the residence gets built or whether the solar collectors continue to receive sunlight?

4. *Partial Equilibrium Analysis:* If the use of solar collectors is widespread, recognizing the right to bring a nuisance action for blocking sunlight will have effects beyond parties to the suit and beyond bargains between future adjacent landowners whose uses conflict. Among those effects is a decrease in the value of undeveloped land located near homes with solar collectors. The use to which such land can be put is diminished by recognizing the right and so the land's value is diminished; the portions of the land on which large homes can be built are limited. Recognizing the right will also affect the market for undeveloped land and will have corresponding distributional effects, benefitting those who already have already built homes and harming those who would like to develop property. Those effects are externalities, harms and benefits resulting from the assignment of rights that are not taken into account in the process of assigning the right.

When determining whether a reallocation is efficient, economists frequently ignore external effects, such as price changes in a market other than the one under consideration, and wealth redistribution effects. These effects may be significant. Analysis focuses on the allocation of resources in a single market after bargaining has taken place, when the market is in *equilibrium*. Economists often ignore distributional effects or effects on the allocation of other resources, referring to them as secondary or "second order" effects. Examining effects in one market at a time simplifies analysis that otherwise would be too complicated. Sometimes it is necessary to focus on just part of a question, do a *partial* analysis, in order to gain any useful answer at all. Recognizing that the analysis of a single market in equilibrium is only part of the larger picture, economists describe such analysis as *partial equilibrium analysis*.

The analysis of each of the cases thus far has been partial equilibrium analysis that ignores many effects of property rights assignments on wealth distribution and on markets for other resources. While partial equilibrium analysis is useful, many apparently efficient bargains between individuals have effects other than those considered in the partial analysis.

5. *General Equilibrium Analysis:* An assignment of rights has effects that ripple out beyond a single market. A *general equilibrium analysis* considers the wealth effects of a property rights assignment in numerous markets. Even if changes in the parties' wealth resulting from being assigned or denied the property right are not sufficiently large to influence the final allocation of the resource in question, those changes still affect the parties' purchasing habits in two ways. First, since a wealth transfer between parties occurred, the winner now has command over resources that formerly the loser commanded. If the winner and loser spend their money differently, the allocation of other resources shifts in favor of those the winner values. The allocation is still efficient, but who is valuing those uses has changed. If winner and loser have different values, different preferences, the allocation of resources will change.

In addition, the winner's increase in wealth may alter the winner's preferences. Wealthy people are more likely to acquire yachts than are poor people. A poor person must satisfy her nautical desires by renting rowboats. As an individual becomes wealthier, she may be willing and able to devote more resources to luxuries than to basics. The winner's demand for fine wine increases while her demand for jug wine decreases. The loser's altered preferences may exactly compensate for the changes in the winner's tastes, but an exact match is extremely unlikely.

Thus, from both general and partial equilibrium perspectives, the ultimate allocations of resources resulting from alternative property rights assignments will all be efficient (assuming there are no transaction costs) but the allocations may be different.

6. Reexamine Sturges v. Bridgman and Bryant v. Lefever in light of the Coase Theorem, recognizing the limitations of the Invariance Hypothesis. The possibility of bargaining eliminates the need for the court to find who is the best cost avoider of the injuries. Whoever is assigned liability for injuries caused by the conflicting land use will negotiate with the other to find who could avoid the injury at least cost and then pay that person (if it is the other party) to take the appropriate precautions. Where bargaining is possible, the bargaining rather than the court determines the best cost avoider of the injury.

Questions: Would bargaining have ensured that the most valuable use prevailed in each of those cases regardless of how the court ruled? Assume that the plaintiff in *Bryant,* the owner of the fireplace, was poor. Would his ultimate ability to use the fireplace depend on whether he was granted the injunction? Would the character of the ultimate use have been invariant regardless of how the court ruled?

BOOKER v. OLD DOMINION LAND CO.

Supreme Court of Appeals of Virginia, 1948.
188 Va. 143, 49 S.E.2d 314.

BUCHANAN, JUSTICE.

* * *

In 1937, Old Dominion Land Company subdivided about 114 acres of its land, lying north of Newport News, in Warwick county, into lots, named the subdivision Parkview and made a map thereof, which was recorded. There were about 164 of these lots, laid off along and abutting on the east and west sides of what was called Jefferson avenue on the map, and which is now U.S. Highway No. 168. The company thereupon proceeded to sell these lots and at the time of the institution of this suit had sold all of them. Twelve of the lots were marked "business" and a few as "sold" or "reserved," and the rest were for residential purposes. The deeds for the residential lots contained identical restrictions [restricting their development to dwelling houses costing not less than $1,500.00 each and prohibiting commercial uses of the land until January 1, 1959.]

* * *

Plaintiffs are the owners of [two lots] in this subdivision, conveyed to them June 13, 1946, by deed reciting that it was subject to the restrictions, covenants and conditions contained in the original deeds from the Old Dominion Land Company.

The ground alleged by the plaintiffs as entitling them to a cancellation of the restrictions is a change of conditions "so radical as to destroy the essential objective and purposes of the covenants, conditions and restrictions originally contained in the Old Dominion Land Company deeds.

* * *

The former sales manager [for Old Dominion] testified that the lots were sold by the map; when the lots marked "business" were sold, it was represented to the purchasers that the lots not so marked could be used only for residences, and that the company received a higher price for the business lots because of the residential restrictions. By the same token, he testified, the values of the lots designated as residential were enhanced by the residential restrictions.

Thus it would occur that elimination of these restrictions would result in taking away a value bought and paid for by the owners of both business and residential properties, and in many instances without so much as a "by-your-leave," because many of the owners are not before the court.

* * *

* * * [I]n a building development plan the creation of an area restricted to residences contemplates the continued existence of such an area from which business is excluded. It is to prevent the anticipated encroachment of business on the protected area that the restrictions are created. Purchasers of lots in such an area buy in reliance upon the fact that all other lots in the area are subject to the same restriction, and the entire development will retain its character as a purely residential district. The very purpose of the restriction is to prevent the property from being converted to business use if it should become more valuable for that use.

* * * The relief here sought, if granted, would nullify the covenants, at least in plaintiff's title, for all time and all purposes even though future changes might completely remove the ground for doing so. More is required to warrant such a decree * * *. It must be established that the whole plan has become inoperative and that its objects can no longer be carried out.

The decree [denying the relief sought] is

Affirmed.

Notes and Questions

1. The materials in this section explore the efficiency implications of bargaining between parties to impose limits on each other's use of their property. Courts often must decide whether to enforce these restrictions once the parties have agreed upon them. That decision will also involve an allocative choice. In *Booker,* Judge Buchanan stated "The very purpose of the restriction is to prevent the property from being converted to business use if it should become more valuable for that use." He makes it sound like the restriction is designed to prevent allocative efficiency and then upholds the restriction.

Question: Is the restriction's purpose to prevent property from going to its most valuable use and, if so, are such restrictions inherently inefficient?

2. Judge Buchanan referred to evidence that the real estate developer received a higher price for both the business lots and the residential lots because of the residential restrictions. This means that the development as a whole is more valuable with the restrictions than without and that the restrictive covenants enhance the allocative efficiency of the use of this resource. Judge Buchanan was concerned that elimination of these restrictions would result in taking away a value bought and paid for by both business and residential property owners.

Question: Why would any buyer of either business or residential land be willing to pay more for restricted use land?

3. If purchasers are willing to pay more for land where restrictions on use ensure that the externalities some uses create do not occur, then for a court to lift the restrictions or refuse to enforce the contractual restrictions appears inefficient. Judge Buchanan held that "It must be established that the whole plan has become inoperative and that its objects can no longer be carried out" before the restrictions would be removed.

Questions: Is this test consistent with the underlying efficiency rationale for such restrictions? When should these restrictions be removed?

4. A similar restrictive covenant was discussed in Mountain Springs Ass'n of N.J. Inc. v. Wilson, 196 A.2d 270 (N.J. 1963). In *Mountain Springs,* the court voided terms of the covenant restricting property owners' rights to sell to people who were not members of the association because the restriction was unlimited in duration, unreasonable in the limitation of the number of permitted purchasers, and granted the association too much power to control prospective purchasers. It is sometimes argued that the price of land in such a community reflects the nature of the restrictions imposed on the land and that some buyers will be willing and able to pay more for stricter limitations. Voiding terms of a restrictive covenant must therefore be inefficient, since it substitutes a lower-valued (unrestricted) use for a higher-valued (restricted) use. Each of the three grounds for voiding the covenant in *Mountain Springs,* however, suggests a set of restrictions unnecessarily broad to achieve the purposes of the covenant.

Questions: If the terms of a restrictive covenant are more restrictive than necessary to achieve the desired purpose, will the price of the land necessarily be higher than if the restrictions were more precisely drafted? Who bears the cost of an unnecessarily restrictive covenant, the members of the association or society as a whole?

5. While the previous cases have explored the efficiency implications of private agreements resolving conflicting land uses, *Booker* presents questions involved in the enforcement of such agreements.

Questions: If all of the parties to an agreement wished to remove the restrictive covenant, then would removing the restriction be a Pareto superior reallocation and allocatively efficient? If a group of people can agree privately to restrict their property to residential use, should the court enforce the restriction until private negotiations produce agreement on eliminating the restrictions?

C. TRANSACTION COSTS AND IMPEDIMENTS TO BARGAINING

1. THE COASE THEOREM AND TRANSACTION COSTS

The Coase Theorem states that as long as there are no obstacles to transactions between affected parties, bargaining will ensure an efficient allocation of resources regardless of how property rights are initially assigned. The key to appreciating the Coase Theorem is understanding the implications of the assumption that there are no obstacles to transactions between affected parties. The following cases examine when obstacles to bargaining arise, the efficiency implications of those transaction costs, and legal mechanisms for promoting allocative efficiency when transaction costs are substantial.

PLOOF v. PUTNAM

Supreme Court of Vermont, 1908.
81 Vt. 471, 71 A. 188.

MUNSON, J.

It is alleged as the ground of recovery that on the 13th day of November, 1904, the defendant was the owner of a certain island in Lake Champlain, and of a certain dock attached thereto, which island and dock were then in charge of the defendant's servant; that the plaintiff was then possessed of and sailing upon said lake a certain loaded sloop, on which were the plaintiff and his wife and two minor children; that there then arose a sudden and violent tempest, whereby the sloop and the property and persons therein were placed in great danger of destruction; that, to save these from destruction, or injury, the plaintiff was compelled to, and did, moor the sloop to defendant's dock; that the defendant, by his servant, unmoored the sloop, whereupon it was driven upon the shore by the tempest, without the plaintiff's fault; and that the sloop and its contents were thereby destroyed, and the plaintiff and his wife and children cast into the lake and upon the shore, receiving injuries. This claim is set forth in two counts * * * charging that the defendant by his servant * * * willingly and designedly unmoored the sloop [and] alleging that it was the duty of the defendant by his servant to permit the plaintiff to moor his sloop to the dock, and to permit it to remain so moored during the continuance of the tempest, but that the defendant by his servant, in disregard of this duty, negligently, carelessly, and wrongfully unmoored the sloop. [The defendant objected to both claims on the grounds that he had the right to eject trespassers from his property.]

There are many cases in the books which hold that necessity, as an inability to control movements inaugurated in the proper exercise of a strict right, will justify entries upon land and interferences with personal property that would otherwise have been trespasses. * * *

This doctrine of necessity applies with special force to the preservation of human life. One assaulted and in peril of his life may run through the close of another to escape from his assailant. One may sacrifice the personal property of another to save his life or the lives of his fellows. * * *

It is clear that an entry upon the land of another may be justified by necessity, and that the declaration before us discloses a necessity for mooring the sloop. But the defendant questions the sufficiency of the counts because they do not negative the existence of natural objects to which the plaintiff could have moored with equal safety. The allegations are, in substance, that the stress of a sudden and violent tempest compelled the plaintiff to moor to defendant's dock to save his sloop and the people on it. The averment of necessity is complete, for it covers not only the necessity of mooring, but the necessity of mooring to the dock * * * .

[The judgment of the trial court denying the defendant's motion for summary judgment on the grounds that the allegations were insufficient to state a cause of action was affirmed.]

Notes and Questions

1. *Ploof* presents another case of conflicting uses of resources—in this instance, the defendant's dock. Mr. Putnam, through his servant, was protecting his right to exclusive possession of the land and dock. The plaintiff, Mr. Ploof, valued the dock as a means of preventing harm to his family and boat. Property owners like Mr. Putnam are normally protected against interference with their right to exclusive possession by the law of trespass. Under the doctrine of trespass by necessity, however, Mr. Ploof's intrusion is not only allowed but protected; Ploof was awarded damages because his sloop was unmoored from defendant Putnam's dock. The court permitted the plaintiff to use the dock, in furtherance of a public policy valuing human life more than the right to exclusive possession of property.

Applying the private necessity doctrine involved the court in the question of which party's use of the dock is more valuable. As the Coase Theorem suggests, it may have been necessary for the law to assign the right to one of the parties so that they would have a reference point for bargaining about departures from that assignment of rights. This does not explain why the law should recognize a private necessity defense.

Questions: If the defendant has a right to exclusive possession, would bargaining between the parties lead to an efficient outcome? What are the transaction costs in private necessity cases generally?

2. To arrange a mutually beneficial exchange of rights, parties must become aware of the potential gains of exchange, identify the other party with whom they hope to exchange, establish communication with that party, negotiate the terms of the exchange, and then perform the exchange. At each stage, impediments may arise and costs may be incurred.

When discussing the court's opinion in *Sturges,* Coase argued that "[i]t was of course the view of the judges that they were affecting the working of the economic system—and in a desirable direction. * * * The judges' view that they were settling how the land was to be used would be true only in the case in which the costs of carrying out the necessary market transactions exceeded the gains which might be achieved by any rearrangement of rights." Coase recognized that sometimes the costs of bargaining to reallocate rights exceed the efficiency benefits of reallocation. In such a case, the least expensive course of action is to suffer the inefficiency, unless rights can be redefined to facilitate bargaining or an efficient outcome.

In reality, market transactions almost always involve some costs, and sometimes substantial ones. In many factual circumstances like the one in *Ploof,* transaction costs prevent the efficient reallocation of rights through bargaining and the initial allocation of rights made by the court may be the final allocation. In such cases, the court's decision matters very much to the efficient allocation of resources.

3. If transaction costs prevent bargaining from allocating resources efficiently, then substitutes for bargaining may maximize societal welfare. One substitute might be legal rules that permit a party who values a resource more highly to take that resource from its owner and pay damages. Another alternative would employ a court or other decisionmaker to allocate the resource directly to those who (the decisionmaker believes) value the resource most highly and forbid bargaining over reallocations. In the following excerpt, Calabresi and Melamed describe rules requiring bargaining before rights can be exchanged as *property rules*. The alternatives are characterized as *liability rules* and *inalienability rules*, respectively. The discussion of Vincent v. Lake Erie Transport Co., which follows the excerpt from Calabresi and Melamed, employs that nomenclature in evaluating the efficiency implications of the private necessity doctrine introduced in *Ploof*.

CALABRESI AND MELAMED, PROPERTY RULES, LIABILITY RULES, AND INALIENABILITY: ONE VIEW OF THE CATHEDRAL *

85 Harv.L.Rev. 1089, 1092–93, 1105 (1972).

Only rarely are Property and Torts approached from a unified perspective. Recent writings by lawyers concerned with economics and by economists concerned with law suggest, however, that an attempt at integrating the various legal relationships treated by these subjects would be useful both for the beginning student and the sophisticated scholar. By articulating a concept of "entitlements" which are protected by property, liability, or inalienability rules, we present one framework for such an approach. * * *

* * *

An entitlement is protected by a property rule to the extent that someone who wishes to remove the entitlement from its holder must buy it from him in a voluntary transaction in which the value of the entitlement is agreed upon by the seller. * * *

Whenever someone may destroy the entitlement if he is willing to pay an objectively determined value for it, the entitlement is protected by a liability rule. This value may be what it is thought the original holder of the entitlement would have sold it for. But the holder's complaint that he would have demanded more will not avail him once the objectively determined value is set. * * *

An entitlement is inalienable to the extent that its transfer is not permitted between a willing buyer and a willing seller. * * *

It should be clear that most entitlements to most goods are mixed. Taney's house may be protected by a property rule in situations in

which Marshall wishes to purchase it, by a liability rule where the government decides to take it by eminent domain, and by a rule of inalienability in situations where Taney is drunk or incompetent.
* * *

* * *

Whenever society chooses an initial entitlement it must also determine whether to protect the entitlement by property rules, by liability rules, or by rules of inalienability. In our framework, much of what is generally called private property can be viewed as an entitlement protected by a property rule. No one can take the entitlement to private property from the holder unless the holder sells it willingly and at the price at which he subjectively values the property. Yet a nuisance with sufficient public utility to avoid an injunction has, in effect, the right to take property with compensation. In such a circumstance the entitlement to the property is protected only by what we call a liability rule: an external, objective standard of value used to facilitate the transfer of the entitlement from the holder to the nuisance. Finally, in some instances we will not allow the sale of the property at all, that is, we will occasionally make the entitlement inalienable.

VINCENT v. LAKE ERIE TRANSPORT CO.

Supreme Court of Minnesota, 1910.
109 Minn. 456, 124 N.W. 221.

O'BRIEN, J.

The steamship Reynolds, owned by the defendant, was for the purpose of discharging her cargo on November 27, 1905, moored to plaintiff's dock in Duluth. While the unloading of the boat was taking place a storm from the northeast developed, which at about 10 o'clock p.m., when the unloading was completed, had so grown in violence that the wind was then moving at 50 miles per hour and continued to increase during the night. There is some evidence that one, and perhaps two, boats were able to enter the harbor that night, but it is plain that navigation was practically suspended from the hour mentioned until the morning of the 29th, when the storm abated, and during that time no master would have been justified in attempting to navigate his vessel, if he could avoid doing so. After the discharge of the cargo the Reynolds signaled for a tug to tow her from the dock, but none could be obtained because of the severity of the storm. If the lines holding the ship to the dock had been cast off, she would doubtless have drifted away; but, instead, the lines were kept fast, and as soon as one parted or chafed it was replaced, sometimes with a larger one. The vessel lay upon the outside of the dock, her bow to the east, the wind and waves striking her starboard quarter with such force that she was constantly being lifted and thrown against the dock, resulting in its damage, as found by the jury, to the amount of $500.

We are satisfied that the character of the storm was such that it would have been highly imprudent for the master of the Reynolds to have attempted to leave the dock or to have permitted his vessel to drift a way from it.   * * *

The appellant contends * * * that, because its conduct during the storm was rendered necessary by prudence and good seamanship under conditions over which it had no control, it cannot be held liable for any injury resulting to the property of others, and claims that the jury should have been so instructed. An analysis of the charge given by the trial court is not necessary, as in our opinion the only question for the jury was the amount of damages which the plaintiffs were entitled to recover, and no complaint is made upon that score.

The situation was one in which the ordinary rules regulating property rights were suspended by forces beyond human control, and if, without the direct intervention of some act by the one sought to be held liable, the property of another was injured, such injury must be attributed to the act of God, and not to the wrongful act of the person sought to be charged. If during the storm the Reynolds had entered the harbor, and while there had become disabled and been thrown against the plaintiffs' dock, the plaintiffs could not have recovered. Again, if while attempting to hold fast to the dock the lines had parted, without any negligence, and the vessel carried against some other boat or dock in the harbor, there would be no liability upon her owner. But here those in charge of the vessel deliberately and by their direct efforts held her in such a position that the damage to the dock resulted, and, having thus preserved the ship at the expense of the dock, it seems to us that her owners are responsible to the dock owners to the extent of the injury inflicted.

* * *

Theologians hold that a starving man may, without moral guilt, take what is necessary to sustain life; but it could hardly be said that the obligation would not be upon such person to pay the value of the property so taken when he became able to do so. And so public necessity, in times of war or peace, may require the taking of private property for public purposes; but under our system of jurisprudence compensation must be made.

Let us imagine in this case that for the better mooring of the vessel those in charge of her had appropriated a valuable cable lying upon the dock. No matter how justifiable such appropriation might have been, it would not be claimed that, because of the overwhelming necessity of the situation, the owner of the cable could not recover its value.

This is not a case where life or property was menaced by any object or thing belonging to the plaintiff, the destruction of which became necessary to prevent the threatened disaster. Nor is it a case where, because of the act of God, or unavoidable accident, the infliction of the injury was beyond the control of the defendant, but is one where the defendant prudently and advisedly availed itself of the plaintiffs' property for the purpose of preserving its own more valuable property, and the plaintiffs are entitled to compensation for the injury done.

Order affirmed.

Lewis, J.

I dissent. It was assumed on the trial before the lower court that appellant's liability depended on whether the master of the ship might, in the exercise of reasonable care, have sought a place of safety before the storm made it impossible to leave the dock. The majority opinion assumes that the evidence is conclusive that appellant moored its boat at respondent's dock pursuant to contract, and that the vessel was lawfully in position at the time the additional cables were fastened to the dock, and the reasoning of the opinion is that, because appellant made use of the stronger cables to hold the boat in position, it became liable under the rule that it had voluntarily made use of the property of another for the purpose of saving its own.

In my judgment, if the boat was lawfully in position at the time the storm broke, and the master could not, in the exercise of due care, have left that position without subjecting his vessel to the hazards of the storm, then the damage to the dock, caused by the pounding of the boat, was the result of an inevitable accident. If the master was in the exercise of due care, he was not at fault. The reasoning of the opinion admits that if the ropes, or cables, first attached to the dock had not parted, or if, in the first instance, the master had used the stronger cables, there would be no liability. If the master could not, in the exercise of reasonable care, have anticipated the severity of the storm and sought a place of safety before it became impossible, why should he be required to anticipate the severity of the storm, and, in the first instance, use the stronger cables?

I am of the opinion that one who constructs a dock to the navigable line of waters, and enters into contractual relations with the owner of a vessel to moor at the same, takes the risk of damage to his dock by a boat caught there by a storm, which event could not have been avoided in the exercise of due care, and further, that the legal status of the parties in such a case is not changed by renewal of cables to keep the boat from being cast adrift at the mercy of the tempest.

Notes and Questions

1. *Vincent* establishes that the right to trespass on another's property in a private emergency does not include the right to cause physical damage to the property. According to the majority, the ship owner is liable for damages if he acted to save his own property at the expense of another's, regardless of whether it was prudent. Using the terminology of Calabresi and Melamed, in an emergency, the dock owner's right to the dock was protected by a liability rule rather than a property rule. If protected by a property rule, the dock owner would be entitled to forbid any boat from using his dock during a storm. A boat in distress would have to bargain with the dock owner. If protected by a liability rule, the dock owner would not be entitled to forbid any boat owner from tying up at his dock during a storm but would be able to collect from the boat owner any damages to the dock caused by the boat's presence.

Questions: What would it mean to assign the right to the boat owner and protect it by a property or liability rule? What kind of rule was adopted in *Ploof?* To whom was the right assigned and how was it protected in *Vincent?* Are the legal rules in *Ploof* and *Vincent* inconsistent?

2. If no obstacles to bargaining existed between the parties in *Vincent,* the party with the greater willingness and ability to pay to protect his property could exclude the other party. If bargaining cannot occur and there is no obligation to pay damages, one party would be able to impose external costs on the other.

Questions: Given the factual circumstances, was there any reason to protect the dock owner's right by a liability rule rather than a property rule? Are the incentives created for the boat owners by making them pay damages likely to lead to an efficient result? In these factual circumstances, are the incentives created by a liability rule more likely to give an efficient result than those created by the property rule?

3. *Vincent* illustrates how, when substantial impediments to bargaining exist between the parties, liability rules may be superior to property rules as a means of internalizing costs that would otherwise be external to one of the decisionmakers. Having decided on a liability rule rather than a property rule, it still must be decided who should be liable to whom. If the dock owner bears the costs of incompatible uses, he will be forced to choose between suffering injury to his dock or setting the boat adrift and risking liability under the rule in *Ploof.* Alternatively, if the boat owner bears the costs of incompatible uses, the boat owner (or captain) must choose between the risks of letting the boat drift and liability for damage to the dock under *Vincent.*

Question: Are the two parties in equivalent positions to evaluate the risk or is one party in the better position to evaluate the risks and act so as to minimize the risk?

4. In his dissent, Justice Lewis argued that the situation in *Vincent* differed from the usual emergency because the parties had a contractual relationship. That suggests that they had an opportunity to negotiate the allocation of the risks presented by potential emergencies. He believed that the risk of dock damage was part of the dock owner's cost of doing business.

Question: Should the contractual relationship between the parties make any difference to the assignment of liability in this case?

2. IMPEDIMENTS TO BARGAINING AND THE CHOICE OF REMEDIES

The *Ploof* and *Vincent* cases deal with trespass, a one-time invasion of another's property right to exclusive use of a resource. In the ordinary trespass, the parties have little opportunity to bargain. The trespasser may not have anticipated the trespass, and the person whose resource is invaded frequently is not even present for bargaining when the trespass occurs. Nuisance cases that involve a chronic, continuing invasion of another's right present different problems. The fundamental inquiry, however, is still whether there is any reason why, when one person's enjoyment of her resource is disturbed on a continuing basis by another's noise, vibration, or pollution, the parties cannot get together and bargain themselves into an efficient outcome. The following cases explore various transaction costs that may prevent allocative efficiency and raise questions about the efficiency of alternative remedies available to courts.

BOOMER v. ATLANTIC CEMENT COMPANY

Court of Appeals of New York, 1970.
26 N.Y.2d 219, 309 N.Y.S.2d 312, 257 N.E.2d 870.

BERGAN, JUDGE.

Defendant operates a large cement plant near Albany. These are actions for injunction and damages by neighboring land owners alleging injury to property from dirt, smoke and vibration emanating from the plant. A nuisance has been found after trial, temporary damages have been allowed; but an injunction has been denied. * * *

* * *

* * * The total damage to plaintiffs' properties is * * * relatively small in comparison with the value of defendant's operation and with the consequences of the injunction which plaintiffs seek.

The ground for the denial of injunction, notwithstanding the finding both that there is a nuisance and that plaintiffs have been damaged substantially, is the large disparity in economic consequences of the nuisance and of the injunction. This theory cannot, however, be sustained without overruling a doctrine which has been consistently reaffirmed in several leading cases in this court and which has never been disavowed here, namely that where a nuisance has been found and where there has been any substantial damage shown by the party complaining an injunction will be granted.

* * *

Although the court at Special Term and the Appellate Division held that injunction should be denied, it was found that plaintiffs had been damaged in various specific amounts up to the time of the trial and damages to the respective plaintiffs were awarded for those amounts. * * *

The court at Special Term also found the amount of permanent damage attributable to each plaintiff, for the guidance of the parties in the event both sides stipulated to the payment and acceptance of such permanent damage as a settlement of all the controversies among the parties. The total of permanent damages to all plaintiffs thus found was $185,000. * * *

This result at Special Term and at the Appellate Division is a departure from a rule that has become settled; but to follow the rule literally in these cases would be to close down the plant at once. This court is fully agreed to avoid that immediately drastic remedy; the difference in view is how best to avoid it. [The defendant's investment in the plant is in excess of $45,000,000. There are over 300 people employed there.]

One alternative is to grant the injunction but postpone its effect to a specified future date to give opportunity for technical advances to permit defendant to eliminate the nuisance; another is to grant the injunction conditioned on the payment of permanent damages to plaintiffs which would compensate them for the total economic loss to their property present and future caused by defendant's operations. For reasons which will be developed the court chooses the latter alternative.

* * *

[T]echniques to eliminate dust and other annoying by-products of cement making are unlikely to be developed by any research the defendant can undertake within any short period, but will depend on the total resources of the cement industry nationwide and throughout the world. The problem is universal wherever cement is made.

For obvious reasons the rate of the research is beyond control of defendant. If at the end of 18 months the whole industry has not found a technical solution a court would be hard put to close down this one cement plant if due regard be given to equitable principles.

On the other hand, to grant the injunction unless defendant pays plaintiffs such permanent damages as may be fixed by the court seems to do justice between the contending parties. All of the attributions of economic loss to the properties on which plaintiffs' complaints are based will have been redressed.

* * *

It seems reasonable to think that the risk of being required to pay permanent damages to injured property owners by cement plant owners would itself be a reasonable effective spur to research for improved techniques to minimize nuisance.

* * *

Thus it seems fair to both sides to grant permanent damages to plaintiffs which will terminate this private litigation. * * *

The judgment, by allowance of permanent damages imposing a servitude on land, which is the basis of the actions, would preclude future recovery by plaintiffs or their grantees.

* * *

The orders should be reversed, without costs, and the cases remitted to Supreme Court, Albany County to grant an injunction which shall be vacated upon payment by defendant of such amounts of permanent damage to the respective plaintiffs as shall for this purpose be determined by the court.

JASEN, JUDGE, dissenting.

* * *

It has long been the rule in this State, as the majority acknowledges, that a nuisance which results in substantial continuing damage to neighbors must be enjoined. To now change the rule to permit the cement company to continue polluting the air indefinitely upon the payment of permanent damages is, in my opinion, compounding the magnitude of a very serious problem in our State and Nation today.

The harmful nature and widespread occurrence of air pollution have been extensively documented. Congressional hearings have revealed that air pollution causes substantial property damage, as well as being a contributing factor to a rising incidence of lung cancer, emphysema, bronchitis and asthma.

* * *

I see grave dangers in overruling our long-established rule of granting an injunction where a nuisance results in substantial continuing damage. In permitting the injunction to become inoperative upon the payment of permanent damages, the majority is, in effect, licensing a continuing wrong. It is the same as saying to the cement company, you may continue to do harm to your neighbors so long as you pay a fee for it. Furthermore, once such permanent damages are assessed and paid, the incentive to alleviate the wrong would be eliminated, thereby continuing air pollution of an area without abatement.

* * *

This kind of inverse condemnation may not be invoked by a private person or corporation for private gain or advantage. Inverse condemnation should only be permitted when the public is primarily served in the taking or impairment of property. The promotion of the interests of the polluting cement company has, in my opinion, no public use or benefit.

* * *

I would enjoin the defendant cement company from continuing the discharge of dust particles upon its neighbors' properties unless, within 18 months, the cement company abated this nuisance.

* * *

Notes and Questions

1. Prior to *Boomer*, New York law recognized a right to injunction whenever a nuisance imposed significant costs on the plaintiff, without regard to any offsetting benefits from the nuisance-causing activity. Judge Bergan's opinion for the majority focused on the wastefulness of shutting down the defendant's $45 million plant just to avoid $185,000 in damages to the eight plaintiffs involved in this suit. Rather than shut down the plant, the injunction was conditioned upon the payment of damages. In effect, the plaintiff's property right to be free of the polluting nuisance was

transformed into a liability right to receive compensation for the injuries caused by the nuisance.

According to the Coase Theorem, if there are no impediments to bargaining between the homeowners and the cement plant, the parties will bargain their way to the efficient allocation no matter where the court initially assigns the right. The Coase Theorem focuses attention on the efficiency justification for a judicial decision that allows a resource, formerly protected by a property right, to be protected now only by a liability right. Suppose the cement plant was worth $45 million as an ongoing business but would be worthless if shut down.

> *Questions:* If an injunction had been issued as dissenting Judge Jasen wished, what is the maximum the cement plant's owners would offer to avoid being shut down? What is the minimum the homeowners would demand to allow it to continue operating? Could transaction costs have prevented the plant's owners from successfully bargaining with the plaintiffs to refrain from enforcing the injunction?

2. Because the injunctive remedy is the traditional relief accorded in nuisance cases, courts often focus on a balancing of harms and benefits from shutting down the polluter. For instance, in Koseris v. J.R. Simplot Co., 352 P.2d 235, 237 (Idaho 1960), the court found the following evidence relevant to its analysis of whether operation of the defendant's fertilizer plant created a nuisance:

> That in the operation of its fertilizer plant it carries on a leading industry in southeastern Idaho, with a capital investment of approximately $5,500,000; that its investment in inventory at the fertilizer plant in Power County as of November 1, 1957, was $1,627,207; that as of the same date its investment at the Gay Mine * * * exceeded $1,644,000; that payments to local businesses amounted to $1,030,000; that its other purchases and sales exceeded $8,500,000; that for the year 1956 it paid over $130,000 in taxes; that nearly 1,000 employees and their dependents rely for their livelihood upon the operations of the Simplot plant, and that it has an annual payroll of more than $1,242,000.

> That it had spent $223,688.00 for a fume and dust control system which constituted only a part of the total moneys expended in its attempts to control dust and fumes; that only 0.1% of any dust which is emitted from its plant due to its operations is discharged from its stacks.

The plaintiff's injured property contained only an abandoned night-club, which had been closed in 1951 under order of the sheriff and had been vacant until the time of trial except for the storage of small items. The trial court enjoined continued operation of the plant. The Idaho Supreme Court reversed on appeal, relying on the following policy argument from York v. Stallings, 341 P.2d 529, 534 (1959), where the Supreme Court of Oregon said:

> This court heretofore has accepted the balancing doctrine in cases involving the public convenience. In Fraser v. City of Portland, this court stated: " * * * sometimes a court of equity will decline to raise its restraining arm and refuse to issue an injunction * * * even though

an admitted legal right has been violated, when it appears that * * * the issuance of an injunction would cause serious public inconvenience or loss without a correspondingly great advantage to the complainant."

The balancing test applied by the Idaho Supreme Court in *Koseris* appears to encourage judges to reassign property rights to pollute, or to be free from pollution, to the user who values the right most highly (see *Ploof*). If Judge Bergan was certain the economic benefits of cement production outweighed the harms, he could simply have refused to grant an injunction.

> *Questions:* What is the justification for awarding damages in *Boomer?* What are the risks of awarding damages instead of granting an injunction? Consider dissenting Judge Jasen's point that pollution not only causes property damage, but also is "a contributing factor to a rising incidence of lung cancer, emphysema, bronchitis and asthma."

3.   The previous questions have developed the rationale for selecting a liability rule over a property rule in nuisance cases but have not addressed whether the cement plant or the homeowners should be given the incentive to investigate ways to reduce the costs of pollution.

> *Questions:* Is there any efficiency reason to provide this incentive to one party rather than the other in *Boomer?* Does the permanent damages solution provide incentives for finding ways to reduce future pollution?

SPUR INDUSTRIES, INC. v. DEL E. WEBB DEVELOPMENT CO.

Supreme Court of Arizona, In Banc., 1972.
108 Ariz. 178, 494 P.2d 700.

CAMERON VICE CHIEF JUSTICE.

From a judgment permanently enjoining the defendant, Spur Industries, Inc., from operating a cattle feedlot near the plaintiff Del E. Webb Development Company's Sun City, Spur appeals.   * * *

* * *

In 1956, Spur's predecessors in interest, H. Marion Welborn and the Northside Hay Mill and Trading Company, developed feed-lots, about 1/2 mile south of Olive Avenue, in an area between the confluence of the usually dry Agua Fria and New Rivers. The area is well suited for cattle feeding and in 1959, there were 25 cattle feeding pens or dairy operations within a 7 mile radius of the location developed by Spur's predecessors. In April and May of 1959, the Northside Hay Mill was feeding between 6,000 and 7,000 head of cattle and Welborn approximately 1,500 head on a combined area of 35 acres.

In May of 1959, Del Webb began to plan the development of an urban area to be known as Sun City. For this purpose, the Marinette and the Santa Fe Ranches, some 20,000 acres of farmland, were purchased for $15,000,000 or $750.00 per acre. This price was considerably less than the price of land located near the urban area of Phoenix, and along with the success of Youngtown[, a retirement community nearby,] was a factor influencing the decision to purchase the property in question.

* * *

Accompanied by an extensive advertising campaign, homes were first offered by Del Webb in January 1960 and the first unit to be completed was south of Grand Avenue and approximately 2 1/2 miles north of Spur. By 2 May 1960, there were 450 to 500 houses completed or under construction. At this time, Del Webb did not consider odors from the Spur feed pens a problem and Del Webb continued to develop in a southerly direction, until sales resistance became so great that the parcels were difficult if not impossible to sell. * * *

By December 1967, Del Webb's property had extended south to Olive Avenue and Spur was within 500 feet of Olive Avenue to the north. Del Webb filed its original complaint alleging that in excess of 1,300 lots in the southwest portion were unfit for development for sale as residential lots because of the operation of the Spur feedlot.

Del Webb's suit complained that the Spur feeding operation was a public nuisance because of the flies and the odor which were drifting or being blown by the prevailing south to north wind over the southern portion of Sun City. At the time of the suit, Spur was feeding between 20,000 and 30,000 head of cattle, and the facts amply support the finding of the trial court that the feed pens had become a nuisance to the people who resided in the southern part of Del Webb's development. * * *

* * *

It is clear that as to the citizens of Sun City, the operation of Spur's feedlot was both a public and a private nuisance. They could have successfully maintained an action to abate the nuisance. Del Webb, having shown a special injury in the loss of sales, had a standing to bring suit to enjoin the nuisance. The judgment of the trial court permanently enjoining the operation of the feedlot is affirmed.

* * *

In addition to protecting the public interest, however, courts of equity are concerned with protecting the operator of a lawful, albeit noxious, business from the result of a knowing and willful encroachment by others near his business.

In the so-called "coming to the nuisance" cases, the courts have held that the residential landowner may not have relief if he knowingly came into a neighborhood reserved for industrial or agricultural endeavors and has been damaged thereby. * * *

* * *

There was no indication in the instant case at the time Spur and its predecessors located in western Maricopa County that a new city would spring up, full-blown, alongside the feeding operation and that the developer of that city would ask the court to order Spur to move because of the new city. Spur is required to move not because of any wrongdoing on the part of Spur, but because of a proper and legitimate regard of the courts for the rights and interests of the public.

Del Webb, on the other hand, is entitled to the relief prayed for (a permanent injunction), not because Webb is blameless, but because of the damage to the people who have been encouraged to purchase homes in Sun City. It does not equitable or legally follow, however, that Webb, being entitled to the injunction, is then free of any liability to Spur if Webb has in fact been the cause of the damage Spur has sustained. It does not seem harsh to require a developer, who has taken advantage of the lesser land values in a rural area as well as the availability of large tracts of land on which to build and develop a new town or city in the area, to indemnify those who are forced to leave as a result.

Having brought people to the nuisance to the foreseeable detriment of Spur, Webb must indemnify Spur for a reasonable amount of the cost of moving or shutting down. * * *

It is therefore the decision of this court that the matter be remanded to the trial court for a hearing upon the damages sustained by the defendant Spur as a reasonably foreseeable and direct result of the granting of the permanent injunction. * * *

Notes and Questions

1. Instead of awarding damages to the land developer who suffered from the nuisance of the feedlot or simply enjoining the feedlot, the court in *Spur* awarded damages to the feedlot company, to compensate it for the expense of moving to a new location. The result has appealing distributional consequences, since the feedlot was doing business in its remote location for years before the Del E. Webb Development Co. decided to develop the area, and to require it to bear the costs of moving seems unfair.

Question: Is there any efficiency justification for requiring the plaintiff to pay damages in *Spur?*

2. At first, it might appear that the court in *Spur* assigned the right to receive damages to the wrong party. Certainly Spur would appear to be the party in the best position to control the insects and odors emanating from its feedlot, perhaps through use of pesticides or chlorophyll-impregnated feeds. Del Webb, however, could best evaluate whether it was worthwhile continuing to expand his residential community southward. If the concept of best cost avoider is interpreted a little more broadly, the efficient assignment of liability would consider whether one party is in the best position to avoid a conflict over uses at all, as well as whether one party can best reduce the costs of conflict.

Question: Does this interpretation of *best cost avoider* assist in choosing whether to impose liability on Spur or Del Webb?

3. Property rules may fail to allocate resources to their most valuable uses when transaction costs prevent bargaining from transferring a re-

source from a lower to a higher-valuing user. In such cases, damages determined by a factfinder act as a surrogate for voluntary exchanges between the parties. Rights protected by liability rules, however, also may fail to allocate resources efficiently where there is reason to doubt the judge's or jury's determination of value (i.e, the calculation of damages).

Impediments to bargaining may occasionally be greater in one direction of reallocation between parties than in the other. For example, suppose an injunction had been granted in *Boomer* and the cement plant found itself having to negotiate with the homeowners to purchase the right to pollute. If even one homeowner held out and refused to sell, the plant would have to shut down. If the injunction were denied, however, the homeowners would have to pay the cement plant to either stop production or to develop pollution control devices. If a few homeowners refused to contribute in the hope of "freeriding" on the others' efforts, the cement plant and the remaining homeowners might still reach a mutually satisfactory agreement. Because it is more difficult for the cement plant to bribe the homeowners than vice versa, a court might prefer to award a property right to the cement plant and refuse to enter the injunction.

Similar considerations may influence a court trying to decide which of two parties making competing claims for a resource should pay damages to the other. Calculating one party's damages may be more difficult than calculating the other's. In such a case, a court may wish to allocate the liability right so as to minimize the chance of an inefficient outcome due to inaccurate damage calculations.

> *Questions:* In Spur, which damage calculation was more reliable: Spur's claim to expenses incurred in moving the feedlot, or the homeowners' claims for losses due to the insects and odors emanating from the feedlot? How might this affect the court's decision as to which party should be required to pay damages?

4. A private nuisance, as in *Boomer,* interferes with a person's use and enjoyment of his property. While the cement particles falling on the plaintiffs' property may have dirtied their lawns, shrubs, and windows, and made their tennis courts slippery, the nuisance is private because it affected the use and enjoyment of their land. In *Spur* the nuisance of the flies and stenches was both private and public. A public nuisance interferes with a right common to the public, such as health, safety, and convenience, and need not be associated with possession of land. In *Spur,* the flies and stenches affected the use and enjoyment of the land Del Webb was developing and presented a health risk. The effect of a public nuisance is often more intangible, harder to quantify than a private nuisance's effect on the value of land.

> *Question:* Should the fact that public nuisances often involve more intangible harms affect the choice of efficient remedies between injunction and damages?

CARPENTER v. DOUBLE R CATTLE COMPANY, INC.

Court of Appeals of Idaho, 1983.
105 Idaho 320, 669 P.2d 643.

BURNETT, JUDGE.

* * *

This lawsuit was filed by a group of homeowners who alleged that expansion of a nearby cattle feedlot had created a nuisance. The homeowners claimed that operation of the expanded feedlot had caused noxious odors, air and water pollution, noise and pests in the area. The homeowners sought damages and injunctive relief. The issues of damages and injunctive relief were combined in a single trial, conducted before a jury. Apparently it was contemplated that the jury would perform a fact-finding function in determining whether a nuisance existed and whether the homeowners were entitled to damages, but would perform an advisory function on the question of injunctive relief. The district judge gave the jury a unified set of instructions embracing all of these functions. The jury returned a verdict simply finding that no nuisance existed. The court entered judgment for the feedlot proprietors, denying the homeowners any damages or injunctive relief. This appeal followed. For reasons appearing below, we vacate the judgment and remand the case for a new trial.

The homeowners contend that the jury received improper instructions on criteria for determining the existence of a nuisance. The jury was told to weigh the alleged injury to the homeowners against the "social value" of the feedlot, and to consider "the interests of the community as a whole," in determining whether a nuisance existed. * * *

* * *

The Second Restatement [of Torts] treats such an "intentional" invasion as a nuisance if it is "unreasonable." Section 826 of the Second Restatement now provides two sets of criteria for determining whether this type of nuisance exists:

An intentional invasion of another's interest in the use and enjoyment of land is unreasonable if

(a) the gravity of the harm outweighs the utility of the actor's conduct, or

(b) the harm caused by the conduct is serious and the financial burden of compensating for this and similar harm to others would not make the continuation of the conduct not feasible.

The present version of § 826, unlike its counterpart in the First Restatement, recognizes that liability for damages caused by a nuisance may exist regardless of whether the utility of the offending activity exceeds the gravity of the harm it has created. This fundamental proposition now permeates the entire Second Restatement. The commentary to § 822, which distinguishes between "intentional" and "unintentional" invasions, and which serves as the gateway for all succeeding sections, emphasizes that the test for existence of a nuisance no longer depends solely upon the balance between the gravity of harm and utility of the conduct. Comment d to § 822 states that, for the purpose of determining liability for damages, an invasion may be regarded as unreasonable even though the utility of the conduct is great and the amount of harm is relatively small. Comment g to the same section reemphasizes that damages are appropriate where the harm from the invasion is greater than a party should be required to bear, "at least without compensation."

* * *

Both the Second Restatement and [this Court's opinion in] *Koseris [v. J.R. Simplot]* recognize that utility of the activity alleged to be a nuisance is a proper factor to consider in the context of injunctive relief; but that damages may be awarded regardless of utility. Evidence of utility does not constitute a defense against recovery of damages where the harm is serious and compensation is feasible. Were the law otherwise, a large enterprise, important to the local economy, would have a lesser duty to compensate its neighbors for invasion of their rights than would a smaller business deemed less essential to the community. In our view, this is not, and should not be, the law in Idaho.

* * *

However, our view is not based simply upon general notions of fairness; it is also grounded in economics. The Second Restatement deals effectively with the problem of "externalities" identified in the [proceedings of the American Law Institute (ALI), which drafted the Second Restatement]. Where an enterprise externalizes some burdens upon its neighbors, without compensation, our market system does not reflect the true cost of products or services provided by that enterprise. Externalities distort the price signals essential to the proper functioning of the market.

This problem affects two fundamental objectives of the economic system. The first objective, commonly called "efficiency" in economic theory, is to promote the greatest aggregate surplus of benefits over the costs of economic activity. The second objective, usually termed "equity" or "distributive justice," is to allocate these benefits and costs in accordance with prevailing societal values. The market system best serves the goal of efficiency when prices reflect true costs; and the goal of distributive justice is best achieved when benefits are explicitly identified to the correlative costs.

Although the problem of externalities affects both goals of efficiency and distributive justice, these objectives are conceptually different and may imply different solutions to a given problem. In theory, if there were no societal goal other than efficiency, and if there were no impediments to exchanges of property or property rights, individuals pursuing their economic self-interests might reach the most efficient allocation of costs and benefits by means of exchange, without direction by the courts. However, the real world is not free from impediments to exchanges, and our economic system operates within the constraints of a society which is also concerned with distributive justice. Thus, the courts often are the battlegrounds upon which campaigns for efficiency and distributive justice are waged.

Our historical survey of nuisance law has reflected the differing emphasis upon efficiency and distributive justice. As noted, the English system of property law placed a preeminent value upon property rights. It was thus primarily concerned with distributive justice in accord with those rights. For that reason the English system favored the injunction as a remedy for a nuisance, regardless of disparate economic consequences. However, when the concept of nuisance was incorporated into American law, it encountered a different value system. Respect for property rights came to be tempered by the tort-related concept of fault, and the demands of a developing nation placed greater emphasis upon the economic objective of efficiency relative to the objective of distributive justice. The injunction fell into disfavor. The reaction against the injunction, as embodied in the First Restatement, so narrowed the concept of nuisance itself that it rendered the courts impotent to deal with externalities generated by enterprises of great utility. This reaction was excessive; neither efficiency nor distributive justice has been well served.

In order to address the problem of externalities, the remedies of damages and injunctive relief must be carefully chosen to accommodate the often competing goals of efficiency and distributive justice. *Koseris* and the Second Restatement recognize the complementary functions of injunctions and damages. Section 826(a) of the Second Restatement allows both injunctions and damages to be employed where the harm created by an economic activity exceeds its utility. Section 826(b) allows the more limited remedy of damages alone to be employed where it would not be appropriate to enjoin the activity but the activity is imposing harm upon its neighbors so substantial that they cannot reasonably be expected to bear it without compensation.

* * *

Each of the parties in the present case has viewed the Second Restatement with some apprehension. We now turn to those concerns.

The homeowners, echoing an argument made during the ALI proceedings, have contended that the test of nuisance set forth in § 826 grants large enterprises a form of private eminent domain. They evidently fear that if the utility of a large enterprise exceeds the gravity of the harm it creates—insulating it from an injunction and subjecting it to liability only in damages—the enterprise might interfere at will with the enjoyment and use of neighboring property, upon penalty only of paying compensation from time to time. Such a result might be consistent with the economic goal of efficiency, but it may conflict with the goal of distributive justice insofar as it violates a basic societal value which opposes forced exchanges of property rights.

Even those legal scholars who advocate the most limited role for injunctions as a remedy against nuisances acknowledge that damages may be inadequate, and injunctions may be necessary, where the harm in question relates to personal health and safety, or to one's fundamental freedom of action within the boundaries of his own property. Ordinarily, plaintiffs in such cases would prevail on the test which balances utility against gravity of the harm. Moreover, in the exceptional cases, the offending activity might be modified or eliminated through legislative or administrative controls such as environmental protection laws or zoning. Therefore, we expect that few cases would remain in need of a judicial remedy. However, we do not today close the door on the possibility that an injunction might lie, to protect personal health and safety or fundamental freedoms, in cases missed by the balancing test and by non-judicial controls. To this extent, our adoption of the Second Restatement's test of nuisance stops short of being absolute.

* * *

We conclude that the entire judgment of the district court, entered upon the verdict of a jury which had been improperly instructed, must be vacated. The case must be remanded for a new trial to determine whether a nuisance exists under the full criteria set forth in § 826 of the Second Restatement.

* * *

Notes and Questions

The trend in modern nuisance law has been to recognize a variety of alternative remedies for nuisance that combine both injunctive and damages components. While damages are typically the only available remedy for injuries already suffered by a plaintiff, the courts may deal with complaints of future harms by four variations of the remedies of damages or injunction:

> (1) granting the plaintiff an injunction, which halts the defendant's activity if the plaintiff enforces it;

> (2) awarding the plaintiff damages, which requires the defendant to compensate the plaintiff for future harm if the activity continues;

> (3) denying the plaintiff an injunction, which allows the defendant's activity to continue unless the plaintiff is willing and able to pay him to stop; or

> (4) awarding the defendant damages, which requires the plaintiff to compensate the defendant if the plaintiff wishes to halt the defendant's activity.

The notes and question following the preceding cases in this section have developed reasons why each of these types of remedies might be appropriate.

When devising a systematic outline of when each type is appropriate you will want to take into account the following considerations:

(1) whether we know for certain which is the more valuable use;

(2) whether we can say which of the parties is in the best position to evaluate the costs and benefits of the activities and act accordingly;

(3) what is the magnitude of transaction costs that would interfere with correcting an incorrect assignment of rights protected by property rules;

(4) what is the magnitude of costs associated with errors in damages calculations required by liability rules;

(5) whether transaction costs or damages calculations are likely to be more of a problem for one party than another; and

(6) what distributional concerns are present.

Questions: Which of the four remedies is appropriate under the facts of *Carpenter?* Which are consistent with Judge Burnett's opinion?

3. PATERNALISM AND INALIENABLE RIGHTS

Property rules prevent the transfer of an entitlement to a valuable resource unless the holder of the entitlement agrees to relinquish it in a voluntary exchange. Liability rules allow involuntary transfers if the person taking or interfering with another's entitlement pays damages in an amount determined by a neutral factfinder. A third rule governing entitlements might prohibit transfers of the entitlement altogether. Criminal rules prohibit the sale of hallucinogenic drugs, skins of rare animal species, or oneself into slavery. Rights to drugs, pelts of endangered species, and oneself cannot be transferred; they are inalienable. The following cases and materials examine whether prohibitions on such transactions are justified by concern for allocative efficiency and the circumstances under which transactions should be prohibited altogether.

SAMPLES v. MONROE

Court of Appeals of Georgia, 1987.
183 Ga.App. 187, 358 S.E.2d 273.

McMURRAY, PRESIDING JUDGE.

This action arises from the unmarried cohabitation of plaintiff and defendant for a period of approximately 14 years. Following the separation of the parties defendant established a residence with another woman.

Plaintiff alleges that during the period of cohabitation (1968–1982) she provided defendant with a residence, food, utilities and "paid all the necessary living expenses" for defendant, based upon the promises of defendant that his earnings would be saved for their mutual benefit. Plaintiff further alleges that the promises and statements of defendant made at the inception and during the course of their cohabitation were intentionally made to deceive plaintiff, resulting in the unjust enrichment of defendant and causing plaintiff to suffer monetary loss and mental pain and suffering. Based on theories of contract and fraud, plaintiff seeks the value of her services rendered defendant, a recovery of one-half of defendant's savings, exemplary damages, attorney fees, and costs.

Following discovery, the superior court granted defendant's motion for summary judgment. Plaintiff appeals the grant of summary judgment in favor of defendant. *Held:*

Insofar as plaintiff's action is predicated upon contract principles, it is barred by OCGA § 13–8–1, which provides in part that: "A contract to do an immoral or illegal thing is void." Plaintiff's deposition acknowledges that sex had always been part of her relationship with defendant, that sex was a part of what she furnished defendant and that defendant probably would not have moved in with her had she indicated to him that she wasn't going to give him any sex. Plaintiff's arrangement with defendant is further illustrated by the following excerpt from her deposition: "Q. Alright. Let me see if I've got this straight now. When he moved in with you, you told him that you'd render all the services to him that a wife would render to a husband, including sex. A. Yes sir. Q. And including takin' care of him? A. Yes. Q. If in consideration for that, if he'd save his money and he'd put it into an account where you two would have a nest egg where you could retire early? A. That's right." In Georgia, sexual intercourse outside of marriage is a criminal offense. *"It is well settled that neither a court of law nor a court of equity will lend its aid to either party to a contract founded upon an illegal or immoral consideration."*

* * * [T]he uncontradicted evidence shows that plaintiff's arrangement with defendant envisioned a meretricious relationship rather than a simple agreement to share living expenses. "A contract founded upon a promise to live in the future in a meretricious state is void."
* * *

* * * The trial court did not err in granting defendant's motion for summary judgment.

Judgment affirmed.

CALABRESI AND MELAMED, PROPERTY RULES, LIABILITY RULES, AND INALIENABILITY: ONE VIEW OF THE CATHEDRAL *

85 Harv.L.Rev. 1089, 1111–15 (1972).

Thus far we have focused on the questions of when society should protect an entitlement by property or liability rules. However, there remain many entitlements which involve a still greater degree of societal intervention: the law not only decides who is to own something and what price is to be paid for it if it is taken or destroyed, but also regulates its sale—by, for example, prescribing preconditions for a valid sale or forbidding a sale altogether. Although these rules of inalienability are substantially different from the property and liability rules, their use can be analyzed in terms of the same efficiency and distributional goals that underlie the use of the other two rules.

While at first glance efficiency objectives may seem undermined by limitations on the ability to engage in transactions, closer analysis suggests that there are instances, perhaps many, in which economic efficiency is more closely approximated by such limitations. This might occur when a transaction would create significant externalities— costs to third parties.

For instance, if Taney were allowed to sell his land to Chase, a polluter, he would injure his neighbor Marshall by lowering the value of Marshall's land. Conceivably, Marshall could pay Taney not to sell his land; but, because there are many injured Marshalls, freeloader and information costs make such transactions practically impossible. The state could protect the Marshalls and yet facilitate the sale of the land by giving the Marshalls an entitlement to prevent Taney's sale to Chase but only protecting the entitlement by a liability rule. It might, for instance, charge an excise tax on all sales of land to polluters equal to its estimate of the external cost to the Marshalls of the sale. But where there are so many injured Marshalls that the price required under the liability rule is likely to be high enough so that no one would be willing to pay it, then setting up the machinery for collective valuation will be wasteful. Barring the sale to polluters will be the most efficient result because it is clear that avoiding pollution is cheaper than paying its cost—including its costs to the Marshalls.

Another instance in which external costs may justify inalienability occurs when external costs do not lend themselves to collective measurement which is acceptably objective and nonarbitrary. This nonmonetizability is characteristic of one category of external costs which, as a practical matter, seems frequently to lead us to rules of inalienability. Such external costs are often called moralisms.

If Taney is allowed to sell himself into slavery, or to take undue risks of becoming penniless, or to sell a kidney, Marshall may be harmed, simply because Marshall is a sensitive man who is made unhappy by seeing slaves, paupers, or persons who die because they have sold a kidney. Again Marshall could pay Taney not to sell his freedom to Chase the slaveowner; but again, because Marshall is not one but many individuals, freeloader and information costs make such transactions practically impossible. Again, it might seem that the state could intervene by objectively valuing the external cost to Marshall and requiring Chase to pay that cost. But since the external cost to Marshall does not lend itself to an acceptable objective measurement, such liability rules are not appropriate.

In the case of Taney selling land to Chase, the polluter, they were inappropriate because we *knew* that the costs to Taney and the Marshalls exceeded the benefits to Chase. Here, though we are not certain of how a cost-benefit analysis would come out, liability rules are inappropriate because any monetization is, by hypothesis, out of the question. The state must, therefore, either ignore the external costs to Marshall, or if it judges them great enough, forbid the transaction that gave rise to them by making Taney's freedom inalienable.

* * *

There are two other efficiency reasons for forbidding the sale of entitlements under certain circumstances: self paternalism and true paternalism. Examples of the first are Ulysses tying himself to the mast or individuals passing a bill of rights so that they will be prevented from yielding to momentary temptations which they deem harmful to themselves. This type of limitation is not in any real sense paternalism. It is fully consistent with Pareto efficiency criteria, based on the notion that over the mass of cases no one knows better than the individual what is best for him or her. It merely allows the individual to choose what is best in the long run rather than in the short run, even though that choice entails giving up some short run freedom of choice. Self paternalism may cause us to require certain conditions to exist before we allow a sale of an entitlement; and it may help explain many situations of inalienability, like the invalidity of contracts entered into when drunk, or under undue influence or coercion. But it probably does not fully explain even these.

True paternalism brings us a step further toward explaining such prohibitions and those of broader kinds—for example the prohibitions on a whole range of activities by minors. Paternalism is based on the notion that at least in some situations the Marshalls know better than Taney what will make Taney better off. Here we are not talking about the offense to Marshall from Taney's choosing to read pornography, or selling himself into slavery, but rather the judgment that Taney was not in the position to choose best for himself when he made the choice for erotica or servitude.

The first concept we called a moralism and is a frequent and important ground for inalienability. But it is consistent with the premises of Pareto optimality. The second, paternalism, is also an important economic efficiency reason for inalienability, but it is not consistent with the premises of Pareto optimality: the most efficient pie is no longer that which costless bargains would achieve, because a person may be better off if he is prohibited from bargaining.

Finally, just as efficiency goals sometimes dictate the use of rules of inalienability, so, of course, do distributional goals. Whether an entitlement may be sold or not often affects directly who is richer and who is poorer. Prohibiting the sale of babies makes poorer those who can cheaply produce babies and richer those who through some non-market device get free an "unwanted" baby. Prohibiting exculpatory clauses in product sales makes richer those who were injured by a product defect and poorer those who were not injured and who paid more for the product because the exculpatory clause was forbidden. Favoring the specific group that has benefited may or may not have been the reason for the prohibition on bargaining. What is important is that, regardless of the reason for barring a contract, a group did gain from the prohibition.

This should suffice to put us on guard, for it suggests that direct distributional motives may lie behind asserted nondistributional grounds for inalienability, whether they be paternalism, self paternalism, or externalities. * * * For example, we may use certain types of zoning to preserve open spaces on the grounds that the poor will be happier, though they do not know it now. And open spaces may indeed make the poor happier in the long run. But the zoning that preserves open space also makes housing in the suburbs more expensive and it may be that the whole plan is aimed at securing distributional benefits to the suburban dweller regardless of the poor's happiness.

Notes and Questions

1. Maximizing the value of the goods produced in society requires that each scarce resource go to the party willing and able to pay the highest price. Maximizing utility or wealth under the Pareto criteria requires that society pursue all exchanges or reallocations that make at least one person better off and no one worse off, in terms of utility or wealth, respectively.

Questions: From the perspective of Ms. Samples and Mr. Monroe, was the agreement to exchange Ms. Sample's sexual and other services in exchange for a one-half interest in Mr. Monroe's savings a Pareto superior exchange? Did the exchange increase the value of the resources involved, as measured by willingness to pay?

2. Throughout Chapters 1 and 2, economic analysis is used to evaluate whether particular rules interfere with allocating resources to their most valuable uses. Even one unacquainted with the logic of economic efficiency would undoubtedly be able to think of (even if unwilling to accept) some policy justification for prohibiting the sale of sexual services, particularly when it takes the form of prostitution. Many such policy arguments can be described as being concerned with the external effects of prostitution on parties not immediately involved in the transaction.

Questions: What are the external costs of prostitution and who bears them? Are paternalistic interests protected by a rule making sexual services inalienable? Are those costs and interests compelling enough to outweigh the benefits to the immediate parties to the transaction?

3. Calabresi and Melamed point out that rules of inalienability have distributional as well as efficiency consequences.

Question: What are the distributional implications of a prohibition on the sale of children or of sexual services?

4. In People v. Daniel, 241 Cal.Rptr. 3 (Cal. Ct. App. 1987), the court denied the defendant the right (a property right) to sell his child to adoptive parents.

Questions: What efficiency justifications support the court's conclusion that this right should be inalienable? How do these efficiency justifications compare to the moral justifications for prohibiting the sale of children?

5. Imagine a community so poor in other resources that all its members found it acceptable to sell their babies to eager buyers in the neighboring wealthy community. All exchanges were voluntary and the babies had the opportunity to grow up in a family with bounteous material resources. Some members of the wealthy community, however, might object to the buying and selling of babies because they are deeply offended by treating babies as property and believe that a market for babies demeans the humanity of not only the babies but those who engage in the transactions. They may believe, contrary to the beliefs of the parties to the transactions, that engaging in the buying and selling is so bad for the participants' morals and standards that the participants are always worse off as a result of the transaction and pass criminal rules to prohibit the transactions.

Questions: Is such a paternalistic rule inconsistent with Pareto optimality? Allocative efficiency?

4. CREATING NEW ENTITLEMENTS: PROPERTY, LIABILITY, OR INALIENABILITY?

Protecting an entitlement to a resource with a property rule encourages the efficient reallocation of the resource through voluntary exchange so long as there are no substantial impediments to bargaining between parties. Where transactions costs are high, liability rules can encourage efficient reallocations when court-ordered damages act as a surrogate for exchange. A rule of inalienability may be appropriate where it prevents costs to third parties, serves paternalistic interests, or has desirable distributional consequences.

When a resource becomes sufficiently scarce to subject it to competing claims, the state resolving those claims must decide whether to protect the claimants' interests with a property, liability, or inalienability rule. In addition, the state must decide to whom the right should be allocated. A court deciding to whom a resource should be allocated may consider: (1) who values the resource most highly, and so would be the most efficient user; (2) who is in the best position to calculate the costs and benefits of using the resource and to act to minimize costs and maximize benefits; and (3) whether transactions costs or inaccurate damages are a greater risk if the right is assigned to one party than to the other.

The following case deals with the evolution of a new form of entitlement. In reading it, consider what form of rule should be used to protect the entitlement—property, liability, or inalienability? To whom should the entitlement be granted?

MOORE v. REGENTS OF THE UNIVERSITY OF CALIFORNIA

Court of Appeal, Second Division, California, 1988.
215 Cal.App.3d 709, 249 Cal.Rptr. 494.

ROTHMAN, ASSOCIATE JUSTICE.

This appeal raises fundamental questions concerning a patient's right to the control of his or her own body, and whether the commercial exploitation of a patient's cells by medical care providers, without the patient's consent, gives rise to an action for damages. This appears to be a case of first impression.

In 1976, plaintiff and appellant sought medical treatment at the Medical Center of the University of California, Los Angeles (UCLA), for a condition known as hairy-cell leukemia. He was seen by Dr. David W. Golde, who confirmed the diagnosis. As a necessary part of the treatment for this disease, plaintiff's spleen was removed at UCLA in October of 1976.

Without plaintiff's knowledge or consent, Dr. Golde and Shirley G. Quan, a UCLA employee, determined that plaintiff's cells were unique. Through the science of genetic engineering, these defendants developed a cell-line from plaintiff's cells which is capable of producing pharmaceutical products of enormous therapeutic and commercial value. The Regents, Golde and Quan patented the cell-line along with methods of producing many products therefrom. In addition, these defendants entered into a series of commercial agreements for rights to the cell-line and its products with Sandoz Pharmaceuticals Corporation (Sandoz) and Genetics Institute, Inc. (Genetics). The market potential of products from plaintiff's cell-line was predicted to be approximately three billion dollars by 1990. Hundreds of thousands of dollars have already been paid under these agreements to the developers. Without informing plaintiff, and in pursuit of their research efforts, Golde and UCLA continued to monitor him and take tissue samples from him for almost seven years following the removal of his spleen.

* * *

In deciding whether plaintiff can state a cause of action for conversion on the facts set forth in his complaint, it is necessary to review the requirements of conversion.

Conversion is "a distinct act of dominion wrongfully exerted over another's personal property in denial of or inconsistent with his title or rights therein, ... without the owner's consent and without lawful justification." It is " 'an act of wilful interference with a chattel, done without lawful justification, by which any person entitled thereto is deprived of use and possession.' "

For conversion, a plaintiff need only allege: "(1) plaintiffs' ownership or right to possession of the property at the time of the conversion; (2) defendants' conversion by a wrongful act or disposition of plaintiffs' property rights; and (3) damages."

* * *

The complaint alleges that plaintiff's tissues, including his spleen, blood, and the cell-line derived from his cells "are his tangible personal property." This is the crux of plaintiff's case for conversion.

* * *

We have approached this issue with caution. The evolution of civilization from slavery to freedom, from regarding people as chattels to recognition of the individual dignity of each person, necessitates prudence in attributing the qualities of property to human tissue. There is, however, a dramatic difference between having property rights in one's own body and being the property of another. To our knowledge, no public policy has ever been articulated, nor is there any statutory authority, against a property interest in one's own body. We are not called on to determine whether use of human tissue or body parts ought to be "gift based" or subject to a "free market." That question of policy must be determined by the Legislature. In the instant case, the cell-line has already been commercialized by defendants. We are presented a fait accompli, leaving only the question of who shares in the proceeds.

* * *

In our evaluation of the law of property, we consider the definition of the word "property" [and] find nothing which negates, and much which supports, the conclusion that plaintiff had a property interest in his genetic material.

"As a matter of legal definition, 'property' refers not to a particular material object but to the right and interest or domination rightfully obtained over such object, with the unrestricted right to its use, enjoyment and disposition. In other words, [in] its strict legal sense 'property' signifies that dominion or indefinite right of user, control, and disposition which one may lawfully exercise over particular things or objects; thus 'property' is nothing more than a collection of rights."

* * *

Plaintiff's spleen, which contained certain cells, was something over which plaintiff enjoyed the unrestricted right to use, control and disposition.

The rights of dominion over one's own body, and the interests one has therein, are recognized in many cases. These rights and interests are so akin to property interests that it would be a subterfuge to call them something else.

* * *

We are told that if plaintiff is permitted to have decisionmaking authority and a financial interest in the cell-line, he would then have the unlimited power to inhibit medical research that could potentially benefit humanity. He could conceivably go from institution to institution seeking the highest bid, and if dissatisfied, "would claim the right simply to prohibit the research entirely."

We concede that, if informed, a patient might refuse to participate in a research program. We would give the patient that right. As to defendants' concern that a patient might seek the greatest economic gain for his participation, this argument is unpersuasive because it fails to explain why defendants, who patented plaintiff's cell-line and are benefiting financially from it, are any more to be trusted with these momentous decisions than the person whose cells are being used. It has been suggested by writers that biotechnology is no longer a purely research oriented field in which the primary incentives are academic or for the betterment of humanity. Biological materials no longer pass freely to all scientists. As here, the rush to patent for exclusive use is rampant. The links being established between academics and industry to profitize biological specimens are a subject of great concern. If this science has become science for profit, then we fail to see any justification for excluding the patient from participation in those profits.

* * *

The judgments of dismissal are reversed with directions to the trial court to take proceedings consistent with the views set forth in the foregoing opinion.

* * *

GEORGE, ASSOCIATE JUSTICE.

I dissent.

* * *

I am greatly concerned about the full implications of the majority's ruling that body fluids and parts constitute a form of property. There are those who believe " 'society will benefit ... from a market in body parts'.... More body parts would be available for recipients, and donors would gain a means to make money." "Some people are revolted by the thought of a woman selling her aborted fetus. Others think it is only fair." (Sherman, *The Selling of Body Parts*, (1987) National L.J. 1.)

Plaintiff himself admits, in his third amended complaint, that had he been aware of the commercial potential of his diseased spleen he "would have considered whether to avail himself of medical, surgical and health care services at other facilities and institutions, where his wishes in this regard would have been inquired into, respected, and carried out. [P]laintiff would have sought to participate in the economic and financial benefit defendants ... are likely to receive, as a result of their research and commercial activities...."

The absence of legislation regulating the trafficking in human body parts (except where transplantation is involved) raises the specter of thriving "used body parts" establishments emulating their automotive counterparts, but not subject to regulation comparable to that governing the latter trade.

I believe we are not authorized, and should not be inclined, to create new rights and remedies in an area which so clearly lies outside the bounds of the legislatively defined cause of action for conversion and is so unsuited to judicial intervention.

* * *

Various "arguments against recognition of property rights" in human bodily substances are listed in Hardiman, *Toward the Right of Commerciality*, [34 UCLA L.Rev. 207,] 236–237 [1987]. They warrant recitation, not because I feel we are in a position to adopt or reject these arguments, but because they illustrate the complexity of the issues before us and the superiority of the Legislature's fact-finding capabilities over our own in resolving these questions: "Although compelling arguments support recognizing property rights in human tissue, arguments against recognition may also be raised. These arguments include: the potential for adverse effects on organ donation for transplantation usage; the moral aversion to treating the body as a commodity; the effect of patient hold-outs and higher transaction costs on research and tissue availability; and the threat of improper motivation in the area of tissue acquisition....

"Several potentially persuasive arguments against property rights arise in the context of organ transplantation. Opponents of organ sales predict a variety of adverse effects should a market in human organs arise: decreases in the number of organs charitably donated; increases in the number of inferior organs; competitive bidding between patients for limited resources; financial pressure on the poor to sell their organs; and unacceptable risks of death for a pecuniary profit. Without question, any adverse effects of property rights on the organ donation system are of critical importance to the health of the populace. If these rights seriously interfere with the availability of life-saving transplantable organs, the cost of recognizing the patient's rights may be too high for society to bear."

If a patient with unusual bodily substances is encouraged (as he or she will be, by today's decision) to shop around for the highest bid on the patient's spleen, tissue, blood, or other bodily substance, the quality of health care and medical research undoubtedly will suffer. By recognizing a property right in such substances, and expanding informed consent to include advisement of potential research and commercial use of the matter removed from the patient's body, the majority clearly establishes a right to bargain over body parts and share in the financial windfall that sometimes ensues from years of expensive medical research.

The right to be advised of research and commercial use of substances taken from one's body implies the right to withhold consent for such use. As one of many illustrations of the potential ramifications of the majority's ruling, we need consider only the current massive effort to eradicate the lethal AIDS virus. Any determination granting a patient the unilateral right to forbid the use of tissues and fluids, already taken from his or her body, in research designed to find a cure to a disease posing a grave threat to public health, should be left to the Legislature. It should also be noted that the problems of consent, and of "profit-sharing," are compounded where specimens from several individuals (or perhaps several hundred or several thousand) are utilized in effecting a cure for a deadly disease.

Much of the New Jersey Supreme Court's characterization of "baby-bartering" in the celebrated case of *Matter of Baby M.* (1988) 109 N.J. 396, 537 A.2d 1227 is equally applicable to "body-part bargaining": "The evils inherent in baby-bartering are loathsome for a myriad of reasons. The child is sold.... Baby-selling potentially results in the exploitation of all parties involved." "Whatever idealism may have motivated any of the participants, the profit motive predominates, permeates, and ultimately governs the transaction. The demand for children is great and the supply small.... The situation is ripe for the entry of the middleman who will bring some equilibrium into the market by increasing the supply through the use of money." "There are, in a civilized society, some things that money cannot buy.... There are, in short, values that society deems more important than granting to wealth whatever it can buy, be it labor, love, or life."

* * *

Notes and Questions

1. In 1990, the Supreme Court of California reversed the Court of Appeals, holding that Mr. Moore did not have a cause of action for conversion but that he had properly stated a cause of action for breach of fiduciary duty and lack of informed consent, thereby keeping alive the property rights questions raised in this Chapter. The line of *Moore* cases clearly presents the issues of who should have the right to a living patient's body parts once removed and, if that right is to be given to the patient, whether that right should be protected by a property rule, a liability rule, or a rule of inalienability.

Question: Taking into account the various considerations raised in this section, what rule is most consistent with the goal of efficiency?

2.   Mr. Moore was alive and competent before and after his spleen was removed.   Many body parts used for transplantation are removed from individuals who are legally dead.   42 U.S.C. § 274e(a) (1989) provides that:

It shall be unlawful for any person to knowingly acquire, receive, or otherwise transfer any human organ for valuable consideration for use in human transplantation if the transfer affects interstate commerce.

Section 274e(a) does not prohibit the use of organs for transplantation. It does, however, prohibit the *sale* of organs.

Questions: What is the effect of this statute on the supply of organs available for transplantation?   Is a rule of inalienability appropriate for organs removed from cadavers?   Does the analysis of such a case differ from the analysis of *Moore?*

Chapter 3

THE ECONOMIC ANALYSIS
OF TORT LAW

A. LIABILITY AS AN INCENTIVE
FOR EFFICIENT BEHAVIOR

People's daily activities inevitably consume scarce resources, at a minimum, human energy or time. It is easy to appreciate that many activities result in the unintentional destruction of property or injury to persons. The economic analysis of tort law focuses on the allocation of the risks of loss due to the destruction of property or injury to persons created by those activities. Tort law may be viewed as a system of rules designed to maximize wealth by allocating risks so as to minimize the costs associated with engaging in daily activities. The materials in this chapter explore how tort law allocates the costs of accidents to those in the best position to minimize those costs. The economic analysis of tort law begins by examining how the law encourages people to allocate resources to accident prevention.

WINN DIXIE STORES, INC. v. BENTON

District Court of Appeal of Florida, Fourth District, 1991.
576 So.2d 359.

STONE, JUDGE.

The appellee was injured in a slip and fall in appellant's market. We affirm a final judgment, entered following a jury verdict for the plaintiff, and find no error in the trial court's denial of Winn Dixie's motions for directed verdict and for judgment notwithstanding the verdict.

At the point of the fall there was a puddle of milk, five to eight inches long and three to four inches wide. There were also milk drops on the floor in a thirty foot trail from the milk container case to the puddle and for another fifty feet from the puddle to the checkout lines.

The drops were in an even pattern, one to one and a half feet apart. A leaky half gallon or gallon milk carton, one quarter empty, was found at the checkout area immediately after the fall. The appellant asserts that the store is normally busy at the time of the accident but appellee argues that this is refuted by the evidence that there were no other customers in the dairy aisle. The floor had not been swept for more than one-half hour prior to the incident. There was evidence that the store manager did not conduct his customary floor inspection that afternoon, and the manager's testimony that he had "inspected" that particular aisle fifteen minutes before the accident was questioned by plaintiff's challenges to the credibility of the witness.

The evidence, any conflicts in the evidence, and all reasonable conclusions which may be drawn from the evidence, must be resolved in favor of the appellee.

It was plaintiff's burden to prove that the milk was on the floor sufficiently long to charge Winn Dixie with notice. Notice may be proved by circumstantial evidence. It has frequently been recognized that the condition of the floor, the nature of the substance on the floor, and the surrounding circumstances, may be sufficient to support an inference by the jury that a dangerous condition existed long enough for the store employees to know, or that they should have known, of the condition. Under such circumstances the issue is for the jury to resolve even where the evidence may be susceptible of more than one reasonable inference.

Resolving whether the store should have discovered the danger in this case did not require the jury to build an inference on an inference. Nor do we consider resolution of the notice issue here to require pure speculation, deemed unacceptable in *Winn Dixie Stores, Inc. v. Gaines Publix Super* and *Markets, Inc. v. Schmidt.*

It was within the province of the jury to decide whether the milk had been dripping for a sufficiently long period to be discovered in the exercise of reasonable care.

WARNER, JUDGE, dissenting.

In my view the evidence shows that a *maximum* of five to ten minutes passed between the last time a store employee walked down the aisle and the injury to appellee occurred. The milk puddle was fresh and there were no tire tracks through it. The evidence is insufficient to show that the management knew or should have known that the dripping milk was on the floor for a sufficient time to be discovered.

Notes and Questions

1. The activities of operating a grocery store and shopping for groceries consume resources and create risks. One of the risks created materialized in *Winn Dixie* when Dorothea Benton slipped and fell on spilt milk. Being made liable for Benton's injury gives Winn Dixie an incentive to think about how to operate this store in the future. Closing down the store

is one way to ensure that no similar accidents occur in the future. If the store is to remain open, however, the owners must choose whether to find other ways to avoid such accidents or accept the financial consequences of letting accidents occur occasionally.

Almost every activity presents the risk of accidents. While the risks in flying airplanes, keeping pet bears, and racing automobiles are obvious, many seemingly harmless activities pose risks as well. Smelling a flower presents the risk of inhaling a bumble bee; serving spaghetti poses the risk of choking to death on a meatball. Accidents impose costs on victims and society would be better off, in both utility and wealth terms, if accidents did not occur.

The risk of accidents can be reduced by investing in precautionary measures. Accident avoidance techniques other than closing down the store in *Winn Dixie* included stationing an employee in every aisle with a mop to clean up immediately or inspecting the floors more frequently to make sure that they are clean and dry. These alternatives vary from relatively inexpensive ways of avoiding injury to customers (regular inspections) to extremely costly ways (closing down). Society would certainly be better off if both the cost of having accidents occur and the cost of safety precautions could be avoided. In his 1970 book, The Costs of Accidents: A Legal and Economic Analysis, Guido Calabresi described the harms resulting from accidents when they occur and the costs of preventing accidents as *primary accident costs*. From a wealth maximizing perspective, one goal of tort law is minimizing primary accident costs, the sum of the cost of having and the cost of avoiding accidents.

2. The possibility of accidents presents a policy dilemma, whether to bear the costs of having accidents or the costs of avoiding accidents. By imposing liability on the grocery store in *Winn Dixie,* the court informed the defendant and owners of other groceries that when they fail to use reasonable care to discover hazards in their stores, they will be required to pay for harm that results. This rule of law internalizes to the stores costs that otherwise would be external to their decisionmaking. This liability rule forces grocery store owners to choose between bearing the costs of such accidents in the future and bearing the costs of taking precautions.

Question: How does the imposition of liability align the profit-making incentives of the grocery store owner with the societal goal of wealth maximization?

3. Accidents resulting from engaging in various activities that pose risks for others can easily be viewed as analogous to the externalities created by the intentional activities discussed in the nuisance cases of Chapter 2. In those nuisance cases, sometimes injunctive relief is the preferred remedy and sometimes damages are preferred. In most torts cases, damages are assumed to be the appropriate remedy.

Question: Reflecting back on the material in Chapter 2, what efficiency justification is there for assessing damages rather than issuing an injunction in the torts context?

4. In American Airlines v. Ulen, 186 F.2d 529 (D.C. Cir., 1949), an airplane flying from Washington D.C. to Mexico City, Mexico crashed into

the top of Glade Mountain in southwest Virginia killing both the pilot and co-pilot and seriously injuring Violet Ulen. While Glade Mountain is 4080 feet high, the pilot's flight plan called for flying at an altitude of 4000 feet on that leg of the flight. The court found that the pilot was negligent as a matter of law.

Questions: What purpose is served by making American Airlines liable in *Ulen?* Is it likely that the imposition of liability will induce pilots to take more care in planning their routes?

DRAKE v. LERNER SHOPS OF COLORADO, INC.

Supreme Court of Colorado, 1960.
145 Colo. 1, 357 P.2d 624.

DOYLE, JUSTICE.

* * * Plaintiff instituted the action seeking damages resulting from a fall suffered as she emerged from the defendant's store. Plaintiff fell to the sidewalk and suffered a fractured hip and other injuries. Trial was had to a jury and at the close of the plaintiff's evidence dismissal was ordered. She seeks review of the judgment.

The defendant operates a clothing store at the corner of 16th and Champa streets in Denver. One entrance is on 16th Street and the other is on Champa. The injury occurred as plaintiff was leaving the store from the Champa Street entrance where there are two sets of heavy glass doors leading to the outside. The inside set of doors were opened inward, and the outside set were closed and had to be pushed open by one making an exit. Beyond the outer set of doors is an area three feet in length leading to the sidewalk and which is some five inches above the sidewalk. This area is terrazzo and is on the floor level of the store. As one exits from the store there are decals on either side of the doors at about eye level. These have the words "Step Down" an them. The opposite side of the decals read "Pull".

Plaintiff testified that as she walked out the sun was shining and its reflection against a white building across the street was such that she could not see well and that she did not observe the "Step Down" signs, and was not aware of the five inch drop-off to the sidewalk. As a consequence she fell and was injured.

The injury occurred on August 6, 1957, and on that day the sun was shining brightly. Photographs introduced in evidence tended to show that the warning signs were difficult to read up close. Another photo introduced by defendant established that the sign was clear from a few feet distance.

In granting the defendant's motion the trial court found the occurrence to have been an accident; that the defendant was free of negligence. In his remarks the judge concluded:

"The Court further finds from the evidence in this case that there was no breach of any duty by the defendant. I believe the evidence unequivocally shows, and the Court so finds, that there is no dangerous condition existing in the Lerner Shops at the entrance on Champa Street; further, that nowhere in the evidence can the Court find that there is any defective condition. Now, the law is pretty well settled on the question that all the duty the defendant has is ordinary care for safe conditions.

* * *

"The Court feels from the evidence in this case that the plaintiff has relied solely on a mere accident and not upon any negligence on the part of the defendant."

In urging that the court erred in holding that the evidence was insufficient as a matter of law, plaintiff argues that the evidence gave rise to conflicting inferences and that the court pronounced its own view—that the facts presented justify a contrary finding that a condition of danger foreseeable to defendant existed, and that defendant failed in its duty to give adequate warning or in any other manner to protect the plaintiff.

The question for determination is whether the maintaining of a step under the circumstances described constitutes sufficient negligence to require submission of the case to a jury. We conclude that it does not.

* * *

In order to establish a prima facie case of negligence, plaintiff's evidence must establish the existence on the premises of an unreasonable risk of harm to her as an invitee. The mere existence of risk is not sufficient. Some degree of risk is present in our every activity and if existence of hazard alone were the standard, it would mean that the happening of an accident would be sufficient to raise a presumption of negligence and the landowner would be an insurer of the safety of his patrons. Such is not the law. The condition created by the conduct or activity of the landowner must pose an *appreciable* risk of harm. The defendant's conduct must threaten harm.

Considering the evidence in a light most favorable to plaintiff, it cannot be said that the condition about which she complains was such as to create an appreciable risk of harm. A step down of five inches is not a hazard which of itself suggests likelihood of harm, and consequently defendant was not required to eliminate it or to provide safeguards other than those which it did provide in order to satisfy the standard required by law. The photographs here indicate that defendant gave a reasonable warning; that the step was plainly visible, and it cannot be said that defendant's failure to provide against the reflection of the sun on the building opposite his own constituted negligence. * * * Here no actionable threat of harm is apparent.

The judgment is affirmed.

Notes and Questions

1. Unlike *Winn Dixie*, where the court required the defendant to pay damages to the injured customer, the court in *Drake* denied compensation

to the customer. If the imposition of liability is designed to give store owners an incentive to avoid accidents, the holding in *Drake* suggests that there must be some accidents that defendants need not avoid. The incentives created by the imposition of liability only result in precautions by the rational maximizer if the cost of those precautions is less than the expected liability from future accidents. Since both having and avoiding accidents impose costs and the wealth of society is maximized by minimizing those costs, the allocative efficiency goal in tort law is described as minimizing primary accident costs. Since primary accident costs include both the costs of having and the costs of avoiding accidents, the efficiency goal explicitly recognizes that, from a societal perspective, some accidents are not worth avoiding. A tort law designed to minimize accident costs is actually encouraging accidents, a heartless perspective that places wealth maximization above safety. Some accidents will be avoided and some will not.

Courts recognize that some precautions are not worth taking. As Judge Breyer said in Rhode Island Hospital Trust National Bank v. Zapata Corp., 848 F.2d 291, 295 (1st Cir. 1988), "One does not, for example, coat the base of the Grand Canyon with soft plastic nets to catch those who might fall in, or build cars like armored tanks to reduce injuries in accidents even though the technology exists."

If Lerner Shops is not going to be liable, then the choice between accident avoidance and accident liability is easy for them. The cost of having accidents is external to their decisionmaking since Grace Drake and any future victims will have to pay their own medical bills. Remember that the court found that there was "no appreciable risk of harm," that the step down was "not a hazard which of itself suggests likelihood of harm." Remember that the sun shining off a bright, white building across the street may make it quite difficult to take precautions against accidents like this one.

Questions: If society's goal is to minimize primary accident costs, does the rule in *Drake* create efficient incentives? Which is the lower of the two sources of primary accident costs, avoidance or the expected losses if the accident occurs?

2. Oliver Wendell Holmes, in The Common Law 77 (1881, Howe ed. 1963), argued that it makes no sense to incur the administrative costs of inserting the government into private disputes unless there is something to be gained: "[T]he prevailing view is that [the state's] cumbrous and expensive machinery ought not to be set in motion unless some clear benefit is to be derived from disturbing the *status quo*. State interference is an evil where it cannot be shown to be a good." The possibility of a more efficient allocation of resources provides an argument that state interference is a "good" in cases where imposing liability gives defendants incentives to minimize primary accident costs. Where liability will not affect primary accident costs, the justification is not present.

The prevailing view described in Holmes's writing reflected a basic distaste for government intervention ("State intervention is an evil where it cannot be shown to be a good."). Calabresi suggests an economic rationale for finding no liability in cases where the accident cannot be avoided at reasonable cost. *Tertiary accident costs* are those costs associated with administering the torts system, including the "cumbrous and expensive machinery" of the courts.

Question: How does denying recovery to Grace Drake minimize tertiary costs?

3. When economists compare accident avoidance cost and accident liability cost, they typically speak of the latter in terms of *expected* costs. If people incur expenditures for avoidance, it is certain that the resources devoted to precaution will be consumed. Once the store manager in *Winn Dixie* pays people to inspect the aisles more frequently, that expenditure of money and time cannot be recaptured. If he decides to risk the accident and bear the cost of liability if the accident occurs, however, he may get lucky and never have another accident. The sun may never blind another customer leaving the Lerner Shops as in *Drake* and no one will ever have to pay for personal injuries resulting. In fact, the court in *Drake* believed that the possibility of a recurrence was so remote that it was not worth considering.

If a rational cost minimizer considers both the likelihood that an accident will occur and the severity of the harm if it occurs, his position is not unlike that of any gambler, who considers the size of the pot and the likelihood he will win it, or a highway speeder, who considers the penalties from being caught and the likelihood of apprehension. State lotteries advertise the probability of winning, either in terms of the probability of winning (about 1 in 3.5 for some instant lotteries) or the percentage of revenues returned in winnings (around 56 cents of each dollar). It is not too farfetched to believe that a rational person betting on accidents (or investing in accident avoidance) will similarly consider the *expected* return from his investment or *expected* cost of liability. Economists sometimes refer to the expected accident liability as the *discounted* cost of letting accidents occur. The cost of an accident occurring is discounted (reduced) by the probability that it will occur. Thus if there is a 25% chance of an accident occurring and the harm if it occurs is valued at $200,000, then the expected or discounted accident liability is only $50,000 (.25 x $200,000). The expected cost of letting accidents occur is the *risk* associated with an activity.

Question: If medical expenses and compensation for pain, suffering, and inconvenience in *Drake* were valued at $25,000 and the probability of one recurrence of this accident in the next year were 1 in 10,000, would it be efficient for a store owner to invest $5.00 a year in avoiding this accident?

SCHOMAKER v. HAVEY
Supreme Court of Pennsylvania, 1927.
291 Pa. 30, 139 A. 495.

PER CURIUM.

* * *

On the night of October 18, 1925, while defendant was driving his coupe automobile along a road in Allegheny county, he was hailed by plaintiff's husband, and, at the latter's request, defendant agreed to give him a lift in his car. The coupe had one other occupant beside defendant, and the deceased elected to stand on the running board, with his head, shoulders, arms, and part of his body inside the window on the side opposite the driver. As the car approached an intersecting road, defendant increased the speed of his car from between 20 and 25 miles to 40 or 45 miles an hour, and, upon reaching the intersection, suddenly swerved his automobile to the left, then to the right, and upset. Schomaker was thrown to the ground sustaining injuries which resulted in his death.

We have held, as a matter of law, that it is contributory negligence to stand on the platform of railroad trains, also to stand on the running boards of street railway cars, and we recently intimated that riding on a running board of a moving motor car constituted contributory negligence.

In Harding v. Philadelphia R. T. Co., we said:

"It is * * * clear that one who takes a position of manifest and imminent danger assumes the risk of his position."

Certainly, standing on the running board of a moving automobile is as dangerous as standing on a similar place on a street car, if not more so, and a person who takes such a position on an automobile is guilty of plain contributory negligence.

In Smith v. Ozark Water Mills Co., the Supreme Court of Missouri properly said:

"The action of the deceased in standing on the running board of an automobile * * * is an act of negligence concerning which reasonable men could not have a difference of opinion. The law is well settled that where a person voluntarily assumes a position of imminent danger when there is at hand and accessible to him a place of comparative safety, and by reason of having taken the dangerous position he is injured, he can have no recovery against another who is also negligent because such person's negligence in taking the dangerous position is one of the direct and proximate causes of the injury and contributes thereto."

As stated by us in Thane v. Scranton Traction Co.:

"Whether [the injured person, had he occupied a different position on the car], would have received some other injury, equal or greater, is conjectural and irrelevant; [since] if he is to recover at all it must be for the injuries received, not for what he might have received under different circumstances."

The order of the court below [denying recovery to the plaintiff] is affirmed.

Notes and Questions

1. Analyzing the efficiency implications of barring recovery when the plaintiff is contributorily negligent, as in *Schomaker*, starts the same way

as the analysis of the implications of holding the defendant liable. If the defendant is not legally liable for the medical bills and other damages, the plaintiff must bear those costs. One or the other will pay; one party will be given the incentive to minimize the costs that the possibility of another similar accident presents. It is unreasonable to expect Schomaker to respond to any incentives; he died from injuries received when he was thrown to the ground. The court in *Schomaker,* by finding that the plaintiff was contributorily negligent, gave other people who find themselves in the same position as Schomaker the incentive to choose between potential medical expenses or the inconvenience of riding *inside* the car. It is the *prospective* application of the incentives that provides the efficiency enhancing benefit of imposing liability.

2. The defendant in *Schomaker* could also have avoided the accident, of course, by insisting that the plaintiff not ride on the running board. Making the defendant liable would have given him, and other drivers similarly situated, incentive to avoid such accidents in the future.

Question: What efficiency reason might there be for making the plaintiff/passenger pay rather than making the driver pay?

B.   THE NEGLIGENCE STANDARD

1.   THE COST–BENEFIT APPROACH TO LIABILITY

One way to structure incentives to minimize primary accident costs is through the definition of reasonable care. In the 1940's, Judge Learned Hand described the negligence standard as a balancing between the two sources of primary accident costs: accident avoidance and accident liability. In United States v. Carroll Towing Co., he defined reasonable care in algebraic terms.

UNITED STATES v. CARROLL TOWING CO.

Circuit Court of Appeals, Second Circuit, 1947.
159 F.2d 169.

L. HAND, CIRCUIT JUDGE.

These appeals concern the sinking of the barge, "Anna C," on January 4, 1944, off Pier 51, North River. [The barge, "Anna C" was owned by Conners Company. On the day in question, it was tied up to a pier along with a flotilla of other barges. The "Carroll," a tug owned by the Carroll Towing Company and chartered by the Grace Lines, attempted to move one of the other barges. In the process, the "Anna C" broke away from the pier and floated down the North River where she collided with a tanker whose propeller broke a hole in her bottom. Because there was no watchman or "bargee" aboard the "Anna C", no one informed the "Carroll" and another nearby tug, the "Grace," that the "Anna C" was leaking. As a result, the "Anna C" sank and her cargo was lost. While there were a number of parties to this suit, including the United States government (for whom the flour was being shipped), the relevant part of this decision relates to the attempt by Conners Company to recover damages from Carroll Towing for the sinking of the "Anna C." Under the admiralty law, the applicable law governing torts on navigable waterways, if defendants Carroll Towing and Grace Lines could demonstrate that the plaintiff Conners' negligence also contributed to the loss, they would be excused from paying a portion of the damage. The opinion addresses whether Conners' failure to have a bargee protecting the barge amounted to negligence.]

We cannot * * * excuse the Conners Company for the bargee's failure to care for the barge, and we think that this prevents full recovery. * * * We do not * * * attribute it as in any degree a fault of the "Anna C" that the flotilla broke adrift. Hence she may recover in full against the Carroll Company and the Grace Line for any injury she suffered from the contact with the tanker's propeller, which we shall speak of as the "collision damages." On the other hand, if the bargee had been on board, and had done his duty to his employer, he would have gone below at once, examined the injury, and called for help from the "Carroll" and the Grace Line tug. Moreover, it is clear that these tugs could have kept the barge afloat, until they had safely beached her, and saved her cargo. This would have avoided what we shall call the "sinking damages." Thus, if it was a failure in the Conner Company's proper care of its own barge, for the bargee to be absent, the company can recover only one third of the "sinking" damages from the Carroll Company and one third from the Grace Line. For this reason the question arises whether a barge owner is slack in the care of his barge if the bargee is absent.

* * * Since there are occasions when every vessel will break from her moorings, and since, if she does, she becomes a menace to those about her; the owner's duty, as in other similar situations, to provide against resulting injuries is a function of three variables: (1) The probability that she will break away; (2) the gravity of the resulting injury, if she does; (3) the burden of adequate precautions. Possibly it serves to bring this notion into relief to state it in algebraic terms: if the probability be called P; the injury, L; and the burden, B; liability depends upon whether B is less than L multiplied by P: i.e., whether $B < PL$. Applied to the situation at bar, the likelihood that a barge will break from her fasts and the damage she will do, vary with the place and time; for example, if a storm threatens, the danger is greater; so it is, if she is in a crowded harbor where moored barges are constantly being shifted about. On the other hand, the barge must not be the bargee's prison, even though he lives aboard; he must go ashore at times. We need not say whether, even in such crowded waters as New York Harbor a barge must be aboard at night at all; it may be that the custom is otherwise and that, if so, the situation is one where custom should control. We leave that question open; but we hold that it is not in all cases a sufficient answer to a bargee's absence without excuse, during working hours, that he has properly made fast his barge to a pier, when he leaves her. In the case at bar the bargee left at five

o'clock in the afternoon of January 3rd, and the flotilla broke away at about two o'clock in the afternoon of the following day, twenty-one hours afterwards. The bargee had been away all the time, and we hold that his fabricated story was affirmative evidence that he had no excuse for his absence. At the locus in quo—especially during the short January days and in the full tide of war activity—barges were being constantly "drilled" in and out. Certainly it was not beyond reasonable expectation that, with the inevitable haste and bustle, the work might not be done with adequate care. In such circumstances we hold—and it is all that we do hold—that it was a fair requirement that the Conners Company should have a bargee aboard (unless he had some excuse for his absence), during the working hours of daylight.

[Accordingly, while recovery of collision damages is not diminished at all, the Conners Company must bear a share of liability for the sinking damages.]

Notes and Questions

1. Under the Learned Hand rule, a party is found negligent and therefor liable for (at least part of) the damages resulting from his actions if $B < PL$. "B," the burden of adequate precautions, is the accident avoidance cost. "P" is the probability that an accident will occur. "L" is the cost of the resulting losses, if the accident does occur. "PL" (the probability of the accident multiplied by the gravity of the resulting injury) is the risk associated with the activity, the expected liability or the discounted accident cost.

Learned Hand suggested that when the costs of preventing an accident are less than the expected loss (properly discounted by the probability of an accident occurring), it is negligent not to take precautionary measures. A corollary of this view is that when the costs of precautions are greater than the expected loss, it is *not* negligent to decline to avoid the accident. In such circumstances, it is not efficient to take precautionary measures. The Learned Hand formula has had great influence on the development of the negligence standard.

2. Learned Hand referred to "P" as the probability that the barge would break away from the dock. Consider what "P" represented in the factual context in *Carroll Towing*.

Question: Is the probability that the barge would break away from the dock the same as the probability that an accident will result?

3. Both the probability of an accident occurring and gravity of harm if an accident does occur vary at different times of the day and night. The decrease in activity in the harbor at night is likely to decrease the likelihood of an injury (fewer barges moving about) and the severity of the harm (fewer other boats to collide with a drifting barge; the barge might run aground instead). The burden of taking precautions may even change from day to night if night bargees cost less. This all makes the calculations quite complicated. It might be impossible for a statistician to calculate even the probability of the accident that actually occurred. And the probability of that precise sequence occurring is likely to have been rather

small. Other likely accidents include the barge colliding into the side of another boat or running aground.

Questions: Must the owner or bargee take all of these possible accidents into account in deciding whether to take precautions? Does an efficient balancing of costs require that the factfinder take all of these possibilities into account in deciding whether the parties were negligent?

4. One goal of the liability system is internalizing the external costs that accidents impose on others. The defendant who fails to take precautions that cost less than the expected loss from an accident is liable for damages if the accident occurs.

Questions: If people are liable for damages whenever they are found to be negligent, why are people ever negligent? Is it because people are not rational?

5. The distributional implications of the right to impose risks on others is clear; victims suffer so that actors may prosper. Whether the distributional implications are troublesome may depend on whether those who are actors are systematically different from those who are victims or whether we all take our turns playing different roles. In automobile accident cases with negligent drivers, for instance, the distributional implications may be slight since almost everyone drives. The implications may be different, however, if the injuries result from use of defective products.

In Hentschel v. Baby Bathinette Corp., 215 F.2d 102, 112 (2d Cir. 1954), the court held that a manufacturer was not negligent for using magnesium strips in constructing a baby bath. The bathinette caught fire for reasons unrelated to its construction. Yet, because of the materials used, it burned intensely and caused bursts of bluish flame to shoot across the hallway from the bathroom in which it was located into a nearby bedroom, burning the plaintiff. Citing another opinion by Judge Learned Hand, Conway v. O'Brien, 111 F.2d 611 (2d Cir. 1940), as an example of how courts take "social welfare" into account, Judge Frank dissented from a finding that the bathinette was reasonably fit for its intended use:

> Today, in this legal province of negligence, considerations of social welfare, or "social value," do (and should) affect the decisions as to a defendant's liability or the duty he owes to a plaintiff. Can anyone really believe * * * that it will promote an important "social value" to protect, from liability to purchasers, the makers and sellers of an article which, in case of fire, will create a hazard far greater than would otherwise exist, a hazard of which they are (or should be) aware but of which the purchasing householders are kept ignorant? What sound social policy inheres in such a rule? * * * My colleagues' ruling will tend to encourage the vending of such commodities perilous to human lives. The social interest in the free trade of goods, the need to avoid legal rules tending unduly to paralyze business initiative, and the fostering of a legitimate profit motive, do not extend that far.

Compare Learned Hand's definition of negligence to the explanation of reasonable care provided by the Restatement (Second) of Torts § 283 comment f: "Where a defendant's negligence is to be determined, the 'reasonable man' is a man who is reasonably 'considerate' of the safety of others and does not look primarily to his own advantage."

Question: Is the Restatement explanation of reasonable care consistent with Learned Hand's definition of negligence?

2. MODERN APPLICATIONS OF THE LEARNED HAND FORMULA

MCCARTY v. PHEASANT RUN, INC.

United States Court of Appeals, Seventh Circuit, 1987.
826 F.2d 1554.

POSNER, CIRCUIT JUDGE.

* * * Dula McCarty, a guest at the Pheasant Run Lodge in St. Charles, Illinois, was assaulted by an intruder in her room, and brought suit against the owner of the resort. The suit charges negligence, and bases federal jurisdiction on diversity of citizenship. The parties agree that Illinois law governs the substantive issues. The jury brought in a verdict for the defendant, and Mrs. McCarty appeals on a variety of grounds.

In 1981 Mrs. McCarty, then 58 years old and a merchandise manager for Sears Roebuck, checked into Pheasant Run—a large resort hotel on 160 acres outside Chicago—to attend a Sears business meeting. In one wall of her second-floor room was a sliding glass door equipped with a lock and a safety chain. The door opens onto a walkway that has stairs leading to a lighted courtyard to which there is public access. The drapes were drawn and the door covered by them. Mrs. McCarty left the room for dinner and a meeting. When she returned, she undressed and got ready for bed. As she was coming out of the bathroom, she was attacked by a man with a stocking mask. He beat and threatened to rape her. She fought him off, and he fled. He has never been caught. Although Mrs. McCarty's physical injuries were not serious, she claims that the incident caused prolonged emotional distress which, among other things, led her to take early retirement from Sears.

Investigation of the incident by the police revealed that the sliding glass door had been closed but not locked, that it had been pried open from the outside, and that the security chain had been broken. The intruder must have entered Mrs. McCarty's room by opening the door to the extent permitted by the chain, breaking the chain, and sliding the door open the rest of the way. Then he concealed himself somewhere in the room until she returned and entered the bathroom.

* * * Her theories of negligence are that the defendant should have made sure the door was locked when she was first shown to her room; should have warned her to keep the sliding glass door locked; should have equipped the door with a better lock; should have had more security guards (only two were on duty, and the hotel has more than 500 rooms), should have made the walkway on which the door opened inaccessible from ground level; should have adopted better procedures for preventing unauthorized persons from getting hold of keys to guests' rooms; or should have done some combination of these things. The suggestion that the defendant should have had better procedures for keeping keys away from unauthorized persons is irrelevant, for it is extremely unlikely that the intruder entered the room through the front door. The other theories were for the jury to accept or reject, and its rejection of them was not unreasonable.

There are various ways in which courts formulate the negligence standard. The analytically (not necessarily the operationally) most precise is that it involves determining whether the burden of precaution is less than the magnitude of the accident, if it occurs, multiplied by the probability of occurrence. (The product of this multiplication, or "discounting," is what economists call an expected accident cost.) If the burden is less, the precaution should be taken. This is the famous "Hand Formula" announced in United States v. Carroll Towing Co., an admiralty case, and since applied in a variety of cases not limited to admiralty.

We are not authorized to change the common law of Illinois, however, and Illinois courts do not cite the Hand Formula but instead define negligence as failure to use reasonable care, a term left undefined. But as this is a distinction without a substantive difference, we have not hesitated to use the Hand Formula in cases governed by Illinois law. The formula translates into economic terms the conventional legal test for negligence. This can be seen by considering the factors that the Illinois courts take into account in negligence cases: the same factors, and in the same relation, as in the Hand Formula. Unreasonable conduct is merely the failure to take precautions that would generate greater benefits in avoiding accidents than the precautions would cost.

Ordinarily, and here, the parties do not give the jury the information required to quantify the variables that the Hand Formula picks out as relevant. That is why the formula has greater analytic than operational significance. Conceptual as well as practical difficulties in monetizing personal injuries may continue to frustrate efforts to measure expected accident costs with the precision that is possible, in principle at least, in measuring the other side of the equation—the cost or burden of precaution. For many years to come juries may be forced to make rough judgments of reasonableness, intuiting rather than measuring the factors in the Hand Formula; and so long as their judgment is reasonable, the trial judge has no right to set it aside, let alone substitute his own judgment.

Having failed to make much effort to show that the mishap could have been prevented by precautions of reasonable cost and efficacy, Mrs. McCarty is in a weak position to complain about the jury verdict. No effort was made to inform the jury what it would have cost to equip every room in the Pheasant Run Lodge with a new lock, and whether the lock would have been jimmy-proof. * * * And since the door to Mrs. McCarty's room was unlocked, what good would a better lock have done? No effort was made, either, to specify an optimal security force for a resort the size of Pheasant Run. No one considered the fire or other hazards that a second-floor walkway not accessible from ground level would create. A notice in every room telling guests to lock all doors would be cheap, but since most people know better than to leave the door to a hotel room unlocked when they leave the room—and the sliding glass door gave on a walkway, not a balcony—the jury might have thought that the incremental benefits from the notice would be slight. Mrs. McCarty testified that she didn't know there was a door behind the closed drapes but the jury wasn't required to believe this. Most people on checking into a hotel room, especially at a resort, are curious about the view; and it was still light when Mrs. McCarty checked in at 6:00 p.m. on an October evening.

* * *

[The jury verdict for the defendant is] Affirmed.

Notes and Questions

1. Thinking about the negligence rule in BPL terms draws attention to the quantitative elements of proof lacking in Dula McCarty's case. While recognizing that many elements of the parties' cases are nonquantifiable, Judge Posner faults the plaintiff for not presenting such evidence as the dollar cost of locks on the hotel room doors or the optimal size of a security force for the hotel grounds. Thinking explicitly about these expenditures as accident avoidance costs rather than trying to judge whether the defendant's behavior was "reasonable" in the abstract requires the factfinder to focus on whether these expenditures really would have prevented the accident. Judge Posner's demand for evidence that these expenditures would have prevented the accident at reasonable cost might be interpreted either as imposing an extra burden on the plaintiff to be specific or as an aid in helping the plaintiff frame her argument. Judge Posner clearly subscribes to the latter interpretation. In Davis v. Consolidated Rail Corp., which follows, the plaintiff has offered satisfactory evidence of the feasibility of accident avoidance measures and the burden shifted to the defendant to use precision in demonstrating the infeasibility of the measures.

2. In *McCarty*, Judge Posner explicitly recognized the social cost-benefit analysis implicit in the Learned Hand test: "Unreasonable conduct is merely the failure to take precautions that would generate greater benefits in avoiding accidents than the precautions would cost." Notice how the formulaic approach enables Posner to take an objective view of the situation without succumbing to the emotional appeal of the plaintiff's case. In another case using the BPL approach, Judge Robertson of the Missouri Supreme Court, Madden v. C & K Barbecue Carryout, Inc., 758 S.W.2d 59, 64 (Mo. 1988), praised the advantages of this perspective:

This method of analysis (which is certainly more complex than is set out here) has been dubbed "law and economics". To its credit, law and economics has been criticized both by those who argue that the tort system favors plaintiffs and those who believe it tilts toward defendants. While I harbor no illusions that law and economics is the holy grail of tort law, it is nonetheless helpful in analyzing cases such as this one which present particularly troubling choices. It is helpful because it allows us to consider cases from a neutral perspective and ex ante, with a view toward determining appropriate rules of law which generate cost-effective behaviors within society. By focusing on these neutral considerations we are freed, to some extent, from the condemnation leveled by those who argue that we now compensate injury without regard to fault. In my credo, the tort system serves responsibly only when it requires a finding of fault as a necessary predicate to any award of compensation.

Questions: Does employing the Learned Hand formula help the jury ignore the distributional implications of the negligence rule? If it helps the jury divorce itself from its passions, does the Learned Hand rule promote the minimization of primary accident costs?

3. The jury in *McCarty* found that the defendant was not negligent and therefore did not reach the question of whether the plaintiff was contributorily negligent.

Question: If neither the Pheasant Run Lodge nor Dula McCarty could have avoided the risk of attack by using reasonable care, are primary and tertiary accident costs minimized by making the defendant or the plaintiff bear the loss?

4. Assume that when she checked into her room at Pheasant Run, Dula McCarty correctly calculated that the probability of being attacked by an intruder was sufficiently low that it did not make economic sense to check to see whether the sliding glass door was locked, even though the costs of being attacked are high. If the resort was similarly not negligent, then one would predict that neither these parties nor similarly situated parties would take precautions to avoid similar accidents in the future.

Questions: Do you suppose that Ms. McCarty checked the lock on the door the next time she checked into a hotel? Do you suppose the resort took any precautions to avoid similar attacks despite winning this case? Would either of these acts be irrational?

DAVIS v. CONSOLIDATED RAIL CORPORATION

United States Court of Appeals, Seventh Circuit, 1986.
788 F.2d 1260.

Posner, Circuit Judge.

* * * The suit arises from an accident that occurred in 1983. The plaintiff, Davis, was 33 years old at the time, an experienced railroad worker who for the past six years had been employed as an inspector of cars by the Trailer Train Company, a lessor of piggyback cars to railroads. He made the inspections in railroad yards, among them

Conrail's marshaling yard in East St. Louis. On the day of the accident, Davis, driving an unmarked van that was the same color as the Conrail vans used in the yard but that lacked the identifying "C" painted on each Conrail van, arrived at the yard and saw a train coming in from east to west. He noticed that several of the cars in the train were Trailer Train cars that he was required to inspect. The train halted, and was decoupled near the front; the locomotive, followed by several cars, pulled away to the west. The remainder of the train was stretched out for three-quarters of a mile to the east; and because it lay on a curved section of the track, its rear end was not visible from the point of decoupling. An employee of Conrail named Lundy saw Davis sitting in his van, didn't know who he was, thought it was queer he was there, but did nothing.

Shortly afterward Davis began to conduct the inspections. This required him to crawl underneath the cars to look for cracks. One of the cars was the third from the end (that is, from the point where the train had been decoupled). Unbeknownst to Davis, a locomotive had just coupled with the other (eastern) end of the train. It had a crew of four. Two were in the cab of the locomotive. The other two, one of whom was designated as the rear brakeman, were somewhere alongside the train; the record does not show just where, but neither was at the western end of the train, where Davis was. The crew was ordered to move the train several car lengths to the east because it was blocking a switch. The crew made the movement, but without blowing the train's horn or ringing its bell. The only warning Davis had of the impending movement was the sudden rush of air as the air brakes were activated. He tried to scramble to safety before the train started up but his legs were caught beneath the wheels of the car as he crawled out from under it. One leg was severed just below the knee; most of the foot on the other leg was also sliced off. * * *

Davis brought this suit against Conrail, charging negligence. * * * A jury found for Davis [and] assessed damages at $3 million[.] * * *

* * *

On the question of Conrail's negligence, Davis presented three theories to the jury. The first was that Conrail's employee Lundy, whose auto was equipped with a two-way radio, should have notified the crew of the train that an unknown person was sitting in a van parked near the tracks. We consider this a rather absurd suggestion. Lundy had no reason to think that the man in the van would climb out and crawl under a railroad car. If he had called the crew and told them there was a man in a van by the tracks, they undoubtedly would have replied, so what? * * *

In the famous negligence formula of Judge Learned Hand, which is recognized to encapsulate the more conventional verbal formulations of the negligence standard, a defendant is negligent only if $B < PL$, meaning, only if the burden of precautions is less than the magnitude of the loss if an accident that the precautions would have prevented occurs discounted (multiplied) by the probability of the accident. If P is very low, elaborate precautions are unlikely to be required even if L is large and here the necessary precautions would have been elaborate.

Davis's second theory of Conrail's negligence is even more fantastic. It is that before the train was moved a member of the crew should have walked its length, looking under the cars. The probability that someone was under a car was too slight, as it reasonably would have appeared to the crew, to warrant the considerable delay in moving the train that would have been caused by having a crew member walk its entire length and then walk back, a total distance of a mile and a half. It might have taken an hour, since the crew member would have had to look under each one of the train's 50 cars, and since the cars were only 12 inches off the ground, so that he would have had to get down on all fours to see under them.

Davis's third theory is more plausible. He argues that it was negligent for the crew to move the train without first blowing its horn (also referred to as the whistle) or ringing its bell. Since no member of the crew was in a position where he could see the train's western end, which was now its rear end, a reasonable jury could find—we do not say we would have found if we had been the triers of fact—that it was imprudent to move the train without a signal in advance. Although the crew had no reason to think that Davis was under a car, someone—whether an employee of Conrail or some other business invitee to the yard (such as Davis)—might have been standing in or on a car or between cars, for purposes of making repairs or conducting an inspection; and any such person could be severely, even fatally, injured if the train pulled away without any warning or even just moved a few feet. Regarding the application of the Hand formula to such a theory of negligence, not only was B vanishingly small—for what would it cost to blow the train's horn?—but P was significant, though not large, once all the possible accidents that blowing the horn would have averted are added together. For in determining the benefits of a precaution—and PL, the expected accident costs that the precaution would avert, is a measure of the benefits of the precaution—the trier of fact must consider not only the expected cost of this accident but also the expected cost of any other, similar accidents that the precaution would have prevented. Blowing the horn would have saved not only an inspector who had crawled under the car (low P), but also an inspector leaning on a car, a railroad employee doing repairs on the top of a car, a brakeman straddling two cars, and anyone else who might have business in or on (as well as under) a car. The train was three-quarters of a mile long. It was not so unlikely that somewhere in that stretch a person was in a position of potential peril to excuse the crew from taking the inexpensive precaution of blowing the train's horn. Or so at least the jury could conclude without taking leave of its senses.

Against this conclusion Conrail and Trailer Train hurl a number of arguments. One is that precautions would not have been effective; Davis himself testified that he would not have heard the train's bell.

But we do not consider this so damaging a concession as the defendants do. Davis would not have heard the bell, no, but it does not mean that he would not have heard the horn. The horn is deafening, and Conrail's assertion (for which no evidence was offered) that the horn would have been inaudible at three-quarters of a mile is as implausible as it is unsubstantiated.

A better point is that there is so much traffic in a marshaling yard that sounding the horn every time a train is moved would cause a cacophony that would deprive the horn of its efficacy as a warning. If horns were blowing all the time, Davis would not know, when the horn sounded, whether it was the horn for this train or some other train. Either he would ignore it or he would be spending all his time scrambling out from under and then back under the cars he was inspecting. The problem with this argument is that Conrail put in no evidence on how busy the marshaling yard was either at the time of the accident or at any other time. We know it is a large (four square miles) and busy yard, but we do not know how frequently trains are actually moved in a large and busy yard. Every 15 minutes? Every hour? Conrail could easily have put in evidence on this point, but did not. Moreover, Davis is not contending that due care requires that the horn be blown before every move. Maybe this move was special, because of the length of the train in combination with the curvature of the track and the fact that all of the crew members were at or near the front of the train. Even if the yard is very busy, if the horn were sounded only in the unusual case where there was more than average danger from a sudden movement the danger of cacophony would be diminished.

* * *

Although the evidence of the defendants' negligence is thin, * * * we can find no reversible error.

Affirmed.

Notes and Questions

1. It is easy to say, after the fact, that precautions should have been taken but, as Judge Robertson, in Madden v. C & K Barbecue Carryout, Inc., 758 S.W.2d 59, 66 (Mo. 1988), insists, "foreseeability must never be measured after the fact; when an injury has occurred, whatever precautions were taken were (obviously) inadequate to prevent that injury." The factfinder in *Davis* must imagine himself in the position of the railroad prior to the accident. If he has any compassion at all, the engineer will regret not having blown the whistle to warn the inspector, but was it unreasonable not to have blown it? Since it was so easy to do, the railroad must provide a specific explanation of why the whistle was not blown. The requirement of specificity has shifted to the defendant in this case, who failed to show either that the precaution would be ineffective or too expensive.

2. In his analysis of the plaintiff's theories of negligence, Judge Posner applied the Learned Hand formula to determine whether Conrail was negligent. The second and third theories offered two accident avoid-

ance measures available to Conrail—having a crew member walk the length of the train checking to see that there was no one under the cars or, alternatively, having the crew blow the train's horn or ring its bell before moving the train to warn people working under the cars.

> *Question:* What differences in the balancing of burdens and risks in the Learned Hand formula support rejection of the second and acceptance of the third theories?

3.   The excerpt from *Davis* illustrates a case where only one party, the defendant, is negligent.   Cases might also arise where the plaintiff rather than the defendant is negligent.   Under traditional rules of tort law, if the only negligent party is the defendant, the plaintiff recovers full damages. If the only negligent party is the plaintiff, the plaintiff recovers no damages.

> *Question:* Are primary and tertiary accident costs minimized by these traditional negligence rules in cases where only one of the parties is negligent?

C.   EFFICIENCY OF DEFENSES TO LIABILITY BASED ON NEGLIGENCE

The principal issue throughout this chapter is whether tort law minimizes accident costs.   The assignment of liability leads to the minimization of accident costs only if people respond to the incentives created by the law.   To provide incentives for parties to minimize primary accident costs, it will be desirable to place liability on the party that is in the best position to evaluate the risks and take cost-justified precautions to avoid them.   Deterrence in tort law relies on the notion that placing liability on a particular type of actor for past acts will deter similarly situated actors in the future.

The cases thus far have focused on how the cost-benefit approach to liability is applied.   It may be easier to appreciate the efficiency of tort law in differing factual contexts if those cases can are classified according to which party could have avoided the accident at reasonable cost, that is, which party was negligent.   In simple, two-party accident cases, there are three categories of accidents: (I) Neither party was negligent, (II) Only one party was negligent, and (III) Both parties were negligent.

Within the first category of accident cases, there are two types of factual circumstances; either the injurer was in the best position to avoid the accident or the victim was.   Because neither was negligent, neither of them had a cost of avoidance that was less than the expected accident cost, but there still may have been a difference in their relative ability to avoid the accident.   It may be that the injurer was the best cost avoider, in which case similarly situated potential injurers in the future also are likely to be the best cost avoiders.   Alternatively, the victim may have been the best cost avoider, in which case similarly situated potential victims in the future also are likely to be the best cost avoiders. Any factual circumstances in this Category falls into one of the two situations.

CATEGORY I: NO NEGLIGENCE

A. INJURER IS BEST COST AVOIDER

B. VICTIM IS BEST COST AVOIDER

For Category IA and IB cases, neither party, if paying strict attention to the costs involved and responding rationally, would avoid the accident, even if he had to pay the costs if the accident occurred. As discussed in the notes and questions following *Drake,* above, the assignment of liability will not affect primary accident costs as long as the parties rationally evaluate their options according to the Learned Hand formula.

In circumstances where only one party is negligent (has available cost-justified precautions), the factual circumstances fall into Category II. Category IIA describes situations where only the injurer is negligent and Category IIB describes situations where only the victim is negligent.

CATEGORY II: ONLY ONE PARTY NEGLIGENT

A. INJURER IS BEST COST AVOIDER

B. VICTIM IS BEST COST AVOIDER

If only one party is negligent, the best cost avoider in Category II must be the negligent party; for the best cost avoider B is less than PL. Since the other party is not negligent, his cost of avoidance, B, must be greater than the risk presented, PL.

In Category IIA, the injurer, but not the victim, could avoid the accident by taking cost-justified precautions. Holding the injurer (defendant) liable in Category IIA gives him and similarly situated others an incentive to avoid accidents in the future, since he and similarly situated defendants know that they will have to bear the higher expected accident cost if they do not.

In Category IIB cases, the defendant would not be liable under a negligence theory, because he had no cost-justified precautions available. In Category IIB cases the denial of recovery to the victim gives him and similarly situated others an incentive to avoid the accident in the future. Since the victim (plaintiff) is the lower cost avoider of accidents, it is efficient to give him the incentive. The task of the factfinder faced with Category II situations is determining which party has cost-justified precautions available and making him bear the costs of the accident.

In this section, the analysis is about to become more complicated. The cases in this section present situations in which both parties have reasonable precautionary measures available to them. In order to minimize primary accident costs, it makes sense in such cases to encourage the person with the least costly method of avoiding the accident to do so. Where both parties are negligent, the cases fall into Category III.

CATEGORY III: BOTH PARTIES ARE NEGLIGENT
A. INJURER IS BEST COST AVOIDER
B. VICTIM IS BEST COST AVOIDER

Category IIIA describes those situations in which both parties are negligent, but the injurer can avoid the accident at lower cost. Category IIIB describes those situations in which both parties are negligent, but the victim is the best cost avoider. The economic analysis of defenses in tort law focuses on whether the law provides incentives that lead to the minimization of accident costs.

1. CONTRIBUTORY NEGLIGENCE

BUTTERFIELD v. FORRESTER

Court of King's Bench, 1809.
11 East's Reports 59, 103 Eng.Rep. 926.

This was an action on the case for obstructing a highway, by means of which obstruction the plaintiff, who was riding along the road, was thrown down with his horse, and injured. At the trial * * *, it appeared that the defendant, for the purpose of making some repairs to his house, which was close by the road side at one end of the town, had put up a pole across this part of the road, a free passage being left by another branch or street in the same direction. That the plaintiff left a public house not far distant from the place in question at 8 o'clock in the evening in August, when they were just beginning to light candles, but while there was light enough left to discern the obstruction at 100 yards distance: and the witness, who proved this, said that if the plaintiff had not been riding very hard he might have observed and avoided it: the plaintiff however, who was riding violently, did not observe it, but rode against it, and fell with his horse and was much hurt in consequence of the accident; and there was no evidence of his being intoxicated at the time. On this evidence Bayley J. directed the jury, that if a person riding with reasonable and ordinary care could have seen and avoided the obstruction; and if they were satisfied that the plaintiff was riding along the street extremely hard, and without ordinary care, they should find a verdict for the defendant: which they accordingly did.

* * *

LORD ELLENBOROUGH C.J.

A party is not to cast himself upon an obstruction which has been made by the fault of another, and avail himself of it, if he do not himself use common and ordinary caution to be in the right. In cases of persons riding upon what is considered to be the wrong side of the road, that would not authorize another purposely to ride up against them. One person being in fault will not dispense with another's using ordinary care for himself. Two things must concur to support this action, an obstruction in the road by the fault of the defendant, and no want of ordinary care to avoid it on the part of the plaintiff.

[Judgment for the defendant was affirmed.]

Notes and Questions

1. *Butterfield* is generally accepted as the case in which the English courts adopted the doctrine of contributory negligence, which relieves a negligent defendant of any liability if he can prove that the plaintiff was also negligent.

> *Questions:* For which party in *Butterfield* was $B<PL$? Following the court's decision, are potential injurers or potential victims given an incentive to avoid such accidents in the future?

2. Contributory negligence cases necessarily involve situations in which both the plaintiff and the defendant could avoid the accident at reasonable cost.

> *Questions:* If cost-justified precautionary measures are available to two or more parties, which should be given the incentive to avoid the accident if primary accident cost minimization is our goal? Is there any way to tell from the facts of *Butterfield* which party can avoid the accident at least cost?

3. The opinion in *Butterfield* clearly indicates that both parties were at fault. Factual circumstances like this fall into Category III of tort cases, for which there are two subcategories reflecting which party could have avoided the accident at least cost. For primary accident costs to be minimized, the least cost avoider of accidents must be given an incentive to take precautionary measures whenever they are less costly than the risks presented by the activity. The law must be structured so that the incentive is given to potential injurers in Category IIIA cases and to potential victims in Category IIIB cases. The following cases and notes illustrate alternative interpretations of reasonable care that create different incentives for injurers and victims.

HAEG v. SPRAGUE, WARNER & CO., INC.

Supreme Court of Minnesota, 1938.
202 Minn. 425, 281 N.W. 261.

HOLT, JUSTICE.

Plaintiff got the verdict in this automobile collision case. Defendant appeals from the order denying its motion in the alternative for judgment notwithstanding the verdict or a new trial.

The impact occurred in daylight at the right-angle intersection, three miles south of the southern limits of the City of Minneapolis, of County Highway No. 52, also known as Nicollet Avenue, and rural Hennepin County Road, known as Eighty-Sixth Street South. The former lies north and south; the latter east and west. Plaintiff approached from the west, on Eighty–Sixth Street, in his ton and one-half Chevrolet truck; Harry Thompson, employee of defendant, and owner of a Chevrolet sedan, came from the south on Highway No. 52. Eighty–Sixth Street is a rough gravel road from 9 to 14 feet wide. Highway No. 52 has a smooth, bituminous-treated surface. Its "black top" is about 27 feet wide. From shoulder to shoulder its width is 36 to 37 feet. The country is flat. There is a clear view in all directions. There were no distracting circumstances on either road at the time of the collision.

We adopt defendant's argument that plaintiff was guilty of contributory negligence as a matter of law. So we must and do put the evidence in the light most favorable to plaintiff. Plaintiff testified to having seen Thompson's car at least four times at various distances south of the point of collision, and that it was traveling from 50 to 60 miles per hour until the collision. The first time plaintiff was about 200 feet west and going at about 30 miles an hour. Then Thompson was 400 to 500 feet to the south. When plaintiff was 30 feet from the intersection he saw Thompson's car 150 to 175 feet away. At that point plaintiff released his accelerator and let his truck coast at the rate, as he says, of about 20 miles an hour into the intersection.

Plaintiff's testimony is that as he entered the intersection Thompson's automobile was still about 100 to 125 feet south of it and apparently not slackening its speed. He testified that "I entered the intersection first, and I expected him to slack up and let me through." The next view plaintiff had of the oncoming car took place when the former was in the center of the intersection, halfway across, and the latter about 50 to 60 feet south. It does not appear at what speed Thompson's car was then going. The impact occurred about 13 feet east of the center line of the highway, on its eastern edge.   * * *

* * *

It is important that, coming as it was, from plaintiff's right, Thompson's car had the statutory right of way unless the latter had forfeited such right by reason of excessive speed. The latter, as to both right of way and the forfeiture of it, were given to the jury by the charge. Thompson admits a speed of about 45 miles per hour until the moment when he saw plaintiff was not going to yield him the right of way. Then, so he testified, he applied the brakes until he got the machine down to "half speed" at the time and place of the collision. The jury must have chosen not to believe Mr. Thompson's testimony on that point. But this much is clear—plaintiff never entertained the thought of yielding the right of way, his intention all along being to get across Nicollet Avenue ahead of Thompson's car.

Plaintiff's case, all through, stresses reliance upon plaintiff's supposed right to assume that Mr. Thompson would have exercised ordinary care to avoid a collision. The latter's negligence must be taken as established by the verdict. Plaintiff's supposed reliance upon Mr.

Thompson's exercise of due care is of no moment for the simple reason that this is a case, if ever there can be one, where such reliance was itself negligence. We stress again the obvious truth of fact and law that it is not due care to depend upon the exercise of care by another when such dependence is itself accompanied by obvious danger. Without binding plaintiff by his own testimonial estimate of speed, or by that of any other witness, we are not yet able to ignore this alternative. Either Thompson's car had the right of way or it was being driven in excess of 45 miles per hour. So when plaintiff entered Nicollet Avenue, Thompson's car was so close and going at such rate of speed that it was the clearest kind of negligence for plaintiff not to stop. If Thompson was driving at 50 miles per hour, he was traveling 73 1/2 feet a second. He could not have stopped his car within 125 feet with instantaneous application of the brakes. And that stopping distance would be increased in proportion to the so-called reaction time needed by Mr. Thompson to apply the brakes after discovering the emergency. We do not hold plaintiff chargeable as with knowledge of such exact figures, or with consciousness, at the moment, of their import. But it is clear that the circumstances were such as to make a collision inescapable if he persisted, as he did, in his attempt to cross Nicollet Avenue ahead of Thompson.

* * *

No one can appreciate more than we the hardship of depriving plaintiff of his verdict and of all right to collect damages from defendant; but the rule of contributory negligence, through no fault of ours, remains in our law and gives us no alternative other than to hold that defendant is entitled to judgment notwithstanding the verdict. It would be hard to imagine a case more illustrative of the truth, that in operation, the rule of comparative negligence would serve justice more faithfully than that of contributory negligence. We but blind our eyes to obvious reality to the extent that we ignore the fact that in many cases juries apply it in spite of us. But as long as the legislature refuses to substitute the rule of comparative for that of contributory negligence we have no option but to enforce the law in a proper case. We cannot escape the conclusion that this case compels its application.

The order must be reversed with directions to enter judgment for defendant notwithstanding the verdict.

So ordered.

Notes and Questions

1. In *Haeg* it was clear that both parties were negligent. The jury found that the defendant's employee, Thompson, was negligent, when it awarded the verdict to the plaintiff. Thompson had apparently been driving too fast for the prevailing conditions. The court found that the plaintiff, Haeg, was contributorily negligent. Haeg had failed to adjust his behavior to take into account the negligence of Thompson, incorrectly relying on a "supposed right to assume that Mr. Thompson would have exercised ordinary care to avoid a collision." The court held that relying

on the other's exercise of due care "was itself negligence." As a result, the court reversed the jury's verdict for the plaintiff and entered judgment for the defendant. The comparative negligence rule to which the court referred would have apportioned liability between the two parties rather than assigned all the liability to the plaintiff. (Comparative negligence is discussed further in the materials following Scott v. Alpha Beta Company, below.)

2. Apparently either party, acting alone, could have avoided the accident in *Haeg* by slowing down. Either could have *unilaterally* prevented the collision. Consistent with minimizing primary accident costs, it would be efficient to have that party who could avoid the accident most easily be the one to take precautions. It would be duplicative and wasteful for both to take precautions if one party alone could avoid the accident. Following the accident discussed in *Haeg*, Thompson may very well want to sue Haeg for damages to his Chevrolet. But whichever party is the plaintiff will lose in this contributory negligence state, whether he is the best cost avoider of the accident or not.

> *Questions:* Under the contributory negligence rule as applied in Minnesota when *Haeg* was decided, would the incentives lead to primary accident cost minimization if the plaintiff was the least cost avoider of the accident? If the defendant was the least cost avoider?

3. The rule in *Haeg*, no absolute right to assume that other people are being careful, is clearly the dominant rule. See, *e.g.*, Prosser and Keeton on the Law of Torts (Keeton gen. ed. 5th ed. 1984) 198–199 ("[A] person is required to realize that there will be a certain amount of negligence in the world." "The duty to take precautions against the negligence of others thus involves merely the usual process of multiplying the probability that such negligence will occur by the magnitude of the harm likely to result if it does, and weighing the result against the burden upon the defendant of exercising such care."). The Restatement (Second) of Torts, § 466, says, "The plaintiff's contributory negligence may be * * * (a) an intentional and unreasonable exposure of himself to danger created by the defendant's negligence, of which danger the plaintiff knows or has reason to know." Section 302A is generally in accord, though it is addressed to the duty to protect others: "An act or an omission may be negligent if the actor realizes or should realize that it involves an unreasonable risk of harm to another through the negligent or reckless conduct of the other or a third person."

At least one judge appears to have a different interpretation of how the reasonable person is expected to behave. While the reasonable person will still avoid accidents only if the cost of avoidance is less than the risk presented, people are entitled to assume that other people are acting reasonably. Interpreting Illinois law in Pomer v. Schoolman, 875 F.2d 1262, 1268 (7th Cir. 1989), Judge Posner said, "A person cannot be deemed negligent for failing to take precautions against an accident that potential victims could avoid by the exercise of elementary care; negligence is failing to take the care necessary and proper to prevent injury to reasonably careful persons." And in a portion omitted from the excerpt of McCarty v. Pheasant Run, Inc., above, Posner said, "It is a bedrock principle of negligence law that due care is that care which is optimal given that the potential victim is himself reasonably careful; a careless person cannot by his carelessness raise the standard of care of those he encounters." While the first quote and beginning of the second may be interpreted as allowing injurers to assume that potential victims are acting reasonably, the latter part of the quote from *McCarty* makes it clear that potential victims are also entitled to assume that potential injurers will act reasonably. In his treatise, Economic Analysis of Law 155 (3d ed. 1986), Posner says that the law defines due care as "the care that is optimal if the other party is exercising due care."

> *Questions:* If Haeg were entitled to assume that Thompson would act reasonably, how would that affect the legal outcome in *Haeg?* Would this entitlement affect the efficiency of the incentives provided in negligence cases fitting into Categories I (no negligence) and II (one person negligent)? Would including this entitlement in the definition of reasonable care affect the efficiency of incentives provided in contributory negligence cases, subcategories IIIA and IIIB?

4. The facts in *Haeg* are a bit unusual, in that the plaintiff actually observed the defendant acting carelessly. The rule in the Restatement (Second) of Torts § 466 is that plaintiffs have a duty to protect themselves from the negligence of others about which they know or *have reason to know.* The Restatement (Second) of Torts § 302A holds defendants to a stricter standard. A potential injurer is negligent if he realizes or *should* realize that his act involves an unreasonable risk of harm to another because of the other's negligent or reckless conduct. Levi v. Southwest Louisiana Electric Membership Cooperative illustrates the application of such a rule.

LEVI v. SOUTHWEST LOUISIANA ELECTRIC MEMBERSHIP COOPERATIVE

Supreme Court of Louisiana, 1989.
542 So.2d 1081.

DENNIS, JUSTICE.

* * *

The plaintiff, Giovanni Levi, an oil field roustabout-pumper for Amoco Oil Company, sustained near fatal permanently disabling injuries when the erected mast of a paraffin removal truck rig upon which he was working came in contact or close proximity with an uninsulated 14,400 volt electric distribution line being operated by Southwest Louisiana Electric Membership Cooperative (Slemco). The accident occurred on February 16, 1982 at the E.C. Stuart # 2 Well in the Section 28 Dome Field, in St. Martin Parish, an oil field owned by Amoco Oil Company. In the 1960's Slemco had constructed an uninsulated electrical distribution line to serve most of the 22 wells producing in the field. The power company routed the line so as to avoid crossing a well driveway or coming in close proximity to the well by placing the line either across the main road from the well or behind the well, with the exception of the E.C. Stuart # 2 Well where the line crossed the access road leading to the well 40.5 feet from the well head and 25.7 feet overhead. Slemco failed to avoid a driveway traversal or a close encounter between its line and the E.C. Stuart # 2 Well because that well was omitted from the power company's original construction plan due to oversight or to the fact that no electricity was supplied to this well or both.

* * *

On the day of the accident Levi and another Amoco employee, while servicing wells in the field, found it necessary to dismantle the lubricator to make a repair. After borrowing some tools they looked for a dry place to work on the device. They did not intend to service the E.C. Stuart # 2 Well that day but in order to get off the main road and find a dry place to repair the rig they drove the truck into that well site and parked. The truck was headed toward the well with its front end approximately 3–4 feet from the well and its rear end approximately 15–16 feet from the point at which the high power line crossed the access road. It was necessary for the workers to raise the mast off the truck and lower the lubricator to the ground to make the repairs. Using control levers on the side of the truck, Levi raised the mast tip up, over the truck and back toward the power line. Levi had noticed the distribution line at this location on previous occasions but failed to pay attention to it on the day of the accident. Levi recalled only that he last saw the mast when it was at a 45 degree angle in front of the truck. Shortly thereafter, the mast either touched the power line or came close enough for electrical arcing to occur. 14,400 volts of electricity escaped from the power line and coursed through the mast, the truck and Levi's body.

As a result of the accident, Levi suffered the amputation of both legs just below the knees and severe burns over 25% of his body. At the time of the trial, he had been hospitalized 10 times for 11 different surgical procedures.

Levi filed suit against Slemco and its insurer. The case was tried before a jury. In response to written interrogatories, the jury found that Slemco's conduct did not fall below the reasonable standard of care. The trial court denied plaintiff's motions for a judgment notwithstanding the verdict and for a new trial. Levi appealed, and the court of appeal affirmed. This court granted writs to determine whether the principles of law had been applied correctly below * * * .

* * *

In the present case there is no dispute as to the fact that the power company had actual knowledge of the oil company's regular use of trucks with erectable high masts around its wells. Because this activity had continued on a regular basis over a long period of time the power company should have been aware of the physical characteristics of this equipment and any electrical hazard it might create. * * * Since the power company knew that its uninsulated 14,400 volt electric line passed near the oil wells at a level of only 25 to 26 feet above ground, the company should have known that electrical hazards would be created if masts were raised near the line.

* * *

We do not think reasonable minds can disagree with the conclusion that the power company, particularly with its superior knowledge, skill and experience in electrical safety, should have recognized that its conduct under these circumstances involved a risk of harm to oil field workers. Aside from the obvious serious possibility that an inattentive worker might raise the mast while parked on the access road too near the power line, there were similar chances that a falling mast could pass dangerously close to the line or that a careless roustabout might attempt to drive under the line on his way to another well without fully lowering his mast. The power company complains that it should not be charged with recognition of any risk that takes effect through a victim's negligence. But the ordinary reasonable person, and even more so the power company, is required to realize that there will be a certain amount of negligence in the world. When the risk becomes serious, either because the threatened harm is great, or because there is an especial likelihood that it will occur, reasonable care may demand precautions against "that occasional negligence which is one of the ordinary incidents of human life and therefore to be anticipated." It is not due care to depend on the exercise of care by another when such reliance is accompanied by obvious danger.

Moreover, the power company had actual knowledge of previous instances of oil field workers' negligence or inattentiveness in moving erect masts under or near the uninsulated power lines. Its own employee testified that he had warned other roustabout crews of danger on two previous occasions when they drove under the uninsulated electric line on a board road with their masts partially or fully erect.

* * *

When the components of the evidence are brought into relief and weighed in the light of their interrelationships, reasonable minds must agree that the minimal burden of adequate precautions was clearly outweighed by the product of the chance and the gravity of the harm. Accordingly, the power company was guilty of negligence that was a legal cause of plaintiff's injuries, or, in other words, the company breached its duty to take precautions against the risk that took effect as those injuries, and the lower courts committed manifest error in not reaching this conclusion.

* * *

Reversed and Remanded to the Court of Appeal.

Notes and Questions

1. *Levi* is a Category III case where the court viewed both parties as negligent. The court did not consider the legal implications of that

conclusion because it focused on the jury's finding that Slemco had acted reasonably. Louisiana is a comparative negligence state where a finding that both parties were negligent would permit Mr. Levi to recover at least some of his damages. The court held that Slemco had a duty to reduce risks to even a careless employee and that duty applied even when the probability of carelessness was less than certain, as it was in *Haeg*. The court's interpretation of due care required Slemco to take precautions to avoid harm to Mr. Levi despite his carelessness—in fact, because of his likely carelessness.

2. Either party in *Levi* could have unilaterally prevented the electrocution. Slemco could have insulated the overhead wire. Mr. Levi could have avoided the accident by carefully scrutinizing the site and perhaps choosing another location for the repair of his lubricator. Either of these *unilateral avoidance measures* would have avoided the accident. If Levi had been careless, the insulation would have protected him. If Levi had been careful, the insulation would have been unnecessary. If we could ensure that one party would avoid the accident, it would be wasteful for both to bear the burden of avoiding the accident. Duplicative avoidance would more than double the cost compared to the least cost avoider doing so alone.

> *Questions:* Where unilateral avoidance by one party is the least costly way to avoid accidents, does the contributory negligence rule ever provide incentives for both parties to avoid the accident? Does the possibility of duplication depend on whether the defendant or plaintiff can avoid the accident at least cost? Does the possibility of duplication depend on whether Judge Posner's interpretation or the *Haeg* and *Levi* interpretation of reasonable care is followed?

3. In the full opinion in *Levi*, the court identified another precautionary technique, putting a warning sign on the power pole and an orange ball warning on the power line. The court concluded that the warning sign and orange ball would have called Mr. Levi's attention to the warning at the E.C. Stuart well, causing him to be more attentive to danger. This precaution requires that both parties work together to avoid the harm. *Cooperative precautionary measures* may be less expensive than the unilateral measures described in the previous question. Instead of insulating the wire or driving to another lubricating location (the more costly unilateral avoidance measures), a warning combined with greater attentiveness could produce the same result. Levi could use the more convenient location for repairing the lubricator and avoid the overhead wire by noting the location of the bright orange ball.

> *Questions:* Do contributory negligence rules provide proper incentives for both parties to take cooperative precautionary measures when they are a less costly means of avoiding the accident than unilateral means? Does your conclusion depend on whether Judge Posner's interpretation or the *Haeg* and *Levi* interpretations of "due care" apply?

4. Studying the efficiency characteristics of the contributory negligence rules naturally raises the issue of whether negligence law would be more efficient if there were no contributory negligence defense.

Questions: Would a pure negligence rule (defendant is liable whenever he is negligent) lead to efficient results in Category I, II, and III cases? Does your conclusion depend on which interpretation of "due care" is followed?

2.   LAST CLEAR CHANCE

PERIN v. NELSON & SLOAN

California District Court of Appeal, Fourth District, 1953.
119 Cal.App.2d 560, 259 P.2d 959.

MUSSELL, JUSTICE.

This is an action for damages for personal injuries sustained by the plaintiff when a truck operated by one of the defendants' employees was backed onto plaintiff's foot. At the time of the accident plaintiff, who was a cement finisher, was engaged in smoothing and finishing a slab of cement which had been poured from defendants' transit mix truck. The area being poured was about 20 feet square. Plaintiff was on his knees at the south edge of the square reaching out to the north as far as he could, his feet approximately 24 inches from the cement, when the driver backed the truck onto the plaintiff's foot, imbedding it in the ground and injuring it. Plaintiff heard the noise of the truck and an order to "back it up", but he was intent on his work and did not see the truck when it was being backed.

The driver testified that after he had poured the cement in the east side of the square, he was told to back up; that he then backed his truck slowly; that as he started backing, he saw the plaintiff smoothing off the cement and "figured he had plenty of room to back up;" that it appeared to him that plaintiff was out of range of the wheels; that during all the time he was backing, he was watching plaintiff; that plaintiff was then on his knees on the ground smoothing the cement and did not look up at him.

The cause was tried before a jury and a verdict was returned in favor of plaintiff. Defendants appeal from the judgment thereupon entered.

While defendants state in their brief that a reversal of the judgement is sought on the grounds that the evidence is insufficient to sustain the judgment and that plaintiff was guilty of contributory negligence as a matter of law, their argument is directed to the contention that the trial court committed prejudicial error in instructing the jury on the doctrine of last clear chance.

The elements of this doctrine are set forth in Daniels v. City & County of San Francisco, where it said:

> "Whether or not the doctrine of last clear chance applies in a particular case depends entirely upon the existence or nonexistence of the elements necessary to bring it into play. Such question is controlled by factual circumstances and must ordinarily be resolved by the

fact-finder. An instruction stating the doctrine is proper when there is evidence showing: '(1) That plaintiff has been negligent and, as a result thereof, is in a position of danger from which he cannot escape by the exercise of ordinary care; and this includes not only where it is physically impossible for him to escape, but also in cases where he is totally unaware of his danger, and for that reason unable to escape; (2) that defendant has knowledge that the plaintiff is in such a situation, and knows, or in the exercise of ordinary care should know, that plaintiff cannot escape from such situation, and (3) has the last clear chance to avoid the accident by exercising ordinary care, and fails to exercise the same, and the accident results thereby, and plaintiff is injured as the proximate result of such failure.' "

In the instant case the uncontradicted evidence shows that plaintiff was in a position of danger. There is also evidence to support an inference that he was totally unaware of his danger and for that reason unable to escape. Plaintiff was not required to show that his ability to escape from his threatened danger was a physical impossibility. The doctrine applies equally if he was wholly aware of his danger, and for that reason unable to escape.

* * *

There was also substantial evidence that the truck driver had the last clear chance to avoid the accident by the exercise of ordinary care. Under the circumstances and conditions described in the record before us, the jury was entitled to determine whether the driver was aware, or in the exercise of the ordinary care should have been aware, of plaintiff's danger and had the last clear chance to avoid the accident.
* * *

Defendants contend that plaintiff was guilty of contributory negligence as a matter of law and that his negligence was continuing up to the time of the accident. However, where as here, all of the elements of the last clear chance doctrine are present, the continuous negligence rule does not operate to the exclusion of the last clear chance doctrine.

Judgment affirmed.

Notes and Questions

1. In *Perin*, the temporal element presents a new analytical dimension to the contributory negligence defense. Perin may very well have been negligent for failing to look up from his cement finishing when he heard the order for the truck to back up in his direction. Although California, at the time, followed the contributory negligence rule, the court concluded that recovery by the plaintiff would not be barred. When the particular factual circumstances described in the case occur, the last clear chance doctrine gives the defendant an incentive to avoid accidents by making him liable for all damages. As in *Haeg* and *Levi*, the defendant must take reasonable precautions to avoid risks created by the (here, known) negligence of others.

2. While it is clear that defendant was negligent in these cases (and therefore the cases belong in either Category II or III), describing the

plaintiff's situation is not as simple. When trying to categorize last clear chance cases according to the classification scheme suggested in this chapter, it is critical to recognize that the cases are of two sorts. The plaintiff may be in danger either because he is aware of the danger and it has become extraordinarily difficult for him to escape (a very high avoidance cost) or because he is unaware of the danger and therefore cannot avoid it until it is too late. Once the plaintiff has negligently put himself in peril and is unable to extricate himself, the factual circumstances sound very much like a Category II situation. At the time of the accident, only the defendant has available reasonable means to avoid the accident. The second type of case sounds very much like a Category III case; the plaintiff could avoid the accident at reasonable cost if only he would look up and notice the danger.

Questions: If the case is of the Category II variety, which of the parties is likely to be the best cost avoider of the accident? If the case is of the Category III variety, which of the parties is likely to be the best cost avoider of the accident? Does the last clear chance rule provide efficient incentives in both of these cases to minimize primary accident costs?

3. The last clear chance doctrine originated in the 1842 English case of Davies v. Mann, 10 M. & W. 546, 152 Eng. Rep. 588. The defendant negligently ran into the plaintiff's donkey, which the plaintiff had (also negligently) left tethered in the road. The plaintiff's negligence was held not to bar recovery because the defendant had the "last clear chance" to avoid the accident.

The facts of *Davies* and the considerable confusion surrounding the precise factual requirements and doctrinal reasons for the last clear chance rule have resulted in the rule being referred to as the "jackass" doctrine. There is no widely accepted single explanation for this exception to the general rule barring recovery in contributory negligence cases. Some courts allow the exception on grounds that the temporal element makes the plaintiff's negligence more remote, less proximate, to the injury and that the defendant's negligence is therefore a more substantial factor in producing the injury. Others have justified the rule on the grounds that the defendant's conduct amounted to gross negligence compared to plaintiff's ordinary negligence and that therefore recovery would not be barred. Despite the doctrinal confusions, the motivation for the doctrine is clear. Courts found that denying recovery was unduly harsh to plaintiffs, who might have been only slightly careless, and inappropriately generous to defendants, who were totally excused from the consequences of their own negligence.

Eventually, courts and legislatures responded to the apparent inequities and perhaps the inefficiencies in the contributory negligence doctrine by replacing it with comparative negligence. All but a very few of the comparative jurisdictions have eliminated the last clear chance doctrine altogether.

3. APPORTIONED COMPARATIVE NEGLIGENCE

SCOTT v. ALPHA BETA COMPANY

California Court of Appeal, Second District, 1980.
104 Cal.App.3d 305, 163 Cal.Rptr. 544.

ASHBY, ASSOCIATE JUSTICE.

Plaintiff Phameline Scott slipped and fell in a grocery store of defendant Alpha Beta Company. A jury found defendant 60 percent negligent and plaintiff 40 percent negligent and awarded plaintiff $120,000 damages after reduction on account of her negligence. The trial court denied defendant's motions for judgment notwithstanding the verdict and for new trial. Defendant appeals from the judgment and the denial of its motion for judgment notwithstanding the verdict, contending there is no substantial evidence of negligence on its part. Plaintiff also appeals from the judgment, contending there is no substantial evidence of contributory negligence on her part.

At about 7 p. m. on September 10, 1976, plaintiff walked into defendant's grocery store at 3581 Century Boulevard in Lynwood. It was raining "kind of heavy" at the time, and had been raining all day.

Defendant's employees had placed a 20–foot long rubber mat inside the entrance to the store, because defendant's terrazzo floor was known to become slippery when wet. Normally the store has about 2,000 customers per day.

When plaintiff stepped off the rubber mat, she slipped; her leg went out from underneath her and she fell down. Lying on the floor, plaintiff noticed that the floor was wet.

Plaintiff suffered injury to her left knee and had surgery shortly after the accident. Her knee will never be normal and she may require further surgery or an artificial knee in the future.

* * *

Dr. Silver testified on behalf of defendant that based upon a review of plaintiff's medical records in his opinion plaintiff had a weakness of the left leg and a "trick knee" prior to the accident, and that such condition was compounded by plaintiff's obesity. In his opinion it was possible plaintiff's knee gave out on her to cause her fall.

This evidence is relevant not only on the issue of proximate cause but also on the issue of contributory negligence, the theory being that persons with known handicaps may have to exercise a greater degree of care in particular circumstances than other persons.

It was raining rather heavily and according to the defense witnesses plaintiff was wearing pink furry house slippers. A person in plaintiff's position might reasonably be expected to know that the floor adjacent to the mat could be wet, even without negligence on defendant's part, or that her slippers might remain wet when she reached the end of the mat. In her testimony plaintiff made no claim to having taken any special cautions in stepping from the mat to the floor. The jury might have thought plaintiff should have seen water on the floor. Under all the circumstances, we think the jury might reasonably conclude that plaintiff failed to exercise due care for her own safety.

* * *

The judgment is affirmed. The order denying defendant's motion for judgment notwithstanding the verdict is affirmed.

Notes and Questions

1. The jury in *Scott* applied the comparative negligence doctrine, which has replaced contributory negligence in the vast majority of states. In California, the damages are divided or apportioned between the parties in proportion to fault; whichever party is more negligent bears a larger portion of the damage. In *Scott,* the jury apparently thought that the store was more negligent, attributing 60% of the negligence to it, though it may be that the jury simply wanted the store to pay the larger share of the damages.

> *Questions:* Under the comparative negligence system, which party has incentive to make the cost-benefit analysis involved in deciding whether or avoid the accident? Under the contributory negligence system, who would have been given the incentive to make the cost-benefit analysis in *Scott?*

2. In *Scott,* the defendant's 60% share of liability amounted to $120,-000; Phameline Scott's total damages were $200,000. Unlike a pure negligence rule or a contributory negligence rule, where all of the loss falls on one party, each party in a comparative negligence jurisdiction must compare the cost of avoidance to the expected *share* of liability he will bear. A party's share is 100% if he or she alone is negligent, less than 100% if both are negligent.

> *Questions:* Assume that each fall by a customer would present the same damage and apportionment of damages as in *Scott.* If the probability of a customer slipping is .01 and the cost of providing a safe surface is 50 cents per customer, would comparative negligence give the Alpha Beta store an incentive to provide a safe surface? If Ms. Scott's accident avoidance cost (the inconvenience of owning a pair of rubber soled shoes and wearing them instead of the pink furry house slippers) was 75¢ per trip to the store and the shoes would eliminate her 1% chance of slipping, would Ms. Scott have an incentive to avoid such accidents in the future? Do these incentives lead to the minimization of primary accident costs?

3. Opponents of comparative negligence often argue that the switch from contributory negligence will increase tertiary accident costs, the costs of administering the torts system.

> *Question:* How is comparative negligence likely to increase tertiary costs borne by the victim, the injurer, the courts, and juries?

4. In a comparative negligence jurisdiction, the jury must determine which party was more negligent and how much more. It seems reasonable

to conclude that of two parties facing the same risk and doing nothing to prevent it, the party that could avoid the risk at lower cost is more negligent. If a store could avoid an accident with an expected cost of (.01 x $200,000) $2000 for 50 cents per customer and a customer could avoid it for 75 cents, the store appears to be more negligent.

It is less obvious how the jury decides "how much more" negligent one party is than the other. Justice Faulkner, in his dissent in Golden v. McCurry, offers a model of jury decisionmaking that is as appealing as any.

GOLDEN v. McCURRY

Supreme Court of Alabama, 1980.
392 So.2d 815.

PER CURIAM.

The significant issue presented by this appeal is whether this Court should abolish the common law rule of contributory negligence and replace it with the rule of comparative negligence.

The basic facts giving rise to the lawsuit are as follows: Plaintiff Correll Golden had ridden home from work in a truck. He alighted from the truck and was crossing Highway 164 to reach his home which was located across the highway. Golden was struck by defendant McCurry's automobile while he was still on the travelled portion of the highway. Golden claimed in his lawsuit that his injuries were proximately caused by McCurry's negligence or wantonness. McCurry claimed that Golden's own negligence contributed to his injuries. Golden asked the court to strike McCurry's contributory negligence defense and adopt the doctrine of comparative negligence. The trial court refused; Golden then stipulated that he was 1% negligent; McCurry stipulated that he would contend throughout the trial that Golden was contributorily negligent and that Golden's negligence proximately contributed to his injuries. Both parties conducted pre-trial discovery.

Claiming that he was entitled to a judgment as a matter of law based upon the pleadings and discovery of record, defendant McCurry filed a motion for summary judgment, which the trial court granted. Golden appeals.

* * *

After due and deliberate consideration, we hold that, even though this Court has the inherent power to change the common law rule of contributory negligence, it should, as a matter of policy, leave any change of the doctrine of contributory negligence to the legislature.

* * *

FAULKNER, JUSTICE, dissenting in part and concurring in part.

* * *

The question of whether contributory or comparative negligence should be adopted in this state is riddled with economic considerations. Judge Learned Hand formulated an algebraic equation to determine negligence: The defendant is liable if the loss (injury) caused by the accident multiplied by the probability of its occurrence is greater than the cost of avoiding the accident. *United States v. Carroll Towing Co.* The economically efficient solution, therefore, is to require the smaller cost to be incurred if it will prevent the larger accident cost.

In application to contributory negligence, if the plaintiff can prevent a $1000 accident at a cost of $50 and the defendant's avoidance cost is $100, the economically efficient solution is to refuse the plaintiff any recovery for failure to avoid the total loss at the lesser cost. If the defendant is liable in all instances without regard to the precautionary measures the plaintiff could have taken, there is no economic incentive for the plaintiff to avert the accident.

On the other hand, if the defendant is able to avoid the $1000 loss at a cost of $50 and the plaintiff's cost is $100, the defense of contributory negligence (assuming it is applicable) still mandates that the plaintiff cannot recover at all. In essence, therefore, this defense sanctions the least economically efficient solution because it provides no incentive for the defendant to spend the lesser avoidance cost cognizant that, if the plaintiff contributed even a little bit, the defendant will incur no liability (expense) at all.

The doctrine of comparative negligence—where the plaintiff's damages are diminished by the percentage of his own negligence that contributed to the accident—is not the panacea either. This doctrine tacitly advocates that more than the economically efficient amount of precautionary measures be taken. Using the same figures immediately above, if the defendant would be two-thirds liable and the plaintiff one-third liable, incurring $666.67 and $333.33 of the $1000 loss respectively, then both parties would opt for the lesser avoidance cost at an aggregate prevention cost of $150. This results in economic *inefficiency* because either amount alone would have been sufficient to avoid the total loss.

Conversely, neither party may decide to opt for the lesser avoidance cost in reliance upon the fact that the other party has an economic incentive to take precautionary measures. This results in compensating a total loss of $1000 that could have been avoided at the lesser amount of $50 or $100, individually, or at a collective amount of $150. Even though the combined expense of $150 is over precautionary, economically speaking, it is at least more economically efficient than incurring the total or partial accident expense.

This economic analysis becomes more intricate as we approach an examination of the respective forms of comparative negligence. I feel that we do this area of the law—and the public—a great disservice by failing to recognize, work through and resolve the economic issues endemic to this dilemma.

Notes and Questions

1. It is quite possible that this case was intended to provoke a change in the law. Presumably knowing that the contributory negligence rule

would completely bar him from recovering any damages, Golden, the plaintiff, agreed ahead of time that he was negligent. If the contributory negligence rule was upheld, as it was by the Supreme Court of Alabama, Golden would get no damages at all. The trial court, under the contributory negligence rule, had no choice but to rule for McCurry. If the court decided to opt for comparative negligence, Golden had limited his risk by agreeing that he was only slightly negligent, 1%, compared to the defendant. Had the Supreme Court abandoned the contributory negligence rule in favor of comparative negligence, his recovery would have been diminished by only 1%.

2. When a state abandons the contributory negligence defense and adopts some form of the comparative negligence defense, the plaintiff's damage award is reduced by some proportion determined by the factfinder. Since the amount of damages each party must pay affects their incentives to avoid accidents in the future, it is important to know how that proportion is determined. Justice Faulkner offered the basic idea that since both parties were at fault they should divide damages in proportion to their fault, with the most careless person paying the most. Justice Faulkner thought that if one party could avoid the accident at half the cost of another then his failure to avoid the accident made him twice as negligent and his liability should be twice as great.

Using Faulkner's approach, each party's share of liability is determined by a ratio of his cost or burden of avoidance ("B" in the Learned Hand formula) to the other's burden of avoidance. In one of Faulker's examples, the potential injurer's burden of avoidance, $B_{injurer}$ was $50 and the potential victim's burden of avoidance, B_{victim}, was $100. The ratio of the two burdens is $50/$100, which is 1/2 (1 to 2). If the person who can avoid the accident at half the price should pay twice as much damages, as Faulkner suggests, then the ratio indicates that the injurer should pay $2 for every $1 to be paid by the victim.

Questions: If the total damages are $60,000, how much would each party pay, using Faulkner's approach and numbers? If the ratio of victim's burden of avoidance to the injurer's was only 1% (1/100), as Golden stipulated, and if Golden's damages were $15,000, what would be McCurry's liability?

3. Employing Judge Faulkner's model for allocating shares of liability between parties, one can compare the relative efficiency of contributory and comparative negligence in any particular case. Assume that the following facts describe the situation faced by the parties in *Golden*. Either party can avoid using unilateral avoidance measures. If the accident occurs the loss to the plaintiff will be $15,000. The probability of the accident occurring if no precautions are taken is .01. The respective costs of avoidance for the injurer and victim are $1 and $100.

Questions: Which party in *Golden* has an incentive to avoid future accidents of this sort? Is the comparative negligence rule efficient in this case? Are primary accident costs likely to be higher if a contributory negligence rule or comparative negligence rule is applied in this case?

4. Judge Faulkner offers the example of an expected loss of $1000 that can be avoided by the plaintiff for $100 and by the defendant for $50. He calculated correctly that the defendant would have to pay $666.67 and the plaintiff would have to pay $333.33, because the defendant would be two-thirds liable and the plaintiff one-third liable, and then concluded that both parties would opt for the lesser avoidance cost at an aggregate prevention cost of $150. "This" he claimed "results in economic inefficiency because either amount alone would have been sufficient to avoid the total loss." To check his conclusion that both would take precautions to avoid the accident, we need to know not only the loss and the burdens for both parties, but also the probability that this accident will occur again, P.

Questions: Is Judge Faulkner's example correct if the probability of an accident occurring is 12%? Is his analysis correct if the probability of an accident occurring is 36%? Are primary accident costs minimized by a contributory or comparative negligence rule if the probability is 12%? What if the probability is 36%?

5. Following Judge Faulkner's model of jury decisionmaking, the efficiency of the incentives provided by the comparative negligence rule depends on the relationships between PL and the burdens for the parties. Notes 3 and 4 illustrated that changing the probability that the accident will occur changes the efficiency of the incentives provided by the comparative negligence rules, assuming that the loss remains constant. Similar changes can be seen by changing the magnitude of the loss if the accident occurs or changing the burdens of the parties. The following question offers one last illustration of this property of comparative negligence.

Questions: Would application of the comparative negligence rule be efficient if P equals .001, L equals $10,000, $B_{injurer}$ equals $9 and B_{victim} equals $8? Would comparative or contributory negligence minimize primary accident costs in this case?

6. Repeated examples would demonstrate that if avoidance costs for both parties are high relative to the risk, PL, then, as long as the parties have no right to assume that others will act carefully, neither has an incentive to avoid the accident and an insufficient amount is spent on accident avoidance. When avoidance costs for both parties are low relative to the risk, then both have an incentive to avoid the accident and an excessive amount is spent on accident avoidance. In all cases in between, the comparative negligence rule provides efficient incentives.

Question: Given their relative strengths and weaknesses in minimizing primary accident costs, is contributory negligence or comparative negligence the preferred doctrine?

4. NONAPPORTIONED COMPARATIVE NEGLIGENCE

GALENA AND CHICAGO UNION RAILROAD COMPANY v. JACOBS

Illinois Supreme Court, 1858.
20 Ill. 478.

[Frederick Jacobs, a four and one-half year old boy, was run over by a locomotive on the tracks running past his parents home. Jacobs, through his lawyers, claimed that the accident was the result of the carelessness of the employees of the railroad company. The railroad claimed that the contributory negligence of the plaintiff prevents his recovery of any damages. The court reviewed a variety of cases where the defendant had claimed that the plaintiff was careless and adopted its own version of the contributory negligence defense.]

BREESE, J.

* * *

It will be seen, from these cases, that the question of liability does not depend absolutely on the absence of all negligence on the part of the plaintiff, but upon the relative degree of care or want of care, as manifested by both parties, for all care or negligence is at best but relative, the absence of the highest possible degree of care showing the presence of some negligence, slight as it may be. The true doctrine, therefore, we think is, that in proportion to the negligence of the defendant, should be measured the degree of care required of the plaintiff, that is to say, the more gross the negligence manifested by the defendant, the less degree of care will be required of the plaintiff to enable him to recover. Although these cases do not distinctly avow this doctrine in terms, there is a vein of it very perceptible, running through many of them, as, where there are faults on both sides, the plaintiff shall recover, his fault being to be measured by the defendant's negligence, the plaintiff need not be wholly without fault.

We say then, that in this, as in all like cases, the degrees of negligence must be measured and considered; and wherever it shall appear that the plaintiff's negligence is comparatively slight, and that of the defendant gross, he shall not be deprived of his action.

Notes and Questions

1. For thirty years during the mid–1800's, Illinois, Tennessee, and Kansas experimented with the *Galena* rule. Also characterized as a "nonapportioned comparative negligence" rule, the *Galena* rule allowed plaintiffs to recover whenever their negligence was slight compared to defendant's. The courts' inability to define "slight" negligence along with the rise of traditional contributory negligence and other factors led to the eventual demise of the rule. But the economic characteristics of the *Galena* rule make it a particularly interesting object of study. For the purpose of this study, the rule is interpreted to mean that the plaintiff will not be denied full recovery unless his negligence is greater than that of the defendant. Another way to explain this rule is to say that the defendant is liable if he is negligent and his negligence is greater than that of the plaintiff.

Consider the six types of factual circumstances that have been discussed above:

CATEGORY I: NO NEGLIGENCE

     A. INJURER IS BEST COST AVOIDER

          B. VICTIM IS BEST COST AVOIDER

     CATEGORY II: ONLY ONE PARTY NEGLIGENT

          A. INJURER IS BEST COST AVOIDER

          B. VICTIM IS BEST COST AVOIDER

     CATEGORY III: BOTH PARTIES ARE NEGLIGENT

          A. INJURER IS BEST COST AVOIDER

          B. VICTIM IS BEST COST AVOIDER

Question: In which categories does the *Galena* rule provide efficient incentives?

2. The discussion following *Levi* introduced the distinction between unilateral and cooperative precautionary measures. Imagine that the *Galena* rule was applied to the facts of *Levi* and that the least costly method of preventing the accident was the cooperative efforts of the company suspending an orange warning ball on the wire and the employee using extra care (and the guidance provided by the ball).

Question: Would the *Galena* rule give the incentive for the parties to use the cooperative precautionary measures rather than the unilateral measures?

3. The South Dakota Comparative Negligence Statute reads in part:

In all actions brought to recover damages for injuries to a person or to his property caused by the negligence of another, the fact that the plaintiff may have been guilty of contributory negligence shall not bar a recovery when the contributory negligence of the plaintiff was slight in comparison with the negligence of the defendant, but in such case, the damages shall be reduced in proportion to the amount of plaintiff's contributory negligence.

Under this rule, the plaintiff's recovery is barred if he is more than slightly careless; if he is only slightly careless, his recovery is diminished slightly. This statute was presumably written to modify the harshness of the traditional contributory negligence statute, which denied all recovery even if the plaintiff was only slightly negligent.

Question: What are the efficiency implications of the South Dakota rule?

5. ASSUMPTION OF RISK

ORDWAY v. SUPERIOR COURT

Court of Appeal, Fourth District, Division 3, 1988.
198 Cal.App.3d 98, 243 Cal.Rptr. 536.

CROSBY, ASSOCIATE JUSTICE.

* * *

     Judy Casella, a veteran jockey who had ridden in 500 professional horse races without incident, was thrown from her mount and further injured when the equine fell and rolled over her during a quarterhorse race at Los Alamitos Race Course on January 3, 1983. The tragic chain of events began when Over Shadow, owned by petitioner Homer Ordway, tangled with another steed, Speedy Ball, who then stumbled in front of Casella's horse. The California Horse Racing Board determined the jockey riding Over Shadow violated a board rule by "crossing over without sufficient clearance, causing interference," and he was suspended for five racing days. Alleging "negligence, carelessness and unlawful conduct," Casella sued the riders, trainers, and owners of Over Shadow and Speedy Ball.

* * *

* * * The correct rule is this: If the defendant's actions, even those which might cause incidental physical damage in some sports, are within the ordinary expectations of the participants—such as blocking in football, checking in hockey, knock-out punches in boxing, and aggressive riding in horse racing—no cause of action can succeed based on a resulting injury. It is of no moment that the participants may be penalized for these actions by the officials. Routine rule violations, such as clipping in football, low blows in boxing, and fouls in horse races are common occurrences and within the parameters of the athletes' expectations.

Here defendant jockeys were attempting to win a horse race. There has never been any suggestion that they, much less the owners of their horses, were motivated by a desire to injure plaintiff. Defendants' conduct, while perhaps negligent, was within the range to be anticipated by the other riders, or should have been. As a professional rider, Casella reasonably assumed the risk of her tragic injury. As with other persons who reasonably assume similar risks, her remedy was to purchase insurance from her athletic income beforehand, not to pursue a lawsuit against her counterparts in the sport afterward. The action, accordingly, is barred as a matter of law. Defendants are entitled to summary judgment.

Notes and Questions

1. In *Ordway*, the jockey, Judy Casella, was denied recovery because she had knowingly and voluntarily assumed the risks inherent in horse racing. The economic analysis of defenses to liability based on negligence requires a determination of whether the jockey was the best cost avoider of the accident. Denying liability would then give the best cost avoider the incentive to avoid the accident. The difficulty in *Ordway* is that the injured jockey had apparently been riding carefully, while Over Shadow's jockey was careless enough to be sanctioned by the California Horse Racing Board.

Not racing at all is one precaution an individual can take to avoid being injured in a professional horse race. This may be the only available precaution, which is why people say that the risks are "inherent" in the sport. If so, then the race organizers and the horse owners can only avoid all injuries by not racing (or so drastically changing the rules that sport is fundamentally changed).

Questions: If these are the only available precautions, to what category of factual circumstances do such tort cases belong? What rule of liability minimizes primary and tertiary accident costs for this category of cases? Is the assumption of risk doctrine, which completely bars recovery in cases like this, an efficient rule?

2. *Ordway* falls into a group of assumption of risk cases commonly denominated *primary assumption of risk.* In this group of cases, it is not necessary to discuss either actor's negligence. Rather, the fact that the injured party was aware of and voluntarily accepted the risks presented relieves the defendant of any obligation to protect her. A typical example of such acceptance of risk and relief from responsibility is the baseball stadium, where the spectators' knowledge of the possibility of balls being hit into the stands relieves the stadium owner from having to screen in the entire stadium. The defendant is, therefore, not negligent for failing to take precautions and there is no fault on his part to balance against the victim's behavior. The plaintiff simply cannot recover.

3. Aggressive sporting activities and dangerous occupations may involve risks the participants do not knowingly and voluntarily assume.

Question: If a football player, angry at an opponent for tackling him just shy of a touchdown, jerks his opponent's helmet off and kicks him in the head, is it efficient to apply the doctrine of primary assumption of risk to prevent the opponent from recovering damages?

4. Justice Crosby distinguishes two dog bite cases. In one situation, the actual facts in Nelson v. Hall, 165 Cal.App.3d 709, 211 Cal.Rptr. 668 (1985), a rabid dog bit a veterinary assistant in the course of her work. In the other, a victim was bitten while foolishly attempting to pet a rabid dog negligently allowed to remain in a veterinarian's waiting room. The law would give different results in the two cases, denying recovery to the veterinary assistant and merely reducing the recovery (under comparative negligence) of the victim in the waiting room.

Question: Is there any economic basis for the distinction between these two cases?

KELLY v. CHECKER WHITE CAB

Supreme Court of Appeals of West Virginia, 1948.
131 W.Va. 816, 50 S.E.2d 888.

HAYMOND, JUDGE.

The plaintiff, Violet Kelly, instituted this action of trespass on the case in the Circuit Court of Kanawha County to recover from the defendants Checker White Cab, Inc., a corporation, and its employee, Don Withrow, damages for personal injuries sustained by her when a taxicab owned by the company, driven by Withrow and in which she was riding as his guest, skidded and ran off a public highway in that county in the early morning of January 1, 1946. At the time of the wreck the taxicab was returning from Spencer to Charleston.

* * *

The plaintiff and her companion testified that, on the trip from Charleston to Spencer, Withrow drove the taxicab at a speed of thirty five to forty miles per hour, that the taxicab skidded three or four times, and that each time the plaintiff protested the speed at which he was driving she told him that if he did not reduce the speed she would get out. They also testified that on the return trip, between Spencer and Clendenin, a distance of about thirty miles, he drove at a speed of from fifty to sixty five miles per hour, that the taxicab slipped and skidded on the slippery road, and that they told him eight or nine times in that distance that he was driving too fast, that they were "scared to death," and that unless he slowed down they would get out. Their version was that after each protest he would reduce the speed until he thought they had forgotten but that in a short time he would again resume his excessive speed. They said that despite their protests he was driving on an icy stretch of road at the rate of sixty to sixty five miles per hour when they saw the truck approaching in front of them and that at that time both vehicles were traveling in the center of the highway.

* * *

The conduct of the defendant Withrow, in driving the taxicab from Charleston to the place at which it skidded from the highway, and especially from Spencer to that point, constituted clear and almost continuous negligence * * *.

* * *

The testimony of the plaintiff is that she observed the careless and dangerous manner in which the driver of the taxicab operated it between Charleston and Spencer and between Spencer and the scene of the wreck and that she protested vigorously against the speed at which he was driving three or four times before they arrived at Spencer and eight or nine times between Spencer and Clendenin. At both of those places he stopped a sufficient length of time to enable her to leave the taxicab if she had wanted to do so. She told him that she was "scared to death" and threatened to get out unless he reduced the speed. She knew that he gave no effective heed to any of her protests, that they were uttered in vain, that he had resumed the excessive speed after only temporarily reducing it following each protest, and that he would and did continue to travel at a speed which caused her to believe that her safety was endangered. She had realized her danger when she actually got out of the taxicab at Spencer and at Clendenin and she must have known that the threat to her safety would continue, as it did, if she did not finally leave it at either place. Yet, despite the fear which she expressed for her own safety, she again voluntarily entered the taxicab at Spencer and at Clendenin and continued to ride in it until the accident which she feared, and in which she was injured, actually occurred. The inconvenience or the hardship of retiring from the taxicab at an unseasonable hour of the morning and of remaining in Spencer or in Clendenin was ignored or declined by her at the fully apprehended risk of her own personal safety. Her decision to reject the one and to accept the other was not a legal excuse for her willingness to continue to ride toward her destination in Charleston. Her failure to quit the taxicab and remain out of it at Spencer or at Clendenin, which she had the fair and reasonable opportunity to do, defeats her right of recovery against the driver of the taxicab and relieves him of liability for her injury.

Notes and Questions

1. Like Judy Ordway's, Violet Kelly's recovery was barred because she knowingly confronted and (apparently) willingly accepted a risk. The cases are different from both a legal and economic perspective, however, because in *Kelly* the defendant's negligence was proved. In *Ordway,* the court found that the defendant had no duty to protect Judy Ordway from the risk. Cases like *Kelly* are placed in the category of *secondary assumption of risk* cases. In secondary assumption of risk cases, the attention shifts from whether the defendant had a duty to protect the plaintiff to the character of the plaintiff's behavior.

2. The court characterized Violet's behavior saying "The inconvenience or the hardship of retiring from the taxicab at an unseasonable hour of the morning and of remaining in Spencer or in Clendenin was ignored or declined by her at the fully apprehended risk of her own personal safety." It does not seem to matter whether her behavior was reasonable or not. In this case, whether the victim was reasonable in assuming the risk did not seem to matter; the fact that she knowingly and voluntarily accepted it was enough. Under the modern view, however, the plaintiff's secondary assumption of a risk is a complete bar to recovery (in contributory negligence states) or a factor to be balanced against the defendant's conduct (in comparative negligence states), only if it was unreasonable to have assumed the risk.

> *Question:* Is the modern rule, requiring that a knowing and voluntary assumption of the risk be unreasonable, more efficient at reducing primary accident costs than a rule that reduces (or bars) recovery even if the assumption of the risk was reasonable?

D. STRICT LIABILITY

1. STRICT LIABILITY AND THE BEST COST AVOIDER

From an economic perspective, liability based on negligence involves establishing, case by case, which parties failed to take cost-justified precautions to avoid accidents. Economic analysis of negligence defenses considers how to assign liability when the fault of several persons coincided to produce an accident. An alternative to the case by case approach is to develop categories of activities in which one type of actor is almost always the best minimizer of primary accident costs. If, after looking at the various factual circumstances giving rise to accidents, some actors could be isolated for special treatment in this way, the liability system could be streamlined. Liability could be imposed on the party who was usually the best cost minimizer without having to go through the cumbersome process of establishing fault or apportioning liability. In the following cases, consider whether people in the position of the defendant are usually in the best position to minimize accident costs.

SPANO v. PERINI CORPORATION

Court of Appeals of New York, 1969.
25 N.Y.2d 11, 302 N.Y.S.2d 527, 250 N.E.2d 31.

FULD, CHIEF JUDGE.

The principal question posed on this appeal is whether a person who has sustained property damage caused by blasting on nearby property can maintain an action for damages without a showing that the blaster was negligent. Since 1893, when this court decided the case of Booth v. Rome, W. & O.T.R.R. Co., it has been the law of this State that proof of negligence was required unless the blast was accompanied by an actual physical invasion of the damaged property—for example, by rocks or other material being cast upon the premises. We are now asked to reconsider that rule.

The plaintiff Spano is the owner of a garage in Brooklyn which was wrecked by a blast occurring on November 27, 1962. There was then in that garage, for repairs, an automobile owned by the plaintiff Davis which he also claims was damaged by the blasting. Each of the plaintiffs brought suit against the two defendants who, as joint venturers, were engaged in constructing a tunnel in the vicinity pursuant to a contract with the City of New York.

* * *

It is undisputed that, on the day in question (November 27, 1962), the defendants had set off a total of 194 sticks of dynamite at a construction site which was only 125 feet away from the damaged premises. Although both plaintiffs alleged negligence in their complaints, no attempt was made to show that the defendants had failed to exercise reasonable care or to take necessary precautions when they were blasting. Instead, they chose to rely, upon the trial, solely on the principle of absolute liability either on a tort theory or on the basis of their being third-party beneficiaries of the defendants' contract with the city. * * *

In our view, the time has come for this court to * * * declare that one who engages in blasting must assume responsibility, and be liable without fault, for any injury he causes to neighboring property.

* * *

Although the court in *Booth* drew a distinction between a situation * * * where there was "a physical invasion" of, or trespass on, the plaintiff's property and one in which the damage was caused by "setting the air in motion, or in some other unexplained way," it is clear that the court, in the earlier cases, was not concerned with the particular manner by which the damage was caused but by the simple fact that any explosion in a built-up area was likely to cause damage. Thus, in Heeg v. Licht, the court held that there should be absolute liability where the damage was caused by the accidental explosion of stored gunpowder, even in the absence of a physical trespass:

"The defendant had erected a building and stored materials therein, which from their character were liable to and actually did explode, causing injury to the plaintiff. The fact that the explosion took place tends to establish that the magazine was dangerous and liable to cause damage to the property of persons residing in the vicinity. * * * The fact that the magazine was liable to such a contingency, which could not be guarded against or averted by the greatest degree of care and vigilance, evinces its dangerous character, * * * In such a case, the rule which exonerates a party engaged in a lawful business, when free from negligence, has no application."

Such reasoning should, we venture, have led to the conclusion that the *intentional* setting off of explosives—that is, blasting—in an area in which it was likely to cause harm to neighboring property similarly results in absolute liability. However, the court in the *Booth* case rejected such an extension of the rule for the reason that "(t)o exclude the defendant from blasting to adapt its lot to the contemplated uses, at the instance of the plaintiff, would not be a compromise between conflicting rights, but an extinguishment of the right of the one for the benefit of the other." The court expanded on this by stating, "This sacrifice, we think, the law does not exact. Public policy is sustained by the building up of towns and cities and the improvement of property. Any unnecessary restraint on freedom of action of a property owner hinders this."

This rationale cannot withstand analysis. The plaintiff in *Booth* was not seeking, as the court implied, to "exclude the defendant from blasting" and thus prevent desirable improvements to the latter's property. Rather, he was merely seeking compensation for the damage which was inflicted upon his own property as a result of that blasting. The question, in other words, was not *whether* it was lawful or proper to engage in blasting but *who* should bear the cost of any resulting damage—the person who engaged in the dangerous activity or the innocent neighbor injured thereby. Viewed in such a light, it clearly appears that *Booth* was wrongly decided and should be forthrightly overruled.

* * *

[The jury verdict awarding Spano $4,400 and Davis $329 was affirmed.]

Notes and Questions

1. In *Spano,* the court recognized two activities as appropriate candidates for assigning liability without fault: blasting with dynamite and

storing gunpowder. The court had found in Heeg v. Licht that the danger presented by the storage of gunpowder "could not be guarded against or averted by the greatest degree of care and vigilance" and in *Spano* suggested that the same was true of blasting, at least near existing structures. This conclusion implies that the burden of eliminating all risks associated with these activities is greater than the associated risks. Because it would be inefficient to take the precautions necessary to avoid the risk that materialized, the defendants were not at fault.

Although not at fault, people who blast with dynamite or store gunpowder may always be better evaluators than potential victims of the risks inherent in those activities and in a better position to take whatever cost-justified precautions are or become available.

> *Question:* Given this difference between the plaintiff's position and the defendant's, is any economic purpose served by assigning liability to the defendants in these cases?

2. When liability is based on negligence, a defendant is liable only if he was at fault. If no one was at fault, the plaintiff must bear the costs of the accident. Strict liability shifts this burden to the defendant; even if not at fault, the defendant must pay for the damage suffered by the plaintiff.

> *Questions:* When liability is based on negligence and neither party was negligent, does denying recovery to the plaintiff create incentives for her to avoid accidents that are not worth avoiding? Under strict liability, does shifting the burden of liability to the defendant even if he is not negligent create incentives to overinvest in accident avoidance?

3. In Booth v. Rome (overruled by *Spano*) the court applied strict liability only if there was an actual physical invasion of the plaintiff's land. If the damage from blasting was caused by vibration underground or in the air, the plaintiff was required to prove that the defendant was negligent in order to be awarded damages. While recovery for tort damages usually required proof of negligence, blasting cases fell into the category of the tort of "trespass." Proof of a trespass traditionally required evidence of physical invasion of another's right to exclusive enjoyment of one's land. Because the damage from blasting was often caused by rocks, dust, or other objects physically intruding onto the plaintiff's land, the tort of trespass applied to blasting cases. Recovery of damages for trespass had historically been on a strict liability basis, which is why the *Booth* court required the actual physical invasion.

> *Question:* From an efficiency perspective, should the decision to impose strict liability depend on whether the damage from blasting is caused by rocks flying through the neighbor's garage roof rather than vibration in the earth that caused the garage's foundation to crumble?

4. Under the general tort rule governing liability for injuries caused by domesticated animals, a plaintiff must prove that the animal's owner was negligent in order to recover damages unless the animal had shown, or was known to have, dangerous propensities. A plaintiff seeking damages for a dog bite must ordinarily prove that the dog's owner was negligent in

permitting the dog to attack. After the dog has bitten one person, however, the owner will be strictly liable to all future plaintiffs under the "One Bite Rule."

Question: What is the economic justification for applying strict liability in selected domesticated animals cases?

5. Occasionally a plaintiff is injured as a result of another's abnormally dangerous activity and the plaintiff is at fault. Suppose that despite the blaster's clear warnings, an adult sneaks up to the blasting site in order to watch the pyrotechnics and is injured. Prohibiting the defense would turn strict liability into absolute liability, effectively insuring the plaintiff against harms from blasting.

Question: Given the economic justification for holding the blaster strictly liable, should recovery be denied to the careless plaintiff?

SHAVELL, STRICT LIABILITY VERSUS NEGLIGENCE *
9 J. Legal Stud. 1, 2–3 (1980).

* * *

By definition, under the negligence rule all that an injurer needs to do to avoid the possibility of liability is to make sure to exercise due care if he engages in his activity. Consequently *he will not be motivated to consider the effect on accident losses of his choice of whether to engage in his activity or, more generally, of the level at which to engage in his activity;* he will choose his level of activity in accordance only with the personal benefits so derived. But surely any increase in his level of activity will typically raise expected accident losses (holding constant the level of care). Thus he will be led to choose too high a level of activity; the negligence rule is not "efficient."

Consider by way of illustration the problem of pedestrian-automobile accidents (and, * * * let us imagine the behavior of pedestrians to be fixed). Suppose that drivers of automobiles find it in their interest to adhere to the standard of due care but that the possibility of accidents is not thereby eliminated. Then, in deciding how much to drive, they will contemplate only the enjoyment they get from doing so. Because (as they exercise due care) they will not be liable for harms suffered by pedestrians, drivers will not take into account that going more miles will mean a higher expected number of accidents. Hence, they will do too much driving; an individual will, for example, decide to go for a drive on a mere whim despite the imposition of a positive expected cost to pedestrians.

However, under a rule of strict liability, the situation is different. Because an injurer must pay for losses whenever he is involved in an accident, he will be induced to consider the effect on accident losses of both his level of care *and* his level of activity. His decisions will therefore be efficient. Because drivers will be liable for losses sustained by pedestrians, they will decide not only to exercise due care in driving but also to drive only when the utility gained from it outweighs expected liability payments to pedestrians.

Notes and Questions

1. To avoid accidents, actors can regulate not only *how* they carry on a particular activity, but also *how often*. A jockey like Judy Casella in *Ordway*, for instance, can reduce the risk of being injured in a horse race by wearing a helmet and protective body armor. Such precautions allow the jockey to ride more safely, assuming she is going to ride at all. Perini Corporation similarly may be able to take steps to minimize damage from blasting, perhaps by careful placement of the dynamite or the use of protective barriers. Such strategies reduce the expected losses from risky activities by increasing the actor's *level of care* in engaging in the activity.

A second strategy for minimizing primary accident costs is to reduce expected losses from risky activities by reducing one's level of participation in the activity. Casella could ride in fewer races or none at all; Perini Corporation could plan to blast less often or dispense with blasting altogether. Automobile drivers can reduce the risk of accidents by driving less, as well as by driving more carefully. In other words, actors can reduce the risks of an activity by reducing their *level of activity* as well as by increasing their level of care when they do act.

Once a defendant decides to pursue an activity that poses a risk of accidents, Learned Hand's "B<PL" negligence test requires the defendant to invest in all precautionary measures that could reduce the risk of accidental loss at less cost than the expected cost of the risk. Thus, under the negligence standard, Perini Corporation would be liable only if it failed to undertake preventative measures that cost less than the expected damage from blasting.

But suppose preventative measures are impossible or prohibitively expensive? The court found in Heeg v. Licht that the danger presented in storing gunpowder "could not be guarded against or averted by the greatest degree of care and vigilance." *Spano* suggested that the same might sometimes be true for blasting. Assuming that blasting was to be done, the defendants apparently did it with an appropriate and efficient level of care.

Shavell states that the negligence rule is not efficient because potential injurers will be led to choose too high a level of activity.

Questions: How does this argument apply to the Perini Corporation in *Spano?* How does strict liability correct inefficient incentives in *Spano?* How does Shavell's argument apply to primary assumption of the risk cases like *Ordway?*

2. At least in theory, judges measuring "B" while applying the BPL formula can consider the burden to the defendant of preventing the accident by simply forgoing the risk-creating activity. For example, a court might find an automobile driver involved in an accident to be negligent if the driver had gone driving "on a mere whim", where the driver would not be negligent if driving to work or on an important errand.

As Professor Shavell notes in Strict Liability versus Negligence at pp. 22–23:

A question which is in a sense logically prior to the analysis of this article must be mentioned, namely, *"Why isn't the level of activity usually considered in the formulation of the due care standard?"* After all, the inefficiencies discussed here were viewed in the main as deriving from the fact that in order to avoid being found negligent (or contributorily negligent), parties are not motivated to alter their level of activity. The answer to the question appears to be that the courts would run into difficulty in trying to employ a standard of due care expanded in scope to include the level of activity. In formulating such a broadened due care standard, courts would, by definition, have to decide on the appropriate level of activity, and their competence to do this is problematic. How would courts decide the number of miles an individual ought to drive or how far or how often a pedestrian ought to walk? How would courts decide the level of output an industry—much less a firm within an industry—ought to produce? To decide such matters, a court would likely have to know much more than would normally have to be known to decide whether care, conventionally interpreted, was adequate.

The implication of Professor Shavell's argument is that strict liability may create better incentives for efficient behavior than negligence in circumstances where the defendant is in a better position to evaluate the costs and benefits of a particular *level of activity* than either the plaintiff or the finder of fact.

We have recognized that there might be certain activities where the defendant is clearly the best evaluator of the efficient level of *care.*

Questions: Are there activities where the defendant is the best evaluator of the efficient level of *activity?* Are there activities where she is not? If the defendant is always the best evaluator of the efficient level of activity should negligence-based liability be abandoned altogether in favor of strict liability?

3. Blasting and the storage of gunpowder are only two examples of activities that tort law describes as being "abnormally dangerous activities" or "ultrahazardous activities" and for which it imposes strict liability. In *Spano,* the court described this category of activities as those in which the activity was "dangerous and liable to cause damage to the property of persons residing in the vicinity" and in which the dangers "could not be guarded against or averted by the greatest degree of care and vigilance" and "located in an area in which it was likely to cause harm to neighboring property." Most states follow the criteria set out in the Restatement (Second) of Torts, § 520, which characterizes an "abnormally dangerous activity" according to whether certain factors are present. Those factors are:

(a) the existence of a high degree of risk of some harm to the person, land or chattels of others;

(b) the likelihood that the harm that results from it will be great;

(c) the inability to eliminate the risk by the exercise of reasonable care;

(d) the extent to which the activity is not a matter of common usage;

(e) the inappropriateness of the activity to the place where it is carried on; and

(f) the extent to which its value to the community is outweighed by its dangerous attributes.

As generally applied, no one of these factors is necessarily sufficient of itself and, ordinarily, several of them are required for strict liability. It is not necessary, however, that all of them be present, especially if others weigh heavily. See, Restatement (Second) of Torts, § 520, Comment f. The following types of activities have been characterized as abnormally dangerous: storing large amounts of gasoline in a residential area, operating a nuclear fuel processing plant, storing chemical waste near a community's water source, operating a propane gas storage yard, and maintaining a liquified manure lagoon.

Question: Do these seem like the kind of activities in which the defendants are in a better position than the plaintiffs to evaluate how the risks should be avoided and how much they should engage in the activity?

GREENMAN v. YUBA POWER PRODUCTS, INC.

Supreme Court of California, In Bank, 1962.
59 Cal.2d 57, 27 Cal.Rptr. 697, 377 P.2d 897.

TRAYNOR, JUSTICE.

Plaintiff brought this action for damages against the retailer and the manufacturer of a Shopsmith, a combination power tool that could be used as a saw, drill, and wood lathe. He saw a Shopsmith demonstrated by the retailer and studied a brochure prepared by the manufacturer. He decided he wanted a Shopsmith for his home workshop, and his wife bought and gave him one for Christmas in 1955. In 1957 he bought the necessary attachments to use the Shopsmith as a lathe for turning a large piece of wood he wished to make into a chalice. After he had worked on the piece of wood several times without difficulty, it suddenly flew out of the machine and struck him on the forehead, inflicting serious injuries. * * *

* * * The jury returned a verdict for the retailer against plaintiff and for plaintiff against the manufacturer in the amount of $65,000. * * *

Plaintiff introduced substantial evidence that his injuries were caused by defective design and construction of the Shopsmith. His expert witnesses testified that inadequate set screws were used to hold parts of the machine together so that normal vibration caused the tailstock of the lathe to move away from the piece of wood being turned permitting it to fly out of the lathe. They also testified that there were other more positive ways of fastening the parts of the machine together, the use of which would have prevented the accident. The jury could therefore reasonably have concluded that the manufacturer negligently constructed the Shopsmith. * * *

* * *

* * * A manufacturer is strictly liable in tort when an article he places on the market, knowing that it is to be used without inspection for defects, proves to have a defect that causes injury to a human being. Recognized first in the case of unwholesome food products, such liability has now been extended to a variety of other products that create as great or greater hazards if defective.

* * *

* * * The purpose of such liability is to insure that the costs of injuries resulting from defective products are borne by the manufacturers that put such products on the market rather than by the injured persons who are powerless to protect themselves. * * * To establish the manufacturer's liability it was sufficient that plaintiff proved that he was injured while using the Shopsmith in a way it was intended to be used as a result of a defect in design and manufacture of which plaintiff was not aware that made the Shopsmith unsafe for its intended use.

The judgment is affirmed.

Notes and Questions

1. *Greenman* is one of the early cases holding manufacturers strictly liable for injuries caused by defective products. The purpose of holding manufacturers strictly liable, according to Justice Traynor, "is to insure that the costs of injuries resulting from defective products are borne by the manufacturers that put such products on the market rather than by the injured persons who are powerless to protect themselves." The movement towards strict products liability extends the application of strict liability from activities that are abnormally dangerous or ultrahazardous, as in *Spano,* to the designing and manufacturing of products.

Questions: Is the purpose for the extension of strict liability to products articulated by Justice Traynor consistent with the efficiency justification for strict liability for injuries caused by abnormally dangerous activities? Are manufacturers always the parties in the best position to engage in risk evaluation and avoidance? Are consumers always "powerless to protect themselves?"

2. In *Greenman,* and in products liability generally, there are primarily two types of defects: defects in manufacturing and defects in design.

The workbench bought by Mr. Greenman's wife may have been different from the general run of workbenches produced by Shopsmith; screws inadequate to hold the machinery together were installed during the manufacturing process. If the workbench had been designed to have stronger screws and someone on the assembly line installed the wrong ones, then the error would be a manufacturing error. Evidence of a manufacturing error may include a comparison of the construction of the unit that caused the injury to other units producer by the same manufacturer. Often, as in the case of a half gallon of ice cream containing a machine spring or a ten dollar bill printed on only one side, the product quality is obviously different from the usual output.

If the design of the workbench called for inadequate screws, then there is no error in manufacturing because the assembly line followed the specifications correctly. The defect is in the design process instead. Since the design process inherently requires tradeoffs between cost and quality, proof of a design defect may include evidence of costs of alternative, safer designs and risks presented by the design selected. Courts also accept evidence that the designed produced was more dangerous than a reasonable consumer would expect.

Question: Does the conclusion that the manufacturer is usually the best cost avoider for product-related accidents depend on whether the characteristic of the product producing the accident is a design defect or a manufacturing defect?

3. Implicit in Justice Traynor's opinion is the conclusion that products will be safer if manufacturers are liable for the cost of injuries resulting from defective products.

Question: Is the substitution of strict liability for liability based on negligence likely to result in safer products?

2. STRICT LIABILITY AND ALLOCATIVE EFFICIENCY

DOE v. MILES LABORATORIES, INC.

United States District Court, District of Maryland, 1987.
675 F.Supp. 1466.

RAMSEY, DISTRICT JUDGE.

A plague inflicts society and this Court is called upon to adjudicate the extent to which the effects will be visited upon its victims. The facts are tragic. In the autumn of 1983, plaintiff Jane Doe, who a week previous had given birth, sought emergency medical treatment for vaginal bleeding. During the course of treatment, the attending physician ordered the administration of 500 units of "Konyne," a blood-coagulation-factor concentrate produced by Cutter Laboratories, a division of Miles. Treatment appeared successful and plaintiff eventually was discharged.

Over the course of the months to follow, plaintiff suffered from a succession of ailments, ultimately being diagnosed as infected by the HTLV-III virus, and as having Acquired Immune–Deficiency Syndrome–Related Complex (ARC), a predecessor of AIDS. On July 6, 1986, plaintiffs Jane and John Doe filed suit, alleging claims for strict liability in tort [among others]. Defendant Miles, following other procedural actions, filed this motion for summary judgment on plaintiffs' counts * * *.

* * *

Implicit in the [justifications] for strict products liability, though perhaps not clearly articulated, is [the argument] that strict products liability can promote the efficient allocation of resources. Society has chosen to allow market forces to set the price for goods and thus to determine their availability and distribution. In some respects the market is very efficient. The price purchasers pay invariably reflects direct costs such as raw products, capital investment, labor, plus a reasonable rate of return. However, in other respects the market is not efficient. Prices often do not reflect indirect costs. These hidden costs can include the effects of pollution or the expenses of accidents, and are what economists refer to as "externalities."

When the price of an item does not reflect both its direct costs and its externalities, the price will be lower than its actual cost. This lower price will stimulate an inefficient allocation of resources, for persons will be encouraged to buy more of the product than they might if they were paying its true price. Society thus may increase the consumption of the very goods that create pollution, and thus have indirect cleanup costs, or that are defective, and thus have indirect accident costs. Strict products liability shifts the cost back to manufacturers, who will then reprice the goods to reflect their actual costs. Strict products liability therefore affords society a mechanism for a rational allocation of resources. Absent it, the costs of externalities are thrust upon victims or upon society through its governmental welfare programs. In essence, without it there is a subsidy given to the polluting or defective products.

* * *

It is argued that providers of blood and blood products are promoting the general welfare by making possible improved health. It is argued that it is a fundamental social policy of the State of Maryland to promote the supply of blood and blood products. And it is argued that to allow strict products liability, which given the wide exposure to AIDS due to transfusions could create potentially substantial liability, would so raise costs of production that the supply of blood could be choked off.

The arguments are unpersuasive. * * * Those who choose to operate in the economic marketplace play by the rules applicable to all.

The arguments in favor of strict products liability apply as persuasively to blood and blood products as they do to any other product. * * * [I]t makes for a more efficient allocation of social resources when the price of a transfusion of blood or blood products reflects its true costs.

Entrepreneurs by their nature are risk taking individuals. To the extent they need an incentive to engage in socially beneficial activities, the law already provides it in the form of a corporate shield on personal liability. To do as defendant argues, and exempt blood from strict liability would be to subsidize the product by forcing either victims or government through its social welfare programs to bear accident costs. In the absence of a clear expression on the part of the legislature of an intent to subsidize a particular product, it is not this Court's role to create the subsidy indirectly by carving out a Judge made exemption to strict products liability.

Accordingly, the Court will deny defendant's motion for summary judgment on plaintiffs' claim for strict products liability.

* * *

Notes and Questions

1. In *Doe,* Judge Ramsey recognized that the failure of an actor to internalize the costs of his activity may result in allocative inefficiency. A manufacturer of products derived from blood charges a price sufficient to cover the costs of supplying that product, including some profit. The sale of this product to a buyer who is willing and able to pay the cost of the resources that went into producing that product is allocatively efficient, because the buyer values the product more highly.

Judge Ramsey considered the injuries resulting from use of the blood coagulant to be part of the cost of manufacturing the product. If the manufacturer is not required to bear all of the costs associated with the product and the price does not reflect that cost, then "[s]ociety cannot make rational decisions concerning the allocation of resources." If the price consumers pay is less than the full social costs then too many resources are allocated to the production of this good. The inefficiency that results is similar to the inefficiency that results when polluters produce an inefficiently large output of their product because they are not forced to take into account the costs they impose on others. By imposing liability on the manufacturers, the cost of accidents becomes a cost they must pass on through higher prices, which discourages buyers and reduces production to the efficient level. (See the discussion following *Orchard Views Farms* in Chapter 2.)

2. The efficiency concern Judge Ramsey identified is ensuring that manufacturers choose the proper level of activity. The activity in which Miles Laboratories is engaged is producing blood coagulants. By ensuring that the price of blood coagulants includes all of their costs, Judge Ramsey intended to ensure that the efficient quantity of that product is produced.

Generally people buy less of a product when the price rises. However, the amount of decrease in use resulting from a given increase in price varies from product to product. When the quantity demanded varies relatively little in response to a change in price, the demand for that product is said to be *inelastic.* The demand for blood coagulants is likely to be inelastic. Patients in Jane Doe's position may want blood coagulant at any price because without it they may bleed to death. If a price change has a relatively great effect on the quantity people demand, demand for that product is *elastic.* The demand for the Shopsmith in *Greenman* is likely to be more elastic than the demand for coagulants. (Chapter 6 discusses the concept of elasticity in greater detail.)

Question: For which products, those with elastic or those with inelastic demand, does the failure to include in the price the cost of externalities lead to greater inefficiencies?

3. Judge Ramsey argued that strict liability forces manufacturers to internalize all the costs associated with their productive activity and to raise their prices accordingly. If there were no liability for dangerous products, manufacturers could charge lower prices and consumers would buy more. The result is the inefficient overproduction of dangerous products because the manufacturer's prices do not reflect the true social costs.

But why conclude that the risk of injury is a cost of supplying the product? Why isn't it a cost of using the product? Coase's theory of reciprocal causation, discussed in Chapter 2, suggests that the risk is associated with both activities. Generally the user can take the risk into account in deciding how much he is willing and able to pay to use a dangerous product, *if he is aware of the risks.* If the user must bear the costs of injury, the risk is reflected in the maximum price he will be willing to pay. The reduced willingness to pay generally results in fewer units of the product being bought, reducing production to an efficient level.

A comparison of the relative abilities of the manufacturer and user may direct the imposition of liability to one or the other. If both the manufacturer and the user have complete information about the risks and are equally able to adjust their behavior to account for the risk, there is no reason to prefer manufacturer liability over no liability. Unless consumers are preferred to manufacturers or vice versa, it does not matter whether the level of activity is reduced to an efficient level by increased prices reflecting greater risks borne by manufacturers or by decreased willingness to pay reflecting the greater risks borne by consumers.

There is reason to believe, however, that manufacturers have a greater ability to evaluate the risks associated with their products and to reflect those costs in their prices accurately. The buyer may investigate carefully every product he buys and still not know as much about it as the manufacturer. The manufacturer is much more likely to know the design characteristics of a product and the probability of a manufacturing defect as a result of repeated, daily experience with the product and its characteristics. After a certain number of defects appear, the manufacturer may be able to project the frequency with which consumers will be injured and reflect potential judgment costs in its prices. The consumer, on the other hand, may have only a single experience with a product, may be unfamiliar with prior defects, and be unable to evaluate how much less he is willing to pay.

Questions: How does the imbalance in the availability of information to consumers and manufacturers affect the choice between no liability and strict liability for product defects? Is fault-based or strict liability a superior method for ensuring that dangerous products are neither over- nor under-produced?

4. Sometimes the injured party is not the purchaser but a third party or bystander. Because these parties do not respond to the price charged for the product, proper incentives for allocatively efficient behavior can be created only by imposing liability on the manufacturer or purchaser. Consider the case of Richman v. Charter Arms Corp., 571 F.Supp. 192 (E.D. La. 1983). The plaintiff was the victim of a shooting by a handgun. Unable to recover her damages from the shooter, the victim sued the

manufacturer claiming that the manufacturer should be strictly liable, on the theory that the defendant's activity should be classified as ultrahazardous.

> *Question:* If the price of handguns is to reflect the external costs imposed by their use, should the gun manufacturer be held strictly liable for damages associated with shootings involving its guns?

5. In *Spano,* Chief Judge Fuld overruled the holding of Booth v. Rome, W. & O.T.R.R. Co., which had limited the liability of blasters. The rationale in *Booth* was that "[p]ublic policy is sustained by the building up of towns and cities and the improvement of property. Any unnecessary restraint on freedom of action of a property owner hinders this."

> *Questions:* Does the imposition of strict liability on blasters interfere with the building up of towns and cities and the improvement of property by making it more expensive? Is interference desirable?

6. In a footnote in *Doe,* Judge Ramsey considered the argument that strict products liability has the potential to drive some manufacturers into bankruptcy, 675 F.Supp. at 1471 n. 3:

> The argument is often made that strict products liability has the potential to bankrupt manufacturers. Such an argument misses the salutary economic role strict products liability plays. Understood properly, it can be seen that strict liability promotes a rational market place. Society cannot make rational decisions concerning the allocation of resources unless the price reflects the true costs. When the price rises greatly, reflecting the fact the product produces either substantial direct costs or creates widespread externalities, it is rational to discourage or even abandon consumption of that product. Strict products liability thus allows the marketplace to make better informed decisions.

> *Question:* When is a manufacturer likely to be driven into bankruptcy as a result of a switch from negligence-based liability to strict products liability? Is it allocatively efficient to eliminate such a manufacturer?

3. RISK–AVERSION AND LOSS SPREADING

ESCOLA v. COCA COLA BOTTLING CO.

Supreme Court of California, 1944.
24 Cal.2d 453, 150 P.2d 436.

GIBSON, CHIEF JUSTICE.

Plaintiff, a waitress in a restaurant, was injured when a bottle of Coca Cola broke in her hand. She alleged that defendant company, which had bottled and delivered the alleged defective bottle to her employer, was negligent in selling "bottles containing said beverage which on account of excessive pressure of gas or by reason of some defect in the bottle was dangerous * * * and likely to explode." This appeal is from a judgment upon a jury verdict in favor of plaintiff.

[The majority of the court affirmed the judgment in favor of the plaintiff concluding that the jury could have reasonably inferred that the defendant was negligent.]

TRAYNOR, JUSTICE, concurring.

I concur in the judgment, but I believe the manufacturer's negligence should no longer be singled out as the basis of a plaintiff's right to recover in cases like the present one. In my opinion it should now be recognized that a manufacturer incurs an absolute liability when an article that he has placed on the market, knowing that it is to be used without inspection, proves to have a defect that causes injury to human beings. * * * Even if there is no negligence * * * public policy demands that responsibility be fixed wherever it will most effectively reduce the hazards to life and health inherent in defective products that reach the market. It is evident that the manufacturer can anticipate some hazards and guard against the recurrence of others, as the public cannot. Those who suffer injury from defective products are unprepared to meet its consequences. The cost of an injury and the loss of time or health may be an overwhelming misfortune to the person injured, and a needless one, for the risk of injury can be insured by the manufacturer and distributed among the public as a cost of doing business. It is to the public interest to discourage the marketing of products having defects that are a menace to the public. If such products nevertheless find their way into the market it is to the public interest to place the responsibility for whatever injury they may cause upon the manufacturer, who, even if he is not negligent in the manufacture of the product, is responsible for its reaching the market. However intermittently such injuries may occur and however haphazardly they may strike, the risk of their occurrence is a constant risk and a general one. Against such a risk there should be general and constant protection and the manufacturer is best situated to afford such protection.

* * *

As handicrafts have been replaced by mass production with its great markets and transportation facilities, the close relationship between the producer and consumer of a product has been altered. Manufacturing processes, frequently valuable secrets, are ordinarily either inaccessible to or beyond the ken of the general public. The consumer no longer has means or skill enough to investigate for himself the soundness of a product, even when it is not contained in a sealed package, and his erstwhile vigilance has been lulled by the steady efforts of manufacturers to build up confidence by advertising and marketing devices such as trade-marks. Consumers no longer approach products warily but accept them on faith, relying on the reputation of the manufacturer or the trade mark. Manufacturers have sought to justify that faith by increasingly high standards of inspection and a readiness to make good on defective products by way of replacements and refunds. The manufacturer's obligation to the consumer must keep pace with the changing relationship between them; it cannot be escaped because the marketing of a product has become so complicated as to require one or more intermediaries. Certainly there is greater reason to impose liability on the manufacturer than on the retailer who is but a conduit of a product that he is not himself able to test.

The manufacturer's liability should, of course, be defined in terms of the safety of the product in normal and proper use, and should not extend to injuries that cannot be traced to the product as it reached the market.

Notes and Questions

1. One of the arguments raised by Justice Traynor in *Escola* in favor of strict products liability is the ability of manufacturers to "anticipate some hazards and guard against the recurrence of others, as the public cannot." This characteristic of the manufacturer makes it the best minimizer of primary accident costs.

Traynor makes a second argument in favor of strict products liability. He points out that those injured by defective products may find that "[t]he cost of [the] injury and the loss of time or health may be an overwhelming misfortune." If manufacturers pay for such injuries under a strict liability regime, however, "the risk of injury can be insured by the manufacturer and distributed among the public as a cost of doing business." In other words, even if strict liability does not affect the level of primary accident costs society incurs, it changes the *distribution* of those costs in a desirable manner. The costs of accidents are dispersed evenly among consumers in the form of higher product prices, rather than borne entirely by the injured individual. Strict liability thus serves to "spread the losses" associated with injuries from defective products.

2. *Risk-Aversion.* In this context, risk means uncertainty. The study of the implications of "risk-aversion" involves examining how people's distaste for uncertainty affects their behavior. Consider a products liability risk as an example. Suppose that the probability of being injured by a defective bottle of Coca Cola is 1 in 100,000, and that the expected cost of the injury (if it occurs) is $5,000. Would you rather pay $.05 (.0001 x $5000) more for each bottle of Coca Cola you drink and know that the manufacturer is strictly liable for any injuries, or would you rather pay less and bear the cost of any injury that occurs yourself? The expected loss in each case is five cents per bottle, but the outcome in the second case is more uncertain; you may suffer $5,000 in accident costs or zero accident costs.

If a consumer is *risk-neutral,* she will be indifferent between paying $.05 more per Coca Cola or bearing the probable loss associated with drinking each Coke (also $.05). A risk-neutral individual is indifferent between the sure thing and an uncertain thing with the same probability-discounted outcome: indifferent between receiving $100, or receiving a lottery ticket with a 10% chance of winning $1,000.

But are consumers really risk-neutral? The practice of gambling indicates that some individuals appear to enjoy risk; they are *risk-preferrers.* Still, most people most of the time seem to prefer to avoid risk, whether risky gains or risky losses. People seem to be *risk-averse* rather than risk-neutral. The existence of a large and highly-developed insurance industry may be sufficient proof that people dislike risk and are willing to pay money to avoid it.

3. *The Declining Marginal Utility of Money.* There is a theoretical explanation for risk-aversion. Many economists believe that as an individual becomes wealthier each additional dollar of wealth adds smaller increments to that individual's total utility. In other words, individuals have "declining marginal utility" for extra income. If you doubt this assumption, ask yourself which would mean more to you, the first million dollars you make—or the second?

The declining marginal utility of money works in reverse, as well. As one loses wealth, each additional dollar lost imposes a greater sacrifice. A $50,000 loss resulting from an accident inflicts a harm more than 50,000 times greater than the loss of one dollar.

4. *Products Liability and Risk–Spreading.* The examples in the previous paragraphs address the principle of declining marginal utility of income for a single individual, but extending the theory to numerous individuals is straightforward. If everyone has declining marginal utility of income, then one person's loss of $5000 is quite possibly a greater subjective loss than 5000 people each losing one dollar (though one cannot be certain, since one cannot systematically compare one person's loss in utility to another's). The possibility that individuals are risk-averse suggests that the risk-spreading that results from strict products liability is a significant benefit. People are better off paying slightly higher prices for products under a strict liability regime, than bearing the risk of large, uncompensated losses from defective products. Notice that this is true even if the expected losses from defective products are the same under strict liability as under a rule of negligence.

5. The costs of having and avoiding accidents are primary accident costs and the administrative costs of the tort system are tertiary accident costs. In The Costs of Accidents, p. 27 (1970), Guido Calabresi referred to the dislocation costs incurred when the lives of the parties to an accident are disrupted, the "societal costs resulting from accidents," as *secondary accident costs.* The distinction between primary and secondary costs is not always clear, but secondary costs are usually associated with two theories of accident cost reduction: The Deep Pocket Theory and the Risk–Spreading Theory. Imposing liability on manufacturers may reduce secondary accident costs in either of two ways. First, it may place liability on the wealthier party, who derives less utility from the money at stake and so suffers a lesser subjective loss than a poorer individual. Second, it distributes the loss as widely as possible, so that many individuals suffer a small loss rather than one victim suffering a large loss.

The Deep Pocket Theory: Placing liability on the wealthiest party is justified on more than simply a distributional equity basis that favors the poor or injured over the wealthy. Under the theory of declining marginal utility, a dollar is worth less to a wealthy person than to a poor person. With their first dollars people buy the things that matter most to them; the later dollars are spent on things that matter less. People still value those later dollars, but not so highly as the initial ones.

In cases where there is no foundation for believing that one party is the better minimizer of accident costs, the law must inevitably decide whether the defendant or the victim will bear the costs of an accident that has occurred. If the wealthy manufacturer pays, then the judgment is paid out of dollars that are valued less highly than if the poor victim must pay. Thus, society's total level of well-being declines less if liability is placed on the wealthier party.

This theory has numerous problems. The most obvious one is that manufacturers are not always wealthy. The accumulation of judgments against manufacturers can drive them into bankruptcy. In addition, it is not clear whether a company has any "utility" of its own at all. A corporation is made up of its officers, employees, and stockholders. Any loss to the corporation must be a loss to them and the deep pocket theory says nothing about their level of wealth compared to the victim's. Moreover, we do not know how the loss will be distributed among these constituent groups. These problems make the deep pocket theory the less favored of the two approaches to minimizing secondary accident costs.

Risk–Spreading and Insurance: Under this theory of spreading, manufacturers can raise prices so that accidental losses are spread over a larger group. Judge Mentz relied on this argument in Richman v. Charter Arms Corp., 571 F.Supp. 192, 203–04 (E.D. La. 1983), which involved strict liability under the theory of abnormally dangerous activities for damages to a woman who was kidnapped, robbed, raped, and murdered by a man using a handgun manufactured by the defendant:

> Perhaps the most significant fact the defendant ignores is that increased insurance costs can be passed on to consumers in the form of higher prices for handguns. The people who benefit most from marketing practices like the defendant's are handgun manufacturers and handgun purchasers. Innocent victims rarely, if ever, are beneficiaries. Consequently, it hardly seems unfair to require manufacturers and purchasers, rather than innocent victims, to pay for the risks those practices entail. Furthermore, economic efficiency seems to require the same result. In an important article on ultrahazardous activities and risk allocation, Professor Clarence Morris makes just this point. Morris, "Hazardous Enterprises and Risk Bearing Capacity", 61 Yale L.J. 1172 (1952). In his view, "the avowed goal of the absolute liability approach is allocation of loss to the party better equipped to pass it on to the public: the superior risk bearer." Professor Morris discusses a variety of examples to show that the defendant is not always the superior risk bearer in an ultrahazardous activity case. Here is what he says, however, about bodily injury and risk-bearing capacity:
>
> > The financial burden of disabling personal injury overwhelms most people. While many can bear the cost of minor injury, prolonged infirmity and extended medical expense often exceed the financial competence of common men. Unless [common man] happens to be rich or covered by one of the more generous workmen's compensation plans, he will probably bear the risk less easily than Enterpriser. The preponderant

likelihood is that Enterpriser is the better risk bearer of the two.

* * * Thus, both fairness and economic efficiency suggest that the community would be better off if the defendant's marketing practices were classified as ultrahazardous. * * *

The court in *Charter Arms* apparently believed that even if the manufacturer was not the best party to minimize primary accident costs, secondary accident costs would be minimized by requiring the manufacturer to spread the loss through higher prices.

The manufacturer may be able to insure against losses by charging higher prices and holding a reserve against future liability or buying a liability insurance policy. The consumer might also be able to obtain insurance, of course.

Questions: Would the consumer's insurance ("first party" insurance) spread the loss just as effectively as imposing liability on the manufacturer? Might there be a difference between the ability of the consumer and the manufacturer to obtain insurance at low cost? If so, what impact should this difference have on the efficiency of strict liability?

SHEPARD v. SUPERIOR COURT

Court of Appeal, First District, Division 2, 1977.
76 Cal.App.3d 16, 142 Cal.Rptr. 612.

KANE, ASSOCIATE JUSTICE, dissenting.

* * *

* * * To start with, it is noted that the avowed purpose of imposing strict liability upon the manufacturer is twofold: (1) loss-distribution or risk-spreading and (2) injury-reduction by enhanced safety. The first rationale, risk-spreading, holds the manufacturer liable for injuries resulting from the use of his product because he is in the best position to distribute the loss either by insurance or by increasing the price of his product. As stated in *Greenman v. Yuba Power Products, Inc.*, the purpose of strict tort liability is to insure that the costs of injuries resulting from defective products are borne by the manufacturers who put such products on the market rather than by the injured persons who are powerless to protect themselves. Echoing the same idea, the court in *Vandermark v. Ford Motor Co.* reemphasized that strict liability on the manufacturer affords protection to the injured person and works no injustice because the manufacturers can protect themselves through obtaining insurance and dispersing the cost through the prices of the products. The second rationale, the theory of injury reduction, holds the manufacturer liable because he is in the best position to discover and correct the dangerous aspects of his products before any injury occurs. Again, the manufacturer may pass on to the consumer the increased product costs by incorporating them in the purchase price of the merchandise.

Although since its inception the courts have generally tended to broaden the scope of products liability, there are few cases, if any, which have embarked on a thorough and delicate analysis to explore whether the above stated policy goals are indeed promoted by the ever-expanding scope of enterprise liability. It is time for such an examination.

The basic facts of economy teach us that the fashionable trend of a wholesale extension of strict liability proves to be counterproductive in many instances by hampering and arresting, rather than promoting, the policy objectives underpinning the doctrine. Thus, it requires no special economic expertise to realize that the double demand posed by the law, i. e., to make the product absolutely safe on the one hand, and to spread the cost of the ever increasing insurance premiums together with the expense of safety measures to the consumer on the other, becomes increasingly difficult, if not entirely impossible, to meet. It is well to remember that economic forces do not work in a vacuum, but rather in a strict and realistic economic environment where prices of merchandise are greatly influenced (if not entirely determined) by economic rivalry and competition. Under these circumstances, the fundamental assumption of spreading the risk of the enterprise to the consumers at large cannot be attained and materialized. While some portion of the ever growing safety and insurance cost may pass directly to the consumer by way of a higher dollar price, the remainder will take the form of decreased quality not affecting safety and decreased profits. The decreased profits affect the manufacturers first (among them mainly the large segment of small businessmen with limited or marginal capital who have to shoulder the strict enterprise liability side by side with the huge corporations), then society as a whole. The motion and realistic operation of economic forces have been graphically described by one observer as follows: *"Decreased profits, however, do not stop with the manufacturer.* He distributes them to the shareholders of his corporation, just as he distributes increased prices to the consumers of his product. Moreover, decreased profits do not stop with the shareholders. *Rather, in more or less attenuated form, they pass on to other, broader classes.* The major distribution of decreased profits occurs when shareholders switch their investment to other, more profitable enterprises. When this happens, the liability-bearing manufacturer's enterprise loses its ability to attract investment capital resulting in decreased industrial activity. *This decreased activity results in losses to several categories. First, the consumer will feel the loss because the manufacturer's ability to produce a better, safer product will diminish. Second, reduced industrial activity will affect labor. Severely diminished profits may force the manufacturer out of business. Even less drastic reductions, however, could reduce the number of new jobs. Finally, reduced economic activity will affect the entire society, in a more or less attenuated form, through lower tax revenues, lower wages, and lower profits for distribution."* (Alden D. Holford, The Limits of Strict

Liability for Product Design and Manufacture (1973) 52 Tex.L.Rev. 81, 87, emphasis added.)

Paying heed to economic realities rather than our own fancy, the courts as a matter of judicial policy must stop the further extension of the strict liability of entrepreneurs, at least to areas where, as here, the determination of damages is speculative and conjectural rather than real and definable. In doing so, we are in line with established law which holds that the manufacturer is not an insurer of the product and that the strict liability of entrepreneurs may not be equated with absolute, limitless liability. As has been emphasized time and time again, in determining the parameters of enterprise liability we must draw a proper balance between the need for adequate recovery and the survival of viable enterprises. The guiding principles to achieve these goals are judicial temperance, evenhandedness and, first and foremost, fairness to all.

* * *

Notes and Questions

1. In *Shepard,* Justice Kane's dissent raises the question of who actually bears the costs of liability when strict liability requires the manufacturer to compensate victims without regard to the manufacturer's fault. Several possible candidates exist: consumers, who may pay more for the manufacturer's products; stockholders in the corporation, who may receive a lower return on the investment in the corporation due to lessened profitability; and employees of the corporation, who may be forced to accepted lower wages as a result of the higher costs. Economic theory provides tools for analyzing how these losses are distributed.

It is not usually true that the manufacturer can increase the price of its product dollar for dollar to reflect the increased judgment costs. There are several ways in which increased prices reduce the amount of output the manufacturer can sell. The most obvious are that the price of the product will be too high for some buyers to afford and that some buyers will not be willing and able to buy as much of the product as they did before. As a result the manufacturer will not be able to sell as much as before. The extent to which people curtail their purchases depends, among other things, on how expensive the product is initially and what substitutes there are for the product. The more expensive the product, other things being equal, the greater is the percentage cut in purchases associated with a given percentage price increase. The more desperately people need the product (that is, the fewer the substitutes) the less people will reduce their purchases. The manufacturer may be willing to raise its price by less than the full amount of the increased costs to avoid losing a large volume of sales. This willingness results in a sharing of the increased costs between manufacturer and buyers.

The share of increased costs borne by the manufacturer decreases the profitability of the investment of assets in the corporation. One way to minimize this decrease in profitability is to reduce costs of inputs, such as labor and raw materials. It is not usually true, however, that the manufacturer can reduce the amount it pays for inputs dollar for dollar to reflect its share of increased liability costs. The willingness of employees to take pay cuts is analogous to the willingness of consumers to pay higher prices for the product; it is affected by the size of the pay cut and the other job opportunities available to them. This is also true of the suppliers of other inputs such as raw materials.

After the manufacturer has raised prices as high as it profitably can and reduced the prices it pays for inputs to the production process, there remain the stockholders. To some extent, the manufacturer can reduce the amount it pays to stockholders in return for their investment. Like the other possible sharers of the burden, however, stockholders may have substitute investments available and low rates of return may make raising new capital more difficult or expensive.

Who actually bears the loss is a difficult question. While Chapter 6 develops the methodology for answering these distributional questions in a systematic way, many related issues are not empirically answerable.

2.   To get some idea of how the costs associated with strict liability are distributed, consider the various products involved in the strict liability cases in this chapter.

Questions: For which products would the manufacturer be able to pass on the largest percentage of the costs to the customer? In other words, for which products is consumer demand likely to be inelastic?

4.   STRICT LIABILITY AND DUTY TO RESCUE

OSTERLIND v. HILL

Supreme Judicial Court of Massachusetts, 1928.
263 Mass. 73, 160 N.E. 301.

BRALEY, J.

This is an action of tort, brought by the plaintiff as administrator of the estate of Albert T. Osterlind to recover damages for the conscious suffering and death of his intestate. There are four counts in the original declaration and five counts in the amended declaration, to each of which the defendant demurred. The first count of the original declaration alleges that, on or about July 4, 1925, the defendant was engaged in the business of letting for hire pleasure boats and canoes to be used on Lake Quannapowitt in the town of Wakefield; that it was the duty of the defendant to have a reasonable regard for the safety of the persons to whom he let boats and canoes; that the defendant, in the early morning of July 4, 1925, in willful, wanton, or reckless disregard of the natural and probable consequences, let for hire, to the intestate and one Ryan, a frail and dangerous canoe, * * * that, in consequence of the defendant's willful, wanton, or reckless disregard of his duties, the intestate and Ryan went out in the canoe, which shortly afterwards was overturned and the intestate, after hanging to it for approximately one-half hour, and making loud calls for assistance, which calls the defendant heard and utterly ignored, was obliged to release his hold, and was drowned; that in consequence of the defendant's willful, wanton, or reckless conduct the intestate endured great conscious mental anguish and great conscious physical suffering from suffocation and drowning. Count 2 differs materially from count 1 only in so far as negligent conduct is alleged as distinguished from willful, wanton, or reckless conduct. In count 3 the acts of the defendant set forth in the previous counts are relied upon as stating a cause of action for death as a result of the defendant's willful, wanton, or reckless conduct.   * * *

The trial court sustained demurrers to both the original and amended declarations and reported the case for the determination of this court.

* * * The declaration must set forth facts which, if proved, establish the breach of a legal duty owed by the defendant to the intestate. * * *

In the case at bar, * * * it is alleged in every count of the original and amended declaration that after the canoe was overturned the intestate hung to the canoe for approximately one-half hour and made loud calls for assistance. * * *

* * * The failure of the defendant to respond to the intestate's outcries is immaterial. No legal right of the intestate was infringed. The allegation common to both declarations that the canoe was "frail and dangerous" appears to be a general characterization of canoes. It is not alleged that the canoe was out of repair and unsafe.

It follows that the order sustaining each demurrer is affirmed.

Notes and Questions

1. Apply the Learned Hand "BPL" formula to the conduct of defendant Hill. While Albert Osterlind (who apparently could not swim) was clinging to the overturned canoe and calling for help, the probability of an accident—a drowning—was quite high, unless the defendant came to the plaintiff's rescue. The burden of the rescue seemed quite low, perhaps requiring no greater effort than Hill's simply rowing one of his other canoes out to get the defendant. Since the burden to Hill of rescuing Osterlind was much lower than the expected loss to Osterlind if Hill did not intervene, one might expect that Hill would be found negligent for his failure to rescue.

Osterlind illustrates the common law rule that an individual generally has no duty to rescue another, even when the cost of rescue is negligible and the victim's situation is extremely perilous. The rule against a duty to rescue often is explained as one of causation or responsibility: since the defendant played no part in endangering the plaintiff, the defendant owes no duty to minimize that risk.

Questions: From an economic perspective, is the causal explanation appealing? Does it make sense to hold defendants responsible when their actions impose a harm on plaintiffs, but not when their inaction withholds a potential benefit—rescue?

2. A categorical rule that defendants have no duty to rescue is equivalent to a rule that plaintiffs are strictly liable for their injuries when

the defendant did not cause those injuries but simply declined to prevent them. Recasting the rule as one of strict liability may shed some light on its rationale.

> *Questions:* Applying the analysis of strict liability developed in the preceding materials, is there an economic explanation for the common law's failure to impose a duty of rescue? Which party is in the best position to minimize the sum of the costs of accidents and the costs of rescues?

3. The common law recognizes an exception to the general rule of no duty to rescue in cases where the defendant's negligence created the plaintiff's perilous situation. If Hill had been negligently piloting the canoe when it overturned, he would have had a duty to use all reasonable efforts to rescue his passenger, Osterlind.

> *Question:* Is that exception consistent with the economic rationale of the rule against a duty to rescue?

4. Establishing a duty to rescue would affect secondary and tertiary accident costs. When considering the tertiary costs of a duty to rescue consider the application of rule in the following circumstances. If a person on the street tells you that he needs food or will go hungry, do you have a duty to provide him food? If a charitable organization informs you that thousands are starving in another country, must you write a large check? Would a medical doctor violate her duty to rescue if she took the weekend off rather than working in the hospital? It is hard to determine where the duty to rescue stops.

E. EFFICIENT DEFENSES
TO STRICT LIABILITY

1. UNFORESEEABLE MISUSE

DANIELL v. FORD MOTOR CO.

United States District Court, District of New Mexico, 1984.
581 F.Supp. 728.

BALDOCK, DISTRICT JUDGE.

* * *

In 1980, the plaintiff became locked inside the trunk of a 1973 Ford LTD automobile, where she remained for some nine days. Plaintiff now seeks to recover for psychological and physical injuries arising from that occurrence. She contends that the automobile had a design defect in that the trunk lock or latch did not have an internal release or opening mechanism. * * *

* * *

The overriding factor barring plaintiff's recovery is that she intentionally sought to end her life by crawling into an automobile trunk from which she could not escape. This is not a case where a person inadvertently became trapped inside an automobile trunk. The plaintiff was aware of the natural and probable consequences of her perilous conduct. Not only that, the plaintiff, at least initially, sought those dreadful consequences. Plaintiff, not the manufacturer of the vehicle, is responsible for this unfortunate occurrence.

Recovery under strict products liability and negligence will be discussed first because the concept of duty owned by the manufacturer to the consumer or user is the same under both theories in this case. As a general principle, a design defect is actionable only where the condition of the product is unreasonably dangerous to the user or consumer. Under strict products liability or negligence, a manufacturer has a duty to consider only those risks of injury which are foreseeable. A risk is not foreseeable by a manufacturer where a product is used in a manner which could not reasonably be anticipated by the manufacturer and that use is the cause of the plaintiff's injury. The plaintiff's injury would not be foreseeable by the manufacturer.

The purposes of an automobile trunk are to transport, stow and secure the automobile spare tire, luggage and other goods and to protect those items from elements of the weather. The design features of an automobile make it well near impossible that an adult intentionally would enter the trunk and close the lid. The dimensions of a trunk, the height of its sill and its load floor and the efforts to first lower the trunk lid and then to engage its latch, are among the design features which encourage closing and latching the trunk lid while standing outside the vehicle. The court holds that the plaintiff's use of the trunk compartment as a means to attempt suicide was an unforeseeable use as a matter of law. Therefore, the manufacturer had no duty to design an internal release or opening mechanism that might have prevented this occurrence.

* * *

WHEREFORE,

IT IS ORDERED that the defendant's Motion for Summary Judgment is granted.

Notes and Questions

1. One of the justifications for imposing strict liability on manufacturers in products cases is that they are usually the party in the best position to minimize primary accident costs and to internalize external costs. The court in *Daniell* held that use of the trunk compartment as a means of attempted suicide was unforeseeable and, therefore, the manufacturer had no duty to design an internal release mechanism. In the law, "unforeseeable" does not mean that people are literally unable to foresee an event. Rather, to be "unforeseeable" in a legal sense, the event must be sufficiently improbable that a reasonable person would not take it into account in his decisions.

Questions: What does the foreseeability of someone using the trunk to commit suicide have to do with whether the manufacturer is the best cost avoider for this accident? Does the customary rationale for strict liability support recovery by Ms. Daniell after she locked herself in the trunk of her LTD?

2. The 1973 LTD was a very large car with a big trunk. It is reasonably foreseeable that someone might climb into the trunk to get a small piece of luggage or some groceries that had rolled out of the shopping bag into the back of the trunk, or to fix some wiring, or a hinge.

Questions: Is the possibility of the lid accidently closing on such a person so remote that the need to escape from the closed trunk is unforeseeable? If Ms. Daniell had climbed into her trunk to retrieve a grapefruit that had fallen from her shopping bag and the wind had slammed the trunk shut, would holding Ford liable be efficient? Why should this change in facts make a difference?

3. In some states, unforeseeable misuse of a product is a complete defense in a strict products liability action.

Question: How does freeing the manufacturer from liability for unforeseeable risks further the goal of minimizing tertiary accident costs?

CRYTS v. FORD MOTOR COMPANY

Missouri Court of Appeals, St. Louis District, Division Three, 1778.
571 S.W.2d 683.

GUNN, PRESIDING JUDGE.

This appeal arises from a civil action in tort based on a two car collision in which plaintiff, David Cryts, suffered paraplegia. The jury returned a verdict in the amount of $150,000, and the judgment was entered against defendants Ford Motor Company (Ford), the manufacturer of the car plaintiff was driving, and Robert Uttendorfer, the driver of the car with which he collided. Uttendorfer's liability is premised on negligence in the operation of his vehicle, while Ford's liability is premised on strict liability for a defectively designed armrest which caused plaintiff's back to be broken when he was thrown against his door in the collision. Each defendant has appealed. * * *

* * *

Plaintiff predicates his theory of recovery on the principle of strict liability in tort for the defective design and condition of the 1957 Thunderbird armrest as applied in the so-called "second collision" or "injury enhancement" doctrine. * * *

* * * In this case, the second collision was plaintiff's body striking the armrest after the first collision between the Thunderbird and the Uttendorfer vehicle. The second collision doctrine differs from the typical § 402A case, in that the defect would not have produced any injury in the absence of an intervening cause which sets the injury producing cycle into action. The source of the original or intervening cause is irrelevant so long as the plaintiff's particular use of the product is reasonably foreseeable. The Eighth Circuit, in applying Missouri law and in adopting the second collision doctrine, specifically held that a manufacturer could be held liable for injuries shown to

have been caused or enhanced by the defective condition of its product which was being used in a manner reasonably anticipated in the course of an accident brought about by an independent cause.

* * *

In this case, plaintiff produced evidence from his expert witness that the 1957 Thunderbird armrest was defective, in that it was constructed of hard plastic with minimal energy-absorbing capacity; that it was lightly padded; and that its pointed shape was such as to concentrate the force of energy absorbed by the body. In light of this evidence the jury could have reasonably found that the armrest was defective and that it was unreasonably dangerous for its anticipated use.

Ford's other arguments that a collision with another vehicle was not an anticipated use * * * [is] not persuasive to the outcome of this case. It has been held that even misuse of a product may be reasonably foreseeable. Further, it has been specifically held that a collision is a foreseeable incident of normal use of a motor vehicle. Ford argues that it built the safest armrest possible under the technology existing in 1957. Such a contention has no bearing on the outcome of a strict liability claim, where the sole subject of inquiry is the defective condition of the product and not the manufacturer's knowledge, negligence or fault. * * *

* * *

Judgment Affirmed.

Notes and Questions

1. In *Cryts,* as in *Daniell,* the consumer was using the product in a manner not intended by the manufacturer. Unlike *Daniell,* the consumer in *Cryts* was using the product in a manner he did not intend and the consumer does not appear to be in a better position than the manufacturer to anticipate the idiosyncratic use. As the majority of courts make clear, however, the manufacturer's liability is not limited to risks resulting from intended uses of the product. See, e.g., Larsen v. General Motors Corp., 391 F.2d 495, 502 (8th Cir. 1968):

> * * * While automobiles are not made for the purpose of colliding with each other, a frequent and inevitable contingency of normal automobile use will result in collisions and injury-producing impacts. No rational basis exists for limiting recovery to situations where the defect in design or manufacture was the causative factor of the accident, as the accident and the resulting injury, usually caused by the so-called "second collision" of the passenger with the interior part of the automobile, all are foreseeable. Where the injuries or enhanced injuries are due to the manufacturer's failure to use reasonable care to avoid subjecting the user of its products to an unreasonable risk of injury, general negligence principles should be applicable. The sole function of an automobile is not just to provide a means of transportation, it is to provide a means of safe transportation or as safe as is reasonably possible under the present state of the art.

We do agree that under the present state of the art an automobile manufacturer is under no duty to design an accident-proof or fool-proof vehicle or even one that floats on water, but such manufacturer is under a duty to use reasonable care in the design of its vehicle to avoid subjecting the user to an unreasonable risk of injury in the event of a collision. Collisions with or without fault of the user are clearly foreseeable by the manufacturer and are statistically inevitable.

2. Suppose that Cryts' injuries had resulted from some intentional, but foreseeable, misuse of the product. For example, Cryts might have lost control of the car while driving in excess of the posted speed limit. Note the language in *Cryts* that "[t]he source of the original or intervening cause [of the plaintiff's injury] is irrelevant so long as the plaintiff's particular use of the product is reasonably foreseeable."

Question: Is it efficient for Cryts to be able to recover on the theory that the car he negligently crashed was defectively designed?

3. Like the State of Missouri in *Cryts,* all states but one apply the language of § 402A of the Restatement 2d of Torts in strict products liability cases:

> § 402A. Special Liability of Seller of Product for Physical Harm to User or Consumer
>
> (1) One who sells any product in a defective condition unreasonably dangerous to the user or consumer or to his property is subject to liability for physical harm thereby caused to the ultimate user or consumer, or to his property, if
>
>> (a) the seller is engaged in the business of selling such a product, and
>>
>> (b) it is expected to and does reach the user or consumer without substantial change in the condition in which it is sold.
>
> (2) The rule stated in Subsection (1) applies although
>
>> (a) the seller has exercised all possible care in the preparation and sale of his product, and
>>
>> (b) the user or consumer has not bought the product from or entered into any contractual relation with the seller.

2. UNREASONABLE ASSUMPTION OF RISK

WILLIAMS v. BROWN MANUFACTURING COMPANY

Supreme Court of Illinois, 1970.
45 Ill.2d 418, 261 N.E.2d 305, 46 A.L.R.3d 226.

UNDERWOOD, CHIEF JUSTICE.

James Williams was injured while operating a trenching machine manufactured by defendant, Brown Manufacturing Company, Inc. Williams brought an action against defendant under a theory of strict product liability in tort, essentially alleging an unreasonably dangerous design, and was awarded damages in the amount of $40,000 by a Madison County circuit court jury. The judgment was affirmed by the Appellate Court for the Fifth Judicial District, and we granted leave to appeal.

* * *

Plaintiff's recovery was based upon a count alleging that while he was operating the trencher, "the machine bucked and unexpectedly jumped a number of feet to the rear, knocking the plaintiff to the ground and running over him, thereby causing serious and permanent injuries * * *." This count enumerated several respects in which the condition of the trencher was "unreasonably dangerous", alleged that the condition existed when the trencher left defendant's control, and claimed that plaintiff's injuries were a direct and proximate result of the condition. * * * Defendant's answer included two affirmative defenses: the action was barred by the statute of limitations, and plaintiff had "assumed all risk in relation to use and operation" of the trencher. Both defenses were stricken by the trial court on plaintiff's motion because of the court's opinion that the proof was insufficient to support either defense.

* * *

The evidence indicated that, while plaintiff was operating the machine from a position between the handlebars at its rear, the digging teeth of the trencher momentarily caught on an underground pipe; when the teeth suddenly slipped off the pipe, the machine lurched backward. Plaintiff maintained that the power unit should have been equipped with some safety device, such as a "throw out clutch", to prevent such a build-up of force. Alternatively, he argued that the drive-belt should have been easily adjustable to a tension which would allow satisfactory digging normally, but would allow slippage when an obstruction was encountered. * * * An instruction booklet had accompanied the machine, and, though it did not advise as to the proper position for an operator, it did state in the two pages concerned with operation and maintenance:

"ADJUSTMENTS AND MAINTENANCE

The engine is bolted stationary to the machine, and when the drive belts become loose enough to slip, adjust them by the threaded shaft on the right hand clutch lever. Caution—do not adjust the belts too tight; they must be able to slip under shock load. * * * "

On cross-examination, plaintiff acknowledged having read the manual prior to his injury, although it is unclear how completely he read it. He did admit to reading at least a portion of the maintenance section, in which section the quoted language appeared.

In resolving the case before us the appellate court relied upon § 402A of the Restatement (Second) of Torts, comment (n), which reads as follows: "*n. Contributory negligence.* Since the liability with which this Section deals is not based upon negligence of the seller, but is strict liability, the rule applied to strict liability cases (see § 524) applies. Contributory negligence of the plaintiff is not a defense when such negligence consist merely in a failure to discover the defect in the product, or to guard against the possibility of its existence. On the other hand the form of contributory negligence which consists in voluntarily and unreasonably proceeding to encounter a known danger, and commonly passes under the name of assumption of risk, is a defense under this Section as in other cases of strict liability. If the user or consumer discovers the defect and is aware of the danger, and nevertheless proceeds unreasonably to make use of the product and is injured by it, he is barred from recovery."

* * *

All authorities agree that plaintiffs in tort actions may so conduct themselves as to bar recovery for injuries suffered by them. This recovery-barring conduct, while given different labels, is ofttimes treated within the general concept of "contributory negligence." * * * In determining where the loss should fall as between the nonnegligent manufacturer, distributor or retailer and the less than careful plaintiff, it has generally been recognized in Illinois and elsewhere that plaintiffs who "misuse" a product—use it for a purpose neither intended nor "foreseeable" (objectively reasonable) by the defendant—may be barred from recovery. There is likewise general agreement that a plaintiff who knows a product is in a dangerous condition and proceeds in disregard of this known danger (often termed "assumption of risk") may not recover for resulting injuries.

The question before us is whether, in a strict product liability in tort action, the concept of contributory negligence as it prevails in this State shall bar a plaintiff's recovery, or whether that recovery will be barred only when the nature of plaintiff's misconduct has reached the point at which he has misused the product or has assumed the risk of its use. We are persuaded that the policy considerations which led us to adopt strict tort liability in [Suvada v. White Motor Co.] compel the elimination of "contributory negligence" as a bar to recovery. We also note that all other jurisdictions which have adopted the theory of strict liability have reached substantially the same conclusion, for, even though some of the opinions speak in terms of "contributory negligence", the actual conduct there held to bar recovery would by us be classified as misuse or assumption of risk.

* * *

[S]ubstantial evidence was presented which could reasonably support a jury determination that plaintiff recognized and voluntarily accepted the danger posed by improper drive-belt adjustment. Plaintiff was an experienced "operating engineer", with proficiency in a wide range of machinery; a jury could have believed him aware of the trencher's obvious design features. Indeed, he admittedly "checked out" the new machine to be sure it was in order. Since he was an experienced machinery operator, a jury could reasonably believe that he understood the general characteristics of belt-drive systems, and it was obvious that the trencher utilized such a system. * * *

* * * In any event, plaintiff admits having read, prior to his injury, portions of the manual relating to maintenance. As earlier noted, that was the section of the manual which contained the cautionary instructions relating to the drive-belt. It also appears that plaintiff may have contemplated the possibility of encountering an underground obstruction, but discounted the danger since, as he related on cross-examination, he had understood there was no underground obstruction in the area.

We emphasize that "assumption of risk" is an affirmative defense which does bar recovery, and which may be asserted in a strict liability action notwithstanding the absence of any contractual relationship between the parties. Furthermore, while the test to be applied in determining whether a user has assumed the risk of using a product known to be dangerously defective is fundamentally a subjective test, in the sense that it is *his* knowledge, understanding and appreciation of the danger which must be assessed, rather than that of the reasonably prudent person * * *.

A determination of the propriety of the trial court's action in striking the affirmative defense of assumption of risk must be predicated upon consideration of the totality of the evidence in its aspect most favorable to defendant. Viewed in this light, we cannot say that the evidence as a whole so overwhelmingly favors plaintiff that a jury finding for defendant on this issue could never stand. It is therefore necessary that this cause be remanded for a new trial under proper instructions in accordance with this opinion.

* * *

Reversed and remanded.

Notes and Questions

1. Unforeseeable misuse cases can be explained by the fact that it is pointless to ask manufacturers to guard against risks that are extremely unlikely to materialize. The plaintiff's injury in *Williams,* however, resulted from a defect reasonably foreseeable to the manufacturer, one addressed in the manufacturer's instruction booklet.

Questions: If the manufacturer is aware of and appreciates the risks associated with a defect in the product, why should the plaintiff bear the entire loss resulting from use of the defective product? Does the assumption of the risk defense to products liability resemble the doctrine of last clear chance?

2. Some courts require that the plaintiff's assumption of the risk in products liability cases be *unreasonable* in addition to being knowing and voluntary. Not all jurisdictions add this requirement.

Questions: When can a plaintiff "reasonably" assume the risk of using a product with an obvious and known defect? From an efficiency perspective, does the requirement of unreasonableness improve the incentives provided by strict products liability?

3. COMPARATIVE NEGLIGENCE

MURRAY v. FAIRBANKS MORSE

United States Court of Appeals, Third Circuit, 1979.
610 F.2d 149.

ROSENN, CIRCUIT JUDGE.

This appeal raises several issues, including novel and important questions as to whether a comparative negligence statute may be applied and, if so, to what extent, in an action for personal injuries brought under twin theories of strict products liability and common law principles of negligence. The jury returned a verdict in favor of the plaintiff, Norwilton Murray, in the sum of two million dollars against the manufacturer, Beloit Power Systems, Inc. (Beloit). The jury, in response to special interrogatories, found that plaintiff's negligence was a proximate cause of his injuries and that he was at fault to the extent of five percent. The trial judge reduced the verdict accordingly and judgment was thereupon entered for the plaintiff. Beloit's motion for a new trial was denied and it appealed. Murray has also cross-appealed contending that the trial court erred in applying contributory negligence as a defense to a products liability action grounded on section 402A of the Restatement (Second) of Torts and that it should not have reduced his verdict because of his own contributory negligence. We find no error on Beloit's appeal and we reject Murray's cross-appeal. Accordingly, we affirm the judgment of the district court.

* * *

Strict products liability evolved by stripping away certain problems of proof plaintiffs encountered under either negligence or warranty theories. By focusing the legal inquiry on the product defect rather than the defendant's conduct and thereby easing the plaintiff's burden of proof, strict liability theory endeavors to place the risk of economic loss on the manufacturers of defective products, thereby spreading the loss and not saddling it solely on an innocent injured consumer. * * *

The elimination of the need to prove defendant's negligence has led some to view strict products liability as a "no-fault" doctrine to which the application of comparative negligence principles is simply not conceptually feasible. * * *

* * * The key conceptual distinction between strict products liability theory and negligence is that the plaintiff need not prove faulty *conduct* on the part of the defendant in order to recover. The jury is not asked to determine if the defendant deviated from a standard of care in producing his product. There is no proven faulty conduct of the defendant to compare with the faulty conduct of the plaintiff in order to apportion the responsibility for an accident. Although we may term a

defective product "faulty," it is qualitatively different from the plaintiff's conduct that contributes to his injury. A comparison of the two is therefore inappropriate. The characterization of both plaintiff's negligent conduct and the defect as faulty may provide a semantic bridge between negligence and strict liability theories, but it provides neither a conceptual nor pragmatic basis for apportioning the loss for a particular injury.

We believe that if the loss for a particular injury is to be apportioned between the product defect and the plaintiff's misconduct, the only conceptual basis for comparison is the causative contribution of each to the particular loss or injury. In apportioning damages we are really asking how much of the injury was caused by the defect in the product versus how much was caused by the plaintiff's own actions.
* * *

* * *

Once a conceptually viable way of apportioning damages in section 402A actions is established, the key inquiry is whether such a system is consistent with the policy goals of strict products liability. As we have indicated already, a central goal of the strict liability action is to relieve the plaintiff of proof problems associated with existing negligence and warranty theories. A system of comparative fault which proceeds to apportion damages on the basis of causation in no way disturbs the plaintiff's burden of proof. The plaintiff still need only prove the existence of a defect causally linked to the injury. The defendant's burden is to prove plaintiff's contributory fault.

A second goal of strict products liability is to place the "burden of loss on manufacturers rather than ... injured persons who are '*powerless to protect themselves* ....' " Under traditional strict products liability law, the ordinary contributory negligence of the plaintiff has been held not to be an available defense. Contributory negligence may occur in two ways in products liability cases. The plaintiff may be negligent in his actual use of the product or he may be negligent in failing to discover the product defect. Because the defendant exposes the plaintiff to a risk of harm by placing a dangerous product on the market, traditional thinking is that he alone should bear the loss despite the presence of such contributory negligence. The rationale is that the manufacturer is in a better position to absorb the economic loss by spreading the risk of loss through the chain of distribution. Eventually the cost is passed on to society as a whole in the form of an increased cost of the product.

The problem with this "deep pocket" rationale is that the manufacturer may be paying for a part of the loss which is attributable not to the product defect, but to plaintiff's conduct. If contributory negligence is ignored in determining the extent of plaintiff's loss, then the future cost of the manufacturer's product will be artificially inflated and will not accurately represent the actual risk posed by the defective product. Although individual plaintiffs may benefit from the immunity currently given for their contributory negligence, the consuming public at large may be adversely affected. If the future cost of a product does not accurately reflect the risk posed, then consumers may actually choose cheaper, less safe products because the cost of the manufacturer's product is artificially high.

The recognition of contributory fault as an absolute bar to recovery would improperly shift the total loss to the plaintiff. Under a system of comparative fault, however, there are good reasons for allowing some form of contributory fault to be considered in reducing damages. When plaintiff's conduct is faulty, *i.e.,* he exposes himself to an unreasonable risk of harm which causes part of his injuries, the manufacturer should not be required to pay that portion of the loss attributable to the plaintiff's fault. Under a comparative system, the future cost of the defendant's product will accurately represent the danger it has caused and not the danger caused by plaintiff's own fault.

* * *

The foregoing analysis leads us to conclude that a system of comparative fault may effectively operate in strict products liability cases and will result in a more equitable apportionment of the loss for product related injuries while furthering the valid policy goals behind the strict products liability action. * * *

* * *

Notes and Questions

1. States have taken different positions on whether contributory negligence should limit a plaintiff's recovery in strict liability cases. Some states allow only specified types of conduct to be raised as a defense (such as voluntarily and unreasonably proceeding in the face of a known risk) while others consider the full range of plaintiff's conduct. In *Murray,* the product defect was faulty welding of iron bars supporting an electrical control panel. The plaintiff was installing the panel when the accident occurred. His contributory negligence consisted of putting his weight on one of the bars while leaning dangerously over an open space at the bottom of the panel. When the bar gave way, Murray fell ten feet to a concrete floor suffering severe spinal injuries. His negligence consisted of failing to use a safer method of installation, such as a scaffolding, which would have prevented his fall. The court reduced Murray's recovery by 5% ($100,000) to give people in his position an incentive to be more careful. Because the jury found that the defect was 95% responsible for the accident, the manufacturer was liable for $1,900,000.

If contributory negligence completely bars a plaintiff's recovery in a strict liability case, the strict liability system may be characterized as one in which defendants bear the costs of accidents unless they can prove that the plaintiff was negligent. This is the exact reverse of the rule of pure negligence, under which plaintiffs must bear their own losses unless the defendant was negligent. The rule of negligence combined with contributory negligence gives desirable incentives in all categories of cases except Category IIIA.

Question: When is a strict liability system with contributory negligence as a complete bar inefficient?

2.   In *Murray,* Judge Rosenn demonstrated his concern for the allocative efficiency of the market for electrical control panels. He reasoned that if consumers do not bear the portion of the risk attributable to their own behavior, they will fail to take efficient precautions and the price of the product must rise to reflect such inefficient losses. But apportioning risk to different parties is an even more conceptually difficult task under strict liability than under a rule of negligence. Because in strict liability there is no "fault" on the part of the manufacturer to balance against the fault of the plaintiff, Judge Rosenn concluded that "the only conceptual basis for comparison is the causative contribution of each to the particular loss or injury."

Questions: If society's goal is to minimize accident costs, does it matter who caused the injury? If society's goal is to ensure that prices properly reflect the risks associated with a product, does it matter who caused the injury?

3.   Faced with the problem of allocating risks between two parties each capable of preventing accidents, the court in *Murray* opted for comparative apportioning of damages on the basis of relative causation, as a means of creating incentives for both to minimize primary accident costs. As discussed in the notes following Golden v. McCurry, comparative negligence can lead to duplicative overavoidance or to mutual nonavoidance.

Question: Are the factual situations that give rise to those possibilities present in *Murray,* suggesting that apportioning liability in strict liability cases may be inefficient?

F.   PROBLEMS IN CALCULATING DAMAGES

This chapter focuses primarily on the economic analysis of who should be liable for the costs of accidents. This section briefly examines how that liability should be measured, the question of damages.

1.   THE COLLATERAL SOURCE RULE

ANHEUSER–BUSCH, INC. v. STARLEY

Supreme Court of California, in Bank, 1946.
28 Cal.2d 347, 170 P.2d 448.

SCOTT, J.

* * *

Plaintiff appeals from a judgment for defendant entered on a directed verdict.

Denver–Chicago Trucking Company, hereinafter referred to as carrier, was engaged as a common carrier, in the transportation by truck of personal property owned by plaintiff. In the course thereof defendant's car collided with the carrier's truck containing the property, resulting in a partial destruction of the property. Prior to the commencement of this action the carrier paid plaintiff's claim for the damage to the property presumably under the law providing: "Unless the consignor accompanies the freight and retains exclusive control thereof, an inland common carrier of property is liable * * * for the loss or injury thereof from any cause whatever, except: 1. An inherent defect, vice, or weakness, or a spontaneous action, of the property itself; 2. The act of a public enemy of the United States, or of this state; 3. The act of the law; or, 4. Any irresistible superhuman cause." Civ. Code, § 2194. Evidence was adduced that the claim was paid without reference to any negligence or tortious conduct on the part of the carrier. No release was given to the carrier by plaintiff.

In the instant action plaintiff seeks to recover damages to its property flowing from the collision, asserting that defendant's negligence was the cause of it. Defendant's motion for a directed verdict was granted solely upon the ground that plaintiff had been fully compensated for its loss by the carrier and that it was not a proper party plaintiff in this action.

Where a person suffers personal injury or property damage by reason of the wrongful act of another, an action against the wrongdoer for the damages suffered is not precluded nor is the amount of the damages reduced by the receipt by him of payment for his loss from a source wholly independent of the wrongdoer. The rule has been applied where the independent source is pension systems or charity. The most typical case is where the person suffering the damage has procured insurance protecting him against the loss, to which the wrongdoer did not contribute in procuring, and his insurer pays him for the loss suffered. In the insurance cases its application is not prevented by the circumstances that the insurer is subrogated to the rights of the insured person suffering the damage as against the tort feasor. The analogy between that rule and the instant case is close.

The liability of the carrier to the owner for damage to property in transit under the contract to transport is practically absolute. The few exceptions are stated in the statutory law. His liability is that of a limited insurer whether it be said to be contractual (the statute forming part of the contract), statutory or in tort. The recovery of the loss by the owner from the carrier comes from a source wholly independent of the tort feasor whose negligence caused the loss. Therefore under this rule plaintiff's action is not barred unless there are some other factors which compel it.

* * *

The judgment is reversed.

TRAYNOR, JUSTICE, dissenting.

I dissent. In my opinion plaintiff's action is barred on the ground that plaintiff has been fully compensated by the carrier for the injury to its goods and would be unjustly enriched by a double recovery.

"When the plaintiff has accepted satisfaction in full for the injury done him, from whatever source it may come, he is so far affected in equity and good conscience, that the law will not permit him to recover again for the same damages." Whether the persons who are responsible to the plaintiff have acted jointly or separately is immaterial, for the controlling questions are whether the loss for which they are responsible is identical and whether the payment by one of them has fully compensated the plaintiff.   * * *

* * *

Notes and Questions

1. Under applicable California law, the Denver–Chicago Trucking Company as a common carrier had to compensate Anheuser–Busch fully for the merchandise damaged in the accident, even though the Denver–Chicago driver might not have been at fault.

Questions: How does such a strict liability provision minimize primary, secondary, and tertiary accident costs? What is the economic effect of the statutory exceptions to carrier strict liability?

2. The "collateral source rule" applied in *Anheuser–Busch* permits plaintiffs to recover damages from defendants even when a third party fully compensated them for their losses.

Question: Does allowing the plaintiff to collect double compensation encourage the defendant to invest too much in preventative measures, resulting in inefficient accident avoidance?

3. If she must pay *someone* for the damage she inflicts, the defendant will avoid that damage when doing so is cost-justified. Defendant Maud Starley would have faced the same incentives if, instead of paying damages to plaintiff Anheuser–Busch, she had been required to compensate the carrier, Denver–Chicago Trucking Company, or even to pay a fine to the California Highway Commission in the amount of the cost of the damaged goods.

Question: What interests are served by requiring defendants to pay their damages to plaintiffs, rather than to a third party?

4. Suppose that plaintiff Anheuser–Busch could have taken precautionary measures to avoid or reduce the damage to its property in the event of a shipping accident, perhaps by investing in special protective packaging.

Questions: In cases where both the plaintiff and the defendant could take cost-justified precautions to minimize accident losses, how does the collateral source rule affect the plaintiff's incentives to take such precautions?

2. MEASURING FUTURE LOSSES

If a defendant is to face appropriate incentives for accident avoidance, legal damages must fully and accurately reflect the plaintiff's losses. Many of the losses plaintiffs suffer fall into a category described as "economic" or "pecuniary" loss, losses easily measured in monetary terms. Pecuniary losses include lost earnings, property damage, or medical expenses.

It is relatively easy to measure a plaintiff's pecuniary losses when those losses have already been incurred. Often, however, a seriously injured plaintiff may expect to incur additional medical expenses for years into the future. Similarly, a severe injury may render an individual unable to work and earn wages for a substantial period of time, perhaps for life. How are such future losses measured?

KACZKOWSKI v. BOLUBASZ

Supreme Court of Pennsylvania, 1980.
491 Pa. 561, 421 A.2d 1027.

NIX, JUSTICE.

Appellant instituted a complaint in trespass in Allegheny County Court of Common Pleas. The suit arose from an automobile accident in which the decedent, Eric K. Kaczkowski, was riding as a passenger in a vehicle operated by appellee. At the original trial of this matter, the jury established the liability of the appellee. Upon appellant's Motion For a New Trial, the case was returned to the trial court for a retrial on the issue of damages.

* * *

* * * [T]he plaintiff relied upon the trial court's charge of impairment of future earning power for the guidance of the jury. The lower court charged the jury to consider the decedent's personal characteristics to: calculate the potential gross earnings of the decedent for the period of decedent's work life expectancy; to determine the maintenance costs of the decedent for the period of decedent's work life expectancy; to deduct the personal maintenance costs from the gross earnings to produce net earnings; and to discount the net earnings to present value by six percent (6%) simple interest. Based upon the judge's instructions, the jury returned a verdict of $30,000. on behalf of the estate of Eric K. Kaczkowski. * * *

The issue raised by appellant is whether the trial court erred in excluding reliable economic testimony showing the impact of inflation and increased productivity[5] on decedent's future earning power. * * *

* * *

Personal injury awards are usually lump-sum payments, and are not paid in weekly or monthly installments. Thus, all damages for personal injuries, including damages expected to accrue in the future,

---

5. Economists recognize that there are at least four major elements which influence the rate of increase of an employee's income. These factors are: (1) the educational attainment of the participant prior to his entry into the labor marker; (2) the influence of age upon the earnings of participants over their life cycle; (3) the significance of productivity and growth; and (4) the impact of inflation. In our analysis, we will isolate the inflation element from the other three factors, collectively called "merit" increases, which are consumed in productivity. * * *

must be proved and calculated at trial. The loss of future wages is discounted to its present value by using the six percent (6%) simple interest figure.[10]

* * *

There are three significant approaches, traditional, middle ground, and evidentiary which the judiciary has adopted in considering the impact of future inflation and productivity on lost future earning capacity. The traditional approach ignores altogether the effects of future productivity and future inflation as being "too speculative." This view was previously adhered to by this Commonwealth, but for reasons stated above, it is hereby rejected.

The middle ground approach is anomalous in that it permits the factfinder to consider the effects of productivity and inflation on lost future earning capacity, but prohibits expert testimony on either of these issues. The proponents of this approach argue that expert testimony on future economic trends is "speculative," yet acknowledge that such facts are within the "common experience" of all jurors and, therefore, jurors should not be prohibited from applying their common knowledge in reaching a verdict. However, it has been consistently demonstrated that expert evidence is essential to accurate economic forecasting. Since it is apparent that the middle-ground approach contributes little to the accuracy or predictability of lost future earnings, and paradoxically allows a judge or jury to determine what an acknowledge[d] expert cannot, we decline to adopt it.

The evidentiary approach in its several variants allows the factfinder to consider productivity and inflation in awarding damages. * * * Recognizing that there are myriad of ways to incorporate such economic data we find that there are two versions appropriate for our consideration.

The first of these two variants of the evidentiary approach was developed by the court in Feldman v. Allegheny Airlines. In *Feldman,* a surviving husband brought a wrongful death action as the administrator of his wife's estate. The defendant airline stipulated as to its liability and the trial was confined to the issue of damages. The court assumed that recovery for lost future earnings included the victim's lost earning capacity. In order to demonstrate the bases for the court's conclusions relative to what course the deceased's life probably would have taken, the court extrapolated the evolving pattern of Mrs. Feldman's life. The court detailed the deceased's college grades, her employment history, the opinion of the deceased held by her fellow

10. The rationale for reducing a lump-sum award to its present value is that:

it is assumed that the plaintiff will invest the sum awarded and receive interest thereon. That interest accumulated over the number of relevant years will be available, in addition to the capital, to provide the plaintiff with his future support until the total is exhausted at the end of the period. The projected interest must therefore be allowed in reduction of capital lest it be claimed that the plaintiff is overcompensated. Fleming, Inflation and Tort Compensation, 26 Am. J.Comp.Law 51, 66 (1977).

* * *

workers, the expressed employment goals of the deceased and the potential jobs for which the deceased was qualified. The court also examined the employment history of another individual who had remarkably similar credentials as the deceased. The defendant produced one witness who testified as to the decedent's employment prospects. Based upon the above factors, the court predicted the incremental salary (productivity) increases of the decedent over her work-life expectancy.

The court was then faced with the inflation component and the task of discounting the award to its present value. The court developed a formula known as the "offset present value method" in which it subtracted the estimated inflation rate from the discount rate to calculate the inflation adjusted or "real" rate of interest. Each year's earnings were then discounted to present value by this "real" discount rate. The "real" discount rate employed by the court was 1.5%. * * *

The second variant of the evidentiary method was adopted by the Alaska Supreme Court in Beaulieu v. Elliott. * * *

In order to account for the inflationary component's impact on lost future earnings and the effect of future interest rates on lump-sum payment, the Alaska court applied that "total offset method." Under the total offset method, a court does not discount the award to its present value but assumes that the effect of the future inflation rate will completely offset the interest rate, thereby eliminating any need to discount the award to its present value.

* * *

Mindful of our goal that a damage award formula should strive to be efficient, predictable as well as accurate, in computing lost future earning capacity this Commonwealth adopts the *Feldman* court's approach to calculating lost productivity and the Alaska court's total offset approach to inflation and discounting to present value. We believe that this eclectic method best computes a damage award which will fairly compensate a victim to the full extent of his or her injuries and avoids unnecessary complexities likely to produce confusion although in reality contributing little to the degree of accuracy to be obtained. * * * After laying a proper foundation, expert and lay witnesses are called upon to testify as to the victim's past and future employment possibilities. The defense may cross-examine the plaintiff's witnesses and present evidence on their own behalf. Upon a thorough evaluation of all the evidence presented, the factfinder makes an informed estimation of the victim's lost earning capacity. Although this approach may be time consuming, and like all estimations of future events may be subject to a degree of speculation, it is exceedingly more accurate to assume that the future will not remain stagnant with the past.

* * *

In support of our adoption of the "total offset method" in allowing for the inflationary factor, we note that it is no longer legitimate to assume the availability of future interest rates by discounting to present value without also assuming the necessary concomitant of future inflation. * * *

* * *

Since over the long run interest rates, and, therefore, the discount rates, will rise and fall with inflation, we shall exploit this natural adjustment by offsetting the two factors in computing ·lost future earning capacity. We are satisfied that the total offset method provides at least as much, if not greater, accuracy than an attempt to assign a factor that would reflect the varying changes in the rate of inflation over the years. Our experiences with the use of the six percent discount rate suggest the difficulties inherent in such an approach. As to the concomitant goals of efficiency and predictability, the desirability of the total offset method is obvious. There is no method that can assure absolute accuracy. An additional feature of the total offset method is that where there is a variance, it will be in favor of the innocent victim and not the tortfeasor who caused the loss.

* * *

An additional virtue of the total offset method is its contribution to judicial efficiency. Litigators are freed from introducing and verifying complex economic data. Judge and juries are not burdened with complicated, time consuming economic testimony. Finally, by eliminating the variables of inflation and future interest rates from the damage calculation, the ultimate award is more predictable.

* * *

Henceforth, in this Commonwealth, damages will be awarded for lost future earnings that compensate the victim to the full extent of the injury sustained. Upon proper foundation, the court shall consider the victim's lost future productivity. Moreover, we find as a matter of law that future inflation shall be presumed equal to future interest rates with these factors offsetting. Thus, the courts of this Commonwealth are instructed to abandon the practice of discounting lost future earnings. By this method, we are able to reflect the impact of inflation in these cases without specifically submitting this question to the jury.

In view of the trial court's refusal to permit appellant to introduce evidence relating to a future productivity factor and our formulation of a new standard to be used for accommodating inflation in these cases, we reverse the judgment below and remand the cause for a new trial as to the damage question.

FLAHERTY, JUSTICE, concurring and dissenting.

* * * I must dissent to the majority's adoption of what it calls the "total offset method", a "per se rule" of doubtful validity. True, such an approach is a simple one, but it does not achieve justice, and, has only been adopted in one jurisdiction, i.e., Alaska. We should simply

permit expert testimony on the issues of inflation and productivity. Such testimony, on both sides of the issue, is, of course, subject to cross-examination and argument as to its validity and weight. Thus, the jury is free to weigh the evidence before it and render its verdict. This is also simple, and provides justice in accordance with our time honored principles.

Notes and Questions

1. As the Pennsylvania Supreme Court noted in *Kaczkowski,* damages for continuing medical expenses or future lost wages normally take the form of a lump-sum damages award rather than a requirement that the defendant pay the plaintiff damages as long as the plaintiff remains incapacitated.

> *Questions:* Is there an economic reason to prefer lump-sum payments? What would be the likely effect on primary and tertiary accident costs of a rule requiring a defendant to pay the plaintiff's lost wages until the plaintiff recovers from his injury?

2. In a wrongful death case like *Kaczkowski,* pecuniary loss normally is measured by the plaintiff's expected future wages less the expected costs of the plaintiff's maintenance (rent, groceries, transportation, and so forth). However, if Kaczkowski had survived and brought an action for lost wages due to personal injury, the defendant would not have been entitled to deduct the cost of the plaintiff's maintenance from lost wages.

> *Questions:* Why shouldn't defendants in personal injury cases deduct maintenance costs from lost future wages? What incentives does this aspect of damage law create for defendants?

3. Many jurisdictions require that lost future wages be discounted to their "present value" in damages awards. Discounting allows a defendant to pay an amount of damages that is less than the amount of wages the plaintiff stands to lose in the future.

> *Questions:* Why should defendants be able to discount lost future wages to present value? In other words, why might $100 today be full compensation for a loss of $106 next year?

4. As the *Kaczkowski* opinion notes, an individual's salary may rise over his working life for reasons apart from inflation in the general economy. People tend to be paid higher inflation-adjusted salaries later in life. Moreover, the average salaries of American workers have tended to increase over time.

> *Question:* What are the causes of productivity increases, both for individual workers and for society as a whole?

5. Inflation requires a defendant to make a larger payment now to give a plaintiff the same purchasing power in the future. Discounting to present value allows a defendant to make a smaller payment now in full compensation for a larger future loss. *Kaczkowski* held that as a matter of Pennsylvania law, the rate of inflation and the discount rate used to reduce future losses to present value would be presumed to be the same, so that the factors of inflation and present value "cancel each other out."

Question: Calculate the damage award a defendant must pay under the *Kaczkowski* rule in the following circumstances. The injured plaintiff is a 50–year old plumber currently earning $20,000 who had planned to work fulltime until her retirement at age 65. As a result of her injury the plaintiff is completely incapacitated. Assume that the plumber had no reason to expect her salary to increase other than to keep pace with inflation—in other words, assume no productivity increase. What amount should the defendant pay for lost wages?

6. The Pennsylvania Supreme Court defended the *Kaczkowski* "total offset rule" on the ground that "over the long run interest rates, and, therefore, the discount rates, will rise and fall with inflation." The Court also claimed that "where there is a variance, it will be in favor of the innocent victim and not the tortfeasor."

Questions: Is it correct to assume that the interest rate and the discount rate are identical? When would that assumption favor plaintiffs and when would it favor defendants? As a practical matter, which party is most likely to benefit from the total offset rule? What are the rule's advantages?

3. VALUING HUMAN LIFE

In addition to past and future pecuniary losses, plaintiffs may suffer physical pain and suffering, mental distress, loss of a spouse's consortium, or even loss of enjoyment of life itself. The problem of attaching monetary values to such non-pecuniary losses raises interesting and perhaps insurmountable questions, some of which are considered below.

SHERROD v. BERRY

United States District Court, Northern District of Illinois, E.D., 1985.
629 F.Supp. 159.

LEIGHTON, DISTRICT JUDGE.

This civil rights suit was brought by a father to recover for the death of his son who was shot and killed by a City of Joliet police officer. A jury returned verdicts and defendants have filed post-trial motions. One of the issues raised is whether this court erred in admitting evidence which allowed the jury to consider "the hedonic value of a human life" when it decided the damages to be awarded plaintiff for the wrongful death of his son.

An expert in economics was permitted to testify that in determining the value of a human life in such a case, a factor to be considered is the hedonic value which, according to qualified economists, is worth more than the economic value of that person. The jury awarded the father $450,000 for the loss of parental companionship with his son, $300,000 for economic loss to the estate, $1,700 for funeral expenses, and $850,000 for the value of the son's life. Defendants contend they were prejudiced by the testimony of the expert and that consequently, they are entitled either to a judgment notwithstanding the verdict, a remittitur, or a new trial. This court does not agree. When a jury is shown that a person was wrongfully killed, and it is asked to award damages, evidence, including the testimony of an expert, is admissible to enable the jury to consider the hedonic value of the life thus taken.

* * *

At the trial, in order to prove the damages he suffered from the death of his son, Lucien Sherrod called as an expert witness, Stanley Smith, an economist, holder of a master's degree in economics from the University of Chicago. * * *

Accordingly, Smith, after explaining what he did and the information he used, testified to the amount of loss Lucien Sherrod suffered when he was deprived of his son's association and companionship. Smith described and explained how he had calculated the economic loss which Ronald Sherrod's estate incurred from his death. Smith told the jury the basis of his opinions, and the economic theories which supported his conclusions.

Apart from his testimony concerning the economic value of life, he gave the jury some "insight into the guidelines that economists use in looking at how society values what we call the hedonic aspect, the hedonic value of life, separate from economic productive value of an individual." He said there had been studies by economists which "indicate that a human life has value separate from the economic productive value that a human being would have." Of course, Smith said, the economic aspect of life valuation presents what may appear to be imponderable difficulties in those cases when the individual, because of infancy, old age, or physical incapacity, has no measurable economic productivity. These difficulties, however, did not apply to the case before the jury because Ronald Sherrod was gainfully employed up to the day he was killed by Berry.

Smith told the jury that in the last 10 years economic literature showed some 15 studies "with respect to the value of life." There "was a study by Blomquist here in Illinois" which in turn considered all the other studies and found that there was a relationship somewhere in the dimension of three times up to 30 times their economic productive income. Smith expressed agreement with Blomquist's conclusions, considering him an authoritative source of knowledge on the subject of the hedonic value of life. At the end of Smith's testimony, which included extensive direct and intensive crossexamination, this court asked Smith to define for the jury the word "hedonic" as it is used in the expression "the hedonic value of life." Smith said:

> It derives from the word pleasing or pleasure. I believe it is a Greek word. It is distinct from the word economic. So it refers to the larger value of life, the life at the pleasure of society, if you will, the life—the value including economic, including moral, including philosophical, including all the value with which you might hold life, is the meaning of the expression "hedonic value".

* * * A § 1983 action is a suit for tort damages, even though the duty a defendant is alleged to have breached is created by the Constitution or federal law. * * * The basic purpose of a § 1983 damages award should be to compensate persons for injuries caused by the deprivation of constitutional rights.

In this case, Ronald Sherrod's death was caused by the constitutional deprivation for which compensation was sought. Section 1983, and the applicable provisions of the Fourteenth Amendment, protect life. It is well established in this and other circuits that on the facts alleged, and on the evidence the jury heard, the estate of Ronald Sherrod could sue and recover damages for the loss of his life.

"Life," Blackstone has reminded us, "is the immediate gift of God, a right inherent by nature in every individual...." The deprivation of life that is prohibited by the Fourteenth Amendment includes "not only of life [itself], but of whatever God has given to everyone with life for its growth and enjoyment...." In other words, the loss of life means more than being deprived of the right to exist, or of the ability to earn a living; it includes deprivation of the pleasures of life.

This is the point that Smith discussed with the jury when he told them about "the hedonic value of life." As he explained to them, "hedonic" refers "to the larger value of life...." This includes the pleasure of living which is destroyed by the blow that is lethal; in this case, the fatal pistol shot that Berry fired into the temple of Ronald Sherrod, a mere youth; and thus taking from him what all the wealth in the world could never purchase. Smith's expert testimony enabled the jury to consider this important aspect of injury which the estate of Ronald Sherrod suffered, an aspect they should have considered in the event they determined that Lucien Sherrod, as administrator, was entitled to a judgment against the defendants.

* * *

Contrary to what may be the popular view, the idea that an estate can recover for the hedonic value of the life of the person killed is not new in Anglo American law. In England, for example, hedonic damage awards have been allowed since 1976. Section 1 of the Law Reform (Miscellaneous Provisions) Act of 1934 has been construed by English judges so that the estate of a person killed can recover for "loss of expectation of life." In this country, legal scholars, economists, and social scientists have grappled with the task of formulating a method by which the value of a human life can be measured in terms understood by a jury. Therefore, the concept, although novel, is not unknown. The testimony of Stanley Smith as an expert in economics enabled the jury to perform its function in determining the proper measure of damages in this case. This court's ruling allowing him to testify concerning "the hedonic value of life" was not error.

So ordered.

Notes and Questions

1. The question of valuing human life often raises an emotional response. Many find the idea that life can be valued repugnant. Some people assert that life is "priceless." On reflection, that cannot be true. If life were truly priceless, no potentially fatal accident would ever be worth risking. People would not fly on airlines, drive cars, or cross the street without a helmet and protective armor. When an individual declines to purchase an airbag for her car because it is "too expensive", she is implicitly saying that she can fix a finite price on the risk of dying prematurely.

Questions: If human life cannot, as a practical matter, be treated as priceless, what is the correct price? In *Sherrod,* the jury valued Lucien Sherrod's life at $850,000. Does that figure seem too high? Too low?

2. One way to answer "What is life worth?" is to ask, "What are you willing to pay for it?" At first, a person's ability to pay for life would appear to be limited by his wealth—for the average individual, his earning capacity. Nevertheless, the court in *Sherrod* held that the "hedonic" value of human life can exceed the "economic" value of a person's expected earnings.

Judge Leighton's opinion makes more sense when one considers that most individuals do not attempt to earn as much money as they possibly could if they sacrificed all non-monetary rewards. The average individual does not spend all her waking hours working overtime, taking a second job, and so forth. Many people earn less money than they could because, after they work a forty-hour week, they find that they gain more utility (more "hedonic" pleasure) from using their time for leisure activities instead of working. Others choose lower-paying jobs they enjoy over higher-paid positions that are more unpleasant or stressful.

If an individual knew she was going to be put in the position of having to pay to keep her life (a payment that must be made in dollars, rather than in the utility gained from leisure), she could alter her pattern of employment and work longer and harder hours, or perhaps choose a less-rewarding occupation with a higher salary. Even if life should be valued according to the amount an individual is willing and able to pay to keep it, lost earnings is too low a measure.

3. The hedonic theory of valuing life may raise as many questions as it answers. The fact that most people choose a mixture of leisure and work over constant working suggests that they value their lives more highly than the maximum amount of money they could earn by spending all their waking hours employed at the highest possible salary. But while people may value their lives more highly than the maximum amount they could earn during their lifespans, they can never pay more than that amount because they can never earn more than that amount. There is no convenient way for the individual to "tap into" the value of leisure time, in terms of utility, in offering to pay for life.

When an individual only works forty hours per week and spends the rest of her time on non-paying leisure activities, that decision may indicate a declining marginal utility for money. The money paid in damages may be paid by a tortfeasor out of earnings that still have a high marginal utility to the tortfeasor.

Question: Under what circumstances will payment of hedonic damages lead to a decline in total utility?

4. A second approach to valuing life is to focus on how much an individual would be willing to accept in return for her life, instead of asking how much she would be willing to pay to keep it. It should be apparent that the two figures are not identical. An individual's ability to pay for life is limited by her wealth and future income. Presumably, however, only a suicidal person would accept even an infinite amount of money in return for sure death, for after death the money has no value.

Questions: Should life be valued according to willingness to pay or willingness to accept? Which criteria more accurately values life?

5. A third approach to valuing life is to shift from an *ex post* evaluation of the loss associated with death to an *ex ante* evaluation of the loss associated with facing a *risk* of death. Even if life is valued according to a willingness to accept criterion, people may be willing to accept a finite amount of money in return for a risk of death because there is a chance of spending the money—money no longer has a zero utility.

Questions: Suppose a car buyer declines to purchase an optional airbag for $500 even though the airbag would reduce her lifetime risk of a fatal auto accident from 1 in 5,000 to 1 in 10,000. What implicit cost does the buyer assign to an additional 1 in 5,000 risk of death? What implicit value does she attach to her life? Would she accept half of that amount in return for facing a 50% risk of death? Would she accept the full amount in return for certain death?

6. In a society where people enjoy different levels of wealth and income, valuing life according to economic principles inevitably raises distributional concerns.

Questions: What are the distributional implications of both the ability-to-pay and willingness-to-receive-for-risk approaches to valuing life? Are the lives of the rich or the poor likely to be valued more highly under each approach?

4. PUNITIVE DAMAGES AND OVERDETERRENCE

To minimize primary accident costs, the defendant must pay an amount at least equal to the loss the plaintiff suffered from the defendant's failure to take preventative measures. Only full compensation ensures that the defendant has completely internalized the otherwise-external costs his conduct imposes on others. What happens if damages not only equal the loss suffered, but exceed it?

STURM, RUGER & CO., INC. v. DAY

Supreme Court of Alaska, 1979.
594 P.2d 38.

CONNOR, JUSTICE.

* * *

Appellee Michael James Day bought a .41 magnum single action revolver on June 1, 1972. The gun had been manufactured two years before by appellant Sturm, Ruger and Company, in August of 1970, but was purchased new by Day.

On July 30, 1972, Day was sitting in the cab of his small pickup truck with two young friends when he decided to unload his gun. As he was unloading the revolver, the gun slipped out of his hands. When he grabbed for the gun it fired, the bullet striking his leg and causing serious injuries.   * * *

Day filed suit against Sturm, Ruger and Company. His second amended complaint * * * included a claim for punitive damages.   * * *

The jury returned a verdict for the plaintiff, finding specifically that the revolver was designed defectively and that it had a manufacturing defect as well. The jury awarded $137,750.00 in compensatory damages and $2,895,000.00 in punitive damages to the plaintiff.

* * *

* * * [I]n order to recover punitive or exemplary damages, the plaintiff must prove that the wrongdoer's conduct was "outrageous, such as acts done with malice or bad motives or a reckless indifference to the interests of another." Actual malice need not be proved. Rather, "[r]eckless indifference to the rights of others, and conscious action in deliberate disregard of them ... may provide the necessary state of mind to justify punitive damages."

* * *

* * * Where * * * plaintiff is able to plead and prove that the manufacturer knew that its product was defectively designed and that injuries and deaths had resulted from the design defect, but continued to market the product in reckless disregard of the public's safety, punitive damages may be awarded.

Punitive damages are designed not only to punish the wrongdoer, but also to deter him and others like him from similar wrongdoing in the future. We believe that as a matter of public policy, punitive damages can serve several useful functions in the products liability area. For example, the threat of punitive damages serves a deterrence function in cases in which a product may cause numerous minor injuries for which potential plaintiffs might decline to sue, or in cases in which it would be cheaper for the manufacturer to pay compensatory damages to those who did present claims then it would be to remedy the product's defect. In addition, if punitive damages could not be awarded in the products liability context, a reckless manufacturer might gain an unfair advantage over its more socially responsible competitors. On balance, we find the arguments advanced by appellant in favor of its position to be outweighed by the sound public policy considerations supporting the imposition of punitive damages in appropriate cases. We therefore decline to jettison the doctrine of punitive damages in this area of the law.

We turn next to Sturm, Ruger's claim that there was insufficient evidence to sustain the jury's award of punitive damages. The evidence presented at trial indicated that top officials at Sturm, Ruger knew that the safety and loading notches of their single action revolver presented a danger of accidental discharge because of the propensity of the engaging middle parts to fail or break. The evidence also reflects knowledge on the part of Sturm, Ruger management that serious injuries had resulted from this deficiency, coupled with procrastination in changing the basic design, at an increased cost of $1.93 per gun. Because we find that fair-minded jurors in the exercise of reasonable judgment could differ as to whether Sturm, Ruger's actions amounted to reckless indifference to the rights of others, and conscious action in deliberate disregard of them, thereby evidencing a state of mind which could justify the imposition of punitive damages, we will not upset the jury's conclusions that punitive damages were warranted.

* * *

The compensatory damages awarded to Michael Day and against Sturm, Ruger amounted to $137,750, exclusive of costs, prejudgment interest, and attorney's fees. The punitive damage award of $2,895,000 appears to be so out of proportion to the amount of actual damages as to suggest that the jury's award was the result of passion or prejudice. The jurors apparently responded to an invitation to punish Sturm, Ruger for all wrongs committed against all purchasers and users of its products, rather than for the wrong done to this particular plaintiff. Under the circumstances, it was a mistake and an abuse of discretion for the trial judge not to have reduced the punitive damages or to have ordered a new trial.

* * *

[The court remanded the case for a new trial with respect to punitive damages as well as a number of other issues.]

BURKE, JUSTICE, dissenting in part.

* * *

The evidence showed that Sturm, Ruger manufactured over 1,501,-000 revolvers of the type causing Day's injury. Sturm, Ruger's profit from the manufacture and sale of those firearms alone was enormous, totalling many millions of dollars. At trial, William Ruger, the president and founder of Sturm, Ruger, testified that redesign of the revolver to cure the defect cost approximately $199,000 and that the increased manufacturing cost per revolver was $1.93. The figure agreed upon by the jury as an appropriate award for punitive damages equalled the amount of the increased manufacturing cost per item multiplied by the approximate number of revolvers sold: $1.93 X 1,500,000 = $2,895,000. Thus, the amount of the award is roughly equal to the profit directly attributable to Sturm, Ruger's callous disregard for the safety of its customers. Such being the case, I think there is no merit to the contention that the figure was the result of improper passion or prejudice. Certainly, the amount of the punitive damage award far exceeded Day's actual damages. However, given the purpose of punitive damages, the award was not excessive.

Notes and Questions

1. In *Sturm, Ruger,* the jury required the defendant to pay the plaintiff punitive damages as well as compensatory damages, in order both to punish and deter the defendant's reckless conduct. The gun manufacturer had chosen to accept the known risk of serious injuries with "reckless indifference" and "deliberate disregard" of the consequences. A rational actor engaged in an activity that presents a risk of harm balances the cost of avoiding accidents with the expected cost of letting them occur. Punitive damages increase the defendant's costs of accidents. Adding $2,895,-000 to a $137,750 damage award certainly helps to get the attention of an actor considering the primary accident costs associated with his activity.

The jury in *Sturm, Ruger* apparently concluded that the benefits of reduced risk outweighed the costs of redesigning the handgun ($1.93 per gun). Suppose the original unsafe hammer design resulted in injury from one gun out of a thousand, and each injury caused an average of $1000 damage. In that case a prospective defendant would expect to pay $1.00 in compensatory damages for each gun manufactured.

> *Questions:* Would expected punitive damages of $25 per gun create incentives for inefficient accident avoidance in that situation? Does the analysis change if average actual damages are $3000 per injury?

2. Awarding punitive damages poses the danger of encouraging accident avoidance when avoidance is inefficient. The likelihood of inefficient accident avoidance depends on the legal standard applied. Although *Sturm, Ruger* was a product liability case, the claim of design defect involves balancing the risks and benefits of alternative designs and resembles the analysis found in negligence cases. Compare the *Sturm, Ruger* test of "reckless indifference" (which follows the Restatement (Second) of Torts § 908) to the test adopted in Reynolds Metals Co. v. Lampert, 316 F.2d 272, 275 (9th Cir. 1963):

> To justify an award of punitive damages, it is not necessary that the act have been done maliciously or with bad motive. Where it has become apparent, as it has here, that compensatory damages alone, while they might compensate the injured party, will not deter the actor from committing similar trespasses in the future, there is ample justification for an award of punitive damages.

> *Question:* Which of the two tests creates incentives more likely to minimize primary accident costs?

3. Questions 1 and 2 focus on incentives to engage in the efficient *level of care.* Consider Shavell's argument that internalizing externalities through strict liability also leads to an efficient *level of activity.*

> *Question:* What is the impact of punitive damages on gun manufacturers' level of gun production?

4. Justice Connor argues that "the threat of punitive damages serves a deterrence function in cases in which a product may cause numerous minor injuries for which potential plaintiffs might decline to sue." Connor's opinion calls attention to the problem of *underenforcement* of liability rules; not all plaintiffs injured by a negligent tortfeasor bother to sue.

Questions: Why might an injured plaintiff decline to sue a negligent defendant? How does potential plaintiffs' failure to sue for their injuries affect defendants' incentives to adopt efficient levels of care and activity? What measure of punitive damages would correct for the problem of underenforcement?

5. Justice Burke supported a measure of punitive damages "roughly equal to the profit directly attributable to the Sturm, Ruger's callous disregard for the safety of its customers." In *Sturm, Ruger,* that amounted to $1.93 x 1,500,000, the savings per gun times the number of guns sold.

Question: Which measure of punitive damages—Justice Connor's or Justice Burke's—is more likely to lead to efficient incentives?

6. Under the Learned Hand formula, an injurer is liable to her victim if she failed to take preventative measures that cost less than the expected costs of the accident. Knowing that she will be liable, no rational injurer would ever be negligent. If negligent behavior is inconsistent with rationality, grossly negligent behavior seems even more peculiar.

Questions: Why are people grossly negligent? Is gross negligence always irrational? Considering the motivations that may underlie grossly negligent behavior, can punitive damages modify such behavior?

Chapter 4

ECONOMICS OF CONTRACT LAW

Resources are allocated among competing uses by negotiation among interested parties, by incentives created by liability rules, and by government fiat. To the casual observer, contract law would seem to involve only the first, since buyers and sellers bargain over who will have the right to use particular resources. Obstacles to bargaining may interfere with the efficient allocation of rights by contract, however, just as they prevent parties from efficiently resolving conflicting uses of land through negotiations. Contract law spells out when and how the legal system will intervene in the contracting process to reduce bargaining costs and to promote the efficient allocation of resources.

This Chapter explores the economic rationale for many of the rules of contract law. It begins with the question of why and when the legal system should involve itself in contracts, then considers how the law should be structured to maximize the benefits and minimize the costs of contracts.

A. THE ECONOMIC FUNCTIONS OF CONTRACT

If two parties contract voluntarily and with full information, both must expect the contracted-for exchange to improve their welfare. If both parties wish to fulfill their contractual obligations when the time comes for performance, judicial involvement is unnecessary. Only when voluntary cooperation breaks down does the law intervene. Thus, contract law usually is brought into play only when one of the parties no longer believes performance is in his self-interest. If an exchange is not voluntary, we cannot be certain it maximizes wealth. Why then should contracts be enforced? What economic role does the law of contracts play?

REXITE CASTING CO. v. MIDWEST MOWER CORP.

St. Louis Court of Appeals, Missouri, 1954.
267 S.W.2d 327.

HOUSER, COMMISSIONER.

Action on a written contract. Plaintiff corporation, Rexite Casting Company, and defendant Midwest Mower Corporation entered into a contract based upon a letter dated November 19, 1947 and an attached purchase order for 100,000 cast aluminum side frames for use in the manufacture of lawn mowers, at a unit price of 52¢ each. * * * After approximately 17,000 to 20,000 castings had been shipped, and on August 16, 1948, William F. Reck, Jr., vice-president of plaintiff company, notified Sigmund Rudman and Harry Bobroff, officers of defendant corporation, that it was necessary to increase the price of the castings due to increased metal costs which plaintiff's officers could not foresee when the contract was negotiated in November, 1947; that unless plaintiff increased the price it would be losing money every time it made a casting; and that defendant could "take it or leave it," i.e., either pay the increase or plaintiff would not make delivery. According to plaintiff's evidence defendant's officers opposed the increased price but, after discussing the "pros and cons" of the upward price, finally "acquiesced" and told Reck to write a letter to that effect. Plaintiff's letter "confirmed" the parties' conversation "regarding adjusting price on future delivery of permanent mold castings" at the "adjusted price" of 78¾¢, the new price to become effective after delivery of the castings already finished and awaiting delivery on plaintiff's floor, which were to be invoiced to defendant at the old price.

* * * Defendant had a substantial number of orders for lawn mowers for which delivery had been contracted at a fixed, established price. An officer of defendant testified that plaintiff raised the price of the castings (approximately 50%) at a time when defendant was in heavy production in an amount which, if paid, would absorb enough of the contemplated profit to make the operation unprofitable. The frame castings were an essential part of the lawn mower, without which the whole manufacturing operation would have to shut down. It was too late to contract for castings from other sources for delivery during that production year. It takes months to make the necessary molds. If defendant did not agree to pay the increased price the plant could no longer operate—they would not be able to deliver and therefore would lose all of their customers. According to defendant's officers defendant was "over a barrel" on the matter; plaintiff had put defendant in an untenable position and defendant had no choice but to agree; had "no other recourse, to stay in business." Defendant's officer felt that plaintiff had "gone back on the original deal." Defendant did not reply in writing to plaintiff's letter of August 16 but did order, receive and pay at the increased price for several lots of castings which were delivered by plaintiff during the fall of 1948 and until it had enough

castings to carry it through that season. * * * On January 5, 1949, after three or four month of negotiating, defendant entered into a contract with Missouri Die Casting Company for the manufacture of side frames * * * to be supplied at the cost of 57¢ per unit. Defendant refused to take more castings from plaintiff as soon as Missouri Die Casting Company had assured defendant that it would produce the castings in sufficient quantity during the coming season. Thereupon defendant made demand for reimbursement for overcharges, claiming the difference between the contract and the "adjusted price" on all deliveries made under the increased price. After defendant refused to take more castings plaintiff demanded payment for castings furnished but not paid for * * *.

* * *

Rexite Casting Company then brought suit against Midwest Mower Corporation * * * for the balance due for castings made and delivered but not paid for, in the sum of $783.22, figured at the rate of 78¾¢ each, based upon the written contract as amended and modified. * * *

* * *

* * * The trial court filed a memorandum opinion holding that plaintiff's refusal to deliver castings at the contract price constituted a breach of contract, relieving defendant of all obligations to make further payments under the contract; that there was no consideration for any agreement to pay a higher price, and that "It would be strange law if plaintiff could commit a flagrant breach of contract and thus recover the cost of these molds which it declined to use under the terms of this contract." * * * Plaintiff casting company has appealed to this court from the judgment directing a verdict for the mower corporation on Count II of the petition.

* * *

* * * [I]t is well settled that while an agreement made in substitution of a prior executory contract annuls the former contract and is itself a sufficient consideration for a release from its obligations, the substituted agreement must contain a change of the obligation of each party in order to constitute a consideration. In [Mt. Vernon Car Mfg. Co. v. Hirsch Rolling Mill Co.], the court said, "If the obligation of one party only is affected by the new arrangement, and the other party receives nothing additional and is relieved of no duty, then there is a want of consideration." That is exactly the situation in the instant case. The only change in the contract was the change in the price of the castings. This merely increased the obligation of defendant. Defendant received nothing additional and was relieved of no duty. The obligation of plaintiff was not increased. " * * * when a party merely does what he has already obligated himself to do, he cannot demand an additional compensation therefor, and although by taking advantage of the necessities of his adversary he obtains a promise for more, the law will regard it as nudum pactum, and will not lend its process to aid in the wrong."

* * *

Thus plaintiff is relegated to whatever rights it may have had under the original contract * * *. All of the evidence, including that of plaintiff's officers, shows that plaintiff refused to furnish any more castings unless defendant consented to the raising of the price from 52¢ to 78¾¢ each. Plaintiff's refusal to further perform the partly executed contract unless defendant consented to a modification constituted a total breach of the original contract.

* * *

* * * [P]laintiff, having breached the indivisible contract in respect to the castings in a material manner, is precluded from recovering thereon * * *.

* * *

The judgment of the circuit court [holding for the defendant] is, accordingly, affirmed.

Notes and Questions

1. The exchange in *Rexite Casting* involved 100,000 cast aluminum side frames for lawn mowers. At the time of the original agreement, Midwest Mower valued each casting more than 52¢, and Rexite valued 52¢ more than it valued each casting. The contracted-for exchange appeared both Pareto superior and wealth-increasing. Although a Rexite officer claimed that an unforeseeable rise in the cost of metal required the price increase from 52¢ to 78¾¢, Midwest Mower obtained a commitment from Missouri Die Casting to supply the castings for 57¢, a price close to Rexite's original price. Suppose that Rexite had not suffered a cost increase but was trying to take advantage of Midwest Mower by behaving "opportunistically."

   Questions: Why would Rexite expect Midwest Mower to agree to pay a price higher than the original contract price? Although Midwest Mower naturally would object to an increase to 78¾¢, would an exchange at that price still be Pareto superior and wealth-increasing? If the exchange remained efficient at 78¾¢, why enforce the original contract?

2. When parties promise to perform in the future, often it is necessary for one or both to invest resources in preparation for performance or to alter their behavior in expectation of performance in order to extract the maximum benefit from the exchange. Consider how Midwest Mower changed its position in reliance on Rexite's promise to deliver the castings. Having received Rexite's commitment, Midwest committed itself to sell lawn mowers at a specified price to its customers. Rexite Casting also relied on the contract by designing and building customized molds to produce Midwest Mowers' castings.

   While relying on each other's performance allowed both Midwest and Rexite to extract greater benefit from their exchange, their reliance put them in a vulnerable position. Consider how Rexite tried to exploit Midwest's customer commitments by demanding a higher price.

Questions: If a promisor does not perform his contractual promise, any preparations he made for performance are wasted. If the promisee relied on the promise by investing resources or otherwise altering its position, the promisee's reliance expenditures are also wasted. In the absence of enforceable contract, which of those potential costs are internal costs to the promisor? Which are external costs to the promisor? If contracts were not enforceable, would parties be more or less willing to invest resources and rely on each others' promises? Would deferred exchanges be more or less likely?

3. There was some evidence in *Rexite Casting* that the price increase was justified by an increase in the cost of the raw materials for castings. Suppose Rexite's officers were not taking advantage of Midwest Mower's predicament but told the truth when they claimed that, without the price increase, they would lose money producing castings for only 52¢ each. Suppose also that Rexite was careless in agreeing to sell the castings for 52¢, because it was apparent when it entered the contract that the price of raw materials would increase substantially in the near future.

Questions: If a rise in the cost of raw materials made it unprofitable for Rexite to sell castings for 52¢, would it be Pareto superior to require Rexite to comply with the original contract terms? Would it be wealth-increasing? Is there any economic reason to require Rexite to live up to the terms of the agreement?

4. By preventing a promisor from exploiting a promisee who changes position in reliance on the promise and by discouraging the promisor from carelessly inducing the promisee to rely on a contract that turns out not to be mutually beneficial, contract law encourages wealth-increasing exchanges that require one or both parties to rely on the other's performance. But enforceable contract is not an absolute requirement for such exchanges. Other mechanisms can protect a promisee from opportunistic or careless defaults. For example, one can avoid making contracts with persons who have previously proven unreliable. Such an informal approach avoids the expense of judicial intervention but requires a great deal of information about potential contracting parties. Whether the costs of legal enforcement are greater or less than the costs of private mechanisms is an empirical question.

Questions: What private arrangements can encourage people to live up to their promises in the absence of formal contract? For example, how might Rexite and Midwest Mowers have structured their transaction if no law of contract existed?

UNITED STATES v. BEHAN

United States Supreme Court, 1884.
110 U.S. 338, 4 S.Ct. 81, 28 L.Ed. 168.

BRADLEY, JUSTICE.

[Under contract with the government, the claimant, Behan, engaged in a project to lay down an artificial covering of cane-mats over the sloping portion of the riverbed of the Mississippi in the harbor of

New Orleans. After examining the progress, the government engineers decided that the objectives to be achieved by the project could not be obtained and notified Behan to discontinue work, which he did immediately. The Court of Claims awarded Behan compensation for expenses that had been incurred up to the time of the notice to discontinue work.]

The [Court of Claims] further finds as follows:

"The contract was of such a character as to require extensive preparations and a large initial expenditure. The claimant made the necessary preparations for carrying on the work to completion and in procuring boats, tools, materials, and apparatus for its prosecution. He engaged actively in carrying out the contract on his part, incurred large expenditure for labor and materials, and had for some time proceeded with the work when the undertaking was abandoned by the defendants and the work stopped without fault of the claimant, as set forth in the following letters."

* * *

"The claimant thereupon closed up his work and sold the materials which he had on hand. Nothing has been paid to him for work, materials, or losses.

"The actual and reasonable expenditures by the claimant in the prosecution of his work, together with his unavoidable losses on the materials on hand at the time of the stoppage by the defendants, were equal to the full amount claimed therefor in his petition, $33,192.20.

* * *

"Upon the foregoing findings of facts the court decides as a conclusion of law that the claimant is entitled to recover the sum of $33,192.20."

* * *

We think that these views, as applied to the case in hand, are substantially correct. The claimant has not received a dollar, either for what he did, or for what he expended, except the proceeds of the property which remained on his hands when the contract was stopped. Unless there is some artificial rule of law which has taken the place of natural justice in relation to the measure of damages, it would seem to be quite clear that the claimant ought at least to be made whole for his losses and expenditures. So far as appears, they were incurred in the fair endeavor to perform the contract which he assumed. If they were foolishly or unreasonably incurred, the government should have proven this fact. It will not be presumed. The court finds that his expenditures were reasonable. * * *

* * *

Notes and Questions

1. When the government engineers notified Mr. Behan that he should stop work on the New Orleans harbor project, Mr. Behan had already

irretrievably committed resources to the project. If no further work was to be done and the work already done failed to accomplish the engineers' objectives, those resources would be wasted. If Mr. Behan was not compensated for his expenses, he would be poorer as a result of his contractual relationship with the government. If compensation was paid, the government would be poorer as a result of its contractual relationship with Mr. Behan.

Oliver Wendell Holmes argued, in the torts context, that it makes no sense to incur the expense of setting the judicial machinery in motion if the only effect is to shift money from one party's pocket to another's.

Questions: Does enforcing this contract by requiring the government to pay Behan's expenses affect the government's behavior in the formation of future contracts? Would failure to enforce this contract affect Mr. Behan's behavior in the formation of future contracts?

2. While the Supreme Court agreed that Behan should be compensated for his expenses, it is fairly clear that if the government had shown that the expenses were foolishly or unreasonably incurred Behan would not have been compensated.

Question: What efficiency purpose is served by enforcing the contract only with regard to reasonable expenses?

3. If contracts like the one in *Behan* are not enforced, contractors might decline to engage in risky, experimental projects—like covering the sides of the harbor bottom with cane matting. If the government offered to pay enough to compensate for the risk, however, it is quite likely that a contractor could be found even if payment was contingent on success. Such an arrangement would shift the risk from the government to the contractor. The government would be willing to shift the risk by a contractual arrangement of this sort only when it is cheaper than agreeing to accept the risk.

Questions: When is the government likely to shift the risk involved with an experimental project to the contractor? Does permitting the parties to allocate risks in this way serve any efficiency objectives?

WOOD v. LUCY, LADY DUFF–GORDON

Court of Appeals of New York, 1917.
222 N.Y. 88, 118 N.E. 214.

CARDOZO, J.

The defendant styles herself "a creator of fashions." Her favor helps a sale. Manufacturers of dresses, millinery, and like articles are glad to pay for a certificate of her approval. The things which she designs, fabrics, parasols, and what not, have a new value in the public mind when issued in her name. She employed the plaintiff to help her to turn this vogue into money. He was to have the exclusive right, subject always to her approval, to place her indorsements on the designs of others. He was also to have the exclusive right to place her own designs on sale, or to license others to market them. In return she was to have one-half of "all profits and revenues" derived from any contracts he might make. The exclusive right was to last at least one year from April 1, 1915, and thereafter from year to year unless terminated by notice of 90 days. The plaintiff says that he kept the contract on his part, and that the defendant broke it. She placed her indorsement on fabrics, dresses, and millinery without his knowledge, and withheld the profits. He sues her for the damages, and the case comes here on demurrer.

The agreement of employment is signed by both parties. It has a wealth of recitals. The defendant insists, however, that it lacks the elements of a contract. She says that the plaintiff does not bind himself to anything. It is true that he does not promise in so many words that he will use reasonable efforts to place the defendant's indorsements and market her designs. We think, however, that such a promise is fairly to be implied. The law has outgrown its primitive stage of formalism when the precise word was the sovereign talisman, and every slip was fatal. It takes a broader view today. A promise may be lacking, and yet the whole writing may be "instinct with an obligation," imperfectly expressed. If that is so, there is a contract.

The implication of a promise here finds support in many circumstances. The defendant gave an exclusive privilege. She was to have no right for at least a year to place her own indorsements or market her own designs except through the agency of the plaintiff. * * * We are not to suppose that one party was to be placed at the mercy of the other. Many other terms of the agreement point the same way. We are told at the outset by way of recital that:

> "The said Otis F. Wood possesses a business organization adapted to the placing of such indorsements as the said Lucy, Lady Duff–Gordon, has approved."

The implication is that the plaintiff's business organization will be used for the purpose for which it is adapted. But the terms of the defendant's compensation are even more significant. Her sole compensation for the grant of an exclusive agency is to be one-half of all the profits resulting from the plaintiff's efforts. Unless he gave his efforts, she could never get anything. Without an implied promise, the transaction cannot have such business "efficacy, as both parties must have intended that at all events it should have." But the contract does not stop there. The plaintiff goes on to promise that he will account monthly for all moneys received by him, and that he will take out all such patents and copyrights and trade-marks as may in his judgment be necessary to protect the rights and articles affected by the agreement. It is true, of course, as the Appellate Division has said, that if he was under no duty to try to market designs or to place certificates of indorsement, his promise to account for profits or take out copyrights would be valueless. But in determining the intention of the parties the promise has a value. It helps to enforce the conclusion that the plaintiff had some duties. His promise to pay the defendant one-half of the profits and revenues resulting from the exclusive agency and to render accounts monthly was a promise to use reasonable efforts to bring profits and revenues into existence. * * *

The judgment of the Appellate Division should be reversed, and the order of the Special Term affirmed, with costs in the Appellate Division and in this court.

Notes and Questions

1. The Lady Duff–Gordon agreed to give up her exclusive right to endorse other products and market designs in exchange for Otis Wood's promise to pay Duff–Gordon one-half of any profits he made from selling her endorsements and designs. Apart from the requirement that Wood share his profits (if any), the contract contained no explicit provisions describing Wood's obligations. Rather than declare the contract void for lack of consideration, the court implied an additional term that Wood "use reasonable efforts" to sell Duff–Gordon's endorsements and designs.

Questions: If the court had declared the contract in Wood void, future parties negotiating similar transactions would have incentive to specify that the party entitled to market endorsements and designs must actually make some effort to do so. Suppose the court had insisted on strictly reading the contract according to its literal terms. Would such formalism motivate future parties negotiating contracts to specify the exact nature of their reciprocal obligations and to provide for contingencies? Is it desirable to encourage such detailed negotiations?

2. A court that wishes to imply a missing contract term needs some guide for determining what the implied term should be.

Questions: Where did Justice Cardozo look for guidance in determining Wood's implied contractual obligations? What standard did he apply?

3. In addition to encouraging deferred exchanges by protecting parties who invest resources and otherwise rely on contractual promises, contract law provides a standard set of terms—such as the obligation to use reasonable efforts in services contracts—that saves the parties time and effort when negotiating their contract. Some rules of contract law cover contingencies that may not have occurred to the parties. If a natural disaster destroyed the supply of metal used to manufacture mower castings in Rexite, making Rexite's performance impossible, contract law provides terms describing the parties' obligations even if that possibility was not covered in the contract. See Eastern S.S. Lines, below. Other rules of contract law apply to circumstances that the parties might have foreseen but not covered explicitly in their contractual arrangements. When Midwest sells mowers to its customers, those mowers may be covered by implied warranties of fitness for their particular purpose even if Midwest's contracts with its customers do not refer to warranties. Since contract law provides standard implied terms where the actual contract remains silent, it is important that those standard terms provide appropriate incentives.

Suppose the implied terms a court would read into a contract are not the terms the parties themselves would have found mutually beneficial. For example, suppose that Otis Wood and Lady Duff–Gordon did not want

Wood to have an obligation to use reasonable efforts—perhaps Duff–Gordon had employed other agents to sell her designs, and Wood did not want to commit himself to make sales efforts on Duff–Gordon's behalf because his other business ventures might claim too much time.

Question: How could the parties avoid the court's imposing implied terms they do not wish to adopt?

B. EXCHANGE, EFFICIENCY AND UNENFORCEABILITY

As the Coase Theorem demonstrates, voluntary exchange can play an important role in allocating goods and services to those who value them most highly. A particular exchange is most likely to result in an efficient allocation of resources when it enjoys several characteristics: the parties voluntarily entered the exchange; there are no transaction costs; the parties have complete information about, and ability to appreciate, the consequences and implications of the exchange; and no one other than the bargaining parties is affected by the transaction. If any of those conditions are not met, an exchange—or contract for exchange—may not further the fundamental economic goal of maximizing wealth. Since enforcement of contracts is costly, perhaps contracts failing those conditions should not be enforced. From an economic perspective, why should the contracts described in the following cases be unenforceable?

1. CONTRACTS CONTRARY TO PUBLIC POLICY

MILTENBERG & SAMTON, INC. v. MALLOR

Supreme Court of New York, Appellate Division, 1956.
1 A.D.2d 458, 151 N.Y.S.2d 748.

BOTEIN, JUSTICE.

Plaintiff seeks to enforce a "guaranty" by defendant to be responsible for the consequences if a bare-faced scheme to deceive the consuming public went awry.

Defendant, a food broker, sold 2,000 cartons of canned Atlantic Coast river herring to plaintiff, who bought the herring for resale to a customer in Egypt. The negotiations and the written terms of sale contemplated that the cans of herring should be labeled as California mackerel. At that time mackerel was in short supply and sold for about twice the price of herring. Concededly, this mislabeling was agreed or insisted upon by all the participants in the transaction—plaintiff, defendant, the packer and the Egyptian customer. The only persons touched by the sale who would be unaware of the deception would be the ultimate consumers in Egypt.

However, in attaching the false labels, the packer negligently failed to remove the herring labels from a number of the cans, and merely pasted the mackerel labels over them. This double labeling was discovered upon inspection at dockside. Plaintiff nevertheless accepted delivery, loaded the cans aboard ship and sent them to the Egyptian purchaser.

Plaintiff, expressing apprehension that discovery of the underlying herring labels would cause the Egyptian purchaser to reject the shipment, refused payment. Finally, to secure payment, defendant and the packer signed the so-called guaranty upon which plaintiff bases this action, in which defendant agreed to be "responsible for any and all consequences due to the fact that the River Herring label was not removed from the tins".

As apprehended by plaintiff, the Egyptian purchaser withheld payment because of the double labeling, complaining that "According to local regulations, we cannot sell canned herrings under the name of Mackerel". Plaintiff gave its Egyptian customer an allowance of about $8,000, and upon refusal of defendant to pay that sum under the guaranty agreement, it commenced this action.

Both parties moved for summary judgment, and Special Term granted judgment for plaintiff, rejecting the defense of illegality on the ground that the Federal statutes did not proscribe the arrangement, since the goods were packed for export and were never introduced into intrastate or interstate commerce for domestic use.

Defendant contends that the complaint must be dismissed because the guaranty agreement is repugnant to public policy * * *.

Sometimes a transaction is so plainly prejudicial to the public good, so clearly repulsive to every concept of morality and fair dealing, that a court need not look further to ascertain whether it is also proscribed expressly by some statute. * * *

> "In many of its aspects, the term 'public policy' is but another name for public sentiment; and, as that is often transitory or shifting, it lacks the permanency upon which fixed principles of law are, or should be, based. There are, however, other phases of public policy which are as enduring and immutable as the law of gravity. One of them is that, as applied to the law of contracts, courts of justice will never recognize or uphold any transaction which, in its object, operation, or tendency, is calculated to be prejudicial to the public welfare. That sound morality and civic honesty are corner stones of the social edifice is a truism which needs no re-enforcement by argument."

Our task is made easier by the fact that the parties make no effort to place a patina of propriety on the transaction. The complaint possibly permits of an inference that payment was refused in Egypt because of the unmerchantable quality of the herrings themselves; but plaintiff, with disarming candor, rejects so honorable a condition and alleges in its bill of particulars that "The fact that the canned fish contained double labels which were contradictory rendered it not fit, suitable or merchantable in Egypt". This would appear to reduce the complaint to the proposition that by reason of the inept labeling the merchandise was unfit for the purpose of deception of the public.

Surely, it is too fundamental to require elaboration that the public welfare demands that consumers be properly informed as to the type and quality of the food they eat and that they not be mulcted by gross misrepresentations. The Government affords some measure of protection to the public by discouraging contracts that contemplate cheating or defrauding members of the public through refusing to enforce them.

"As has been frequently said, the courts, in refusing to enforce these agreements, does so, not because it desires to relieve one of the parties to such an agreement from the obligation that he assumes, but because of the fact that the making of such an agreement is an injury to the public, and that the only method by which the law can prevent such agreements from being made is to refuse to enforce them."

In such a case a court will leave the parties as it found them.

* * *

* * * Materne v. Horwitz, a case markedly similar to this one, involved an agreement by the plaintiff to sell the defendant domestic sardines, which, however, were to be labeled as French sardines. The Court of Appeals made short shrift of the contract:

"It is, therefore, apparent that it was part of the contract that an unlawful object was intended, of which both parties were cognizant, and that it was designed by them, under the contract to commit a fraud and thus promote an illegal purpose by deceiving other parties. In such a case the courts will not aid either party in carrying out a fraudulent purpose."

* * *

The order granting plaintiff's motion for summary judgment should be reversed and the defendant's motion for summary judgment dismissing the complaint should be granted.

* * *

Notes and Questions

1. The contract to relabel herring as "mackerel," including the guaranty clause, was agreed to by all the participants in the transaction: the plaintiff, the defendant food broker, the packer, and the Egyptian purchaser. The defendant failed to meet his contractual obligation to reimburse the plaintiff for any losses resulting from the mislabeling. The court refused to require him to do so since the contract was contrary to public policy.

Questions: Should public policy support bargaining, which leads to efficient use of resources? Does refusing to enforce the contract in *Mallor* interfere with the goal of wealth maximization?

2. As the court noted in *Mallor,* the law declines to enforce not only "illegal" contracts involving direct violations of criminal law, but also contracts repugnant to "public policy." Contracts declared unenforceable

as against public policy include contracts to consent in advance to suffer assault and battery, United States v. King, 840 F.2d 1276 (6th Cir. 1988); "surrogate parenting" agreements to bear a child and then surrender it for adoption, Matter of Baby M, 537 A.2d 1227 (N.J. 1988); and contracts for the sale of sexual services such as the one involved in Samples v. Monroe, discussed in Chapter 2.

> *Question:* Unlike the contract in *Mallor,* the unenforceable contracts described above do not seem to affect large numbers of other people directly. What economic reasons might support their unenforceability?

2. INCOMPLETE INFORMATION AND MISTAKE

WILKIN v. 1ST SOURCE BANK

Court of Appeals of Indiana, 1990.
548 N.E.2d 170.

HOFFMAN, JUDGE.

Respondents-appellants Terrence G. Wilkin and Antoinette H. Wilkin (the Wilkins) appeal from the judgment of the St. Joseph Probate Court in favor of petitioner-appellee 1st Source Bank (Bank). * * *

* * * The findings of fact may be summarized as follows.

Olga Mestrovic died on August 31, 1984. Her last will and testament was admitted to probate on September 6, 1984, and the Bank was appointed personal representative of the estate.

At the time of her death, Olga Mestrovic was the owner of a large number of works of art created by her husband, Ivan Mestrovic, an internationally-known sculptor and artist. By the terms of Olga's will, all the works of art created by her husband and not specifically devised were to be sold and the proceeds distributed to members of the Mestrovic family.

Also included in the estate of Olga Mestrovic was certain real property. In March of 1985, the Bank entered into an agreement to sell the real estate to the Wilkins. The agreement of purchase and sale made no mention of any works of art, although it did provide for the sale of such personal property as the stove, refrigerator, dishwasher, drapes, curtains, sconces and French doors in the attic.

Immediately after closing on the real estate, the Wilkins complained that the premises were left in a cluttered condition and would require substantial cleaning effort. The Bank, through its trust officer, proposed two options: the Bank could retain a rubbish removal service to clean the property or the Wilkins could clean the premises and keep any items of personal property they wanted. The Wilkins opted to clean the property themselves. At the time arrangements were made concerning the cluttered condition of the real property, neither the Bank nor the Wilkins suspected that any works of art remained on the premises.

During their clean-up efforts, the Wilkins found eight drawings apparently created by Ivan Mestrovic. They also found a plaster sculpture of the figure of Christ with three small children. The Wilkins claimed ownership of the works of art, based upon their agreement with the Bank that if they cleaned the real property then they could keep such personal property as they desired.

The probate court ruled that there was no agreement for the purchase, sale or other disposition of the eight drawings and plaster sculpture. According to the lower court, there was no meeting of the minds, because neither party knew of the existence of the works of art.

On appeal, the Wilkins contend that the court's conclusions of law were erroneous. * * *

Mutual assent is a prerequisite to the creation of a contract. Where both parties share a common assumption about a vital fact upon which they based their bargain, and that assumption is false, the transaction may be avoided if because of the mistake a quite different exchange of values occurs from the exchange of values contemplated by the parties. There is no contract, because the minds of the parties have in fact never met.

The necessity of mutual assent, or "meeting of the minds," is illustrated in the classic case of *Sherwood v. Walker* (1887). The owners of a blooded cow indicated to the purchaser that the cow was barren. The purchaser also appeared to believe that the cow was barren. Consequently, a bargain was made to sell at a price per pound at which the cow would have brought approximately $80.00. Before delivery, it was discovered that the cow was with calf and that she was, therefore, worth from $750.00 to $1,000.00. The court ruled that the transaction was voidable:

> "[T]he mistake was not of the mere quality of the animal, but went to the very nature of the thing. A barren cow is substantially a different creature than a breeding one. There is as much difference between them ... as there is between an ox and a cow...."

Like the parties in *Sherwood,* the parties in the instant case shared a common presupposition as to the existence of certain facts which proved false. The Bank and the Wilkins considered the real estate which the Wilkins had purchased to be cluttered with items of personal property variously characterized as "junk," "stuff" or "trash". Neither party suspected that works of art created by Ivan Mestrovic remained on the premises.

As in *Sherwood,* one party experienced an unexpected, unbargained-for gain while the other party experienced an unexpected, unbargained-for loss. Because the Bank and the Wilkins did not know that the eight drawings and the plaster sculpture were included in the items of personalty that cluttered the real property, the discovery of those works of art by the Wilkins was unexpected. The resultant gain to the Wilkins and loss to the Bank were not contemplated by the parties when the Bank agreed that the Wilkins could clean the premises and keep such personal property as they wished.

* * * The probate court properly concluded that there was no agreement for the purchase, sale or other disposition of the eight drawings and plaster sculpture, because there was no meeting of the minds.

The judgment of the St. Joseph Probate Court is affirmed.

Notes and Questions

1. In Sherwood v. Walker, cited in *Wilkin,* the parties negotiated about a cow both believed to be barren. If the cow was barren, its most valuable use was probably as meat. If fertile, the cow could produce both calves and milk and was worth from $750 to $1000.

Questions: Suppose the sellers in *Sherwood* were dairy farmers and the buyer was a meat packer. Once the cow was discovered to be fertile, who probably valued the cow most highly? According to Coase, the cow will end up with the highest-valuing user no matter to whom the court assigns her, so why shouldn't the legal system enforce the contract? How does the analysis of *Sherwood* support the court's determination in *Wilkin* that there was no enforceable contract between the Wilkins and the Bank with respect to the artwork?

2. The *Wilkin* case is an example of *mutual mistake*—both parties were mistaken about a vital fact upon which the bargain was based. As a result, both the Wilkins' gain and the bank's loss were "unexpected" and "unbargained-for."

Suppose instead that the Wilkins had inspected the house and discovered the artwork *before* they contracted to buy the house from the bank. In other words, there was a *unilateral mistake* concerning the subject of the contract. While the bank mistakenly believed that the Mestrovic house contained only junk, the Wilkins knew it contained valuable artworks by Ivan Mestrovic.

Questions: What are the potential costs of enforcing contracts based on unilateral mistake? Suppose the President of 1st Source Bank, an ardent Mestrovic fan, would love to display the Mestrovic art in her office. What are the costs of refusing to enforce such contracts? Suppose the Wilkins purchased a burglar alarm for their home in the expectation of owning the Mestrovic masterpieces. Is there any reason to believe that such costs can be more readily controlled in unilateral mistake cases than in mutual mistake cases?

3. Suppose that *Sherwood* was not a mutual mistake case, but a unilateral mistake case.

Question: From an economic perspective, in which of the following circumstances should the contract be enforced?

(a) The seller sends the buyer a contract of sale for "one cow, infertile, price $80." The buyer signs without looking at the contract. Later the buyer claims the contract is voidable because he mistakenly assumed the cow was fertile.

(b) The buyer verbally agrees to purchase the cow for $800. The seller sends the buyer a contract of sale for "one cow, price $80.00." The buyer notices the typographical error and gleefully signs the contract. The seller claims the contract is voidable because both he and the buyer intended the sale to be for $800.

(c) The seller, knowing the cow is sterile, tells the buyer the cow is fertile. The written contract says "one cow, fertile, price $800." The buyer, discovering the cow is infertile, sues the seller claiming the contract is voidable for misrepresentation.

HARRIS v. TYSON

Supreme Court of Pennsylvania, 1855.
24 Pa. 347.

BLACK, J.

This action depends on the defendant's right to dig and take away chrome from the land of the plaintiff. The defendant claims that right under the plaintiff's deed, giving and granting it in due form. But the plaintiff asserts that the deed is fraudulent and void because, 1. The defendant suppressed the truth; 2. He suggested a falsehood; 3. He paid a totally inadequate consideration * * *.

A person who knows that there is a mine on the land of another may nevertheless buy it. The ignorance of the vendor is not of itself fraud on the part of the purchaser. A purchaser is not bound by our laws to make the man he buys from as wise as himself. The mere fact, therefore, that Tyson knew there was sand chrome on Harris's land, and that Harris himself was ignorant of it, even if that were exclusively established, would not be ground for impugning the validity of the deed. But it is not by any means clear that one party had much advantage over the other in this respect. They both knew very well that chrome could be got there, which one wanted and the other had no use for. But the whole extent of it in quantity was probably not known to either of them for sometime after the deed. When it was discovered that sand chrome was as valuable as the same mineral found in the rock, and that large quantities of the former could be got in certain parts of the fast land as well as by the streams, it was natural enough that the plaintiff should repent and the defendant rejoice over the contract: but this did not touch its validity. Every man must bear the loss of a bad bargain legally and honestly made. If not, he could not enjoy in safety the fruits of a good one. Besides, we do not feel sure that the contract has made the plaintiff any poorer, for it is not improbable that he would never have discovered the value of the mineral deposit on his land if he had not granted to the defendant the privilege of digging.

If the defendant, during the negotiation for purchase, wilfully made any misstatement concerning a material fact, and then misled the plaintiff and induced him to sell it at a lower price than he otherwise would, then the contract was a cheat and the deed is void utterly. But in all cases where the evidence brings the parties face to face, the language and conduct of the defendant seem to have been unexceptionable.   * * *

Mere inadequacy of price is not sufficient to set aside a deed.   * * * [T]he plaintiff had a right to sell at what price he pleased or keep his property. Having chosen to do the the former, he cannot undo it by changing his own mind.

* * *

Judgment affirmed.

Notes and Questions

1. In Harris v. Tyson, Harris apparently believed that his land was not suitable for profitable commercial sand chrome mining. Tyson, a professional chrome miner, may have known better. After selling his mining rights to Tyson, Harris tried to claim that the contract was void because Tyson had failed to disclose the value of the chrome sand on Harris' land. *Harris* can be characterized as a case of unilateral mistake; Harris, the mistaken party, would not have agreed to the contract had he had full information. Consider Justice Black's comment that "we do not feel sure that the contract has made the plaintiff any poorer, for it is not improbable that he would never have discovered the value of the mineral deposit on his land if he had not granted to the defendant the privilege of digging."

Questions: Who was the best avoider of the negotiation, reliance, and enforcement costs associated with this mistaken contract? From an economic perspective, should the best avoider of mistakes lose this case in order to give him and similarly situated people an incentive to reveal information necessary to avoid a mistake?

2. Suppose that Wilkins v. 1st Source Bank was a unilateral mistake/nondisclosure case rather than a mutual mistake case, and that the Wilkins knew the house contained the Mestrovic masterpieces before they contracted to buy it from the bank.

Question: From an economic perspective, in which of the following circumstances should the contract be enforced?

(a) The Wilkins knew the "junk" was really art because they hired an appraiser to examine and authenticate it.

(b) The Wilkins knew the "junk" was art because it was readily apparent that the paintings and sculptures were masterpieces (they were very attractive, bore Mestrovic's conspicuous signature, and so forth). In order to hide the existence of the art from the Bank, the Wilkins placed them under a pile of trash where the Bank was unlikely to discover them.

(c) The Wilkins knew the "junk" was art because it was readily apparent that the paintings and sculptures were masterpieces. Although the Wilkins took no affirmative action to hide the art from the Bank, rather than informing the Bank of the existence of the art they chose to remain silent.

3. Section 161 of the Restatement (Second) of Contracts provides:

When Non–disclosure Is Equivalent to an Assertion

A person's non-disclosure of a fact known to him is equivalent to an assertion that the fact does not exist in the following cases only:

(a) where he knows that disclosure of the fact is necessary to prevent some previous assertion from being a misrepresentation or from being fraudulent or material.

(b) where he knows that disclosure of the fact would correct a mistake of the other party as to a basic assumption on which that party is making the contract and if non-disclosure of the fact amounts to a failure to act in good faith and in accordance with reasonable standards of fair dealing.

(c) where he knows that disclosure of the fact would correct a mistake of the other party as to the contents or effect of a writing, evidencing or embodying an agreement in whole or in part.

(d) where the other person is entitled to know the fact because of a relation of trust and confidence between them.

Questions: How would *Harris* have been decided under the Restatement (Second) of Contracts? Does § 161 make sense from an economic perspective?

3. LACK OF CAPACITY

ORTELERE v. TEACHERS' RETIREMENT BOARD OF THE CITY OF NEW YORK

Court of Appeals of New York, 1969.
25 N.Y.2d 196, 303 N.Y.S.2d 362, 250 N.E.2d 460.

BREITEL, JUDGE.

This appeal involves the revocability of an election of benefits under a public employees' retirement system and suggests the need for a renewed examination of the kinds of mental incompetency which may render voidable the exercise of contractual rights. The particular issue arises on the evidently unwise and foolhardy selection of benefits by a 60–year–old teacher, on leave for mental illness and suffering from cerebral arteriosclerosis, after service as a public schoolteacher and participation in a public retirement system for over 40 years. The teacher died a little less than two months after making her election of maximum benefits, payable to her during her life, thus causing the entire reserve to fall in. She left surviving her husband of 38 years of marriage and two grown children.

* * *

The husband and executor of Grace W. Ortelere, the deceased New York City schoolteacher, sues to set aside her application for retirement without option, in the event of her death. It is alleged that Mrs. Ortelere, on February 11, 1965, two months before her death from natural causes, was not mentally competent to execute a retirement application. By this application, effective the next day, she elected the maximum retirement allowance. She thus revoked her earlier election of benefits under which she named her husband a beneficiary of the unexhausted reserve upon her death. Selection of the maximum allowance extinguished all interests upon her death.

* * *

Mrs. Ortelere, an elementary schoolteacher since 1924, suffered a "nervous breakdown" in March, 1964 and went on a leave of absence expiring February 5, 1965. She was then 60 years old and had been happily married for 38 years. On July 1, 1964 she came under the care of Dr. D'Angelo, a psychiatrist, who diagnosed her breakdown as involutional psychosis, melancholia type. * * *

* * *

Following her taking a leave of absence for her condition, Mrs. Ortelere had become very depressed and was unable to care for herself. As a result her husband gave up his electrician's job, in which he earned $222 per week, to stay home and take care of her on a full-time basis. She left their home only when he accompanied her. Although he took her to the Retirement Board on February 11, 1965, he did not know why she went, and did not question her for fear "she'd start crying hysterically that I was scolding her. That's the way she was. And I wouldn't upset her."

* * *

Dr. D'Angelo stated "[a]t no time since she was under my care was she ever mentally competent"; that "[m]entally she couldn't make a decision of any kind, actually, of any kind, small or large." He also described how involutional melancholia affects the judgment process: "They can't think rationally, no matter what the situation is. They will even tell you, 'I used to be able to think of anything and make any decision. Now,' they say, 'even getting up, I don't know whether I should get up or whether I should stay in bed.' Or, 'I don't even know how to make a slice of toast any more.' Everything is impossible to decide, and everything is too great an effort to even think of doing. They just don't have the effort, actually, because their nervous breakdown drains them of all their physical energies."

* * *

The well-established rule is that contracts of a mentally incompetent person who has not been adjudicated insane are voidable. * * *

Traditionally, in this State and elsewhere, contractual mental capacity has been measured by what is largely a cognitive test. Under this standard the "inquiry" is whether the mind was "so affected as to render him wholly and absolutely incompetent to comprehend and understand the nature of the transaction." * * *

These traditional standards governing competency to contract were formulated when psychiatric knowledge was quite primitive. They fail to account for one who by reason of mental illness is unable to control his conduct even though his cognitive ability seems unimpaired. * * *

* * *

On this analysis it is not difficult to see that plaintiff's evidence was sufficient to sustain a finding that, when she acted as she did on February 11, 1965, she did so solely as a result of serious mental illness, namely, psychosis. * * * Mrs. Ortelere's psychiatrist testified quite flatly that as an involutional melancholiac in depression she was incapable of making a voluntary "rational" decision. * * * [T]here should be a new trial under the proper standards frankly considered and applied.

Accordingly, the order of the Appellate Division should be reversed, without costs, and the action remanded to Special Term for a new trial.

JASEN, JUDGE, dissenting.

Where there has been no previous adjudication of incompetency, the burden of proving mental incompetence is upon the party alleging it. I agree with the majority at the Appellate Division that the plaintiff, the husband of the decedent, failed to sustain the burden incumbent upon him of proving deceased's incompetence.

The evidence conclusively establishes that the decedent, at the time she made her application to retire, understood not only that she was retiring, but also that she had selected the maximum payment during her lifetime.

* * *

The generally accepted test of mental competency to contract which has thus evolved is whether the party attempting to avoid the contract was capable of understanding and appreciating the nature and consequences of the particular act or transaction which he challenges. This rule represents a balance struck between policies to protect the security of transactions between individuals and freedom of contract on the one hand, and protection of those mentally handicapped on the other hand. In my opinion, this rule has proven workable in practice and fair in result. * * *

As in every situation where the law must draw a line between liability and nonliability, between responsibility and nonresponsibility, there will be borderline cases, and injustices may occur by deciding erroneously that an individual belongs on one side of the line or the other. To minimize the chances of such injustices occurring, the line should be drawn as clearly as possible.

The Appellate Division correctly found that the deceased was capable of understanding the nature and effect of her retirement benefits, and exercised rational judgment in electing to receive the maximum allowance during her lifetime. I fear that the majority's refinement of the generally accepted rules will prove unworkable in practice, and make many contracts vulnerable to psychological attack.

Any benefit to those who understand what they are doing, but are unable to exercise self-discipline, will be outweighed by frivolous claims which will burden our courts and undermine the security of contracts. The reasonable expectations of those who innocently deal with persons who appear rational and who understand what they are doing should be protected.

Accordingly, I would affirm the order appealed from.

Notes and Questions

1. By contracting for the maximum allowable retirement benefit, Mrs. Ortelere increased her monthly retirement allowance from $375 to $450 per month but gave up her husband's right to receive anything should she predecease him. 250 N.E.2d at 462. Because she died less than three months after electing the maximum payment, her total gain from changing the contract was no more than $225. Meanwhile, Mr. Ortelere was left without a job and without any retirement benefits of his own. It is understandable that the court would decline to enforce the change in Mrs. Ortelere's retirement contract on fairness grounds, given that the Orteleres' losses from the change far outweighed their gains. From an economic perspective, however, any loss suffered by the Orteleres is a gain to the retirement fund.

> *Question:* Apart from distributional concerns, are there efficiency grounds for refusing to enforce contracts entered into by people unable to appreciate the consequences of their acts?

2. According to *Ortelere,* the common law courts applied a "cognitive test" in deciding whether to excuse a party from a contract on the ground of incapacity. If a party to a contract appeared to understand the nature and consequences of her actions, she had capacity to contract. In *Ortelere,* the New York court added an alternative "volitional test" for incapacity. Under the volitional test, a party may be excused from a contract if she had the cognitive or intellectual ability to understand what she was doing but was unable to control her own behavior or exercise volition.

> *Questions:* From an economic perspective, should parties be able to avoid their contractual obligations if they fail the volitional test? If they fail the cognitive test? Is the law in New York following *Ortelere* consistent with enforcing contracts only when they are likely to be wealth-increasing?

3. As Judge Jasen's dissent noted, in the absence of a previous adjudication of incompetency, the burden of proving contractual incapacity remains on the party alleging it. In many states, incapacity must be shown by "clear, precise, and convincing evidence." See McGovern's Estate v. Commonwealth of Pennsylvania State Employee's Retirement Bd., 512 Pa. 377, 517 A.2d 523, 526 (1986).

> *Questions:* Why should the law presume that every adult not adjudicated incompetent is mentally sound and put the burden on the party alleging the contrary? What are the potential costs of a legal rule that defines incapacity broadly and reduces the evidentiary burden of

proving incapacity? What are the potential costs of a rule that defines incapacity narrowly and makes it difficult to prove?

4. LACK OF CONSIDERATION

STELMACK v. GLEN ALDEN COAL CO.

Supreme Court of Pennsylvania, 1940.
339 Pa. 410, 14 A.2d 127.

BARNES, JUSTICE.

This is an appeal from the order of the court below entering judgment for the defendant in an action of assumpsit brought by plaintiffs to recover the cost of repairs to their building which was damaged as a result of mining operations conducted by the defendant. The suit is upon an oral agreement, and the sole question is whether the contract is supported by a consideration.

On July 3, 1922, plaintiffs purchased a certain lot of ground situated in the city of Scranton, upon which was erected a building containing stores and residential apartments. The deed to them incorporated by reference, and was made subject to certain reservations, conditions and releases respecting the mineral rights in the land, which appeared in prior conveyances in the chain of title of the property. Among them was the following provision: "It is also expressly understood and agreed by and between the parties to this deed that the right to surface support to the said surface or right of soil is not hereby conveyed.... That in no event whatever shall the parties of the first part, their heirs or assigns, be liable for any injury or damage that may be caused or done to the said surface or right of soil, or to the buildings or improvements that are now or hereafter may be put thereon, by reason of the mining and removing of said coal and minerals." * * *

The defendant company is the present owner of the coal and mineral rights in the premises, and is actively engaged in mining operations. The plaintiffs aver that they were informed in 1927 by a duly authorized agent of the defendant that mining was about to begin under their property which would cause a subsidence of the soil. He is alleged to have made an oral agreement with them, on behalf of defendant, that if they would permit the coal company's employees to enter upon their land and prop up their building to prevent its collapse, or to minimize any damages which might occur, the company would make all repairs necessary to restore the property to its original condition.

Plaintiffs permitted ties and supports to be erected about their building which rendered it "unsightly" and resulted in some loss of rents, although it is not contended that the work was performed negligently. As mining operations continued during the period from 1928 to 1935, it became necessary, according to plaintiffs, to reconstruct the building, due to the further subsidence of the surface. From time to time the defendant made repairs to the property, but later refused to restore it to its previous condition.

In the present action for the breach of the alleged oral agreement, plaintiffs seek to recover the sum of $3,185, representing the amount expended by them for the repair and restoration of their property. * * *

That consideration is an essential element of an enforceable contract is one of our fundamental legal concepts, and there are but few exceptions to the rule. "Consideration is defined as a benefit to the party promising, or a loss or detriment to the party to whom the promise is made." The terms "benefit" and "detriment" are used in a technical sense in the definition, and have no necessary reference to material advantage or disadvantage to the parties.

It is not enough, however, that the promisee has suffered a legal detriment at the request of the promisor. The detriment incurred must be the "quid pro quo," or the "price" of the promise, and the inducement for which it was made. "Consideration must actually be bargained for as the exchange for the promise". Restatement, Contracts, § 75, Comment (b). If the promisor merely intends to make a gift to the promisee upon the performance of a condition, the promise is gratuitous and the satisfaction of the condition is not consideration for a contract. The distinction between such a conditional gift and a contract is well illustrated in Williston on Contracts, (Rev. Ed.) Vol. 1, § 112, where it is said: "If a benevolent man says to a tramp, 'if you go around the corner to the clothing shop there, you may purchase an overcoat on my credit,' no reasonable person would understand that the short walk was requested as the consideration for the promise, but that in the event of the tramp going to the shop the promisor would make him a gift."

In the present case it clearly appears that the defendant's offer to repair the plaintiffs' building was entirely gratuitous. The permission to enter upon the land and to erect props and ties was sought by defendant merely for the purpose of conferring a benefit upon plaintiffs as a voluntary act, and not as the price or consideration of its alleged promise to restore the building to its original condition. The placing of supports about the structure was of no conceivable advantage to the defendant, for, as we have seen, it had no liability whatever "for any injury or damage that may be caused or done to the said surface or right of soil, or to the buildings or improvements" under the provisions of the deeds in plaintiffs' chain of title. The interest of plaintiffs alone was served by the defendant's efforts to prevent the collapse of the structure and to minimize the damages resulting from the mining operations. As this was done at the expense of the defendant, and solely for the protection of the plaintiffs, we are unable to see how it could have constituted a consideration for the defendant's promise, and converted a purely gratuitous undertaking into a binding contract.

* * *

* * * We are satisfied that there is nothing in the present record to bring this case within any recognized exception to the well settled principle of contract law, that a promise unsupported by consideration is nudum pactum, and unenforceable.

The judgment of the court below is affirmed.

Notes and Questions

1. In *Stelmack*, the coal company promised that if the owners of the building allowed the company to come onto their land and prop up the building so as to minimize damage during the mining operations, the company would make all repairs necessary to restore the building to its original condition after the mining operations were complete. The company devoted labor and materials to the project.

Generally, contract law enforces agreements between parties that reallocate resources, in order to encourage value-increasing exchanges requiring one or both parties to invest resources beforehand to reap the benefits of exchange.

Questions: Did *Stelmack* involve a value-increasing exchange? What is the efficiency basis for the court's refusal to enforce the coal company's promise?

2. Just as it is costly for the legal system to enforce the rules of property and tort liability, it is costly to enforce contracts. Judges, lawyers, and courts are expensive. Moreover, in any situation where an outside decisionmaker substitutes his estimate of value for the outcome determined by bargaining, there is the possibility of legal error. In the context of contracts, error results if the court enforces an exchange that allocates resources inefficiently, perhaps because the court found a promise where none was actually made or misinterpreted a promise that had been made. Those costs, as well as the benefits from enforcing contracts, should be considered in deciding whether a particular type of contract should be enforced.

Question 1, above, suggests that determining whether enforcing gratuitous promises improves allocative efficiency may be difficult, implying that the benefits of enforcing contracts without consideration are likely to be small. Given the possibility that the benefits from enforcement of gratuitous promises are likely to be small, the administrative costs and the costs of legal error associated with enforcement become particularly significant.

Question: Are the administrative costs and costs of legal error associated with enforcing contracts without consideration likely to be higher than those associated with contracts with consideration?

3. Lon Fuller offers a different perspective on the enforcement of gratuitous promises, Fuller, Consideration and Form, 41 Colum.L.Rev. 799, 821 (1941):

Moral Obligation as Consideration. Courts have frequently enforced promises on the simple ground that the promisor was only promising to do what he ought to have done anyway. These cases have either been condemned as wanton departures from legal principle, or reluctantly accepted as involving the kind of compromise logic must inevitably make at time with sentiment. I believe that these decisions are capable of rational defense. When we say the defendant was morally obligated to do the thing he promised, we in effect assert the existence of a substantive ground for enforcing the promise. In a broad sense, a similar line of reasoning justifies the special status accorded by the law to contracts of exchange. Men *ought* to exchange goods and services; therefore when they enter contracts to that end, we enforce those contracts.

Questions: Does Fuller's approach to consideration recommend enforcement of the agreement in *Stelmack?* Was the coal company morally obliged to protect the building from the risks posed by the mining operations?

MILLS v. WYMAN

Supreme Judicial Court of Massachusetts, 1825.
20 Mass. (3 Pick.) 207.

This was an action of assumpsit brought to recover a compensation for the board, nursing, etc. of Levi Wyman, son of the defendant, from the 5th to the 20th of February, 1821. * * *

* * *

PARKER, C. J.

General rules of law established for the protection and security of honest and fair-minded men, who may inconsiderately make promises without equivalent, will sometimes skreen [sic] men of a different character from engagements which they are bound *in foro conscientiae* to perform. This is a defect inherent in all human systems of legislation. The rule that a mere verbal promise, without any consideration, cannot be enforced by action, is universal in its application, and cannot be departed from in its application, and cannot be departed from to suit particular cases in which a refusal to perform such a promise may be disgraceful.

The promise declared on in this case appears to have been made without any legal consideration. The kindness and services towards the sick son of the defendant were not bestowed at his request. The son was in no respect under the care of the defendant. He was twenty-five years old, and had long left his father's family. On his return from a foreign country, he fell sick among strangers, and the plaintiff acted the part of the good Samaritan, giving him shelter and comfort until he died. The defendant, his father, on being informed of this event, influenced by a transient feeling of gratitude, promises in writing to pay the plaintiff for the expenses he had incurred. But he has determined to break this promise, and is willing to have his case appear on record as a strong example of particular injustice sometimes necessarily resulting from the operation of general rules.

It is said a moral obligation is a sufficient consideration to support an express promise; and some authorities lay down the rule thus broadly; but upon examination of the cases we are satisfied that the universality of the rule cannot be supported, and that there must have been some pre-existing obligation, which has become inoperative by positive law, to form a basis for an effective compromise. The cases of debts barred by the Statute of Limitations, of debts incurred by infants, of debts of bankrupts, are generally put for illustration of the rule. Express promises founded on such pre-existing equitable obligations may be enforced; there is a good consideration for them; they merely remove an impediment created by law to the recovery of debts honestly due, but which public policy protects the debtors from being compelled to pay. In all these cases there was originally a *quid pro quo,* and according to the principles of natural justice the party receiving ought to pay; but the legislature has said he shall not be coerced; then comes the promise to pay the debt that is barred, the promise of the man to pay the debt of the infant, of the discharged bankrupt to restore to his creditor what by the law he had lost. In all these cases there is a moral obligation founded upon an antecedent valuable consideration. These promises, therefore, have a sound legal basis. They are not promises to pay something for nothing; not naked pacts, but the voluntary revival or creation of obligations which existed before in natural law, but which had been dispensed with, not for the benefit of the party obliged solely, but principally for the public convenience. If a moral obligation, in its fullest sense, is a good substratum for an express promise, it is not easy to perceive why it is not equally good to support an implied promise. What a man ought to do, generally he ought to be made to do whether he promise or refuse. But the law of society has left most of such obligations to the *interior* forum, as the tribunal of conscience has been aptly called. * * *

Without doubt there are great interests of society which justify withholding the coercive arm of the law from these duties of imperfect obligation, as they are called; imperfect, not because they are less binding upon the conscience than those which are called perfect, but because the wisdom of the social law does not impose sanctions upon them.

A deliberate promise in writing, made freely and without any mistake, one which may lead the party to whom it is made into contracts and expenses, cannot be broken without a violation of moral duty. But if there was nothing paid or promised for it, the law, perhaps wisely, leaves the execution of it to the conscience of him who makes it. It is only when the party making the promise gains something, or he to whom it is made loses something, that the law gives the promise validity. * * *

* * *

The cases of instruments under seal * * * in which considerations need not be proved, do not contradict the principles above suggested. [These] import a consideration in themselves * * *.

* * *

For the foregoing reasons we are all of opinion that the nonsuit directed by the Court of Common Pleas was right, and that judgment be entered thereon for costs for the defendant.

Notes and Questions

1.   *Mills* confirms the general rule that promises without consideration are enforced only by the tribunal of the conscience.   Comparing *Stelmack* to *Mills,* however, there appears to have been an exchange in the latter case; the good Samaritan Mills cared for the defendant's son while the defendant father promised money to Mills.   The father apparently believed he had received something of value and Mills would certainly be better off if the promise was enforced.   Since the promise was in writing there was solid evidence to reduce the cost of factfinding and the likelihood of legal error.

Question: From an efficiency perspective, why should the fact that the good Samaritan performed his part of the exchange before the father promised to pay prevent the court from enforcing the contract?

2.   The court in *Mills* identified several situations where gratuitous promises are enforceable: promises to pay debts barred by the Statute of Limitations;   promises to pay otherwise-unenforceable debts incurred when the debtor lacked capacity;   and promises to pay debts discharged in bankruptcy proceedings.

Question: Given the benefits and costs associated with enforcing contracts, what economic rationale supports the above exceptions to the general rule of nonenforcement of gratuitous promises?

3.   The common law enforced gratuitous promises made under seal.   A promise under seal was a written promise signed with an individual's personal seal, which meant "and I really mean it."

Questions: What economic rationale supports the enforcement of promises under seal?   Many states no longer enforce promises under seal. Is that efficient?

POSNER, GRATUITOUS PROMISES IN ECONOMICS AND LAW *

6 J. Legal Stud. 411, 411–13 (1977).

* * *

Why would "economic man" ever make a promise without receiving in exchange something of value from the promisee, whether it be money, promise of future performance beneficial to the promisor, or something else of value to him?   It is tempting to answer this question simply by invoking "interdependent utilities."   Since people may indeed derive utility or welfare from increases in the utility or welfare of family members, or for that matter of strangers, interdependence may explain why (some) gifts or transfers are made.   But it cannot explain why a *promise* to make a transfer in the future is made.   Promises, as distinct from transfers, seem related to situations of bilateral performance, of exchange. A promises B $25,000 in exchange for B's building a house for A. B will not build without a promise of payment in advance; A will not pay in advance without B's promise to build. But if A wanted merely to transfer $25,000 to B (his favorite charity), why would he *promise* B to make the transfer in the future? Why not wait until he is ready to make the transfer and just do it? The purpose of a promise seems to be to induce performance of some sort by the promisee; if reciprocal performance is not desired, there seems no reason to make a promise.

* * * [A] gratuitous promise, to the extent it actually commits the promisor to the promised course of action (an essential qualification), creates utility for the promisor over and above the utility to him of the promised performance. * * * [I]t does so by increasing the present value of an uncertain future stream of transfer payments.

To illustrate, suppose A promises to give $1000 a year for the next 20 years to the B symphony orchestra. The value of the gift to B is the discounted present value of $1000 to be paid yearly over a 20–year period in the future. Among the factors that will be used by B in discounting these expected future receipts to present value is the likelihood that at some time during the 20–year period A will discontinue the annual payments. Depending on B's estimation of A's fickleness, income prospects, etc., the present value of the gift of $1000 a year may be quite small; it may not be much more than $1000. But suppose the gift is actually worth more to B because A is certain to continue the payments throughout the entire period, though this fact is not known to B. If A can make a binding promise to continue the payments in accordance with his intention, B will revalue the gift at its true present worth. The size of the gift (in present-value terms) will be increased at no cost to A. Here is a clear case where the enforcement of a gratuitous promise would increase net social welfare.

This can be seen even more clearly by considering A's alternatives if his promise is not enforceable. One possibility would be for A to promise a larger gift, the discounted value of which to B would equal the true value as known to A. * * * Another possibility would be for A to substitute for the promised series of future transfers a one-time transfer the present value of which would be the same as that of the series of enforceable future transfers. However, the fact that A preferred making a future gift to a present one suggests that they are not perfect substitutes; there are many reasons (including tax and liquidity considerations) why they might not be.

* * *

Notes and Questions

1. In Webb v. McGowin, 27 Ala. App. 82, 168 So. 196 (1935), McGowin promised to give Webb $15 every two weeks for the remainder of Webb's life after Webb suffered serious injuries while saving McGowin's life.

When McGowin's heirs tried to renege, the court enforced the promise, saying "McGowin was benefitted. [Webb] was injured. Benefit to the promisor or injury to the promisee is a sufficient legal consideration for the promisor's agreement to pay."

> *Questions:* According to Posner, how would McGowin be made better off by making his promise enforceable? Assuming Webb also would be better off if the promise were enforced, was the court's decision in Webb v. McGowin efficient?

2. Posner's justification for enforcing gratuitous promises relies on the conclusion that, whatever the promisor's reason for wanting to benefit the promisee, the promisor can give a greater value to the promisee if his promise is enforceable. Webb would value McGowin's promise to pay over a period of years more highly if it was enforceable.

> *Questions:* Is there an analogous economic argument for enforcing a pledge to pay a lump sum next year? Next week? Are the facts of *McGowin* sufficiently different from the facts of *Mills* in this regard to justify the different outcomes in the cases?

3. Another form of gratuitous promise that is enforced in many states is the charitable subscription. In Salsbury v. Northwestern Bell Tel. Co., 221 N.W. 2d 609 (Iowa 1974), the Iowa Supreme Court enforced a promise by Northwestern Bell to pay $5000 each year for three years, noting the following policy concerns:

> Cases throughout the country clearly reflect a conflict between the desired goal of enforcing charitable subscriptions and the realities of contract law. The result has been strained reasoning which has been the subject of considerable criticism. This criticism is directed toward efforts by the courts to secure a substitute for consideration in charitable subscriptions. These efforts were thought necessary to bind the subscriber on a contract theory. Yet, in the nature of charitable subscriptions, it is presupposed the promise is made as a gift and not in return for consideration.   * * *

>   * * *

> Charitable subscriptions often serve the public interest by making possible projects which otherwise could never come about.   * * * [W]here a subscription is unequivocal the pledgor should be made to keep his word.

> *Question:* Whose reasoning do you think best explains the enforceability of charitable subscriptions: Posner's or Fuller's? (See *Stelmack* Question 3, above.)

RICKETTS v. SCOTHORN

Supreme Court of Nebraska, 1898.
59 Neb. 51, 77 N.W. 365.

SULLIVAN, J.

In the district court of Lancaster county the plaintiff, Katie Scothorn, recovered judgment against the defendant, Andrew D. Ricketts, as executor of the last will and testament of John C. Ricketts, deceased. The action was based upon a promissory note, of which the following is a copy: "May the first, 1891. I promise to pay to Katie Scothorn on demand, $2,000, to be at 6 per cent. per annum. J.C. Ricketts." * * * The material facts are undisputed. They are as follows: John C. Ricketts, the maker of the note, was the grandfather of the plaintiff. Early in May—presumably on the day the note bears date—he called on her at the store where she was working. What transpired between them is thus described by Mr. Flodene, one of the plaintiff's witnesses: "A. Well, the old gentleman came in there one morning about nine o'clock, probably a little before or a little after, but early in the morning, and he unbuttoned his vest, and took out a piece of paper in the shape of a note; that is the way it looked to me; and he says to Miss Scothorn, "I have fixed out something that you have not got to work any more." He says, none of my grandchildren work, and you don't have to. Q. Where was she? A. She took the piece of paper and kissed him, and kissed the old gentleman, and commenced to cry." It seems Miss Scothorn immediately notified her employer [Mayer Bros.] of her intention to quit work, and that she did soon after abandon her occupation. * * * The testimony of Flodene and [the plaintiff's mother], taken together, conclusively establishes the fact that the note was not given in consideration of the plaintiff pursuing, or agreeing to pursue, any particular line of conduct. There was no promise on the part of the plaintiff to do, or refrain from doing, anything. Her right to the money promised in the note was not made to depend upon an abandonment of her employment with Mayer Bros., and future abstention from such service. Mr. Ricketts made no condition, requirement, or request. He exacted no quid pro quo. He gave the note as a gratuity, and looked for nothing in return. So far as the evidence discloses, it was his purpose to place the plaintiff in a position of independence, where she could work or remain idle, as she might choose. * * * The instrument in suit, being given without any valuable consideration, was nothing more than a promise to make a gift in the future of the sum of money therein named. Ordinarily, such promises are not enforceable, even when put in the form of a promissory note. But it has often been held that an action on a note given to a church, college, or other like institution, upon the faith of which money has been expended or obligations incurred, could not be successfully defended on the ground of a want of consideration. In this class of cases the note in suit is nearly always spoken of as a gift or donation, but the decision is generally put on the ground that the expenditure of money or assumption of liability by the donee on the faith of the promise constitutes a valuable and sufficient consideration. It seems to us that the true reason is the preclusion of the defendant, under the doctrine of estoppel, to deny the consideration. * * *

Under the circumstances of this case, is there an equitable estoppel which ought to preclude the defendant from alleging that the note in controversy is lacking in one of the essential elements of a valid contract? We think there is. An estoppel is pais is defined to be "a right arising from acts, admissions, or conduct which have induced a change of position in accordance with the real or apparent intention of the party against whom they are alleged." * * * Having intentionally influenced the plaintiff to alter her position for the worse on the faith of the note being paid when due, it would be grossly inequitable to permit the maker, or his executor, to resist payment on the ground that the promise was given without consideration. The petition charges the elements of an equitable estoppel, and the evidence conclusively established them. If errors intervened at the trial, they could not have been prejudicial. A verdict for the defendant would be unwarranted. The judgment is right, and is affirmed.

Notes and Questions

1. The court's reason for enforcing the grandfather's promise in *Ricketts* was explicitly equitable rather than economic: having caused his granddaughter to give up her salary of $10 a week at Mayer Bros. and "abandon her occupation" by his promise of $2000, it would be unfair for him or his executor to claim the contract was unenforceable because it lacked consideration. From a contracting perspective, because the promisor apparently did not seek anything in exchange for his promise, the promisor did not need to bind his granddaughter in order to induce her to enter a mutually satisfactory exchange.

> *Questions:* If the traditional economic theory of contract does not apply because there is no bargained-for, wealth maximizing exchange, is there any other economic rationale for enforcing grandfather Ricketts' promise? Consider how the granddaughter altered her position in reliance upon her grandfather's promise. If Scothorn had not quit her job or otherwise altered her conduct in reliance on the promise, should the court have enforced the promise?

2. Section 90 of the Restatement (Second) of Contracts describes the doctrine of promissory estoppel:

> § 90. Promise Reasonably Inducing Action or Forbearance

> (1) A promise which the promisor should reasonably expect to induce action or forbearance on the part of the promisee or a third person and which does induce such action or forbearance is binding if injustice can be avoided only by enforcement of the promise. The remedy granted for breach may be limited as justice requires.

> *Questions:* Suppose that Katie Scothorn was married, and that after her grandfather promised her $2,000 she and her husband both quit work. Could Scothorn's husband successfully sue to enforce the promise as a traditional contract? Could he sue under Section 90? From an economic perspective, should he be allowed to sue for enforcement?

3. The court in *Ricketts* interprets the grandfather's promise as gratuitous; there was no *quid pro quo.* In other "gratuitous" promise cases the promisor may impose a precondition to performance. Satisfying the precondition is often interpreted as the equivalent to consideration. In

Hamer v. Sidway, 124 N.Y. 538, 27 N.E. 256, 257 (1891), an uncle promised $5000 to a nephew on condition that the nephew refrain from drinking, using tobacco, swearing, and playing cards or billiards for money until he reached 21 years of age. The nephew complied but, upon reaching the age of 21, was denied the money. The court held that "[i]n general a waiver of any legal right at the request of another party is a sufficient consideration for a promise."

Katie Scothorn did not waive a legal right at the request of another party; her grandfather's promise merely enabled her to quit her job. Agreeing to give up something of value (like using tobacco or playing cards for money) in exchange for money sounds like a wealth maximizing exchange.

Question: From an efficiency perspective, does the nephew's waiver of his legal rights distinguish *Hammer* from *Ricketts*?

4. Profesor Fuller, in Consideration and Form, 41 Colum.L.Rev. 799, 800 (1941), describes the justifications for requiring consideration and concludes that consideration provides "evidence of the existence and purport of the contract, in case of controversy."

Question: What evidence in *Ricketts* fulfilled the evidentiary function of consideration?

C. EFFICIENT BREACHES

Voluntary exchange generally reallocates resources from less to more valuable uses. When parties contract to exchange in the future, however, circumstances may change after contracting and before performance so that the values of competing uses alter and the contracted-for exchange becomes inefficient. In such cases, the promisor will be tempted to breach, not for opportunistic reasons, but because changed circumstances make performance inefficient. The cases in this section explore in various contexts how the law deals with changed circumstances and efficient breach.

1. EFFICIENT BREACHES

CAMPBELL SOUP CO. v. WENTZ

United States Court of Appeals, Third Circuit, 1948.
172 F.2d 80.

GOODRICH, CIRCUIT JUDGE.

These are appeals from judgments of the District Court denying equitable relief to the buyer under a contract for the sale of carrots. * * *

The transactions which raise the issues may be briefly summarized. On June 21, 1947, Campbell Soup Company (Campbell), a New Jersey corporation, entered into a written contract with George B. Wentz and Harry T. Wentz, who are Pennsylvania farmers, for delivery by the

Wentzes to Campbell of all the Chantenay red cored carrots to be grown on fifteen acres of the Wentz farm during the 1947 season. Where the contract was entered into does not appear. The contract provides, however, for delivery of the carrots at the Campbell plant in Camden, New Jersey. The prices specified in the contract ranged from $23 to $30 per ton according to the time of delivery. The contract price for January, 1948 was $30 a ton.

The Wentzes harvested approximately 100 tons of carrots from the fifteen acres covered by the contract. Early in January, 1948, they told a Campbell representative that they would not deliver their carrots at the contract price. The market price at that time was at least $90 per ton, and Chantenay red cored carrots were virtually unobtainable. The Wentzes then sold approximately 62 tons of their carrots to the defendant Lojeski, a neighboring farmer. Lojeski resold about 58 tons on the open market, approximately half to Campbell and the balance to other purchasers.

On January 9, 1948, Campbell, suspecting that Lojeski was selling it "contract carrots," refused to purchase any more, and instituted these suits against the Wentz brothers and Lojeski to enjoin further sale of the contract carrots to others, and to compel specific performance of the contract. The trial court denied equitable relief. We agree with the result reached, but on a different ground from that relied upon by the District Court.

* * *

We think that on the question of adequacy of the legal remedy the case is one appropriate for specific performance. It was expressly found that at the time of the trial it was "virtually impossible to obtain Chantenay carrots in the open market." This Chantenay carrot is one which the plaintiff uses in large quantities, furnishing the seed to the growers with whom it makes contracts. It was not claimed that in nutritive value it is any better than other types of carrots. Its blunt shape makes it easier to handle in processing. And its color and texture differ from other varieties. The color is brighter than other carrots. * * * It did appear that the plaintiff uses carrots in fifteen of its twenty-one soups. It also appeared that it uses these Chantenay carrots diced in some of them and that the appearance is uniform. The preservation of uniformity in appearance in a food article marketed throughout the country and sold under the manufacturer's name is a matter of considerable commercial significance and one which is properly considered in determining whether a substitute ingredient is just as good as the original.

* * *

Judged by the general standards applicable to determining the adequacy of the legal remedy we think that on this point the case is a proper one for equitable relief. There is considerable authority, old and new, showing liberality in the granting of an equitable remedy. We see no reason why a court should be reluctant to grant specific relief when it can be given without supervision of the court or other time-consuming processes against one who has deliberately broken his agreement. Here the goods of the special type contracted for were unavailable on the open market, the plaintiff had contracted for them long ahead in anticipation of its needs, and had built up a general reputation for its products as part of which reputation uniform appearance was important. We think if this were all that was involved in the case specific performance should have been granted.

* * *

Notes and Questions

1. The changed circumstances in *Campbell Soup* are typical fluctuations in market conditions that induce breach. From June 1947, when the contract to supply carrots was signed, to January of 1948, the price of Chantenay carrots more than tripled. In some cases, prices fall so much the buyer refuses to pay the contract price. Whether the changed circumstances create a windfall or a loss, the question is whether the parties' promises should be enforced. The opinion in *Campbell Soup* discusses one way promises may be enforced: by ordering specific performance. Specific performance, analogous to an injunction, would require that the Wentzes stop selling to Lojeski and others and sell all of their Chantenay carrots to Campbell Soup at the contract price of $30. The alternative remedy— ordering the Wentzes to pay damages—is discussed in the questions following *Eastern S.S. Lines, Inc.*, below.

Question: In the two following factual situations, is it efficient to order the Wentzes to perform their obligation under the contract and sell their carrots to Campbell Soup at $30 per ton?

(a) Campbell Soup has promised to pay $30 per ton for all the Wentzes' Chantenay carrots. After promising to deliver all of their carrots to Campbell Soup at that price, the Wentzes find a third party willing to pay $85 per ton.

(b) Campbell Soup has promised to pay $30 per ton for all the Wentzes' Chantenay carrots. The carrots are worth no more than $30 per ton to Campbell Soup because Campbell can substitute other types of carrots at that price. After promising to deliver all their carrots to Campbell Soup, the Wentzes find a third party willing to pay $85 per ton.

2. Apply the Coase Theorem to the problem of efficient breach.

Questions: Will failing to enforce the Wentzes' promise to sell the carrots lead to an inefficient allocation of carrots if there are no obstacles to bargaining among parties interested in the carrots? Will breaching the promise to sell carrots have any distributional or resource allocation effects if there are no obstacles to bargaining?

EASTERN S.S. LINES, INC. v. UNITED STATES

United States Court of Claims, 1953.
112 F.Supp. 167, 125 Ct.Cl. 422.

MADDEN, JUDGE.

* * *

The Steamship *Acadia,* owned by the plaintiff, had been for some time * * * chartered by the plaintiff to the United States Maritime Commission and used as an Army Transport. * * * [The charter required the government either to restore the *Acadia* to her original class and condition before returning her to the plaintiff, or to pay the plaintiff "the amount reasonably expended to place the Vessel in such class and condition, and to perform the work of restoration * * *."]

* * *

From October 16, 1942, to February 7, 1946, the *Acadia* was used by the Army Transport Service as a troop transport and hospital ship. After February 7, 1946, she was used for the carriage of dependents of service men from the United States, and the carriage of troops returning to the United States. Early in 1947 discussions began between the plaintiff and the United States Maritime Commission looking to the redelivery of the *Acadia* to the plaintiff. * * *

On May 16, 1947 the plaintiff received a telegram from a representative of the Maritime Commission offering, subject to the approval of the Commission, to pay the plaintiff $3,590,000 as a lump sum settlement of all the Government's redelivery obligations with respect to the *Acadia.* On May 19 the plaintiff by telegram advised that it was willing to accept that sum. The Maritime Commission then telegraphed that it would approve the settlement only if the plaintiff would agree to use the $3,590,000 for restoring the vessel. The plaintiff refused to so agree, saying that the sum was not sufficient to cover the actual costs of the restoration.

On July 3, 1947, the Commission telegraphed the plaintiff that it would redeliver the *Acadia,* unrestored, on July 23, 1947. The telegram further stated [that the government would only pay amounts actually expended in restoration, and would not in any case pay any amount in excess of the value of the *Acadia,* which it estimated to be $2,575,000.]

* * *

We think we may assume, from the general aura of the case, that the costs of restoration of the *Acadia* would be greatly in excess of the value of the restored ship. * * * We assume, therefore, in order to expose the question for examination, that after some $4,000,000 had been spent in restoring the ship, it would be worth $2,000,000. * * *

* * * *

We must determine, then, which of the parties, if either, has interpreted the charter agreement correctly. According to the plaintiff's interpretation the Government has now become obligated to pay it $4,000,000. Candor compels the plaintiff to say that it will not feel obliged to spend the $4,000,000 when it gets it, to restore the *Acadia*. Common sense and reality tell us that it will not so spend the money, since after the expenditures it would have only a $2,000,000 ship. The result would be that the Government would pay out $2,000,000 more than the plaintiff had lost by the Government's chartering and use of its ship. The extra $2,000,000 would not be a subsidy to get ships built or sailing. The *Acadia* would still rust at anchor. We decline to * * * produce such a result.

The Government's position is that it will not reimburse the plaintiff for the expenditure of $4,000,000 to produce a $2,000,000 ship. There is economic sense in that, and if the contract requires such an expenditure of public funds to produce such a result, the contract should never have been made. But the Government says that it will not pay even the $2,000,000, which is the value of what it took from the plaintiff when it used up the plaintiff's ship, unless the plaintiff in the first instance pays out $4,000,000 of its own funds, of which $2,000,000 will be completely wasted and will not be recovered. If the contract means that, it is a harsh and unconscionable contract which the plaintiff should not have agreed to and which the Government should be ashamed to insist upon.

We conclude that neither party is offering us a reasonable interpretation of the charter contract. We think that neither party anticipated what actually happened, *viz.* that the market for old ships on the one hand, and the market for labor and materials, on the other, would be such as to make the restoration of old ships a useless and wasteful expenditure of public funds.

The charter contained Clause D which * * * said that "in the event of the actual or constructive total loss of the Vessel as provided in Part II of this charter, the Charterer shall pay to the Owner * * * just compensation for the loss of the Vessel". * * * We assume that the loss provision of Clause D does not fit the situation which is before us. But when the fact is that, to restore the ship, either the Government or the owner or the two combined must wastefully and uselessly pay out twice as much as the ship will be worth when restored, the ship is worse than a total loss, and falls within the reason of the total loss clause of the charter. We have concluded that it is not covered by other provisions of the charter, as interpreted by the parties in their contentions before us. The truth is that what happened was not anticipated by the parties, and hence not expressly provided for in the charter. In that situation, we may assume that the parties would, if they had anticipated the event, have desired that the problem be fairly resolved. We think that the loss provision of Clause D solves it with perfect fairness. The plaintiff recovers what it has lost. The Government pays what its use of the vessel cost the plaintiff. No money, either of the plaintiff or the public is wasted.

* * *

The motions for summary judgment of both the Government and the plaintiff are denied. The case will be assigned to a commissioner of this court for trial upon the question of the value of the *Acadia*.

It is so ordered.

Notes and Questions

1. In *Eastern Steamship*, a contractual exchange that appeared efficient when the parties contracted became inefficient when circumstances changed. Requiring the promisor to perform his obligations under the contract would have imposed a burden on the promisor greater than the benefits the promisee would have realized from performance. Breaching became efficient.

A contract creates an entitlement to the contracted-for performance. In *Campbell Soup*, the Third Circuit declared that it might be appropriate under the facts of the case to protect the promisee's entitlement by requiring the promisor to perform. Such a rule gives the promisee a property right in performance; the promisor must perform unless he can convince the promisee to waive his rights. In *Eastern Steamship*, the court excused the defendant from performance where breach was efficient and instead required the defendant to pay damages, which were less than the cost of either performing or purchasing a substitute performance. The promisee's entitlement to contracted-for performance was protected by a liability rule rather than a property rule.

The damage remedy tests whether a breach is desirable from an efficiency viewpoint. In Patton v. Mid–Continent Systems, Inc., 841 F.2d 742, 750–51 (7th Cir. 1988), Mid–Continent awarded a franchise to Truck–O–Mat in breach of its promise to Patton that Patton would have exclusive right to that territory. Judge Posner described the relationship between damages and efficient breach as follows:

> [I]t is important to bear in mind certain fundamentals of contractual liability. First, liability for breach of contract is, prima facie, strict liability. That is, if the promisor fails to perform as agreed, he has broken his contract even though the failure may have been beyond his power to prevent and therefore in no way blameworthy. The reason is that contracts often contain an insurance component. The promisor promises in effect either to perform or to compensate the promisee for the cost of nonperformance; and one who voluntarily assumes a risk will not be relieved of the consequences if the risk materializes.
>
> Even if the breach is deliberate, it is not blameworthy. The promisor may simply have discovered that his performance is worth more to someone else. If so, efficiency is promoted by allowing him to break his promise, provided he makes good the promisee's actual losses. If he is forced to pay more than that, an efficient breach may be deterred, and the law doesn't want to bring about such a result. Suppose that by franchising Truck–O–Mat in the plaintiffs' territory,

Mid–Continent increased its own profits by $150,000 and inflicted damages of $75,000 on the plaintiffs. That would be an efficient breach. But if Mid–Continent had known that it would have to pay in addition to compensatory damages $100,000 in punitive damages, the breach would not have been worthwhile to it and efficiency would have suffered because the difference between Mid–Continent's profits of $150,000 and the plaintiffs' losses of $75,000 would (certainly after the plaintiffs were compensated) represent a net social gain.

2. Under the charter's terms, the plaintiff in *Eastern Steamship* was entitled to have the *Acadia* fully restored when it was returned. Even if the court was unwilling to require the defendant to perform under the contract, monetary damages of $4 million would have allowed the plaintiff to purchase substitute performance from another ship restorer. The court did not grant $4 million but held that the plaintiff was entitled to damages not exceeding the value of the *Acadia,* which was approximately $2 million.

Question: From an economic perspective, why should the court grant $2 million rather than $4 million damages?

3. The court excused the government from performing its contractual obligations in *Eastern Steamship* on the ground that restoring the vessel would not make "economic sense." The court went on to note that "if the contract requires such [wasteful] expenditure of public funds to produce such a result, the contract should never have been made."

But the contract *was* made, and by its terms required the government either to restore the ship or pay for its restoration. When declining to order specific performance of the contractual obligations, the court reasoned that when the government and Eastern Steamship Lines first arranged to charter the *Acadia* as a troopship, both parties expected the rental agreement (including the redelivery clause) to be in their self-interest. Neither party foresaw that circumstances would change by the time for performance. Strict compliance with the redelivery clause would require the government to incur renovation expenses of $4,000,000 to produce a ship with an approximate value of $2,000,000. When deciding that the government's obligation was only to pay the value of the *Acadia,* not the cost of restoration, the court reasoned that such a resolution would have been adopted by the parties *if only they had anticipated* that the market for ships might drop to the point where restoration was uneconomic.

The court's analysis in *Eastern Steamship* illustrates again how contract law provides efficient "default" contract terms for situations and circumstances the parties did not consider or address in their bargaining. A system of implied efficient contractual terms, resembling those the parties would have selected if they had only addressed the matter, reduces the costs of bargaining. Consider whether that role of contract law can explain the decision in Peevyhouse v. Garland Coal & Mining Co., below.

PEEVYHOUSE v. GARLAND COAL
& MINING COMPANY

Supreme Court of Oklahoma, 1962.
382 P.2d 109.

JACKSON, JUSTICE.

* * *

Briefly stated, the facts are as follows: plaintiffs owned a farm containing coal deposits, and in November, 1954, leased the premises to defendant for a period of five years for coal mining purposes. A "stripmining" operation was contemplated in which the coal would be taken from pits on the surface of the ground, instead of from underground mine shafts. In addition to the usual covenants found in a coal mining lease, defendant specifically agreed to perform certain restorative and remedial work at the end of the lease period. * * *

During the trial, it was stipulated that all covenants and agreements in the lease contract had been fully carried out by both parties, except the remedial work mentioned above; defendant conceded that this work had not been done.

Plaintiffs introduced expert testimony as to the amount and nature of the work to be done, and its estimated cost [about $29,000]. Over plaintiffs' objections, defendant thereafter introduced expert testimony as to the "diminution in value" of plaintiffs' farm resulting from the failure of defendant to render performance as agreed in the contract— that is, the difference between the present value of the farm, and what its value would have been if defendant had done what it agreed to do [about $300].

* * *

* * * It is highly unlikely that the ordinary property owner would agree to pay $29,000 (or its equivalent) for the construction of "improvements" upon his property that would increase its value only about ($300) three hundred dollars. The result is that we are called upon to apply principles of law theoretically based upon reason and reality to a situation which is basically unreasonable and unrealistic.

* * *

We * * * hold that where, in a coal mining lease, lessee agrees to perform certain remedial work on the premises concerned at the end of the lease period, and thereafter the contract is fully performed by both parties except that the remedial work is not done, the measure of damages in an action by lessor against lessee for damages for breach of contract is ordinarily the reasonable cost of performance of the work; however, where the contract provision breached was merely incidental to the main purpose in view, and where the economic benefit which would result to lessor by full performance of the work is grossly disproportionate to the cost of performance, the damages which lessor may recover are limited to the diminution in value resulting to the premises because of the non-performance.

* * *

Under the most liberal view of the evidence herein, the diminution in value resulting to the premises because of non-performance of the remedial work was $300.00.   * * *

* * *

We are of the opinion that the judgment of the trial court for plaintiffs should be, and it is hereby, modified and reduced to the sum of $300.00, and as so modified it is affirmed.

IRWIN, JUSTICE, dissenting.

* * *

Defendant admits that it failed to perform its obligations that it agreed and contracted to perform under the lease contract and there is nothing in the record which indicates that defendant could not perform its obligations.   Therefore, in my opinion defendant's breach of the contract was wilful and not in good faith.

Although the contract speaks for itself, there were several negotiations between the plaintiffs and defendant before the contract was executed.   Defendant admitted in the trial of the action, that plaintiffs insisted that the above provisions be included in the contract and that they would not agree to the coal mining lease unless the above provisions were included.

In consideration for the lease contract, plaintiffs were to receive a certain amount as royalty for the coal produced and marketed and in addition thereto their land was to be restored as provided in the contract.

Defendant received as consideration for the contract, its proportionate share of the coal produced and marketed and in addition thereto, the *right to use* plaintiffs' land in the furtherance of its mining operations.

The cost for performing the contract in question could have been reasonably approximated when the contract was negotiated and executed and there are no conditions now existing which could not have been reasonably anticipated by the parties.   Therefore, defendant had knowledge, when it prevailed upon the plaintiffs to execute the lease, that the cost of performance might be disproportionate to the value or benefits received by plaintiff for the performance.

* * *

In Great Western Oil & Gas Company v. Mitchell, we held:

"The law will not make a better contract for parties than they themselves have seen fit to enter into, or alter it for the benefit of one party and to the detriment of the others; the judicial function of a court of law is to enforce a contract as it is written."

* * *

In the instant action defendant has made no attempt to even substantially perform. The contract in question is not immoral, is not tainted with fraud, and was not entered into through mistake or accident and is not contrary to public policy. It is clear and unambiguous and the parties understood the terms thereof, and the approximate cost of fulfilling the obligations could have been approximately ascertained. There are no conditions existing now which could not have been reasonably anticipated when the contract was negotiated and executed. The defendant could have performed the contract if it desired. It has accepted and reaped the benefits of its contract and now urges that plaintiffs' benefits under the contract be denied. If plaintiffs' benefits are denied, such benefits would inure to the direct benefit of the defendant.

* * *

I therefore respectfully dissent to the opinion promulgated by a majority of my associates.

Notes and Questions

1. *Peevyhouse* presented another situation where performing the promise to restore the lessor's property to its original condition seemed inefficient. Restoration would have cost about $29,000 and added only $300 to the market value of the land. From a social perspective, it appears wealth maximizing to use the resources that would have been consumed in restoring the land for some other purpose. However, one difference from the preceding two cases is that in *Peevyhouse* no change in circumstances had arisen to alter the parties' original expectations regarding the benefits and costs of their bargain. If performance was inefficient, it had been inefficient from the very beginning.

> *Questions:* Is it fair to assume that at the time of contracting the parties believed that the exchange of rights to stripmine the land for a percentage of royalties plus restoration of the land increased the wealth of both parties? If the parties knew the promise to restore would not be enforced, how would the royalty amount likely have been changed? Could Peevyhouse possibly have valued the restoration at $29,000 when the market value of the restoration was only $300? If so, did the court's refusal to enforce the promise authorize an inefficient breach?

2. In *Eastern Steamship Lines*, the court justified its decision to excuse the government from its obligation to perform its promise and instead pay damages on the theory that "such a resolution would have been adopted by the parties *if only they had anticipated*" the change in circumstances that made performance inefficient (emphasis in original). That reasoning does not hold up under the facts of *Peevyhouse*. As Justice Irwin's dissent pointed out, the parties are likely to have anticipated the high cost of performance and still choose to contract for restoration of the land. The *Peevyhouse* opinion went beyond anticipating what terms rational parties would have negotiated had they foreseen a change in circum-

stances that would render performance economically wasteful, and implied that damages are always the best remedy for an efficient breach even where there is no evidence that the parties would have agreed to a damages provision had they negotiated the matter.

2. IMPRACTICABILITY AND IMPOSSIBILITY OF PERFORMANCE

In the previous efficient breach cases, it was not economical for one of the parties to perform its promise. Those cases suggest that breach sometimes is justified on efficiency grounds, particularly when there is a change in circumstances the parties could not have predicted or avoided.

The Uniform Commercial Code § 2–615 recognizes the importance of changed circumstances as evidence that one party should be excused from its contractual performance. Section 2–615 provides that "[d]elay in delivery or non-delivery in whole or in part by a seller * * * is not a breach of his duty under a contract for sale if performance as agreed has been made impracticable by the occurrence of a contingency the non-occurrence of which was a basic assumption on which the contract was made." If § 2–615 is interpreted to promote allocative efficiency, should the court excuse the seller's promise to deliver molasses in Canadian Industrial Alcohol Co. v. Dunbar Molasses Co.?

CANADIAN INDUSTRIAL ALCOHOL CO. v. DUNBAR MOLASSES CO.

Court of Appeals of New York, 1932.
258 N.Y. 194, 179 N.E. 383.

CARDOZO, C.J.

A buyer sues a seller for breach of an executory contract of purchase and sale.

The subject matter of the contract was "approximately 1,500,000 wine gallons Refined Blackstrap [molasses] of the usual run from the National Sugar Refinery, Yonkers, N.Y., to test around 60% sugars."

The order was given and accepted December 27, 1927, but shipments of the molasses were to begin after April 1, 1928, and were to be spread out during the warm weather.

After April 1, 1928, the defendant made delivery from time to time of 344,083 gallons. Upon its failure to deliver more, the plaintiff brought this action for the recovery of damages. The defendant takes the ground that, by an implied term of the contract, the duty to deliver was conditioned upon the production by the National Sugar Refinery at Yonkers of molasses sufficient in quantity to fill the plaintiff's order. The fact is that the output of the refinery, while the contract was in force, was 485,848 gallons, much less than its capacity, of which amount 344,083 gallons were allotted to the defendant and shipped to the defendant's customer. The argument for the defendant is that its own duty to deliver was proportionate to the refinery's willingness to supply, and that the duty was discharged when the output was reduced.

The contract, read in the light of the circumstances existing at its making, or more accurately in the light of any such circumstances apparent from this record, does not keep the defendant's duty within boundaries so narrow. We may assume, in the defendant's favor, that there would have been a discharge of its duty to deliver if the refinery had been destroyed, or if the output had been curtailed by the failure of the sugar crop, or by the ravages of war, or conceivably in some circumstances by unavoidable strikes. We may even assume that a like result would have followed if the plaintiff had bargained not merely for a quantity of molasses to be supplied from a particular refinery, but for molasses to be supplied in accordance with a particular contract between the defendant and the refiner, and if thereafter such contract had been broken without fault on the defendant's part. * * *

* * * The defendant asks us to assume that a manufacturer, having made a contract with a middleman for a stock of molasses to be procured from a particular refinery, would expect the contract to lapse whenever the refiner chose to diminish his production, and this in the face of the middleman's omission to do anything to charge the refiner with a duty to continue. Business could not be transacted with security or smoothness if a presumption so unreasonable were at the root of its engagements. There is nothing to show that the defendant would have been unable by a timely contract with the refinery to have assured itself of a supply sufficient for its needs. There is nothing to show that the plaintiff, in giving the order for the molasses, was informed by the defendant that such a contract had not been made, or that performance would be contingent upon obtaining one thereafter. If the plaintiff had been so informed, it would very likely have preferred to deal with the refinery directly, instead of dealing with a middleman. The defendant does not even show that it tried to get a contract from the refinery during the months that intervened between the acceptance of the plaintiff's order and the time when shipments were begun. It has wholly failed to relieve itself of the imputation of contributory fault. So far as the record shows, it put its faith in the mere chance that the output of the refinery would be the same from year to year, and finding its faith vain, it tells us that its customer must have expected to take a chance as great. We see no reason for importing into the bargain this aleatory element. The defendant is in no better position than a factor who undertakes in his own name to sell for future delivery a special grade of merchandise to be manufactured by a special mill. The duty will be discharged if the mill is destroyed before delivery is due. The duty will subsist if the output is reduced because times turn out to be hard and labor charges high.

* * *

The judgment [entered on a jury verdict in favor of the plaintiff] should be affirmed, with costs.

Notes and Questions

1. The facts of *Dunbar Molasses* appeared to meet the requirements of U.C.C. § 2–615. Both the defendant middleman and the plaintiff Canadian Industrial Alcohol Company assumed that the National Sugar Refinery would continue its high level of production; that assumption was basic to the contract; and the refinery's reduced production made it impracticable to supply molasses from that refinery. Despite the fundamental change in conditions, Justice Cardozo found that the middleman had breached his promise to supply molasses.

Questions: What was the legal basis for Cardozo's conclusion? Was it sound from an efficiency perspective?

2. Cardozo distinguished *Dunbar Molasses* from situations where the refinery was destroyed, the crop of sugar (the basic component of molasses) failed, or war prevented the seller from supplying his customer. Unlike those situations, the molasses middleman in *Dunbar Molassas* might have prevented the harm to the plaintiff from breach by contracting with the refinery to ensure the supply.

The logic of giving promisors incentive to make reasonable efforts to avoid breach and attendant damage to promisees from nonperformance should be familiar from the study of tort law. As is true in the economic analysis of torts, in some cases the promisee might also be able to avoid the damage. Excusing Dunbar Molasses from its duty to supply molasses to its customer places the burden of any loss on the customer and gives the customer incentive to avoid potential damage from contract breach.

Questions: Which party was in the best position to avoid the damages in *Dunbar Molasses?* Which party could avoid the losses resulting from nonperformance at lower cost?

3. The 1920's were years of prosperity and economic growth in the United States. There were two economic recessions, but they have been described as "so mild that many if not most of those who lived and worked at the time were unaware that they had occurred." Friedman and Schwartz, A Monetary History of the United States, 296 (1963). If the sugar refining business was as prosperous as the rest of the country during the 1920's, the middleman might not have foreseen that the National Sugar Refinery would ever operate at less than full capacity; it might have been reasonable to assume that there would be plenty of molasses for all buyers.

Question: Should the fact that the risk was not reasonably foreseeable relieve the middleman of his duty to supply molasses to the customer?

4. Justice Cardozo would not excuse the middleman from his contractual promise to supply molasses in the event that "output is reduced because times turn out to be hard and labor charges high." Suppose such an event raised the cost of molasses to the middleman so high that he could no longer profitably fulfill his promise to his customer.

Questions: Should an increase in labor charges beyond either of the parties' control relieve the middleman of his obligation? Should it make any difference if labor costs rose much higher than could reasonably have been foreseen by either party?

TRANSATLANTIC FINANCING CORPORATION
v. UNITED STATES

United States Court of Appeals District of Columbia Circuit, 1966.
363 F.2d 312.

J. SKELLY WRIGHT, CIRCUIT JUDGE:

This appeal involves a voyage charter between Transatlantic Financing Corporation, operator of the SS CHRISTOS, and the United States covering carriage of a full cargo of wheat from a United States Gulf port to a safe port in Iran. The District Court dismissed a libel filed by Transatlantic against the United States for costs attributable to the ship's diversion from the normal sea route caused by the closing of the Suez Canal. We affirm.

On July 26, 1956, the Government of Egypt nationalized the Suez Canal Company and took over operation of the Canal. On October 2, 1956, during the international crisis which resulted from the seizure, the voyage charter in suit was executed between representatives of Transatlantic and the United States. The charter indicated the termini of the voyage but not the route. On October 27, 1956, the SS CHRISTOS sailed from Galveston for Bandar Shapur, Iran, on a course which would have taken her through Gibraltar and the Suez Canal. On October 29, 1956, Israel invaded Egypt. On October 31, 1956, Great Britain and France invaded the Suez Canal Zone. On November 2, 1956, the Egyptian Government obstructed the Suez Canal with sunken vessels and closed it to traffic.

On or about November 7, 1956, Beckmann, representing Transatlantic, contacted Potosky, an employee of the United States Department of Agriculture, who appellant concedes was unauthorized to bind the Government, requesting instructions concerning disposition of the cargo and seeking an agreement for payment of additional compensation for a voyage around the Cape of Good Hope. Potosky advised Beckmann that Transatlantic was expected to perform the charter according to its terms, that he did not believe Transatlantic was entitled to additional compensation for a voyage around the Cape, but that Transatlantic was free to file such a claim. Following this discussion, the CHRISTOS changed course for the Cape of Good Hope and eventually arrived in Bandar Shapur on December 30, 1956.

Transatlantic's claim is based on the following train of argument. The charter was a contract for a voyage from a Gulf port to Iran. Admiralty principles and practices, especially stemming from the doctrine of deviation, require us to imply into the contract the term that the voyage was to be performed by the "usual and customary" route. The usual and customary route from Texas to Iran was, at the time of contract, via Suez, so the contract was for a voyage from Texas to Iran via Suez. When Suez was closed this contract became impossible to perform. Consequently, appellant's argument continues, when Transatlantic delivered the cargo by going around the Cape of Good Hope, in compliance with the Government's demand under claim of right, it conferred a benefit upon the United States for which it should be paid * * *.

The doctrine of impossibility of performance has gradually been freed from the earlier fictional and unrealistic strictures of such tests as the "implied term" and the parties' "contemplation." It is now recognized that "A thing is impossible in legal contemplation when it is not practicable; and a thing is impracticable when it can only be done at an excessive and unreasonable cost." The doctrine ultimately represents the ever-shifting line, drawn by courts hopefully responsive to commercial practices and mores, at which the community's interest in having contracts enforced according to their terms is outweighed by the commercial senselessness of requiring performance. When the issue is raised, the court is asked to construct a condition of performance based on the changed circumstances, a process which involves at least three reasonably definable steps. First, a contingency—something unexpected—must have occurred. Second, the risk of the unexpected occurrence must not have been allocated either by agreement or by custom. Finally, occurrence of the contingency must have rendered performance commercially impracticable. Unless the court finds these three requirements satisfied, the plea of impossibility must fail.

The first requirement was met here. It seems reasonable, where no route is mentioned in a contract, to assume the parties expected performance by the usual and customary route at the time of contract. Since the usual and customary route from Texas to Iran at the time of contract was through Suez, closure of the Canal made impossible the expected method of performance. But this unexpected development raises rather than resolves the impossibility issue, which turns additionally on whether the risk of the contingency's occurrence had been allocated and, if not, whether performance by alternative routes was rendered impracticable.

Proof that the risk of a contingency's occurrence has been allocated may be expressed in or implied from the agreement. Such proof may also be found in the surrounding circumstances, including custom and usages of the trade. * * *

If anything, the circumstances surrounding this contract indicate that the risk of the Canal's closure may be deemed to have been allocated to Transatlantic. We know or may safely assume that the parties were aware, as were most commercial men with interests affected by the Suez situation, that the Canal might become a dangerous area. No doubt the tension affected freight rates, and it is arguable that the risk of closure became part of the dickered terms. We do not deem the risk of closure so allocated, however. Foreseeability or even recognition of a risk does not necessarily prove its allocation. Parties to a contract are not always able to provide for all the possibilities of which they are aware, sometimes because they cannot agree, often simply because they are too busy. Moreover, that some abnormal risk was contemplated is probative but does not necessarily establish an allocation of the risk of the contingency which actually occurs. In this case, for example, nationalization by Egypt of the Canal Corporation and formation of the Suez Users Group did not necessarily indicate that the Canal would be blocked even if a confrontation resulted. The surrounding circumstances do indicate, however, a willingness by Transatlantic to assume abnormal risks, and this fact should legitimately cause us to judge the impracticability of performance by an alternative route in stricter terms than we would were the contingency unforeseen.

We turn then to the question whether occurrence of the contingency rendered performance commercially impracticable under the circumstances of this case. The goods shipped were not subject to harm from the longer, less temperate Southern route. The vessel and crew were fit to proceed around the Cape. Transatlantic was no less able than the United States to purchase insurance to cover the contingency's occurrence. If anything, it is more reasonable to expect owner-operators of vessels to insure against the hazards of war. They are in the best position to calculate the cost of performance by alternative routes (and therefore to estimate the amount of insurance required), and are undoubtedly sensitive to international troubles which uniquely affect the demand for and cost of their services. The only factor operating here in appellant's favor is the added expense, allegedly $43,972.00 above and beyond the contract price of $305,842.92, of extending a 10,000 mile voyage by approximately 3,000 miles. While it may be an overstatement to say that increased cost and difficulty of performance never constitute impracticability, to justify relief there must be more of a variation between expected cost and the cost of performing by an available alternative than is present in this case, where the promisor can legitimately be presumed to have accepted some degree of abnormal risk, and where impracticability is urged on the basis of added expense alone.

We conclude, therefore, as have most other courts considering related issues arising out of the Suez closure, that performance of this contract was not rendered legally impossible. * * *

Affirmed.

Notes and Questions

1. In *Transatlantic*, neither party reasonably could have avoided the Canal closing that prevented performance according to the (implied) terms of the contract. Unlike *Dunbar Molasses*, it would be fruitless to create an incentive for either party to attempt to prevent performance from becoming impossible.

The monetary losses associated with contract breach, however, are only one type of cost associated with nonperformance. The uncertainty or "risk" created by the *possibility* of nonperformance is also a burden imposed on contracting parties. Recall the discussion of risk in Chapter 3.

Risk must impose real costs, otherwise people and businesses would be unwilling to incur the expense of buying insurance or self-insuring by maintaining larger savings or higher inventories. If the burden of risk could be minimized by shifting uncertainty to the least risk-averse party, both parties could arrange the deal to make themselves better off. Thus society could be made better off by minimizing the costs imposed by the risk of breach even if it could not avoid the breach.

Question: In impossibility cases like *Transatlantic,* neither party can reasonably avoid the contingency that makes performance impossible and causes breach. Can either party take steps to minimize the costs associated with the risk of impossibility?

2. If a contract explicitly allocates the risk of breach to one party, economics presumes that letting that party bear the uncertainty produced by the possibility of breach is efficient. From a contract law perspective, that means enforcing explicit contract terms allocating risks to one party rather than the other.

Question: Why is it efficient to enforce contract terms that explicitly allocate risk?

3. Even where a contract does not allocate the risk of breach explicitly, it may do so implicitly. Often contractual terms are inferred from the customary practice in the industry. Consider how admiralty principles and practices required the court in *Transatlantic* to "imply into the contract" the term that the voyage was to be performed through the Suez Canal.

Questions: Does the expense of bargaining over contract terms provide an economic justification for "implying" terms into a contract? What economic justification is there for implying an allocation of risk only when no explicit allocation can be found?

4. When a contract fails to allocate losses from breach due to impossibility either explicitly or implicitly, the court must look beyond the contract to determine how the parties would have allocated those losses had they bothered to do so. First, the court will want to maintain incentives to minimize losses from nonperformance by imposing those losses on the party in the best position to avoid nonperformance. When neither party can efficiently prevent the contingency which rendered performance impossible, the court should try to impose the loss on the party who can best bear the uncertainty of the risk of impossibility, the *best risk bearer* or *best insurer.* The best insurer will be the party in the best position to appraise the risk (by determining the probability that disastrous contingencies will arise and the losses that will result) and to act on that determination (perhaps by buying insurance). The above analysis closely resembles the *best cost avoider* analysis from previous chapters, except that its purpose here is to minimize the harm associated with the uncertainty rather than with the monetary losses.

Question: Which party did Judge Wright believe was the better insurer in *Transatlantic?*

5. It was obviously too late for either party in *Transatlantic* to minimize the harm associated with the risk of the Suez Canal's closure in response to the incentives created by the court's holding. As precedent, however, the case gives guidance concerning how courts will allocate risks. Future parties might respond by purchasing insurance or bargaining over explicit contract terms that would avoid the court's approach. The court's decision provides a starting point for bargaining, so the decision itself reduces uncertainty.

6. Robert Birmingham, in A Second Look at the Suez Canal Cases: Excuse for Nonperformance of Contractual Obligations in the Light of Economic Theory, 20 Hastings L.J. 1393 (1969), suggested that courts do more than allocate risks when they determine whether a promise should be discharged in an impossibility or impracticability case. The Suez Canal's closure resulted in extra profits for carriers charging for shipments all the way around the Cape of Good Hope, and merchants selling commodities from stocks acquired before the canal's closing greatly increased prices. Birmingham recommended a more complex analysis of the parties' economic status following the unexpected contingency. That exploration is not solely of distributional or equitable interest. If one party benefits indirectly from an unforeseen contingency, it has no reason to insure against the risk of that contingency and the best insurer analysis is less appropriate.

PHELPS v. SCHOOL DIST. NO. 109, WAYNE COUNTY

Supreme Court of Illinois, 1922.
302 Ill. 193, 134 N.E. 312.

FARMER, J.

This is an appeal, on a certificate of importance, from a judgment of the Appellate Court affirming a judgment of the circuit court for $100 in favor of appellee. Appellee is a school-teacher and was regularly employed by appellant to teach school at a salary of $50 per month. It is stipulated that during 2 months of the period for which she was employed the school was closed by order of the state board of health on account of the influenza epidemic; that she was ready and willing to teach during all the time, and did teach 14 days of said two months, and regularly made and filed schedules as provided by law. She claimed pay for the entire 2 months the school was closed. Appellant refused payment and tendered her $33 for the 14 days she actually taught. She refused to accept it and sued for $100—the salary for the 2 months. * * *

* * *

* * * Both parties are presumed to have known when the contract was made that the state board of health had authority to order the school to be closed, if an epidemic occurred which rendered such action necessary for the protection of the lives and health of the people of the community. Neither one of them could know whether such a contingency would arise during the period covered by the contract. If

appellant had desired to be relieved of liability in the event such a contingency arose and cause the school to be closed, it could have accomplished that result by so stipulating in the contract. No such qualification was placed in the contract, but it was an unconditional contract of employment for a definite period at $50 per month. It was no fault of appellee that the school was closed a portion of the time she was employed to teach, neither was it the fault of appellant. Some one was required to suffer loss resulting from an unforeseen contingency which caused the school to be closed, and the rule is that the loss will rest on the party who has contracted to bear it, for if he did not intend to bear it he should have stipulated against it. If the performance of the contract had been legally impossible, it would have been unenforceable, but its performance was not legally impossible. When made, the contract was lawful and valid. Its performance was rendered impossible by the subsequent happening of a contingency, which could not be foreseen or known when the contract was made, and the rule is that, if one of the parties desires not to be bound in the event of such a contingency, he must so provide in the contract.

The general doctrine is well settled that, when a party contracts to do a thing without qualification, performance is not excused because by inevitable accident or other contingency not foreseen it becomes impossible for him to do that which he agreed to do. This rule, so far as we are informed, has been universally applied to cases where a schoolhouse was destroyed by fire during the period for which the teacher was employed. Unless it was otherwise stipulated in the contract, the district was not relieved from liability to pay the teacher. Another illustration of the application of the rule is that, in absence of a provision in the lease of a building to the contrary, the destruction of the building does not discharge the tenant from liability to pay the rent for the full term. * * * It works no hardship on any one to require school authorities to insert in the contract of employment a provision exempting them from liability in the event of the school being closed on account of a contagious epidemic. As said by the Supreme Court of Ohio, courts will not insert by construction, for the benefit of one of the parties, a condition which they have omitted from their own contract.

The judgment is affirmed.

Notes and Questions

1. The court in *Phelps* intended that parties not wanting to be bound to their promises in the event of the occurrence of some contingency would so provide in the contract. Economists often view contract law as supplying contractual terms that the parties would have agreed on, had they confronted the contingencies that ultimately occurred. If one assumes that parties are willing to decide what terms maximize the value of the transaction to them, it would be sensible to enforce all of the terms to which they agreed. When a term is omitted, such as what to do if one of the promises is impossible to perform or the purpose of the contract is frustrated, as it was in *Phelps,* the role of contract law is to supply the omitted term. The

court in *Phelps* would simply force the party who is unwilling to perform to bear the risk.

> *Questions:* How are the parties to the contract in *Phelps* likely to have allocated the risk of school closure? Is the court's approach likely to lead to an efficient allocation of risk in most cases?

2. In their influential article, Impossibility and Related Doctrines in Contract Law, 6 J. Legal Stud. 83 (1977), Posner and Rosenfield offer the following hypothetical. The plaintiff is a manufacturer of printing machinery who has promised a printer that he will build a printing machine to the printer's unique and idiosyncratic specifications and install it on the printer's premises. After the machine is built, but before installation, a fire destroys the printer's plant, frustrating the purposes of the contract. The printer declines to accept delivery of the machine and refuses to pay for it. The machine is of no use to anyone else and the manufacturer sues for the contract price. From a legal perspective, the issue is whether the promise of the printer should be discharged.

> *Question:* From an economic perspective, which party should be required to bear the risk of a contingency that makes acceptance impossible?

D. EFFICIENT REMEDIES

1. THE FULL COMPENSATION TEST FOR EFFICIENT BREACH

REDGRAVE v. BOSTON SYMPHONY ORCHESTRA

United States District Court, District of Massachusetts, 1985.
602 F.Supp. 1189.

KEETON, DISTRICT JUDGE.

Plaintiffs, Vanessa Redgrave (Redgrave) and Vanessa Redgrave Enterprises, Ltd., sued the Boston Symphony Orchestra, Inc. (BSO) for breach of contract * * *. All the asserted claims arose from BSO's cancellation of its performances of Oedipus Rex in Boston and New York, in which Vanessa Redgrave was scheduled to appear as narrator. Plaintiffs contend that BSO cancelled the performances in retaliation for Redgrave's public expressions on political issues. BSO argues primarily that the performances were cancelled because of a concern for physical security and a decision that risks of disruption would impair the artistic integrity of the performances. * * *

* * *

The law does not forbid an entity organized to promote a form of art—or those who function as its managerial agents—from taking account of recognized differences among its members and patrons regarding controversial political issues. For example, it is not illegal for a private entity to make a choice not to contract with an artist for a performance if its agents believe that the artist's appearance under their sponsorship would be interpreted by others as in some degree a political statement. Thus, BSO was entirely free not to make a contract with Redgrave for such reasons even though its agents considered her a superb actress and exceptionally qualified to perform as narrator in Oedipus Rex.

Once BSO contracted for Redgrave to appear in the production of Oedipus Rex, BSO gave up part of its freedom. By contracting with a party, however, an entity does not entirely surrender all of its freedom to act. * * * The freedom that BSO retained may even include freedom to break the contract (subjecting itself of course to liability for damages under the law) for any reason other than one specially forbidden by the law (for example, discrimination on grounds of sex or race). The suggested freedom to break a contract and suffer liability only for the legally recognized damages is within the scope of the idea often referred to as Holmes' bad man theory of contract law—that one who is willing to pay the penalty of such damages as the law assesses is free to break the contract and pay. As to contracts not specifically enforceable in equity, the law provides no other remedy. Even if it is inappropriate to say that one has a legal "right" to break the contract and pay the assessed damages, legal redress is limited to those damages. Of course, if this point of view is accepted, one must determine the critical question as to the measure of damages under the law. * * *

* * *

* * * Under the contract, plaintiffs were to receive a performance fee of $31,000, but were responsible for paying all travel expenses incidental to the engagement. The parties have stipulated that the net amount after expenses would have been $27,500. * * *

* * *

Judgment will be entered for plaintiffs, on the breach of contract claim, in the amount of $27,500 * * *.

* * *

Notes and Questions

1. Ms. Redgrave was an outspoken supporter of the Palestine Liberation Organization. See 602 F.Supp. at 1192. Following the announcement of Ms. Redgrave's planned performance, the Orchestra received anonymous calls from individuals threatening the BSO with "severe adverse consequences" if it did not cancel the performance. See 557 F.Supp. 230, 233.

2. The discussion of Holmes' "bad man" theory of contract law in *Redgrave* makes explicit what was implicit in *Peevyhouse;* contract law normally does not bind contracting parties to perform their promised obligations. Rather, the law requires that parties perform or pay damages. Using the analysis of property, liability, and inalienability rules developed in Chapter 2, contract law protects the promisee's entitlement to performance with a liability rule.

It need not be so. Another possibility would be to give the beneficiaries of contractual promises an absolute right to the contracted-for performance, to be given up only in voluntary exchange. A promisee's rights then would be protected by a property rather than a liability rule. In certain cases, contract rights are enforced through property rules rather than liability rules. The choice between liability (monetary damages) and property (specific performance) remedies for contract breach is explored in the notes and questions following Madariaga v. Morris, below.

> *Questions:* If the Boston Symphony Orchestra was required to permit Ms. Redgrave to perform unless she voluntarily agreed not to, what is the minimum price Ms. Redgrave would demand to give up her right to perform? What maximum price might she demand? What are the economic advantages of enforcing Ms. Redgrave's right with damages rather than specific performance? What are the disadvantages of a liability rule?

3. Applying the Pareto criteria to any reallocation of resources requires a *status quo,* an initial allocation from which subsequent reallocations can be made and evaluated. Once the court determines that there is a contract, the contractual rights establish the status quo. That status quo is the baseline to which reallocations resulting from breach are compared. Pareto superior reallocations are promoted when the legal remedy for breach encourages only those breaches leaving at least one party better off and no one worse off. Such breaches are described as *efficient breaches.* From a Kaldor–Hicks perspective, efficient breaches are those creating sufficient benefits that the promisor could breach, fully compensate the promisee, and still be better off breaching than performing.

In *Redgrave,* the BSO was obliged to pay $31,000 and Redgrave was obliged to perform. The adverse publicity surrounding Redgrave changed the benefits each party expected to obtain from the contract and the BSO determined it was no longer in its interest to have Redgrave appear with the orchestra. If the BSO was so eager to cancel Redgrave's appearance that it was willing to compensate Redgrave fully for her losses, cancelling the performance would make at least one party better off while leaving no one worse off, and breach would be efficient.

As the court noted in *Redgrave,* the critical question is what amount of damages would compensate Redgrave. Full compensation means leaving the injured party no worse off than if the contract was performed. While Vanessa Redgrave lost her $31,000 performance fee when her performance was cancelled, she saved $3,500 in travel expenses, making her worse off by a net of $27,500 as a result of the breach. After this case, promisors in the position of the Boston Symphony Orchestra know they will be required to pay full compensation if they breach.

> *Questions:* Will requiring promisors to pay full compensation always deter them from breaching their promises? Under what circumstances will promisors breach despite the full compensation requirement? In circumstances like *Redgrave,* will full compensation encourage only efficient breaches?

4. Suppose that Vanessa Redgrave's future earning potential was damaged as a result of the Boston Symphony Orchestra's cancelling her performance.

Question: Would it be efficient to include in the damages an estimate of the present value of the decline in Redgrave's future income? Consider both the incentives for efficient breach as well as the possible costs of error in calculating damages.

5. Suppose Ms. Redgrave had already incurred the $3,500 in travel expenses before the BSO cancelled her performance.

Question: Would the full compensation test require payment of $31,000 to provide incentive for efficient breaches?

2. EXPECTATION, RESTITUTION, AND RELIANCE DAMAGES

The full compensation measure of damages described in the notes and questions following *Redgrave* is more familiar to students of contract law as the *expectation* measure of damages. The idea is to make the promisee as well off as the promisee had expected to be after the promise was performed, considering both the benefits and the burdens associated with performance. With respect to expectation damages, the Restatement (Second) of Contracts provides:

§ 361. MEASURE OF DAMAGES IN GENERAL

Subject to the limitations stated in §§ 364–367, the injured party has a right to damages based on his expectation interest as measured by

(a) the loss in the value to him of the other party's performance caused by its failure or deficiency, plus

(b) any other loss, including incidental or consequential loss, caused by the breach, less

(c) any costs or other loss that he has avoided by not having to perform.

Does this measure of damages encourage only efficient breaches in cases like Neri v. Retail Marine Corp.?

NERI v. RETAIL MARINE CORPORATION

Court of Appeals of New York, 1972.
30 N.Y.2d 393, 334 N.Y.S.2d 165, 285 N.E.2d 311.

GIBSON, JUDGE.

* * *

The plaintiffs contracted to purchase from defendant a new boat of a specified model for the price of $12,587.40, against which they made a deposit of $40. They shortly increased the deposit to $4,250 in consideration of the defendant dealer's agreement to arrange with the manufacturer for immediate delivery on the basis of "a firm sale", instead of the delivery within approximately four to six weeks as originally specified. Some six days after the date of the contract plaintiffs' lawyer sent to defendant a letter rescinding the sales contract for the reason that plaintiff Neri was about to undergo hospitalization and surgery, in consequence of which, according to the letter, it would be "impossible for Mr. Neri to make any payments". The boat had already been ordered from the manufacturer and was delivered to defendant at or before the time the attorney's letter was received. Defendant declined to refund plaintiffs' deposit and this action to recover it was commenced. Defendant counterclaimed, alleging plaintiff's breach of the contract and defendant's resultant damage in the amount of $4,250, for which sum defendant demanded judgment. * * *

Upon the trial so directed, it was shown that the boat ordered and received by defendant in accordance with plaintiff's contract of purchase was sold some four months later to another buyer for the same price as that negotiated with plaintiffs. From this proof the plaintiffs argue that defendant's loss on its contract was recouped, while defendant argues that but for plaintiffs' default, it would have sold two boats and have earned two profits instead of one. Defendant proved, without contradiction, that its profit on the sale under the contract in suit would have been $2,579 and that during the period the boat remained unsold incidental expenses aggregating $674 for storage, upkeep, finance charges and insurance were incurred. Additionally, defendant proved and sought to recover attorneys's fees of $1,250.

The trial court found "untenable" defendant's claim for loss of profit, inasmuch as the boat was later sold for the same price that plaintiffs had contracted to pay; found, too, that defendant had failed to prove any incidental damages * * * .

The issue is governed in the first instance by § 2–718 of the Uniform Commercial Code which provides, among other things, that the buyer, despite his breach, may have restitution of the amount by which his payment exceeds * * * the seller['s] * * * right to recover damages under the provisions of [the Uniform Commercial Code].

Among [those provision] are those to be found in § 2–708, which the courts below did not apply. Subsection (1) of that section provides that "the measure of damages for non-acceptance or repudiation by the buyer is the difference between the market price at the time and place for tender and the unpaid contract price together with any incidental damages provided in this Article (§ 2–710), but less expenses saved in consequence of the buyer's breach." However, this provision is made expressly subject to subsection (2), providing: "(2) If the measure of damages provided in subsection (1) is inadequate to put the seller in as good a position as performance would have done then the measure of damages is the profit (including reasonable overhead) which the seller would have made from full performance by the buyer, together with any incidental damages provided in this Article (§ 2–710), due allowance for costs reasonably incurred and due credit for payments or proceeds of resale."

* * *

It is evident, first, that this retail seller is entitled to its profit and, second, that the last sentence of subsection (2), as hereinbefore quoted, referring to "due credit for payments or proceeds of resale" is inapplicable to this retail sales contract. Closely parallel to the factual situation now before us is that hypothesized by Dean Hawkland as illustrative of the operation of the rules: "Thus, if a private party agrees to sell his automobile to a buyer for $2000, a breach by the buyer would cause the seller no loss (except incidental damages, i.e., expense of a new sale) if the seller was able to sell the automobile to another buyer for $2000. But the situation is different with dealers having an unlimited supply of standard-priced goods. Thus, if an automobile dealer agrees to sell a car to a buyer at the standard price of $2000, a breach by the buyer injures the dealer, even though he is able to sell the automobile to another for $2000. If the dealer has an inexhaustible supply of cars, the resale to replace the breaching buyer costs the dealer a sale, because, had the breaching buyer performed, the dealer would have made two sales instead of one. The buyer's breach, in such a case, depletes the dealer's sales to the extent of one, and the measure of damages should be the dealer's profit on one sale. § 2-708 recognizes this, and it rejects the rule developed under the Uniform Sales Act by many courts that the profit cannot be recovered in this case." (Hawkland, Sales and Bulk Sales [1958 ed.], pp. 153–154.)

The record which in this case establishes defendant's entitlement to damages in the amount of its prospective profit, at the same time confirms defendant's cognate right to "any incidental damages provided in this Article (§ 2-710)" (Uniform Commercial Code, § 2-708, subsection [2]). From the language employed it is too clear to require discussion that the seller's right to recover loss of profits is not exclusive and that he may recoup his "incidental" expenses as well.
* * *

The trial court correctly denied defendant's claim for recovery of attorney's fees incurred by it in this action. * * *

It follows that plaintiffs are entitled to restitution of the sum of $4,250 paid by them on account of the contract price less an offset to defendant in the amount of $3,253 on account of its lost profit of $2.579 and its incidental damages of $674.

* * *

Notes and Questions

1. Calculating damages based on the promisee's expectations protects an interest some describe as the promisee's "benefit of the bargain." A right to the benefit of the bargain is the economic equivalent of accepting the allocation of rights in the contract as the status quo from which reallocations are evaluated.

Questions: Plaintiff Anthony Neri breached his promise to purchase a boat when his financial circumstances changed as a result of an illness requiring surgery. What loss did the seller in *Neri* suffer as a result of

Neri's breach? Accepting Neri's assertions as true, is it efficient to force the hospitalized Neri to pay damages to the boat seller, who was able to sell the boat to someone else?

2. In addition to its lost profit, the court awarded Retail Marine $674 for incidental damages: storage, upkeep, and finance charges.

Question: Are incidental damages necessary to ensure that promisors have incentive to breach only when breach is efficient?

3. The court in *Neri* interprets § 2–710 of the Uniform Commercial Code as allowing recovery of lost profits even though the seller has resold the same article to another buyer for the same price. Judge Gibson accepts the distinction between the facts of *Neri* and a case where a buyer breaches his contract to buy a car from a private party and the seller subsequently sells the car for the same price to another buyer. In the automobile case, the buyer would be liable only for the costs associated with the resale, not the lost profits from the thwarted first contract.

Questions: What is the economic rationale for different measures of damages in these two cases? Are the facts of *Redgrave* more like the automobile case or the boat case?

4. The previous questions have focused attention on whether the damage remedy provides incentives to breach only when it is efficient to do so. A related question involves the ability of parties to take precautions to avoid breaches and whether alternative contract remedies provide incentives to take cost-justified precautions. This issue was first raised in the materials following *Dunbar Molasses,* above. In that case, a middleman who promised to supply molasses from a specified factory was forced to breach when the factory cut back on its production. The court stated that he was negligent for failing to prevent the decrease in production by contracting with the factory to supply his needs.

If the costs arising from breach can be minimized by taking precautions to avoid the breach, then efficient remedies for breach must provide appropriate incentives to take cost-justified precautions. The efficiency of precautions to avoid breach are judged by the associated costs and expected benefits. The benefit from such precautions is reducing the risk of breach just as the benefit from precautions in tort law is reducing the risk of accidents. In contracts, the risk of breach is measured by the damage that results if a breach occurs discounted by (multiplied by) the probability that a breach will occur. As in torts, it is not wealth maximizing to avoid all risks, only those risks that can be avoided at a cost that is less than the expected benefit.

Dunbar Molasses may be interpreted as a case where the middleman was held liable for causing a breach that he could have avoided at reasonable cost, for failing to take efficient precautions to avoid the risk of breach.

Questions: Does the expectation measure of damages provide incentives for the middleman to take efficient precautions to avoid the risk of breach in *Dunbar Molasses?* Does the expectation measure of damages provide incentives for Anthony Neri to avoid the risk of breach?

DEITSCH v. MUSIC COMPANY

Hamilton County Municipal Court, Ohio, 1983.
6 Ohio Misc.2d 6, 453 N.E.2d 1302.

PAINTER, JUDGE.

This is an action for breach of contract. Plaintiffs and defendant entered into a contract on March 27, 1980, whereby defendant was to provide a four-piece band at plaintiffs' wedding reception on November 8, 1980. The reception was to be from 8:00 p.m. to midnight. The contract stated "wage agreed upon—$295.00," with a deposit of $65, which plaintiffs paid upon the signing of the contract.

Plaintiffs proceeded with their wedding, and arrived at the reception hall on the night of November 8, 1980, having employed a caterer, a photographer and a soloist to sing with the band. However, the four-piece band failed to arrive at the wedding reception. Plaintiffs made several attempts to contact defendant but were not successful. After much wailing and gnashing of teeth, plaintiffs were able to send a friend to obtain some stereo equipment to provide music, which equipment was set up at about 9:00 p.m.

* * *

The court finds that defendant did in fact breach the contract and therefore that plaintiffs are entitled to damages. The difficult issue in this case is determining the correct measure and amount of damages.

Counsel for both parties have submitted memoranda on the issue of damages. However, no cases on point are cited. Plaintiffs contend that the *entire* cost of the reception, in the amount of $2,643.59, is the correct measure of damages. This would require a factual finding that the reception was a total loss, and conferred no benefit at all on the plaintiffs. Defendant, on the other hand, contends that the only measure of damages which is proper is the amount which plaintiffs actually lost, that is, the $65 deposit. It is the court's opinion that neither measure of damages is proper; awarding to plaintiffs the entire sum of the reception would grossly overcompensate them for their actual loss, while the simple return of the deposit would not adequately compensate plaintiffs for defendant's breach of contract.

Therefore, we have to look to other situations to determine whether there is a middle ground, or another measure of damages which would allow the court to award more than the deposit, but certainly less than the total cost of the reception.

* * *

The case that we believe is on point is *Pullman Company v. Willett*. In that case, a husband and wife contracted with the Pullman Company for sleeping accommodations on the train. When they arrived, fresh from their wedding, there were no accommodations, as a result of which they were compelled to sit up most of the night and change cars several times. The court held that since the general measure of damages is the loss sustained, damages for the deprivation of the comforts, conveniences, and privacy for which one contracts in reserving a sleeping car space are not to be measured by the amount paid therefor. The court allowed compensatory damages for the physical inconvenience, discomfort and mental anguish resulting from the breach of contract, and upheld a jury award of $125. The court went on to state as follows:

"It is further contended that the damages awarded were excessive. We think not. The peculiar circumstances of this case were properly [a] matter for the consideration of the jury. The damages for deprivation of the comforts, conveniences and privacy for which he had contracted and agreed *are not to be measured by the amount to be paid therefor.* He could have had cheaper accommodations had he so desired, but that he wanted these accommodations under the circumstances of this case was but natural and commendable, and we do not think that the record fails to show any damages, but, on the contrary it fully sustains the verdict and would, in our opinion, sustain even a larger verdict had the jury thought proper to fix a larger amount." (Emphasis added.)

* * *

The court holds that in a case of this type, the out-of-pocket loss, which would be the security deposit, or even perhaps the value of the band's services, where another band could not readily be obtained at the last minute, would not be sufficient to compensate plaintiffs. Plaintiffs are entitled to compensation for their distress, inconvenience, and the diminution in value of their reception. For said damages, the court finds that the compensation should be $750. Since plaintiffs are clearly entitled to the refund of their security deposit, judgment will be rendered for plaintiffs in the amount of $815 and the costs of this action.

Judgment accordingly.

Notes and Questions

1. An alternative to expectation damages is *restitution,* which simply requires the breaching promisor to return any benefits the promisee has conferred on him. The defendant in *Deitsch* was arguing for restitution when it claimed that the plaintiffs' damages should be $65, the amount of the plaintiffs' deposit to engage the band's performance.

Question: Does the restitution measure of damages encourage efficient breach and discourage inefficient breach? Consider the incentives created in cases like *Redgrave* and *Neri* if the promisor who breaches must pay only restitution.

2. Suppose that the value of the band to the Deitschs was exactly $295, the contract price, and that they had paid that full amount in advance. In that case, the expectations measure and the restitution

measure of damages would result in the same damage award, $295, which equals both the amount necessary to make the Deitschs as well off as if performance had occurred and the prepaid amount.

Questions: If the value of the band and the contract price were both $295 but the deposit was only $65, what would be the awards under the expectations and restitution measures of damages? Is the initial assumption that the value of the band to the Deitschs was equal to the contract price likely to be accurate? If not, will restitution and expectations damages still be identical?

3. The underlying principle of expectation damages is to give the promisee the benefit of the bargain. If the promisee contracted for the purpose of making a profit, then the expectation loss equals the profit that would have been made (from which the promisee expected to pay any costs actually incurred in connection with performance), plus any incidental damages arising from the promisor's breach. Thus, in *Redgrave*, the damages were equivalent to the performance fee minus the travel expenses avoided by Redgrave as a result of the BSO's breach, expenses she would have paid out of her fee had the contract been performed. In *Neri*, the damages were lost profits plus incidental storage and insurance expenses incurred as a result of Neri's breach.

When there are no lost profits it is more difficult to calculate expectation damages. Still, the expectation loss for a consumer is analytically identical to that of a business—the total benefit from performance less the costs that would have been incurred (but were not) had the contract been performed. It is as difficult for an external factfinder to calculate this benefit as it is to monetize any loss in utility. One place to start is to determine the maximum the Deitschs would be willing to pay to have the band play at their wedding. From this amount one can determine the expectation loss by subtracting the amount they actually agreed to pay for the band. If the Deitschs would have been willing to pay up to $500 but found an acceptable band for only $295, their "profit" or expectation from the deal would $205. Economists call the surplus value the consumer enjoys when she is required to pay less than the maximum she would be willing to pay—$205 in this example—*consumer surplus*. The Deitschs' expectation damages are the lost value of the band's performance (equal to the contract price plus their consumer surplus), less the costs of obtaining performance (the contract price). Thus, in this case, the expectations damages must be $500–$295 or $205. When, as here, there is a pre-paid amount ($65), it must also be returned. If the $65 is not returned along with the $205 in expectations, the Deitschs will be undercompensated, netting ($205–$65=) $140 as a result of the contract instead of $205 as anticipated.

Questions: Are the damages awarded in *Deitsch* consistent with the expectation measure? Do they provide incentives for the Music Company to breach only when it is efficient to do so?

4. In addition to requiring The Music Company to return the Deitschs' $65 deposit, and awarding damages for the diminution in value of

their reception (lost expectations), the court awarded the Deitschs a sum to compensate them for their "distress" and "inconvenience."

Question: Is it necessary to compensate the Deitschs for distress and inconvenience to achieve the goal of efficient breach?

5. The Deitschs were able to minimize the diminution in the value of their reception by arranging for a friend to set up his stereo equipment. Suppose they had not done so.

Questions: Would a measure of damages that allowed the Dietschs to recover the diminution in value between a reception with music provided by the Music Company and a reception with no music create incentives for the couple to minimize the damage after the breach? Would the expectation measure of damages give the couple any incentive to take advance precautions to minimize damages in the event of a breach?

6. The Restatement (Second) of Contracts § 350 limits an injured promisee's damages:

§ 350. Avoidability as a Limitation of Damages

(1) Except as stated in Subsection (2), damages are not recoverable for loss that the injured party could have avoided without undue risk, burden or humiliation.

(2) The injured party is not precluded from recovery by the rule stated in subsection (1) to the extent that he has made reasonable but unsuccessful efforts to avoid loss.

Question: Does § 350 provide incentives for the promisee to minimize damages from the promisor's breach?

7. The plaintiffs in *Dietsch* argued that the proper measure of damages was $2,643.59, the cost of the reception. In effect the plaintiffs were arguing for a third measure of damages, known as *reliance* damages. While restitution returns any benefit the promisee has given the promisor, and expectation damages seek to make the promisee as well off as if the contract had been performed, reliance damages seek to make the plaintiff as well off *as if the contract had never been entered.* The goal is restoring the promisee to her position prior to formation of the contract.

The court rejected the Dietschs' claim to reliance damages because it found that the expense of the reception had not been incurred entirely in anticipation of the band's performance. Even without the band, the plaintiffs derived some enjoyment from their reception—it was not a total loss. However, in Security Stove & Mfg. Co. v. American Ry. Express Co., the court adopted the reliance measure in lieu of expectation damages on the theory that the injured party could not establish with sufficient certainty what its benefit from the bargain would have been. When reading *Security Stove,* consider the incentives created by the reliance measure of damages.

SECURITY STOVE & MFG. CO. v. AMERICAN RY. EXPRESS CO.

Kansas City Court of Appeals, Missouri, 1932.
227 Mo.App. 175, 51 S.W.2d 572.

BLAND, J.

This is an action for damages for failure of defendant to transport, from Kansas City to Atlantic City, New Jersey, within a reasonable time, a furnace equipped with a combination oil and gas burner. The cause was tried before the court without the aid of a jury, resulting in a judgment in favor of plaintiff in the sum of $801.50 and interest, or in a total sum of $1,000.00. Defendant has appealed.

The facts show that plaintiff manufactured a furnace equipped with a special combination oil and gas burner it desired to exhibit at the American Gas Association Convention held in Atlantic City in October, 1926. The president of plaintiff testified that plaintiff engaged space for the exhibit for the reason "that the Henry L. Dougherty Company was very much interested in putting out a combination oil and gas burner; we had just developed one, after we got through, better than anything on the market and we thought this show would be the psychological time to get in contact with the Dougherty Company"; that "the thing wasn't sent there for sale but primarily to show"; that at the time the space was engaged it was too late to ship the furnace by freight so plaintiff decided to ship it by express, and, on September 18th, 1926, wrote the office of the defendant in Kansas City, stating that it had engaged a booth for exhibition purposes at Atlantic City, New Jersey, from the American Gas Association, for the week beginning October 11th; that its exhibit consisted of an oil burning furnace, together with two oil burners which weighed at least 1,500 pounds; that, "In order to get this exhibit in place on time, it should be in Atlantic City not later than October the 8th. What we want you to do is tell us how much time you will require to assure the delivery of the exhibit on time."

Mr. Bangs, chief clerk in charge of the local office of the defendant, upon receipt of the letter, sent Mr. Johnson, a commercial representative of the defendant, to see plaintiff. Johnson called upon plaintiff taking its letter with him. Johnson made a notation on the bottom of the letter giving October 4th, as the day that defendant was required to have the exhibit in order for it to reach Atlantic City on October 8th.

On October 1st, plaintiff wrote the defendant at Kansas City, referring to its letter of September 18th, concerning the fact that the furnace must be in Atlantic City not later than October 8th, and stating what Johnson had told it, saying, "Now Mr. Bangs, we want to make doubly sure that this shipment is in Atlantic City not later than October 8th and the purpose of this letter is to tell you that you can *have your truck call for the shipment between 12 and 1 o'clock on*

Saturday, October 2nd for this." (Italics plaintiffs.) On October 2d, plaintiff called the office of the express company in Kansas City and told it that the shipment was ready. Defendant came for the shipment on the last mentioned day, received it and delivered the express receipt to plaintiff. The shipment contained 21 packages. Each package was marked with stickers backed with glue and covered with silica of soda, to prevent the stickers being torn off in shipping. Each package was given a number. They ran from 1 to 21.

Plaintiff's president made arrangements to go to Atlantic City to attend the convention and install the exhibit, arriving there about October 11th. When he reached Atlantic City he found the shipment had been placed in the booth that had been assigned to plaintiff. The exhibit was set up, but it was found that one of the packages shipped was not there. This missing package contained the gas manifold, or that part of the oil and gas burner that controlled the flow of gas in the burner. This was the most important part of the exhibit and a like burner could not be obtained in Atlantic City.

Wires were sent and it was found that the stray package was at the "over and short bureau" of the defendant in St. Louis. Defendant reported that the package would be forwarded to Atlantic City and would be there by Wednesday, the 13th. Plaintiff's president waited until Thursday, the day the convention closed, but the package had not arrived at the time, so he closed up the exhibit and left. About a week after he arrived in Kansas City, the package was returned by the defendant.

* * *

Plaintiff asked damages, which the court in its judgment allowed as follows: $147.00 express charges (on the exhibit); $45.12 freight on the exhibit from Atlantic City to Kansas City; $101.39 railroad and pullman fares to and from Atlantic City, expended by plaintiff's president and a workman taken by him to Atlantic City; $48.00 hotel room for the two; $150.00 for the time of the president; $40.00 for wages of plaintiff's other employee and $270.00 for rental of the booth, making a total of $801.51.

* * *

Defendant contends that plaintiff "is endeavoring to achieve a return of the status quo in a suit based on breach of contract. Instead of seeking to recover what he would have had, had the contract not been broken, plaintiff is trying to recover what he would have had, had there never been any contract of shipment"; that the expenses sued for would have been incurred in any event. It is no doubt the general rule that where there is a breach of contract the party suffering the loss can recover only that which he would have had, had the contract not been broken, and this is all the cases decided upon which defendant relies. But this is merely a general statement of the rule and is not inconsistent with the holdings that, in some instances, the injured party may recover expenses incurred in relying upon the contract, although such expenses would have been incurred had the contract not been breached.

In Sperry v. O'Neill–Adams Co., the court held that the advantages resulting from the use of trading stamps as a means of increasing trade are so contingent that they cannot form a basis on which to rest a recovery for a breach of contract to supply them. In lieu of compensation based thereon the court directed a recovery in the sum expended in preparation for carrying on business in connection with the use of the stamps. The court said:

"Plaintiff in its complaint had made a claim for lost profits, but, finding it impossible to marshal any evidence which would support a finding of exact figures, abandoned that claim. Any attempt to reach a precise sum would be mere blind guesswork. Nevertheless a contract, which both sides conceded would prove a valuable one, had been broken and the party who broke it was responsible for the resultant damage. In order to carry out this contract, the plaintiff made expenditures which otherwise it would not have made. * * * The trial judge held, as we think rightly, that plaintiff was entitled at least to recover these expenses to which it had been put in order to secure the benefits of a contract of which defendant's conduct deprived it."

* * *

While, it is true that plaintiff already had incurred some of these expenses, in that it had rented space at the exhibit before entering into the contract with defendant for the shipment of the exhibit and this part of plaintiff's damages, in a sense, arose out of a circumstance which transpired before the contract was even entered into, yet plaintiff arranged for the exhibit knowing that it could call upon defendant to perform its common law duty to accept and transport the shipment with reasonable dispatch. The whole damage, therefore, was suffered in contemplation of defendant performing its contract, which it failed to do, and would not have been sustained except for the reliance by plaintiff upon defendant to perform it. It can, therefore, be fairly said that the damages or loss suffered by plaintiff grew out of the breach of the contract, for had the shipment arrived on time, plaintiff would have had the benefit of the contract, which was contemplated by all parties, defendant being advised of the purpose of the shipment.

The judgment is affirmed.

Notes and Questions

1. The manufacturer in *Security Stove* did everything possible to inform the carrier, American Railway Express, of the importance of promptly delivering all of the stove's parts. To avoid slip-ups, the manufacturer even applied silica of soda over the labels to prevent their being torn off. The carrier, on the other hand, was almost certainly negligent. In an omitted portion of the opinion the court in *Security Stove*, 51 S.W.2d at 575, stated:

As we view the record this negligence is practically conceded. The undisputed testimony shows that the shipment was sent to the over and short department of the defendant in St. Louis. As the packages were plainly numbered this, prima facie, shows mistake or negligence on the part of the defendant. No effort was made by it to show that it was not negligent in sending it there, or not negligent in not forwarding it within a reasonable time after it was found.

Given the carrier's potential liability for expectation damages, one would expect the carrier to take greater care. Still the negligence occurred.

If the manufacturer fully informed the carrier of its purposes (as the facts suggest), the carrier knew that the manufacturer had no contracts of sale for the stove and merely hoped to encourage sales by exhibiting the stove's merits at the show. The manufacturer had no firm expectations for which the carrier could be held liable.

> *Questions:* Given the rule that expectation damages must be proved with reasonable certainty, was the incentive of expectation damages really present in *Security Stove?* If the court awards no damages, does the carrier have incentive to take reasonable precautions against breach and to avoid a repeat of these unfortunate circumstances?

2. If an injured party cannot establish lost expectations with reasonable certainty, the court may allow the promisee to recover out-of-pocket expenditures incurred in reliance on the expected performance, those "expenses to which it had been put in order to secure the benefits of a contract of which defendant's conduct deprived it." In *Security Stove,* reliance expenditures included express charges paid to the carrier, travel, hotel, and booth rental expenses incurred by the manufacturer, and lost wages and salaries. The *reliance* measure of damages restores the manufacturer to its financial position before it entered into the contract with the carrier.

Suppose that Security Stove arranges to sell a stove to a New Jersey customer and expects to clear a $2,000 profit on the sale after all expenses, including packing and shipping. If the stove does not arrive within three days the order will be cancelled. In reliance on the carrier's promise to deliver the stove within three days, Security Stove spends $500 on packing materials to ensure that the stove is not damaged in shipping.

> *Questions:* Does the reliance measure of damages, interpreted as recovery of out-of-pocket expenditures, provide incentives for the carrier to engage only in efficient breach? Does the expectation measure of damages ($2000 lost profit) provide incentives for the carrier to engage only in efficient breach?

3. A broader interpretation of the reliance interest might include more than out-of-pocket expenditures. Reliance damages generally restore to the promisee the cash it had before the contract but do not restore the opportunities the promisee had before the contract. Before contracting with American Railway Express, the manufacturer had the opportunity to hire another carrier to ship the model stove to the convention on time. Relying on American Railway's promise, the manufacturer not only in-

curred out-of-pocket expenditures but also gave up the valuable opportunity to hire another carrier.

Questions: Is the value of that lost opportunity equal to the expectations loss? If so, would awarding the value of the lost opportunity as part of the promisee's reliance damages result in a damages award in the same amount as the expectations measure? Would this award of the value of lost opportunities have the efficiency properties of the expectations measure?

4. Previous notes examine the role of damages in discouraging the promisor from breaching inefficiently and imposing undue losses on the promisee. The materials following *Redgrave, Neri,* and *Deitsch* illustrate the incentive effect of expectation damages on the promisor's decision to breach when the costs and benefits associated with performance of a promise change. The materials following *Dunbar Molasses* and *Neri* illustrate the incentive effect of expectation damages on the promisor when there are available cost-justified precautions that will reduce the risk of breach. But the promisor is not always the only party who can reduce or avoid the harms resulting from the breach.

One of contract's principal economic functions is to encourage promisees to invest resources to increase the expected value and reduce the cost of performing an exchange. Consider how, in *Rexite Casting,* society's wealth is increased by reassuring Rexite that it can build custom molds to produce Midwest Mower's castings because it can rely on Midwest's promise to purchase the custom castings. But one can have too much of a good thing. Perhaps Security Stove relied too much on American Railway's promise when it was foreseeable the carrier might not perform. Security Stove could have taken steps to reduce the losses likely to follow from delayed delivery, perhaps by building a second model stove to be shipped by air in event of emergency. While promisors can minimize the losses that follow from breach by not breaching, promisees can minimize losses from breach by not relying too heavily on the promise to perform and, in some cases, by taking precautions that reduce the probability of a breach.

Questions: What precautions did Security Stove take to reduce the possibility that American Railway would fail to deliver the stove on time? Does the award of expectations provide an incentive to encourage promisees, like Security Stove, to take precautions?

5. As in torts, when both parties have the ability to avoid a loss, the relative ability of each is important to efficiency analysis. When both parties can avoid a harm we want the best cost avoider to do so. Section 350 of the Restatement (Second) of Contract, discussed in the notes following *Deitsch,* requires promisees to mitigate their damages but applies only to measures that minimize losses *after* the promisee has reason to know that breach will occur. Frequently the promisee can take steps *before* breach becomes likely to minimize the promisee's loss if breach occurs. Efficient damage remedies should not only discourage inefficient breach by promisors, but also discourage *inefficient reliance* by promisees.

Questions: Does the expectation measure of damages discourage inefficient reliance by promisees? Does the reliance measure discourage inefficient reliance by promisees?

3. LIMITATIONS ON DAMAGES

HADLEY v. BAXENDALE

In the Court of Exchequer, 1854.
9 Exch. 341.

[The plaintiffs' milling business was suspended May 11 when the crankshaft that drove the mill broke. The plaintiffs arranged for the defendant carrier to ship the broken crankshaft to engineers in Greenwich who would use the broken shaft as a pattern for a new shaft. One of the plaintiffs' employees informed a clerk in the defendant's office that the shaft should be sent immediately. The clerk replied that the shaft could be delivered to Greenwich in a day. The plaintiffs delivered the broken shaft to the defendant's office and paid the shipping fee on May 14. The defendant negligently delayed the shipment to Greenwich and the plaintiff sued for lost profits resulting from the delay.]

ALDERSON, B. * * *

* * *

Now we think the proper rule in such a case as the present is this:—Where two parties have made a contract which one of them has broken, the damages which the other party ought to receive in respect of such breach of contract should be such as may fairly and reasonably be considered either arising naturally, i.e., according to the usual course of things, from such breach of contract itself, or such as may reasonably be supposed to have been in the contemplation of both parties, at the time they made the contract, as the probable result of the breach of it. Now, if the special circumstances under which the contract was actually made were communicated by the plaintiffs to the defendants, and thus known to both parties, the damages resulting from the breach of such a contract, which they would reasonably contemplate, would be the amount of injury which would ordinarily follow from a breach of contract under these special circumstances so known and communicated. But, on the other hand, if these special circumstances were wholly unknown to the party breaking the contract, he, at the most, could only be supposed to have had in his contemplation the amount of injury which would arise generally, and in the great multitude of cases not affected by any special circumstances, from such a breach of contract. For, had the special circumstances been known, the parties might have specially provided for the breach of contract by special terms as to damages in that case; and of this advantage it would be very unjust to deprive them. * * * [W]e find that the only circumstances here communicated by the plaintiffs to the defendants at the time the contract was made, were, that the article to be carried was the broken shaft of the mill, and that the plaintiffs were the millers of that mill. But how do these circumstances show reasonably that the profits of the mill must be stopped by an unreasonable delay in the delivery of the broken shaft by the carrier to the third person? Suppose the plaintiffs had another shaft in their possession put up or putting up at the time, and that they only wished to send back the broken shaft to the engineer who made it; it is clear that this would be quite consistent with the above circumstances, and yet the unreasonable delay in the delivery would have no effect upon the intermediate profits of the mill. Or, again, suppose that, at the time of delivery to the carrier, the machinery of the mill had been in other respects defective, then, also, the same results would follow. Here it is true that the shaft was actually sent back to serve as a model for a new one, and that the want of a new one was the only cause of the stoppage of the mill, and that the loss of profits really arose from not sending down the new shaft in proper time, and that this arose from the delay in delivering the broken one to serve as a model. But it is obvious that, in the great multitude of cases of millers sending off broken shafts to third persons by a carrier under ordinary circumstances, such consequences would not, in all probability, have occurred; and these special circumstances were here never communicated by the plaintiffs to the defendants. It follows, therefore, that the loss of profits here cannot reasonably be considered such a consequence of the breach of contract as could have been fairly and reasonably contemplated by both the parties when they made this contract. For such loss would neither have flowed naturally from the breach of this contract in the great multitude of such cases occurring under ordinary circumstances, nor were the special circumstances, which, perhaps, would have made it a reasonable and natural consequence of such breach of contract, communicated to or known by the defendants.   * * *

Notes and Questions

1. Hadley v. Baxendale limits damages to those reasonably foreseeable because they "flow naturally from the breach" or because they "may reasonably be supposed to have been in the contemplation of both parties." A promisor can foresee damages that are the natural consequence of the breach. The promisor can also foresee more unusual damages about which the promisee informs him, for they are then "within the contemplation of both parties". In *Hadley,* the defendant was held not liable for the plaintiff's losses because those loses arose from circumstances neither naturally foreseeable nor communicated to the defendant.

Questions: The miller's lost profits, while unforeseeable, resulted from the defendant's failure to ship the crankshaft promptly as promised. If the plaintiff's losses were the result of the defendant's breach, why shouldn't the breaching defendant be strictly liable for such losses? Consider whether the miller could have done anything to prevent losses from stopping the mill. If the defendant was liable for all damages resulting from nondelivery, does the miller have any incentive to avoid those losses?

2. The *Hadley* rule applies to both expectation damages and other losses (both incidental and consequential) resulting from a breach. The court found that lost profits would not have flowed naturally from the breach, because a carrier taking an objective view of the situation would

not anticipate that lost profits might result from delay. Since lost profits were not a reasonably foreseeable *type* of damage in that case, they were not recoverable. Unusual types of damages must come under the "within the contemplation of the parties" part of the rule; the possibility of lost profits resulting from the delay would had to have been raised at the time the contract was formed. Note that it is the general type of damage rather than the amount of damage that is subject to this rule. While the amount of lost profits must be proved with reasonable certainty at trial, that amount need not have been reasonably foreseeable at the time of contracting.

The materials following *Security Stove* raised the issue of whether expectation damages give promisees incentive to take cost-justified precautions to minimize losses associated with breach. Consider how the *Hadley* rule of reasonable foreseeability changes the parties' incentives in the following circumstances:

> *Questions (a):* The carrier knows that because of poor roads and foul weather, there is a 10% chance that the crankshaft will be delayed three days unless the carrier doubles the usual number of horses, which would cost $200. If the plaintiff loses $1000 each day the mill is shut down and has no way of minimizing that loss, would it be desirable from an efficiency perspective for the carrier to incur the cost of hiring the extra horses? If the defendant was aware of these facts, would the expectations measure of damages as modified by *Hadley* provide an incentive for the carrier to take that precaution against breach?

> *Questions (b):* Suppose the miller could avoid shutting the mill by renting a spare crankshaft for $50 a day, but must reserve the spare ahead of time and must commit himself to pay three days' rental. Suppose the carrier has no means of minimizing the losses. Would it be efficient for the plaintiff to incur the cost of reserving the rental crankshaft? If both parties are aware of all facts, will the reasonable miller reserve a replacement crankshaft prior to shipping his own crankshaft away for repairs given the incentives provided by *Hadley?*

> *Questions (c):* Suppose both parties have available to them the precautionary measures described in situations (a) and (b) above, and are fully aware of each other's loss prevention options and their associated costs as well as the expected losses from breach. Under the reasonably foreseeable expectations rule described in *Hadley,* which party has the incentive to avoid the losses? Is that efficient?

3. In Question 2(c), the miller could avoid the losses associated with breach at a lower cost than the carrier could. The miller could avoid the probable $300 loss from breach at a cost of $150 ($50 rental per day times three days) while the extra horses would cost the carrier $200.

> *Question:* If those costs were reversed, so that the miller could avoid the loss for $200 while the carrier could avoid the loss for $150, would the answer to Question 2(c) change?

4. *Hadley* limits the expectations measure of damages to "general" damages that are reasonably foreseeable as a natural consequence of

breach, on the theory that breaching promisors should not be strictly liable for costs they are neither aware of nor likely to foresee. The *Hadley* rule also permits liability for "special" damages "fairly or reasonably contemplated by both the parties when they made this contract." The *Hadley* rule thus encourages parties to bargain about foreseeable risks and allocate responsibilities in a way that maximizes mutual benefit from the bargain. The rule forewarns parties who face unusual risks that they had better communicate any special circumstances that may affect the damages from breach so the contract terms can allocate those risks efficiently.

If the parties have actually allocated the risks in the contract, however, the rule of *Hadley* is irrelevant. So long as the court does not construe the damage measure provided by the contract as a penalty (see the discussion of liquidated damages, below), it will uphold the contractual provisions. The reasonably foreseeable damages limitation applies when the parties have not explicitly allocated the risks. Once again, contract law endeavors to supply efficient implied terms where the parties have neglected to address the matter expressly.

FLORIDA EAST COAST RAILWAY CO. v. BEAVER STREET FISHERIES, INC.

District Court of Appeal of Florida, First District, 1989.
537 So.2d 1065, 14 Fla. L. Week. 226.

JOANOS, JUDGE.

Florida East Coast Railway Company (FEC) appeals a final judgment following a bench trial holding it liable for all costs associated with damage to two containers of food consigned to Club Med in the British West Indies. The issues for our review are: (1) whether the trial court erred in awarding Beaver Street Fisheries, Inc. (BSF) all costs associated with an emergency reshipment of goods by chartered aircraft * * * .

The two containers which form the subject of this appeal were loaded in Jacksonville, Florida, on July 31, 1985, for transport by FEC to Fort Lauderdale, Florida. Container 336 was loaded by BSF employees with frozen meats and other frozen food products. The container was then closed and sealed, and the temperature gauge was set at zero degrees Fahrenheit. Container 336 left Jacksonville on July 31, 1985, at 5:30 p.m. by FEC train * * * and arrived in Fort Lauderdale on August 1, 1985, at 2:45 a.m. * * *.

Container 337 was loaded by Movsovitz & Sons, Inc., a supplier for BSF, with produce and other perishable food items. Employees of both BSF and Movsovitz supervised the packing of the container, and both BSF and Movsovitz employees checked the temperature setting of the container before it left the Movsovitz premises. * * * The container was set and operating at thirty-eight degrees Fahrenheit when it left the Movsovitz premises at 6:17 p.m. on July 31, 1985. Container 337 left Jacksonville on July 31, 1985, at 9:45 p.m., by FEC train * * * and arrived in Fort Lauderdale on August 1, 1985, at 9:00 a.m. * * *.

* * *

* * * On August 6, 1985, the containers were placed on the BAL barge MOBRO 1207, for ocean carriage to Providenciales, British West Indies. The containers arrived in Providenciales on August 10, 1985, and were delivered to the consignee Club Med, sometime between 3:00 a.m. and 8:00 a.m. on August 10, 1985. When the containers were opened, they revealed that the frozen meat in container 336 had thawed and deteriorated, and the produce in container 337 had frozen solid. * * *

* * *

In the final judgment, BSF was awarded the sum of $68,871.90, together with prejudgment interest of $18,780.00, for a total of $87,-651.90. * * * [O]ur examination of the record leads us to conclude that the amount assessed against FEC contemplates the replacement cost of the damaged shipment, the ocean freight charges [for barge shipment of the ruined food beyond Fort Lauderdale], and the cost of the replacement shipment by jet charter.

* * *

The purpose of damages for breach of contract is to restore the injured party to the position he would have been in had the contract been performed according to its terms. In the process, "the common law also seeks to protect the defendant from unforeseeable large losses to the plaintiff."

Under the rule articulated in Hadley v. Baxendale, the damages recoverable for breach of contract are: (1) such as may fairly and reasonably be considered as arising in the usual course of events from the breach of contract itself, or (2) such as may reasonably be supposed to have been in contemplation of the parties at the time they made the contract. In other words, "general damages are awarded only if injury were foreseeable to a reasonable man and ... special damages are awarded only if actual notice were given to the carrier of the possibility of injury. Damage is foreseeable by the carrier if it is the proximate and *usual consequence* of the carrier's action." [Emphasis supplied by this court]. Thus, knowledge is a prerequisite for liability for special damages.

* * *

In the instant case, it is undisputed that FEC was on notice that the ultimate destination of containers 336 and 337 was Club Med, Providenciales, British West Indies. Nevertheless, it is also undisputed that (1) FEC's contract of carriage contemplated only the transport of the containers from FEC's Jacksonville rail yard to its Fort Lauderdale rail yard, and (2) FEC was without knowledge that loss or damage to the shipment would mean that Club Med would be completely without food for its six hundred guests. Thus, there is no competent substantial evidence to support a finding of FEC liability for the special damages associated with the replacement shipment by jet charter.

* * *

In summary * * * we consider that a carrier's liability for damages due to loss or injury to a food shipment slated for a facility in the British West Indies should contemplate the inconvenience occasioned by the loss or the attendant delay for a replacement shipment. On the other hand, we do not consider it reasonable that a carrier would foresee circumstances such as those which obtained in this case, i.e., that loss of the food shipment would leave Club Med completely without food for its guests. Rather, a reasonable person could consider that a large resort hotel situated on a Caribbean Island would maintain a reserve food supply, in anticipation of late shipments or an emergency situation such as a hurricane. By the same token, BSF agrees that FEC was without knowledge that Club Med would be completely without food for its guests if the food in containers 336 and 337 did not arrive in good condition. Therefore, we conclude that special damages are not warranted in the circumstances of this case, and reverse on this issue.

* * *

Notes and Questions

1. *Florida East Coast* raises the question of what precautions the breaching promisor may presume the injured promisee has taken to minimize losses from breach. The court appears to permit the promisor to assume the promisee has taken reasonable precautions against undue reliance, without regard to which party is the best cost avoider.

Questions: After this case, resorts like Club Med have incentive to maintain large food reserves. Is that an efficient outcome if the carrier's cost of ensuring safe and timely deliveries is less than the resort's cost of maintaining large food supplies in the hot climate of the British West Indies? What limitations on expectation damages would create incentives for the best cost avoider of losses from breach to avoid those losses?

2. Making promisors liable for all losses resulting from breach discourages inefficient breach, but encourages promisees' inefficient reliance. Making promisees bear their own losses in the event of breach discourages inefficient reliance, but encourages promisors to breach inefficiently. Because both parties can mitigate the losses that flow from breach, losses cannot be unilaterally assigned to one party without creating undesirable incentives for the other.

Questions: Suppose that both parties had to bear the full cost of breach. A breaching promisor must pay full expectation damages, but those damages would go into a trust to reduce the national debt. The injured promisee is paid no compensation in the event of breach but must bear his own losses. Would such a system create incentives for efficient breach and efficient reliance? Would such a system create incentives leading to primary accident cost minimization? What might be the disadvantages of such a liability system?

ROCHESTER LANTERN CO. v. STILES & PARKER PRESS CO.

Court of Appeals of New York, 1892.
135 N.Y. 209, 31 N.E. 1018.

EARL, C.J.

* * *

* * * On the 19th day of March, 1887, James H. Kelly entered into a contract with the defendant, whereby it was to make and deliver to him certain dies, to be used by him in the manufacture of lanterns. That it agreed to make and deliver the dies within a reasonable time,—that is, within five weeks from the time of the order, to manufacture and deliver the same. That the plaintiff was incorporated shortly prior to the 27th day of August, 1887, and on the 29th day of that month Kelly duly assigned to the plaintiff his contract with the defendant, and all his rights and claims thereunder. * * * That the defendant failed to carry out the contract, and to furnish dies as thereby required. That the plaintiff, for the sole purpose of carrying on the business of manufacturing the lanterns which it was intended that these dies should make, entered into certain obligations and incurred certain liabilities as follows: It paid one Butts, for rent of room from October 3 to November 1, 1887, the sum of $31.86; it paid one Broad, an employe, for his wages from October 3, 1887, to March 24, 1888, the sum of $250, and one Bristow, an employe, for his wages during the same time, the same sum; it paid to Crouch & Sons, for the rent of premises from November 1, 1887, to March 24, 1888, $278.46. That by reason of defendant's failure to perform the contract as agreed by it, the plaintiff was unable to manufacture any lanterns for the market until after the commencement of this action on the 24th day of March, 1888; and that the plaintiff, by reason of such failure, sustained loss in the sums above mentioned, which it actually paid, and the referee awarded judgment for the amount of the items above specified.

* * * It is frequently difficult in the administration of the law to apply the proper rule of damages, and the decisions upon the subject are not harmonious. The cardinal rule undoubtedly is that the one party shall recover all the damage which has been occasioned by the breach of the contract by the other party. But this rule is modified in its application by two others: the damages must flow directly and naturally from the breach of the contract, and they must be certain, both in their nature and in respect of the cause from which they proceeded. Under this latter rule, speculative, contingent, and remote damages which cannot be directly traced to the breach complained of are excluded. Under the former rule, such damages only are allowed as the parties may fairly be supposed when they made the contract to have contemplated as naturally following its violation.

* * * No fact is found showing that the defendant had any reason to suppose that he would hire any workmen or persons before the dies were furnished, and it cannot be said that it was a natural and proximate consequence of a breach of the contract that he would have idle men or unused real estate causing him the expenses now claimed. Much less can it be supposed that the defendant could, when the contract was made, anticipate that the contract would be assigned, and that the assignee would employ men and premises to remain idle after the defendant had failed to perform the contract, and in consequence of such failure. Such damages to the assignee could not have been contemplated as the natural and proximate consequence of a breach of the contract. If we should adopt the rule of damages contended for by the plaintiff, what would be the limits of its application? Suppose, instead of employing two men, the plaintiff had projected an extensive business in which the dies were to be used, and had employed one hundred men, and had hired or even constructed a large and costly building in which to carry on the business, and had kept the men and the building unemployed for months, and perhaps years, could the whole expense of the men and building be visited on the defendant as a consequence of its breach of contract? If it could, we should have a rule of damages which might cause ruin to parties unable from unforeseen events to perform their contracts. The damages allowed by the referee in this case are special damages not flowing naturally from the breach of the contract, and we think the only damages such an assignee in a case like this can recover is the difference between the contract price of these dies and the value or cost of the dies if furnished according to the contract. Even if Kelly could have recovered special damages, we see no ground for holding that his assignee, of whose connection with the contract the defendant had no notice, could recover special damages not contemplated when the contract was made. We are therefore of opinion that the award of damages made by this judgment was not justified by the facts found, and that the judgment should be reversed, and a new trial granted, costs to abide event. All concur.

Notes and Questions

1. As discussed in the notes following *Security Stove*, promisees injured by a breach are limited to recovering out-of-pocket expenses if they cannot establish their "benefit of the bargain" with reasonable certainty. Allowing promisees to recover all out-of-pocket expenses gives them no incentive to take into account the possibility of a breach when incurring those expenses. Precluding the promisee from recovering any out-of-pocket expenses preserves the promisee's incentive to take precautions against breach by engaging in efficient reliance.

Recall the facts of *Security Stove*. Relying on the model stove's timely delivery to the convention, the president of the stove manufacturing company incurred expenses for exhibition space, travel, and employee's wages. If he expected all those expenses to be repaid if the carrier breached, the president would have no incentive to consider the possibility of a breach before incurring those expenses.

Question: How does the rule applied in *Rochester Lantern* modify the incentives to engage in efficient reliance by promisees and efficient breach by promisors provided by the two following possible rules: (a) recovery of all out-of-pocket expenses and (b) recovery of no out-of-pocket expenses?

2. The paucity of cases like *Rochester Lantern* and *Security Stove* makes it difficult to predict how the reliance measure of damages would be applied in other contexts. Conceivably, reliance expenditures "within the contemplation of the parties" are those that are reasonable rather than extravagant or foolish. Foolish out-of-pocket expenditures might include those a reasonable person would not make if he thought there was a significant probability the promisor would breach. If *Rochester Lantern* is interpreted in that fashion, the rule may provide incentives for efficient reliance. Recall that efficient reliance expenditures produce a benefit (increased value from performance discounted by the probability the defendant will perform) greater than their cost (loss in the event of breach discounted by the probability the defendant will breach).

Questions: Assume that the lantern manufacturer in *Rochester Lantern* could hire workers and rent space either before, or after, delivery of the dies. Hiring afterwards would result in production delays that would reduce first-year profits from $2,000 to $1000. If there is a 20% chance of breach and the out-of-pocket expenses wasted in the event of breach totaled $810.32, is it efficient for the manufacturer to rely on the promisor's performance? Does denying recovery for those expenses provide correct incentives? Under our interpretation of the rule, would recovery be denied?

4. SPECIFIC PERFORMANCE

From an economic perspective, specific performance is the contract law equivalent to protecting the promisee's entitlement to performance with a property rule; the promisee is entitled to performance unless he willingly waives that right. As we have seen, liability is usually the preferred remedy for contract breach. What are the advantages and disadvantages of property and liability in contracts?

MADARIAGA v. MORRIS

Court of Appeals of Texas, 1982.
639 S.W.2d 709.

SUMMERS, CHIEF JUSTICE.

This is an appeal from a judgment granting specific performance of an option to purchase a business.

Plaintiff/appellee James Morris brought this suit against defendants/appellants Albert Madariaga and wife Mae Madariaga, seeking specific performance of an option to purchase a business contained in a written lease agreement between the parties. The Madariagas answered with a general denial. After a nonjury trial, the court decreed specific performance of the option. The Madariagas have perfected this appeal.

We affirm.

The Madariagas had a business in Kilgore, Texas, for "making, manufacturing and selling 'Albert's Famous Mexican Hot Sauce.'" They owned the formula for this sauce. On or about December 9, 1970, they entered into a written contract whereby they leased said business, including the formula and goodwill of said business, to Morris * * * for a consideration of $54,000.00. [The contract also provided that after the $54,000.00 had been paid, Morris had an option to buy the business and formula for Albert's Famous Mexican Hot Sauce for an additional payment of $1,000.00].

* * *

It is undisputed that on December 10, 1979, Morris had made the following payments to the Madariagas as provided in the contract: (1) the sum of $54,000.00 as consideration for the lease in monthly installments of $500.00 as due under the contract, (2) all royalty payments called for during the rental payment period, and (3) the sum of $1,000.00 in cash as consideration for a conveyance of the business under the option granted in the contract.

After paying the $1,000.00, Morris requested that the Madariagas convey him the business. This, they refused to do unless he would continue paying the royalty perpetually.

The Madariagas have appealed asserting four points of error. In their first point they complain that the pleadings and proof did not support a judgment for specific performance. They contend that Morris has not pleaded nor offered any evidence that money damages were inadequate.

The equitable remedy of specific performance is not ordinarily available when the complaining party can be fully compensated through the legal remedy of damages.

Where, however, the personal property contracted for has a special, peculiar, or unique value or character, and the plaintiff would not be adequately compensated for his loss by an award of money damages, specific performance may be decreed. Similarly, special performance of a contract involving personal property may be granted where the subject matter of the contract is of a special and peculiar nature and value, and damages are not measurable.

Under Tex.Bus. & Com.Code Ann. § 2.716, it is provided that specific performance may be decreed where the goods are unique or in other proper circumstances.

Equity will generally decree specific performance at the instance of the buyer of personal property, which property he needs and which is not obtainable elsewhere. The scarcity of a chattel has been recognized as an important factor in determining whether specific performance of a contract for its sale will be granted.

Although plaintiff's petition must show that he does not have an adequate remedy at law, it is not necessary for him to allege in express terms that plaintiff does not have an adequate legal remedy or that the breach cannot be adequately compensated in damages. It is sufficient if the facts brought out in the pleadings show such to be the case.

In the case at bar, we hold that the plaintiff, by the facts brought out in his pleadings and evidence show that he does not have an adequate remedy at law and cannot be adequately compensated in damages. This is apparent from the subject matter of the sale. The business, including the hot sauce formula and goodwill, has a special, peculiar, unique value or character; it consists of property which Morris needs and could not be obtained elsewhere.

* * * Madariagas' first point is overruled.

The judgment of the trial court is affirmed.

Notes and Questions

1. As the court notes in *Madariaga*, specific performance is available as a remedy only when damages are "inadequate" to protect the injured party. According to Section 360 of the Restatement (Second) of Contracts, courts should consider the following factors in deciding whether legal damages are adequate: (a) the difficulty of proving damages with reasonable certainty, (b) the difficulty of procuring a suitable substitute performance with monetary damages, and (c) the likelihood that monetary damages could not be collected. The first factor suggests a situation where expectation damages cannot be recovered because the plaintiff cannot establish them with sufficient certainty.

> *Question:* Expectation damages fully compensate the injured party for the lost benefit of the bargain and create incentives for the promisor to breach only when breach is efficient. Does specific performance fully compensate the injured party and create incentives for efficient breach?

2. The Coase Theorem states that absent obstacles to bargaining, it does not matter to whom rights are assigned since bargaining will ensure an efficient allocation of resources. Consider the scenario that might follow an award of specific performance in *Madariaga*. We do not know why the Madariagas demanded more royalty monies for their secret. They may have been breaching opportunistically, taking advantage of Morris' prepayment of thousands of dollars. They may have had another offer for the business that was higher than Morris' original offer, raising the possibility their breach was efficient.

> *Questions:* Suppose breach was efficient because another potential buyer valued the business more highly than Morris. If Morris valued the business $10,000 more than the Madariagas, and the third party valued the business $25,000 more than the Madariagas, would an award of specific performance requiring the Madariagas to sell to Morris prevent the efficient reallocation of the business to the third

party who values the business more highly? Would an award of expectation damages to Morris prevent an efficient reallocation of the business? Assume no transaction costs.

3. The choice of remedies between specific performance and damages is the choice between property and liability rules. Property rules are more likely to lead to an efficient allocation of resources when parties can bargain and exchange freely; when obstacles to bargaining exist, liability rules may be preferred as a surrogate for exchange. Liability rules may be unreliable, however, when it is more difficult for the court accurately to assess a resource's value to the parties than for the parties to do so themselves. The choice between property and liability rules in a particular case thus depends on whether transaction costs are likely to be high (in which case damages may be preferred) and whether there is a high risk of legal error in valuing resources (in which case specific performance may be preferred).

Why should contract law generally favor liability? It might appear that transaction costs would be slight for two parties who have already contracted. Morris and the Madariagas had bargained before. Consider, however, how the Madariagas and Morris might bargain once the court established Morris' right to specific performance. Using the facts of Question 2, suppose the Madariagas want to pay Morris to waive his right to specific performance so they can sell to the third party for $25,000 more. Morris is better off waiving his right in return for any payment over $10,000. However, if Morris suspects that there is a third party willing to pay more for the business (or, more generally, interprets the breach as a signal that the Madariagas would be willing to pay more than $10,000 to keep the business) he will hold out for more than $10,000. The Madariagas, in turn, want to pay as little as possible. Any settlement between $10,000 and $25,000 leaves both parties better off, but each party has incentive to haggle in order to reap a larger share of the potential gains.

The bargaining situation in specific performance cases is often described as a *bilateral monopoly.* Each party has no alternative but to bargain with the other and there is a large stake of potential gains to split by bargaining. When goods are not unique, buyers have many sellers from which to choose, and sellers may have many buyers. But if Morris has the right to the business and the recipe for Albert's Famous Mexican Hot Sauce and the Madariagas want it back, they must bargain with him. In addition, they must keep him from discovering and bargaining with the third party without paying him so much that the benefit they would derive from reselling to the third party disappears. The resulting haggling has two possible outcomes: the Madariagas buy back the business and subsequently resell it to the third party, or the hard bargaining prevents any bargain and the business goes to Morris, who does not value it as highly as the third party.

Questions: Does bargaining over the potential gains confer any social benefit or does it simply waste time and resources? Does the possibility of bilateral monopoly recommend specific performance or damages equal to the benefit of the bargain?

4. The second factor the Restatement considers in awarding specific performance is the difficulty in procuring a suitable substitute performance by means of money awarded as damages. The comparable provision in Texas and most jurisdictions is that specific performance is appropriate when the goods are "unique".

> *Questions:* When parties contract over unique goods like the secret recipe for Albert's hot sauce, is the probability of legal error in assessing the good's value likely to be high or low? Is haggling and strategic behavior likely to occur if specific performance is granted? Do these considerations recommend specific performance or damages as the better remedy?

5. As the preceding questions suggest, specific performance and expectation damages both have limitations as methods for encouraging efficient breach. A remedy that produces too many inefficient breaches encourages *excessive breaching.* A remedy that discourages breach when breach is efficient leads to *excessive performance.*

> *Questions:* Which form of excessive behavior is more likely to arise from the bilateral monopoly associated with specific performance? Which form is more likely to result from the legal error associated with expectations damages? Is there any reason to prefer excessive breaching to excessive performance?

6. The economic analysis of specific performance and expectations damages must recognize the faults of both. Besides the incentive effects discussed above, specific performance can involve the court in continual and expensive supervision of the quality of the reluctant promisor's performance. Yet precise expectation damages calculations also involve the court in expensive and complex factfinding. And while awarding specific performance interferes with the promisor's individual liberty by requiring the promisor to perform when she does not desire to, awarding less than full compensation in a case where valid expectations cannot be established with reasonable certainty is unfair to the promisee.

5. LIQUIDATED DAMAGES.

LAKE RIVER CORPORATION v. CARBORUNDUM COMPANY

U.S. Court of Appeals, Seventh Circuit, 1985.
769 F.2d 1284.

POSNER, CIRCUIT JUDGE.

This diversity suit between Lake River Corporation and Carborundum Company requires us to consider questions of Illinois commercial law, and in particular to explore the fuzzy line between penalty clauses and liquidated-damages clauses.

Carborundum manufactures "Ferro Carbo," an abrasive powder used in making steel. To serve its midwestern customers better, Carborundum made a contract with Lake River by which the latter agreed to provide distribution services in its warehouse in Illinois.

Lake River would receive Ferro Carbo in bulk from Carborundum, "bag" it, and ship the bagged produce to Carborundum's customers. The Ferro Carbo would remain Carborundum's property until delivered to the customers.

Carborundum insisted that Lake River install a new bagging system to handle the contract. In order to be sure of being able to recover the cost of the new system ($89,000) and make a profit of 20 percent of the contract price, Lake River insisted on the following minimum-quantity guarantee:

> In consideration of the special equipment [i.e., the new bagging system] to be acquired and furnished by LAKE–RIVER for handling the product, CARBORUNDUM shall, during the initial three-year term of this Agreement, ship to LAKE–RIVER for bagging a minimum quantity of [22,500 tons]. If, at the end of the three-year term, this minimum quantity shall not have been shipped, LAKE–RIVER shall invoice CARBORUNDUM at the then prevailing rates for the difference between the quantity bagged and the minimum guaranteed.

If Carborundum had shipped the full minimum quantity that it guaranteed, it would have owed Lake River roughly $533,000 under the contract.

After the contract was signed in 1979, the demand for domestic steel, and with it the demand for Ferro Carbo, plummeted, and Carborundum failed to ship the guaranteed amount. When the contract expired late in 1982, Carborundum had shipped only 12,000 of the 22,500 tons it had guaranteed. Lake River had bagged the 12,000 tons and had billed Carborundum for this bagging, and Carborundum had paid, but by virtue of the formula in the minimum-guarantee clause Carborundum still owed Lake River $241,000–the contract price of $533,000 if the full amount of Ferro Carbo had been shipped, minus what Carborundum had paid for the bagging of the quantity it had shipped.

When Lake River demanded payment of this amount, Carborundum refused, on the ground that the formula imposed a penalty. * * *

* * *

The hardest issue in the case is whether the formula in the minimum-guarantee clause imposes a penalty for breach of contract or is merely an effort to liquidate damages. Deep as the hostility to penalty clauses runs in the common law, we still might be inclined to question, if we thought ourselves free to do so, whether a modern court should refuse to enforce a penalty clause where the signator is a substantial corporation, well able to avoid improvident commitments. Penalty clauses provide an earnest of performance. The clause here enhanced Carborundum's credibility in promising to ship the minimum amount guaranteed by showing that it was willing to pay the full contract price even if it failed to ship anything. On the other side it can be pointed out that by raising the cost of a breach of contract to the contract breaker, a penalty clause increases the risk to his other creditors; increases (what is the same thing and more, because bankruptcy imposes "deadweight" social costs) the risk of bankruptcy; and could amplify the business cycle by increasing the number of bankruptcies in bad times, which is when contracts are most likely to be broken. But since little effort is made to prevent businessmen from assuming risks, these reasons are no better than makeweights.

A better argument is that a penalty clause may discourage efficient as well as inefficient breaches of contract. Suppose a breach would cost the promisee $12,000 in actual damages but would yield the promisor $20,000 in additional profits. Then there would be a net social gain from breach. After being fully compensated for his loss the promisee would be no worse off than if the contract had been performed, while the promisor would be better off by $8,000. But now suppose the contract contains a penalty clause under which the promisor if he breaks his promise must pay the promisee $25,000. The promisor will be discouraged from breaking the contract, since $25,000, the penalty, is greater than $20,000, the profits of the breach; and a transaction that would have increased value will be forgone.

On this view, since compensatory damages should be sufficient to deter inefficient breaches (that is, breaches that cost the victim more than the gain to the contract breaker), penal damages could have no effect other than to deter some efficient breaches. But this overlooks the earlier point that the willingness to agree to a penalty clause is a way of making the promisor and his promise credible and may therefore be essential to inducing some value-maximizing contracts to be made. It also overlooks the more important point that the parties (always assuming they are fully competent) will, in deciding whether to include a penalty clause in their contract, weigh the gains against the costs—costs that include the possibility of discouraging an efficient breach somewhere down the road—and will include the clause only if the benefits exceed those costs as well as all other costs.

On this view the refusal to enforce penalty clauses is (at best) paternalistic—and it seems odd that courts should display parental solicitude for large corporations. But however this may be, we must be on guard to avoid importing our own ideas of sound public policy into an area where our proper judicial role is more than usually deferential. The responsibility for making innovations in the common law of Illinois rests with the courts of Illinois, and not with the federal courts in Illinois. And like every other state, Illinois, untroubled by academic skepticism of the wisdom of refusing to enforce penalty clauses against sophisticated promisors, continues steadfastly to insist on the distinction between penalties and liquidated damages. To be valid under Illinois law a liquidation of damages must be a reasonable estimate at the time of contracting of the likely damages from breach, and the need for estimation at that time must be shown by reference to the likely difficulty of measuring the actual damages from a breach of contract after the breach occurs. If damages would be easy to determine then, or if the estimate greatly exceeds a reasonable upper estimate of what the damages are likely to be, it is a penalty.

* * *

Mindful that Illinois courts resolve doubtful cases in favor of classification as a penalty, we conclude that the damage formula in this case is a penalty and not a liquidation of damages, because it is designed always to assure Lake River more than its actual damages. The formula—full contract price minus the amount already invoiced to Carborundum—is invariant to the gravity of the breach. When a contract specifies a single sum in damages for any and all breaches even though it is apparent that all are not of the same gravity, the specification is not a reasonable effort to estimate damages; and when in addition the fixed sum greatly exceeds the actual damages likely to be inflicted by a minor breach, its character as a penalty becomes unmistakable. This case is within the gravitational field of these principles even though the minimum-guarantee clause does not fix a single sum as damages.

* * *

The fact that the damage formula is invalid does not deprive Lake River of a remedy. The parties did not contract explicitly with reference to the measure of damages if the agreed-on damage formula was invalidated, but all this means is that the victim of the breach is entitled to his common law damages. In this case that would be the unpaid contract price of $241,000 minus the costs that Lake River saved by not having to complete the contract (the variable costs on the other 45 percent of the Ferro Carbo that it never had to bag). The case must be remanded to the district judge to fix these damages.

* * *

Notes and Questions

1. *Lake River* illustrates contract law's refusal to enforce penalty clauses even when negotiated by rational parties. Judge Posner suggests that hostility arose because penalty clauses interfere with efficient breach. To determine whether the penalty clause in *Lake River* would likely lead to inefficient breach, it is necessary to calculate Lake River's expectation loss. Lake River expected to bag at least 22,500 tons and receive a total payment of $533,000. If their expected profit was 20% of the contract price, they would have earned $106,600.

To calculate Lake River's loss according to the Restatement (Second) § 361, subtract from the contract price the costs Lake River avoided by not performing. Lake River spent $89,000 on bagging equipment that was useless without any Ferro Carbo to bag. Subtracting Lake River's expected profit ($106,600) and the cost of the bagging equipment ($89,000) from the total payment ($533,000), the other costs of production must have been $337,400 or $14.99 a ton. Lake River received $292,000 for bagging the 12,000 tons shipped before market demand for Ferro Carbo plummeted and

Carborundum stopped shipping. Lake River saved $14.99 on each of the 10,500 tons it did not have to bag.

> *Questions:* If the court awards Lake River expectations damages, what will the damage award be? If lost expectations calculated under § 361 were $85,000, would a liquidated damages clause requiring Carborundum to pay $241,000 in damages interfere with efficient breach? Would it encourage over- or underperformance?

2. While damages exceeding the full compensation measure seem to create incentives for inefficient performance, a party contemplating breach and faced with a penalty clause can always bargain to avoid inefficient performance. Suppose it would cost Carborundum $200,000 to perform and performance would benefit Lake River by $85,000. If the penalty provision was enforced, Carborundum must pay $241,000.

> *Questions:* Can bargaining reduce the likelihood of inefficient performance? If it costs Carborundum less to perform than Lake River's expectation loss from breach, will Carborundum perform? If the cost of performance is greater than the penalty, will Carborundum perform?

3. Although penalty clauses generally are unenforceable, liquidated damages clauses are not. Judge Posner notes that under Illinois law a liquidated damages clause must be "a reasonable estimate at the time of contracting of the likely damages from breach," and the parties must show the need for an estimate by showing "the likely difficulty of measuring the actual damages from a breach of contract after the breach occurs." If those requirements are not met, the clause is labelled a penalty clause and will not be enforced.

Generally, a promisee may recover only those expectation losses provable with reasonable certainty. If the promisee cannot recover a full measure of compensation the promisor has incentive for inefficient breach. Judicial resolution of contract disputes also has costs, including the administrative costs of deciding cases and the costs of legal error when miscalculated expectation damages lead to inefficient behavior.

> *Question:* How do the two requirements for liquidated damages minimize inefficient breach and the costs of judicial enforcement of contracts?

ARDUINI v. BOARD OF EDUCATION

Appellate Court of Illinois, Fourth District, 1981.
93 Ill.App. 3d 925, 49 Ill. Dec. 460, 418 N.E.2d 104.

MILLS, JUSTICE.

* * *

Here is the sequence of events that led to the instant litigation:

August 6, 1979 Defendant adopted its liquidated damages policy;

August 27, 1979 Plaintiff, a tenured teacher, began his duties for the 1979–80 school year;

September 13, 1979 Plaintiff received a "Contractual Continued Service Notification" from defendant, stating the salary plaintiff would receive for the 1979–80 school year, with a copy of the liquidated damages policy attached;

October 19, 1979 Plaintiff resigned from his teaching position in defendant's schools.

Pursuant to the liquidated damages policy, defendant withheld $715.92—4% of plaintiff's contract salary—from his final paycheck. Plaintiff filed a complaint seeking recovery of that amount, and defendant subsequently filed a counterclaim for declaratory judgment asking the court to determine the validity of its liquidated damages policy. The trial court held that the policy was valid and entered judgment in favor of the defendant.

* * *

Plaintiff contends that 4% of his salary bears no relationship to defendant's actual damages. In this regard he points out that defendant presented no evidence that it incurred any losses whatever. But a party seeking to enforce a liquidated damages clause does not need to present evidence of his actual damages. Such a clause would be of no use if a party still had to prove up his losses. The reasonableness of a liquidated damages provision is to be determined as of the time of contracting, not at some time following a breach when "the evidence is in" on actual damages.

Looking at the provision from that locus, we agree that defendant could be expected to incur considerable expense in finding a suitable replacement for plaintiff. In addition, defendant's school system would likely be disrupted by a resignation occurring in midyear. Plaintiff makes much of the fact that he was an experienced teacher and that defendant probably saved money by hiring a less experienced teacher who would earn a lower salary. First, the record does not indicate whether that in fact occurred or even whether plaintiff was actually high on the salary scale. But more importantly, paying a lower salary to a less experienced teacher would still not compensate defendant for having to bring onto its staff—in midyear—a teacher unfamiliar with the school system and thus perhaps less effective in his teaching than someone who had filled the position from the beginning of the school year. These losses were ones to which it would be difficult to assign a precise monetary amount. As such, they are particularly amenable to being compensated through a liquidated damages provision.

We find that 4% of plaintiff's salary is an eminently reasonable estimate, in advance, of the losses defendant could be expected to suffer in the event of plaintiff's breach. It is not so large that it appears on its face to be a penalty. Also, the percentage method of computing liquidated damages is particularly appropriate in a teacher's contract. A higher salary denotes more experience and/or education. Thus, the higher a teacher's salary, the more difficult it would be to find a comparable replacement, and the more disruptive his departure likely would be to the school system.

Plaintiff attacks the reasonableness of the provision by pointing out that it would exact the same damages from a teacher whether he resigned the first week or the last week of the school year. That argument, however, misses the mark, for the kinds of losses defendant could be expected to suffer would tend to change very little from one time of year to another. Perhaps if a teacher were to resign in the last week of school, defendant would be spared the expense of seeking a replacement. However, that saving could arguably be offset by the added disruption caused by a resignation at that time in terms of deciding whether students should pass or fail and accomplishing the teacher's statutory year-end duties.

* * *

[The trial court judgment upholding the validity of the liquidated damages clause is] Affirmed.

Notes and Questions

1. *Lake River* instructs that under Illinois law, liquidated damages must bear a reasonable relationship to the likely damages from breach, and actual damages must be difficult to measure.

Questions: Does the liquidated damages clause upheld in *Arduini* meet those requirements? Are the liquidated damages more likely to reflect the damages that would fully compensate the school district than the amount it would likely recover under the expectations measure? Are liquidated damages more likely than expectation damages to give resigning teachers incentives to engage only in efficient breaches?

2. Besides supplying a more accurate measure of actual loss than a court's calculation of expectations in some circumstances, liquidated damages clauses can help promisors convince promisees of their trustworthiness. A disproportionately high liquidated damages provision benefits those trying to overcome a bad reputation or those unknown to potential contracting partners. The promise of liquidated damages resembles a payment to the promisee in exchange for his accepting the risk of dealing with the promisor.

If liquidated damages are viewed as a risk premium, the school board in *Arduini* may have insisted on the liquidated damages clause as insurance against teachers disrupting the educational process by resigning during the school year. For this analogy to work, the teacher would have to receive a "premium" for providing insurance, perhaps in the form of a higher salary or being hired over someone else. If the teacher agrees to bear the loss should the risk materialize in return for a premium, it is efficient to enforce the parties' risk allocation because if they are rational maximizers, the teacher is the best cost avoider of the resulting losses, or is less risk-averse.

Questions: Is it plausible that the liquidated damages provision in *Arduini* minimized the losses associated with breach by allocating losses to the least cost avoider? That it allocated risk to the least risk-averse party?

3. For liquidated damages provisions to fulfill insurance purposes, the amount of the damages specified in the contract must exceed expectation damages to take account of the "premium" paid the insurer. For example, the premium for fire insurance should approximate the expected loss from a fire discounted by the probability that a fire will occur. Insurance against a one percent chance of fire should cost roughly one percent of the likely losses resulting from the fire. When a fire does occur, the payout to a single claimant will thus be much larger than his premium for a given period. Similarly, a liquidated damages clause with an insurance function may be substantially disproportionate to the expectation losses of the promisee who paid the "premium". A half-percent increase in pay may fully compensate a teacher for agreeing to pay four percent of his annual salary in the event of his mid-year resignation.

Question: Does the insurance function make the liquidated damages clause in *Arduini* look less like a penalty clause? Arduini earned $3579.60 for 38 days of teaching and was required to pay damages of $715.92 (twenty percent of his earnings) when he resigned.

E. THE LIMITS OF CONTRACT

The beginning of this chapter identified characteristics of the contracting process that might interfere with the allocation of resources to their most valuable uses. Contractual exchanges may not maximize wealth, and perhaps should not be enforced, when they are not voluntary or when there is incomplete information about or ability to appreciate their consequences and implications. In the cases below, courts apply the doctrines of duress and unconscionability to excuse individuals who entered contractual arrangements from their obligations. The court in Peter Matthews, Ltd. v. Robert Mabey, Inc. describes the fault in the contracting process as a lack of voluntary agreement. The court in Williams v. Walker–Thomas Furniture Co. declares that the contract's terms are too one-sided and suggests that the contracting process was flawed by lack of information and the plaintiff's inability to appreciate the consequences of the exchange.

From an economic standpoint, contracts inevitably involve varying degrees of voluntariness, fairness, completeness of information, and appreciation of economic consequences of an exchange. The discussions of duress and unconscionability that follow explore the economic rationale for those defenses and the limits of courts' willingness to enforce contracts.

1. DURESS

A party to a contract may claim the defense of duress if he agreed to the contract's terms because of an "improper" threat by the other party that left him no reasonable alternative. See Restatement (Second) of Contracts § 175 (1979). To appreciate the economics of duress, focus on the contracting process to determine what aspect of the bargaining makes the contract unenforceable.

PETER MATTHEWS, LTD. v. ROBERT MABEY, INC.

Supreme Court, Appellate Division, 1986.
117 A.D.2d 943, 499 N.Y.S.2d 254.

YESAWICH, JUSTICE.

* * *

Plaintiffs Peter and Sarah Matthews, husband and wife, own and operate plaintiff Peter Matthews, Ltd. (hereinafter the corporation). The corporation is organized under the laws of the United Kingdom and is engaged internationally in dealing in fine art. In 1979, plaintiffs hired defendants to move the contents of their New York City apartment, including corporate property (paintings), to a house they had rented in East Chatham, Columbia County. The move occurred on May 7, 1979. After defendants' employees had fully loaded plaintiffs' possessions into a moving truck, Peter Matthews was presented with a bill of lading to sign. A provision of the bill limited the carrier's liability in the event of loss to the greater of a lump sum value to be declared or an amount based on the poundage transported; Peter Matthews specified $15,000 as the lump sum value and signed the bill. En route to East Chatham, a fire in the truck destroyed or damaged many of plaintiffs' belongings.

Plaintiffs thereafter instituted the instant negligence and breach of contract suit seeking damages substantially in excess of the $15,000 contract limit. * * * [P]laintiffs claimed that the bill of lading was invalid, having been signed under duress * * *.

Defendants urge that plaintiffs' proof does not, as a matter of law, raise a question of duress in the execution of the bill of lading. Duress sufficient to render a contract voidable exists where contract concessions are elicited "by means of a wrongful threat precluding the exercise of [the aggrieved's] free will". In this regard, the affidavit of Peter Matthews states that at 7:00 P.M. on the day of the move, "the atmosphere of hostility and impatience was extreme" and the crew, "three angry and exhausted working men", "were frantic to leave in order to get back to Chatham that night. The Bill of Lading was thrust at me with a demand for a signature—'without this we can't leave'." With respect to the declaration of a lump sum limit on liability, Peter Matthews swears as follows:

> [The workers] said any figure above a nominal one would have to be cleared and agreed by [defendant Robert] Mabey. If we insisted on a higher figure they said they could not and would not leave. Their insistence that Mabey could not be reached out of office hours left us no choice. To get them on the road, we put $15,000 in desperation.

According to plaintiffs, at that juncture it was early evening and their apartment was empty; their goods were all in the truck on a busy Manhattan street, with no agreement consigning the goods to the movers. In addition, the movers refused to proceed until the bill of lading was signed. Nothing in the record suggests that plaintiffs had any practical alternative to compliance. That facts sufficient to withstand summary judgment on the duress issue were raised is self-evident.

* * *

Order [denying defendants' motion for summary judgment on the duress issue] affirmed, with costs.

Notes and Questions

1. Consider Peter and Sarah Matthews' alternatives on their Manhattan street that early evening. They could ship the contents of their apartment with $15,000 in lump sum insurance, substantially underinsuring the artwork, or leave their valuables in the truck in the street overnight until the boss of the three impatient and exhausted working men could be found the next day to approve a higher insurance figure. It is not literally true that they had "no choice"; the alternative to signing the bill of lading was merely unattractive. The Matthews did not deny that they preferred signing to the less attractive alternative.

Question: Given the parties' positions at the time they agreed to the insurance term, did the agreement leave both parties better off than they would have been without the agreement?

2. *Peter Matthews* describes duress as extracting a contract "by means of a wrongful threat precluding the exercise of the [aggrieved's] free will." In a sense, Peter and Sarah Matthews exercised free choice when they agreed to the $15,000 limitation of liability in order to get the three angry truck drivers started on their way. Although the defendants' threat may have drastically limited the range of attractive choices, the Matthews were able to evaluate their options intelligently, appreciated the consequences and implications of their agreement, and all of the parties affected by the exchange were involved in the bargaining. Ordinarily contracts made under those conditions are enforced.

Question: Why should the court decline to enforce a contract entered under threat of an illegal or wrongful act? Consider the case of two people bargaining over a horse. When the buyer first offers $100, the owner refuses to sell; the buyer then puts a gun to the owner's head and the owner agrees to sell the horse for $100.

3. Duress requires an illegal or wrongful threat. Although Matthews described the defendants' employees as "hostile" and "angry," the defendants never threatened violence. Their only clear threat was a threat not to perform their obligations under the contract until the plaintiffs signed the bill of lading.

Contract law generally protects a promisee's entitlement to performance with a liability rule. A promisor is free to breach and pay damages. Of course, a rational promisor who is liable for the promisee's damage will only breach when the cost of performance exceeds the damage from nonperformance.

> *Questions:* If the Matthews had refused to sign and the shipping company had breached the contract, would that have been an efficient or inefficient breach? In what sense might the defendants' threat of nonperformance have been "wrongful"?

4. A growing number of states recognize the doctrine of "economic duress" or "business compulsion." Courts generally have found three elements necessary to a prima facie case of economic duress: (1) wrongful acts or threats by the defendant; (2) financial distress caused by the wrongful acts or threats; (3) the absence of any reasonable alternative to the terms presented by the wrongdoer. See International Paper Co. v. Whilden, 469 So.2d 560, 562 (Ala. 1985) (striking down third party's agreement to indemnify International Paper as executed under duress, because International Paper wrongfully refused to pay accounts due to third party unless it signed indemnity agreement).

Like classic duress, economic duress involves an element of extortion, in the sense that the defendant is a cause of the plaintiff's distress. In Hackley et al. v. Headley, 45 Mich. 569, 8 N.W 511 (1881), the court overturned a trial court finding of duress where the defendant had not created but merely exploited the plaintiff's vulnerability. Hackley and his partners owed Headley $4260 and offered $4000 in full settlement of the debt, knowing that Headley was in dire financial straits and could not refuse the offer. Hackley's breach of the promise to repay $4260 was certainly a wrongful act, but it was not the cause of Headley's financial woes. Part of the court's justification is as follows, 8 N.W. at 514:

> The same contract which would be valid if made with a man easy in his circumstances, becomes invalid when the contracting party is pressed with the necessity of immediately meeting his [own debts]. But this would be a most dangerous, as well as a most unequal doctrine; and if accepted, no one could well know when he would be safe in dealing on the ordinary terms of negotiation with a party who professed to be in great need.

> *Questions:* When the defendant is *not* the cause of the plaintiff's distress, is there any economic reason not to enforce a contract where the defendant takes advantage of the plaintiff's weak bargaining position? Suppose the owner of a fine horse worth $100 suddenly finds himself destitute. He needs money to buy food and decides to sell the horse immediately. Unfortunately he can only find one potential buyer. The buyer, who knows the seller's predicament, offers only $10. The owner sells. Should the contract be enforceable?

5. Two years later, the Michigan Supreme Court again considered the facts of *Hackley* in Headley v. Hackley et al., 50 Mich. 43, 14 N.W. 693 (1883). This time the court held that the original promise to pay the plaintiff $4200 *was* enforceable. Instead of arguing distress, the plaintiff argued that he received no consideration for agreeing to settle for only $4000.

Recall that in *Rexite Casting*, above, the court held that a modification of a contract is unenforceable unless it modifies the obligations of *both* parties: "If the obligation of one party only is affected by the new arrangement, and the other party receives nothing additional and is relieved of no duty, then there is a want of consideration."

The Uniform Commercial Code permits enforcement of unilateral contract modifications: § 2–209(1) states that "[a]n agreement modifying a contract within this Article needs no consideration to be binding." Section 2–209 appears to be contrary to the *Rexite Casting* rule, but, as the Official Comments to the U.C.C. reveal, only for good faith modifications to which both parties agree. Comment 2 reads:

> 2. Subsection (1) provides that an agreement modifying a sales contract needs no consideration to be binding.

> However, modifications made thereunder must meet the test of good faith imposed by this Act. The effective use of bad faith to escape performance on the original contract terms is barred, and the extortion of a "modification" without legitimate commercial reason is ineffective as a violation of the duty of good faith. Nor can a mere technical consideration support a modification made in bad faith.

Questions: Does the rule allowing only "good faith" modifications without consideration encourage the efficient allocation of resources? How does that rule apply to the facts of Headley v. Hackley?

2. UNCONSCIONABILITY

Thus far, the economic analysis of contract law in this book has ignored the substantive terms of contracts themselves. It has examined the issues of efficient breach, efficient remedies, and problems in formation while assuming that the allocation of rights selected by the parties is an acceptable starting point for analysis. The unconscionability doctrine calls that assumption into question and requires an inquiry into when that allocation of rights itself should be examined.

The Uniform Commercial Code § 2–302 permits the court to refuse to enforce a contract (or any clause of a contract) it finds unconscionable. The challenge for economic analysis is to find an efficiency rationale for the unconscionability rule, a way of applying the doctrine of unconscionability rules consistent with the principle of wealth maximization.

WILLIAMS v. WALKER–THOMAS FURNITURE COMPANY (I)

District of Columbia Court of Appeals, 1964.
198 A.2d 914.

QUINN, ASSOCIATE JUDGE.

Appellant, a person of limited education separated from her husband, is maintaining herself and her seven children by means of public assistance. During the period 1957–1962 she had a continuous course of dealings with appellee from which she purchased many household articles on the installment plan. These included sheets, curtains, rugs, chairs, a chest of drawers, beds, mattresses, a washing machine, and a stereo set. In 1963 appellee filed a complaint in replevin for possession of all the items purchased by appellant, alleging that her payments were in default and that it retained title to the goods according to the sales contracts. By the writ of replevin appellee obtained a bed, chest of drawers, washing machine, and the stereo set. After hearing testimony and examining the contracts, the trial court entered judgment for appellee.

Appellant's principal contentions on appeal are (1) there was a lack of meeting of the minds, and (2) the contracts were against public policy.

Appellant signed fourteen contracts in all. They were approximately six inches in length and each contained a long paragraph in extremely fine print. One of the sentences in this paragraph provided that payments, after the first purchase, were to be prorated on all purchases then outstanding. Mathematically, this had the effect of keeping a balance due on all items until the time balance was completely eliminated. It meant that title to the first purchase, remained in appellee until the fourteenth purchase, made some five years later, was fully paid.

At trial appellant testified that she understood the agreements to mean that when payments on the running account were sufficient to balance the amount due on an individual item, the item became hers. She testified that most of the purchases were made at her home; that the contracts were signed in blank; that she did not read the instruments; and that she was not provided with a copy. She admitted, however, that she did not ask anyone to read or explain the contracts to her.

We have stated that "one who refrains from reading a contract and in conscious ignorance of its terms voluntarily assents thereto will not be relieved from his bad bargain." "One who signs a contract has a duty to read it and is obligated according to its terms." "It is as much the duty of a person who cannot read the language in which a contract is written to have someone read it to him before he signs it, as it is the duty of one who can read to peruse it himself before signing it."

A careful review of the record shows that appellant's assent was not obtained 'by fraud or even misrepresentation falling short of fraud.' This is not a case of mutual misunderstanding but a unilateral mistake. Under these circumstances, appellant's first contention is without merit.

Appellant's second argument presents a more serious question. The record reveals that prior to the last purchase appellant had reduced the balance in her account to $164. The last purchase, a stereo set, raised the balance due to $678. Significantly, at the time of this and the preceding purchases, appellee was aware of appellant's financial position. The reverse side of the stereo contract listed the name of appellant's social worker and her $218 monthly stipend from the government. Nevertheless, with full knowledge that appellant had to feed, clothe and support both herself and seven children on this amount, appellee sold her a $514 stereo set.

We cannot condemn too strongly appellee's conduct. It raises serious questions of sharp practice and irresponsible business dealings. A review of the legislation in the District of Columbia affecting retail sales and the pertinent decisions of the highest court in this jurisdiction disclose, however, no ground upon which this court can declare the contracts in question contrary to public policy. * * * We think Congress should consider corrective legislation to protect the public from such exploitative contracts as were utilized in the case at bar.

Affirmed.

WILLIAMS v. WALKER–THOMAS FURNITURE COMPANY (II)

United States Court of Appeals District of Columbia Circuit, 1965.
350 F.2d 445, 121 U.S.App.D.C. 315.

J. Skelly Wright, Circuit Judge:

Appellee, Walker–Thomas Furniture Company, operates a retail furniture store in the District of Columbia. During the period from 1957 to 1962 each appellant in these cases purchased a number of household items from Walker–Thomas, for which payment was to be made in installments. The terms of each purchase were contained in a printed form contract which set forth the value of the purchased item and purported to lease the item to appellant for a stipulated monthly rent payment. The contract then provided, in substance, that title would remain in Walker–Thomas until the total of all the monthly payments made equaled the stated value of the item, at which time appellants could take title. In the event of a default in the payment of any monthly installment, Walker–Thomas could repossess the item.

* * *

Appellants' principal contention, rejected by both the trial and the appellate courts below, is that these contracts, or at least some of them, are unconscionable and, hence, not enforceable. * * *

* * *

We do not agree that the court lacked the power to refuse enforcement to contracts found to be unconscionable. In other jurisdictions, it has been held as a matter of common law that unconscionable contracts are not enforceable. While no decision of this court so holding has been found, the notion that an unconscionable bargain should not be given full enforcement is by no means novel. In Scott v. United States, the Supreme Court stated:

" * * * If a contract be unreasonable and unconscionable, but not void for fraud, a court of law will give to the party who sues for its breach damages, not according to its letter, but only such as he is equitably entitled to. * * * "

Since we have never adopted or rejected such a rule, the question here presented is actually one of first impression.

Congress has recently enacted the Uniform Commercial Code, which specifically provides that the court may refuse to enforce a contract which it finds to be unconscionable at the time it was made. The enactment of this section, which occurred subsequent to the contracts here in suit, does not mean that the common law of the District of Columbia was otherwise at the time of enactment, nor does it preclude the court from adopting a similar rule in the exercise of its powers to develop the common law for the District of Columbia. In fact, in view of the absence of prior authority on the point, we consider the congressional adoption of § 2–302 persuasive authority for following the rationale of the cases from which the section is explicitly derived. Accordingly, we hold that where the element of unconscionability is present at the time a contract is made, the contract should not be enforced.

Unconscionability has generally been recognized to include an absence of meaningful choice on the part of one of the parties together with contract terms which are unreasonably favorable to the other party. Whether a meaningful choice is present in a particular case can only be determined by consideration of all the circumstances surrounding the transaction. In many cases the meaningfulness of the choice is negated by a gross inequality of bargaining power.[7] The manner in which the contract was entered is also relevant to this consideration. Did each party to the contract, considering his obvious education or lack of it, have a reasonable opportunity to understand the terms of the contract, or were the important terms hidden in a maze of fine print and minimized by deceptive sales practices? Ordinarily, one who signs an agreement without full knowledge of its terms might be held to assume the risk that he has entered a one-sided bargain. But when a party of little bargaining power, and hence little real choice, signs a commercially unreasonable contract with little or no knowledge of its terms, it is hardly likely that his consent, or even an objective manifestation of his consent, was ever given to all the terms. In such a case the usual rule that the terms of the agreement are not to be questioned should be abandoned and the court should consider whether the terms of the contract are so unfair that enforcement should be withheld.

7. Inquiry into the relative bargaining power of the two parties is not an inquiry wholly divorced from the general question of unconscionability, since a one-sided bargain is itself evidence of the inequality of the bargaining parties. This fact was vaguely recognized in the common law doctrine of intrinsic fraud, that is, fraud which can be presumed from the grossly unfair nature of the terms of the contract. * * *

In determining reasonableness or fairness, the primary concern must be with the terms of the contract considered in light of the circumstances existing when the contract was made. The test is not simple, nor can it be mechanically applied. The terms are to be considered "in the light of the general commercial background and the commercial needs of the particular trade or case." Corbin suggests the test as being whether the terms are "so extreme as to appear unconscionable according to the mores and business practices of the time and place." [12] We think this formulation correctly states the test to be applied in those cases where no meaningful choice was exercised upon entering the contract.

Because the trial court and the appellate court did not feel that enforcement could be refused, no findings were made on the possible unconscionability of the contracts in these cases. Since the record is not sufficient for our deciding the issue as a matter of law, the cases must be remanded to the trial court for further proceedings.

So ordered.

DANAHER, CIRCUIT JUDGE, dissenting.

The District of Columbia Court of Appeals obviously was as unhappy about the situation here presented as any of us can possibly be. Its opinion in the Williams case, quoted in the majority text, concludes: "We think Congress should consider corrective legislation to protect the public from such exploitative contracts as were utilized in the case at bar."

My view is thus summed up by an able court which made no finding that there had actually been sharp practice. Rather the appellant seems to have known precisely where she stood.

There are many aspects of public policy here involved. What is a luxury to some may seem an outright necessity to others. Is public oversight to be required of the expenditures of relief funds? A washing machine, e.g., in the hands of a relief client might become a fruitful source of income. Many relief clients may well need credit, and certain business establishments will take long chances on the sale of items, expecting their pricing policies will afford a degree of protection commensurate with the risk.   * * *

I mention such matters only to emphasize the desirability of a cautious approach to any such problem, particularly since the law for so long has allowed parties such great latitude in making their own contracts. I dare say there must annually be thousands upon thousands of installment credit transactions in this jurisdiction, and one can only speculate as to the effect the decision in these cases will have.

I join the District of Columbia Court of Appeals in its disposition of the issues.

12. The traditional test * * * is "such as no man in his senses and not under delusion would make on the one hand, and as no honest or fair man would accept, on the other."

Notes and Questions

1. Under *Williams*, the doctrine of unconscionability requires an evaluation of (1) the process by which the agreement was reached, and (2) the fairness or reasonableness of the resulting agreement. The procedural inquiry focuses on the "absence of a meaningful choice." The court may also consider the relative bargaining power of the parties and the manner in which the contract was entered. The substantive inquiry explores whether procedural defects produced a contract with unfair terms. Thus, the court looks to whether the terms of the contract were unreasonably favorable to one party. Only if the contract suffers from both procedural defects and resulting substantive unfairness will the doctrine of unconscionability apply.

2. Both the District of Columbia Court of Appeals and the United States Court of Appeals for the District of Columbia Circuit (which heard appeals from the local District of Columbia courts at the time) believed Mrs. Williams had entered a contract with extremely unfavorable terms. Nevertheless, apart from a brief mention of her "limited education," neither case suggested she be excused from the contract because she was not a rational maximizer competent to pursue her own best interests.

Question: Why should the law presume that individuals are competent even when they enter unfavorable contracts that suggest otherwise?

3. The D.C. Court of Appeals decision in *Williams* held that the contract was not obtained by fraud or deliberate misrepresentation. The case was one of "unilateral mistake"—presumably, Mrs. William's mistake in failing to read the long paragraph "in extremely fine print" containing the proration provision.

The U.S. Court of Appeals did not analyze *Williams* as a unilateral mistake case but instead focused on potential procedural defects in the contract's formation. The court was particularly concerned that important contractual terms were "hidden in a maze of fine print and minimized by deceptive sales practices." The comments to § 2–302 of the Uniform Commercial Code indicate that one of the principles underlying the doctrine of unconscionability is protecting parties against "unfair surprise." If a party is confronted with contract terms she cannot reasonably be expected to understand or concerning which she has a reasonable but mistaken understanding, and the other party knows she is mistaken, it is the same as if the other party had misrepresented those terms, whether innocently or intentionally.

Questions: From an economic perspective, how might "unfair surprise" affect the efficiency of contractual agreements? Should such contracts be enforced?

4. In evaluating procedural defects, the U.S. Court of Appeals noted that there may be an "absence of meaningful choice" when there is "gross inequality of bargaining power" between the parties.

Questions: In what sense might Mrs. Williams have had no choice but to sign the contract? Would Mrs. Williams have been able to raise a successful defense of economic duress?

5. The doctrine of unconscionability is unnecessary when a party can prove duress, fraud, or incompetence. Unconscionability does permit the court to set aside contracts when such procedural defects are suspected but unprovable by dispensing with the need to prove them.

But potential procedural defects, alone, are not enough to make a contract unconscionable. Unlike cases of fraud, incompetence, and duress, which do not require a separate inquiry into the fairness of the contract's substantive terms, a claim of unconscionability only succeeds when the contract is substantively unfair as well as procedurally suspect. Unconscionability is not just a watered-down version of the rules applying to fraud, duress, or incompetence because, in addition to showing procedural defects that created "the absence of meaningful choice on the part of one of the parties," the doctrine includes the additional element that the "contract terms were unreasonably favorable" to the other party "in light of circumstances existing when the contract was made." The requirement of substantive unfairness at the time of the agreement eliminates cases where changed circumstances create particular hardships for one of the parties. The substantive analysis focuses on whether the contract terms were reasonable when the deal was struck.

Economic analysis suggests a role for the two parts of the unconscionability inquiry. Procedural defects in the form of fraud, duress, or incompetence may result in contracts whose efficiency is suspect. If evidence of procedural defects is not sufficiently strong to make a case for one of the traditional defenses, additional proof of the severity of the defect may be required. Substantively unfair contract terms supply that additional proof.

Some unconscionability cases emphasize the significance of procedural defects and slight the substantive defects while others emphasize the substantive defects. This suggests that if one of these two defects is particularly serious, less evidence is needed to establish the existence of the other.

Question: What are the efficiency implications of such an approach to claims of unconscionability?

6. Substantively unfair contracts may result when the exploiting party has an advantage because of circumstances internal to the transaction (characteristics of the transaction or of the victim). If the victim is unaware or unable to understand her options, if the nature of the bargaining impairs the victim's ability to exercise her judgment, or if other procedural defects arise, one party may be able to make an unreasonably favorable deal. Economic analysis might assist in determining whether the deal is unreasonably skewed by seeking a legitimate business justification for the contract terms. A legitimate business justification would help negate the inference that the terms were unfair or exploitative.

Substantively unfair contracts may also result from factors external to the immediate transaction, such as characteristics of the market as a whole. A seller would be able to insist on particularly favorable terms if there was no competition in its geographic area for the product or service involved. The lack of competition may be due to the fact that there are no other sellers in the area to whom the buyer can turn, or that all sellers tacitly follow each other's practices in order to avoid competition or agree not to compete (which in this case would mean that they agree to adopt the same contractual term). Where there is only one seller, that seller acts as a monopolist and is not constrained in setting price or other terms by the possibility that other sellers will offer terms the buyer would prefer. Agreements not to compete, tacit or explicit, result in "term fixing" where all firms set similar contract terms. Lack of competition is customarily the concern of antitrust law, examined in Chapter 6, but one can imagine that the furniture store in *Williams* might have been the only seller of furniture in the area, or that all of the sellers in the area where Mrs. Williams shopped either explicitly agreed to employ the same term or simply followed each other's practice to avoid competition.

7. A legitimate business justification for harsh contract terms helps negate the inference that the terms were substantively unfair or exploitative. Consider the proration or "add-on" term in the *Williams* contract. By this term, the seller/creditor was permitted to apply the buyer's payments on any article purchased on credit to the buyer's outstanding balances on all items. The seller could make certain that the buyer did not pay off any of the items until all were paid off. The result was that all of the items purchased on credit served as security until the buyer paid off the debt on all the items.

Questions: Could Walker–Thomas reasonably argue that the add-on term was justified? Consider that Mrs. Williams apparently had little else to offer as security and that the value of used furniture usually is substantially less than its purchase price and potentially less than the credit extended to buy it. If the proration clause was financially necessary from a business perspective, does that mean it was substantively reasonable?

8. Consider the efficiency characteristics of a purely substantive unconscionability test, one that would allow a party to overturn any contractual term that was unreasonably favorable to the other party at the time the contract was made. Such an unconscionability rule would have consequences for consumers.

Questions: Consider the *Williams* decision. Buyers in Mrs. Williams' position who sign similar contracts will not be bound by them and businesses will be unable to use them. Will consumers be better off as a result? Does the answer to this question depend on whether the add-on clause is a business necessity justified by the risks inherent in extending credit for furniture to people like Mrs. Williams?

Chapter 5

THE EFFICIENCY OF THE COMMON LAW

Previous chapters explore the notion that the common law rules of property, tort, and contract serve the economic goal of efficiency by creating incentives for individuals to behave in a fashion that maximizes total wealth. That possibility raises the question: if the common law *is* efficient, how did it become so?

Chapter 5 considers two explanations for why the common law should tend toward efficient rules. The first explanation is that judges recognize efficiency as a value and pursue efficiency when formulating legal rules. The second explanation is that the litigation process may create evolutionary pressures favoring efficient over inefficient rules even when judges are insensitive to, or hostile towards, economic analysis.

A. JUDICIAL VALUES AND ECONOMIC ANALYSIS
UNION OIL COMPANY v. OPPEN
United States Court of Appeals, Ninth Circuit, 1974.
501 F.2d 558.

SNEED, CIRCUIT JUDGE.

This is another case growing out of the Santa Barbara oil spill of 1969. The plaintiffs are commercial fishermen. Each of their complaints alleges that * * * the defendants joined in an enterprise, the day-to-day operation of which was within the control and under the management of defendant Union Oil Company, to drill for oil in the waters of the Santa Barbara Channel; that during the period commencing on or about January 28, 1969, vast quantities of raw crude oil were released and subsequently carried by wind, wave and tidal currents over vast stretches of the coastal waters of Southern California; and that as a consequence the plaintiffs have suffered various injuries for which damages are sought. * * *

* * *

In May of 1972, the defendants moved for partial summary judgment * * * to strike from plaintiffs' prayers "that item of damage usually denominated as 'ecological damage'." More specifically, the defendants sought to eliminate from the prayers any element of damages consisting of profits lost as a result of the reduction in the commercial fishing potential of the Santa Barbara Channel which may have been caused by the occurrence. According to the defendants, such longterm ecological damage is not compensable under the law * * *.

The motion was denied * * *.

* * *

* * * As we see it, the issue is whether the defendants owed a duty to the plaintiffs, commercial fishermen, to refrain from negligent conduct in their drilling operations, which conduct reasonably and foreseeably could have been anticipated to cause a diminution of the aquatic life in the Santa Barbara Channel area and thus cause injury to the plaintiffs' business.

In finding that such a duty exists, we are influenced by the manner in which the Supreme Court of California has approached the duty issue in tort law. * * *

* * *

* * * [U]nder California law the presence of a duty on the part of the defendants in this case would turn substantially on foreseeability. That being the crucial determinant, the question must be asked whether the defendants could reasonably have foreseen that negligently conducted drilling operations might diminish aquatic life and thus injure the business of commercial fishermen. We believe the answer is yes. The dangers of pollution were and are known even by school children. The defendants understood the risks of their business and should reasonably have foreseen the scope of its responsibilities. To assert that the defendants were unable to foresee that negligent conduct resulting in a substantial oil spill could diminish aquatic life and thus injure the plaintiffs is to suppose a degree of general ignorance of the effects of oil pollution not in accord with good sense.

* * *

The same conclusion is reached when the issue before us is approached from the standpoint of economics. Recently a number of scholars have suggested that liability for losses occasioned by torts should be apportioned in a manner that will best contribute to the achievement of an optimum allocation of resources. See e.g., Calabresi, The Cost of Accidents, 69–73 (1970) (hereinafter Calabresi); Coase, The Problem of Social Cost, 3 J. Law & Econ. 1 (1960). This optimum, in theory, would be that which would be achieved by a perfect market system. In determining whether the cost of an accident should be borne by the injured party or be shifted, in whole or in part, this approach requires the court to fix the identity of the party who can avoid the costs most cheaply. Once fixed, this determination then controls liability.

It turns out, however, that fixing the identity of the best or cheapest cost-avoider is more difficult than might be imagined. In order to facilitate this determination, Calabresi suggests several helpful guidelines. The first of these would require a rough calculation designed to exclude as potential cost-avoiders those groups/activities which could avoid accident costs only at an extremely high expense. While not easy to apply in any concrete sense, this guideline does suggest that the imposition of oil spill costs directly upon such groups as the consumers of staple groceries is not a sensible solution. Under this guideline, potential liability becomes resolved into a choice between, on an ultimate level, the consumers of fish and those of products derived from the defendants' total operations.

To refine this choice, Calabresi goes on to provide additional guidelines which, in this instance, have proven none too helpful. * * *

Calabresi's final guideline, however, unmistakably points to the defendants as the best cost-avoider. Under this guideline, the loss should be allocated to that party who can best correct any error in allocation, if such there be, by acquiring the activity to which the party has been made liable. The capacity 'to buy out' the plaintiffs if the burden is too great is, in essence, the real focus of Calabresi's approach. On this basis there is no contest—the defendants' capacity is superior.

* * *

* * * The plaintiffs in the present action lawfully and directly make use of a resource of the sea, *viz.* its fish, in the ordinary course of their business. This type of use is entitled to protection from negligent conduct by the defendants in their drilling operations. Both the plaintiffs and defendants conduct their business operations away from land and in, on and under the sea. Both must carry on their commercial enterprises in a reasonably prudent manner. Neither should be permitted negligently to inflict commercial injury on the other. We decide no more than this.

Affirmed.

Notes and Questions

1. Judge Sneed's opinion in Union Oil Company v. Oppen explicitly used economic analysis in determining the appropriate rule of law to apply to the commercial fishermen's claim against Union Oil for oil spill damage to the fish in the Santa Barbara channel.

Questions: How does Judge Sneed's attitude towards, and use of, economic analysis compare with other judicial opinions appearing in this book? In other words, what values and concerns do courts typically appear to consider in making legal rules?

2. In *Union Oil*, the Ninth Circuit decided whether the commercial fishing fleet or the oil company should bear the cost of oil spill damage to schools of commercially-harvested fish in the Santa Barbara channel. In assigning the loss to the oil company, the court attempted to determine which party was in the best position to minimize the combined costs of damage to fish if drilling continued, or lost oil production if drilling were halted to prevent another spill. However, the Court observed that "fixing the identity of the best or cheapest cost-avoider is more difficult than might be imagined" and concluded that "[u]nder this guideline, potential liability becomes resolved into a choice between, on an ultimate level, the consumers of fish and those of products derived from the defendants' total operations." The court thus concluded that the question of who should bear the loss came down to a choice between consumers of fish caught in the channel, and consumers of oil and gasoline products.

Questions: Would consumers who purchase oil and gasoline products be likely to bear all the costs if Union Oil paid damages to the plaintiff fisherman? Would fish consumers be likely to bear all the costs if the fishermen received no compensation for the injury to the fish harvest?

3. The Ninth Circuit found especially compelling Calabresi's suggestion that in assigning accident costs, policymakers should be sensitive to allocating losses to "that party who can best correct any error in allocation." In The Costs of Accidents: A Legal and Economic Analysis 150 (1970), Calabresi describes his guideline as follows:

The third guideline for picking the cheapest cost avoider is * * * to allocate accident costs in such a way as to maximize the likelihood that errors in allocation will be corrected in the market. This criterion assumes that despite transactions costs, a tendency exists for the market to find the cheapest cost avoider and influence him by bribes. It therefore urges us, to the extent we are unsure of who the cheapest cost avoider is, to charge accident costs to that loss bearer who can enter transactions most cheaply. This means that if the initial loss bearer chosen is not in fact the cheapest cost avoider, we have minimized the obstacle transaction costs impose on the market's finding and influencing the behavior of the cheapest cost avoider. Obviously this criterion does not suggest picking a party that clearly is not the cheapest cost avoider simply because he can bribe easily. It suggests that to the extent we are unsure of our choice among possible cheapest cost avoiders, the best briber in the group is our best bet.

Judge Sneed concluded that Calabresi's test required the court to allocate accident costs to the party that could best correct an error in allocation by "acquiring the activity to which the party has been made liable. The capacity 'to buy out' the plaintiffs if the burden is too great is, in essence, the real focus of Calabresi's approach. On this basis there is no contest—the [oil company's] capacity is superior * * *."

Question: Does the court accurately apply Calabresi's guidelines for the efficient allocation of accident costs?

4. In the vast majority of American and English courts, plaintiffs like the commercial fishermen in *Union Oil* who suffered lost profits may not recover those economic losses unless they also suffered property damage or

personal injury, on the theory that otherwise the defendants' liability might be boundless. In addition to harming the commercial fishing fleet, the Santa Barbara spill injured recreational fishers, boaters, and businesses operating restaurants and marinas on the channel. The spill also harmed those who sell supplies to recreational boaters and fishers and businesses on the channel.

Questions: Should such potential plaintiffs receive damages from Union Oil? Does economic analysis offer any insight into the threshold question of who is entitled to recover damages for environmental injury?

SAINT BARNABAS MEDICAL CENTER v. COUNTY OF ESSEX

Supreme Court of New Jersey, 1988.
111 N.J. 67, 543 A.2d 34.

STEIN, JUSTICE.

The novel question for decision in this case is the extent to which a county is responsible for the hospitalization costs of an indigent county jail inmate where the inmate remains hospitalized past the termination of his sentence. The Appellate Division held that an implied contract existed between the parties obligating defendant Essex County to pay to plaintiff, Saint Barnabas Medical Center (Saint Barnabas), the full amount owing for the inmate's hospitalization, here nearly $54,000, provided Saint Barnabas could prove that the entire duration of the patient's stay was necessary. We reverse. * * *

On July 13, 1982, Jessie Williams was committed to the Essex County Jail Annex, located in Caldwell, to begin serving a fifteen-day sentence. On July 16, Williams set himself on fire and required emergency treatment. Although Essex County had an existing arrangement with University Hospital for the treatment of its prisoners, corrections officers transported Williams to Saint Barnabas because of its specialized burn unit. * * *

Three days later, on July 19, 1982, Ray Grimm of Saint Barnabas phoned Elizabeth Neff in the Jail Annex's business office to confirm Williams' status as an inmate and to ascertain whether the County would be responsible for the treatment costs. * * * Neff informed Grimm that Williams was being "released," but acknowledged that the County would pay for the hospitalization costs incurred thus far, from Williams' admission to the hospital on the sixteenth through the end of the day. * * *

* * * After roughly seven weeks of treatment, Williams was released from the hospital on September 2, 1982; the total cost of his treatment and hospitalization came to $53,725.59, and an invoice in that amount was forwarded to the County. Consistent with its stated position, the County refused to acknowledge liability except for the first four days of Williams' treatment, an amount stipulated to be $5,401.

* * *

The basic issue in this case can be stated simply: As between a county and a hospital, which entity should bear the cost associated with the medical treatment of an indigent initially requiring such treatment while a ward of the county? Its resolution derives partially from principles of contract law, but is based primarily on the legal duties imposed on counties, with respect to the health care of indigent county jail inmates, and on hospitals, with respect to the health care of indigents generally.

* * *

* * * [T]he Appellate Division erred in finding an implied contract in this case since the circumstances did not sufficiently "negative the idea that [the services] were gratuitous." We hold that no liability to pay for Williams' care in part or in full can be imposed on defendant County based on a contract implied in fact.

However, Saint Barnabas need not shoulder the entire burden of providing the indigent inmate with medical treatment. Because Saint Barnabas fulfilled the County's duty to provide or obtain treatment for Williams during the tenure of his sentence, the County has been enriched at plaintiff's expense. To the extent the County benefitted from plaintiff's discharge of its duty, recovery may be had based on quasi-contract, or a contract implied-in-law.

* * *

The regulations governing the administration of county correctional facilities clearly imposed the responsibility for an inmate's health care on the county, but only during the period of incarceration. * * *

* * * Nothing * * * indicates that counties are to be treated as insurers for the future medical needs of indigent inmates any time a condition necessitating treatment arises during the period of confinement. The implausibility of imposing insurer-like duties on a county is evinced by positing the case of an indigent prisoner who, during the pendency of a county jail term, discovers he has cancer or AIDS, requiring extensive medical treatment for the rest of his life. In the absence of a tortious relationship between the county's incarceration of the inmate and the medical condition necessitating treatment, the existing legislative allocation of fiscal health care obligations compels the conclusion that county taxpayers are not the appropriate source of funding for such treatment. * * *

From Saint Barnabas's perspective, it is entirely within the ambit of its legal and fiscal responsibilities to accept the costs associated with indigent health care. * * * [T]he Legislature [has] established the Uncompensated Care Trust Fund and directed the computation of a uniform statewide "uncompensated care add-on" to be used in rate-setting at all hospitals. Hospitals that collect more through the add-on than necessary to cover their uncompensated care costs then "remit the net difference to the Fund," while hospitals whose indigent health care costs exceed the amount collected are authorized "to receive the net difference from the Fund." * * *

The Legislature has thus clearly established as the public policy of this State a system that imposes the costs of indigent medical care not on county taxpayers but on "all payers of health care services." Accordingly, we hold that the cost of the inmate's health care subsequent to the expiration of his [fifteen-day] sentence cannot be passed on to Essex County, but is to be borne by Saint Barnabas subject to its right to spread the loss through appropriate statutory and regulatory mechanisms. We recognize that this allocation of responsibility between a county and a private hospital does not follow inevitably from existing statutory or regulatory commands. It is significant, however, that in these cases the duration of the care may bear no relationship to the duration of the custodial term. We are convinced that our resolution of this issue is one that is both pragmatic and fully consistent with the public policies underlying the pertinent statutes and regulations.

* * *

POLLOCK, J., concurring.

* * *

The Court concludes that Essex County is responsible for the medical care of the prisoner for a period of time co-extensive with the prisoner's original sentence, and that St. Barnabas is responsible for the balance of the prisoner's medical care. In reaching that result, the Court * * * considers the costs of the prisoner's medical care and the consequences of the allocation of those costs. I concur. Courts should be aware of the costs and consequences of their decisions.

Implicit in the Court's opinion is recognition that the County is better able to control the risk of loss resulting from injuries to prisoners while they are in the County Jail. As between the County and St. Barnabas, the County, which maintains the jail, is better able to prevent prisoners from setting themselves on fire. Furthermore, the Court considers whether the County or the hospital is better able to allocate the cost of that risk. The parties did not present facts on the economic aspects of the distribution of the risk of loss or of the cost of that risk. Nonetheless, the [New Jersey] statutory scheme makes clear that a hospital must provide emergency treatment to an indigent patient and that the cost of that treatment is to be spread among the ratepayers of other hospitals throughout the State. Here, the effect would be to spread the cost among citizens, albeit those who are hospital patients, located throughout New Jersey, not simply those who reside in Essex County. * * * In this context, the court sensibly concludes that the County should bear the cost of treatment during the period of the prisoner's original sentence and that the hospital should thereafter be responsible. Both entities can spread the risk of loss: the County by transmitting the risk to the taxpayers, and the hospital by transmitting the risk to other ratepayers.

* * *

A court need not be committed to economic determinism to appreciate that an economic analysis can reveal and effectuate policy choices. As the Court acknowledges, its decision is not compelled by economic considerations but "is based primarily on the legal duties imposed on counties, with respect to the health care of indigent county jail inmates, and on hospitals with respect to the health care of indigents generally." In effect, the Court invokes economic reasoning to disclose policy choices implicit in legislatively imposed legal duties. Rather than predicate the decision on an independent economic analysis, the Court defers to the legislative and regulatory judgment on policy choices. Nonetheless, an economic analysis reveals the costs and subsidies implicit in the Court's decision.

This, I believe, is an appropriate use of economic analysis in the judicial process. Economics and law are different, but each discipline can illuminate the other. Economic analysis not only recognizes a decision's costs and benefits, but makes more predictable the effect of the decision. To appreciate that use of economic analysis, one need not subscribe to the proposition that the right rule of law is necessarily the one that is the most efficient. An economic analysis may be more appropriate in some cases, such as those involving rights that are traditionally measured by a monetary standard, than in others, such as those that involve fundamental or deeply personal rights. Some rights are not readily susceptible to an economic evaluation. Deciding cases remains an exercise in judgment, and an economic analysis, although it sheds light on a just decision, need not predetermine the outcome of a case.

Notes and Questions

1. The injuries Jessie Williams incurred when he set himself on fire were not the fault of the Essex County jail; there was no claim of negligence. The New Jersey Supreme Court consequently faced a choice of which of two potential defendants, if either, should be strictly liable for William's medical bills. The Court eventually determined that the Essex County jail was liable as William's custodian for those expenses incurred during the fifteen days that Williams was originally sentenced to incarceration. The Medical Center was responsible for all expenses incurred after Williams was originally scheduled to be released.

     Question: While the majority opinion in *Saint Barnabas* does not discuss economic considerations explicitly, Justice Pollock believed that the rule of law eventually adopted by the court was the efficient and correct rule under an economic analysis. How can judges select economically efficient rules without explicit consideration or use of economic analysis?

2. Earlier chapters include a number of examples of cases where a court has applied economic analysis either explicitly, as in *Union Oil,* or implicitly, as in *Saint Barnabas'* majority opinion. Economic analysis leads to efficient rules only if done correctly. Complex formulations such

as Calabresi's and Melamed's criteria give guidance but also create opportunities for misunderstanding. An alternative is for judges to apply common sense in recognizing the economic implications of legal rules.

Question: What economic principles and distributional choices are reflected in the majority's decision in *Saint Barnabas?*

3. Justice Pollock's concurrence in *Saint Barnabas* suggests that "[a]n economic analysis may be more appropriate in some cases * * * than in others."

Questions: In what areas of law might judges be more willing and able to adopt efficient rules? In what areas might economic analysis be more likely to be ignored, dismissed, or misapplied?

B. THE EFFICIENT EVOLUTION OF THE COMMON LAW

The cases examined thus far suggest that some judges are willing to use explicit economic analysis, some consider efficiency only implicitly, and others ignore or are hostile towards efficiency concerns. Even those courts willing to use economic analysis show varying degrees of competence in doing so.

A judicial preference for efficient rules therefore seems a weak explanation for the strong tendency toward efficiency observed in the common law doctrines of property, torts, and contract. Some additional explanation seems required. The following two sections consider theories of common law efficiency that focus not on judicial behavior, but on the behavior of the litigants who determine which cases are brought before the courts. Courts are essentially reactive rather than active; judges can only make law when litigants choose to bring disputes before them. To understand how litigant behavior can influence the development of the law, one must consider the factors that influence a party's decision to bring a case, settle it, try it, or appeal a trial court's decision.

1. THE LEGAL PROCESS AND LITIGANT BEHAVIOR

WEEKS v. BARECO OIL CO.

Circuit Court of Appeals, Seventh Circuit, 1941.
125 F.2d 84.

EVANS, CIRCUIT JUDGE.

This is a civil, statutory action to recover treble damages for injuries caused by an unlawful combination violative of the Anti–Trust Laws, and is an aftermath of a criminal prosecution therefor.

Plaintiffs are two Illinois jobbers of gasoline. They sue on their own behalf, and as representatives of a class of approximately 900 Illinois jobbers. The nineteen defendants are oil companies which were charged by indictments, with violating the Sherman Act.

The gist of the alleged conspiracy and injury is that defendants, in 1934, 1935, and 1936, lessened the jobbers' margin of profit, from 7½ cents to 5 cents per gallon. This illegal object was achieved by defendants' combining to raise and fix the spot tank car market price of gasoline, which price was, in the contracts between the respective plaintiffs and defendants, made the basis of the jobbers' cost price.

Motions to strike, and to quash, and to dismiss, were made by the defendants, and the District Court dismissed the complaint and dissolved the temporary restraining order which it had theretofore entered enjoining other jobbers in Illinois from instituting similar suits. The bases for the dismissal order were: (1) the plaintiffs do not constitute a "class" within Rule 23, of the Federal Rules of Civil Procedure, because they do not seek a "common relief." (2) The plaintiffs do not insure the adequate representation of all members of the class. * * *

Plaintiff Weeks, a former jobber at Wilmington, Illinois, claims specific damages to himself of $11,937.30 (to be trebled) incurred in the sale of 477,492 gallons in said three years. Plaintiff Sterling Corporation, a jobber at Chicago, handled 2,515,197 gallons in the same period, with a damage of $62,879.92 (untrebled). The 900 jobbers are alleged to have suffered $37,500,000 damages (2½ cents on 1,500,000,000 gallons).

The first sharply controverted issue is the propriety of this class action, instituted by two jobbers on behalf of nine hundred others.

* * *

The history of class suit litigation, its development over a century of growth, the origin and status of present Rule 23 of the Federal Rules of Civil Procedure, are all persuasive of the necessity of a liberal construction of this Rule 23, and its application to this class of litigation. It should be construed to permit a class suit where several persons jointly act to the injury of many persons so numerous that their voluntarily, unanimously joining in a suit is concededly improbable and impracticable. Under such circumstances, injured parties who are so minded, may present the grievance to a court on behalf of all, and the remaining members of the class may join as they see fit.

There are, it seems, more than the usual or ordinary reasons for permitting a class action here.

The difficulties inherent in the obtaining and presentation of proof by individual small jobbers, as contrasted by able, financially powerful companies, must be considered and appreciated. If there be a single conspiracy between all the codefendants here charged, and said single conspiracy were directed at *all* jobbers, a single trial would obviously expedite and simplify the achievement of justice. Each jobber should not be put to the tremendous task of ferreting out the evidence indicative of the existence of the alleged conspiracy. In all probability, the individual jobber could not do so. But, through a joinder of forces they might, between them, uncover such evidence as may lead to the proof of the conspiracy, if there be such proof. Nor is the financial aspect to be overlooked—that is, the plaintiffs' and defendants' relative financial ability. The relative financial interest in the outcome of this litigation is such, that greater parity of ability is obtained by a joinder of plaintiffs.

To permit the defendants to contest liability with each claimant in a single, separate suit, would, in many cases give defendants an advantage which would be almost equivalent to closing the door of justice to all small claimants. This is what we think the class suit practice was to prevent. Like many another practice, necessity was its mother. Its correct limitations must be ascertained by the experiences which brought it into existence.

* * *

Whether plaintiffs meet the [adequate representation] requirements of Rule 23 is the precise question we must answer. * * *

In the instant case we have two plaintiffs suing for and on behalf of nine hundred. This, on its face, seems small, but nevertheless a suit may be welcomed and supported, in fact, by a large percentage of said nine hundred, although many would not care to start separate, individual suits. Others, because of fear of costs and any other good reason, may not favor the class suit. May it be said that the two, therefore, did insure an adequate representation of the others?

* * *

There should be no obstruction thrown in the way of plaintiffs by the defendants, whose interests may well be to obstruct and impede the enforcement of claims against them. They would, undoubtedly, prefer to defend against each one of these claimants, separately. The chances of tiring the litigant or putting him to such large expense that his right of action would be a remediless one, may be part of the defensive tactics of a combination of such large companies as are here sued. On the other hand, the court should not tie the hands of a large number of individuals of one class, by an action brought by a few members of the class, whom they do not care to have represent them, or to whom they do not wish to entrust the prosecution of their claim. The number, the *character,* the size of the claimants of this class, as well as the nature of the defense (that is dilatory and expense-creating, or on the merits) must be considered, and then intelligent action will be more probable.

Because we cannot say that the two plaintiffs herein, insured the adequate representation of all, we are not justified in setting aside the order of the District Court in this respect.

* * *

The judgment of the District Court is reversed with directions to enter one in accordance with these views. Appellants shall recover their costs.

Notes and Questions

1. In *Weeks,* two Illinois wholesale "jobbers" of gasoline faced off against a powerful cartel of nineteen oil-producing companies charged with antitrust violations. Although the Seventh Circuit eventually upheld the district court's dismissal of the class suit on the ground that the individual plaintiffs had not demonstrated they would represent the class adequately, the Seventh Circuit also held that a class suit could be brought if appropriate representatives were found. In finding a class action appropriate, the Seventh Circuit noted that "[t]he difficulties inherent in the obtaining and presentation of proof by individual small jobbers, as contrasted by able, financially powerful companies, must be considered and appreciated. * * * To permit the defendants to contest liability with each claimant in a single, separate suit, would, in many cases give defendants an advantage which would be almost equivalent to closing the door of justice to all small claimants."

> *Question:* If the plaintiffs' claims had merit, why should the district court's refusal to allow the case to proceed as a class action "close the door of justice to all small claimants?"

2. Like other economic actors, rational litigants deciding whether to pursue a claim must weigh the potential benefits against the potential costs. Suppose a jobber like plaintiff Weeks believed he had lost $11,937 in profits as a result of the defendants' illegal price-fixing.

> *Questions:* What are Weeks' expected benefits from bringing his claim as an individual? What are Weeks' expected costs? Why might Weeks choose not to sue?

3. Rational individuals will not pursue even meritorious legal claims if their expected recovery is less than the attorney's fees, costs, and other expenses involved. As a result, individuals tend not to pursue relatively small claims. That can result in the inefficient allocation of resources when an injurer inefficiently continues to impose relatively small external costs on a large number of potential plaintiffs, none of whom has sufficient incentive to invest the time and resources necessary to bring a lawsuit.

Justice Connor referred to that problem in his opinion in Sturm, Ruger & Co., Inc. v. Day, 594 P.2d 38, 47 (Alaska 1979), in which the Supreme Court of Alaska upheld the award of punitive damages against the manufacturer of a poorly-designed handgun:

> We believe that as a matter of public policy, punitive damages can serve several useful functions in the products liability area. For example, the threat of punitive damages serves a deterrence function in cases in which a product may cause numerous minor injuries for which potential plaintiffs might decline to sue, or in cases in which it would be cheaper for the manufacturer to pay compensatory damages to those who did present claims than it would be to remedy the product's defect. * * *

The American legal system has developed a several mechanisms to encourage meritorious lawsuits when a defendant's conduct injures a large number of small claimants who otherwise might not sue. Punitive damages such as those awarded in *Sturm, Ruger,* and treble damages awarded under the antitrust laws to plaintiffs like Weeks, encourage plaintiffs to bring smaller claims by increasing each plaintiff's recovery. Other devices encourage small claims by decreasing the costs of litigation. For example, some statutes allow a successful plaintiff to recover his attorney's fees from the defendant as well as any judgment. See § 9 of the Securities Exchange Act of 1934, 15 U.S.C. § 78i(e) (allowing court to assess attorney's fees).

Questions: How does the Rule 23 class action device encourage lawsuits by small claimants? With respect to the tertiary costs of administering the legal system (see Chapter 3), how does the class action device compare to statutes that encourage lawsuits by allowing small litigants to recover their attorney's fees?

4. Suppose a plaintiff suffered a $100,000 injury as a result of a defendant's conduct. The plaintiff estimates that he has a 50% chance of prevailing against the defendant at trial. His lawyer offers to take the case either for a $20,000 flat fee to be paid whether the plaintiff wins or loses, or for a 40% contingent fee to be paid out of the damages won, if any.

Questions: Which fee arrangement will the plaintiff choose, and what factors are relevant to his choice? How might the plaintiff's wealth or poverty affect his choice of fee structure or his decision to sue?

5. Bringing a claim is a risky business. If the plaintiff wins, he may recover substantial damages; if he loses, he may have to pay substantial attorney's fees. Recall the discussion of risk in Chapter 3.

Questions: When a lawyer accepts a plaintiff's case on a contingent basis, part of the risk of suing is shifted from the plaintiff to the lawyer. Does that arrangement minimize the costs of risk as well as shifting those costs? Does it matter whether the lawyer is a solo practitioner or a member of a large firm?

6. The contingency fee system is sometimes thought to encourage small claims; a plaintiff is willing to bring a claim with a small expected return because he does not have to pay his lawyer unless he wins. However, even a risk-neutral attorney will demand that the expected contingency fee be as large as the flat fee she would require to cover her costs and earn a reasonable return on her time. She therefore would be unwilling to accept a contingent case with too small an expected return.

Question: The American system of requiring even successful plaintiffs to pay their own attorney's fees discourages rational plaintiffs from bringing lawsuits when the potential recovery is small. Do similar factors affect a party's decision to pursue an appeal in a case?

SISSON & ACKER v. THE MAYOR AND CITY COUNCIL OF BALTIMORE

Supreme Court of Maryland, 1879.
51 Md. 83.

ALVEY, J.

This is an action brought by the appellants against the appellees, for an alleged balance due on contract for extra work on the new City Hall in the City of Baltimore.

The appellants were the contractors for supplying the marble and doing the marble work on the new City Hall; and the marble was furnished and the work all done in accordance with the requirements of the contract. The work and materials were all accepted by the appellees, through their Building Committee, and the contract price, amounting to a sum between $900,000 and $1,000,000, was paid, according to the terms of the contract, excepting only the price for the extra work which had been done.

In the specifications for the building, in reference to which the proposals of the appellants for the work were made, and which proposals are referred to and made part of the contract between the parties, this provision occurs: "All extra work, additions or omissions, not referred to in the following lists, shall be valued by the architect, with reference and in proportion to the contract price."

It is admitted that after all the work was done, the extra work, embraced by the provision just cited, was measured by Mr. Frederick, the regular architect of the building, and was valued by him at the sum of $46,852.29. This valuation, however, was not satisfactory to the Building Committee, and they refused to certify to its correctness, or to give an order for the amount thus ascertained, without which the money could not be obtained from the city treasury. * * *

* * * [T]here was still another question of difference between the appellants and the Building Committee, and that was as to who should pay the cost of a railway track, laid by the Northern Central Railway Company, under the authority of an ordinance of the city, by which stone and other material were taken to the building whilst in progress of erection. * * * This question of difference, however, was subsequently agreed between the parties; and it is admitted, that on the 9th of January, 1874, the Building Committee paid the appellants, by an order drawn on the Comptroller of the city, the sum of $32,040.96, which was all the appellants were entitled to receive for the extra work and materials furnished * * * less * * * the cost of the railway track. This latter amount was retained by the agreement of the appellants, and the sum of $32,040.96, was received by them in full settlement of all claim under the contract for marble work, and a receipt was given to that effect. The appellants proved at the trial below that they agreed to these terms of settlement [because] they could not get the money thus awarded them, without resort to litigation, except upon the condition of allowing for the cost of the railway; and that they were "willing to settle the dispute by accepting the conditions to get rid of the whole matter."

This being the state of the case, there are two questions presented: 1. Whether the appellants are concluded by their acts * * * upon the claim for the extra work; and, 2. Whether they are bound by their agreement that the cost of the railway track should be retained out of the money found to be due them by the award. * * *

* * * The law always favors compromises and amicable adjustments of disputes, rather than compel parties to resort to litigation and it would be strange if, in the absence of clear evidence of fraud or mistake, the parties were not bound and concluded after what has taken place in respect to this award.

* * * The award was fully acquiesced in by the parties to the reference, and the money has been paid to the appellants on the faith of it, which they were willing and actually agreed to accept in full settlement of their claim under the original contract. After such dealing, it does not lie with either party to make question of the legality of what has been done. * * * We think it clear that both parties are concluded with respect to the amount ascertained to be due by the award.

Then, as to the cost of the railroad track retained by the Building Committee, with the consent of the appellants, from the amount ascertained to be due for the extra work. * * * This was certainly a proper question for adjustment between the parties concerned; and, as was said by the Supreme Court of the United States, in the case of Sweeny vs. U.S., "Parties may adjust their own disputes, and when they do so voluntarily and understandingly, no appeal lies to the Courts to review their mutual decision." There is no suggestion here that the appellants did not understand all the facts under which they were acting at the time of the settlement; and it was to avoid litigation that they agreed to settle the dispute in the manner they did. It is said that the appellants were coerced to make the settlement, inasmuch as they could not get the money due them without agreeing to be charged with the cost of the road track. However that may be, there is nothing in the case that brings it within the legal definition of duress. Repeating again in the language of the Supreme Court, used in the case of U.S. vs. Childs & Co., "If the principle contended for here be sound, no party can safely pay by way of compromise any sum less than what is claimed of him, for the compromise will be void as obtained by duress. The common and generally praiseworthy procedure by which business men every day sacrifice part of claims which they believe to be just to secure payment of the remainder would always be duress, and the compromise void." * * *

In view of these well-settled principles of the law, we think the Court below was entirely right in rejecting the several prayers offered by the appellants, and in entering judgment for the appellees, and that judgment will be affirmed.

Judgment affirmed.

Notes and Questions

1. According to Mr. Frederick, the architect who evaluated the extra work done by the plaintiffs on the Baltimore City Hall, the plaintiffs were entitled to compensation of $46,852.29 for that work. The plaintiffs also asserted that they were not responsible for the cost of the railroad track

laid to carry materials to and from the building site. According to the Baltimore City Council, $46,852.29 was too high a figure for the extra work and the plaintiffs should bear the cost of the track. Both sides eventually agreed to settle both claims for a total payment of $32,040.96 to the plaintiffs. The plaintiffs tried, unsuccessfully, to overturn that settlement.

> *Question:* The opinion indicates that the plaintiffs agreed to accept the $32,040.96 payment "to avoid litigation" and to "get rid of the whole matter." What particular considerations might lead the plaintiffs to accept a $32,040.96 settlement when they believed they were entitled to the full $46,852.29?

2. Suppose that the plaintiffs, Sisson & Acker, believed that they had a 50% chance of winning a judgment of $100,000 against the City of Baltimore, and the City of Baltimore also believed that the plaintiffs had a 50% chance of winning $100,000. If the case had gone to trial, each side would have had to spend approximately $10,000 on attorney's fees and other litigation expenses.

> *Question:* Considering the minimum the plaintiffs would have accepted and the maximum the defendant would have offered to settle the case, what is the bargaining range of settlement amounts the parties might have found mutually acceptable?

3. A lawyer's rule of thumb is that fewer than one in ten civil cases ever goes to trial. The prevalence of pre-trial settlement is another example of the Coase Theorem and the power of voluntary exchange. Because a trial requires both parties to invest substantial sums in attorney's fees that cannot be recovered, there is usually a range of settlement amounts that both parties perceive would leave them better off than if the case were litigated to the bitter end. Under such circumstances, rational parties will settle.

Not every case is settled, however. A number of factors might prevent parties from reaching a mutual agreement on a case's settlement value. Consider the following possibility. The plaintiff believes he has a 50% chance of winning a judgment of $100,000 against the defendant. The defendant thinks the plaintiff only has a 25% chance. Each party will have to spend $10,000 on attorney's fees and other litigation expenses if the case goes to trial.

> *Questions:* Will the case settle? What will happen if the plaintiff believes he has a 25% chance of winning, and the defendant believes the plaintiff has a 50% chance of prevailing?

4. Weeks v. Bareco Oil suggested that the likelihood that the plaintiff will file a lawsuit is related to the amount of the plaintiff's claim. The size of the plaintiff's claim is also relevant to the decision to settle rather than litigate. Consider two situations. In the first, the plaintiff thinks his probable recovery is $25,000 while the defendant believes the plaintiff is overestimating by 25% and the claim is only worth $20,000. Each side expects to pay $5,000 in attorneys' fees if the case goes to trial. In the second, the stakes are increased by a multiple of four; the plaintiff believes his claim is worth $100,000 while the defendant again thinks the plaintiff is

overestimating by 25% and is only entitled to $80,000. Again, the cost of trial is $5,000 for each party.

Question: Which case will settle?

2. THE LEGAL PROCESS AND THE EVOLUTION OF EFFICIENT RULES

The previous section considered how the size of a potential plaintiff's claim might influence the plaintiff's decision to sue and the parties' decision to settle rather than proceeding to trial or appeal. Decisions of that sort, made by litigants rather than judges, can direct the law's development. This section examines an "evolutionary" theory of common law efficiency positing that rational litigant behavior drives the common law toward more efficient rules regardless of judicial attitudes towards efficiency.

PRIEST, THE COMMON LAW PROCESS AND THE SELECTION OF EFFICIENT RULES *

6 J. Legal Stud. 65 (1977).

* * * I shall argue that the tendency of the set of all legal rules to become dominated by rules achieving efficient as opposed to inefficient allocative effects is substantially more pervasive than might be thought. It will be shown that efficient rules will be more likely to endure as controlling precedents regardless of the attitudes of individual judges toward efficiency, the ability of judges to distinguish efficient from inefficient outcomes, or the interest or uninterest of litigants in the allocative effects of the rules. Furthermore, it will be shown that this tendency toward efficiency is a characteristic of the common law process so that the content not only of the common law itself, but also of the legal interpretation of statutes or of the Constitution, is subject to forces pressing toward efficiency. The only assumption necessary for the hypothesis is that transaction costs in the real world are positive.
* * *

* * *

Various recent articles have developed a model [of] the major determinants of the decision of two parties either to settle their dispute out of court or to litigate * * *. An implication of this model is that, if all other factors are held constant, those cases in which the stakes are higher are more likely than those in which the stakes are lower to be litigated rather than settled.

For the set of all legal disputes, the stakes will be greater for disputes arising under inefficient rules than under efficient rules. Inefficient assignments of liability by definition impose greater costs on the parties subject to them than efficient assignments. For example, where the marginal cost of reducing the likelihood of an accident by a given amount is greater for one party than for the other, to place liability on the party whose cost is greater will lead in general to more accidents or more severe accidents than if the assignment were reversed. Where the cost of avoidance is made greater, the amount invested in avoidance generally will be lower. Even where it is possible for the party legally liable to pay the other party to assume the burden of prevention, it will be necessary to invest resources to achieve this reallocation. Thus the costs imposed by inefficient rules will always be higher than the costs imposed by efficient rules.

It follows, therefore, that other factors held equal, litigation will be more likely for disputes arising under inefficient rules than for those arising under efficient rules. Once promulgated, inefficient rules are more likely than efficient rules to be reexamined by courts because they will come up in litigation more often. This conclusion follows directly from the fact that inefficient rules impose higher costs than efficient rules on the parties subject to them, and thus that the value to the parties from overturning the judgments that result—which is what I call the stakes of the litigation—is higher.

* * *

[Thus,] if the disputes that proceed to judgment consist of a disproportionately large share which contest the appropriateness of inefficient rules, then the set of rules not contested, those remaining in force, will consist of a disproportionately large share of efficient rules. * * * Even where the judiciary exercises a strong hostility to efficient outcomes, it will be unable to fully impose its bias on the total set of legal rules in force. In fact, as we shall see, it is possible for the total set of rules to be predominantly efficient, despite a preference of the judges promulgating the rules for inefficient outcomes.

An arithmetical example will illustrate the point. Imagine that judges decide cases on some basis unrelated to efficiency of outcome, so that, with respect to allocative effects, judicial decisionmaking may be described as random. Assume for simplicity that all rules can be characterized as (equally) efficient or inefficient. The likelihood in any given case of the rule being efficient or inefficient then will be .5. Imagine that 100 disputes go to judgment. By definition, the rules announced for 50 of these cases will be inefficient and for 50 will be efficient. Now assume that further litigation ensues concerning some of these rules. It is unnecessary to place any restrictions on the distribution of the other characteristics that determine the litigation-settlement ratio, but imagine that they are distributed so that 30 of the initial 50 inefficient rules are relitigated. By our previous finding (and this is essential to the theory), it follows that a smaller proportion of efficient rules will be relitigated, say 20 of the initial 50. By assumption, the judges will decide the 50 relitigated cases again randomly with respect to allocative effects. Thus 25 of the new rules will be inefficient and other 25 efficient. But when the new rules are added to the uncontested rules, it is clear that the stock of legal rules has become in sum more efficient. The number of efficient rules has increased from 50 to 55.   * * *

The tendency of the proportion of efficient rules to increase does not depend on the assumption of decision making that is random with respect to allocative effects. The proportion of efficient rules may increase over time even where each judge has a strong bias against efficient outcomes. Amend the previous example by assuming that judges promulgate inefficient rules in 90 percent of all cases, so that at period 1, 90 of the rules are inefficient, 10 efficient. Assume even greater relitigation: 80 of the 90 inefficient rules are relitigated and 7 (again a smaller proportion) of the 10 efficient rules, so that 10 inefficient and 3 efficient rules remain in force unchallenged. Of the 80 relitigated inefficient rules, 72 of the new rules will remain inefficient while 8 will be changed to become efficient. Of the 7 relitigated efficient rules, 6.3 will become inefficient and .7 will remain efficient. Again the totals following relitigation favor efficiency: at the subsequent period, 88.3 as opposed to 90 rules are inefficient but 11.7 as opposed to the previous 10 are now efficient.

In this simple model the proportion of efficient rules in force at any period is a function of the stock of efficient and inefficient rules in force at the previous period, the respective rates of relitigation of efficient and inefficient rules, and the proportion of efficient rules announced by judges (the judicial bias toward efficiency). If the rates of relitigation and the judicial bias remain constant over time, the share of efficient rules will reach an equilibrium level. The proportion of efficient rules at equilibrium will be greater than the proportion of efficient rules promulgated by judges in any given period, regardless of the relitigation rates or the level of the judicial bias.

* * *

It is important to appreciate the implications of this model on the exercise of judicial authority. It is true, of course, that greater judicial hostility to efficiency will lead to a lower equilibrium level of efficient rules. But the difference in the rates of relitigation between efficient and inefficient rules places an important restriction on the extent to which judges who prefer inefficiency can implement their preferences. Table 2 shows equilibrium levels of efficient rules, holding the rate of relitigation of efficient rules constant, for plausible values of judicial attitudes toward efficiency (within a range of 40 percent of the mean) and for selected relitigation rates of inefficient rules. Note that "judicial bias" represents the proportion efficient of all rules promulgated by all of the judges within a given jurisdiction over a long period of time. Thus a .3 judicial bias measure could not be achieved if only a small set of judges were hostile to efficiency or if judges were to exercise their hostility in only a selected set of cases. Rather such a measure would require deep and systematic hostility.

TABLE 2
EQUILIBRIUM PROPORTION OF EFFICIENT RULES (%)
Relitigation Rate of Efficient Rules Held Constant (.02%)

Relitigation Rate, Inefficient Rules

		.04	.06	.08	.09
	.7	82.4%	87.5%	90.3%	91.3%
JUDICIAL	.6	75.0	81.8	85.7	87.1
BIAS	.5	66.7	75.0	80.0	81.8
(% EFFI-	.4	57.1	66.7	72.7	75.0
CIENT)	.3	46.2	56.3	63.2	65.9

* * *

The tendency of legal rules to become efficient over time is independent of judicial bias or the method of judicial decisionmaking. It follows rather from the limitations on the opportunity set of cases available for judicial decision, limitations imposed by independent economic variables that determine the cases that are litigated. Efficient rules "survive" in an evolutionary sense because they are less likely to be relitigated and thus less likely to be changed, regardless of the method of decision. Inefficient rules "perish" because they are more likely to be reviewed and review implies the chance of change whatever the method of judicial decision. * * * It is evident, furthermore, that the tendency of the common law over time to favor efficient rules does not depend on the ability of judges to distinguish efficient from inefficient outcomes. Even where judges are ignorant of the allocative effects of their judgments, they will be led by the litigation decisions of individual parties to promulgate rules that increase the relative proportion of efficient rules.

* * * [E]fficient outcomes will tend to dominate for all disputes resolved by this process including not only rules derived from the common law itself but also rules interpreting legislation and construing provisions of the Constitution. To the extent that a statute or an interpretation of a statute imposes inefficiencies, it will be more likely to be overturned because of the greater likelihood of relitigation. Similarly, within the class of possible constructions of a given constitutional provision, those constructions with relatively more efficient allocative effects will tend over time to survive. It is immaterial to this result that one of the parties to a dispute regarding a statute or a constitutional provision may itself be the government (such as the Justice Department or an administrative agency) whose investment in litigation may be determined by the maximization of something other than dollar returns. Where government suits are brought under legal rules that are inefficient, the stakes will be higher and defendants will be more likely to resist the suits and force litigation.

* * *

It is important to appreciate that this paper has not shown that the rules of the common law are or ever will be completely efficient. It has suggested only that the common law process incorporates a strong tendency toward efficient outcomes. It is an implication of this theory that the rate at which efficient outcomes will be achieved will be a function of the nature of the judicial bias for or against efficiency, the frequency of relitigation of inefficient rules (itself determined by the costs of litigation versus settlement, the precedential effect of the rules, and the extent of their inefficiency), the rate of change of the social conditions that underlie various disputes, and the adaptability of earlier surviving precedents to the efficient resolution of new disputes. It is a further implication that areas of the law within which characteristic disputes have remained relatively consistent over time, such as admiralty, sales, or procedure, are more likely today to be dominated by efficient rules; and there is evidence supporting this hypothesis. Perhaps a more important suggestion of the paper, however, is that the predictive ability of attempts to explain the character of common law decision making is likely to be enhanced by more careful attention to the forces that systematically affect the amount of litigation.

LEMLE v. BREEDEN

Supreme Court of Hawaii, 1969.
51 Haw. 426, 51 Haw. 478, 462 P.2d 470.

LEVINSON, JUSTICE.

This case of first impression in Hawaii involves the doctrine of implied warranty of habitability and fitness for use of a leased dwelling. The plaintiff-lessee (Lemle) sued to recover the deposit and rent payment totalling $1,190.00. Constructive eviction and breach of an implied warranty of habitability and fitness for use were alleged as the basis for recovery. The defendant-lessor (Mrs. Breeden) counterclaimed for damages for breach of the rental agreement. The trial court, sitting without a jury, held for the plaintiff and the case comes to us on appeal from that judgment.

The facts in this case are relatively simple and without substantial conflict. The rented premises involved are owned by the defendant, Mrs. Breeden, and are located in the Diamond Head area of Honolulu. The house fronts on the water with the surrounding grounds attractively landscaped with lauhala trees and other shrubbery. * * * The house is relatively open without screening on windows or doorways.

* * * On September 21, 1964 during the daylight hours, the realtor showed the home to the plaintiff and his wife, newcomers to Hawaii from New York City, and told them that it was available for immediate occupancy. The plaintiff saw no evidence of rodent infestation during the one-half hour inspection.

That evening the rental agreement was executed. * * * The rental was $800.00 per month fully furnished. * * * The plaintiff tendered a check to the defendant's agent for $1,190.00 at that time.

The very next day, September 22, 1964, the plaintiff, his wife and their four children, who had been staying in a Waikiki hotel, took possession of the premises. That evening it became abundantly evident to the plaintiff that there were rats within the main dwelling and on the corrugated iron roof. It was not clear whether the rats came from within the house or from the rocky area next to the water. During that night and for the next two nights the plaintiff and his family were sufficiently apprehensive of the rats that they slept together in the downstairs living room of the main house, thereby vacating their individual bedrooms. Rats were seen and heard during those three nights.

On September 23, 1964, the day after occupancy, the defendant's agent was informed of the rats' presence and she procured extermination services from a local firm. The plaintiff himself also bought traps to supplement the traps and bait set by the exterminators. These attempts to alleviate the rat problem were only partially successful and the succeeding two nights were equally sleepless and uncomfortable for the family.

On September 25, 1964, three days after occupying the dwelling, the plaintiff and his family vacated the premises after notifying the defendant's agent of his intention to do so and demanding the return of the money which he had previously paid. Subsequently this suit was brought.

The trial judge ruled that there was an implied warranty of habitability and fitness in the lease of a dwelling house, that there was a breach of warranty, that the plaintiff was constructively evicted, and that the plaintiff was entitled to recover $1,110.00 plus interest.

We affirm.

* * *

At common law when land was leased to a tenant, the law of property regarded the lease as equivalent to a sale of the premises for a term. The lessee acquired an estate in land and became both owner and occupier for that term subject to the ancient doctrine of *caveat emptor*. * * * Predictably enough, this concept of the lessee's interest has led to many troublesome rules of law which have endured far beyond their historical justifications.

Given the finality of a lease transaction and the legal effect of *caveat emptor* which placed the burden of inspection on the tenant * * * [o]nly if there were fraud or mistake in the initial transaction would the lessee have a remedy. * * * In the absence of statute it was generally held that there was no implied warranty of habitability and fitness.

The rule of *caveat emptor* in lease transactions at one time may have had some basis in social practice as well as in historical doctrine. At common law leases were customarily lengthy documents embodying the full expectations of the parties. There was generally equal knowledge of the condition of the land by both landlord and tenant. The land itself would often yield the rents and the buildings were constructed simply, without modern conveniences like wiring or plumbing. Yet in an urban society where the vast majority of tenants do not reap the rent directly from the land but bargain primarily for the right to enjoy the premises for living purposes, often signing standardized leases as in this case, common law conceptions of a lease and the tenant's liability for rent are no longer viable. * * *

* * *

* * * [T]he general rule of *caveat emptor* [must] be re-examined.

In the law of sales of chattels, the trend is markedly in favor of implying warranties of fitness and merchantability. The reasoning has been (1) that the public interest in safety and consumer protection requires it, and (2) that the burden ought to be shifted to the manufacturer who, by placing the goods on the market, represents their suitability and fitness. The manufacturer is also the one who knows more about the product and is in a better position to alleviate any problems or bear the brunt of any losses. This reasoning has also been accepted by a growing number of courts in cases involving sales of new homes. The same reasoning is equally persuasive in leases of real property.

The Supreme Court of New Jersey recently re-examined the doctrine of *caveat emptor* in a case involving a tenant who vacated leased business premises after being consistently flooded during every rain. In assessing the relative positions of the parties, that court said:

> It has come to be recognized that ordinarily the lessee does not have as much knowledge of the condition of the premises as the lessor. Building code requirements and violations are known or made known to the lessor, not the lessee. He is in a better position to know of latent defects, structural and otherwise, in a building which might go unnoticed by a lessee who rarely has sufficient knowledge or expertise to see or to discover them. A prospective lessee, such as a small businessman, cannot be expected to know if the plumbing or wiring systems are adequate or conform to local codes. Nor should he be expected to hire experts to advise him. Ordinarily all this information should be considered readily available to the lessor who in turn can inform the prospective lessee. These factors have produced persuasive arguments for re-evaluation of the *caveat emptor* doctrine and, for imposition of an implied warranty that the premises are suitable for the leased purposes and conform to local codes and zoning laws. Reste Realty Corporation v. Cooper, 53 N.J. 444, 452, 251 A.2d 268, 272 (1969).

The application of an implied warranty of habitability in leases gives recognition to the changes in leasing transactions today. * * * It is a doctrine which has its counterparts in the law of sales and torts and one which when candidly countenanced is impelled by the nature of the transaction and contemporary housing realities. Legal fictions and artificial exceptions to wooden rules of property law aside, we hold that in the lease of a dwelling house, such as in this case, there is an implied warranty of habitability and fitness for the use intended.

* * *

* * * We affirm the judgment for the plaintiff on the ground that there was a material breach of the implied warranty of habitability and fitness for the use intended which justified the plaintiff's rescinding the rental agreement and vacating the premises.

Affirmed.

Notes and Questions

1. In the 1960's and 1970's, American property law underwent a sea change. One by one, the supreme courts of a number of states adopted the doctrine of "implied warranty of habitability" for residential leases. Following the lead of New Jersey and Hawaii, courts held that the doctrine of *caveat emptor* (and its analogue applying to leases, *caveat lessee*) did not apply to housing rentals and that residential contracts included an implied warranty that tenants were renting housing fit for residential purposes.

Questions: Apply Priest's evolutionary theory to the alternate rules of *caveat lessee* and the implied warranty of habitability. Either rule imposes costs. Under *caveat lessee*, renters must bear the costs of repairing premises and of moving into unfit premises they would not have rented had known of their defects. The implied warranty of habitability requires landlords to repair and rent only fit premises unless the parties explicitly agree otherwise. Is the landlord or the lessee likely to be in the best position to estimate and minimize the sum of those costs? Does the implied warranty of habitability create better incentives to minimize those costs than the doctrine of *caveat lessee?*

2. Priest's model assumes that "transaction costs in the real world are positive." One obstacle to efficient bargaining between landlord and tenant is tenant ignorance of hidden defects in the premises.

Question: Why is the assumption of positive transactions costs necessary to Priest's theory?

3. Priest concludes that "the rate at which efficient outcomes will be achieved will be a function of the nature of the judicial bias for or against efficiency, the frequency of relitigation of inefficient rules * * * [and] the rate of change of the social conditions that underlie various disputes * * * ."

Question: In *Lemle*, the Supreme Court of Hawaii pointed out that the nature of landlord-tenant relations had changed since the original formulation of the *caveat emptor* doctrine in residential leases. What are the implications of a rapidly-changing modern society for the evolution of efficient rules?

4. Like many other evolutionary theories, Priest's model depends on "differential litigation," the notion that parties are more likely to litigate some kinds of rules than others. Priest argues that parties are more likely to litigate inefficient rules that impose large costs and give rise to large

claims than efficient rules that impose small costs and lead to small claims. Recall, however, that rational litigants who agree on a case's likely outcome will prefer to settle to avoid the cost of a trial. See Notes and Questions following *Sisson & Acker,* above. When parties settle cases, courts have no opportunity to reconsider and change legal rules. If unchallenged, even the most inefficient rules can survive.

Rules are challenged and evolution occurs only when the parties disagree on the probable outcome of litigation. In particular, the plaintiff's view of her likelihood of success must be higher than the defendant's estimate of the plaintiff's chances.

Questions: Are parties more likely to disagree and litigate claims arising under inefficient or efficient rules? Priest notes that another factor which will effect the rate of evolution is "the precedential effect" of rules. How does strong precedent influence the parties' decision to settle?

5. If litigants ever challenge efficient rules, and if judges are at all insensitive to efficiency, there always remains the chance that occasionally an efficient rule will be challenged and changed to an inefficient one. Thus Priest's model does not suggest that the common law is, or ever will be, completely efficient. A number of factors influence how far the law is likely to develop towards efficiency: judicial attitudes toward efficiency, the frequency of litigation, the presence or absence of precedent, and the rate of change of society as a whole.

Questions: Considering those factors, what areas of law might be more likely to develop a high proportion of efficient rules? What areas might be less likely to do so?

6. If parties agree on how a court will decide their case should they proceed to trial and/or appeal, they will make similar estimates of the probable outcome of litigation and be more likely to settle. If judges prefer efficient rules and litigants know of that preference, they will not challenge inefficient rules but instead will settle their disputes according to the efficient terms they believe the court would have adopted.

In a subsequent article, Professor Priest applied the above reasoning to suggest that "litigation is likely to occur chiefly when the parties disagree over what the court will find the efficient outcome to be," and that "unless a court is superior to the parties at determining the efficient outcome, it is likely to render an efficient decision roughly as many times as an inefficient one." Priest, Selective Characteristics of Litigation, 9 J. Legal Stud. 399, 410 (1980). See also Priest & Klein, The Selection of Disputes for Litigation, 13 J. Legal Stud. 1 (1984). That suggestion is an application of Priest's "selection hypothesis." In layman's terms, the selection hypothesis predicts that whenever parties to a lawsuit can predict which substantive rule of law the court is likely to apply in their case, they are likely to reach similar conclusions about the probable result of a trial and so settle. It does not matter whether the court's decision would be based on precedent, efficiency, or personal taste; so long as the parties can predict which rule the court would apply they will settle before the court actually applies that rule. As a result the class of litigated disputes is not a representative sample of the set of all legal disputes.

The selection hypothesis suggests that the only cases that go to trial (or appeal) are those so difficult or novel that the parties cannot predict what precedent, efficiency, or the judge's personal tastes will dictate. The court's decision similarly will appear to bear an unpredictable relationship to precedent, efficiency, or the judge's tastes. The substantive basis of the law will appear indeterminate. Because only hard cases are litigated, only bad law is reported.

Priest's selection hypothesis is not necessarily inconsistent with the notion that the law favors efficiency. Appellate decisions are not the only means of judging the legal system's impact. Consider Priest's point that "[t]he common law will appear indeterminate * * * only with respect to the substantive basis of judgments and decisions * * * [and not] with respect to other indicia of the common law system of rules, such as the parties' settlement terms or their behavior." 9 J. Legal Stud. 416, 420 (1980). However, an obvious tension exists between the selection hypothesis and the claim that appellate opinions show a marked tendency to favor efficiency. Indeed, in his later article Priest argued that "it is a true puzzle how study of common law decisions from an economic standpoint could have so uniformly discovered efficiency" in the law as expressed in appellate cases. 9 J. Legal Stud. at 412 (1980).

JAVINS v. FIRST NATIONAL REALTY CORP.

U. S. Court of Appeals, District of Columbia Circuit, 1970.
428 F.2d 1071, 138 U.S.App.D.C. 369.

J. SKELLY WRIGHT, CIRCUIT JUDGE.

These cases present the question whether housing code violations which arise during the term of a lease have any effect upon the tenant's obligation to pay rent. The Landlord and Tenant Branch of the District of Columbia Court of General Sessions ruled proof of such violations inadmissible when proffered as a defense to an eviction action for nonpayment of rent. The District of Columbia Court of Appeals upheld this ruling.

Because of the importance of the question presented, we granted appellants' petitions for leave to appeal. We now reverse and hold that a warranty of habitability, measured by the standards set out in the Housing Regulations for the District of Columbia, is implied by operation of law into leases of urban dwelling units covered by those Regulations and that breach of this warranty gives rise to the usual remedies for breach of contract.

* * *

* * * Courts have a duty to reappraise old doctrines in the light of the facts and values of contemporary life—particularly old common law doctrines which the courts themselves created and developed. * * *

* * *

* * * Recent decisions * * * have relied without discussion upon the old common law rule that the lessor is not obligated to repair unless

he covenants to do so in the written lease contract. However, the Supreme Courts of at least two states, in recent and well reasoned opinions, have held landlords to implied warranties of quality in housing leases. In our judgment, the old no-repair rule cannot coexist with the obligations imposed on the landlord by a typical modern housing code, and must be abandoned in favor of an implied warranty of habitability. In the District of Columbia, the standards of this warranty are set out in the Housing Regulations.

* * *

The common law rule absolving the lessor of all obligation to repair originated in the early Middle Ages. Such a rule was perhaps well suited to an agrarian economy; the land was more important than whatever small living structure was included in the leasehold, and the tenant farmer was fully capable of making repairs himself. These historical facts were the basis on which the common law constructed its rule; they also provided the necessary prerequisites for its application.

* * *

It is overdue for courts to admit that these assumptions are no longer true with regard to all urban housing. Today's urban tenants, the vast majority of whom live in multiple dwelling houses, are interested, not in the land, but solely in "a house suitable for occupation." Furthermore, today's city dweller usually has a single, specialized skill unrelated to maintenance work; he is unable to make repairs like the 'jack-of-all-trades' farmer who was the common law's model of the lessee. Further, unlike his agrarian predecessor who often remained on one piece of land for his entire life, urban tenants today are more mobile than ever before. A tenant's tenure in a specific apartment will often not be sufficient to justify efforts at repairs. In addition, the increasing complexity of today's dwellings renders them much more difficult to repair than the structures of earlier times. In a multiple dwelling repair may require access to equipment and areas in the control of the landlord. Low and middle income tenants, even if they were interested in making repairs, would be unable to obtain any financing for major repairs since they have no long-term interest in the property.

* * *

* * * [T]he relationship of landlord and tenant suggests further compelling reasons for the law's protection of the tenants' legitimate expectations of quality. The inequality in bargaining power between landlord and tenant has been well documented. Tenants have very little leverage to enforce demands for better housing. Various impediments to competition in the rental housing market, such as racial and class discrimination and standardized form leases, mean that landlords place tenants in a take it or leave it situation. The increasingly severe shortage of adequate housing further increases the landlord's bargaining power and escalates the need for maintaining and improving the existing stock. Finally, the findings by various studies of the social impact of bad housing has led to the realization that poor housing is detrimental to the whole society, not merely to the unlucky ones who must suffer the daily indignity of living in a slum.

Thus we are led by our inspection of the relevant legal principles and precedents to the conclusion that the old common law rule imposing an obligation upon the lessee to repair during the lease term was really never intended to apply to residential urban leaseholds. Contract principles established in other areas of the law provide a more rational framework for the apportionment of landlord-tenant responsibilities; they strongly suggest that a warranty of habitability be implied into all contracts for urban dwellings.

* * *

In the present cases, the landlord sued for possession for nonpayment of rent. Under contract principles, however, the tenant's obligation to pay rent is dependent upon the landlord's performance of his obligations, including his warranty to maintain the premises in habitable condition. In order to determine whether any rent is owed to the landlord, the tenants must be given an opportunity to prove the housing code violations alleged as breach of the landlord's warranty.

* * *

So ordered.

Notes and Questions

Both *Javins* and *Lemle* modify the rental contract negotiated between the parties by adding an implied term that the premises leased are fit for habitation. However, *Lemle* does not appear to *preclude* the parties from knowingly and explicitly contracting to rent unfit premises. In contrast, the District of Columbia building code implied into the parties' contract in *Javins* requires landlords (and tenants) to rent only premises that conform to the code's requirements.

Question: Is the *Javins* rule of nonwaivable implied warranty of habitability efficient?

———

Priest argued that his evolutionary model applied not only to judicial decisions interpreting and developing the common law, but also to decisions interpreting the meaning of a statute or the Constitution. The following case involves just such a question of statutory interpretation. While reading it, consider the factors that affect litigants' decisions to bring a case, settle, or litigate. In what directions other than efficiency might the law tend to evolve? What other interests and values might it tend to favor?

PALMER v. LIGGETT GROUP, INC.

United States Court of Appeals, First Circuit, 1987.
825 F.2d 620.

JOHN R. BROWN, SENIOR CIRCUIT JUDGE.

This interlocutory appeal presents one highly disputed issue: whether the Federal Cigarette Labeling and Advertising Act (the Act), preempts the Palmers' smoking and health related claims that challenge either the adequacy of the federal warning on cigarette packages or the propriety of Liggett's advertising and promotion of cigarettes. In deference to the congressional declaration that (i) cigarettes be labeled uniformly and (ii) a balance be struck between the priority given to tobacco commerce and to our national health policy, we hold that the Act does preempt the Palmers' state law claims, and reverse the decision of the District Court.

* * *

Joseph C. Palmer died on August 26, 1980, at the age of 49, allegedly from lung cancer. The Palmers allege that Palmer smoked between three and four packs of Liggett's cigarettes per day until his death.

On August 19, 1983, Ann M. Palmer, individually and as administrator of the estate of her late husband, and her mother-in-law, Daphne S. Palmer, filed this diversity action in the District Court. In their amended complaint, the Palmers contended that liability should be imposed on Liggett because of its failure to warn adequately of the health consequences of cigarette smoking. * * * At bottom, the Palmers complained that Liggett negligently gave inadequate warnings about the dangers of cigarette smoking and that this negligence proximately caused Palmer's death.

In response, Liggett filed a motion to dismiss all inadequate warning claims on the ground that they were preempted by the Act. After a thorough review of the record, Judge Mazzone denied Liggett's motion to dismiss. The court concluded that "Congress [could not have] meant, by its silence on the issue of common law claim preemption, to do away with all means of obtaining compensation for those hurt by inadequate cigarette warnings in advertising." * * *

* * *

The District Court, the defendants, and the plaintiffs agree that the issue of the Act's preemptive force controls the disposition of virtually the entire case. If the Labeling Act is found to preempt state law actions, either expressly or impliedly, the Palmers lose. If Congress did not intend for the Act to be so preemptive, Liggett loses the appeal. The line thus drawn, we proceed now to a discussion of how Congress constructed the Labeling Act.

In 1964, the Surgeon General released the now famous "Smoking and Health: Report of the Advisory Committee to the Surgeon General." That initial report was one of the first official, scientifically approved statements linking cigarette smoking to lung cancer, bronchitis, and emphysema. The public response was immediate and vocal; clearly, some form of governmental action was imminent.

In a rush to protect and inform its citizens, several states proposed and adopted mandatory warning labels for cigarette packages to be sold in their individual states. Given the potential maze of conflicting state regulations, Congress stepped in in 1965 to set up a uniform, nationally consistent system of warning labels for cigarettes. Further, it did so with the express intention of striking a balance between its concern for the national health policy of smoking education and its protection of the trade and commerce aspects of the tobacco industry.

After much internal and external debate, with classic confrontations between North and South, rural and urban states, together with vigorous lobbying by all forms of interested groups and businesses, the members of Congress negotiated a hard-fought compromise with the passage of the Federal Cigarette Labeling and Advertising Act * * *.

This case, like so many we are called on to decide, turns on a question of statutory construction and interpretation. It is by definition a frustrating task, for if the law's meaning is truly "plain" enough or its effect clear-cut enough, there is no need for us to pronounce what we discern its meaning or effect to be. * * *

Nevertheless, that is the task assigned to us, and having acknowledged the inherently unsatisfying nature of it, we come now to the actual words of the law. * * *

* * *

[Section] 1334 sets out the section most relevant to our preemption analysis—the preemption section:

(a) No statement relating to smoking and health, other than the statement required by section 1333 of this title, shall be required on any cigarette package.

(b) No requirement or prohibition based on smoking and health shall be imposed under State law with respect to the advertising or promotion of any cigarettes the packages of which are labeled in conformity with the provisions of this chapter.

* * *

In its thoughtful and detailed scrutiny of this case, the District Court considered at length the reasoning in the three major opinions rendered to date in these cigarette products liability cases—the two *Cipollone* decisions [Cipollone v. Liggett Group, 593 F.Supp. 1146 (D.N.J.1984), rev'd, 789 F.2d 181 (3d Cir.1986), cert. denied, 479 U.S. 1043, 107 S.Ct. 907, 93 L.Ed.2d 857 (1987)] and Roysdon v. R.J. Reynolds Tobacco Co., 623 F.Supp. 1189 (E.D.Tenn.1985). The Third Circuit and *Roysdon* courts held that the Act preempted state law tort claims, while the District Court in *Cipollone* held the claims were not preempted.

After reviewing the basic approaches to preemption analysis, the District Court considered and rejected the argument that either express or any of the forms of implied preemption were present in this case. We reverse and hold that the Act impliedly preempts the Palmers' claim.

* * *

* * * As discussed earlier, Congress ran a hard-fought, bitterly partisan battle in striking the compromise that became the Act. It is inconceivable that Congress intended to have that carefully wrought balance of national interests superseded by the views of a single state, indeed, perhaps of a single jury in a single state. Contrary to the District Court's view, we therefore hold that a suit for damages on a common law theory of inadequate warning—if the warning given complies with the Act—disrupts excessively the balance of purpose set by Congress, and is thus preempted.

To permit the interposition of state common law actions into a well-defined area of federal regulation would abrogate utterly the established scheme of health protection as tempered by trade protection. The Supremacy Clause of the Constitution, as enforced through the doctrine of preemption, prohibits this.

* * *

* * * The Palmers disingenuously maintain that any monetary damages awarded would not compel a manufacturer to change its label for, after all, "the choice of how to react is left to the manufacturer." This "choice of reaction" seems akin to the free choice of coming up for air after being underwater. Once a jury has found a label inadequate under state law, and the manufacturer liable for damages for negligently employing it, it is unthinkable that any manufacturer would not immediately take steps to minimize its exposure to continued liability. The most obvious change it can take, of course, is to change its label. Effecting such a change in the manufacturer's behavior and imposing such additional warning requirements is the very action preempted by § 1334 of the Act. Indeed, it arrogates to a single jury the regulatory power explicitly denied to all fifty states' legislative bodies.

* * *

Accordingly, having dismissed the Palmers' arguments against preemption as meritless, and having determined the effects of state tort liability to be seriously disruptive to the congressionally calibrated balance of national interests, we hold the Palmers' state-based claim of inadequate warning to be preempted by the Act. The decision of the District Court must be reversed and remanded for proceedings consistent with this opinion.

Notes and Questions

1. As the First Circuit observed, *Palmer* was one of a series of cases in which cigarette smokers sued the tobacco industry claiming that it did not adequately inform them of the hazards of smoking cigarettes. In each case, the tobacco industry either obtained at trial, or persevered and obtained on appeal, a ruling that any claim of inadequate warning dating after the 1965 passage of the Federal Cigarette Labeling and Advertising Act was preempted by the Act.

> *Questions:* The Act initially required the cigarette industry to print the following warning on cigarette packages: "Warning: Cigarette Smoking May Be Hazardous to Your Health." Analyzing the *Palmer* rule in light of the economic theory of tort law developed in Chapter 3, was that warning sufficient to ensure that the person who smoked cigarettes, rather than the tobacco company that produced, packaged, and advertised them, was in the best position to minimize the primary, secondary and tertiary costs of smoking? Was the holding in *Palmer* efficient?

2. Priest's evolutionary theory of common law efficiency holds that because inefficient rules impose greater costs than efficient rules, they are challenged—and changed—more often. Other factors might affect how frequently a rule is challenged. In his article Why is the Common Law Efficient?, 6 J. Legal Stud. 51, 55 (1977), Professor Rubin suggests that:

> If only one party to a dispute is interested in future cases of this sort, there will be pressure for precedents to evolve in favor of that party which does have a stake in future cases, whether or not this is the efficient solution. This is because a party with a stake in future decisions will find it worthwhile to litigate as long as liability rests with him; conversely, a party with no stake in future decisions will not find litigation worthwhile.

To appreciate the evolutionary implications of "repeat players" who expect to litigate a series of similar cases, consider the following situation. Assume smoking causes Palmer to suffer $100,000 in damages which the tobacco industry could prevent at an expected cost of $80,000. Whatever liability rule applies, if either party sues there is a 50% chance of overturning the prevailing rule. Litigation would cost each party $60,000. The difference between the parties is that Palmer is interested only in the outcome of his case while the defendant tobacco company faces nine identical pending cases for which the outcome of Palmer's case will be precedent. Rubin's analysis suggests that this difference will affect incentives to sue.

> *Questions:* If the prevailing rule requires smokers to bear their own costs, will Palmer sue and challenge that rule? If the prevailing rule holds the tobacco industry liable, will the industry sue and challenge the rule? Which rule assigns the costs of smoking efficiently?

3. The presence of repeat players may also influence settlement behavior. In answering the following question, use the numbers in Question 2 but assume that the cost of litigation is $20,000 for each party.

Questions: If the prevailing legal rule requires Palmer to bear his own smoking costs, what minimum would Palmer be willing to accept and what maximum would the tobacco industry be willing to pay to settle the case, assuming a 50% chance of overturning the rule and gaining a $100,000 verdict? If the prevailing rule requires the tobacco company either to avoid Palmer's injury or pay damages, what minimum would Palmer be willing to accept and what maximum would the tobacco industry be willing to pay to settle, again assuming a 50% chance of a $100,000 verdict? Is settlement more or less likely when precedent favors the repeat player?

4. In Alvis v. Ribar, 85 Ill.2d 1, 52 Ill.Dec. 23, 25, 421 N.E.2d 886, 888 (1981), the Supreme Court of Illinois offered the following explanation for the adoption of the doctrine of contributory negligence:

> The doctrine was swiftly adopted in American jurisprudence, commencing with the case of *Smith v. Smith* (1824), 19 Mass. (2 Pick.) 621, 13 Am.Dec. 464. Legal scholars attribute the swift and universal acceptance of the doctrine to newly formed industry's need for protection "against the ravages which might have been wrought by over-sympathetic juries." Judicial concern was particularly evident in the area of personal injury suits brought by railroad employees against the railroads. The courts realized that, in the pervading public view that saw railroads as "harmful entities with deep pockets", juries' sympathies toward plaintiffs could wreak financial disaster upon that burgeoning industry.

Question: What other areas of legal doctrine might be influenced by the litigation of repeat players?

5. As this edition goes to print, the Supreme Court is reviewing the preemption doctrine in another tobacco case, Cipollone v. Liggett Group, Inc., 893 F.2d 541 (3d Cir. 1990), *cert. granted* ___ U.S. ___, 111 S.Ct. 1386, 113 L.Ed.2d 443 (1991). Numerous organizations and individuals filed *amicus* briefs in support of the grant of certiorari in that case, including the Ralph Nader-organized Public Citizen Litigation Group; the American Cancer Society; the American Medical Association; and the plaintiff's-attorney organization Association of Trial Lawyers of America.

Question: How might the involvement of such groups overcome the tobacco industry's "repeat player" advantage in influencing the evolution of the law?

6. If rules that are challenged often tend to perish, in what other directions might the common law evolve? Consider how the wealth of the tobacco industry might be related to its success in establishing controlling precedent on the preemption doctrine as a defense to claims of inadequate warning in smoking cases. The typical tobacco lawsuit might well be titled David v. Goliath; the plaintiffs are usually individuals of modest means, while the defendants are giant companies with tremendous legal and financial resources at their disposal.

Questions: What impact might wealth distribution patterns have on the evolution of legal rules, and why? What role does the contingency fee play in that process?

7. This Chapter has focused on the evolution of judge-made law as influenced by litigants' decisions to sue, settle, go to trial and appeal, as well as by judges' values. Perhaps the same sort of analysis can be applied to statutory law created through the legislative process. Consider the adoption of the Federal Cigarette Labeling and Advertising Act as described by the First Circuit in *Palmer*.

Questions: Do the factors that influence the evolution of the common law have analogs in the legislative process? In what directions might statutory law tend to evolve?

Chapter 6

ECONOMIC ANALYSIS
OF REGULATION

This chapter discusses the basic economic tools necessary to analyze the impact and desirability of government regulation of economic activity and to understand and apply selected basic regulatory techniques.

A. ECONOMIC THEORY OF DEMAND AND SUPPLY

The first section of this chapter explores the economic theories of demand and supply, essential basic building blocks for analysis of the efficiency implications of regulation.

1. THE THEORY OF DEMAND

Analysis of the efficiency implications of legal rules and policy choices begins with an assumption that resources *should* be allocated to those whose willingness and ability to pay for those resources is the greatest. The theory of demand describes how individuals' willingness and ability to pay for goods and services changes in response to changes in their economic surroundings. In Mescalero Apache Tribe v. State of New Mexico, the legality of the state's regulation of hunting on the Mescalero Apache reservation turns, in part, on the effect of that regulation on hunters' willingness and ability to pay for hunting licenses, a significant source of revenue for the Mescalero Apache Tribe. The opinion introduces the *demand curve,* a graphic representation of the relationship between the price charged for licenses and the number of licenses hunters demand. The demand curve illustrates the effect of state regulation on revenue derived by the Tribe from license sales.

MESCALERO APACHE TRIBE v.
STATE OF NEW MEXICO

United States Court of Appeals, Tenth Circuit, 1980.
630 F.2d 724.

McKAY, CIRCUIT JUDGE.

This case involves a challenge to the State of New Mexico's attempt to regulate the management and harvesting of wildlife resources within the boundaries of the Mescalero Apache reservation.   *   *   *

[As part of a program to promote tourism, the Tribe adopted hunting and fishing ordinances that were inconsistent with state laws. By imposing "bag limits" on the number of animals or fish sportspeople could take that are different from the State's and by permitting hunting on reservation lands when hunting on State land was forbidden, for instance, the Tribe offered unique and valuable recreational opportunities. The Tribe had erected a resort complex with recreational facilities where many sportspeople stay while on the reservation along with many nonhunters who accompany them. The Tribe argued that the State's regulations reduced the attractiveness of hunting and fishing on reservation lands and thereby reduced both the attractiveness of the hunting and fishing licenses the Tribe sold and the income derived from use of its resort.]

* * * The State challenges, as it unsuccessfully did below, the Tribe's right to bring this suit. The State asserts that the Tribe has no standing and that the suit is otherwise not justiciable.

On the standing issue, the State argues that "[t]he Tribe is seeking to enjoin the enforcement of State penal statutes which do not apply to it and which do not threaten it or its members in any real, direct and immediate sense." In the State's view, a challenge to the state regulations may be prosecuted only by an aggrieved non-member sportsman. Since the Tribe has sold nearly all of its available hunting and fishing permits, the Tribe has allegedly suffered no revenue losses and no other "injury in fact" by the regulations the State would impose on non-member sportsmen.

The State's understanding of standing requirements is overly narrow. For purposes of standing, federal courts may certainly consider the principles of elementary economics. The State's imposition of higher costs on individual sportsmen clearly limits the Tribe's ability to raise the prices of its own licenses. We have no reason to assume that the demand curve for reservation hunting and fishing is so inelastic that the Tribe could charge and receive any imaginable price for its licenses. Even though all tribal licenses are now sold, and applications for licenses exceed the number available, that fact merely reflects the Tribe's conservative adjustment to market forces in devising its own fee structure. Similarly, other conflicts between the tribal and state regulatory structures-e.g., variations in hunting seasons-necessarily deter some non-member hunters from entering the reservation at some times. These conflicts affect the Tribe's own regulatory scheme. They also influence the prices the Tribe may charge and impinge on the Tribe's revenue-raising powers. These effects are not merely speculative, but are the straightforward and immediate results of economic forces.

* * *

No other barrier to justiciability is present. The impact of the state regulation upon the Tribe is "sufficiently direct and immediate as to render the issue appropriate for judicial review at this stage." The limits of state jurisdiction on the reservation is an issue now as ripe for resolution as it will ever be. The State has made clear that prosecution of non-member violators of state game laws, with the attendant effects on tribal regulation and revenue-raising, is intended and probable.

* * *

Notes and Questions

1. In Mescalero Apache Tribe v. State of New Mexico, the court examined the impact of state regulation on the Mescalero Apache Tribe's ability to raise revenue from selling licenses to hunt on its reservation. Two types of regulations may be analyzed to appreciate the effect of the regulation on the Tribe: the requirement that hunters on reservation lands also have state hunting licenses, and regulations that restrict how, where, and what the hunters may hunt and so reduce the pleasure hunters obtain from hunting. The former increases the effective price hunters have to pay to hunt on the reservation while the latter reduces the willingness of hunters to pay for licenses. The analysis begins with consideration of the effect of a price increase on the number of hunting licenses sold.

The court in Mescalero Apache Tribe v. State of New Mexico recognized the basic theory of demand when it stated that it is unlikely that the Tribe could charge and receive any imaginable price for its licenses. A higher asking price is likely to result in a decline in the quantity demanded by buyers. As the price rises above the maximum a particular hunter is willing and able to pay, the total quantity demanded is reduced by one. It might be that the hunter can no longer afford the license or that the high price makes substitute forms of recreation more attractive. Whatever the reason, higher prices are associated with reductions in the total quantity demanded.

Table 6–1 presents hypothetical numbers of licenses demanded by people wishing to hunt the reservation lands of the New Mexico Mescalero Apaches during a given time period at various prices. In accord with the theory of demand, fewer hunting licenses are demanded at higher prices; 200 hunters are willing and able to pay $100 each for a license while 500 hunters are willing and able to pay $25. The *demand schedule* in Table 6–1 reveals that the $100 price is greater than the maximum price many of the hunters are willing and able to pay.

Table 6–1
Demand for Hunting Licenses

Price for Each License	Number of Licenses Demanded
$125	100
$100	200
$75	300
$50	400
$25	500

Figure 6–1 presents these data in graphic form. Numbers along the horizontal axis, labeled "Number of Licenses Demanded," indicate the quantity of licenses demanded at various prices. The prices are indicated along the vertical axis, labeled "Price for Each License." The *demand curve* reveals the relationship between price and the quantity demanded. It indicates the quantity demanded during the time period at various prices as well as the maximum price that can be charged to sell various quantities during the time period.

Figure 6–1
Demand for Hunting Licenses

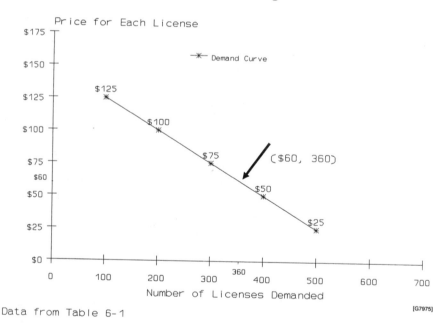

Data from Table 6–1   [G7975]

On Figure 6–1, the quantity demanded at prices not shown on Table 6–1 is estimated by connecting the points representing the information available (the price and quantity pairs for prices $25, $50, $75, $100, and $125). By referring to the demand curve, one can estimate how many licenses will be demanded at any price between those prices indicated. For instance, if the Mescalero Apache Tribe asks a price of $60 per license, one can estimate a quantity demanded of 360 licenses from the demand curve.

2. Economists have devised a term for describing buyers' responsiveness to changes in price that now pervades legal opinions on economic matters. Judge McKay concluded "We have no reason to assume that demand for reservation hunting and fishing is so *inelastic* that the Tribe could charge and receive any imaginable price for its licenses." The *price elasticity of demand* is a measure of how much the quantity demanded changes as the price changes. If demand is *inelastic,* then a price change will produce a relatively small change in quantity demanded. If demand is *elastic,* the change in quantity demanded in response to a price change is relatively large. As Judge McKay pointed out, very inelastic demand means that there would be relatively little decline in the quantity of hunting licenses demanded even if the Mescalero Apache Tribe dramatically increased the price of their hunting licenses. The notes following *Hospital Corp.,* below, discuss the price elasticity of demand in greater detail.

3. State regulation of hunting on reservation land may not only increase the effective price that hunters pay; it may also affect the benefits obtained from hunting. Hunters' willingness to buy licenses may be affected by a state regulation that reduces the number of elk they may kill. The demand curve in Figure 6–1 and the demand schedule in Table 6–1 reflect people's preferences, preferences that may be influenced by changes in circumstances that affect people's willingness and ability to purchase this particular good. A hunter's preference for hunting on state or reservation land may depend on the "bag limits" on those lands. The demand curve is a snapshot of people's willingness and ability to pay at a given time and under a specific set of circumstances.

A critical assumption underlying the demand curve is that nothing relevant to the desire of purchasers to buy a particular quantity changes except the price. This assumption is called the *ceteris paribus* assumption; *ceteris paribus* means "other things equal" or "unchanged." However, people's tastes and preferences may change for reasons unrelated to price. For example, hunting may become less fashionable or the reduced "bag limit" may make hunting less rewarding. When changes that alter people's preferences do occur, the demand schedule and the demand curve change, as an economic analysis of the regulations in Mescalero Apache Tribe v. State of New Mexico indicates.

The State of New Mexico argued that its application of state hunting and fishing laws to the reservation lands of the Apache did not threaten the Tribe in any real, direct, and immediate sense and, therefore, the Tribe had no standing to challenge the application of the regulations to tribal land. The court found that because the regulations restricted the pleasure sportspeople would get from hunting and fishing on the reservation, the maximum sportspeople would be willing to pay for those licenses was reduced. The reduced willingness to pay was likely to have a real, direct, and immediate effect on the Mescalero's ability to raise revenues by selling licenses.

The decline in demand for licenses that accompanies the restriction on the freedom of sportspeople can be illustrated by a shift in the demand curve that reflects the decreased willingness to pay. As Table 6–2 illustrates, the regulation reduced the number of individuals who were willing and able to buy licenses at any given price. The maximum price at least some hunters were willing and able to pay declined due to the reduced attractiveness of those licenses. Figure 6–2 compares the demand curve without regulation to the demand curve with regulation and shows the decline in demand. At a price of $100 per license, for example, demand declined from 200 licenses to 100 licenses. The estimate for the number of sportspeople willing and able to pay $60 for a license has declined from 360 to 260.

Table 6–2
Demand Shift with State Regulation

Price	Quantity Demanded without Regulation	Quantity Demanded with Regulation
$125	100	0
$100	200	100
$ 75	300	200
$ 50	400	300
$ 25	500	400

Figure 6–2
Demand Shift with State Regulation

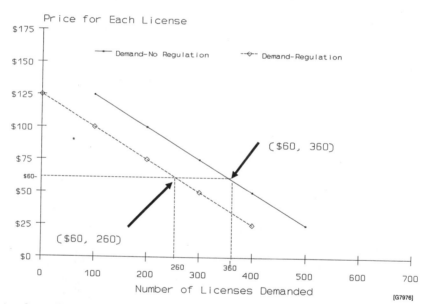

Data from Table 6–2

4. Demand curves can illustrate two types of variation in purchasers' behavior. Note 1 illustrated *changes in quantity demanded.* Changes in price cause changes in quantity demanded. The downward sloping nature of the demand curve means that as prices fall quantity demanded increases and as prices rise quantity demanded decreases. Any movement along the same demand curve is a change in quantity demanded. In this example, a decrease in the number of hunting licenses hunters wish to buy resulting from an increase in price is a change in quantity demanded.

While changes in quantity demanded result only from changes in price, *changes in demand* may result from changes in purchasers' tastes and preferences, changes in their incomes, or changes in the prices of other items the purchaser desires (which affect the relative attractiveness of the item in question and the wealth the purchaser has available to allocate among competing resources). These three sources of changes in demand are the "other things" that are assumed to be "unchanged" under the *ceteris paribus* assumption. When any one of them changes, a *change in demand* results. In our example, demand for hunting licenses may decrease if killing animals becomes distasteful to more people, demand may increase as people become wealthier, and the demand for hunting licenses may be affected by an increase in the cost of a substitute leisure activity, such as boating.

Note 3 illustrates a change in demand for hunting licenses that is due to a decrease in hunters' desire to hunt on the Mescalero Apache reservation if the state regulations restricting the manner of hunting are imposed. A change in demand is reflected by a shift in the demand curve. On Figure 6–2, for instance, the shift in the demand curve due to a decrease in the desirability of the hunting licenses reduced the demand for hunting licenses at the price of $60 from 360 to 260 licenses. Decreases in demand are reflected in a shift of the demand curve downward and to the left. Increases in demand are reflected in a shift of the demand curve upwards and to the right.

HOSPITAL CORPORATION OF AMERICA v. FEDERAL TRADE COMMISSION

United States Court of Appeals, Seventh Circuit, 1986.
807 F.2d 1381.

POSNER, CIRCUIT JUDGE.

Hospital Corporation of America, the largest proprietary hospital chain in the United States, asks us to set aside the decision by the Federal Trade Commission that it violated Section 7 of the Clayton Act, by the acquisition in 1981 and 1982 of two corporations, Hospital Affiliates International, Inc. and Health Care Corporation. Before these acquisitions (which cost Hospital Corporation almost $700 million), Hospital Corporation had owned one hospital in Chattanooga, Tennessee. The acquisitions gave it ownership of two more. In addition, pursuant to the terms of the acquisitions it assumed contracts, both with four-year terms, that Hospital Affiliates International had made to manage two other Chattanooga-area hospitals. So after the acquisitions Hospital Corporation owned or managed 5 of the 11 hospitals in the area.   * * *

* * *

When an economic approach is taken in a Section 7 case, the ultimate issue is whether the challenged acquisition is likely to facilitate collusion.   * * *

* * *

In showing that the challenged acquisitions gave four firms control over an entire market so that they would have little reason to fear a competitive reaction if they raised prices above the competitive level, the Commission went far to justify its prediction of probable anticompetitive effects. Maybe it need have gone no further. But it did. First it pointed out that the demand for hospital services by patients and their doctors is highly inelastic under competitive conditions. This is not only because people place a high value on their safety and comfort and because many of their treatment decisions are made for them by their doctor, who doesn't pay their hospital bills; it is also because most hospital bills are paid largely by insurance companies or the federal government rather than by the patient. The less elastic the demand for a good or service is, the greater are the profits that providers can make by raising price through collusion. A low price elasticity of demand means that raising price will cause a relatively slight fall in demand, with the result that total revenues will rise sharply. For example, if the price elasticity of demand throughout the relevant portion of the demand curve is .2, meaning that within that area every 1 percent increase in price will result in a two-tenths of 1 percent decrease in the quantity demanded, then a 10 percent increase in price will cause only a 2 percent reduction in quantity sold, and hence an almost 8 percent increase in total revenue. And since less is being produced, costs will fall at the same time that revenue is rising, resulting in an even greater percentage increase in profit than in revenue.

Second, there is a tradition, well documented in the Commission's opinion, of cooperation between competing hospitals in Chattanooga. Of course, not all forms of cooperation between competitors are bad. But a market in which competitors are unusually disposed to cooperate is a market prone to collusion. * * *

* * *

All these considerations, taken together, supported—we do not say they compelled—the Commission's conclusion that the challenged acquisitions are likely to foster collusive practices, harmful to consumers, in the Chattanooga hospital market. * * *

* * *

The Commission's order is affirmed and enforced.

Notes and Questions

1. Section 7 of the Clayton Act prohibits mergers that are likely to result in increased prices. The court applied the theory of demand to an evaluation of the probable anticompetitive effects of the merger. In *Hospital Corp.*, the price increases would be a result of a new unified pricing policy among the now jointly-controlled hospitals and the elimination of whatever price competition there may have been between the formerly independent hospitals.

Question: How does the inelasticity of demand for hospital services affect the profitability of price increases?

2.   A demand curve similar to that in Figure 6–1 could be drawn describing the relationship between the price of hospital services and the quantity demanded.   Economists customarily express the elasticity of demand in numerical terms.   When calculating the price elasticity of demand, changes in quantity demanded and in price are calculated in percentage terms.   Thus, when Judge Posner described a price elasticity of demand of 0.2, he indicated that a 1% increase in price would result in a 0.2% decrease in quantity demanded.   As his example illustrates, calculating the price elasticity involves determining the percentage change in quantity demanded that accompanies a specified percentage change in prices.

Referring to the demand curve in Figure 6–1, we find that the price elasticity of demand for an increase in price from $100 to $125 is three. The calculation of price elasticity of demand, shown below, requires three relatively simple steps:

(1) Calculating the numerical changes in price and quantity demanded,

(2) Using the result in (1) to calculate the percentage changes in price and quantity demanded, and

(3) Dividing the percentage change in quantity demanded by the percentage change in price.

Of these calculations, only the second is conceptually difficult.   The percentage change compares the numerical change (in price or quantity) to a base amount.   As shown below, the numerical change in quantity demanded is from 200 to 100 licenses, a difference of 100 units.   The percentage change compares this difference to a base amount, which is, by convention, the average of the two quantities, (200 + 100)/2 or 150.   The percentage change in quantity demanded is, then, 100/150 = .66 or 66%. A similar calculation gives a percentage change in price of .22 or 22%. The price elasticity of demand between these two points on the demand curve is .66/.22 = 3.

Calculation of Price Elasticity of Demand
Data

At Lower Price		At Higher Price	
Price	$100	Price	$125
Quantity	200	Quantity	100

(1)   Numerical Changes in Price and Quantity:
Price Difference = $100 − $125 = −$25
Quantity Difference = 200 − 100 = 100

(2)   Percentage Changes in Price and Quantity:
Price: Base for Price is average of $100 and $125,
($100 + $125)/2 = $112.50.
Percentage Change is −$25/$112.50 = −.22.

Quantity: Base for Quantity is average of 200 and 100,
(200 + 100)/2 = 150.
Percentage Change is 100/150 = .66.

(3)   Dividing the Percentage Changes:
        Price Elasticity of Demand = .66/−.22 = −3.
        (Note that economists frequently ignore the minus sign and simply report the price elasticity of demand as 3.)

A price elasticity of three implies that a 1% increase in price results in a 3% decrease in quantity demanded. Using this method, you can confirm that the demand curve is more inelastic in its lower regions. For instance, for the portion of the demand curve in Figure 6–1 between the prices of $50 and $25, the price elasticity of demand is .17 indicating that a 1% increase in price in that portion of the demand curve will result in a .17% decrease in demand on average.

> *Question:* What is the price elasticity of demand for the portion of the demand curve between the prices of $50 and $60?

3.   When the price elasticity of demand is greater than one, economists describe demand as being *elastic* because the percentage change in quantity demanded is greater than the percentage change in price. When the price elasticity of demand is less than one, economists, and judges such as Posner in *Hospital Corp.* and McKay in Mescalero Apache Tribe v. State of New Mexico, describe demand as being *inelastic*. When the price elasticity of demand is equal to one, demand is described as having "unitary" elasticity.

> *Question:* Referring to Table 6–1 and Figure 6–1, is demand elastic, inelastic, or unitary for the portion of the demand curve between the prices of $50 and $100?

4.   It should not be surprising that demand is more elastic at higher prices. As prices rise, substitutes become more attractive and the buyers' ability to pay for various quantities of the item decreases. A price change of 10% will involve more dollars for a high price than a low price and a greater percentage decline in demand can therefore be anticipated for the upper regions of a demand curve.

Because the price elasticity varies all along the demand curve, becoming more and more elastic as prices increase, the result of the calculation will depend on the particular portion of the demand curve examined. Calculating the price elasticity of demand as shown above yields the average or *arc price elasticity* of demand throughout the portion examined. Because this calculation of price elasticity is an "average" throughout a portion of the curve, the elasticity for the portion between $50 and $100 (calculated in Question 2), which included higher prices, was greater than for the portion between $50 and $60 (calculated in Question 3).

5.   Unless firms are controlled by the same management or agree (explicitly or tacitly) on what prices to charge, they cannot ordinarily raise prices with impunity. In a competitive market, if one firm raises its price while others keep their prices at a lower level, customers will abandon it and buy from the lower-priced firms. For this reason, demand for the product of a competitive firm is usually considered to be elastic; even a small increase in price will cause a relatively large decrease in the quantity demanded from that firm. If a firm that raises its price even a little loses all of its customers, the demand for that firm's product is said to be

perfectly elastic. The ability of a firm to raise prices profitably depends on the elasticity of the demand for its product.

Just as the elasticity of a firm's demand curve dictates its ability profitably to raise price, the elasticity of demand for a particular product affects the incentives for the firms in an industry to raise prices by agreeing to do so together. In *Hospital Corp.,* the Federal Trade Commission expressed particular concern at the incentives for hospitals in Chattanooga to collude and raise prices. The fact that demand for hospital services is inelastic increases the incentives to collude by making the price increases more profitable.

> *Question:* According to the opinion in *Hospital Corp.,* "[a] low price elasticity of demand means that raising price will cause a relatively slight fall in demand, with the result that total revenues will rise sharply." Is it correct that raising price will affect demand? Or does raising price affect quantity demanded?

6. Three factors influence the price elasticity of demand. The first is familiar—price. Demand is likely to be inelastic if the price is low. An inexpensive good, like salt, takes such a small portion of any consumer's budget that consumers would not be expected to alter their consumption of salt very much even if the price of salt doubled from its current level of 22 cents a pound to 44 cents.

Of at least equal importance to price is the availability of substitutes to consumers of the product, *substitutes in consumption.* The decision to buy less of a product depends on whether there is another product that has similar attributes, that satisfies the same need. If consumers find english muffins a good substitute for bagels, then a small change in the price of bagels will cause people to substitute english muffins in their diet; the demand for bagels would be elastic. If they did not believe there was any close substitute for bagels, then the demand for bagels would be more inelastic.

Time is the third factor that influences the elasticity of demand. Elasticities tend to increase over time because buyers have an opportunity to adjust to price changes. A demand curve is likely to be more elastic in any price range if it is measuring quantity demanded over a longer time period. When the first oil shortage occurred in the 1970's and the price of gasoline rose dramatically, the quantity of gasoline demanded did not decline very quickly. Over time, however, users of gasoline changed their driving habits and purchased more fuel-efficient cars. For a short time period, demand was inelastic, but as time allowed consumption habits to change, the decline in quantity demanded was greater. The passage of time influences both increases and decreases in quantity demanded. When oil prices fell in the 1980's, quantity demanded did not suddenly increase. Instead, oil consumption increased only after a long period of stable and then gradually declining oil prices in the 1980's.

> *Question:* Did the FTC's rationale for concluding that demand for hospital services was inelastic reflect either the price of hospital services or the availability of substitutes?

2. THE THEORIES OF COST AND SUPPLY

The prices actually charged for goods and services depend not only on individuals' willingness and ability to pay for them but also on the willingness and ability of individuals to supply them. According to economic theory, the willingness of producers to supply products depends primarily on the cost of supplying them and the price they receive for doing so. The following cases explore the theories of cost and supply and the graphic representation of the relationship between price and quantity supplied.

GOLD PLACER MINING

EFFLUENT LIMITATIONS GUIDELINES AND NEW SOURCE PERFORMANCE STANDARDS

Environmental Protection Agency, 1987.

52 Fed.Reg. 9414.

[Gold placer mining involves running water through gold-bearing sand and gravel to carry away lighter materials leaving behind heavy minerals including gold. The effluent water carrying away the waste materials pollutes other water and is subject to regulation by the Environmental Protection Agency under the Clean Water Act. In those regulations, the Agency has proposed limits on the amount of effluent that may be discharged from various types of placer mining operations. Executive Order 12291 requires the Agency to analyze the regulatory impact of major rules (those which impose a cost on the economy of $100 million or more). To determine whether the gold placer mining regulation requires a regulatory impact analysis, the Agency studied the costs of the pollution control regulations. The analysis involved comparing the cost of production prior to the adoption of the regulations (pre-compliance operating costs) with projections of costs of production after the regulations in force (post-compliance operating costs) for various types of mines.]

The application of the [methodology employed] resulted in the development of "representative" mines for each mine type in each region where that mine type is found. For each representative mine, the Agency calculated pre-compliance operating costs based on dollars-per-cubic-yard of ore processed and then converted this value into dollars-per-fine-ounce of gold production; that is, the cost in dollars of producing a fine ounce of gold prior to imposing any regulatory controls and related expenses. In this way, the Agency developed a systematic method of comparing mining costs under a variety of conditions for the gold placer mining industry.

The Agency then used this data to generate supply curves for each mine size in each region. The supply curves represent the total quantity of gold produced by each mine type in each region. In order to estimate the supply curves, the Agency derived total operating costs of the lowest and highest cost mine for each mine type in each region. Interpretation of the supply curve is based on the economic principle that a gold placer mining operation's cost per fine ounce of gold produced must be lower than the 1986 average price of gold in order for the mine to continue operating as a [profitable] entity.

The Agency estimated total cumulative gold production by summing all gold produced by active gold placer mining operations in Alaska and the lower 48 states for the 1986 mining season. * * * Cumulative gold production at any particular point on the supply curves is equal to the sum of the production of all mines that can deliver gold at a cost less than or equal to that which occurs at that point on the supply curve.

To determine the amount of gold production lost and the number of mine closures resulting from implementing effluent guideline limitations, a post-compliance supply curve is estimated which takes into account the costs of meeting the effluent guideline. All mines with total post-compliance operating costs (on a per-ounce of gold recovered basis) greater than the 1986 price of gold per ounce are projected to close (i.e., would not operate in the 1987 season) due to regulatory controls. * * *

* * *

* * * The regulation for gold placer mining activities is not expected to be a major rule. The costs expected to be incurred by this industry (<$12 million annually) are significantly less than $100 million. Therefore, a formal Regulatory Impact Analysis is not required. * * *

Notes and Questions

1. As the EPA Request for Comments in *Gold Placer Mining* indicates, supply curves describe how much of a particular product suppliers are willing and able to provide at different prices. Producers' willingness and ability to supply a product depends on the cost of producing the product and the price they can obtain in the market. In an example like placer mining, it is reasonable to suppose that producers would first seek out the alluvial or glacial deposits of gold that were most easily mined. Owners of mines where costs were lowest would be willing to supply gold at the lowest prices and higher prices would be necessary to encourage extracting gold from more inaccessible deposits.

Unlike the theory of demand, which proposes an inverse relationship between price and quantity demanded, the theory of supply assumes that price and quantity supplied are directly related; as price increases, the quantity supplied increases. Table 6–3 and Figure 6–3 present hypothetical data reflecting the direct relationship between price and quantity supplied for a large gold mine. As was true in the discussion of the demand curve, the relationship between price and quantity supplied relies on the *ceteris paribus* assumption; the relationship holds as long as other relevant factors are unchanged. The table and graph reveal that as the price of gold rises, the producer is willing to supply increasing quantities of gold.

Table 6–3
Supply of Gold

Price Received per ounce of Gold	Ounces of Gold Supplied
$30	60,000
$90	180,000
$200	400,000
$300	600,000
$500	1,000,000

Figure 6–3
Supply of Gold

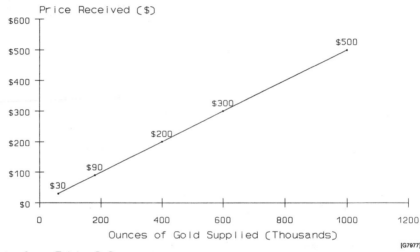

Data from Table 6-3

2. *Deriving the Supply Curve:* The supply curve describing total cumulative gold production calculated by the Environmental Protection Agency is made up of supply curves for each mine size and reflects the output of high cost and low cost mines of each size. The EPA adds the output each mine contributes to the total output for mines of its size to the output from each other similar mine, keeping track of how much it costs to produce that output. This results in a schedule of how much is produced at each cost level for a given mine type.

Table 6–4 presents a listing of amounts supplied for a sample of small mines and shows the cost per ounce of producing gold in those mines. Table 6–5 summarizes this data by displaying first how much *additional* output is produced at each cost level and then the total output produced at each cost level.

Table 6–4
Output of Gold Mines

Mine Designation	Ounces Supplied	Cost per Ounce
A	1,000	$ 80
B	5,000	$130
C	4,000	$130
D	2,000	$ 40
E	7,000	$100
F	20,000	$100
G	50,000	$300
H	4,000	$250
I	17,000	$250

Table 6–5
Supply Schedule for Small Mines

Cost Level	Additional Production (from mines indicated)	Total Production Ounces
$40	2,000(D)	2,000
$80	1,000(A)	3,000
$100	27,000(E,F)	30,000
$130	9,000(B,C)	39,000
$250	21,000(H,I)	60,000
$300	50,000(G)	110,000

Figure 6–4
Supply from Small Gold Mines

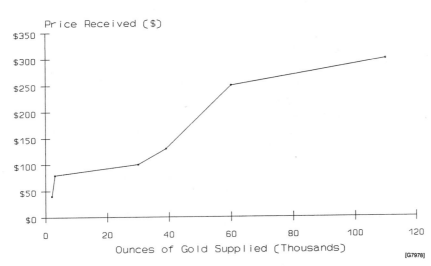

Data from Table 6-5

As Table 6–5 reveals, total production of 110,000 ounces is available from the small mines listed at costs per ounce of $300 or less. Only 39,000 ounces can be produced in these small mines at a cost of $130 or less. Figure 6–4 is a supply curve for the output of small mines from which the same information can be read.

As the EPA reported in this excerpt, the total cumulative gold production is estimated by adding up the quantity supplied by mines of all types at each cost. The supply curve in Figure 6–4, reflecting only the output of small mines, represents just a portion of the data collected to estimate the supply curve for the entire industry.

3. *Normal Economic Profit.* Economists typically include in the definition of "cost" enough of a return on the entrepreneur's investment of time and capital to make engaging in the enterprise worthwhile relative to other opportunities. This portion of cost is referred to as *normal economic profit.* The normal economic profit is added to the other expenses, such as materials, labor, or loan payments, that make up the "accounting costs" of doing business. It is important to realize that the economic concept of cost includes not only the cost of other inputs to the production process, such as machinery and raw materials, but also the cost of the owners' and investors' time and money. It may happen that prices are so high that the business earns more than enough to cover its accounting costs plus its normal economic profit, the return that is just enough to keep it in business. This excess profit is sometimes referred to as *pure profit, monopoly profit,* or *economic rent.*

Since the economic concept of cost includes a normal economic profit—just enough of a return to make it worthwhile to keep the business going—any price greater than *or equal to* cost is high enough to entice a supplier to produce.

Question: With this principle in mind, consider the following statement by the EPA: "Interpretation of the supply curve is based on the economic principle that a gold placer mining operation's cost per fine ounce of gold produced must be lower than the 1986 average price of gold in order for the mine to continue operating as a [profitable] entity." Has the bureaucrat responsible for this report chosen a definition of cost that is more consistent with the traditional economic definition or with the notion of accounting costs?

4. This book follows the traditional economic definition in which cost includes enough of a return to encourage the supplier to produce the output at a price equal to cost. The reasons for this definition and the logic of including normal economic profit in cost are explored further in the following case, Crown v. Commissioner of Internal Revenue.

Questions: Apply the concepts of cost and supply to the following questions, which refer to the data presented in Figure 6–4:

a. At a price of $130, how many ounces of gold will be supplied from the small placer mines in the sample?

b. How much does the quantity of gold supplied increase as price increases from $130 to $250?

c. What price is required to induce suppliers to produce 30,000 ounces of gold?

d. How much of a price increase is necessary to call forth an increase of 21,000 ounces if the current level of production is 39,000 ounces?

5. By requiring changes in the production process, the effluent rules proposed by the Environmental Protection Agency would increase the cost of production for miners. As a result, miners would require a higher price to induce them to supply the same quantity of gold. That would result in a *change in supply*, reflected in a shift in the supply curve, just as a change in demand would result in a shift in the demand curve.

Questions: Referring to the supply curves in Figure 6–5, answer the following questions:

a. How much of an increase in cost per ounce would the regulation impose?

b. If producers were willing and able to supply 800,000 ounces at a price of $400 per ounce, what price would be necessary to induce them to supply 800,000 ounces after complying with the effluent rules?

c. If the world price of gold remained at $450 an ounce, how much would the quantity of gold supplied by placer mines in the United States decline after producers complied with the effluent rules?

d. If the world price of gold remained at $450 an ounce and other countries did not impose similar environmental protection regulations, would the EPA's regulatory scheme increase or decrease the share of the world market supplied by producers in the United States?

Figure 6–5
Supply Shift with Effluent Regulation

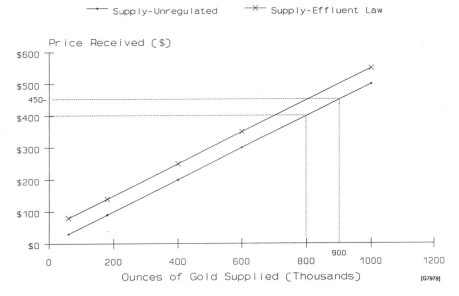

6. When the costs of supplying a product change, the result is a shift in the supply curve, which is referred to as a *change in supply*. Movements

along the supply curve, which result from changes in price, are referred to as *changes in quantity supplied.* This nomenclature parallels that developed for changes in demand and changes in quantity demanded.

Changes in supply may result from changes in the cost of inputs to the production process, developments in the technology used to produce the output, or changes in other opportunities available to the entrepreneur or investor. Just as demand is often interpreted as the maximum people are willing and able to pay to receive a given quantity of a good, supply is interpreted as the minimum people are willing and able to accept to provide a quantity of a good. It is easy to see how an increase in wages (an input) might affect the minimum producers are willing and able to provide. Increases in wages raise costs, reducing profits at any given price. Producers are willing to supply less at the old price and the supply curve shifts upward reflecting the fact that a higher price is necessary to call forth the same quantity as before the wage increase. Analogously, a new technology might reduce the costs of production and shift the supply curve downwards.

> *Questions:* If the price of another ore that is mined by the placer method increases and makes mining of the other ore more profitable than it was before, how would this affect the normal economic profit necessary to keep the gold placer mines in operation? How would this change the supply of gold from placer mines?

7. The price elasticity of the supply curve is a concept analogous to the price elasticity of demand discussed in the materials following *Hospital Corp.* The more elastic the supply curve, the greater is the response of producers to a change in price. An inelastic supply curve is one in which the quantity supplied changes very little in response to a price change. Like the price elasticity of demand, price elasticity of supply is computed by dividing the percentage change in quantity (supplied) by the corresponding percentage change in price. Supply is considered to be elastic if the elasticity is greater than one and inelastic if the elasticity is less than one.

> *Question:* Using the same approach as that outlined for the price elasticity of demand in Note 2 following *Hospital Corp.,* calculate the price elasticity of supply for the portion of the supply curve in Figure 6–4 between the prices of $100 and $130.

8. Since the willingness of producers to increase supply in response to a price increase depends on the cost of producing additional gold, an elastic supply curve indicates that the cost of increasing quantity supplied is relatively low. This is likely to be true in an industry where there is potential for inexpensive expansion of output, where, for instance, factories or mines are operating at less than full capacity. When there is potential for inexpensive expansion of output, then there will be little upward pressure on prices as quantity supplied increases.

The elasticity of supply in an industry is an important consideration when analyzing the effect on domestic producers of the imports of competing goods. The United States International Trade Commission has jurisdiction to prevent unfair competition by foreign producers that threatens injury to United States industry. In Copperweld Corp. v. United States, 682 F.Supp. 552 (Ct. Int'l Trade 1988), domestic producers of carbon steel pipe complained that Canadian producers were selling pipe in the United

States at such a low price that the profits of domestic producers were significantly reduced. The court referred to expert testimony on the elasticity of supply in the industry to determine the effect of imports on domestic profits.

Figure 6–6 presents an elastic supply curve and an inelastic supply curve for carbon steel pipe. The relatively flat or horizontal elastic supply curve in Figure 6–6 illustrates that there will be little upward pressure on prices as volume (quantity supplied) increases. On the elastic curve, for instance, 20 million feet of pipe will be supplied at a price closer to $3 than $4. An increase in quantity supplied from 20 million feet of pipe to 30 million feet can be induced by increasing price very little, 20 or 30 cents. While the price for 20 million feet of pipe may be low on the inelastic supply curve, less than one dollar per foot, increasing output to 30 million feet would require a much greater price increase, to over five dollars.

Figure 6–6
Elastic and Inelastic Supply Curves

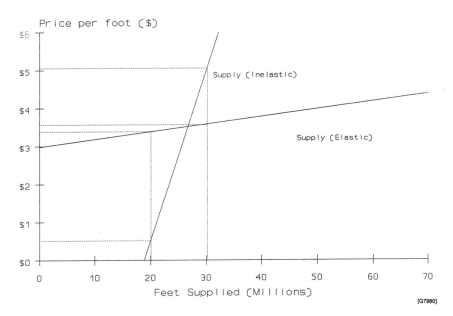

Expert testimony in *Copperweld* established that the supply curve in the carbon steel pipe industry was elastic before Canadian producers started competing in the United States. The expert testified that, when supply is elastic, competition in an industry is likely to be intense and profits are likely to be low. He concluded that if these conditions were observed in the absence of Canadian competition, then Canadian imports could not have been the cause of the low profits. Relying (in part) on this testimony, the court denied the domestic producers' claims.

Question: Why is elastic supply likely to lead to intense competition and low profits?

9. The ability of producers to increase supply, either by expanding their capacity to produce the product in question or by switching from the production of a similar product to the product in question, determines the elasticity of supply. The elasticity of supply for steel pipes will depend, for instance, on how willing and able producers of iron pipes are to change their production to steel pipes in response to an increase in the price of steel pipes. Products among which a producer may choose to produce are *substitutes in production* and affect the price elasticity of supply just as *substitutes in consumption* affect the price elasticity of demand. See *Hospital Corp.* Question 6. Supply may also be increased by new entrants to the industry, who are attracted by the higher prices.

Time influences the elasticity of supply, just as it affects the elasticity of demand. A supply curve describes the quantities producers are willing and able to supply at different prices within a given time period. A supply curve for a longer time period is likely to be more elastic.

Question: A demand curve is likely to be more elastic if it describes changes in demand over a long period of time, reflecting the increased ability of consumers to adjust their consumption patterns to changes in price. Why does the elasticity of supply increase with time?

CROWN v. COMMISSIONER OF INTERNAL REVENUE

United States Court of Appeals, Seventh Circuit, 1978.
585 F.2d 234.

HARLINGTON WOOD, JR., CIRCUIT JUDGE.

The primary question presented in this appeal is whether a taxpayer who lends money to his children and other close family members in the form of no-interest loans and open accounts payable on demand must include in the computation of gifts taxable during a particular tax year the value of the interest foregone on the indebtedness outstanding during that year. The tax court ruled in favor of the taxpayer's argument that no taxable gift occurred. We affirm.

* * *

The Commissioner begins his argument for finding a gift in these loans with the proposition that the granting of a loan over a period of time at less than the true economic rate of interest bestows an economic benefit on the recipient. As with any productive asset the ability to employ that asset in productive activity gives rise to "income" in an economic sense. When money is loaned at zero interest over a period of time the recipient is enriched by the amount of income that the money generates for him. At the same time, the person who lends the money is poorer by the amount of interest foregone. His nominal wealth may not decline, but he misses out on a chance to increase his net worth. This is the "opportunity cost" of his loan. In order for an economic benefit to be transferred to the recipient, it is not necessary that the interest rate be set at zero, but only that the interest rate on the loan be less than the appropriate market rate of interest at the time.

* * * Appellee's counter-argument, which was accepted by the majority in the Tax Court, is that

> our income tax system does not recognize unrealized earnings or accumulations of wealth and no taxpayer is under any obligation to continuously invest his money for a profit. The opportunity cost of either letting one's money remain idle or suffering a loss from an unwise investment is not taxable merely because a profit *could have been made* from a wise investment.

It is true that under our system a taxpayer is not under any duty to cultivate the fruits of his capital (or labor) and will not be taxed as if he had when he hasn't. However, by actively placing others in a position to enjoy the fruits of his capital, the taxpayer in a sense vicariously "realizes" the economic potential thereof. Permitting others to enjoy the economic benefits of an asset can be seen as one means of exerting control over the asset's economic potential. This might serve as a theoretical basis for distinguishing gifts such as those involved here from situations where the taxpayer lets his productive properties lie totally fallow. However, whatever the value of this consideration as a policy factor favoring the gift taxation of loans such as those present in the instant case, the Commissioner has not been able to point to any authority suggesting that the congressional purpose of protecting the estate tax was concerned with the use of gifts to diminish a taxpayer's potential estate as well as his actual one.

* * *

In conclusion, although we are sympathetic to the Commissioner's desire to fill in what may be a significant loophole in the gift tax laws, a number of theoretical and practical problems make it undesirable to do so by judicial construction. We express no view here as to whether a prospective regulation making such loans taxable would be valid or whether, on the other hand, the problem would best be left to Congress.

The judgment of the Tax Court is affirmed.

———

In the Tax Reform Act of 1984, Congress amended the Internal Revenue Code to include the opportunity cost of the interest foregone among those items taxable as gifts:

§ 7872: Treatment of loans with below-market interest rates

(a) Treatment of gift loans and demand loans.

(1) In General.—For the purposes of this title, in the case of any below-market loan to which this section applies and which is a gift loan or a demand loan, the foregone interest shall be treated as—

(A) transferred from the lender to the borrower, and

(B) retransferred by the borrower to the lender as interest.

Notes and Questions

1. For the taxpayer in *Crown*, the opportunity cost of the loan given at a below-market rate arose from the fact that he "miss[ed] out on a chance to increase his wealth." An estimate of this opportunity cost would be the difference between the interest he would have earned at the market rate and the interest earned at the rate actually charged, in the taxpayer's case, zero. In theory, Judge Wood decided, this is an opportunity the taxpayer had given up and equivalent to wealth transferred to the recipient of the gift. From the recipient's viewpoint, it is easy to see this as a transfer of wealth. The recipient could either invest the money, earn the market rate of interest, and increase his wealth or, by using the money instead of borrowed money, save the expense of paying interest to someone else.

Judge Wood reasoned that since the gift tax system was designed to tax transfers of wealth between taxpayers, the gift of free interest should be taxed. Nevertheless, he concluded that the tax code provided no authority for taxing the opportunity cost of the gift as if it were like any other transfer of wealth. History shows that either the logic of opportunity costs or the revenue raising opportunity was so compelling that the tax code was amended. Section 7872 of the Internal Revenue Code now taxes the foregone interest from a below market rate loan to the lender.

2. Opportunity cost is the value of the benefit foregone by choosing one alternative rather than another. In the interest-free loan context, the two alternatives are making an interest-free loan and making a market rate loan. For a law student, the opportunity cost of being in law school is the value of benefits that could be obtained by engaging in the most beneficial alternative activity, such as earning money as a paralegal. For a consumer, the opportunity cost of buying a VCR is the value of the benefit that could be derived from buying the most valuable alternative item, such as a stereo. A rational entrepreneur is assumed to be engaged in the activity that earns her the highest return.

Question: What is the opportunity cost of choosing to engage in the business of gold placer mining?

3. The notes following *Gold Placer Mining* described normal economic profit as sufficient return on their investment of time and capital to keep entrepreneurs or investors engaged in a particular line of business. Since that "sufficient return" will depend on what other opportunities are available, the notion of normal economic profit is identical with that of opportunity cost. The entrepreneur or investor must earn more in gold placer mining than she would earn in her next best available opportunity or it would be irrational to stay in that business. Thus, it would be accurate to describe costs as including both accounting costs (such as the costs of raw materials, labor, and other expenses) and opportunity costs.

Like any other business, gold placer mining involves the cost of inputs to the production process (pipes, workers, etc.) as well as giving up other opportunities. Choosing to placer mine for gold in a particular location requires giving up the opportunity to mine in other locations.

Question: If the specialized equipment employed is only useful in gold mining, how would one determine the normal economic profit necessary to keep the miner working at that location?

3. THE INTERACTION OF SUPPLY AND DEMAND

The prevailing price in a market is determined by both supply and demand and therefore influenced by all of the factors that affect the willingness and ability of individuals to buy and sell. The notice of rulemaking from the Department of Labor and the Tenth Circuit tax case excerpted in this section illustrate the relevance of demand and supply, the costs that affect supply, and the price elasticities of demand and supply to the prevailing market price.

OCCUPATIONAL NOISE EXPOSURE: FINAL RULE

Department of Labor Occupational Safety and Health Administration, 1981.
46 Fed.Reg. 4078.

Summary: This final rule establishes a hearing conservation program, including exposure monitoring, audiometric testing, and training, for all employees who have occupational noise exposures equal to or exceeding an 8–hour time-weighted average of 85 dBA. [In this notice, OSHA explains the rationale for its regulation, including its analysis of the impact of the regulation on prices of the products produced by those subject to the regulation.]

* * *

Noise is one of the most pervasive occupational health problems. It is a by-product of many industrial processes. Exposure to high levels of noise causes temporary or permanent hearing loss and may cause other harmful health effects as well. The extent of damage depends primarily on the intensity of the noise and the duration of exposure.

There is an abundance of epidemiological and laboratory evidence that protracted noise exposure above 90 decibels (dB) causes hearing loss in a substantial portion of the exposed population, and that more susceptible individuals will incur hearing loss at levels below 90 dB.
* * *

* * *

OSHA's existing standard for occupation exposure to noise specifies a maximum permissible noise exposure level of 90 dB for a duration of 8 hours, with higher levels allowed for shorter duration. Employers must use feasible engineering or administrative controls, or combinations of both, whenever employee exposure to noise in the workplace exceeds the permissible exposure level. Personal protective equipment may be used to supplement the engineering and administrative controls where such controls are not able to reduce the employee exposures to within permissible limits. The standard also requires employers to administer a "continuing, effective hearing conservation program" for overexposed employees, but the standard does not define such a program.

* * *

* * * Information in the record indicates that many employees are not receiving the benefits of engineering controls to reduce their exposures to within the permissible exposure limits. In fact, there are some 2.9 million workers in American production industries with [time-weighted average sound levels] in excess of 90 dB, and an additional 2.3 million whose exposure levels exceed 85 dB. These workers, who face a significant risk of material impairment of health or functional capacity, will receive greatly increased protection from the promulgation and enforcement of these hearing conservation requirements, which amend certain provisions of the present noise standard. * * *

* * *

PRICE IMPACT

Economic reasoning indicates that firms will attempt to pass on higher production costs by increasing the selling price of their products. If an industry faces a perfectly inelastic demand for its output, the manufacturers would shift the entire cost of complying with the amendment to their customers through a price increase without a contraction of industry sales. This market condition, however, is seldom the case. On the other hand, if the industry supply curve is perfectly elastic, product prices will rise by the full amount of the cost increase, but industry output will fall to the extent that sales are inversely related to price. Except for over very long time periods, this industry response would also be considered unusual.

In general, firms will try to pass on cost increases by raising product prices, and consumers will respond by reducing their purchases of the industry's products. Most firms, therefore, will find that they cannot quickly recoup all of their profits through price hikes, but must settle for price increases allowing less than a full cost passthrough. If firms could pass on their entire cost increase, however, the maximum expected price rise can be calculated by dividing the estimated compliance cost for each industry by the sales of that industry, and expressing the result as a percentage. [OSHA has calculated] the percentage price increase that would be attributable to the amendment if the entire cost is passed on solely and exclusively in the form of price increases.

[Those calculations show] that the overall impact of the proposed amendment, if all of the costs were passed on, would be to increase prices by 0.01 percent, i.e. one hundredth of a percent in the 19 industrial sectors studied. This clearly implies a negligible change to any of the nation's more aggregated price index series. While there is variation among industries, in only a few cases are the estimated price increases greater than a few hundredths of a percent. The largest increase in price, 0.078 percent, is recorded for the lumber and wood sector, an industry estimated to have over 94 percent of its production workers exposed to noise levels above 85 dB. However, even this price increase is of such a small magnitude that its effect would be hardly noticeable among all of the other cyclical factors affecting the industry product prices.

Notes and Questions

1. Neither the buyers' willingness and ability to pay nor the sellers' willingness and ability to supply, taken alone, determines market price. Both demand and supply conditions influence the price at any given time and both must be considered when evaluating changes in prices that result from changed conditions.

The OSHA Rule establishing monitoring, testing, and training requirements for employees exposed to loud noises will cost the employers money. Raising their costs changes their supply curves, shifting them upwards to indicate a willingness to supply a smaller quantity of goods at any given price or, what is equivalent, to indicate the higher price necessary to cover the cost of producing any given quantity. While the regulation is unlikely to have any effect on demand for the goods, the ability of suppliers to pass on the costs of the hearing conservation program is limited by the buyers' willingness and ability to pay increased prices. By examining the supply and demand curves for any affected industry, we can determine the effect of the regulation on prices and on quantities demanded and supplied in that industry.

The OSHA analysis assumes that firms are able to pass on all of their costs and notes that this will be true only if demand is perfectly inelastic or if supply is perfectly elastic. The OSHA recognizes that both are unlikely, but proceeds with this assumption anyway. This is a worst-case scenario for price increases, as the following notes reveal. Even at worst, OSHA concluded, the price increases are likely to be less than one hundredth of one percent in most of the industries studied.

2. Figure 6–7 illustrates the traditional economic analysis of how demand and supply conditions determine the price at which goods will be exchanged. At a price such as P1, the quantity sellers are willing and able to supply, QS1, is less than the quantity buyers demand, QD1; there is a shortage. Since there are buyers willing and able to pay more than P1 and sellers who would be willing to supply more at a higher price, there is a tendency for prices to rise as long as shortages exist.

Figure 6–7
Demand and Supply Equilibrium

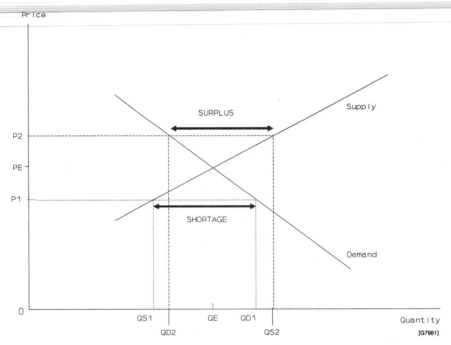

At a price such as P2, the quantity sellers are willing and able to supply, QS2, exceeds the quantity demanded, QD2; there is a surplus. Since sellers are unable to find enough buyers at P2 but could sell the surplus at a lower price, there is downward pressure on prices as long as surpluses exist.

Only where the quantities demanded and supplied are equal, where the demand and supply curves intersect, will there be no pressure for prices to rise or fall. The price at which this balance occurs is referred to as the *equilibrium price,* PE. At the equilibrium price there is no unsatisfied demand or excess supply. The quantity demanded and supplied at this price is the *equilibrium quantity,* QE.

3. Whenever demand or supply changes, the balance represented by the equilibrium price and quantity is upset. Figure 6–8 illustrates the effect on price and output of a decrease in supply. The decrease in this illustration is due to the increased costs associated with the hearing conservation program established in *Occupational Noise.* The market in which the effects are analyzed is the market for gold. Neither demand nor supply is perfectly inelastic in this market; both the quantity demanded and quantity supplied are responsive to price.

Figure 6–8
Market Price for Gold

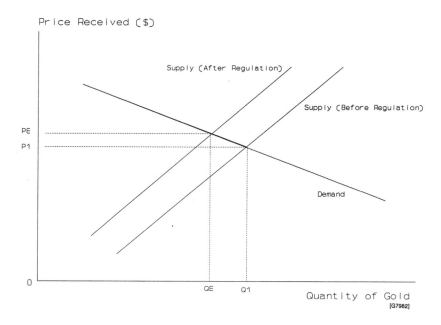

Before regulation the equilibrium price is P1, but the increased costs have shifted the supply curve up and to the left, creating a shortage at the old price. The shortage creates pressure for an increase in price, leading ultimately to a new equilibrium price, PE (higher than the old price, P1), and a new equilibrium quantity, QE (lower than the old quantity, Q1).

Figure 6–9 describes the analysis performed by OSHA. The price increases estimated by OSHA in *Occupational Noise* were calculated following the assumption that either demand is perfectly inelastic or supply is perfectly elastic. In Figure 6–9, demand is perfectly inelastic.

Figure 6–9
Prices for Gold (Inelastic Demand)

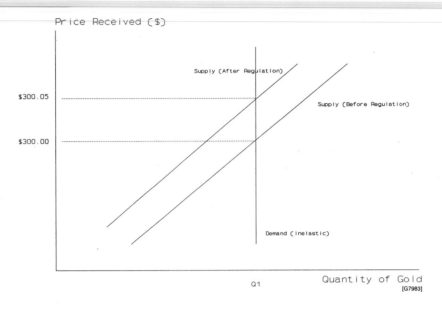

Questions: Why does perfectly inelastic demand result in the maximum possible price increase? Why does perfectly elastic supply result in the maximum possible price increase?

4. The tables in the full notice in *Occupational Noise* reveal that the maximum price increase for the primary metals industry is .0164%. If this figure applies to gold production and the preregulation equilibrium price was $300 per ounce, the postregulation equilibrium price would be .0164% higher, or about $300.05 per ounce.

Question: If OSHA had made the more realistic assumption that there was some responsiveness of quantity demanded and supplied to price, would the equilibrium price after regulation be higher or lower than $300.05?

5. If the cost of regulation per ounce of gold is 5 cents per ounce, as in the illustration in Note 4, and the new equilibrium price is only 2 cents higher than the preregulation price, then the producers will have to absorb 3 cents of cost increase while the buyers will absorb 2 cents of the increase. The relative shares of any cost increase that are borne by buyers and sellers depend on the elasticity of demand and supply.

Questions: Are sellers able to pass on more of their costs when demand is elastic or inelastic? How does the elasticity of supply affect the proportion of costs borne by the buyer and seller?

MESCALERO APACHE TRIBE v. O'CHESKEY

United States Court of Appeals, Tenth Circuit, 1980.
625 F.2d 967.

SETH, CHIEF JUDGE.

The State of New Mexico sought to impose its gross receipts tax on the several contractors who had done construction work for the Mescalero Apache Tribe on a resort complex and other projects within the boundaries of the State of New Mexico. The work was performed for the Mescaleros and on reservation lands. The trial court held that the tax was imposed on the contractors and they were liable for it to the State of New Mexico. The trial court held that the Tribe had purchased materials on [a] housing job * * * and these purchases were not within the gross receipts tax by reason of a specific exemption.

* * *

This court considered the same tax in *United States v. State of N.M.* and decided that the sovereignty of the United States did not prevent the imposition of this tax on a contractor providing services to the federal government on federal lands. We there also necessarily considered the incidence of this tax.

* * *

"The Act specifically makes the gross receipts tax applicable to the doing of business in New Mexico without reference to whether that business is with the United States and, with uniformly applied exceptions, assesses the tax upon anyone receiving compensation. There is no evidence that the tax interferes with the performance of federal functions. The tax is not directly imposed on the United States and, although the contractors pass the tax on to the United States they are not required by the Act to do so."

The incidence of this tax cannot be different here just because Indians are involved. The tax is the same, the incidence remains the same, and it is clearly on the contractor. The Indians here are in no different a position than was the federal government in *United States v. State of N. M.*

* * *

* * * The gross receipts tax on contractors, and all others, obviously is a cost of doing business as are the employment security taxes, social security taxes, income taxes, and all the overhead that goes into the jobs, and must be recovered from the work charges. The tax nevertheless is on the seller. An indirect burden obviously is initially on the one for whom the services are performed thus on the Tribe or the Government. However, it is equally apparent that this indirect burden is again passed on to the users of the resort and again by them. The tax becomes dispersed. There is no way of telling where the ultimate economic burden falls. This is the reason why the initial

incidence of the tax must be the determinative factor. It is the only significant matter for our consideration.

* * *

The judgment of the trial court is AFFIRMED.

Notes and Questions

1. The Mescalero Apache Tribe is exempt from paying gross receipt taxes in New Mexico. While the Tribe is not required to pay taxes on items it purchases, it is not exempt from higher charges resulting from a contractor's payment of taxes on materials used for a project on Tribal lands. The court reasons that since the tax is initially assessed against the contractor, rather than the Tribe, the ability of the contractor to pass on the cost to the Tribe is immaterial.

The initial incidence of a tax is referred to by economists as the *statutory incidence,* indicating the party from whom the government collects the tax. As the opinion in this case indicates, however, it is widely recognized that the statutory incidence is not necessarily the same as the *economic incidence,* indicating the parties who ultimately pay the tax. The reason for ignoring who actually pays the tax is administrative convenience. The court notes that an indirect burden is placed on the Tribe, but this burden is again passed on to users of the Tribal resort and hunting lands and then again by those users, widely dispersing the tax. "There is no telling where the ultimate economic burden falls. This is why the initial incidence of the tax must be the determinative factor."

The ability of contractors to pass on taxes can be analyzed in the same way as increases in costs due to regulation, as discussed in the materials following *Occupational Noise.* The price elasticities of demand and supply for the products bought by the Tribe will determine the economic incidence of the tax, that is, who bears the tax burden. To determine the tax burden borne by the Tribe, for instance, we would want to determine first how much of the tax the contractor passed on to the Tribe. Then, we would want to know how much of that tax burden the Tribe was able to pass to purchasers of its resort services. Determining the ultimate incidence of the tax is approached through three distinct steps evaluating two distinct markets, the market for resort construction and the market for resort services to guests.

A. Figures 6–10 and 6–11 describe the demand and supply conditions in two markets: the market for resort construction on the reservation and the market for the Tribe's resort services. The tax is imposed on construction materials and, by shifting the supply curve for resort construction, raises the price the Tribe pays for construction. Figure 6–10 describes the demand and supply conditions in the market for resort construction. The equilibrium price per square foot of construction before the tax was $51. The tax increase is assumed to be $5 per square foot of construction. This cost increase for the contractors is reflected in shifting the supply curve up and to the left. The vertical distance between the supply curves with and without the tax is five dollars, as indicated on the graph.

Questions: How much of the $5 tax is passed on to the Tribe by the contractors and how much of the tax burden is borne by the contractors themselves? If a typical hotel room in the resort is 500 square feet, how much is the Tribe's cost of adding another room to the hotel increased by the tax?

Figure 6–10
Market for Resort Construction

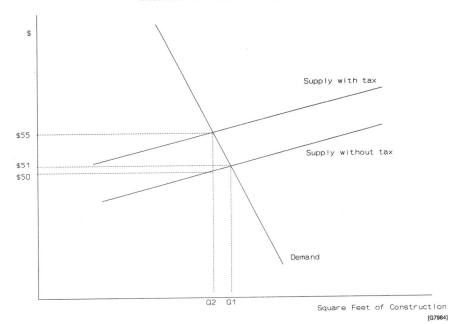

[G7984]

Figure 6–11
Market for Resort Services

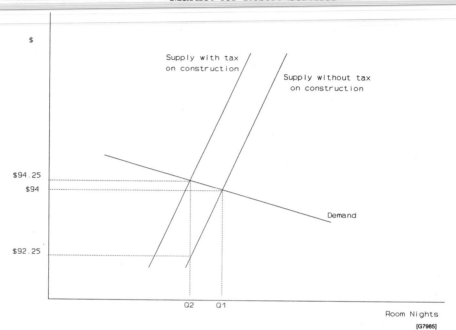

B. The Tribe, faced with higher construction costs, will attempt to pass on as much of those increased costs as possible to the purchasers of resort services. Figure 6–11 describes demand and supply conditions in the market for resort services. Note that this is a distinct market from the market for construction. The tribe paid more for each square foot of construction, but does not sell rooms by the square foot. They sell rooms by the night. The entire cost of construction is not passed on to a customer in one night; it is spread throughout the useful life of the room. The shift in the supply curve for "room-nights" reflects the increased cost of providing one room-night, hypothetically $2.00.

Before the tax, the equilibrium price per room night was $94. The increased construction costs raise the supply curve up and to the left to reflect the amount of the increase in costs. Suppose that the cost increase translates into an increase of $2 in the cost of providing a room for one night. The vertical distance between the supply curves for resort services with and without the tax in Figure 6–11 is then equal to $2.

Questions: How much of this $2 cost increase is the Tribe able to pass on to the buyers of resort services? In terms of percentages, how much of the cost increase is the Tribe able to pass on?

C. The previous calculations revealed what percentage of the amount passed on to the Tribe is borne by the Tribe and what percentage is passed on to the guests. The ultimate question is how much of the total amount of the tax is borne by the various parties.

Question: How much of the burden of the $5 tax on construction materials is ultimately borne by the Tribe, the contractors, and the guests at the resort?

2. It is a violation of federal antitrust law for two competitors to agree to fix their selling price at a level higher than the prevailing market price. Under federal law, the purchaser of goods for which the price has been fixed has a right to recover damages, which are based on the amount of enhancement of the price. Under state law (in California, for instance), the person to whom the first purchaser sells those goods may have a right to recover damages for any enhancement of the price he pays as a result of the price fixing.

Questions: If price fixing raised the price to the first purchaser by $10 per unit, how would demand and supply curves be used to estimate the price increase paid by the subsequent purchaser?

3. One of the motives for imposing strict liability on manufacturers in torts is the ability of manufacturers to spread the cost of injuries across their customers.

Question: How might demand and supply curves be used to determine the ability of manufacturers to spread the costs to their customers by raising prices?

4. In each of the preceding examples, there are additional factors that affect the ability of parties to pass on costs. In addition to passing on the costs to customers in the form of higher prices, the manufacturers in the strict liability question may be able to pass on these costs to workers in the form of lower wages or to stockholders in the form of lower dividends. People who buy anything from or sell anything to the manufacturer may be affected by the increased costs imposed on the manufacturer. That makes finding the economic incidence of the increase in costs very difficult because a complete answer would require an examination of the demand and supply relationships in each of the markets involved.

Question: What additional relationships would have to be examined in order to determine the economic incidence in the antitrust and gross receipts tax cases described above?

B. MARGINAL ANALYSIS AND ALLOCATIVE EFFICIENCY

In order to maximize wealth, resources must be devoted to their most valuable uses. Using the theory of demand, economists analyze how highly people value various goods and services. Using the theory of supply, economists consider the cost of supplying those goods and services. Putting the theories together, policymakers can maximize the wealth of society by allocating goods and services to those who value them more highly than the cost of supplying them. This section contains cases in which courts consider whether governmental involvement in price-controlled or regulated industries does or should promote the goal of allocative efficiency.

STANDARD OIL COMPANY OF OHIO v. FEDERAL ENERGY ADMINISTRATION

Temporary Emergency Court of Appeals, 1979.
612 F.2d 1291.

LACEY, JUDGE.

The defendant Federal Energy Administration (FEA) appeals from a decision of the district court that a Remedial Order and an Appeal Decision and Order issued by the FEA conflicted with regulations administered by the FEA and exceeded the scope of the FEA's authority. We affirm.

Plaintiff Standard Oil Company of Ohio (Sohio) is an independent refiner of petroleum products. [At issue is a question of Sohio's method for setting the price of oil. The Government supervision of pricing involved in this case began when the Economic Stabilization Act of 1970 granted authority to the Cost of Living Council to promulgate regulations restricting refiners' freedom to set the price of oil according to market forces. Congress transferred this authority to a variety of different agencies and departments during the years when the regulations were enforced. The Federal Energy Administration was the agency with the greatest involvement in this litigation. The particular regulation involved was the "two-tier" pricing rules. The "two-tier" pricing system was originated by the Cost of Living Council during the fourth phase of the program designed to stabilize prices. The aim of the system was to minimize the inflation caused by higher worldwide prices, while still providing an incentive for increasing domestic production.]

* * * In November and December 1973 and January 1974, Sohio bought domestic crude. Under the two-tier pricing system, "old" oil was subject to a ceiling price [of $5.25 per barrel], but "new" oil could be sold at the prevailing market price, which, of course, was higher. Thus, when Sohio made these purchases domestic oil did not sell at a uniform price. The sellers of this crude oil invoiced Sohio at the "old" oil ceiling price, for they did not know at the time of sale how much was "old" and how much was "new" oil.

This made it impossible for Sohio when it received a shipment to know for sure the ultimate cost. Only later—sometimes as much as five months later—would the supplier ascertain the proportions of "old" and "new" oil and bill Sohio the true amount. Sohio, however, did not wait to get the suppliers' figures of the exact proportion of "new" and "old" oil before passing to its customers the higher price of the "new" oil. Based on production records, known "new" oil supplies, and industry reports, Sohio calculated the probable amount of "new" oil in a purchase, and then estimated the extra costs later to become payable and added those costs to its base price of May 1973. According to the FEA, using estimates violated the regulations. The FEA does not criticize the accuracy of the estimates or the manner of calculation.

On August 3, 1974 the FEA issued to Sohio a Notice of Probable Violation of the regulations. In that notice the FEA ordered Sohio to recompute its increased product costs in a way that excluded the higher prices anticipated from the "new" oil premium and the increase in foreign oil prices. Sohio was also ordered to submit a "plan outlining in detail the method by which Sohio will compensate for the effects of the violations...." * * *

* * *

The question is whether the FEA exceeded its authority in determining that under [the regulation governing the permissible pricing of products by a refiner] a cost is incurred only when known, or whether Sohio is correct in saying that the regulation permits estimating the future costs of present obligations.

* * *

Besides equitable pricing, the [Emergency Petroleum Allocation Act] calls for the "preservation of an economically sound and competitive petroleum industry," "economic efficiency," and "minimization of economic distortion, inflexibility, and unnecessary interference with market mechanisms." The FEA's interpretation of the regulations does not foster economic efficiency or minimize economic distortion. The key to the smooth operation of a free market economy is that buyers and sellers through the forces of demand and supply find the equilibrium price where demand equals supply. At that point the economy operates most efficiently. See Samuelson, Economics 67–68, 630–32 (10th ed. 1976); Dorfman, Prices and Markets 128–36 (1st ed. 1967). It is at this price that resources will best be allocated. As Samuelson states:

> The final competitive equilibrium is an "efficient" one. Because prices equal marginal costs, output is being maximized, inputs are being minimized;.... From so efficient a final point, you can no longer make everyone better off. You can help (A) only by hurting (B).

Under the FEA's interpretation of the regulations, for several months the price charged for some refined products should have been set by assuming that it was refined only from "old" crude oil (which it was not) or that the price of foreign crude oil had not risen (which it had). Thus, the real cost of producing the refined product would be higher than the price the FEA would allow Sohio to charge. The price of the products would be set, not by the free market, but by an insistence that costs be fixed before they be used in establishing a price. Inaccurate economic information would be conveyed; truthful information suppressed. Yet the key to the price system "is its power to elicit and transmit essential economic information and to stimulate appropriate decisions by producers and consumers." Dorfman, *supra,* at 136.

Thus, the FEA's interpretation of its regulations, by causing a deviation from free market price, neither enhances economic efficiency nor minimizes economic distortion. It is also doubtful that preventing

Sohio from recouping its actual expenses helps preserve a sound petroleum industry. Moreover, one can question whether the FEA's position promotes equitable pricing vis-a-vis consumers. Adopting the FEA's interpretation could mean that the prices paid for refined products by Sohio's customers would differ even though the cost to Sohio of making the product was the same. For example, compare the prices paid by two consumers who purchase at different times a refined product made from the same crude oil: One buys after the percentage of "new" oil is known, and the other buys when the proportion is still uncertain. Under the FEA's view, the former consumer pays more, although the cost to Sohio of the product is identical in either case. This can scarcely be considered equitable. That such a result is possible also illustrates the kinds of economic distortions that the FEA's system renders possible. Therefore, after weighing the relevant objectives listed by Congress, this court finds that the FEA's reliance on [its interpretation of the Emergency Petroleum Allocation Act] is misplaced.

* * *

Notes and Questions

1. The Emergency Petroleum Allocation Act discussed in *Standard Oil* recognized the relationship between equilibrium price and output, discussed in the previous section of this chapter, and allocative efficiency, which is a primary focus of law and economics. The economy operates most efficiently where demand equals supply. The court quoted Paul Samuelson, an eminent economist, who described the optimal demand and supply relationship in terms of price and cost. The efficient competitive equilibrium Samuelson described is characterized by prices equal to *marginal cost*.

"Marginal cost" is an economist's way of measuring the value of the additional resources required to produce an additional unit of output. The term "incremental" cost is also used to capture the essence of the idea. When economists discuss marginal cost, they usually assume that some quantity of output, whether of oil, bicycles, or gold, is being produced. The marginal cost is the cost of going from that level of output to the production of one more unit, another barrel, bicycle, or ounce. Marginal cost measures how much is added to total costs if one more unit of output is added to the total quantity of output already produced.

For some products and services, marginal costs are low. Unless a law school is at its maximum capacity, the marginal cost of adding one more law student to its output of law graduates is very low, since no new teachers or staff or courses or buildings or chairs would have to be added to accommodate that additional student. The addition to total cost of increasing the total output of graduates by one is small, because little, if any, additional resources need to be consumed. By contrast, the marginal cost of producing one more concert-quality handmade violin is relatively high. It may be that the workbench and tools of the craftsperson and that person's skills are already in place, but increasing the total output of handmade violins by one violin takes a substantial increment of valuable time and materials.

Questions: If oil is pumped out of an oil field by pumps operating at less than full capacity, would the marginal cost of pumping one more barrel of oil be relatively high or low?

2. *Allocative Efficiency and Marginal Cost:* To appreciate the efficiency implications of charging prices equal to marginal costs, it is helpful to think of balancing costs and benefits. The marginal cost of producing a particular item is a measure of the value of the resources sacrificed to produce it. The price of a particular item is a measure of the value of the resources a buyer must be willing to give up in order to obtain the item. From a societal perspective, it does not make sense to produce an item if it takes more resources to produce than people are willing to give up to buy it. It would be allocatively inefficient to do so because production would sacrifice resources whose value in an alternative use exceeds its value in this use. Thus, price must be at least as high as marginal cost in order to justify production of the good. Moreover, a producer would not be willing to produce an item if the price charged did not cover the additional costs of producing it.

A price in excess of marginal cost may also be allocatively inefficient. The theory of demand described in the previous section states that as price increases, *ceteris paribus,* the quantity of output demanded by buyers declines. At a price greater than marginal cost, some buyers who value the item more than they value the resources going into producing it may not be able to make the purchase. Imagine that the cost of increasing the production of bicycles by one unit is $100. That means that $100 of scarce resources are given up to produce the bike. From a wealth maximizing perspective, society will be better off if an individual who is willing and able to pay $100 for that bicycle is given the opportunity to do so. A price greater than marginal cost, such as a price of $120 for the bicycle, reduces social welfare. Prices in excess of marginal cost result in fewer sales of produced items than would occur if prices equalled marginal cost.

Question: Taking into account all of the additional costs of supplying one additional barrel of oil, how does establishing a price that is equal to the marginal cost of oil production lead to allocative efficiency?

3. The distortions in resource allocation resulting from prices in excess of marginal cost may be better appreciated by looking beyond the price/cost relationship in a single industry. Imagine that the marginal costs of producing oil and kerosene are identical and that, at a price equal to the marginal costs, an individual prefers oil to kerosene. If oil is selling for a price that exceeds marginal cost, the consumer may substitute kerosene for oil. The individual consumer is made worse off and more of the substitute good is produced than would be justified by consumers' preferences. Prices in excess of marginal cost thus distort consumer's purchases in both the oil and kerosene industries and the allocation of resources among competing uses, substituting less valuable for more valuable uses.

Questions: Suppose that a consumer would rather purchase oil at its marginal cost of $1 per gallon than kerosene at 90 cents per gallon but would switch to kerosene if the supplier of oil charged any amount greater than $1.40 per gallon. If the supplier charged $1.50, how is the consumer made worse off by switching to kerosene at 90 cents per gallon? How is social welfare injured by this price in excess of marginal cost?

4. Since marginal cost is the cost of increasing output by one unit, marginal cost and supply are directly related. A marginal cost curve, such as the one pictured in Figure 6–12, indicates the marginal cost (including normal economic profit) for various levels of output. A supply curve indicates the price necessary to induce the producer to expand output. For those prices high enough so that it is worthwhile for the producer to be in business, a competitive firm's supply curve is identical to its marginal cost curve; the price necessary to induce a competitive supplier to expand output by one unit *is* the marginal cost of producing that unit. By adding together the supply curves for individual firms, as discussed in the notes following *Gold Placer Mining,* economists obtain the supply curve for the market as a whole.

Figure 6–12
Marginal Cost Curve

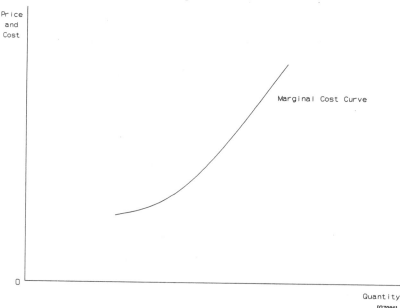

The demand curve may also be interpreted as a "marginal" curve. For an individual, the demand curve indicates the value that person assigns to various quantities of a product. The demand curve is typically downward sloping because individuals assign more value to the initial units of a product obtained than to additional units. Because the demand curve for an individual reveals the value that person assigns to obtaining an additional unit at any given point, the demand curve is sometimes described as a *marginal valuation curve.* The demand curve for the entire market is the sum of all individuals' marginal valuations.

Following these interpretations of the demand and supply curves as marginal valuation and marginal cost curves, it makes sense to increase the output of a product as long as the additional or marginal value obtained by members of society from its production exceed the marginal cost of its production. The point where additions to value no longer exceed additions to cost is the equilibrium price and quantity.

5. Understanding the relationship between marginal cost and allocative efficiency facilitates an appreciation for the goals underlying the Emergency Petroleum Allocation Act and the reasons for the court's opinion in *Standard Oil.*

Questions: How does allowing Standard Oil to estimate actual costs of crude oil and to take these estimates into account in establishing prices further the goals of "economic efficiency" and the "minimization of economic distortion?" How does the ruling further the other goals of "equitable pricing" and "preservation of an economically sound and competitive petroleum industry?"

6. *Average variable, fixed, and total cost:* Marginal costs include only the additional costs of producing one more unit. If the law school is in place or the violin maker has already acquired his tools and workbench, those are not "additional costs" associated with producing one more unit. If you understand which costs are marginal, you might wonder how a supplier can ever make a profit charging a price that only covers his marginal costs. How does the violin craftsman pay for his workbench and tools if he is only charging enough to cover his incremental costs? How does the oil company pay for its drilling and wells and pipelines if the per unit price is only as great as the cost of supplying the last unit? Profitability depends not on covering marginal costs but covering all costs per unit, including those expenses that do not vary when total output is increased.

In economics, *total cost* refers to all of the costs going into the production process. Total cost includes both those costs that vary depending on how much is produced, the *total variable cost* (the total time, wood, and varnish for all the violins the craftsman makes), and the costs that do not vary, the *total fixed cost* (the cost of the craftsman's workbench and tools). Since *average total cost* or cost per unit is calculated by dividing total cost by the number of units of output produced, it is logically the sum of the *average variable cost* plus the *average fixed cost.*

As long as the marginal cost of producing one more unit of output is greater than or equal to average total cost, marginal cost pricing will be profitable because revenue per unit will be at least as great as cost per unit. If marginal cost is less than average total cost, then marginal cost pricing will be unprofitable because the revenue per unit will be less than the cost per unit. Firms must minimize costs to maximize profits. In a competitive market, firms are forced eventually to produce at as low a cost as possible because only by doing so can they keep customers and make a profit.

The *theory of eventually increasing average total cost* states that as the level of output expands, cost per unit (average total cost) declines, but that at some point the level of activity is so busy that one machine cannot keep up with another or workers get in each other's way or coordination of activity becomes difficult. When the level of activity gets beyond its most productive point, the cost per unit starts to increase. A firm subject to competitive pressure and seeking to minimize cost will be best off over time if it ceases expanding its output from a particular productive facility before average total cost starts to rise.

Questions: Would normal economic profit be a fixed or variable cost? Does it vary with the amount of output produced? How does the theory of eventually increasing average total cost apply to the violin craftsman?

7. Figure 6–13 illustrates the relationship between marginal cost and average total cost for a hypothetical producer. The average total cost curve reflects the theory of eventually increasing average total cost. As output expands and the firm becomes more efficient, average cost falls. At some point, labeled the "minimum ATC" point on Figure 6–13, average total cost starts to rise as the level of productive activity gets beyond its most efficient point.

Figure 6–13
Average Total and Marginal Cost Curves

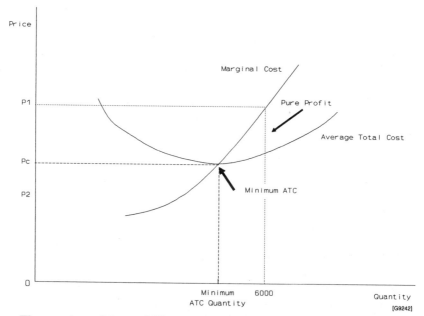

The precise point at which average total cost is at a minimum and then starts to rise is also the point where marginal cost equals average total cost. This is inevitably true whenever the description of the production process in the previous paragraph applies. As long as the cost of producing one more item, the marginal cost, is below the average total cost, producing it will bring the average down; average total cost will be declining. Average total cost rises when the cost of expanding output by one more unit is greater than the average total cost of the previously produced units. As long as a competitive firm has expanded its output to the point where average total cost just begins to rise, marginal cost pricing will ensure a normal economic profit.

At prices greater than the minimum average total cost, the firm can expand output and earn a greater-than-normal profit. P1 on Figure 6–13 is such a price. The marginal cost curve shows that a competitive firm would be willing to supply 6000 units. The pure profit per unit is the difference between the price and the average total cost at that level of output. P2 is lower than the minimum average total cost. At any such price, production will result in a loss rather than a profit.

Questions: If P1 equals $12 and the average total cost of producing 6000 units is $8, what is the total pure profit earned by the firm whose production costs are described in Figure 6–13? How much profit is earned at the price Pc?

NATIONAL ASSOCIATION OF METAL FINISHERS v. ENVIRONMENTAL PROTECTION AGENCY

United States Court of Appeals, Third Circuit, 1983.
719 F.2d 624.

HUNTER, CIRCUIT JUDGE.

Section 307 of the Clean Water Act directs the Administrator of the Environmental Protection Agency ("EPA") to promulgate regulations requiring industrial facilities to pretreat the pollutants that they discharge into public sewage treatment systems. The Administrator has promulgated both general pretreatment regulations and regulations establishing categorical pretreatment standards for existing electroplating sources. The petitioners in these consolidated cases seek review of the Administrator's actions in promulgating certain provisions of those regulations. Under section 509 of the Clean Water Act we have jurisdiction to exercise a limited review of the Administrator's actions. We may overturn those actions only if they are arbitrary, capricious or otherwise contrary to law.   * * *

* * *

NAMF [The National Association of Metal Finishers] contends that the 1979 electroplating standards are not "economically achievable." It points in particular to the Administrator's estimate that approximately 20% of indirectly discharging job shops, employing almost 10,000 workers, may close as a result of the standards. Because the Act requires that pretreatment standards be "economically achievable," NAMF argues, the electroplating standards are thus arbitrary and capricious.

* * *

In *Weyerhaeuser Corp. v. Costle,* the petitioners argued that the Administrator had to make an incremental balancing of costs and benefits in promulgating certain * * * effluent limitations. The court replied:

A requirement that EPA perform the elaborate task of calculating incremental balances would bog the Agency down in burdensome proceedings on a relatively subsidiary task. Hence the Agency need not on its own undertake more than a net cost-benefit balancing to fulfill its obligation under section 304.

> However, when an incremental analysis has been performed by industry and submitted to EPA, it is worthy of scrutiny by the Agency, for it may "avoid the risk of hidden imbalances between cost and benefit."

The *Weyerhaeuser* court examined the marginal analysis submitted by the petitioners and found no hidden imbalances between the marginal costs and benefits.

> [B]oth cost and benefit remain factors that the Administrator must consider and compare. Such comparison is meaningless unless conducted on a marginal basis. Marginal analysis may indeed be an elaborate task, but Congress anticipated that the Administrator would have to engage in "complex balancing." Moreover, while we agree that only marginal analysis will reveal hidden imbalances between cost and benefit, we cannot understand why the Act would require such analysis only on request. We therefore conclude that the Administrator on his own must undertake a sufficient marginal analysis to indicate that the marginal cost is not wholly out of proportion to the marginal effluent reduction benefit.

We note that despite his legal position in this case the Administrator apparently employed marginal cost-benefit analysis in setting the electroplating standards. He stated:

> Although the Clean Water Act does not require consideration of alternative timing, or alternative methods of ensuring compliance, EPA has considered alternative stringency levels, and alternative types of regulations.

The Administrator lifted many requirements from electroplaters with smaller flows, finding that his action would "greatly [reduce] the projected economic impact of the standards while relaxing controls on less than one percent of the flow." He set the required flow rate at 10,000 gallons per day by balancing the marginal economic impact against the effluent reduction benefits. Similarly, the Administrator eliminated the hexavalent chromium limits because it reduced the cost of the electroplating standards without significant environmental effect.

* * *

We are thus left with NAMF's assertion that the net costs of the 1979 electroplating standards are wholly out of proportion to the net effluent reduction benefits. We cannot say that the Administrator was arbitrary and capricious when he determined that the removal of 140 million pounds per year of toxic pollutants was worth $1.34 billion plus $425 million annually, with the loss of 737 firms and 12,584 jobs.

* * *

Notes and Questions

1. In *Metal Finishers,* the court compared two methods of determining the appropriate extent to which producers of electroplated products must reduce their discharge of toxic metals, such as cadmium, lead, cyanide, chromium, copper, nickel, and zinc, into the nation's waterways. The two methods were described by the *Weyerhaeuser* court as the "net cost-benefit" analysis and the "incremental" analysis. The *Metal Finishers* court described the incremental analysis as a *marginal analysis,* a way of ensuring that the marginal cost of pollution control is not wholly out of proportion to the marginal effluent reduction benefit.

The concepts of marginal cost and marginal benefit should be familiar from the notes following *Standard Oil,* even though the application to pollution reduction is somewhat different. Figure 6–14 presents curves that describe the marginal costs and benefits from various amounts of reduction of discharge of toxic metals from no reduction at the far left to 100% reduction at the far right. The *marginal benefit* curve has a meaning similar to that of the marginal valuation or demand curve described in the notes following *Standard Oil.* The marginal benefit curve describes the additional benefit obtained by members of society from each additional increase in the percentage of toxins removed from the discharge from electroplating plants. The marginal benefit curve in Figure 6–14 reveals that greater benefits are obtained from removing the initial toxins than from removing the later toxins. That may be because different organisms have different threshold levels of toxins they can tolerate in the water they consume. Thus, removing even small amounts of toxins generates great benefits to human but further amounts of clean-up generate benefits only to aquatic lives, which society values less highly than human lives.

Figure 6–14
Marginal Benefit and Cost Curves

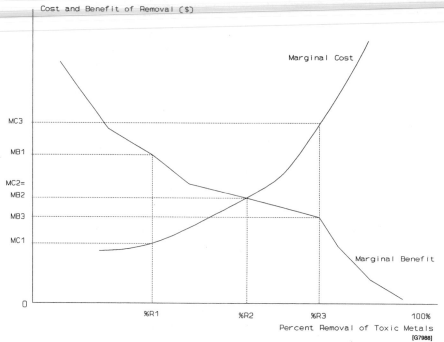

The marginal cost curve reveals the additional cost required to in-crease the percentage of toxins removed from the discharge by 1%. The upward sloping nature of the marginal cost curve indicates that it is less costly to remove the first pounds of toxins from polluted water than to remove a pound of toxins from water that is cleaner. It makes sense that electroplaters would first take steps to remove those toxins that could be removed at lowest cost.

Marginal analysis leads to a level of removal of pollutants that is justified by the incremental costs and benefits of removal. At the lowest removal level pictured on Figure 6–14, %R1, the additional benefits from increasing the percentage of removal, MB1, greatly exceed the additional costs of doing so, MC1. At that point, it is allocatively efficient to increase the severity of the regulation by requiring that electroplaters remove a higher percentage of the toxic metals from their effluent. It is efficient to increase the percentage of removal until the incremental benefits no longer exceed the additional costs of doing so, at the percentage of removal indicated by %R2, where MB2 is equal to MC2. At the highest removal level pictured, %R3, the additional costs of removal far outweigh the additional benefits obtained thereby. It makes sense, from an efficiency perspective, to relax the stringency of the regulations at that point because money is being wasted. As long as the increase in cost from increasing the severity of the regulation (the marginal cost) exceeds the incremental benefits (the marginal benefits), it is efficient to reduce the percentage removal required. From this marginal analysis comes the rule that the optimal or efficient amount of pollution control is where the marginal cost equals the marginal benefit.

2. The discussion of the optimal level of pollution control in Note 1 assumed that the optimal level could be determined by a comparison of the marginal benefits of pollution discharge with the marginal cost of removing pollutants. In fact, there are additional costs to be considered. Downing and Watson, in The Economics of Enforcing Air Pollution Controls, 1 J. Envtl. Econ. & Mgmt. 219 (1974), recommend including not only the costs to the emitting firms but also the costs of enforcing the regulations. The enforcement costs are also likely to increase as the regulations impose higher costs on the polluters, so the marginal cost of enforcement curve is likely to be upward-sloping. The sum of the firms' costs and the governments' costs equals the social cost of increasing pollution reduction through the clean water program.

   Question: Figure 6–15 depicts the marginal cost to the firm, the marginal cost of enforcement, and the marginal social cost of pollution reduction. What is the efficient level of removal of pollutants?

Figure 6–15
Marginal Benefit and Social Cost Curves

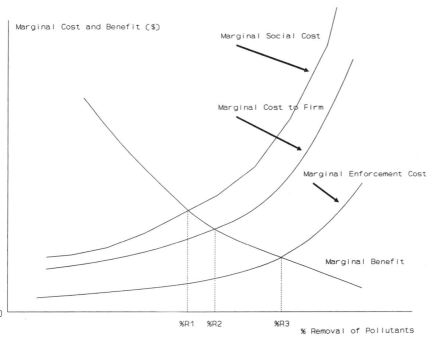

[G7989]

3. The marginal cost-benefit analysis substitutes for what the court described as "net cost-benefit" analysis. The test for increasing the severity of regulations under net cost-benefit analysis is whether total benefits exceed total costs rather than whether marginal benefits exceed marginal costs. The net cost-benefit approach may lead to excessively severe regulations, as the hypothetical data in Table 6–6 reveal:

Table 6–6
Comparison of Net and Marginal Cost–Benefit Analysis
(Figures in Millions of Dollars)

% Remov-al	Total Benefit	Total Cost	Marginal Benefit	Marginal Cost
0	0	0	—	—
1	4.0	1.0	4.0	1.0
2	7.0	2.2	3.0	1.2
3	8.9	4.1	1.9	1.9
4	10.5	6.1	1.6	2.0
5	11.1	8.5	0.6	2.4
6	11.5	11.5	0.4	3.0
7	11.7	15.2	0.2	3.7
8	11.8	19.2	0.1	4.0

Graphing the Total Benefit, Marginal Benefit, and Marginal Cost curves, as in Figure 6–16, allows us to depict the percentage of pollutant removal selected under each approach. Note that the percentage removal selected under the marginal cost-benefit approach is at the maximum difference between total cost and total benefits and maximizes wealth.

Figure 6–16
Net and Marginal Cost-Benefit Analysis

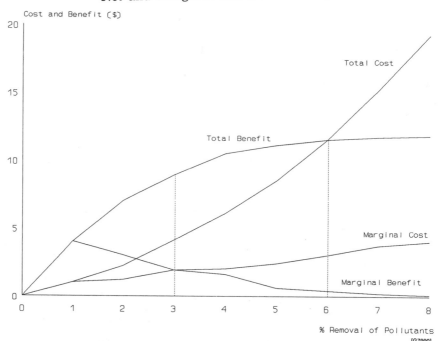

Questions: Referring to Table 6–6 and Figure 6–16, what percentage of removal will result under the net and marginal approaches? Which is the efficient level of removal?

4. The court in *Metal Finishers* found that the Administrator of the EPA had engaged in marginal cost-benefit analysis, relying on the following evidence:

[1] The Administrator lifted many requirements from electroplaters with smaller flows, finding that his action would "greatly [reduce] the projected economic impact of the standards while relaxing controls on less than one percent of the flow." [2] He set the required flow rate at 10,000 gallons per day by balancing the marginal economic impact against the effluent reduction benefits. [3] Similarly, the Administrator eliminated the hexavalent chromium limits because it reduced the cost of the electroplating standards without significant environmental effect.

Question: How is each of these actions consistent with the rule that it is efficient to chose a level of pollution reduction that equates marginal benefits and marginal costs?

UNITED STATES v. ATLANTIC RICHFIELD COMPANY

United States District Court, Eastern District of Pennsylvania, 1977.
429 F.Supp. 830.

BECKER, DISTRICT JUDGE.

These cases raise issues concerning the proper construction and the constitutionality of the "civil penalty" provision of the oil and hazardous substance sections of the Federal Water Pollution Control Act Amendments of 1972 (FWPCA), § 1321(b)(6) of 33 U.S.C. §§ 1251 *et seq.* (Supp.1976). * * *

* * * In each case either Arco or Gulf owned or operated a vessel or facility from which oil was discharged in harmful quantity into the navigable waters of the United States. The discharges were "accidental" or "unintentional," but, perforce, they violated the prohibition on discharge of (b)(3); hence, without more, they subjected the owners (defendants) to liability for the civil penalty under (b)(6). However, the appropriate defendant (or its agent) promptly reported each spill and cleaned it up within the limits of technological feasibility and to the satisfaction of the Coast Guard. Despite defendants' compliance with their reporting and clean up duties, the Coast Guard, following the prescribed administrative procedure, assessed a civil penalty in each case. Upon defendants' refusal to pay, the government sued.

* * *

Most of defendants' statutory argument is designed to convince us that we should construe the phrase "criminal case" in (b)(5) as including the instant (b)(6) actions. * * * [D]efendants claim that, as applied to accidental, reporting, self-cleaners, (b)(6) is really criminal rather than civil because, where defendants are not at fault, the penalty serves none of the ends of civil regulation, but acts only as a punishment. * * *

* * *

The * * * defendants' argument goes as follows: The stipulated facts would not survive a motion to dismiss for failure to state a claim under the common law of negligence; *i.e.,* although the facts reveal "accidental" spills, they do not reveal a basis for inferring that defendants caused the spills through a lack of due care; but "negligence" is the lowest level of "fault" recognized by our law; *i.e.,* non-negligent conduct is reasonable conduct; therefore, if the spills were not negligent, we can infer that there was no reasonable means for defendants to prevent the spills.

We find that defendants' argument makes most sense when translated into simple economic terms. A rational owner of an oil facility, recognizing his potential liabilities for clean ups under § 1321 (and for damages under common law damage remedies which § 1321 leaves untouched), will attempt to minimize the costs of spills. To accomplish this he will calculate the marginal costs of preventing spills and of potential liabilities. He will thereupon engage in prevention to the point where the marginal cost of prevention equals his marginal liability for spills. Because that point defines *reasonable* spill prevention, a reasonable person will spend money for just that much prevention and no more. To spend less would be negligent. To spend more would be wasteful or inefficient.

On this basis we can make some sense of defendants' argument that (b)(6) serves no regulatory purpose when applied to "faultless" spillers. But defendants move from the claim that they were "faultless" to the claim that no regulatory purpose would be served by imposing a(b)(6) penalty, an argument we reject because it proceeds from a faulty premise. While it is true that the stipulated facts about the spills themselves would not be sufficient to support an action in negligence, this is not such an action, but rather an action to enforce a penalty.

The elements of this statutory action are only that defendant violated (b)(3) and that the Coast Guard following the appropriate procedure assessed the (b)(6) penalty. The statute does not make "fault" an element of the cause of action, but rather a factor in the administrative penalty setting procedure. This is proper because there is no principle of law which requires that civil regulability through imposition of penalty be predicated upon a finding of fault. Moreover, a number of factors support civil regulability here in the absence of fault. First, as we explain more fully in our discussion of the Constitutional issues, *infra,* the principal goal of (b)(6) is to *deter* spills. Second, the Congressional purpose here was to impose a standard of conduct higher than that related just to economic efficiency. Additionally, the Congress obviously believed: (a) that no clean up effort could be complete because, after discharge, it is impossible to guarantee against residual harm from quantities of oil too small or too well dispersed to be detectable; and (b) that even the transitory pollution of waters was deleterious to the environment.

* * *

In view of the foregoing analysis we must reject defendant's contention that, as applied to accidental, reporting, self-cleaners, (b)(6) is really criminal rather than civil because, (1) the statutory language is not ambiguous; and (2) even where defendants are not at fault, the penalty does not act only as a punishment but serves the ends of civil regulation.

* * *

The constitutional guarantee of "due process" has been applied by the courts in myriad situations. Defendants argue that the application of the (b)(6) penalty [up to $5000 in this case] to persons who have spilled oil, irrespective of whether the spill was accidental or not, of whether the spiller reported or not, and of whether the spiller cleaned up or not, is unfair and "shocking to the conscience."

The Supreme Court has, of course, held that "conduct that shocks the conscience" can reach the level of a due process violation. However, for forty years that Court has consistently applied only a rationality test to economic regulation of business. * * *

* * *

We believe, however, that there is a rational nexus between the behavior being penalized and the purpose of the revolving fund [supported by the penalties], in part because of the use of the fund to supervise clean up, but mainly because of the magnitude of the Coast Guard's surveillance task, given the length and breadth of our coastline and navigable waterways, and the need for a fund to support that effort. We note too that an accidental, reporting, self-cleaner might not always be so. However, the principal rational basis for (b)(6) as we see it lies not in the creation and use of the fund but in its deterrent purpose and the goal of preventing spills.

Earlier in the opinion we discussed briefly the notion of economic efficiency and its relationship to the legal notions of fault and deterrence. At that point we posited that the defendants' claim that they were faultless meant, in economic terms, that the marginal cost of prevention exceeded the marginal cost of clean up and damages. That posit rested on the "more is better" value concept which is central to classical economics. In that discussion we were trying to explain defendants' contention about fault, though we rejected them as being repugnant to the statutory intent. Now, however, we are not considering rationality as an economic notion but as a requirement of due process. We do not believe that the two are identical; *i.e.*, we believe that Congress has the power to elevate other values over economic efficiency and that it can properly design statutes to promote such values. Moreover, while the test of whether the statute is rationally designed will often take the form of an economic efficiency analysis, that analysis may itself be subordinated to the ultimate non-efficiency goal.

It is widely recognized that the FWPCA policy subordinates economic efficiency to the goals of clean water. The general declaration of "goals and policy" includes the elimination of all polluting discharges by 1985. And § 1321 announces an immediate no discharge policy for oil and hazardous substances. On the level of abstract policy neither section yields to simple claims of economic efficiency or accepts pollution on the ground that its prevention would be unreasonably expensive. Indeed, Dean Wildavsky, *[Economy and Environment/Rationality and Ritual*, 29 Stan.L.Rev. 183, 191 (1976)] has presciently analyzed the clash of values that has led to the frustration which the defendants in our case express:

> The exasperation with which [they] regard the behavior of the environmentalists and their political allies would be justified if everyone agreed the goals could be expressed in terms of economic rationality. Then the means to this end would indeed be perverse—spending much to gain little.... But it is precisely this mode of thinking in terms of opportunity costs to which environmentalists object.

> If purification is what you are after, more is better than less and you would expect to pay more for each increment. Confusion enters because the transactions occur between two worlds, so that homage must still be paid to the old economic costs and benefits while choices are predicated on quite different environmental values.

It is clear that Congress has rejected the economic efficiency or rationality test as the ultimate test of value under the FWPCA. Nonetheless, it has chosen to use economic means—the (b)(6) penalty in order to deter spills. It is only in evaluating whether the economic sanctions are reasonably calculated to deter, hence to achieve the noneconomic values that Congress has selected, that the test of economic rationality is appropriate. It is our judgment that the economic sanction of the (b)(6) penalty *is* reasonably calculated to deter and to achieve those values. Defendants' due process claim must therefore be denied.

* * *

Notes and Questions

1. As the court points out in *Atlantic Richfield,* environmental purists find efficiency analysis abhorrent. By paying attention to the cost of clean-up, efficiency analysis often results in policy prescriptions that stop short of recommending complete removal of pollutants from emissions or effluents. To some extent, the critique is appropriately addressed not to the methodology of equating marginal costs and marginal benefits but rather to the values assigned to the benefits to be achieved. The problem of not assigning enough value to the benefits of clean-up can be rectified simply by reassessing the numbers underlying the marginal benefit curve. From this perspective, environmental purists assign such high value to the benefits that marginal costs are always less than the marginal benefits and efficiency analysis would always recommend 100% removal of pollutants.

A second problem with efficiency analysis is that it is distributionally neutral with respect to who would bear the cost and who would reap the benefits of pollution reduction. The costs are borne by polluters, who profit from polluting the nation's waterways and air, while private individuals (and plants, animals, birds, and fish) are the ones who would benefit from the clean-up. From an efficiency perspective, it makes no difference who bears the costs or reaps the benefits; all are members of society and the net increase or decrease in the wealth of society as a whole is all that is relevant. However, plants, animals, birds, and fish have no opportunity to indicate the value they place on additional pollution reduction and are forced to rely on humans to argue their case for them. From a distributional perspective, it may make perfectly good sense to sacrifice one dollar of the polluter's wealth in order to confer 50 cents of benefit on individuals. Efficiency analysis typically fails to consider the policy significance of a willingness to redistribute wealth from producers to consumers.

2. When it chose to eliminate all polluting discharges by 1985, Congress implicitly decided that it was worthwhile to clean up more than is justified by economic efficiency. In terms of marginal analysis, Congress apparently decided that it was worthwhile to continue to clean up even though the additional costs of doing so exceed the additional benefits.

Questions: Could any rational decisionmaking body actually intend to clean up more than is cost-justified using a marginal analysis? Could Congress have done so?

3. In *Atlantic Richfield,* the court described negligence as failing to take precautions that are cost-justified. Having studied the efficiency implications of equating marginal costs and benefits, one can appreciate this interpretation of fault in those situations where accident avoidance is not an all-or-nothing choice (that is, to avoid or not to avoid) but is an incremental choice (that is, how much to avoid).

The curves in Figure 6–17 reflect two costs associated with accidents in industries producing toxic substances, the cost of avoiding accidents and the cost of having them. In Chapter 3, these are described as *primary accident costs.* As more precautions are taken to avoid accidents, the cost of taking additional precautions increases in Figure 6–17, reflecting increasingly expensive removal of pollutants, either from effluents or accidental spills. The benefit from precautions is reducing the risk of harm. The marginal benefit from precautions declines as the additional precautionary measures produce less incremental reduction in risk.

Figure 6–17
Minimizing Primary Accident Costs

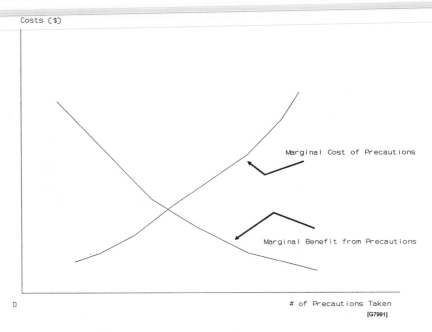

The efficiency rule requiring the equality of marginal benefits and costs mandates taking precautions until the marginal costs exceed the marginal benefits, that is, until the additional burden of taking precautions exceeds the additional accident avoidance benefit.

Questions: At what point on Figure 6.17 are the primary costs of accidents minimized?

C. REGULATION AND CONSUMER WELFARE ECONOMICS

Regulation that increases or decreases prices affects allocative efficiency and consumers. In 1981, President Reagan's Executive Order 12,291 required regulators to describe the potential benefits and costs of major rules and determine the net benefits of such rules. The published notice of the ban of lawn darts by the Consumer Product Safety Commission illustrates the balancing of costs and benefits.

BAN OF LAWN DARTS
Consumer Product Safety Commission.
Rules and Regulations, November 18, 1988.
53 Fed.Reg. 46828.

SUMMARY: Lawn darts are devices with elongated tips that are used in an outdoor game by being thrown upward and striking the ground tip first. In this notice, the Commission bans lawn darts because they present a risk of puncture wounds, including skull punctures.

* * *

An analysis by the Commission's Directorate for Epidemiology indicates that about 670 lawn-dart-related injuries have occurred annually over the last ten years. Economic studies indicate that the average cost of these injuries was about $7,500 per occurrence. The estimated total yearly cost of injuries associated with lawn darts is about $5 million.

The Commission is aware of 3 deaths associated with lawn darts over the period 1970–1987. If it is assumed that other variables, such as exposure and use characteristics, have remained constant and that the Commission is aware of all such deaths, the darts may present a 17 percent risk of one death in a given year. If a statistical valuation of $2 million for loss of life were assigned, lawn darts would have additional expected losses of about $300,000 per year.

Therefore, the estimated total yearly costs of death and injury associated with lawn darts are about $5.4 million. A reduction of these injuries and of the risk of death will make up the benefits accruing from the rule. * * *

* * *

The impact of lost sales of lawn darts will be the loss of net profit associated with production and marketing of these products, less any profit derived from other products marketed in their stead. [Lost revenues were estimated at $2.5 million per year but lost profits were not determined. The Commission noted that lost profits will depend on the ability to use the production machinery to manufacture other products for which there is a demand.]

* * *

Costs borne by consumers will take two forms. Consumers will be unable to purchase a game which has a proven popularity and will be induced to purchase alternate games to fill that demand. There are ready substitutes available, at approximately the same price; however, it is not clear whether these substitutes provide a similar level of utility (enjoyment) as the products they would replace. If consumers are compelled to purchase more costly games in order to receive the same utility as that provided by prohibited lawn darts, the rule may result in increased costs to consumers. Further, there may be a loss in consumer surplus associated with the unavailability of lawn darts if consumers were willing to pay more than they now pay at retail for the game in order to acquire it, thus indicating that they value the product in excess of the retail price. The extent of any lost consumer surplus is unknown, but is expected to be small.

* * *

After considering the costs and benefits of the rule, the Commission concludes that the benefits of the rule will bear a reasonable relationship to its costs.

* * *

Notes and Questions

1. The *consumer surplus* loss associated with a regulation such as that in *Lawn Darts* measures the benefits lost by consumers due to the elimination of a product from the marketplace. Since there are substitutes for lawn darts, people will not be totally without lawn games to play once lawn darts are banned. Nevertheless, those who were willing and able to pay more for lawn darts than for substitute games suffer a loss if they are forced to purchase a less desirable product. Regulatory economics takes this loss into account as a cost of the regulation to be balanced against the benefits.

2. The *market demand curve* for the product reflects the willingness of consumers to buy a particular game. The amount people are willing to spend for a product measures the benefit society derives from that product. To determine whether production of the product is worthwhile from a cost-benefit point of view, one must balance those benefits against the costs of supplying the product. The net benefit is the difference between the maximum people are willing and able to pay and the cost of supplying the product to them.

If the demand curve for lawn darts is downward-sloping, it is likely to be because some consumers are willing to pay more for lawn darts than others. If all consumers pay the same price for the game, some consumers will get more benefit from their purchase than others. A consumer who is willing to pay twelve dollars for a set of lawn darts is four dollars better off if he pays only eight dollars than if he has to pay the full twelve dollars. A second consumer, who is willing to pay up to nine dollars a set, gains one dollar in surplus value if he only has to pay eight dollars. The difference between the maximum each consumer is willing and able to pay for a set and the amount he actually pays is the surplus value for that consumer. For each individual, that net benefit is his *consumer surplus*. For the market as a whole, the consumer surplus is the sum of the individual consumer surpluses for all consumers.

Economists measure consumer surplus in dollars by calculating the difference between the maximum each consumer is willing to pay (as reflected by the demand curve) and the amount each is required to pay (the price each is charged). Graphically, the amount of consumer surplus is represented by the area between the demand curve and a horizontal line indicating the price the consumers pay. On Figure 6–18, that area is the triangle labeled "Consumer Surplus."

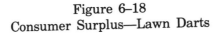

Figure 6–18
Consumer Surplus—Lawn Darts

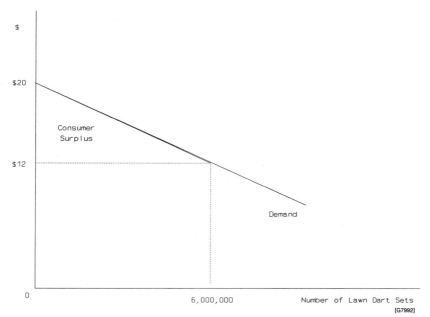

Question: Using the numbers shown on Figure 6–18, what is the consumer surplus loss from banning the sale of lawn darts?

3. In Red Drum Fishery of the Gulf of Mexico, 53 Fed. Reg. 12790, the National Oceanic and Atmospheric Administration (NOAA) of the Department of Commerce announced a proposed rule banning recreational and commercial fishing for red drum in a portion of the Gulf. Evaluating the benefits and costs of the rule, NOAA concluded that "[c]onsumers of red drum are not expected to be significantly impacted by the ban on commercial fishing because red drum appear to have good substitutes, indicating a highly elastic demand curve and, therefore, a small loss in consumer surplus."

Question: Illustrate graphically and explain in words why the presence of substitutes and elasticity of demand for the product influence the amount of the consumer surplus lost by such a ban.

4. If supply changes, *ceteris paribus,* equilibrium price will change and that will affect the amount of consumer surplus. Consider, as an example, a technological innovation that lowers costs of production. A shift in the market supply curve, downwards and to the right, reflects this decrease in cost.

Figure 6–19 describes the increase in supply that results from the savings of $17 per unit in the cost of supplying the good or service at all levels of output. Figure 6–19 shows a new equilibrium quantity of 6000 units sold at the reduced price of $56, an increase from the 4400 units demanded at the higher price of $65.

Figure 6–19
Consumer Surplus Gain from Cost Savings

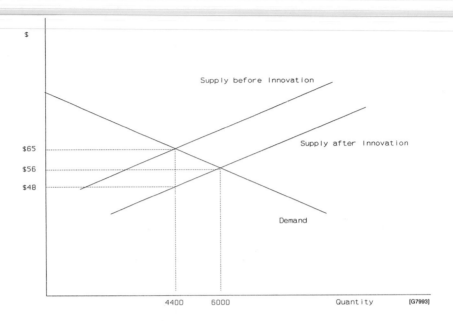

Questions: What consumer surplus increase results from this innovation if the price falls as shown? How much of the increase is due to the change in supply and how much is due to the drop in price? Will the elasticity of supply affect the increase in consumer surplus obtained by any given cost savings?

5. Regulation that increases costs may decrease supply and decrease consumer surplus. As a result of the regulation in *Occupational Noise,* for instance, the increase in the cost per ounce of producing gold was estimated to be 5 cents. (See notes following *Occupational Noise.*) There are three pertinent results from this regulation. The first is that workers in gold mines are exposed to less noise. The second is that this benefit is paid for by gold suppliers who make less profit and gold consumers who pay higher prices. Third, some purchasers of gold are no longer willing and able to buy and some producers are no longer willing and able to produce. They have been forced out of the market by the enhanced price or cost resulting from the regulation. Figure 6–20 illustrates the cost of the regulation, the buyers' burden or share of the cost and the sellers' burden or share of the cost, and the consumer welfare loss as a result of regulation.

Figure 6–20
Consumer Surplus in Regulated Markets

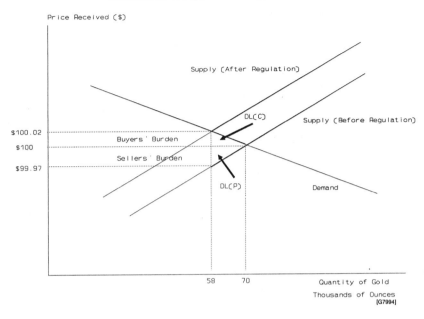

Calculation of the shares of the cost borne by buyers and sellers should be familiar from the materials following *O'Cheskey.* The respective shares are determined by the elasticities of supply and demand. The 5¢ of increased cost is shared by the remaining consumers of gold, who pay 2¢ more than before, and the remaining sellers, who earn 3¢ less per ounce than before. The buyers who continue to buy gold pay their share in higher prices, which represents a reduction in consumer surplus. Because each buyer who remains in the market pays a higher price and her willingness to pay for gold has not changed, each has a lower consumer surplus. It would appear that as long as the health benefits from noise reduction are greater than the burden borne by these remaining buyers and sellers, society is better off as a result of the regulation.

The entire amount of the consumer surplus lost as a result of the regulation, however, is more than simply the rectangle in Figure 6–20 labeled "Buyers' Burden." It also includes the small triangle labeled "DL(C)." Due to the higher price, the quantity of gold demanded declined. The consumer surplus lost as a result does not go towards paying for noise reduction, it just disappears. There is no transfer of this consumer surplus from buyers of gold to those who benefit from noise limitations; the consumer surplus is simply lost to society. This loss is referred to as a *deadweight loss* because it is not transferred to anyone else, as is the benefit from the "Buyers' Burden." Because these excluded buyers are forced to spend their money on resources they value less highly than gold, this is an allocative efficiency loss.

Questions: Given the numbers provided on Figure 6–20, how large is the deadweight loss associated with the loss of consumer surplus?

How large is the wealth transfer from buyers who remain in the market to those who benefit from the noise reduction regulation? How large is the wealth transfer from sellers to those who benefit from the noise reduction regulation?

6. Economists refer to profits earned in excess of normal economic profits as *economic rents* or *producer surplus*. It is apparent from the upward sloping supply curve (before regulation) in Figure 6–20 that some gold would have been supplied at prices below $100 per ounce. If all gold is sold for the same price, however, those who would have been willing to sell for a price below $100 earn a surplus, the producer surplus or economic rent.

Producers suffer losses as a result of the regulation analogous to those consumers suffer. The increased costs reduce profits of those who continue to produce and sell gold (by an estimated three cents per ounce of gold produced) as well as those who cease or reduce their production of gold because of the increased cost. The rectangle labelled "Sellers' Burden" on Figure 6–20 indicates the reduced profits on that gold that is produced after the regulation. These lost profits, along with the buyers' contribution (two cents per ounce) go towards paying for the noise reduction. There is a second geometric area on Figure 6–20, labelled DL(P). That triangle represents the lost profits due to decreased sales of gold. The profits represented by that triangle do not go towards paying for the costs of the regulation. It is the *deadweight loss* associated with the loss of producer surplus, analogous to the deadweight loss associated with the loss of consumer surplus. The allocative efficiency loss associated with the regulation is the total of the deadweight losses associated with both the consumer and producer surplus losses.

Questions: Given the numbers provided on Figure 6–20, how large is the deadweight loss associated with the loss of producer surplus? How large is the total reduction in economic rents as a result of the regulation? How great is the allocative efficiency loss associated with this regulation?

7. Regulation may also raise prices without a readily identifiable corresponding benefit. A Congressionally-mandated study of the effects of federal regulation analyzed the effects of regulation of airlines by the Civil Aeronautic Board and of trucking by the Interstate Commerce Commission. Examination of those regulatory episodes suggested that rates were 20 percent higher than they would have been without regulation. The effects on consumer welfare of those regulations can be examined using the analytical tools developed in the preceding notes.

Consider the regulation of the trucking industry. In 1973, a period of regulated rates for trucking, common carrier truck revenues were $20.7 billion. If these revenues were 20 percent higher than they would have been without regulation, then consumers paid $4.1 billion more for the trucking services they purchased than they would have paid for that service without regulation. The wealth that buyers of trucking services would have retained with the lower price was transferred to sellers as a result of the regulation. The Department of Agriculture studies found evidence that higher prices did not actually result in a transfer of wealth from consumers to producers, since costs of providing trucking services rose as a result of excess capacity, empty backhauls, circuitous routes and other impacts of the regulatory process. If so, then the wealth transfer became increased costs rather than a gain in wealth by the sellers.

Questions: Is $4.1 billion a correct estimate of the consumer surplus lost from regulation? If the $4.1 billion was merely transferred from one segment of society to another, was there any reason to be concerned about the enhanced price?

D. ECONOMICS OF ANTITRUST LAW

The analytical techniques of consumer welfare economics described in the previous section are the fundamental tools for understanding the efficiency justifications for prohibiting certain types of conduct by firms. The Sherman and Clayton Acts, which are the backbone of the antitrust statutes, prohibit activities whose effects include decreasing allocative efficiency. The antitrust cases in this chapter describe two ways in which firms can eliminate the competition that ensures that firms earn no more than a normal economic profit: merging with competitors and conspiring with competitors to fix prices.

1. ACTIVITIES AFFECTING PRICE AND OUTPUT

When numerous firms compete in a market, the ability of each firm to earn more than a normal economic profit is typically quite limited. Unless a firm has loyal customers who will continue to buy its product even when it raises its prices, competition will keep that firm's price down to the level of its competitors. The pressure of competition for customers throughout the market keeps prices down to the point where they just cover costs, including a normal economic profit.

In order to earn more than a normal economic profit, a firm can attempt to eliminate its competitors or attempt to coordinate its pricing policy with its competitors. The first strategy eliminates the pressure to keep prices low. The second allows competitors to raise their prices together. Some of the ways of attempting to eliminate competitors are desirable, such as producing higher quality or more innovative products or producing at lower cost (which allows the firm to charge a lower, but still profitable, price and seduce away all of the other firms' customers). Of the various ways of eliminating competitors that are undesirable, the most obvious is by merging, combining the assets of the competing firms under a single business entity. Section 7 of the Clayton Act prohibits mergers where the effect "may be substantially to lessen competition or to tend to create a monopoly."

If a firm can eliminate all of its competitors by merging with them, then there is no competing producer to whom a customer faced with an increased price can turn. Only a single seller remains, a *monopoly.* The "tend to create a monopoly" language of Section 7 prohibits such mergers. More typically, mergers merely decrease the number of competitors. This situation is dealt with in the "lessen competition" language. In some markets and in some industries, when the number of competitors is sufficiently small, coordination of pricing policy (or "price fixing," as it is called in antitrust law) becomes much easier. This latter situation is the one that arises in Hospital Corporation of America v. FTC. As you read the case, take particular note of the characteristics of the market for hospital services that make coordination of pricing policy easier. The facts of this case appear in the excerpt reproduced above in Section A.I.

HOSPITAL CORPORATION OF AMERICA v. FEDERAL TRADE COMMISSION

United States Court of Appeals, Seventh Circuit, 1986.
807 F.2d 1381.

POSNER, CIRCUIT JUDGE.

[Mergers resulted in Hospital Corporation owning or managing 5 of the 11 hospitals in the Chattanooga, Tennessee area. This reduced the number of firms acting independently from 11 to 7. The issue arising under § 7 of the Clayton Act was whether the acquisitions facilitated cooperation among the defendant and other competitors on reducing or limiting output or increasing prices.]

If all the hospitals brought under common ownership or control by the two challenged acquisitions are treated as a single entity, the acquisitions raised Hospital Corporation's market share in the Chattanooga area from 14 percent to 26 percent. This made it the second largest provider of hospital services in a highly concentrated market where the four largest firms together had a 91 percent market share compared to 79 percent before the acquisitions. * * *

* * *

The reduction in the number of competitors is significant in assessing the competitive vitality of the Chattanooga hospital market. The fewer competitors there are in a market, the easier it is for them to coordinate their pricing without committing detectable violations of section 1 of the Sherman Act, which forbids price fixing. This would not be very important if the four competitors eliminated by the acquisitions in this case had been insignificant, but they were not; they accounted in the aggregate for 12 percent of the sales of the market. As a result of the acquisitions the four largest firms came to control virtually the whole market, and the problem of coordination was therefore reduced to one of coordination among these four.

Moreover, both the ability of the remaining firms to expand their output should the big four reduce their own output in order to raise the market price (and, by expanding, to offset the leading firms' restriction of their own output), and the ability of outsiders to come in and build completely new hospitals, are reduced by Tennessee's certificate-of-need law. Any addition to hospital capacity must be approved by a state agency. The parties disagree over whether this law, as actually enforced, inhibits the expansion of hospital capacity. The law may indeed be laxly enforced. Not only is there little evidence that it has ever prevented a hospital in Chattanooga from making a capacity addition it wanted to make, but empirical studies of certificate of need regulation nationwide have found little effect on hospital expenditures. Yet the Tennessee law might have some effect under the conditions that would obtain if the challenged acquisitions enabled collusive pricing of hospital services. Should the leading hospitals in Chattanooga collude, a natural consequence would be the creation of excess hospital capacity, for the higher prices resulting from collusion would drive some patients to shorten their hospital stays and others to postpone or reject elective surgery. If a noncolluding hospital wanted to expand its capacity so that it could serve patients driven off by the high prices charged by the colluding hospitals, the colluders would have not only a strong incentive to oppose the grant of a certificate of need but also substantial evidence with which to oppose it—the excess capacity (in the market considered as a whole) created by their own collusive efforts. At least the certificate of need law would enable them to delay any competitive sally by a noncolluding competitor. Or so the Commission could conclude * * *. We add that at the very least a certificate of need law forces hospitals to give public notice, well in advance, of any plans to add capacity. The requirement of notice makes it harder for the member of a hospital cartel to "cheat" on the cartel by adding capacity in advance of other members; its attempt to cheat will be known in advance, and countermeasures taken.

All this would be of little moment if, in the event that hospital prices in Chattanooga rose above the competitive level, persons desiring hospital services in Chattanooga would switch to hospitals in other cities, or to nonhospital providers of medical care. But this would mean that the Chattanooga hospital market, which is to say the set of hospital-services providers to which consumers in Chattanooga can feasibly turn, includes hospitals in other cities plus nonhospital providers both in Chattanooga and elsewhere; and we do not understand Hospital Corporation to be challenging the Commission's market definition, which is limited to hospital providers in Chattanooga. Anyway, these competitive alternatives are not important enough to deprive the market shares statistics of competitive significance. Going to another city is out of the question in medical emergencies; and even when an operation or some other hospital service can be deferred, the patient's doctor will not (at least not for reasons of price) send the patient to another city, where the doctor is unlikely to have hospital privileges. Finally, although hospitals increasingly are providing services on an out-patient basis, thus competing with nonhospital providers of the same services (tests, minor surgical procedures, etc.), most hospital services cannot be provided by nonhospital providers; as to these, hospitals have no competition from other providers of medical care.

* * *

Second, there is a tradition, well documented in the Commission's opinion, of cooperation between competing hospitals in Chattanooga. Of course, not all forms of cooperation between competitors are bad. But a market in which competitors are unusually disposed to cooperate is a market prone to collusion. The history of successful cooperation establishes a precondition to effective collusion—mutual trust and forbearance, without which an informal collusive arrangement is unlikely to overcome the temptation to steal a march on a fellow colluder by undercutting him slightly. That temptation is great. A seller who makes a profit of $10 on each sale at the cartel price, and then cuts price by $1 and thereby (let us suppose) doubles his output, will increase his total profits by 180 percent.

The management contracts between Hospital Affiliates (itself an owner as well as manager of hospitals) and two other hospitals in Chattanooga—contracts that when taken over by Hospital Corporation gave it virtual control over the pricing and other decisions of two of its competitors, at least for a time—illustrate the unusual degree of cooperation in this industry; imagine Ford's signing a management contract with General Motors whereby General Motors installed one of its officers (who would remain an officer of GM) as Ford's manager. Hospitals routinely exchange intimate information on prices and costs in connection with making joint applications to insurers for higher reimbursement schedules. Such cooperation may be salutary but it facilitates collusion and therefore entitles the Commission to worry even more about large horizontal acquisitions in this industry than in industries where competitors deal with each other at arm's length.

* * *

All these considerations, taken together, supported—we do not say they compelled—the Commission's conclusion that the challenged acquisitions are likely to foster collusive practices, harmful to consumers, in the Chattanooga hospital market. Section 7 does not require proof that a merger or other acquisition has caused higher prices in the affected market. All that is necessary is that the merger create an appreciable danger of such consequences in the future. A predictive judgment, necessarily probabilistic and judgmental rather than demonstrable, is called for. * * *

* * *

The Commission's order is affirmed and enforced.

Notes and Questions

1. The Federal Trade Commission's primary concern in *Hospital Corp.* was the hospitals' increased ability to agree to reduce output and raise prices above the competitive level. This is also the primary concern of the Antitrust Division of the United States Department of Justice, which has issued guidelines describing the circumstances under which it will challenge mergers. According to the United States Department of Justice Merger Guidelines (1984) § 1, reprinted in 46 Antitrust & Trade Reg. Rep.

(BNA) N. 1169 (Special Supp. June 14, 1984), the reason for this focus is as follows:

> The unifying theme of the Guidelines is that mergers should not be permitted to create or enhance "market power" or to facilitate its exercise. A sole seller (a "monopolist") of a product with no good substitutes can maintain a selling price that is above the level that would prevail if the market were competitive. Where only a few firms account for most of the sales of a product, those firms can in some circumstances either explicitly or implicitly coordinate their actions in order to approximate the performance of a monopolist. This ability of one or more firms profitably to maintain prices above competitive levels for a significant period of time is termed "market power." Sellers with market power also may eliminate rivalry on variables other than price. In either case, the result is a transfer of wealth from buyers to sellers and a misallocation of resources.

In the context of *Hospital Corp.,* the transfer of wealth would have been from buyers of medical services (patients and their insurers) to providers (the hospitals) and the resources misallocated would have been those resources devoted to the provision of hospital services. The tools of consumer welfare economics developed in the previous section can be used to evaluate the extent of the wealth transfer and misallocation that results from artificially enhanced prices.

> *Questions:* Imagine that the hospitals in Chattanooga conspire to raise their semi-private room charges by 10% from $300 to $330 per night and that this reduces the quantity of room nights demanded from 180,000 per year to 178,000. How much of the loss is wealth transferred from patients (and their insurers) to hospitals? How great is the deadweight loss associated with the loss of consumer surplus? What resources are misallocated as a result of this conspiracy? What is the consumer surplus loss associated with this violation of the antitrust laws?

2. Since ability to conspire to raise prices is the key to evaluating the legality of the merger in *Hospital Corp.,* it is important to identify the critical pieces of evidence that led the Federal Trade Commission to conclude that conspiracy would be likely. In *Hospital Corp.,* much of the evidence falls into one of four categories: (1) the market concentration, (2) barriers to entry into the market, (3) the lack of substitutes for the product that is the subject of the conspiracy, and (4) the history of collusion in the industry.

The Department of Justice 1984 Merger Guidelines Section 3.1 describes the significance of market concentration as follows:

> Market concentration is a function of the number of firms in a market and their respective market shares. Other things being equal, concentration affects the likelihood that one firm, or a small group of firms, could successfully exercise market power. The smaller the percentage of total supply that a firm controls, the more severely it must restrict its own output in order to produce a given price increase, and the less likely it is that an output restriction will be profitable. If collective action is necessary, an additional constraint applies. As the

number of firms necessary to control a given percentage of total supply increases, the difficulties and costs of reaching and enforcing consensus with respect to the control of that supply also increase.

Question: What evidence of market concentration was found in *Hospital Corp.?*

3. If existing competitors in a market raise prices and make profits in excess of normal economic profits, other entrepreneurs may be enticed to enter the market. The profitability of collusion depends on the ease with which entry can occur.

Question: What was the evidence in *Hospital Corp.* with respect to ease of entry? Did that evidence suggest that collusion would be profitable or not?

4. The existence of substitutes for the product that is the subject of price fixing limits the ability of colluding suppliers to raise prices without losing many customers. The existence of substitutes for hospital services has both geographic and product dimensions. Geographic substitutability would involve patients seeking hospitals in other geographic areas in response to a price increase in Chattanooga. Product substitutability by consumers involves switching from the purchase of hospital services to the purchase of another product or service in response to a price increase in hospital services.

Questions: What substitutes were available for hospital services in Chattanooga? What evidence in *Hospital Corp.* suggested that there were few *practical* geographic or product substitutes? If the elasticity of demand for hospital service was .2, as hypothesized by Judge Posner in the excerpt from *Hospital Corp.* appearing earlier in this chapter, does that indicate that so many consumers would abandon the hospitals in Chattanooga in response to a price increase that collusion would have been unprofitable?

5. All of these critical pieces of evidence are interrelated and each must be taken in the context of the others. A high degree of concentration, for instance, may not be dispositive of a case if entry into the industry is easy. In United States v. Waste Management, Inc., 743 F.2d 976, 983–84 (2d Cir. 1984), for instance, the merger of two waste disposal companies in Dallas, Texas gave the combined firm, WMI, a 48.8% market share. Despite the high resulting concentration, the Second Circuit concluded that there was no threat to competition:

> Turning to the evidence in this case, we believe that entry into the relevant product and geographic market by new firms or by existing firms [from neighboring cities] is so easy that any anti-competitive impact of the merger before us would be eliminated more quickly by such competition than by litigation. [District Court] Judge Griesa specifically found that individuals operating out of their homes can acquire trucks and some containers and compete successfully "with any other company." * * *

> * * * Ease of entry constrains not only WMI, but every firm in the market. Should WMI attempt to exercise market power by raising prices, none of its smaller competitors would be able to follow the price

increases because of the ease with which new competitors would appear. WMI would then face lower prices charged by all existing competitors as well as entry by new ones, a condition fatal to its economic prospects if not rectified.

Similarly, the difficulty of entry is less significant if the industry is not concentrated or if there are many substitutes for the product in question. The lack of practical substitutes alone is of less significance if there are many competitors. If there are only a few competitors, that fact is less significant if there are many substitutes.

Question: What was the relevance of the history of cooperation between Chattanooga's hospitals in the past to the probability of collusive pricing in the future, given the concentrated market, the difficulty of entry, and the lack of practical substitutes?

6. Some economists question the likelihood that competitors will be able to stick to an agreement to raise prices. Consider the incentives to defect from a cartel and lower prices. If buyers can easily switch from one seller to another in response to a price change, one firm may increase sales tremendously by lowering its price. Similarly, if there are only a few buyers or if each order placed is large relative to a firm's annual sales, there are great incentives to cheat on the agreement because there are tremendous gains to be made each time the firm does so.

Question: Given the incentives to cheat on a cartel agreement, are hospitals likely to adhere to a price fixing agreement?

UNITED STATES v. CONTAINER CORPORATION OF AMERICA

Supreme Court of the United States, 1969.
393 U.S. 333, 89 S.Ct. 510, 21 L.Ed.2d. 526.

Douglas, Justice.

This is a civil antitrust action charging a price-fixing agreement in violation of § 1 of the Sherman Act. * * *

* * *

Here all that was present was a request by each defendant of its competitor for information as to the most recent price charged or quoted, whenever it needed such information and whenever it was not available from another source. Each defendant on receiving that request usually furnished the data with the expectation that it would be furnished reciprocal information when it wanted it. That concerted action is of course sufficient to establish the combination or conspiracy, the initial ingredient of a violation of § 1 of the Sherman Act.

There was of course freedom to withdraw from the agreement. But the fact remains that when a defendant requested and received price information, it was affirming its willingness to furnish such information in return.

There was to be sure an infrequency and irregularity of price exchanges between the defendants; and often the data were available from the records of the defendants or from the customers themselves. Yet the essence of the agreement was to furnish price information whenever requested.

Moreover, although the most recent price charged or quoted was sometimes fragmentary, each defendant had the manuals with which it could compute the price charged by a competitor on a specific order to a specific customer.

Further, the price quoted was the current price which a customer would need to pay in order to obtain products from the defendant furnishing the data.

The defendants account for about 90% of the shipment of corrugated containers from plants in the Southeastern United States. While containers vary as to dimensions, weight, color, and so on, they are substantially identical, no matter who produces them, when made to particular specifications. The prices paid depend on price alternatives. Suppliers when seeking new or additional business or keeping old customers, do not exceed a competitor's price. It is common for purchasers to buy from two or more suppliers concurrently. A defendant supplying a customer with containers would usually quote the same price on additional orders, unless costs had changed. Yet where a competitor was charging a particular price, a defendant would normally quote the same price or even a lower price.

The exchange of price information seemed to have the effect of keeping prices within a fairly narrow ambit. Capacity has exceeded the demand from 1955 to 1963, the period covered by the complaint, and the trend of corrugated container prices has been downward. Yet despite this excess capacity and the downward trend of prices, the industry has expanded in the Southeast from 30 manufacturers with 49 plants to 51 manufacturers with 98 plants. An abundance of raw materials and machinery makes entry into the industry easy with an investment of $50,000 to $75,000.

The result of this reciprocal exchange of prices was to stabilize prices though at a downward level. Knowledge of a competitor's price usually meant matching that price. The continuation of some price competition is not fatal to the Government's case. The limitation or reduction of price competition brings the case within the ban, for as we held in *United States v. Socony–Vacuum Oil Co.*, interference with the setting of price by free market forces is unlawful *per se*. Price information exchanged in some markets may have no effect on a truly competitive price. But the corrugated container industry is dominated by relatively few sellers. The product is fungible and the competition for sales is price. The demand is inelastic, as buyers place orders only for immediate, short-run needs. The exchange of price data tends toward price uniformity. For a lower price does not mean a larger share of the available business but a sharing of the existing business at a lower return. Stabilizing prices as well as raising them is within the ban of § 1 of the Sherman Act. As we said in *United States v. Socony–*

Vacuum Oil Co., "in terms of market operations stabilization is but one form of manipulation." The inferences are irresistible that the exchange of price information has had an anticompetitive effect in the industry, chilling the vigor of price competition. * * *

Price is too critical, too sensitive a control to allow it to be used even in an informal manner to restrain competition.

Reversed.

MARSHALL, JUSTICE, dissenting.

* * *

I do not believe that the agreement in the present case is so devoid of potential benefit or so inherently harmful that we are justified in condemning it without proof that it was entered into for the purpose of restraining price competition or that it actually had that effect. The agreement in this case was to supply, when requested, price data for identified customers. Each defendant supplied the necessary information on the expectation that the favor would be returned. The nature of the exchanged information varied from case to case. In most cases, the price obtained was the price of the last sale to the particular customer; in some cases, the price was a current quotation to the customer. In all cases, the information obtained was sufficient to inform the defendants of the price they would have to beat in order to obtain a particular sale.

Complete market knowledge is certainly not an evil in perfectly competitive markets. This is not, however, such a market, and there is admittedly some danger that price information will be used for anticompetitive purposes, particularly the maintenance of prices at a high level. If the danger that price information will be so used is particularly high in a given situation, then perhaps exchange of information should be condemned.

I do not think the danger is sufficiently high in the present case. Defendants are only 18 of the 51 producers of corrugated containers in the Southeastern United States. Together, they do make up 90% of the market and the six largest defendants do control 60% of the market. But entry is easy; an investment of $50,000 to $75,000 is ordinarily all that is necessary. In fact, the number of sellers has increased from 30 to the present 51 in the eight-year period covered by the complaint. The size of the market has almost doubled because of increased demand for corrugated containers. Nevertheless, some excess capacity is present. The products produced by defendants are undifferentiated. Industry demand is inelastic, so that price changes will not, up to a certain point, affect the total amount purchased. The only effect of price changes will be to reallocate market shares among sellers.

In a competitive situation, each seller will cut his price in order to increase his share of the market, and prices will ultimately stabilize at a competitive level—*i.e.,* price will equal cost, including a reasonable return on capital. Obviously, it would be to a seller's benefit to avoid such price competition and maintain prices at a higher level, with a corresponding increase in profit. In a market with very few sellers, and detailed knowledge of each other's price, such action is possible. However, I do not think it can be concluded that this particular market is sufficiently oligopolistic, especially in light of the ease of entry, to justify the inference that price information will necessarily be used to stabilize prices. Nor do I think that the danger of such a result is sufficiently high to justify imposing a *per se* rule without actual proof.

In this market, we have a few sellers presently controlling a substantial share of the market. We have a large number competing for the remainder of the market, also quite substantial. And total demand is increasing. In such a case, I think it just as logical to assume that the sellers, especially the smaller and newer ones, will desire to capture a larger market share by cutting prices as it is that they will acquiesce in oligopolistic behavior.

* * *

Notes and Questions

1. *Container Corp.* was a Sherman Act § 1 case illustrating a more subtle kind of price fixing than that hypothesized by Judge Posner in *Hospital Corp.*. Rather than explicitly agreeing on a specific high price for its products, the defendants in *Container Corp.* exchanged price information in an apparent attempt to keep prices from falling as quickly as they would otherwise. Notes following the previous case analyze the welfare effects of conspiracies to raise prices.

Question: What are the consumer welfare effects of a practice that slows down the rate of price decline?

2. In contrast to *Hospital Corp.*, where the court assessed the implications of changing the industry structure by merger, the court in *Container Corp.* investigated the implications of the conduct of the firms. As both majority and dissenting opinions reveal, however, the economic implications of conduct may depend on the industry structure.

Several structural characteristics of the cardboard container industry were identified in the majority and dissenting opinions. These structural characteristics can be used to evaluate the likely effect of the defendants' conduct on competition for sales of cardboard in the Southeastern United States. They include the following findings:

a. The defendants accounted for 90% of the shipment of corrugated containers from plants in the Southeastern United States.

b. The containers were substantially identical, no matter who produces them, when made to particular specifications. The product was fungible.

c. Capacity had exceeded demand and demand had been increasing dramatically.

d. In the eight years covered by the complaints, the industry had expanded in the Southeast from 30 manufacturers with 49 plants to 51 manufacturers with 98 plants.

e. An abundance of raw materials and machinery made entry into the industry easy with an investment of $50,000 to $75,000.

f. Demand was inelastic, as buyers placed orders only for immediate, short-run needs.

g. A few sellers controlled a substantial share of the market. A large number of firms competed for the remainder of the market, also quite substantial.

h. The trend of container prices had been downward.

Each piece of evidence tended to prove or disprove the allegation that the exchange of price information either *had affected* the price of cardboard or *was likely to affect* the price of cardboard or to establish a motivation for the defendants to engage in the practice.

Question: What was the relevance of each datum?

3. One of the ironies of this case is that it is generally assumed that for the competitive system to work, each firm must know what others are charging in order to have an incentive to undercut that price and increase its market share. The difficult task faced by the court in information exchange cases is to determine whether the particular facts of the case offer an exception to the general rule.

4. Both opinions concluded that entry was easy because materials and machinery were abundantly available at a low cost. It is tempting to conclude, as Justice Marshall did in the dissent, that if entry is easy, so that any new entrant can produce the type of cardboard desired by any existing buyer of the product at a low cost, then the other evidence should not matter.

Question: Are there costs of entry other than raw materials and machinery that Justice Marshall may have ignored? Is it sufficient to look at the absolute cost of obtaining machinery and materials or must one also look at the cost to the larger firms of obtaining those requirements and the relative costs of production of the existing and entering firms?

2. THE PRODUCTIVE EFFICIENCY TRADEOFF

Merging may give a firm the power to raise prices above the level of marginal costs causing allocative inefficiencies measured by the deadweight loss in wealth. However, merging may permit firms to reduce costs by combining their operations. Economists refer to cost savings as *productive efficiencies*. The social benefit from an increase in productive efficiency is measured by the value of the resources saved by changing production methods, or, in the case of mergers, combining operations. If allocative inefficiency losses might be offset by productive efficiency gains, then policy makers must determine when productive efficiency gains are an appropriate justification for otherwise anticompetitive conduct. State of California v. American Stores Company is one of the cases in which the "productive efficiencies defense" was raised.

STATE OF CALIFORNIA v. AMERICAN
STORES COMPANY

United States District Court, Central District of California, 1988.
697 F.Supp. 1125.

KENYON, DISTRICT JUDGE.

* * *

Plaintiff, State of California, through its Attorney General, John K. Van de Kamp, ("State") brought this action to enjoin the merger of the assets and businesses of Lucky Stores, Inc. ("Lucky") and American Stores Company, Alpha Beta Acquisition Corporation, and their respective subsidiaries ("Alpha Beta").

The parties to this proposed merger are the first and fourth largest supermarket chains in California and two of the ten largest grocery chains in the United States. Both Alpha Beta and Lucky are principally engaged in the retail sale of food and related products for off-premises consumption. In California, Alpha Beta operates "Alpha Beta" and "Skaggs Alpha Beta" retail supermarkets. Lucky operates 340 "Lucky Stores" and "Lucky Food Basket" retail supermarkets. The proposed Lucky/Alpha Beta acquisition follows on the heels of a merger by the second and third largest grocery chains in California, Vons and Safeway.

The State's purpose in seeking the preliminary injunction is "to maintain the status quo for consumers—the existence of at least three competing supermarket chains." The State maintains that the effect of the Lucky/Alpha Beta proposed merger may be substantially to lessen competition in violation of Section 7 of the Clayton Act.

* * *

Case law has established guidelines for determining whether the effect of a proposed merger may be "substantially to lessen competition" in violation of the Clayton Act.

> [A] merger which produces a firm controlling an undue percentage share of the relevant market, and results in a significant increase in the concentration of firms in that market, is so inherently likely to lessen competition substantially that it must be enjoined in the absence of evidence clearly showing that the merger is not likely to have such anticompetitive effects.

The Court further stated that "if concentration is already great, the importance of preventing even slight increases in concentration and so preserving the possibility of eventual deconcentration is correspondingly great." Statistical evidence of market share and concentration resulting from a merger can establish a prima facie case or the presumption that the proposed merger would substantially lessen competition in violation of the Clayton Act. The presumption of a Clayton Act violation based on the post-merger market statistics is not conclusive and can be overcome, but only by a showing that the statistics do not accurately reflect the probable effect of the proposed merger on competition.

Recent cases use a variety of statistical indicators to determine whether a proposed merger can be presumed to substantially lessen competition. Post-merger market share is one indicator. * * *

* * *

The Court finds that the statistical evidence concerning post-merger market shares and concentration, as well as market concentration trends, overwhelmingly creates the presumption that the increased concentration in the relevant markets which would result from the proposed merger between the Lucky and Alpha Beta supermarket chains would substantially lessen competition in those markets, and presents a prima facie violation of Section 7 of the Clayton Act.

* * *

The presumption that a proposed merger violates the Clayton Act if it results in a certain percentage of market share is not irrebuttable. The presumption can be overcome by evidence that the market share statistics give an inaccurate account of the merger's probable effect on competition. * * *

* * *

As the Supreme Court stated in [United States v. Marine Bancorporation Inc.], the burden is on defendants to rebut the presumption of illegality demonstrated by the market share percentage. Defendants have failed to demonstrate evidence of low entry barriers. Although defendants assert that entry into the California market is easy, their lack of evidence to support this contention produces an inference to the contrary. According to defendants, supermarkets in California can be opened rapidly and without obstacles in response to any opportunity to earn a good level of return. Yet, defendants have produced no evidence of such an occurrence. Moreover, defendants' declarations assert that sites for new construction or remodeling are readily available but fail to explain who has taken advantage of this abundance of available space. * * *

The defendants advance the additional argument that the merger can be justified because it allows greater efficiency of operation. John M. Lillie, chairman of the board and chief executive officer of Lucky, declared that the blending of Alpha Beta and Lucky's manufacturing plants, warehouses and transportation system coupled with further efficiencies and synergies will result in approximately $50 million in annual shelf price reductions to California consumers. Edgar H. Grubb, senior vice president and chief financial officer of Lucky, stated that efficiencies resulting from the combination of Lucky and Alpha Beta will generate annual cost savings of at least $78.1 million. The Supreme Court has clearly rejected this efficiency argument in [United States v. Philadelphia National Bank] and the Ninth Circuit reiterated the rejection in [RSR Corp. v. FTC]. In *RSR*, the court stated, "RSR argues that the merger can be justified because it allows greater efficiency of operation. This argument has been rejected repeatedly." Moreover, even assuming these efficiency savings do result, the Court is not convinced that defendants will invariably pass these savings on to consumers. As the State queried, "And, most importantly, is it really true that the new firm can achieve $50 million in savings after servicing the debt they assumed in leverage [sic] this $2.5 billion buy-out?" The State asserts, to the contrary, that prices will rise since there exists a direct correlation between increased concentration and high prices. The Court concludes that defendants have not met their burden of demonstrating that the statistics do not accurately reflect the probable effect of the proposed merger on competition.

* * *

The overwhelming statistical evidence has demonstrated a strong probability that the proposed merger will substantially lessen competition in violation of Section 7 of the Clayton Act. This showing has not been rebutted by clear evidence that the proposed merger will not, in fact, substantially lessen competition. Defendants have failed to demonstrate ease of entry into the retail grocery industry. This Court finds that unless defendants are enjoined, the citizens of California will be substantially and irreparably harmed. While the Court in no way belittles the harm defendants may suffer as a result of this preliminary injunction, the Court concludes that it is substantially less than the harm plaintiff would suffer if the merger is not enjoined.

* * *

WILLIAMSON, ECONOMIES AS AN ANTITRUST DEFENSE REVISITED *
125 U. Pa. L.Rev. 699, 704, 706–08 (1977).

The merger of two firms is commonly viewed from an antitrust standpoint in terms of its anticompetitive effects on price. Sometimes, however, a merger will also result in real increases in efficiency that reduce the average cost of production of the combined entity below that of the two merging firms. The neglect, obfuscation, or even perverse interpretation of such economies was characteristic of antitrust enforcement in the early sixties and beyond. Indications exist, however, that economies are now being valued more positively.

* * *

A net-benefit approach to the economies-defense issue is to be contrasted with common admonitions that "[w]herever non-competitive markets exist, government should operate to lead them to the competitive solution." This latter position appears to be consistent with a literal reading of section 7 of the Clayton Act, which prohibits mergers "where in any line of commerce in any section of the country, the effect of such acquisition . . . may be substantially to lessen competition, or to tend to create a monopoly." To be sure, the need to make hard choices is avoided by literal interpretations of passages of this kind. But ought the conflict between competition and merger economies always be resolved in favor of competition, even if current and prospective competitive effects are slight and the merger would yield substantial cost savings?

* * *

For purposes of developing the tradeoff model, I will assume that the merging firms in question are duopolists of either a local or a national sort, that the product is homogeneous, and the degree of price increase is "margin restricted" by the prospect that geographically remote rivals will ship into the region or that potential entry will be activated locally. The argument may be simplified by assuming further that only competitive returns were being realized before the merger. The effects on resource allocation of a merger that yields both economies and postmerger market power can then be investigated in a partial equilibrium context with the help of Figure 1. The horizontal line labeled AC_1 represents the level of average costs of each duopolist before combination, while AC_2 shows the level of average costs after the merger. The price before the merger is given by P_1 and is equal to AC_1. The price after the merger is given by P_2 and is assumed to exceed P_1; if it were less than P_1, the immediate economic effects of the merger would be strictly positive.

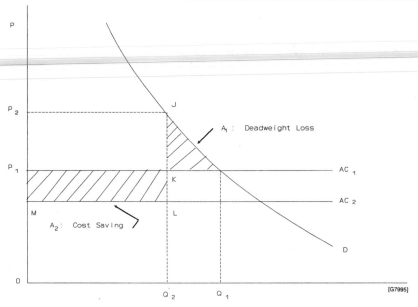

Figure 1

The net welfare effects of the merger are represented by the two shaded areas in the Figure. The area designated A_1 is the familiar deadweight loss that would result if price were increased from P_1 to P_2, assuming that costs remain constant. But because average costs are actually reduced by the merger, the area designated A_2, which represents cost savings, must also be taken into account. Geometrically, the net allocative-efficiency effect of the price increase and cost reduction resulting from the merger (judged in naive terms) is positive if the area represented by A_2 is greater than the area represented by A_1; the effect is negative if A_1 is greater than A_2; and the merger has a neutral effect if A_1 and A_2 are equal.

* * *

UNITED STATES DEPARTMENT OF JUSTICE, MERGER GUIDELINES

(1984)

3.5 Efficiencies

The primary benefit of mergers to the economy is their efficiency-enhancing potential, which can increase the competitiveness of firms and result in lower prices to consumers. Because the antitrust laws, and thus the standards of the Guidelines, are designed to proscribe only mergers that present a significant danger to competition, they do not present an obstacle to most mergers. As a consequence, in the majority of cases, the Guidelines will allow firms to achieve available efficiencies through mergers without interference from the Department.

Some mergers that the Department otherwise might challenge may be reasonably necessary to achieve significant net efficiencies. If the parties to the merger establish by clear and convincing evidence that a merger will achieve such efficiencies, the Department will consider those efficiencies in deciding whether to challenge the merger.

Cognizable efficiencies include, but are not limited to, achieving economies of scale, better integration of production facilities, plant specialization, lower transportation costs, and similar efficiencies relating to specific manufacturing, servicing, or distribution operations of the merging firms. The Department may also consider claimed efficiencies resulting from reductions in general selling, administrative, and overhead expenses, or that otherwise do not relate to specific manufacturing, servicing, or distribution operations of the merging firms although, as a practical matter, these types of efficiencies may be difficult to demonstrate. In addition, the Department will reject claims of efficiencies if equivalent or comparable savings can reasonably be achieved by the parties through other means. The parties must establish a greater level of expected net efficiencies the more significant are the competitive risks identified in Section 3.

Notes and Questions

1. According to the Department of Justice Merger Guidelines, § 3.5, enhanced *productive efficiency* is the primary benefit of mergers. Productive efficiency means providing goods or services at lower cost than could be obtained without the merger. The Guidelines refer to numerous sources of cost saving, including better integration of production facilities, lower transportation costs, and efficiencies relating to specific distribution operations of the kind claimed by the Alpha Beta and Lucky stores. As Judge Kenyon states in *American Stores,* this defense has been rejected repeatedly. In Federal Trade Commission v. Proctor and Gamble, 386 U.S. 568, 580, 87 S.Ct. 1224, 1231, 18 L.Ed.2d 303 (1966), Justice Douglas specifically stated that "[p]ossible economies cannot be used as a defense to illegality. Congress was aware that some mergers which lessen competition may also result in economies but it struck the balance in favor of protecting competition." Nevertheless, according to the Department of Justice's Statement Accompanying Release of Revised Merger Guidelines (1984), reprinted in 46 Antitrust & Trade Reg. Rep. (BNA) No. 1169 at S–13 (Special Supp. June 14, 1984), "[i]n practice, the Department never ignores efficiency claims."

The explanation for this obvious anomaly lies in the historical development of antitrust law and economic theory. In Allocative Efficiency and the Limits of Antitrust, 59 Am.Econ.Rev. 105 (1969), and Economies as an Antitrust Defense Revisited, 125 U.Pa.L.Rev. 699 (1977), Professor Oliver Williamson explored the tradeoff between the deadweight loss and the productive efficiency gains associated with mergers. The timing of the second article coincided with a reformulation of the goals of antitrust law in the academic literature and the Justice Department. During the 1970's and 1980's the antitrust laws were interpreted as designed to promote wealth maximization. In a number of cases, the Supreme Court lent support to this view, without addressing the question of productive efficiencies specifically. This emboldened the President Reagan's Department of Justice, which was sympathetic to the wealth maximization orientation, to incorporate an "efficiencies defense" into its enforcement strategy.

2. Professor Williamson's tradeoff analysis relies on the consumer welfare approach used in the preceding sections of this Chapter. A firm that acquires market power as a result of a merger may increase prices above the level of marginal costs, causing a deadweight loss. However, if that same merger produces a lower-cost way of doing business that cannot be produced in any way that has a less detrimental effect on consumer welfare, the cost savings may outweigh the wealth loss through misallocation.

Imagine that the cost savings that would result from Alpha Beta and Lucky Stores' ability to combine their warehousing facilities amounted to 18¢ per gallon of milk, that, as a result of the lack of competition, the merged stores were able to raise their price of milk from 64¢ per gallon to 92¢, and that, as a result of the price increase, the quantity of milk demanded would fall from 2,000,000 gallons to 1,500,000 gallons per year. Graphing these figures on a chart similar to Professor Williamson's Figure 1, one can determine the magnitude of the deadweight loss and the cost savings. Assume, as Professor Williamson did, that average costs are constant. This means that marginal costs are constant and that there is no producer surplus loss associated with decreasing output.

Question: Would the productive efficiency gain outweigh the deadweight loss?

3. In Question 2, a 28% cost savings outweighed the deadweight loss associated with a decline in quantity demanded of 500,000 gallons. If the quantity demanded drops more dramatically, which it would if demand were more elastic, then the deadweight loss would be greater and the cost savings would be spread over fewer units.

Question: If the quantity of milk demanded fell to 1,000,000 as a result of the increase in price to 92¢, would the 18¢ per unit cost savings outweigh the deadweight loss?

4. As Questions 2 and 3 reveal, the elasticity of demand has a considerable influence on the magnitude of the deadweight loss and the cost savings realized from a merger. Professor Williamson, 125 U.Pa. L.Rev. 699, 709, reported encouraging estimates for how much of a cost savings is needed to offset price increases of various magnitudes. The necessary cost savings depend, as the following table reveals, on the elasticity of demand.

Table 6–7

Elasticity of Demand	Percentage Price Increase		Percentage Cost Decrease Required
Relatively Elastic	3	5	.44
		10	2.00
		20	10.38
	2	5	.27
		10	1.21
		20	5.76

Elasticity of Demand	Percentage Price Increase		Percentage Cost Decrease Required
Unitary	1	5	.13
Elastic		10	.55
		20	2.40
Relatively	.5	5	.06
Inelastic		10	.26
		20	1.10

Questions: Given the relationship between the elasticity of demand and the cost savings necessary to offset the deadweight loss created by the enhanced price, would you expect the Antitrust Division of the Department of Justice to pursue more vigorously mergers in industries producing products for which there are many close substitutes or in industries producing products for which there are few close substitutes? Of what additional relevance is the elasticity of demand to the decision of whether to a merger should be challenged? (See *Hospital Corp.* Question 4 and *Container Corp.* Question 2.)

5. The deadweight loss associated with prices that are greater than marginal cost results from the reduction in quantity demanded. Some of those who would have purchased at a lower price are not willing and able to pay the enhanced price. If a seller could charge a lower price to those whose willingness and ability to pay was low and a higher price to those whose willingness and ability to pay was high, the deadweight loss could be avoided. This pricing strategy is called *price discrimination*. A seller engaged in *perfect price discrimination* charges each buyer the maximum the buyer is willing and able to pay.

Questions: How much of the buyers' consumer surplus is transferred to a seller engaging in perfect price discrimination? What is the deadweight loss resulting from a strategy of perfect price discrimination? Should antitrust law be concerned with perfect price discrimination? What obstacles prevent monopolists from engaging in this strategy?

3. THE EFFICIENCY/EQUITY TRADEOFF

When producers restrict supply in order to extract economic rents, resources are inefficiently misallocated. However, the ability to raise prices above marginal cost raises distributional as well as efficiency concerns.

CROWN ZELLERBACH CORPORATION v. FEDERAL TRADE COMMISSION

United States Court of Appeals, Ninth Circuit, 1961.
296 F.2d 800.

POPE, CIRCUIT JUDGE.

In June 1953, the petitioner Crown Zellerbach Corporation acquired the stock and assets of St. Helens Pulp and Paper Company. On

February 15, 1954, the Federal Trade Commission filed a complaint
against the petitioner charging that such acquisition of St. Helens by
Crown Zellerbach was a violation of § 7 of the Clayton Act in that "the
effect of the aforesaid acquisition by respondent (Crown Zellerbach) of
control of St. Helens may be substantially to lessen competition or to
tend to create a monopoly in the lines of commerce * * *."

* * *

As was noted in United States v. E. I. du Pont de Nemours & Co.,
often the participants in a merger take such action with the best of
motives and with no thought or intention of restraint of trade or
monopoly. The Court there said: "It is not requisite to the proof of a
violation of § 7 to show that restraint or monopoly was intended.' In
the instant case, Crown may have seen in the acquisition of St. Helens
an opportunity to provide itself with a more efficient, more useful set of
production facilities. Thus St. Helens was developing a new bleaching
plant. Acquiring that plant could save Crown from building a similar
plant elsewhere. When a large company increases its size, it has an
opportunity to lower its costs of operation; it may by acquiring plants
near certain markets save transportation costs. As a concern grows it
may accomplish other economies: in purchases, in setting up research
and legal staffs, and in increasing its advertising and promotion bud-
gets. Such growth may well result in enabling it to offer its goods at
lower prices. That might well be a positive benefit to ultimate consumers.

It is plain however from the Act and its legislative history that
concern with such considerations was no part of the Congressional
thought. Congress was not concerned about increased efficiency; it
was concerned about the competitor, the small business man whose
"little, independent units are gobbled up by bigger ones," and about
other competitors whose opportunities to meet the prices of the larger
concern and hence compete with it might be diminished by a merger
which increased the concentration of power in the large organization.
Thus the House Report described as one of the unlawful effects which
the legislation was designed to avoid an "increase in the relative size of
the enterprise making the acquisition to such a point that its advantage
over its competitors threatens to be decisive.   * * *" As stated in the
Senate Report, the purpose of the legislation was "to limit future
increases in the level of economic concentration resulting from corporate mergers and acquisitions."

As the legislation was under consideration by Congress it was duly
appreciated that decentralized and deconcentrated markets are often
uneconomic and provide higher costs and prices. All this it laid aside
in its concern over the "curse of bigness" and the concentration of
power in the nation's markets which Congress thought advantaged the
big man and disadvantaged the little one.

Anyone attempting to formulate the tests to be applied in determining whether a given merger is one whose effect "may be substan-

tially to lessen competition, or to tend to create a monopoly" should begin with a reading of the House and Senate reports that accompanied the bill which brought about the amended section. Thus the House Report contained an extensive discussion of the evils of business concentration. It noted 445 corporations owned 51percent of the country's gross assets. In many great industries three or four firms controlled most of the business. Thus concentration was still increasing, and much of this was through mergers. Small industries, small businesses, were rapidly being wiped out by mergers through which they were being absorbed by big firms. Those in charge of the bill considered that "these mergers are usually the forerunners of collectivism and socialism", and noted the lessons from other countries where opportunity had been vested in the hands of a few: "The result has been that either socialization or a totalitarian form of government has taken over."

The most certain thing about the case before us is that its facts, in a striking manner, disclose exactly the sort of thing which the Congressional Reports said should be prohibited. This sort of merger was precisely the kind which was portrayed as an evil to be avoided. In considering, then, the meaning of those words, phrased with such generality and lack of concrete specification: "may be substantially to lessen competition, or to tend to create a monopoly", we must assume that this strongly stated purpose of the Reports throws much light upon the meaning of the statutory phraseology. It would be strange indeed if it were to be held that the words of the amended section had no impact whatever upon a typical instance of the evils sought to be cured.

* * *

Crown, with its leadership in production and sales of the product-line papers, its great disparity in size as compared with other competitors in the area, and its position as a price leader in the market, was already in a dominant position before the merger. Its acquisition of St. Helens could not help but substantially increase that dominance. It significantly added to its concentration of power.

* * * It is its tendency to concentration of power that condemns this merger.

This alone justified the Commission's finding that the reasonably probable result of the acquisition would be substantially to lessen competition and to tend to create a monopoly.

* * *

STANDARD OIL COMPANY OF NEW JERSEY v. UNITED STATES

United States Supreme Court, 1911.
221 U.S. 1, 31 S.Ct. 502, 55 L.Ed. 619.

WHITE, CHIEF JUSTICE.

* * *

The debates [surrounding the Sherman Antitrust Act] show that doubt as to whether there was a common law of the United States which governed the subject in the absence of legislation was among the influences leading to the passage of the act. They conclusively show, however, that the main cause which led to the legislation was the thought that it was required by the economic condition of the times, that is, the vast accumulation of wealth in the hands of corporations and individuals, the enormous development of corporate organization, the facility for combination which such organizations afforded, the fact that the facility was being used, and that combinations known as trusts were being multiplied, and the wide-spread impression that their power had been and would be exerted to oppress individuals and injure the public generally. * * *

* * *

Without going into detail and but very briefly surveying the whole field, it may be with accuracy said that the dread of enhancement of prices and of other wrongs which it was thought would flow from the undue limitation on competitive conditions caused by contracts or other acts of individuals or corporations, led, as a matter of public policy, to the prohibition or treating as illegal all contracts or acts which were unreasonably restrictive of competitive conditions * * * thus restraining the free flow of commerce and tending to bring about the evils, such as enhancement of prices, which were considered to be against public policy. * * *

HORIZONTAL MERGER GUIDELINES OF
THE NATIONAL ASSOCIATION OF
ATTORNEYS GENERAL

March 10, 1987.

§ 2. Policies Underlying These Guidelines

The federal antitrust law provisions relevant to horizontal mergers, most specifically section 7 and analogous state law provisions, have one primary and several subsidiary purposes. The central purpose of the law is to prevent firms from attaining market or monopoly power, because firms possessing such power can raise prices to consumers above competitive levels, thereby affecting a transfer of wealth from consumers to such firms.

* * *

Other goals of the law were the prevention of excessive levels of industrial concentration because of the political and social effects of concentrated economic power and the fostering of productive efficiency, organizational diversity, technological innovation and the maintenance of opportunities for small and regional businesses to compete.

Goals such as productive efficiency, though subsidiary to the central goal of preventing wealth transfers from consumers to firms possessing market power, are often consistent with this primary purpose. When the productive efficiency of a firm increases (its cost of production is lowered), the firm may pass on some of the savings to consumers in the form of lower prices. However, there is little likelihood that a productively efficient firm with market power would pass along savings to consumers. To the limited extent that Congress was concerned with productive efficiency in enacting these laws, it prescribed the prevention of high levels of market concentration as the means to this end. Furthermore, the Supreme Court has clearly ruled that any conflict between the goal of preventing anticompetitive mergers and that of increasing efficiency must be resolved in favor of the former explicit and predominant concern of the Congress.

The Congress evidenced little or no concern for allocative efficiency when it enacted section 7 and the other antitrust laws. Nevertheless, preserving allocative efficiency is generally considered an additional benefit realized by the prevention of market power, because the misallocative act of restricting output has the concomitant effect of raising prices to consumers. It is counterintuitive, however, to primarily base merger policy on the analysis of these efficiency effects, which are inconsequential in the statutory scheme, and are insignificant in relation to the wealth transfers associated with the exercise of market power.

Notes and Questions

1. *Crown Zellerbach, Standard Oil,* and the excerpt from the Horizontal Merger Guidelines of the National Association of Attorneys General [NAAG] identify a multiplicity of goals underlying the antitrust laws.

Questions: What are the nonefficiency goals of antitrust identified in these excerpts? Which are consistent and which are inconsistent with the wealth maximization goal?

2. An ongoing debate in antitrust law is which of the competing goals should have priority in enforcement. In many respects, the conflict among competing goals reflects the differences between utility maximization and wealth maximization identified in the first chapter of this casebook. Society might, for instance, choose to restrain large firms from realizing economies of scale in order to provide greater competitive opportunities. The existence of the Small Business Administration in the federal government is evidence of the desire to preserve opportunities for individual entrepreneurs. Society might also wish to restrict the size of corporations in order to prevent them from acquiring too much political power. In the legislative history from the debates surrounding the amendments to the Clayton Act after the Second World War, one of the sponsors of the bill, Representative Celler, quoted from a report from the Secretary of War who identified the rise of industrial monopolies and their increasing control of Germany with the rise of Hitler and the initiation of World War II. Many such goals defy economic analysis and the increasing emphasis on economic theory has meant that these concerns are routinely ignored in antitrust enforcement.

3. The National Association of Attorneys General identifies "the central purpose" of the antitrust law as preventing the transfer of wealth from consumers to firms that charge higher than competitive prices. An antitrust enforcer whose first concern was the transfer of wealth might have different enforcement priorities than an enforcer whose main concern was allocative efficiency.

Question: What would be the relevance to each type of enforcer of the elasticity of demand for the product with the artificially enhanced price?

4. *Standard Oil* is typical of those cases identifying the "enhancement of prices" as the primary concern of the antitrust laws. It is unclear, however, whether the concern with enhanced prices is because of a concern with allocative efficiency or with the distribution of wealth. On one hand, there is no evidence that the notion of allocative efficiency was specifically understood by any legislator whose comments were recorded in the relevant legislative history or any judge who recorded a decision in an early antitrust case. On the other hand, there is specific reference to concern for the decline in output that accompanies an enhancement of price, the decline that accounts for the direct "restraint upon the trade in the article" prohibited by § 1 of the Sherman Act. See, for instance, Addyston Pipe and Steel Co. v. United States, 175 U.S. 211, 20 S.Ct. 96, 44 L.Ed. 136 (1899). That decline in output is the source of the deadweight loss.

Question: Are these two goals, minimizing the deadweight loss and minimizing the wealth transfer that results from enhanced prices, incompatible?

5. The opinion in *Crown Zellerbach* makes it seem as if the productive efficiency goal is antithetical to preventing the transfer of wealth from buyers to sellers. If the cost savings are passed on to consumers in the form of lower prices, however, there is no conflict. The conflict only arises when a merger that produces cost savings also produces market power on the part of the productively efficient firm and the cost savings are not passed on. Then the policy maker is confronted with a more complex tradeoff than the balancing between allocative efficiency and productive efficiency discussed in the previous section. A merger may produce cost savings but, if the merger creates market power, enhanced prices will result in both a wealth transfer and a deadweight loss. The equity/efficiency tradeoff takes the distributional effects of the enhanced prices into account.

According to the underlying premises of consumer welfare economics, it does not matter in whose hands the wealth of society rests. As stated by Harberger in his article Three Basic Postulates for Applied Welfare Economics, 9 J. Econ. Lit. 785 (1971):

"[W]hen evaluating the net benefits or costs of a given action (project, program, or policy), the costs and benefits accruing to each member of the relevant group (e.g., a nation) should normally be added without regard to the individual(s) to whom they accrue."

Consumer welfare economics is concerned with deadweight losses but not wealth transfers. The NAAG Horizontal Merger Guidelines explicitly recognize this conflict in goals (see 52 Antitrust and Trade Reg. Rep. (BNA) No. 1306 (Special Supp. Mar. 12, 1987) S–4 notes 14 and 15):

> * * * Allocative efficiency can be achieved in an economy with massive inequalities of income and distribution, e.g., 1% of the population can receive 99% of the economy's wealth and 99% of the population can receive 1%. A massive transfer of wealth from consumers to a monopolist does not of itself decrease allocative efficiency. * * *

In most mergers creating market power, the effect of the wealth transfer from consumers will be many times as great quantitatively as the effect on allocative efficiency (dead-weight loss). It is important to re-emphasize that wealth transfer is irrelevant to the issue of allocative efficiency. The term of art "consumer welfare," often used when discussing the efficiency effects of mergers and restraints of trade, refers to the concept of allocative efficiency. A transfer of wealth from consumers to firms with market power does not diminish "consumer welfare." For the unwary Judge or practitioner stumbling upon this term it is important to understand this fact and to further understand that "consumer welfare," when used in this manner, has nothing to do with the welfare of consumers.

6. Professor Williamson recognized that, if the social significance of the transfer of wealth from consumers to producers can be quantified, economists can systematically evaluate the tradeoff between equity and efficiency. To evaluate this tradeoff systematically, one must decide how much one would be willing to reduce the wealth of society in order to prevent $1 of transferred wealth.

Assume that society would be willing to pay 25¢ to prevent a transfer of $1 from consumers to producers. In terms of the tradeoff, this means that society would be willing to forego 25¢ in cost savings if realizing that savings would result in $1 of monopolistic price increase. With this measure of the social significance of the wealth transfer, one can analyze the desirability of a merger that produces productive efficiencies. The magnitude of the wealth transfer in Professor Williamson's Figure 1 is equal to the area of rectangle P_2JKP_1. That wealth transfer is a loss to society, under the equity approach, while the net wealth gain, under the efficiency approach, is the difference between the area of the deadweight loss triangle, A_1, and the cost savings rectangle, A_2. When comparing the net efficiency gain to the net wealth transfer loss, remember that 25¢ of cost savings offsets $1 of wealth transfer.

Question: Referring to the numerical example in Question 2 following *American Stores,* the excerpt from Williamson, and the Department of Justice Merger Guidelines, does the equity loss outweigh the net efficiency gain? In that example, the cost savings resulting from the merger was 18¢ per gallon of milk while the price rose from 64¢ to 92¢ per gallon and the quantity demanded fell from 2,000,000 gallons to 1,500,000 gallons per year.

E. REGULATION OF NATURAL MONOPOLIES

1. ECONOMIC AND SOCIAL JUSTIFICATIONS FOR REGULATION

Both the law and economic theory recognize that there are some industries in which the competitive model will not achieve either the wealth maximizing or equitable goals described in the preceding sections. In these industries, enforcement of the antitrust laws will be unproductive because there is insufficient demand to support multiple competitors of efficient size. Where demand is insufficient to purchase the output of more than one efficient producer, the market is described as naturally monopolistic. As in other markets where there is only one supplier, policy makers are concerned with enhanced prices that result in allocative inefficiencies and the transfer of wealth from consumers to the monopolistic producer on one hand and with the economies of large scale operations associated with large single firm size on the other. The administrative solution to these problems in natural monopoly markets is regulation rather than antitrust supervision—regulation of entry into the market and of the price charged by the monopolist. Justice Brandeis' dissent in New State Ice v. Liebmann explores the economic and equitable justifications for regulation of natural monopolies. The majority had struck down the Oklahoma statute as an arbitrary and oppressive interference with a useful business.

NEW STATE ICE CO. v. LIEBMANN

United States Supreme Court, 1932.
285 U.S. 262, 52 S.Ct. 371, 76 L.Ed. 747.

BRANDEIS, JUSTICE, dissenting.

Chapter 147 of the Session Laws of Oklahoma 1925, declares that the manufacture of ice for sale and distribution is "a public business"; confers upon the Corporation Commission in respect to it the powers of regulation customarily exercised over public utilities; and provides specifically for securing adequate service. The statute makes it a misdemeanor to engage in the business without a license from the commission * * *.

Under a license, so granted, the New State Ice Company is, and for some years has been, engaged in the manufacture, sale, and distribution of ice at Oklahoma City, and has invested in that business $500,000. While it was so engaged, Liebmann, without having obtained or applied for a license, purchased a parcel of land in that city and commenced the construction thereon of an ice plant for the purpose of entering the business in competition with the plaintiff. To enjoin him from doing so this suit was brought by the ice company. * * *

* * *

* * * Our function is only to determine the reasonableness of the Legislature's belief in the existence of evils and in the effectiveness of

the remedy provided. In performing this function we have no occasion
to consider whether all the statements of fact which may be the basis of
the prevailing belief are well-founded; and we have, of course, no right
to weigh conflicting evidence.

(A) In Oklahoma a regular supply of ice may reasonably be considered a necessary of life, comparable to that of water, gas, and
electricity. The climate, which heightens the need of ice for comfortable and wholesome living, precludes resort to the natural product.
There, as elsewhere, the development of the manufactured ice industry
in recent years has been attended by deep-seated alterations in the
economic structure and by radical changes in habits of popular thought
and living. Ice has come to be regarded as a household necessity,
indispensable to the preservation of food and so to economical household management and the maintenance of health. * * *

* * *

The business of supplying ice is not only a necessity, like that of
supplying food or clothing or shelter, but the Legislature could also
consider that it is one which lends itself peculiarly to monopoly.
Characteristically the business is conducted in local plants with a
market narrowly limited in area, and this for the reason that ice
manufactured at a distance cannot effectively compete with a plant on
the ground. In small towns and rural communities the duplication of
plants, and in larger communities the duplication of delivery service, is
wasteful and ultimately burdensome to consumers. At the same time
the relative ease and cheapness with which an ice plant may be
constructed exposes the industry to destructive and frequently ruinous
competition. Competition in the industry tends to be destructive because ice plants have a determinate capacity, and inflexible fixed
charges and operating costs, and because in a market of limited area
the volume of sales is not readily expanded. Thus, the erection of a
new plant in a locality already adequately served often causes manag-
ers to go to extremes in cutting prices in order to secure business.
Trade journals and reports of association meetings of ice manufacturers
bear ample witness to the hostility of the industry to such competition,
and to its unremitting efforts, through trade associations, informal
agreements, combination of delivery systems,and in particular through
the consolidation of plants, to protect markets and prices against
competition of any character.

That these forces were operative in Oklahoma prior to the passage
of the act under review is apparent from the record. Thus, it was
testified that in only six or seven localities in the state containing, in
the aggregate, not more than 235,000 of a total population of approximately 2,000,000, was there "a semblance of competition"; and that
even in those localities the prices of ice were ordinarily uniform. The
balance of the population was, and still is, served by companies enjoying complete monopoly. * * *

(B) The statute under review rests, not only upon the facts just detailed, but upon a long period of experience in more limited regulation dating back to the first year of Oklahoma's statehood. For 17 years prior to the passage of the act of 1925, the Corporation Commission under section 13 of the Act of June 10, 1908, had exercised jurisdiction over the rates, practices, and service of ice plants, its action in each case, however, being predicated upon a finding that the company complained of enjoyed a "virtual monopoly" of the ice business in the community which it served. The jurisdiction thus exercised was upheld by the Supreme Court of the state in *Oklahoma Light & Power Co. v. Corporation Commission.* The court said, "The manufacture, sale and distribution of ice in many respects closely resembles the sale and distribution of gas as fuel, or electric current, and in many communities the same company that manufactures, sells, and distributes electric current is the only concern that manufactures, sells and distributes ice, and by reason of the nature and extent of the ice business it is impracticable in that community to interest any other concern in such business. In this situation, the distributor of such a necessity as ice should not be permitted by reason of the impracticability of any one else engaging in the same business to charge unreasonable prices, and if such an abuse is persisted in the regulatory power of the state should be invoked to protect the public."

* * *

In 1916, the commission urged, in its report to the Governor, that all public utilities under its jurisdiction be required to secure from the commission "what is known as a 'certificate of public convenience and necessity' before the duplication of facilities."

"This would prevent ruinous competition resulting in the driving out of business of small though competent public service utilities by more powerful corporations, and often consequent demoralization of service, or the requiring of the public to patronize two utilities in a community where one would be adequate."

Up to that time a certificate of public convenience and necessity to engage in the business had been applied only to cotton gins. In 1917 a certificate from the commission was declared prerequisite to the construction of new telephone or telegraph lines. In 1923 it was required for the operation of motor carriers. In 1925, the year in which the Ice Act was passed, the requirement was extended also to power, heat, light, gas, electric, or water companies proposing to do business in any locality already possessing one such utility.

* * *

* * * There must be power in the States and the Nation to remold, through experimentation, our economic practices and institutions to meet changing social and economic needs. I cannot believe that the framers of the Fourteenth Amendment, or the States which ratified it, intended to deprive us of the power to correct the evils of technological unemployment and excess productive capacity which have attended progress in the useful arts.

* * *

Notes and Questions

1. In *New State Ice*, there were a variety of rationales for permitting a single, regulated firm to monopolize the ice business in a particular locality. They included:

    a. Ice was a necessary of life.

    b. The business lent itself peculiarly to monopoly because the market was limited in area and competition from a distance was infeasible.

    c. Entry into the industry was easy but duplication of plants and duplication of delivery was wasteful.

    d. Entry into the industry was easy but duplication was ultimately burdensome to consumers.

    e. Competition in the industry tended to be destructive, with managers going to [unprofitable] extremes in price cutting in order to secure business.

    f. Ice suppliers actually were monopolists in many areas and the impracticability of competition allowed them to charge unreasonable prices unless regulated.

These rationales illustrate four of the general justifications for regulating an industry: (1) equitable notions of the kinds of products that should be subject to regulation, (2) recognition of the productive efficiencies achieved by large scale operation, (3) concern for the inappropriate transfer of wealth from buyers to sellers, and (4) consideration of whether the competitive process will result in competitive prices.

Question: Which of the preceding six rationales fit into which of the general justifications?

2. In a competitive market, the ability of consumers to find alternative sources of supply keeps prices close to costs. Whether there will be numerous alternative sources of supply in a particular geographic area depends on how great demand is in the area and how many firms are needed to meet that demand. The ability of one firm to satisfy a given amount of demand depends on the technology of producing and delivering the product in question. As discussed in the materials following *Standard Oil*, a firm's average total cost of producing a product declines over some ranges of output as more units of the good are produced. At some point, identified as the minimum average total cost point, average total costs start to rise as the level of productive activity gets beyond its most efficient point. See Figure 6–13. If the demand for the product in the relevant geographic area is small enough relative to the level of output at which the firm's average total costs are minimized, one firm may be able efficiently to supply the entire demand.

Imagine what will happen if an existing firm in a naturally monopolistic market is able efficiently to meet the demand for ice and another firm enters that market, using the same technology to produce ice. The entering firm must charge a price lower than the existing firm in order to win customers. A particularly aggressive entrant might even offer a price that was below its costs, hoping to drive the existing firm out of business, and then raise price to a monopoly level and recover its losses. If entry into the market is easy, however, only the willingness of the winning firm to suffer losses will discourage potential competitors from trying the same tactic. This explains Justice Brandeis' willingness to allow regulation that "would prevent ruinous competition resulting in the driving out of business of small though competent public service utilities by more powerful corporations." The result of such competition would be the substitution of one monopoly for another, hardly an improvement from the consumers' perspective.

An entering firm may not have to charge prices below its costs in order to win customers away from the existing monopolist. It may charge a price greater than its average cost of production but lower than the monopoly price. The monopolist is likely to respond to this threat by lowering its prices.

> *Question:* Can an entrant profitably charge a lower price than an existing firm is able profitably to charge if both are using the same technology?

3. It is possible for two firms to share a naturally monopolistic market. They would, however, have to agree not to compete to avoid the "ruinous competition" described in the previous paragraph and such an agreement would violate the antitrust laws.

> *Question:* Imagine that two firms, each of which could efficiently supply the entire demand for ice, agree instead to divide the market in half. If average costs are declining throughout the entire range of demand in the relevant geographic area, would the costs of producing ice in this market be higher or lower than if there were a monopolist? How great are the incentives for the two firms to cheat on their agreement?

4. Consider the characteristics of ice manufacturing and ice delivery that make those two activities naturally monopolistic.

> *Questions:* Does the natural monopoly justification for regulation also apply to power, heat, light, gas, electric and water companies? Telephone and telegraph companies? The operation of trucks as motor carriers?

OMEGA SATELLITE PRODUCTS COMPANY
v. CITY OF INDIANAPOLIS

United States Court of Appeals, Seventh Circuit, 1982.
694 F.2d 119.

POSNER, CIRCUIT JUDGE.

This is an appeal from the denial of a preliminary injunction in a suit under the First Amendment and the Sherman Act to prevent the City of Indianapolis * * * from enforcing the provisions of its cable television ordinance that relate to the award of cable television franchises. [The ordinance denied plaintiff, Omega Satellite Products Company, the right to run a satellite television cable through the public ways of the City in competition with the cable company to which an exclusive franchise had been awarded.]

* * *

The cost of the cable grid appears to be the biggest cost of a cable television system and to be largely invariant to the number of subscribers the system has. We said earlier that once the grid is in place—once every major street has a cable running above or below it that can be hooked up to the individual residences along the street—the cost of adding another subscriber probably is small. If so, the average cost of cable television would be minimized by having a single company in any given geographical area; for if there is more than one company and therefore more than one grid, the cost of each grid will be spread over a smaller number of subscribers, and the average cost per subscriber, and hence price, will be higher.

If the foregoing accurately describes conditions in Indianapolis— again a question on which the record of the preliminary injunction proceeding is sketchy at best—it describes what economists call a "natural monopoly," wherein the benefits, and indeed the very possibility, of competition are limited. You can start with a competitive free-for-all—different cable television systems frantically building out their grids and signing up subscribers in an effort to bring down their average costs faster than their rivals—but eventually there will be only a single company, because until a company serves the whole market it will have an incentive to keep expanding in order to lower its average costs. In the interim there may be wasteful duplication of facilities. This duplication may lead not only to higher prices to cable television subscribers, at least in the short run, but also to higher costs to other users of the public ways, who must compete with the cable television companies for access to them. An alternative procedure is to pick the most efficient competitor at the outset, give him a monopoly, and extract from him in exchange a commitment to provide reasonable service at reasonable rates. In essence Omega's antitrust allegations accuse the City of Indianapolis of having taken this alternative route to the monopoly that may be the inevitable destination to which all routes converge.

Although there is language in some Supreme Court opinions to the effect that the only thing to consider in deciding whether a practice violates the Sherman Act is the effect on competition, it is unlikely that the Court meant to overturn the established proposition that the antitrust laws do not require the impossible—a competitive market under conditions of natural monopoly. If a market has room for only one firm, it would be an effort worthy of King Canute to keep two firms in it. True, a cartel among the competing firms in such a market would be illegal per se, even if the alternative was the destruction, through unbridled competition, of all but one. But that is because the cartel, by holding a price umbrella over the least efficient firms, would retard the evolution of the market toward its optimal state, which would be to have only one firm.

It is also true that the antitrust laws protect competition not only in, but for, the market—that is, competition to be the firm to enjoy a natural monopoly, and by a modest extension competition to replace the existing natural monopolist. If the most efficient method of determining which firm should have the natural monopoly is a competitive process that will inevitably destroy the other firms, the antitrust laws presumably would forbid interference with that process. If, therefore, Omega were challenging an agreement between Indianapolis Cablevision and American Cablevision not to invade each other's territories, or to cooperate in repelling an invasion of either territory by a third party such as Omega, the antitrust laws would condemn the agreement as an artificial interference with a natural, if in a sense destructive, competitive process. * * *

But that is not Omega's complaint. It is rather that officials of the City of Indianapolis—the representatives of the consumers of cable television—have granted the existing franchisees de facto exclusive franchises. * * * There is no precedent for condemning an exclusive franchise in these circumstances, at least out of hand, and it would be perilous to assume that this or any other court will soon create one. But that is not to say that Omega will not prevail on its Sherman Act count at trial. It may be able to prove that the City officials were not acting in the consumer interest, that cable television in Indianapolis is not a natural monopoly, that exclusive franchising is a needlessly restrictive way of dealing with natural monopoly, or other propositions that separately or together might establish a violation of the Sherman Act under the Rule of Reason. All we hold is that on this record Omega has not established a sufficient probability of prevailing to persuade us that it is entitled to a preliminary injunction on the basis of its Sherman Act claim.

* * *

Affirmed.

Notes and Questions

1. In *Omega Satellite Products,* Judge Posner took an explicitly economic approach to the relationship between regulation and antitrust. In a natural monopoly market, the optimal state is to have only one firm. Either competition will eliminate all competitors except the most efficient firm or the City will "pick the most efficient competitor at the outset, give him a monopoly, and extract from him in exchange a commitment to provide reasonable service at reasonable rates." Figure 6–21 illustrates the relationship between market demand and average costs in a naturally monopolistic market.

> *Questions:* Why does the declining average total cost curve mean that competition in a natural monopoly market will ultimately lead to the survival of only one firm? What costs are imposed on society by using antitrust remedies to keep the market competitive?

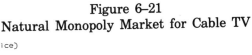

Figure 6–21
Natural Monopoly Market for Cable TV

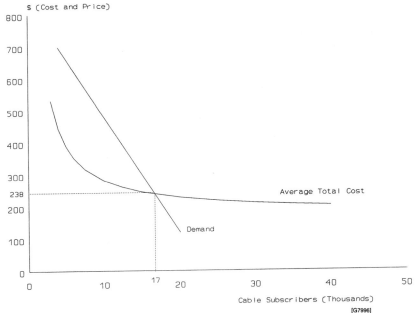

   2.   The market illustrated in Figure 6–21 is a hypothetical small town with a willingness to pay for cable television indicated by the demand curve. Maintaining a cable grid capable of servicing the town costs about $1,020,000 a year, including debt to pay off the costs of engineering and constructing the system. In addition, it costs $50,000 per year to operate the system and $175 to maintain and service the connection of each home to the cable.

   Questions: If a single cable company were to supply the market, what is the lowest price it could profitably charge to cable subscribers? If there were two identical cable companies in the market, each with a 50% market share and each capable of servicing the entire town, would the lowest price each could profitably charge be greater or less than that charged by the monopolist?

   3.   From a consumer welfare perspective, society is concerned not only with the price charged to subscribers but also with the efficiency characteristics of the market. Compare the quantity demanded and the productive efficiency characteristics of two alternative structures of the industry described in Figure 6–21. The first alternative is a duopoly in which two firms share the market (50% each) earning only a normal economic profit. The second alternative is a monopolist, earning a normal economic profit.

   Question: Would quantity demanded be greater or smaller in the duopoly or monopoly structure? Would productive efficiency be better served by having one firm or two in a naturally monopolistic market?

   4.   The problem in Note 2 described a variety of costs associated with providing cable services. The debt, for instance, covers the cost of mapping

and designing the system and the engineering as well as the construction of the cable grid. In addition, there are the costs of operating the system and the costs of maintaining the service to individual homes.

> *Questions:* Which of these costs are variable and which are fixed? If price is set equal to marginal cost, what would be the annual price for cable service?

2. REGULATION OF PRICES

To allocate resources to their most valuable uses, prices should be equal to marginal costs. In a competitive industry, firms will compete to offer the lowest price by searching for the lowest cost way to produce and deliver their products. When producing at the minimum point of its average total cost curve and selling at a price that just covers cost, including normal economic profit, a competitive firm is charging a price that is equal to the marginal cost of producing its last unit of output. See the discussion following Standard Oil Company of Ohio v. Federal Energy Administration, above.

In a natural monopoly industry, there is no competitive pressure to keep costs down or to price at a level that returns only a normal economic profit. Government regulation of natural monopolies often involves control over the price charged by the monopolist. In *Greeting Cards*, which follows, the court considered a plan for pricing postal services, a monopoly on the national level. The particular problem was determining the appropriate prices for different classes of mail when the costs of delivering them were difficult to apportion among classes. The method evaluated by the court is a common regulatory variation on marginal cost pricing that has significant allocative efficiency characteristics.

NATIONAL ASSOCIATION OF GREETING CARD PUBLISHERS v. UNITED STATES POSTAL SERVICE
(Part I)

United States Court of Appeals, District of Columbia Circuit, 1979.
607 F.2d 392.

Leventhal, Circuit Judge.

In this case the court again has occasion to consider the response of the United States Postal Service ("USPS" or "Postal Service") to the "special, and quite demanding, ratemaking requirements" of the Postal Reorganization Act of 1970 and to this court's views concerning those requirements.

This case arises from the fourth general ratemaking proceeding under the Act. Our principal focus here, as in our cases reviewing earlier ratemaking proceedings, is on the methods by which the Postal Service, in setting the rates for the various classes of mail, allocates its costs among those classes.   * * *

* * *

In its first two rate proceedings under the Act, the Commission adopted a two-step approach to the allocation of the costs of operation of the Postal Service among the classes of mail. The Commission first "attributed" to the various mail classes and postal services only those costs demonstrably caused by providing the particular service, thereby establishing a rate floor for each class and service. The key to determining causation was a strict requirement of a showing of cost variability—that a particular cost varied with a change in volume of the service provided. * * *

* * *

As to "marginal cost pricing," traditional economic theory, if we may sketch our general understanding, holds that in a system of "pure" or "perfect" competition the most efficient allocation of resources occurs when the price of a good or service equals its marginal cost—the cost to the economy of producing one additional unit. The marginal cost concept includes variable costs but not historic fixed costs ("sunk" costs), though it does include the cost of capital if capital investment is required to increase capacity for additional production. Traditional economic theory concludes that a price set at marginal cost achieves the optimum equalization of the current cost to society of employing scarce resources and the value to consumers of using those resources. In a system of perfect competition, an individual producer will employ his productive capacity to the degree that he can recover his variable costs, thereby minimizing average cost and maximizing attainable profit at the market price.

* * *

The transfer of marginal cost pricing theory to regulated monopolies presents obvious difficulties, including the inapplicability of the basic free-market assumptions. However, it is appropriate to note that in the view of some economists, economic efficiency is similarly enhanced when the prices charged by regulated utilities are set at the long run marginal costs of the enterprise, including not only the variable cost of producing an additional unit with existing capacity, but the costs of adding additional capacity to meet increases in volume. Traditional ratemaking principles require, however, that total revenues generated by the regulated utility cover the historic costs of the enterprise, including a return on useful investment, as well as current operating and future capacity costs. In return for the guarantee of such a return the utility forgoes opportunities to charge the "market prices" that might be exacted from consumers. There is not a free market but a market under the constraint of what is, in effect, a long-range regulatory bargain. There is no certainty that the total revenues guaranteed by the regulatory understanding will equal the revenues that would be generated by pricing at marginal cost—which is prospective in nature even though long run marginal cost embraces capital additions. (Of course the risk implicit in that lack of certainty is taken into account by the regulator in determining permissible rate of return.)

* * *

Notes and Questions

1. In *Greeting Card* (Part I), Judge Leventhal introduced a temporal element into the discussion of marginal costs:

> The marginal cost concept includes variable costs but not historic fixed costs ("sunk costs"), though it does include the cost of capital if capital investment is required to increase capacity for additional production.

The discussion following *Standard Oil,* above, described marginal cost as including those incremental costs necessary to expand output by one unit. Marginal costs did not include the violin maker's workbench or tools nor the wells and pipelines of the oil company. Judge Leventhal, however, took a longer run perspective. At some point, the craftsman's workshop is going to become so crowded that no amount of additional variable costs will produce another violin; the workshop must be expanded. At that point the marginal cost increases drastically. As long as an electricity-generating plant designed to produce a maximum of 2000 megawatts is operating at less than full capacity, 1900 megawatts, for instance, the additional cost of producing one more watt is only the cost of additional fuel needed to generate that additional watt. The marginal cost of producing the additional watt at less than full capacity is relatively low compared to the situation where the plant is already operating at full capacity. If the plant is operating at full capacity, generating 2000 megawatts, then in order to produce one more watt a new plant must be built. In the full capacity case, the marginal cost of producing an additional unit of output would be relatively high and include "the capital investment" required to build a new plant.

Economists describe the situation where demand is not so great that new plants have to be built as the *short run.* It is not unreasonable to expect, however, that as demand changes, over the *long run,* productive capacity will change. Old plants may be abandoned; new plants may be built. The concept of *long run marginal cost* takes the cost of changing capacity into account.

Always omitted from the two concepts of marginal cost in the regulatory context are those fixed costs for which unalterable commitments have been made, such as paying off the debt on plants that have already been constructed. Judge Leventhal referred to those as *historic fixed costs* or *sunk costs.* Since those costs have already been incurred, the decisionmaker, whether business manager or regulator, cannot decide whether to incur them or not; they do not vary depending on output decisions.

The difference between short run and long run marginal costs becomes significant in the regulatory context whenever it can reasonably be anticipated that the entrepreneur, in this case the Postal Service, is going to be required to make additions to capacity. These costs must be covered in order for the enterprise to cover its total cost and for the price of additional mail services to reflect the cost to society of providing it. It was, therefore, appropriate for Judge Leventhal to focus on long run marginal costs. In setting rates for postal services, regulators necessarily had to consider covering the costs of increases in capacity.

Question: Which of the costs incurred by the Postal Service in delivering special delivery mail were likely to be historic fixed costs, short run marginal costs, and long run marginal costs?

2. In a competitive market, firms expand output to the point where marginal cost is equal to minimum average total cost, allowing the firm to earn a normal economic profit. (See the notes following *Standard Oil.*) The transfer of marginal cost pricing theory to regulated monopolies like the Postal Service presents difficulties because the level of output produced by the regulated firm may not be great enough that the point of minimum average total costs has been reached. In that case, even long run marginal cost will be less than average total cost and the regulated firm will be unable to earn a normal economic profit at a price equal to marginal cost.

When the marginal cost is less than the average total cost, total revenues earned by a price equal to marginal cost will fall short of being profitable by the amount of average fixed cost, which is the only cost not not included among the marginal costs of increasing output. As Judge Leventhal describes it, "[t]raditional ratemaking principles require * * * that total revenues generated by the regulated utility cover the historic costs of the enterprise, including a return on useful investment, as well as current operating and future capacity costs." Unless something is done to the pricing scheme to adjust for the shortfall, no firm will want to produce in a regulated industry where the price is fixed and equal even to long run marginal costs.

Reconsider the effect of marginal cost pricing in *Omega Satellite Products.* The cost of adding an additional subscriber to the system, $175, is the marginal cost. Because average costs include both that cost and the fixed costs of debt and operation, average total costs exceed marginal costs. Setting a price equal to marginal cost would not provide sufficient revenue to cover average total costs, and the regulated cable monopolist would be unable to earn a profit. Figure 6–22 illustrates that as the number of subscribers increases, marginal cost approaches but never quite equals average total cost. At no point on the marginal cost curve is there a profitable price.

Figure 6–22
Pricing in a Regulated Industry

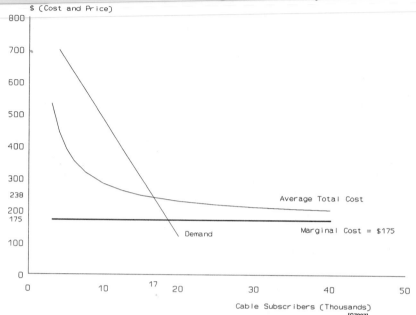

Cable Subscribers (Thousands)
[G7997]

NATIONAL ASSOCIATION OF GREETING CARD PUBLISHERS v. UNITED STATES POSTAL SERVICE (Part II)

United States Court of Appeals, District of Columbia Circuit, 1979.
607 F.2d 392.

LEVENTHAL, CIRCUIT JUDGE.

* * *

What economists frequently advance as the solution [to the problem arising when a price equal to long run marginal cost does not cover average total costs] is the selective use of price discrimination—permitting deviation from marginal costs in inverse proportion to the elasticity of demand for the utility service of various classes of users. The concept is that this minimizes inefficient allocation of resources, because those consumers who would, relatively speaking, consume the same amount of resources regardless of price pay the greatest differential from marginal costs, while those whose level of consumption is most susceptible to price considerations are charged the price closest to marginal costs.

This is the kind of thinking that apparently informed the PRC in its first two ratemaking decisions, although it did not elaborate on its view. The PRC first established an initial rate floor in the process of determining "attributed" costs by ascertaining variable (or marginal) costs. Because strictly variable costs generated only about half the revenues necessary to recover the costs of the Postal Service, the PRC then sought to "assign" the remaining unattributed costs in inverse proportion to the elasticities of demand of the various classes.

In terms of economic efficiency, the advantage of [this two-step] pricing for regulated utilities is that it serves as a means of "encouraging the maximum economic use of a company's services consistent with the so-called 'full-cost' requirement." A corollary is its potential for close control of consumer demand, by assuring that consumption choices reflect the current costs to society of providing the resource. [This two-step] pricing has attained some currency in electric power ratemaking, where efficient utilization of increasingly scarce energy resources is a matter of primary concern.

In the context of postal ratemaking, however, the dominant objective of Congress, as ascertained by the court in [National Association of Greeting Card Publishers v. United States Postal Service, 116 U.S.App. D.C. 331, 569 F.2d 570 (1976), vacated as to other issues, 434 U.S. 884, 98 S.Ct. 253, 54 L.Ed.2d 169 (1977) (*NAGCP I*)], was not so much the regulation of demand for postal services, as the prevention of discrimination among the mail classes. In any event, the concern for maximization of use of capacity is less compelling where demand is inelastic. The court in *NAGCP I* noted that the Postal Service had conceded that demand for all classes of mail was essentially inelastic at foreseeable rates. It rejected the effort to assign almost half the costs of USPS on the basis of relative inelasticities of demand as inappropriate, as in effect permitting a discretion barred by the Act, and as unduly burdening first class mail, the most inelastic of the classes. *NAGCP I* certainly did not command a complete jettison of economic principles. It approved cost variability as an appropriate starting point for cost determinations. The path to be followed from that point on differed from that of the PRC in view of the congressional intent. This is not the only context in which a concern for equal or fair treatment yields results different from those obtainable if economic efficiency in the allocation of resources were the exclusive or even the dominant goal. The choice of goals and objectives is a policy choice of the legislature, and the court's function is to ascertain the legislature's choice and to apply it, including the assurance of faithful application by agencies which make decisions subject to judicial review.

* * *

* * * [W]e affirm the cost allocation decisions.

Notes and Questions

1. The relationship between marginal cost pricing and allocative efficiency should be clear by now. Marginal cost pricing tests consumers' valuations of the item produced. The goal of marginal cost pricing is to ensure that the level of production is allocatively efficient. The regulatory dilemma is to maintain that level of output while covering total costs, which were, in *Greeting Card,* as in other regulatory areas, greater than the marginal cost of providing the mail services to any class of customers.

The price elasticity of demand measures the degree to which a given collection of customers will change the quantity of service they demand in response to a price rise. Assigning fixed costs in inverse proportion to the elasticities of demand of various classes of consumers means that a class whose price elasticity of demand is relatively inelastic, a price elasticity of 0.5, for instance, will have a price for postal services that includes six times as much of the fixed costs than as class whose demand is relatively price elastic, a price elasticity of demand equal to 3 (because three is six times greater than 0.5). The class with the lower elasticity of demand pays a higher percentage of the fixed costs.

Question: How does the inverse elasticity rule reconcile the goals of minimizing allocative inefficiency and ensuring a profit to the provider of the service?

2. In *Greeting Card,* the court rejected the two-step price setting process, noting that demand for postal services is generally inelastic and that this makes efficiency concerns less important.

Questions: Did the court reject the two step price setting process on equity or efficiency grounds? What is the logical basis for the court's conclusion that the inelasticity of demand for postal services makes application of the inverse elasticity rule in this industry less important?

3. The court in *Greeting Card* asserted that the dominant objective of Congress was not so much the regulation of demand for postal services as the prevention of discrimination among classes of users.

Questions: Did the court in *Greeting Card* completely reject the allocative efficiency approach to pricing? How much of the approach survives this opinion?

Chapter 7

CONSTITUTIONAL LAW AND
PUBLIC CHOICE

Economic analysis is usually associated with markets, which allocate resources through the voluntary actions of rational buyers and sellers exchanging goods and services. But not all goods are allocated through markets. Modern societies allocate many resources through political rather than market systems. Governments require auto manufacturers to install seatbelts and consumers to buy them, impose property, sales, and income taxes, provide police protection and public education, and pay farmers to keep agricultural land out of production. The government giveth and the government taketh away.

The tools of economics—the assumptions of utility maximization and rational choice—can be applied to political allocations as well as market allocations. The emerging discipline of "public choice" studies political decisionmaking through just such an economic lens. Among the questions public choice addresses are: why might rational individuals choose to have a political state? What sort of state and what sort of constitution are they likely to choose? How will individual preferences be translated into group preferences and social choices? And how can a government made up of egoistic, rational maximizing individuals pursue such group goals? The following materials examine these and other questions.

A. THEORY OF THE STATE

1. AN INTRODUCTION TO THE SOCIAL CONTRACT

Economists assume that rational maximizers voluntarily exchange resources in market transactions because exchange leaves both parties better off. Thus, market reallocations increase society's overall level of well-being. The efficiency of government allocations is more questionable. When the state requires a promisor to pay damages for breach of contract, imprisons a mugger for criminal assault, or requires a monopolist to charge competitive prices, the objects of such government coercion clearly are less well off than they would have been had the state not interfered. Nevertheless, there are reasons why rational maximizers might prefer a coercive state to the absence of government authority.

T. HOBBES, LEVIATHAN
(1651).

* * *

Hereby it is manifest, that during the time men live without a common power to keep them all in awe, they are in that condition which is called war; and such a war, as is of every man, against every man. * * *

* * * In such condition, there is no place for industry; because the fruit thereof is uncertain: and consequently no culture of the earth; no navigation, nor use of the commodities that may be imported by sea; no commodious building; no instruments of moving, and removing such things as require much force; no knowledge of the face of the earth; no account of time; no arts; no letters; no society; and which is worst of all, continual fear, and danger of violent death; and the life of man, solitary, poor, nasty, brutish, and short.

* * *

The final cause, end, or design of men (who naturally love liberty, and dominion over others) in the introduction of that restraint upon themselves (in which we see them live in commonwealths) is the foresight of their own preservation, and of a more contented life thereby; that is to say, of getting themselves out from that miserable condition of war, which is necessarily consequent * * * to the natural passions of men, when there is no visible power to keep them in awe, and tie them by fear of punishment to the performance of their covenants * * *.

For * * * covenants, without the sword, are but words, and of no strength to secure a man at all. * * *

* * *

* * * [T]herefore it is no wonder if there be somewhat else required (besides covenant) to make their agreement constant and lasting; which is a common power, to keep them in awe, and to direct their actions to the common benefit.

The only way to erect such a common power, as may be able to defend them from the invasion of foreigners, and the injuries of one another, and thereby to secure them in such sort, as that by their own industry, and by the fruits of the earth, they may nourish themselves and live contentedly; is, to confer all their power and strength upon one man, or upon one assembly of men, that may reduce all their wills, by plurality of voices, unto one will * * * and therein to submit their wills, every one to his will, and their judgments, to his judgment. This is more than consent, or concord; it is a real unity of them all, in one and the same person, made by covenant of every man with every man, in such manner, as if every man should say to every man, *I authorize and give up my right of governing myself, to this man, or to this assembly of men, on this condition, that thou give up thy right to him, and authorize all his actions in like manner.* This done, the multitude so united in one person, is called a COMMONWEALTH, in latin CIVITAS. This is the generation of that great LEVIATHAN, or rather (to speak more reverently) of that *mortal God,* to which we owe under the *immortal God,* our peace and defence. For by this authority, given him by every particular man in the commonwealth, he hath the use of so much power and strength conferred on him, that by terror thereof, he is enabled to perform the wills of them all, to peace at home, and mutual aid against their enemies abroad. And in him consisteth the essence of the commonwealth; which (to define it) is *one person, of whose acts a great multitude, by mutual covenants one with another, have made themselves every one the author, to the end he may use the strength and means of them all, as he shall think expedient, for their peace and common defence.*

And he that carrieth this person, is called SOVEREIGN, and said to have *sovereign power;* and every one besides, his SUBJECT.

* * *

JACOBSON v. COMMONWEALTH OF MASSACHUSETTS

Supreme Court of the United States, 1905.
197 U.S. 11, 25 S.Ct. 358, 49 L.Ed. 643.

HARLAN, JUSTICE.

This case involves the validity, under the Constitution of the United States, of certain provisions in the statutes of Massachusetts relating to vaccination.

* * *

* * * [T]he plaintiff in error, Jacobson, was proceeded against by a criminal complaint in one of the inferior courts of Massachusetts. The complaint charged that on the seventeenth day of July, 1902, the Board of Health of Cambridge, being of the opinion that it was necessary for the public health and safety, required the vaccination and revaccination of all the inhabitants thereof who had not been successfully vaccinated since the first day of March, 1897, and provided them with the means of free vaccination, and that the defendant, being over twenty-one years of age and not under guardianship, refused and neglected to comply with such requirement.

* * *

* * * [F]or nearly a century most of the members of the medical profession have regarded vaccination, repeated after intervals, as a preventive of smallpox; that while they have recognized the possibility of injury to an individual from carelessness in the performance of it, or even in a conceivable case without carelessness, they generally have considered the risk of such an injury too small to be seriously weighed as against the benefits coming from the discreet and proper use of the preventive * * *.

* * *

The authority of the State to enact this statute is to be referred to what is commonly called the police power * * *. According to settled principles the police power of a State must be held to embrace, at least, such reasonable regulations established directly by legislative enactment as will protect the public health and the public safety. * * * The mode or manner in which those results are to be accomplished is within the discretion of the State, subject, of course, so far as Federal power is concerned, only to the condition that no rule prescribed by a State, nor any regulation adopted by a local governmental agency acting under the sanction of state legislation, shall contravene the Constitution of the United States, or infringe any right granted or secured by that instrument. * * *

We come, then, to inquire whether any right given, or secured by the Constitution, is invaded by the statute as interpreted by the state court. The defendant insists that his liberty is invaded when the State subjects him to fine or imprisonment for neglecting or refusing to submit to vaccination; that a compulsory vaccination law is unreasonable, arbitrary, and oppressive, and, therefore, hostile to the inherent right of every freeman to care for his own body and health in such way as to him seems best; and that the execution of such a law against one who objects to vaccination, no matter for what reason, is nothing short of an assault upon his person. But the liberty secured by the Constitution of the United States to every person within its jurisdiction does not import an absolute right in each person to be, at all times and in all circumstances, wholly freed from restraint. There are manifold restraints to which every person is necessarily subject for the common good. On any other basis organized society could not exist with safety to its members. Society based on the rule that each one is a law unto himself would soon be confronted with disorder and anarchy. Real liberty for all could not exist under the operation of a principle which recognizes the right of each individual person to use his own, whether in respect of his person or his property, regardless of the injury that may be done to others. * * * In the constitution of Massachusetts adopted in 1780 it was laid down as a fundamental principle of the social compact that the whole people covenants with each citizen, and each citizen with the whole people, that all shall be governed by certain laws for "the common good," and that government is instituted "for the common good, for the protection, safety, prosperity and happiness of the people, and not for the profit, honor or private interests of any one man, family or class of men." The good and welfare of the Common-wealth, of which the legislature is primarily the judge, is the basis on which the police power rests in Massachusetts.

* * * If the mode adopted by the Commonwealth of Massachusetts for the protection of its local communities against smallpox proved to be distressing, inconvenient or objectionable to some—if nothing more could be reasonably affirmed of the statute in question—the answer is that it was the duty of the constituted authorities primarily to keep in view the welfare, comfort and safety of the many, and not permit the interests of the many to be subordinated to the wishes or convenience of the few. There is, of course, a sphere within which the individual may assert the supremacy of his own will and rightfully dispute the authori-ty of any human government, especially of any free government exist-ing under a written constitution, to interfere with the exercise of that will. But it is equally true that in every wellordered society charged with the duty of conserving the safety of its members the rights of the individual in respect of his liberty may at times, under the pressure of great dangers, be subjected to such restraint, to be enforced by reason-able regulations, as the safety of the general public may demand. * * * The liberty secured by the Fourteenth Amendment, this court has said, consists, in part, in the right of a person "to live and work where he will", and yet he may be compelled, by force if need be, against his will and without regard to his personal wishes or his pecuniary inter-ests, or even his religious or political convictions, to take his place in the ranks of the army of his country and risk the chance of being shot down in its defense. It is not, therefore, true that the power of the public to guard itself against imminent danger depends in every case involving the control of one's body upon his willingness to submit to reasonable regulations established by the constituted authorities, under the sanction of the State, for the purpose of protecting the public collectively against such danger.

* * *

We are not prepared to hold that a minority, residing or remaining in any city or town where smallpox is prevalent, and enjoying the general protection afforded by an organized local government, may thus defy the will of its constituted authorities, acting in good faith for all, under the legislative sanction of the State. If such be the privilege of a minority then a like privilege would belong to each individual of the community, and the spectacle would be presented of the welfare and safety of an entire population being subordinated to the notions of a single individual who chooses to remain a part of that population. We are unwilling to hold it to be an element in the liberty secured by the Constitution of the United States that one person, or a minority of persons, residing in any community and enjoying the benefits of its local government, should have the power thus to dominate the majority when supported in their action by the authority of the State. * * *

* * *

The judgment of the court below must be affirmed.

It is so ordered.

Notes and Questions

1. In *Jacobson,* the Supreme Court held that Massachusetts could require an individual to submit to smallpox vaccination against his will. Jacobson claimed that vaccination was likely to harm him because "he had suffered seriously from previous vaccination, thus indicating that his system was sensitive to the poison of the vaccination virus." 197 U.S. at 17. The Supreme Court pointed out that it was within the state's police power not only to force Jacobson to submit to vaccination, but to require him to serve in the military and face the risk of death or crippling injury. *Jacobson's* discussion of the limits of the police power serves as a reminder that the law is a system of behavioral rules that individuals follow not because they choose to, but because the human agents of an amorphous "commonwealth" compel them to. Behind every legal judgment lies the coercive power of the state.

> *Questions:* When the state forces an individual to do something she would rather not do, or prohibits her from doing something she would like to do, by definition the coerced individual suffers a loss of utility as a result of the government's interference. Does that mean government coercion is inefficient? Consider the facts of *Jacobson,* and assume that while smallpox vaccination poses a small risk to the vaccinated individual, a vaccinated person cannot transmit the disease to anyone else and complete vaccination of a population will eradicate the disease. Why might a rational individual like Jacobson refuse immunization? If there were no immunization requirement, would the risk of a smallpox epidemic likely increase or decrease? Was the compulsory vaccination statute involved in *Jacobson* inefficient?

2. Writing centuries apart, Harlan and Hobbes describe a contractual relationship between the individual and the state. Entering the "covenant of every man with every man," rational persons voluntarily agree to submit to government coercion in return for government protection. The notion of the "social contract" has proven one of the most powerful and persistent ideas in political theory and is reflected in both the classic writings of Hobbes, Locke, and Rousseau and the modern work of Kant, Nozick, and Rawls.

A rational maximizer will choose to enter a social contract only if doing so increases her level of well-being. That implies that a social contract, like other exchanges, is efficient. However, most discussion of contractarian theory has focused on its moral rather than its economic implications.

> *Questions:* How does the notion of a social contract provide a moral justification for intrusive state action? Why might Massachusetts claim that requiring Jacobson to submit to vaccination was not only within its legal authority but also within its moral authority?

3. While citing contractarian theory, Justice Harlan also argued that Cambridge's compulsory vaccination program was justified because "it was

the duty of the constituted authorities primarily to keep in view the welfare, comfort, and safety of the many, and not permit the interests of the many to be subordinated to the wishes or convenience of the few."

Questions: Compare the contractarian and "public welfare" justifications for the coercive state. Which more closely resembles Pareto's perspective? Which reflects the Kaldor–Hicks criteria?

4. Thomas Hobbes argued in *Leviathan* that state compulsion was essential to rein in individuals' "natural passions," which if uncontrolled would lead to a state of nature in which man's life was "nasty, brutish, and short." Justice Harlan similarly believed that a "[s]ociety based on the rule that each one is a law unto himself would soon be confronted with disorder and anarchy." Such statements imply that without a coercive government, individuals will impose external costs on and withhold external benefits from each other to an intolerable degree.

Questions: Is the state of nature necessarily as unpleasant as Hobbes and Harlan imply? Using the facts of *Jacobson,* suppose there were no coercive state to require immunization. Could Cambridge's residents reach a voluntary, informal agreement to submit to a vaccination program? (Recall Hobbes' view that "covenants, without the sword, are but words, and of no strength to secure a man at all.") In the absence of state intervention or informal agreement, would a smallpox epidemic necessarily ensue? Consider whether there might be circumstances under Jacobson might voluntarily seek vaccination.

5. The *Jacobson* opinion concludes that "[w]e are not prepared to hold that a minority, residing or *remaining* in any city or town where smallpox is prevalent, and enjoying the general protection afforded by an organized local government, may thus defy the will of its constituted authorities" (emphasis added). That language raises the possibility that Jacobson might have escaped vaccination by simply moving away from Cambridge and settling in some other town that did not have a vaccination requirement.

Question: Given that many factors may influence an individual's opinion of Cambridge's desirability as a place to live, does Jacobson's decision to remain in Cambridge say anything about the efficiency of the Cambridge statute?

PEREZ v. BROWNELL

Supreme Court of the United States, 1958.
356 U.S. 44, 78 S.Ct. 568, 2 L.Ed.2d 603.

FRANKFURTER, JUSTICE.

Petitioner, a national of the United States by birth, has been declared to have lost his American citizenship by operation of the Nationality Act of 1940 * * *. Section 401 of that Act provided that

"A person who is a national of the United States, whether by birth or naturalization, shall lose his nationality by:

"(e) Voting in a political election in a foreign state or participating in an election or plebiscite to determine the sovereignty over foreign territory * * *."

Petitioner was born in Texas in 1909. He resided in the United States until 1919 or 1920, when he moved with his parents to Mexico, where he lived, apparently without interruption, until 1943. * * *

Petitioner brought suit in 1954 in a United States District Court for a judgment declaring him to be a national of the United States. The court, sitting without a jury, found * * * that he had voted in a "political election" in Mexico in 1946. The court, concluding that he had thereby expatriated himself, denied the relief sought by the petitioner. The United States Court of Appeals for the Ninth Circuit affirmed. We granted certiorari because of the constitutional questions raised by the petitioner.

* * *

It cannot be said * * * that Congress acted without warrant when, pursuant to its power to regulate the relations of the United States with foreign countries, it provided that anyone who votes in a foreign election of significance politically in the life of another country shall lose his American citizenship. To deny the power of Congress to enact the legislation challenged here would be to disregard the constitutional allocation of governmental functions that it is this Court's solemn duty to guard.

* * *

Judgment affirmed.

WARREN, CHIEF JUSTICE, dissenting.

The Congress of the United States has decreed that a citizen of the United States shall lose his citizenship by performing certain designated acts. The petitioner in this case, a native-born American, is declared to have lost his citizenship by voting in a foreign election. Whether this forfeiture of citizenship exceeds the bounds of the Constitution is the issue before us. The problem is fundamental and must be resolved upon fundamental considerations.

Generally, when congressional action is challenged, constitutional authority is found in the express and implied powers with which the National Government has been invested or in those inherent powers that are necessary attributes of a sovereign state. The sweep of those powers is surely broad. In appropriate circumstances, they are adequate to take away life itself. The initial question here is whether citizenship is subject to the exercise of these general powers of government.

What is this government, whose power is here being asserted? And what is the source of that power? The answers are the foundation of our Republic. To secure the inalienable rights of the individual, "Governments are instituted among Men, deriving their just powers from the consent of the governed." I do not believe the passage of time has lessened the truth of this proposition. It is basic to our form of government. This Government was born of its citizens, it maintains itself in a continuing relationship with them, and, in my judgment, it is without power to sever the relationship that gives rise to its existence. I cannot believe that a government conceived in the spirit of ours was established with power to take from the people their most basic right.

Citizenship is man's basic right for it is nothing less than the right to have rights. Remove this priceless possession and there remains a stateless person, disgraced and degraded in the eyes of his countrymen. He has no lawful claim to protection from any nation, and no nation may assert rights on his behalf. * * * This government was not established with power to decree this fate.

* * *

There is no question that citizenship may be voluntarily relinquished. * * *

* * *

The fatal defect in the statute before us is that its application is not limited to those situations that may rationally be said to constitute an abandonment of citizenship. In specifying that any act of voting in a foreign political election results in loss of citizenship, Congress has employed a classification so broad that it encompasses conduct that fails to show a voluntary abandonment of American citizenship. * * *

* * * If the Government determines that certain conduct by United States citizens should be prohibited because of anticipated injurious consequences to the conduct of foreign affairs or to some other legitimate governmental interest, it may within the limits of the Constitution proscribe such activity and assess appropriate punishment. But every exercise of governmental power must find its source in the Constitution. The power to denationalize is not within the letter or the spirit of the powers with which our Government was endowed. The citizen may elect to renounce his citizenship, and under some circumstances he may be found to have abandoned his status by voluntarily performing acts that compromise his undivided allegiance to his country. The mere act of voting in a foreign election, however, without regard to the circumstances attending the participation, is not sufficient to show a voluntary abandonment of citizenship. The record in this case does not disclose any of the circumstances under which this petitioner voted. We know only the bare fact that he cast a ballot. The basic right of American citizenship has been too dearly won to be so lightly lost.

* * * As I see my duty in this case, I must dissent.

Notes and Questions

Like Justice Harlan's opinion in *Jacobson*, Chief Justice Warren's dissent in *Perez* refers to the "consent" theory of government—the notion that a state may legitimately coerce its citizens because they have consented, implicitly or explicitly, to that coercion. Justice Warren's emphasis on consent theory was so strong that he argued that implicit consent is necessary not only to bring an individual within the shadow of the state but also to expel him from it.

Questions: An individual's decision to remain within a particular jurisdiction may be evidence that she has consented to that jurisdiction's laws, presumably because she expects to be better off under those laws than she would be in another jurisdiction with a different social contract. Of course, one's ability to contract depends on several factors, including the existence of other parties interested in contracting and the costs of contracting. Do these considerations undermine the notion of implied consent as a justification for state coercion? Is consent a more plausible argument in *Perez,* which involved a "choice" of nationality, or in *Jacobson,* which involved a "choice" of municipal residence?

2. GOALS OF THE SOCIAL CONTRACT

Economic analysis explains why rational individuals might prefer a coercive government authority over the freedom of the "state of nature." Rational maximizers in the state of nature impose external costs on and withhold external benefits from each other in a wasteful, inefficient fashion that prevents society from reaching the much higher level of well-being possible when a government controls externalities. By mutually agreeing to submit to a coercive state, individuals force themselves to behave more responsibly and efficiently, improving the well-being of all.

The theory of the social contract may be more accurately described as a normative statement of the basis for an efficient and legitimate government than a positive description of the state's origins. Nevertheless, the idea has proven to be powerful and enduring. More than three centuries after Thomas Hobbes published *Leviathan,* Chief Justice Warren still regarded "government by the consent of the governed" as the foundation of the state's authority.

To suggest that rational individuals can improve their well-being by creating a political state only begins the inquiry into the notion of constitution as contract. Although many possible political states might be preferable to none, rational individuals would prefer some governments over others. The remainder of Chapter 7 considers how rational individuals might fashion the constitution for a coercive state—*i.e.,* draft the terms for the social contract. This section begins with the fundamental issue of what goal rational maximizers would want the social contract to serve.

a. Utilitarianism

If individuals prefer a coercive political state over the state of nature because they expect to be made better off, it seems natural that they should also prefer the political structure that makes them *best* off, *i.e.,* provides the most utility. Extrapolating from the principle of individual utility maximization leads naturally to *utilitarianism*—the notion that the social contract should seek the greatest happiness for the greatest number.

J. BENTHAM, AN INTRODUCTION TO
THE PRINCIPLES OF MORALS
AND LEGISLATION
(1832 ed.).

* * *

The principle of utility is the foundation of the present work: it will be proper therefore at the outset to give an explicit and determinate account of what is meant by it. By the principle of utility is meant that principle which approves or disapproves of every action whatsoever, according to the tendency which it appears to have to augment or diminish the happiness of the party whose interest is in question * * * .

* * *

The interest of the community is one of the most general expressions that can occur in the phraseology of morals: no wonder that the meaning of it is often lost. When it has a meaning, it is this. The community is a fictitious *body,* composed of the individual persons who are considered as constituting as it were its *members.* The interest of the community then is, what?—the sum of the interests of the several members who compose it.

* * *

An action then may be said to be conformable to the principle of utility, or, for shortness sake, to utility, (meaning with respect to the community at large) when the tendency it has to augment the happiness of the community is greater than any it has to diminish it.

* * *

Pleasures then, and the avoidance of pains, are the *ends* which the legislator has in view: it behoves him therefore to understand their *value.* * * *

* * *

To take an exact account then of the general tendency of any act, by which the interests of a community are affected, proceed as follows. Begin with any one person of those whose interests seem most immediately to be affected by it * * *.

* * *

Sum up all the values of all the *pleasures* on the one side, and those of all the *pains* on the other. The balance, if it be on the side of pleasure, will give the *good* tendency of the act upon the whole, with respect to the interests of that *individual* person; if on the side of pain, the *bad* tendency of it upon the whole.

Take an account of the *number* of persons whose interests appear to be concerned; and repeat the above process with respect to each.

Sum up the numbers expressive of the degrees of *good* tendency, which the act has, with respect to each individual, in regard to whom the tendency of it is *good* upon the whole: do this again with respect to each individual, in regard to whom the tendency of it is *bad* upon the whole. Take the *balance;* which, if on the side of *pleasure,* will give the general *good tendency* of the act, with respect to the total number of community of individuals concerned; if on the side of pain, the general *evil tendency,* with respect to the same community.

* * *

The end of law is, to augment happiness. The general object which all laws have, or ought to have, in common, is to augment the total happiness of the community * * * .

Notes and Questions

1. Since at least Bentham's day, the idea that the state's sole purpose should be maximizing its citizens' utility has sparked a heated and enduring debate. See generally J. Smart & B. Williams, Utilitarianism: For and Against (1973).

Questions: How does utilitarian theory compare with religious or ethical theories of the state? Is Marxism or Islamic fundamentalism consistent with utilitarianism?

2. Bentham argued that total happiness should be calculated by adding together the utilities and disutilities of all the individual members of society.

Question: How do the goals of a utilitarian state, as described by Bentham, relate to the economic goals of Pareto optimality and wealth maximization under the Kaldor–Hicks criteria?

———

To the economist concerned with efficiently maximizing utility, utilitarian theory has obvious attractions. However, a truly utilitarian society might adopt legal rules that many find troubling. The following cases explore some of the less-attractive aspects of utilitarianism.

BOWERS v. HARDWICK

Supreme Court of the United States, 1986.
478 U.S. 186, 106 S.Ct. 2841, 92 L.Ed.2d 140.

WHITE, JUSTICE.

In August 1982, respondent Hardwick was charged with violating the Georgia statute criminalizing sodomy by committing that act with another adult male in the bedroom of respondent's home. After a preliminary hearing, the District Attorney decided not to present the matter to the grand jury unless further evidence developed.

Respondent then brought suit in the Federal District Court, challenging the constitutionality of the statute insofar as it criminalized consensual sodomy. * * *

* * *

This case does not require a judgment on whether laws against sodomy between consenting adults in general, or between homosexuals in particular, are wise or desirable. * * * The issue presented is whether the Federal Constitution confers a fundamental right upon homosexuals to engage in sodomy and hence invalidates the laws of the many States that still make such conduct illegal and have done so for a very long time. * * *

* * *

Respondent * * * relies on *Stanley v. Georgia*, where the Court held that the First Amendment prevents conviction for possessing and reading obscene material in the privacy of his home: "If the First Amendment means anything, it means that a State has no business telling a man, sitting alone in his house, what books he may read or what films he may watch."

Stanley did protect conduct that would not have been protected outside the home, and it partially prevented the enforcement of state obscenity laws; but the decision was firmly grounded in the First Amendment. The right pressed upon us here has no similar support in the text of the Constitution, and it does not qualify for recognition under the prevailing principles for construing the Fourteenth Amendment. * * *

Even if the conduct at issue here is not a fundamental right, respondent asserts that there must be a rational basis for the law and that there is none in this case other than the presumed belief of a majority of the electorate in Georgia that homosexual sodomy is immoral and unacceptable. This is said to be an inadequate rationale to support the law. The law, however, is constantly based on notions of morality, and if all laws representing essentially moral choices are to be invalidated under the Due Process Clause, the courts will be very busy indeed. Even respondent makes no such claim, but insists that majority sentiments about the morality of homosexuality should be declared inadequate. We do not agree, and are unpersuaded that the sodomy laws of some 25 States should be invalidated on this basis.

Accordingly, the judgment of the Court of Appeals is reversed.

BURGER, CHIEF JUSTICE, concurring.

I join the Court's opinion, but I write separately to underscore my view that in constitutional terms there is no such thing as a fundamental right to commit homosexual sodomy.

* * * Decisions of individuals relating to homosexual conduct have been subject to state intervention throughout the history of Western Civilization. Condemnation of those practices is firmly rooted in Judeo–Christian moral and ethical standards. Homosexual sodomy was a capital crime under Roman law. During the English Reformation when powers of the ecclesiastical courts were transferred to the King's Courts, the first English statute criminalizing sodomy was passed.

Blackstone described "the infamous *crime against nature* " as an offense of "deeper malignity" than rape, an heinous act "the very mention of which is a disgrace to human nature," and "a crime not fit to be named." The common law of England, including its prohibition of sodomy, became the received law of Georgia and the other Colonies. In 1816 the Georgia Legislature passed the statute at issue here, and that statute has been continuously in force in one form or another since that time. To hold that the act of homosexual sodomy is somehow protected as a fundamental right would be to cast aside millennia of moral teaching.

This is essentially not a question of personal "preferences" but rather of the legislative authority of the State. I find nothing in the Constitution depriving a State of the power to enact the statute challenged here.

Blackmun, Justice, dissenting.

This case is no more about "a fundamental right to engage in homosexual sodomy," as the Court purports to declare, than *Stanley v. Georgia* was about a fundamental right to watch obscene movies * * *. Rather, this case is about "the most comprehensive of rights and the right most valued by civilized men," namely, "the right to be let alone."

* * *

In a variety of circumstances we have recognized that a necessary corollary of giving individuals freedom to choose how to conduct their lives is acceptance of the fact that different individuals will make different choices. For example, in holding that the clearly important state interest in public education should give way to a competing claim by the Amish to the effect that extended formal schooling threatened their way of life, the Court declared: "There can be no assumption that today's majority is 'right' and the Amish and others like them are 'wrong.' A way of life that is odd or even erratic but interferes with no rights or interests of others is not to be condemned because it is different." The Court claims that its decision today merely refuses to recognize a fundamental right to engage in homosexual sodomy; what the Court really has refused to recognize is the fundamental interest all individuals have in controlling the nature of their intimate associations with others.

* * *

The Court's failure to comprehend the magnitude of the liberty interests at stake in this case leads it to slight the question whether petitioner, on behalf of the State, has justified Georgia's infringement on these interests. * * *

* * *

The core of petitioner's defense of § 16–6–2 * * * is that respondent and others who engage in the conduct prohibited by § 16–6–2 interfere with Georgia's exercise of the " 'right of the Nation and of the States to maintain a decent society.' " Essentially, petitioner argues, and the Court agrees, that the fact that the acts described in § 16–6–2 "for hundreds of years, if not thousands, have been uniformly condemned as immoral" is a sufficient reason to permit a State to ban them today.

I cannot agree that either the length of time a majority has held its convictions or the passions with which it defends them can withdraw legislation from this Court's scrutiny. * * * [B]ecause the issue raised by this case touches the heart of what makes individuals what they are * * * we should be especially sensitive to the rights of those whose choices upset the majority.

* * *

Nor can § 16–6–2 be justified as a "morally neutral" exercise of Georgia's power to "protect the public environment". Certainly, some private behavior can affect the fabric of society as a whole. * * * [But p]etitioner and the Court fail to see the difference between laws that protect public sensibilities and those that enforce private morality. Statutes banning public sexual activity are entirely consistent with protecting the individual's liberty interest in decisions concerning sexual relations: the same recognition that those decisions are intensely private which justifies protecting them from governmental interference can justify protecting individuals from unwilling exposure to the sexual activities of others. But the mere fact that intimate behavior may be punished when it takes place in public cannot dictate how States can regulate intimate behavior that occurs in intimate places.

This case involves no real interference with the rights of others, for the mere knowledge that other individuals do not adhere to one's value system cannot be a legally cognizable interest, let alone an interest that can justify invading the houses, hearts, and minds of citizens who choose to live their lives differently.

* * *

* * * I can only hope that * * * the Court soon will reconsider its analysis and conclude that depriving individuals of the right to choose for themselves how to conduct their intimate relationships poses a far greater threat to the values most deeply rooted in our Nation's history than tolerance of nonconformity could ever do. Because I think the Court today betrays those values, I dissent.

Notes and Questions

1. The Georgia statute challenged in *Bowers* provides that "[a] person commits the offense of sodomy when he performs or submits to any sexual act involving the sex organs of one person and the mouth or anus of another." The statute's language is not limited to homosexual conduct but appears to extend to consensual sex between married, heterosexual partners. The punishment for conviction of a single offense is "imprisonment for not less than one nor more than 20 years." Ga. Code Ann. § 16–6–2 (1984).

2. The State of Georgia's justification for its antisodomy statute, accepted by the Supreme Court, was the "presumed belief of a majority of the electorate in Georgia that homosexual sodomy is immoral and unacceptable." A utilitarian would agree that the majority's notions of morality are a legitimate justification for regulating conduct, even if that conduct does not affect others directly. If the "moral majority's" utility from prohibiting offensive and immoral conduct outweighs the disutility suffered by those who would prefer to engage in immoral acts, morality statutes are utility maximizing.

The idea that A's notions of morality justify regulating B's private conduct is in tension with the libertarian (or, as it is sometimes called, liberal) view that individual dignity and autonomy demand there be some areas where others' preferences are irrelevant to the individual's decision how to conduct herself. John Stuart Mill was one of the leading proponents of that view, J.S. Mill, On Liberty 552 (Dolphin ed. 1961) (first publication 1859):

> What, then, is the rightful limit to the sovereignty of the individual over himself? Where does the authority of society begin? * * *
>
> * * *
>
> * * * As soon as any part of a person's conduct affects prejudicially the interests of others, society has jurisdiction over it, and the question whether the general welfare will or will not be promoted by interfering with it, becomes open to discussion. But there is no room for entertaining any such question when a person's conduct affects the interests of no persons besides himself, or need not affect them unless they like (all the persons concerned being of full age, and the ordinary amount of understanding). In all such cases, there should be perfect freedom, legal and social, to do the action and stand the consequences.

In Jacobson v. Massachusetts, above, Justice Harlan expressed a similar view that "[t]here is, of course, a sphere within which the individual may assert the supremacy of his own will and rightfully dispute the authority of any human government."

> *Question:* Justice Blackmun's dissent in *Bowers* differentiated between laws protecting "public sensibilities" and laws enforcing "private morality." Mills also distinguished between conduct that prejudiced others' interests and conduct that need not affect others "unless they like," *i.e.,* unless they allowed themselves to be affected. Does utilitarianism provide any basis for Blackmun's and Mill's distinctions?

3. Amartya Sen has provided a proof of the conflict between liberal values and utility maximization using the following example. Mr. Lewd and Mr. Prude share a single copy of D.H. Lawrence's Lady Chatterley's Lover. Mr. Prude prefers that no one reads the book, but if it must be read, he would rather endure reading it himself than allow Mr. Lewd to wallow in such filth. Mr. Lewd would prefer that they both read the book, but if only one can read it he would give up the pleasure of reading it himself for the glee of knowing that Mr. Prude must read it. The optimal result from the point of utility maximization is that Mr. Prude reads Lady Chatterley's Lover while Mr. Lewd does not. Yet that is exactly the

opposite of what the liberal value system says should occur, *i.e.,* each should make his own decision to read the book or not while ignoring the other's decision—in which case Mr. Lewd will read the book and Mr. Prude won't. See A. K. Sen, Collective Choice and Social Welfare 79–88 (1970).

The conflict between utility maximization and liberalism arises from Mr. Lewd and Mr. Prude both having "nosy" preferences; each experiences utility and disutility from the other's private behavior. Sen suggests one way out of the "liberal paradox" is for Mr. Lewd and Mr. Prude to impose upon themselves liberal values and to ignore their preferences relating to others' private behavior.

Question: Is Sen's solution to the liberal paradox consistent with utilitarianism?

4. In *Bowers,* the Supreme Court refused to find the sexual conduct prohibited by the Georgia statute to be constitutionally protected. However, in other cases the Court has recognized an individual's fundamental right to privacy and applied strict scrutiny to strike down, under Due Process or Equal Protection theories, statutes regulating individuals' choices in "private" matters. See, e.g., Griswold v. Connecticut, 381 U.S. 479, 85 S.Ct. 1678, 14 L.Ed.2d 510 (1965) (right to use contraceptives); Roe v. Wade, 410 U.S. 113, 93 S.Ct. 705, 35 L.Ed.2d 147 (1973) (woman's right to abortion in first trimester); Cruzan v. Director Missouri Department of Health, ___ U.S. ___, 110 S.Ct. 2841, 111 L.Ed.2d 224 (1990) (implying vegetative patient's right to die rather than receive extraordinary medical care).

Question: Is a fundamental right to privacy inconsistent with utilitarianism and utility maximization?

KOREMATSU v. UNITED STATES

Supreme Court of the United States, 1944.
323 U.S. 214, 65 S.Ct. 193, 89 L.Ed. 194.

[The majority opinion in this "Japanese Internment Case" focused on the constitutional validity of a military order forbidding any United States citizen of Japanese descent to remain in certain areas of the Pacific coast. That order was part of an overall plan for the forced detention of Japanese–Americans in internment camps. Another military order, which the majority declined to review, prohibited Japanese–Americans from *leaving* the restricted zone. As Justice Roberts noted in his dissent in *Korematsu,* "[t]he predicament in which the petitioner [found] himself was this: He was forbidden, by Military Order, to leave the zone in which he lived; he was forbidden, by Military Order, after a date fixed, to be found within that zone unless he were in an Assembly Center located in that zone. General DeWitt's report to the Secretary of War concerning the programme of evacuation and relocation of Japanese makes it entirely clear * * * that an Assembly Center was a euphemism for a prison." 323 U.S. at 230.]

BLACK, JUSTICE.

The petitioner, an American citizen of Japanese descent, was convicted in a federal district court for remaining in San Leandro, California, a "Military Area," contrary to Civilian Exclusion Order No. 34 of the Commanding General of the Western Command, U.S. Army, which directed that after May 9, 1942, all persons of Japanese ancestry should be excluded from that area. No question was raised as to petitioner's loyalty to the United States. The Circuit Court of Appeals affirmed, and the importance of the constitutional question involved caused us to grant certiorari.

It should be noted, to begin with, that all legal restrictions which curtail the civil rights of a single racial group are immediately suspect. That is not to say that all such restrictions are unconstitutional. It is to say that courts must subject them to the most rigid scrutiny.   * * *

* * *

* * * [W]e are unable to conclude that it was beyond the war power of Congress and the Executive to exclude those of Japanese ancestry from the West Coast war area at the time they did. True, exclusion from the area in which one's home is located is a [great] deprivation * * *. Nothing short of apprehension by the proper military authorities of the gravest imminent danger to the public safety can constitutionally justify [it]. But exclusion from a threatened area * * * has a definite and close relationship to the prevention of espionage and sabotage. The military authorities, charged with the primary responsibility of defending our shores, concluded that curfew provided inadequate protection and ordered exclusion. They did so * * * in accordance with Congressional authority to the military to say who should, and who should not, remain in the threatened areas.

* * *

We uphold the exclusion order as of the time it was made and when the petitioner violated it. In doing so, we are not unmindful of the hardships imposed by it upon a large group of American citizens. But hardships are part of war, and war is an aggregation of hardships. All citizens alike, both in and out of uniform, feel the impact of war in greater or lesser measure. Citizenship has its responsibilities as well as its privileges, and in time of war the burden is always heavier. Compulsory exclusion of large groups of citizens from their homes, except under circumstances of direst emergency and peril, is inconsistent with our basic governmental institutions. But when under conditions of modern warfare our shores are threatened by hostile forces, the power to protect must be commensurate with the threatened danger.

* * *

Affirmed.

JACKSON, JUSTICE, dissenting.

Korematsu was born on our soil, of parents born in Japan. The Constitution makes him a citizen of the United States by nativity and a citizen of California by residence. No claim is made that he is not loyal to this country. There is no suggestion that apart from the matter involved here he is not law-abiding and well disposed. Korematsu, however, has been convicted of an act not commonly a crime. It consists merely of being present in the state whereof he is a citizen, near the place where he was born, and where all his life he has lived.

* * *

Now, if any fundamental assumption underlies our system, it is that guilt is personal and not inheritable. * * * But here is an attempt to make an otherwise innocent act a crime merely because this prisoner is the son of parents as to whom he had no choice, and belongs to a race from which there is no way to resign. * * *

* * *

* * * I would reverse the judgment and discharge the prisoner.

Notes and Questions

1. The *Korematsu* decision makes it clear that the Constitution permits the government to impose severe deprivations upon innocent individuals when the public need is great enough. In *Korematsu,* the perceived threat was one to national security. The military authorities on the Pacific Coast believed that the uncontrolled movement of Japanese–Americans posed an unavoidable threat of sabotage that might be disastrous to the war effort. The Supreme Court accepted that argument and held that the perceived threat to the nation's security justified the effective imprisonment of all American citizens of Japanese descent living on the West Coast.

Utilitarian theory supports the *Korematsu* decision. A state action that prevents significant harm to the vast majority of society's members may maximize utility even though a small minority suffers greatly. As Justice Harlan noted in Jacobson v. Massachusetts, above, "[i]f the mode adopted by the Commonwealth of Massachusetts for the protection of its local communities against smallpox proved to be distressing, inconvenient or objectionable to some * * * the answer is that it was the duty of the constituted authorities primarily to keep in view the welfare, comfort and safety of the many, and not permit the interests of the many to be subordinated to the wishes or convenience of the few."

2. There was some suggestion in *Korematsu* that the principal "benefit" West Coast residents derived from the Japanese–Americans' internment was not freedom from sabotage but the opportunity to acquire the internees' property at bargain prices and to eliminate Japanese–American competition in the marketplace. Justice Murphy also wrote a dissent in *Korematsu,* in which he noted that "[s]pecial interest groups were extremely active in applying pressure for mass evacuation. Mr. Austin E. Anson, managing secretary of the Salinas Vegetable Grower–Shipper Association, has frankly admitted that 'We're charged with wanting to get rid of the Japs for selfish reasons. We do. * * * They undersell the white man in the markets. * * * They work their women and children while the white farmer has to pay wages for his help. If all the Japs were removed tomorrow, we'd never miss them in two weeks, because the white farmers

can take over and produce everything the Jap grows. And we don't want them back when the war ends, either.'" 323 U.S. at 239 n.12.

Under utilitarian theory such sentiments legitimately may be considered in calculating whether the harm state action imposes on the minority is outweighed by the benefit to the majority. Because all preferences are equally acceptable, any reallocation is justified if the calculus of utilities suggests total utility is increased. Taken to an extreme, utilitarian theory would allow a society to torture an innocent individual to entertain a large sadistic audience, provided the mob's total glee outweighed the victim's agony. Of course, that scenario is unlikely. The more realistic problem posed by utilitarian values is that utilitarianism allows social rules under which most individuals prosper, but a few live in wretched conditions.

b. Rawls' Theory of Justice

J. RAWLS, A THEORY OF JUSTICE *
(1971).

Justice is the first virtue of social institutions, as truth is of systems of thought. A theory however elegant and economical must be rejected or revised if it is untrue; likewise laws and institutions no matter how efficient and well-arranged must be reformed or abolished if they are unjust. Each person possesses an inviolability founded on justice that even the welfare of society as a whole cannot override. For this reason justice denies that the loss of freedom for some is made right by a greater good shared by others. It does not allow that the sacrifices imposed on a few are outweighed by the larger sum of advantages enjoyed by many.

* * *

My aim is to present a conception of justice which generalizes and carries to a higher level of abstraction the familiar theory of the social contract as found, say, in Locke, Rousseau, and Kant. In order to do this we are not to think of the original contract as one to enter a particular society or to set up a particular form of government. Rather, the guiding idea is that the principles of justice for the basic structure of society are the object of the original agreement. They are the principles that free and rational persons concerned to further their own interests would accept in an initial position of equality as defining the fundamental terms of their association. * * *

* * *

* * * No society can, of course, be a scheme of cooperation which men enter voluntarily in a literal sense; each person finds himself placed at birth in some particular position in some particular society, and the nature of this position materially affects his life prospects. Yet

a society satisfying the principles of justice * * * comes as close as a society can to being a voluntary scheme, for it meets the principles which free and equal persons would assent to under circumstances that are fair. In this sense its members are autonomous and the obligations they recognize self-imposed.

* * *

I shall maintain [that] the persons in the initial situation would choose two rather different principles: the first requires equality in the assignment of basic rights and duties, while the second holds that social and economic inequalities, for example inequalities of wealth and authority, are just only if they result in compensating benefits for everyone, and in particular for the least advantaged members of society. These principles rule out justifying institutions on the grounds that the hardships of some are offset by a greater good in the aggregate. It may be expedient but it is not just that some should have less in order that others may prosper. But there is no injustice in the greater benefits earned by a few provided that the situation of persons not so fortunate is thereby improved. The intuitive idea is that since everyone's well-being depends upon a scheme of cooperation without which no one could have a satisfactory life, the division of advantages should be such as to draw forth the willing cooperation of everyone taking part in it, including those less well situated. * * * The two principles mentioned seem to be fair agreement on the basis of which those better endowed, or more fortunate in their social position, neither of which we can be said to deserve, could expect the willing cooperation of others when some workable scheme is a necessary condition of the welfare of all. * * *

* * *

My aim is to work out a theory of justice that represents an alternative to utilitarian thought * * * that society is rightly ordered, and therefore just, when its major institutions are arranged so as to achieve the greatest net balance of satisfaction summed over all the individuals belonging to it.

* * *

* * * [T]he two principles read as follows.

First: each person is to have an equal right to the most extensive basic liberty compatible with a similar liberty for others.

Second: social and economic inequalities are to be arranged so that they are * * * reasonably expected to be to everyone's advantage * * *

* * * As their formulation suggests, these principles presuppose that the social structure can be divided into two more or less distinct parts, the first principle applying to the one, the second to the other. They distinguish between those aspects of the social system that define and secure the equal liberties of citizenship and those that specify and establish social and economic inequalities. The basic liberties of citizens are, roughly speaking, political liberty (the right to vote and to be

eligible for public office) together with freedom of speech and assembly; liberty of conscience and freedom of thought; freedom of the person along with the right to hold (personal) property; and freedom from arbitrary arrest and seizure as defined by the concept of the rule of law. These liberties are all required to be equal by the first principle, since citizens of a just society are to have the same basic rights.

The second principle applies, in the first approximation, to the distribution of income and wealth * * *. While the distribution of wealth and income need not be equal, it must be to everyone's advantage * * * One applies the second principle * * * [by arranging] social and economic inequalities so that everyone benefits.

* * *

* * * [I]t should be observed that the two principles (and this holds for all formulations) are a special case of a more general conception of justice that can be expressed as follows.

All social values—liberty and opportunity, income and wealth, and bases of self-respect—are to be distributed equally unless an unequal distribution of any, or all, of these values is to everyone's advantage.

* * *

Thus, the parties start with a principle establishing equal liberty for all, including equality of opportunity, as well as an equal distribution of income and wealth. But there is no reason why this acknowledgment should be final. If there are inequalities in the basic structure that work to make everyone better off in comparison with the benchmark of initial equality, why not permit them? The immediate gain which a greater inequality might allow can be regarded as intelligently invested in view of its future return. If, for example, these inequalities set up various incentives which succeed in eliciting more productive efforts, a person in the original position may look upon them as necessary to cover the costs of training and to encourage effective performance. * * * A person in the original position would, therefore, concede the justice of these inequalities. Indeed it would be shortsighted of him not to do so. Inequalities are permissible when they maximize, or at least all contribute to the long-term expectations of the least fortunate group in society.

* * *

* * * [I]t is useful as a heuristic device to think of the two principles as the maximin solution to the problem of social justice. * * * The maximin rule tells us to rank alternatives by their worst possible outcomes: we are to adopt the alternative the worst outcome of which is superior to the worst outcomes of the others. * * *

Notes and Questions

1. Rawls' analysis is rooted firmly in the tradition of the social contract, yet he proposes contractual terms that differ significantly from traditional utilitarian theories. Rawls argues that rational individuals

drafting a social contract from "the original position" (a hypothetical condition corresponding to a state of nature in which no one knows what position he will occupy in society) would choose a society that distributes goods according to two principles of justice. The *equality principle* requires basic political freedoms and liberties to be distributed perfectly equally. The *difference principle* allows differences among individuals in the distribution of economic rights like wealth and income, but only so long as those differences improve the economic position of the worst-off in society.

Rawls describes both principles as an extension of the general rule that all social goods "are to be distributed equally unless an unequal distribution of any, or all, of these values is to everyone's advantage." That is Rawls' rule of "maximin;" inequalities are tolerated when they operate to *maximize* the rights of those who enjoy the *minimum* in society. Rawls argues that there is no reason to tolerate inequalities in basic political liberties because there is no way disparities in political liberties can increase the degree of political liberty enjoyed by those worst-off in society. On the other hand, he believes that allowing differences in wealth and power can improve the economic position of the least-advantaged.

> *Question:* Rawls seems to assume that the supply of basic political liberties like voting rights is fixed, so that increasing one person's political liberty necessarily decreases another's. In contrast, Rawls presumes that the supply of economic wealth is not fixed and allowing inequality can increase total wealth in a fashion that benefits all the members of society. Are Rawls' technological assumptions about the supply of wealth and political liberties sensible?

2. Rawls describes his theory as a theory of "justice." Nevertheless, his analysis has an economic flavor.

> *Question:* Rawls presents his theory as an alternative to utilitarianism. While utilitarians are concerned only with the total amount of utility in society and not with its distribution, Rawls' theory does not allow the interests of an individual to be sacrificed for the greater good. What is the relationship between utilitarianism and Rawls' theory as political ideas, and Kaldor–Hicks wealth maximization and the Pareto criteria as economic ideas?

UNIVERSAL DECLARATION OF HUMAN RIGHTS

General Assembly Resolution 217(III).
Dec. 10, 1948.

* * *

ARTICLE 25

1. Everyone has the right to a standard of living adequate for the health and well-being of himself and of his family, including food, clothing, housing and medical care and necessary social services, and the right to security in the event of unemployment, sickness, disability, widowhood, old age or other lack of livelihood in circumstances beyond his control.

* * *

Notes and Questions

1. As Bowers v. Hardwick, above, illustrates, the Supreme Court normally upholds state action if it is rationally related to some legitimate government purpose. The rational relation standard is easily met and statutes reviewed under that standard are rarely struck down. In cases involving "fundamental rights," however, the Court applies the more severe standard of strict scrutiny. Under the Due Process Clause, strict scrutiny requires that government action burdening a fundamental right be necessary to a compelling state objective. See Roe v. Wade, 410 U.S. 113, 93 S.Ct. 705, 35 L.Ed.2d 147 (1973). The Equal Protection Clause similarly requires classifications involving fundamental rights to be narrowly tailored to promote a compelling state interest. See Kramer v. Union Free School District, 395 U.S. 621, 89 S.Ct. 1886, 23 L.Ed.2d 583 (1969).

Which rights, then, are fundamental? The Supreme Court has held that the Constitution explicitly guarantees a number of political rights to U.S. citizens, including the rights to peaceable assembly, to free speech, and to trial by jury. The Court has found other fundamental rights implicit in the Constitution, including the rights to vote (under the Equal Protection clause) and to travel from state to state.

In Shapiro v. Thompson, 394 U.S. 618, 89 S.Ct. 1322, 22 L.Ed.2d 600 (1969), the Court struck down as unconstitutional state statutes that denied welfare assistance to residents who had not resided within a state's jurisdiction for at least one year prior to applying for assistance. The principal focus of Justice Brennan's opinion for the majority was the burden the statutes imposed upon the judicially-recognized fundamental right to interstate travel. However, Brennan also hinted that the residency requirements might be unconstitutional because the statutes precluded new residents from receiving "welfare aid upon which may depend the ability of the families to obtain the very means to subsist—food, shelter, and other necessities of life." 394 U.S. at 627, 89 S.Ct. at 1889. Justice Harlan's dissent in *Shapiro* protested Brennan's "cryptic suggestion" that strict scrutiny applied because the classification affected the appellees' access to food or shelter, 394 U.S. at 661–62, 89 S.Ct. at 1345–46:

> Virtually every state statute affects important rights. * * * When the right affected is one assured by the Federal Constitution, any infringement can be dealt with under the Due Process Clause. But when a statute affects only matters not mentioned in the Federal Constitution and is not arbitrary or irrational, I must reiterate that I know of nothing which entitles this Court to pick out particular human activities, characterize them as "fundamental," and give them added protection under an unusually stringent equal protection test.

Lindsey v. Normet, 405 U.S. 56, 92 S.Ct. 862, 31 L.Ed.2d 36 (1972), involved a challenge to procedural limitations imposed on tenants' suits against landlords under Oregon's Forcible Entry and Wrongful Detainer Law. The complainants urged the Court to examine the statute under a stricter standard than mere rationality review because the statute affected the poor's fundamental interest in shelter. Justice White's opinion for the Court instructed, 405 U.S. at 74, 92 S.Ct. at 874:

> We do not denigrate the importance of decent, safe and sanitary housing. But the Constitution does not provide judicial remedies for every social and economic ill. We are unable to perceive in that document any constitutional guarantee of access to dwellings of a particular quality. * * * Absent constitutional mandate, the assurance of adequate housing and the definition of landlord-tenant relationships are legislative, not judicial, functions.

Similarly, in Dandridge v. Williams, 397 U.S. 471, 90 S.Ct. 1153, 25 L.Ed.2d 491 (1970), the Court held that the fact that public welfare assistance affected the most basic economic needs of the poor did not justify strict scrutiny.

In San Antonio Independent School District v. Rodriguez, 411 U.S. 1, 93 S.Ct. 1278, 36 L.Ed.2d 16 (1973), it became clear that Harlan's view that the Constitution did not recognize fundamental economic rights to food, shelter or education had won out. *Rodriguez* was a class action brought on behalf of poor and minority children challenging Texas' system of financing public education. Powell's opinion for the majority admitted that education was essential to the individual's progress in life, including the ability to exercise political liberties, but nevertheless upheld the Texas system under a mere rationality standard, 411 U.S. at 33–37, 93 S.Ct. at 1296–99.

> It is not the province of this Court to create substantive constitutional rights in the name of guaranteeing equal protection of the laws. Thus, the key to discovering whether education is 'fundamental' is not to be found in comparisons of the relative societal significance of education as opposed to subsistence or housing. * * * Rather, the answer lies in assessing whether there is a right to education explicitly or implicitly guaranteed by the Constitution.

> Education, of course, is not among the rights afforded explicit protection under our Federal Constitution. Nor do we find any basis for saying it is implicitly so protected. * * * It is appellees' contention * * * that education is distinguishable from other services and benefits provided by the State because it bears a peculiarly close relationship to other rights and liberties accorded protection under the Constitution. Specifically, they insist that education is itself a fundamental personal right because it is essential to the effective exercise of First Amendment freedoms and to intelligent utilization of the right to vote. * * *

* * *

> * * * [T]he logical limitations on appellees' nexus theory are difficult to perceive. How, for instance, is education to be distinguished from the significant personal interests in the basics of decent food and shelter? Empirical examination might well buttress an assumption that the ill-fed, ill-clothed, and ill-housed are among the most ineffective participants in the political process, and that they derive the least enjoyment from the benefits of the First Amendment. If so, appellees' thesis would cast serious doubt on the authority of *Dandridge v. Williams* and *Lindsey v. Normet*.

We have carefully considered each of the arguments supportive of the District Court's finding that education is a fundamental right or liberty and have found those arguments unpersuasive. * * *

Shapiro and *Rodriguez* mark the rise and fall of the notion that the Constitution protects "economic" rights to a share of society's resources as well as political liberties. See also DeShaney v. Winnebago County Dept. of Social Services, 489 U.S. 189, 109 S.Ct. 998, 103 L.Ed.2d 249 (1989) ("[The Due Process Clause] is phrased as a limitation on the State's power to act, not as a guarantee of certain minimal levels of safety and security. * * * [O]ur cases have recognized that the Due Process Clauses generally confer no affirmative right to governmental aid, even where such aid may be necessary to secure life, liberty, or property interests.").

> *Questions:* Compare the United States Supreme Court's view of entitlements to political and economic rights with the United Nation's aspirations in the *Declaration of Human Rights.* To what extent are the Supreme Court's and the United Nation's theories of rights consistent with Rawls' equality principle? With Rawls' difference principle?

2. In Rawls' "original position," individuals negotiate the social contract in ignorance of the role they are likely to play in their future society. They do not know if they are going to belong to the best-off or worst-off classes. Rawls believed rational persons choosing a social contract under such circumstances would choose to distribute social goods according to the maximin principle because (A Theory of Justice 154 (1971)):

> the person choosing * * * cares very little, if anything, for what he might gain above the minimum stipend that he can, in fact, be sure of by following the maximin rule. It is not worthwhile for him to take a chance for the sake of a further advantage, especially when it may turn out that he loses much that is important to him. * * * [T]he rejected alternatives have outcomes one can hardly accept. The situation involves grave risks.

> *Questions:* What does Rawls assume about people's willingness to accept risk in the original position? Is that assumption realistic?

3. As Rawls himself admitted, "[c]learly the maximin rule is not, in general, a suitable guide for choices under uncertainty. * * * Offhand, the most natural rule of choice would seem to be to compute the expectation of monetary gain for each decision and then to adopt the course of action with the highest prospect." A Theory of Justice 153 (1971). A utilitarian society that does not care particularly about the worst-off in society but only about maximizing the sum of all its members' utility would probably adopt the second rule, which can be characterized as maximizing the individual's expected *average* utility.

> *Question:* If persons drafting a social contract from Rawls' original position choose the principle of maximizing expected average utility, what does that imply about their attitudes towards risk?

4. The jurisprudence of rights reflected in *Rodriguez* indicates that, at least on the Constitutional level, the United States economic system is not organized to benefit the worst-off in society. At the legislative level, however, federal and state governments have adopted a number of institu-

tions designed to benefit those who are less well off, including welfare, Medicaid, and free public education at the primary and secondary levels.

Question: What do such programs suggest about human attitudes towards risk and preferences for rules for allocating wealth and income?

3. SOCIAL CONTRACT AND STATUS QUO: WHOSE CONSTITUTION?

A Theory of Justice attracted the widespread attention of both economists and political philosophers not only because of Rawls' claim that rational individuals drafting a social contract would choose the maximin principle for the distribution of economic goods but also because of his arguments concerning the circumstances under which that choice should be made. Rawls' theory depends on his assumptions concerning the "original position" from which rational individuals negotiate the terms of the social contract. In reading the following materials, consider how a change in the circumstances of the original position might change the likely terms to which rational individuals would consent.

J. RAWLS, A THEORY OF JUSTICE *
(1971).

* * * [T]he original position of equality corresponds to the state of nature in the traditional theory of the social contract. This original position is not, of course, thought of as an actual historical state of affairs, much less as a primitive condition of culture. It is understood as a purely hypothetical situation characterized so as to lead to a certain conception of justice. * * *

* * *

The idea of the original position is to set up a fair procedure so that any principles agreed to will be just. * * * Now in order to do this I assume that the parties are situated behind a veil of ignorance. They do not know how the various alternatives will affect their own particular case and they are obliged to evaluate principles solely on the basis of general considerations.

It is assumed, then, that the parties do not know certain kinds of particular facts. First of all, no one knows his place in society, his class position or social status; nor does he know his fortune in the distribution of natural assets and abilities, his intelligence and strength, and like. * * * More than this, I assume that the parties do not know the particular circumstances of their own society. That is, they do not know its economic or political situation, or the level of civilization and culture it has been able to achieve. * * *

* * *

The restrictions on particular information in the original position are * * * of fundamental importance. Without them we would not be able to work out any definite theory of justice at all. We would have to be content with a vague formula stating that justice is what would be agreed to without being able to say much, if anything, about the substance of the agreement itself. * * * The veil of ignorance makes possible a unanimous choice of a particular concept of justice. Without these limitations on knowledge the bargaining problem of the original position would be hopelessly complicated. Even if theoretically a solution were to exist, we would not, at present anyway, be able to determine it.

* * *

* * * [T]he reasons for the veil of ignorance go beyond mere simplicity. We want to define the original position so that we get the desired solution. If a knowledge of particulars is allowed, then the outcome is biased by arbitrary contingencies. As already observed, to each according to his threat advantage is not a principle of justice. If the original position is to yield agreements that are just, the parties must be fairly situated and treated equally as moral persons. The arbitrariness of the world must be corrected for by adjusting the circumstances of the initial contractual situation. * * *

Notes and Questions

1. Rawls gives two reasons why individuals in the original position should be denied information concerning their likely place in society as well as their likely abilities, talents, and advantages. The first reason is that ignorance is necessary in order to ensure that the terms of the social contract are just. Rawls believes that those who are strongest or most capable should not be allowed to exploit those advantages while negotiating the social contract. Recall Rawls' suggestion, above, that his two principles of justice "seem to be fair agreement on the basis of which those better endowed, or more fortunate in their social position, *neither of which we can be said to deserve,* could expect the willing cooperation of others" (emphasis added). The veil of ignorance ensures that persons in the original position bargain from a posture of equality as moral persons. "If no one knows his situation in society nor his natural assets * * * no one is in a position to tailor principles to his advantage." A Theory of Justice 139 (1971).

Question: Does the justice of the social contract negotiated behind a veil of ignorance depend on whether one agrees with Rawls' assertion that individuals do not deserve their social positions or natural endowments?

2. Rawls' second reason for arguing that the social contract should be drafted behind the veil of ignorance is that ignorance is a practical necessity to achieve unanimous agreement on the contract's terms.

Questions: How will bargaining among people who know their likely advantages and disadvantages differ from bargaining among people in a position of ignorant equality? In which case will unanimous agreement be harder to achieve?

DRED SCOTT v. SANDFORD

Supreme Court of the United States, 1856.
60 U.S. (19 How.) 393, 15 L.Ed. 691.

TANEY, CHIEF JUSTICE.

* * *

The plaintiff in error, who was also the plaintiff in the court below, was, with his wife and children, held as slaves by the defendant, in the State of Missouri; and he brought this action in the Circuit Court of the United States for that district, to assert the title of himself and his family to freedom.

The declaration * * * contains the averment necessary to give the court jurisdiction; that he and the defendant are citizens of different States; that is, that he is a citizen of Missouri, and the defendant a citizen of New York.

* * *

The question is simply this: Can a negro, whose ancestors were imported into this country, and sold as slaves, become a member of the political community formed and brought into existence by the Constitution of the United States, and as such become entitled to all the rights, and privileges, and immunities, guaranteed by that instrument to the citizen? One of which rights is the privilege of suing in a court of the United States in the cases specified in the Constitution.

* * *

The words "people of the United States" and "citizens" are synonymous terms, and mean the same thing. They both describe the political body who, according to our republican institutions, form the sovereignty, and who hold the power and conduct the Government through their representatives. They are what we familiarly call the "sovereign people," and every citizen is one of this people, and a constituent member of this sovereignty. The question before us is, whether the class of persons described in the plea in abatement compose a portion of this people, and are constituent members of this sovereignty? We think they are not, and that they are not included, and were not intended to be included, under the word "citizens" in the Constitution, and can therefore claim none of the rights and privileges which that instrument provides for and secures to citizens of the United States. On the contrary, they were at that time considered as a subordinate and inferior class of beings, who had been subjugated by the dominant race, and, whether emancipated or not, yet remained subject to their authority, and had no rights or privileges but such as those who held the power and the Government might choose to grant them.

It is not the province of the court to decide upon the justice or injustice, the policy or impolicy, of these laws. The decision of that question belonged to the political or law-making power; to those who formed the sovereignty and framed the Constitution. The duty of the court is, to interpret the instrument they have framed, with the best lights we can obtain on the subject, and to administer it as we find it, according to its true intent and meaning when it was adopted.

* * *

In the opinion of the court, the legislation and histories of the times, and the language used in the Declaration of Independence, show, that neither the class of persons who had been imported as slaves, nor their descendants, whether they had become free or not, were then acknowledged as a part of the people, nor intended to be included in the general words used in that memorable instrument.

* * *

The language of the Declaration of Independence is equally conclusive:

It begins by declaring that, "when in the course of human events it becomes necessary for one people to dissolve the political bands which have connected them with another, and to assume among the powers of the earth the separate and equal station to which the laws of nature and nature's God entitle them, a decent respect for the opinions of mankind requires that they should declare the causes which impel them to the separation."

It then proceeds to say: "We hold these truths to be self-evident: that all men are created equal; that they are endowed by their Creator with certain unalienable rights; that among them is life, liberty, and the pursuit of happiness; that to secure these rights, Governments are instituted, deriving their just powers from the consent of the governed."

The general words above quoted would seem to embrace the whole human family, and if they were used in a similar instrument at this day would be so understood. But it is too clear for dispute, that the enslaved African race were not intended to be included, and formed no part of the people who framed and adopted this declaration * *,*.

* * *

* * * [T]here are two clauses in the Constitution which point directly and specifically to the negro race as a separate class of persons, and show clearly that they were not regarded as a portion of the people or citizens of the Government then formed.

One of these clauses reserves to each of the thirteen States the right to import slaves until the year 1808, if it thinks proper. * * * And by the other provision the States pledge themselves to each other to maintain the right of property of the master, by delivering up to him any slave who may have escaped from his service, and be found within their respective territories. * * * And these two provisions show, conclusively, that neither the description of persons therein referred to, nor their descendants, were embraced in any of the other provisions of the Constitution; for certainly these two clauses were not intended to confer on them or their posterity the blessings of liberty, or any of the personal rights so carefully provided for the citizen.

* * *

Upon the whole, therefore, it is the judgment of this court, that it appears by the record before us that the plaintiff in error is not a citizen of Missouri, in the sense in which that word is used in the Constitution; and that the Circuit Court of the United States, for that reason, had no jurisdiction in the case, and could give no judgment in it. Its judgment for the defendant must, consequently, be reversed, and a mandate issued, directing the suit to be dismissed for want of jurisdiction.

Notes and Questions

1. In Rawls' vision of the original position, individuals are stripped to their moral beings and negotiate the basic terms of society in ignorance of their future places in it. Such an arrangement necessarily leads to concern for those less well off in society, since each party to the agreement risks ending up in that position.

The Constitution of the United States was drafted by individuals aware of their own circumstances, which included: a large portion of the population lived in slavery and were regarded as property rather than citizens; women were presumed unfit to govern themselves or enjoy the full rights of citizenship, including the right to vote; and a small propertied class enjoyed a disproportionate amount of wealth, power, and privilege.

Question: How are those circumstances reflected in the Constitution?

2. In addition to arguing that individuals in the original position should have no knowledge of their likely place in the society they are forming, Rawls also argued (A Theory of Justice 137 (1971)):

> The persons in the original position [should] have no information as to which generation they belong. These broader restrictions on knowledge are appropriate in part because questions of social justice arise between generations as well as within them, for example, the questions of the appropriate rate of capital saving and of the conservation of natural resources and the environment of nature. * * * [I]n order to carry through the idea of the original position, the parties * * * must choose principles the consequences of which they are prepared to live with whatever generation they turn out to belong to.

Questions: Members of future generations could not participate in the U.S. Constitution's drafting. What provision does the Constitution make for future generations' interests? Must tomorrow's Americans rely upon the altruism and generosity of today's? Consider future Americans' interests in present policy on education, the federal deficit, and the environment. If future generations do not participate in negotiating the social contract, how is that likely to affect society's structure?

3. A compelling aspect of Rawls' theory is his normative claim that individuals should choose a social contract behind a veil of ignorance so that "no one is advantaged or disadvantaged in the choice of principles by the outcome of natural chance or the contingency of social circumstances" and all negotiate as equal "moral persons". A Theory of Justice 12 (1971). Individuals should not be allowed to exploit their natural advantages such as strength, energy, or intelligence. Those are acquired only through "chance;" they are not "deserved."

In Sierra Club v. Morton, 405 U.S. 727, 92 S.Ct. 1361, 31 L.Ed.2d 636 (1972), the Sierra Club challenged a U.S. Forest Service plan to allow Walt Disney Enterprises, Inc. to build a ski resort and summer recreation area in the Mineral King Valley adjacent to Sequoia National Park. Sierra Club alleged that the development "would destroy or otherwise adversely affect the scenery, natural and historic objects and wildlife of the park and would impair the enjoyment of the park for future generations." 405 U.S. at 734, 92 S.Ct. at 1365. The Supreme Court upheld the Ninth Circuit's determination that the Club lacked standing under the Administrative Procedure Act because none of the Club's individual members had alleged injury, and the Club could not sue as a general representative of the public interest.

In an impassioned dissent, Justice Douglas declared, 405 U.S. at 741–43, 752, 92 S.Ct. at 1369–70, 1374:

> The critical question of "standing" would be simplified and also put neatly in focus if we fashioned a federal rule that allowed environmental issues to be litigated before federal agencies or federal courts in the name of the inanimate object about to be despoiled, defaced, or invaded by roads and bulldozers * * *

> Inanimate objects are sometimes parties in litigation. A ship has a legal personality * * * The ordinary corporation is a "person" for purposes of the adjudicatory processes, whether it represents proprietary, spiritual, aesthetic, or charitable causes.

> So it should be as respects valleys, alpine meadows, rivers, lakes, estuaries, beaches, ridges, groves of trees, swampland, or even air that feels the destructive pressures of modern technology and modern life. * * *

* * *

> * * * [E]nvironmental issues should be tendered by the inanimate object itself. Then there will be assurances that all of the forms of life which it represents will stand before the court—the pileated woodpecker as well as the coyote and bear, the lemmings as well as the trout in the streams. * * *

Questions: The Administrative Procedure Act, like many federal statutes, provides a cause of action for "a *person* suffering legal wrong." 5 U.S.C. § 702. As Justice Douglas pointed out, the American legal system recognizes as "persons" not only natural persons but also certain legal personalities such as corporations. The concept of person is not, however, normally extended to wildlife, vegetation, or natural wonders. From an economic perspective, does that make sense? Does it matter if society's goal is wealth maximization or utility maximization? Does Justice Douglas' dissent in *Sierra* imply that trout and coyotes are also moral persons behind the veil of ignorance?

4. Because Rawls' original position of ignorant equality is not a real state, it is a normative act to draft a social contract as if it were. How far one wants to proceed towards ignorant equality in constitutional bargaining is a question for the philosopher more than the economist. The economist takes preexisting distributions of advantages and disadvantages as given. She is concerned with allocating resources efficiently given the status quo, not with the justice of the status quo.

B. TRANSLATING INDIVIDUAL PREFERENCES INTO PUBLIC CHOICES: VOTING RULES AS INDICIA OF SOCIAL WELFARE

Identifying the goal of state coercion is only the first step in drafting a social contract. The next is deciding which resource allocations best accomplish that goal. Consider a beneficial but polluting technology like the internal combustion engine. How should a utilitarian state regulate such a technology? The aim is the greatest possible increase in utility (or, at least, the minimum decrease). The difficulty is determining which allocation of resources produces the most utility. How much disutility does society suffer from dirty air, and how much utility does it gain from the automobile? Individual preferences for clean air and mobility must somehow be translated into optimal social choices.

In markets, individuals express their preferences for goods and services through their willingness and ability to pay. In the political arena, individuals express their preferences for the goods produced by government—pollution regulation, police protection, public education—through voting. This section examines from an economic perspective the problems associated with using votes to translate individual preferences into social choices.

The discussion below divides voting rules into two broad categories. The first is unanimity voting, which requires that each member of a group consent to a proposed group action. The second category includes any rule that allows action based on less-than-unanimous agreement, such as plurality voting, traditional majority voting, and "supermajority" provisions requiring two-thirds or three-quarters approval. Under the rule of unanimity the group will only act if no one is left worse off as a result. Unanimity voting ensures that social choices pass Pareto's strict criteria. Unfortunately, reaching unanimous agreement can be difficult and time consuming and sometimes impossible. Allowing group action based on majority rule makes group decisionmaking easier and simpler and increases the range of actions that the group can approve. However, as discussed below, less-than-unanimity voting creates a risk of group action that actually decreases overall utility.

The cases presented below provide contexts for discussing the efficiency implications of group decisions under unanimity and less-than-unanimity voting. Those implications are important because the United States political system relies heavily on voting rules (and especially less-than-unanimity rules) for making public choices. For example, citizens vote to elect Representatives to Congress under a plurality system; Congress in turn votes on public legislation, generally under traditional majority rule. Rational maximizers drafting a social contract would want to consider the costs and risks of voting rules in deciding how group decisions should be made. The final section of this Chapter applies public choice analysis to the United States Constitution and considers how that document's provisions may minimize the costs of group action and the risk of erroneous social choices.

1. THE RULE OF UNANIMITY

A series of Supreme Court cases decided in the first half of the twentieth century appeared to assume that the Sixth Amendment right to a jury trial in federal criminal cases included a right to a unanimous jury verdict for conviction. See Andres v. United States, 333 U.S. 740, 748–49, 68 S.Ct. 880, 884–85, 92 L.Ed. 1055 (1948); Patton v. United States, 281 U.S. 276, 288–90, 50 S.Ct. 253, 254–55, 74 L.Ed. 854 (1930); Hawaii v. Mankichi, 190 U.S. 197, 211–12 (1903). That question was revisited in Apodaca v. Oregon and a related case, Johnson v. Louisiana, 406 U.S. 356, 96 S.Ct. 1620, 32 L.Ed.2d 152 (1972), where the Court addressed directly whether the Constitution required a unanimous verdict for criminal conviction and whether, if such a right existed under federal law, it should be incorporated under the Fourteenth Amendment and applied to criminal convictions in State courts as well.

APODACA v. OREGON

Supreme Court of the United States, 1972.
406 U.S. 404, 92 S.Ct. 1628, 32 L.Ed.2d 184.

WHITE, JUSTICE.

Robert Apodaca, Henry Morgan Cooper, Jr., and James Arnold Madden were convicted respectively of assault with a deadly weapon, burglary in a dwelling, and grand larceny before separate Oregon juries, all of which returned less-than-unanimous verdicts. The vote in the cases of Apodaca and Madden was 11–1, while the vote in the case of Cooper was 10–2, the minimum requisite vote under Oregon law for sustaining a conviction. After their convictions had been affirmed by the Oregon Court of Appeals, and review had been denied by the Supreme Court of Oregon, all three sought review in this Court upon a claim that conviction of crime by a less-than-unanimous jury violates the right to trial by jury in criminal cases specified by the Sixth Amendment and made applicable to the States by the Fourteenth. We granted certiorari to consider this claim, which we now find to be without merit.

* * *

Like the requirement that juries consist of 12 men, the requirement of unanimity arose during the Middle Ages and had become an accepted feature of the common-law jury by the 18th century. But * * * "the relevant constitutional history casts considerable doubt on the easy assumption * * * that if a given feature existed in a jury at common law in 1789, then it was necessarily preserved in the Constitution." * * *

* * *

Our inquiry must focus upon the function served by the jury in contemporary society. * * * [T]he purpose of trial by jury is to prevent oppression by the Government by providing a "safeguard against the corrupt or overzealous prosecutor and against the compliant, biased, or eccentric judge." * * * Requiring unanimity would obviously produce hung juries in some situations where nonunanimous juries will convict or acquit. But in either case, the interest of the defendant in having the judgment of his peers interposed between himself and the officers of the State who prosecute and judge him is equally well served.

* * *

Petitioners also cite quite accurately a long line of decisions of this Court upholding the principle that the Fourteenth Amendment requires jury panels to reflect a cross section of the community. They then contend that unanimity is a necessary precondition for effective application of the cross-section requirement, because a rule permitting less than unanimous verdicts will make it possible for convictions to occur without the acquiescence of minority elements within the community.

There are two flaws in this argument. One is petitioners' assumption that every distinct voice in the community has a right to be represented on every jury and a right to prevent conviction of a defendant in any case. * * * No group * * * has the right to block convictions; it has only the right to participate in the overall legal processes by which criminal guilt and innocence are determined.

We also cannot accept petitioners' second assumption—that minority groups, even when they are represented on a jury, will not adequately represent the viewpoint of those groups simply because they maybe outvoted in the final result. They will be present during all deliberations, and their views will be heard. We cannot assume that the majority of the jury will refuse to weigh the evidence and reach a decision upon rational grounds, just as it must now do in order to obtain unanimous verdicts, or that a majority will deprive a man of his liberty on the basis of prejudice when a minority is presenting a reasonable argument in favor of acquittal. * * *

* * *

Judgment affirmed.

POWELL, JUSTICE, concurring.

* * *

In an unbroken line of cases reaching back into the late 1800's, the Justices of this Court have recognized, virtually without dissent, that unanimity is one of the indispensable features of *federal* jury trial. * * * It therefore seems to me, in accord with both history and precedent, that the Sixth Amendment requires a unanimous jury verdict to convict in a federal criminal trial.

* * *

The question, therefore, that should be addressed in this case is whether unanimity is in fact so fundamental to the essentials of jury trial that this particular requirement of the Sixth Amendment is necessarily binding on the States under the Due Process Clause of the Fourteenth Amendment. An affirmative answer * * * would give unwarranted and unwise scope to the incorporation doctrine as it applies to the due process right of state criminal defendants to trial by jury.

* * *

* * * In an age in which empirical study is increasingly relied upon as a foundation for decisionmaking, one of the more obvious merits of our federal system is the opportunity it affords each State, if its people so choose, to become a "laboratory" and to experiment with a range of trial and procedural alternatives. * * * [This] might well lead to valuable innovations with respect to determining—fairly and more expeditiously—the guilt or innocence of the accused.

* * * I see no constitutional infirmity in the provision adopted by the people of Oregon. It * * * appears to be patterned on a provision of the American Law Institute's Code of Criminal Procedure. A similar decision has been echoed more recently in England where the unanimity requirement was abandoned by statutory enactment. Less-than-unanimous verdict provisions also have been viewed with approval by the American Bar Association's Criminal Justice Project. Those who have studied the jury mechanism and recommended deviation from the historic rule of unanimity have found a number of considerations to be significant. Removal of the unanimity requirement could well minimize the potential for hung juries occasioned either by bribery or juror irrationality. Furthermore, the rule that juries must speak with a single voice often leads, not to full agreement among the 12 but to agreement by none and compromise by all, despite the frequent absence of a rational basis for such compromise. Quite apart from whether Justices sitting on this Court would have deemed advisable the adop-

tion of any particular less-than-unanimous jury provision, I think that considerations of this kind reflect a legitimate basis for experimentation and deviation from the federal blueprint.

* * *

DOUGLAS, JUSTICE, dissenting.

* * *

The plurality approves a procedure which diminishes the reliability of a jury. First, it eliminates the circumstances in which a minority of jurors (a) could have rationally persuaded the entire jury to acquit, or (b) while unable to persuade the majority to acquit, nonetheless could have convinced them to convict only on a lesser-included offense. * * *

The diminution of verdict reliability flows from the fact that nonunanimous juries need not debate and deliberate as fully as must unanimous juries. As soon as the requisite majority is attained, further consideration is not required either by Oregon or by Louisiana even though the dissident jurors might, if given the chance, be able to convince the majority. * * * Indeed, if a necessary majority is immediately obtained, then no deliberation at all is required in these States. (There is a suggestion that this may have happened in the 10—2 verdict rendered in only 41 minutes in Apodaca's case.) To be sure, * * * initial majorities normally prevail in the end, but about a tenth of the time the rough-and-tumble of the jury room operates to reverse completely their preliminary perception of guilt or innocence. The Court now extracts from the jury room this automatic check against hasty factfinding by relieving jurors of the duty to hear out fully the dissenters.

It is said that there is no evidence that majority jurors will refuse to listen to dissenters whose votes are unneeded for conviction. Yet human experience teaches that polite and academic conversation is no substitute for the earnest and robust argument necessary to reach unanimity. As mentioned earlier, in Apodaca's case, whatever courtesy dialogue transpired could not have lasted more than 41 minutes. * * *

* * *

Moreover, even where an initial majority wins the dissent over to its side, the ultimate result in unanimous-jury States may nonetheless reflect the reservations of uncertain jurors. I refer to many compromise verdicts on lesser-included offenses and lesser sentences. Thus, even though a minority may not be forceful enough to carry the day, their doubts may nonetheless cause a majority to exercise caution. Obviously, however, in Oregon and Louisiana, dissident jurors will not have the opportunity through full deliberation to temper the opposing faction's degree of certainty of guilt.

The new rule also has an impact on cases in which a unanimous jury would have neither voted to acquit nor to convict, but would have deadlocked. In unanimous-jury States, this occurs about 5.6% of the time. * * *

* * *

Notes and Questions

1. In his concurrence in *Apodaca,* Justice Powell argued that, while the Sixth Amendment required a unanimous verdict in federal criminal cases, that requirement should not be imposed on states under the Fourteenth Amendment because it would discourage state experimentation with different means of determining the defendant's guilt or innocence "more expeditiously."

> *Question:* What advantages of allowing 10–2 convictions rather than requiring unanimity does *Apodaca* suggest?

2. The requirement of unanimity was once typical of shareholder voting on "fundamental" corporate changes. Under nineteenth-century common law, a corporation could not dissolve, merge, amend its charter, or sell substantially all its assets unless each and every shareholder agreed to such action. The Supreme Court discussed the traditional rule of shareholder unanimity in Voeller v. Neilston Co., 311 U.S. 531, 535 n. 6, 61 S.Ct. 376, 377 n. 6, 85 L.Ed. 322 (1941): "At common law, unanimous shareholder consent was a prerequisite to fundamental changes in the corporation. This made it possible for an arbitrary minority to establish a nuisance value for its shares by refusal to cooperate. To meet the situation, legislatures authorized the making of changes by majority vote."

> *Question:* To appreciate what the Court meant by the "nuisance value" of refusing to cooperate, consider the following example. A corporation has ten shareholders, each of whom owns one share. Each share has a market value of $8. A third party offers to buy the firm for $20 per share. What strategic opportunities would a requirement of unanimity present to each of the shareholders?

3. In the nineteenth century, the typical corporation was a relatively small entity controlled by a single individual or group of individuals who ran the business together and dealt regularly with one another. In the twentieth century the typical corporation became larger, with a greater number of shareholders, some of whom might not be involved in the business at all. Under the typical modern state corporation statute, a corporation may dissolve, merge, or sell all its assets with the approval of from 50% to 75% of the firm's shareholders.

> *Questions:* How does increasing the size of a decisionmaking body affect the time spent in decisionmaking? The likelihood of deadlock? The probability of strategic hold-out behavior? Can the increased size and complexity of twentieth century corporations explain why state legislatures abandoned shareholder unanimity in favor of less-than-unanimity rules? How are decisionmaking time, deadlock, and hold-out behavior changed by reducing the voting requirement from unanimity to 75% group approval? From 75% to 51% approval?

4. A footnote to Justice White's opinion in *Apodaca,* at 406 U.S. at 407–08 n.2, 92 S.Ct. at 1631–32 (1971), noted that while the origins of the common-law rule requiring jury unanimity rule were obscure, one possible explanation was:

[J]ury unanimity arose out of the medieval concept of consent. Indeed, "(t)he word consent (*consensus*) carried with it the idea of concordia or unanimity * * * ." Even in 14th century Parliaments there is evidence that a majority vote was deemed insufficient to bind the community or individual members of the community to a legal decision; a unanimous decision was preferred. It was only in the 15th century that the decisionmaking process in Parliament became avowedly majoritarian, as the ideal of unanimity became increasingly difficult to attain.

Compare the medieval focus on unanimity with Justice Harlan's argument in Jacobson v. Massachusetts, 197 U.S. 11, 37–38, 25 S.Ct. 358, 366–69, 49 L.Ed. 643 (1905):

> We are not prepared to hold that a minority * * * may thus defy the will of its constituted authorities, acting in good faith for all, under the legislative sanction of the State. If such be the privilege of a minority then a like privilege would belong to each individual of the community, and the spectacle would be presented of the welfare and safety of an entire population being subordinated to the notions of a single individual who chooses to remain a part of that population.

Question: From the perspective of utility maximization, how does the distinction between unanimity and less-than-unanimity voting rules resemble the distinction between the Pareto and the Kaldor–Hicks criteria?

5. Justice White's opinion for the majority in *Apodaca* suggested that allowing less-than-unanimous jury verdicts did not necessarily exclude the views of minority dissenters, as they might still voice their opinions during the jury deliberation process. Justice Brennan wrote a dissent in *Apodaca*, in which he argued, 406 U.S. at 596, 92 S.Ct. at 1651:

> When verdicts must be unanimous, no member of the jury may be ignored by the others. When less than unanimity is sufficient, consideration of minority views may become nothing more than a matter of majority grace. In my opinion, the right of all groups in this Nation to participate in the criminal process means the right to have their voices heard. A unanimous verdict vindicates that right. Majority verdicts could destroy it.

Question: Whose arguments are more persuasive on the issue of minority participation in the decisionmaking process, Justice White's or Justice Brennan's?

6. Justices Powell and Douglas subscribed in their opinions to belief that divided juries often produce "compromise verdicts," convicting the defendant of a lesser-included offense or convicting the defendant but imposing a relatively light sentence. Justice Powell appeared to regard compromise verdicts as undesirable, while Justice Douglas regarded them as beneficial.

Questions: What are the advantages and disadvantages of encouraging compromise? Is compromise more likely under a rule of unanimity or under a rule allowing less-than-unanimous verdicts?

7. Where jury unanimity is required, unanimous agreement is essential for *either* acquittal or conviction. Under the double jeopardy clause, if a jury fails to reach a unanimous verdict a prosecutor is free to treat the verdict as a nullity rather than as an acquittal and to seek a new trial. While a deadlock does not preclude a second trial, it does mean that the first trial was in a sense "wasted."

> *Questions:* Who is more likely to benefit from the requirement that criminal jury verdicts be unanimous, the prosecution or the accused? If hung juries squander the resources allocated to trial, why should Justice Douglas be concerned that allowing less-than-unanimous jury verdicts might produce *fewer* deadlocks?

2. SUPERMAJORITY, MAJORITY, AND PLURALITY VOTING RULES

Given the practical difficulties of requiring unanimity, especially when large numbers are involved, it should not be surprising that unanimity voting is the exception in most circumstances where groups are called upon to make decisions. The United States political system makes great use of less-than-unanimity voting rules, including plurality, traditional majority, and supermajority rules. Less-than-unanimity rules share common characteristics that distinguish them sharply from decisions reached unanimously. This section considers some of the economic implications of state action over a dissenting minority's protests.

a. *Arrow's Theorem and Solutions to the Indeterminacy of Majority Rule*

One political authority that frequently uses less-than-unanimous decisions as a basis for group action is the appellate court. When appellate judges disagree, the judgment normally is determined by what a majority of the panel sitting on the case believe the case's outcome should be. The court's opinion will be the opinion with the support of the largest number of judges concurring in the judgment.

The less-than-unanimity voting rules applied by appellate courts allow courts to reach more decisions more quickly than a rule of unanimity would. At the same time, appellate decisionmaking suggests some of the problems associated with majority rule.

F. EASTERBROOK, WAYS OF CRITICIZING THE COURT *
95 Harv.L.Rev. 802 (1982).

* * *

Everyone thinks that the Court should be consistent. Consistency is, it seems, an essential attribute of any institution that decides on the basis of statutes, constitutions, and criteria other than the Justices' preferences. The Court cannot logically say in December that a criminal defendant has a "valued right" to a jury verdict and in May that the deprivation of this right is irrelevant. Similarly, it cannot say that freedom of speech is a more important constitutional value than a defendant's right to a fair trial, that fair trial is more important than military preparedness, and that military preparedness is more important than free speech. To do so is to say that at least one decision is wrong or that they do not rest on the same document. Thus the propositions that decisions must be consistent, that principles must be followed unless the decisions announcing them are overruled, and that decisions rest on principles of general applicability are put by the Court's critics as logical implications of the proposition that the Court is supposed to follow statutes and a written Constitution. If this is so, an inconsistent Court is a willful, irresponsible Court.

Yet while admitting that it is bound by the written documents, the Court continues to hand down inconsistent decisions, to dishonor precedents, and to change the weight attached to particular constitutional and statutory provisions or the values derived from them. * * *

I * * * offer a different perspective. Inconsistency is inevitable, in the strong sense of that word, no matter how much the Justices may disregard their own preferences, no matter how carefully they may approach their tasks, no matter how skilled they may be. * * * [D]emands for perfect consistency can not be fulfilled, and it is inappropriate to condemn the Court's performance as an institution simply by pointing out that it sometimes, even frequently, contradicts itself.

The argument in the following pages is based on the developing theory of public choice. The theory is an outgrowth of the work of Kenneth Arrow, whose book *Social Choice and Individual Values,* published in 1951, prompted an explosion of work by economists and political scientists that has become a separate discipline. Arrow's followers began to examine with great care the operation of all systems for making collective choices: that is, methods of pooling individual preferences and decisions to arrive at a decision for the group. This work almost always concerns voting mechanisms * * *.

* * *

The Court decides cases by majority vote. Its ability to make consistent, principled decisions therefore depends on the existence of a system of voting that produces such outcomes. Yet voting systems are subject to many problems. First, decisions produced by voting will tend to be unstable even when the same voters participate in all decisions; second, the sequence in which issues are decided frequently controls the outcome of the process * * *.

* * *

Suppose the Justices have studied the establishment clause, and different Justices reach different conclusions about the meaning of that provision. * * * Three Justices conclude that all public acts that directly or indirectly aid religion violate the clause; call this Position A for absolutism. Three more conclude that any public act is constitutional if it is neutral between religious and nonreligious associations (N for neutrality). The remaining three conclude that the clause requires balancing, in which the purpose of the act, its effect on religion, and the extent of entanglement between state and religion all play a role (B for balancing). It is a detail that three Justices have each position; the problem would be the same (although the presentation would be more complicated) if the numbers were different and there were more than three interpretations of the clause.

Each group of Justices, moreover, has a preference between the two positions taken by the others. The Justices who take position N (neutrality) [group 1] may believe that position B (balancing) more accurately reflects the design of the framers an the Court's cases than does position A (absolute ban on aid). The Justices who take position B [group 2] may conclude that A is more nearly correct than N. And the Justices who take position A [group 3] may conclude that N is more nearly correct than B. This last is not as odd as it first appears: these Justices conclude that the clause embodies a bright line test and that any attempt at balancing is worse than either bright line test because it immerses the Court in the details of a process properly left to the legislature.

* * * When a case under the establishment clause comes before the Court, the Justices always vote according to their conclusions. But this voting will not lead them to agree on a rule, no matter how they go about the task. They cannot settle on rule A, because the Justices in groups 2 and 3 (a majority) believe that rule B is a more accurate construction of the clause than rule A. Yet rule B cannot be chosen either, because a majority (those in groups 1 and 3) would select rule N over rule B. And, to complete the cycle, a majority (in groups 1 and 2) would select rule A over rule N. No matter what the Court does, a majority would always vote to change the rule.

* * *

* * * One of the most interesting findings of the public choice literature is that the decisions of any group are sensitive to the order in which it considers the options. One theorem states that it is possible to construct a decision path that ends with *any* rule, as long as each step is taken by majority vote and, at every step, earlier decisions are respected. * * *

* * *

The conclusion of this analysis is unsettling, as any application of Arrow's Theorem is unsettling. * * * Any general criticism of the Court, as an institution, for rendering inconsistent decisions is untenable. At least some inconsistency, and probably a great deal of inconsistency, is inevitable.

* * *

Notes and Questions

1. One of the most important developments in public choice theory was Kenneth Arrow's 1951 publication of his General Possibility Theorem, which is now widely known, because of his conclusions, as "Arrow's Impossibility Theorem." Arrow demonstrated that under certain conditions, groups attempting to choose among three or more alternatives by majority voting may be unable to reach a consistent decision.

Consider the following example. Larry, Curly, and Mo have to decide what they are going to do together Sunday afternoon. The friends have three options; tour an art gallery, go to the baseball game, or attend a matinee symphony concert. Larry prefers art to baseball and baseball to concerts; Curly prefers baseball to concerts and concerts to art; and Mo prefers concerts to art and art to baseball. In other words, the three friends' preference rankings are as follows:

Larry: art > baseball > concert
Curly: baseball > concert > art
Mo: concert > art > baseball

If Larry, Curly, and Mo attempt to choose an alternative by voting between art, baseball, and a concert in a series of pairwise votes, they will be unable to reach a stable decision. When they vote between a trip to the art gallery and baseball, a majority (Larry and Mo) will prefer the art gallery. When they vote between baseball and a concert, a majority (Larry and Curly) will prefer baseball. And when they vote between a concert and art, a majority (Curly and Mo) will prefer a concert. But how can this be, if baseball is preferred to a concert, and art preferred to baseball? The results of majority voting in this case are an unstable "cycle" in which the group first chooses the art gallery, then the baseball game, then the concert, then art again, and so on *ad infinitum.*

Questions: What does cycling suggest about the accuracy of majority voting as a method of deciding which option maximizes group welfare? Does unanimity voting share this characteristic of majority voting?

2. Arrow's proof examined whether a voting system could aggregate individual orderings (rankings) of preferences into a social ordering exhibiting the five following desirable characteristics:

(1) *Unanimity* (the Pareto postulate): If an individual's preferences are unopposed by any other group member, that individual's preferences will be respected in the social ordering. That is, the social ordering will prefer any change that makes at least one person better off while making no one worse off.

(2) *Nondictatorship:* No individual's preference may be the preference of the social ordering if it is opposed by all other individuals. That means no single individual may dictate society's choice, no matter how strongly that individual may feel about the matter.

(3) *Range* (unrestricted domain): Individuals may rank alternatives in any order they choose; in other words, individuals may prefer

any one of the many possible orderings of art, baseball, and a concert. There are no restrictions on the kinds of orderings that are possible.

(4) *Independence of Irrelevant Alternatives:* Individuals' choices between two alternatives are based solely on their relative preferences for those alternatives and not on their opinions of other "irrelevant" alternatives not being voted on at the time. This condition is designed in part to ensure that individuals do not strategically misrepresent their choices in order to influence voting in subsequent elections.

(5) *Transitivity:* The social ordering produced by voting is a stable and consistent ordering of all alternatives. If art is preferred to baseball and baseball is preferred to concerts, then concerts cannot be preferred to art. When the social ordering is intransitive (as in the example presented in the preceding question), voting systems produce unstable results or "cycling."

Arrow demonstrated that it was impossible to produce a social preference ranking based on individual rankings meeting all five of the above characteristics, hence the modern label "Impossibility Theorem." For a relatively simple exposition of the proof, see K. Arrow, Social Choice and Individual Values (2d ed.1963) 96–100; D. Mueller, Public Choice II 385–87 (1989).

3. On July 1, 1981, the Supreme Court handed down two Fourth Amendment search and seizure cases: New York v. Belton, 453 U.S. 454, 101 S.Ct. 2860, 69 L.Ed.2d 768 (1981) and Robbins v. California, 453 U.S. 420, 101 S.Ct. 2841, 69 L.Ed.2d 744 (1981). In *Belton,* a New York State trooper stopped a car for speeding, found marijuana on the floor of the vehicle, arrested the occupants, and then found cocaine when he unzipped and searched the pockets of a jacket one of the passengers had left on the car's back seat. Justices Stewart, Burger, Powell, Blackmun, Rehnquist, and Stevens believed the search was constitutional, while Justices Brennan, Marshall, and White dissented.

In *Robbins,* California Highway Patrol officers stopped the petitioner's stationwagon because he was driving erratically and then found marijuana inside the passenger compartment of the car. The officers searched the car further by opening the tailgate and lifting up the door to a recessed luggage compartment that contained two packages wrapped in opaque plastic. The officers unwrapped the packages and found 15 pounds of marijuana. Justices Stewart, Burger, Powell, Brennan, Marshall, and White believed the search and seizure should be struck down as a Fourth Amendment violation, while Justices Blackmun, Rehnquist, and Stevens dissented that the search was constitutional.

Justice Steven's dissent in *Robbins* declared that "[i]t is quite clear to most of us that this case and *New York v. Belton* should be decided in the same way. Both cases involve automobile searches. In both cases, the automobiles had been lawfully stopped on the highway, the occupants had been lawfully arrested, and the officers had probable cause to believe that the vehicles contained contraband." 453 U.S. at 444, 101 S.Ct. at 2855. Justice Stevens went on to observe in a footnote that "Justice Blackmun, Justice Rehnquist, and I would uphold the searches in both cases; Justice Brennan, Justice White, and Justice Marshall would invalidate both searches. Only The Chief Justice [Burger], Justice Stewart, and Justice Powell reach the curious conclusion that a citizen has a greater privacy interest in a package of marihuana enclosed in a plastic wrapper than in the pocket of a leather jacket." 453 U.S. at 444 n.1, 101 S.Ct. at 2855 n.1.

Suppose that the justices' preferences were as follows. Justices Blackmun, Rehnquist, and Stevens preferred upholding both searches to striking down both but preferred striking down both searches to upholding one and striking down the other. Justices Brennan, White, and Marshall preferred striking down both searches to upholding one and striking down the other and preferred upholding one and striking down the other to upholding both searches. And Chief Justice Burger and Justices Stewart and Powell preferred upholding one and striking down the other to upholding both searches but preferred upholding both to striking down both.

Question: How might the opinions in *Robbins* and *Belton* illustrate Arrow's Theorem?

4. Although Arrow proved cycling is *possible* under majority voting when the conditions of unanimity, range, nondictatorship, and independence of irrelevant alternatives apply, cycling is not the *inevitable* result of majority voting. Returning to the facts presented in Question 1, suppose that Larry, Curly and Mo ranked their options as follows:

> Larry: art > baseball > concert
> Curly: baseball > concert > art
> Mo: concert > baseball > art

In such a case, baseball consistently wins in pairwise voting against either the art gallery or the symphony concert. An extreme example of the same point is three individuals who favor the same option—the art gallery, for instance—so that art wins consistently under majority voting. The more homogeneous voter preferences are, the more likely majority voting will produce stable results.

Questions: On what sorts of issues are voter preferences likely to be homogeneous? On what issues might preferences be very diverse, so that majority voting leads to unstable cycling? What effect has the number of available alternatives on voter homogeneity of preference?

———

Judge Easterbrook suggests that majority voting leads appellate courts to dishonor precedent and hand down inconsistent and unstable decisions. Yet another political authority that relies on majority voting—the representative legislature—appears to produce reasonably consistent and stable decisions. Legislatures rarely vote for a 65 m.p.h. speed limit this year, no speed limit at all the next, a 55 m.p.h. limit the third year, and a return to 65 m.p.h. the fourth. New laws tend to be passed in response to changing social conditions (for example, a gasoline shortage) rather than an inexplicable change of legislative heart.

It is puzzling that legislation exhibits such stability, especially when one considers that while judges are supposed to defer to precedent, legislators are free not to. Legislative stability hints at the limits of Arrow's Theorem. The three following cases provide contexts for discussing legislative solutions to cycling under majority rule. In reading them, consider whether the factors that lead to stable voting results also improve the *accuracy* of majority voting as a measure of social preferences.

KRAMER v. UNION FREE SCHOOL DISTRICT NO. 15

Supreme Court of the United States, 1969.
395 U.S. 621, 89 S.Ct. 1886, 23 L.Ed.2d 583.

WARREN, CHIEF JUSTICE.

In this case we are called on to determine whether § 2012 of the New York Education Law is constitutional. The legislation provides that in certain New York school districts residents who are otherwise eligible to vote in state and federal elections may vote in the school district election only if they (1) own (or lease) taxable real property within the district, or (2) are parents (or have custody of) children enrolled in the local public schools. Appellant, a bachelor who neither owns nor leases taxable real property, filed suit in federal court claiming that § 2012 denied him equal protection of the laws in violation of the Fourteenth Amendment. With one judge dissenting, a three-judge District Court dismissed appellant's complaint. Finding that § 2012 does violate the Equal Protection Clause of the Fourteenth Amendment, we reverse.

* * *

* * * Appellant agrees that the States have the power to impose reasonable citizenship, age, and residency requirements on the availability of the ballot. The sole issue in this case is whether the *additional* requirements of § 2012—requirements which prohibit some district residents who are otherwise qualified by age and citizenship from participating in district meetings and school board elections—violate the Fourteenth Amendment's command that no State shall deny persons equal protection of the laws.

* * * "(S)ince the right to exercise the franchise in a free and unimpaired manner is preservative of other basic civil and political rights, any alleged infringement of the right of citizens to vote must be carefully and meticulously scrutinized." This careful examination is necessary because statutes distributing the franchise constitute the foundation of our representative society. Any unjustified discrimination in determining who may participate in political affairs or in the selection of public officials undermines the legitimacy of representative government.

* * *

* * * Accordingly, when we are reviewing statutes which deny some residents the right to vote, the general presumption of constitutionality afforded state statutes and the traditional approval given state classifications if the Court can conceive of a "rational basis" for the distinctions made are not applicable. The presumption of constitutionality and the approval given "rational" classifications in other types of enactments are based on an assumption that the institutions of state government are structured so as to represent fairly all the people. However, when the challenge to the statute is in effect a challenge of this basic assumption, the assumption can no longer serve as the basis for presuming constitutionality. * * *

* * *

Appellant asserts that excluding him from participation in the district elections denies him equal protection of the laws. He contends that he and others of his class are substantially interested in and significantly affected by the school meeting decisions. All members of the community have an interest in the quality and structure of public education, appellant says, and he urges that "the decisions taken by local boards ... may have grave consequences to the entire population." Appellant also argues that the level of property taxation affects him, even though he does not own property, as property tax levels affect the price of goods and services in the community.

We turn therefore to question whether the exclusion is necessary to promote a compelling state interest. First, appellees argue that the State has a legitimate interest in limiting the franchise in school district elections to "members of the community of interest"—those "primarily interested in such elections." Second, appellees urge that the State may reasonably and permissibly conclude that "property taxpayers" (including lessees of taxable property who share the tax burden through rent payments) and parents of the children enrolled in the district's schools are those "primarily interested" in school affairs.

* * *

We need express no opinion as to whether the State in some circumstances might limit the exercise of the franchise to those "primarily interested" or "primarily affected." * * * For, assuming, *arguendo*, that New York legitimately might limit the franchise in these school district elections to those "primarily interested in school affairs," close scrutiny of the § 2012 classifications demonstrates that they do not accomplish this purpose with sufficient precision to justify denying appellant the franchise.

Whether classifications allegedly limiting the franchise to those resident citizens "primarily interested" deny those excluded equal protection of the laws depends, *inter alia,* on whether all those excluded are in fact substantially less interested or affected than those the statute includes. In other words, the classifications must be tailored so that the exclusion of appellant and members of his class is necessary to achieve the articulated state goal. Section 2012 does not meet the exacting standard of precision we require of statutes which selectively distribute the franchise. The classifications in § 2012 permit inclusion of many persons who have, at best, a remote and indirect interest, in school affairs and, on the other hand, exclude others who have a distinct and direct interest in the school meeting decisions.

    * * * The requirements of § 2012 are not sufficiently tailored to limiting the franchise to those "primarily interested" in school affairs to justify the denial of the franchise to appellant and members of his class.

    The judgment of the United States District Court for the Eastern District of New York is therefore reversed. The case is remanded for further proceedings consistent with this opinion.

    It is so ordered.

    STEWART, JUSTICE, dissenting.

* * *

    * * * So long as the classification is rationally related to a permissible legislative end, therefore—as are residence, literacy, and age requirements imposed with respect to voting—there is no denial of equal protection.

    Thus judged, the statutory classification involved here seems to me clearly to be valid. New York has made the judgment that local educational policy is best left to those persons who have certain direct and definable interests in that policy: those who are either immediately involved as parents of schoolchildren or who, as owners or lessees of taxable property are burdened with the local cost of funding school district operations. True, persons outside those classes may be genuinely interested in the conduct of a school district's business—just as commuters from New Jersey may be genuinely interested in the outcome of a New York City election. But unless this Court is to claim a monopoly of wisdom regarding the sound operation of school systems in the 50 States, I see no way to justify the conclusion that the legislative classification involved here is not rationally related to a legitimate legislative purpose. "There is no group more interested in the operation and management of the public schools than the taxpayers who support them and the parents whose children attend them."

    With good reason, the Court does not really argue the contrary. Instead, it strikes down New York's statute by asserting that the traditional equal protection standard is inapt in this case, and that a considerably stricter standard—under which classifications relating to "the franchise" are to be subjected to "exacting judicial scrutiny"— should be applied. But the asserted justification for applying such a standard cannot withstand analysis.

* * *

    * * * I am at a loss to understand how such reasoning is at all relevant to the present case. The voting qualifications at issue have

been promulgated, not by Union Free School District No. 15, but by the New York State Legislature, and the appellant is of course fully able to participate in the election of representatives in that body. There is simply no claim whatever here that the state government is not "structured so as to represent fairly all the people," including the appellant.

* * *

* * * I respectfully dissent from the Court's judgment and opinion.

Notes and Questions

1. Courts normally uphold state classifications of persons against challenges under the Equal Protection Clause if the classification is rationally related to a legitimate government objective. When a classification burdens an individual's fundamental rights, however, the court applies the more exacting standard of strict scrutiny and will strike down the classification scheme unless it is necessary to promote a compelling state objective. *Kramer* held that voting was a fundamental right under the Equal Protection clause and that § 2012's classification did not stand up to the strict scrutiny test.

Questions: According to the defendants in *Kramer,* the state objective promoted by § 2012 was restricting voting in rural school board elections to those community members most interested in the elections' outcomes. What sort of interests did plaintiff Kramer—a 31–year–old, childless, bachelor stockbroker living rent-free in his parents' home— claim in his district's school board elections? How do Kramer's interests compare with the interests of a homeowner with three school-age children?

2. Justice Stewart's dissent in *Kramer* observed that the plaintiff was fully able to participate in the election of members to the New York State Legislature, which passed § 2012's voting restriction.

Questions: Why might the New York State Legislature have wanted to restrict voting in school board elections? Could restricting voting on particular issues to those most directly affected improve the accuracy of voting outcomes so that voting decisions are more likely to maximize utility?

3. The appellants in *Kramer* did not dispute that states have the power to impose reasonable citizenship, age, and residency requirements for voting.

Question: How might such traditional voting restrictions serve the economic goal of maximizing utility?

4. Although the majority opinion in *Kramer* avoided the question of whether restricting elections to interested voters was a "legitimate" state objective, in subsequent cases the Court has upheld voter restrictions in elections to a limited-purpose governmental units.

Salyer Land Co. v. Tulare Lake Basin Water Storage District, 410 U.S. 719, 93 S.Ct. 1224, 35 L.Ed.2d 659 (1973), upheld a state voting restriction providing that only landowners within the Tulare Lake Basin Water

Storage District could elect officers to the District. The statute also determined the number of the landowner's votes according to the assessed value of his land. The Court emphasized that the water district had an extremely limited purpose and also that the district's decisions disproportionately affected the landowners who received nearly all the water benefits of the project but also bore all the costs, which were assessed against each landowner according to the benefits received.

Ball v. James, 451 U.S. 355, 101 S.Ct. 1811, 68 L.Ed.2d 150 (1981), upheld a similar provision restricting voting in elections to the Salt River Project Agricultural Improvement and Power District to landowners and apportioning votes according to the number of acres owned. However, unlike the Tulare Lake Basin District, the Salt River District raised the money for its water operations not by landowner assessments but primarily by selling electricity to hundreds of thousands of persons living in the metropolitan Phoenix area. The opinion in *Ball* emphasized the district's narrow purpose but appeared far less concerned about the impact of the district's policy decisions on non-voters, electricity consumers in particular. The Court upheld the restriction on the ground that it was a rational means for the state to pursue its objectives.

Question: From an economic perspective, which is more relevant to the accuracy of voting as a measure of group preferences, the limited purpose of a special government unit or the fact that the unit's impact is restricted to a particular group primarily affected by its policies?

5. Traditional voting is a binary process; the voter can express whether he is for or against a proposal, but cannot express *how much* he supports or opposes it. "Yea" may mean either enthusiastic endorsement or mild preference; "nay" may mean passionate opposition or slight disapproval.

Traditional voting's failure to reflect individuals' intensity of feeling makes voting a potentially inaccurate measure of group preferences and leads to the cycling possibilities implied by Arrow's Theorem. Attaching equal weight to the votes of the individual who slightly favors a proposal and the individual who vehemently opposes it presents an unavoidable risk of inefficient decisions. Consider how society's overall utility is reduced when a 51% majority approves an action which benefits each of them slightly but imposes great costs on each person in the 49% minority.

To measure the sum of individual preferences accurately, individuals must be able to express the degree of utility or disutility they associate with proposed actions. Suppose Larry, Curly and Mo could express the exact amount of utility (measured in utils [u.]) they derive from art, baseball, and concerts in the following fashion:

Larry: art (14 u.) > baseball (2 u.) > concert (1 u.)
Curly: baseball (8 u.) > concert (4 u.) > art (1 u.)
Mo: concert (3 u.) > baseball (2 u.) > art (1 u.)

Questions: Given cardinal information about individual preferences, can one determine which activity maximizes the total utility of the small society composed of Larry, Curly, and Mo? If the votes of each person were weighed by the amount of utility to be obtained by each outcome, would the results of pairwise voting be transitive or intransitive? Which activity would be selected under traditional binary pairwise majority voting?

6. Some voting methods attempt to take account of the intensity of voters' preferences. Consider cumulative or "point" voting schemes. Each voter is given a supply of votes and permitted to use them as she chooses. The voter may decide to cast a small number of ballots for a number of different proposals or candidates. Alternatively, the voter may pass on issues about which, or candidates about whom, she has no strong feelings and save her votes in order to cast them all at once for the single proposal or candidate she favors most strongly.

Corporate charters often provide for cumulative voting in directors' elections. For California corporations, this requirement is statutory. Section 708 of the California Corporations Code provides:

> [E]very shareholder * * * entitled to vote at any election of directors may cumulate such shareholder's votes and give one candidate a number of votes equal to the number of directors to be elected multiplied by the number of votes to which the shareholder's shares are normally entitled, or distribute the shareholder's votes on the same principle among as many candidates as the shareholder thinks fit * * *.

Suppose a California corporation has four shareholders. Each owns one share and is entitled to one vote. At the annual shareholders' meeting, an election is held to fill the four positions on the board of directors. One shareholder, John, desperately wants to elect Mary to the board. The other three shareholders—who hold a majority of shares and votes—agree to conspire against John and try to elect a slate of four other candidates to the Board.

Questions: What would be the result of an election under traditional majority rule? How does cumulative voting incorporate John's intense preference for Mary as a director?

7. Voting in legislative bodies such as the U.S. Congress generally takes the form of traditional majority voting rather than point or cumulative voting. Nevertheless, individual legislators can express the intensity of their feelings on proposed legislation to some degree when the legislature is faced with a series of votes on differing issues. In such a case, a representative can concentrate her voting power not by saving and pooling her own votes (an impossibility under traditional majority rule) but by pooling her votes with other representatives'. The intensely concerned representative can persuade other representatives to vote with her on the bills about which she feels most strongly if she agrees to vote with them on the bills about which they feel most strongly.

The practice of trading votes—also known as *logrolling*—allows a legislator to accumulate voting strength on an issue about which she cares deeply. By voting in favor of proposals she mildly dislikes, she buys allies to support the proposal she strongly favors. Exchanging votes thus provides an indirect means of reflecting the intensity of preferences.

Questions: Can logrolling improve the accuracy of majority voting in legislative bodies? Can logrolling improve the accuracy of general elections in which voters select representatives to the legislature?

8. A third method for voters to express their intensity of preference— the simple buying and selling of votes—is expressly forbidden by law. If votes were sold on the market, voting power on a particular issue would end up in the hands of the person who valued it most highly as measured by willingness to pay.

Questions: From an economic perspective, what are the advantages of allowing a market in votes? What are the distributional implications of the inalienability of voting rights and the "one-person-one-vote" norm?

GREGG v. GEORGIA

Supreme Court of the United States, 1976.
428 U.S. 153, 96 S.Ct. 2909, 49 L.Ed.2d 859.

STEWART, JUSTICE.

* * *

The petitioner, Troy Gregg, was charged with committing armed robbery and murder. In accordance with Georgia procedure in capital cases, the trial was in two stages, a guilt stage and a sentencing stage. The evidence at the guilt trial established that on November 21, 1973, the petitioner and a traveling companion, Floyd Allen, while hitchhiking north in Florida were picked up by Fred Simmons and Bob Moore. * * * A short time later the four men interrupted their journey for a rest stop along the highway. The next morning the bodies of Simmons and Moore were discovered in a ditch nearby.

* * *

* * * The jury found the petitioner guilty of two counts of armed robbery and two counts of murder.

At the penalty stage, which took place before the same jury, neither the prosecutor nor the petitioner's lawyer offered any additional evidence. Both counsel, however, made lengthy arguments dealing generally with the propriety of capital punishment under the circumstances and with the weight of the evidence of guilt. The trial judge instructed the jury that it could recommend either a death sentence or a life prison sentence on each count. The judge further charged the jury that in determining what sentence was appropriate the jury was free to consider the facts and circumstances, if any, presented by the parties in mitigation or aggravation.

* * *

* * * [T]he jury returned verdicts of death on each count.

* * *

We address initially the basic contention that the punishment of death for the crime of murder is, under all circumstances, "cruel and unusual" in violation of the Eighth and Fourteenth Amendments of the Constitution. * * *

* * * [U]ntil *Furman v. Georgia,* the Court never confronted squarely the fundamental claim that the punishment of death always, regardless of the enormity of the offense or the procedure followed in imposing the sentence, is cruel and unusual punishment in violation of the Constitution. Although this issue was presented and addressed in *Furman,* it was not resolved by the Court. Four Justices would have held that capital punishment is not unconstitutional *per se;* two Justices would have reached the opposite conclusion; and three Justices, while agreeing that the statutes then before the Court were invalid as applied, left open the question whether such punishment may ever be imposed. We now hold that the punishment of death does not invariably violate the Constitution.

* * *

We now consider whether Georgia may impose the death penalty on the petitioner in this case.

While *Furman* did not hold that the infliction of the death penalty *per se* violates the Constitution's ban on cruel and unusual punishments, it did recognize that the penalty of death is different in kind from any other punishment imposed under our system of criminal justice. Because of the uniqueness of the death penalty, *Furman* held that it could not be imposed under sentencing procedures that created a substantial risk that it would be inflicted in an arbitrary and capricious manner. * * * [T]he death sentences examined by the Court in *Furman* were "cruel and unusual in the same way that being struck by lightening is cruel and unusual. * * * [T]he Eighth and Fourteenth Amendments cannot tolerate the infliction of a sentence of death under legal systems that permit this unique penalty to be so wantonly and freakishly imposed."

Furman mandates that where discretion is afforded a sentencing body on a matter so grave as the determination of whether a human life should be taken or spared, that discretion must be suitably directed and limited so as to minimize the risk of wholly arbitrary and capricious action.

* * *

Jury sentencing has been considered desirable in capital cases in order "to maintain a link between contemporary community values and the penal system * * * ." But it creates special problems. Much of the information that is relevant to the sentencing decision may have no relevance to the question of guilt, or may even be extremely prejudicial to a fair determination of that question. This problem, however, is scarcely insurmountable. Those who have studied the question suggest that a bifurcated procedure—one in which the question of sentence is not considered until the determination of guilt has been made—is the best answer.

* * *

For the reasons expressed in this opinion, we hold that the statutory system under which Gregg was sentenced to death does not violate the Constitution. Accordingly, the judgment of the Georgia Supreme Court is affirmed.

It is so ordered.

Notes and Questions

1. In upholding Georgia's death penalty statute, the majority in *Gregg* gave great weight to the fact that, under the bifurcated sentencing procedure, the jury first determined guilt or innocence and then, in a second proceeding, decided whether to impose the death penalty. The Court held that the bifurcated procedure, combined with other statutory provisions guiding the jurors' discretion, eliminated any substantial risk that the penalty would be inflicted in an "arbitrary and capricious" or "freakish" manner.

Consider the implications of Arrow's Theorem for whether a bifurcated trial would help ensure that the death penalty is not imposed capriciously in a hypothetical case where majority rule decides the outcome. Suppose a defendant is being tried by a jury of twelve in a case where the death penalty is an option and where the defendant can be convicted and sentenced on the basis of a two-thirds vote. There are three possible outcomes. The defendant may be acquitted; may be sentenced to life imprisonment; or may receive the death penalty.

Four of the jurors (Group 1) believe that the defendant probably did not commit the crime. If the defendant *did* commit the crime, however, they believe the death penalty should be imposed. Another four (Group 2) believe the defendant is guilty and should be imprisoned but loathe the notion of capital punishment and would rather let a guilty man go free than inflict it. The remaining four jurors believe the defendant is guilty and also believe capital punishment should be imposed. The preferences of the three groups can be described as follows:

> Group 1: acquittal > death > imprisonment
> Group 2: imprisonment > acquittal > death
> Group 3: death > imprisonment > acquittal

The jury determines guilt and sentencing in a bifurcated proceeding like the one approved in *Gregg*. First, the jury votes on whether the defendant is innocent, or should be at least be imprisoned (acquittal versus imprisonment). A majority favor imprisonment. The jury next considers whether the death penalty should be imposed (imprisonment versus death). A majority prefer the death penalty to imprisonment, and the defendant is sentenced to death.

Questions: What would happen if the order of proceedings were reversed? In other words, suppose the jury chooses *first* between the death penalty and life imprisonment should the defendant be convicted (imprisonment versus death), and *then* decides guilt or innocence (death versus acquittal)?

2. The previous question suggests that the order of bifurcated proceedings in death penalty cases can affect the outcome of cases decided under majority rule. As a practical matter, states that allow the jury to recommend or demand the death penalty generally also require the jury's decision on that issue to be unanimous. But see Proffitt v. Florida, 428 U.S. 242 (1976) (upholding Florida death penalty statute where judge sentences defendant after hearing jury's advisory verdict based on majority vote).

Question: Does bifurcation affect the outcome of voting under a rule of unanimity?

3. Arrow predicted that under certain conditions, majority voting leads to unstable cycling of results. However, cycling cannot occur when the individuals voting respect earlier decisions. For example, having decided that the defendant is guilty and should not be acquitted, and having chosen the death penalty over imprisonment, the jury refuses to revisit the issue of their preferences for acquittal versus the death penalty.

Question: Deciding to call a halt to voting and not revisit old issues is one way of overcoming cycling. Does respecting earlier decisions make voting a more accurate measure of social preferences or simply a more stable measure?

4. Judge Easterbrook noted in Ways of Criticizing the Court, above, that "[o]ne of the most interesting findings of the public choice literature is that the decisions of any group are sensitive to the order in which it considers the options." That characteristic of majority voting under Arrow's Theorem is sometimes described as "path dependence." If the group respects past decisions, the outcome of majority voting can depend on the path of group decisionmaking. Whether the defendant is executed or set free depends on whether guilt or penalty is decided first.

When the results of voting are path dependent, an individual can control the outcome of voting if he or she can control the agenda, the path of decisionmaking, by deciding the order in which issues are considered. By determining where the group begins, and where it calls a halt to voting, the agenda controller can break the cycling pattern at the most advantageous point.

The power to determine outcome by setting the agenda exists even when a series of pairwise votes would produce a consistently favored outcome instead of cycling. Suppose Larry, Curly, and Mo have the following preferences:

```
Larry:   art > baseball > concert
Curly:   baseball > art > concert
Mo:      concert > baseball > art
```

In a series of pairwise votes, baseball will always defeat both the art gallery and the symphony concert. An option which triumphs over all other options in pairwise voting is called a *Condorcet winner,* after the Marquis de Condorcet, an eighteenth-century nobleman who may have been the first public choice theorist to discover the cycling implications of majority voting.

Suppose, however, that Larry, a public choice theorist, controls the agenda. He can ensure that the group picks his favorite option (the art gallery) by setting the following agenda. First, the three friends will vote baseball "up or down." In effect, the choice is between baseball and "not-baseball" (the art gallery or concert). If baseball is *not* chosen, the second vote will be between the remaining two options, the art gallery and the concert.

Larry will triumph under such an agenda. In effect, Larry has managed to have his option chosen by first defeating the most-popular Condorcet winner, baseball, with a coalition of less-favored options. *See* Levine & Plott, Agenda Influence and Its Implications, 63 Va.L.Rev. 561, 581 (1977) (reporting results of an actual experiment in which authors imposed their preferences upon their recreational club by arranging agenda to defeat Condorcet winner in favor of program preferred by authors).

5. Another fashion in which voters can manipulate the results of majority voting is to misrepresent their preferences strategically. Suppose that Larry, Curly, and Mo have the preferences diagrammed in Question 4 above. If, in a vote between baseball and the concert, Larry votes for the concert even though he really prefers baseball, baseball will lose to the concert. Then, in a subsequent vote between the art gallery and the concert, art will win.

Question: Arrows' Theorem assumes that such strategic misrepresentation will not occur. Which one of Arrow's five conditions—transitivity, the Pareto postulate, range, nondictatorship, or the independence of irrelevant alternatives—is violated by strategic voting?

6. Agenda-setting may help explain the relative stability of legislative decisions. Consider the example of decisionmaking in the U.S. House of Representatives.

Any Representative may submit proposed legislation. The House Speaker routinely refers such bills to the relevant standing committee charged with examining legislation on that particular subject. When more than one committee has jurisdiction, the Speaker may order sequential referral, *i.e.,* may determine the order in which relevant committees consider a bill.

Once a bill is "in committee," the Committee Chair has the power to schedule hearings on the bill, refer it to a (potentially hostile) subcommittee, or simply let the matter languish. In the U.S. Congress, approximately 80% to 90% of all proposed bills "die in committee." A majority vote of the committee's members is necessary to override the Chair's decision to kill a bill by placing it on the Committee's agenda. The Chair retains the power to determine the order in which the Committee considers particular issues and amendments to the bill.

After the committee has "marked up" the bill to its satisfaction, it is sent to the House floor. At this point, the House Rules Committee determines when the bill shall be considered, how much debate will be allowed, and most particularly whether consideration will be "open rule" (floor amendments permitted), "closed rule" (no floor amendments), or "modified closed rule" (only specified floor amendments allowed). After debate and possible amendment, the entire House votes the bill up or down, usually by a majority vote.

Of course, once the bill is approved, it must be sent to the Senate for approval. If the Senate does not agree with the bill, the two Houses begin reconciliation procedures designed to come up with a proposal which can be approved by a majority of both houses. Once both houses agree on a reconciled bill, it must be presented to the President for signature or veto. See W. Eskridge & P. Frickey, Cases and Materials on Legislation: Statutes and the Creation of Public Policy 28–36 (1988).

Questions: What opportunities for agenda control does such a system create? In particular, which individuals or groups have the greatest power to control the outcome of voting, and how? Is the system rigged to favor changes in legislation or the status quo?

———

Arrow's Theorem proves that social choices can be intransitive under any decisionmaking rule characterized by the Pareto postulate, nondictatorship, free range of choice, and the independence of irrelevant alternatives. If one or more of those conditions is dropped, Arrow's Theorem no longer applies. The questions following *Kramer,* above, explored how logrolling (which violates the independence of irrelevant alternatives) leads to stable results and greater accuracy in measuring social preference. Tashjian v. Republican Party of Connecticut illustrates what happens when another of Arrow's conditions is violated—the condition of "free range of choice."

The condition of free range requires that individuals may rank alternatives in any order they choose. A person may prefer tennis to skiing and skiing to swimming; she may also prefer skiing to swimming and swimming to tennis. Any kind of ordering of preferences is possible.

On many issues, the preferences of individuals choosing among three or more alternatives do seem to be free ranging. On other issues, however, individuals' preferences seem to fall into a "natural" ordering. Suppose someone is trying to choose among three alternative positions on abortion: (a) abortions should never be permitted; (b) abortion should be allowed only in cases of rape or incest; and (c) abortion should be available on demand. The person choosing may rank those alternatives a > b > c, or she may rank them b > c > a. It seems implausible, however, that she would rank them a > c > b. Someone whose first choice is a total ban on abortions is unlikely to prefer abortion on demand to allowing abortion only in cases of rape or incest.

On some issues, like abortion, preferences seem to form a "spectrum" of positions. Each individual has a favorite point on the spectrum. The closer any given alternative is to that optimum, the more the individual prefers it. Public choice scholars refer to preferences that are not free-ranging but have a natural ordering as "single-peaked." To understand the derivation of that term, note that if options lie along a spectrum from one extreme to another, people with single-peaked preferences will not prefer both extremes over the middle. If the middle is least preferred (a > c > b), the ordering is free-ranging or multipeaked; the two ends of the spectrum are higher than the middle, a valley with two peaks. The plausible abortion orderings are single-peaked, with the middle being the peak (b > c > a) or one of the extremes being the highest point on the peak (a > b > c), as illustrated in Figure 7–1.

Figure 7–1
Single and Multipeaked Preferences

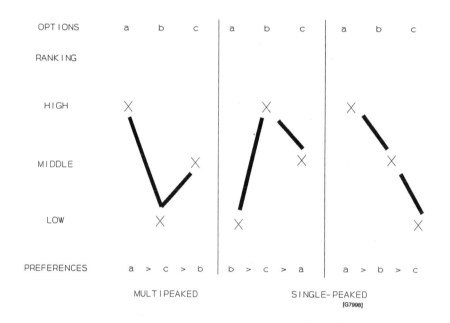

The following case explores the implications of single-peaked preferences for the accuracy and stability of majority voting.

TASHJIAN v. REPUBLICAN PARTY OF CONNECTICUT

Supreme Court of the United States, 1986.
479 U.S. 208, 107 S.Ct. 544, 93 L.Ed.2d 514.

MARSHALL, JUSTICE.

Appellee Republican Party of the State of Connecticut (the Party) in 1984 adopted a party rule which permits independent voters—registered voters not affiliated with any political party—to vote in

Republican primaries for federal and state-wide offices. Appellant Julia Tashjian, the Secretary of the State of Connecticut, is charged with the administration of the State's election statutes, which include a provision requiring voters in any party primary to be registered members of that party. Conn.Gen.Stat. § 9–431 (1985). Appellees, who in addition to the Party include the Party's federal officeholders and the Party's state chairman, challenged this eligibility provision on the ground that it deprives the Party of its First Amendment right to enter into political association with individuals of its own choosing. * * *

* * *

* * * Motivated in part by the demographic importance of independent voters in Connecticut politics * * * [the Republican Party] adopted the Party rule now at issue, which provides:

"Any elector enrolled as a member of the Republican Party and any elector not enrolled as a member of a party shall be eligible to vote in primaries for nomination of candidates for the offices of United States Senator, United States Representative, Governor, Lieutenant Governor, Secretary of the State, Attorney General, Comptroller and Treasurer."

During the 1984 session, the Republican leadership in the [Connecticut] state legislature, in response to the conflict between the newly enacted Party rule and § 9–431, proposed to amend the statute to allow independents to vote in primaries when permitted by Party rules. The proposed legislation was defeated, substantially along party lines, in both houses of the legislature, which at that time were controlled by the Democratic Party.

The Party and the individual appellees then commenced this action in the District Court, seeking a declaration that § 9–431 infringes the appellees' right to freedom of association for the advancement of common political objectives guaranteed by the First and Fourteenth Amendments, and injunctive relief against its further enforcement. * * *

* * *

The Party here contends that § 9–431 impermissibly burdens the right of its members to determine for themselves with whom they will associate, and whose support they will seek, in their quest for political success. The Party's attempt to broaden the base of public participation in and support for its activities is conduct undeniably central to the exercise of the right of association. * * *

* * *

* * * The statute here places limits upon the group of registered voters whom the Party may invite to participate in the "basic function" of selecting the Party's candidates. The State thus limits the Party's associational opportunities at the crucial juncture at which the appeal to common principles may be translated into concerted action, and hence to political power in the community.

* * *

Appellant contends that § 9–431 is a narrowly tailored regulation which advances the State's compelling interests * * *.

* * *

[Appellant argues] that the closed primary system avoids voter confusion. Appellant contends that "[t]he legislature could properly find that it would be difficult for the general public to understand what a candidate stood for who was nominated in part by an unknown amorphous body outside the party, while nevertheless using the party name." Appellees respond that the State is attempting to act as the ideological guarantor of the Republican Party's candidates, ensuring that voters are not misled by a "Republican" candidate who professes something other than what the State regards as true Republican principles.

* * *

In arguing that the Party rule interferes with educated decisions by voters, appellant [disregards] the substantial benefit which the Party rule provides to the Party and its members in seeking to choose successful candidates. Given the numerical strength of independent voters in the State, one of the questions most likely to occur to Connecticut Republicans in selecting candidates for public office is, how can the Party most effectively appeal to the independent voter? By inviting independents to assist in the choice at the polls between primary candidates selected at the Party convention, the Party rule is intended to produce the candidate and platform most likely to achieve that goal. The state statute is said to decrease voter confusion, yet it deprives the Party and its members of the opportunity to inform themselves as to the level of support for the Party's candidates among a critical group of electors. * * * The State's legitimate interests in preventing voter confusion and providing for educated and responsible voter decisions in no respect "make it necessary to burden the [Party's] rights."

Finally, appellant contends that § 9–431 furthers the State's compelling interest in protecting the integrity of the two-party system and the responsibility of party government. Appellant argues vigorously and at length that the closed primary system chosen by the state legislature promotes responsiveness by elected officials and strengthens the effectiveness of the political parties.

* * *

Under these circumstances, the views of the State, which to some extent represent the views of the one political party transiently enjoying majority power, as to the optimum methods for preserving party integrity lose much of their force. The State argues that its statute is well designed to save the Republican Party from undertaking a course of conduct destructive of its own interests. But on this point "even if the State were correct, a State, or a court, may not constitutionally substitute its own judgment for that of the Party." The Party's determination of the boundaries of its own association, and of the structure which best allows it to pursue its political goals, is protected by the Constitution. * * *

We conclude that the State's enforcement, under these circumstances, of its closed primary system burdens the First Amendment rights of the Party. The interests which the appellant adduces in support of the statute are insubstantial, and accordingly the statute, as applied to the Party in this case, is unconstitutional.

* * *

Notes and Questions

1. Voter preferences for candidates for political office may be single-peaked if candidates are viewed as falling on a spectrum from radical left through liberal to moderate to conservative to ultra-conservative. Whatever the voter's favorite point on that spectrum, the further a candidate departs from that optimum, the less desirable she will be. A voter is unlikely to prefer a conservative candidate to a liberal and a liberal to a moderate.

Arrow's Theorem predicts that when preferences are multipeaked (free-ranging), majority voting can produce cycling results. That is no longer true when preferences are single-peaked. Suppose Larry, Curly and Mo are voting on candidates for office. Their choices are a liberal (L), a conservative (C), and a middle-of-the-road moderate (M). Conservative Curly prefers C > M > L; Leftist Larry prefers L > M > C; and Muddled Mo prefers M > C > L.

Questions: What happens when the friends vote first between L and C, and then the winner goes up against M? Choose first between M and C, and the winner goes against L? Choose first between L and M, and the winner goes against C?

2. In *Tashjian*, the Republican party challenged a Connecticut statute precluding independents from voting in Republican primaries. The Party claimed that the statute burdened its fundamental freedom of association and harmed its chances of political success through broadening its base of public support.

Question: How did the Republican Party expect to benefit from allowing independents to vote in its primary?

3. United States politics is a two-party system; winning candidates tend to be either Democrats or Republicans. Consider the campaign strategies of two political candidates, one a liberal Democrat (D), and the other a conservative Republican (R). D and R both believe that voter preferences in campaign elections tend to be single-peaked, falling in a continuum between the far left and the far right as illustrated below.

Voters' Political Preferences

D	M	R
Left	(50%)	Right

"M" is the median of voter preferences. Exactly 50% of the electorate have a political philosophy more liberal than the median (to the left of M); 50% have a more conservative philosophy (to the right of M). Thus, M represents the preferences of the median voter.

Before the election, the political philosophies of D and R lie to the left and to the right, respectively, of the median position. However, both D and R realize that to win the election they must put together a campaign platform that attracts the support of more than half of all voters. Voters with philosophies more conservative than R's are sure to vote for R over D, just as voters who lie to the left of D are trapped into picking D over R. But to win, D or R must capture the votes of the individuals whose political philosophies lie between them. In particular, each candidate must try to capture the "median" voter whose vote puts the candidate over the 50% threshold of victory.

> *Questions:* How will the need to gain the support of the median voter affect the political position each candidate is likely to espouse? Why are two-party system politics dominated by the median voter's preferences?

4. When the conditions of Arrow's Theorem apply, majority voting can produce cycling results. This not only implies that the results of majority voting may be unstable, but also raises serious doubt about the accuracy of majority voting as a means of weighing social preferences.

When voter preferences are single-peaked, Arrow's Theorem is inapplicable and voting produces a stable outcome. But stability is not necessarily accuracy.

> *Question:* A voting system is accurate when it produces social choices that maximize social welfare or utility. Are single-peaked preferences sufficient to ensure that the outcome of majority voting is accurate as well as stable?

5. In *Tashjian,* the State argued that closed primaries are essential to "protect the integrity of the two-party system." Previous questions suggest that an open primary tempts both parties to appeal to the political preferences of the median voter.

> *Question:* How do closed primaries contribute to preserving two distinct parties with two distinct political platforms?

6. When voter preferences are single-peaked, majority voting produces stable outcomes determined by the median voter. The legislative branch of the United States government involves two types of voting. Citizens vote in general elections to choose representatives to the legislature, and representatives in turn vote on particular pieces of legislation. Question 1 suggested that if candidates for the legislature fall on an ideological spectrum from left to right, citizens' preferences in general elections are likely to be single-peaked.

> *Question:* Is the assumption that voter's preferences in general elections are single-peaked sensible given the phenomenon of "single-issue" candidates who put particular emphasis on issues such as abortion or gun control?

7. Representatives chosen in general elections themselves vote on proposed statutes in the legislature. Most state constitutions contain a provision to the effect that proposed legislation must address a single subject. For example, the Minnesota Constitution provides that "No law shall embrace more than one subject, which shall be expressed in its title." Minn. Const. Art. IV, § 27 (1857). Such requirements effectively preclude the passage of omnibus bills on a number of unrelated matters. In contrast, the U.S. Congress permits omnibus bills.

Question: What are the implications of single-subject and omnibus bills for the stability of legislative voting?

b. Wealth Redistribution Under Majority Rule

The public choice analysis of voting has assumed thus far that the coercive state's goal is identifying and pursuing policies that efficiently improve its citizens' well-being. Under a rule of unanimity rational citizens are unlikely to agree to anything else. Under majority rule, however, the state's coercive power can be turned to satisfying the desires of a segment of society rather than the collective needs of all.

The Framers of the U. S. Constitution were sensitive to the possibility that a legislature governed by majority rule might serve the interests of part of society rather than the whole. Consider Article I of the Constitution, which provides:

> Representatives and direct Taxes shall be apportioned among the several States which may be included within this Union, according to their respective Numbers, which shall be determined * * * within three Years after the first Meeting of the Congress of the United States, and within every subsequent Term of Ten Years * * * .

In 1894, after lengthy and heated debate, Congress imposed a 2% tax on individual and corporate income from real property, personal property such as stocks or bonds, and business or employment. Shortly after the tax statute became effective, the Supreme Court agreed to hear *Pollock v. Farmer's Loan & Trust Co.,* in which a corporate shareholder sought to enjoin his corporation from paying the income tax on the ground that the tax was unconstitutional under Article I.

POLLOCK v. FARMERS' LOAN & TRUST COMPANY

Supreme Court of the United States, 1895.
157 U.S. 429, 15 S.Ct. 673, 39 L.Ed. 759.

FULLER, CHIEF JUSTICE.

* * *

The contention of the complainant is:

First. That the law in question, in imposing a tax on the income or rents of real estate, imposes a tax upon the real estate itself; and in imposing a tax on the interest or other income of bonds or other personal property, held for the purposes of income or ordinarily yielding income, imposes a tax upon the personal estate itself; that such tax is a direct tax, and void because imposed without regard to the rule of apportionment; and that by reason thereof the whole law is invalidated.

* * *

The constitution provides that representatives and direct taxes shall be apportioned among the several States according to numbers, and that no direct tax shall be laid except according to the enumeration provided for * * *.

The men who framed and adopted that instrument had just emerged from the struggle for independence whose rallying cry had been that "taxation and representation go together."

The mother country had taught the colonists, in the contests waged to establish that taxes could not be imposed by the sovereign except as they were granted by the representatives of the realm, that self-taxation constituted the main security against oppression. * * * The principle was that the consent of those who were expected to pay it was essential to the validity of any tax.

The States were about, for all national purposes embraced in the Constitution, to become one, united under the same sovereign authority, and governed by the same laws. But as they still retained their jurisdiction over all persons and things within their territorial limits * * * they were careful to see to it that taxation and representation should go together, so that the sovereignty reserved should not be impaired, and that when congress, and especially the house of representatives, where it was specifically provided that all revenue bills must originate, voted a tax upon property, it should be with the consciousness, and under the responsibility, that in so doing the tax so voted would proportionately fall upon the immediate constituents of those who imposed it.

* * * All the thirteen were Seaboard States, but they varied in maritime importance, and differences existed between them in population, in wealth, in the character of property and of business interests. * * *

* * *

Nothing can be clearer than that what the Constitution intended to guard against was the exercise by the general government of the power of directly taxing persons and property within any State through a majority made up from the other States. It is true that the effect of requiring direct taxes to be apportioned among the States in proportion to their population is necessarily that the amount of taxes on the individual taxpayer in a State having the taxable subject-matter to a larger extent in proportion to its population than another State has, would be less than in such other State, but this inequality must be held to have been contemplated, and was manifestly designed to operate to restrain the exercise of the power of direct taxation to extraordinary emergencies, and to prevent an attack upon accumulated property by mere force of numbers.

* * *

* * * [T]he acceptance of the rule of apportionment was one of the compromises which made the adoption of the Constitution possible, and secured the creation of that dual form of government, so elastic and so strong, which has thus far survived in unabated vigor. If, by calling a tax indirect when it is essentially direct, the rule of protection could be frittered away, one of the great landmarks defining the boundary between the Nation and the States of which it is composed, would have disappeared, and with it one of the bulwarks of private rights and private property.

We are of opinion that the law in question, so far as it levies a tax on the rents or income of real estate, is [an unapportioned direct tax] in violation of the Constitution, and is invalid.

* * *

Notes and Questions

1. Whether a particular tax is a direct tax that must be apportioned among the states in proportion to their census population or is "indirect" may be far from obvious. Case law on the question shows confusion. See Hylton v. United States, 3 U.S. (3 Dall.) 171, 1 L.Ed. 556 (1796) (annual tax on carriages held indirect); Springer v. United States, 102 U.S. (12 Otto) 586, 26 L.Ed. 253 (1880) (Civil War income tax upheld as indirect); see generally 1 Bittker, Federal Taxation of Income, Estates and Gifts ¶ 1.2.2 (1981) (discussing difficulty of determining what is direct tax under Constitution). In Pollock, the Supreme Court concluded that a tax on income from real estate was equivalent to a direct tax on the real estate itself and was unconstitutional unless apportioned among the states according to their census populations.

2. According to Chief Justice Fuller, Article I was intended to guard against "the exercise by the general government of the power of directly taxing persons and property within any state through a majority made up from the other states" or "an attack upon accumulated property by mere force of numbers." Fuller observed that the original thirteen colonies differed substantially "in population, in wealth, [and] in the character of property and of business interests."

Questions: Under majority rule, how can interstate differences in wealth, property and population lead to taxes that redistribute wealth from one state to another? The Constitution provides two protections against disparate taxation: the Apportionment Clause, and the requirement that tax legislation originate in the House of Representatives rather than the Senate. How do those provisions discourage redistributive taxation?

3. The possibility that a coercive government may transfer wealth rather than create it suggests another explanation for the state; the state may exist because one subgroup in society wants to exploit the remainder.

Questions: How does the wealth-transfer theory of the state compare with contractarian theory premised on citizen consent to state coercion? Consider Justice Fuller's claim in *Pollock* that "the consent of those who [are] expected to pay it [is] essential to the validity of any tax." Which model best describes British government of the American colonies in the late eighteenth century?

4. In a subsequent opinion in *Pollock,* the Supreme Court held that the unconstitutional provisions of the income tax statute rendered the statute invalid as a whole. See Pollock v. Farmer's Loan & Trust Co., 158 U.S. 601, 634–35, 15 S.Ct. 912, 919–20, 39 L.Ed. 1108 (1895). Again writing for the majority, Chief Justice Fuller noted:

> If it be true that the Constitution should have been so framed that a tax of this kind could be laid, the instrument defines the way for its amendment. In no part of it was greater sagacity displayed. Except that no state, without its consent, can be deprived of its equal suffrage in the Senate, the Constitution may be amended upon the concurrence of two-thirds of both houses, and the ratification of the legislatures or conventions of the several States, or through a Federal convention when applied for by the legislatures of two-thirds of the States, and upon like ratification.

The Sixteenth Amendment authorizing a federal income tax without apportionment was ratified in 1913.

Question: How do the requirements of two-thirds Congressional concurrence and ratification by three-fourths of the states decrease the likelihood that a federal tax would redistribute wealth among the states in a fashion that did not increase overall utility?

5. The modern Internal Revenue Code provides for "progressive" income taxation. Individuals' *proportionate* tax burdens increase with income. For example, a progressive tax system might impose no tax on the first $10,000 an individual earns, impose a 10% tax on the next $10,000, take 20% of the third $10,000 earned, and so forth. Even a flat-rate system requires high-income individuals to pay more taxes than persons with low incomes. But the wealthy bear an even larger share of the tax burden under progressive taxation.

Assume that tax revenues pay for government services that benefit rich and poor equally. (Question 8, below, reexamines that assumption.) If the government collects more from the rich than the poor but spends those funds on projects that benefit rich and poor equally, government redistributes wealth from the rich to the poor.

Question: Why might all members of society, rich and poor, prefer a progressive income tax? Recall Rawls' arguments in support of the maximim principle discussed earlier in this Chapter.

6. Wealthy individuals moved by pity or empathy for the poor can (and do) give to charities that help the worst-off in society.

Question: If the wealthy have a "taste for charity," why might a coercive progressive income tax serve such altruistic preferences for wealth redistribution more effectively than a voluntary system that permits rich individuals to give when they feel like doing so?

7. A redistributive tax unanimously approved by rich and poor alike meets Pareto's strict criteria for the desirability of a reallocation. The efficiency implications of a redistributive tax imposed by majority rule are less clear.

Questions: Is a progressive tax system favored by a majority consisting of the poor and middle-class, but disfavored by the rich, utility maximizing? Wealth maximizing?

8. Majority rule by definition permits state action that benefits one group (the approving majority) but leaves another (the dissenting minority) worse off. Any action based on less-than-unanimous consent thus potentially involves an element of "redistribution." Majority rule's redistributive possibilities are most obvious when the state takes wealth from (imposes taxes on) a subgroup of society. However, providing disparate benefits can redistribute wealth just as imposing disparate costs does.

Question 5 assumed that the revenues raised under a progressive tax system were spent on projects benefiting rich and poor equally. In reality, government programs often benefit some individuals or groups more than others.

Question: What are the redistributive effects of the following government activities: building a federally-funded "supercollider" research facility in a particular location; imposing strict pollution controls on smokestack industries; creating entitlement programs to provide medical and income-support benefits for low-income individuals; and federally insuring deposits in savings and loan institutions?

9. Because a coercive state can redistribute wealth through both uneven taxation and uneven provision of benefits, both sides of the equation must be considered to calculate the net redistribution of wealth from government action.

Questions: Consider the following three government activities: providing free (but low quality) education at the primary and secondary levels; compulsory vaccination for polio; and maintaining a police force. If those programs are paid for by a poll tax imposed on rich and poor alike, who benefits most and who benefits least from government intervention? If they are paid for by a flat 10% tax on all property? Paid for by a progressive tax system?

10. Any group that hopes to profit by extracting wealth from others under majority rule must put together a redistributing program that benefits (and so has the support of) more than half the individuals entitled to vote on the measure. Once a majority coalition is created, however, there is no reason to try to gain an even larger percentage of support for the redistributive proposal. To the contrary. The greater the percentage of voters who gain from the proposal, the greater the number to share the spoils and the smaller the number to be exploited. A coalition of 51% exploiting the remaining 49% enjoys greater average gains than a coalition

of 95% exploiting the remaining 5%. Thus individuals who hope for the maximum gain from redistribution under majority rule will put together the *minimum winning coalition* necessary to pass the measure under whatever voting rule applies. See W.H. Riker, The Theory of Political Coalitions (1962).

Bargaining among potential coalition members can destabilize redistributive coalitions. Suppose Poor Peter, Rich Richard and Middle–Class Mary buy a lottery ticket together and are thrilled when they win $300. They agree to divide the winnings according to majority rule. Poor Peter proposes that he get the entire $300. Not surprisingly, Richard and Mary form a coalition and propose that Peter receive nothing and they receive $150 each. Peter, trying to make the best out of a bad situation, approaches Richard and offers to form a coalition under which Richard will get $200, Peter will get $100, and Mary will receive nothing. When Mary finds out she also approaches Richard and suggests that Richard get $201, she get $99, and Peter get nothing. At this point Peter approaches Mary and suggests a coalition under which Peter gets $200, Mary gets $100, and Richard gets nothing—a deal that gives Mary more than the coalition she is trying to form with Richard.

When redistributive coalitions are unstable, it is difficult for one group in society systematically to exploit another. Calculations of the overall amount of wealth redistribution resulting from all government programs in the United States in 1984 indicate that, while the direction of redistribution was generally from the rich to the poor, the amount involved was fairly small. See D. Mueller, Public Choice II 453, Table 23.2 (1989).

C. RENT–SEEKING AND THE ECONOMIC THEORY OF LEGISLATION

Earlier chapters assumed that government's goal is improving society's welfare (whether measured in utility or wealth) by controlling excessive external costs and other market failures. The preceding discussion suggests that the state may fail to achieve that end when majority voting proves an inaccurate means of identifying and measuring social preferences, or permits one group in society to exploit the remainder. This section considers a second obstacle to efficient government intervention—the self-interested, rational maximizing behavior of the individual voters and elected representatives who comprise the political state.

HARPER v. VIRGINIA BOARD OF ELECTIONS
Supreme Court of the United States, 1966.
383 U.S. 663, 865 S.Ct. 1079, 16 L.Ed.2d 169.

Douglas, Justice.

These are suits by Virginia residents to have declared unconstitutional Virginia's poll tax. * * *

* * *

Long ago in *Yick Wo v. Hopkins,* the Court referred to "the political franchise of voting" as a "fundamental political right, because preservative of all rights." Recently in *Reynolds v. Sims,* we said, "Undoubtedly, the right of suffrage is a fundamental matter in a free and democratic society. Especially since the right to exercise the franchise in a free and unimpaired manner is preservative of other basic civil and political rights, any alleged infringement of the right of citizens to vote must be carefully and meticulously scrutinized." * * *

It is argued that a State may exact fees from citizens for many different kinds of licenses; that if it can demand from all an equal fee for a driver's license, it can demand from all an equal poll tax for voting. But we must remember that the interest of the State, when it comes to voting, is limited to the power to fix qualifications. Wealth, like race, creed, or color, is not germane to one's ability to participate intelligently in the electoral process. * * * To introduce wealth or payment of a fee as a measure of a voter's qualifications is to introduce a capricious or irrelevant factor. The degree of the discrimination is irrelevant. In this context—that is, as a condition of obtaining a ballot—the requirement of fee paying causes an "invidious" discrimination that runs afoul of the Equal Protection Clause. * * *

* * *

We have long been mindful that where fundamental rights and liberties are asserted under the Equal Protection Clause, classifications which might invade or restrain them must be closely scrutinized and carefully confined.

Those principles apply here. For to repeat, wealth or fee paying has, in our view, no relation to voting qualifications; the right to vote is too precious, too fundamental to be so burdened or conditioned.

Reversed.

HARLAN, JUSTICE, dissenting.

* * *

The Equal Protection Clause prevents States from arbitrarily treating people differently under their laws. Whether any such differing treatment is to be deemed arbitrary depends on whether or not it reflects an appropriate differentiating classification among those affected; the clause has never been thought to require equal treatment of all persons despite differing circumstances. The test evolved by this Court for determining whether an asserted justifying classification exists is whether such a classification can be deemed to be founded on some rational and otherwise constitutionally permissible state policy. * * * This standard reduces to a minimum the likelihood that the federal judiciary will judge state policies in terms of the individual notions and predilections of its own members, and until recently it has been followed in all kinds of "equal protection" cases.

* * *

* * * Is there a rational basis for Virginia's poll tax as a voting qualification? I think the answer to that question is undoubtedly "yes."

* * *

* * * [I]t is certainly a rational argument that payment of some minimal poll tax promotes civic responsibility, weeding out those who do not care enough about public affairs to pay $1.50 or thereabouts a year for the exercise of the franchise. It is also arguable, indeed it was probably accepted as sound political theory by a large percentage of Americans through most of our history, that people with some property have a deeper stake in community affairs, and are consequently more responsible, more educated, more knowledgeable, more worthy of confidence, than those without means, and that the community and Nation would be better managed if the franchise were restricted to such citizens. * * *

* * *

I would affirm the decision of the District Court.

Notes and Questions

1. Both the majority and the minority opinions in *Harper* apparently assumed that a $1.50 poll tax would deter at least a few voters from voting. The theory seems to be that voting becomes less attractive when the costs of voting are increased. One study has shown that a $6.00 poll tax imposed in 1960 did, indeed, reduce the average individual's probability of voting by 42%. See Ashenfelter & Kelley, Determinants of Participation in Presidential Elections, 18 J. L. & Econ. 695, 698 (1975).

Harlan's dissent argued that Virginia's poll tax was intended to discourage certain citizens from voting as much as to raise revenue. Among the persons likely to be discouraged from voting were the poor (who Harlan suggested might not have as deep a stake in the community) and the indifferent (who do not care deeply about exercising their franchise).

Questions: Does the absence of a poll tax mean that voting is a costless activity? What other costs are associated with voting? Are those burdens greater for the rich or the poor?

2. A rational voter will vote only if the costs of doing so are less than the benefits.

Question: Given that voting imposes costs, what are its benefits?

3. Applying the model of rational maximization to why voters vote raises a quandary known as the *paradox of voting*. If individuals vote to affect election outcomes, any rational voter should realize quickly that the odds of her vote making a difference in results are negligible. The benefit of voting is therefore the expected difference in the voter's utility from electing one candidate over another, multiplied by the infinitesimal chance that the voter's vote will determine which candidate wins. At the same time, voting involves significant costs in terms of time, money, and inconvenience. For the average person, any possible net benefit from voting is

substantially outweighed by the risk the voter will be run down by a truck on the way to the polls.

The paradox of voting suggests that it is irrational for the average person to vote. See A. Downs, An Economic Theory of Democracy 11–14 (1957). Nevertheless, many individuals who appear rational vote regularly. Some economists speculate that people have a "taste for voting" so that voting, as political participation, provides utility even when voters have no real expectation that their vote will make a difference to the election's outcome.

4. Suppose individuals vote only to influence outcome. In that case, very few indeed might bother to vote.

Questions: How might very low voter turnout affect a rational maximizer's decision whether or not to vote? Does it matter how close the vote is likely to be, that is, whether the election is hotly contested or has a clear frontrunner?

5. Consider Justice Harlan's argument that poll taxes "[weed] out those who do not care enough about public affairs to pay $1.50 or thereabouts a year for the exercise of the franchise."

Questions: How might a poll tax improve voting's ability to assist the state in maximizing utility? Wealth?

6. In some states and municipalities citizens occasionally vote directly on referenda addressing specific government policies. Most often, however, citizens express their policy preferences by electing representatives to state and federal legislatures charged with the authority to make law. It seems reasonable to assume that representatives, like the voters who elect them, are self-interested rational maximizers. That raises the risk that representatives will vote in a fashion that ignores their constituents' interests but furthers the representatives' personal goals.

The voter who wishes to guard against a representative's running amok must first investigate candidates for office to select the candidate most likely to vote in accord with the voter's preferences and then monitor the candidate's voting record after election to ensure that the representative is, in fact, furthering the voter's interests.

Questions: Given the uncertain benefits of voting, how much effort is the rational voter likely to spend educating herself on candidates' positions and overseeing elected representatives' voting performance? On what sources of information are rational voters likely to rely in selecting and monitoring representatives?

BUCKLEY v. VALEO

Supreme Court of the United States, 1976.
424 U.S. 1, 96 S.Ct. 612, 46 L.Ed.2d 659.

PER CURIAM.

These appeals present constitutional challenges to the key provisions of the Federal Election Campaign Act of 1971 (Act) * * *.

* * *

* * * The major contribution and expenditure limitations in the Act prohibit individuals from contributing more than $25,000 in a single year or more than $1,000 to any single candidate for an election campaign and from spending more than $1,000 a year "relative to a clearly identified candidate." Other provisions * * * limit the overall amount that can be spent by a candidate in campaigning for federal office.

* * *

The Act's contribution and expenditure limitations operate in an area of the most fundamental First Amendment activities. Discussion of public issues and debate on the qualifications of candidates are integral to the operation of the system of government established by our Constitution. * * * In a republic where the people are sovereign, the ability of the citizenry to make informed choices among candidates for office is essential, for the identities of those who are elected will inevitably shape the course that we follow as a nation. * * *

* * *

A restriction on the amount of money a person or group can spend on political communication during a campaign necessarily reduces the quantity of expression by restricting the number of issues discussed, the depth of their exploration, and the size of the audience reached. This is because virtually every means of communicating ideas in today's mass society requires the expenditure of money. The distribution of the humblest handbill or leaflet entails printing, paper, and circulation costs. Speeches and rallies generally necessitate hiring a hall and publicizing the event. The electorate's increasing dependence on television, radio, and other mass media for news and information has made these expensive modes of communication indispensable instruments of effective political speech.

* * *

By contrast with a limitation upon expenditures for political expression, a limitation upon the amount that any one person or group may contribute to a candidate or political committee entails only a marginal restriction upon the contributor's ability to engage in free communication. A contribution serves as a general expression of support for the candidate and his views, but does not communicate the underlying basis for the support. The quantity of communication by the contributor does not increase perceptibly with the size of his contribution, since the expression rests solely on the undifferentiated, symbolic act of contributing. At most, the size of the contribution provides a very rough index of the intensity of the contributor's support for the candidate. A limitation on the amount of money a person may give to a candidate or campaign organization thus involves little direct restraint on his political communication * * *.

* * *

Appellees argue that the Act's restrictions on large campaign contributions are justified by three governmental interests. According to the parties and *amici*, the primary interest served by the limitations and, indeed, by the Act as a whole, is the prevention of corruption and the appearance of corruption spawned by the real or imagined coercive influence of large financial contributions on candidates' positions and on their actions if elected to office. Two "ancillary" interests underlying the Act are also allegedly furthered by the $1,000 limits on contributions. First, the limits serve to mute the voices of affluent persons and groups in the election process and thereby to equalize the relative ability of all citizens to affect the outcome of elections. Second, it is argued, the ceilings may to some extent act as a brake on the skyrocketing cost of political campaigns and thereby serve to open the political system more widely to candidates without access to sources of large amounts of money.

It is unnecessary to look beyond the Act's primary purpose—to limit the actuality and appearance of corruption resulting from large individual financial contributions—in order to find a constitutionally sufficient justification for the $1,000 contribution limitation. Under a system of private financing of elections, a candidate lacking immense personal or family wealth must depend on financial contributions from others to provide the resources necessary to conduct a successful campaign. The increasing importance of the communications media and sophisticated mass-mailing and polling operations to effective campaigning make the raising of large sums of money an ever more essential ingredient of an effective candidacy. To the extent that large contributions are given to secure a political *quid pro quo* from current and potential office holders, the integrity of our system of representative democracy is undermined. * * *

* * *

We find that, under the rigorous standard of review established by our prior decisions, the weighty interests served by restricting the size of financial contributions to political candidates are sufficient to justify the limited effect upon First Amendment freedoms caused by the $1,000 contribution ceiling.

* * *

The Act's expenditure ceilings impose direct and substantial restraints on the quantity of political speech. The most drastic of the limitations restricts individuals and groups, including political parties that fail to place a candidate on the ballot, to an expenditure of $1,000 "relative to a clearly identified candidate during a calendar year."
* * *

* * *

We find that the governmental interest in preventing corruption and the appearance of corruption is inadequate to justify [the] ceiling

on independent expenditures [relative to a clearly identified candidate].
* * *

* * *

It is argued, however, that the ancillary governmental interest in equalizing the relative ability of individuals and groups to influence the outcome of elections serves to justify the limitation on express advocacy of the election or defeat of candidates imposed by [the independent] expenditure ceiling. But the concept that government may restrict the speech of some elements of our society in order to enhance the relative voice of others is wholly foreign to the First Amendment, which was designed "to secure 'the widest possible dissemination of information from diverse and antagonistic sources,' " and " 'to assure unfettered interchange of ideas for the bringing about of political and social changes desired by the people.' " The First Amendment's protection against governmental abridgment of free expression cannot properly be made to depend on a person's financial ability to engage in public discussion.

* * *

Section 608(c) places limitations on overall campaign expenditures by candidates seeking nomination for election and election to federal office. Presidential candidates may spend $10,000,000 in seeking nomination for office and an additional $20,000,000 in the general election campaign. The ceiling on senatorial campaigns is pegged to the size of the voting-age population of the State with minimum dollar amounts applicable to campaigns in States with small populations. * * * The Act imposes blanket $70,000 limitations on both primary campaigns and general election campaigns for the House of Representatives * * *

No governmental interest that has been suggested is sufficient to justify the restriction on the quantity of political expression imposed by § 608(c)'s campaign expenditure limitations. * * *

* * *

The campaign expenditure ceilings appear to be designed primarily to serve the governmental interests in reducing the allegedly skyrocketing costs of political campaigns. * * * [T]he mere growth in the cost of federal election campaigns in and of itself provides no basis for governmental restrictions on the quantity of campaign spending and the resulting limitation on the scope of federal campaigns. The First Amendment denies government the power to determine that spending to promote one's political views is wasteful, excessive, or unwise. * * *

In sum, the provisions of the Act that impose a $1,000 limitation on contributions to a single candidate, a $5,000 limitation on contributions by a political committee to a single candidate, and a $25,000 limitation on total contributions by an individual during any calendar year, are constitutionally valid. These limitations * * * constitute the Act's primary weapons against the reality or appearance of improper influence stemming from the dependence of candidates on large campaign contributions.   The contribution ceilings thus serve the basic governmental interest in safeguarding the integrity of the electoral process without directly impinging upon the rights of individual citizens and candidates to engage in political debate and discussion.   By contrast, the First Amendment requires the invalidation of the Act's independent expenditure ceiling * * * and its ceilings on overall campaign expenditures.   These provisions place substantial and direct restrictions on the ability of candidates, citizens, and associations to engage in protected political expression, restrictions that the First Amendment cannot tolerate.

* * *

Affirmed in part and reversed in part.

WHITE, JUSTICE, concurring in part and dissenting in part.

* * *

* * * [I dissent] from the Court's view that the expenditure limitations * * * violate the First Amendment.

* * *

I have little doubt * * * that limiting the total that can be spent will ease the candidate's understandable obsession with fundraising, and so free him and his staff to communicate in more places and ways unconnected with the fundraising function.   There is nothing objectionable—indeed it seems to me a weighty interest in favor of the provision—in the attempt to insulate the political expression of federal candidates from the influence inevitably exerted by the endless job of raising increasingly large sums of money.   I regret that the Court has returned them all to the treadmill.

It is also important to restore and maintain public confidence in federal elections.   It is critical to obviate or dispel the impression that federal elections are purely and simply a function of money, that federal offices are bought and sold or that political races are reserved for those who have the facility—and the stomach—for doing whatever it takes to bring together those interests, groups, and individuals that can raise or contribute large fortunes in order to prevail at the polls.

* * *

Notes and Questions

1.   To understand the consequences of representatives' self-interest for legislative voting, one must form a theory of what representatives desire. Among representatives' many likely sources of utility is election itself. Campaigning for political office involves substantial time, effort, and risk of failure.   No rational individual would incur such costs unless she expected to derive utility from election.

Both the majority opinion in *Buckley* and Justice White's dissent noted that campaigning requires large amounts of money.   Consider how financing can improve a candidate's likelihood of election.   Since it is illegal to buy votes outright, campaign dollars tend to be used to purchase posters, leaflets, campaign buttons, television and radio time, and polling and political consulting services.

Questions: Given the theory of the rational voter developed in the notes following *Harper,* how is advertising likely to affect the rational voter's preferences? How can using the media improve a candidate's chances? Does political advertising improve the accuracy of election outcomes?

2. The fact that political campaigns usually are financed from contributions and that Congress felt compelled to pass legislation limiting such contributions raises interesting economic questions. Not the least is why so many people are trying so hard to give so much money to politicians in the first place. The economist would assume contributors are buying something.

The majority opinion in *Buckley* mentioned two types of goods and services contributors might be trying to purchase. The first, less troubling, reason for contributing to a candidate's campaign is to support "the candidate and his views." If a contributor believed that one candidate's platform would provide her with substantially more utility than the other candidate's platform would, the contributor might find it in her interest to help finance her ideologically-favored candidate's campaign. The second, less attractive, motive is to exert a "coercive influence * * * on candidates' positions and on their actions if elected to office." The first motive seems to presume that candidates want to win elections to implement their preferred policies. The second suggests that candidates choose their policies to woo contributors and win elections.

Both theories suggest that making contributions increases the likelihood that the representative elected will vote in a fashion that serves the contributor's interests. However, the two theories lead to very different predictions for contributor behavior. Consider a contributor trying to decide whether to make campaign contributions to one candidate or to both. Consider also a contributor trying to decide to whether to give a contribution in a very close election or in an election where one candidate is a clear frontrunner.

Question: Which contribution strategy does each theory predict in the two circumstances?

3. If elected representatives cater to big contributors' interests at the expense of their constituents' when voting in the legislature, they run the risk that voters will detect their defection and refuse to reelect them. Accepting contributions is self-defeating if it loses more votes than it gains.

Question: What factors reduce the likelihood that the rational voter will detect that a representative's vote on an issue favors contributors' interests rather than constituents'?

4. The questions following *Kramer* examined how majority voting's accuracy as a measure of social preferences is improved by allowing voters to express their intensity of preference. In the legislature, representatives can express their preference intensity to some extent by "logrolling." However, logrolling is not practicable in general elections where a large population of citizens elects representatives to the legislature.

Question: Although the majority in *Buckley* upheld the limitation on campaign contributions, it noted that "the size of the contribution provides a very rough index of the contributor's support for the candidate." From an economic perspective, isn't such a means of expressing intensity of preference in general elections desirable?

5. In addition to finding that the Federal Election Campaign Act of 1971 (FECA) implicated First Amendment interests in free expression, *Buckley* held that "[t]he Act's contribution and expenditure limitations also impinge on protected associational freedoms. Making a contribution, like joining a political party, serves to affiliate a person with a candidate. In addition, it enables like-minded persons to pool their resources in further-ance of common political goals."

Federal law invites individuals to pool resources in making campaign contributions. While the FECA prohibits individual contributions of more than $1,000 to a individual candidate or $25,000 overall, the statute permits individuals to give up to $5,000 to a political action committee (PAC). PACs in turn are free to contribute up to $5,000 to individual candidates and unlimited amounts overall. The 1970s and 1980s saw a proliferation in the number of PACs and a corresponding increase in their importance to campaign finance. See W. Eskridge and P. Frickey, Legisla-tion: Statutes and the Creation of Public Policy 218–21 (1988).

Concerted group action is common not only at the campaign finance stage but also after election when special interest groups lobby legislators to vote one way or another on particular issues. Lobbyists influence legislative voting both through implied promises of political support and contributions in future campaigns, and by providing selective information to legislators trying to determine which way to vote. Business interests seem particularly likely to form industry-wide groups to lobby on legisla-tion affecting the industry. The American Petroleum Institute (API) and the Motor Vehicles Manufacturers Association (MVMA) are typical exam-ples. However, organizations such as the Sierra Club and the National Rifle Association representing non-business interests lobby as well.

Question: Why might individual persons and businesses find it advan-tageous to form a group to lobby rather than relying on solitary efforts?

WILLIAMSON v. LEE OPTICAL OF OKLAHOMA

Supreme Court of the United States, 1955.
348 U.S. 483, 75 S.Ct. 461, 99 L.Ed. 563.

DOUGLAS, JUSTICE.

This suit was instituted in the District Court to have an Oklahoma law declared unconstitutional and to enjoin state officials from enforc-ing it, for the reason that it allegedly violated various provisions of the Federal Constitution. * * *

The District Court held unconstitutional portions of three sections of the Act. First, it held invalid under the Due Process Clause of the Fourteenth Amendment the portions of [the Act] which make it unlawful for any person not a licensed optometrist or opthalmologist to fit lenses to a face or to duplicate or replace into frames lenses or other optical appliances, except upon written prescriptive authority of an Oklahoma licensed opthalmologist or optometrist.

An ophthalmologist is a duly licensed physician who specializes in the care of the eyes. An optometrist examines eyes for refractive error, recognizes (but does not treat) diseases of the eye, and fills prescriptions for eyeglasses. The optician is an artisan qualified to grind lenses, fill prescriptions, and fit frames.

The effect of [the Oklahoma law] is to forbid the optician from fitting or duplicating lenses without a prescription from an ophthalmologist or optometrist. In practical effect, it means that no optician can fit old glasses into new frames or supply a lens, whether it be a new lens or one to duplicate a lost or broken lens, without a prescription. The District Court conceded that it was in the competence of the police power of a State to regulate the examination of the eyes. But it rebelled at the notion that a State could require a prescription from an optometrist or ophthalmologist "to take old lenses and place them in new frames and then fit the completed spectacles to the face of the eyeglass wearer." It held that such a requirement was not "reasonably and rationally related to the health and welfare of the people." The court found that through mechanical devices and ordinary skills the optician could take a broken lens or a fragment thereof, measure its power, and reduce it to prescriptive terms. The court held that "Although on this precise issue of duplication, the legislature in the instant regulation was dealing with a matter of public interest, the particular means chosen are neither reasonably necessary nor reasonably related to the end sought to be achieved." It was, accordingly, the opinion of the court that this provision of the law violated the Due Process Clause by arbitrarily interfering with the optician's right to do business.

* * *

The Oklahoma law may exact a needless, wasteful requirement in many cases. But it is for the legislature, not the courts, to balance the advantages and disadvantages of the new requirement. It appears that in many cases the optician can easily supply the new frames or new lenses without reference to the old written prescription. It also appears that many written prescriptions contain no directive data in regard to fitting spectacles to the face. But in some cases the directions contained in the prescription are essential, if the glasses are to be fitted so as to correct the particular defects of vision or alleviate the eye condition. The legislature might have concluded that the frequency of occasions when a prescription is necessary was sufficient to justify this regulation of the fitting of eyeglasses. Likewise, when it is necessary to duplicate a lens, a written prescription may or may not be necessary. But the legislature might have concluded that one was needed often enough to require one in every case. Or the legislature may have concluded that eye examinations were so critical, not only for correction of vision but also for detection of latent ailments or diseases, that every change in frames and every duplication of a lens should be accompanied by a prescription from a medical expert. To be sure, the present law does not require a new examination of the eyes every time the frames are changed or the lenses duplicated. For if the old prescription is on file with the optician, he can go ahead and make the new fitting or duplicate the lenses. But the law need not be in every respect logically consistent with its aims to be constitutional. It is enough that there is an evil at hand for correction, and that it might be thought that the particular legislative measure was a rational way to correct it.

The day is gone when this Court uses the Due Process Clause of the Fourteenth Amendment to strike down state laws, regulatory of business and industrial conditions, because they may be unwise, improvident, or out of harmony with a particular school of thought. We emphasize again what Chief Justice Waite said in Munn v. Illinois, "For protection against abuses by legislatures the people must resort to the polls, not to the courts."

* * *

Affirmed in part and reversed in part.

Notes and Questions

1. When the state allocates a scarce resource among parties with conflicting claims to that resource, inevitably some parties win and others lose. The scarce resource allocated in *Lee Optical* was the right to sell replacement prescription lenses and eyeglass frames to the public. Two groups pressed claims to that right: the optometrists and the opticians.

The optometrists had much to gain from legislation preventing opticians from providing lenses or frames without a prescription on file. The optometrists' nationwide policy was never to issue a prescription for corrective lenses without insisting that the patient also use the optometrist to fill that prescription. Most of the opticians' business therefore came from patients who had gotten prescriptions from a medical doctor specializing in eye care (opthalmologist), and from providing, without prescription, duplicate eyeglasses, replacement lenses, and new frames. The opticians feared that the Oklahoma statute, by prohibiting the latter transactions, would deprive the opticians of a substantial portion of their total business. See Brief for Respondents–Appellants Lee Optical of Oklahoma, Inc., at 17–18, 21–22. To whom would that business go? The optometrists.

Lee Optical argued that "optometrists in Oklahoma and elsewhere are in direct competition with opticians in the sale of eyeglasses, frames, and lenses." *Id.* at 20. The Guild of Prescription Opticians and other *amici* also argued that "[t]he inevitable thrust of the statute is optometric monopoly of both refracting and dispensing [eyeglasses]." Brief Amici Curiae of The Guild of Prescription Opticians of America, Inc., et. al., at 384.

Question: Optometrists obviously gained at the expense of opticians under the Oklahoma statute. Who else might have been harmed?

2. The Oklahoma legislature did not happen to pass a statute benefiting optometrists by coincidence. The Oklahoma Optometric Association was involved deeply in having the legislation introduced and steering its passage through the legislature. In its appellate brief, Lee Optical complained about the district court's decision to exclude from evidence a letter dated March 13, 1953 that the Oklahoma Optometric Association had sent to its membership. The letter said the optometrists were "off to war" and that the "spreading menace of the dispensing opticians has forced us to introduce" the challenged bill into the Oklahoma legislature. The letter concluded that "we do not want the dispensing opticians licensed to practice." Brief for Respondents–Appellants Lee Optical of Oklahoma, Inc., at 206.

At the national level, the American Optometric Association had displayed a similar initiative in restricting competition. At the 1954 Annual Congress, the Association adopted a Resolution to recommend "to its affiliated state associations the desirability of causing the introduction of legislation to prevent the indiscriminate sale of ready-made eyeglasses as merchandise so that the unsuspecting and unknowing public may be protected against the dangers which may flow through the use of these articles." Brief in Support of Motion of Pennsylvania Optical Company to file a Brief *Amicus Curiae,* at 4 n.1.

The opportunity under majority rule to profit from legislation that simply reallocates wealth inevitably creates incentives for individuals and groups to attempt just that. Economists use the phrase *rent-seeking* to refer to special interest groups' efforts to promote legislation that redistributes wealth in their favor.

Question: Consider a typical interest group such as the American Petroleum Institute (API), which represents petroleum producers, refiners, and distributors. For what sorts of rent-seeking legislation might the API lobby?

3. From an economic perspective, a pure wealth transfer is a neutral transaction. If society takes $100 from one individual and gives it to another, the loser is poorer and the gainer is richer, but society's overall level of wealth remains unchanged, absent transaction costs. The Oklahoma statute challenged in *Lee Optical* might have involved a pure wealth transfer. If the gains enjoyed by optometrists plus the public benefits of the statute equalled the losses imposed on optometrists and consumers and there were no transaction costs involved, the optometrists' rent-seeking behavior would be neutral from a social welfare perspective.

Questions: Did the special interest legislation passed by the Oklahoma legislature at the optometrists' behest result in a neutral wealth transfer? When might special-interest legislation increase society's wealth? Decrease wealth?

4. Even when rent-seeking legislation results in a pure wealth transfer, the practice may ultimately be destructive of wealth. To understand why, consider the steps a group of optometrists would have to take to

secure protective legislation excluding opticians from making replacement glasses. First, the optometrists must meet and organize for group action. Next a lobbying group like the Oklahoma Optometric Association must be formed, staffed, and given office space and supplies. Then the lobbyists must begin to lobby—drafting proposed legislation, wining and dining State representatives to persuade them to introduce and pass it, perhaps running a media campaign extolling the virtues of the legislation. At the same time, the opticians may be pursuing similar measures.

The opportunity to profit from rent-seeking legislation invites interest groups to compete fiercely to get it. Optometrists and opticians fight over regulation of their respective professions; unions face off against employers on mandatory employment benefits; domestic and foreign auto producers wrestle over import quotas and tariffs; defense contractors squabble over contracts to build nuclear warheads; and the Fraternal Order of Police and the National Rifle Association battle over handgun legislation. But because securing wealth-transferring legislation is a zero-sum game, the costs of competing for such legislation are a deadweight loss to society, a waste. The more competition, the greater the waste. Rent-seeking by special interest groups thus may decrease society's overall wealth and well-being. Moreover, some economists argue that in an efficient rent-seeking market, the superior gains offered by favorable legislation will be competed away until the costs of effective lobbying begin to approach the gains expected from it.

Mancur Olson has argued that in wealthier societies, efforts to redistribute wealth under majority rule grow to overshadow and replace efforts to increase productivity. See M. Olson, The Rise and Decline of Nations (1982).

Question: Does the rule of unanimity pose similar risks of wealth-decreasing rent-seeking behavior?

5. The discussion following Pollock v. Farmer's Loan & Trust Co., above, examined how majority rule invites majority attempts to profit by taking wealth from the minority. *Lee Optical* illustrates how, in a representative democracy peopled by rationally ignorant and apathetic voters and special interest groups willing to lobby and make campaign contributions, it is also possible for the minority to profit by taking wealth from the majority. To determine what sorts of groups are most likely to be successful in securing legislation that redistributes wealth in their favor, consider two of the groups with interests at stake in *Lee Optical:* the optometrists who sold replacement eyewear and the nearsighted consumers who purchased it.

Rational maximizers decide to form an interest group just as they make any other decision, by comparing the costs with the benefits. The benefit of joining an interest group is the individual's expected increase in utility if joining allows the group to lobby successfully for favorable legislation. Thus, the more intense the interest of individual group members, the more likely a group will be formed. Certainly optometrists have a greater stake in excluding opticians from competition than the average nearsighted consumer has in more competitive prices for the occasional pair of replacement glasses she must purchase.

The costs of interest group lobbying include the administrative costs of forming the group as well as the lobbying costs themselves. The Oklahoma Optometric Association was a pre-existing organization originally intended to serve a variety of optometrists' needs in addition to lobbying. Thus, the marginal cost of using the group for lobbying was relatively small. In contrast, the start-up cost of organizing nearsighted Oklahomans into a lobbying group would be very large. Groups already formed to achieve another joint purpose (like labor unions formed to bargain with management or professional organizations such as the ABA) have a distinct cost advantage when it comes to lobbying.

Finally, because a single lobbyist's office can represent ten individuals or ten thousand, it would appear that the individual cost of lobbying is reduced (and lobbying made more attractive) when lobbying costs can be spread among a group with a large membership, rather than a group with a small membership. But such an analysis ignores the freerider effects so often inherent in group action. Successful lobbying is a public good; all optometrists benefitted from the Oklahoma statute, whether they were members of the Oklahoma Optometric Association or not. Mancur Olson argued that because smaller groups can control freeriding more readily, small groups have a lobbying advantage over large ones, and both types have incentive to try to find a way to prevent freeriding. M. Olson, The Logic of Collective Action 11, 21 (1965). A union, for example, might bargain for a "closed shop" contract with management.

The problem of freeriding leads to a phenomenon Olson referred to as "the exploitation of the great by the small." When two individuals are both interested in certain legislation but one has a much greater financial interest than the other, the individual with the lesser interest is likely to sit back and freeride on the efforts of the person with a large amount at stake. Thus, the largest producers in an industry have the greatest incentive to lobby for legislation favorable to the industry while smaller producers are tempted to coast on their efforts. In lobbying against pollution controls or fuel economy standards, General Motors works while Chrysler smirks.

> *Questions:* What other factors might affect a group's success in lobbying for special interest legislation? In particular, how does the relative wealth of groups affect their power in gaining favorable legislation?

6. When groups spend time and money lobbying for particular legislation, they in effect are trying to "buy" a favorable law. According to the economic theory of legislation, Landes & Posner, The Independent Judiciary in an Interest–Group Perspective, 18 J. L. & Econ. 875, 877 (1975):

> Legislation is supplied to groups or coalitions that outbid rival seekers of favorable legislation. The price that the winning group bids is determined by both the value of the legislative protection to the group's members and the group's ability to overcome the free-rider problems that plague coalitions. Payments take the form of campaign contributions, votes, implicit promises of future favors, and sometimes outright bribes. In short, legislation is "sold" by the legislature and "bought" by the beneficiaries of the legislation.

Questions: Assuming that the groups that lobby the hardest are the most likely to succeed, laws, like other market goods, will be channelled to those willing and able to pay the most for them. Isn't that wealth maximizing? How does the "economic theory of legislation" resemble the evolutionary theory of common law efficiency examined in Chapter 5?

7. The Framers of the U.S. Constitution recognized the temptation for individuals under majority rule to devote scarce resources to the negative-sum game of redistributing wealth. In the Federalist No. 10, Madison argued that individuals are inevitably tempted to be "united and actuated by some common impulse or passion, or of interest, adverse to the rights of other citizens, or to the permanent and aggregate interests of the community," so that "[t]he latent causes of faction are thus sown in the nature of man."

This Chapter's final section examines how one might go about the task faced by the Framers—crafting a Constitution to ensure that government improves, rather than decreases, society's overall level of well-being. As an introduction to that section, consider the Due Process Clauses of the Fifth and Fourteenth Amendments, which provide that neither the federal government nor the states may deprive any person "of life, liberty, or property, without due process of law."

In the early part of this century, the Supreme Court declared that due process required that legislative action bear a "real and substantial relationship" to the public welfare. Under that standard the Court inquired into the merits of legislation and struck down statutes the Justices felt to be unwise, unreasonable, or insufficiently connected to the public interest. See Lochner v. New York, 198 U.S. 45, 25 S.Ct. 539, 49 L.Ed. 937 (1905) (striking down law limiting hours that bakery employees could work during week); Coppage v. Kansas, 236 U.S. 1, 35 S.Ct. 240, 59 L.Ed. 441 (1915) (striking down statute prohibiting employers from requiring employee to agree they would not join unions); Adkins v. Children's Hospital, 261 U.S. 525, 43 S.Ct. 394, 67 L.Ed. 785 (1923) (striking down minimum wage law).

The *Lochner* era of "substantive due process" might be thought of as a judicial attempt to use the Due Process Clauses to check legislative action furthering private redistributive interests more than the public welfare. By the mid-century, however, the Supreme Court had backed away from the *Lochner* philosophy and showed increasing reluctance to second-guess the wisdom of legislative action. Recall Justice Douglas' announcement in *Lee Optical* that "[t]he day is gone when this Court uses the Due Process Clause of the Fourteenth Amendment to strike down state laws, regulatory of business and industrial conditions, because they may be unwise, improvident, or out of harmony with a particular school of thought." The modern Court will uphold state action that does not burden a fundamental right against a Due Process challenge so long as the government's action meets the minimal requirement of being "rationally related" to a "legitimate" government purpose.

Question: Can the rational relation standard effectively deter the use of the legislative process for redistributive ends? Consider Justice Douglas' opinion in *Lee Optical.*

D. CHOOSING OPTIMAL RULES OF DECISION: THE CRAFTING OF A CONSTITUTION

Previous sections of this Chapter explored the relative advantages and disadvantages of unanimity and less-than-unanimity voting rules. Under a rule of unanimity, group action will always improve group welfare because it is always to the advantage of each group member. Otherwise, there would be no unanimous consent. Unfortunately, reaching unanimous agreement can be difficult, not only because of the need for argument and discussion but also because of individuals' incentives to engage in strategic hold-out behavior.

Majority rule reduces opportunities for strategic behavior and allows more decisions to be reached more quickly. However, majority rule carries its own risks. Arrow's Theorem demonstrates that decisions reached under majority voting may not accurately reflect social preferences. Projects approved by a majority may reduce group welfare when dissenters' losses are taken into account. A related problem is the opportunity that majority rule creates for one group to benefit by taking wealth from another. Rational maximizers will exploit the redistributive opportunities of majority rule even when the deadweight losses of redistribution reduce society's overall wealth or utility.

Recognizing that different decisionmaking rules pose different risks leads naturally to the question of constitutions. How can rational individuals entering a social contract tailor decisionmaking rules to maximize social welfare while protecting themselves from harmful redistributive government coercion?

1. EXTERNAL COSTS, DECISIONMAKING COSTS, AND THE ECONOMIC ARGUMENT FOR A CONSTITUTION

J. BUCHANAN & G. TULLOCK, THE CALCULUS OF CONSENT *

(1965)

* * * The possible benefits from collective action may be measured or quantified in terms of reductions in the costs that the private behavior of other individuals is expected to impose on the individual decision-maker [externalities]. However, collective action, if undertaken, will also require that the individual spend some time and effort in making decisions for the group, in reaching agreement with his fellows. More importantly, under certain decision-making rules, choices contrary to the individual's own interest may be made for the group. In any case, participation in collective activity is costly to the individual, and the rational man will take this fact into account at the stage of constitutional choice.

* * * [W]e may develop two cost functions or relationships that will prove helpful.   In the first, which we shall call the *external-costs* function, we may relate, for the single individual with respect to a single activity, the costs that he expects to endure as a result of the actions of others to the number of individuals who are required to agree before a final political decision is taken for the group.   * * * It is clear that, over the range of decision-making rules, this will normally be a decreasing function: that is to say, as the number of individuals required to agree increases, the expected costs will decrease.   When unanimous agreement is dictated by the decision-making rule, the expected costs on the individual must be zero since he will not willingly allow others to impose external costs on him when he can effectively prevent this from happening.

This function is represented geometrically in Figure 1.   * * *

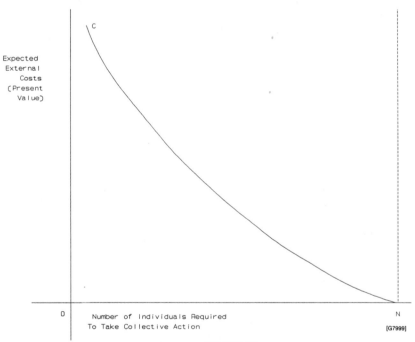

FIGURE 1

* * * Suppose that the decision-making rule is such that a collective action can be taken at any time that any one member of the group dictates it.   The single individual can then authorize action for the State, or in the name of the State, which adversely affects others in the group.   It seems evident that under such a rule the individual must anticipate that many actions taken by others which are unfavorable to him will take place, and the costs of these actions will be *external costs* in the same sense that the costs expected from private activity might be external.   The fact that collective action, under most decision-making rules, involves external costs of this nature has not been adequately

recognized. The private operation of the neighborhood plant with the smoking chimney may impose external costs on the individual by soiling his laundry, but this cost is no more external to the individual's own private calculus than the tax cost imposed on him unwillingly in order to finance the provision of public services to his fellow citizen in another area. Under the extreme decision-making rule which allows any individual in the whole group to order collective action, the expected external costs will be much greater * * *.

* * * We shall employ a simple illustration. Assume that all local public services are financed from property-tax revenues and that the tax rate is automatically adjusted so as to cover all public expenditures. Now assume further that any individual in the municipal group under consideration may secure road or street repairs or improvements when he requests it from city authorities. It is evident that the individual, when he makes a decision, will not take the full marginal costs of the action into account. He will make his decision on the basis of a comparison of his individual marginal costs, a part of total marginal costs only, with individual marginal benefits, which may be equal to total marginal benefits. The individual in this example will be able to secure external benefits by ordering his own street repaired or improved. Since each individual will be led to do this, and since individual benefits will exceed individual costs over a wide extension of the activity there will surely be an over investment in streets and roads, relative to other public and private investments of resources. The rational individual will expect that the general operation of such a decision-making rule will result in positive external costs being imposed on him.

* * *

As we move to the right from point C in Figure 1, the net external costs expected by the individual will tend to fall. If two persons in the group, *any* two, are required to reach agreement before collective action is authorized, there will be fewer decisions that the individual expects to run contrary to his own desires. In a similar fashion, we may proceed over the more and more inclusive decision-making rules. If the agreement of three persons is required, the individual will expect lower external costs than under the two-person rule, etc. * * * So long as there remains any possibility that the individual will be affected adversely by a collective decision, expected net external costs will be positive. These costs vanish only with the rule of unanimity. * * *

* * *

If collective action is to be taken, someone must participate in the decision-making. Recognizing this, we may derive, in very general terms, a second cost relationship or function. * * * If two or more persons are required to agree on a *single* decision, time and effort of another sort is introduced—that which is required to secure agreement. Moreover, these costs will increase as the size of the group required to agree increases. As a collective decision-making rule is changed to include a larger and larger proportion of the total group, these costs may increase at an increasing rate. As unanimity is approached, dramatic increases in expected decision-making costs may be predicted. In fact, when unanimity is approached, the situation becomes radically different from that existing through the range of less inclusive rules. * * * Individual investment in strategic bargaining becomes highly rational, and the costs imposed by such bargaining are likely to be high.

* * * [T]he rewards received by voters in any such agreement would be directly proportionate to their stubbornness and apparent unreasonableness during the bargaining stage. If we include (as we should) the opportunity costs of bargains that are never made, it seems likely that the bargaining costs might approach infinity in groups of substantial size. * * * Thus our bargaining-cost function operates in two ranges: in the lower reaches it represents mainly the problems of making up an agreed bargain among a group of people, any one of whom can readily be replaced. Here, as a consequence, there is little incentive to invest resources in strategic bargaining. Near unanimity, investments in strategic bargaining are apt to be great, and the expected costs very high.

* * * Figure 2 illustrates the relationship geometrically.

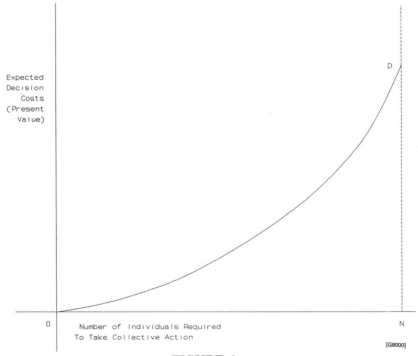

FIGURE 2

* * * For a given activity the fully rational individual, at the time of constitutional choice, will try to choose that decision-making rule which will *minimize* the present value of the expected costs that he

must suffer. He will do so by minimizing the *sum* of the expected external costs and expected decision-making costs, as we have defined these separate components. Geometrically, we add the two costs functions vertically. The "optimal" or most "efficient" decision-making rule, *for the individual whose expectations are depicted and for the activity or set of activities that he is considering,* will be that shown by the lowest point on the resulting curve. Figure 3 is illustrative: the individual will choose the rule which requires that K/N of the group agree when collective decisions are made.

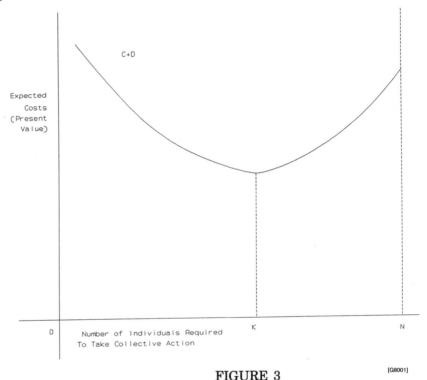

FIGURE 3   [G8001]

* * *

* * * The rational individual, at the stage of constitutional choice, confronts a calculus not unlike that which he must face in making his everyday economic choices. By agreeing to more inclusive rules, he is accepting the additional burden to decision-making in exchange for additional protection against adverse decisions. In moving in the opposing direction toward a less inclusive decision-making rule, the individual is trading some of his protection against external costs for a lowered cost of decision-making.

* * *

What are some of the implications of the analysis of individual choice of constitutional rules that has been developed? First of all, that analysis suggests that it is rational to *have a constitution.* By this is meant that it will be rational for the individual to choose more than one decision-making rule for collective choice-making under normal circumstances. If a single rule is to be chosen for all collective decision, no constitution in the normal sense will exist.

The second, and most significant, implication of our analysis is that at no point in the discussion has it seemed useful or appropriate to introduce the *one* particular decision-making rule that has traditionally been very closely associated with theories of democracy. We have not found occasion to refer specifically to the rule of majority decision, or, in more definite terms, to the rule described by $(N/2 + 1)/N$. The analysis has shown that the rule of unanimity does possess certain special attributes, since it is only through the adoption of this rule that the individual can insure himself against the external damage that may be caused by the actions of other individuals, privately or collectively. However, in our preliminary analysis, once the rule of unanimity is departed from, there seems to be nothing to distinguish sharply any one rule from any other.

Notes and Questions

1. A person in the state of nature, without government, can freely impose his external costs on others but also must suffer the externalities others impose on him. Social theorists from Hobbes to Rawls have assumed that the likely result is a world where society's overall level of well-being falls well below the level possible when a coercive state keeps order and controls externalities.

Buchanan and Tullock point out that a state also imposes at least two kinds of costs. One is the "external cost" of state coercion itself. Citizens suffer costs whenever the government forces them to do something they would rather not do: pay taxes, refrain from stealing from their neighbors' property, serve in the military. A second cost of state action is the "decisionmaking cost" of meeting, discussing, and voting over what state action is appropriate. The expected external costs of government coercion decrease as the proportion of group support required to take state action increases; when unanimous consent is required, no one suffers coercion. But the decisionmaking costs of government action increase as decision-making rules become more inclusive. Decisions by a single individual are easy to make. Unanimous group decisions are sometimes impossible.

The rational individual calculating the costs of government intervention will take account of both types of costs. Rational maximizers will choose the decisionmaking rule that permits action to be taken at least cost, including decisionmaking costs and potential external costs from state coercion.

2. The rule of unanimity is qualitatively different from any non-unanimous rule because only the former eliminates all risk of external costs from government coercion. Buchanan and Tullock suggest that once unanimity is abandoned, rules allowing group action on less-than-unanimous agreement differ only quantitatively, in the degree of decisionmaking and external costs they impose. In particular, there is nothing special

about "traditional" majority rule (greater than 50% approval). One might just as well require 30%, 40%, or 60% approval.

There may, however, be some advantage to requiring at least 50%-plus approval for group action. Suppose a group adopts a decisionmaking rule requiring the support of 40% of group members to authorize group action. Approximately 55% of the group support daylight savings time; 45% want to abolish it.

> *Questions:* Will a motion to abolish daylight savings pass? Will a subsequent motion to reverse that decision pass? What are the advantages of requiring 50%-plus approval?

3. The U. S. Constitution provides for a representative government rather than a true democracy where all citizens vote on all issues.

> *Question:* How does representative government reflect the decision-making costs associated with group action?

4. Within the context of a representative system, the Constitution provides different decisionmaking rules for different social decisions. Citizens elect members of Congress by plurality vote. Once elected, the legislators use traditional majority rule and statutes are passed only if supported by more than half the members of both House and Senate. It takes a two-thirds vote of both Houses to override a Presidential veto, and a two-thirds vote of both Houses followed by three-quarters state ratification to amend the Constitution.

> *Question:* Buchanan and Tullock suggest a less-inclusive decisionmaking rule is appropriate when decisionmaking costs are high and/or the risk of inefficient external costs from government action is low, and a more inclusive rule is appropriate when the reverse is true. Is the pattern of decisionmaking rules presented in the U.S. Constitution consistent with their analysis?

5. Buchanan and Tullock approach choosing optimal decisionmaking rules from a single individual's perspective. But different state actions pose different risks for different individuals. Persons with high incomes may be particularly sensitive to the potential external costs of a progressive income tax; farmers may be concerned about decisions to eliminate agricultural subsidies; workers and employers each may worry (for different reasons) about minimum wage laws. Thus, different individuals may demand more-inclusive decisionmaking rules for different issues. The problem for constitutional formation is molding such differing preferences into a single recipe for group action.

The now-familiar solution is to place individuals at the constitutional stage in an "original position" where they do not know which forms of government intervention pose the greatest risk to their particular interests. All individuals choose decisionmaking rules from the same perspective— that of the "average" member of the society-to-be. That average individual will choose the decisionmaking rule that imposes the lowest decisionmaking and external costs, on average, for a particular type of issue.

Buchanan's and Tullock's solution in The Calculus of Consent 77–78 resembles Rawls':

Agreement seems more likely on general rules for collective choice than on the later choices to be made *within* the confines of certain agreed-upon rules. * * * Essential to the analysis is the presumption that the individual is *uncertain* as to what his own precise role will be in any one of the whole chain of later collective choices that will actually have to be made. * * * [T]he individual will not find it advantageous to vote for rules that may promote sectional, class, or group interests because, by presupposition, he is unable to predict the role that he will be playing in the actual collective decision-making process at any particular time in the future. He cannot predict with any degree of certainty whether he is more likely to be in a winning or a losing coalition on any specific issue.

Question: Buchanan and Tullock assert that "[t]he uncertainty that is required in order for the individual to be led by his own interest to support constitutional provisions that are generally advantageous to all individuals and to all groups seems likely to be present at any constitutional state of discussion." *Id.* Is that a valid assumption?

———

Varying the degree of inclusiveness of voting rules is just one of many potential devices rational individuals drafting a constitution might use to encourage a coercive state to serve the public welfare rather than to engage in wealth-destroying redistributive schemes. The remainder of this Chapter examines other constitutional doctrines that may channel state action towards welfare maximization and away from intervention and rent-seeking that makes society worse off.

2. EFFICIENT STATE INTERVENTION

DeSHANEY v. WINNEBAGO COUNTY DEPARTMENT OF SOCIAL SERVICES

Supreme Court of the United States, 1989.
489 U.S. 189, 109 S.Ct. 998, 103 L.Ed.2d 249.

REHNQUIST, CHIEF JUSTICE.

Petitioner is a boy who was beaten and permanently injured by his father, with whom he lived. Respondents are social workers and other local officials who received complaints that petitioner was being abused by his father and had reason to believe that this was the case, but nonetheless did not act to remove petitioner from his father's custody. Petitioner sued respondents claiming that their failure to act deprived him of his liberty in violation of the Due Process Clause of the Fourteenth Amendment to the United States Constitution. We hold that it did not.

* * *

The Due Process Clause of the Fourteenth Amendment provides that "[n]o State shall ... deprive any person of life, liberty, or property, without due process of law." Petitioners contend that the State deprived Joshua of his liberty interest in "free[dom] from ... unjustified intrusions on personal security," by failing to provide him with adequate protection against his father's violence. * * *

But nothing in the language of the Due Process Clause itself requires the State to protect the life, liberty, and property of its citizens against invasion by private actors. The Clause is phrased as a limitation on the State's power to act, not as a guarantee of certain minimal levels of safety and security. It forbids the State itself to deprive individuals of life, liberty, or property without "due process of law," but its language cannot fairly be extended to impose an affirmative obligation on the State to ensure that those interests do not come to harm through other means. * * * Its purpose was to protect the people from the State, not to ensure that the State protected them from each other. The Framers were content to leave the extent of governmental obligation in the latter area to the democratic political processes.

* * *

* * * Petitioners concede that the harms Joshua suffered did not occur while he was in the State's custody, but while he was in the custody of his natural father, who was in no sense a state actor. While the State may have been aware of the dangers that Joshua faced in the free world, it played no part in their creation, nor did it do anything to render him any more vulnerable to them. * * * Under these circumstances, the State had no constitutional duty to protect Joshua.

* * *

Judges and lawyers, like other humans, are moved by natural sympathy in a case like this to find a way for Joshua and his mother to receive adequate compensation for the grievous harm inflicted upon them. But before yielding to that impulse, it is well to remember once again that the harm was inflicted not by the State of Wisconsin, but by Joshua's father. The most that can be said of the state functionaries in this case is that they stood by and did nothing when suspicious circumstances dictated a more active role for them. In defense of them it must also be said that had they moved too soon to take custody of the son away from the father, they would likely have met with charges of improperly intruding into the parent-child relationship * * *.

The people of Wisconsin may well prefer a system of liability which would place upon the State and its officials the responsibility for failure to act in situations such as the present one. They may create such a system, if they do not have it already, by changing the tort law of the State in accordance with the regular lawmaking process. But they should not have it thrust upon them by this Court's expansion of the Due Process Clause of the Fourteenth Amendment.

AFFIRMED.

Notes and Questions

1. Uncontrolled individuals in the state of nature often either engage in activities that impose external costs on others or decline to act in a fashion that would confer external benefits. Social contract theory suggests that the principal function of a coercive state is to regulate individual behavior in order to minimize costs and maximize benefits.

It was undoubtably welfare-reducing as well as cruel for the State of Wisconsin to allow Joshua's father to beat him until "he suffered brain damage so severe that he is expected to spend the rest of his life confined to an institution for the profoundly retarded." 489 U.S. at 193, 109 S.Ct. at 1002. Although Mr. DeShaney presumably derived some utility from beating his son, his pleasure probably was far outweighed by the pain of Joshua's severe and permanent injury. The State could have prevented the tremendous pecuniary and nonpecuniary costs arising from Joshua's injury if it had taken a more active role in supervising Mr. DeShaney's childrearing practices and intervened when it appeared Joshua might be harmed.

Nevertheless, there is no Constitutional requirement that the State of Wisconsin protect Joshua from his father. Nor, as Justice Rehnquist's opinion notes, did the Wisconsin voters feel it worthwhile to pass a statute requiring more active State supervision of childrearing and custody decisions. Wisely or unwisely, the vast majority of children in Wisconsin and elsewhere are raised with little or no state intervention.

> *Questions:* Are there economic reasons why the state should decline to monitor parents closely in order to prevent harmful childrearing practices? Recalling Buchanan's and Tullock's discussion of the costs of group action, what costs would have been incurred preventing Joshua's injury? More generally, why might rational maximizers drafting a social contract balk at requiring the state to eliminate all external harms?

2. Individuals suffering from external harms have a third option other than simply enduring the harm or submitting to coercive government intervention. That option is to reduce or eliminate the inefficiency through *voluntary* arrangements. One area where capitalist societies tend to rely on voluntary arrangements instead of government directives to allocate resources efficiently is the commercial market for goods and services. Individuals can channel resources to higher-valued uses through exchange without need for government intervention.

> *Question:* Goods and services can be allocated by government directive rather than through a free market. Indeed, many of the formerly communist governments allocated by directive. Why might it be advantageous to rely on voluntary arrangements instead?

3. The potential for private voluntary arrangements to reduce externalities extends far beyond the simple case of an exchange between two individuals. Homeowner's associations and recreational clubs are other examples of voluntary arrangements designed to increase group well-being by overcoming externalities.

Buchanan and Tullock suggest that the costs of government intervention include decisionmaking costs plus the external costs that government coercion imposes on the coerced individuals. Previous chapters examined some of the costs of using voluntary exchange to correct inefficient allocations.

Question: How do the costs of correcting externalities through voluntary arrangements resemble, and differ from, the costs of state intervention?

4. Individuals faced with external harms in the state of nature have three options: do nothing and suffer the costs others impose, as in Hobbes' state of nature (SON); undertake voluntary action which reduces those external costs but imposes its own transactions costs (V); and employ a government authority that reduces or eliminates the external costs that others impose but imposes its own operating costs and the risk of external costs from state coercion (G). Rational individuals will choose the option— SON, V, or G—that minimizes the *sum* of those varying costs. Sometimes it is cheapest to do nothing; sometimes state regulation is best; and sometimes costs are best minimized through voluntary transactions.

Question: Consider the following activities involving external costs or benefits: choosing a car color, allocating consumer goods, and arranging police protection and a national defense. Which option—SON, V, or G—is the most appropriate response to the externalities associated with those activities?

3. THE INDEPENDENT JUDICIARY

MARBURY v. MADISON
Supreme Court of the United States, 1803.
5 U.S. (1 Cranch) 137, 2 L.Ed. 60.

MARSHALL, CHIEF JUSTICE.

* * * [A] rule was granted in this case, requiring the secretary of state to show cause why a mandamus should not issue, directing him to deliver to William Marbury his commission as a justice of the peace for the county of Washington, in the District of Columbia.

* * *

Mr. Marbury * * * was appointed; * * * the appointment was not revocable, but vested in the officer legal rights, which are protected by the laws of his country.

* * *

The government of the United States has been emphatically termed a government of laws, and not of men. It will certainly cease to deserve this high appellation, if the laws furnish no remedy for the violation of a vested legal right.

* * *

This, then, is a plain case for a mandamus, either to deliver the commission, or a copy of it from the record: and it only remains to be inquired,

Whether it can issue from this court.

The act to establish the judicial courts of the United States authorizes the Supreme Court "to issue writs of mandamus in cases warranted by the principles and usages of law, to any courts appointed, or persons holding office, under the authority of the United States."

The Secretary of State, being a person holding an office under the authority of the United States, is precisely within the letter of the description, and if this court is not authorized to issue a writ of mandamus to such an officer, it must be because the law is unconstitutional, and therefore absolutely incapable of conferring the authority, and assigning the duties which its words purport to confer and assign.

The constitution vests the whole judicial power of the United States in one Supreme Court, and such inferior courts as congress shall, from time to time, ordain and establish. * * *

In the distribution of this power it is declared that "the Supreme Court shall have original jurisdiction in all cases affecting ambassadors, other public ministers and consuls, and those in which a state shall be a party. In all other cases, the Supreme Court shall have appellate jurisdiction."

* * *

To enable this court, then, to issue a mandamus, it must be shown to be an exercise of appellate jurisdiction * * *.

* * *

It is the essential criterion of appellate jurisdiction, that it revises and corrects the proceedings in a cause already instituted, and does not create that cause. * * * [T]o issue such a writ [of mandamus] to an officer for the delivery of a paper, is in effect the same as to sustain an original action for that paper, and, therefore, seems not to belong to appellate, but to original jurisdiction. * * *

The authority, therefore, given to the Supreme Court, by the act establishing the judicial courts of the United States, to issue writs of mandamus to public officers, appears not to be warranted by the constitution; and it becomes necessary to inquire whether a jurisdiction so conferred can be exercised.

The question, whether an act, repugnant to the constitution, can become the law of the land, is a question deeply interesting to the United States; but, happily, not of an intricacy proportioned to its interest. It seems only necessary to recognize certain principles, supposed to have been long and well established, to decide it.

That the people have an original right to establish, for their future government, such principles, as, in their opinion, shall most conduce to their own happiness is the basis on which the whole American fabric has been erected. * * *

* * *

Certainly all those who have framed written constitutions contemplate them as forming the fundamental and paramount law of the nation, and, consequently, the theory of every such government must be, that an act of the legislature, repugnant to the constitution, is void.

* * *

If an act of the legislature, repugnant to the constitution, is void, does it, notwithstanding its invalidity, bind the courts, and oblige them to give it effect? * * *

It is emphatically the province and duty of the judicial department to say what the law is. Those who apply the rule to particular cases, must of necessity expound and interpret that rule. If two laws conflict with each other, the courts must decide on the operation of each.

So if a law be in the opposition to the constitution; if both the law and the constitution apply to a particular case, so that the court must either decide that case conformably to the law, disregarding the constitution; or conformably to the constitution, disregarding the law; the court must determine which of these conflicting rules governs the case. This is of the very essence of judicial duty.

If, then, the courts are to regard the constitution, and the constitution is superior to any ordinary act of the legislature, the constitution, and not such ordinary act, must govern the case to which they both apply.

* * *

* * * [I]t is apparent, that the framers of the constitution contemplated that instrument as a rule for the government of courts, as well as of the legislature.

Why otherwise does it direct the judges to take an oath to support it? * * *

It is also not entirely unworthy of observation, that in declaring what shall be the supreme law of the land, the constitution itself is first mentioned; and not the laws of the United States generally * * *.

Thus, the particular phraseology of the constitution of the United States confirms and strengthens the principle, supposed to be essential to all written constitutions, and that a law repugnant to the constitution is void; and that courts, as well as other departments, are bound by that instrument.

The rule must be discharged.

Notes and Questions

1. *Marbury* held that legislation that conflicts with the U.S. Constitution is void and unenforceable, and that it is the court's role rather than the legislature's to "say what the law is" and determine when constitution and statute conflict.

Questions: Why might rational maximizers drafting a constitution want to ensure that the constitution's provisions trump inconsistent legislation subsequently passed under majority rule? Why might they create an independent government branch to determine when legislation conflicts with constitutional provisions rather than leave the question of constitutionality to the legislature?

2. The economic theory of legislation supposes that statutes are the product of interest group lobbying in the legislature. A court that strikes down legislation on constitutional grounds would appear to interfere with that process and to curb legislative catering to special interests.

In The Independent Judiciary: An Interest–Group Perspective, 18 J. L. & Econ. 875, 879 (1975), William Landes and Richard Posner argued that rather than interfering with competition for legislation, an independent judiciary actually benefits interest groups hoping to extract favorable laws. They note that the economic theory of legislation portrays statutes as "bargains" between legislators and interest groups who lobby legislators and promise them political support. Unlike private contracts, however, bargains between politicians and interest groups are not binding.

> Legislation is not self-enforcing, however. If the people subject to a law refuse to obey it, recourse to the courts is necessary to enforce the law. A judiciary that was subservient to the current membership of the legislature could nullify legislation enacted in a previous session of the legislature. * * * Insofar as judges are merely agents of the current legislature, they will utilize their considerable interpretive leeway to rewrite the legislation in conformity with the views of the current rather than the enacting legislature and they will thereby impair the "contract" between the enacting legislature and the group that procured this legislation.

> If we assume that an independent judiciary would, in contrast, interpret and apply legislation in accordance with the original legislative understanding (an assumption examined shortly) it follows that an independent judiciary facilitates rather than, as conventionally believed, limits the practice of interest-group politics.

Questions: How does an independent judiciary further bargaining between legislators and interest groups by enforcing the terms of the original bargain underlying a statute? Can Landes' and Posner's view of the court's role be reconciled with the notion that the courts are a check on legislative authority? Consider the different roles courts play when they strike down statutes on constitutional grounds, and when they resolve issues of statutory interpretation between parties who disagree on a statute's meaning.

3. Article III of the U.S. Constitution provides that federal judges enjoy life tenure, and that Congress may not reduce judges' salaries while they remain in office.

Questions: How might Article III's provisions help the judiciary better serve the goal of maximizing society's well-being? How might those provisions threaten social welfare?

4. SEPARATION OF POWERS AND BICAMERALISM

IMMIGRATION AND NATURALIZATION
SERVICE v. CHADHA

Supreme Court of the United States, 1983.
462 U.S. 919, 103 S.Ct. 2764, 77 L.Ed.2d 317.

BURGER, CHIEF JUSTICE.

* * * [This case] presents a challenge to the constitutionality of the provision in § 244(c)(2) of the Immigration and Nationality Act, authorizing one House of Congress, by resolution, to invalidate the decision of the Executive Branch, pursuant to authority delegated by Congress to the Attorney General of the United States, to allow a particular deportable alien to remain in the United States.

[Chadha was born in Kenya and lawfully admitted to the United States in 1966 on a nonimmigrant student visa. His visa expired in 1972. Pursuant to § 244(c)(1), an immigration judge suspended Chadha's deportation and Attorney General conveyed to Congress a report recommending against deportation. A resolution opposing granting permanent United States residence to six aliens, including Chadha, was introduced in the House of Representatives and passed. Pursuant to § 244(c)(2), the resolution was not submitted to the Senate for a vote, nor to the President for signing. After the House vetoed the Attorney General's decision to allow Chadha to remain in the United States, the immigration judge reopened deportation proceedings. Chadha moved to terminate the proceedings on the ground that the Congress' veto of the Attorney General's decision under § 244(c)(2) was unconstitutional.]

* * *

* * * [T]he fact that a given law or procedure is efficient, convenient, and useful in facilitating functions of government, standing alone, will not save it if it is contrary to the Constitution. Convenience and efficiency are not the primary objectives—or the hallmarks—of democratic government and our inquiry is sharpened rather than blunted by the fact that congressional veto provisions are appearing with increasing frequency in statutes which delegate authority to executive and independent agencies * * *.

* * *

Explicit and unambiguous provisions of the Constitution prescribe and define the respective functions of the Congress and of the Executive in the legislative process. Since the precise terms of those familiar provisions are critical to the resolution of this case, we set them out verbatim. Art. I provides:

"All legislative Powers herein granted shall be vested in a Congress of the United States, which shall consist of a Senate *and* a House of Representatives." (Emphasis added).

"Every Bill which shall have passed the House of Representatives *and* the Senate, *shall,* before it becomes a Law, be presented to the President of the United States * * * " (Emphasis added).

"*Every* Order, Resolution, or Vote to which the Concurrence of the Senate and House of Representatives may be necessary (except on a question of Adjournment) *shall* be presented to the President of the United States; and before the Same shall take Effect, *shall* be approved by him, or being disapproved by him, *shall* be repassed by two thirds of the Senate and House of Representatives, according to the Rules and Limitations prescribed in the Case of a Bill." (Emphasis added).

These provisions of Art. I are integral parts of the constitutional design for the separation of powers.   * * *

* * *

The President's role in the lawmaking process [reflects] the Framers' careful efforts to check whatever propensity a particular Congress might have to enact oppressive, improvident, or ill-considered measures. The President's veto role in the legislative process was described later during public debate on ratification:

"It establishes a salutary check upon the legislative body, calculated to guard the community against the effects of faction, precipitancy, or of any impulse unfriendly to the public good which may happen to influence a majority of that body * * *." The Federalist No. 73, *supra,* at 458 (A. Hamilton).

The Court also has observed that the Presentment Clauses serve the important purpose of assuring that a "national" perspective is grafted on the legislative process:

"The President is a representative of the people just as the members of the Senate and of the House are, and it may be, at some times, on some subjects, that the President elected by all the people is rather more representative of them all than are the members of either body of the Legislature whose constituencies are local and not countrywide * * *."

The bicameral requirement of Art. I, §§ 1, 7 was of scarcely less concern to the Framers than was the Presidential veto and indeed the two concepts are interdependent.   * * *

* * *

However familiar, it is useful to recall that apart from their fear that special interests could be favored at the expense of public needs, the Framers were also concerned, although not of one mind, over the apprehensions of the smaller states. Those states feared a commonality of interest among the larger states would work to their disadvantage; representatives of the larger states, on the other hand, were skeptical of a legislature that could pass laws favoring a minority of the people. It need hardly be repeated here that the Great Compromise, under which one House was viewed as representing the people and the other the states, allayed the fears of both the large and small states.

We see therefore that the Framers were acutely conscious that the bicameral requirement and the Presentment Clauses would serve essential constitutional functions. * * * It emerges clearly that the prescription for legislative action in Art. I represents the Framers' decision that the legislative power of the Federal government be exercised in accord with a single, finely wrought and exhaustively considered, procedure.

* * *

* * * After long experience with the clumsy, time-consuming private bill procedure, Congress made a deliberate choice to delegate to the Executive Branch, and specifically to the Attorney General, the authority to allow deportable aliens to remain in this country in certain specified circumstances. It is not disputed that this choice to delegate authority is precisely the kind of decision that can be implemented only in accordance with the procedures set out in Art. I. Disagreement with the Attorney General's decision on Chadha's deportation—that is, Congress' decision to deport Chadha—no less than Congress' original choice to delegate to the Attorney General the authority to make that decision, involves determinations of policy that Congress can implement in only one way; bicameral passage followed by presentment to the President. Congress must abide by its delegation of authority until that delegation is legislatively altered or revoked.

* * *

The veto authorized by § 244(c)(2) doubtless has been in many respects a convenient shortcut; the "sharing" with the Executive by Congress of its authority over aliens in this manner is, on its face, an appealing compromise. In purely practical terms, it is obviously easier for action to be taken by one House without submission to the President; but it is crystal clear from the records of the Convention, contemporaneous writings and debates, that the Framers ranked other values higher than efficiency. * * *

The choices we discern as having been made in the Constitutional Convention impose burdens on governmental processes that often seem clumsy, inefficient, even unworkable, but those hard choices were consciously made by men who had lived under a form of government that permitted arbitrary governmental acts to go unchecked. * * * With all the obvious flaws of delay, untidiness, and potential for abuse, we have not yet found a better way to preserve freedom than by making the exercise of power subject to the carefully crafted restraints spelled out in the Constitution.

We hold that the Congressional veto provision in § 244(c)(2) is severable from the Act and that it is unconstitutional. Accordingly, the judgment of the Court of Appeals is

Affirmed.

Notes and Questions

1. The constitutional requirements that legislation be passed by both Houses and then presented to the President are inconvenient and cumber-

some. In Buchanan's and Tullock's terms, those requirements increase decisionmaking costs. A rational maximizer might still prefer to adopt such a system.

Consider the Presidential veto. Suppose a society decided to make public decisions according to majority rule in a national legislature of nine representatives. Each representative is elected by majority vote from a district with nine voters. The total number of voters in the nation is therefore 81. Consider the effect of adding a president with power to veto legislation, who is elected by a simply majority of all 81 voters.

Questions: What is the smallest number of voters who could push through legislation in the absence of a presidential veto? With a presidential veto? In economic terms, what purpose is served by a veto that increases decisionmaking costs?

2. Article I's bicameral requirement ensures that no federal legislation is passed without the approval of both a majority of the Senate and of the House. Two different classes of representative politicians—House members and Senators—have group power to veto legislation proposed by the other House.

Questions: What interests or constituencies are likely to be served by Senators and Representatives, respectively? What possible advantage might follow from giving those constituencies a veto over proposed legislation?

5. RATIONALITY REVIEW AND THE REQUIREMENT OF PUBLIC PURPOSE

HAWAII HOUSING AUTHORITY v. MIDKIFF

Supreme Court of the United States, 1984.
467 U.S. 229, 104 S.Ct. 2321, 81 L.Ed.2d 186.

O'CONNOR, JUSTICE.

The Fifth Amendment of the United States Constitution provides, in pertinent part, that "private property [shall not] be taken for public use, without just compensation." These cases present the question whether the Public Use Clause of that Amendment, made applicable to the States through the Fourteenth Amendment, prohibits the State of Hawaii from taking, with just compensation, title in real property from lessors and transferring it to lessees in order to reduce the concentration of ownership of fees simple in the State. We conclude that it does not.

The Hawaiian Islands were originally settled by Polynesian immigrants from the western Pacific. These settlers developed an economy around a feudal land tenure system in which one island high chief, the ali'i nui, controlled the land and assigned it for development to certain subchiefs. * * *

Beginning in the early 1800's, Hawaiian leaders and American settlers repeatedly attempted to divide the lands of the kingdom among the crown, the chiefs, and the common people. These efforts proved largely unsuccessful, however, and the land remained in the hands of a few. In the mid–1960's, after extensive hearings, the Hawaii Legislature discovered that while the State and Federal Governments owned almost 49% of the State's land, another 47% was in the hands of only 72 private landowners. * * * The legislature concluded that concentrated land ownership was responsible for skewing the State's residential fee simple market, inflating land prices and injuring the public tranquility and welfare.

To redress these problems, the legislature decided to compel the large landowners to break up their estates. * * * [T]he Hawaii Legislature enacted the Land Reform Act of 1967 (Act), which created a mechanism for condemning residential tracts and for transferring ownership of the condemned fees simple to existing lessees. * * *

* * *

* * * [T]he Court of Appeals [for the Ninth Circuit] determined that the Act could not pass the requisite judicial scrutiny of the Public Use Clause. It found that the transfers contemplated by the Act were unlike those of takings previously held to constitute "public uses" by this Court. The court further determined that the public purposes offered by the Hawaii Legislature were not deserving of judicial deference. The court concluded that the Act was simply "a naked attempt on the part of the state of Hawaii to take the private property of A and transfer it to B solely for B's private use and benefit." * * *

* * *

The starting point for our analysis of the Act's constitutionality is the Court's decision in *Berman v. Parker.* In *Berman,* the Court held constitutional the District of Columbia Redevelopment Act of 1945. That Act provided both for the comprehensive use of the eminent domain power to redevelop slum areas and for the possible sale or lease of the condemned lands to private interests. In discussing whether the takings authorized by that Act were for a "public use," the Court stated:

> "We deal, in other words, with what traditionally has been known as the police power. * * * [W]hen the legislature has spoken, the public interest has been declared in terms well-nigh conclusive. In such cases the legislature, not the judiciary, is the main guardian of the public needs to be served by social legislation * * * This principle admits of no exception merely because the power of eminent domain is involved * * *."

The Court explicitly recognized the breadth of the principle it was announcing, noting:

> "Once the object is within the authority of Congress, the right to realize it through the exercise of eminent domain is clear. For the power of eminent domain is merely the means to the end.... Once the object is within the authority of Congress, the means by which it

will be attained is also for Congress to determine. Here one of the means chosen is the use of private enterprise for redevelopment of the area. Appellants argue that this makes the project a taking from one businessman for the benefit of another businessman. But the means of executing the project are for Congress and Congress alone to determine, once the public purposes has been established."

The "public use" requirement is thus coterminous with the scope of a sovereign's police powers.

There is a role for courts to play in reviewing a legislature's judgment of what constitutes a public use, even when the eminent domain power is equated with the police power. But the Court in *Berman* made clear that it is "an extremely narrow" one. * * *

To be sure, the Court's cases have repeatedly stated that "one person's property may not be taken for the benefit of another private person without a justifying public purpose, even though compensation be paid." * * * But where the exercise of the eminent domain power is rationally related to a conceivable public purpose, the Court has never held a compensated taking to be proscribed by the Public Use Clause.

On this basis, we have no trouble concluding that the Hawaii Act is constitutional. The people of Hawaii have attempted, much as the settlers of the original 13 Colonies did, to reduce the perceived social and economic evils of a land oligopoly traceable to their monarchs. The land oligopoly has, according to the Hawaii Legislature, created artificial deterrents to the normal functioning of the State's residential land market and forced thousands of individual homeowners to lease, rather than buy, the land underneath their homes. Regulating oligopoly and the evils associated with it is a classic exercise of a State's police powers. We cannot disapprove of Hawaii's exercise of this power.

Nor can we condemn as irrational the Act's approach to correcting the land oligopoly problem. * * *

Of course, this Act, like any other, may not be successful in achieving its intended goals. But "whether *in fact* the provision will accomplish its objectives is not the question: the [constitutional requirement] is satisfied if ... the ... Legislature *rationally could have believed* that the [Act] would promote its objective." When the legislature's purpose is legitimate and its means are not irrational, our cases make clear that empirical debates over the wisdom of takings—no less than debates over the wisdom of other kinds of socioeconomic legislation—are not to be carried out in the federal courts. Redistribution of fees simple to correct deficiencies in the market determined by the state legislature to be attributable to land oligopoly is a rational exercise of the eminent domain power. Therefore, the Hawaii statute must pass the scrutiny of the Public Use Clause.

* * *

The State of Hawaii has never denied that the Constitution forbids even a compensated taking of property when executed for no reason other than to confer a private benefit on a particular private party. A purely private taking could not withstand the scrutiny of the public use requirement; it would serve no legitimate purpose of government and would be void. But no purely private taking is involved in these cases. The Hawaii Legislature enacted its Land Reform Act not to benefit a particular class of identifiable individuals but to attack certain perceived evils of concentrated property ownership in Hawaii—a legitimate public purpose. Use of the condemnation power to achieve this purpose is not irrational. Since we assume for purposes of these appeals that the weighty demand of just compensation has been met, the requirements of the Fifth and Fourteenth Amendments have been satisfied. Accordingly, we reverse the judgment of the Court of Appeals, and remand these cases for further proceedings in conformity with this opinion.

It is so ordered.

Notes and Questions

1. The state may exercise its coercive "police power" to require vaccination (*Jacobson*); to take property (*Midkiff*); and even to imprison innocent individuals (*Korematsu*). Nevertheless, the Constitution circumscribes the state's authority. Among other limitations, state action is confined by a requirement that it serve more than purely private interests.

In *Midkiff,* Justice O'Connor found the requirement of "public use" in the language of the Takings Clause itself. A similar limitation is implied in Supreme Court cases under the Due Process and Equal Protection clauses requiring state actions and classifications to be rationally related to a legitimate "public purpose." See discussion following *Bowers* and *U.N. Declaration of Human Rights,* above.

The requirement that state action be directed to public rather than private ends may be recharacterized as a requirement that state intervention operate to increase society's level of well-being rather than simply redistribute wealth or utility from one group or individual to another.

> *Question:* Suppose that, in *Midkiff,* the Court had *not* found that the concentration of Hawaiian lands in the hands of a few large landowners created monopoly power distorting land and rental prices. Instead, the Hawaiian legislature simply felt that large landholdings were inequitable and should be broken up and redistributed to a broader segment of the public. Would such a motivation be a "public purpose" justifying the exercise of the state's police power?

2. *Midkiff* indicates that a government taking must bear a "rational" relationship to the legislature's intended public purpose. The Due Process Clause similarly requires that state action be rationally related to a legitimate public objective. See *Lee Optical,* above. The Supreme Court also has read the Equal Protection Clause to require state classifications to be rationally related to a public purpose. See United States Department of Agriculture v. Moreno, 413 U.S. 528, 93 S.Ct. 2821, 37 L.Ed.2d 782 (1973) (striking down federal law restricting foodstamp eligibility to households of related individuals on the ground that the restriction bore no rational

connection to the foodstamp statute's public purposes, but only to the impermissible purpose of discriminating against "hippies").

Professor Cass Sunstein has argued that "[t]he rationality requirement may * * * be understood precisely as a requirement that regulatory measures be something other than a response to political pressure" by rent-seeking interest groups. Sunstein, Interest Groups in American Public Law, 38 Stan.L.Rev. 29, 49 (1985).

> *Question:* How much protection does the rationality requirement provide against welfare-reducing redistributive state action?

6. TAKINGS AND THE REQUIREMENT OF COMPENSATION

LORETTO v. TELEPROMPTER MANHATTAN CATV CORP.

Supreme Court of the United States, 1982.
458 U.S. 419, 102 S.Ct. 3164, 73 L.Ed.2d 868.

MARSHALL, JUSTICE.

This case presents the question whether a minor but permanent physical occupation of an owner's property authorized by government constitutes a "taking" of property for which just compensation is due under the Fifth and Fourteenth Amendments of the Constitution. New York law provides that a landlord must permit a cable television company to install its cable facilities upon his property. N.Y. Exec.Law § 828. In this case, the cable installation occupied portions of appellant's roof and the side of her building. The New York Court of Appeals ruled that this appropriation does not amount to a taking. Because we conclude that such a physical occupation of property is a taking, we reverse.

* * *

On appeal, the Court of Appeals * * * ruled that the law serves a legitimate police power purpose—eliminating landlord fees and conditions that inhibit the development of CATV, which has important educational and community benefits. Rejecting the argument that a physical occupation authorized by government is necessarily a taking, the court stated that the regulation does not have an excessive economic impact upon appellant when measured against her aggregate property rights, and that it does not interfere with any reasonable investment-backed expectations. Accordingly, the court held that § 828 does not work a taking of appellant's property. * * *

* * *

In *Penn Central Transportation Co. v. New York City,* the Court surveyed some of the general principles governing the Takings Clause. The Court noted that no "set formula" existed to determine, in all cases, whether compensation is constitutionally due for a government restriction of property. Ordinarily, the Court must engage in "essentially ad hoc, factual inquiries." But the inquiry is not standardless.

The economic impact of the regulation, especially the degree of interference with investment-backed expectations, is of particular significance. "So, too, is the character of the governmental action. A 'taking' may more readily be found when the interference with property can be characterized as a physical invasion by government, than when interference arises from some public program adjusting the benefits and burdens of economic life to promote the common good."

As *Penn Central* affirms, the Court has often upheld substantial regulation of an owner's use of his own property where deemed necessary to promote the public interest. At the same time, we have long considered a physical intrusion by government to be a property restriction of an unusually serious character for purposes of the Takings Clause. Our cases further establish that when the physical intrusion reaches the extreme form of a permanent physical occupation, a taking has occurred. In such a case, "the character of the government action" not only is an important factor in resolving whether the action works a taking but also is determinative.

* * *

Teleprompter's cable installation on appellant's building constitutes a taking under the traditional test. The installation involved a direct physical attachment of plates, boxes, wires, bolts, and screws to the building, completely occupying space above and upon the roof and along the building's exterior wall.

* * *

Our holding today is very narrow. We affirm the traditional rule that a permanent physical occupation of property is a taking. In such a case the property owner entertains a historically rooted expectation of compensation * * *. We do not, however, question the equally substantial authority upholding a State's broad power to impose appropriate restrictions upon an owner's *use* of his property.

* * *

The judgment of the New York Court of Appeals is reversed, and the case is remanded for further proceedings not inconsistent with this opinion.

It is so ordered.

BLACKMUN, JUSTICE, dissenting.

* * *

Before examining the Court's new takings rule, it is worth reviewing what was "taken" in this case. At issue are about 36 feet of cable one-half inch in diameter and two 4" X 4" X 4" metal boxes. Jointly, the cable and boxes occupy only about one-eighth of a cubic foot of space on the roof of appellant's Manhattan apartment building. * * *

* * *

The Court's recent Takings Clause decisions teach that *nonphysical* government intrusions on private property, such as zoning ordinances and other land-use restrictions, have become the rule rather than the exception. Modern government regulation exudes intangible "externalities" that may diminish the value of private property far more than minor physical touching. Nevertheless, as the Court recognizes, it has "often upheld substantial regulation of an owner's use of his own property where deemed necessary to promote the public interest."

* * *

* * * [Section] 828 differs little from the numerous other New York statutory provisions that require landlords to install physical facilities "permanently occupying" common spaces in or on their buildings. As the Court acknowledges, the States traditionally—and constitutionally—have exercised their police power "to require landlords to * * * provide utility connections, mailboxes, smoke detectors, fire extinguishers, and the like in the common area of a building." * * *

* * * For example, New York landlords are required by law to provide and pay for mailboxes that occupy more than five times the volume that Teleprompter's cable occupies on appellant's building. If the State constitutionally can insist that appellant make this sacrifice so that her tenants may receive mail, it is hard to understand why the State may not require her to surrender less space, *filled at another's expense*, so that those same tenants can receive television signals.

For constitutional purposes, the relevant question cannot be solely *whether* the State has interfered in some minimal way with an owner's use of space on her building. Any intelligible takings inquiry must also ask whether the *extent* of the State's interference is so severe as to constitute a compensable taking in light of the owner's alternative uses for the property. * * *

* * *

I would affirm the judgment and uphold the reasoning of the New York Court of Appeals.

Notes and Questions

1. *Loretto* held that when the state physically and permanently occupied a citizens' property, a taking had occurred and the state must pay just compensation under the Fifth and Fourteenth Amendments. Outside the context of a permanent physical occupation, however, the question of what amounts to a taking demanding compensation is muddled. As Justice Blackmun noted in his dissent, virtually every state regulation interferes with private property to some degree. Regulatory restrictions on the use one can make of one's property can impose a far greater degree of hardship than the minimal physical occupation in *Loretto*. At the same time, "[g]overnment could hardly go on if to some extent values incident to property could not be diminished without paying for every such change in the general law." Pennsylvania Coal Co. v. Mahon, 260 U.S. 393, 413, 43 S.Ct. 158, 67 L.Ed. 322 (1922).

In Penn Central Transportation Co. v. New York City, 438 U.S. 104, 98 S.Ct. 2646, 56 L.Ed.2d 631 (1978), the Supreme Court reviewed a New York statute designed to preserve architectural landmarks by restricting the owner's ability to remove or alter landmark features without the approval of the New York Landmarks Preservation Commission. Penn Central, the owner of Grand Central Terminal in New York City, arranged a long-term lease with a developer which planned to build a 55–story tower atop the Terminal. Penn Central was to receive $3 million a year under the lease. However, the Landmark Preservation Commission refused to grant permission for such an alteration and Penn Central sued, claiming that the Commission's decision deprived it of property without compensation.

Justice Brennan's opinion for the majority noted that the question of whether or not such regulation amounted to a taking was an "essentially ad hoc, factual" inquiry. Among the relevant factors to be considered were "[t]he economic impact of the regulation, especially the degree of interference with investment-backed expectations" and "the character" of the governmental action: a physical invasion was more likely to be found a taking than regulatory interference with an owner's use. Ultimately, the Court held that Penn Central's loss did not amount to a taking requiring compensation.

> *Question: Penn Central* suggests that the state can adopt regulations that impose severe economic losses on groups or individuals without paying for those losses. From an efficiency perspective, what risks are presented by such a rule?

2. In Nollan v. California Coastal Commission, 483 U.S. 825, 107 S.Ct. 3141, 97 L.Ed.2d 677 (1987), property owners sought to overturn a decision by the Coastal Commission that conditioned the granting of a permit to rebuild their beach home upon their providing the public with a right-of-way across their beach. The owners claimed that the state's action was not mere regulation but instead amounted to a taking requiring compensation. Justice Scalia, writing for the majority, held that the permit system amounted to a taking. He also indicated that when reviewing state regulation of land uses, the Court ought to apply a standard of review higher than the mere rationality required by the Due Process and Equal Protection Clauses. In particular, the Court ought to examine whether the regulation "substantially advances" (rather than being merely "rationally related to") legitimate state interests. See 483 U.S. at 835 & n.3.

3. When the state does take property in a fashion that requires compensation, that compensation must be "full." In a dissent in *Penn Central,* Justice Rehnquist stated that "[t]he Fifth Amendment does not allow simply an approximate compensation but requires 'a full and perfect equivalent for the property taken.'" 438 U.S. at 150, 98 S.Ct. at 2672.

> *Question:* Why is it important that compensation for a government taking of private property be a "perfect equivalent"?

4. Recall the Supreme Court's declaration in Midkiff v. Hawaiian Housing Authority, above, that even with full compensation, takings may only be made for a public use.

Question: Assuming as Justice O'Connor did in *Midkiff* that "the weighty demand of just compensation has been met," does requiring a public justification for a government taking improve the efficiency of state action?

5. The U.S. Constitution was drafted by prosperous, propertied individuals with full knowledge of their relative place in society.

Question: If the Takings Clause does not serve efficiency goals, is there another reason why the Framers might have included that provision in their Constitution?

7. STRICT SCRUTINY AND FUNDAMENTAL RIGHTS

SHAPIRO v. THOMPSON

Supreme Court of the United States, 1969.
394 U.S. 618, 89 S.Ct. 1322, 22 L.Ed.2d 660.

BRENNAN, JUSTICE.

These three appeals were restored to the calendar for reargument. Each is an appeal from a decision of a three-judge District Court holding unconstitutional a State or District of Columbia statutory provision which denies welfare assistance to residents of the State or District who have not resided within their jurisdictions for at least one year immediately preceding their applications for such assistance. We affirm the judgments of the District Courts in the three cases.

* * *

There is no dispute that the effect of the waiting-period requirement in each case is to create two classes of needy resident families indistinguishable from each other except that one is composed of residents who have resided a year or more, and the second of residents who have resided less than a year, in the jurisdiction. On the basis of this sole difference the first class is granted and the second class is denied welfare aid upon which may depend the ability of the families to obtain the very means to subsist—food, shelter, and other necessities of life. * * * [A]ppellees' central contention is that the statutory prohibition of benefits to residents of less than a year creates a classification which constitutes an invidious discrimination denying them equal protection of the laws. We agree. The interests which appellants assert are promoted by the classification either may not constitutionally be promoted by government or are not compelling governmental interests.

Primarily, appellants justify the waiting-period requirement as a protective device to preserve the fiscal integrity of state public assistance programs. It is asserted that people who require welfare assistance during their first year of residence in a State are likely to become continuing burdens on state welfare programs. Therefore, the argument runs, if such people can be deterred from entering the jurisdiction by denying them welfare benefits during the first year, state programs to assist long-time residents will not be impaired by a substantial influx of indigent newcomers.

* * *

We do not doubt that the one-year waiting-period device is well suited to discourage the influx of poor families in need of assistance. An indigent who desires to migrate, resettle, find a new job, and start a new life will doubtless hesitate if he knows that he must risk making the move without the possibility of falling back on state welfare assistance during his first year of residence, when his need may be most acute. But the purpose of inhibiting migration by needy persons into the State is constitutionally impermissible.

This Court long ago recognized that the nature of our Federal Union and our constitutional concepts of personal liberty unite to require that all citizens be free to travel throughout the length and breadth of our land uninhibited by statutes, rules, or regulations which unreasonably burden or restrict this movement. * * *

We have no occasion to ascribe the source of this right to travel interstate to a particular constitutional provision. It suffices that, as Mr. Justice Stewart said for the Court in *United States v. Guest:*

"The constitutional right to travel from one State to another ... occupies a position fundamental to the concept of our Federal Union. It is a right that has been firmly established and repeatedly recognized.

"... (The) right finds no explicit mention in the Constitution. The reason, it has been suggested, is that a right so elementary was conceived from the beginning to be a necessary concomitant of the stronger Union the Constitution created. In any event, freedom to travel throughout the United States has long been recognized as a basic right under the Constitution."

Thus, the purpose of deterring the in-migration of indigents cannot serve as justification for the classification created by the one-year waiting period, since that purpose is constitutionally impermissible. * * *

* * *

* * * [A] State may no more try to fence out those indigents who seek higher welfare benefits than it may try to fence out indigents generally. Implicit in any such distinction is the notion that indigents who enter a State with the hope of securing higher welfare benefits are somehow less deserving than indigents who do not take this consideration into account. But we do not perceive why a mother who is seeking to make a new life for herself and her children should be regarded as less deserving because she considers, among others factors, the level of a State's public assistance. Surely such a mother is no less deserving than a mother who moves into a particular State in order to take advantage of its better educational facilities.

* * *

Appellants next advance as justification certain administrative and related governmental objectives allegedly served by the waiting-period requirement. They argue that the requirement (1) facilitates the planning of the welfare budget; (2) provides an objective test of residency; (3) minimizes the opportunity for recipients fraudulently to receive payments from more than one jurisdiction; and (4) encourages early entry of new residents into the labor force.

At the outset, we reject appellants' argument that a mere showing of a rational relationship between the waiting period and these four admittedly permissible state objectives will suffice to justify the classification. * * * [I]n moving from State to State or to the District of Columbia appellees were exercising a constitutional right, and any classification which serves to penalize the exercise of that right, unless shown to be necessary to promote a *compelling* governmental interest, is unconstitutional.

* * *

Under this standard, the waiting-period requirement clearly violates the Equal Protection Clause.

* * *

Accordingly, the judgments in [these three appeals] are

Affirmed.

Notes and Questions

1. Following the demise of *Lochner* substantive due process, the Supreme Court has generally upheld legislative action under the Due Process Clause if it was rationally related to a legitimate public objective. The Court usually has applied a similar rational relation standard to government classifications under the Equal Protection Clause. See *Lee Optical* Question 7 and *Midkiff* Questions 1 and 2, above.

However, under both the Due Process and Equal Protection Clauses, state action or classifications that burden the exercise of a "fundamental right" have been held to the higher standard of strict scrutiny. The Equal Protection Clause also has required strict scrutiny when the state employed a "suspect classification." The strict scrutiny standard requires that legislation and classifications be "necessary" to a "compelling" government objective. Strict scrutiny appears to require both a greater degree of public interest to justify state intervention *and* a tighter causal link between that interest and the legislature's chosen means of pursuing it.

Justice Brennan's opinion for the majority in *Shapiro* struck down the welfare statutes at issue under strict scrutiny because their minimum residency requirements burdened a fundamental "right to travel" implied in the Constitution. What rights are or are not "fundamental" is not always obvious. The Court regularly has held that rights explicitly guaranteed by the Constitution, such as the First Amendment freedoms of assembly and of speech, are fundamental and legislation burdening those rights is subject to strict scrutiny under the Due Process and Equal Protection Clauses. However, the Court also has held that the Constitution implies other fundamental rights not expressly provided for in that document. See *Shapiro*, above (right to travel); Skinner v. Oklahoma, 316 U.S. 535, 62 S.Ct. 1110, 86 L.Ed 1655 (1942) (fundamental right to marriage and procreation); Griswold v. Connecticut, 381 U.S. 479, 85 S.Ct. 1678, 14 L.Ed.2d 510 (1965) (right to privacy in use of contraceptives); Cruzan v. Director Missouri Department of Health, ___ U.S. ___, 110 S.Ct. 2841, 111 L.Ed.2d 224 (1990) (implied right to die rather than continue in persistent vegetative state). Still other rights have been held "fundamental" in the sense that, while the state had no obligation to provide that right, having elected to do so it could not discriminate among classes in a manner inconsistent with the Equal Protection Clause. See Harper v. Virginia Board of Elections and Kramer v. Union Free School District, above (discriminatory voter qualifications).

The Warren Court inclined toward broadening the concept of fundamental rights. The modern Court has been reluctant to expand the concept of fundamental rights beyond the cases that form the Warren Court's legacy. See *U.N. Declaration of Human Rights* Question 1, above.

2. Consider whether there might be economic justifications for according fundamental rights greater protection against legislative incursion than other rights. Rawls has argued that individuals negotiating a social contract behind a veil of ignorance will allocate political liberties equally, and will not tolerate differences in the level of political liberty society's members enjoy. See *U.N. Declaration of Human Rights* Question 1, above. Arrow's Theorem suggests that a legislature acting under majority rule may pass laws that impose greater disutility on the dissenting minority than the utility those laws provide to the approving majority. See *Kramer* Questions 3 and 5, *Bowers* Question 4, above. Judge Posner has argued that "[t]he nonpolitical rights in the Constitution (some of them are in it, though, only by judicial interpretation) are more plausibly regarded as a particularly durable form of legislative protection obtained by particularly effective interest groups * * *." R. Posner, Economic Analysis of Law 585 (3d ed. 1986). As an example, Posner suggested that the First Amendment may be viewed as "a form of protective legislation on behalf of an interest group consisting of intellectuals, publishers, journalists, pamphleteers, and others who derive pecuniary and nonpecuniary income from publication and advocacy." *Id.*

> *Question:* How do each of the above approaches explain strict judicial scrutiny for statutes burdening fundamental rights while statutes burdening other rights need only meet the rational relation standard?

3. *Shapiro* held that a fundamental right to travel freely from one state to another was implicit in the U.S. Constitution. Justice Brennan argued that the right to interstate travel applied without regard to a citizen's motive for moving: a mother who moves to obtain a higher level of public assistance is "no less deserving than a mother who moves into a particular State in order to take advantage of its better educational facilities."

> *Question:* How might a fundamental right to travel promote overall social welfare? Consider the differing implications of a right freely to exit any state and a right freely to enter any state.

8. STRICT SCRUTINY AND SUSPECT CLASSIFICATION

REGENTS OF UNIVERSITY OF CALIFORNIA v. BAKKE

Supreme Court of the United States, 1978.
438 U.S. 265, 98 S.Ct. 2733, 57 L.Ed.2d 750.

POWELL, JUSTICE.

This case presents a challenge to the special admissions program of the petitioner, the Medical School of the University of California at Davis, which is designed to assure the admission of a specified number of students from certain minority groups. * * *

* * *

Allan Bakke is a white male who applied to the Davis Medical School in both 1973 and 1974. In both years Bakke's application was considered under the general admissions program, and he received an interview. [In both years Bakke's applications were rejected.] * * *

* * * In both years, [black, Mexican–American, and Asian] applicants were admitted under the special program with grade point averages, MCAT scores, and benchmark scores significantly lower than Bakke's.

After the second rejection, Bakke filed the instant suit in the Superior Court of California. He sought mandatory, injunctive, and declaratory relief compelling his admission to the Medical School. He alleged that the Medical School's special admissions program operated to exclude him from the school on the basis of his race, in violation of his rights under the Equal Protection Clause of the Fourteenth Amendment * * *.

* * *

* * * Because the special admissions program involved a racial classification, the [California] Supreme Court held itself bound to apply strict scrutiny. * * * [T]he California Court held that the Equal Protection Clause of the Fourteenth Amendment required that "no applicant may be rejected because of his race, in favor of another who is less qualified, as measured by standards applied without regard to race." * * *

* * *

The guarantees of the Fourteenth Amendment extend to all persons. Its language is explicit: "No State shall ... deny to any person within its jurisdiction the equal protection of the laws." * * * The guarantee of equal protection cannot mean one thing when applied to one individual and something else when applied to a person of another color. If both are not accorded the same protection, then it is not equal.

Nevertheless, petitioner argues that the court below erred in applying strict scrutiny to the special admissions program because white males, such as respondent, are not a "discrete and insular minority" requiring extraordinary protection from the majoritarian political process. *Carolene Products Co.,* 304 U.S., at 152–153 n. 4. This rationale, however, has never been invoked in our decisions as a prerequisite to subjecting racial or ethnic distinctions to strict scrutiny. Nor has this Court held that discreteness and insularity constitute necessary preconditions to a holding that a particular classification is invidious. These characteristics may be relevant in deciding whether or not to add new types of classifications to the list of "suspect" categories or whether a particular classification survives close examination. Racial and ethnic classifications, however, are subject to stringent examination without regard to these additional characteristics. * * * Racial and ethnic distinctions of any sort are inherently suspect and thus call for the most exacting judicial examination.

This perception of racial and ethnic distinctions is rooted in our Nation's constitutional and demographic history. The Court's initial view of the Fourteenth Amendment was that its "one pervading purpose" was "the freedom of the slave race, the security and firm establishment of that freedom, and the protection of the newly-made freeman and citizen from the oppressions of those who had formerly exercised dominion over him."

* * * [It is] no longer possible to peg the guarantees of the Fourteenth Amendment to the struggle for equality of one racial minority. * * * [T]he United States [has] become a Nation of minorities. Each had to struggle—and to some extent struggles still—to overcome the prejudices not of a monolithic majority, but of a "majority" composed of various minority groups of whom it was said—perhaps unfairly in many cases—that a shared characteristic was a willingness to disadvantage other groups. As the Nation filled with the stock of many lands, the reach of the Clause was gradually extended to all ethnic groups seeking protection from official discrimination. * * *

* * *

* * * Because the landmark decisions in this area arose in response to the continued exclusion of Negroes from the mainstream of American society, they could be characterized as involving discrimination by the "majority" white race against the Negro minority. But they need not be read as depending upon that characterization for their results. It suffices to say that "[o]ver the years, this Court has consistently repudiated '[d]istinctions between citizens solely because of their ancestry' as being 'odious to a free people whose institutions are founded upon the doctrine of equality.' "

* * *

We have held that in "order to justify the use of a suspect classification, a State must show that its purpose or interest is both constitutionally permissible and substantial, and that its use of the classification is 'necessary ... to the accomplishment' of its purpose or the safeguarding of its interest." The special admissions program purports to serve the purposes of: (i) "reducing the historic deficit of traditionally disfavored minorities in medical schools and in the medical profession," (ii) countering the effects of societal discrimination; (iii) increasing the number of physicians who will practice in communities currently underserved; and (iv) obtaining the educational benefits that flow from an ethnically diverse student body. It is necessary to decide which, if any, of these purposes is substantial enough to support the use of a suspect classification.

If petitioner's purpose is to assure within its student body some specified percentage of a particular group merely because of its race or ethnic origin, such a preferential purpose must be rejected not as insubstantial but as facially invalid. Preferring members of any one group for no reason other than race or ethnic origin is discrimination for its own sake. This the Constitution forbids. * * *

The State certainly has a legitimate and substantial interest in ameliorating, or eliminating where feasible, the disabling effects of identified discrimination. * * *

We have never approved a classification that aids persons perceived as members of relatively victimized groups at the expense of other innocent individuals in the absence of judicial, legislative, or administrative findings of constitutional or statutory violations. * * * Without such findings of constitutional or statutory violations, it cannot be said that the government has any greater interest in helping one individual than in refraining from harming another. Thus, the government has no compelling justification for inflicting such harm.

* * *

Petitioner identifies, as another purpose of its program, improving the delivery of health-care services to communities currently underserved. It may be assumed that in some situations a State's interest in facilitating the health care of its citizens is sufficiently compelling to support the use of a suspect classification. But there is virtually no evidence in the record indicating that petitioner's special admissions program is either needed or geared to promote that goal. * * *

* * *

* * * As the interest of diversity is compelling in the context of a university's admissions program, the question remains whether the program's racial classification is necessary to promote this interest.

* * *

The experience of other university admissions programs, which take race into account in achieving the educational diversity valued by the First Amendment, demonstrates that the assignment of a fixed number of places to a minority group is not a necessary means toward that end. * * *

* * *

It has been suggested that an admissions program which considers race only as one factor is simply a subtle and more sophisticated—but no less effective—means of according racial preference than the Davis program. A facial intent to discriminate, however, is evident in petitioner's preference program and not denied in this case. No such facial infirmity exists in an admissions program where race or ethnic background is simply one element—to be weighed fairly against other elements—in the selection process. * * *

In summary, it is evident that the Davis special admissions program involves the use of an explicit racial classification never before countenanced by this Court. It tells applicants who are not Negro, Asian, or Chicano that they are totally excluded from a specific percentage of the seats in an entering class. No matter how strong their qualifications, quantitative and extracurricular, including their own potential for contribution to educational diversity, they are never afforded the chance to compete with applicants from the preferred groups for the special admissions seats. At the same time, the preferred applicants have the opportunity to compete for every seat in the class.

The fatal flaw in petitioner's preferential program is its disregard of individual rights as guaranteed by the Fourteenth Amendment. Such rights are not absolute. But when a State's distribution of benefits or imposition of burdens hinges on ancestry or the color of a person's skin, that individual is entitled to a demonstration that the challenged classification is necessary to promote a substantial state interest. Petitioner has failed to carry this burden. For this reason, that portion of the California court's judgment holding the petitioner's special admissions program invalid under the Fourteenth Amendment must be affirmed.

* * *

BRENNAN, JUSTICE, concurring in the judgment in part and dissenting in part.

* * *

* * * Since we conclude that the affirmative admissions program at the Davis Medical School is constitutional, we would reverse the judgment below in all respects. Mr. Justice Powell agrees that some uses of race in university admissions are permissible and, therefore, he joins with us to make five votes reversing the judgment below insofar as it prohibits the University from establishing race-conscious programs in the future.

* * *

Unquestionably we have held that a government practice or statute which restricts "fundamental rights" or which contains "suspect classifications" is to be subjected to "strict scrutiny" and can be justified only if it furthers a compelling government purpose and, even then, only if no less restrictive alternative is available. But no fundamental right is involved here. Nor do whites as a class have any of the "traditional indicia of suspectness: the class is not saddled with such disabilities, or subjected to such a history of purposeful unequal treatment, or relegated to such a position of political powerlessness as to command extraordinary protection from the majoritarian political process."

* * *

On the other hand, the fact that this case does not fit neatly into our prior analytic framework for race cases does not mean that it should be analyzed by applying the very loose rational-basis standard of review that is the very least that is always applied in equal protection cases. * * * Instead, a number of considerations—developed in gender-discrimination cases but which carry even more force when applied to racial classifications—lead us to conclude that racial classifications designed to further remedial purposes " 'must serve important governmental objectives and must be substantially related to achievement of those objectives.' "

* * *

[R]ace, like gender and illegitimacy, is an immutable characteristic which its possessors are powerless to escape or set aside. While a classification is not *per se* invalid because it divides classes on the basis of an immutable characteristic, it is nevertheless true that such divisions are contrary to our deep belief that "legal burdens should bear some relationship to individual responsibility or wrongdoing," and that advancement sanctioned, sponsored, or approved by the State should ideally be based on individual merit or achievement, or at the least on factors within the control of an individual.

* * * [I]t is clear from our cases that there are limits beyond which majorities may not go when they classify on the basis of immutable characteristics. Thus, even if the concern for individualism is weighed by the political process, that weighing cannot waive the personal rights of individuals under the Fourteenth Amendment.

In sum, because of the significant risk that racial classifications established for ostensibly benign purposes can be misused, causing effects not unlike those created by invidious classifications, it is inappropriate to inquire only whether there is any conceivable basis that might sustain such a classification. Instead, to justify such a classification an important and articulated purpose for its use must be shown. In addition, any statute must be stricken that stigmatizes any group or that singles out those least well represented in the political process to bear the brunt of a benign program. * * *

Davis' articulated purpose of remedying the effects of past societal discrimination is, under our cases, sufficiently important to justify the use of race-conscious admissions programs where there is a sound basis for concluding that minority underrepresentation is substantial and chronic, and that the handicap of past discrimination is impeding access of minorities to the Medical School.

* * *

Accordingly, we would reverse the judgment of the Supreme Court of California holding the Medical School's special admissions program unconstitutional and directing respondent's admission, as well as that portion of the judgment enjoining the Medical School from according any consideration to race in the admissions process.

MARSHALL, JUSTICE.

* * *

Three hundred and fifty years ago, the Negro was dragged to this country in chains to be sold into slavery. Uprooted from his homeland and thrust into bondage for forced labor, the slave was deprived of all legal rights. It was unlawful to teach him to read; he could be sold away from his family and friends at the whim of his master; and killing or maiming him was not a crime. The system of slavery brutalized and dehumanized both master and slave.

* * *

While I applaud the judgment of the Court that a university may consider race in its admissions process, it is more than a little ironic that, after several hundred years of class-based discrimination against Negroes, the Court is unwilling to hold that a class-based remedy for that discrimination is permissible. In declining to so hold, today's judgment ignores the fact that for several hundred years Negroes have been discriminated against, not as individuals, but rather solely because of the color of their skins. It is unnecessary in 20th-century America to have individual Negroes demonstrate that they have been victims of racial discrimination; the racism of our society has been so pervasive that none, regardless of wealth or position, has managed to escape its impact. The experience of Negroes in America has been different in kind, not just in degree, from that of other ethnic groups. It is not merely the history of slavery alone but also that a whole people were marked as inferior by the law. And that mark has endured. The dream of America as the great melting pot has not been realized for the Negro; because of his skin color he never even made it into the pot.

These differences in the experience of the Negro make it difficult for me to accept that Negroes cannot be afforded greater protection under the Fourteenth Amendment where it is necessary to remedy the effects of past discrimination. * * *

* * *

It is because of a legacy of unequal treatment that we now must permit the institutions of this society to give consideration to race in making decisions about who will hold the positions of influence, affluence, and prestige in America. For far too long, the doors to those positions have been shut to Negroes. If we are ever to become a fully integrated society, one in which the color of a person's skin will not determine the opportunities available to him or her, we must be willing to take steps to open those doors. I do not believe that anyone can truly look into America's past and still find that a remedy for the effects of that past is impermissible.

* * *

BLACKMUN, JUSTICE.

* * *

It is worth noting, perhaps, that governmental preference has not been a stranger to our legal life. We see it in veterans' preferences. We see it in the aid-to-the-handicapped programs. We see it in the progressive income tax. We see it in the Indian programs. We may excuse some of these on the ground that they have specific constitutional protection or, as with Indians, that those benefitted are wards of the Government. Nevertheless, these preferences exist and may not be ignored. And in the admissions field, as I have indicated, educational institutions have always used geography, athletic ability, anticipated financial largess, alumni pressure, and other factors of that kind.

I add these only as additional components on the edges of the central question as to which I join my Brothers Brennan, White, and Marshall in our more general approach. It is gratifying to know that the Court at least finds it constitutional for an academic institution to take race and ethnic background into consideration as one factor, among many, in the administration of its admissions program. * * *

* * *

Notes and Questions

1. Justice Powell announced the judgment in *Bakke* affirming the California Supreme Court's ruling that the Davis special admissions program was unlawful and that Bakke should be admitted to the medical school. However, Powell also reversed the California court's order enjoining Davis from ever giving any consideration whatsoever to race in its admission process. Only Justice Powell thought that the California Supreme Court should be reversed in part and affirmed in part. Justices Burger, Stewart, Rehnquist and Stevens concurred in the first part of the judgment but would have upheld the California Court's finding that race should never be a factor in medical school admissions. Justices White, Brennan, Marshall and Blackmun agreed with Powell that under some circumstances race might constitutionally be considered in admissions, but thought that Davis' particular special admissions program should be upheld. As a result Justice Powell had a majority (five votes, including his own) on each issue.

Question: How does the *Bakke* decision reflect the median voter theorem? See *Tashjian* Question 3, above.

2. Under the Equal Protection Clause, judges have applied strict scrutiny not only to state acts that burden "fundamental rights" but also to programs employing "suspect classifications." Racial classifications are

the paradigm of "suspectness." See Loving v. Virginia, 388 U.S. 1, 87 S.Ct. 1817, 18 L.Ed.2d 1010 (1967). The Court has also suggested that classifications based on national origin are suspect, Hernandez v. Texas, 347 U.S. 475, 74 S.Ct. 667, 98 L.Ed. 866 (1954), as are some classifications based on alienage, Graham v. Richardson, 403 U.S. 365, 91 S.Ct. 1848, 29 L.Ed.2d 534 (1971). In addition, the Court has identified certain classifications as "quasi-suspect." See Craig v. Boren, 429 U.S. 190, 97 S.Ct. 451, 50 L.Ed.2d 397 (1976) (gender), Levy v. Louisiana, 391 U.S. 68, 88 S.Ct. 1509, 20 L.Ed.2d 436 (1968) (illegitimacy). While quasi-suspect classifications have not been held to strict scrutiny, the Court has applied an intermediate level of review requiring the state's action to be "substantially" related to an "important" governmental objective. Craig v. Boren, above. Justices Brennan, Marshall, White and Blackmun thought the intermediate standard appropriate for classifications that worked to the disadvantage of whites.

As Justice Blackmun's concurrence noted, government preferences are common in American political life. When a classification is not suspect or quasi-suspect, it need only meet the rational relation standard. The Court has held that classifications based on age or wealth are not "suspect" and need not meet strict scrutiny. See Massachusetts Board of Retirement v. Murgia, 427 U.S. 307, 96 S.Ct. 2562, 49 L.Ed.2d 520 (1976) (age); San Antonio Ind. School District v. Rodriguez, 411 U.S. 1, 93 S.Ct. 1278, 36 L.Ed.2d 16 (1973) (wealth).

> *Question:* Is there any reason to believe that preferences based on suspect classifications like race are more likely to be redistributive than wealth maximizing? Consider Justice Powell's assertion that the United States is a nation of "various minority groups of whom it was said * * * that a shared characteristic was a willingness to disadvantage other groups."

3. *Bakke* discusses a number of competing rationales for when a classification should be regarded as suspect. The petitioner in *Bakke* argued that the Court should test "suspectness" according to the famous footnote four of United States v. Carolene Products Co., 304 U.S. 144, 152 n.4, 58 S.Ct. 778, 783 n.4, 82 L.Ed. 1234 (1938). Justice Stone observed in that note that "prejudice against discrete and insular minorities may be a special condition, which tends seriously to curtail the operation of those political processes ordinarily to be relied upon to protect minorities, and which may call for correspondingly more searching judicial inquiry."

> *Question:* Recall the analysis of interest groups' roles in the political process in the questions following *Lee Optical,* above. Is Justice Stone correct in arguing that the fact that a minority is "discrete and insular * * * tends seriously to curtail the operation of those political processes ordinarily to be relied upon to protect minorities?"

4. Another factor the *Bakke* Court considered in deciding whether or not a classification was suspect was whether the classification was based on an "immutable" characteristic. See concurring opinion of Justices Brennan, Marshall, White, and Blackmun. Race, gender, and illegitimacy are immutable; wealth, veteran's status, residence, and smoking are not.

Question: From an economic perspective, is there any reason to suspect that classifications based on immutable characteristics are more likely to be welfare-reducing than classifications based on characteristics over which the individual has more control?

5.   Justice Marshall's concurring opinion emphasized another factor in weighing suspectness—history. Marshall argued that because of the legacy of slavery, classifications that discriminate against blacks in favor of whites or other groups were more suspect than classifications that discriminate against whites in favor of blacks. Extrapolating from Marshall's historical analysis, the Court should uphold classification schemes that benefit Americans of African descent while it should strike down similar programs to benefit Americans of European, Hispanic, or Asian descent.

Question: Does Justice Marshall's analysis lead to welfare-enhancing rules?

*

Index

References are to Pages

531

†

Wild Wishes
and
Windswept Kisses

MAYA PRASAD

HYPERION
Los Angeles   New York

First Edition, October 2023
10 9 8 7 6 5 4 3 2 1
FAC-004510-23236
Printed in the United States of America

This book is set in Adobe Caslon/Monotype.
Designed by Marci Senders

Library of Congress Cataloging-in-Publication Data

Names: Prasad, Maya, author.
Title: Wild wishes and windswept kisses / by Maya Prasad.
Description: Los Angeles : Hyperion, 2023. • Audience: Ages 12–18. •
Audience: Grades 10–12. • Summary: "The four teen Singh sisters navigate
romance, coming of age, and chasing their dreams over the course of one
windy November day"— Provided by publisher.
Identifiers: LCCN 2022057833 • ISBN 9781368081245 (hardcover)
Subjects: CYAC: Sisters—Fiction. • Coming-of-age—Fiction. • East Indian
Americans—Fiction.
Classification: LCC PZ7.1.P6974 Wi 2023 • DDC [Fic]—dc23
LC record available at https://lccn.loc.gov/2022057833

Reinforced binding

Visit www.HyperionTeens.com

Logo Applies to Text Stock Only

For the diaspora kids, the queer kids,
the kids who don't quite know
what to call themselves.
You're more than enough; you're perfect.
You're a star!

Part One:
The Wind Is
Stirring

Prologue

The Songbird Inn loomed on the edge of a craggy cliff, mist rising over its decks, winds howling, the sea churning and thrashing below. A starless November sky engulfed the place into its shadowy folds. It had been a little over a year since a Douglas fir had fallen through the roof of the cozy little inn, tearing apart one attic bedroom and rattling one Singh sister in ways she never expected.

Now that fierce and searching wind had returned to shake up those Singh sisters once more. Because every once in a while, when the clouds are thickening and wishes are crowding you with what you think you need, you'll forget what it's like just to feel the spray of the sea on your face, to hear the rustle of pines, to inhale the scent of lavender from the nearby farm.

This was one of those moments for the Singh sisters. Three of them tossed and turned inside the restored inn, the windows rattling like old bones rising from a graveyard of unsaid things. Meanwhile, the eldest was slowly making her way back to the islands, over thousands of miles, even as circumstances sought to thwart her with each step.

Nidhi:

> Yay! My flight to Paris finally arrived—after a six-hour delay. I can't wait to see you all!

Dad:

> Glad you're on your way! Safe travels!

Amir:

> Can't wait to see you and hear all about your adventures in India!

Rani:

> Ooh, let us know if you meet any cute Parisians at the airport. And if you do, be sure to document it thoroughly—it could be inspiration for my next short film after Remeet-Cute goes gangbusters! Kisses.

Avani:

> omg, can you stop talking about your short film for just one second? Nidhi, we have A LOT to discuss. Srsly. Get home soon. Love you.

Sirisha:

Yeah, would love some tips from big sis about this murder-mystery party I have to go to. For one thing, how the heck does a murder-mystery party even work? Bethany did not provide any details. xo

Nidhi:

Haha, and I thought my little sisters didn't need me anymore. Don't worry, I'll be there soooooon! xx

Chapter One

Nidhi

When Nidhi's international flight touched down on US soil at LAX, all the passengers clapped. She didn't know why exactly, whether:

- it was the exuberance of touching down to any ground after a twelve-hour flight

- they were really patriotic

- or this was all for Nidhi—and the fact that she was no longer a virgin

She smiled to herself. It was her secret, something that she was perfectly fine not sharing with anyone. Not even her dear sisters.

It had happened a couple of months ago—but it certainly wasn't the only thing that had changed her during her time in New Delhi. She lingered in the memories of the warm days spent with her cousins and aunt and uncle, her first trip to the motherland. The Diwali celebration. The book market that took over a street and was full of rare finds. The unapologetic coffee shop where intellectuals like Nehru had once hung out. The poet's historic mansion. The gully rap scene. The art collective she was hoping to work with.

She loved seeing that other side of Delhi, the one that people in the US knew nothing about. Oh, she'd done some of the more obvious stuff, too. She couldn't go to India and not see the white marble grandeur of the Taj Mahal. Riding a camel in the Thar Desert had been an admittedly touristy delight. And those palaces of old—in Jaisalmer, in Udaipur, in Jaipur—had been full of the kind of gorgeous and intricate architecture that was a photographer's dream. But Nidhi wasn't a photographer, and more than anything else, she'd loved some of the ideas circulating among people her age in New Delhi.

As the plane continued to glide along the runway, Nidhi smiled at the student newspaper in her lap. Suresh had mailed her the article he'd written about the night they'd danced to Deity and Hailstorm.

The headline: "Gully Rap Is Hitting Its Stride—But What Happens When Politicians Don't Like the Lyrics?"

It was a great piece, really, and Nidhi was so impressed. At the same time, it was strange to think that right this very moment, Suresh could be getting engaged through the matchmaker his family had hired. Strange to think they'd probably never see each other again—though Nidhi was actually fine with that. His article showed he was well on his way to pursuing his dreams. Now she just had to figure out hers. Even planning next term seemed so hard. Her dreams always seemed to be shifting and changing, like puffy clouds across blue skies.

She was nervous about telling her sisters and the Dads that she didn't want to come back to the US just yet. She knew they'd support her, of course, but this was already the longest she'd been away from them.

The plane's captain interrupted her thoughts. "We have arrived at our destination," he said warmly. "If you're home, welcome back! Visitors, we hope you enjoy your stay! And if you're just passing through, safe travels."

Was she home?

What was home?

She knew it had once unquestionably been the Songbird Inn on Orcas Island, where she had grown up with her father and sisters. But now she wanted so much more, a yearning that felt like the pull of an ocean current. Only she wasn't getting dragged under, she was sailing over. Or at least that was how she thought of it, and that flight—that movement itself—was maybe her home now.

Nidhi yawned, unbuckling her seat belt and stuffing the newspaper back in her bag. She'd been traveling a full twenty-eight hours straight. There had been delays upon delays in the world of commercial airlines, and she was still only in Los Angeles. Yet, adrenaline pulsed through her. It was currently 2:40 a.m. local time; in India, it would be Saturday afternoon.

Nidhi had always been a girl of two worlds, but now more than ever. Since she'd spent the last few months in India, she'd become much more fluent in Hindi, and felt at home in temperatures she'd never imagined when growing up in the Pacific Northwest. But for now, she was excited to see her sisters, Dad, and Amir after so long, to huddle together in the dining room of the Songbird Inn, at the table by the bay window, stormy weather outside.

Passengers began filtering slowly off the plane, and the customs line was long and slow. Nidhi scrolled through photos from her trip as she waited. Snaps of her family and sites all over the city. Too many food pics, because Nidhi could never resist trying anything and everything. She'd gotten sick eating street food—her cousins had warned her about her "delicate American stomach"—but it had been worth it. Maybe if she stuck around in India long enough, she could toughen her gut bacteria up.

Eventually, she made it to the bored customs agent who was checking passports, found her baggage among all the others, and got in yet another line to have it scanned again.

Behind her, a cute guy fumbled with his phone. He was tall, Black, and square-jawed. He also wore a familiar down vest, the kind that was way too popular in the PNW. She wondered if he too was headed to Seattle.

"Crap. I'm not going to make it to my flight," he muttered.

Nidhi glanced at the time. Oof! Maybe she wasn't either.

Overall, customs had taken an hour and a half, and her next flight was leaving in twenty-five minutes—which sounded like plenty of time, but LAX was a maze and she needed to get out of the international terminal. She was huffing and puffing when she finally made it to the gate, right on the heels of the guy in the down vest.

The gate agent's voice boomed on the speakers: "This is the final boarding call for Flight 766 to Seattle. Passengers, please make your way to the gate."

"Nidhi!" someone said behind her, her name a low rumble.

It was a voice of moonlit adventures. Of smoke and dragons and night whispers. Of art and shadows and sailing across a fantastical, uncharted sea.

She turned. There he was. That sandy hair and those stormy-sea eyes and that handsome face that often flitted unexpectedly into her thoughts.

Grayson.

Chapter Two

Avani

Avani awoke that morning to her alarm buzzing on her phone and velvety dark November skies outside. The wind screeched, rain lashed against the windowpanes, the bones of the inn creaked and groaned. Normally, she would have been all for the atmosphere since it was perfect for scribbling in her journal. But even though she was snuggled up in her soft bed, her cozy gray comforter curled around her,

for some reason
she felt a little bit B.L.U.E.
everything was fine—
great, in fact!

and yet something ached inside her

and come to think of it

she missed her big sis

It was strange, since Nidhi had been so bossy and annoying when she still lived at the Songbird. Did Avani actually sort of miss the patented Concerned Sister™ look when she was late for breakfast duty in the restaurant? Did she miss a good scolding when she accidentally messed up an order or took too long delivering drinks because she was chatting away with the guests?

Nah, of course not. (It was called being friendly, *Nidhi*.)

Yet, she could use some advice. Relationship advice, specifically. (The kind that seemed to come best from a big sis.)

At least Avani didn't have long to wait. Nidhi was due to return to the islands today—her first visit home since she'd gone to India. Unfortunately, she would arrive while Avani and Fernando were attending an all-day salsa workshop. Nidhi had originally been scheduled to return yesterday, but she'd had some delayed flights and missed connections. It was all so frustrating.

Sigh. Waiting. Avani could do that. And maybe there would be nothing to ask at all. Maybe the workshop with Fernando would fix everything broken between them. Maybe between a spin and a dip, he and Avani would click again in a way that they hadn't for a while.

Wow, Avani hated admitting that. Even to herself.

Senior year had been busier than she'd expected. Avani was on a mission to decide her future—or at least what she wanted to major in next year. She'd signed up for debate and journalism and creative writing and horticulture club and even photography. But despite busting her butt all semester long, she was still desperately waiting for that epiphany that was supposed to come to her about what she should do for the rest of her life. All those coming-of-age movies promised it would happen, so Avani was certain that it would, given she tried enough things! Though singer-songwriter/radio host/professional beer pong player was still tempting.

As she doodled in her journal, an annoying click-clacking from a keyboard started up. Rani was up now too, humming a poppy Bollywood tune (with terrible pitch, as usual).

"How can you still be working on your script?" Avani moaned. "You're filming today."

"I know, I know." Rani typed away, her fingers on a mission. "But I dreamed the perfect zinger for Layla when Nate comes into the café!"

Rani was entering a short film contest today, her script transparently based on her relationship with Raj. Avani was happy for them, of course. They'd even managed to overcome the whole long-distance thing. They were cute together—well, if she was being honest, they were a little too cute for her taste. But if Avani felt just a smidgen of jealousy that Raj and Rani seemed to embody Perfect Couple status, she certainly wasn't planning to say anything about it.

Instead, she leaned over Rani's shoulder and chuckled at her twin's new script updates.

"Perfect," she agreed.

"Thank you," Rani said primly, and then set the file to print. "I wish you were filming with me today, though."

Avani nudged her shoulder. "It would've been fun. But I really just wanted to spend some time with Fernando, you know? We've both been so busy lately. He's taking that college prep class really seriously—he studies all the time!"

"Uh-huh." Rani nudged her back. "What about the ten zillion clubs you joined this year?"

"Yeah, okay. I've been busy, too." She threw an arm around her twin. "What should I do?"

"About what?"

"About Fernando!"

"Sounds like you've got it figured out." Rani set her laptop on her desk. "Go to this dance class with him. I'll see you both at the One Day Shoot-Out award ceremony after. It'll be great."

"Yeah, the thing is—"

"This machine is so ancient. We really need to upgrade, don't you think?" Rani glowered at the printer. Then, without waiting for an answer, she flounced into their shared bathroom.

Avani deflated. This was what all senior year had felt like so far: half-finished conversations, unsaid things hanging in the air with no time for them to actually get said. She wanted to tell her twin everything, but there never seemed to be a good time. It wasn't easy to get the words out, to tell anyone about all those swirling feelings inside her.

She reached for the figurine of a goat that she kept on her nightstand. It was a gift from Fernando: a reminder of the baby goat that had brought them together. Usually, when she held it, her heart swelled with all those best moments they'd shared. Chicken raising. Dancing. Kissing in snow-storms in the winter and drizzle in the spring and in the long, lingering shadows of warm summer twilight.

But right now, echoes from their fight the weekend before battered her ears like the rain outside.

ONE WEEK EARLIER

Fernando's parents had been away on an overnight trip to San Juan Island for some business. Perfect, since Fernando and Avani had been looking for some time alone. It was hard to come by when you both had family responsibilities and jobs and school and college applications.

The second they'd gotten to Fernando's house after school, she'd grabbed him, kissed him hard. Late-afternoon light had streamed in through the windows. She loved his place: the cabin-style wood paneling; huge exposed log beams; and the eighteen-foot vaulted ceilings in the living room. Lots of windows. Very romantic.

She kissed him like their lives depended on it, like they hadn't kissed in years, in ages. And he returned her intensity.

> His lips swollen
> > and dark
> > > full of yearning
> > full of *want*

The kind of kiss you didn't have in front of friends and family. The kind of kiss that only happened on a stormy November night without anyone else around. All those senior-year worries melted away, and Avani sank into Fernando. Concentrating on the feel of his lips against hers. Fernando stopped to switch on the gas fireplace, which ignited with a purr.

She pulled him down to the couch. His hands gripped her hips, then swept in beneath her shirt.

> His fingers were chilly
> > from outside

but she liked it
　　a tingle shot up her spine
　　electric and urgent
　her chest heaved next to his
the fabric of their clothes
　between them
　　too many clothes . . .

"Your turn!" Rani singsonged as she came out of the steamy bathroom, wrapped in a towel. "Better get a move on! Breakfast and then we have to catch that ferry. Fernando's picking us up, right?"

Avani forced herself to get up and shuffle into the bathroom.

In the steam of the shower,
　her fingers still tingled
　　at the memory
Fernando's fingers on her back
　his breath in her ear
　　his lips like petals
　　　his moth brown eyes
　　the way he knew how to
touch her here
　and there
　　and omg *there*

But that night hadn't gone how she'd hoped, far from it. It was why she wanted to talk to Nidhi so desperately. What had gone wrong between her and Matt last year? And were Avani and Fernando doomed to make the same mistakes?

Through the door, she could hear Rani humming as she picked out her clothes—that infernal humming that was seriously getting on Avani's nerves. That humming said: *Oh, I'm just so happy with my life and my relationship. Everything is perfect.*

Avani tried her best to mind meld with her twin: *Well, I'm not happy. Senior year sucks! Just tell me what I'm doing wrong with Fernando already!*

But Rani remained oblivious.

Avani tried to silently scream one more time: *Help! My relationship is going up in smoke!*

Rani didn't get the SOS.

Chapter Three

Rani

As Rani hopped in the shower that morning, she closed her eyes. Let the steam wrap around her. She sometimes had her best ideas in the shower; it was how she'd come up with the premise for her short film, *Remeet–Cute*.

INT. CAFÉ - DAY

LAYLA
(reading a romance novel)
I'll never meet a guy like this Highland warrior. He's so
brave and strong but also incredibly sensitive.

A bell dings. NATE enters the café. He immediately notices LAYLA but heads to the counter and chitchats with the barista. LAYLA hides behind her book. She notices him too but pretends not to. NATE finally brings his coffee over to her table.

NATE

Can I talk to you?

LAYLA

Do I know you?

NATE

Come on, don't be like that. I'm sorry I didn't keep in touch like I promised to.

LAYLA

You should be.

LAYLA turns back to her book, pointedly ignoring him.

Okay, so *Remeet-Cute* was not-so-secretly about Rani and her perfect boyfriend, Raj. They'd met two summers ago, but Raj hadn't had the guts to make a move at the time. Afterward, they'd lost contact for almost an entire year—until he'd shown up at the Songbird Inn. At first, she hadn't been too impressed since he hadn't called or texted for so long. But when she'd taken the time to listen to him, all those old feelings had come tumbling back. Now they were together, they were the perfect couple, and their romance was completely and utterly epic.

(What? It was true!)

Naturally, it all made for the best rom-com. Raj had even tracked down the email address of Rani's absolute favorite director's assistant. Sadly, Olivia Lee's team had yet to get back to her about making the "based on a true story" romantic comedy about Raj Mehta and Rani Singh. Rani was sure she'd hear from them *very* soon, but she was excited about making her own short film, too.

When she'd first spotted the flyer for the One Day Shoot-Out film contest on the bulletin board at school, she hadn't thought much about it. Just walked on by.

But then she'd walked by it a second day.

And a third.

At the end of the week, she finally took a snapshot of it on her phone. That night, she started googling "how to make a short film." She'd learned that people actually spent months just to make a five-minute movie. But . . . there was also someone on the internet who went around making short films in an hour. That didn't count pre-production or post-production, but whatever. If someone could shoot one in an hour, then surely Rani and her team could make one in a whole day. Okay, so it was really only eight hours, but Rani thought that was plenty of time.

Today was the big event.

Rani had been prepping her crew as much as she could so they'd be as efficient as possible. They'd rehearsed, figured out the blocking, and planned out their shots. They had an arsenal of sound and music ready. Raj had volunteered to be her cameraman, and JJ Doherty was great at editing. They had everything planned out, though Rani was open to some improv, too.

She'd never thought of herself as an artist before, but in this last month, she'd embraced the role. After consuming so many romances in books, movies, and songs, she was finally creating her own. Telling the world all she knew about life and love. She never would have gone for it if not for Raj's encouragement either. (See also: perfect boyfriend.)

Stepping out of the steamy shower, Rani wrapped a towel snugly around herself, another one around her hair, and popped back into the bedroom only to find Avani staring at the ceiling.

"Your turn!" Rani singsonged cheerfully. "Better get a move on! Breakfast and then we have to catch that ferry. Fernando's picking us up, right?"

She didn't want to sound like a certain older sister who had always nagged them about being on time to things, but she also couldn't afford to be late for the ferry. If they missed it, they'd have to wait a whole hour for the next one. They'd miss orientation—and obviously, time was of the essence.

As Rani rummaged through her closet for the perfect directorial outfit, Avani slunk into the bathroom. What was with that girl? Rani suspected that she and Fernando had gotten into some kind of tiff recently. She'd definitely noticed a bit of awkwardness between them at school this last week.

Normally, the Official Love Guru would demand every detail. Rani wanted to, she really did. But her focus had strictly been on pre-production with her team and perfecting that script. Avani kept telling her to stop tinkering, but Rani knew that dialogue was key. It was the difference between a great Olivia Lee film and the countless others that fell away to mediocrity.

Plus, it was so hard to fit everything she wanted to say about romance and love in a mere seven minutes, per contest rules! But she had to. She had to do it all: be funny and poignant and speak truths about humanity and love and teenagerdom.

Sigh. Now she knew why there were so few Nora Ephrons and Olivia Lees. Accomplishing all of that was hard, but those icons of film had managed to do it—not just once but several times. Rani thought back to her recent favorite Olivia Lee film, *A Girl, a Boy, and a Dozen Puppies*. It was about two teenagers who were complete opposites, but they shared the mutual goal of finding homes for a dozen abandoned puppies. The film had stolen Rani's heart. (And made her wonder if she should add puppies to her story.)

But Raj—her wonderful, amazing, perfect boyfriend—said her script stood on its own. He'd even located some fancy camera equipment for her. Right now, he should already be driving to Anacortes. It was *so sweet*—he was waking up extra early to meet her in Friday Harbor. He lived on the mainland, but they'd somehow made this long-distance thing work. How did she get so lucky? The two of them were going to be *such* a powerhouse Hollywood couple someday.

She shot him a quick text:

So excited for today! Red carpet, here we come!

SEPTEMBER

Rani and Raj were cuddled up at the cove on a warm evening under the stars, a moonlit picnic spread in front of them. Waves lapped gently against the sand, the sea breeze tickled, and peppermint hot cocoa steamed in their hands. Dad had made them a special dinner of finger foods to share:

samosas and chutney, mushroom and spinach mini-quiche, and a few kebobs with grilled meat and veggies.

"Your dad is the best," Raj said, inhaling his second samosa.

"I know," Rani said, biting into an exquisitely grilled tomato on her kebob. The bell peppers were so good, too. Only Dad could char bell peppers just right.

"You look beautiful tonight," Raj said.

"Thanks." Rani was wearing a delicate pink and frilly shift-dress she'd found at a boutique in Eastsound. "You don't look bad yourself. I love your haircut by the way."

"I'm glad you like it." He grinned at her. "Remember you sent me that pic of that boy band guy you like?"

Her eyes lit up. "You had your stylist copy it?"

Raj looked a little embarrassed. "Kind of. So you think I pull it off, right?"

"Totally," Rani agreed. "Wait—that black T-shirt and gray jacket look a lot like what he was wearing, too."

"Yeah well, you're always teasing me about my video game shirts."

"Teasing you is our thing," Rani said, swatting the air as if swatting away the idea that she was being serious. "You know I secretly love your geek shirts."

He perked up. "Yeah, I know. I just wanted you to admit it."

Rani giggled. "Okay, okay, I admit it. I like your geeky T-shirts! I like it when you do the robot dance! I could live without the floss, though."

He nudged her lightly. "Is that so?"

"Okay, whatever, fine. I think everything you do is hot. Including how you look in this leather jacket."

"I aim to please." Raj leaned in for a kiss.

Even their banter was perfect. Rani tried to keep herself grounded, but sometimes she couldn't help but let her imagination run away with her. Raj was her prince, her captain, her hero in a Bollywood film . . .

EXT. BEACH COVE - EVENING

>   RAJ
>
> My love is brighter than the moon and the stars. It's
> wider than the entirety of the ocean. If an asteroid were
> coming to obliterate the earth, I would have no regrets.
> You are perfect.

>   RANI
>
> Oh, Raj. I feel the same about you. Aren't we the
> luckiest?

>   RAJ
>
> Yes, I feel sorry for everyone else who doesn't have a love
> as grand as ours.
>   (kisses RANI with a burning passion)

Rani kissed Raj as if an asteroid really was coming to Earth and they had only hours left to live. That was how she always kissed him.

When they came up for air, she said, "You know, our love story is truly epic. It's as good as that new Olivia Lee movie, don't you think?"

"The one you've made me watch three times?" Raj said. "Yeah, I think I remember it, but it's a bit hazy."

She elbowed him. "Just to be sure, we'll watch it a fourth time tonight."

"Actually, I meant I remember it perfectly. Every word."

"You're not getting out of watching it again."

"But you said our love was better." Raj raised his brows. "So why should we watch an inferior romance?"

Rani paused. Why *should* they watch an inferior romance?

And then she got really excited. "Raj, you're onto something, you know that?"

"I am?"

"Yes!" Rani said. "Instead of watching someone else's romance, we should write our own love story! As a screenplay—and then send it to Olivia Lee. She'll love it!"

Raj laughed, cuddling up against her. "Great idea, babe. But we could just lie out here under the stars and make out instead."

"I mean, that does sound good." Rani leaned in to kiss him again.

He had really nice lips. Soft and firm at once, plump and perfect for kissing. But her head was whirring. She had to share this story—she just had to!

"Okay, enough of that," she said, pulling away. "Let's go. We could totally write it this weekend."

Raj groaned. "But what about all the other stuff you had planned? Kayaking? Berry picking? Going on a hike with your dads?"

"We can brainstorm while doing all that stuff. I'll take notes. But I think we should at least write that very first scene—remember, when you showed up at the inn after a whole year without a single text?"

"I explained about the texts," Raj said. "My parents were having issues. . . ."

"Yeah, I know," Rani said. "But honestly, the whole year without contact thing made for good drama. Perfect beginning for our script, too."

She started stacking the dishes and napkins and cups haphazardly back in the picnic basket. Raj, of course, took everything out and restacked the dishes so they all fit properly. Rani didn't mind—she thought it was cute how much of a neat freak he was. She rolled up the picnic blanket in a ball. Raj handed her the repacked picnic basket and then folded the picnic blanket tidily. She rolled her eyes but seriously—his obsession was so cute!

As they hiked up the trail, she couldn't stop talking about everything that would go into the screenplay. The ideas were flowing, slamming her like waves against a rocky cliff.

"Seems like you've got everything figured out," Raj said. "So what do you need me for?"

She bumped his shoulder playfully. "Well, your first task is to find Olivia Lee's email address."

"I doubt she just has that publicly available."

"Fine," Rani grumped. "I'll settle for her assistant's."

Chapter Four

Sirisha

A starless night. A screeching wind that threatened to tear apart anything and everything. Creaking pines, groaning old windows, and the heaviness that came with planned social engagements.

Sirisha couldn't sleep. Her veins thrummed: with anticipation, with anxiousness, and—could it be?—a bit of excitement. It had been a while since she'd felt much of anything, honestly. Ever since her breakup with Brie, Sirisha had been feeling kind of numb. Which was preferable to being heartbroken, she supposed.

But did it have to come in the middle of the night? She tossed, she turned, she stuffed a pillow over her head. Sleep continued to elude her, but it was also too early to go to breakfast. Too dark to take any good photos. She got up anyway, grabbed her camera from the nightstand, and snapped away with her best low-light lens. A shot of her hands. Her feet. And, of course, the nefarious invitation.

The silver-tipped edges sparkled in the darkness. It was a challenge, a dare, a whisper in the night that called to her. (Or it was just her friend Bethany's birthday party invitation and she was letting the November windstorm outside go to her head.) Sirisha picked it up. A pattern of magnifying glasses and fingerprints dotted the back of the card and the borders. The front read:

Dear Sirisha,

You're invited to the Château Belmont at 301 Lonely Pines Place for Bethany's birthday luncheon—served with a side of intrigue and murder! Bring your sleuthing skills to help solve the nefarious crime in this interactive mystery game. Costumes and character cards will be provided upon arrival.

To save your spot at a luncheon that is sure to thrill, please RSVP at . . .

Dress up in a costume? Play a part? Solve some fictional mystery? It really wasn't her type of thing at all.

She should have made up some excuse. A big event at the inn, maybe. Or an illness. It all sounded like far too much, especially since Sirisha had become extra reclusive lately. But Bethany was a good friend, one who had really been there for her after the breakup with Brie. Still, Sirisha vacillated between despair that she was totally going to embarrass herself, and maybe, just maybe, being a tiny bit intrigued? At least she was feeling *something*.

Outside, something screeched at the window. A hiss.

No, a hoot.

An owl perched on a fat and gnarled tree limb. Stared at her with big, knowing eyes.

"Don't you judge me," Sirisha muttered. While simultaneously feeling foolish for talking to an owl.

Owl: *Hoo-Hoo-who me?*

This owl was definitely judging her. She could feel it.

Owl: *Hoo-hoo-who would be scared of a party?*

It didn't really say that, but it *felt* like it was saying it. Sirisha wasn't the superstitious type, but an owl staring her down suddenly felt like a portent, an omen. A warning.

In a flash, it soared into the night sky, past a break in the clouds where the crescent moon peeked out, before swooping down and disappearing into the shadows of the trees swaying in the wind. Apparently, its message had been delivered. A judgy look.

The wind screeched in its wake, a wail of loneliness and lost days.

If Nidhi were here, she'd remind Sirisha that there was no such thing as a portent, that she was just nervous about being around so many people and having to potentially speak to them. Which was probably true. Maybe if she was lucky, her character card would be for someone who was quiet and fearful. The perfect fit.

Whenever Sirisha had gone to parties with Brie, things had been different. Brie was the spotlight that drew people, and Sirisha could simply nod along. No one really noticed when she didn't say a word. But those days were gone. Sirisha still couldn't believe that her very first relationship was over.

It was right; a part of her knew that. She and Brie had once burned like a flame. Until the wick ran out.

SEPTEMBER

A delayed ferry. A blue feather. An evening performance.

Bethany, her girlfriend Paola, and Sirisha had gone to Lopez Island to watch Brie's opening night for a new play. But since the ferry had been forty minutes late, they'd arrived at the small community theater a few minutes after the show was supposed to start.

Luckily, the curtain hadn't yet lifted.

An usher took their coats and cheerfully opened the doors for them. "There's a seat. There's another two back there. Another two in the far corner."

Sirisha took a spot between two couples, and Bethany and Paola weaved into the row behind her. They'd become quite the friendly four-some since early August when Sirisha and Brie had spotted Bethany and Paola at a farmer's market—passionately kissing in front of a cherry stand. It had been a surprise; neither Bethany nor Paola had ever dated another girl before. Sirisha had naturally been delighted to have more queer friends. Brie had suggested a double date, and the friendship had sprung from there.

Even when Brie wasn't around, Sirisha had started spending more and more time with Bethany and Paola. They never made her feel like a third wheel, though she was careful to give them plenty of alone time. Her introverted nature made that part easy.

The theater was a little chilly, even with her sweater. Sirisha crossed her legs, uncrossed them. The burgundy curtains remained closed and expectant. Bethany and Paola whispered something Sirisha couldn't quite hear.

At last, someone came onstage to welcome them and remind everyone to turn off their phones. The lights dimmed, the curtains lifted, and the teen cast appeared on the stage. They were seated in a row at a long table, the background set painted with bookshelves to create a library. The play was about die-hard academic students viciously backstabbing each other in their quest for the Ivy League, and Brie had the part of one of the most diabolical students. Sirisha had gone through lines with her, been entranced by Brie's effortless portrayal of a twisted academic.

She'd surprised herself, too, reading the lines of Brie's rival with a cattiness that was kind of fun. She'd never be able to speak like that in real life; she was far too shy to let go in public that way. But alone with Brie, she'd actually gotten into it.

Now, as the audience gasped at yet another twist, Sirisha twirled a feather in her hands. It was a delicate, lovely little thing. Black with a streak of electric blue. Brie still tended to get nervous before each play, so Sirisha had started a ritual where whenever she came to one of her shows, she brought Brie something small and pretty—a good luck charm. A polished pebble, a bead, a seashell. Brie always tucked the item somewhere on her, in a pocket maybe, or pinned beneath her collar.

Since they were late that evening, there hadn't been time to give Brie the feather. But she was ready to hold it up when her girlfriend looked her way, a reminder that Sirisha was there, that she believed in Brie.

Yet Brie didn't scan the crowd for Sirisha. Her character was full of fury over a lazy grade from a lazy teacher. Even Sirisha was entranced. Because with Brie, fury was beautiful.

The first act went by. And then the second.

At last, there came a moment when Brie turned to the audience.

Addressed them directly. Sirisha held up the feather. And sure enough, Brie's eyes caught hers.

But something was different.

Her smile wavered. For just a moment. Then, it was pasted right back on.

Brie didn't glance her way again, not until the bows at the very end. It was a small community theater, and the audience was invited to mingle with the cast after the show. Sirisha, Bethany, and Paola helped the crew fold up the chairs and stack them along the walls to make room.

A twelve-year-old ran up, chattering excitedly about Brie's performance. Completely starstruck. Brie was great with her, very friendly. They took a selfie together. More members of the community came to share encouragement and enthusiasm for Brie and the show.

When at last Brie had a moment to herself, Sirisha gave her the blue feather. "Sorry we got here too late to give it to you before."

"That's okay," Brie returned, touching her arm softly. "Thanks for coming out."

"Of course."

They entwined their fingers, yet somehow Sirisha felt miles apart from Brie. They usually didn't need words, spoke in silences. But today, Sirisha had no idea what Brie might be thinking. She felt unsettled. Something was coming—but what?

"Want to grab dinner at the bar and grill across the street?" Bethany asked after the place had emptied.

Brie nodded and squeezed Sirisha's hand. They all walked outside, where dusk was falling like bits of indigo and silver confetti. A few steps ahead, Bethany whispered something to Paola, and Paola's laughter swirled with the September breeze. The trees rustled, and the very first autumn leaves took the plunge from their safe little branches.

Brie slowed to a shuffle. "We'll be right there," she called to Bethany, and the other two went in to grab a table.

"It was a great play," Sirisha said. She knew she wasn't speaking to whatever it was between them. She didn't want to speak to it. She wanted Brie to forget it.

What she should probably say: "Is something going on?"

What she actually said: "Honestly, I . . . I was definitely afraid of you. Your character was so cutthroat—and you totally pulled off the evil look." She gulped, trying to swallow away her anxiety. She wasn't usually a rambler, but today wasn't like other days.

"I'm glad you liked it. But, Sirisha, I've been thinking . . ." Now, finally, Brie looked a little nervous. Uncertain. "I have loved being with you," she whispered.

"Loved?" Sirisha echoed.

Brie grazed her finger along Sirisha's jawline. "I love your lips. Your hair. Your eyes. The way you look at me when I'm performing and I know everything will be okay. That you've got my back."

Sirisha felt that old fire inside her, the flame that warmed her toes as if she was walking across coals.

"But I don't know if I'm in love with you," Brie finished sadly. "I don't know if I'm ready for love, really. I . . . I don't want to hurt you, but I think we should just be friends."

Even though Sirisha had suspected something was coming, the words were still a shock. Like being plunged in ice suddenly when you thought you were just having a water fight. What did it mean that Brie didn't know if she was in love with her? They were in high school. Were they supposed to be *in love*? What did that even mean?

Wasn't being in *like* with each other enough?

A part of her knew that maybe it wasn't. A part of her knew that Brie was a butterfly who had landed on her shoulder one day but was destined to flit away. A part of her knew that someone else would come; another butterfly would flutter into her life again. Maybe several. And one day, a magical day, one who wanted to stay.

But in that moment, it hurt. She hated goodbyes. She hated endings. Tears started creeping down Sirisha's face. Oh, wonderful. She was such a baby. As the youngest of four sisters, she often felt that way, but now especially.

"Don't cry," Brie whispered, kissing her forehead.

The evening air was cool, and the streetlights glowed golden. A couple more leaves rustled and fell, flitting around them. As Brie's lips left her skin, Sirisha forced herself to let go of Brie's hand, to take a step back.

"It's okay. I'm okay." She did her best to smile, though it was probably a wayward grimace. "Yes, let's stay friends."

Chapter Five

Nidhi

Let's keep things casual.

As the plane's engine roared to life, Nidhi recalled the agreement she and Grayson had made each other so many months ago. She clutched the seat rest as they traveled down the runway. She wasn't a nervous flier; she knew she was statistically more likely to die in a traffic accident than in an airplane. But her stomach flip-flopped like it was on the moon and still trying to find its way back to Earth.

It was obviously because she:

- hadn't flown that many times in her life

- was jet-lagged

- and had been eating questionable airline food

It was definitely not because of the guy seated a few rows back. Or should she say *man*? It was so strange to think that she was now the age to be dating men at all, but here she was. An adult. In college. A woman.

Yes, she—Nidhi—was a woman.

A woman who was furiously clutching the armrest as the plane began to gently lift off the ground. The plane jolted a bit as it ascended through some clouds. Suddenly, Nidhi felt too cold from the frigid air being blasted at her through the little circular vents, and yet she started sweating, too. Lovely. It was probably a reaction to all the grime since she'd already been traveling nearly thirty hours now without a shower.

At last, the plane straightened out. Nidhi's shoulders sagged in relief. One thing less to worry about. Yet there was still a prickling in the back of her neck. There was still Grayson. On this plane.

How had things gotten so weird between them?

When they'd agreed not to go for a long-distance relationship, Nidhi had thought that was the grown-up thing to do. After all, they were both trying to open themselves up to new worlds and new experiences. Having a boyfriend just couldn't be a part of that; she'd realized it with Matt last year. He'd wanted everything to stay the same, and she hadn't. She hadn't wanted to repeat her mistakes, and even though Grayson was so easygoing, she knew making it "official" would change things. Change the ties in her heart and what she owed him.

She remembered that first day in Delhi. The overwhelming feeling of being alone in a new country. She'd had her relatives, of course, but the newness loomed large all the same. . . .

NEW DELHI—EARLY AUGUST

The first moment Nidhi stepped outside the airport, she blinked at the unyielding sunshine. It was nine in the morning and already sweltering hot.

"Welcome to India," her uncle said cheerfully, grabbing her suitcase and leading her to his parked car.

"Thanks!"

She hurried behind him, hoisting her heavy tote bag on one shoulder. She wanted to soak it all in, to start her adventure now now now. As they pulled out of the airport lot and onto the highway, she gawked at all the varieties of cars and buses and motorcycles roaring past. Everything looked different than in the US. The shapes of cars. The buildings. The crushing tangle of traffic. On Orcas Island, a traffic jam was when three cars were stopped because some deer were crossing the road, nothing like this.

New Delhi was a whole new world, one that she was anxious to sink into.

But she was also just plain anxious. Most of her life, Nidhi had played it safe. She was the girl who followed the rules, the girl who did her homework on time and filled out her college applications months ahead of the due date. She was the girl whose big dreams were to start her own bakery on Orcas. Nothing wrong with that. After all, Dad's lifelong passion had led him to running his own inn.

But then that fateful Douglas fir had come crashing down on her—literally. And she'd met dear Grayson. Discovered his delicious secret—that he was the mysterious street artist called the Skull. She'd gone along with him on one of his late-night adventures. And she'd seen the stars, the sky, the big universe beyond.

She'd wanted to conquer that universe, wanted to experience it to the fullest.

It had been the first spark that led her to this moment. Here she was: in India. And she realized she had no idea how to make it hers.

Deepak Phupha pointed out different places they passed, promising to take her to Chandni Chowk and the Red Fort and India Gate. And a bunch of other sites that were mentioned in her guidebook.

But seeing the pictures in the guidebook hadn't prepared her for what it was really like here. She'd never seen so many people all together like this. She'd never sweated like this either, even though Phupha was blasting the car's AC. When they pulled off the main road, they were engulfed in narrow streets, vendors and pedestrians crowding both sides. Stalls with all kinds of things—fruits and scarves and cellphone cases. Sunglasses and jewelry.

"You'll love shopping in India," Phupha promised her. "Haggling is an art. And your phua is a master."

Haggling? It sounded intimidating.

She pulled out her guidebook, something she'd picked up in the one and only bookshop on Orcas. She'd been surprised to find it at all. She knew most of the information was online, but there was something about flipping through the glossy photos that was just so tactile and lovely. She'd so desperately wanted to see all those places in person, to feel the dust in her face and inhale the aromas of street food. Of course, now that she was actually here, she realized that she'd be lucky to get through a fraction of everything.

Where was the part about haggling again? Oh yes—page 33.

Haggling

Haggling is an integral part of the culture in India. Vendors will expect
you to negotiate prices with them. Some might even feel insulted if you
don't. But if you suggest a price too low, it might also cause offense.
They expect that foreigners will be able to pay more than a local. You will
be respected if you haggle a little bit but pay a reasonable price.

But how would Nidhi know what a reasonable price to pay was? She
quickly tucked the book back in her bag, as it would be absolutely mortifying if her uncle saw her reading a tourist's guidebook for advice. This
was supposed to be her homeland!

As the traffic slowed to nearly a crawl, Nidhi texted Grayson.

> Just landed. It's beautiful. And hot. High of 46
> degrees Celsius today, can you believe it?

Grayson:

> Let me check the conversion to Fahrenheit.
> 115 degrees? That's intense. Can't wait
> to get there and see you, though.

Nidhi:

> We can melt in a pile of sweat together for
> those couple of days you're here.

Grayson:

That sounds hot.

Nidhi flushed, flustered and overwhelmed by this big new world—and suddenly realizing her text could be interpreted much more sexily than she'd intended.

Nidhi:

Er, yep. Definitely hot.

She burned as she said it. She was such a dork. Even though she and Grayson had been dating for nearly a year, they'd stayed fairly PG with their intimate moments. They'd never done anything that involved taking off their clothes, that was for sure. She supposed she'd been keeping a part of her heart to herself, but still—how could she be worldly when she was so inexperienced? At life, at love, at haggling over prices.

Three dots appeared in her messages, indicating Grayson was about to respond. But after a few minutes, nothing happened. The three dots disappeared. There. He agreed. She was a dork.

Or he was just busy. Was he in Australia right now? He'd emailed his intended itinerary, but he didn't always stick with it (not that she was planning to spend her time in India obsessing over his travel schedule or anything).

He was all about standby flights at the last second, picking a spot and traveling there when the mood hit him. She envied his relaxed attitude, but at the same time she wondered if he was maybe missing out on something by moving around so much. Was he ever really sinking into any place, seeing anything beyond the usual tourist traps?

Chandni Chowk and the Red Fort and India Gate were all well and good, but she yearned for more on this trip. She didn't know exactly *what* more, but in the last year, she'd learned to be more okay with leaving things open. She'd never be as unrestrained as Grayson, probably. But there was an untamable yearning inside her, and she had to give herself the space to explore.

As she pondered how to make the most of these next months, Phupha pulled the car up to a locked gate. The watchman waved them in. Nidhi had never been to a place that had a watchman before, but her uncle didn't explain. It was just a normal part of life to him, it seemed. They parked in the drive, in front of a charming three-story bungalow painted a fresh white, with balconies on each of the upper levels. They didn't have a lot of garden space, but there were some neatly planted bushes and trees within the encompassing eight-foot-tall wall. Similar bungalows neighbored each side and continued down the street.

"This is a newer neighborhood," he said. "All the buildings were constructed in the last five years, and more are going up every day. It's a little far from my job in the government district, and I have to sit in traffic for too much of my life. But we like it here. It's peaceful."

Lalita Phua came outside to welcome Nidhi, wrapping her in a warm hug and fussing over whether she'd eaten, as aunties were wont to do. (At least, Nidhi figured. Aside from Dad's recent wedding, she'd never spent time with extended relatives before.) Her cousins Sona and Prakash greeted her, too, and they all ushered her into the house. She wasn't hungry at all, but their cook Shiv had already prepared a hearty lunch. Poori bhujia, raita, biryani, goat curry, and more. Shiv had also made the most exquisite rasgulla with a lovely cardamom aftertaste.

From that single aromatic rasgulla, it was obvious that Shiv would be someone she could learn a lot from in the kitchen. Nidhi's study abroad proposal had been centered on the mentorship of a professional chef. Nidhi had to present regular reports and essays about culinary culture in New Delhi to her advisor at UW, but that seemed fair considering she was getting college credit for being here.

Her new mentor, Shiv, was a bit shy at first, but Sona and Prakash insisted he sit and chat with her about his cooking. He was forty-five, had studied at a prestigious program, and also currently worked several nights in a popular restaurant. With a little coaxing, Nidhi was able to get him to open up, and she found he had lots of ideas about blending flavors: what he adamantly believed needed to stay traditional and what could use just a bit of experimentation. He reminded Nidhi of her dad a bit, and soon they were swapping stories of meals they'd made that had gone awry.

"My sister Rani said my paratha looked like roadkill," Nidhi confessed.

"Roadkill?" Shiv asked.

Although he spoke English very well, Nidhi realized that maybe he hadn't heard that term.

"A dead animal," she clarified.

"Ah." Shiv chuckled. "Well, let me see if I can help you make something a bit more appealing."

Cooking had always been a comfort to Nidhi. And though the tools in an Indian kitchen were different than what she was used to, she found herself getting lost in spices and smells, in the scent of onions sizzling in ghee, in taking a bite of fresh mango as she listened to Shiv explain how to make the perfect paratha. The taste of mango blossomed in her mouth, a riot of sweet flavor that was nothing like the mangoes she'd ever tasted before.

That taste wasn't something you could infer from a guidebook either.

"Excuse me, sir." Grayson's voice interrupted Nidhi's memories. He was talking to the guy sitting beside her on the plane. "Would you mind switching seats with me so I can sit next to my friend? I'm happy to buy you a drink for your trouble."

He offered that dimpled smile of his, his stance relaxed and cheerful.

That cheerfulness was so infectious that the guy next to her—who had looked pretty grizzled and tired earlier—seemed suddenly relaxed. "It's kind of early in the day, but whatever. I could use that drink, thanks."

Ah, Grayson. Always seemed to know how to read people. And now, Nidhi:

- had to confront her kind-of sort-of ex (they'd never broken up because they'd never been official)

- had to do it while sleep-deprived and over twenty-four hours since her last shower, her hair a greasy wild mess, her blouse coffee-stained

- also had to pretend that the bit of facial scruff on his chin didn't ignite a tiny fire inside her

Of course, he'd always been hot, with that sandy hair that seemed to catch light no matter where he stood and those stormy-sea eyes and that dimple in his smile that made a girl melt. Somehow, even after months of traveling all over the world, he still smelled like a ship's captain, a fragrance of salt water and blustery gales and misty mornings.

Nidhi grabbed her cardigan from the bag at her feet and tried to strategically place it to cover up the coffee stain.

"Imagine running into you!" he said, sliding into the seat and filling it up with not just his body but all that signature unbridled charm.

"Imagine that," she replied coolly.

Oops. Maybe slightly too coolly. She really didn't have a problem with the way things had gone with Grayson. She hadn't thought about him much in the past couple of months either, as she'd slowly started to get used to life in New Delhi.

"Sorry I haven't had the chance to text in a while," Grayson said. "It's just been so wild. Did I tell you I got pickpocketed in Paris? So much for the most romantic city in the world."

"Oh no! I'm sorry. What did they take?"

"Just my wallet." Grayson scratched that scruff on his face. "Luckily I had another credit card in my backpack, or it would have really been bad."

Oh my. Why was his facial hair so damn sexy? Was this because of Nidhi's first and only sexual encounter? Was she now doomed to constantly be thinking about sex?

Sex. Sex. Sex.

Even though she'd experienced it, the word still felt so awkward to say out loud. Though it happily echoed in her brain.

"I'm glad it wasn't worse," Nidhi managed to say sympathetically. "Besides getting pickpocketed, what have you been up to?"

He listed an impressive string of countries that made Nidhi smile. His wanderlust resonated with her, too—that need to do more than what she was doing. She'd thought that this trip would appease that feeling.

Instead, it had only grown stronger.

"What about you?" Grayson said. "How's Delhi? Your aunt, your uncle, your cousins?"

"They're great," Nidhi said.

Grayson may have surfed in Namibia, but she'd had her fun, too. She almost didn't know where to begin with the things she'd seen and done.

"It's been great," she repeated awkwardly. "I've seen so many things in India. The touristy stuff—but also some of the less touristy stuff. It's been really nice, actually. Did I tell you I've fallen in love with gully rap now?"

"Gully rap?"

"It means street rap," Nidhi told him. "I met this rapper called Hailstorm. She's really funny and cool, and I'm completely in awe of her."

"Nice." He smiled. "You look like you've gotten a lot of sun."

"More than you know." Nidhi chuckled, relaxing a little bit. "It's so weird. That first day I landed, I felt overwhelmed by everything. It was so different there, you know? Nothing like quiet, rainy Orcas. When you came for those few days in Jaisalmer, I didn't say anything, but I was considering calling it quits and going back to the US early."

"You?" Grayson looked shocked. "You looked totally at home. Not like me, with the evil camel who definitely hated me."

Nidhi giggled. Back in August, they'd met up for a weekend in the desert city, accompanied by Sona and Prakash. While there, Nidhi and Grayson had gone on the most touristy camel ride, and her cousins had taken lots of pictures of them looking like goofballs.

"That camel was definitely not happy about something that day," she agreed.

"He's probably still out there spitting on other tourists." Grayson agreed. Then paused. "There's something different about you. I think all this time in Delhi has really suited you. You look . . . happy."

Nidhi nodded. He got it. "Now that I've been there for a few months, I think I kind of . . . love it?"

Grayson flashed his dimple. "I knew you would."

Oh, those quiet words. Why did he know her so well? She wished . . . Well, she wished for things she couldn't have. No point in lingering on them.

"So. How're you planning on getting back to the San Juans from the airport?" Grayson asked. "Maybe we can go together."

"Actually, I have a meeting with my advisor at UW today," Nidhi said. She didn't mention that she was nervous about bringing up staying in India for another semester. It wouldn't feel real until she said it out loud, and she was still working up the courage. "After that, Rita and I planned to head to the ferry together. Actually, I'm going to Friday Harbor, too—Rani's shooting a short film for a contest today, and I really want to make it to the screening tonight."

"Rita, huh? Maybe I could stop at UW with you and say hi, too? We could all head to Friday Harbor together?"

Nidhi blinked at him. If he stuck with her, they'd be together for a lot longer than just this two-hour flight. She couldn't exactly say no; that would be weird. But spending the day together all of a sudden was a little weird, too.

Sigh.

"Yeah, sure. I bet Rita would love to see you."

"It's been a while since we talked," Grayson said. "It's been a while since you and I talked, too."

His eyes searched hers, and Nidhi was momentarily transported back to a misty night from a little over a year ago. A dark seascape of smoke and dragons and night whispers. The world had seemed theirs that night.

"Yeah, it has been a while," Nidhi said finally. "I missed you."

Wow, she hadn't planned on saying that.

"I missed you, too," he returned huskily.

Nidhi sucked in a breath. She couldn't deny that this boy—this man—had the ability to tug on her heartstrings like no one else. She hastily cleared her throat. "So—I think I saw that one of your murals went viral? The one you did in Amsterdam?"

He laughed, running a hand through his hair. "Yeah, it was wild. I didn't realize it would get so much attention, but then suddenly people were forwarding it to me."

"People who have no idea you're actually the Skull?"

"Yep."

He laughed again, and this time she laughed with him. Even if they weren't destined to be, they both still shared his secret.

"Have you told anyone else?" she asked. Suddenly, it felt very important that he hadn't. Especially not with some random *girl*. But that was a problem, too, wasn't it? Nidhi needed to find a way to let go. Again.

"Nope," he said. "Although I could have used a helper. I don't get nearly as much done in a night as I did with you."

Nidhi didn't like the relief she felt at that.

"Then why don't you recruit someone new in every city?" she asked.

They weren't really talking about murals anymore, were they?

"I . . ." He faltered for a moment. And she read in his eyes that he certainly *could* have recruited someone new. "It has to be someone I trust, okay? Besides, I didn't tell you; you figured it out on your own. That's part of the fun."

"No one else has figured it out?"

Grayson shook his head. "Nope. Not even when I snuck out of bed with someone to do it."

So he *had* been in bed with someone. And he'd snuck out. She didn't know who that someone was—and she didn't want to. She had no intention of telling Grayson about Suresh, either.

Chapter Six

Avani

At breakfast that morning in the Songbird's dining room, Avani picked at her pumpkin pancakes. The orange-gourd regime had been going strong since October. Dad was hardcore pumpkin, and Nidhi wasn't around to insist on switching it up with delicata squash.

Not that Avani minded. She was totally cool with pumpkin, especially since Dad, with Amir as his sous chef, had created an entire decadent pancake topping bar. (Not just for the family, but for the restaurant. But they were getting first crack at it, so it felt pretty VIP.) Avani had opted for bananas, chocolate chips, crushed hazelnuts, and a generous dollop of whipped cream.

"Eat up!" Dad said, dumping some bacon on her plate. "You'll need your strength for your dance workshop!"

"Thanks!" Avani stuffed a mouthful down her throat.

She expected it all to taste like autumn, like cozy mornings curled up by the fire. In reality, the sweet flavors tasted a bit too rich for 6:25 a.m. Maybe she should have left off the chocolate chips.

It was still dark out, the sea through the bay window nothing but deep shadows. The Dads had insisted on a family breakfast before everyone went off and did their thing for the day. (The Singh sisters still called Amir "Amir" and Dad "Dad," but as a plural they were definitely "the Dads.")

After the wedding in July, Amir had moved into the Songbird, and he felt like an essential part of the family. He was kind, he was funny, and Dad lit up from within when they were together. Avani felt very lucky to have them both. She still missed Pop, of course, but she'd tucked her love for him in the fuzzy folds of her heart, and there she kept it safe.

"How many dancers does it take to change a lightbulb?" Amir asked, sprinkling chocolate shavings over his own pancakes.

The Dads had been cracking dad jokes all morning.

"How many?" Avani tried her best to play along, despite that nagging feeling she'd woken up with.

That good ol' feeling of impending doom that would hopefully clear up by noon. (*Please let it be so.*)

"Five, six, seven, eight!" Amir said, grinning.

Avani snorted.

"Nice!" Dad chuckled. "Sirisha, your turn. What falls a long way but doesn't get hurt?" He topped his own pumpkin pancakes with crushed pecans, a dollop of crème fraîche, and of course maple syrup.

Sirisha stopped listlessly stirring her chai. "Oh, I don't know. An inanimate object thrown off the Empire State building?"

"That wasn't where I was going with that one," Dad said. "But good guess."

Sirisha fussed with her hair, a wild bramble. Avani had never cared too much about her own (she considered a ponytail fashionable enough, much to Rani's dismay), but even she thought Sirisha should try running a brush through hers.

Ever since Brie had dumped her a couple months back, Sirisha had seemed to stop caring about basic things like taming her hair. Avani was kind of shocked that Sirisha had actually agreed to go to a murder-mystery birthday party at some swanky mansion.

But then again, maybe the youngest Singh sister was changing and growing. Avani wished she could say the same about herself. Instead, she felt woefully stuck in place, floundering as everyone around her was becoming more mature and growing new interests and learning how to cope with things like college.

Avani plucked at her sleeve. For the dance workshop, she'd donned leggings and a tank top layered under a long-sleeved, loose tee. An outfit she could move in, that she could sweat in, that she'd feel comfortable in. Too bad it was her own skin that felt uncomfortable today. Sigh.

Outside, the wind howled again, and water droplets splattered against the windows. Speaking of which . . . Dad's joke. *What falls a long way but doesn't get hurt?*

"Rain falls but doesn't get hurt," Avani said.

"You got it!" Dad said, laughing.

Avani laughed along, too, even if it was a bit forced. At her elbow, Rani furiously scribbled blocking notes on her printed script, a cup of black coffee in the other hand. Her twin had never been into black coffee before, but apparently it was a vital component of becoming a film auteur. Avani leaned in to get a closer look at the changes.

"Oh, don't tell me you went back to that corny joke about Pikachu?"

"Well, it was really in character for him . . ." Rani bit her lip. She'd changed this same joke so many times. "Do you think I should go for something else? Did you like the one about the three poodles who entered the bar?"

"Personally, I don't think you can go wrong with three poodles entering a bar."

"Oh yeah, that was my favorite, too," Amir agreed.

He'd taken a serious interest in Rani's film, going so far as to read every draft. Avani was impressed that he'd taken the time when everyone else, including Dad, had politely declined after the fifth rewrite. Avani could hardly keep track of the changes, but Rani would insist they were vital improvements.

"More chai anyone?" Dad asked.

"Please and thank you." Avani pushed her cup forward. "Caffeine is necessary today."

"What happened to that bottomless Avani energy?" Dad refilled the cup carefully, steam curlicues rising satisfyingly above.

What *had* happened? She was honestly exhausted, and not just from that fight with Fernando.

"Dads, I'm deep in a pit of my own making," Avani admitted for the first time. "Why did you let me sign up for yearbook? And journalism? And debate club? I was up so late last night working on an article."

Dad and Amir glanced at each other.

"We did mention maybe you were taking on a bit too much," Dad said gently. "Back in September?"

"But we wanted to encourage you, too," Amir added. "And we've never seen you fail yet."

Amir was a solid guy. A great 50 percent of the Dads. And Avani appreciated the support, but maybe she could have used a larger dose of reality earlier in the year from both of them? Of course, Amir tended follow Dad's lead when it came to parenting stuff—which made sense since he was new to it. And Dad had always let them make their own mistakes. Which might be wise in the long run, but currently she was swimming in them.

A reminder popped up on her phone. *Horticulture Podcast Thingy with Zadie, 11 a.m.*

Wait, what? There was no way Avani could have scheduled that for today. She'd have noticed it in her calendar when she'd signed up for the workshop. And yet—both items were there on her phone.

She quickly texted Zadie:

> Sorry, can we talk plants tomorrow? Totally spaced, but I have other plans today.

Zadie:

> No problem. I've got ADHD so I'm often guilty of overbooking. Of course, now I have no excuse to procrastinate on my college applications, so thanks for that.

Avani responded with:

> Yikes! Now I really feel bad.

Zadie:

> You're the worst.

Avani:

Come over to the Songbird tomorrow.

Coffee on the house.

Zadie:

Throw in some pastries and you might be forgiven.

Avani:

You got it.

There, crisis averted. Phew. Good thing Zadie was so chill.

Avani shoved too much pancake in her mouth at once. Suddenly, her throat was super dry. She took a big swig of chai, then another bite of delicious, too-rich-for-6-a.m. pancake. Of course, she wasn't just chewing on bananas and chocolate chips and hazelnuts. She was chewing on that word. ADHD. She hadn't known that Zadie had it. She also didn't know a lot about it. She'd thought that people with ADHD usually had problems with schoolwork, but Zadie was a decent student. And honestly, a lot more organized in general than Avani.

Hmm. She chewed on more banana hazelnut pumpkin pancake. (With chocolate chips.) Was it possible that Avani maybe—

"What did the tide say to the shore?" Dad asked. "What do you think, Rani?"

Rani shrugged. "I have no idea. What?"

"Nothing, it just waved."

Avani laughed-coughed-choked on too much pancake. Spit out chai everywhere, including on Rani's script. Dad pounded her on the back.

That only made her laugh-choke-cough harder. Oh dear. And now Rani was yelling at her.

"I'm sorry!" Avani said. She felt like she did everything wrong these days, and she'd just—ugh.

Chapter Seven

Rani

"Ackkkkk!" Rani screeched, frantically trying to clean up her script.

"I'm sorry!" Avani looked genuinely contrite.

Rani was annoyed, but she couldn't resist her twin's apologetic face. "It's okay. I'll just print another copy." It would give her a chance to put in some of her edits anyway.

At least the chai spit-up hadn't gotten on her pantsuit. *Nobody* had better mess with Rani's directorial debut pantsuit. She'd paired it with black pumps and light pink beads that she hoped screamed "serious director" and not "casket bearer."

Despite the now-soggy script, Rani loved that the Dads had made this special pancake breakfast for her. (It was obviously for her, and not her other sisters. After all, *she* was the one entering the One Day Shoot-Out today. Sure, Sirisha had her murder-mystery party, but that was Bethany's celebration, not hers. And Avani had her dance workshop thingy—and yes, it had required an audition to get into, but still. Rani was making a *film*. And that warranted pancakes. Pumpkin ones.)

Unfortunately, Rani could hardly eat. She was nervous and jittery and excited all at once. (Or maybe that was because she was already on her second cup of coffee.) Her feet shook with too much energy. She only half listened to the Dads' dad jokes. Yes, this special breakfast was obviously for her, but she was also very busy and important. She hovered over her soggy script with a red pen, second-guessing her dialogue. The film was only going to be seven minutes long, so she really had to get the most out of each and every word.

INT. CAFÉ - DAY

NATE

Hey, you have every right to be mad at me. I know I haven't kept in touch like I promised.

LAYLA

Who are you again? Because I think you've got the wrong girl. I have tons of admirers. Ones with yachts, even.

NATE

Yachts? Who are you dating with a yacht?

LAYLA slides a copy of *Wired* magazine toward him, open to a page with a handsome seventeen-year-old activist.

Rani chuckled to herself. She really had dated a guy with a yacht—Vikram Chaudary of *the* Chaudarys. Yes, the bike app Chaudarys—Vikram's parents had sold the app for roughly a zillion dollars. Vikram's sister was a best-selling novelist, and Vikram himself was an internet politico with half a million subscribers.

When Raj had come to find her that fateful day in that café, she hadn't actually had a copy of *Wired* magazine to thrust at him. In real life, he'd been wildly jealous without it. But Rani knew that film wasn't exactly like real life. Some visual flair was required.

JJ—her producer and the person who handled every detail that Rani couldn't—was making a prop copy of *Wired*. Instead of Vikram, it would have a picture of Raj smiling a very pretentious smile. His impression of how a rich kid would smile.

It was hilarious.

"You're giggling at your script again," Sirisha said, leaning down to look.

Rani quickly flipped the tea-stained pages. "Yeah, yeah. So I think I'm funny. Is that a bad thing?"

"It's great," Sirisha said.

"You need a haircut, by the way," Rani said, taking in her little sister's tangled bird's nest. "You're really going to a party like that?"

"I know it's been a while since I cut it, but it doesn't look that bad, does it?" Sirisha touched her hair, looking a little hurt.

Oops.

"I mean," Rani said, "you might want to wear a hat."

What? It was good advice. But obviously Sirisha was feeling a bit sensitive, because that didn't seem to go over well. So touchy.

Chapter Eight

Sirisha

*D*id Sirisha really look that bad? She didn't exactly remember brushing her hair that morning, nor did she particularly care, but Rani's words still stung. Oof. She just wanted to crawl back into bed. She'd known that getting out of it that freezing November morning was a mistake. The inn was well heated but somehow Sirisha could still feel the chill of that gale that kept rattling the windows.

"Well, I'm sure nobody will notice," Rani said. "Besides, people will be more focused on your camera than your hair. But let me cut it later this week, okay? After today, I'll finally have more time."

What Sirisha should probably say: "Thanks, but the comment was still unnecessarily rude. You know I've been having a rough time since Brie dumped me."

What Sirisha actually said: "Sure."

Sigh.

She couldn't help but think back to last spring, when she'd been so happy. Not just because she'd had her very first kiss, and got into her very first relationship. But because of the promotional photography work she'd done with the Thousand Shores theater troupe, which had felt so incredibly meaningful to her. She'd felt like she'd made a real contribution to boosting the show on social media—and therefore boosting the brown and queer voices that were a part of it.

She'd even placed in the San Juan Snaps photography contest with her pictures from the production. But the troupe had only been on Orcas for Spring Fest, where plays and musicals and ballet recitals were performed in venues all over the island in May. Now they were gone, and had left a void behind. She'd tried to recreate the excitement she'd felt, volunteering to take promotional photos for a school play, but somehow the experience just didn't have the same energy.

Or maybe *Sirisha* who didn't have the same energy.

She tried to muster up some enthusiasm for Bethany's party. At least she'd get some good photos out of it. Bethany would appreciate that, even if Sirisha was terrible at actually acting out a part. Her heart raced a bit just thinking about it, but outwardly, she just sipped her chai and smiled through breakfast as the Dads tried to distract the twins from bickering with more jokes.

A text popped up on her phone.

Brie:

Surprise! I'm staying on Orcas this week! So sorry for the last minute notice—but are you up for brunch with Liza and me? I'd love to catch up.

Oh dear. Brunch with her ex? Sirisha was already sweating the birthday party. She wasn't ready for this. Of course, she was also really bad at saying no to things. And if Brie was actually making an effort at being friends, she should go, shouldn't she?

Chapter Nine

Nidhi

Nidhi blearily blinked her eyes open. Over the speakers, the captain was saying something about 70 mph winds. She didn't remember falling asleep, but here she was, her cheek squished against Grayson's shoulder. A little bit of drool in the corner of her mouth. She quickly rubbed at it with her sleeve. Hopefully, he hadn't noticed.

When her chin felt sufficiently dry, she croaked, "What were they announcing?"

She tried not to stare too intently at Grayson, even though:

- his gray, long-sleeved cable-knit sweater looked a little too autumn-adorable

- he still smelled good—even after multiple flights (how?)

- his lips were quirked and his eyes were faraway, and a part of her wanted to bring him back to her, no matter how dangerous that felt.

Before he could answer, the captain's voice blared again: "Air traffic control has confirmed that heavy winds in Seattle will prevent us from touching down there. We're diverting to Portland. I apologize for the inconvenience. You can speak to a representative at the gate about reaching your final destination, wherever that may be."

Nidhi groaned. "Seriously?"

Grayson rubbed the scruff on his chin.

It's just facial hair, Nidhi. Geez.

"Yeah, sorry," he said. "Not sure you'll be able to make that meeting with your advisor. Do you think you'll be able to reschedule?"

"I don't know," Nidhi said. "I really need to see her."

A part of her almost wanted to skip the meeting because she was so nervous. But she'd been gearing herself up for this, practicing in her head all the points she wanted to make. Mostly, she just wanted to say the words aloud, to make it all official.

Saying it would mean the decision was made, after all.

Grayson reached for Nidhi's hand. "What's the meeting for?"

Nidhi hadn't even told her sisters and Dad yet. It wasn't just that she wanted to stay in India longer. It was that she was rethinking what she wanted to do with her life. Again.

Not ready to explain all this to Grayson, she said, "Just wanted to go over some stuff. You know, to get credit for the term."

"It doesn't have to be today, does it?"

Nidhi shrugged. "Once we land, I'll email and ask if we can reschedule for later this week—but who knows what her holiday plans are. She probably doesn't want to . . . Why are you looking at me like that?"

He had a goofy look on his face. "Nothing. You just look cute when you're worried. Not that I think you need to be. I'm sure it'll work out. You're so studious and you've probably been documenting every recipe you've made and every museum you've seen. I bet you're the most serious study abroad student they've ever had."

She narrowed her eyes at him. "You make me seem so fun."

"Hey, it's a compliment." Grayson winked. "We both know there's more to you."

That wink. Grayson was just too charming, too full of promises of adventure. And there was still an awful jealous feeling inside Nidhi as she wondered who else had experienced that Grayson charm these last months. Who else had been in that bed with him as he'd snuck out.

She shook those silly thoughts away. It wasn't fair of her to be so possessive—she'd wanted to focus on new experiences, not boyfriends. She'd been the one to suggest they keep things casual. Actually, twice. First, after she had just broken up with her previous boyfriend, Matt. And then again when they were discussing their summer plans.

And Grayson had been fine with it. Why wouldn't he be? He was so good-looking, he probably had a line of girls waiting their turn to be with him.

Casual was fine. Casual was good.

Casual was definitely what she felt about his new facial hair, too.

The line to talk to the customer service representatives snaked past several gates in the airport.

"If there's some huge windstorm, will there even be any flights to Seattle?" Nidhi wondered.

"Probably not," Grayson said. "This feels really pointless."

The cute guy in the down vest Nidhi had noticed at customs in LA came grumbling past them, on his phone. "Mom, I know. I had it all planned out, and now there's no way it's happening. They gave me a hotel voucher and a flight for tomorrow afternoon. And I'm lucky I even got that—they said it was the last seat on that plane. Thanksgiving is coming up, and everything is sold out."

"Wait, there aren't even any flights tomorrow?" Nidhi's stomach plummeted.

She'd come all the way from India to see her family for the week. Forget the advisor appointment; it sounded like she'd be spending most of her trip in the airport. She'd really been looking forward to hanging out with her sisters, catching up on everything that was going on with them—the short calls and texts just weren't enough. Plus, despite everything, despite all the new dreams and wants and yearnings, she also felt homesick. She longed to ground herself back in the Songbird, to linger in the chill of Salish Sea air and take quiet walks down to the cove and sip hot cocoa on the porch hammock.

How could she make any life decisions if she hadn't done those things first?

Grayson ran a hand through his hair. "Maybe we should rent a car. It's only three hours to Seattle. You could even make it to your appointment."

"But we're not old enough, are we?" Nidhi pulled out her phone, searching for the age for renting a car in Oregon. "No, you have to be twenty-one."

Nidhi and Grayson were still only nineteen.

"Dang it," Grayson said. "That's so obnoxious!"

They stared at each other, momentarily flummoxed. Meanwhile, the guy with the down vest had finally hung up the phone and was now looking glumly at his shoes. He looked like he needed a friend.

Grayson seemed to think so, too, because he said, "Hey, you okay?"

The guy bit his lip. "Not really. It's important for me to get to Seattle."

"Well, we were thinking of renting a car, but we're not old enough. Don't suppose you'd be willing to drive?"

The guy looked bemused. "Renting a car? Yeah, that might not be a bad idea. But how old are you? I don't want to kidnap any minors."

"We're both nineteen," Grayson assured him. "Officially adults, though apparently not adult enough to rent a car."

Nidhi had to admit that it was kind of ridiculous. They could vote and travel the world, but not rent a car. Sigh.

"I'm guessing it won't be cheap to rent one last-minute, so we'll definitely chip in," she added.

The guy thought about it for a moment, then nodded. "Okay, I guess that works. I wouldn't want to leave you two stranded."

Nidhi felt like hugging him. Finally, they had a plan. Despite all the changes she'd gone through, she still very much liked having one—especially when things were chaotic. "Yay, thank you so much! I have to get to a meeting with my advisor at UW, so this will be a huge help."

"I get it," the guy said. "I really don't have time to be stranded in Portland. I've been planning to surprise my boyfriend and propose today!

I have every detail worked out, but I need to be in Seattle by two this afternoon."

Nidhi blinked.

Oh wow. Marriage. It all seemed very grown up and far away to her. She honestly wasn't sure she'd ever be ready for it, not with that storm inside her that kept her so restless all the time.

Grayson, on the other hand, shook the guy's hand enthusiastically. "Congrats, man! There's no way we can let a windstorm stand in the way of true love, right, Nidhi?"

The words *true love* echoed in her head. Did Grayson believe in such a thing? Did she? Of course, Rani would chide her if she knew the thoughts Nidhi was having. But all that stuff about soulmates and there only being one other person in the world for you had never really felt right to Nidhi. Because after all, what if that one other person never met you? What if they were already married?

Rani would say that fate would bring you together. But Nidhi wasn't so sure that real life was like that. Suresh certainly hadn't been her one true love. He was cool and fun and nice—and she'd been wildly attracted to him. It hadn't been the right time and place to fall in love, but it had been the right time and place to have a quick fling.

She tried not to let all her warring thoughts show, but the down-vest guy laughed.

"Don't worry," he said. "Marriage isn't contagious."

Nidhi felt her face heating up. Was she that obvious? Her eyes flicked unwillingly to Grayson.

He laughed a little louder than necessary. "Don't worry, no one is tying you down."

Nidhi's face heated further. "That's not what I was thinking at all. It's cute that you're proposing. I'm Nidhi, by the way." She held out her hand.

"Lucas," down-vest guy replied. "Good to meet you."

The lady at the car rental agency laughed at them. She literally *laughed*.

"It's the holidays," she said. "Everything is reserved. And even if I had anything, I couldn't authorize a one-way out-of-state rental on a week this busy."

So that was out.

Lucas slumped. "But I need to propose to my boyfriend! I have it all planned out."

The lady perked up. "You're proposing? That's so cute! Tell me everything. Where are you going to do it? When? How? I love proposals so much!"

There was a gigantic line snaking behind them, and this lady wanted to know Lucas's life story.

Lucas just chuckled. "If I tell you, will you have a car for us?"

The woman shook her head sadly. "I'm so sorry. I really would give you one if I could. But I sincerely doubt any of the rental agencies will have anything unless you have a reservation. It's just that busy right now, and the canceled flights aren't helping. Have you checked Amtrak?"

Nidhi perked up at that idea. "Ooh, that sounds fun."

Grayson nodded. "I loved taking trains in Europe. You really get to take everything in. I bet the ride to Seattle from here would be beautiful."

The chatty agent, paying no attention to the disgruntled people in line, leaned forward. "Oh, it really is. I did it once when I was visiting some girlfriends up in Seattle. Highly recommend it."

Nidhi had never taken a train in the US, but she'd done it in India and sort of adored it as a mode of travel. They'd taken the high-speed train from Delhi to Agra so Nidhi could see the Taj Mahal on a day trip with Sona. She'd also taken a train to Jaipur and Udaipur. Those were much longer, and flying would have taken less time. But there was something about being forced to relax, forced to enjoy the moment. Nidhi was restless, but on a train she knew she was going somewhere, and that helped her settle in for a long ride.

Lucas smiled at the woman. "Amtrak it is. Thanks for the idea. For that, I'll answer one of your questions. I'm going to propose at a concert later—if I can make it in time. My boyfriend's in a band, and they're playing today."

"Aww, that's so cute. But you have to tell me more. What's your plan? How will you get his attention?"

Lucas just laughed. "Maybe it'll go viral and you'll find out."

"You're cruel for not telling me!" she said as they walked away. "But good luck!"

"Thanks!"

As they walked past the line, they definitely got a few glares for holding things up. But Grayson just flashed that dimpled grin of his and people seemed to relax. He'd always been handsome, but now he had a great tan from all that surfing in Namibia, his sandy hair looked bedhead perfect, and his collared shirt showed just a bit of chest hair poking out. Naturally, the women in the line were swoony, and the men seemed to think he was their best friend.

As they got near the door, they passed an East Asian couple fumbling with their bags, which had tags indicating they were flying in from Beijing.

"Took you long enough," the woman grumbled, seemingly immune to Grayson's smile. She was petite with long black hair, in her fifties, and wore a cute belted gray trench and knee-high boots.

"Sorry," Grayson said to her. "We were trying to butter up the lady to give us a car. But she said there aren't any unless you have a reservation."

He shrugged his good-natured shrug, and the woman softened a bit.

"See? We're wasting our time," said the man with her, adjusting his black fedora. He too was probably in his fifties, and just as stylish with his camel-colored wool jacket that made him look a bit like Sherlock Holmes.

"We're going to try Amtrak," Lucas said cheerfully.

The couple looked at each other and then at them. "Good idea!" "We're coming, too."

Chapter Ten

Sirisha

The wind howled outside, and the joints of the Songbird creaked under pressure from the gale. Yikes! Sirisha wondered if it was all a sign, like that owl that had given her the judgy look that morning.

She was torn about the text from Brie. Should she go? When they'd broken up in September, they'd promised to stay friends. Yet the texts and calls had died off, and since Brie lived on another island, it wasn't as if they ran into each other randomly.

Well, except when Brie was visiting her longtime family friend Liza, on Orcas. Which apparently she was this week. Of course, if Brie had really wanted to remain friends, shouldn't she have mentioned to Sirisha that she was planning to spend fall break here? But maybe Brie too had felt awkward about it. It wasn't as if Sirisha was the only one who ever felt awkward in certain situations. (Though maybe she was the only one who felt awkward in *every* situation.)

What she wanted to text: *We're not friends, Brie. I don't know how to be just friends with you. You didn't love me, remember?*

What she actually texted:

> I'm not sure, I have a thing later . . .

Brie:

> I'd really love to see you. Can you stop in for just a few minutes?

As Sirisha's stomach twisted in knots, Dad suddenly gasped.

"Oh no!" He stared at his phone.

"What is it?" Sirisha asked.

He looked really disappointed. "Nidhi's flight was diverted to Portland. She's trying to get on another one, but with the windstorm, she might just be stuck."

Sirisha soaked in the news, putting Brie out of mind for a moment. Nidhi was delayed *again*. What bad luck. She'd really been looking forward to some time with her big sis.

"But . . . but . . . she just has to come!" Rani moaned. "The screening is this evening!"

Sirisha couldn't help but notice that Rani was making this all about *her*. She felt a twinge of annoyance, because they all needed Nidhi.

"I'm sure she wants to come," Dad said, getting up to put an arm around her. "And she'll watch your film when she arrives. I mean, we want her to be safe, right? It's good they made the call."

"Ugh, the world stinks," Rani muttered, her fist clenching her soggy script. "We have cell phones and satellites, but we still can't stop a simple windstorm?"

Everyone laughed at that. And Sirisha felt her annoyance recede. Rani could be kind of self-absorbed sometimes, but her over-the-topness was something that Sirisha actually sort of admired. Rani really went for things she was excited about—and she pushed Sirisha to do the same. Sirisha probably never would have had the confidence to talk to Brie in the first place if not for Rani's pestering—and her Official Love Guru romance lessons and makeover.

Also, Rani had been working so hard on *Remeet-Cute*. It really would be a shame if Nidhi missed the screening.

"Don't worry," Sirisha said. "The rest of us will be there to cheer on your film. It's going to be amazing. I'll hop on the ferry to Friday Harbor right after the party."

"Thanks." Rani's gaze softened. "And sorry about the comment about your hair. I'll help you tame it a bit—I've got an amazing new hair serum. Let's hurry up though—Fernando will be coming over soon to take Avani and me to the ferry."

Dad looked worriedly at his phone again. "I just hope the ferry system doesn't get shut down. The weather says we might get seventy mile per hour winds."

"It'll be fine," said Avani. "The ferries are really stable. I'm actually surprised they canceled any flights. Airplanes can still take off and land with wind."

"Just our luck that they changed their minds today," Rani grouched.

"Everything will be okay." Amir rubbed Dad's shoulder comfortingly. "They wouldn't run the ferries unless it was safe, right?"

"I suppose . . ."

Sirisha smiled at the Dads. Dad was definitely the worrier of the two, and Amir ever the optimist. They balanced each other out so nicely.

"I can't wait for tonight, Rani!" Amir exclaimed. "Our very own celebrity director. I hope you'll remember us when you walk down the red carpet."

Rani beamed. "I'll try. Now, Sirisha, let's see what we can do about your hair."

Rani:

Nidhi, windstorm or not, you'd better get your butt to Friday Harbor in time for my film screening. This is the start of my whole career! You can't miss it.

Sirisha:

What Rani means to say is: safe travels! We hope we see you tonight!

Avani:

Yeah, we miss you. But don't let it go to your head or anything.

Chapter Eleven

Avani

After breakfast, Avani and Rani waited on the porch outside reception. The wind was screaming, the skies a mix of periwinkle and slate with a heavy dose of charcoal gray. And Fernando was already ten minutes late.

"Where is he?" Rani said. "We can't miss the ferry!"

Her pumps clattered against the pavement as she paced back and forth.

(So impractical. Avani was wearing sneakers, but she had a duffel bag with her dance shoes and a change of clothes for the film screening.)

"He'll be here," Avani returned.

She checked her phone again. It wasn't like him not to at least text and give her a heads-up if he was running off schedule. In that fight last week, he'd called her the flaky one, but here he was: missing.

Sometimes he got caught up in things on the farm, and there were parts of his family's property that didn't have great cell reception. Avani had always understood; she'd grown up helping Dad at the inn, and it was cool that she and Fernando had both been so thoroughly shaped by their families' businesses. Also, it had been proof that she wasn't alone in sometimes forgetting things. Everyone did, right?

Right?

Then again, Zadie's text still lingered in her mind. ADHD. Could that explain everything? Maybe everyone forgot things, but did they forget them as often as Avani did?

She didn't think so.

A text from Fernando finally popped up:

> Hey, Frida's sick and my mom can't get her to take her medicine. I'm trying to wrangle her.

Avani loved Frida, the baby goat that had brought them together last winter when they'd accidentally gotten trapped in a barn in a snowstorm. (It had been really romantic, actually.) But Fernando knew that today was important—both to her and to Rani. Couldn't he let his parents handle this crisis?

Avani:

> Maybe Sirisha can give us a ride to your farm to save time. Will you be ready by then?

Fernando:

> Great idea! Yes, this won't take long.

76

ONE WEEK EARLIER

With the fireplace still glowing, Avani and Fernando kissed with urgency, with heat.

And then
    it was a little more
        than just kissing
A trail of
    parkas and sweaters
        gloves and scarves
    oh and there, her T-shirt
a trail of
    kisses
        down his chest
as she popped open
    each button
of his collared shirt
    and then his
lips on that spot
    on the crook of her neck
        his hands
    on her lacy
black bra . . .

Yet a swarm of stray thoughts were like moths fluttering in all directions in the night. Avani ignored them because she didn't need that buzzing, the flapping of wings in the darkness—just everything warm and wonderful in front of her.

And then

    a ping

        a text

    a distraction

"Can't you ignore it?" Fernando asked, his breath coming fast as she fumbled with her phone.

"I would, but I have this feeling—"

Sirisha:

> Do you still have my big telephoto lens?
> Because I really need it for this wildlife shoot.

Avani:

> Hey, kinda busy at the moment.

That was the understatement of the year. Avani's heart was still pounding. Why had she even bothered to look at the text?

Okay, maybe because she'd known in the pit of her stomach that she'd forgotten something.

Sirisha:

> It's just that there are eagles circling right now and I
> need this for my portfolio for that summer internship
> I'm applying to. It's really important to me.

Avani:

I put it in your bag, didn't I?

Sirisha:

You said you did, but nope, it's not here.

Avani grabbed her backpack. She'd been so certain she had put it away. It had been on her to-do list. But then—oh yes, she'd been about to return it when she'd gotten a sexy text from Fernando. Shirtless and photo attached. Ironically, now that text was ruining her alone time with him.

"Shoot," she said to Fernando. "Is it okay if we run this over? I'm really sorry—apparently there are eagles and Sirisha needs to get the shot for her portfolio for that internship she's applying to. I should have given it to her earlier, but you sent me this . . ."

She flashed him the photo. S.E.X.Y.

Fernando just sighed. Put his shirt back on. "Sure, blame me."

"I'm not blaming you, I'm just trying to explain . . ."

"You're always explaining why you forgot this or that." His voice was tight. "You knew this was our night—finally—to hang out together. And now we have to interrupt it."

Avani swallowed. "It should be a compliment that you distracted me that much."

"I'm glad you liked the pic. Anyway, I don't want to be the bad guy, so let's just go."

He was saying one thing, but his tone said something else.

"You're not the bad guy," Avani said. "Spending time together is important. I know that."

He raised his brows. "Do you? You've signed up for so many clubs this semester that I barely see you."

A twinge of annoyance prickled Avani. "Wait a minute, you're the one who decided to take a college prep course that was at the same time as our dance class."

Okay, so she was more than a little bitter at that. Salsa time had been their time. She'd never felt more connected to him than when they'd swished and turned together. Well, except when his lips and hands were hot against her.

"I'm not a brilliant writer like you," he returned. "Writing essays doesn't come easily to me. I'm just trying to give myself the best chance I have to get into college. You'd think you could understand that."

"You'd think you could understand why I signed up for so many clubs!" Avani said. "I'm trying to figure out what to do with my life!"

Fernando brushed a hand in his hair. "Whatever. Let's just go."

Avani grabbed her bag, and they trundled along the island roads in Fernando's SUV, the heavy air of resentment between them. Avani put a playlist on to distract them from the fact that they seemed to have nothing at all to say to each other these days.

A few minutes later, they'd arrived, and Avani found Sirisha with several others from the photography club. Everyone else was clicking away at the eagles, which were now in a tree. "Here's the lens."

"Thanks," Sirisha said. "You should have seen them swooping around earlier. It was really something."

Avani nodded, feeling guilty for making Sirisha miss the best shots. Why hadn't she just put the darn lens back in Sirisha's camera bag in the first place? Now nobody was happy. Fernando was still sulking when they got back to the SUV.

She reached over. Put a hand on his leg. "Well, now we can get back to what we were doing."

Fernando didn't answer.

When they got back, she grabbed him and kissed him. His lips were on hers. His hands were roaming. But something felt off.

"Are you still mad?" she said.

"I'm just waiting for the next text that will interrupt us," Fernando said.

"There's not going to be another text."

"You sure? You haven't flaked on horticulture club? Or maybe you suddenly need to practice for debate?"

Avani didn't even hear the rest.

Flaked.

Oh, that cut deep. That was what other people always said about her, not Fernando. Or even if they didn't say it out loud, it was often implied. But Fernando should know she always had a reason when she missed things.

And all those
>hurts
>>she'd been
>>>holding in
>>came rising
>up through her
all those doubts
>and maybe a few tears
>>welling up
>but the tears
>>quickly crystalized
into words

sharp ones
meant to cut
He too had missed things
He too had been
busy
distracted
grouchy
this semester
The words flew from there
weapons designed to dig
beneath flesh
to burrow into bone
to strike where it hurt most
but like all weapons
once the first ones flew
the return strike was imminent
until neither side knew how to stop
until there was no stopping

Chapter Twelve

Nidhi

Unfortunately for Nidhi and her stranded traveler friends, Amtrak was also completely booked up. It was clear that:

- travel delays during the holiday break were an absolute nightmare

- the weather had a personal vendetta against her

- she would have to live in Portland now

At least she was in good company. Grayson, Lucas, and the couple from the rental car place—whose names turned out to be Lena and John Liu—were all twiddling their thumbs glumly beside her. The station was gorgeous, with dangling chandeliers hanging from intricately coffered ceilings. Morning light filtered in the airy space, but none of that beauty could counteract everyone's disappointment.

Well, maybe it did for Lena, who snapped a picture with her phone. "I'm starving. Anybody else?"

"Me!" Lucas cried.

Nidhi then realized she'd been running on empty all morning and now she was going to positively collapse if someone didn't get some food soon.

"I have a buddy who lives in Portland," Grayson said. "He'll probably have some good recommendations. Let me text him."

"Okay," said Nidhi. "I'm going to go freshen up a bit."

She grabbed her bag and headed to the bathroom. Luckily, she had packed light for this short trip home and didn't have to deal with checked-in luggage. Her carry-on had plenty of extra clothes. And a jacket.

"I'll join you," Lena called.

Nidhi felt slightly better after brushing her teeth, changing into fresh clothes, washing her face, and swiping some deodorant under her arms. She pulled her hair into an efficient top knot, a hairstyle she'd perfected over the past year. Her pins would actually stay in place now, and the only loose wisps were the ones she wanted that way, to soften the look.

Underneath her clothes, there was still a layer of Chanel's Eau de Airport Grime, but at least it was less obvious. She sniffed herself again just to be sure.

Lena sniffed her, too. "You're fine. I like that shirt. Did you get it in India?"

"Thanks," Nidhi said. "Yeah, it's a salwar top."

The tunic-length paisley top had come from one of the Delhi boutiques where you didn't need to haggle; the prices were set. The vibrant bustle of the open-air markets was exhilarating, but she had to admit that sipping complimentary lemonade in an air-conditioned shop could be quite pleasant. Plus, she didn't need Sona's help agreeing on a price.

"It looks lovely on you." Lena fussed with her hair in front of the mirror. She'd changed into an extremely chic magenta dress. It was the kind that screamed at people to notice you. The kind that Nidhi still avoided like sugar-free baked goods. But Lena could totally pull it off.

When they arrived back in the lobby, Grayson grinned at them. "Good news—Brad's coming to pick us up. He says he knows a great place."

"Will he have room for all of us?" Nidhi asked.

Lena and John might be fine on their own, but Lucas was sitting with his head in hands, muttering about how his proposal had to be today or it would be a bust.

"Don't worry," Grayson said. "Brad's got a station wagon. It's old but reliable—and huge. Three rows."

Apparently, the station wagon had stopped being reliable when it reached the grand old age of thirteen. And Brad had traded it in for a Mini Cooper. Which was adorable. And very, very tiny.

"Oops," Brad said sheepishly, getting out of the car. "I didn't realize you had so many friends." With his sunny smile and surfer blond hair, he looked like he could be Grayson's brother. They both had that "everything's chill" vibe.

"We can take a cab," Lena offered.

"No, no," Brad insisted. "We'll make it work."

Apparently, Brad was also one of *those* guys. The ones that took everything as a challenge.

"What about our luggage?" Lena asked.

Lena and John each had roller suitcases, Nidhi had her carry-on bag, and Grayson and Lucas both had duffels. It wasn't that much stuff, but the Mini Cooper was extremely Mini.

"No problem," said Brad, "I've got bungee cords."

"I'll help you!" Lucas added enthusiastically.

"This is silly," Lena protested. "I'll just get us a ride share."

But now Grayson and John were at it, too. They all wanted to show how capable they were as men apparently because they were quickly loading all the luggage on top of the Mini Cooper and fiddling with bungee cords.

Lena grinned ruefully at Nidhi. "The world's strangest macho display."

Nidhi had to giggle. "But how in the world are we all going to fit in there?"

She glanced doubtfully at the back seat.

"Oh, we'll fit," said Lena. "Now that these guys are determined, I can tell we're going to fit even if they have to tie one of us to the roof. And I'm way too famished to argue right now."

Although it didn't quite come to that, John ended up on Lena's lap and Nidhi was on Grayson's. Lucas with his extra-long legs got the cushy front passenger seat.

"I hope the restaurant isn't far," Nidhi muttered, squirming awkwardly.

Grayson wrapped his arm around her waist. "Come on now, isn't this great?"

"Absolutely great."

His scruff rubbed against her shoulder, sending tingles all over her body. And there was that scent again, of pines and sea. Of midnight and murals and magic. It had been four months since their last kiss. Four months since they'd last held each other.

"I just hope we don't hit traffic," John muttered next to her.

"Oh, I'm sorry, dear," Lena said. "Are you uncomfortable?"

Even though John was the one who had originally been enthusiastic, now that he was wriggling in Lena's lap, he seemed a little less zealous. He kept trying to rearrange his legs, but there was literally zero space for them.

Meanwhile, Lena grinned like she was having the time of her life. From the front, Brad just laughed and turned on some music—catchy hip-hop that was way too nightclub for 8:00 a.m. Apparently, it was a popular song because Lucas started singing the words. Then Lena joined in. Grayson, Brad, and John added their voices. Nidhi had never heard it, probably because she'd been busy getting caught up on Bollywood hits and gully rap in India these last months.

The thought made her smile, and different lyrics came to mind. Lyrics she'd heard at a club in India, lyrics that had crept into her soul, that had made her stop and think and listen.

NEW DELHI—SEPTEMBER

Though the early days in New Delhi had been an adjustment, after a few weeks, time started to fly by. Nidhi visited ancient, crumbling forts. Gorgeous palaces with intricately carved marble and jewel-toned mosaics. Old marketplaces where she picked up a few of her aunt's amazing haggling abilities. As someone with an American accent, Nidhi would never be given the best prices. But with some practice, she could at least talk them down a bit.

Her aunt and uncle insisted that she always had a chaperone wherever she went, and Nidhi felt so lost in this big bustling city that she didn't mind. She tagged along with Sona and Prakash whenever she could. Hung out with their friends. She was curious about what their everyday lives were like, what people her age got up to in New Delhi

With all her exploring, not to mention the heat, Nidhi would fall dead asleep each night, the fan whirring above her. Her nose still tickled with the scent of spices from her cooking sessions with Shiv. Her heart still aflutter with this place that was so unfamiliar and yet seemed to call to her soul.

One night, Prakash took her to a party with friends from his university. Nidhi dressed carefully, in linen pants and a loose-fitting long-sleeved blouse. Dangly twenty-four-karat gold earrings that Lalita Phua had gifted her, assuring her that in India nobody wore anything less than twenty-four karat.

Since she'd arrived, Nidhi had been following the directions from her guidebook—which she kept hidden in her bag and only nosed through when her cousins weren't around to make fun of her. (She'd pulled it out once, and they'd both been very curious about what it said and also mentioned that a lot of the advice was out of date, at least in their urban New Delhi circles.)

What to Wear

Loose fitting clothes with breathable fabrics are your best bet in the heat. Local customs may vary, but keeping your arms and legs covered is recommended. You would do best to avoid shorts, skirts, or dresses

unless they are ankle-length. Avoid tank tops, but short sleeves may still
be acceptable . . .

Deep-throated laughter filled the house when she and Prakash
arrived. (Sona wasn't invited because, at sixteen, Prakash thought she was
too young for a college party.). The place was another bungalow, with
minimalist furnishing and sparkling white walls. Splashes of color in tap-
estries and toss pillows, plants growing in all the windows.

There were definitely girls at the party wearing tank tops and skirts.
Others wore shorts or jeans. The male uniform seemed to be polos, jeans,
and trendy sneakers. Although Lalita Phua wore saris nearly all the time,
Nidhi had already noticed that a lot of girls her age tended to wear a fusion
of East and West—hints of traditional Indian patterns and embroidery,
often paired with jeans.

Of course, she had no clue how anyone could wear jeans in the intense
heat. Dealing with it was one of the hardest things to adjust to. She
didn't miss home as much as she had at first, but she could kill for a cool
sea breeze.

Prakash introduced her to his friends, who were very nice and polite
and asked her lots of questions. Mostly. There was one guy who was both
drunk and rather aggressive. Even though she tried to mingle with others,
he kept following her around.

"Do you have a boyfriend?" he asked. "Is he American?"

In India, she'd noticed that *American* usually meant *white* depending
on the context. Which rankled a bit, since Nidhi was American, too. But
then again, her cousins often teased her about being "American" also—
especially when it came to food and drink. She swore to herself that

her gut bacteria would be able to handle street food one of these days.

"Come on," the annoying guy insisted. "Tell us about your boyfriend. Or boyfriends."

Prakash had disappeared into the kitchen, and Nidhi was starting to feel uncomfortable.

"Oh, buzz off," said a girl with flowing long hair, a nose ring, and four-inch heels. "She doesn't need all your rude questions."

Her glare was enough to get him to stalk off. Thank goodness.

"Thanks," Nidhi said. "It was getting a little creepy."

"Yeah, some guys just don't understand that whole idea of *not* being creepy," the girl replied. "I'm Sheela, by the way."

Nidhi stuck by Sheela or Prakash for the rest of the party. But she felt like there were eyes on her the whole evening. Lots of male attention. It could have been because of her clothes or makeup or because she'd ditched the braids for good. But Nidhi had the sudden feeling that maybe it was more than that?

At school, she'd always felt awkward and gangly. Her nose longer and less pert than other girls', her features sharper than what American beauty magazines emphasized. But here, her nose wasn't unusual at all.

Maybe it was beautiful?

It was nearly one in the morning when someone got a text saying that some hot young Bollywood actor—who Nidhi hadn't heard of—was at some bar. Prakash, Sheela, and a bunch of others decided they simply *had* to go meet him.

Nidhi had never cared much for celebrities. But she also wasn't ready for sleep yet.

"I'm in," she said, reveling in the words.

Chapter Thirteen

Rani

Rani was surprised that Fernando hadn't picked them up on time. But she was even more surprised at Avani's anger. After all, it was Rani who needed to be on the ferry to meet her cast—she was the director of their film! Avani was just going to a dance workshop. Why the angst over that? It wasn't even a showcase or anything.

It certainly didn't seem worth picking a fight with Fernando over. But Avani and Fernando bickered when Sirisha dropped them off at the Gutiérrez Farm. They bickered as they got into the SUV. Now they were bickering in the front as they raced toward the ferry terminal. About silly things, too. Avani wanted music, Fernando didn't. Avani said he was being grumpy. He accused her of the same. Geez. At least she and Raj never bickered like that.

She felt immediately terrible for thinking that. She shouldn't be comparing their relationship with hers. After all, not everyone found their soulmate in high school. Some relationships were destined to end.

Rani decided to tune them out, focusing on her printout instead.

INT. CAFÉ - DAY

                              NATE
            I know I was supposed to keep in touch and I didn't. Can
            I make it up to you? Take you out?

                              LAYLA
            I told you, I'm seeing other people.

                              NATE
            Yacht guy, yeah, I remember.

                              LAYLA
            Yeah, and someone else, too.

                              NATE
            Let me guess, he owns an island?

Rani smiled. She was proud of this scene, how Layla stayed so cool and aloof. How she was making Nate work for it. True love required a little bit of effort.

Up front, Avani and Fernando had finally stopped their bickering, but the chilly silence between them was somehow worse. Avani's lips were pursed, and Fernando was clutching the steering wheel so hard his fingers were turning red. Okay, even though Rani had put aside her Official Love Guru hat to focus on the Shoot-Out, she couldn't just ignore this.

"You know, communication is key to a good relationship," she said. "Avani, do you have something constructive to say to Fernando?"

Avani shot her a withering glare. "Look, I'm really not in the mood for your Official Love Guru stuff right now. Let's just get on the ferry."

Ouch. She was just trying to help.

Fernando's fingers stayed tight on the wheel. He too looked annoyed, but he didn't say anything.

"We're going to miss it," Avani muttered as they sped along the road.

"No we're not," he returned.

"Yes we are."

The sea was churning furiously below them, and when they rounded the last curve, cars were already driving onto the ferry. They parked in the lot on the hill, grabbed their bags, and scrambled to the dock. They were literally the last foot passengers to get on, just seconds before the ferry eased away from shore.

"There. We made it." Fernando's shoulders slumped in relief.

"Barely," Avani muttered.

"We appreciate you hurrying up even though Frida was sick," Rani said, trying to mediate.

"Your mom could've taken care of her," Avani said, heading toward the stairs that led to the passenger lounge.

"She tried, but you know how Frida is. She'll escape if she can."

Avani huffed and walked faster, clutching her dance bag. The ferry lurched, and Rani stumbled. Fernando offered her a hand to steady her.

"Thanks," Rani said.

Her twin had already disappeared, so Rani and Fernando made their way up to the lounge together.

"What's with Avani?" Rani asked. "She's not usually so tense."

Fernando rubbed his forehead. "Things . . . have been kind of rocky between us."

Rani patted his shoulder. "Maybe get her something to make up for it?"

Fernando sighed. "I have something planned, but I'm not sure it will work out."

They found Avani in a booth, her nose stuck in a book about the judicial system—one that looked rather long and dense and boring. Probably something she was reading for debate club. No wonder the girl was so grumpy. Like the Dads, Rani had warned her she was overcommitting at the beginning of the year, and Avani had ignored that warning.

Now Avani was reading about court precedent instead of enjoying fall break with her boyfriend. Fernando sat down across from her and pulled out an SAT prep book. Wow. Apparently, they both planned to spend their Saturday morning studying and ignoring each other and making occasional huffing sounds. Lovely.

But they'd figure it out; the Official Love Guru was sure of it. Just like Layla and Nate.

INT. BEACH - DAY

NATE

Look, I'm saying everything all wrong. I'm happy for you
that you have other . . . friends.

LAYLA

They're not just friends. They're my many admirers.

NATE

Right. Obviously. Let's start over. I came here to explain
why I didn't keep in touch.

LAYLA

Your broke your fingers so you couldn't type? You moved
to Antarctica?

NATE

Yep, I live in Antarctica now.

LAYLA

I'm sure you'll enjoy the company of all the penguins.

NATE

Okay, for real, it's not Antarctica. It's just that my
parents have been fighting a lot. It's been really rough. I
wanted to reach out, but then I'd hear them screaming or
see my mom crying, and then I just didn't know what to
say anymore.

LAYLA

(looks sheepish for the first time)
Wow. Okay, I guess that makes sense. I'm sorry you've
been going through all that.

After dispensing some more relationship gems to Avani and Fernando (such as "Your relationship is a journey, not a destination. Enjoy the twists and turns!"), Rani felt she'd done her bare minimum duties as Official Love Guru. Not that they were listening to her anyway, but at least she'd tried.

JJ texted that the cast was waiting on the outdoor deck. When Rani stepped out, the wind was blowing everyone's hair into disarray, and she was glad she'd at least remembered her heather-gray trench coat, which fit perfectly over the pantsuit. It was extremely cold, and her lips felt parched from the unrelenting gale. Brrr.

Near the railing, Dominic Evans (*Remeet-Cute*'s leading actor) and Sara Goldstein (minor parts and makeup) were making out while Parker McCormick (leading lady) and JJ Doherty (producer) chatted a few feet away.

The five of them had been spending a whole lot of time together in the past month, scrambling to get ready for the Shoot-Out. It had been pretty amazing, actually. Rani's crew had been incredibly dedicated to the project, and that touched her heart. They must truly think it was something special!

"Ugh, get a room, you two," Rani called to Dominic and Sara.

Sara stopped tongue-wrestling long enough to say, "Hey, Rani!"

Dominic mumbled something too, and then they were back at it. Rani, of course, wished it were her and Raj making out wildly on a ferry, the wind blustering around them, the choppy waves a symphony to their love. They'd have time for that later, she supposed. She couldn't wait to see him—it had been literal weeks since they'd been together! Such torture, but Rani would never let such a silly thing as time and space come between them.

"Ignore them," JJ said, slouching as always, which made their petite build look even shorter.

It was honestly freezing, but JJ only wore a black, long-sleeved T-shirt under a gray down vest and jeans. Rani noted cute silver cloud clips glittering from their pixie cut—and the prop copy of *Wired* magazine in their hands.

"Oh my gosh, it looks so good," Rani said, grabbing it. She'd seen Raj's rich-kid smirk in digital form, but holding it in her hands like a real magazine was a whole other thing.

"Thanks." JJ grinned. "Raj looks perfect. It's all in the eyes. Anyway, I've got everything in order. I signed us up for slots at all the available indoor locations: the library, the café, the auditorium. We really don't have a lot of time if we want to edit anything—"

JJ was interrupted by the sound of Parker retching over the side of the railing, her shampoo-commercial blond hair flying in the wind. (Though somehow it looked great anyway; thus were her powers.) She wiped her mouth and fussed with her cream-colored scarf. Her pale peach winter coat was beautiful—but probably wouldn't look great with vomit.

"Oh my gosh, are you okay?" Rani said, rubbing her back.

"It's too choppy," Parker moaned. "I've never been on a ferry like this."

The wind and waves were slamming into the side of the boat. It wasn't some dinky river-crossing ferry either—this thing had three stories and was normally extremely stable. Rani felt a smidgen worried about some of the outdoor scenes she had planned for the day. She'd known it was risky to have any in November, but she'd figured they could just put an umbrella over the camera and that it would be perfectly romantic. Drizzly and dreamy.

She hadn't accounted for all this darn wind. An umbrella would snap into pieces in seconds. What genius had decided to have the Shoot-Out in November anyway? Ah, well. Adversity was what helped great artists create, right?

JJ glanced at their phone. "I hope they don't call off the whole competition due to the weather."

Rani's eyes nearly popped out of her head. Canceling the One Day Shoot-Out was inconceivable. "They'd better not! We've been working for months on this!"

"Seriously!" Dominic and Sara echoed, apparently at a stopping point with their tonsil hockey.

Dominic smiled his boy-band smile. He had sparkling amber eyes and floppy hair and wore a vintage bomber jacket. Very leading-man worthy, if Rani did say so herself. Also, he was the only guy in her class who'd been interested in the part, but that wasn't really the point.

"Relax, everyone," he said in that leading-man voice. "We can make the film anyway. And just upload it online directly. We'll be huge in no time."

He winked at an imagined camera behind them. Such a ham.

JJ raised their brows. "You do realize we're not actually *in* a movie right now, don't you, Dominic?"

"Of course," Dominic said, winking at an imaginary camera again.

Rani chuckled. "That would be ridiculous. And I definitely don't have a secret theory that we're all trapped inside a rom-com either. Or that Raj and I are the stars. Nope, definitely not."

"Uh-huh," JJ retorted.

"Excuse me!" Dominic cut in. "Obviously, Sara and I are the stars of this movie we're in!"

"Yeah," Sara huffed, tossing her brunette ringlets.

"Whatever," Rani said. The two of them being so happy and cute together was fine—when Raj was around. But at the moment, she wished they'd cut it out.

Instead, they were making out again. Maybe the chop would throw them overboard. (No, no. She needed them, despite their annoying cuteness.) The ferry rumbled and Parker moaned, clutching the railing. Rani also stumbled—right into someone's bulky backpack.

"Hey, watch it!" said a haughty voice behind her.

She knew that snobbish voice. Rani whirled, her hackles raised. Sure enough, Ed Yi was there on the ferry. A Korean American senior who had recently moved to Orcas Island from LA. He was skinny and not particularly tall, but he carried himself with such an air of importance that people tended to think he really was. (Not Rani, obviously.)

He seemed to have a sneer pasted across his face at all times, his eyebrows permanently arched as if he couldn't believe how absolutely banal the world around him was. Today he wore dark jeans with a collared white button-down that showed off his lightly tanned skin, a gray bowler hat, and pretentious brown leather loafers. What kind of teenager wore loafers?

Okay, Rani might normally think it was hot, if Ed weren't so constantly obnoxious.

"This camera equipment is very expensive," he added with a sniff.

"Camera equipment?"

He'd *better* not say it was for the One Day Shoot-Out.

"Yes, I'm entering a film competition," he answered. "The One Day Shoot-Out."

Dang it.

Chapter Fourteen

Avani

Avani:

Hey Nidhi, if you're stuck in the airport and have nothing to do, text me okay? I want to chat about something.

Avani:

You there?

Avani:

Seriously, need your advice.

"Your relationship is a journey, not a destination. Enjoy the twists and turns!" Rani said, before flouncing off.

Avani was in a M.O.O.D. and her twin's pat advice wasn't exactly helping. Nor was the fact that the ferry was rocking hard from the ferocity of the wind and the waves, and she wondered if she was seriously going to hurl.

"Rani sure has all the answers, doesn't she?" Fernando commented over his SAT prep book. "I wish I could be that sure of myself."

That made Avani smile. "The Official Love Guru on the job, ladies and gentlemen! Did you know that we should enjoy the twists *and* the turns? The twists alone are not sufficient."

"Apparently, it's about the journey," Fernando added. "Not the destination. Of course, what exactly would the destination be? Side-by-side gravestones?"

Avani snorted. "Very romantic."

She turned back to her judicial systems book, but the ferry was rocking so hard, the words swam on the page in front of her. Talk about a fruitless endeavor. But then again, she was supposed to enjoy the "twists," and she supposed this windstorm was one of those.

THUMP. BUMP. THUMP.

The chop sent her books and papers sliding off the table. Avani scrambled to pick them up, a pencil rolling down the aisle before she could grab it.

Fernando sprinted after it, but the pencil seemed to have a mind of its own. Finally, it stopped at the sneaker of a little girl blowing a giant gum bubble. As Fernando knelt down, the kiddo stumbled. In the end, Fernando came back to their booth with the pencil—and bubble gum smeared all over his shirt.

The girl's mom came running up behind him. "I'm so sorry about your clothes! Can I buy you a coffee to make up for it?"

"It wasn't her fault," Fernando said. "The ferry is really rocking."

"True. But I'll get you something anyway. What do you like? You too, dear." She smiled at Avani.

"Thanks," Avani returned. Despite all the chai from that morning, she still felt like she needed more caffeine.

By the time the woman brought back two lattes, Avani no longer felt like reading about horticulture or gun control or writing an article about the school's pea patch. She twirled the pencil in her hands and doodled beside her unfinished article.

"Thanks again," Avani said to the woman, taking a grateful swig. It was definitely nothing like the lattes that Nidhi brewed up, but it was still warm and comforting and achingly sweet with vanilla syrup.

"No problem." The mom glanced at all the books on their table. "Aren't you two a studious pair! I hope Mia grows up to be as responsible."

Then she was gone, and Avani and Fernando were left with two lattes and a whole lot of unsaid things hanging in the air between them.

"Look," Fernando finally said. "I'm sorry about making us late this morning."

"It's okay," she said. "I know it wasn't your fault that Frida was sick. I get it. Sorry for being so crabby about it."

He sipped his coffee. "What's going on with you? It feels like you're always mad."

That got her hackles up. "I'm not always mad. I'm just overwhelmed!"

She gestured at her books, waiting for Fernando to tell her that she'd overcommitted. She couldn't help but think about all those times that people had judged her for forgetting things or for not being organized enough. Maybe she really did have ADHD.

The more she thought about it, the more it felt like it might explain everything: why her brain seemed so different from everyone else's, why other people never seemed to understand the way she did things.

Fernando held up his hands. "Okay, okay. I know we're both stressed right now. Anyway, I have a brilliant idea."

She smiled tentatively. It was hard to get over that impending sense of doom, but she never could resist those cheekbones cheekboning. Plus, his bubble-gum-covered T-shirt was pretty endearing. "What brilliant idea?"

"Well," he said. "The Cloud Grifters are playing tonight in Friday Harbor. I got us tickets! Isn't that awesome?"

They weren't one of Avani's favorite bands, but she knew Fernando loved them. They were from Seattle and tended to come out to the islands every few months. "That sounds fun, but what time are they on? We have to go to Rani's film screening, remember?"

Fernando looked at his phone. "Doors open at seven-thirty p.m. Can't we just skip out a little early?"

"Oh no. The screening will just be getting started then," Avani said. "I honestly don't know how long it will be."

"Are you sure?" Fernando said. "This is important to me."

Avani blinked. She didn't need the Official Love Guru to tell her that when the person you're in a relationship with says those five words—"This is important to me"—you're supposed to pay attention. Especially, when you've been going through a bit of a rough patch

especially when
the echoes of a fight

are still haunting
your dreams
especially when
the two of you
are on the edge
of a chasm
dark and deep
with no bridge to cross it.

But—how could he ask her to choose between him and her sister? How could he not understand that missing Rani's film was nonnegotiable?

"I can't commit to leaving early." Avani swallowed. "Why don't you go to the concert, and I'll catch up with you when the screening is over?"

It seemed like a perfectly reasonable compromise, but Fernando didn't look happy. "That's not what I had in mind."

He got up and stalked off, outside to the back deck.

This was really weird, actually. When she'd said she wanted to spend the day together, she'd definitely told Fernando that they had to attend the screening. He'd agreed. So why did he think he was going to get out of it?

Avani took a deep breath. There had to be some miscommunication, though she was racking her brain and couldn't figure out how it had happened. She'd been clear; she was sure of it. But then again, was she sure of anything? A lump formed in her throat.

Letters danced in her mind: *ADHD, ADHD, ADHD.*

But if she had it, what did it really change? Wasn't it just a label?

All she knew was that she needed to figure things out with Fernando. She got up and sprinted after him, out to the deck at the back of the ferry. There weren't many people out there. His back was to her, and he was looking out at the islands retreating in the distance. She put her arms around him from behind. Something squished against her arm.

"Ew, the bubble gum!" she said, pulling back from the sticky mess.

He turned around. "Sorry. I should probably change."

"Did you bring an extra shirt?"

"Yeah," he said. "I've got the button-down I was planning to change into for the concert. I mean, um. The film thing."

Right.

His moth-brown eyes searched hers. And when he looked at her that way, she didn't know what to think. There was something there, and it wasn't anger. She didn't know what it was. But she still heard his voice all scratchy, how it had been that night as his house . . .

"Remember the way we used to love to dance?" Avani asked softly.

The wind and waves blustered around them, the silver air thick with wishes.

"It was always just the two of us." His voice was a rumble, a purr, a dance on its own.

They'd started taking salsa lessons together last spring. They'd wanted to do everything together back then; they were raising chickens and going on hikes and Fernando would come over for dinner with the family every Sunday.

Spring had turned into summer and summer had turned into fall. And suddenly those moments twirling in the little dance studio in Eastsound seemed so far away. Avani no longer felt like that girl from the previous spring. Senior year had put new pressures on her, made her feel that every moment was as ephemeral as ocean spray, that she could never linger in the present the way she wanted to.

She stood now on tiptoe, her ponytail swishing on a chilly blast, and brought her lips to his. There was heat between them, the kind that came from

    the ember of their relationship
        a flame lit from so many twigs
            gathered over the years . . .
    they held each other
        for a long while
   in that in-between place
        surrounded by thrashing slate grays
          and yearning blues
        hints of silver and periwinkle
          that would
              soon
                 be lost

Part Two:
The Leaves Are
Swirling

Chapter Fifteen

Rani

On the outdoor ferry deck, Rani stared at Ed Yi with his bulky camera bag. *Do not panic. Do not panic.*

"Oh." She was unable to keep the dismay out of her voice. "You're entering, too?"

"Didn't I just say so?" he retorted snootily.

Everything he said came out snootily. He probably even ate a sandwich snootily.

It was then that she noticed all her least favorite seniors from school were milling about on the deck. Could they be . . . Ed's cast? There was Fiona—the drummer for the Cuts, a folksy rock band that played at most school events. They were good, but did that mean Fiona had to constantly be talking about her "influences" as if she was being interviewed for a rockumentary? So obnoxious.

Near Fiona, Rani also spotted Ricky, a kid who was mostly a loner and was always reading things like *Infinite Jest* and other thousand-page literary novels. Of course he'd be on Ed Yi's crew.

Finally, there was Adam, a jock who played soccer in the fall, basketball in the winter, and baseball in the spring. He was really popular, with his sunny smile and surfer-boy hair, but also super fake. He was always pretending to be interested in what you had to say but would stop talking literally midsentence if someone he deemed "better than you" showed up.

Team Better-Than-Thou, she dubbed the lot of them.

"Well, good luck," Rani said, but what she was truly thinking was: *I will crush you.*

"Same to you," Ed said. "And I have to thank you."

"For what?"

"I wouldn't have heard about the competition if not for you and your cast rehearsing after school."

"Oh. It wasn't from the flyer in the hallway?"

"There was a flyer?" He scratched his head. "I must have missed that. Nope, I just asked Dominic what he was up to when I saw him rehearsing with Parker one time. He told me all about the Shoot-Out, and I thought it sounded cool."

Dang it. The Shoot-Out wasn't a secret or anything—after all, the flyer had been hanging right there in the hallway. But seriously, did Dominic have to tell *Ed Yi* with those ridiculous loafers about it?

(She hoped he stepped in a giant muddy puddle. A really squishy one.)

"Anyway," Ed continued, "when I saw the prize was a consultation with Helmuth Gerhardt, I knew I *had* to enter. I mean, he's basically my idol."

"Right," Rani said. "Of course."

She'd *tried* to watch a Helmuth Gerhardt film before. But it moved so slowly—so many panned shots of windmills, why?—and her eyes just would not stay open. She'd finally managed to wake herself up . . . by scrolling on her phone and catching up on the latest celebrity gossip.

But obviously panned shots of windmills would drive Ed wild.

Ugh. Every time he raised his hand in AP English Lit, Rani winced. Like most *normal* people her age, the so-called "classics" weren't her favorite reading—sure, she loved the drama of *Wuthering Heights*, but would it kill anyone to call something Indian a classic? (She knew that the true classics were romance novels by Nalini Singh and Alisha Rai.)

But Ed wasn't like other kids. The way he droned on and on about nineteenth-century dark romanticism and its roots in the transcendentalism movement . . . Snore! First of all, it had become disappointingly clear that dark romanticism had nothing to do with two people falling in love and was just some literary term to describe extremely mediocre (non-romantic!) books. Seriously, the best part about being a senior was that Rani could escape Ed Yi and AP English in a few months.

Of course, with escape so imminent, maybe she should start thinking about which colleges to apply to? She'd been avoiding it because of that big question of whether she and Raj would end up in the same place next year. But that was silly, too—destiny with a capital *D* would take care of that. She had no reason to worry.

"I've won a few short film festivals before back in LA," Ed continued, shifting his weight from foot to foot. "But I've never done a one-day shoot.

That's definitely going to be a challenge. I tend to tinker with editing a lot, and we won't have the time. But personally, I think that editing is where the true artistry comes in. . . ."

The ferry began rocking precariously once more, forcing Rani to clutch the railing for dear life. Somehow, Ed managed to keep his footing despite the rolling waves. Worse, he continued to yammer on about editing. (Why? They were mortal enemies, and she was planning to crush him and the rest of the Better-Than-Thous. Didn't he know that?) Rani considered the merits of jumping overboard just to get away.

"You've entered other film contests?" JJ cut in (thankfully). "Got any tips?"

Rani elbowed them. "You can't ask for tips from the competition! He could try to sabotage us with misinformation!"

Ed smiled. Snootily. Definitely snootily. (Just like the way he would eat a sandwich.) "Hardly. And I'm okay with a little bit of healthy competition."

Rani was secretly thinking she was okay with a bit of *unhealthy* competition. Normally, it was her twin who was the competitive one, but Ed and the Better-Than-Thous really brought out the fighting spirit in Rani—and the urge to crush them.

"Firstly, it helps to have watched a lot of short films," Ed answered. "I mean, in the hundreds. You can start with the Oscar winners, of course, but there are so many that are in indie festivals that are brilliant, too. . . ."

(Rani had watched a grand total of three short films in preparation. But so what? She had a lifetime of experience watching romantic comedies. Was a shorter version really so different?)

"There are so many styles," Ed gushed, obviously in film geek heaven.

"I'm most drawn to the ones with great visuals though. There's not much time for dialogue in a short film, you know. . . ."

(Showed what he knew. Rani's script was mostly dialogue, which was obviously key to a great film!)

While Ed rattled on about an exploration of the sublime in everyday things, Rani wondered if perhaps it would be fun to have her leading male character, Nate, be a bit more insufferable. Not like Ed, obviously, because he was *too* insufferable. But maybe Nate could be slightly insufferable but also lovable? It could be good conflict to up the tension.

EXT. BEACH - MOONLIGHT

Flashback to Nate and Layla hanging out the summer before.

LAYLA

Isn't the night sky incredible? It really inspires me.

NATE

Oh yes, man's insignificance in the face of the infinite is certainly something to give one pause.

LAYLA

Um yeah . . . also, look at the moon tonight. It's just hanging there, totally perfect.

NATE

I agree! The phases of the moon are fascinating. Did you know that it helps stabilize the earth's rotation, which helps stabilize our climate as well?

LAYLA

I've heard that. But look at the romantic glow.

NATE

It's not actually glowing, it's reflecting—

LAYLA

—the sun's light. Yeah, I'm aware.

Nah. Rani loved Raj's goofball sense of humor. She couldn't possibly change that!

"So," Ed said. "What's your film about? Some kind of romance, I heard?"

Rani didn't like the way he said *romance*. As if it was a seed stuck between his teeth. "Like I would tell the competition."

Ed nodded. "Right. You wouldn't want me to know what genre of film you're working on."

She should have just let the conversation end there. But something in her made her keep talking. "Okay, yes, it's a romance. Specifically, a rom-com. Two people getting together after some misunderstandings."

Ed blinked. "Oh. How very . . . commercial."

It was the way he said *commercial* that made Rani's blood boil. And suddenly, today's film competition wasn't just something she was doing for practice before meeting Olivia Lee. Suddenly, Rani had an even more specific purpose. To stand up for the kind of stories she loved. "Yeah, I like commercial movies," she retorted fiercely. "There's a reason why they have a wider audience than movies about windmills."

Ed blinked. "I'm guessing you mean *The Howlers at Dawn*. It's about a lot more than windmills. It's a look into the way poverty and lack of education . . ."

Rani's eyes were already glazing over. "Yeah, yeah. But people need some joy in their life, too."

His dark brows shot up. "Not disputing that."

He'd probably never heard of the word *joy* in his life.

"Gerhardt *is* a judge, and I'm not sure rom-coms are his thing, but obviously it's not all about winning," he said. "This is great experience for you. Making your first short film is a big step."

Could he be any more patronizing? Rani narrowed her eyes. "He's one judge, but not the only one. And they told us any genre of film was allowed. I know it's not exactly avant-garde, but I think it's really funny and has a lot of heart."

"I'm sure it does." Ed smiled (snootily). "Good luck with that."

Good luck with that?

"Um . . . thanks," Rani said. "I suppose you're doing something . . ." She searched for a word other than pretentious, but nothing was coming to mind.

"Abstract?" JJ supplied.

"Yeah, I guess you could say that." Ed held out his hand. "May the best team win."

Rani shook his hand a little harder than necessary. "Exactly. And that will be *us*."

Ed just smiled faintly. "It's on."

Rani:

OMG. Ed Yi is on the ferry. Apparently he's gonna be in the film festival too! How can I compete? He's all cool and from LA. For all I know his dad is some Hollywood producer.

Avani:

If his dad's a Hollywood producer, why would he move to Orcas?

Rani:

I have no idea! Celebrities buy mansions here sometimes. Probably for the produce. We have excellent produce.

Avani:

True, true. Especially Gutiérrez tomatoes.

By the time the ferry arrived in Friday Harbor, everyone was glad to be stepping off onto solid land again.

"I can't remember the waves ever being as bad as that," Parker declared.

"I'm glad you're feeling better, though," Rani said. "Ready to play Layla?"

Parker rolled her eyes. "I only threw up twice, but yeah, I'm fine, Rani."

Okay, so maybe that had sounded insensitive. But Rani was the director, and the whole purpose of this trip was to shoot the film. Rani decided to ignore Parker's grouchiness. She'd get into it once the camera was rolling.

"Hope you feel better soon," Avani said to Parker sympathetically, her hand in Fernando's.

At least the two of them weren't bickering at the moment. Rani could tell that her twin was feeling more relaxed now that they'd made it to San Juan Island.

Rani patted Avani's shoulder. *Try to enjoy the day with your boyfriend. He's too good a guy to lose over being late one morning.*

Avani gave her a small, tight smile back. *Whatever. Like you care.*

Avani and Fernando left for their dance workshop, Rani felt somewhat relieved to escape their downer mood, along with a smidgen of guilt for *wanting* to escape. Sigh. Twinning was hard sometimes.

She and her cast went to grab a coffee at a nearby spot. Despite the ferocious weather, the place was hopping. Most of the locals were chattering about the windstorm, arguing whether the news reports were overblowing it or whether it would be something historic.

"They closed down SeaTac," a lady said. "They almost never do that just for wind."

"I think I heard it was more for the safety of the ground crew than an issue with the airplanes," someone else said.

Rani paid them no mind. Wind, shmind. Nidhi would get here, somehow. She just knew her big sis wouldn't let her down.

"Raj's ferry is arriving half an hour from now," Rani said as they inched forward in line.

"The schedule says it's running on time," JJ said, checking their phone. "Which is good since we're supposed to be at the auditorium by nine. We should be able to make it, no problem."

It was really nice to have another detail-oriented person on her crew. JJ was the best.

Rani sent a quick text to Raj:

> Can't wait to see you! Our film is going to be awesome!
> And you will be the most handsome cameraman!

Three dots showed up, indicating he was typing, but then they were gone a moment later. Rani pushed aside that niggling doubt that something had gone wrong. He would have told her if he'd missed the ferry or something important like that. He was probably just juggling his breakfast and coffee from the ferry café and would text back in a moment.

Once Rani and her cast had put in their orders, they sat at a table with a view of the harbor. They'd know exactly when the ferry arrived.

"You and Raj were so cute at the Fall Festival," Parker commented. "And now he's your camera guy. You're so lucky to have such a devoted boyfriend." She sighed, cupping her chin with her hands. "Someday I'll get one of those."

Rani patted Parker's shoulder. "You'll find the right guy. Just give it time."

Dominic shrugged, leaning against his chair. "Okay, let's go over the plan again. When do we need to finish filming?"

"By four at the latest," JJ said. "That'll give me two hours to edit before the deadline at six. Which is really not enough time, either. Ed says—"

"That editing is where the artistry is," Rani interrupted. "Yeah, yeah. I get it. But the judges are expecting a rough cut. It doesn't have to be perfect."

"I know, but still." JJ took out their laptop and started messing with editing software. "I can't believe Helmuth Gerhardt is going to be watching and I have to do such a hatchet job. *The Howlers at Dawn* was amazing."

"Uh-huh," Rani said. If all the panned shots of windmills impressed JJ, Rani wasn't about to disagree.

Dominic didn't try to hide his skepticism though. "Not really my kind of thing? But I believe you."

"Try extremely boring," Parker said.

"Never heard of it." Sara shrugged, looking it up on her phone. "But if Gerhardt's super artsy, is he really going to like our rom-com?"

That was exactly what Ed had said, too. Rani had put on a brave face, but she had to admit that it was kind of worrying.

JJ laughed. Not unkindly, but still. "It's hard to say if a guy like him has actually ever seen one before. But that's fine. I'm just happy to be making our own film. We don't need to win."

"What?" Rani's voice got so shrill, the words came out as somewhere between a squawk and a shriek. "Of course we need to win! That's what we're here for!"

"Totally," Parker said vehemently. "How dare you imply that my acting won't charm Gerhardt?"

"I didn't say that . . ." JJ hedged. "Look, I think it's cute. But we just have to be realistic."

Time to put on that brave face again.

"Like I told Ed," Rani cut in, "Gerhardt is giving the prize consultation, but he's also just one of the judges. The contest organizers said any genre short film qualifies."

"Besides, who could resist this smile?" Dominic grinned at his imaginary camera for his imaginary audience.

"Not me," Sara said, planting a wet one on his cheek.

"Thanks, babe."

And then, of course, they were making out again. Some older folks at the coffee shop looked a bit scandalized at the full-tongue PDA going on. Rani ignored them. She believed in rom-coms as an art form. They made people happy. They made them hopeful. And they were true to life, too—sort of. (Okay, sadly usually not the "just one bed" trope, unfortunately.) Still, Rani knew that sometimes people were thrown together by the whims of fate. She knew that sizzle from the very first meet-cute could lead to a Happily Ever After. How else could you explain that the Mehtas had chosen to stay at the Songbird Inn, bringing Rani and Raj together? Now Rani couldn't imagine life without his goofball dance moves. (Raj liked to do the robot. A lot.)

"I'm not worried," Rani lied, trying to strike the exact right motivational tone. "Our script is really good; Parker and Dominic's acting is fantastic; Sara's a makeup genius; and if the artistry really is in the editing, JJ will totally blow everyone away!"

She held out her hand to the center of the table. "Come on, we can do this. On three."

They all placed their hands on hers and she called, "One, two, three— GO TEAM!"

"GO TEAM!" they echoed with determination.

"That's better," Rani said with approval. "And don't forget—once we've totally crushed the competition, the award is something we could put on our college applications!"

Lately, Rani had been thinking film school would be pretty fun. If she could get in. She'd even confessed the dream to Raj, and he hadn't laughed or anything. He was so supportive and lovely and perfect. Rani could see it now—the lights, the glamor, the red carpet. She'd be there soon enough. With her devoted, amazing boyfriend Raj to hold her purse, of course.

As they sipped their coffees, she kept an eye out for the ferry. They went over her most recent changes to the dialogue, which everyone was fine with. Rani tuned out a bit while JJ talked about camera shots. Raj was obviously going to handle all that.

When the ferry finally arrived, Rani bounded up, excited to get going. "Come on, let's go meet Raj."

Chapter Sixteen

Sirisha

An ex who wanted to meet up. A party that sounded like torture. And a windstorm that seemed to be screaming *Stay home, Sirisha!* The powerful gusts felt like they might blow the car off the twisty island road, right into the waters of East Sound.

The howling of the wind certainly fit the morning mood. A little too well. Nidhi was delayed for who knew how long. Rani, Avani, even Fernando had been grumpy and impatient when she'd dropped off her sisters at his farm. At least the Dads had been reasonably calm and cheery. The newlyweds usually were.

Sirisha could use another dad joke just about now. Why had she agreed to meet Brie again? She really needed to learn to say no.

She was rounding a curve in the road when three deer dashed in front of the car. Her brakes squealed in protest as she tried to slow without swerving. Luckily, the deer made it safely to the other side, but—in a blink—a girl appeared in the middle of the road.

A girl in overalls, holding a basket. A girl who looked shell-shocked at the car hurtling toward her. A girl with large brown eyes, a tangled nest of dark hair that reminded Sirisha of her own unruly waves, and brown russet skin that matched the leaves lining the side of the road.

Sirisha managed to screech to a stop just in time. She opened her window and leaned out. "Hey, are you okay?"

The girl stood frozen for a moment longer, before shaking it off. "Yeah, I might need heart resuscitation, but other than that, I'm good."

"Fair," Sirisha said, climbing out of the car. "Though I don't think you looked both ways before crossing the street, either."

She noticed now that the girl had impossibly long lashes.

"Yeah, I guess not." The girl shrugged. "But you were going pretty fast. Did you just rob a bank?"

"Fast?" Sirisha sputtered. "I was not! It's just that you pick up a lot of momentum in that turn. . . ."

"Sure, if you're reckless."

Reckless? When had anyone ever called Sirisha reckless? She was the opposite of reckless!

What she wanted to say: "That's ridiculous! I am utterly responsible!"

What she actually said: ". . ."

The girl shook her head and gestured for Sirisha to go. "Well, I'm fine now, so you can be on your—"

The wind howled, drowning out the rest. Then—

Trees swaying. A horrible creaking. Time slowing as if it were wading through sticky maple syrup. A tall cedar falling . . .

The girl. The basket. Sirisha didn't think. She moved. Yanked at the other girl's hand. Dragged her out of the way.

"What're you doing— Oh!"

A whoosh. A loud, echoing thud. A crashed cedar tree lying where they'd been standing only moments before. A vortex of leaves and pine needles and dust.

"Did that just really happen?" The girl stared at the spot where she'd only just been standing as the wind continued to ravage everything around them in a howling fury.

"I think so?" Sirisha said. This all felt a little too familiar. Trees really didn't seem to like the Singh sisters. Was it some kind of karma? Had the Singhs angered some unearthly force?

"My mushrooms," the girl said with dismay.

Sirisha only then noticed all the foraged mushrooms that the girl had dropped. A variety of species. Sirisha bent down to help gather them. "Well, some of these are still good."

The other girl didn't answer, but they both worked on picking up all the mushrooms that weren't ruined. Once they had them back in her basket, Sirisha searched for words.

What she wanted to say: "I can't believe we both had a near-death experience. We're lucky to be alive. There's so much adrenaline running through me that I feel like I just had eighteen cups of coffee."

What she actually said: "I'm Sirisha."

"I'm Lavi," the other girl said. "New to the island. Do you go to Orcas Island High School?"

"Yeah," Sirisha said.

"I'm starting there on the Monday after fall break," Lavi told her.

"Cool." Sirisha's tongue tied itself in the usual knots. Words sprang around in her mind, but they would not be tamed into sentences. Trees. Hazards. Near-death experiences.

"Guess your car is blocked," Lavi said eventually.

Sirisha realized Lavi was correct. The treacherous cedar may not have claimed their lives, but it had fallen directly across the road. And the trees alongside it were too thick for Sirisha to drive around.

"Huh," Sirisha said.

Actually, maybe this was the excuse she was looking for. She could probably manage a U-turn and head home. For just a moment, she gleefully thought of the faux-regretful texts she could send.

Sorry, Brie, there was a giant tree blocking the road so I couldn't come see you.

Sorry, Bethany, a tree that nearly killed me was blocking the road down to your end of the island.

Too bad that there actually was a different way. Sure, it was a longer route and would make her late to meet Brie, but it wouldn't prevent her from getting to Bethany's party. Sigh.

"I know another way through this property," Lavi said. "Give me a ride back to my house and I'll tell you where to go. It would be the least I could do—since, you know, you saved my life."

Had I really? Sirisha thought in wonder. Sirisha, the lifesaver. That was new.

Shivers crawled up her skin, both for what might have happened—what they'd both escaped from—and also the sense that now she and Lavi were irrevocably connected. Or was she putting too much significance on a moment of chance?

The girl sauntered toward the passenger seat of the car. "You coming?"

She didn't seem like she was too worried about some mystical connection.

"Yeah," Sirisha said, still in a bit of a daze. A shortcut through the property would be a lot faster than working her way to the other main road on the peninsula between East and West Sounds. So much for her excuse to get out of seeing her ex.

As she unlocked the car and slipped behind the wheel, Lavi got in on the passenger side. Gave her directions to a small cabin nestled in the thick woods. It wasn't far, and when they pulled into the drive, Sirisha didn't want to say goodbye yet.

What she wanted to say: "Hey, I know this was an odd way to meet, but um, tell me your life story because I really want to avoid this murder-mystery birthday party I'm supposed to go to."

What she actually said: "I guess I'll see you at school in a week!"

Lavi squirmed beside her. "Yeah, I guess so."

Sirisha noted Lavi's listlessness. Had she sounded weird? Her throat tickled with more words. She forced herself to get them out. "What brought you to Orcas Island, by the way?" That was totally a normal thing to ask, right?

"My mom fell in love, got remarried, and now we live here. Maybe you know my new stepdad? Paul Rivers?"

Sirisha nodded. "Yeah, I've met him once or twice. It's a small island."

"Yeah," Lavi said. "It's going to be a bit of an adjustment. I'm from Chicago."

"Awesome," Sirisha said. She had no idea what life was like in big cities. She'd been five when Dad had bought the Songbird and brought them to Orcas. But they had something else in common. "My dad recently got remarried, too."

"Oh yeah?" Lavi said. "Small world. It's nice to see another brown face, by the way. I wasn't sure how many people of color were on this island."

"There aren't that many, really," Sirisha said. "But I feel like we tend to find each other. My dad's from India and his new husband is from Pakistan."

Lavi raised her brows. "It's nice to know there are actually queer South Asians here. Maybe I'll fit right in. My mom's Indian, too. My dad—they got divorced a while ago—is from Singapore."

"Nice," Sirisha said. And it was.

"Well, I have to get cleaned up for a thing later," Lavi said. "But thanks for saving my life and all." She rattled off directions on how to get back to the main road, waved, and ran into the cabin.

Sirisha stared after her, her heart feeling . . . something, though she wasn't quite sure what.

White-crested waves smashing into a tiny rocky island in the sound. An eerie tune whistling through the trees. Gray skies like the feathers of a judgmental owl.

A Singh sister late to meet her ex.

"I didn't think you were coming," Liza admitted as Sirisha slid into the corner booth in the quiet little café that overlooked the thrashing sea.

"Oh, Sirisha wouldn't bail," Brie said, smiling. "Right?"

Sirisha found herself bristling a bit. Was that really what they thought of her? Someone who did as she was told? Who went along with anything, including brunching with an ex?

What she wanted to say: "Don't make assumptions about me."

What she actually said: "Sorry I'm late. A tree fell in front of my car."

"Wow," Brie said. "I'm glad you're okay, at least."

The café was fairly quiet, but a few other customers nearby were discussing the windstorm, too. Apparently, one had a shed that had been damaged. Another told a story of a windstorm a few years ago that left their car smashed beneath a tree. At the end of that one, everyone instinctively looked outside, as if to make certain their own cars were still okay.

Sirisha took in her ex, who was wearing a snug sweater and jeans, a thick scarf circled around her neck several times. She looked cute bundled up so warmly, and plenty happy, her dark cedar skin glistening, her cheeks maybe a little warm from the heated café. Her hair in neat braids.

Their relationship had only lasted through the warm seasons. Now here was a new Brie, the Brie of the colder months. One that Sirisha would never get to know.

Sirisha, too, had changed her way of dressing, but she couldn't say it was purely because of the weather. She just didn't care anymore. There was no one to impress, so she wore whatever old leggings and shirts and sweaters she found in her closet and threw on a parka when necessary. Today's red sweater had a long curling thread hanging loose and plenty of pilling. It had probably gotten scratched by low-hanging branches while Sirisha was traipsing the woods with her camera, the place where she felt the most peaceful. After all, the deer and bunnies never pointed out that her hair was a disaster.

At least after breakfast Rani had, as promised, helped tame her hair somewhat with some kind of magical detangling serum.

The waitress came and took their orders. Brie and Liza were apparently starving since they ordered three dishes to share between them: an omelet, biscuits and gravy, and French toast.

"I'll just have the yogurt and fruit bowl, unsweetened," Sirisha said. "And a latte."

The yogurt would definitely be a good palate cleanser from all the rich foods of the morning. While they waited for their dishes, Brie and Liza chitchatted the way old friends do. Sirisha managed to surmise that Brie was spending fall break on Orcas because her mom was visiting a sick aunt in San Antonio.

"I hope your aunt feels better soon," Sirisha said.

"Thanks," Brie said. "I hope so, too. I would have told you I was going to be on the island sooner, but it was really hectic and last-minute."

Sirisha nodded. At least that explained the impromptu invite. She felt bad about the sick aunt, but she still didn't know what to feel about Brie. This was, after all, the first person she'd ever kissed. The first person she'd had enough guts to go after—in her own weird, quiet way.

The first girl she'd almost, sort of, kind of *loved*?

But Brie hadn't thought it was love. And to be honest, Sirisha still didn't know what that meant, or if there was really even one definition. Maybe their relationship had never been what all those songs were about. Still, plenty of raw emotions were swirling in her, whispering fiercely: *You were dumped. You weren't enough. Of course, Brie didn't love you. No one ever will.*

"What are you up to today?" Brie asked, taking a bite of French toast.

Without overthinking it, Sirisha quickly swiped a bite from Brie for herself.

Brie grinned at her. "Take as much as you want. We ordered way too much."

Sharing a bite with them made Sirisha feel slightly less on the outside. So she took a second one. "I'm going to Bethany's birthday party."

It suddenly occurred to her that Bethany was supposed to be friends with both of them. In theory. "Are you . . . going?"

Please say no, please say no, please say no.

"No," Brie said. "I wasn't invited."

Okay, that was awkward. But it wasn't a total surprise, right? Even though they'd all hung out until Brie had dumped her, Bethany had been Sirisha's friend from school, just as Liza had been Brie's friend originally.

"Oh," Sirisha said. "Well, I guess she couldn't really invite that many people. It's a murder-mystery party, you know the kind with the character cards?"

Brie smiled. "And you're going to act out a part? That's so cool. I love that!"

That's what she said. But they'd always been able to communicate without words, and what Sirisha suspected she was really saying was: *You have no idea what you're doing, do you?*

Well, what did Brie know? Not about the tree that had nearly flattened her like a pumpkin pancake. Not about the mysterious mushroom girl either.

What she wanted to say: "Yeah, it'll be fun!"

What she actually said: "Yeah, it'll be . . . fun?"

She didn't sound very convincing. Liza and Brie burst into giggles.

"That's the spirit!" Brie said. "Did she go with Devious Party Planners like I suggested?"

"Um, I don't know. . . . How did you— I mean when did you . . ." Sirisha was confused.

"She actually had the idea way back in August, I think," Brie said. "I told her the Devious team is amazing. I have some theater friends who work for them. I was thinking about applying, too—it's a really good acting gig! But I got too busy with other plays during the summer."

Brie had been in four separate productions over the summer. Sirisha didn't know how she did it, honestly. But somehow Brie made it work. She was fantastic at memorizing lines, and she gave her all to every role.

"I bet it'll be a great opportunity for your photography," Brie continued. "Lots of costumes and decor."

Sirisha had thought the same. But the comment rubbed her the wrong way; made her feel as if Brie didn't think there was anything more to Sirisha than her photography. And even though Sirisha had always been shy at parties, she didn't want Brie thinking of her as some sad wallflower.

"Actually," Sirisha found herself saying, "I wasn't planning to take pictures."

Brie raised her brows. "You weren't?"

What her ex didn't need to say: *But how will you hide from all the people?*

"No," Sirisha said, taking a bite of yogurt and blackberry to hide the wobbling of her chin.

"Why not?" Liza asked.

Brie shot Liza a look. Then nodded for Sirisha to continue when she was ready. She'd always been fine with waiting for Sirisha to fill in the silences. And despite everything, despite how she rankled at Brie's assumption, Sirisha's heart ached at that small gesture. Could anyone else wait for her words the way Brie always had?

What Sirisha wanted to say: "Because there's more to me than just my photography, you know."

What she actually said: "I guess I want to be more . . . present?"

Okay, so it came out like a question. But the more she thought about it, the more it felt like the truth.

Chapter Seventeen

Avani

The salsa workshop was being held in a beautiful four-story brick building with art deco fixtures. A boy and a girl stepped inside the lobby, holding hands, full of wishes and doubts that something would change inside this space.

They'd always loved to dance, after all.

"We're here for Señora Vasquez's salsa workshop," Avani said to the man at the reception desk.

"Fourth floor." He waved them toward the elevators, preoccupied with his phone.

Fernando pushed the up button, and Avani tapped her toes with impatience. It was way too quiet. She and Fernando hadn't really talked on the walk over, just let the opera of wind and waves and creaking trees be their soundtrack. The quiet had felt a little bit like possibilities, and Avani was feeling hopeful again. It came and it went. Sometimes she felt on the edge of despair, and then she reminded herself that nothing bad had truly happened. A few harsh words and a few odd silences would not be the end of them.

The elevator dinged, and when they stepped inside, she gasped. She'd been in elevators before—sterile gray boxes that took you up and down to different floors. She usually preferred the stairs, to let out all her excess energy. But this spacious elevator was something else entirely: glittering with gold trim and old-fashioned bronze push-buttons and gorgeously patterned wood panels. A ceiling wallpapered to look like a midnight sky dotted with stars.

"It's so pretty," Avani said. "I feel like I'm going to a speakeasy, and there should be an elevator attendant in a very dapper uniform."

Fernando squeezed her hand. "Yeah. It's nice."

But he didn't say anything more, and the silence was back to being decidedly U.N.C.O.M.F.O.R.T.A.B.L.E., stretching across the seconds as if across a lifetime of homework assignments and parties and jobs and dinners. Avani shivered at the thought, that many silences spanning across years and decades. No, this silence could not be what was left between them.

They'd find their rhythm again. They had to.

"Hello, class!" A woman with bright red lipstick and thick black hair pinned up in a cloud above her face smiled brightly. "Welcome to today's Dips, Tricks, and Lifts Salsa Workshop. I'm Lisa Vasquez, and this is my husband, Rodrigo."

She and her husband danced a few quick steps together, showing off the smooth way they moved their hips and arms, as if they didn't have bones at all.

Avani took Fernando's hand, her feet itching to move with the rhythm, too. To return to that magical place where they'd always connected. But Lisa was instead going into the history of the dance for some reason. . . .

"Salsa music originated from Cuba but has since become a global phenomenon. Puerto Ricans in New York in the 1960s helped popularize it in the United States. Colombians developed their own style. There are now thriving scenes all over the world. In Tokyo and India and . . ."

It was interesting and all, but Avani's knees were already bending, her arms, already loosening

Anticipating
    how it felt
to spin
    to move her body
with someone else

Lisa and Rodrigo continued their demonstration, picking up the heat with a showier number. It was fast; it was sexy; there was a whirlwind of tricks and dips and spins that made Avani dizzy just watching.

"In this workshop, we'll be teaching LA-style salsa with some studio styling as well. LA style is known for being fast and energetic, with plenty of Hollywood flair. . . ."

Just when Avani didn't think they could get any flashier, they pulled out the lifts. A quick one, then one that was a bit higher, and then Lisa was flying in the air. Her landing was impeccable, too. They finished with a simple basic step.

Everyone clapped and cheered. Avani hooted enthusiastically. That kind of lift was for people who had trained all their lives, probably.

"And you're going to do that same dance today," Lisa said with a big smile.

There was nervous tittering among the students. She was joking, right? The music was still swirling inside Avani, and a part of her felt she could dance anything. Anything . . . except that number she'd just seen. She could spin, she could dip, but could she fly?

Avani surveyed the rest of the students. There were about twenty people, mostly young adults, college age or older. She wondered how good they were. The workshop had been listed as "intermediate level," which she'd thought she and Fernando qualified for. But this felt like a stretch.

The teachers told them to pair up, and Fernando reached his hand out to hers.

"Do you really think we can do this?" Avani asked.

He gave her a devastating smile. Full of swagger and chiseled cheekbones. "Us? Do you even have to ask?"

And then, with just a quick flick of his wrist, he twirled her. And she remembered the feel

of following
    but also leading
        of being one
    with the music and each other

"Hang on," she said, "let's get our dance shoes on."

She kicked off her sneakers and pulled her patent leather dance shoes out from her duffel. With kitten heels and a strap across the ankles, they were soft and supple and let her feet move. Something inside her changed as she stood up in them and slid a foot across the gleaming wood floor.

"Let's warm up with some freestyle," Lisa called.

> The boy held out a hand
> and the girl put hers in his
> something electric charged between them
> their anger something
> that could morph into
> a wildfire

Avani sucked in a breath. She could do this. Fernando spun her and she twirled,

> letting that electricity
> course through her
> remembering that the two of them
> had something
> worth keeping
> the steps were easy
> he was leading
> but so was she
> and for a moment they weren't a girl and a boy
> but a whirling tornado
> a phenomenon
> all its own

Another couple went twirling by. Avani recognized the girl—she'd been at Fernando's cousin's wedding last February. Fernando had danced with her, and they'd shown off a few moves of their own at that event. At the time, the girl had been a fiery redhead, but now she sported jet-black hair and bangs, her arms wrapped around the nape of a cute guy. They both looked a little older, college age. And they were spinning and dipping with sure footing.

"Fernando!" the girl said, recognizing him and twirling their way. "How are you?"

"Greta!" Fernando dropped Avani's arms and ran over to her. "Wait, when did you get here? How did I miss you?"

"We snuck in a little late," Greta admitted. "Our ferry was delayed—the windstorm. Fancy seeing you here, though! This is Trent, by the way."

Trent was a very tall and skinny white dude, even taller and leaner than Fernando. He had three visible tattoos and several piercings and black eyeliner—and he was totally pulling it off. In fact, he and Greta were actually a really gorgeous couple, almost a little too picture-perfect together.

"Hi! This is Avani," Fernando said. "You were at Manuel's wedding—remember, in that barn? That was at Avani's family's inn."

"Oh yeah, that place was adorable!" Greta said. "Nice to meet you."

But Trent was obviously impatient, because he just grunted at them and started twirling Greta away.

"We'll catch up later!" Greta promised as she followed Trent's lead.

"She's an old family friend. So funny to run into her," Fernando said.

Avani felt a stirring of jealousy, recalling how good the two of them had looked together at that wedding. On the other hand, Avani probably didn't need to worry since Greta seemed pretty involved with her partner. From the way they held their heads close together, their bodies perfectly in sync and sizzling with smoky heat, it was clear that they were more than just dance partners. Their freestyling was excellent and beautiful and awe-inducing.

And that extremely competitive part of her—the part that drove her to kick unstoppable soccer goals, the part that crushed her opponents in both beer pong and debate—needed to show them that she and Fernando had the moves.

Now she took the lead
        and it was no longer a give and a take
                but a general
                        giving marching orders
                at first Fernando followed along
        and as she forced him to dip her low
his face came close
        and she thought maybe
he'd kiss her passionately
        right there in the studio
                forgetting about everyone around them

But instead, he said, "Ow! What're you doing?"

He clutched his back in pain. Avani realized that in her enthusiasm she'd pulled him down into an awkward position.

"Sorry!" She straightened, reaching for him.

"Can you take it easy?" Fernando winced, rubbing the muscles on his lower back. "Actually, I think I need to sit down."

But Avani didn't want to stop, not with the music swirling inside her, not with feelings brewing like a potion, boiling and crackling in tempo to the song. Why was it that whenever she found her focus, something always got in the way?

Chapter Eighteen

Nidhi

The Portland restaurant that Brad took them to had a mod 60s look: a cross between a spaceship and a club. White walls and tables with neon-purple accents. Everything was sleek and rounded. The hostess had big hair and wore a long, slim skirt paired with go-go boots. Most of the other customers were dressed to the nines, looking as if they'd been up all night partying at nearby clubs. "Love Shack" played loudly over the speakers.

"Cool place, right?" Brad shouted over the music.

"I feel slightly old for the crowd!" Lena yelled, but she didn't look it. The trench coat over the magenta dress somehow looked perfect for 8:00 a.m. clubbing.

At least Nidhi wasn't still wearing that stained blouse, even if her salwar top and jeans didn't quite fit with the vibe here.

"Lena, you'll always be young," John shouted over the music to his wife, and the two of them kissed.

Honestly, they were adorable together. Even though marriage was the opposite of what Nidhi wanted at the moment, she still loved to see couples who'd obviously weathered plenty of storms together. It gave her hope that someday, she might find the same.

In the far, far future.

While they waited for a table, Lucas and Grayson looked over a bunch of event flyers taped to the wall. Concerts and open mic events were plastered everywhere. She spotted an especially moody and cute one, with misty seas and a band whose members were sporting a mix of suspenders and square-rimmed glasses and cravats. They were called the Cloud Grifters and had a bunch of tour dates all over the Pacific Northwest. There was even one happening in Friday Harbor that very night.

Which reminded Nidhi to check her texts. Her sisters and the Dads had sent a ton of messages, concerned about her diverted flight, asking lots of questions about what she was doing next. Rani was pressuring her to get there in time for her film awards ceremony. But Nidhi wasn't one to make promises she wasn't certain she could keep. She offered Rani some encouragement, then turned to the texts from Avani.

Nidhi didn't know what was going on between Avani and Fernando, but her usually confident and bubbly sis was feeling so down. That was one of the things that was making her hesitate about her plan to stay in India. She really, really missed her sisters, and it seemed like they really, really missed her, too.

She shot Avani a text:

> I'm trapped in Portland at the moment, but I promise, we'll talk. Just as soon as I can figure out how to get home.

Nidhi also updated Professor Cunningham. It was looking less and less likely that they'd be able to meet today. Sigh. Why did registration dates for next term have to be so soon?

A man in flared white pants and a neon-orange shirt waved at their group. "Your table is ready. Right this way!"

As they looked over the menu, the waiter told them there was a special on bottomless mimosas. From the look of the crowded tables around them—full of energetic people shouting cheerfully over the music—it was a liquid breakfast kind of situation.

"I'll take one!" Lucas yelled over an Abba song.

The waiter glanced at everyone else, and the others nodded, except Brad, who explained he was driving. Nidhi didn't say anything, but moments later there was a champagne flute of juice that wasn't just juice in front of her.

Apparently, no one would be checking her or Grayson's IDs. Well, she was used to that from her time in New Delhi, and it wasn't as if she'd never had a drink before.

John held out his glass. "To the wind taking you somewhere unexpected."

"Hear, hear!" Lena raised her own.

Lucas clinked his glass against theirs. "When in Portland . . ."

What the heck. Sure:

- it was eight in the morning

- she still needed to figure out some miracle to get to her advisor meeting

- and she had no idea where she was sleeping tonight

But none of those things could be fixed right at that moment. Hence, Nidhi raised her own glass. "To thwarted travels and new friends!"

The funny thing about declaring them as friends was that suddenly, it felt like they were. The drinks came, and so did their food, and everyone let their worries go for a bit. Nidhi had a Croque Madame that was absolutely to die for. Of course, given how tired and hungry she was, even an old piece of toast from the garbage probably would have tasted like salvation in that moment.

"So, Lena and John," she asked between bites, "where have you been traveling, and what takes you to Seattle?"

Lena smiled. "We had the best time in China. Lots of family, lots of good food. We live in Vancouver, but we were planning to spend a few days in Seattle to visit our son at UW."

"Oh, really?" Nidhi said. "I go to UW, too."

"Well, I know it's a really big school, but I suppose there's a chance you know David?" John pulled out a picture from his wallet. It showed a good-looking young man at a UW football game, decked out in Huskies gear.

"Actually, I've been studying abroad in India all semester." Nidhi wondered if she was missing out on some ineffable life experience that required dressing up in purple and gold and rooting for the football team.

Not that she knew a thing about football. Dad and Avani watched the occasional Seahawks game, but Nidhi had always found it kind of boring. Then again, there was probably a whole different energy when you were watching it live in a crowded stadium.

Even though she was 93 percent certain about her decision to stay in India, there was that storm inside her, the one that didn't want to miss a thing. Not one darn thing. Right then, she had a whole new sense of empathy for Avani—her sister who hated to choose just one option for fear of all she would miss out on.

Apparently, Nidhi had been holding on to that photo of their son for too long because Lena raised her brows. "He's single."

Nidhi's face heated. "Um, I'm sure not for long."

Grayson chuckled, nudging her. "You're cute when you're flustered."

She shot him an annoyed look. "Who says I'm flustered?"

He just laughed.

"Studying abroad is so fun," Lena said. "Is your family from India originally?"

"Yeah, though I was actually born here in Portland," Nidhi replied. "Not that I remember it. I grew up on Orcas Island and—"

"Orcas Island is so beautiful!" Lena cut in. "You're so lucky."

Nidhi nodded. "I am. But it's been so cool spending time in India. I've been staying with my relatives and just really had a chance to connect with this part of me that I've always wondered about."

"That's fabulous!" Lena said, "It's great you've had this opportunity to get in touch with your heritage. It's funny, but I felt almost like a tourist in Beijing this time because I don't have any family there right now. But we were able to get out to the country and visit my mom and siblings and

a whole bunch of other relatives. There, I really felt home. But not home."
She laughed. "It's complicated. I've lived all over the world, though I've been
in Vancouver for the last ten years. I never quite know where to call home."

"Believe me," Nidhi said. "I totally get that."

Nearby, a group of post-clubbers got even more loud and silly and flirtatious.

"Ah, to be young again," John commented.

Lucas smiled. "I'm going to get exactly that ridiculous if Keith says
yes. Because you don't even know what a catch he is."

"Photo?" Lena asked.

Lucas scrolled through his phone for a second and then passed it to
Lena. Nidhi squeezed in closer to get a good look.

"What a handsome young man!" Lena smiled. "You're lucky."

"He's gorgeous," Nidhi agreed. "But he's lucky, too."

Lucas grinned. "Aww, thanks. He's amazing, everything I ever wanted
in a guy—and I'm worried that if I don't get there today, I don't know.
That I won't get the same chance again. It feels like this windstorm is the
dragon I need to slay to earn the love of my prince, you know?"

Nidhi understood. In theory, he could propose anytime, but there are
moments in your life when the urgency and passion of a decision is at its
peak. And you don't want to miss that window. She felt like that about
India, that if she didn't hold on to the opportunity, it would blow away in
a chaotic windstorm.

"Hey, we're going to figure it out, Lucas," Nidhi said, determined.
"Because Keith is too hot to wait."

Grayson nudged her. "Hey! How many guys are you going to find
attractive that aren't me?"

Nidhi nudged him back and batted her lashes. "Calm down. I still
think you're cute."

Was she . . . flirting? Was this the new her? Or maybe it was the mimosa.

"I'm glad you still think so," he said with an easy grin. "You look gorgeous, by the way."

That made Nidhi let out a sputtering laugh. Mimosa droplets went spraying. She wiped at her chin with a napkin. How mortifying.

"You've got to be kidding," she said. "I've been traveling for like thirty-five hours straight. I feel like moldy cheese."

Grayson tucked a curly ringlet behind her ear. "You have a glow."

"That's sweat." Something stirred in Nidhi at his touch. He was the boy that made her want to let everything loose, not just a few ringlets from her top knot. But she had plans, plans that didn't involve him.

This day was so confusing.

"Then you make perspiration look good," Grayson returned.

Lena started laughing. "Listen to these two banter."

"Seriously, get a room you two," Brad concurred.

"The way they look at each other reminds me of us," John said, clasping Lena's hand.

"They are sweet together," Lucas said, smiling.

"Whatever," Nidhi said, her cheeks burning. "Let's move on."

Lena pounded the table. "I'm a little buzzed, people. And when I get buzzed, I talk too much. Fair warning."

She launched into a story about a fling she'd once had with a Spanish politician when she'd worked as a flight attendant.

"She won't stop telling this story," John said, shaking his head with a mock sigh. And downing another mimosa.

The waiter seemed more than happy to pour them, but Nidhi nursed hers. She still needed to get home somehow, after all! The others didn't seem quite so worried. The mimosas kept flowing, and everyone at the table started telling stories. War stories, really. Stories about love and life. Lucas told them about the time he'd been arrested for stealing a chinchilla, and his mom refused to post bail. John told them how he'd once helped a Chinese movie star escape the paparazzi by ushering her into an alley and then into the kitchen of a restaurant he worked at.

"I thought I was going to have my own *Roman Holiday* adventure with her," John said. "But instead, she scarfed down some noodles, gave me a generous tip, and then disappeared in a limo. It was over way too fast."

"I'm sure she was very attracted to you, darling," Lena said, patting his hand.

"Don't patronize me!" he huffed. "We had a connection."

All their stories reminded Nidhi that she still had so much growing up to do. Would she one day have as many tales of love and life and adventure as they did? Would she ever feel as if she'd made the most of the time she had? Last year, she'd been so frightened that she'd end up simply going through the motions of life, without ever really passionately engaging in it. That fear had pushed her. Maybe it would always keep pushing her.

But she wished she could push herself without the fear, too.

Lucas drummed his fingers on the table. "I was so wild in my younger days. Keith is more of a homebody."

"But does that bother you?" Nidhi asked.

"Not at all," Lucas said. "With him, chilling with a movie feels like an utterly perfect night."

"That sounds lovely," Lena said.

"Sounds like you need to lock it down," John added.

Nidhi wondered if she could ever feel that kind of peace with someone, if she could ever settle down and just enjoy the small moments with them. Right now, though, she wanted art, she wanted passion, she wanted the world several times over. Wishes whirled inside her like an untamed windstorm.

She caught Grayson watching her. Maybe a little too intensely.

And she downed her second mimosa.

What?

- The waiter was always right there, ready to pour

- Nidhi had no idea if she'd make it Seattle so she might as well

- She was working up to sharing her own stories

But not quite yet.

"What about you, Grayson?" Lena asked. "Have you ever been arrested? Get into trouble?"

"Me?" Grayson offered his swoony dimpled smile. "Nah, I usually go to bed at nine p.m."

Nidhi snorted. "Right."

"Come on, share with us your post-nine-p.m. adventures," Lena begged.

"Everyone has to tell at least one story," Lucas agreed. "This is truth or truth now."

Grayson raised his hands. "Okay, then. If it's truth or truth, I guess I have no choice. There was this one night in Prague . . ."

Grayson recounted a story about how he met an airline tycoon who invited him to his country estate late one night to paint his wife. Grayson's friends offered to come with him, just to be safe. The tycoon agreed that they should, and at four in the morning, they all drove out of the city, through very abandoned roads. Even Grayson's friends started to seem nervous. Eventually, they came to a creepy old mansion in the country.

"It was right out of a haunted movie," Grayson said. "I assumed I was definitely getting sucked into a vortex by a poltergeist. But the guy just offered us our own rooms. Don't know about my friends, but I barely slept.

"At around noon, a maid knocked on my door to invite me down to lunch. It was an amazing meal, a totally lavish spread. Lobster tails. Fresh oysters. Caviar."

"And then?" Nidhi asked.

"And then I met his wife. I was expecting some kind of femme fatale, but she was pretty down to earth. I painted her, and the tycoon paid me—enough to live it up for the next few cities on my trip. I got to stay in actual hotels, not just hostels, so that was definitely nice."

"And that's it?" Lena asked.

"That's barely a story." Lucas shook his head.

"That time you didn't get murdered," Nidhi concluded.

"Or sucked into a vortex by a poltergeist," John added.

"I was seriously worried!" Grayson insisted.

They all laughed.

"Okay, your turn, Nidhi," Grayson said. "What wild things did you get up to in India?"

This was her chance. To share something of her own.

"Me?" She grinned. "Nah, I went to bed at nine p.m., too."

Grayson stage-whispered to the rest of them, "Don't believe her!"

Everyone was looking at her expectantly.

"Come on, Nidhi, don't hold back," Lucas said.

"Don't hold back! Don't hold back!" Lena chanted. John, Brad, and Grayson started chanting, too.

Well, if they insisted . . .

"How about the time I met a Bollywood celebrity?"

Chapter Nineteen

Nidhi

Nidhi, Prakash, and the other partygoers ended up at the rooftop bar in a fancy hotel, with a canopy of lights and soft music playing and lots of beautiful people milling around in what were probably designer clothes. You wouldn't know it was the middle of the night because the place was still hopping.

The hot young Bollywood star they'd come to see, Alok Anand, was in a generous mood and took selfies with anyone who came up to him at the bar, including most of the kids from the party.

"Come on," Sheela insisted, gesturing Nidhi to her side as she posed next to Alok.

The star winked at her. "Yeah, get in here."

Was this really happening? Rani would absolutely die when she saw the pic. Here was a story to tell her friends back home.

Nidhi handed her phone to Prakash, fluffed her hair, and hopped over next to Sheela. Alok definitely had that star quality, chatting easily with everyone, never getting overwhelmed with the crowd.

"Hope you all can come to this event next weekend," Alok said, handing each of them a silver invitation.

"Thanks!" Sheela said. "We wouldn't miss it!"

Nidhi glanced at the invite as she and Sheela wandered to a quieter part of the bar. *Club Hello. Enjoy a rap battle and concert, hosted by Alok Anand.*

"Oh yeah, I've heard of the place." Sheela waved to the nearby bartender. "Can I get a Manhattan?"

"Of course," he said, then turned his eyes to Nidhi. "And you?"

A jolt went through Nidhi as she gazed into those henna-dark eyes. There was something about him that caught Nidhi by surprise. He was young, with a little bit of stubble and a curve in his smile that seemed to say that he was keeping a secret from the world. A small mole on the side of his cheek that somehow made his face look more sculpted.

He was cute, sure. But not ridiculously attractive.

Yet she *noticed* him. Her whole body noticed him. This was something she'd never experienced before—something blazing and lustful. Pheromones maybe. Nidhi had never thought that she would be the type to react so strongly to her libido, something utterly primordial.

"Would you like anything?" he asked, flashing that secretive smile again.

Oof. She realized she'd just been standing there, gaping like a fool. Her face heated in embarrassment.

"Um, I'll have a Coke." She felt even more embarrassed saying it.

She was a little girl ordering a Coke. The legal drinking age in India varied from city to city, but technically in New Delhi, it was twenty-one (recently lowered from twenty-five!). Yet few places actually seemed to check ID. Still, Nidhi was a rule-follower.

"Rum and Coke?" the cute bartender asked.

"Um . . ."

"Because I can make you something much better," he said with a wink.

Oh, oh, had he really just winked at her? Nidhi's heart was racing, her hands were clammy. She must have nodded yes, because soon enough he was handing Sheela her Manhattan and Nidhi her mystery drink in a martini glass, a slice of lime hanging off the side.

Whatever it was, it was delicious. Nidhi—the rule-follower, the girl who avoided trouble, the girl who overthought everything—downed it.

"Do you approve?" the bartender asked.

"This is the best Manhattan I've ever had," Sheela declared.

Nidhi just nodded shyly.

"Another round?" he asked.

"Sure," Sheela said. Then she turned to Nidhi. "Alok Anand is even hotter in person! I'm so excited we'll get to see him again." She waved at the invite for Club Hello. "Ooh, Deity will be there!"

"Who's Deity?" Nidhi asked idly. Definitely not noticing the bartender washing his hands and wiping the table with a washcloth.

"A gully rapper," Sheela said. "Street rap. It's gotten so big. It started with these kids from the slums in Mumbai, but now it's everywhere. There are some great artists in New Delhi. Alok is going to star in a movie that's loosely based on Deity's life."

The bartender snorted. "If it doesn't get banned."

"Why would it?" Nidhi asked curiously.

She was also trying not to notice that he was definitely noticing *her* as he shook their next drinks. She hadn't realized that a black shirt and black pants could be so sexy. And she was suddenly regretting the fashion choices she'd made from the outdated guidebook. She'd blame the woozy way she was feeling on the alcohol, except she'd felt it the second she'd looked into those silky henna eyes.

And yet . . . he was still peeking at her from beneath long lashes.

"Oh yeah," Sheela said. "I heard about that. Apparently, some of the lyrics that Deity wrote for the movie are pretty critical of the government. There's some talk that the censor board might be influenced by angry politicians. But you'd think they'd just cut the lyrics so the movie can go forward."

"Deity won't do it," the bartender said. "He's threatened to back out of the whole project if his lyrics are chopped."

"You seem to know a lot about it," Sheela said.

The bartender looked slightly abashed. "Sorry, I didn't mean to eavesdrop. I'm just a big fan of Deity and excited about this movie."

Sheela nodded. "I can tell. Anyway, you'll come to the rap battle, right, Nidhi?"

"Um . . . sure, I guess," she answered. "It sounds fun."

The bartender handed them their second rounds, and then he had to go serve some other customers. But not before flashing one more devastating smile at Nidhi. Did she say he wasn't ridiculously attractive? Maybe she'd been wrong about that. His features were too chiseled, that mole a little too perfectly placed.

"He's cute, huh?" Sheela said.

Nidhi finally tore her eyes away from the bartender. "Umm . . ."

Sheela burst out laughing. "Maybe you should get his number."

Nidhi shook her head, even though she wanted to. But that was ridiculous. She barely knew this bartender. He could be an ax murderer. He could be a creep. He could even be—horror of horrors—one of those monsters who liked plain vanilla cake with plain vanilla frosting.

Yikes.

"Hey, Nidhi," Prakash said. "We're heading out. Ready to go?"

"Yeah," she said with regret. Could she ever be the kind of girl who just asked a guy for his number?

Not tonight. She said her goodbyes to Sheela, waved to the possible ax murderer bartender, and got in the taxi with Prakash.

It was the night of the rap battle, and Nidhi didn't have anything appropriate to wear, so Sona had offered her an outfit. One that didn't leave much to the imagination.

"You're sure I can go out like this?" Nidhi asked, fiddling with the straps of the little black dress that wrapped tightly around her figure. She kept wanting to snatch it down to cover more of her legs.

Sona smirked and snapped a photo. "Finally, you decided to give up on that silly guidebook you keep reading! Relax, you're gorgeous and I can't believe Alok Anand invited you to a concert! If only I could go, too!"

Like Sirisha, Nidhi's younger cousin was an avid photographer, and very talented. The familiar *click, click, click* was a bit of home here in New Delhi.

Nidhi laughed. "I can try to convince your parents. . . ."

"There's no way they'll okay it," Sona said. "Not until I'm in college at least. But have fun!"

"Thanks," Nidhi said, hugging her cousin. "And thanks for lending me the dress."

It was one of those sticky hot nights, the air thick with humidity. Even in the skimpy dress, Nidhi was impatient to get into the club—and into sweet, sweet air-conditioning. Then again, the crush of warm bodies still might be suffocating.

She clutched the invite, and Sheela nudged her shoulder. "How cool is this?"

Prakash and a bunch of his friends were ahead of them, debating their favorite gully rappers.

"Of course, Alok Anand doesn't know anything about the streets," Prakash commented.

"Neither do you," one of his friends replied.

"True," Prakash admitted. "I'm just wondering if he can pull it off."

While they were waiting, a black Hummer limousine pulled up to the club. Out stepped Alok, and everyone in line cheered and whistled. Alok handled it all with ease, waving at them. Winking at the girls.

Nidhi swore he was looking right at her for a moment, his eyebrows raised in appreciation. It was the dress—the little black dress—and she felt her whole body heat up.

But in a second, the star was inside.

Not long later, the line finally started moving. Nidhi had no idea what to expect. Orcas Island was a sleepy place, and her idea of a concert was a couple folk singers playing acoustic guitar at the back of a coffee shop. This was something else altogether. Thumping music, drinks flowing, people dressed in only the trendiest of clothes. (Thank goodness for

Sona—Nidhi would have been mortified to wear anything she owned.)

She was just stepping inside, when she heard the bouncer say, "Sorry, guy. But this event is invitation only."

"Please, I'm a journalist" was the reply. "I promise to write up something positive about the club."

That voice—it was a rumble of secrets and sexiness.

Nidhi turned around to find the bartender from the other night. He wasn't wearing his bartender uniform this time, though. He too was dressed to fit in, in dark jeans, shiny, expensive-looking sneakers, and a T-shirt emblazoned with Deity's name.

"If you don't have an invite, you can't come in," the bouncer repeated.

Nidhi stepped back, grabbing the bartender's hand. She looked the bouncer squarely in the eyes. "He's with me."

The bouncer blinked. Then nodded. "Okay, then."

The bartender grinned at her, and they walked hand in hand into the crowd. Nidhi couldn't believe her fingers were entwined with his. Unbidden, she imagined intertwining much more.

Sheesh. Nidhi needed to calm down. She couldn't believe the way her entire body so viscerally responded to him.

He was just a stranger. A possible ax murderer or plain-vanilla-cake lover.

"Oh, hello again," Sheela said when she noticed them.

Her eyes, of course, went right to their linked hands.

Nidhi hastily let go. "The bouncer wasn't letting him in, so I said we were together. Of course"—she turned to him—"I don't even know your name."

"Suresh," he said, his eyes sparkling in the dim club lighting. "Thanks for your help."

"Are you really a journalist?" Nidhi asked. "Or just a rabid rap fan?"

He chuckled. "I'm a rap fan. And a student journalist. I want to write a piece for my college newspaper—something about censorship and authenticity and who gets to tell these stories."

"That sounds cool," Sheela said. "Look, Prakash and the others are over there."

Their group had staked out a spot near the stage. Nidhi didn't know what came over her, but she just looked at Suresh and said, "You coming?"

She didn't check to see if he was following as she and Sheela made their way to the others. But she hoped he was.

Nidhi had never seen a rap battle before, but it was so fun—watching the rappers take one another down with rhyming insults. Alok Anand acted as the host and emcee, introducing the different rappers and commenting on their styles. He even hopped into battle himself. His lines sounded practiced, but he got in a few good blows. Besides, his star quality superseded any lackluster rhymes.

After the battle, there were performances by the different rappers. They were obviously heavily influenced by American rappers, but they rhymed in their home languages. Nidhi only spoke Hindi (and even following that was difficult at rap speeds), but Urdu was really similar and she could glean some meaning from other languages, too.

Their lyrics opened a window into life in their neighborhoods, their big dreams, their run-ins with the police, and how they held on to their individual faiths. They weren't afraid to call out local political issues, government corruption, and even a few politicians by name.

Nidhi remembered what Suresh had said about Deity's lyrics

potentially getting censored for the movie with Alok Anand. Whatever happened with the film, she knew the songs she was hearing would get out anyway. Sheela had told her that most of the rappers here had gotten so much local acclaim just by posting music videos directly online.

"Wow," Nidhi commented. "I only understand about half of what they're saying, but they're amazing."

"Don't worry," Sheela said. "Even I have trouble following some of their slang. But I love how they just get up there and tell their truths. There's an authenticity here that people really respond to."

"Not all of them," Suresh disagreed. "Some of them just rap about the things they think makes them 'street.' But Deity should be up soon, and he's the real deal. You'll see. Want anything to drink?"

"Just water for me," Nidhi said, hoping it didn't sound terribly uncool. But she still wasn't used to the whole drinking thing. And this place was such a crush that water sounded amazing.

"I'll take a beer," Sheela said.

"Got it," Suresh said, and disappeared to the bar.

Onstage, one of the very few female rappers of the night came on, dressed casually in a black hoodie and jeans, her hair cropped into a blunt bob. She was introduced as Hailstorm. And words came spewing, fast and hard like hail, her rhymes with clipped edges that made you listen. She'd been through a lot, but she was determined to take control of her life.

Nidhi didn't understand most of the lyrics, but she understood the chorus.

I'll get OUT.
My life isn't THIS.

My life is MORE.

Watch, kid. I'll get OUT.

As Hailstorm left the stage, Nidhi knew she had to listen to more. That girl had a voice that demanded your full attention. The internet said she was eighteen years old, but she made nineteen-year-old Nidhi feel so much younger. Because she didn't have half the experiences or the wisdom of this girl. She felt her privilege then, the fact that she'd grown up in an idyllic inn on Orcas Island, where she'd mainly worried about things like having enough tomatoes in the restaurant pantry and the next big math test.

But Hailstorm had already found a way *OUT*. With her music. Nidhi wished her nothing less than wild success.

When the headliner, Deity, finally came on, the crowd cheered and screamed passionately. With the easy way his lyrics sprang forward, it was obvious why he was so popular. He knew how to tell a story, how to make you listen, how to call out hypocrisy and zero in to the heart of the matter.

As she bounced up and down, screaming with the crowd, Nidhi happened to lock eyes with Suresh. He smiled. And that was all it took.

Chapter Twenty

Nidhi

*N*idhi smiled to herself as she recalled that night at the club. The night she'd fallen in love—not with a guy but with an art form.

"You're smiling like you have a secret," Lena accused.

Nidhi chuckled. "What? I told you everything."

Okay, so she definitely had *not* told them everything. But she had told them about meeting Alok Anand, pulling up the pic she had with him and Sheela on her phone. She was grinning so hard, and even though she was wearing that overly modest outfit prescribed by the guidebook, she glowed.

"You look like you're just where you want to be," Grayson commented.

There was a bit of wistfulness in his voice, his words catching a little.

And Nidhi's heart lodged in her throat. Why did she have to feel this tug-of-war between two continents?

"You look like you're about to get into trouble." Lena waggled her brows.

Nidhi felt her cheeks heat. How did Lena know that? She hadn't even known it in the moment. But she'd met Suresh just minutes later.

"Speaking of which," John said. "I wonder what kind of trouble our son is getting into."

"Oh, I'm sure he's not getting into any," Nidhi replied, thinking that was what they wanted to hear.

But Lena and John looked at each other and snorted.

"We hope he's getting into a teensy bit of trouble," Lena said. "Because bending the rules and taking a few risks are a part of life."

Nidhi sort of liked that.

Nearby, three girls were giggling. And definitely checking out Grayson. The girls were decked out in slinky dresses, blown out hair, and bright shades of eyeshadow. When Grayson finally offered them a little wave, they launched into another fit of giggles.

And then they came over.

"Hi, I'm Hannah!" one of the girls said. "This is Shawna and Anna. We met at the club last night, remember?"

Grayson shook his head. "Nope, you got the wrong guy. . . ."

"Are you sure?" Hannah pouted. "We were the girls celebrating Shawna's birthday?"

"Nope, couldn't have been me," Grayson said. "I was on a flight back from Brazil. Actually, except for Brad here, we were all headed to Seattle. But the windstorm left us stranded."

"Oh!" Hannah said. She and the other girls burst into giggles again.

"I'd lend you all my car," Brad said, "but I have to drive to work. Also, I don't think you want to squeeze together in it all the way to Seattle."

Hannah, Shawna, and Anna exchanged glances.

"Actually . . ." Anna said. "We're going to Seattle, too. Our band has a bus. Want to come with? There's plenty of room."

Hannah and Shawna gushed in agreement.

"It would be so fun!"

"Please come!"

"Oh my gosh, that would be incredible!" Lucas jumped out of his chair—he was that excited. "I need to propose to my boyfriend today, or I know I'll never have the guts again."

"Are you sure you have enough room?" Grayson asked. "For all of us?"

The girls nodded. "Oh yeah, there's plenty of room. No problem at all."

It was a school bus.

Hannah and Shawna and Anna had offered them a ride on a freaking school bus.

Brad had followed their car into a parking lot, where the school's marching band was lining up to get on. Nidhi had thought those girls looked young despite all the makeup and slinky dresses.

"Is this for real?" Lucas's jaw hung open at the scene.

Nidhi scrambled out of the Mini Cooper, anxious to stretch her legs but also worried she was about to have to get right back in. She now saw that the building nearby had a big sign—NATHAN HALE HIGH SCHOOL.

Hannah, Shawna, and Anna waved at them. Their nightclub clothes were now covered with costumes. They were . . . vegetables?

Why were these girls dressed as vegetables?

"See?" said Anna. "We've got plenty of room. Our band is playing at the Harvest Parade in Seattle."

"We can't go on your high school bus!" Lucas sounded exasperated. "We're not students. How old are you three, anyway, if you were out partying last night?"

Hannah pouted. "We're plenty old. We were celebrating Shawna's eighteenth birthday and the fact that all of us are finally clubbing age!"

"It was the best birthday," Shawna added.

"Are you sure you weren't there?" Anna asked Grayson suspiciously.

"I'm sure," Grayson said. "But I don't think your teachers will just let some random strangers on this bus."

"Why not?" Hannah said. "They're always telling us we're supposed to help people and stuff. I'll go ask."

As the three girls ran to talk to their teachers, Grayson ran a hand through his hair. "Why does this seem like a terrible idea?"

"There's no way this is going to work," Lucas agreed.

"What're we going to do?" Nidhi moaned.

Her phone pinged with a notification for a new email. It was from Professor Cunningham.

Hi Nidhi,

I'm so sorry to hear about your delay! But I'm leaving town tomorrow for a conference, so today is really the only day we can meet before you return to India. I'll be on campus until 5 p.m. Let me know if you can make it by then. But if you can't, don't worry! I've already sent you my recommendations for next term's classes. Don't forget that registration is due a week from Tuesday!

Best,

Professor Cunningham

Of course, Nidhi was perfectly aware that registration was due a week from Tuesday; in fact, that was the problem! She needed to get approval for another term abroad, and that meant getting Professor Cunningham on her side.

Nidhi squared her shoulders. Maybe she needed to get on this school bus, after all.

Shawna, Hannah, and Anna returned with a group of parent chaperones and teachers, identified by their badges. The teachers seemed bored, but the parents were extra suspicious.

"This is highly unusual," said a man with glasses who probably thought adding flavored syrup to a latte was *highly unusual.*

"How do we know that you're not criminals?" asked another woman sternly.

Lena held up her phone. "Look, here I am volunteering at the library with kids. You have to have a background check to do that."

"Hmmph," said the man with glasses, "This says it's from a Canadian library. Who knows what they do in Canada?"

"My wife is not a criminal!" John huffed. "And I've volunteered at the library, too."

"I've volunteered at Habitat for Humanity!" Lucas offered.

"What does that have to do with anything?" another parent demanded.

"I don't know!" Lucas shrugged. "Look, I just need to get to Seattle to propose to my boyfriend. I'll do anything! We'll buy Girl Scout cookies or wrapping paper to support your school!"

"We're not the Girl Scouts," one of the teachers said.

"And we're not currently selling wrapping paper," another one added.

"Wait a minute," a woman said. "You're proposing to your boyfriend? That's so sweet! Tell us all the details!"

"Oh yes, we want to know," said another parent.

In fact, suddenly everyone was staring at Lucas, enthralled and waiting for his proposal story. It was a special kind of magic that left Nidhi a little bit in awe.

"I have a whole thing planned," Lucas said. "My boyfriend is playing a concert this afternoon, and I got his band in on it. They're going to put me in the spotlight at just the right moment. It'll be really hard to re-create on another day."

"That's so sweet!"

"Adorable!"

"I love that idea for a proposal!"

"You have to send us a recording!"

They were like putty in Lucas's hands. If it could help Nidhi make her meeting with Professor Cunningham, she couldn't complain.

"Wait a minute!" said the man who thought this was all highly unusual. "If you're so into this proposal, why was your flight today? Isn't that kind of last minute?"

Lucas held up his hands. "Trust me, this wasn't what I had planned. I was supposed to have plenty of time. My initial flight got canceled and then there were just so many delays . . ." He gestured to Nidhi, Grayson, Lena, and John. "We've all been affected. Nidhi's supposed to meet her advisor today. Lena and John are supposed to see their son for his birthday. And Grayson—well, I guess Grayson doesn't have anything urgent."

Grayson shrugged. "Okay, so I don't. But come on, my buddy needs help! You can't stand in the way of love, can you?" He patted Lucas's back and gave them his charm-'em-and-leave-'em smile.

And that was all it took. Well . . . and they had to buy some marching band T-shirts specially made for the Harvest Parade. They would forever be "Nathan Hale High School Veggie Lovers."

Nidhi:

Good news all, I've got a ride! I'm finally heading to Seattle. Will try to make it to see your film, Rani!

Rani:

Woohoo! I knew you could do it!

Sirisha:

Oh, that's wonderful, Nidhi. Can't wait to see you!

Nidhi:

Oh, and you'll never guess what! Grayson was on my flight from LA. So . . . yeah. Weird, right?

Rani:

Nidhi! It's obviously Destiny! When are you going to learn?

Nidhi:

Haha, if you say so.

Rani:

Whatever, I can't help you if you don't help yourself.

Chapter Twenty-One

Rani

Rani watched excitedly as the passengers disembarked. She couldn't wait to see Raj's goofy grin. She always tried not to dwell on the negative, but long distance really was hard. So many people had told her it couldn't possibly work out. Nidhi. Avani. Parker. JJ.

Even the Dads seemed a bit skeptical.

But she'd proven them all wrong. She and Raj had been going strong since the summer. He texted or called her nearly every day. And when he didn't—well, it was usually because his parents were back to fighting again. Their trip to Orcas in July had done them some good, but the peace hadn't lasted, unfortunately. Poor Raj. He was lucky to have Rani to show him what a loving relationship looked like.

As more and more people got off, Rani felt that prickle of unease return. Where was he? He was coming, right? He had to. He was the perfect boyfriend, and perfect boyfriends showed up. Especially when it was important. Especially when you were chasing your dreams.

And yet . . .

All the foot passengers had gotten off.

"Maybe he decided to drive?" Rani said.

"Oh yeah," Parker agreed. "That must be it."

They watched as all the cars unloaded next. But soon every car had gotten off the ferry. And still no Raj.

"Maybe he's on the next one," JJ said. "He didn't text you?"

Rani swallowed and shook her head. All that she'd gotten from him was those three dots that had gone away. Remembering it made that prickle of unease bloom into a full panic. She broke into a sweat. It was suddenly hard to breathe.

"I'm sure he's coming," Sara said, patting Rani's shoulder. "He's not the type to flake."

JJ looked at their phone. "Well, let's head over to the auditorium. Raj knows where to find us, right?"

Rani nodded, swallowing. Trying to regain her composure, even though she felt as if the windstorm had blown her straight out to sea. Still, she had to be strong for her cast and crew. This was her directorial debut, after all. She bit her lip. "Yeah, let's do it."

OCTOBER

The Saturday of the school's Fall Festival had begun with a brief drizzle, but luckily it had cleared up around noon. The early evening was warm, and the school grounds were buzzing with students and teachers and volunteers. The leaves were just turning colors, it wasn't parka weather yet, and the days were still long enough to have light until 7 p.m.

Rani and Raj held hands, wandering the booths, inhaling the scents of burgers and funnel cakes. The French club sold the best frozen lemonade, and the photography club had put together a dunk tank. Rani had her eye on an adorable stuffed octopus at a dart-throwing game.

She batted her lashes. "You'll win me it for me, won't you?"

"I guess I do owe you," Raj said, giving his three tickets to the freckled, redheaded kid manning the booth. "Since I showed up late and everything."

Rani nodded. She didn't want to get into a fight or anything, but Raj had originally promised to arrive on Orcas last night. He always stayed at the inn on his weekend visits. But at the last second, he'd said he'd needed to do something with his mom (no details forthcoming) and that he'd come in the morning instead. And then he'd missed the earliest ferry and ended up only getting here a couple of hours ago. Rani suspected there was something going on with his family, and she didn't want to pry. She trusted him—but this didn't leave them with much time since he'd have to head back tomorrow. Weekends were too short.

They'd have to make the most of it, she supposed.

In the dart-game booth, there were tons of cardboard creatures moving along a conveyer belt. To win a giant stuffed animal, you had to hit a tiny cardboard version of it that was zipping around. The marching band was playing showtunes not far away, and Rani tapped her foot to the rhythm as Raj took aim, biting his lip in determination. (Such an adorable lip, too.)

The first dart went flying.

Miss.

"You'll get the next one," Rani said confidently.

His second dart also missed. Finally, his third hit a large cardboard rabbit. Of course, the bigger the target, the easier it was to hit, and therefore the smaller the prize.

"Congratulations." The bored freckled kid handed Raj a lollipop.

"That is so not what I asked for!" Rani exclaimed teasingly.

"Oh yeah? Well, I was going to offer this to you, but now I'm going to keep it for myself!" Raj unwrapped the lollipop and stuck it in his mouth.

Rani gasped. "So unchivalrous."

"It's modern times, honey," Raj returned, smiling through his lollipop. "Maybe you should try to win yourself."

Rani tossed her hair. "Fine, I will."

She loved the way they bantered; it was so very rom-com worthy. But this was a feminist rom-com, and she didn't need Raj to win an octopus for her! She handed over three tickets, then waited patiently for the small cardboard octopus to get close on the conveyer belt. When the timing was right, she let her first dart loose.

Miss.

Second dart.

Hit another useless giant rabbit.

The freckled kid started to hand her a lollipop, but she waved him off. "I get one more try!"

"Okay," the kid said, shrugging.

Rani narrowed her eyes. Even though she had a perfect, amazing boyfriend, she was definitely going to get that octopus. *Hey, universe, you owe this to me for making Raj miss half our planned weekend!*

She thought she felt a tingle in her fingers. It was obviously the universe telling her she was right. She let the dart fly with a fury.

Only she'd whipped her hand too hard, and it went straight toward the freckled kid's forehead. Luckily, he dove out of the way just in time.

"Hey!" he said. "Watch it!"

Rani's cheeks heated up. "Oops, sorry."

The kid's eyes narrowed. "You do *not* get a lollipop."

That was maybe a bit embarrassing. She knew it was just a game, but she'd really thought the universe was going to give her that one. Oh well. She reached out for Raj's hand and squeezed tight. He squeezed back.

They played some more games, ate some corn dogs, and tried the frozen lemonade. Most of the school was there, and whenever they ran into friends, Raj seemed a natural at getting the jocks to laugh, the girls to wish he was their own goofball boyfriend. He looked cute tonight in jeans, trendy new sneakers, and a pale blue polo with a small Link from Zelda stitched on the front pocket. She didn't know where he'd found it, but the video game reference was surprisingly discreet compared to the T-shirts he usually wore. She thought it was a perfect nod to his interests, while also looking a little dressy.

"You look cute tonight," she told him.

He squeezed her hand. "Thanks. You look cute, too."

She smiled. At the dunk tank, he managed to plunge Mr. Wallace, the PE teacher who had tortured Rani with too many laps during her freshman year.

"I guess that makes up for not winning me the octopus." Rani kissed his cheek.

"I was hoping you'd say that," Raj answered, kissing her on the lips.

The sun was setting now, rosy hues filling the sky, and it seemed the perfect moment to wander beyond the booths to a cluster of birch trees with golden leaves, branches bending down to provide a curtain of privacy.

She grabbed his hand and he went with it, running with her. Pressing his lips against hers in the shadows. It was perfect, the kind of moment she wished she could freeze in time, that could last forever.

"I have something for you," he said when they came up for air.

"A giant stuffed octopus?"

"Let it go already." He grinned and pulled from his pocket a small black box with a red bow. It looked fancy—the kind that held jewelry.

Rani had never received jewelry from a boy before. She knew it was kind of cliché, but she could tell that Raj had thought a lot about it. He looked earnest as she carefully untied the bow.

"It's not expensive," he said. "I mean, I couldn't afford anything that expensive."

She smiled at him. "I don't care."

In the twilight, he looked like a prince. One that smelled a bit like corn dog, but that was to be expected. She carefully opened the box. Inside, there was a pair of earrings. Colorful beads and crystals were arranged in the shape of an ocean wave below crystal stars and a white-stoned moon.

"They're beautiful," she said, putting them on deftly.

"I'm glad you like them," he said.

"You have taste, Raj."

He looked a bit sheepish. "Okay, so maybe my mom helped me pick them out."

"She did?" Rani had never been sure if Raj's mom really supported their relationship. She was kind of standoffish.

"I keep telling you, my mom likes you," Raj said, reading her thoughts.

"She's only invited me over to your place once," Rani reminded him. "That was all the way back in August."

Raj looked really sad. "Yeah, that's probably because she's embarrassed.

My parents are really trying, you know. I thought all the counseling and that vacation over the summer would help. But they still get into weird fights. It's not screaming like before. It's more just . . . I don't know. Quiet. Sad."

Rani decided to let go of that nugget of resentment she'd had over him canceling last night to spend time with his mom. There was just so much going on with him. And he'd come today, after all. He was always there when it counted. She wanted to be there for him, too.

She sank down onto the grass and patted the space beside her. "I'm listening if you want to talk."

Chapter Twenty-Two

Rani

Rani entered the auditorium with trepidation. Her team was giving her worried looks, and she still felt like her pulse was racing. She was sweating, too. She trusted that Raj had a good reason for being late, but the knot in her stomach hadn't gone away. It probably wouldn't until he got here.

She forced a smile on her face anyway. "We're so going to kick ass. Raj didn't need to be here for the orientation—he's our camera guy and he already knows what to do."

"True," JJ said. "Yesterday, I sent him a complete list of all the shots we would need, suggested angles, etc. He even gave me some feedback on it, and they were good thoughts."

That made Rani feel better. He'd been in contact with JJ. He was as invested in this movie as she was.

Dominic and Sara led the way to an empty row not far from the stage, Parker following after. The auditorium was mostly empty, but people were still filtering in. Rani scoped out the competition—it wasn't just Ed Yi she had to crush.

Her hackles raised when she heard his voice.

"Okay, you've got the shot list, right?" he asked Fiona as he took a seat directly behind Rani. An entire empty auditorium and that's where he had to sit.

"Yes, for the zillionth time," Fiona answered. "I know it's supposed to be artsy and all, but I think we could use maybe just a tiny amount of plot."

"Plot is overrated," Ed returned. "Trust me, I've won—"

"Three short film contests," Fiona returned. "Yeah, yeah, you've mentioned it one or twenty-seven times."

Ed coughed. "Oops. Sorry about that. I don't mean to sound immodest."

Rani snorted. Who used the word *immodest* that was actually immodest? She turned around in time to see Fiona rolling her eyes. Ed hunched his shoulders down and started flipping through a printout of the rules.

Well, at least they had that in common. Rani had her own copy tucked in her bag, and she pulled it out. She probably had it memorized by now, but she didn't want to get accidentally disqualified on some technicality.

More people were entering the room, sitting in clusters with their cast and crew. JJ started chatting with Fiona. Rani narrowed her eyes. Didn't they see that Fiona and the rest of Ed's cast were the enemy? So much for loyalty. Rani slumped in her seat.

By the time an organizer stood on the stage, it looked like there were about twelve groups competing. Okay, that wasn't too bad. She only had to be the best out of twelve to meet a famous director. Totally doable. Of course, at the moment she didn't even have a camera, which might be a bit of a problem.

Raj would show, though. He had to.

A woman wearing a maxi dress and oversize purple glasses cleared her throat at the microphone in the front.

"Welcome, welcome!" she said. "My name is Rowan, and I'm the coordinator for today's Youth One Day Shoot-Out. I'm very excited to see what all you young filmmakers come up with! Remember to have fun out there!

"I understand that many of you are interested in going on to study film in college. That's wonderful, and I think today's grand prize will be a great step toward your future career—a consultation with Helmuth Gerhardt, the critically acclaimed director of *The Howlers at Dawn*. Gerhardt—" There was a lot of clapping and cheering from the crowd. Rowan smiled. "Yes, I can tell that many of you are fans. His work has been recognized by the Sundance Film Festival, the Toronto International Film Festival—"

Another staff member came onstage and whispered something in her ear. Rowan looked very taken aback.

"Oh, I am so sorry," she said. "It appears that Mr. Gerhardt has been unavoidably delayed. Apparently, all incoming flights at SeaTac have been canceled."

Yikes. The freaking windstorm struck again. First, Nidhi had gotten stranded in Portland. Now even Gerhardt couldn't make it? Angry murmurs rippled through the auditorium.

Ed cursed softly behind her. "He was the whole reason I was interested in this!"

"Oh, this isn't worthy of you now?" Adam muttered. "Tell us again about the three contests you've won."

At least Ed's crew also found him slightly insufferable. (Sufferable enough to work with, though.) Rani's stomach gurgled. Gerhardt wasn't her favorite director or anything, but he was really big. Meeting him could open the door to unknown opportunities. There was more discussion onstage as a third staff member came up to consult with the others.

Finally, Rowan turned back to the microphone. This time, she had a big smile pasted back on her face. "I am so pleased to tell you that we will have another guest director today! It appears that Olivia Lee is in the area, and she has agreed to come judge the Shoot-Out. She's the director of the romantic comedies *A Girl, a Boy, and a Dozen Puppies*; *Love in a Nutshell*; *Last Stop on the Muni*; and more. What a delight!"

WHAT.

Rani was stunned. Maybe the windstorm was actually on her side. After all, her idol was coming, her idol would judge the contest, her idol would be breathing the same air as her . . .

"Who?" Ed muttered.

"Oh yeah, I watched *Love in a Nutshell* with my girlfriend," Adam said. "Not bad for a chick flick."

Not bad for a chick flick? *Not bad for a chick flick?*

Rani had half a mind to smack him down, but she was too busy imagining the shining moment when she would meet *the* Olivia Lee. And then, naturally, they'd become really good friends and co-write and co-direct a ton of amazing rom-coms together.

INT. SOMEWHERE FANCY - EVENING

RANI is making her way down the red carpet in a stunning dress.
REPORTER #1
Rani, here!

(flashbulbs as reporter takes multiple photos)
REPORTER #2
Rani, your new film is a sensation! What do you have to
say to your fans?

RANI
I couldn't have done it without my amazing colleague
Olivia Lee.

(waves at Olivia, who approaches and hugs her)
OLIVIA LEE
Rani, our latest film is a smash. I'm so glad I met you
at that Youth Film contest. You understand love for the
younger generation.

RANI
Oh, Olivia, I'm so glad I met you, too. You're the best
mentor and friend. It's been an honor to work with you.

OLIVIA LEE
No, it's been an honor to work with you. You're the best.

RANI

No, you are.

OLIVIA LEE

You are!

". . . I think that's all I have." Rowan shuffled her papers once more, and then nodded to herself. "Yes, that's it! I'm around if you have any questions, but everything we've discussed has been emailed to you. Good luck and be safe!"

As everyone filtered out of the auditorium, Rani felt a surge of renewed determination. *Remeet-Cute* was going to blow Olivia away!

Outside, she quickly checked her phone in case she'd missed a text. Sure enough, there were some.

Raj:

Hey, really sorry but I wasn't able to get on the ferry. Something came up. I can't make it today.

Raj:

Rani? Did you get my message?

Raj:

Seriously, I'm sorry.

The texts from Raj were from fifteen minutes ago. The knot in her stomach tightened. Something came up? Why didn't he say what had come up? He was supposed to be her camera guy. But maybe something terrible had happened.

Oh gosh, she hoped he was all right.

Rani:

Is something wrong? Are you and your family okay? Is this an emergency?

Those three dots came up.

She waited.

They disappeared and reappeared. And then finally a response.

Raj:

Yeah, we're fine. It's not a medical emergency—but still kind of an emergency? Will explain later. Good luck with the competition.

Rani was devastated. Whatever was happening, it must be something big. Still a part of her was just a tiny bit resentful. Couldn't he just tell her what was going on? Wasn't this worth a phone call, not just a text?

Should she call?

She should call.

But . . . Raj didn't answer. Rani thought she was going to scream. She wanted to kick her phone to the ground and smash the screen and throw a toddler-esque tantrum. It wasn't just Rani who had relied on him either. JJ, Parker, Dominic, and Sara had all worked hard in pre-production. What was she going to tell them?

Rani:

OMG Raj just texted that he's not coming.

Sirisha:

What? I thought he was your camera person.

Rani:

He was supposed to be! This is a disaster!! He didn't tell me why, though I'm sure he has a good reason. But what am I supposed to do? Use a camera phone?

Nidhi:

Oh no! I'm so sorry. I hope you figure something out!

Rani:

There is one good thing that happened this morning . . . Helmuth Gerhardt couldn't make it, so Olivia Lee is going to judge and give the consultation!!! Can you believe it?

Sirisha:

Omg, it's your idol. That's so cool! Don't worry, Rani. You can totally make a short film using just a camera phone. Here, I'm sending you some links with tips on how to make it work. Oh, and also an example short film. It's brilliant!

Rani:

Thanks, Sirisha. It won't be the same, but I'll check them out.

Nidhi:

Good luck! I know you can do it. Ack, I'm getting a headache from this marching band's singing.

Sirisha:

Marching band?

Nidhi:

Er, yes. I'm on a school bus (long story).

Rani:

Hmm. I guess Avani's too busy with her workshop to care about my crisis, but whatever.

Sirisha:

She's probably dancing away. I'm sure she'll respond when she gets a chance.

Rani:

You'd think she could read my mind, but I guess our twin powers are failing. But I'll keep sending the mental SOS.

Chapter Twenty-Three

Avani

They say that twins can sense when there's something wrong with the other one, and Avani had the urge to check her phone to see how Rani's morning was going. She and Fernando were sitting on the benches that lined one of the studio walls, since he'd said he'd needed a minute to recover from that dip. Avani had offered to massage the spot on his lower back, but he'd just winced and shook his head.

She reached for her bag. Maybe nothing was wrong, actually. Maybe she was just addicted to checking her phone. It was a possibility.

But Lisa caught her sneaking it out. "No devices in this workshop, dear. Please put that away!"

Caught by the teacher. Avani reluctantly dropped it in her bag.

Lisa clapped her hands for attention. "Awesome freestyling, everyone. Now that we're loosened up, we're going to practice the actual routine."

She and Rodrigo demonstrated in a slow rhythm. "Just the basic here. Quick, quick, slow. Quick, quick, slow. Cross body lead, a spin, another basic, and then a dip. Remember, the focus today is to trust each other, to be in sync with each other. This isn't a dance you can learn with your head. It requires you to learn it with your heart."

Easy for her to say. Avani had done her best to stay in the moment, to follow her instincts, and she'd just ended up hurting Fernando.

She was always hurting him, and not just with dance. They were always hurting each other. How had it become like this?

They'd danced together in gym class in the eighth grade—when they'd first learned a bit of salsa—and they'd seemed to be so in sync in an unexpected way. They weren't a couple back then, just friends, but even then, they'd intuitively moved together. With a touch of his fingers, she knew when to turn. And most importantly, they'd had *fun*.

Last year, they'd finally gotten together. They'd signed up for salsa in the spring, and reveled in it, reveled in how it was almost like she knew where he was going with a move just by him thinking it. She'd loved that feeling, that connection with him.

But now she felt all helter-skelter. She couldn't calm her mind, she couldn't calm her heart, she couldn't tame the windstorm inside her. She fidgeted, stretching her neck muscles. Her boyfriend was right there in front of her, breathing the same dance studio air as she was. And yet . . .

They had never been so far from each other.

He took her right hand in his left. He put his other hand on her waist, and she rested her left hand on his shoulder. They waited for the right beat. And then they moved together.

"Let's just practice the basic and some cross body leads for a bit," he said, "before we try that first dip."

"Sounds good." Avani sucked in a breath. Tried to relax into the steps, the ones she already knew by heart. Quick, quick, slow. Quick, quick, slow. Cross body lead. Cross body lead. Fernando had them repeat it several more times. It was so boring not to spin or dip or add any flair that Avani's mind wandered back to that twinge she'd felt and whether Rani's film was doing okay and whether Nidhi would be able to make it back to the islands and how Sirisha was doing with her murder-mystery party.

"Come on," Fernando said. "Focus on me."

There was an edge to his voice, and his moth-brown eyes were glittering with something she couldn't quite name. She wanted to focus on him, she did. She was generally only as good as her partner made her look, and Fernando had always made her look good.

"Quick, quick, slow," Lisa called out loudly. "Quick, quick, slow. Yes! Beautiful."

Avani was intensely aware of Lisa and Rodrigo circulating the room, commenting on how everyone was doing. Greta and Trent were flying: They'd basically already mastered the entire dance. Greta did an amazing flip, and they managed the first several lifts. It was only the last one, the one that was the most difficult, that they were having a bit of trouble with.

"I'm sure they've had a lot of training," Rodrigo said to Avani and Fernando. He had a soft, melodic voice, the kind that made you lean in to listen. "Don't be intimidated, though! I promise that you can learn this dance. Show me the beginning few steps again."

Fernando and Avani swept into the opening of the routine again. That part was easy.

"You two have some natural chemistry together," he said, nodding in approval.

The words were a balm to Avani's ears, and she relaxed slightly.

"You're thinking too much, though," Rodrigo said. He held out his hand to Avani, inviting her to dance with him.

Of course, she knew she was thinking too much! But she didn't know how to stop. For approximately the zillionth time that day, Avani again wondered about the possibility she had ADHD. But what would that mean for her? That she could never focus when she wanted to? No, Avani knew that she'd done this before, that she and Fernando had danced as one. Just because her brain worked differently didn't meant that she couldn't master this.

Rodrigo let her take her time, and somehow that calmed her. She stepped up and put one hand in his, the other on his shoulder. He wasn't particularly tall, about the same height as Avani, which somehow made the dance more intimate. He squeezed her hand slightly, as if to remind her to straighten up and get in proper position. She arched her back, fixed her elbows into place, bent her knees slightly.

Then, he gently guided her through the routine, but with slower steps than what the music called for. It was much easier with a professional since he knew how to correct her when she was going wrong. He even went through the lifts with her, his arms firm and steady as he made her feel like she could fly. When he picked up the pace, Avani flubbed a few steps, but she was able to cover up her mistakes with a few extra flashy kicks.

Rodrigo chuckled. "Nice. I like your style."

Next, he danced with Fernando. Rodrigo was just as comfortable following as he was leading. He talked Fernando through the routine, including the motions of the lift.

"You need to support her back here," he said. "And then cup her knee quickly here."

Fernando nodded, somehow managing the lifts in slow motion with Rodrigo. Lisa came up to watch them and clapped. They looked . . . really good together.

"Now, that's sexy." Lisa winked at Avani.

It was.

"Time for you two to try it together," Rodrigo said. "You both know what to do."

Avani locked eyes with Fernando. They got the first few basic moves and turns easily. Then Fernando went for the first lift, and Avani leapt up a little bit early and he didn't quite have a grip on her.

They both teetered.

"You've got this," Rodrigo said. "Try closing your eyes. Listen to each other's breathing. Feel the beat. And then go."

Avani exchanged a skeptical look with Fernando.

"Let's just do it," he said.

And so she closed her eyes
    and the world was dark
        with bright patches that filtered in
    through her lids
she saw stars and nebulas
    and felt the warmth of a sun
        close to her

He was leading, and this time she let him do so, didn't press him ahead. He twirled her, and she let herself spin. Repeat. Now his hands gripped her more tightly for the first lift. She waited for the right moment, then leapt. He supported her back and it felt right, but there was no time to think, just move to the next one.

"We can do this," Fernando whispered.

"Yeah, of course," she said,

> pushing all those doubts back
>> this was *them*
>>> this was *him*
> he spun her
>> and she twirled
> and then the third lift
>> where he had to support her waist and her knee
>>> only she tilted too much
> and . . .
>> SPLAT.

The more they practiced, the worse they were getting. That wasn't the way it was supposed to be, was it?

"Okay," Lisa said. "Before we break for lunch, let's mix things up a bit. It's good to practice with a variety of partners. When I stop the music, you'll find a new partner. Got it?"

Everyone nodded. Avani started off with Fernando as usual, only getting in a few spins before the music stopped. Another student offered her his hand, and they moved together. While she liked this guy's sharp, staccato style, his steps seemed a bit too jerky.

When they switched again, her next partner confessed he was trained in New York style.

"I don't mind switching things up," she said. It took them a few bars, but she was able to follow his lead and go with the "on two" beat that was popular on the other coast. It was a smoother, slower style—very romantic, actually. (Should she and Fernando try it? Could simply starting on a different beat solve their problems?)

Her following partner was a petite woman with glasses. "I like to lead. Is that cool?"

"Totally," Avani said, and let her be the guide of when to move and where.

The woman even picked up Avani in the lifts with ease. It wasn't that she was particularly strong; she just had the balance and control. And though she didn't know why exactly, with this woman, Avani was finally able to let the music seep into her bones. She loved the rhythm of it; she loved salsa. She felt sexy as she swished her hips, added a flourish of a wide sweeping arm or an extra kick. It was how she'd always felt with Fernando—except today.

The music stopped again, and Avani ended up face-to-face with Trent. He'd rudely ignored her and Fernando earlier, but as she danced with him, it became clear that he liked to give his full attention to his partner. The way he moved his hips—daaaang! He dipped her with panache, and Avani somehow felt completely secure.

The music turned off for the last time.

"Excellent," Lisa said. "You've all earned your lunch break. Let's take forty-five minutes. There's a deli across the street, a coffee shop, and a pizza place if you want to grab a slice. Cafés and restaurants tend to move on island time here in Friday Harbor, so it's best if you get something simple to go." She glanced out through the big windows, where leaves were blustering and swirling in the wind. "In the afternoon, we'll record everyone's routine and give you specific tips to help you improve."

Avani grabbed her water bottle and chugged what was left in it. This was already her third refill of the morning—salsa was an intense workout. Actually, that was one of the things she loved about it, since she always seemed to have an excess of frenetic energy.

She was sweating wildly, but at least her deodorant was working. She sprayed herself generously with a rose-scented spritz she had in her bag, then leaned against the window, looking out at swirling leaves. Red, gold, orange. It was gorgeous, but there probably wouldn't be any left after today's windstorm. Just naked branches.

Despite the heat of the studio, it made her feel incredibly cold.

Chapter Twenty-Four

Sirisha

Another twisty road. More wind and rain and groaning trees.

It was a dark and stormy night. Or rather, it was a dark and stormy 11 a.m. as Sirisha pulled through the gated drive of Bethany's family property. Her parents were definitely well off, and their mansion was nestled away down a long, hidden road that wound through a veritable forest. Celebrities had bought properties in this area before, vacation homes that they rarely visited.

The rain had come in stops and starts the whole morning, and suddenly it was intense again. The windshield wipers couldn't keep up, and Sirisha slowed to a crawl, determined not to hit any random beautiful girls foraging for mushrooms. The tires squealed over mud, puddle water sloshing everywhere. The wind shrieked with warnings and fury and the possibility of epiphanies. Eventually, the mansion leapt out from under a thunderous sky. Glinting with beauty and danger. Three stories with tall windows and many eaves. A circular drive, several cars parked around it.

It was the moment of truth.

She'd told Brie that she wanted to be more present, that she wasn't planning to spend the whole party taking photos. But was that something she'd said just in the moment, to defy Brie? Or was that something she really yearned for?

Ever since the breakup, Sirisha had only been going through the motions. Doing her homework, going to school, working at the inn. Bethany and Paola had invited her on hikes and beach walks and coffee dates to get her out of her funk. She'd gone along with them, but in her heart, she'd felt detached from everyone. It was an intensely lonely feeling, and a part of her had carried around that loneliness like a cloak. Nothing had seemed to really call to her except photography. The challenge of capturing the perfect shot was the only thing that kept her going.

Right now, her camera was in the back seat, where it always was. Snug in its case, ready. She thought longingly of what she could do with it in this dark and stormy mansion. She liked making people look good. Was there anything wrong with that?

The wind whistled an unintelligible answer.

She reached into the back and pulled her camera out of the bag. It felt comforting just to hold it in her hands. It had always made her feel powerful, in control. As if she had purpose. But she couldn't go through life never interacting with anyone. Her camera her sole companion. What if she was putting too much of herself in her photography? After all, she had more to offer than just that, didn't she?

She missed what she had with Brie, but she'd never find it again with someone new if she kept hiding. She yearned for those butterflies in her stomach, for her heart to pitter-patter once more. Mostly, she just wanted a connection with someone, one that made the whole world seem bigger and more beautiful and rife with endless joys.

Sirisha forced herself to put the camera back in the case. She'd give this whole "being present" thing a try. Before she could second-guess herself, she pulled the hood of her parka over her face and ran toward the enormous barrel front doors.

A spacious foyer. A glittering chandelier. A circular staircase that looked like the kind young debutantes would traipse down in ballgowns. Down the hallway: art deco gas lamps and building facades, a faux moon and stars hanging above.

"May I have your name, please?" said a woman with a clipboard. She was in her forties, her brown hair clipped shoulder-length, her nails painted burgundy to match her lipstick. She wore a black butler's uniform.

"Sirisha," Sirisha murmured, pushing back her damp hair. She hoped the rain hadn't ruined Rani's magic.

"Fantastic," the woman said, crossing off her name on the checklist. "I'm Mrs. Fowler, by the way. You'll see me again at the Jade Club."

She handed Sirisha a Devious Party Planning business card. The company that Brie had said was amazing. Sirisha slipped the card into her wet jeans pocket. Maybe Dad would want it for events at the Songbird.

"I can take your coat for you, thanks," Mrs. Fowler continued, accepting the wet parka. "Now, just take the stairs and look for the yellow rose room. Enjoy your evening!"

"Evening?" Sirisha said.

The woman nodded, pointing to a big grandfather clock, which said it was 7:11. "It's just past seven now. We hope to wrap up the festivities by midnight."

Ah. Sirisha would have to get used to this game of pretend, where even day was night. She did the mental math—it was a five-hour party, and it was 11 a.m. now in the real world, so it should be wrapped up by 4 p.m. Which was good because she had to drive to the ferry terminal and head over for Rani's film screening afterward.

"Thanks." Sirisha took a deep breath and ascended the stairs.

A long row of rooms with cards on them stretched in front of her. The first had a picture of a red peony on the door. The next one had a purple hydrangea, and then a pink tulip. At the end of the hallway, Sirisha came to the room with the yellow rose. She stepped inside.

A sumptuous four-poster king-size bed, an elaborately detailed antique vanity, and an enormous fireplace crackling merrily. A small sitting area next to a large window with a balcony. There was even an opulent en suite bathroom with beautiful green-and-white tile work.

A garment bag with an envelope on it lay on the bed. Inside the envelope, she found her character sheet.

Welcome to the Murder at the Jade Club party! Our fictional story takes place at an illegal speakeasy during the 1920s Prohibition Era. A number of people are gathering at the Jade Club tonight: the mayor and his wife, a pair of rival crime bosses and their minions, a couple of Prohibition agents from the Department of Justice, the speakeasy owner and staff, a former silent film star, a pilot, a newspaper reporter, and more. They all have secrets that they're hiding, and nearly all have motives to kill the person who ultimately dies.

You are encouraged to mingle with the other guests in order to learn their secrets while subtly revealing your own. You will receive character cards with clues to dispense.

Please stay in character at all times for maximum enjoyment.

Oh dear. This already sounded hard. Sirisha was supposed to mingle? Share clues? What if she couldn't get the words out? On top of that, she was supposed to maintain her character—and pick up on everyone else's clues? Avani would be so much better at this. So would Rani. The twins both had a ton of flair.

Suddenly, Sirisha was even less sure about her decision to leave behind her camera. But she couldn't give in to her fears. Not this early in the game. Steeling herself, she hurried into the beautiful bathroom and splashed some water on her face. There was some lovely lavender-scented soap, so she lathered it up in her hands and let the fragrance calm her.

She was going to do this, and she was going to do this *right*. She returned to the packet and pulled out the next card.

Character Card: "Scarlett Singh"
You're the daughter of one of the biggest bootleggers in the Midwest. Your father, Sandeep Singh, is currently in prison, serving a sentence after being convicted for violating Prohibition laws, bribing officials, and more. He's still running his business from his cell, and you're his second-in-command.

In his absence, you've discovered you have a knack for organized crime. You've made some improvements in the pipeline, and business is booming.

Tonight, you've been told that the city's rival bootlegger, Randall Johnson, wants to talk. Your father has no respect for Randall, who sells sub-quality liquor and backstabs anyone who works for him. But Randall claims he has some information that is of interest to you.

Sirisha smiled. She loved that she got to keep Singh as her name. She hadn't realized that the characters would be personalized this way— what a wonderful surprise! And she supposed it was good that she hadn't faked an illness, or someone else would be playing Scarlett Singh. That wouldn't do.

She glanced at the last card.

Objective: Identify the murderer and their motivation.

Your character could also be the murderer, and you are allowed to "confess" and explain your own motive as well to win the game.

If you guess or confess incorrectly, you will be out of the game. That means you will no longer be able to gather or dispense clues, nor make further accusations.

We have a small prize for your effort! We are also providing a lovely luncheon that accommodates different dietary needs. Eat, drink, and solve a murder at your leisure.

Hmm. Well, Sirisha didn't care too much about winning. She just wanted to get through the party without completely making a fool of herself. Hands trembling, she unzipped the garment bag to reveal her costume.

A black suit with scarlet piping, a matching fedora, a long string of pearls, hair pins, and a cigarette holder with a fake cigarette. As she put on the costume, a tingle went through her body. It was just a suit, but it felt like it was made for her, and when she modeled it in front of the full-length mirror, she couldn't help but admire her reflection. A scarlet handkerchief was tucked into the breast pocket, and it had her character name embroidered on it—Scarlett Singh.

On the vanity, Sirisha found a brush to run through her hair, which had become frizzy due to the rain. She managed to tame it though (Rani's serums were probably helping) and even added a cluster of pins to create a side-swept style. Now for a dash of lipstick from her purse. A bit of smoky eyeliner. A quick brush of bronzer. The Official Love Guru had taught her well.

She felt suddenly powerful. Beautiful and dangerous. Maybe even a little bit deadly.

The suit came with one other accessory—a small fake silver pistol, and instructions on its use for the game. It was lightweight and had a faux-pearl handle flourish. Tucking it into the inner pocket of her suit helped her feel even more in character. She was the daughter of the biggest bootlegger in the Midwest, after all. She'd taken over his criminal empire. And she'd done it with panache.

She thought back to all the movies she'd seen from this era. While real life may have been gritty and violent, she enjoyed gangsters and noir on screen. But those films rarely included any people of color.

Sirisha had learned in history class that during the 1920s, South Asians were still being excluded from immigrating to the US under the Chinese Exclusion Act. In fact, it had actually restricted almost all Asian immigration. Still, that didn't mean there were zero immigrants—some had arrived before the Exclusion Act. Media and history books tended to erase the BIPOC who had existed, making it seem as if the world had only come to color recently.

This was her chance to play a part so rarely given to brown people— and come to think of it, she looked pretty dang good in her fedora. Finally, she got to be someone with plenty of derring-do. Someone who wouldn't hide but would *live*. She locked eyes with herself in the mirror. Tilted her fedora just so. Held her cigarette holder between her fingers with surprising ease.

Beautiful and dangerous.

"Heya," she said in faux-gangster accent. "I'm Scarlett Singh. Oh, you've heard the name, have ya? Those coppas can't prove a thing."

Okay, she needed to lose the accent.

"You can't prove a thing," she said again, this time with a whisper of untold ferocity. And then she blew a kiss at her reflection.

Chapter Twenty-Five

Sirisha

It was a dark and stormy night, and Scarlett Singh had a sneaking suspicion it was about to get dangerous. The Feds were already out and about, lurking.

Under the faux streetlights, Paola grinned at Sirisha in a black suit. That grin quickly transformed into a scowl, though, and she flashed her Department of Justice badge.

Sirisha closed her eyes. Tried to sink into her character. This was for Bethany. But also, for herself? She was more than her camera. More than Brie's former sidekick. She was Scarlett Singh, daughter of a notorious bootlegger and second in command of an organized criminal enterprise.

Scarlett had Agent Miller in her pocket of course, but there were new agents popping up like gophers every day. Agent Miller had always been reliable, though.

"What do you have for me?" Scarlett asked, slipping some cash to the DOJ agent.

Miller kissed the wad and tucked it into her pocket. "There's buzz that something's going down at the Jade Club tonight. I'll look the other way, but I can't guarantee that the new kid will. Agent Klein's the idealistic type."

There it was. Yet another gopher.

"Everyone can be bribed," Scarlett said. "You just have to find the right price."

Miller shrugged. "Klein isn't like the others. I'd be careful with her."

Scarlett nodded. "Thanks for the tip."

Okay, that wasn't so bad—but Sirisha felt comfortable around Paola. Could she pull this off with the other kids? Or would she clam up as she usually did in class? She felt a surge of trepidation as she came to the doorway with a sign that read THE JADE CLUB.

Sirisha wished she could write down her first clues—there were a lot of names to remember in this game! Paola was Agent Miller. Someone else would play Agent Klein, the idealistic new rookie. Noted.

You can do this. You can do this. You can do this.

Or, she could run back to her car and drive away in shame.

No, that would be ridiculous. What would she tell the Dads? Her sisters? She imagined making up some elaborate story about the party, pretending she'd gone.

I won—I solved the murder! she'd say.

Really? Avani would answer with skepticism.

You? Rani would echo.

I'm sure you did your best, Dad might say.

Good for you for giving it the old college try, Amir might add.

Okay, no. Everyone's extremely low expectations of her were not enough. She was sixteen now, not the shy baby of the family anymore.

Scarlet Singh knocked on the Jade Club door, impatient to get the night's business over with. The problem with being the head of one of the largest bootlegging operations in the Midwest was that she rarely got a night off. But hopefully her father could take the reins back soon. She'd hired the best lawyers, and an appeal for his case was in motion. Until then, she'd have to take care of dangerous situations herself—like meeting her father's rival, Randall Johnson.

The door opened partly, and a man peeked out. "Password?"

"Horned owl."

The man swung the door wide and gestured for her to come in.

The Jade Club was a mixture of seedy and classy, and everyone from the mayor and his wife to Scarlett's underlings frequented the place. Jade-green velvet curtains covered all the windows, shutting out the real world.

Sirisha took in the transformed living room. It looked truly amazing. She marveled at her classmates and the Devious crew mingling around her.

A singer crooned onstage, a girl in a tux played piano, waitstaff in jade-green uniforms circled the room carrying drinks and appetizers. Flapper dresses, fancy jewelry, tuxedoes in a range of dapper colors. Long cigarettes and feather boas. Fedoras and bowler hats. Handbags and T-strap heels.

The Jade Club glittered and shone. It thrummed with energy—and a hint of underlying violence. At least the music was consistently good and they knew how to deal with the occasional police raid (which were usually for show since Scarlett had the chief of police in her pocket.)

Scarlett's ex-lover, Tomás, brushed past her on the way to the stage. He looked flashy in a silver tux, glittery eyeshadow, and rings on each finger. Their affair had been brief but smoldering. Tomás was great in bed but unreliable in general. Besides, Scarlett's heart was too hardened to stay in any relationship for long.

"Good evening, friends and foes," he said into the mic. "I'm Tomás Knight. Please relax and enjoy the offerings at the bar. All completely legal of course; no alcohol here tonight." He winked and smiled. "Definitely none of the offerings of Randall 'the King' Johnson"—he looked pointedly at a table in a shadowy corner, where Scarlett spotted the inferior bootlegger with his minions—"and none from Ms. Scarlett 'Say Your Prayers' Singh, either." Now he looked directly at her, and there was a murmuring as the club patrons noticed that the rival bootleggers were in the venue at the same time.

Scarlett wasn't keen on the situation either.

Tomás started singing in a warm baritone that sounded like golden honey.

Sirisha hadn't known that her classmate Tomás could sing at all—but Bethany must have known. Must have tailored the role for him.

Surreptitiously, she pulled out her Round 1 card, and reread it.

You are to reveal the following clues in Round 1 (pre-death):
1. You've heard that the mayor has a new initiative to crack down on organized crime.

2. You're meeting with rival bootlegger Randall Johnson to discuss what
can be done.
Your underling JONESY will also be coming to give you a business report.
(Look out for a blue feather headband.)

Sure enough, another classmate—Lily—came up to her. She was
wearing a beaded flapper dress that draped elegantly over her petite frame
and a cute blue feather hairband rested in her dark wavy hair.

Scarlett spotted her underling, Jonesy, loitering near the bar.

"Jonesy," Scarlett said. "What do you have to report to me?"

*"Boss, more bad news," Jonesy said. "Another one of our own is out of
the game."*

"Arrested?" Scarlett asked.

*"No." Jonesy played with a strand of black beads that wrapped her throat.
"Maria Santiago was found washed up in the river."*

*"Maria Santiago?" Scarlett asked. "Is that someone whose name I
should know?"*

*"She worked in the warehouse," Jonesy said. "We think maybe Johnson is
responsible. It could be a warning."*

*"If he killed her," Scarlett said, "he's going to pay. But why Maria? Was she
important to our supply chain?"*

*"Not really. He would have had more impact if he hit . . ." Jonesy
gulped. "Me."*

Scarlett stepped forward. "He wouldn't dare."

*"One last thing," Jonesy said. "I got word that Johnson has a proxy he's
sending."*

"What, he won't face me himself?" Scarlett asked. She patted the pistol tucked in her coat pocket. "Coward. Who's this proxy?"

"The dame by the bar." Jonesy nodded across the room. "Name's Lola Vandermeer. And watch out. She may once have been a fickle silent film star, but now she's as ruthless as any gangster."

Lola had her back turned to them, but Scarlett could see a gold fringe dress with a low back.

Sirisha took a deep breath. Had she dropped her clues as she was supposed to? It seemed like Jonesy already knew the same things she did. Sirisha wanted to play the game as it was meant to be played, but she wasn't sure if she was doing it right. Still, energy thrummed through her. This was just the beginning. Her next task was obviously to meet this Lola person. As she walked toward the bar, the girl in the gold dress turned.

Sirisha froze. She wasn't Scarlett in that moment. She was a shy girl at a party in a swanky mansion on a dark and stormy day.

And the girl in front of her was none other than Lavi.

Part Three:
The Sea Is
Churning

Chapter Twenty-Six

Sirisha

Gone were the overalls. Gone was the basket of mushrooms. Gone was the wild hair blowing in the wind.

Instead, the girl in front of Sirisha was dressed to the nines. She had a faux-diamond bracelet that shimmered in the dazzling lights of the Jade Club, her low-cut fringed flapper gown draped her every curve as if it had been made for her, and her hair was now clipped into a style that had been popular in the era.

Lavi extended a white-gloved hand.

The dame was gorgeous—deadly gorgeous. With a smile that asked you to kill for her.

"I've been waiting for you." she said. "I'm Lola Vandermeer. Of course, we've met before. When you saved my life."

Wait, was that part of the storyline? No, Sirisha realized. Lavi was ad-libbing, blending real life with their characters. Very clever.

Sirisha's toes were suddenly toasty. It had been a long time since she'd felt that. Since she'd felt much of anything.

But suddenly, her heart pitter-pattered.

Her breath came a little too fast.

It was happening again! Sirisha almost wanted to cry with the joy of feeling something. Anything.

What she wanted to say: *(something snappy)*

What she actually said: ". . ."

Lavi cocked a single eyebrow.

It was another challenge. A call to adventure. And Sirisha was determined to meet it head on.

"Yes—you're lucky I was able to stop that tree from falling on you," Scarlett said, thinking back to that unexpected moment of heroism. She was a bootlegger, a gangster, the daughter of one of the most notorious men in the country. But that day, she'd done some good.

"Very lucky," Lola admitted. "We'd been shooting that silent film I was starring in, remember? It was before you'd become a criminal mastermind."

Lola was right. It had been a more innocent time for Scarlett. She'd always known her father was a bootlegger, but she hadn't had to get her hands dirty with the family money back then. Now every day felt heavy. She'd had to harden herself to the way things really worked, the darker side of humanity. And if she was honest with herself, she didn't know if she had it in her to save anyone anymore.

But Scarlett wasn't about to share all that.

"I don't know what you're talking about," Scarlett said. "I'm not involved in anything illegal."

"Sure, if you say so." Lola just smiled. "Care to have a drink with me?"

Scarlett felt herself being reeled in by the dame against her will. Something made her sit down at the bar, even though she had a hunch this game was too dangerous to play. Scarlett needed to keep her wits about her. She couldn't trust Lola. Not with the company she kept.

"I hear you've taken up with Randall Johnson," she said. "I must admit, it comes as something of a surprise."

Lola leaned forward and batted her eyelashes. "I'm open to better offers."

Sirisha felt her heart thump. Lavi was flirting with her.

Lavi was *flirting* with her.

She wanted to run screaming; she wanted to stay put; she wanted everything and nothing at once. She was scared to put her heart on the line again, but another part of her was more than ready to give romance another chance.

Her heart pitter-pattered.

Her toes were still toasty.

She desperately wished she could text her sisters and ask for help. But there was no time. If she didn't speak up now, she'd lose her chance.

Scarlett smirked. "I think I can make you a better offer than that scoundrel."
She waved at the bartender—Mandy Blossom. "A drink for the lady?"
Mandy and her husband were the owners of the Jade Club. When Scarlett's

father had been free, they wouldn't have dared serve Johnson liquor in the establishment. Now Scarlett scanned the bar, vowing revenge as she noted the bottles from her father's rival.

Lola perused the cocktail menu. "A Quick Hit, please."

"Excellent choice," Mandy said. "And for you, Ms. Singh?"

"I'll take a Pick Your Poison," Scarlett said. "With Singh whiskey and no substitutes."

"Coming right up," Mandy said. She leaned down to whisper, "Oh also, I wanted to warn you—there may soon be more competition in your business. Rumor has it that another bootlegger has entered the scene. Not Randall Johnson. A third party."

"And will you be serving this interloper's wares?" Scarlett demanded.

Mandy shrugged. "Without protection, what choice do I have? I've heard this new person is ruthless. You'd better watch your back."

"And you'd better watch yours," Scarlett returned, downing her whiskey.

Sirisha knew she was supposed to be circulating the room to learn more clues—and to drop her own. But she was having so much fun with Lavi—no, *Lola.*

Lola was a welcome amusement. Despite being a silent film star, she liked to talk and gleefully shared wild stories about everyone in the club. Her arsenal of secrets could come in handy, but Scarlett wanted to know a bit more about the dame herself.

"What brought you to the Midwest?" Scarlett said. "You were living the life of a star in California."

Lola nodded. "It was lovely. Actually, I came out here because of my mom.

She was getting remarried. I know I'm an adult and everything, but I wanted to be near her."

The way Lavi blended reality with the game made Sirisha's head spin. But she forged ahead.

"Do you like your mom's new beau?" Scarlett asked.

Lola shrugged. "He's nice enough. No complaints. It's just a new life here."

Scarlett nodded. "Big changes. But hopefully you've met some good people? And you'll meet a few more?"

"Oh, yes. There are people out here that have me intrigued. Girls with handguns tucked into their pockets. Girls who run big businesses and aren't afraid of anything." Lola batted her lashes again. "Girls who look gorgeous in a suit."

Sirisha's breath caught. Lavi was really laying it on thick. But was this just part of the game, or did it mean something more? Was the pitter-pattering of a heart hers alone, or was Lavi feeling something, too?

Lola was a relentless flirt, and Scarlett felt herself getting caught in the Hollywood starlet's grip. But that wouldn't do. Scarlett had business to attend to.

Footsteps came up behind them. It was Tennison, the chief of police. He thumped the bar. "I'll have a Police Raid."

Scarlett wasn't worried about him, though. His police raids were like the cocktail—mainly for show. He played the game: took bribes and looked the other way. Like Agent Miller, he was reliable.

"Hello, Chief," Scarlett said.

"Hello, ma'am." Tennison hesitated. He must have news to share.

Scarlett got up. As amusing as Ms. Lola Vandermeer was, Scarlett needed to keep her head cool. Gesturing for Tennison to follow her, she moved to a quieter corner.

"What's the word?" she asked.

"A couple things that may interest you. Mayor Blackburn keeps digging and digging, but his investigation isn't turning up much." He grinned.

"Thank you for your loyalty," Scarlett said. "You'll be rewarded."

Tennison nodded. "But that new Prohibition agent has been sniffing around. Real idealistic gal. She thinks she's single-handedly going to take down Singh Liquor. I tried to dissuade her, but you can tell that money isn't the way. She's hoping to create a reputation with the DOJ, and she wants to use you and your father's business to do it."

Scarlett nodded. She knew the type. It wasn't about right or wrong. Everyone had a motive, and this agent wanted to build her career. "We'll deal with her. Now, what can you tell me about the death of Maria Santiago?"

Sirisha had a hunch that the death Jonesy had mentioned was an important clue. And even though she wasn't in it to win it, she had to at least try, right?

"It was no accident," Chief Tennison said. "But maybe Ms. Vandermeer would know more about it."

Scarlett felt something in the pit of her stomach sink. She knew that Lola was involved with Randall but had hoped that she wasn't directly involved in his business.

She shouldn't judge Lola. It wasn't as if Scarlett's hands were clean. But she didn't want to have to kill the silent film star either.

Chief Tennison gave her a last nod, and then disappeared at the other end of the bar.

Onstage, Tomás leaned into the microphone. "What a beautiful night it is!
Too beautiful to go to waste." He looked like he was tearing up for a moment, but
then he got a hold of himself. "Lovely folks, get yourselves on this here dance floor!"
Then he started singing again, his voice like melted butter.
Lola tapped her shoulder. "Want to dance?"

Sirisha gulped, her head swimming. Even though the drinks weren't
actually alcoholic, reality was definitely getting a bit fuzzy. She tried to
remember she barely knew Lavi, that falling too hard, too fast might be a
bad idea, even if she was ready to feel those big feelings again.

But something about Lavi made her want to leave caution behind—
perhaps it was the sparkle in her eyes as she came up with another one of
her stories that mixed truth and fiction. Perhaps it was the way her smile
tilted a little as she waited for Sirisha to respond.

What Sirisha would have said: "Um, no thanks. I'll just sit here quietly by the bar."

What Scarlett said: "I'd love to."

Scarlett hadn't meant to say that. She was a gangster, a bootlegger, a crim-
inal with a dark past. But Lola wasn't the type to take no for an answer. She
dragged Scarlett out to the dance floor. Soon, the music of the nightclub was the
only thing that mattered, and Lola's delicate perfume the only thing that Scarlett
could focus on.

Until she spotted Johnson get up and move to the bar. He was watching
them. And Lola knew it.

"What do you see in him?" Scarlett asked. "Johnson, I mean?"

"Oh, he's got a heart of gold, once you get to know him," Lola said, squeezing
Scarlett's waist. Bringing them even closer together.

Sirisha was dancing with a girl. A beautiful girl in a gold dress that took her breath away. And despite the game, the warmth of Lavi's hand on her waist was real. The scent of her perfume and the shampoo she used. Sirisha inhaled. Gave herself to this role, to this femme fatale.

Actually maybe they were both femmes fatales?

Sirisha sort of liked that.

"I'm really glad I ran into you here," Lola continued. "And before. You know, that time you pushed me out of the way of a moving truck."

"Wasn't it a falling tree?" Scarlett asked.

"Oh, no—it was a truck. And it was no accident—someone wanted me out of the way. But you saved me."

"I don't normally go around saving people's lives," Scarlett whispered as they swayed. "It was luck."

"Maybe it was," Lola said. "But you were there at the right time and the right place. And now we wind up here together. The right time and the right place."

The music was slow, the lights were dizzying. They danced some more, twirling about the room. That fuzzy feeling was back again.

The Jade Club blinked in and out of existence. Sometimes they were all wearing silly costumes in what was still actually the middle of the day. Other times, Scarlett and Lola truly existed in their own little world, and no gangsters or murders were going to come between them.

Everyone else just faded away.

"Maybe I can help you get out," Scarlett eventually said. "You don't have to be with Johnson if you don't want to. Maybe . . . I'd be better for you."

Lola stopped dancing. "Why, Ms. Singh. Are you asking me out?"

Scarlett didn't know what she was playing at. None of this was part of her plan for the night. None of this was smart. But the dame had entranced her.

Before she could answer, there was a choking noise. A scream.

They whirled to find the mayor's wife, Edith Blackburn, lying on the floor next to one of the tables. A sickly foam gurgled out of the side of her mouth, as she clutched her throat.

"Help! Help!" yelled Mayor Blackburn. "My wife has been poisoned. Get a doctor!"

Devious actors came hustling into the Jade Club. Dressed as police, dressed as paramedics. Someone pronounced Edith dead.

"I guess we know who gets murdered now, at least," Lavi murmured.

Everyone started talking at once, some of them dropping character for a moment to squeal about how excited they were that the murder had finally happened.

"I'm so gonna win this thing," Rob/Chief Tennison said.

"Yeah, right," Tomás/Tomás returned.

"I'll win it," declared Mark/Randall Johnson.

A Devious crew member passed each of them a red card, and a bell clanged loudly. It was Mrs. Fowler from earlier, and she grabbed the mic from the stage. "If you're holding a red card, it's because you've been caught breaking character. Please come to the stage."

Tomás and Mark and several others who had been boasting about their murder-mystery solving prowess stepped up.

Mrs. Fowler smirked at them. "Obviously, you need a tonic to help you stay in character."

Another Devious crew member handed each of them a shot glass with green-brown liquid that did not look appetizing.

Tomás sniffed at it. "Ugh, is this wheatgrass?"

"In case of any allergies, the Devious crew members can provide you with a complete ingredient list."

Tomás shook his head. "That's cool." He made a face and then shouted, "Bottoms up!"

All the other red-card kids followed his lead, making retching faces as they swallowed.

Except Mark, who smiled. "Dudes, wheatgrass is awesome." He flexed his biceps to show the amazing powers of wheatgrass.

The game was back on. The actress playing Edith lay back in place on the floor.

Bethany waltzed forward, wearing a Prohibition agent suit. She flashed her badge at Sirisha and Lavi, which named her "Agent Klein."

"Well, well, well. A gangster dancing with her rival's dame," Agent Klein said, glancing between Scarlett and Lola. "I gather there's more going on here than it looks like. Not that your romantic liaisons are of any interest to me. Empty your pockets, please. And your purses."

Lola did as she was told, spilling out the contents in her clutch onto a nearby table. Nothing incriminating.

"Your turn," Agent Klein said, turning to Scarlett.

Scarlett slowly emptied her pockets, revealing lipstick. And the pearl-handled pistol. At least Edith had been poisoned, not shot.

"And?" Agent Klein said, pointing to an outer pocket that Sirisha hadn't even noticed was there. But something bulged in it.

She pulled it out slowly. It was a small glass bottle . . . labeled CYANIDE.

Scarlett knew that it hadn't been in her pocket earlier. She glanced at Lola, who cocked her eyebrow once again. Had she planted it? If so, Scarlett wasn't mad. She was impressed.

Chapter Twenty-Seven

Rani

Rani felt a little better after texting with Sirisha and Nidhi. It sounded like her eldest sis was doing what she could to make it up here, and Rani appreciated the effort. Plus, Rani wanted to hear more about this school bus Nidhi was on—and this chance encounter with Grayson. She'd always thought Nidhi was a fool for letting that hottie go. But maybe that was part of their journey, just as whatever emergency had come up today was part of hers and Raj's.

Also, Sirisha was so sweet to send the short film that had been filmed on a phone camera. It actually did manage to make the most of the medium; it was homey but also very personal.

Rani showed it to her cast. "What do you think? We can do this, right?"

JJ nodded. "Totally. It helps that I have the latest greatest phone. It has beautiful high-resolution video and even pretty decent sound."

"Yeah, but is it going to work over all that wind?" Parker asked.

It was shrieking menacingly, howling the way Rani secretly wanted to.

"That I can't guarantee," JJ admitted. "But we have a slot in the library first. Let's focus on that."

"Right." Rani's knees were still shaking a bit. Her hands were trembling. She was starting to perspire underneath her blazer and trench. But she was the director. With or without Raj. "The show must go on."

The library was only a block away. They wandered past the Better-Than-Thous, where Fiona was looking confused as Ed pointed at a crack on the sidewalk.

"It represents the fragility of our society. How civilization is slowly crumbling . . ."

Riveting stuff.

Rani smirked. Ed's style might have been perfect for Gerhardt. But Olivia Lee? Rani's idea was much more up her alley. They were totally going to kill this—and demolish the competition.

"We're totally going to demolish the competition," Ed Yi said, his voice carrying on the wind.

What? How exactly did he figure that?

"How do you figure?" Fiona asked.

"Come on, my experience means something. Yeah, Rani's script might appeal to Olivia Lee with her *rom-com*"—his voice dripped with disdain—"but she's not the only judge. I've checked out the film winners from previous years, and they were always heavy with symbolism and broad, worldly themes. So I think we're on solid ground."

Rani shook her head. Whatever. Ed Yi *thought* he was so great, and she couldn't wait to wipe the floor with him. Did he have an extremely snooty loser face? Because that was what he'd be wearing tonight!

JJ signed them in at the library. They had just a half-hour slot to shoot so other groups could get time.

"You have to keep your filming to that corner with the big windows by the children's section," the librarian said. "Good luck!"

"Thanks." Rani clutched her script and sauntered toward the back.

"Is it weird we're going to have a bunch of kids' books in the background of our scene?" Sara asked as they dropped their backpacks next to a rack full of Berenstain Bears books.

"We can work something into the dialogue," Rani muttered.

Parker glanced at her phone. "Oh, also one of the items on the list is incorporating *Catcher in the Rye*."

"The list?" Dominic asked.

Rani rolled her eyes. "Maybe if you and Sara weren't always making out, you'd have heard them talk about this at orientation this morning. Or you could have read the rules ahead of time."

Sara had the grace to look a little guilty. "Um, sorry!"

"Well," Parker said, "Since I actually care about *Remeet-Cute*, I was paying attention. And they said we have to incorporate at least five items from their list into the film. I guess it's to make sure we're really all filming today."

Rani nodded. "I don't think it should be much of a problem to fit them into the script."

"Maybe *Catcher in the Rye* is one of Layla's favorite books," Parker suggested.

"It's not exactly a romance," Rani hedged. "I don't think that fits with her character."

Dominic grinned. "It could be Nate's favorite book."

"He is a bit of a goober," Rani said, unsure whether she was talking about Nate or Raj. Okay, maybe she was feeling a teensy bit resentful that he'd abandoned her. But a good girlfriend trusted her partner. She could do that. She *would* do that.

"Excuse me," Dominic huffed. "Nate is *not* a *goober*. Whatever that means. I'll go find a copy."

As he left, Sara took out her makeup kit and started applying eye shadow to Parker's lids.

"Help me practice my lines?" Parker asked.

"You should already know them by now!" Rani said.

"I'll help you," Sara said, smudging carefully. "While I do your makeup."

"I'll take some test shots." JJ scanned the area and then went to work with their phone. "The lighting isn't great, but maybe if I adjust some settings. I also have a filter app that makes everything look amazing." They pointed the phone's camera at Rani.

"Get away from me," Rani said, even as she pasted on a big smile and straightened her shoulders. What? She couldn't help it. The camera had always loved her.

"Ooh, maybe we should use this graphic novel filter," JJ said, replaying the video of Rani from a moment before.

"I do look pretty cute animated," Rani said. "But let's keep our options open for now. We can decide what filter to use after we're done filming."

"Got it, boss," JJ said, still fiddling.

There was a filter that made everything look Technicolor. Another one that gave Rani a black-and-white noir look. She felt a little better knowing she had options. Maybe technology would save the day.

"Okay, grabbed a copy." Dominic waved *Catcher in the Rye* in Rani's face. "Also, I hid all the rest of them so the other teams won't be able to find them."

Parker gasped. "You can't do that!"

"What? We want to win, don't we?"

"Not by playing dirty," Sara said. "Put 'em back."

Dominic looked disappointed, but he wasn't going to argue with his girlfriend apparently.

Rani patted his shoulder. "I understand the temptation. But there is a rule about this. They said they purposely picked items that are available at the approved filming locations and removing those items would disqualify you from the contest."

Dominic gave her a sheepish look. "Oh man, so they thought of that already, huh? Harsh."

INT. LIBRARY - DAY

LAYLA
Okay, if you really want to learn about relationships, this
is the place to do it.

NATE
I've heard making out in the stacks is a lot of fun.

LAYLA

Um, not quite what I meant.

NATE

(shrugs)

Ah well, a guy's gotta try. But shouldn't we go to the
nonfiction section for relationship advice?
(gestures to the fiction titles, picking up Catcher in the Rye)

LAYLA

Nonfiction can tell you what to do. But fiction can show
you—it can make you really feel things in ways that no
one can easily explain.

NATE

(scratches head)

Huh. I guess that makes sense.

LAYLA

(passionate)

Haven't you ever been so inspired by a book that it
changed your life?

"This is great," Rani said. "You're both doing great. Let's review that take, JJ."

They'd rehearsed it before, but Rani truly felt like Dominic and Parker were taking it to the next level. Maybe there was something about knowing that today was the big day that made it come to life.

JJ showed them all the video—and it wasn't bad. Especially when they put it through a lighting filter that made it look so much brighter.

"I look good," Parker said, tossing her shampoo-commercial blond hair.

"So do I," Dominic said.

"Yeah, you do," Sara agreed, kissing him.

"This isn't the time, you two," Rani said. "And I don't want Nate to look like he's just been kissing someone. That would send all the wrong signals."

"Oops," Sara said, fixing his hair back in place.

JJ cleared their throat and nodded at a bit of lip gloss on the corner of Dominic's mouth.

"Got it," Sara said, immediately pulling out makeup-removing wipes and dabbing him.

"Let's do another take," Rani said.

"But it was perfect!" Dominic complained.

"Yeah, it was great, and we only have so much time," Parker said. "We should move on."

"It was good, but we're just getting warmed up," Rani said. "We should get ten takes of every scene so we have enough good footage."

"TEN!" Dominic protested. "I thought we only had half an hour to shoot."

"Okay, well, as many as we can fit in," Rani said. "Stop complaining and let's get going. Did you think a one day shoot was going to be easy?"

"Um, yeah," Dominic said, grinning his boy-band grin. "I thought all I'd have to do was smile for the camera. Not repeat the same thing over and over again."

Rani rolled her eyes. "Welcome to show business."

Somehow, she wrangled them into the next take even though Parker and Dominic both clearly wanted to move on. The next two were stiff since her leads were sulking a bit. But by the seventh, they were having fun with it. They even started improvising—and although Rani's script was amazing, she had to admit that their impromptu discussion of how classics had made them feel (like the potent ennui in *Catcher in the Rye*) was pretty hilarious. Mainly because Nate kept making it clear that he had never read a book in his life.

                              NATE
                 The veritude in Fahrenheit 451 was—

                              LAYLA
                   You mean verisimilitude?

                              NATE
                  No, it's veritude. Right?

                              LAYLA
              I think you need to change your veritude about paying
              attention in English class.

But right after that take, the lights flickered. Uh-oh. They'd better not lose power. Rani had enough problems. She motioned for them to keep going. "We'll fix it in post."

JJ rolled their eyes as if they weren't completely convinced that it could be fixed in post. Rani had faith in them though. JJ was an editing genius. Also, they had that magic filter app!

Rani nodded along as they reviewed the take. "That was hilarious. Okay, one more time. From the top."

"No way," Parker said. "Come on. You're a director, not a dictator. We've already done it twenty times."

"Just nine," Rani said.

"There's no way we only did nine." Dominic crossed his arms.

Rani didn't want open revolt from her cast. But didn't they know that doing a lot of takes was normal? It was what professionals did.

"Unfortunately, she's right," JJ said. "This would be our tenth take."

"Come on, it's not that bad," Rani pleaded. "Let's do just one more."

"Ugh," Dominic groaned.

> NATE
>
> Okay, okay, I'm at your service. Teach me all there is to know about love.

> LAYLA
>
> You'd better not be saying that sarcastically.

> NATE
>
> No, no, I'm serious. I need all the help I can get.

The lights continued to flicker as they filmed. Dominic and Parker were having a hard time not looking up at the ceiling.

"Okay, so maybe that last one wasn't so great," Rani said after they'd wrapped up. She knew there was no way she'd get them to try an eleventh take. "But that's why we needed so many!"

Dominic grumbled something about dictatorial directors.

"What's his problem?" Rani asked as they left the library.

"Oh, he gets like this when he's hungry," Sara returned. "Maybe we should have a snack break. I brought granola bars!"

Chapter Twenty-Eight

Rani

Rani and her cast found a picnic table by the harbor. It wasn't exactly pleasant outside, the wind as blustery cold as a spurned love interest, but at least it had stopped raining. Rani wrapped her hair tightly in a scarf to keep it from getting hopelessly tangled while Sara wiped down the benches with a spare towel.

"You're prepared for anything," Rani said with admiration.

As they chomped on the candy and granola bars that Sara had so kindly provided, Rani decided to forgive her for constantly making out with Dominic. Even though a minute later, they were at it again.

Parker stared at them. "I think I'd get a tongue cramp by now."

JJ snorted.

"Quick, get that shot," a familiar voice commanded.

It was Ed Yi and his crew. Ed pointed at a tree with long bare branches. The windstorm had already blown off most of the leaves, but as the blustering continued, Ed watched with odd rapture.

"What shot?" Fiona sounded confused.

"You missed it!" Ed said. "But I want you to try to get a single leaf falling. It represents death—the end of all things."

Rani smirked at JJ. "Can you believe this guy?"

JJ shrugged. "I don't know, I'm into macrophotography. It could be a cool shot."

"Uh-huh." Rani didn't want to argue with JJ, but she couldn't help it. "Look, even if you're into avant-garde stuff, hasn't this been done before?"

"Um, so?" JJ said. "How is it different from *Remeet-Cute*? It's not exactly the first romantic short film ever to be made. In fact, a lot of people would say that all romances are the same. Person meets person. Usually cisgender person meets person of the opposite sex. Hijinks ensue. Then the inevitable HEA."

Rani stared at JJ. "Well, if that's how you feel about it, why are you even working with me? Maybe you should be on Ed's cast of the Better-Than-Thous."

"The Better-Than-Whats?" JJ asked. "Look, I'm happy to be working on *Remeet-Cute*. It actually is really cute! But I'm just saying that we all draw from what's come before. There's nothing wrong with that."

Rani thought about it. "Okay, maaaaybe you have a point. A small one."

"Oh, come on!" Ed shouted to Fiona as another leaf fell. "Don't tell me you missed that one, too."

"I got the last part of the drop. I just didn't know it was going to be the next one to fall. I think that's the best we can do."

"No way," said Ed. "We need to get it from the moment it drops. That one seems loose. Just focus on it."

"We're just going to wait here for a gust of wind?" Fiona asked doubtfully.

"Yes."

"Wait a minute." Ricky crossed his arms. "I thought this film was about the death of *democracy*. Not like *death* death."

"Sure, but it's also about climate change," Ed said. "And that will lead to the end of all things. Or '*death* death' as you call it."

"Whatever. We better get babes out of this," Adam muttered.

Oh man, Rani didn't care what JJ said about macrophotography. Team Better-Than-Thou was beyond pretentious. Following Ed's demands, his crew all stood there, waiting for the perfect gust of wind. Rani inched closer because, as ridiculous as it all was, she was also weirdly fascinated.

"Don't worry," Ed said. "This will be perfect. This leaf is gonna win us first place."

"All so we can get a consultation with Olivia Lee?" Adam asked.

"Look, she's not my favorite director, but I don't like losing," Ed said.

Okay, how dare he? Rani had been pretending not to pay attention, but she couldn't help but stomp over. "Olivia Lee is a master of characterization, and you would be lucky to meet with her."

Ed looked down his nose at her. "Do you mind? We're filming."

Rani rolled her eyes. Fiona continued to stand there with her camera ready. A couple of leaves did eventually fall, though.

"Did you get it?" Ed asked.

"Um . . . not sure . . ." Fiona checked the video. "Definitely got most of the drop."

"No, no, no. We need to get the whole thing, from the moment it falls off the tree," Ed said.

Rani snorted. But then she noticed JJ was now holding their phone up to the tree.

"Seriously?" she whispered to JJ. "We can't copy them. Not that I even want to. Besides, now that we've had our snack, we need to get to our next location. Which is on the beach, skipping rocks, remember?"

"Let me just get this shot quickly," JJ said. "Actually, a leaf falling was one of the items on the email list."

"No, it wasn't."

"Um, yes it was. Check the email."

Rani did. Oh. JJ was right; a falling leaf really was one of the items. She'd missed that part. Of course, in November, it wasn't that hard to find one. But did they have to use the same tree as Ed?

"Parker?" JJ called. "Stand right here. Look pensive. We can stitch it in later—I'm sure there'll be a good moment for it."

"Hey, what are you doing? You can't film this tree!" Ed said. "We were here first."

Rani had to agree. They had been there first—but it was kind of fun to annoy him?

JJ wasn't budging. "You don't own this tree. Don't worry, we'll stay out of your shot."

Ed narrowed his eyes. "I think you could have found your own tree."

"But this one really does have that certain something," JJ said. "The bare branches, the harbor in the background. It just has a great sense of place. You have a good eye."

"Oh." Ed looked surprised but pleased. "Well, thanks. And . . . I suppose we can share this tree."

"Don't worry, I'm going for something totally different than you," JJ added.

Then Rani noticed another problem. Parker was vigorously rubbing her eyes. And they were getting more and more red.

"Are you okay?" Rani asked.

Parker rubbed them some more. "Oh my gosh, the wind is so annoying. Dust keeps getting in my eyes."

When she looked up again, Rani gasped. Her leading lady looked like a zombie literally reawakening from the dead. Although—potential plot twist—she supposed *Remeet-Cute* could have a whole different meaning than what she'd originally intended.

Postapocalyptic remeet-cute, anyone?

Eventually, Rani managed to drag her cast away from the tree and out to the beach. Unfortunately, the wind's blast was even stronger here. Plus, sand.

"This is terrible for my contacts," Parker complained, rubbing her eyes.

Rani grabbed her hand. "You're making it worse. Besides, they look fine."

That was a lie—they looked the opposite of fine. Ghastly. Definitely radioactive-plague-postapocalyptic-zombie bad.

"Um, wear these," Sara said, handing Parker sunglasses.

"She can't wear those!" Rani said. "Her expression is very important to this scene. She'll look too aloof with sunglasses."

"Well, what do you want?" Sara said. "Zombie eyes?"

"You said it didn't look that bad!" Parker wailed.

"I'd date a zombie chick if she was hot," Dominic offered.

Sara swatted him. "Not helpful."

Dominic offered his most suave grin. "Seriously? You'd make a gorgeous zombie. I'd even let you bite me."

How Sara could possibly be into Dominic's ridiculous lines, Rani didn't know. But they were at it again—making out. Okay, if she was honest, Rani would fall for just about any line Raj used.

But thinking of Raj just made her heart ache. She'd called him three more times and sent several more texts, but he hadn't responded. Whatever had come up today was certainly keeping him busy. She just wished that he would confide in her. After all the hours she'd spent listening to his woes with his parents, didn't she deserve that?

But maybe he didn't want to burden her on her big day. Yes, that must be it. He was being considerate.

"Executive decision," Rani said. "Let's do a few takes with the sunglasses and a few without. And anyway, JJ can fix the zombie eyes in post."

JJ rolled their eyes. "We can't fix everything *in post*, Rani."

"I'm sure your filter app must have a touch-up function," Rani insisted. She clapped her hands to get everyone's attention (read: Sara and Dominic and their respective tongues).

EXT. BEACH - DAY

NATE

I lied to you, you know.

LAYLA

You did? About what?

NATE

Huh? What did you say?

LALYA

(indistinguishable muffle)

NATE

I can't hear you with this darn wind.

LAYLA

Yeah, we should go—

(indistinguishable muffle)

NATE

Go where?

LAYLA

(indistinguishable muffle)

They replayed the footage, and it was awful. They couldn't hear a thing.

"Oh no," Rani said. "This is a disaster."

She glanced at JJ with beseeching eyes.

"Don't even think about saying that we'll fix it in post," JJ warned. "Because we can't."

"I wasn't going to!" Rani protested.

Okay, so she totally had been. But they'd work around this. They had to.

Chapter Twenty-Nine

Avani

*D*espite her exhaustion, music was still swirling in Avani's head as she and Fernando made their way into the vintage elevator. It seemed like half the class managed to fit inside it on their way to lunch. Beside her, Fernando looked wiped. Normally, they'd be commiserating about what a workout it had been, but they'd also be totally up for more. Today, they were just quiet.

She'd been so convinced that all she and Fernando needed was a little music and dance to bring them together. But if Avani was honest with herself, she'd had more fun dancing with other people than she had with him. Maybe it was because there was no pressure. Maybe it was the newness of dealing with someone else's style.

Was that it, then? Had her relationship with Fernando run its course?

Avani felt herself panicking, her body flushing with heat, her heart beating too fast. In an elevator full of people, she'd never felt so alone. And so frightened.

When the doors opened and everyone filtered out, Avani stayed. She needed to figure out how to breathe again. She wasn't someone who had a lot of panic attacks (or any, for that matter), and she didn't know why today was the day. Fernando didn't even notice. By the time she got out of the elevator, no one was left in the lobby. She finally spotted him chatting with Greta and Trent outside.

Avani gathered up the pieces of herself, all that confidence she usually wore like salty sea air. "Greta and Trent. You two were amazing!"

"You both looked great, too," Greta returned with a big smile.

Avani chuckled. "You don't have to lie. We were all over the place."

Greta shrugged. "No way! I thought you were great. Sure, it wasn't perfect, but we have the whole rest of the afternoon to figure it out. That last lift was totally kicking our butts, too, by the way."

The wind started howling, making it difficult to continue talking. Greta wrapped a scarf around her head to stop her hair from flying before cheerfully waving goodbye to them. She shouted something Avani couldn't quite make out but was probably the equivalent of *See you after lunch!*

Avani's ponytail kept her own hair in place, but the icy wind slapped at her ears. She pulled the hood of her parka on, but another gust of wind blew it right back off. She couldn't stay warm today.

"Where should we go for lunch?" she asked through chattering teeth.

Fernando rubbed his eyes. "You know, I think I want to take a walk."

"A walk?" Avani moaned. "I'm so tired and sore. We've been moving nonstop since eight in the morning. How can you want more of a workout?"

"That's fine, you can get some rest," Fernando said. "I need to be alone for a bit and clear my head."

"Oh."

He didn't even want to have lunch together? On a day that was supposed to be all about them? That hurt.

"I'll meet you back at the studio, okay?"

"Um. Okay." Avani swallowed. "How long will you be? You want me to grab you a sandwich?"

"Nah, I'll get something," Fernando said. "Don't worry. I'll be back in time for the rest of the workshop."

And then Fernando was walking away, the ends of his cashmere scarf floating like wishes in the wind, all those wishes that Avani wanted to share with him but didn't know how.

All A.L.O.N.E. in a bustling coffee shop, Avani ate a sandwich that tasted like cardboard. She drank a latte that was as bitter as the chill wind outside. She stared at her stacks of books. Why had she brought so many for a dance workshop? Was she really going to read *99 College Essays That Wowed Admissions Staff at Top Universities*? Did she plan to memorize all the court cases she needed to know for the next debate tournament?

She pulled out her journal. (One of three she'd brought.) This one was for all her long-term plans. She'd created pages for all the clubs and organizations she'd decided to join this semester. Full of energy at the beginning of senior year, she'd jotted down thoughts after the first meeting or event for each one. But as the weeks had worn on, she'd stopped having time, despite the fact that the whole reason she'd taken on so many things was to figure out what she wanted to do next year.

As Avani peered at her unfinished grand plans to map out a career for herself, her life stretched out like a desolate highway across nothing but dirt and grass. All she'd accomplished with her numerous clubs was delaying having to think about the future by keeping herself busy—and in the process, she'd completely alienated her boyfriend.

Avani flipped to a fresh page in the journal. Wrote the words that were brewing in her heart. The ones that she knew to be true: *I failed. (At my relationship with Fernando AND deciding what to do with my life.)* She underlined *failed* three times, just to emphasize it. Journaling was truth telling, and she couldn't lie to herself or the pages of her notebook.

She'd been avoiding something else today, too. It was time to face it now. She twirled her pen and began scribbling: *Do I have ADHD? Is that why I can't decide things? Why I get interested in everything at once? Why I have so much energy all the time?*

Okay, so there it was on paper. Not just a fleeting thought. And if it was important enough to articulate that way, it was important enough to give serious consideration to. She pulled out her phone and started researching. There were videos on the web of real-life people who had it, and as she watched, she started to see more and more of herself in them. There were different types of ADHD, and not everyone had all the same symptoms. But Avani checked a lot of the boxes: poor time management, an excess of energy, disorganization, impulsiveness. Even hyperfocus, when she was really into something.

The videos also mentioned that to get a formal diagnosis, she would need to talk to a doctor. From what she could tell, it seemed like a long process, though, and who had time for that? Maybe she would one day. But for now, it made her feel better just to realize that she *might* have ADHD. It was an explanation, and there was a whole community online of people who had it, too. She wasn't alone. She thought differently than most people, certainly, but there were so many others who thought the way she did.

"You okay, honey?" asked a kindly woman as she bussed the next table.

Avani didn't think she could speak, but she managed a nod.

The woman glanced at all of Avani's books. "Wow. Senior?"

"Yep," Avani said. And then, unprompted, she started sobbing. She couldn't stop; it was a river of disgusting snot.

"Oh, honey. You poor baby!" The woman handed her a stack of napkins. "Whatever is the matter?"

Avani blew her nose as loudly as the ferry horn. "I have no idea what college to go to or what I should major in or anything!"

The woman patted her back. "You know, my daughter graduated high school last year, and she had no idea, either. I told her that it's perfectly okay not to have everything figured out yet! It's okay to just be undeclared. Don't pressure yourself too much."

Avani felt embarrassed. "I feel like I'm the only senior I know who is totally overwhelmed."

"I doubt that," the woman said. "Daughters don't often take their moms' advice, but in this case, mine actually did. She's undeclared as a freshman and just having a ball taking whatever classes interest her."

Undeclared. Undeclared?

"But eventually, I'll have to decide," Avani said.

The woman looked thoughtful. "Will you? People change careers even at my age. I used to be a nurse, but it wasn't for me. I actually like serving pie a lot better. In fact, how about a piece right now? Blackberry with ice cream on the side? It's on the house!" She leaned in conspiratorially.

"Don't tell anyone this, but I know our sandwiches aren't the best. The pie is top-notch though."

"That's okay, you don't have to. . . ."

"I insist."

And with that, the woman bustled off. She returned moments later with a slice that smelled like heaven. As Avani worked her way through the sugary delight—which was not at all like cardboard—one thing had become clear: She needed to quit all these clubs. They weren't getting her any closer to deciding on what she wanted to do for college.

After she'd left not a single crumb, she gathered her things. She still had another twenty minutes. Maybe she should return early and practice a bit? But her feet had other ideas. Leaves swirled around her, chasing her down the streets of Friday Harbor. A few tangled in her hair.

She pulled out her phone, realizing she hadn't checked it since that morning. And oh wow, Raj had bailed on Rani? What a jerk. How could he do this to her twin?

Avani considered texting Raj and demanding answers. But then again, if he hadn't offered much of an explanation to Rani, why would he respond to her?

Instead, she messaged her sisters.

Avani:

Rani, I'm so sorry Raj bailed! How's the filming going? Did you find some other equipment, or opt for the phone camera? I'm sure you can come up with something great either way.

Rani:

Thanks. I'm actually having fun—though my cast keeps muttering that I'm a dictator. Can you believe it? Me? I'm totally easygoing! How's the workshop?

Avani:

It's not good. I don't think things are working out between me and Fernando. I think that he's probably going to break up with me. He didn't even want to have lunch with me. He said he needed space!

Rani:

Whoa. We're grabbing lunch right now at a cafe in the marina. I don't have a lot of time, but want to come in for a quick hug?

Chapter Thirty

Rani

Dominic was getting hangry and muttering about dictatorial directors again.

"Let's get some lunch," Sara said diplomatically.

Rani really didn't want to—when she got into something, she really got into it. Food, drink, and rest were mere afterthoughts. But her cast and crew obviously did not feel the same, because the next thing she knew, they were in a cute café near the harbor. She had to admit, it was pretty nice to be back inside where it was warm and dry. Another shower was passing through, the windstorm continued to menace the trees, and the café was crowded with customers.

The place was cozy, but maybe a little bit too cozy. Instead of tables and chairs, it had clusters of sofas. Sara and Dominic were playing footsy while eating their sandwiches. Rani was just glad they weren't making out, though her hopes that it would last were low.

She devoured her sandwich and gulped down her mocha, and then she was restless to get back to it. "Come on guys, let's get going."

JJ patted her shoulder. "Actually, our slot to film at Café Helix is at the hour. It's only a block away, so we have plenty of time."

"We could run through our lines and blocking, then," Rani said.

"I need more of a break," Parker said, craning her neck as if looking for someone in another part of the café.

Rani turned to see whoever Parker might be noticing. Oh. Ed's cast was at the counter, ordering. Parker and JJ both bounced up to go chat with them. Rani couldn't believe they wanted to speak to the enemy, yet Parker was openly flirting with Adam while JJ and Fiona had their heads ducked together, whispering something.

And naturally, now Sara and Dominic were making out.

Something was definitely in the air. Normally, Rani would be happy to play matchmaker, but today she really wished her cast and crew would save it for the big screen. (Okay, probably the small screen, but whatever. Any screen.)

Rani texted Raj again:

> We're making great progress with Remeet-Cute. Turns out modern filter apps can do a lot for phone videos! It's very impressive—not having proper camera equipment won't be that much of a problem after all.

Did that sound passive-aggressive? It probably did. She was just telling the truth, but she was also pointing out how much they'd been counting on him.

Rani backtracked.

> I mean, I just don't want you to feel bad. Your family emergency is obviously important. Hope you're all okay.

She waited breathlessly, hoping that this time he'd respond. Say something, anything. But nope, not even three dots. He was either totally ignoring her or totally absorbed in whatever he was doing. Whatever this non-medical family emergency was.

Then Avani texted. Oh boy. Fernando had said he needed space? Rani didn't exactly have that much time before she had to get back to filming, but she knew her twin needed her. She quickly asked Avani to come meet her. The Official Love Guru was not going to fail her twin this time. She got up to grab a second mocha for herself, and one for Avani—

And nearly ran right into Ed.

"Oh, hey," he said. "How's your filming going?"

"Um, fine," Rani mumbled. "No, I mean, it's great. Really good. You?"

"Um, also fine. Really good." Ed offered her a tight smile.

Rani didn't know what else there was to say. They were rivals. Competitors. Her cast might be fraternizing with the enemy, but she was the fearless leader. She had to set an example. "Well, I was just going to order a second mocha."

"Oh yeah, cool," Ed said. A little awkwardly. He scanned the room for his cast. But Fiona was now at a two-person bistro table with JJ. Parker and Adam were getting sugar packets for their drinks and making eyes at each other. Ricky had plopped down at the cluster of sofas where Rani had been sitting, his nose in a book. Dominic and Sara actually stopped making out for a moment to ask him about his book, though they were holding hands all cutely.

"Um, you can sit with us," Rani heard herself offering.

So much for not fraternizing with the enemy. But right then, as he clutched a metal stand with his order number on it, he looked like a kid searching the cafeteria for a friend.

"Oh," he said, "Thanks."

Did Ed actually sound a little bit relieved? She must have imagined that. He was way too snooty to be wondering if he had anyone to sit with.

Rani ordered her second mocha, passing JJ and Fiona deep in conversation about a band she'd never heard of. Parker and Adam were still flirting. When she returned to the sofas where Ed, Ricky, Dominic, and Sara were sitting, Ed had his laptop out, and she couldn't help but glance at the screen, where he was playing their footage of leaves falling.

He'd narrowed in on one and was editing it to slow it down.

Dang it—his ridiculous leaf was kind of beautiful.

"Not bad," she found herself saying.

What was she doing? She was supposed to crush him and his team. Not give them compliments.

He looked a little embarrassed. "I may have spent way too long getting this footage. And pissed everyone off. I think Fiona is ready to kill me."

Rani had to laugh. "Oh my gosh, Parker and Dominic were getting so angry because I wanted to get so many takes. But I really do think it's a good idea to have plenty of footage so that JJ has options when they edit."

Should she be telling him this? The guy who said the phrase *rom-com* as if it were a dirty word?

"Makes sense," Ed replied. "I will have literally no options. Just one falling leaf."

He looked so forlorn. And maybe not that snooty? Rani had to admit, it felt good to have another director to confide in. She'd been feeling seriously at odds with her cast, which was weird because during their rehearsals, everyone had seemed so focused and into it.

Maybe she should take pity on Ed. He didn't know what he was missing when it came to romances, obviously. Someone needed to show him that there was more to life than depressing movies with long, boring windmill shots.

Plus, he looked so dismayed at his lack of footage.

Rani chuckled, patting his shoulder. "Well, at least a falling leaf is on the list of items to include."

"Luckily," Ed said. "I'll get one point."

"Everyone's gotta start somewhere."

"I guess they do."

Rani realized she still had her hand on his shoulder. WHY WAS HER HAND ON HIS SHOULDER? It was strange how natural it felt, and she quickly snatched it back. Before today, she'd probably be worried about being infected by pretentiousness. But . . . well, maybe he wasn't as bad as she'd thought. Maybe she was overthinking his rom-com comment.

"Why are you worried, anyway?" she asked. "I thought you'd won three film contests already back in 'LA.'" She put LA in air quotes. Because it did sound very Better-Than-Thou.

To her surprise, Ed laughed. "Would it help if I told you they were all teen-only contests, like this one? I've never competed against professionals or anyone who's been to film school."

That did make Rani feel just a tiny bit better. They chatted some more, and to Rani's utter shock, it wasn't terrible. They weren't so different in some ways. Very into their art. Rani smiled to herself. Yes, she was an artist, and the rom-com haters could go jump in the freezing November waters.

Also, Ed could be self-deprecating in a really funny way. Like when he admitted that he didn't entirely get through all of Gerhardt's *The Howlers at Dawn*, either.

"Don't get me wrong, cinema verité has its merits . . ." he said, "but there were *a lot* of windmills." Then he looked embarrassed. "Of course, that's what everyone will think of my leaf."

"At least your film is only seven minutes long. Wasn't *The Howlers at Dawn* like three hours?"

"Three and a half," he returned with a chuckle.

Ed's sandwich and coffee arrived, as did Rani's two mochas. (What had happened to Avani? Her twin still hadn't shown. . . .)

Rani took a sip and tried not to be too obvious about staring at Ed. The moment of truth was upon them. Was he going to eat his sandwich snootily? Like with a knife and fork? With his pinkie in the air?

Just as he reached for it, the café lost power and they were plunged into darkness.

Chapter Thirty-One

Avani

Avani jogged to the café where Rani and her crew were eating. She really wanted her twin's advice. But as she peered into the window of the café, she stopped. Rani was staring at her phone—and she looked so lost. Avani had been totally judging her sister for not getting her mental SOS messages, but she had to admit Rani had her own stuff going on. Clearly.

Also, Rani was offering to meet her now, even when she had her own crisis going on. Shooting a short film was enough of an undertaking, but now she had to deal with no cameraperson and a boyfriend who was possibly being a jerk? Rani would make some excuse for Raj, of course. She always did. Avani knew that Raj's parents had been struggling, and that he had a large family, and that unexpected things sometimes came up. It was just that with Raj, things seemed to come up kind of a lot?

Maybe that wasn't fair, but Avani wanted better for her twin. Maybe if she won this film contest, she'd focus more on her Hollywood career instead of on boys. Romance was wonderful, but it wasn't everything. Then again, what did Avani know? She wasn't exactly doing so well in either romance or life. Plus, she'd been spending a lot of time obsessing about Fernando lately, too.

She stood outside the window, watching as Rani sat down next to her nemesis, Ed Yi. The two of them always had fireworks between them in school—snipping and snarking at each other for things like their interpretations of *Wuthering Heights*. Strangely, right now it looked like she and Ed were . . . playing nice? Ed even sat down at Rani's table. They kept talking. Pleasantly?

Oh. My. Movie tickets.

Rani laughed. She actually *laughed*. At something Ed just said, no less. And now he was chuckling, too. She put her hand on his shoulder.

WHY WAS RANI'S HAND ON ED'S SHOULDER?

Avani had her nose practically pressed up against the glass. She was no Official Love Guru, but if this wasn't a meet-cute or a remeet-cute (or an enemies-to-lovers slow burn or some other trope?), then Avani didn't know what was. All she knew was that her twin looked happy. Rani was probably talking about filmmaking—something she loved—with a guy who loved it, too. Okay, so Ed Yi didn't seem like the rom-com type, but they clearly both loved stories.

Hence their endless bickering about *Wuthering Heights*.

Maybe it was time for Rani to let Raj go and find someone new. Avani couldn't possibly interrupt her chance. She turned around, heading back to the workshop. Unfortunately, she'd gotten so fixated on what Rani was up to that she'd lost track of time. And now she'd be lucky to get back before the class started back up.

Avani ran, wind and leaves and wishes nipping at her heels.

Chapter Thirty-Two

Nidhi

The bus sped along the freeway toward Seattle. As a headache bloomed, Nidhi was definitely regretting the two mimosas she'd had, even with Hannah's water bottle. Or was it Shawna's? The girls looked and acted like triplets.

Well, Nidhi was grateful to them, even if the marching band was very much into cheerfully and relentlessly singing.

So far, they were making their way through:

- their school fight song (at least it was short)

- "The Wheels on the Bus" (wasn't that for kindergarteners?)

- "One Thousand Bottles of Beer" (definitely just to torture her and everyone else)

Would Nidhi ever escape? Both the singing and high school life? The singing grew even louder. Nidhi wanted to stab someone but restrained herself and chugged the rest of her water instead.

Somehow, John had passed out on the seat behind Nidhi and Grayson, and Lena was calmly reading. (How? There were literally 826 more bottles of beer!) Lucas was in the aisle across from them, his back to the window, his knees pulled up since there was no space for his long legs. Hannah, Shawna, and Anna were a few rows ahead, turning around every once in a while to gawk at Grayson.

Nidhi might have thought being back on a school bus would feel nostalgic, but instead it just felt super awkward. She'd never really *felt* like a teen. She'd always been so absorbed with running the inn, her future as a baker, and being a big sister—acting like a de facto adult. The notable exception had been those vulnerable moments where she'd floundered with her feelings over her ex, Matt, and then later, with Grayson.

That had been part of the appeal with Suresh; she'd wanted to get some sexual experiences under her belt. And it had worked—she did feel like less of a fumbling kid in that department now. Strangely, though, she still couldn't imagine what it felt like to do it with someone you maybe, kind of, sort of . . . loved?

Love. Now that was a word Nidhi was still unsure of. A word that sat heavy on her tongue. She could easily say that she loved her sisters and Dad, of course. But a boy? A *man*? No, that still felt very far away, just like a marriage proposal.

Yet fate kept throwing her back together with Grayson. Literally. The bus lurched into a different lane, making her slide into his warmth against her will. Though it wasn't entirely uncomfortable.

"You okay?" he asked.

Did Nidhi imagine it, or was his voice a little husky? Maybe he wasn't entirely uncomfortable, either. But she wasn't here today to rekindle their flame. Her mission was to meet with Professor Cunningham and then book it to Friday Harbor to hopefully catch Rani's film.

"I was not made for buses." Lucas groaned, stretching out his legs a bit and nearly kicking Nidhi from across the aisle. "The things I do for love."

Lena snapped a picture of him on her phone. "There, now you have proof of this bus ride for Keith! Are you excited? We'll be there soon!"

Lucas smiled. "I can't wait! Wanna come with? Keith's playing a two p.m. concert in Capitol Hill today. We should just be able to make it."

"Perfect," Lena said with delight. "Our son has class then anyway."

Nidhi checked her phone. Oh good, Professor Cunningham had gotten her message that she was on her way. "I can make it, too. My advisor said she could meet me at four."

"Fantastic, thank you!" Lucas said. "I could use the moral support!"

"Are we invited?" asked Hannah loudly.

Shawna pouted. "Pleaaaase?"

Lucas laughed. "What about the Harvest Parade? The whole reason you're going to Seattle? And dressed like vegetables? It's at the same time."

Hannah sighed. "Fine, I guess we can't make it. But I love proposals."

Anna sighed, too. "I can't believe we have to miss it."

"We never get to do anything fun," Shawna agreed.

"Yeah," Anna said. Then she grinned secretively, elbowing Hannah. "I mean, except for last night."

Hannah laughed, glanced at the parent chaperones a few rows ahead, and shushed her. "Last night? We didn't do anything last night. Just homework and going to bed early at your place."

All three of them burst into giggles.

Luckily for them, their vegetable costumes really did hide their clubbing outfits.

Grayson paid them no mind. He was quietly drawing in a large sketchbook, seemingly lost to the rest of the silliness around them. She peeked over his shoulder, but he shut it swiftly.

"Come on, I've seen your work before," she reminded him.

Pink tinged his cheeks. "I'm not ready to share this one."

"Not even with me?" She batted her lashes and pouted. Uh-oh, was she flirting with him? She'd gotten a little better at that in recent months, too.

Still, she knew she shouldn't. She wasn't planning to stick around.

But Grayson seemed charmed. "Well, okay. You twisted my arm."

He opened his journal, and Nidhi was back in a secret haven with Grayson, one full of art and light and swirling gorgeous colors. He'd sketched a map of the world, all the places he'd traveled, and overlaid it with sweeping architecture, bustling city streets, and amazing landscapes. There were depictions of quaint villages and colorful festivals and everyday people doing everyday things. He must have spent hours on this one page alone, and now he was still working away at adding texture with a deep blue color pencil.

"It's really hard to get the details in here," he said. "I need a bigger area to work with."

"What you have is amazing," Nidhi said. "I can't believe how much you've included."

"Actually, I've got more pages with close-ups," he said, flipping through the journal. He'd zoomed in on different parts of the map with finer lines and his signature swirling colors.

"These are exquisite," Nidhi said. "It would make such a cool mural on the side of a building. People could stare at it for hours and still not see everything."

She flipped through some more, soaking in the magic of his work, scenes from all over the world. A fountain in Italy. A surfboard in Namibia. A camel in Rajasthan.

"That camel!" She laughed, remembering their day together in the Thar Desert when he'd been there all too briefly.

"He had it in for me." Grayson chuckled.

Nidhi arched her brows. "Well, I think you know what you need to do."

Grayson looked so genuinely confused, with his forehead crinkling up. "Learn how to befriend a camel?"

She chuckled. "Not what I was getting at. Though it's sort of funny how your endless charm doesn't extend to camels. What I meant was that you have to get an official commission. This map is way too detailed to put up in one night."

"First of all, you think I have endless charm?" His dimple flashed sexily.

She punched his arm. "You know you do."

He winked, then got serious. "Do you think I could actually get an official commission? Who would hire me? My only experience is secret."

She thought about it. "Yeah, that might be a problem. Even though I think the pages in your journal should be enough to impress anyone, I'm learning that's not how the art world works."

"You are?"

"Yeah." Nidhi smiled. "I made a friend in New Delhi who works for an art collective. She helps fundraise for the artists, finds them commissions or paid work, and generally just helps raise awareness for them. It's really cool."

"Perfect," Grayson said. "She's hired."

"Actually, she focuses on local artists in New Delhi. But maybe if you went to art school, you'd get mentors who could help you?"

"Art school?" Grayson said. "That sounds like a lot. Besides, you know I don't want to do this professionally."

"Why not?" Nidhi asked. "Why not take something you love and make a career from it? You're so talented. Even if art school isn't your thing, maybe find some other way to get involved in the art world. There must be organizations here in the US that could help you."

"I have no idea how to even get started with that," Grayson said. "Besides, maybe people like the Skull's work because it's so mysterious. They might not care about it if it was just . . ." He shrugged, not finishing.

"Just you?" she guessed.

"Yeah."

For a moment, they listened to the rumble of the bus, the infernal singing, and the giggling of Shawna, Hannah, and Anna.

Nidhi glanced at that handsome face she knew so well. He hid behind that facade of good cheer, but he was actually terrified, she realized. After all this time, after all his success, after even going viral as the Skull, Grayson was still afraid to put his work out there.

NEW DELHI—SEPTEMBER

In between chopping and sautéing with her mentor, Shiv, Nidhi exchanged flirty messages with Suresh. She loved cooking, she loved the heady scents of new spices. But today it was all contributing to something new inside her. Instead of making her hungry, the aromas seemed to have acted as an aphrodisiac. This was a new kind of restlessness, an excess of energy that could only be excised with warm skin against hers.

Nidhi and Grayson had always kept things PG. Whenever things had heated up between them, she'd held a part of herself back. Had always made sure things cooled down before they got too excited. After all, they'd been headed their separate ways, and she didn't want to get entangled in something she couldn't distance herself from. Of course, rationally she understood:

- sex was only something physical

- they already *were* entangled emotionally

- Grayson would always mean something to her, whether or not they slept together

Yet a part of her guessed that making love would change everything irrevocably. And she was afraid of that. Weirdly, she didn't feel the same about a no-strings-attached encounter with Suresh. They'd been texting since the night of the concert.

For now, she nodded and smiled at Shiv's directions, while everything inside of her tingled. For now, she pretended a sumptuous feast with her family was all she wanted—when what she was hungry for was something else entirely.

Nidhi had only one glorious afternoon alone with him, skin to skin. The tingling feelings had been unleashed, had exploded in a passion that was so physical and in the moment that Nidhi could not think of another time when she'd felt so viscerally alive.

Well, perhaps that time she'd stood on a wakeboard.

Both had awakened something inside her that she hadn't expected; she felt like a butterfly rising out of its cocoon. A little uncertain, a little new to this colorful world. But spreading her fledgling, beautiful wings to flutter and fly and make her own way.

As they lay in bed, basking in the aftermath, Nidhi wondered how to tell him that she didn't want anything more. They'd been careful, used a condom. It was double protection, since Nidhi had also gotten on birth control before leaving for India. Maybe a part of her had known she was ready to take this step, even if she hadn't been with Grayson.

Yet now she worried that she might break another heart. She'd done it before, with Matt, and it had left her aching and wishing there was a way to make it all easier. Less messy. But she'd learned the hard way that you couldn't keep everything neat and tidy, no matter how hard you tried.

Better to get it over with. Like a Band-Aid.

She swirled her finger against the hair on his bare chest. "That was fun. But—I just want you to know that I'm . . . not looking for a relationship."

Suresh caught her hand, smiling a small smile. "I kind of figured."

"You did?" she asked.

Phew.

"Yeah, the way this all went down . . ." He gestured at the hotel room they'd rented. "It wasn't screaming commitment. Besides, my mom is probably talking to a matchmaker about my marriage prospects right now."

Hmm. Nidhi felt a little deflated, but she didn't have any right, did she? She hadn't wanted anything more—so why did she expect him to pine after her? Was she the kind of person who *liked* breaking hearts?

No, she couldn't be that way. She wouldn't take it personally. But she would allow herself to be surprised. "Already? You're still in college."

"She thinks it's better we start looking now," he answered, playing with her fingers. "I'm from a conservative family. It's always been the plan."

"You're okay with that?" she asked.

He traced her back gently. Even now, her spine tingled at his touch. "Yeah, I am. Anyway, they wouldn't force me to marry anyone I don't like. I'll meet several prospects and hopefully hit it off with one."

It was how Nidhi's mom and dad had gotten together, a tradition to fall in love after the wedding. Growing up as she had, it was hard to fathom, but she knew that Dad had never regretted it. That her parents had, in fact, fallen in love. She hoped for the same for Suresh.

"I'm glad my first time was with you," she said.

"It was my first time, too," he said. "Thanks."

Thanks. Nidhi thought ruefully how strange that sounded. But they were like ships on the open sea, crossing paths briefly before charting their way to different places. Guided by stars and wind and goals just out of reach.

At long last, the Nathan Hale Veggie Lovers arrived in Seattle. Nidhi watched the skyscrapers go by as they passed downtown and got off the freeway in Capitol Hill. The streets here were busy, twisty, and steep. Buses turned precarious corners, pedestrians jaywalked, and cars honked impatiently. It was dark and cloudy, and the wind shrieked over the city sounds. Yet when the school bus pulled over at Cal Anderson Park, there were still plenty of people loitering and laughing, walking their dogs, and even playing basketball. Wind certainly wasn't bothering these Seattleites.

"We've arrived," one of the teachers announced. "We have time to rest and have a quick lunch before the Harvest Parade begins. It will start here and head along Pike Street into downtown."

It felt freeing to finally be in Seattle. Seeing Grayson's sketchbook and his beautiful mural idea had reminded her that she was here for a reason today. That she had a project of her own that was burning in her soul.

Also, the singing was over—and she hadn't resorted to physical violence. It was an accomplishment.

Everyone made their way off the bus, and the Veggie Lovers spread out in the grass with their sack lunches. While wearing their vegetable costumes. (Apparently, veggies needed sustenance, too.)

Nidhi's stomach rumbled. "Do we have time to grab some food before the concert?"

"Totally," Lucas said. "It's just a ten-minute walk from here."

Hannah, Shawna, and Anna ran up. "Don't leave without saying goodbye!"

"I wouldn't!" Lucas said. "I owe you three."

"In that case," Hannah said, "I want an exclusive."

"An exclusive?" Lucas asked. "For what?"

"Record your proposal and send it to me. I want to post it on social media. It's going to be so adorable! It'll go viral."

Lucas laughed. "I'm not sure I want my proposal to go viral."

"Oh, trust me, you do," Shawna returned. "You'll get free stuff out of it. I'm serious. Besides, Hannah is a major influencer."

Anna chewed her gum loudly. "Seriously. We're the best publicity team you could get."

"I don't doubt it." Lucas chuckled. "Okay, since you helped us, I'll give you the exclusive footage. Nidhi, you'll shoot it, won't you?"

"Sure," Nidhi said. "No problem."

The first floats for the Harvest Parade headed out, while the vegetable marching band of Nathan Hale High waited their turn. At last, the teachers called on the students to take position. They were definitely struggling in their costumes as the wind blew furiously. A girl's kale leaf cap went flying and landed right in front of Nidhi.

"Here you go," Nidhi said, handing it back. The girl pushed the kale cap back on her head, tied the strap so it would stay in place, and kept marching.

Hannah, Anna, and Shawna were bringing up the rear. They waved goodbye to Nidhi and the stranded travelers.

"Good luck, Lucas!" Hannah shouted. "This one's for you!"

They gestured to the rest of the vegetable marching band, who started playing "Marry You" by Bruno Mars.

As the Veggie Lovers marched down the street, even the parent chaperones and teachers waved goodbye, and Mr. Highly Unusual actually shouted, "Go get 'em, tiger!" to Lucas.

Nidhi smiled. "Come on, let's do this."

Chapter Thirty-Three

Nidhi

Lucas led them into an old brick building that housed local classes and productions. Maybe it was the jet lag, but Nidhi hadn't really thought about why Lucas's boyfriend was having a concert in the middle of the day. However, the truth dawned on her when they entered the venue. The concert was in a big space with exposed brick and long, tall windows and gleaming wooden floors. And it was filled with young kids and their parents.

"Is this a kids' rock band?" Nidhi whispered to Lucas for confirmation.

He grinned. "Yeah, Keith's really good, too."

Nidhi was delighted. "Oh my gosh, that's so adorable."

"What's their band name?" Lena asked eagerly.

"The Electric Boogers," Lucas answered with a smile.

They all laughed. The space was packed with restless, roaming kids. Parents who seemed to be glad to let their progeny run around like little monsters. A concession stand kept the kids hopped up on candy and juice boxes.

Children gathered up front near the stage, some sitting criss-cross apple sauce, some lying on their stomachs, some chasing each other. A steady din of babies crying in the background completed the chaos. After a few minutes, the lights dimmed and flashed. Babies continued wailing, but the older kids got excited.

A woman came onstage and said, "Welcome everyone! So glad you could make it! Are you ready for a rocking good time on this very windy and stormy Saturday?"

Kids continued to scream and laugh and shuffle around restlessly, but the woman seemed to know how to corral them. "I didn't hear you! Should I send the band back home? Nobody likes dancing or music?"

"I do!" yelled a little girl.

"Me too!" said another girl.

"Me three!" screamed a boy behind them.

His mom returned, "Jacob, what did we agree about being too loud?"

"But Mom, you're supposed to be loud at a rock concert!"

The woman on the stage overheard. "He might have a point. Let's all scream as loudly and wildly as we can for the Electric Boogers!"

This was their chance to do what they weren't allowed to do at school or at home. To be as boisterous as they wanted. They made the most of it, screaming at the tops of their tiny lungs.

Nidhi got it, got those restless feelings, that push to be that thing nobody wanted you to be. Free and wild and full of chaotic energy. Like that windstorm outside.

When the frenzy was just right, the Electric Boogers stormed the stage.
"Oh, I see him!" Lena said excitedly.

Sure enough, Nidhi recognized Keith from Lucas's picture. He was
playing bass guitar. The group began rocking out, the singer belting his
lyrics with fervor:

You know what's the best time?
It's gotta be screentime
There's really no good time
other than screentime.

Mama says put down that iPad
Mama says turn off the Switch
Mama says forget the cell phone
Or she'll throw them in a ditch

But Mama
Mama
Mama
I gotta have my iPad
Gotta have my Switch
Gotta have my cell phone
Or I'll scream in my highest
Piiiii—iiiiii—iiiiittchhhhhhhhh!

The singer's voice went low, then higher, then into a true squeal. And
the kids followed along with their own musical yelps.

"I need to hide before Keith sees me," Lucas whispered. "I've got it worked out when I'm going to do it—they'll play a couple of songs and then ask for requests. That's when I'll pop in with my own 'request.'"

"That's so sweet," Lena crooned.

"You got this," Grayson said.

"I'll have my cell phone ready," Nidhi said. "For Hannah's exclusive."

John just high-fived him, and then Lucas disappeared to wait for his big moment. Nidhi softly sang along to the song and shook her hips to the beat. (It was really catchy!)

Keith looked like he was having a blast up there, too. Someday—in the extremely far future—if Nidhi ever got married, she knew she'd want her partner to love kids. She'd always adored playing with Anita, her ex's little sister. She was so sweet and funny and couldn't resist bopping to a good tune; in fact, she'd listened to the same Bert and Ernie album over and over again.

And . . . was also a fan of the Electric Boogers?

Yep, Nidhi spotted Anita's tiny face screaming along to the song. Matt was right beside her.

Grayson noticed them, too. "Hey isn't that . . ."

"Yeah, it's Matt," Nidhi said. "I guess I should say hi."

"Want me to come with?" Grayson asked.

"Sure," she said. Nothing like talking to her ex alongside yet another ex. Sort-of ex, she reminded herself. As they walked through the crowd, Grayson sang along to the next song, which was about chores. Another cute and catchy number.

Nidhi tapped Matt's shoulder. "Hey, Matt."

"Nidhi?" he said in surprise. Then he broke into a grin. "Hey!"

It had been a long time, and old feelings came tumbling back. Matt would always be her first boyfriend, her first love. The boy whose heart she knew she'd broken last year.

"Hey back!" She reached for him, and he responded with a big, warm hug.

It felt good and weird at the same time.

"I thought you were in India!" he said, laughing. "Why are you listening to the Electric Boogers?"

She laughed, too. "What? It's great music. Just my style."

Anita—who had been too engrossed in the music to notice their conversation—screamed, just absolutely screamed, and came tumbling into Nidhi's arms. Her excitement was so cute, and Nidhi remembered all the good times they'd had playing together. She and Anita hadn't seen much of each other after the breakup, which was really too bad.

"The Electric Boogers are my favorite band," Anita confided. "Don't you love this song?"

The band had now moved on to a song called "Substitute Teacher":

We'll get him with a whoopie cushion!
A bug in his soup!
A fake spider in his desk!
We'll throw him for a loop!

When it comes to playing pranks
We're the best
And we'll get him to quit
Cuz WE ARE PESTS!
WE ARE PESTS!
WE
ARE
PESTS!!!

Anita cackled and screamed "Pests" and ran off.

Nidhi and Matt both laughed and exchanged a fond look. It was really familiar, and Nidhi had a sense of déjà vu for a moment, as if somehow they'd done this before. They hadn't, of course, not exactly, but they'd definitely exchanged many a look over Anita in the past.

"She's a lot bigger now," Nidhi said.

"And just as much a handful," Matt said ruefully. "But man, it's good to see her enjoy this so much." A small pause. "So, you're back?"

Oh dear. That moment of relaxation was gone, and they'd returned to the awkward place.

"Just for the week," Nidhi said.

"Ah." He nodded. "Well, I'm heading back to Orcas for the break. Maybe we can get coffee sometime?" He glanced at Grayson. "I mean, we all can, if you want."

"Yeah," Nidhi said. "We should."

Things had been weird all senior year, but Nidhi really did want to push past it. Now Matt was in college and she was in India, and it seemed a shame if they couldn't at least have coffee together.

Of course, Matt probably thought she and Grayson were still together. Correcting him would be ever weirder though.

"Well, I'd better go find Anita," he said. "I don't want to lose her in the crowd."

"Of course," Nidhi said, shooing him away. "We'll catch up."

She couldn't help but watch him amble away, her heart squeezing. He wasn't a bad guy; he never had been. She didn't know why things hadn't worked out, except that she'd felt like a butterfly fluttering uselessly inside a glass jar.

The Electric Boogers now had their kindergarten crowd completely riled up, just the way they wanted it.

"Okay, all our fans out there, you know this one, don't you?" the lead singer shouted.

You gotta pick, pick, pick
the lint in your belly
Gotta pick, pick, pick
anything a little bit smelly . . .

Grayson held out his hand. "May I have this dance, Ms. Singh?"

She took it and he led her to the less crowded area in the back of the room. Then they were swirling and twirling to the music, to the wild screams of the kids. Nidhi had never been a great dancer particularly, and she'd always been a bit self-conscious of that fact. But inspired by the kiddos around her, she let go.

"You gotta pick, pick, pick the lint in your belly!" she sang.

"It's smelly and kinda gross!" Grayson returned.

He twirled her away from him, and then back in. Her breath was coming fast, her face was flushed, and when she twirled into him, she let herself fall right into his chest.

"I missed you, Nidhi," Grayson said.

"Missed you too," she breathed.

And she had. Suresh was fun. Matt was her first love. But there was something about Grayson. That first kiss of theirs came back: the one with chalk on their fingers and a smudged skeleton behind them and rain falling fast. The world had been wide open to them, and they'd kissed with abandon. Kissed even though she knew he was going his way, and she was going hers.

And now, with the raucous melodies of the Electric Boogers, he looked at her in the way that he always had. That look made her want to cancel all her big plans. Made her want to give up everything—just to be with him.

"Nidhi," he whispered, and she suddenly, desperately wanted him to kiss her the way he'd always kissed her.

They were warm and flushed, and music and laughter whirled around them.

"And now, we want to ask if anyone has a request," the singer shouted.

It was Lucas's cue. Nidhi sucked in a breath, then quickly pulled out her phone, remembering her promise to record it all.

Right on time, Lucas shouted from the doorway. "I have a request! I have a request!"

"Lucas?" Keith said in surprise.

The rest of the band started playing the tune of "Marry You" by Bruno Mars, just like the Nathan Hale Veggie Lovers. The stage lights flashed in blue and red and purple, and a group of kids threw bright red rose petals into the air and all over the stage.

The spotlight landed at last on Lucas. He got down one knee. "Keith, would you do me the honor of marrying me?"

Lucas's face was something Nidhi would never forget. So full of hope and love and light. And Keith did not disappoint. He was crying, crying like a little kid. And he ran right into Lucas's arms. "Yes, of course I will, you sneaky bastard!"

And they hugged and kissed, and the parents were going wild and the kids felt the excitement and started going wild, too, and the place was so full of energy and happiness. Nidhi squeezed Grayson's hand. This was such a pure moment, one with dancing fairy lights and rose petals and glimmers of magic.

Keith dragged Lucas to the stage. "Who else wants to come up here and sing with us?"

Lena and John pointed at Nidhi and Grayson and shouted, "These two do! These two do!"

Nidhi held on to Grayson with one hand and took Lena's in the other. "If I'm coming, so are you!"

"If you insist," Lena said, laughing.

Moments later they were up on the stage, the crowd cheering. Though Nidhi usually avoided the spotlight, she had to admit this was hardly intimidating since it was mostly a bunch of over-sugared kids. The band got to work vamping the crowd. Anita dragged Matt up onstage, too. Other kids rushed up to join. Even the parents were getting into it, and soon the whole auditorium was scream-singing:

But Mama
Mama
Mama
I gotta have my iPad
Gotta have my Switch
Gotta have my cell phone
Or I'll scream in my highest
Piiiii—iiiiiiiiii—iiiiiitch!

Grayson caught her eye, and she had a floating, magical feeling, up on stage with a bunch of rowdy kids and the Electric Boogers. There are moments in your life that freeze even when they're loud and full of movement. It's a breath, it's a heartbeat, it's the act of living.

And Nidhi knew that for her, this was one of them. A gorgeous, golden frozen moment.

Chapter Thirty-Four

Sirisha

Bethany/Agent Klein read Scarlett her rights and brought her to the jail for questioning. It was actually Bethany's dad's office, but for now it was an interrogation room—if an interrogation room had an extremely fancy mahogany carved desk, lots of plants, and family photos. They'd added a few touches to make it feel like one though: windows with jail bars and Most Wanted signs. There was even a fake newspaper clipping on the arrest of notorious bootlegger Sandeep Singh.

"Take a seat," Agent Klein said. "You may as well make yourself comfortable since we'll be here awhile. Would you like some water?"

"Certainly," Scarlett said. "But I won't talk, you dirty coppa."

"I'm with the Department of Justice," Agent Klein reminded her. She handed Scarlett the water glass. *"I'll give you a moment to get your story straight,"* she added darkly, before slipping out the door.

Before leaving, Bethany had passed Sirisha her next character card, but Sirisha took a moment to relax, to *feel*. It was exhausting, staying tough and witty all the time for the sake of her character. Still, it was better than feeling nothing, than being numb, than trying to protect a broken heart.

Who was she kidding? She was falling in love with the game. Flirting with Lola. Bantering over made-up stories, holding her own in a battle of words. And she thought she was maybe even getting to know the real girl, too. Lavi was obviously feeling lost and lonely after her mom's new marriage and moving to Orcas. It was a huge change from Chicago.

But while the two had danced, Scarlett had said what Sirisha might have been too shy to: "If you're feeling lonely, kid, you know where to find me."

She felt so aflutter around Lavi, and it was like the early days with Brie again. That wanting, the hope that someone else wanted you, too. She wasn't sure when things had fizzled with Brie, couldn't quite put her finger on it. But somewhere along the way, her toes had stopped feeling toasty. Her heart had stopped pitter-pattering. She didn't want to be one of those people that only liked the newness of a relationship, that was always trying to return to those feeling of first kisses and shy glances. She knew the real thing took more than that.

But Brie had made the choice for her, and now Sirisha had to pick herself back up. Try again. Even when her heart felt so tender she wasn't sure what it could take.

She put that aching tenderness away for the moment. Took a look at the latest character card.

MURDER AT THE JADE CLUB

Scarlett Singh Character Card - Round 2
During this phase of the game, you should reveal the following clue:

A few weeks ago, you saw Edith Blackburn kissing a man who wasn't her husband.

Okay, things were definitely getting interesting with this mystery. Edith Blackburn had been fooling around. Maybe Mayor Blackburn learned of her infidelity, and he was actually the one who poisoned her. But that seemed kind of obvious. Sirisha had a feeling she'd have to keep digging.

If Avani were here, she'd be so on top of getting everyone's clues. Would probably somehow manage to get them to reveal the clues that they weren't supposed to reveal, as well.

Something new seized Sirisha then.

She wanted to win.

She wanted to *win*.

She wanted to surprise everyone. They thought she was just the shy girl behind the camera. But she could be more than that. She could be a notorious gangster named Scarlett Singh. She could be the kind of girl who picked up clues that people hadn't meant to drop, the kind of girl who put everything together.

Bethany/Agent Klein came back in. "Are you ready to answer my questions?"

Sirisha tipped the front of her fedora down to hide her eyes for a moment—before jumping up and hugging Bethany as hard as she could. "Happy birthday! This game is really fun! I love the part you gave me!"

Bethany grinned. "Thanks! I was worried it would be a little too out of your comfort zone and you'd hate it."

"I was worried about that, too," Sirisha admitted. "But I'm actually getting into it. I guess I like being someone glamorous and dangerous."

"And hot," Bethany added. "You totally look hot in that costume. And I saw you dancing with my cousin Lavi. Lola in the game. You two looked great together."

Sirisha's cheeks heated. "She's your cousin?"

"Yeah, well, step-cousin," Bethany clarified. "Her mom married my uncle. Now they've moved to Orcas, too."

"I didn't know Paul Rivers is your uncle!"

"Yeah." Bethany laughed. "He is. But he's kind of a recluse and doesn't come over much. We had no idea he was even seeing anyone and suddenly he was like 'Surprise! I got married!'"

Sirisha chuckled. "Love works in mysterious ways."

"Don't I know it," Bethany said. "Anyway, I know this move is probably a lot for Lavi. But I love it here, you love it here. She'll love it here eventually, right?"

"I hope so."

Bethany's eyes glinted. "You two were flirting a lot."

Sirisha felt her cheeks go hot.

"I know things have been rough for you since the breakup with Brie," Bethany continued. "So maybe I'm projecting a bit about you and Lavi because I want you to be happy. But even if that doesn't go anywhere, I hope you know Paola and I are always here for you."

Sirisha hugged her again, tightly, her face crushed against the dark blue Prohibition agent suit. "You're not that intimidating of a DOJ agent, you know that?"

Bethany squeezed her, and then said in a serious voice. "Oh, I haven't even gotten started yet. That was good cop. Now you have to deal with bad cop."

Sirisha offered her a smirk. Seriously, how was she doing this? She wasn't sure she'd ever smirked in her life. Lavi/Lola was a great teacher, though.

"You ain't getting nothing out of me." Scarlett crossed her arms, put her feet up on the desk, and tilted her fedora again.

"Is that right?" Agent Klein gave her a dark stare. "Trying to pin it on the mayor, are you?"

"I didn't say that."

"You said his wife was cheating on him."

"Yes."

"The mayor's an upstanding fellow, unlike some of the scum that walk these streets." Agent Klein pinned one last glare at her. "Besides, maybe it was this feller you saw her with. Who was it?"

"I didn't get a good look," Scarlett hedged. "But I think you should question Mayor Blackburn."

"My job is to focus on Prohibition cases," Agent Klein reminded her.

"Oh, so you'll gather evidence on innocent people like my father and me," Scarlett returned, "but not a true murderer?"

Agent Klein scoffed. "There's nothing innocent about you or your father. As long as you continue your illegal bootlegging operation, I will be after you every step of the way. If I can't prove you're violating the Prohibition Act, I'll prove you murdered Edith Blackburn."

Scarlett stood up. "Because selling a little liquor and murdering someone are exactly the same? I'll have you know that an innocent girl, Maria Santiago, was murdered. And what're you doing about it?"

Agent Klein shrugged. "That's not my jurisdiction."

"Apparently, justice isn't your jurisdiction." Scarlett narrowed her eyes.

There was a knock on the door, then Agent Miller walked in. "Bail has been posted for the suspect."

Agent Klein glared at Scarlett. "Don't think this is over."

"Oh, I won't." Scarlett glared right back.

Chapter Thirty-Five

Sirisha

Sirisha wandered back into the Jade Club, where lunch was being served. Real lunch. The Devious crew wandered the room with trays of delicious-smelling food. Bethany and her family had not skimped, and there was a lovely variety of seafood, sushi, salads, and fancy finger sandwiches.

As Sirisha loaded up her plate, Tomás started singing another song. She was surprised he had any voice left, honestly. But he looked happy up there—and great in gold eyeshadow, too.

Scarlett took a seat at a corner table of the room, alone. She couldn't believe she hadn't caught Lola planting that poison vial in her pocket. But now she knew where Lola's allegiances lay. She didn't doubt that Randall was behind it all. He was serving a warning to the mayor, framing Scarlett, and eliminating the competition with one blow. It was diabolical, it was wretched, and Scarlett wasn't going to let him get away with it.

Lola plopped down on the seat across from her.

"You have some nerve," Scarlett said.

"I didn't plant it on you," Lola returned. "I swear."

Scarlett shook her head. She'd been entranced by Lola, and she was impressed by her sleight of hand. For all Scarlett knew, Lola had probably hired someone to pretend the truck was going to hit her, just to reel Scarlett in. And she'd fallen for it: hook, line, and sinker.

Mandy Blossom appeared at the table. "Can I get you two anything? We're dry at the moment. Feds crawling all over this place. Edith Blackburn's death didn't do us any favors."

"It'll probably die down soon," Scarlett said, then gestured at Lola. "And also, she's not staying."

"Come on, love," Lola said, "There's something between us, don't you think?"

What Scarlett wanted to say: "Go to hell."

What she actually said: "Go to hell."

Mandy glanced between them and then artfully scurried toward other customers.

"I want to help clear your name," Lola said.

Scarlett narrowed her eyes. "Why?"

Lola touched her arm. "Because then maybe you'll trust me."

Scarlett had no intention of trusting anyone but herself. But perhaps she could use Lola.

"Fine," Scarlett said. "Can you talk to Randall and find out if he had anything to do with the murder of one of my people? Name was Maria Santiago."

Lola nodded. "I can do that. But what does it have to do with clearing your name?"

"I don't know. Maybe it's not related. But that poor girl died, and I need to know why."

The Jade Club was suddenly plunged into darkness. Tomás stopped singing, the piano player messed up a few notes before stopping. There were muffled voices and people bumping into each other. Someone dropped a glass onto the hardwood floors.

"Don't panic, everyone," Mrs. Fowler called. "Please, find a place to sit down and be safe for a moment."

Sirisha felt some whiplash at suddenly being thrust back into reality. But the mansion really had lost power—apparently the windstorm couldn't be kept at bay simply by imagining they were in another time and place.

That smirk that came so easily to Scarlett was gone, and Sirisha looked awkwardly across the table at Lavi. Lavi didn't glance at her at all, but instead watched some of the Devious crew open the windows, letting the light of day into the room. What there was of it, anyway. The sky was charcoal, trees thrashed outside the window. Windstorms weren't uncommon on the island—and neither was losing power. But it was a shame that it had to happen in the middle of Bethany's party!

Hopefully it was just a brief interruption, and wouldn't end the game. Sirisha desperately wanted to go back to Scarlett and Lola, to see this thing that was sizzling between them through.

"I'd better go check on Bethany," Lavi said.

"I'll come with you," Sirisha offered.

"Okay."

Suddenly, whatever spark they'd had between them felt completely lost. Sirisha's heart hammered in her chest. She'd thought she was getting to know Lavi, even if it was through the game. But now the other girl was looking at Sirisha as if she were a stranger. Which she kind of was?

It was confusing, and the dousing of daylight wasn't helping. Sirisha followed Lavi to where the birthday girl stood glumly next to one of the windows.

"Hey." Sirisha put a hand on Bethany's shoulder. "I'm sure we can keep going without power."

"We do have a generator," Bethany said. "I'm going to check with my parents about getting it up and running." She nodded over to them—they were playing the club owners, Mandy and Ryan Blossom.

"It's nice that they're playing parts, too," Sirisha said.

Bethany gave a tentative smile. "Yeah, it's cool of them. I really, really wanted this party to be one that people remember, you know?"

Sirisha nodded, even though she couldn't really imagine having a birthday this elaborate, with all the costumes and decorations. But it was lovely, and she had to admit that she was glad to have been invited.

If only Lavi would catch her eye again.

If only that spark between them could be real.

Sirisha's heartbeat pitter-pattered helplessly. She knew it was up to her to make that connection, to make this real. But she didn't know how.

Rani:

> Oh great, the power is out in the cafe where we're supposed to film! This was my most important scene. What do I do? JJ's phone camera can't handle this kind of low light.

Sirisha:

Oh no. Can you change the script? Have it located somewhere else? Btw, the power is out here, too. They're trying to get the generator on.

Rani:

I wish this cafe had a generator. The thing is, I'm pretty sure most of Friday Harbor has lost power. So we can't exactly go anywhere else. And outside it's so windy you can't hear a thing.

Rani:

I did come up with the idea to include the storm in the short film. But do you think it's okay if you literally can't see anything for the whole cafe scene?

Sirisha:

Sure! You could make an artistic statement with the darkness. Just get their voices in the scene, and maybe a few shadows. There's an intimacy to that.

Rani:

LOL, I can't believe I'm saying this but yeah, you're right. It sounds like something Ed Yi would do.

Sirisha:

Haha. Sounds like something I would do, if I'm being honest.

Rani:

Oh sure, take his side.

Sirisha:

I'm ON YOUR SIDE. You can do this. Get your pretentious, artsy dark cafe scene! It's going to be great.

Rani:

Thanks. How's the murder-mystery party going?

Sirisha:

Pretty good actually. Hopefully, things will get rolling again soon, if Bethany's dad can get the generator on.

Rani:

You're having FUN? At a party? There's a pretty girl there, isn't there?

Sirisha:

Hey, I could have fun at a party without a romantic interest involved!

Rani:

Whatever. When I see you tonight, I'll get all the REAL details.

Sirisha:

Why does that sound like a threat?

Rani:

It's a promise. Good luck with your non-love-interest.

Sirisha:

Good luck with your film. I wonder why
Avani and Nidhi aren't responding.

Rani:

AVANI? NIDHI?

A few minutes later . . .

Rani:

Okay, clearly they're in dire trouble. But I have to
finish my film so they'll have to save themselves.

Sirisha:

Glad you've got your priorities straight.

Ten minutes passed. Then twenty. Bethany's parents weren't able to get the generator working. Sirisha and Lavi sat awkwardly at a table by the "bar." Sirisha racked her head for something to say.

"Are you excited about meeting everyone at school on Monday?" Sirisha asked.

Lavi shrugged. "Yeah, I guess so."

Awkward silence. Yikes. As Lola and Scarlett, they hadn't had this problem. Sirisha swallowed, determined to keep trying. Questions were always the key to opening someone up.

"Do you play a sport?"

"Nope, not interested."

"Any clubs you want to join?" Sirisha asked.

"Haven't thought about it."

Sirisha was getting a little frustrated. Couldn't Lavi at least attempt to make conversation? Or maybe the game was just a game, and Lavi was not-so-subtly trying to tell Sirisha that.

She gave it one more shot. "I'm in photography club. I'm usually the one hiding behind a camera."

Lavi glanced at her. "That's cool. Listen, I need to use the restroom. Hopefully, they'll get this party back up soon."

And then the girl that had warmed Sirisha's toes was walking away. Lavi definitely had no interest in her. It had all been part of the game. Suddenly, Sirisha no longer cared about winning.

She also couldn't help but notice that her classmates were getting restless. Mark—the kid from Sirisha's photography club who was playing rival bootlegger Randall Johnson—was grumbling he had better places to be. Rob/Chief Tennison was passing a flask around, and Sirisha didn't think that it was a prop with faux liquor inside. In fact, there were some people getting very silly in the lounge area of the Jade Club.

Paola and Bethany sipped sodas at a table nearby.

"Oh God, this is a disaster," Bethany said. "They're getting wasted. A bunch of other people are going to leave."

"We won't let them," Paola said.

Bethany put her face in her hands. "The whole reason I had the party during the day was because there's some big senior party that Kiera is throwing tonight. I knew I couldn't compete."

"Ugh, who cares about hanging out with a bunch of seniors?" Paola said. "I mean, they're so boring right now. All they talk about is SATs and college applications."

"Thanks for trying to make me feel better, babe," Bethany said. "But I'm pretty sure that's not what anyone will be talking about at Kiera's party tonight. They'll be playing beer pong and hot tubbing. And her parents won't be there."

Sirisha had definitely heard about Kiera's parties from Avani. She had to agree—there probably wouldn't be a lot of college application talk.

What Sirisha wanted to say: "I think your party is so much more unique and fun."

What Scarlett said: "I'll bust their kneecaps if they even think about leaving."

Bethany burst out laughing and hugged her. "Thanks."

Paola dragged Bethany to get some lunch, but Sirisha noticed that Mark actually was heading out the door, a gaggle of girls following after him. She didn't even stop to think—she ran after them. He and the others were heading to his car, but she sprinted in front of them, waving her arms wildly like a kid who thought they could fly.

"Come on, guys," Sirisha said, "You can't leave. This is for Bethany."

"It's not my fault the power went off," Mark said.

"They're working on it!" Sirisha said.

"Look, we waited a long time," Jenna Roberts replied, flipping her hair.

"Yeah!"

"This is boring!"

"The party is over."

"You still have your costumes on," Sirisha pointed out.

Jenna looked down at her peacock-blue flapper dress. "Yeah, it is pretty great. I really don't want to change."

"So don't. It'll be worth it, I promise," Sirisha said. "Mark—you're so good at portraiture. Why don't you keep people entertained by taking their pictures? People will want to remember their costumes."

Jenna perked up. "Ooh, yes, please. This dress is really too nice not to post online."

"Why don't you do it?" Mark returned, crossing his arms. "You're the San Juan Snaps prize winner, remember?"

She hadn't actually won, but she'd placed. And Mark had been weird about it in photography club ever since.

"Don't be bitter about that, Mark." Sirisha said. "Your portfolio was amazing."

He didn't look convinced.

"Seriously!" she said. "Awards are super subjective, but I was really impressed with your work. That one with the sailboat that looked like it was going to tip? You caught it at just the right moment. And the lighting was out of this world. I loved it."

She wasn't lying—she really had been impressed.

"I thought it was good," he muttered. "But I didn't bring my camera anyway."

"You can use mine."

Mark's eyes widened. "You'd really trust me with your precious camera?"

Apparently, flattery would get you everywhere.

Sirisha nodded, grabbing it out of her car and handing it to him. "Thanks, Mark! You're the best!"

Chapter Thirty-Six

Avani

R eady to finish the workshop, Avani rushed into the glittering lobby. She spotted Fernando waiting for the elevator, a tired expression on his face.

"We're late." Avani glanced at her phone to confirm. Yep, it was already five minutes after they were supposed to be back.

He shrugged. "I'm sure it's fine. Just a couple minutes."

They both waited silently. Beautiful vintage elevators weren't exactly fast.

"How was your, uh, walk?" she asked, her voice tight.

It suddenly occurred to her that her thoughts about Rani and Raj might apply to her and Fernando, too. That maybe it was time for them both to move on.

But the idea
    was just a bit
        devastating.

"It was good," Fernando said. "I was thinking—"

DING.

The elevator door opened.

"Yeah?" Avani said, stepping in.

"Well, I—"

"Hold the door, please!" cried Greta from the lobby door, followed by Trent.

"Oh, just go," Avani whispered. "They can catch the next one."

She wanted to hear what Fernando had to say.

"That would be rude," Fernando returned, pushing the door-hold button.

Avani bit back a response as Greta and Trent rushed into the elevator.

"We went to this restaurant that was really slow," Greta explained. "Lisa did warn us about the island time, didn't she? Anyway, at least the food was excellent. Hopefully, she won't hold it against us."

"It'll be fine," Trent said, his voice barely more than a grunt.

The elevator doors closed behind them, and Fernando punched four.

"Yeah, I'm sure it will be." Greta was smiling the smile she seemed to have permanently plastered on her face. Trent reached for her hand.

Even though Greta and Trent were nice, the pure perfection of them as dancers and as a couple made Avani feel like barfing. They looked like they were meant to be onstage together, the perfect height difference between them, both so beautiful they looked like CGI.

Double barf.

As the elevator lurched upward, Avani's thoughts rioted. She and Fernando were supposed to be the perfect couple, not these two. She'd always been overly competitive—she knew that—and now all she wanted to do was obliterate Trent and Greta on the dance floor. (If Fernando was really gearing up to break up with her, they could at least go out with a bang.)

Also why was this elevator so darn slow? It seemed to take forever to reach the second floor. Then, floor three. Somewhere between three and four the lights flickered. And a moment later, the lights went out altogether. It was pitch-dark, and the elevator careened to an awkward stop.

Trent cursed softly. Fernando let out a groan.

Avani set her phone to flashlight mode. Greta's smile was frozen like she was a creepy wax figure. Avani pushed the button to open the door, but nothing happened.

"The lights have been flickering all day," Greta finally said. "I'm sure we'll get the power back in a moment."

Fernando tapped the emergency button. "Just in case."

There was a staticky sound, and then a woman's voice came on. "Hello, this is building management."

"Hi," said Fernando. "We're in the elevator, and it's stuck."

"I'm sorry to hear that," replied building management. "Please remain calm. The power in the building is out, and the elevator requires electricity to run. I'm sure it will return momentarily!"

Avani didn't move, as if remaining as still as possible would make the power come back sooner. A glitch that they could all forget. (Although now maybe she was the one that looked like a creepy wax figure.)

A minute passed, then another. Then fifteen more.

Standing perfectly still didn't appear to help. Avani banged on the emergency button again. "Excuse me, it doesn't seem like the power is coming back on."

More static. And then—"Unfortunately, the power is out in the whole town. We've informed public works of the issue, but it might be a few hours before they're able to fix it."

"A few hours? That's ridiculous!" Avani said. "Can't someone come here and pry open the top? There has to be some kind of emergency exit!"

There was a pause. "I apologize for the inconvenience. We will do our best to get someone to help you. Hopefully, it won't take long."

Hopefully, the woman had said.

But Avani could tell that she didn't think it was likely.

She slumped to the floor. "Sounds like we'll be here a while."

Suddenly, the spacious elevator didn't seem quite so spacious. Greta looked unsure about the floor, but eventually sat as well.

Trent slid down and put his arm around her. "Well, there's no one I'd rather be trapped in an elevator with than you."

The two of them shared a deep, lingering kiss, and then pressed their foreheads together. Triple Barf. They'd better not get into a full make-out session in front of Avani or she was going to absolutely scream.

Especially since Fernando had crouched as far from her as possible in a spacious-but-not-that-spacious elevator. He wouldn't meet her eyes.

This was totally fine. Wonderful, in fact. Exactly what she had been hoping for today.

Cue internal screaming.

Avani:

You will not believe what happened! I'm trapped in an
elevator. No, scratch that. I'm trapped in purgatory.
This is obviously karmic punishment for something, but I
don't know what. Someone please come rescue me!

(!) Message not delivered.

Part Four:
The Clouds Are Thickening

Chapter Thirty-Seven

Avani

Avani wanted to yell
    stomp her feet
        throw an absolute fit
          like a toddler
      this wasn't fair—

Ugh, how had she ever thought this ridiculous elevator was beautiful? Now it only seemed like a death trap. And this whole situation was *not* as romantic as getting stuck in a barn with Fernando last year.

Especially since Greta and Trent were giving each other vomit-inducing googly eyes in the shadows. Avani had left her phone on flashlight mode, pointing the intense beam at an empty spot on the wall so as not to hurt anyone's eyes, but maybe darkness would be preferable.

Meanwhile, Fernando was slumped in his corner. Not even pretending that he wanted to be here with her. He was four feet away, and yet it seemed like an entire ocean was between them. And she didn't know how to sail across it.

Listless, Avani pulled one of her trusty journals out of her bag. It was calming to write her thoughts there, to let the pages soak them in.

And nobody to judge her
    when her mind skipped
        from thought to thought
messy
    and unfiltered
whirling
    like leaves
      in a
        windstorm

"Ooh, have you decided where you're applying?" Greta asked. She gestured at the *99 College Essays* book sticking out of Avani's bag.

Avani tried not to be annoyed by the question. It was only polite chitchat.

She sighed. "I've gotten about a million brochures from all over the country." She rummaged through the bag, pulling out a bunch of them. Glossy photos boasting of historic buildings and tree-lined campuses and an array of strategically diverse students apparently having the time of their life.

Greta leaned forward to rifle through them, too. "Ooh, Chicago looks nice. Or New York. Or Los Angeles. You could really up your salsa game there! I mean—" Greta looked guilty for a moment. "Not that you aren't awesome already."

"Right." Avani didn't want to talk about the disastrous workshop at the moment. "How did you decide where to go to college?"

Greta shrugged. "The in-state tuition kind of sealed the deal. UW is a great school. It was an obvious choice."

Trent nodded. "Yeah, totally. I thought about one of the UC schools, but UW just made a lot of sense."

"That's a good point," Avani returned. "College is so ridiculously expensive. I was hoping to get some financial aid or something."

"You probably will," Greta said. "You should definitely apply to a lot of places. More chance that something will line up. Are you and Fernando coordinating?"

"I mean, not yet . . ." Avani glanced at Fernando, who was still scooted into his own corner. She had no idea what he was thinking. They'd talked about college, in the abstract. But they'd never really made a plan. Which was maybe weird? Shouldn't they talk about coordinating, so they'd have a chance to be together?

"I emailed you a list of where I wanted to apply in September," Fernando said, crossing his legs. "But you never responded."

"You did? I don't remember seeing it." Avani searched her email on her phone but couldn't find it. She added the key word *college* and then— oh, there it was. In a folder she'd marked as RESPOND LATER. The truth was, she had all these mechanisms in place to remind herself of things, but even they weren't perfect. "Oh, okay. Yeah, you did. I guess I forgot."

"Apparently," Fernando said.

There it was, that edge to his voice—that strange distance between them again.

"Why didn't you ask me about it?" Avani asked, annoyed.

"I thought maybe you didn't care," Fernando said.

Avani was hurt. "Of course I care. I just wasn't ready to decide everything that early."

Fernando didn't say anything, but she could tell that she'd hurt him, too.

She lowered her voice. "I'm sorry."

"It's fine," he said. "There was no hurry at the time. I was planning to check back eventually."

"Okay . . ." She looked over his list. UW was in there. So were some other colleges in the area. And a couple more scattered throughout the country. More or less what she was thinking.

"Maybe I should just apply where you're applying," she said. Honestly, it would be a relief not to have to think about it more. With the added bonus that they'd have a chance of being together next year.

"If that's what you want to do," Fernando said. "But I picked a lot of these schools because of their agricultural science programs, just so you know. So I can help with the family business."

"Oh."

Was that what she was supposed to be doing? Choosing a college based on her major? Which totally made sense—if you knew what you wanted to do. Fernando was barreling along with his life plans while she'd been consumed in a fog of panic and debate tournaments and horticulture podcasts. Well, no longer. She was going club-free from here on out.

"I can help you come up with a list if you want," Fernando said gently. "I feel like big colleges with a lot of programs will suit your interests."

She glanced back at him in surprise. Despite the darkness, she could see something of the boyfriend she once thought she knew. The one who really understood her like no one else did.

"Thanks," she said softly. "That's a good idea."

The elevator was quiet again. She didn't want to break that fragile connection between them. Instead, she reached for his hand. He squeezed back.

It was a start.

Time had no meaning. They'd been trapped for at least an hour by now, maybe more. No texts were going through. Building management had reported that they were having trouble contacting the elevator maintenance person.

"I know," said Greta. "We should play a game!"

"A game?" Fernando returned doubtfully.

Avani rested her head on his shoulder. The smells in the elevator were starting to get to her. After all, they'd all been working up a sweat all morning. She now regretted her liberal use of the rose-scented spritz; the mingling scent of rose and perspiration was cloying. Also, she didn't want to say anything, but hot Trent definitely stank the worst.

At least he and Greta didn't have some magic superpower that made them smell like vanilla cupcakes.

"Do we have to?" Trent moaned, rubbing his eyes. "I just want to take a nap."

"Yes!" Greta said emphatically. "We can't just sit here! This is our chance to get to know each other. Maybe the universe brought us together for a reason."

Trent snorted. "The universe didn't bring us together. This building is just really old and there's a windstorm."

Greta elbowed him. "Whatever. We're doing this. So wake up!"

"I vote to nap," Trent said. "Or at the very least, to sit and sulk."

The way he said it tugged a giggle out of Avani. "I mean, sitting and sulking does have its merits."

Greta chuckled, too. "Okay, how about sixty more seconds of sitting and sulking. And then, we'll play a game. Bond. Make the most of this ridiculous situation."

Uh-oh. Avani was detecting all sorts of camp counselor energy. She knew the type—they would not rest until the games had been played, the team building had been completed, the good vibes had been had. Well, Avani was her own type, and that type was the kind who won—at whatever she did. She'd been feeling inferior because Trent and Greta were better dancers. Maybe kicking some Trent and Greta butt would energize her.

"I'm in," Avani said.

Greta squealed with excitement. "Yesss! How about Two Truths and a Lie? Everyone know that one? You have to tell two true statements and one statement that's a lie. Then the rest of us try to guess which one is the lie. Cool?"

Avani exchanged a look with Fernando: *We're stuck with this monster.*

Fernando offered a small smile. *We'd better repay her with winning.*

One thing about Fernando: He was no slouch when it came to competition, either.

Greta didn't wait to see what anyone else said. She just rubbed her hands together, an evil peppy glint in her eye. "This is going to be so fun!"

Oh dear.

Greta went first. "Let's see. Here are my three statements. Number one: When I was little, I wanted to be a teacher because my actual teacher Mrs. Rose was not like a rose at all but very mean and took sick pleasure in yelling at us. Anyway, I wanted to be the opposite of her—a nice teacher who actually liked kids."

She pursed her lips, as if remembering.

"And?" Avani said. "Your other two statements?"

Greta nodded. "Number two: I have a pet rabbit named George that wandered into our yard one day. And number three: Last summer I got involved in extreme ironing and even made the local newspaper."

"What the heck is extreme ironing?" Avani asked.

"You take an ironing board and an iron to an extreme location and then you have to iron some clothes," Greta explained. "Like on the top of Mount Everest or something like that."

Avani laughed. "Okay, that's way too weird not to be true."

Fernando puzzled over it. "Yeah, it's definitely too weird not to be true. But I'm also pretty sure you have a bunny named George. And you still sound mad about Mrs. Rose. And—I think I remember you wanting to be a teacher!"

Avani glanced between them. "How long have you two known each other?"

"We used to be neighbors," Greta said. "When Fernando was really little."

"Yeah, we moved to Orcas when I was in first grade," Fernando confirmed. "But before that, my family was in Maple Valley. Greta and Manuel were always getting into trouble together, and they hardly ever let me hang out with them. So mean."

"You were such a brat," Greta said fondly. "You'd tell your mom whatever we were up to!"

"When I was like three!" Fernando protested.

Avani chuckled. Fernando was definitely the rule-following type. It was funny to think that he'd been that way even when he was three. She snuggled a little closer to him, putting her head on his shoulder.

"Well, what's your answer?" Greta asked. "Which is the lie?"

Avani had to admit that this was a tough one. "I think you're lying about the bunny. Maybe you do have one but it didn't wander into your yard?"

"Oooh, you think the lie is a technicality," Trent said. "That could be a good strategy. But less fun than making up a big ridiculous lie."

"I don't know, I'm rethinking the extreme ironing thing," Fernando said. "I know you're weird, but you're not that weird."

Greta looked at Trent with an eyebrow raised. "And do you have a guess?"

Trent grinned. "Nah, you're totally lying about the teacher thing. Cuz Greta does have a bunny named George that she adopted randomly, and she dragged me—not a lie—scuba diving last summer with, of all things, an ironing board!"

Greta laughed. "You loved it."

"You're a freak," Trent said. But he was grinning. "It's hot."

"It is?"

"Totally, babe."

And then they were kissing. There was definitely tongue hockey involved. (Quadruple barf!)

Jealousy prickled through Avani. She wanted to be just as passionate with Fernando. But little annoying things kept creeping in on her, even as she tried to let them go. How could he have called her a flake in that fight last week? Especially when just this morning he was the one who'd been late to pick them up, without even a text giving them a heads-up. Also, why did he think there was even a remote possibility she would miss Rani's film screening? It made no sense.

Her questions got more and more frantic as her mind raced. Did he really think she was going to blow off her sisters? (Or was that the problem? Did he feel like she always chose her sisters over him?) If that was case, Avani didn't know how to fix that. (Clearly, they were doomed and she should just call it quits now.)

"Do you want to see pics from our scuba dive?" Greta asked.

Apparently, she and Trent had come up for air while Avani's thoughts were racing away like sleds on ice.

"Sure," Avani said.

"Here it is!" Greta said proudly, showing them her phone.

There she was: Greta on the sea floor in full scuba gear, fish swimming around her, furiously ironing with an iron that clearly wasn't plugged in.

"Freak," Trent said. "You're lucky I agreed to take pictures for you."

"Getting the board down to the bottom was not easy!" Greta said.

"Neither was getting it back up to the boat," Trent said. "Such a pain."

"Please." Greta poked him. "You loved it."

"Yeah, kinda . . ."

Ugh. More googly eyes. Avani had to distract them. "You really made up that thing about Mrs. Rose? Because it sounded so real!"

"I swear you wanted to be a teacher!" Fernando added.

Greta shook her head. "Nope. You're remembering that wrong. Even though Mrs. Rose was super mean, my kindergarten class was full of little snot-nosed monsters. I didn't want to deal with them either."

"She still can't stand kids," Trent added.

"You know me so well," she said.

Avani could practically see hearts in each of their eyes. (Infinity-and-beyond barf.)

Chapter Thirty-Eight

Nidhi

After saying goodbye to Lucas and Keith, who were heading out to celebrate their engagement, Nidhi and the remaining stranded traveler crew took the train from Capitol Hill to the U District. While they rode, Nidhi sent the proposal video to Hannah.

Nidhi:

They're so cute!

Hannah:

♥♥♥♥♥

The wind screamed like kids at an Electric Boogers concert, yet nobody on campus paid it much mind. The UW quad was crowded with booths and students milling around. Delicious food truck scents permeated the air, clubs and organizations handed out flyers, and local businesses gave out free swag. The canvas top of one of the booths started flapping, but they swiftly got it under control by tying it to a sandbag.

Nidhi's phone pinged with another text from Hannah.

Hannah:

> Omg, the video already has 20k views. I mean, I knew it would be popular, but that was fast.

She shared the news with Lena, John, and Grayson.

"Not surprising really," Grayson said. "Sweeping gestures get attention."

Nidhi smiled. "Yeah, I guess they do."

"What kind would impress you?" Grayson asked softly.

She glanced at him in surprise.

"I don't know," Nidhi said. "Maybe it's the surprise that's the fun of it."

He nodded. "The surprise, huh. Good to know."

"Of course, some of the best moments aren't really gestures," she added. "It's creating something together."

She hoped he knew that she meant those nights of moonlight and murals and magic she'd shared with him. They'd been frozen golden moments in their own right, just like the Electric Boogers concert. The kind of memories that could keep you warm on the wettest, windiest of days.

Lena glanced between them. "Ooh, something is definitely going on between you two. I *knew* it."

Nidhi's cheeks heated even as a chilly blast of wind tried to blow her into oblivion. "We used to go out. But since we were both going to be traveling and doing our own things, we decided to keep things casual."

"Actually, you said that," Grayson returned.

"What?" Nidhi stared at him. "We both said it."

Grayson just looked at her. "Are you sure about that?"

"Whoa." Lena said. "Um, well we'll leave you two to sort this out. Besides, our son is waiting. We have big plans for his birthday!" She hugged Nidhi, then Grayson.

John did the same. "It was fun getting stranded with you two!"

"Glad we met," Nidhi said. "It *was* fun."

"Don't party too hard," Grayson joked. "Your son wouldn't approve."

Lena and John just laughed. And then they were gone, leaving Grayson and Nidhi with a swirling windstorm of wishes and unspoken things between them.

"I'd better go see Professor Cunningham," Nidhi said finally. "I have a lot to discuss with her."

She started walking past the booths to the building where she was meeting her advisor, but she couldn't stop thinking about Grayson either. About what he'd said. What he hadn't said. And all the things she wanted to say but couldn't quite get out.

She was late, but she turned around anyway. "You were traveling all over the world. Did you really want a girlfriend this whole time?"

Grayson kicked the asphalt with his boot, his hands in pockets. He wasn't looking at her, and he seemed . . . nervous? Was that even possible for Grayson, the guy who always charmed everyone?

Nidhi took another step toward him, but then a scream split through the gray skies.

"Jordan!" someone shrieked. "You're the absolute worst. I don't want to be with you anymore. Why can't you understand?"

"How can you say that? After everything we've been through?"

Nidhi and Grayson exchanged a look. They knew the first voice. They fought through the crowded quad until they found their old friend Rita in tears, mascara streaking down her cheeks, her red hair a cloud of anger around her.

Nidhi touched her shoulder. "Whoa, Rita, are you okay?"

"Nidhi! You made it!" Rita hugged Nidhi tightly, squeezing as if she'd fall through the earth to the other side if she let go. Nidhi squeezed her back.

"Sorry you had to see that." Rita fussed with her hair. "And Grayson? Hi?"

"Hey," he said, offering her a hug, too.

"Come on, let's get you out of this crowd," Nidhi said. "Everyone is staring."

"Let them."

Rita had never been the type to care what anyone else thought, but she followed Nidhi out to a grassy lawn anyway. The wind shrieked again, as if in agony over breakups and old wishes and uncertain futures.

"What was all that about?" Nidhi asked, plopping onto the grass.

Rita sat down beside her. "It's actually not that big a deal."

"It sounded like a big deal."

Rita laughed a sad little laugh. "I'm over it already. Jordan's great and all, but it just wasn't working. He cared more about his dog than he did about me."

Nidhi squeezed her hand. "I'm sorry."

Grayson crouched next to them. "Nidhi, don't you need to go meet your advisor?"

Oh wow. How had she forgotten? But she didn't want to just ditch Rita in her time of need, either.

"Don't worry about me," Rita said, as if reading her thoughts. "I'll be fine."

Grayson nodded. "I'll stay with Rita. She can tell me all about that dog."

"Thanks," Nidhi said, hurrying away. Today was such a whirlwind, and she wished she had more time to just stop and think. To examine all the tumultuous feelings she had for Grayson and decide what she really wanted.

Behind her, she heard Grayson and Rita laughing.

"Are you for real?" he said.

"The dog got the bed. I got the couch. Can you believe it?"

NEW DELHI—LATE OCTOBER

The days were getting cooler. Nidhi got to spend her first Diwali in India, see how it was celebrated in the mother country. The neighborhood transformed as people decorated with twinkle lights and vibrant mandalas drawn with colored sand.

Neighbors visited and brought them gifts and candy. Nidhi, along with her cousins, aunt, and uncle, went to pay their respects to others, too. They braved the New Delhi traffic to have a big dinner at Lakshman Dada's house on the other side of the city. All the relatives gathered: second cousins, third cousins, maybe even fourth cousins. Aunties and uncles.

Nidhi liked the way that in India, her father's cousins were her aunts and uncles, that the generational difference was respected. Somehow it just felt more right.

Nidhi helped with the cooking. Everyone had their beloved recipes, but she was allowed to stir here and chop a vegetable there. And she'd brought some rasgulla that she'd made herself, with Shiv's tips on how to keep it moist and flavorful. They all ate too much and laughed too much and then it was time to go outside. The kids ran with sparklers, and fireworks exploded all over the neighborhood, and Nidhi's family lit a few themselves.

It was a night of light and color. Of music and spices. Of a family too large to remember everyone's name. And Nidhi realized then that New Delhi had settled into her bones, that she belonged here, that her American accent and her terrible attempts at haggling and her delicate gut had their place here, too.

She thought of Suresh now and again, that smoldering heat that had existed between them. Sometimes she could feel it rising within her late at night when she listened to the ceiling fan whirring softly as she tried to sleep. But in the morning, those restless urges were replaced by new wonders.

Professor Cunningham's office was empty when Nidhi arrived. She glanced at a large clock ticking at the end of the hallway. She was a good half an hour late. How? She swore she'd only been talking to Rita for a few minutes.

Nidhi checked her email, and sure enough, there was a message from Professor Cunningham.

Hi Nidhi,

I know you've been doing your best to get here, but you did tell me 4:00 p.m. worked for you. Are you still planning to come? I'm stepping out to grab some food. Email me!

Professor Cunningham

Oops. Nidhi quickly emailed Professor Cunningham, apologizing profusely and letting her know that she'd finally made it on campus.

She waited another twenty minutes there but didn't get a response. Maybe she'd blown her chance. On the other hand, a part of her was doubting her plan again. Maybe she didn't want to stay in India. Maybe all she wanted was an artist boy with the scent of star-tossed seas and untamed nights.

Nidhi's shoulders slumped as she walked in a daze back to the crowded quad, where the wind blustered and rainclouds gathered overhead and yet college kids enjoyed their churros. Rita was sitting on a bench with two plates of tacos. No sign of Grayson.

"Food truck tacos are the best cure for a breakup," Rita said. "How did the meeting with your advisor go?"

"She wasn't there." Nidhi slunk down next to her. "I guess I was pretty late."

"Ugh, this is totally my fault," Rita said. "I'm so sorry."

Nidhi shook her head. "No, I should have paid more attention to the time. Anyway, she said she was just getting food, so maybe she'll email me in a minute." Nidhi put her head in her hands. She had tons of texts from her family piling up, and Rani was still insisting she had to make it to the film screening.

Nidhi felt like a terrible sister. She was letting everyone down. She was even letting herself down. More than ever, she understood why Lucas had to propose today. Sometimes, when you've been working yourself up to say the thing burning up inside you, you really don't want to wait even a second longer. If it doesn't burst out of you right now, you'll never have the nerve to try it again.

"You look like you need a taco," Rita said, shoving a plate toward Nidhi.

Nidhi took one and stuffed it in her mouth. Then another. Rita inhaled three.

"These are really good," Nidhi said with her mouth full. "Can we get more?"

"Let's do it," Rita said.

As they waited in an impossibly long line, Rita kept glancing at her.

"What is it?" Nidhi said. "Do you want to talk about Jordan more?"

"Nah," Rita said. "Breakups are a part of life. I accept that. Honestly, maybe I get off on the drama."

"You're the only person I know who looks gorgeous with mascara running down your face," Nidhi said.

Rita had wiped most of it off, but what was left looked artful and smoky and mysterious.

"It's a gift," Rita returned, tossing her hair. Then an evil gleam came into her eyes. "And anyway, it's your turn to spill. You're back with Grayson?"

"No, we just ran into each other at the airport." Nidhi explained how they'd been on the same flight that got diverted to Portland. "It's honestly a miracle we got here in time for the meeting at all."

"I see," Rita said.

Nidhi didn't understand that look Rita was giving her. As if she were—disappointed? Sure, she and Grayson had been great together, but she had told Rita before about why she was glad they'd kept things casual.

Though Rita seemed to be dying to tell her something.

"What?" Nidhi said. "Just spit it out."

"You know that boy is in love with you, right?"

Nidhi's heart raced. Love? No, they'd never discussed that.

"He said this to you?"

"Not in those words," Rita said. "But just before you left for India, he definitely . . . well, he sounded pretty down about not seeing you as much. We went wakeboarding together one day in July, and yeah. He was really excited for all his traveling, but he said he wished he had someone to share it with. Naturally, I asked if he meant you. He didn't answer, but I think it was clear. He was just . . . really sad. But he hides it, you know."

Nidhi tried to absorb that. She tried to remember that conversation with Grayson about what they wanted. The first time they'd kissed, it had only been a week after she'd broken up with Matt. And she hadn't been ready to call him her boyfriend. He'd seemed to understand without her saying it.

And they'd talked about all their big plans over the next months.

Rita nudged her shoulder. "I think he just went along with that whole 'keeping it casual' thing because he thought that was what you wanted."

"No," Nidhi said. "That's not how it happened. . . ."

Chapter Thirty-Nine

Nidhi

JUNE—GRADUATION EVE

*N*idhi waited for Grayson down at the cove, shivering in the breeze even though it wasn't that cold. It had drizzled earlier, the kind of June rain that was too warm for a raincoat so you just let it dampen your clothes. She felt a little sticky, but the sun had at least come out and now it looked like it was going to be nice after all.

Especially when Grayson's boat arrived on the horizon. It was actually his mom's research schooner, but she let him borrow it once in a while—if he did a lot of hull scraping in return. Nidhi watched his handsome silhouette as he anchored a little way off, then lowered a dinghy to pick her up. He looked so capable and in his element, as if he were a part of the sea itself.

"Hey, gorgeous," he said as he set foot on the beach. The waves lapped gently behind him, the evening sun bright in the June sky. "Ready for dinner?"

"You didn't have to plan all this . . ." Nidhi said.

"Are you kidding? You're graduating tomorrow! I wanted to celebrate." He helped her into the dinghy.

Nidhi's spine always tingled a bit when she got into Grayson's boat, and that evening was no different. The schooner spelled adventure, it spelled romance. And she lived for those enchanting nights of art and secrecy they had before a big holiday. Their first one, the eve before Halloween. Then Diwali. They'd done several more throughout the year. Gorgeous street art that popped up all over Friday Harbor and Eastsound.

"I'm going to miss our midnight adventures," she said to him.

His eyes met hers. "I'll miss them, too."

As he pulled up the dinghy and made sure it was properly secured, she stared out at the sea. Sometimes she didn't want to leave at all. It was so beautiful here in the San Juans, especially in the summer when the sun shone warm on her skin. He gestured for her to follow him into the little interior cabin. And soon they were speeding off over waters sparkling with sapphires and diamonds. Nidhi let the song of the engine wrap around them, loud and operatic.

She was graduating the next day. High school life was over. And this summer, everything would change.

She'd wanted everything to change, but that didn't mean she was ready. It didn't mean that she wasn't slightly terrified about stepping foot in a country she'd never been, all the way on the other side of the world.

Grayson maneuvered the boat expertly through the water and brought them to a quiet, protected place between islands.

"Is this where we went wakeboarding with Rita?" Nidhi asked.

"You remembered." He smiled, dropping anchor and leading them both to the back deck.

"The moment when I stood up on the wakeboard is forever etched in my brain," Nidhi confessed. "Sometimes I worry that nothing else in my life will live up to that. That I peaked at age eighteen."

Grayson laughed. "There's no way. You'll have moments even more beautiful and epic. You were meant for great things, Nidhi. It's written in the stars."

"Oh, do you read stars?" she asked.

"I'm an excellent reader of stars," he returned. "Now, let's get this party started."

He unfolded a small bistro table and two chairs. Draped a linen table-cloth over it and added a vase of fresh chocolate lupines and hollyhocks.

"Wow," Nidhi murmured. "So fancy."

"I wanted this to be special," he said. "Another great moment for your memory book."

And it was. Grayson had gotten takeout from a local restaurant: fresh fish and a light salad and sparkling raspberry cider. Nidhi couldn't help but wonder what the secret ingredient in the vinaigrette was; it was both tangy and sweet—and delicious. They gushed about all their big plans—Nidhi in India and Grayson all over. They both had so many places they wanted to visit, so many things they wanted to see and do.

They talked about it all as the sky softened into rosy, romantic hues and Nidhi again felt that strange urge to stop time. It was the opposite of what she'd been longing for all year, the opposite of all the work she'd put into making this study abroad program happen. But when she was sitting across from Grayson, looking into the star-tossed wishes in his eyes, she wanted nothing more than to be in the here and now. Between the sky and sea.

And that was dangerous. So, so dangerous. She couldn't let her feelings for him undermine everything she wanted for herself.

"This is lovely," she said, then forced a chuckle. "I can't even imagine what kind of dates you'll plan in Paris or Milan or wherever—for whoever you're with."

He gave her a funny look. "Who says I want to plan dates for anyone else?"

That stopped her short.

"Well, we never really said we were going to try long distance," Nidhi reminded him. "Plus, I'm sure you don't want to be tied down to a girlfriend while you're exploring the world. You want to meet people and have fun and live in the moment, right?"

Grayson didn't answer right away, just moved some last bits of salad around on his plate. "Sure. If that's what you think is best."

The sky was even more rosy now, the sea bathed in sunset enchantment, and the waves full of possibilities and maybe even a few mermaids. Nidhi heard their soft sighs on the wind, as if they were telling her to forget all her practical thoughts and confess to this boy in front of her that she maybe, sort of, definitely loved him.

Loved him?

No, no, she couldn't be in love with him. She hadn't even graduated high school yet (she still had another day to go). And she was about to explore and conquer new worlds. She was about to lay claim to her motherland and declare it hers, too.

"Nidhi?" he asked.

His lips were full and pink and gorgeous, and she thought of all those times she'd let herself get lost in them, let herself feel nothing but his urgent kiss.

"Don't you think it's best? For us to keep things casual?" she asked, her heart in her throat.

He shrugged. "I don't know."

"What're you going to do after traveling your forty-two countries?"

She'd asked him this very question so many times before, but he'd always shrugged it off. Nidhi knew he wasn't the type to plan ahead, and yet if they were going to stay together, she needed to know they'd be back in each other's vicinity at some point.

"I told you," Grayson said. "I haven't decided. I want to be open to wherever life leads me. I think traveling will change me in ways I can't really predict right now."

"I feel the same way," Nidhi said. And she did. She didn't begrudge him not knowing his future. But she couldn't fully give him her heart, either. "I'll miss you though."

"I'll miss you, too," he returned, his voice husky and soft. His eyes searching hers for something, some secret he didn't know.

Oh boy.

She steeled herself. "But I think it's for the best that we don't spend all our time pining after each other. Besides, I'm sure you'll meet lots of girls, and . . . I might meet someone, too. We should leave ourselves open to whatever happens, right?"

His eyes were again misty, mermaid-filled seas. But he only nodded. "Sure, let's keep things casual. Ready for dessert? You won't believe this chocolate crème brûlée."

He produced two small bowls of dessert. They were topped with raspberries that matched the sunset painted across the sea and sky.

"This is amazing," Nidhi said.

Losing herself to crème brûlée was much easier than letting Grayson sweep her away.

Nidhi's heart creaked like a tree just before a fall as she recalled that day on the boat. She still didn't know exactly what Grayson wanted. Yes, he'd hesitated a little at going their separate ways, but he hadn't had any answers for what the future might hold for them either.

He hadn't had a plan, or even a vision for what they might be to each other. And nothing had changed, really. Nidhi still wanted to follow her dreams and her heart. Not tie herself to a boy—or a man—or anyone.

"Hey, look, there's something going on over there," Rita said.

Nidhi heard lots of excited exclamations from people around a nearby booth.

"He's the Skull!"

"He's gotta be!"

"I've watched every video with his street work!"

"He's a legend!"

"Uh-oh," Nidhi said. "Looks like Grayson's been found out."

"Found out about what?" Rita asked.

Oh, right. Rita didn't know Grayson's secret, only Nidhi did. And he needed her help now. She rushed over to the booth, where Grayson was standing sheepishly with his sketchbook in hand. A crowd of admirers looking at him as if he was some deity. Nidhi had no idea why he'd opened the sketchbook—he was normally so secretive about it. But maybe he'd thought no one would recognize the Skull's work. (Even though she had, a year ago.)

"Come on, just admit it," said the guy in the booth for the UW art and design program.

"No, no," Grayson said, quickly slapping the sketchbook closed. "It's not me, I swear."

"Your sketches are exactly his style," the guy said. "You can't deny it. But I haven't seen you around the art department. Are you enrolled?"

Grayson shook his head. "No, I'm not a student."

"Well, that makes sense," the guy said. "That last piece was in Amsterdam."

"It's not me!" Grayson said. "Trust me, you've got the wrong guy. Though I did see the piece you're talking about."

"Everyone saw it," the guy returned. "It went totally viral."

"Yeah, so maybe he inspired my art," Grayson returned. "But I can't take credit for what's not mine."

There were a bunch of disbelieving snorts. Nobody was buying it. Nidhi had known Grayson long enough to understand that keeping the Skull's secret was really important to him. That being anonymous gave him the opportunity to create what he wanted without worry about judgment or consequences or being penned in.

The secret set him free.

Nidhi decided that teasing them might be the best way to go. "Well, if my boyfriend has been the Skull all along, that's news to me. But I wouldn't mind dating the Skull." She batted her eyelashes. "Babe, have you been keeping something from me?"

Her performance seemed to confuse everyone, and the crowd backed off a bit. Some of them were still convinced Grayson was really the Skull, but others seemed to believe that maybe he'd just been inspired by his icon. It was plausible.

Grayson shot her a grateful look.

"You know, even if you're not the Skull, you're quite talented," interjected a woman in her forties with glasses and long curly brown hair. It was . . . Nidhi's advisor, Professor Cunningham.

"Thanks, ma'am," Grayson said bashfully. His cheeks were turning the shade of a sunset over the sea. Like the sunset when Nidhi had told him she didn't want to do the long-distance thing.

Her heart still ached at the things between them that could never be.

Professor Cunningham handed him her business card. "I'm not in the art department, but I'm sure the dean would be interested. And no need to mention the Skull. Your work stands on its own."

"Well, thank you," Grayson said, flustered. "But I wasn't planning to study art."

"What were you planning?" she asked.

"I hadn't planned anything," he admitted. "I've been traveling, trying to see the world."

"Aha!" The booth guy with the intense eyes jumped on it. "Exactly. The Skull has been seeing the world."

"He's not the Skull!" Nidhi said loudly. "Lots of people travel around the world."

"Uh-huh," the booth guy said. But he seemed to be the last believer.

Professor Cunningham finally seemed to recognize her. "Nidhi? Oh, you made it, finally!"

Nidhi chuckled ruefully. "Yes, it's been a day, let me tell you."

"Hey!" the art booth guy stared at Nidhi. "Wait a minute, I know you, too."

Nidhi blinked. "What? No, we've never met. . . ."

"No, I do," he said with assurance, pulling out his phone.

Familiar notes played from the tiny phone speaker:

It's smelly and kinda gross
just like the electric boogers
in your electric booger nose

And sure enough, a video had caught Nidhi dancing with Grayson. Some extra footage from Lucas's proposal. Nidhi certainly hadn't taken it—but Lena must have. And Hannah had cut that into the proposal video before uploading it.

Nidhi saw that there were more than 100,000 views already. Wow.

Grayson laughed. "Okay, this time you've actually got us."

He launched into the long-winded story of how they'd stuck together all day up until arriving on campus. "Nidhi just really has to help people. It's something she can't not do."

Professor Cunningham chuckled. "Nidhi, I love this. And I have to admit, it's nice to see you let loose. Your reports have been so meticulous that sometimes I wonder if you're so busy being the perfect study abroad student that you're not having any fun."

Nidhi laughed in surprise. "I didn't include everything in my reports."

(Understatement of the year.)

"Well, I'd love to know what you've really been up to. Are you ready to have that meeting now? I'm going to head out soon."

"Yes, of course!" Nidhi said the words she was supposed to say—just like she wrote the reports she was supposed to write. Even though inside she was questioning if she had any idea what she really wanted at all.

"And you, young man." Professor Cunningham shot Grayson a stern look. "You could take a note from your friend Nidhi and follow through. I hope to hear from you!"

"Yes, ma'am," Grayson said again, shrugging at Nidhi in his aww-shucks way.

And then the professor's heels were clacking against the pavement as she walked toward her office. Nidhi shrugged back at Grayson, giving him a look that said: *Maybe you should think about it.*

"You coming?" Professor Cunningham called.

"Yes, Professor!" Nidhi hurried after her.

Chapter Forty

Avani

*Y*our turn," Greta said to Fernando. And kicked him.

"Hey! You don't need to get violent!" Fernando rolled his eyes, but he smiled.

"You haven't seen violence yet," Greta returned, kicking him again with a big grin.

He chuckled. "Fine, fine. I'm thinking!"

Their whole childhood-besties vibe was seriously getting on Avani's nerves. If she couldn't have that easy repartee with Fernando, she firmly resented that anyone else could. Long-time family friend or not.

Fernando cleared his throat. Avani knew he was a bad liar—and that was a good thing. But her competitive side was on high alert, and she was ready to smash apart any false statements.

"Number one," he said. "I'm struggling with my college applications, especially the essay part. I've been taking a college prep class to help with them, but I can't think of anything college worthy to write about. Number two: Back in the fourth grade, I tried to impress Avani with a joke, but it didn't land at all and she thought it was way too corny. What she didn't know was that I'd practiced that joke a lot. Like for weeks. It was a real disappointment when it flopped."

Wait, what?

Was he for real? She had no recollection of this joke that completely flopped, but his words sounded sincere. Besides, this would be a cruel thing to lie about, and as dense as she'd felt that he was being lately, he surely knew that.

Of its own accord, her heart was completely melting at the thought of him as a little kid practicing some joke just for her. She pointed the phone's flashlight at him to discern the truth, to see for herself that he'd really done that.

"Hey!" he yelped, holding his hand in front of his face to block the light. "My eyes!"

"Sorry," Avani said, putting it back into position to point at the wall.

Fernando blinked several times, then continued. "And number three: Avani and I got together when a baby pig got loose and we had to wrangle her back into the barn, but there was a snowstorm and we got trapped inside."

Ah. Frida the naughty goat had been responsible. Not a pig. But he'd done a good job with burying the lie within the truth.

Trent snorted. "Sorry, dude, but we're supposed to believe you two have been trapped in a barn before and now you're trapped in an elevator? How much bad luck are we supposed to think you've had?"

"I don't know," said Greta, "Not that I put much stock in fate or anything, but for some reason, I believe you. So—that leaves your bad joke or struggling with your college applications as the lie. Don't tell me you're already finished with them? Because that's not exactly a humble brag. Just a brag brag."

Since Avani had already spotted the lie, she knew he wasn't boasting. She felt bad that he was struggling with his college essays, but also a little hurt that he hadn't confided in her about them. She'd told him so many times that she didn't know what to do next year. Why hadn't he mentioned he was having a hard time, too?

Fernando just raised his brows. "Is anyone going to definitively guess which is the lie?"

"College essays," Greta and Trent said at the same time. They smiled at each other, and Trent whispered, "Great minds think alike."

"Well." Fernando nudged Avani's knee with his. "Do you want to tell them?"

It was such a familiar thing, but everything still felt so hot and cold with him. She never knew when he'd be gentle and soft or when there would be fiery anger in his eyes. And it was exhausting.

"We actually were trapped in a barn," she said quietly. "But it wasn't an escaped pig. It was a baby goat named Frida."

Even though she hadn't guessed right, Greta still shot Trent a triumphant look. "I knew something went down."

Trent just shook his head. "Trapped twice, huh. Seems like you two are pretty unlucky together."

Greta swatted him. "Not nice, Trent."

Avani wiggled her feet uncomfortably. Were they unlucky?

She wasn't like Rani; she didn't really think that fate was guiding her.

When they'd been trapped in that barn the first time, she'd been so upset. She'd been worried she'd missed the party she'd planned in honor of Pop, the man who had been a second father to the Singh sisters before he'd died of a stroke. But later, the snowstorm had proved to be a blessing in disguise, the thing that had made her realize her true feelings for Fernando. It was where they'd first kissed.

> It had been
>
>   magic
>
>   in a
>
>   mason
>
>   jar.

Yet here they were, less than a year later. Trapped together again. And even though she loved what Fernando had said about practicing that joke just to impress her, it didn't make all the bad things go away. The fight they'd had the week before was still seared in her memory. The bickering from this morning, too. She wanted to forgive and forget, but she didn't know how. Everything still felt raw and prickly inside.

Maybe Trent had a point. Maybe they actually did bring bad luck onto each other.

Trent stretched his long legs and slouched against the elevator. "Number one: I think David Bowie is superior to Led Zeppelin. Number two: I speak three languages. Number three: The day Greta and I met on campus was the same day my grandfather died, but I didn't want to bum her out, so I didn't tell her."

Avani's thoughts were still swirling, full of doubts and insecurities and fears that wanted to take over her brain. Her possibly ADHD brain. That part she was okay with, actually. More memories were coming back to her, memories that fit with the indicators she'd read about.

How Fernando had once asked her out, and she'd missed the date because she'd been so excitedly nervous she'd entered it wrong in her calendar. Forgetting to return Sirisha's lens because she got distracted by Fernando's sexy text. Mixing up orders in the restaurant because she was mentally putting together the details of the Winter Ball in Pop's honor. So many other times she'd missed things because she was too focused on something else.

It was all clicking in place, and she felt more and more sure.

"Well?" Trent said expectantly. "Is anyone going to guess or what?"

Fernando just grunted.

Avani tried to focus on Trent. "You seem like a Bowie guy."

Greta nodded. "He owns every Bowie album on vinyl."

"The grandfather thing seems real," Avani said. "Unless he's just being sneaky."

Trent grinned a slow, sneaky smile. "So would you care to take a guess?"

Avani tried to think. Greta had used lots of details to cover up the lie. But maybe he was doing the opposite?

"I'm going to guess your lie is speaking three languages," she said.

He grinned. "Yeah. I actually speak four. Portuguese, Spanish, English, and now I'm learning Japanese."

"Ah, so it was a non-humble brag," Avani joked.

Trent grinned. "Hey, I know that people don't think this beautiful face could possibly hold a brain, so I like to surprise them."

Avani chuckled. "Trent has a brain. Noted."

Greta punched him lightly. "Babe, you could have told me about your grandfather!"

He shrugged. "Yeah, but I didn't want you to like me out of pity."

She punched him once more. And then they kissed. Again.

Hmm. This time, Avani didn't feel quite so much like barfing. Somehow, that story about Trent hiding his grief the day he'd met Greta made her look at them differently. It was sweet and also a little bit sad. Just like Fernando's story about the joke he'd practiced—that she'd dismissed as corny.

The things people do for love, how they hide parts of themselves . . . how the air is always so thick with unsaid things.

But what if they actually said them?

It was Avani's turn to tell two truths and a lie.

She felt oddly nervous, and she didn't know why. It was just a game, and she knew she could pull off a lie if she wanted. Greta's strategy was a good one: provide enough details to trick people. But truthfully, this game was a lose-lose situation. Because if she actually pulled off her lie, that meant that Fernando didn't know her.

if she won
    then she lost
if she lost
    then she won
but if she
    made it too easy

it was all
        meaningless
She swallowed
   let her thoughts swirl
     like the leaves outside

"Okay," Avani said slowly. "Number one: I rock at beer pong because my aim is impeccable and I've had a little too much practice. Number two: I'm older than my twin sister Rani by seven minutes, and I try to remind her of my extra seven minutes of lived experience whenever I get the chance. And number three: I've decided what I'm putting for my major on my college applications."

Ten minutes ago, there would have been two lies. But she had decided. It was obvious, really, when she let go of those unrealistic expectations she'd had for herself. That woman at the café had put it all in perspective—why should there be so much pressure to decide her future right now? She was only seventeen, after all.

She glanced at Fernando. It was a little bit tricky, but he should be able to deduce the answer.

He chuckled. "Okay, that's a little too easy. There's no way you've picked out your major—you just told us you didn't even know where you were applying."

And there it was. Whatever connection they once had, it seemed to have disappeared. Avani felt her gut clench. Her throat ache. Her heart plummet.

"What do you think?" she asked Greta and Trent.

"You do seem like you would rock at beer pong," Greta said. "And

Fernando's right—you did just tell us you had no idea what you wanted to do for college."

"I smell a trap," Trent said, suddenly very intent on winning the game. "You said you didn't know where you wanted to go, but that doesn't mean you don't know what you want to major in. Plus, it would be really sneaky of you to try to trip us up like that."

Trent was absolutely right. But how was it that he understood her devious mind and Fernando didn't? Especially when it came to games she wanted to win.

(Even if she actually wanted to lose.)

Avani didn't say anything, but Trent nodded to himself anyway.

"Your twin is the older one, isn't she?" he said.

Sigh.

Avani nodded. "Yep. Rani's the one who's older by seven minutes." She glanced at Fernando. "How could you not remember that Rani brags about how mature she is all the time? She's so obnoxious!"

"That's what I thought!" Fernando protested. "But then I second-guessed myself. And . . . how could you have picked your major? All you've been talking about is how overwhelmed you are by the choices and that's why you've spent the whole term doing all those ridiculous clubs and being so distracted."

Avani blinked at him. Just because she might have ADHD didn't mean she was the only one who ever got distracted.

"You've been distracted by your own things, too," she reminded him. "Frida. Your college essays. SAT prep. Besides, shouldn't you be glad I figured it out?"

Fernando bit his lip. "Okay. You're right. I've been equally caught up in my own stuff. I'm sorry. And I really want to know—what did you decide?"

Despite everything, she was suddenly really excited about her decision. "I'm not going to decide. I'm going forward with undeclared!"

She may only be punting the problem, but it felt so freaking good.

That woman in the café would probably never know what a difference she'd made in Avani's life. Well, someday, some younger person would come to a crossroads and Avani would pay it forward, too.

"Wait a minute," Fernando said. "That's not picking a major. It's the opposite of picking a major."

"Actually," Avani said, "my exact words were *I've decided what I'm putting for my major on my college applications*. I didn't actually say I'd picked a major."

"Tricky," Trent said with appreciation. He held up a hand to high-five her.

Hot Trent wanted to high-five her?

(It wasn't that Avani was obsessed with Trent or anything. She was fine with him being with Greta and not her. It's just that he exuded cool, and if he thought she was cool, then well . . . she must be.)

She had no choice. She high-fived hot Trent.

"Nice one," Greta agreed.

Avani high-fived Greta, too. Okay, maybe this couple that was way too good at dancing wasn't so horrible to hang with. But she still had no idea what to do about Fernando. She needed a sign that they were going to make it, but everything today seemed to say the opposite.

That they were completely doomed.

When they got bored of Two Truths and a Lie, Greta—with way too much peppy energy—suggested moving on to Twenty Questions.

"But instead of everyone guessing like we did before," Greta said. "Let's split into teams. Trent and I will be a team and you two can be the other. We'll compete to see who can guess their partner's item. And it has to be something physical, not abstract or fictional. Got it?"

Avani was secretly thinking of strangling Greta and her peppy vibes. This team building was not working. The walls were S.E.R.I.O.U.S.L.Y. getting closer together. The ceiling was D.E.F.I.N.I.T.E.L.Y. getting lower. Clearly, they were all getting sucked into a dark, dark void where nothing existed but Greta's annoying games.

"Is it a person?" Trent asked Greta.

"Nope."

"Is it an object?" Trent asked.

"Nope."

"Is it a place?"

"Yes."

"Santa Fe!" he said, grinning.

Greta grinned right back. "You know me so well."

What. The. Heck. How could he possibly guess that in just three questions? It was impossible. Clearly, they were freaky mind readers.

Avani took in a breath. If Rani were here, she'd probably say the elevator was a metaphor for how she and Fernando were stuck in a bad place that they needed to escape. Maybe these extremely annoying games could actually help with that (not that she would admit it to Greta).

Focus

focus

FOCUS.

They needed to reconnect. They needed a mind meld. Not the kind twins had, but the kind couples had. The kind Trent and Greta obviously had. (Seriously, *Santa Fe?* What the heck.) There must be something that would remind Fernando of all that was beautiful and joyous between them, of kisses in snowstorms in the winter and entwined hands in the drizzle in the spring, and long, lingering silences that felt just right in the endless summer twilight.

She had it! The goat figurine on her nightstand.

"Okay," Avani said, doing her best to send him a telepathic image. "I've got something in mind."

Fernando quickly established that it was an object, human made, and you could hold it in the palm of your hand.

"Do you have one in the inn?" he asked.

"Yep."

"Is it something in the restaurant?"

"Nope."

"Is it something in one of the guest rooms?"

"Nope."

He kept going—listing the cleaning closet, the storage room, the library, the bathroom. Avani was getting impatient.

"You're using up all the questions," she reminded him.

"Yeah, that's how you play the game," he returned.

How could he not guess Avani's room? Had he forgotten she lived there?

He finally narrowed it down to her bedroom—at question sixteen. This wasn't good. She projected even harder. *Goats, Fernando!* They'd just been talking about them! But, after guessing a stuffed animal, a journal, a book, and jewelry, he was out of questions.

Avani's throat felt like it was closing up. "The baby goat figurine you gave me. Remember, the one on my nightstand?"

"Oh!" he said. "Oh."

She could tell that he felt bad about not guessing it. Their eyes locked. He hadn't gotten the clue, but maybe he could still hear her thoughts.

I miss you. I miss us. Can we find our way across the chasm that seems to have opened up between us?

Chapter Forty-One

Sirisha

The Jade Club had been reinvented with lanterns and candles and strings of battery-powered lights. Mrs. Fowler and the Devious crew were pros, and it looked incredibly romantic—even better than it had before. The curtains were back into place so there wasn't a hint that it was still midafternoon.

Mrs. Fowler called for everyone's attention. "Thanks for your patience! As they say, the show must go on! To make up for lost time, we'll be passing out your round three and round four cards together this time. There will be twice as many clues for you to share, and twice as many to gather. It might be a little chaotic, but do your best."

Sirisha was happy for Bethany that things were back on track. But she still didn't know where she stood with Lavi. Mushroom Girl had been distant ever since the blackout. But maybe the game would bring them back together.

Tomás was singing a sad song. The pianist banged on ivory keys.

Blood had been spilled, but that wouldn't stop the patrons of the Jade Club. Instead they reveled in gossip, and Scarlett was no longer the only one under suspicion. Someone else had spilled the news of Edith's affair. Rumor had it that this supposed third bootlegger might have been the killer, but their identity had yet to be revealed.

Scarlett nursed a drink at the bar. She knew she needed to clear her name, but she was stewing on how.

"Care to dance with me?"

Lola Vandermeer was back in Scarlett's vicinity, with a wink and a flirtatious smirk. A smirk that could penetrate the icy heart of gangsters everywhere.

Another dance. Another sad song. Another chance to pry information out of Lola.

Scarlett wished for more in this life, but she knew she wasn't going to get it.

She twirled Lola, then whispered in her ear. "Did you talk to Randall? Find out if he knows anything about Maria?"

"He said he had no idea who she was."

"And you believed him?"

"Hard to say. He's a liar and a cheat, but I don't know what his motive would be. You told me Maria wasn't important to your operation."

That was true. But Scarlett had a bad feeling that all of this was tied together. And even if it wasn't, she had a responsibility to figure out what had happened to Maria. She couldn't let her people get murdered without taking action. When she'd signed up to take over her father's business, she hadn't expected to be responsible for who lived and who died.

Maybe she wasn't cut out for the gangster life after all. Perhaps her heart wasn't completely hardened yet. Perhaps that was a weakness. Or perhaps it was the only thing keeping her human.

Tomás took a break from singing. Out of the corner of her eye, Scarlett noticed him slink over to the bar, where Mandy and Maxwell Blossom got into some kind of heated conversation with him. Scarlett couldn't make out the words, but he was angry.

Sirisha didn't want to leave Lola/Lavi's arms. But not knowing whether the spark they had in the game could ever translate to anything in real life was getting hard. She was tempted to give up and go home. But the only tenable way to end this was to solve the murder.

"You still don't trust me, do you?" Lola said, her eyes glinting in the club's dim lights.

"I can't," Scarlett said. "And I need to expose Edith's murderer."

With regret, she let Lola go. It was time she questioned Johnny Finch, that no-good reporter who had written so many over-the-top stories about Scarlett's father and all his supposedly violent acts. Scarlett knew Johnny was a fake—someone who pretended to care about Prohibition because it sold well for his paper.

He was sitting at a table with the very person that Scarlett knew had been having an affair with Edith Blackburn.

Sirisha had learned who had been having the affair with Edith from conversation in the club. Her abilities to pick up minutia seemed to have improved the longer she played the game. But she still didn't know who the murderer was. She pressed on.

Eric Bartlett was a former navy pilot. Rumor had it that he'd been relieved of duty due to his habit of drinking on the job. Now he didn't work at all, as far Scarlett knew. He just drank—which was good for business, but why Edith would want to waste her time with the likes of him was anyone's guess.

"Tell your friend to scram," Scarlett said to Johnny Finch, plopping down beside him at a table in the corner of the club. She was determined to get some answers.

Eric Bartlett got up to leave, but Johnny waved him back. "I'd feel more comfortable if he stayed, actually. I'm not used to being in the company of gangsters and murderers."

Scarlett narrowed her eyes. "I didn't have anything to do with Edith's death."

Johnny crossed his arms. "Don't pretend to be some innocent girl. Your father put up this huge act about how he was just bringing the people what they wanted."

"My father never killed anyone."

"Sure, he just had one of his thugs do it. Didn't dirty his own hands. And you're the same. Dumping the body of Maria Santiago in the river, like she was nothing. Why? Was it revenge on your former lover—Tomás Knight? Or did she make some kind of mistake in your so-called organization, and you just didn't care that Maria was Tomás's sister?"

Scarlett stared at him, trying to process everything. "Maria is Tomás's sister? Are you certain?"

"Don't act like you didn't know. And that you didn't have her murdered."

"That's a dirty rotten lie," Scarlett countered, leaning forward so her face was inches from Johnny's. "And you better not publish any of that nonsense, or I'll sue."

"Uh-huh. Why'd you come over here anyway?" he asked.

She glared at him. "Did you know that your friend"—she jerked her head toward Eric—"was having an affair with Edith Blackburn?"

"That's ridiculous!" Johnny said.

"Totally ridiculous," Eric said.

Scarlett pinned Eric with a piercing look. "I saw you with her last night. Coming out of the Blue Carpet Theater. You were arguing about something at first—but then she kissed you and you weren't exactly struggling."

Johnny shook his head. "Eric was home sick last night. We were supposed to meet here at the Jade Club for drinks, but he told me he couldn't make it."

Scarlett stared Eric down. "Were you sick?"

Eric crossed his arms. "I was, not that it's any of your business."

Around them, patrons of the Jade Club were not doing a very good job of pretending not to listen. All eyes and ears were on them. Something was fishy with Eric, and Scarlett was determined to find out what.

But the DOJ stepped in before she could finish her interrogation. Agent Miller flashed her badge. "Eric Bartlett, I've received information that you were with the victim last night. You two were seen at the Blue Carpet Theater."

Eric got up. "That's a lie. I wasn't there. You can't trust this no-good gangster."

"The information didn't come from her," Agent Miller replied.

Chief Tennison arrived on the scene, too. "There are multiple reports, which include an altercation between you and the mayor's wife."

Mayor Blackburn showed up. "You were having an affair with my wife? How dare you!"

And then he leapt on Eric in a fury.

Sirisha stepped out of the club. Clues swirled in her head. Everyone's acting was so good—the mayor's fury had felt so real! She'd also now learned that Edith Blackburn was the new bootlegger trying to get into the scene. Maybe Randall killed her for that. Maybe the mayor had. There were a lot of names, a lot of leads. And yet she didn't feel any closer to the answer.

She checked her phone to see how her sisters were doing. Avani was still MIA. Rani seemed to be making progress on her film. Nidhi had made it to Seattle. Sirisha tapped out some encouraging messages and then tucked her phone back into her suit pocket.

Only, the pocket wasn't empty. Someone had slipped something in there—again.

How did she keep missing that?

She pulled out a message on a Jade Club napkin.

Meet me at the boathouse. I have information that can absolve you.
Signed,
An old friend

A shiver of excitement went through Sirisha. Maybe she was finally making progress in this game! She pulled out her map, which outlined where they were allowed to go on the property as part of the game. Sure enough, the boathouse was included. The actual boathouse down by the pier.

Sirisha had been there before, over the summer. One gorgeous Saturday, she and Brie and Bethany and Paola had taken out a speedboat on the water. That day had been full of laughter and flirting and soaking in the sun. The kind of day she'd thought meant she and Brie were supposed to be together, the kind of day where she didn't want anything to change.

Of course, wishing desperately for time to stay still hadn't kept it from moving forward. And now she was here. In a dark and stormy mansion. Even though her feelings about Lavi were in flux, she had to admit the day had been exhilarating. It had brought out new things in her, things she hadn't known she wanted.

To the boathouse.

Chapter Forty-Two

Avani

"Okay, who's up for another game? Charades?" Greta said.

She wasn't the kind who would let an awkward silence linger.

Trent groaned. "Give it a rest, babe!"

"What? We were having fun!" Greta returned, sounding a little surprised and hurt.

"You don't have to be our kindergarten teacher anymore," Trent said. "Maybe it's time for some peace and quiet. Or we could just listen to some music." His voice was stern in a way that Avani hadn't heard him use before.

Uh-oh. Greta's face indicated she didn't like that tone, either.

Avani was surprised at this sudden tension between them—given the googly eyes they'd been giving each other just moments before. Still, she wasn't going to protest. She was feeling D.O.N.E. with these games, too. She'd hoped they would bring her and Fernando together, but instead she was filled with a sudden, intense sadness. One she couldn't shake.

"Actually, that doesn't sound bad," Fernando said, apparently oblivious to Greta and Trent's couple tension. Of course he was. And worse—he pulled his headphones out of his bag and started listening to something. Then Trent did the same.

Greta poked her boyfriend, in a pretending-to-be-playful-but-really-I'm-pissed kind of way. "Hey, I don't have headphones!"

Trent winced. "Don't tell me you want us all to listen with the phone audio. Because that will be a tragedy."

"Just do it," Greta commanded.

Trent complied with a roll of his eyes.

But Greta was clearly still annoyed. "Not this song again. This is all you ever play."

"Yeah," Trent growled. "Because it's amazing."

"Dude," Fernando said, "I'm obsessed with the Cloud Grifters!"

"Same," Trent said. "So you're going to the concert tonight?"

Fernando glanced at Avani. "Actually, I was hoping to go, but we have a thing."

Avani didn't know what to say. Here they were again. He was clearly still annoyed, and she still didn't get how he could be so clueless about the fact that she had to go to Rani's event!

"Oh, that's too bad," Trent said. "Their new album blew me away. Can't wait to see it live."

"Yeah, they're amazing live," Fernando agreed. "I saw them a couple of years ago, and I thought—these guys are gonna be huge! But it feels like they're still flying under the radar."

"Totally," Trent agreed. "Which is kind of cool, because they probably wouldn't be playing small venues like the one they're at tonight otherwise."

"True. They'd be off on some big tour all over the country."

"What's your favorite song from the new album?"

"It's hard to decide," Fernando said. "They're basically all brilliant. But I have to go with 'Last Night.' The melody, the lyrics, everything . . . is just perfect."

"Just perfect!" Trent said at the same time.

"Sounds like a bromance has started," Greta said, but her tone was off again, full of what was definitely faux cheerfulness.

Which made sense. Avani was beyond sick of being in this elevator. Sure, Greta's games had been distracting for a while,

but the four walls
    and the darkness
were closing in
    on her again
        and what once
felt spacious
    was now
extremely
    claustrophobic

Trent and Greta fought just as intensely as they seemed to love.

Greta poked Trent's chest. "I hate to break it to you, Trent, but you're not as cool as you think you are. This whole skater-tough-guy-emo look is so not it."

"Then what are you doing with me?" Trent asked. "If I'm so unattractive to you." He spoke in a bored voice, which would have completely infuriated Avani if it was directed at her.

"I have no idea!" Greta screamed.

Well, apparently, it had the same effect on Greta. So much for them representing all that was perfection in a couple. Avani wasn't sure how it had come to this—it had started with Greta asking if they could listen to her favorite band after they'd finished the Cloud Grifters' song. Trent had made some snarky comment and then Greta had rebutted with a snarky comment about Trent's taste in shoes, which was apparently a sore spot for him. And soon enough, they were literally screaming at each other.

"Yikes," Avani muttered to herself.

"Double yikes," Fernando agreed.

The elevator had been stopped for hours but suddenly it felt as if the whole world had frozen. Greta was mid-scream. Trent was mid-retort. Their faces were sharp, their foreheads furrowed. Their eyes so angry.

There are a few moments in your life when an epiphany hits you, and the planet and the stars around you rotate completely. Watching the fireworks between Greta and Trent was one of those moments for Avani. And she understood. *The fight wasn't about them as a couple at all—it was actually about their own insecurities.*

Avani decided it was time to set hers aside. She needed to reconnect with Fernando, but maybe dance wasn't enough. Maybe they actually needed to . . . talk to each other? (Okay, yes, that was obvious, but something about watching Greta and Trent screaming made it so much clearer.)

Just as quickly as it had frozen, the scene now unfroze and Trent and Greta continued their argument. But Avani was in a new headspace. Everything and nothing had changed. *She* had changed.

She got out one of her three journals and wrote: *Should we intervene?*

She passed the notebook to Fernando, along with a pen, and waited.

He read the note, then wrote back: *We're all frustrated being stuck here. Let them hash it out.*

Avani: *I doubt they'd listen to what we had to say right now, anyway.*

Fernando: *Exactly.*

Avani: *Well, should you and I hash a few things out? But with less volume?*

Fernando: *Probably. But I feel like when we try to talk, we just get defensive and it turns into a fight.*

Avani: *I pinkie swear that I will stay calm and not get overly defensive, if you'll do the same.*

She held up her pinkie finger. Fernando curled his own around hers, and they pinkie shook on it. Just as they did so, Greta let out another ghastly scream, more violent than the wild squall outside. She was a force of nature, that was for sure.

Avani: *My ears are starting to hurt.*

Fernando: *You can borrow my noise-canceling headphones.*

Avani: *Yes, please!!*

Lending her the headphones to tune out Greta and Trent may have been the single most gallant thing in the history of the universe. After all, now Fernando was stuck listening to them at full volume.

Avani: *I wish I could let things out the way Greta just did.*

Fernando: *Go for it. They're not holding back. Scream!*

Avani: *I don't want to overshadow them. But here's a silent scream. Ahhhhhhhhhhhhhhhhhhhhhhhhhhhhh!!! Senior year suckssssssssssssss!!!!*

Fernando: *Yeah it does.*

Avani: *Okay, to hash it out, I think we should both write a list of our own insecurities. Because I think our hang-ups are what's making us miserable. But maybe if we understand each other, we can do better. What do you think?*

Fernando: *Let's do this.*

Avani's hang-ups
- *not knowing what I'm doing next year*
- *feeling like I'm never going to figure out a career*
- *feeling like I'm never doing enough*
- *feeling like I'm always doing too much*
- *feeling disorganized and all over the place*
- *feeling in the shadow of my sisters*
- *wondering if my brain will ever work the way everyone else's does*
- *wondering if Fernando really sees me anymore*
- *wondering if Fernando's about to dump me*

Fernando's hang-ups
- *not being good enough in school*
- *not being a great writer*
- *wondering if any colleges will actually accept me*
- *letting down my parents*
- *letting down my girlfriend, who is good at literally everything*
- *wondering if my girlfriend is just with me because we got trapped together in a barn once*
- *wondering if Avani will dump me*

As the girl and the boy exchanged notes in the shadowed corner of an unmoving elevator, the world seemed to still. The windstorm stopped its furious bellows, the autumn leaves decided to stay put for a bit.

The girl
   reached for
      the boy's hand
  in the darkness
      as she had so many times before
         but now she knew
    he knew
       everything she
   didn't want him to know
      and everything she did
   they weren't alone
      but a wildfire lit
        inside them
      their lips met
        and something ignited
      that could not
        be doused

Chapter Forty-Three

Sirisha

A dark and stormy mansion. A mysterious note. A pearl-handled pistol. A path to a boathouse, wind-blown trees, drizzly skies.

Scarlett felt for her pearl-handled pistol in her suit's interior pocket. It was still there, at least. Too many hands had been in and out of Scarlett's pockets that day, and those mistakes were costly. She needed to be more alert.

Her heart pounded as she approached the boathouse. A part of her hoped the author of the note was a certain beautiful girl in a gold dress. The girlfriend of a scoundrel rival gangster. Another part wanted the dame to stay as far away as possible.

An unlocked door. Soft gray light spilling in. A boat covered for the winter. Shadows and darkness and an expectant air. The sound of breathing.

"Who's there?" Scarlett said, pulling out her pistol.

Tomás came out from behind the shadows. He raised his own revolver. "You killed my sister, Maria. How could you? I know we're not together anymore, but don't you have any loyalty?"

"I didn't kill her, Tomás. You've got the wrong person."

"I don't believe you. You learned she was planning to defect to Randall Johnson's operation and so you had her offed." He waved the gun angrily.

Scarlett wasn't afraid to die. It was a shame though—she was starting to think she knew who had killed Edith Blackburn.

Tomás pulled out a die. "Shall we roll for it?"

Sirisha stared at the die in his hand. Oh, yes, they weren't actually going to shoot each other—this was just a game. She reviewed the weapons instruction card. Since they both had guns, they would roll to see who won the "shoot-out."

She sat down on the cold boathouse floor.

"Well?"

"I'll roll first," he said, crouching across from her.

He got a two.

"Not good," he said with a sigh, resigned to his fate.

Now it was her turn. It wasn't impossible for her to lose this thing, but what the heck. It was the moment of truth. Her hands trembled. She wanted to win, but this part was pure chance. She even kissed the die in her knuckles.

And then she let it fly.

Tomás lay dead at Scarlett's feet. She didn't feel good about what had happened. He'd only wanted answers about his sister. And she'd killed him.

She knelt beside him. "I'll find out who killed Maria. I'll avenge her."

Wind swept through the boathouse, a furious vengeful thing. Footsteps clacking against the path. A shadow at the door.

"What did you do?" Lola stood silhouetted at the entrance, hair flying. "I thought you and I were working together."

"It was self-defense," Scarlett said.

Lola pulled out her gun, pointing it dead at Scarlett's heart. "Get ready to defend yourself again."

Scarlett waved her pearl-handled pistol. "Are you sure you want to do this?"

Lola smiled, with her usual twinge of irony. "I'll take my chances."

With Tomás still playing faux-dead beside her, Sirisha sat down once more on the cold boathouse floor. As she pulled out her single die, a shiver swept through her. The game was coming to a close—she could feel it in her bones. But what then?

The Jade Club would transform back into a living room. The Devious crew would scatter to their next gigs. Scarlett and Lola would cease to exist.

Sirisha didn't know if she could face that future. But for now, she had to see this game through.

"Ready?" Lavi said, kneeling beside her with her own die.

Sirisha nodded. "Go."

Lola rolled . . . a five.

Scarlett felt a burning inside her, as if she'd been shot. But she needed to get her own bullet in.

So she rolled.

It was a six.

Lavi dropped her gun on the ground. "Looks like I'm dead."

"Bad luck," Sirisha said.

Lavi smirked. It wasn't exactly the same as a Lola smirk; it was its own beautiful thing. The shadows seemed to pulse around them, and the screaming wind became a song that only the two of them could hear.

"Now that I'm out of the game," Lavi said, her voice husky, "can I tell you something?"

Sirisha's breath hitched. "What's that?"

"It's been really fun flirting with you."

Sirisha felt the world tilt and swirl. Lavi had admitted she was flirting. That she'd had fun. And now all Sirisha could focus on was Lavi's lips. The shape of them, like an elongated heart. The slight cleft in her chin. Her hair. Her cheeks. Her smile. Her dark chestnut eyes.

"Um." Tomás cleared his throat and sat up. "I think I'll be going now. . . . It's starting to get a little heated in here. Um—but don't tell Mrs. Fowler. I cannot deal with more wheatgrass."

Sirisha and Lavi both laughed as he scrambled away.

And then they were alone.

Two girls. In a stormy boathouse. The wind rattling outside. A November opera written just for them.

"Thanks for saving my life this morning," Lavi said, her words coming out in a rush like a raging river after a storm. "I'm glad we met. Even though my mushrooms mostly got ruined. And you nearly ran me over. I guess we're even on the lifesaving part, actually. But also, you make a really great gangster. Do you know who the killer is? You can tell me since I'm out of the game. . . ."

Sirisha chuckled. She also always rambled when she was nervous.

"I had fun today, too," she said softly. "Can I kiss you now?"

Lavi quieted. Her big eyes grew even bigger, and her mouth parted just a little bit. She licked her lips. And then she leaned forward with a low moan from the back of her throat. One of wanting, one of desire. "Yes."

Sirisha made her move. Closing the gap between them. The first touch was feather light. Just a brush. She breathed in Lavi's scent, like pines and earth and raindrops. A taste of tangy fruit cocktail in her mouth. Then Lavi put her arms around Sirisha's waist. The kiss deepened, and the boathouse seemed to grow steamy.

The rain battering against the wooden roof crescendoed, a sweeping melody of something new.

Chapter Forty-Four

Avani

"Hello!" Greta said. "Get a room, you two."

Avani desperately wished they could. She'd give anything to be alone with Fernando right now. To be back where they had been a week earlier, at his house, their clothes on the floor. . . .

She was panting. She wanted him. Now.

But Greta and Trent were staring at them. It seemed they'd finally run out of steam and were slouched in their respective corners. They weren't screaming anymore, but the air was still thick with their mutual hostility. Avani searched for a way to ease it. Should she give in and play yet another one of Greta's games? But Trent was sick of them, too. She racked her mind—

But was interrupted when Trent's stomach let out a huge growl. A truly epic one.

Trent looked absolutely mortified, and that crack in his emo-but-also-tough-guy vibe was too funny. He was probably going to be so mad at her, but Avani couldn't help snorting. Then Fernando let out a giggle. The giggle itself was funny, too, and Avani's snort morphed into a full-blown peal of laughter.

Clearly, it was contagious because Greta cracked a smile. "Didn't we just have lunch?"

"That was, like, ages ago!" Trent moaned.

They all laughed again because he sounded *so* miserable. Avani took pity on him and rummaged through her bag. She had a single granola bar in there that she kept for snack emergencies.

"Want this?" She held it out to Trent. "It's a little smushed, but it's still good."

"Thanks," Trent said, ripping it open.

"Hey!" Greta said. "Maybe the rest of us are hungry, too. Have you ever thought of sharing?"

Trent looked mournfully at the granola bar—which wasn't that big. "Um, you want half?"

He sounded like he really did not want to share half.

Just then, Fernando's stomach made a weird noise. And Avani, who had been hungry for something entirely different moments before, was suddenly S.T.A.R.V.I.N.G. And now they were all staring mournfully at the granola bar.

"No, it's okay," Avani said, swallowing. "You can have it."

Trent looked at all of them and made up his mind.

"We'll split it four ways. Hope you don't mind my germs." He broke the bar into four pieces and passed one to each of them.

It was basically one bite apiece. And they each ate theirs as if they were ravenous, as if they'd been trapped in the elevator for days instead of a couple of hours.

"We so would not survive the apocalypse," Avani joked.

"Oh my God, I would be the first to die," Greta said.

"No way, babe," Trent said gallantly. "You're way stronger than I am. You know I lose it at the first signs of low blood sugar. I cannot function."

"You're right," Greta teased. "You would definitely be the first to go. I'd just be really soon after you."

"And I wouldn't be far behind," Fernando agreed. "But Avani's just joking about not surviving. She'd be stockpiling food and hoarding weapons and figuring out how to win the apocalypse. Because only Avani would think you can win an apocalypse."

Avani tossed the crumpled-up granola bar wrapper at him. "Hey! What's that supposed to mean?"

"You're tough," Fernando said. "Own it."

She opened her mouth to retort—but laughed instead. When she let go of her insecurities, she suddenly felt light. He knew who she was. He knew she made mistakes and was disorganized and could dance like a boss. And she *was* tough. She liked being that way.

"Okay, I own it," she said. "I would totally win the apocalypse."

"I know you would."

And then there it was. That heat again. The wildfire that burned between them. Just when Avani felt like her blood was literally going to boil over, the power finally came back on.

The elevator lurched. For a second it felt like it was going to drop down the shaft. They all yelled. Fernando grabbed hold of her. Greta and Trent grabbed each other, too. At least if they were going to die, they'd do it together.

"Hey, are we moving up?" Fernando said with wonder.

"We're going up!" Trent said, high-fiving him.

And then, blessedly, the door opened.

It opened

    it OPENED

       it *opened*.

When they stepped back into the studio, Lisa greeted them each with big hugs. "I was so worried about you four! To be trapped in an elevator—a space so small . . ." She shuddered. "I wouldn't wish that on my worst enemy."

"It wasn't so bad," Avani said, realizing she actually meant it. She'd wanted to spend more time with Fernando, and she had.

"Thank you for being a good sport about it." Lisa patted her shoulder. "Because you missed so much of the class, you four may join me in three weeks, if you like, when I'm offering this workshop again. But in the meantime, you may as well get in a bit more practice."

They all thanked Lisa for the chance to redo the workshop and joined the other students. The rest of the class had been practicing with electric candles and lanterns. It was nice.

Lisa and Rodrigo put the music back on and this time Avani felt the rhythm

it wasn't an ember
    small and sparking
it was a wildfire
    and that heat
was alive
    in her bones
      in her blood
        in her toes
    and somehow
she and Fernando
were moving together
a golden, untamed fire
    in his moth-brown eyes

Their steps weren't perfect, and they fumbled here and there. They couldn't get every trick right; one lift was flawless, another one not so much. But Avani didn't let those flaws bother her

because it didn't mean
    they weren't good together
it didn't mean
    they weren't
      in love

In love? The thought made Avani come to a sudden stop.
Was she in love with Fernando? What was love? What did that even *mean*?
"You okay?" he asked.
"Yeah," she said, breathless, her mind in a million places.

Chapter Forty-Five

Sirisha

Sirisha clutched Lavi's hand. She was afraid that if she let go, the girl would disappear in the windstorm. That perhaps she'd been a figment of Sirisha's imagination all along. That there had never been a falling tree or a basket of mushrooms.

Lavi's fingers stayed warmly entwined with hers though, even as they returned to the Jade Club to find Eric Bartlett accusing Mayor Blackburn of the murder of this wife.

"You found out about us, didn't you? You found out about our affair and in a jealous rage, your murdered her! Isn't that right?" Eric's voice was blunt with grief.

Mrs. Fowler stepped in. "Is this a formal accusation?"

Eric (his real name, too) nodded, crossing his arms. "It is."

Mayor Blackburn shook his fist. "You're wrong, buddy boy. I didn't kill my wife."

Eric looked flabbergasted. "But it has to be you."

"Well, it's not."

Everyone turned to Mrs. Fowler for confirmation. She nodded. "The mayor is telling the truth. He is not the murderer. Would anyone else like to give a guess?"

Lavi was playing with Sirisha's fingers, and it was definitely hard to concentrate. Sirisha glanced at Bethany and Paola, who were both spread across the sofa. Bethany shook her head. The birthday girl wasn't ready to make a guess.

So Sirisha cleared her throat. "I think I know who it was."

Mrs. Fowler smiled. "Please, do share."

The Jade Club was deathly quiet. Scarlett wasn't certain anyone would believe a gangster. But she had to try.

"It wasn't me. It wasn't Randall Johnson. It wasn't any of our goons. And it wasn't a crime of passion, though I wouldn't mind if our self-righteous mayor wound up behind bars."

"Then who was it?" Agent Klein asked, skeptical.

"Yes, do tell," Agent Miller agreed.

There was a smattering more of encouragement. Sirisha felt her face go up in flame. She almost regretted solving the murder, because now she was forced to speak in public. But she'd come a long way since last year. She could definitely do this.

"It was Johnny Finch," Scarlett announced, pointing an accusing finger in the reporter's direction.

Johnny gasped. "Prove it."

"I will," Scarlett returned.

Mrs. Fowler smiled. "If you're making a formal accusation, you must also provide a motive."

"Edith Blackburn was planning to get in on the bootlegging business, with the help of her lover and pilot, Eric Bartlett. They had connections in France. They had several other pilots lined up to help. They had Mandy and Maxwell ready to start selling their liquor at a new club."

Mandy shrugged. "She was paying well."

"But that doesn't explain why Johnny would kill her," Mayor Blackburn said.

"I'm getting to that part," Scarlett said. "You see, Johnny thought Edith was playing his friend Eric for a fool. And then he learned that Edith had killed Maria Santiago—when she refused to defect from the Singh bootlegging pipeline. He knew she was ruthless. He did it to help his friend escape a bad situation."

"Very good." Mrs. Fowler produced the murderer card. She passed it to Sirisha, and sure enough, she was correct.

"That's kind of sweet," the kid playing Eric Bartlett said to the kid playing Johnny Finch. "Thanks, man."

Johnny shrugged. "She had it coming."

A game played. A mystery solved. A kiss and a guess and a new fresh feeling. The kind that came after a storm had passed.

Kids were lingering, enjoying more drinks and an array of appetizers. All that murder and mayhem had made everyone hungry.

Sirisha found herself unwittingly in the spotlight. Her classmates were duly impressed, not just because she'd solved the mystery, but because they'd seen a side of her they hadn't known existed. But now what? Scarlett no longer existed, and Sirisha was sad to see her go.

That left the question of what the kiss with Lavi meant. Were they girlfriends now? Or was it just something that happened in the heat of the moment when you were alone in a boathouse on a dark and stormy day?

She sat down at the faux bar, unsure of herself. Moments later, Lavi sat down next to her. Bethany and Paola joined them. The Devious crew were circulating with hot chocolate, the perfect antidote to the storm outside.

"You were great," Bethany said, taking a sip of her own steaming mug. "And here's your prize!"

She pulled out an enormous basket from beneath the bar. It was piled high with gorgeous Prohibition-era vintage items—tins, magazines, books, an old telephone, and even a vintage camera.

"It probably doesn't actually work," Bethany warned.

"It's adorable," Sirisha said. "Thanks."

"You could go into acting!" Paola added. "Actually, you and Lavi both could."

Sirisha looked at her feet. "Nah. This was a once-in-a-lifetime thing."

"Same." Lavi wrung her hands. "I don't even know how I did it. But I felt like someone else. I'm usually pretty shy."

Sirisha looked over at her in amazement. Could they really be so alike? Was that why Lavi had been so distant when she'd tried to ask her about clubs and school and such? It was hard to believe anyone could be as awkward as Sirisha, but maybe, just maybe, she'd found her match.

Bethany raised her cup in a toast. "This makes me so happy! You two came out of your shells!"

"Yeah," Sirisha said, clinking mugs with her. "But I only do that at parties where murder is involved."

"Then I guess we need more murders around here," Paola joked.

They all laughed. As Bethany and Paola started grilling Lavi about clubs and interests, Sirisha was secretly glad she wasn't the one under interrogation. She pulled out her phone to check what her sisters were up to.

Avani:

You guys, I'm trapped in purgatory. This is obviously karmic punishment for something, but I don't know what. Someone please come rescue me!

Avani:

Is anyone getting these messages?

Avani:

We need help!!!!

Avani:

Ugh, I can't believe this is happening to me. We have no power and apparently no cell service. This thing must be made of lead.

Avani:

I can't believe I've gotten trapped again—just like last year. Only this time, I'm not in a barn with cute baby goats. Instead, there's an annoying other couple with us. Omg. The girl wants to play games to occupy us. She's one of THOSE people. The-let's-make-the-best-of-it people. Kill me now.

Sirisha:

Oh, I just got these texts. I guess they were delayed. Does that mean you're free, Avani?

Avani:

Yes, we finally escaped! I'm okay but can't really talk. Workshop is still going!

Rani:

Avani, I'm glad you've escaped and that you're okay. The thing is . . .I'm not.

Sirisha:

Oh no! What happened?

Rani:

Well—I can't believe I'm typing this. Raj broke up with me. Don't bother coming to Friday Harbor. I'm going home.

Sirisha:

Omg, I'm so sorry. Did he say why?

Rani:

Yeah. I don't want to talk about it though. All I know is, there's no way I'm going to finish this film. It was all about me and Raj, and now it's way too painful. Besides, love is clearly dead.

Sirisha:

Come on, you don't believe that.

Rani:

I do. So don't bother coming to Friday Harbor. The film is OFF.

Sirisha stared at her phone. She couldn't let Rani quit the film. Her sister loved rom-coms and she deserved to be able to compete for this chance to meet Olivia Lee. Why did Raj have to do this today of all days?

Sigh.

Sirisha stood up. "Hey, this was really fun. But Rani needs me, and I have to get to Friday Harbor. It's an emergency!"

"Oh no!" Bethany returned.

"I hope she's okay," Paola added.

Lavi stood up too. "Can I help? What's going on?"

The offer was so sweet and Sirisha felt little hearts bubbling up inside her. "Do you know anything about making a short film?"

Chapter Forty-Six

Rani

All of Friday Harbor seemed to have lost power. And that included Café Helix, where Rani and her cast were supposed to be filming. Also, previous crews were running late and the outage wasn't helping, so Rani's cast had to wait. Forty-five minutes passed by before they got their turn. Still no power, but the last group had just dealt with the low lighting.

Luckily, the café had plenty of windows. Hopefully, that would be enough because no one had any idea when the power would return.

A cheerful man with a bulbous nose and red cheeks pointed to the sign-in sheet when they arrived. "I can't wait to see the short films you kids create! But, man, what a day to have the shoot-out. Maybe next year they should opt for a day in the summer."

"Right?" Dominic said. "Who came up with the idea to do it in November?"

"Not someone who cares about camera equipment," JJ said. "Luckily, we don't have any!"

Rani didn't know whether to laugh or cry about that.

The man looked confused. "How are you filming then?"

JJ held up their phone. "This baby."

He raised his brows. "Well, good luck. I hope it can handle low lighting."

But JJ's phone couldn't in fact pull it off.

It was really dark and gray outside, and despite having Parker and Dominic seated across from each other at a table next to a generously large window, it just wasn't working.

Parker rubbed her temples as if she was getting a headache. Sara hovered aimlessly, JJ fiddled with their phone, and Rani did breathing exercises as she tried not to completely lose it.

Which was really hard, actually.

"Try another filter," Rani said between gritted teeth.

"I've already tried them all," JJ said. "None of them make it look halfway decent. Unless you want to try your phone."

"Mine is older than yours. There's no way the camera is better."

"If only someone reliable had brought the camera equipment." Parker put her hands under her chin and glanced at Rani pointedly.

Oh no. She did *not* just go there.

"I told you." Rani narrowed her eyes dangerously. "Something came up. A family emergency."

Parker seemed unmoved. "Raj said everyone was okay. What kind of an emergency is that?"

"I'm sure he has a good reason," Rani bit out. Of course, Parker was only saying what a part of Rani was feeling, too. That made it worse.

"Whatever. He should have told you what was going on," Parker returned. "You said he was the *perfect* boyfriend, but he certainly doesn't seem like it today."

Rani couldn't believe this. Parker had always been so supportive of her and Raj—so what was with the sudden passive-aggressive tone?

"Nobody's perfect," she said.

"Well, you've been bragging about how *he* is ever since you got together."

"Whoa, whoa, whoa." Dominic waved his hands. "Let's all cool down."

But Rani wasn't cooling down. "If you have something to say about Raj, just say it. Or are you just jealous because you don't have a boyfriend?"

"I'm not sure you do, either."

It was a really low thing to say. Rani stared at her friend. Ex-friend. "Get out."

Parker blinked at her. For a second, Rani thought she might apologize. But then Parker's eyes hardened.

Sara let out a shaky laugh. "Hey, Raj is a good guy, Parker. Don't be so hard on him."

Dominic nodded. "Yeah, I think we're all just tired and frustrated. Maybe we should take five while JJ and Rani decide what to do about lighting. Sound good?"

Rani was so angry in that moment that she honestly did not trust herself to answer. She just gave them a curt nod.

He grinned his boy-band grin, brushing his hair out of his face. "And I'll get you some calming chamomile tea, okay?"

"Thanks," Rani muttered.

She was glad he'd defused the situation, but she was still burning all over. How. Dare. Parker. How could she even think anything bad about Raj? How could she imply that he hadn't done everything he could to be there? He would have crossed galaxies for her. But he had a big heart, and sometimes that meant he was hanging out with his mom after a fight with his dad.

Dominic gently nudged her to sit down and brought her the tea. Ed's cast had arrived—she'd noticed on the sign-in sheet that they were slated to film in this location next.

"Maybe I'll ask Fi if she has any thoughts about what we can do for the lighting," JJ said.

"Fi?"

"Yeah, Fi."

No one called Fiona "Fi." Except apparently JJ.

Rani slumped in her chair as her cast and crew wandered off. It was just a five-minute break. Suddenly, she felt completely and utterly exhausted. She'd been working on *Remeet-Cute* every waking second. She'd been flying high off just the potential of having her work seen and heard.

Time to text her sisters for some serious help. Maybe Sirisha would know what to do for this low-lighting fiasco. Or maybe she too would say real camera equipment would have worked.

No, Sirisha wasn't Parker. Rani pulled out her phone, heart pounding.

374

Rani:

Oh great, the power is out in the cafe where we're supposed to film! This was my most important scene. What do I do? JJ's phone camera can't handle this kind of low light.

Sirisha:

Oh no. Can you change the script? Have it located somewhere else? Btw, the power is out here, too. They're trying to get the generator on.

Rani:

I wish this cafe had a generator. The thing is, I'm pretty sure most of Friday Harbor has lost power. So we can't exactly go anywhere else. And outside it's so windy you can't hear a thing.

Rani:

I did come up with the idea to include the storm in the short film. But do you think it's okay if you literally can't see anything for the whole cafe scene?

Sirisha:

Sure! You could make an artistic statement with the darkness. Just get their voices in the scene, and maybe a few shadows. There's an intimacy to that.

Rani:

LOL, I can't believe I'm saying this but yeah, you're right. It sounds like something Ed Yi would do. . . .

Rani felt better after talking things over with Sirisha. (And kind of amazed that her little sis was actually having fun at Bethany's birthday extravaganza. There MUST be a girl. The Official Love Guru could sense it.)

Even though she was still reeling from the harsh words with Parker, Rani felt slightly more calm, too. Sirisha's ideas swirled in her head—could she really lean into the darkness?

"Rough filming?" a sympathetic voice said.

Rani looked up from her phone to find Ed Yi at her table. "Yeah. We still have this place reserved for a bit longer."

"I know," Ed said. "I mean, we can wait outside—but I just thought I'd see if I could help."

That was awfully nice of him.

"My cameraman didn't show up today," she admitted. Though she was *not* going to tell him that said cameraman was also her boyfriend. Too mortifying. "That's why I'm stuck using a cellphone camera."

"Wow," Ed said, sitting down across from her. "Sorry that happened. I thought you were just doing it because you weren't that serious about the Shoot-Out."

Rani glared at him. "Well, I was serious. I've been working really hard on the script. But anyway, my sister had a great idea for dealing with this power outage. JJ's cellphone camera can't handle this low lighting, but

Sirisha suggested we lean into it. Let it be intimate and dark and emphasize the audio."

Ed scratched his ear. "Actually, that's a really good idea? There's a rule in filming I've heard: Don't try to fight the conditions you have. Work with them."

"Exactly!" Rani said. "The only thing is that artistic aesthetics aren't really my strength."

"Maybe I can help." Ed said. "Let me see your phone."

"Well, JJ has the one we're actually filming with."

"That's okay. Let's try to set up the shot and the audio and get it all ready for when they get back. Where's your script?"

Rani pulled it out, showing him. He'd better not make fun of it, or there was no way she could deal with his help.

But he was reading, and then—surprise of surprises—he actually laughed.

"You're a natural at dialogue," he said. "The sparks are really flying."

Rani bit her lip, remembering what she'd overheard earlier. "I suppose you think it's good . . . for a rom-com."

He blinked. "I think it's good, period."

Okay, she was totally calling him out. "I heard you tell your crew that you didn't think a rom-com could possibly win this contest. That you'd studied past winners and we had no chance."

"I didn't say you had zero chance." Ed had the grace to look a bit sheepish. "And honestly, I was just trying get them motivated."

Hmm. Rani had to admit she'd made some disparaging remarks about Ed's film for the same reason.

"Besides, they were complaining a lot. John thinks I'm going too far with the stylization and that my ideas are too"—Ed made air quotes—"'inaccessible.'"

Rani arched her brows. "I didn't think you would care if your work was accessible or not."

"Well, I do."

"Okay, well, I care about rom-coms. And they're harder to write than you might think."

Ed held up a hand. "Look, I think we all have a story to tell, and it can be told in lots of different ways. Can I keep reading?"

She was flustered and ready to argue more, but also she was low on time. "Well . . . okay."

He returned to the script, reading with rapt attention. He even laughed out loud several times. "It's awesome how you manage to really set up their relationship in just a few pages."

Rani felt as if she were glowing enough to fix all their lighting issues. Ed Yi—Ed Yi the Gerhardt fan, Ed Yi the guy who loved dark romanticism, Ed Yi of the crack in the sidewalk that represents death—yes, *that* Ed Yi was impressed by her script.

She grinned. "So what do you think about the lighting issue?"

"I have some ideas."

Was Rani actually having fun with Ed Yi?

She thought maybe she was.

They were both sitting at the table, their two cell phones simultaneously recording, each one focused on their respective hands. Hers flipping through her book. His fidgeting with a napkin. It was better than looking at grainy faces.

INT. CAFÉ - DAY

> ### NATE
> So, do you mind if I sit down?

> ### LAYLA
> Yeah, actually I do.

> ### NATE
> Come on. It's dark in here — you can't exactly read your book anymore with no power.

> ### LAYLA
> There's a window.

> ### NATE
> I'm concerned for your eyesight. You shouldn't strain your eyes.

> ### LAYLA
> I'm fine. I was planning to leave soon anyway.

> ### NATE
> It's so windy it would probably be dangerous to be wandering about. Besides, you haven't even finished your lunch.

> **LAYLA**
>
> I'm not hungry.

> **NATE**
>
> (sits down anyway)
>
> Did you hear the one about the clam who was sorry?

> **LAYLA**
>
> No. Go away.

> **NATE**
>
> He said he was very shellfish.

> **LAYLA**
>
> (laughs in surprise)
>
> Uh-huh.

> **NATE**
>
> How about the bird who had done a bad thing?

> **LAYLA**
>
> (chuckling)
>
> No idea.

> **NATE**
>
> He had a lot of egrets.

LAYLA

Oh my god, these are terrible. Why are you subjecting me
to this?

NATE

The typewriter was really sorry, too. Know why?

LAYLA

Why?

NATE

He knew it wasn't cool the way he'd really pushed your
buttons.

LAYLA
(laughs)
You're ridiculous.

NATE

In a good way? Because I have more.

Rani's script wasn't exactly noir material. And they weren't able to incorporate the *Wired* magazine prop at all. It was simply impossible with this lighting.

Yet something about the corny jokes while focusing on their shadowed hands was . . . actually kind of working? It made you listen to the dialogue more. Every pause, every intonation. And even though the footage was grainy, the hands told a story, too. Pausing, retreating, fidgeting.

First separate, later inching a little closer together. JJ would have to splice the two separate recordings together, but Rani could already tell that it was going to look great.

"It's weird how well this works," Rani confessed. "Thanks for your help."

Ed smiled. "I think the juxtaposition of your character's goofy puns and the shadowy cinematography will create a really interesting effect."

Usually, when someone said something was *interesting*, they meant it was weird and they didn't like it. But Rani could tell Ed was being sincere.

"Thank you," she said softly.

Ed chuckled. "Somehow, you've managed to make it so we both hate and respect Nate. Trying to win back a girl with terrible puns? Bold, my friend, bold. Honestly, my dialogue game could use some work."

"Maybe I can help?" Rani heard herself saying.

A part of her couldn't believe she was offering to aid Ed Yi and the Better-Than-Thous. But he'd helped her, so obviously it was the least she could do.

Ed raised his brows. "As long as you promise not to include any terrible puns. No offense—just not my style."

Rani laughed. The puns were new from this morning, inspired by the Dads. She thought they were really goofy and perfect. Just like Raj was goofy and perfect.

OCTOBER

"Well, what do you think of the script?" Rani asked Raj eagerly.

"You only handed it to me thirty seconds ago!" Raj returned. "And I'm trying to enjoy this meal with my girlfriend! Isn't it romantic?"

They were having a candlelit dinner in the Songbird restaurant, the sunset splashing across the sky over the sea through the bay windows. Rani had picked Raj up at the ferry dock earlier that afternoon.

Rani smiled. She was eager to have him read her genius work, but she had to admit that the present was pretty nice, too. "Okay, okay. I guess we have plenty of the time for you to read it." She reached across to hold his hand. "And this *is* very romantic."

She stared into the perfectly brown eyes of her perfect boyfriend, searching his soul for the secrets of his tender heart. . . .

"Um, why are you staring at me like that?" he asked.

Rani giggled. "What? I was searching your soul for the secrets of your tender heart."

He let out a big, loud laugh, the kind that made Rani's skin tingle. She loved being ridiculous with him, and that he always—okay, almost always—stepped up to be her Bollywood hero. And that she could be as over-the-top as she wanted, and he never seemed to mind.

"You crack me up," he said. "By the way, this pasta is so good. What did your dad say he put in the sauce?"

Dad must have overheard him because he popped over. "It's butternut squash and figs. A new recipe I'm trying. You like it?"

"It's divine," Raj assured him.

"Seriously, brilliant," Rani agreed.

Dad gave them both a sunny grin. "Amir really likes figs. I can't wait for him to try it."

After Dad wandered off, Raj wrapped some pasta around his fork and stared at it thoughtfully. "It's cute how he wants to impress Amir. They're still in their honeymoon phase, huh?"

Rani nodded. "Yeah, I guess so."

"Hope it lasts."

There was an awkward pause. Raj's mom had lost her job and the financial strain was throwing a wrench in things. Rani and Raj had spent hours on the phone wondering where things had gone wrong, hatching up ideas that might get them back together, *Parent Trap* style. They weren't serious solutions, but they usually made Raj feel better.

"Has anything improved with your parents?" she asked.

Raj launched into a long story about how his dad had thrown a fit over a medical bill they'd received. It hadn't been discretionary; his little sister had fractured her elbow while rollerblading.

"When he saw the bill, Dad basically slammed it on the table and left for a bike ride," Raj said. "But he was back in like fifteen minutes because of a flat tire. And then he was in such a mood that my sister and I decided we needed to leave. We went to see a movie. It was a terrible alien action flick with cheesy dialogue, but it was playing at the right time."

Oh dear. "Could we invite them out to Fernando's barn and then make sure the door gets conveniently stuck? It worked for Avani!"

Raj smiled a small sad smile. "Maybe."

Usually, he laughed. Things must really be getting bad between them. And even she, Official Love Guru, felt at a loss. Maybe there were some people who really weren't meant to be together. But the idea frightened Rani in a way that she didn't want to admit out loud. She hated the idea that his parents couldn't make it work—because what did that mean for everyone else? What did that mean for her and Raj?

Nothing, she told herself. His parents weren't them. She and Raj were perfect together— even with all her big expectations of love and life, he got her. He *knew* her. She loved that.

"Thanks for listening," he added. "I know it's a lot. I know it feels like it's all we ever talk about. I mean, besides your upcoming directorial debut."

"Hey, you help me, and I help you." Rani nudged his knee with hers. "That's why we make such a great team. And you know I'm up for more scheming if it will help. But—seriously, I'm dying. Will you read my screenplay? I need to know what you think. Also, um, I hope you don't mind but I did include some stuff about Nate's parents fighting. Is it too personal? I could change it to something else."

He shrugged. "Nah, it's fine. Even if you changed the reason Nate didn't keep in touch with Layla, I would always know what the real one was. Your film wouldn't change that."

She swallowed, suddenly second-guessing the entire script and how it was based on them. But she'd spent a lot of time on it, and she thought it was a story that deserved to be told. "You're sure?"

"Yeah, totally sure." Raj reached for her hand, the flickering light of the candles reflected in his beautiful deep brown eyes. "And there's no question it'll be amazing. But is it okay if I finish this pasta before reading it? I wasn't lying to your dad—I think this may be the nectar of the gods."

Rani rubbed her thumb against his. "I suppose that would be acceptable."

Chapter Forty-Seven

Rani

Dominic and Sara were the first to wander back, holding hands and smiling all perfect-couple-ish-ly. Rani and Ed showed them the new footage with the shadowed hands.

"I dig it," Dominic said, sitting down at his spot. "Let's get this show on the road."

"Sounds good," Rani agreed. "But the five minutes were over ten minutes ago. Where are JJ and Parker?"

"I think they went for a walk along the harbor. Should be back soon," Dominic said.

Only, they weren't back soon. Their filming time was up, but still no sign of Parker or JJ. Or Adam or Fiona.

"Ugh, they're so irresponsible," Rani said, pacing.

"When they get back, you can have some of our time," Ed offered.

Rani didn't think about it—she just hugged him. And wow—Ed smelled really good. Of course, Raj always smelled good, too, but this caught her off guard. She'd thought he'd smell like musty closets full of old subtitled films, but actually she loved the cologne he was using. It seemed expensive and fresh all at once.

She felt a little embarrassed for noticing though. "Um, thanks. It's really nice of you, since my cast has obviously totally lost track of time."

Ed looked a little flustered at the hug, too. "Um, yeah, I mean . . . of course. My cast was obviously distracting your cast." He ran his hand through his hair, as if at a loss. "Should we go look for them?"

Ricky had been reading in the café all along—he was so quiet! But besides him and Dominic, the rest of their casts were AWOL. Rani wasn't exactly thrilled that she needed to send out a search party, but what choice was there? Ricky and Dominic went to scour the area near the auditorium, and Ed offered to comb the harbor area with her.

"What is with Parker today?" she fumed as they wandered past docked boats. She and Ed had both lost their time slots in the café now; the afternoon was rapidly passing, and they needed to finish their films to have time even for a hatchet edit job.

The wind was still wailing. The sea was still churning. The clouds above were thick and the kind of gray that made you think there was no such thing as sun.

It fit Rani's mood perfectly.

Ed squinted down the street. "Is that Parker and Adam?"

He pointed to a couple of people under the same tree that Ed had been filming earlier. The wind blustered around them, the leaves blowing up from the ground like a flock of birds taking off. But in the midst of all that—yep. It was Parker and Adam.

Making out.

What was in the air today? Clearly that windstorm seemed to be blowing some kind of aphrodisiac over the island. Maybe that was why Rani had thought Ed smelled so good. She had to ignore that traitorous feeling of course, since she had a boyfriend. (One who apparently hadn't gotten the windstorm aphrodisiac memo, clearly.)

The clock was ticking, and Rani had a bad feeling that Ed was also going to miss out on his café shooting slot. She jogged down to the tree where Parker and Adam were in their own little world.

Ed followed, groaning when he stepped in a muddy puddle in his loafers. Rani would have smirked, but she was too busy limping, maybe just slightly regretting the black pumps she'd picked as part of her debut directorial look. She wore heels at school just fine, but she hadn't thought through how much time she'd spend on her feet today.

And now the heels kept sinking into sticky mud. Eventually, the two of them—with extremely muddy shoes—made it to where Parker and Adam were still going at it as if the only oxygen available was in each other's mouths.

"Hey," Rani said. "It was supposed to be a five-minute break! What're you doing?"

Parker didn't stop kissing Adam right away, but she did open her eyes. Took her time coming up for air. Rani was tempted to strangle her, but she certainly couldn't waste any jail time on this traitor. (Yes, she was definitely still feeling raw about what Parker said regarding Raj.)

"Clearly we weren't going to get that shot," Parker said. "It's too dark for JJ's cell phone. We don't have a proper camera. Let's just move on."

"Actually, Ed helped me come up with a brilliant way to handle the low lighting," Rani said. "So if you still want to be the star in an award-winning short film, let's go."

Parker rolled her eyes. "I have my doubts about that."

"What's with you?" Rani demanded. "You were completely into *Remeet-Cute* when we were rehearsing for the past month. Now you're more into making out with this doofus?"

"Hey!" Adam protested.

Parker glared at her. "It isn't my fault that nothing is working out. Wake up! There's no power in Friday Harbor. Your boyfriend stood you up and screwed us. There isn't going to be any *Remeet-Cute!*"

"So you just want to give up?" Rani asked.

Parker clasped Adam's hand. "I think we might as well make the most of the day."

"Honestly, I think they're going to cancel the whole thing," Adam added. "I heard that now Olivia Lee isn't sure she can get here on time. She was supposed to come by seaplane, but her flight got canceled, too."

What?

"She has to come," Rani protested. "She just has to. After all the work I've put into this, after the months of working on the script and practicing . . ."

"Sorry," Adam said. "I was looking forward to it, too. But we need to face the music."

Rani felt like sinking into the mud. (Her heels already were, but this was metaphorical.) What about her big plans? What about meeting Olivia Lee and becoming co-directors and conquering the red carpet together?

Parker finally let go of Adam. "Look, I'm sorry about what I said about Raj. I'm sure he does have a good reason for not being here. But sometimes you just have to let things go."

Rani's heart squeezed. "Are you talking about the film or about Raj?"

Parker shrugged. "Maybe both."

And then, her phone vibrated. Rani pulled it out without thinking. Probably the Dads checking in to see how everything was going.

Only it wasn't the Dads. It was Raj.

"Hey, Raj. What's going on?" Rani spoke breathlessly as she strode quickly away from the others. For once she was glad for the howling wind because they wouldn't be able to overhear.

"Sorry I didn't call you back earlier," Raj replied. "I just . . . couldn't get out of bed this morning."

Rani didn't understand. "Oh no, are you sick? Is it the flu?"

"No." Raj sighed. "My parents are officially getting divorced."

Rani sat down at the picnic table where her cast had snacked earlier. "Wow. That's terrible. I'm so, so sorry."

This was big. No wonder Raj hadn't been able to come; he wouldn't have been able to concentrate anyway. She'd known he had a good reason. Suddenly, she really, really hated Parker for making her doubt him. After all, Rani and Raj had an epic love, one that was meant for the history books.

"Yeah." Raj's voice was dull.

"I know how hard they've been trying . . ."

"Yeah."

"They're really sure they can't work it out? More counseling? Remember the trap-them-in-a-barn idea?"

"I think it's really over," he said.

Rani struggled to respond, but it was difficult for her to understand this. She'd lost a mom to a car crash, Pop to a stroke. But Dad had never gotten divorced. And Rani realized that had been part of what shaped her whole worldview. She saw love as a thing that lasted, especially after you said those words, those big promises: *I do*. But she also understood that not everyone could be as lucky in finding their soulmates as Dad had been.

"The thing is," Raj continued, "I think we should break up."

What?

Rani suddenly felt so cold, like the blues and grays of the sky had invaded her soul and chilled it with permanent November. "Raj, I know you're really sad right now, but your parents' divorce doesn't have anything to do with us."

Raj sighed. "I'm just not in a good place to be in a relationship right now. I know you want a lot in a boyfriend. You want your Bollywood hero, and that's not what I can be right now. I can't deal with all your expectations."

Again, what?

"What do you mean?" Hurt spilled into Rani's voice. "You said you loved being my Bollywood hero. You said we had an epic romance that transcended time and space. . . ."

"Actually, you're the one who always said that," Raj said.

Rani was stunned. "And you just went along with it?"

The silence seemed to fill the entire Salish Sea, all the space between Bellingham and Friday Harbor.

"Look, I do love how much you believe in love," Raj said. "I know you have grand expectations, and to be honest, it did push me to be a better boyfriend. I helped you with your script, I even found Olivia Lee's assistant's email, I did everything I could to be who you wanted me to be. . . ."

"And what?" Rani said. "I never did anything for you? We've spent hours and hours every week talking about your parents. I've always made time to listen to your problems and—"

"You're right," Raj said, cutting her off. "You've been there for me, and I didn't mean to imply you haven't. For a while, I believed what you imagined for us. I wanted to believe that we had an epic romance that would survive time and space."

"Then what's the problem?"

He paused, and when the words came next, they too were choked. "I might be moving to Toronto."

"What? Why?"

"My mom got a new job there. She's moving. I have to decide who I want to live with."

Rani wanted to scream that *obviously* he should live with his dad and stay right where he was. Wouldn't he do that if he really cared about their relationship? She suddenly felt like every moment they'd had together was a complete lie.

Even though he'd never echoed her thoughts about their epic romance out loud, she'd thought he'd felt the same way. That he'd said it not with words but with his eyes. With those gorgeous earrings he'd given her. With his enthusiasm for her screenplay.

"Don't you care about us?" Rani asked quietly.

"Of course I do," Raj said. "I love you. I do. But is it really a forever kind of love? The kind where I decide if I should live here or in Toronto based on it? It might sound nice to say our love is epic and beyond time and space and all that stuff. But really, we're only in high school. We're seniors, and we'll be off to college soon. Who knows where we'll end up?"

Rani sputtered. "If we're meant to be, it'll work out."

"Exactly," Raj countered. "If we're meant to be, we'll find each other again."

Wow. He'd turned her own words around on her. And she didn't know if he really thought it was a possibility or was just telling her the thing she wanted to hear.

"I want to make a decision about Toronto that's all my own," he said. "If we're together, I just couldn't help thinking about what you want. And that's not fair to me and what I want."

A part of Rani understood, she really did. But her heart was broken, just shattered to pieces. She'd waited so long to meet someone like Raj. Someone she clicked with. Someone who was fine with her quirkiness and her over-the-topness—someone who even sort of loved it.

This was so unfair. She hated Raj's parents for making it come to this. If only they had more time, if only they could have spent their senior year together. They'd barely gotten together in July! Just a few short months of the best, most meaningful romance of her life.

"I'm so sorry, Rani," Raj said. "I didn't want to ruin your big day, but since you kept calling, I felt like I owed you an explanation. Also, I really do adore *Remeet-Cute*. It's so funny, and I love the way you took our story and shared it in this really cool way. I hope you'll send me a copy—whether or not you win the contest. I'm proud of you for seeing this through."

The thing was, Rani wasn't sure if she wanted to see the film through anymore. She couldn't answer, mumbled something about talking later, and hung up. She felt physically ill, as if someone had given her three lattes and then punched her. Everything was gurgling up inside her—the pancakes from that morning, the mochas—and she thought she might vomit. Her forehead was clammy, and she felt like she had a fever.

No, she couldn't possibly finish *Remeet-Cute*.

She texted her sisters: *Raj broke up with me. Don't bother coming to Friday Harbor. I'm going home.*

Part Five:
The Moon Is
Glittering

Chapter Forty-Eight

Nidhi

NEW DELHI—EARLY NOVEMBER

It was a Sunday morning, highs in the nineties expected. Nidhi was finally starting to feel at home in the heat, though she still couldn't deal with wearing jeans. Instead, she'd opted for a loose linen dress that she'd picked up a couple of weeks ago, a feminine flirty thing with puffy sleeves and an A-line skirt, her loose curls free.

She felt peaceful that morning, though a little melancholy, too. It was a shame that her term abroad would be ending in December, just when she had gotten used to the snarl of New Delhi traffic and crowded sidewalks and train trips and the melodic sounds of Hindi and Urdu and so many other languages drifting around her.

That morning, she and Sona were wandering the Daryaganj book market, where stacks and stacks of books were displayed across the sidewalks. Books from local small presses. Books from abroad. Rare books. Collector's items. More books than she'd ever seen in one place in her life.

"How do you find anything in this place?" Nidhi asked.

"I love browsing," Sona said. "But there are a few vendors who are my favorites."

They wandered along, pausing to rifle through some zines and comic books from one vendor, then turning to classical Indian poetry at another, and then stopping at place that had a bunch of American young adult fiction. Nidhi glanced at the cover of a summer romance, a girl riding a bike along a boardwalk.

She felt like one of those girls, the ones who changed and grew and came of age over the course of a few significant months. She was so much more comfortable in her skin than she'd ever been before. She'd:

- gotten closer to her relatives

- become more fluent in Hindi

- met a Bollywood actor

- danced to gully rap

- meandered through old palaces

- seen artwork from hundreds of years ago

- fallen in love with the poetry of Rabindranath Tagore

- accepted she'd never be any good at haggling

- lost the guidebook somewhere—and didn't miss it

It was funny how life brought you so much, if only you let it.

"Ooh, there's my friend Rekha," Sona said, waving to a vendor a few paces away. "She runs this art collective called Monster Arts. I'd love to be a part of it someday, but you have to be at least eighteen to join."

Rekha smiled, overhearing Sona. "We'll be excited to have you when you're old enough."

Sona sighed the sigh of every sixteen-year-old anxious to prove themselves in the bigger world out there.

Nidhi squeezed her shoulder. "What does the collective do, exactly?"

"We help promote artists," Rekha said. "We have a rotating exhibit where we display their work. We host fundraisers to provide grants. We connect our artists with paid opportunities. We also publish books that showcase their work. Here's our latest."

Rekha gestured at a large coffee-table book. Nidhi flipped through the glossy pages, filled with shots of murals and graffiti art painted in urban spaces. The artists celebrated local culture even as they called for progress against inequality and civil liberties.

"This is amazing," she said. "I'll take it."

"That's great," Rekha said. "Are you an artist, too?"

Nidhi shrugged. "Someone once told me that my baking is an art."

Sona poked her. "Don't be so modest. Her baking really is an art." She pulled up a photo on her ever-present camera.

It was a platter of burfi that Nidhi had recently made. The recipe had been from Shiv, but she'd decorated them with her own vision. She'd been thinking of the gorgeous mosaics she'd seen at some of the old palaces she'd visited and had used colored sprinkles to recreate them. They'd taken *forever* and her family had protested they were too pretty to eat.

(They really were, but Nidhi had insisted they do so anyway.)

"She's right," Rekha said. "This is incredible work."

"You can eat those?" another voice said in amazement.

They turned to find someone familiar. Nidhi couldn't quite place how she knew this girl. . . .

"Hailstorm!" Rekha said. "Good to see you!"

The female rapper's lyrics had haunted Nidhi for weeks. Now Hailstorm was standing right here in front of her, sunshine on her face. She was dressed casually and yet trendily in dark jeans, a T-shirt, bangles running up her arms.

"Oh my gosh," Nidhi gushed, "I saw you perform a while back. At that concert Alok Anand hosted? What was the name of the club again? Well, anyway, you were amazing. I still have your song 'Get Out' stuck in my head. Seriously, I've watched the video so many times; I'm obsessed. . . ." She was fangirling hard, but she couldn't help it.

Hailstorm chuckled. "It's nice to meet you."

From inside Professor Cunningham's office, Nidhi could hear the windstorm shrieking like Deity's most devoted fans, reminding her that life was never what anyone expected. After all, who knew she'd be singing at the top of her lungs about iPads and lint in your belly this afternoon?

Even though her plans had been completely wrecked, she'd had so much fun today. And that feeling was there again, that feeling that said there were so many forks in the path, and yet she didn't want to miss a thing. Why couldn't she have infinite time in this world, time to explore limitless possibilities? That was where that deep yearning really came from: the knowledge of all that was out there in this universe. Lives and loves and art and books and so many recipes you couldn't make them all. . . .

"So, what did you want to talk to me about?" Professor Cunningham asked, bringing Nidhi out of her reverie.

Maybe Nidhi should just get Professor Cunningham's opinion. Let the decision fall to someone else. Yes, that sounded nice.

"I have this opportunity," Nidhi explained. "There's this art collective in New Delhi. And I've been offered an internship there!"

"I didn't realize you were interested in pursuing a career in art," Professor Cunningham said. "Your interests have been in business and culinary school. I loved your scholarship essay for your term abroad—the one about how you wanted to own a bakery or restaurant one day, how you wanted to try to fuse flavors from the east and the west."

Nidhi had almost forgotten about that essay she'd written last winter, the one that had ultimately gotten her a fellowship to spend a term abroad. Strange how even as her dreams had been changing back then, she'd thought that was the last of it. She'd thought that going to India and seeing the white marble of the Taj Mahal, inhaling the scents of street food, and gobbling pani poori and Indian egg rolls would somehow make that yearning stop. That her unrest would be satiated.

But no, she had bigger dreams even now. A bigger appetite for tasting everything on the menu.

"Actually, I wouldn't be working as an artist myself, but more on the marketing and publicity side," Nidhi said. "I'd be helping raise awareness about different artists, especially those who haven't had access to a formal education or come from financially disadvantaged families. Helping with fundraising, learning how a nonprofit works from the inside. Do you want to pull up the website? It's called the New Delhi Monster Arts Collective. . . ."

As they discussed Hailstorm and the local art scene, all the passion Nidhi had felt for the internship came tumbling back.

"It sounds like a very unique opportunity," Professor Cunningham said as she walked Nidhi out into the hallway. "I'll recommend it, if you write up a formal proposal. Keep in mind that we don't have much time to change your plans for next term, so I'll need it ready and polished a week from Monday."

"I understand. But I'm still thinking it over myself," Nidhi responded, her head in a swirl, her heart aching at what it would mean to be away even longer. "What do you recommend? Should I come back and study in the classroom, or do this?"

Professor Cunningham put a hand on her shoulder. "Nidhi, I can't decide for you. You've made a great case that you'd learn a lot. What's holding you back?"

Nidhi hesitated. She didn't want to admit she was scared:

- that her dreams would forever shift and change

- that she'd never find a way to settle that restlessness inside her

- that she'd lose her chance with a boy with stormy-sea eyes

- that her heart was pounding and her hands were clammy with the weight of so many choices

"Think it over . . . but keep in mind we need to get that proposal in if you want to pursue this," Professor Cunningham said. "And have a good time this week with your family!"

After her meeting, Nidhi found Rita and Grayson back in the quad, still at the art booth. Apparently, Grayson had agreed to draw quick charcoal portraits of anyone who asked, gratis.

"When did you learn to do this?" Rita watched while he quickly sketched a girl with big, curly hair and round glasses.

"Oh, I've been sketching for a while," Grayson said. "I never really thought I was that good, but I practiced during my travels. Plus, Nidhi's always so encouraging."

"Well, she's right. You are really talented," Rita said, watching in admiration—and perhaps remembering what Nidhi had said earlier about Grayson being "found out." Oops. But Nidhi trusted Rita to keep a secret.

"That's what I've been telling him." Nidhi noticed that he was using a distinctly different style than he had in his work as the Skull. More angular lines, an emphasis on the girl's facial features rather than her full profile. Deflecting suspicion, she supposed.

"Thanks!" the girl said as she hopped away with her portrait.

"Do me next!" someone said, striking a pose with hands on hips and a full grin.

"Dude, you're seriously not going to apply to the art school?" the art-booth guy said as more people lined up.

Grayson just shrugged and continued sketching. Nidhi put a hand on his shoulder. "Making a decision like that is a big deal. He'll think about it."

"I will?" Grayson's voice was amused.

"Why not? You've traveled your forty-two countries. Maybe it really is time to start thinking about next term."

It occurred to Nidhi that perhaps he needed a push, just as she had the year before. A night of midnight magic had changed her, made her more confident, made her reach for the stars.

"You're amazing, Grayson," she said softly. And she wasn't just talking about his art. "I believe in you. Will you at least chat with Professor Cunningham about it? Since she gave you her card. She's been a really good advisor to me. Encouraging and down to earth."

Grayson rubbed at the scruff on his chin. (Why did Nidhi get weak in the knees when he did that?)

"Yeah, okay. Maybe she can answer some of my questions about what I can really do with a degree in art."

Nidhi squealed and hugged him.

He chuckled, dropping his pencil. "I didn't know you'd be so excited about it."

She smiled. "I mean, it's totally your choice, of course. But I just think it's great that you're giving it some serious thought."

Grayson pulled her onto his lap. "Well, it would be fun to go to the same college."

Nidhi's heart thudded like wild horses stampeding across an open desert. It was so tempting.

"It would be fun," she admitted. "But . . . well, I was thinking about staying in India for another term." She filled him in on the internship.

He nodded. "That does seem really cool."

Nidhi searched his eyes, wondering what he was truly feeling. She was sitting in his lap for the second time today, and this time it wasn't because of a Mini Cooper. A storm was rustling inside her again, something new pumping through her veins. Why did it feel suddenly hot on this November day?

"Err . . . are you going to finish my sketch?" asked Grayson's current subject.

Nidhi giggled. Grayson winked at her. Reluctantly, she got up, her insides still feeling warm and melty like marshmallows in hot chocolate.

As Grayson finished his drawing, Rita put an arm around her shoulders.

"Girl . . ." Rita whispered. "You two need to get back together."

Nidhi laughed too. "We'll see."

As she wondered what in the world she was going to decide about next term, she noticed she had yet more texts from her family. But there was one message that was clearly the most urgent.

Rani:

> Raj broke up with me. Don't bother coming to Friday Harbor. I'm going home.

Sirisha and Rani had then exchanged a whirlwind of back-and-forth texts, which Nidhi had also missed. Nidhi mentally shoved aside her own doubts and fears of the future; it was time to focus on her sister, who obviously needed her. Rani was obviously devastated.

She showed the text to Rita and then Grayson.

"I want her to know that her film is important," Nidhi said. "That it's all hers whether or not she's still in a relationship with Raj. Mostly, I just want to be there for her. But it'll take three hours to get from here to Friday Harbor."

Rita nodded. "If we drive and take the ferry, yes. We'd get there really late."

"Is there some other alternative?" Nidhi asked.

Chapter Forty-Nine

Nidhi

It turned out that Rita knew a guy with a seaplane. *Well, of course she knew a guy with a seaplane.* Her parents were very well off and their family often flew back and forth from the islands. (They also had a yacht. "A very small yacht!" Rita would always remind her. "Right," Nidhi would always respond.)

But as much as she enjoyed joking about Rita's family's gratuitous wealth, right now it was definitely helpful. The three of them raced down to Lake Union. They'd had to leave behind the line of students hoping for portraits from Grayson, but one girl had insisted they go, whispering to Nidhi, "What a hunk. He's totally the Skull, right?"

Nidhi had just laughed and shook her head.

Now here they were, at a dock on Lake Union. The clouds had

thickened over the sky, an angry canvas with huge slashes of charcoal and slate and inky indigo.

"Pete! Hey!" Rita called to the pilot waiting beside a seaplane on the water.

A fashionable woman in expensive sunglasses, impractical heels, and a heather-gray blazer had been talking to him intensely, gesturing wildly, her voice getting swallowed by the roar of another plane taking off.

Rita hurried forward. "Do you have space for two? My friends really need to get to Friday Harbor."

Pete shook his head. "I'm so sorry, Rita, but I was just telling this lady"—he gestured at the woman in sunglasses—"I'm all booked up."

"Please," said the woman, "I need to be in Friday Harbor. Seriously, I'll pay you a big bonus!"

"I'd love to help you, ma'am. But I told you. I've only got three passenger seats on the plane, and they're all booked."

"I'll sit on the floor," the woman said. "I need to be there. I'm judging a youth film shoot-out. Do you really want to disappoint a bunch of kids who worked hard all day to create a short film? The prize is a consultation with me."

Oh. *Oh.* This must be Olivia Lee, Rani's idol. Which perhaps explained why the woman was wearing sunglasses with such dark skies. (What was with celebrities and their sunglasses?)

Nidhi waved to her. "Hi! You'll never believe this, but my sister is one of the directors for the One Day Shoot-Out!"

Oliva smiled. "Oh, that's wonderful. But I honestly don't know if we can make it."

Rita turned to Pete. "Do you know if any other seaplanes have seats?"

Pete shook his head. "I doubt it. Most companies canceled all flights today. My buddy Jenson just took off"—he gestured at the plane that was slowly ascending—"and I only agreed to this one ride because the wind has finally calmed down, and the family had booked this weeks ago. In fact, that's probably them."

Nidhi whirled around to see . . . John and Lena? And their son David with them.

No way.

"Wow, what a coincidence!" Lena said with a big grin. "Are you going on a sunset flight, too? Not that there will be much of a sunset today— way too many clouds. But the sea still looks gorgeous, so stormy and atmospheric."

David gaped at Olivia. "Wait a minute, aren't you . . ."

"Olivia Lee," Rita said, confirming.

"I'm such a big fan!" David said, eyes wide. "I loved *A Girl, a Boy, and a Dozen Puppies*!"

"Really?" Olivia looked pleased. "Usually men won't admit to liking rom-coms."

"Well, I do," David said. "In fact, would you mind taking a selfie with me?"

"Sure," Olivia said. "Do you want your parents in there with you?"

David smiled. "Yeah, that would be great!"

Nidhi offered to take the photo. They gathered with their arms around each other, Olivia Lee keeping her unnecessary sunglasses on, though her smile was warm. David grinned like it was the best birthday present ever.

"Thanks," Lena said. "Now, what brings you three here?"

"Well," said Nidhi. "There's this short film contest, and . . ."

The seaplane took off over the water, the sunset blotted out by gray clouds. Nidhi squeezed Grayson's hand as they waved to Lena, John, David, and Rita below. Olivia smiled at the two of them from the front. The pilot pointed out the Space Needle, then the islands they were passing. After spending so many hours on flights and buses, it was hard to register that they were finally returning to the San Juans. On a plane with a famous director, no less.

"It was so nice of Lena and John to give us their seats on the plane," Nidhi said.

Despite the loudness of the motor, Olivia heard her. "Yes, it was very nice. Good friends of yours?"

"We actually only met today," Nidhi shouted over the noise, "When our plane got stranded in Portland."

"Really?" Olivia said. "Sounds like you've had an adventure today!"

"Oh, we have," Grayson said. "There were a bunch of stranded travelers, so a group of us sort of banded together. . . ."

"We all piled into this guy's friend's tiny Mini Cooper and then had a ridiculous breakfast at a place that looked like a club. . . ." Nidhi added.

She and Grayson took turns telling the story of their zany day, finishing each other's sentences as they:

- admitted to morning mimosas that left them with midday headaches

- laughed about vegetables on parade

- quoted Electric Boogers lyrics

- pulled up Lucas's now-viral proposal

"Sounds like the premise of a good road trip movie," Olivia said, chuckling. "In fact, I'm getting some ideas. It could be an enemies-to-lovers rom-com about two people who hate each other having to work together to get home. Oh, or they could be exes whose flame is rekindled. Or it could be . . ."

As Olivia brainstormed aloud, Nidhi couldn't think of anything else but the part about the exes whose flame is rekindled.

She looked out at the view. Even in the tempestuous November gray, the San Juans were utterly beautiful. The sea was lined with silver and the pine trees were shrouded in the kind of wet mist that evaded any umbrella. Nidhi rested her head on Grayson's shoulder, and he gave her a brief little kiss on the forehead.

That little kiss was nothing, just a peck. But it was exactly how casual it was, how familiar it felt, that shook Nidhi to her core. And she knew.

No matter how she'd tried to protect her heart, Grayson was the one for her.

He always had been.

Chapter Fifty

Avani

The workshop was coming to an end, and each couple had the opportunity to show off the routine. Avani sat cross-legged with her head on Fernando's shoulder as they watched Greta and Trent run through the steps, their hips moving seamlessly, the passion between them palpable. They even nailed that last lift despite having missed hours of the workshop. (Jerks. Nice jerks, but still.)

The class offered them a standing ovation, and Avani joined in.

"They could compete," someone behind her said.

"They're unstoppable," another voice echoed.

Trent and Greta really did seem to have something special, both in their dancing and with each other. Even if they did get into the occasional screaming match while trapped in an elevator. Avani didn't envy whoever had to go next, but the truth was everyone had their own style. Even the couples that messed things up were cute because they were trying. People seemed exhausted but in good spirits.

And then it was her turn with Fernando.

This was him, the boy she didn't know if she loved, but she knew she loved dancing with him. The first steps were slow and easy, but Avani let herself enjoy them anyway. And then she and Fernando were flying with renewed fervor and she

```
didn't care about
      words
            only how she felt
when she was moving
      with this boy
            and
they
      even
            got
                  that
                        last
                              lift
                                    right.
```

"Wow, you two nailed it," Greta said as the class wandered out of the studio.

"Thanks," Avani said. "Will you be back for the makeup session?"

"Nah," Trent said at the same time that Greta said, "Absolutely."

Then Trent smiled. "Kidding. We'll be here."

"Great," Avani said, tossing her hair. "We'll beat you next time."

They all laughed, and it felt good. As they got to the elevator where other students were already waiting, Greta raised her brows. "Take the stairs?"

The foursome couldn't get down them fast enough.

Fernando and Avani walked back toward the auditorium, hands swinging between them. The windstorm was maybe dying down, though the stormy skies were still gray, gray, gray.

"Want to get some ice cream?" Avani asked. "We have some time before we have to meet everyone for the film thing."

"Ice cream in a freezing November windstorm?" he asked. "You know it."

She laughed and they stopped at the place everyone loved with the line that always went around the block in the summer. The wind outside carried with it the scent of fresh waffle cones. Luckily, there wasn't much wait at the moment.

"Share a cone with me?" Avani asked.

Fernando nodded. Naturally, they had to try at least eight different flavors until they agreed on one, but pumpkin chocolate chip was definitely a winner. (Perhaps Dad's love for all things pumpkin had rubbed off on Avani.) They found a cozy corner and took turns licking the cone. And then their lips found each other's and the kiss mingled with the freshly churned ice cream. It was sweet and dreamy and Avani's head spun.

When they came up for air, Fernando's face was serious.

"Listen, I'm sorry about the concert thing," he said. "I really love the Cloud Grifters, but obviously I don't want to make you choose between us and your sister. And I didn't want to make you do that last week, either. When you had to return the camera lens."

Avani took a deep breath. "Thanks, Fernando. I know my sisters do take up a lot of my time. I know that I can be scatterbrained about things, too."

It was okay if she said it. She hated it when anyone else called her that, but somehow, owning it felt good. Maybe it was time to stop being so defensive.

"You're not scatterbrained," Fernando corrected. "Or flaky. And I'm sorry I said that. You're passionate about a lot of things. I feel lucky that one of them is me."

All she wanted to do was keep kissing him, forget all their fights. But she knew they had to address them or they'd happen all over again.

"Thanks for apologizing.," she said, swallowing. "I'm sorry, too—for making you feel like you're not my focus. You are. And I've been thinking about it. I . . ."

She paused. Could she say these words aloud? But Fernando was looking at her the way he always had, and after sharing all their insecurities, she realized she had to say all the unsaid things.

"I think I might have ADHD."

Fernando paused for a moment. Then, nodded, taking her hand. Squeezing it. "Yeah, I guess I could see that."

"So?" she asked. "Does that change how you think of me?"

She stared into his moth-brown eyes.

"No," he said. "It makes a lot of sense. And the way you're uniquely you is absolutely perfect." His eyes were burning with their own glowing intensity. "Besides, I have my own issues. I get really grouchy when I'm stressed. I need to work on that."

"Same," Avani admitted. "But I did promise to make this day about you. I thought you'd think the screening would be fun though. I know we won't be alone—but Rani's really been working hard on directing it and writing the script, and . . ."

"Wait a minute, I didn't know she was directing it," Fernando said. "Or that she wrote the script? I thought she was just acting in it."

"No, this project is all hers," Avani said. "I thought I'd been talking about it constantly."

It had been such a hectic semester. She had to forgive him if he'd somehow missed it. And she had to forgive herself if it was her fault, if she'd never fully gone into the details. She honestly couldn't remember.

Fernando squeezed her hand again. "We've both been so busy. If I'd known it was such a big deal, I wouldn't have even suggested the concert."

She kissed him again. Another ice-cream-flavored kiss full of sweetness and chocolate and pumpkin. "Clearly, we need to work on our communication more. But we can go to the concert—after the screening and awards. I mean, they're not really going to be finished performing by nine, are they?"

"Hopefully not." Fernando smiled. "If we make it, we make it. I just want to be with you."

"How did I get the best boyfriend?" Avani asked.

A little kid nearby, probably about seven years old, started making gagging sounds. "You both are so gross!"

"Kathy Jane Davidson, that is very rude," her mother said. "We don't say that to people."

Avani chuckled. "It's okay. We kind of are."

She leaned forward to kiss Fernando and forget about everyone else. (Well, okay, so she could hear Kathy Jane pretend-gagging again while her mom shushed her, but it was fine.)

But then her phone pinged with a flurry of texts.

"I can ignore it," Avani murmured between kisses.

"No," Fernando said. "It might be important. Take it."

Chapter Fifty-One

Rani

Ed Yi was the one who found Rani slumped at the picnic table. She thought maybe he'd come to film some more falling leaves, but he just stood there awkwardly, thumbs in the pockets of his jeans. His muddy loafers getting even more muddy. They really weren't meant for wet weather. Or any weather, really.

She started giggling.

"What?" he asked.

"Your loafers," Rani said. "They're so you. I love them."

He smiled a rueful smile, brushed his hair with fingers. "I like what I like. Even if they're not really practical. They were fine in the concrete jungle that is LA."

"I bet they were. And who I am to talk?" She nodded at her directorial-debut pumps, which were also a mess.

The wind seemed to have calmed, but the sky was still slate gray with glints of silver. Rani hadn't thought any leaves were left on the nearby trees, but a few more feathered down. Perhaps just to remind her that winter was coming, that her relationship had ended, that there was no hope left in the world.

"Hey, I don't know what's going on," he said, "but you've been sitting here for a while. May I sit with you?"

She was surprised but nodded. He took a seat on the wet bench beside her.

"Do you want to talk about it?" he asked.

She shrugged. "My boyfriend just broke up with me."

She thought he might tease her. All semester long she'd been bragging about Raj. About how great he was, how perfect they were as a couple. It was honestly embarrassing, now that she'd been summarily dumped.

Maybe that was why Parker had said what she had. And Rani had to admit that her own words about Parker not having a boyfriend hadn't exactly been great friendship material. Sigh.

"That sucks," Ed said, not a hint of teasing in his voice.

"Yeah it does."

He picked up a stick and started poking a muddy patch with it like a kid. "I got dumped earlier this year, too."

"Wow," said Rani. "I'm sorry."

And she was. She'd obviously been judging him too harshly all year. He really wasn't so bad. (Though seriously? Dark romanticism? Why?)

"What happened?" she asked. "I mean, if you want to talk about it."

He continued to poke viciously at the mud in a way that indicated that maybe, possibly, he wasn't completely over it. "We went to the same school in LA, and when I moved here, we did the long-distance thing. She would call and text, but I noticed she'd been hanging with this other guy a lot on Instagram. She told me they were just friends, but then a couple of weeks later, she changed her mind. She decided she liked him after all and dumped me and that was pretty much it."

Rani nodded. "That sucks that you saw it on Instagram first."

"I mean, I believe her that they started out as friends," he said. "But I guess it was inevitable. She was there and I was here."

Rani found her own stick and started poking the puddle, too. It was pretty satisfying, actually, feeling it squish into the mud. "You'll probably think I'm ridiculous, but I always thought that me and Raj would be the ones who lasted. Against all the odds, we'd be together till we were old."

"That's . . . a lot of pressure to put on a high school relationship," he returned.

"Yeah. That's what he said, too. But I just thought—" She choked up. Again. Oh boy, was she about to cry in front of Ed Yi? Um, yes, she was, she was totally crying.

Ed looked a little terrified, but then he patted her back. "It'll be okay, Rani."

That was all it took. She sobbed against his shoulder.

After her embarrassing sobfest—which Ed was being so nice about— Rani finally let go of him. Ed had been there for her, and he really had no reason to. She'd never been particularly friendly to him, but here he was.

Letting her eyes leak all over his jacket. There was a brief drizzle as they'd talked, but now . . . the wind seemed to have decided to stop its ceaseless havoc. Perhaps it had done what it had set out to do.

And although Rani didn't think she was living out a rom-com anymore, it did feel like the skies seemed to have calmed along with her own emotions. She'd let everything out, and now she felt a little bit better.

"I'm done with *Remeet-Cute*," she said to Ed. "But let's get your film finished. I'll help you get everyone together."

"You really don't have to," Ed said. "I'll figure something out with the footage I have. Maybe my whole film will be one falling leaf. It'll be riveting, I swear."

Rani smiled. "Somehow, I believe it wouldn't be bad. But we might as well try to finish your footage."

"RANI!" Avani came dashing down the street. "Are you okay?"

Fernando was just steps behind her. "Rani—seriously, what can we do to help?"

Rani hugged her twin and Fernando. Despite the fact that she was still a bit of a wreck inside, the Official Love Guru noted that the tension between these two seemed to have dissipated.

Even though she still felt shaky, she raised her brows at Avani. Time to see if the twin mind meld was still intact. *How was the workshop?*

Avani shrugged, smiling a goofy smile. *It was good actually. Fernando and I found our way back to each other. Even though you gave us terribly cliché advice.*

Rani nudged her with a shoulder. *Sorry about that. I should have been there for you more.*

Avani nudged her back. *All is forgiven. And I'm sorry about Raj.*

Rani shrugged. *It sucks, but I'm doing okay, I think.*

Avani: *Really? You're not devastated?*

Rani: *Of course I'm devastated. But I can be devastated and still move on.*

Avani: *You can?*

Rani: *I think I might be growing or something. But don't tell anyone.*

Avani: *Wouldn't dream of it.*

Rani: *Thanks, twinsy. I missed our silent talks.*

Avani: *Me too.*

Rani was sad about *Remeet-Cute*, but helping Ed find his cast and finish his film was about all she had energy for. Getting dumped was emotionally exhausting.

"You really don't need to do this," Ed said.

"Yes, I do," Rani insisted. "Let's go find your cast."

They found Ricky first, still listening to music alone in the café. Unfortunately, even after an extended search, nobody could find Parker and Adam. Fi was around but said she was sick of Ed's dictatorial ways. He apologized for being so persnickety about the falling leaf, but apparently it was too late.

"I just can't do this anymore," she said. "I know that the second I pick up the camera, you'll go back to being . . . you."

Ed looked like he wanted to argue, and Rani thought he'd genuinely learned his lesson, but she could see on Fi's face that it wasn't going to happen.

"Maybe I can take the part," Fernando said. "I'm not an actor or anything, but it's better than nothing, right?"

"Yes!" Ed looked like he was about to hug him, but he stopped himself. "Thanks."

Rani chuckled. He still had to keep those aloof airs.

"I can handle the camera," Avani said. "I've been in photography club this semester, so I've learned a few things from Sirisha."

They'd long since lost their filming slot at Café Helix, but another team decided they weren't going to use the location after all, so Ed was able to get another one. The power had returned to Friday Harbor, so hopefully they could get going quickly. Fernando and Avani got to work helping Ed, and—despite everything—it made Rani happy to see Ed happy.

Chapter Fifty-Two

Sirisha

Lavi leaned against the ferry railing. Inky curls fluttered in the breeze. Chestnut cheeks chapped enough to turn ruddy. Lips a dusky mauve that looked way too kissable.

Sirisha sucked in a breath, handed her a coffee from the ferry café. "Careful, it's hot."

Lavi took it with a gloved hand. "You know, I'm beginning to understand what people like about living here."

With a heart pitter-pattering, toes toasty, Sirisha leaned with her back against the railing. "Oh yeah?"

Lavi gestured at the thrashing waves, the islands they were passing. "I mean it's gorgeous, but it's more than that. I love how dense Chicago is, how there's so much to do. But there's something cool about being out here. It feels like you're on the very edge of the world."

Sirisha smiled and inched closer. "If you like edges, you're going to love the Songbird Inn."

"What's that?"

"Didn't I tell you my family runs an inn?" Sirisha said. "It's on a cliff-side that overlooks the water. It truly feels like it's perched on the edge of the world."

"I have to see this place," Lavi said, scooching closer to Sirisha, too.

"I can't wait to show it to you," Sirisha said a little breathlessly.

Then she wasn't thinking of the inn anymore, but of the girl in front of her. And then two girls were kissing, lips soft like pillows, salty sea air curling around them, a fine mist sparkling like fairy dust. Somewhere in the distance, the clouds parted. A stream of sunlight filtered down. And a rainbow ribboned across pearlescent skies.

Chapter Fifty-Three

Rani

The rainbow seemed like a sign.

The Universe was speaking to Rani again, telling her that there would be better days, brighter skies. Moments when the clouds parted to let in a stream of sunshine. She knew that Raj was right—that she did have big expectations for their relationship. But she was looking for that person who felt the same way, the person who really believed in love with the big *L* the way she did.

She'd thought that person was Raj. And maybe it was—maybe they'd find their way back to each other. But for now, she tried to remember those early days with him, when she'd asked him to come to Dad's wedding. At that time, she'd still been feeling things out. She'd promised herself that she would let the relationship be whatever it was going to be.

Somewhere along the way, she'd left behind any reservations and decided Raj was The One.

Sigh.

She was gathered with the Dads at the same café she and her cast had eaten lunch at earlier. Dad and Amir had rushed over when they'd seen her text, and Sirisha had arrived on the ferry with a pretty girl in tow. Rani really felt the love—everyone was so sweet to drop everything and come to her when she was at her lowest. Especially since . . . admittedly, Rani had been pretty self-absorbed lately.

"You can't give up on *Remeet-Cute!*" Amir said, interrupting her thoughts. "It's too adorable. And you're almost finished with the footage!"

Rani was so exhausted, and it felt like heaven to be sipping hot chocolate with her family, cozily in front of a fire and away from the November cold. If only they would stop giving her those concerned looks.

"I don't believe in that script anymore," Rani explained. "When I wrote it, I thought all my relationship problems were over with. I thought I'd reached the Happily Ever After and that I was just documenting the journey. Now it's just too painful to remember all those small moments with Raj."

"That's the thing," Dad said. "There *is* no end. Relationships will always have the next hurdle."

"Or sometimes they come to an end," Sirisha added softly. "But there are always new beginnings."

Rani zeroed in on Sirisha's and Lavi's clasped hands. They were adorable, and she had to admit that it gave her hope. She would always believe in The One, her true soulmate. But maybe it really didn't have to come in high school. After all, tons of people married their college sweethearts.

EXT. COLLEGE CAMPUS - DAY

RANI, wearing a stylish beret, is chatting with a friend, lots of weighty college textbooks in her hands. Then a sudden gust of wind blows off her beret. A GOOD-LOOKING BOY on the quad manages to grab it for her.

> RANI
>
> Thank you so much. That's one of my favorite hats!

> GOOD-LOOKING BOY
>
> You're welcome. You know, there's something about you
> that seems familiar.

> RANI
>
> I don't think we've met before.

> GOOD-LOOKING BOY
>
> Yes, perhaps not in this life. But I feel certain our souls
> have crossed paths before. . . .

> RANI
>
> (staring deeply into his eyes)
> Yes, perhaps you're right. Perhaps our last meeting was
> in a past life. But this is our new beginning. . . .

Endings and beginnings . . . Rani turned the phrase over and over in her mind. And maybe . . . an idea was forming? A thrill pulsed through her. The kind that had nothing to do with finding a new true love. The kind that had to do with art. Rani itched to write a new script.

She didn't need to start over from scratch either. She could add to the footage she already had.

"I'm not going to finish *Remeet-Cute*," Rani said slowly, "But I have another idea. . . ."

Nidhi:

Rani, you cannot go home. Because you'll never guess who I'm on a seaplane with.

Rani:

A guy who will make me forget all about Raj?

Nidhi:

No. This is better than a guy. This is . . . drumroll please . . . Olivia Lee!

Rani:

Are you serious? I heard she wasn't coming. I heard the whole screening might get canceled.

Nidhi:

Well, it better not be because she's on her way. You're welcome.

Rani:

I don't know how you did it, but thank you, thank you, thank you.

Sprawled on the comfy sofa in the coffee shop, Rani completely rearranged her script. Tossed out big parts. Added a bunch of new scenes. Pages went flying as she worked, but the Dads helped her keep track of them. Her new idea was a celebration of how love was sweet even when it was transient—and that it could always bloom again. With the same person or someone different. Yes, it was pretty transparently about Raj and Rani. Again. But it was also universal.

She was excited about it, but . . . it was way too long for a short film. The contest rules were clear that it had to be under seven minutes.

"Can we read it?" Dad asked.

"Please?" Amir added.

Rani sighed. Handed over her pages.

Dad read the first page, then passed it to Amir before moving on to the second page. Amir passed the first page to Sirisha, and when she was done, she passed it to Lavi. Rani held her breath as they read. They'd better like this new envisioning. (Or maybe she was supposed to be okay with their feedback, considering she knew they loved her and wanted her to succeed? That seemed like *a lot* of growth for one day though. They'd better love it.)

"I love it," Sirisha said, finally looking up.

"Yay!" Rani squealed.

Sirisha smiled. "This is so great—showing different couples at different stages of their relationships. Some stay together, some break up. But it's showing it's okay when they move on."

Rani hugged her. "You get it! You really get it!"

Sirisha chuckled. "I think I do."

"But it's too long!" Rani moaned. "And half my cast has disappeared! This is impossible."

Sirisha put a hand on her shoulder. "It'll be a rough cut, but I think

429

we can do a version of this. Some of the scenes are definitely way too long. We'll have to get rid of a lot of the dialogue, make each snippet the briefest possible moment."

"Just short vignettes," Amir said thoughtfully. "I love it. Get ready for the red carpet, Rani!"

Rani squealed and hid her face behind her hands. "You really think we can do this? Today?"

"Absolutely!" "For sure!" "This will be amazing!" Her family was all in.

Sirisha started geeking out about camera shots. "Ooh, we can have them fade into the next one. . . . It'll indicate the passage of time. . . ."

Soon, they'd come up with the plan.

"We need more people," Rani said.

"Well," Sirisha said, "I'd love to be in it."

Rani shot her a skeptical look. "Seriously? You?"

Sirisha laughed. "I played a part today at the birthday party."

"She was really good," Lavi added. "Scarlett Singh was a gangster that I personally wouldn't want to mess with."

"Lola messed with Scarlett constantly," Sirisha returned.

"That was Lola," Lavi reminded her. "But me? No way."

So much banter. Rani glanced between them for about the millionth time, her Official Love Guru senses on high alert. She had no idea what had made Sirisha so bold, but she was happy for her little sis.

And apparently she had a cast?

"You're hired, both of you," Rani said. "And Dad and Amir? You can play an old couple."

"Old!!!" Dad said. "Did you hear her call us old?"

"I'm very offended," Amir said. "We're not old. We're middle-aged."

Rani rolled her eyes. "Fine, a middle-aged couple. It'll be great."

Chapter Fifty-Four

Sirisha

Sirisha:

Brie, you won't believe it. I'm acting in my sister's short film!

Brie:

Oh my gosh, that's awesome! I love that you're doing that. How was Bethany's party?

Sirisha:

It was really fun actually. Playing a part was surprisingly enjoyable.

Brie:

Look at you growing!

Brie:

Did that sound patronizing? I didn't mean it that way. It's just cool to see you let loose.

Sirisha:

No, no, I get it. I probably wouldn't have the nerve before today. Anyway, I'll tell you more later—we're filming now.

Brie:

Yes, later is fine! Enjoy! And you'd better send me that film!

Sirisha:

Haha. Yes, will send. ♥

Chapter Fifty-Five

Nidhi

By the time Nidhi, Grayson, and Olivia landed in Friday Harbor, the sky was dark, the crescent moon shining through a break in the clouds. The air still and quiet, the calm after the literal storm.

Nidhi was incredibly grateful she'd made it here. No matter how much she traveled, where she went, or what she learned, coming back to the San Juans would always mean something. And she was glad.

They thanked Pete the pilot, who waved at them cheerfully and secured the plane. Nidhi had assumed he was based in Seattle, but he told them that he, too, was from the islands. Upon closer inspection, Nidhi realized—yes, he had the look. The one that said time was something that was set by the tides and the ferry schedules. Or in his case, windstorms and seaplane schedules, but certainly not by anything else.

"I'd better run," Olivia said. "But thanks for sharing your story. I'm seriously thinking a road trip movie might be my next calling. Don't worry—it'll be totally different than your day!"

Nidhi laughed. "If you wanted to use some of it, we wouldn't sue you—if that's what you're worried about."

Olivia chuckled. "Good to know. I'll see you at the screening?"

Nidhi nodded. "Definitely. My sister is so excited you're judging!"

"I can't wait to see what everyone came up with!" Olivia trotted away in high heels down the dock.

Nidhi and Grayson shuffled slowly behind. Nidhi knew she should tell Rani that she'd made it. Say hi to her family who she hadn't seen in months. But for some reason, her feet stopped moving.

She looked up at Grayson, who came to a stop, too. He seemed to know she had something to say. Of course, he did.

She swallowed. "You know . . . when I said let's be casual . . . you didn't have to go along with it."

For a moment, she thought he might be like other guys. Scoff. Pretend he hadn't felt anything. But Grayson had never been like that, and his eyes were serious as they glinted in the moonlight.

"I didn't want to tie you down, Nidhi," he said. "I didn't want to be another Matt."

How did he do that—read her like a book? She stepped closer. Looked up at him. "I think I love you for that."

He sucked in a breath. "Did you just say what I think you said?"

Nidhi nodded. "I love you, Grayson. It took me going away and coming back to realize that."

He leaned forward to kiss her, but she stopped him.

"The thing is . . ."

Grayson groaned. "What?"

"I really do want to extend my trip to India. And I don't know if we can survive that."

Grayson leaned close, his eyes peering into hers. "Nidhi. I support you to do whatever you want. But you should know that I love you, too. I have for a long time."

And Nidhi knew with everything in her, her bones and sinews, that he did.

"So, what now?" she asked, her heart fluttering.

"We can be together," Grayson said. "We can make this work. I want you to stay in India. I want you to dream big for yourself. You're such a star, Nidhi, and I would never try to make you shine less brightly."

Nidhi smiled. "That's very poetic."

With those simple words, the jar was no longer closed. The butterfly was free to roam and to wander, to spread its wings as it wanted.

"Thank you." He gave her a wolfish, sexy grin. Scratched his scruff. "Look, I get why you didn't want to commit. Maybe that's how I've been feeling about my art. I thought if I went to art school or tried to do it for a job, all the joy and freedom would be erased. But maybe that's wrong. . . .

"On the quad today, all those people lining up for a portrait—that was amazing. They liked my work even when I wasn't keeping it mysterious. Maybe I was trapping myself by trying to keep it all a secret. I love being the Skull. You know, a shadow in the night . . ."

"A very sexy shadow . . ." Nidhi grinned, clasping the nape of his neck. She inhaled his scent, the scent of the sea and wild promises and desperate wishes floating in the air like dandelion seeds.

He took a ragged breath, holding her around the waist. His voice was husky as he continued. "Um, what was I saying?"

"What were you saying?" Nidhi batted her lashes. A fire was growing inside her, heating up her whole body. She loved the way his jaw clenched a little as he inhaled.

"Um . . ." He laughed shakily. "Oh yeah, art school. I guess sharing my work isn't as scary as I thought. Maybe I can even learn a few things. Thanks for helping me see that. And if you're in India, and I'm in the US, that's okay. We've got phones, right? Besides, who knows? Maybe next year we'll both be at UW together."

Nidhi kissed him then. She simply had to. Their breaths mingled, their chests heaved, and the cold of November in the PNW was no match for the blaze between them.

How could she have been so lucky to meet someone who understood her so well? Someone who wanted as much for her as she wanted for herself? And she wanted everything and more for him, too. She wanted him to shine brightly in the night sky, a star burning with energy and passion and big swirling dreams right beside her.

The clouds shifted, and the moon glittered through the break, and two silhouettes became one over star-tossed seas.

Chapter Fifty-Six

Rani

INT. CAFÉ - DAY

SIRISHA is waiting for her drink order near the counter.

BARISTA

Dark chocolate mocha!

LAVI

(grabs the mocha, starts out the door)

SIRISHA

Wait, that's mine!

LAVI

(whirls around)

No, I ordered the oat milk dark chocolate mocha.

SIRISHA

(looks at the barista)

Is this regular milk or oat milk?

BARISTA

Regular.

LAVI

Oh. OH. Well, thank you for saving me from dairy.

(shudders and hands the mocha to Sirisha)

Let's just say, it would not have been good if I

drank that.

SIRISHA

(smiles shyly)

You're welcome.

"That was perfect!" Rani said.

"Wait, don't you want ten more takes?" Dominic demanded.

Rani sucked in a breath. "Look, I'm sorry if I was too hard on you guys earlier. I'm glad you came back."

Dominic grinned and hammed it up for his imaginary camera again. "What kind of leading man would I be if I abandoned my part?"

Rani just laughed and hugged him. Then she hugged Sara and JJ. It turned out that they'd gone off to some camera store to see if they could rent equipment, and that's why they'd been MIA. It was really sweet. Only Parker had remained adamant that she was done filming for the day, but at least she'd apologized for what she'd said about Raj. In return, Rani had said she was sorry for her own comments. She still didn't know if their friendship would ever really be the same—she'd witnessed a new side of Parker today that she didn't understand. But that was okay. Endings and beginnings applied to friendships, too.

Chapter Fifty-Seven

Sirisha

Endings and Beginnings. Rani's new film idea resonated with Sirisha so much. She was ready to let Brie go. To start something anew. After the scene with her and Lavi, Sirisha took over the camera that JJ and Sara had managed to procure. Since Ed's group had finished filming and Ricky was now editing their stuff, they'd offered their equipment to Rani, so now they had plenty of choices.

Despite that, filming was frenzied as they hurried to get everything together in time. It was ambitious but cool to see everyone come together.

"Dads," Sirisha said. "Over here."

She angled the camera to get them bathed together in the soft glow of twilight that was now shining through the windows. It wouldn't last much longer, though.

"Wait! We still need to include the items in the list," JJ reminded Rani. "But there's one I can't find. I've checked every board game, but there are no dice in them."

"Someone must have cheated," Dominic said. "I told you we should have hidden *Catcher in the Rye*."

"Well, this isn't the official café we were supposed to film at," Rani reminded him. "So maybe the board games are just really old and nobody plays them."

"If you say so." Dominic's eyes narrowed, and he glanced around suspiciously.

"Actually . . ." Sirisha grinned at Lavi, who was happily snacking on a scone. Before heading out from Bethany's party, they'd both changed back into their regular clothes. Sirisha into her red sweater with the loose threads and jeans. Lavi back into her overalls. Sirisha had the prize basket that she'd won to remember the day—but she'd also asked Bethany if it was okay to keep the die. She pulled it out of her pocket now.

"No way," Lavi said, pulling out her own.

Rani screamed and hugged them both. "You're lifesavers!"

"You're welcome." Sirisha chuckled. "But we want those back. They're special."

"Got it," Rani said, and quickly instructed Dad and Amir on what to say next.

As Sirisha filmed, the Dads' characters discussed what they wanted to do for their twentieth anniversary—and decided on the simple pleasure of playing a board game. Sirisha loved that the dice that she and Lavi had kissed over would now forever be a part of the film.

Next, Dominic and Sara had a scene, followed by Fernando and Avani. Then Rani and Ed. But then some of the couples would get mixed up. There would be breakups and heartaches and new relationships. They dashed through the vignettes, each couple getting less than a minute, sometimes only fifteen seconds.

Sirisha couldn't wait to see it all edited together.

"Proud of you, sis," she said to Rani.

"Thanks," Rani said. Her eyes grew soft. "By the way, I really am sorry about the comment about your hair this morning. I was being insensitive."

"You think?" Avani asked, joining them.

Rani chuckled. "Okay, okay. Maybe I've been a *teensy* bit self-involved. I'm working on it!"

Sirisha laughed. "It's okay. I know I've been in a funk. You could have been nicer about it, but at least you did help me get ready for the day. Though with all the stormy weather, my hair's back in a tangle."

Rani looked it over with a critical eye, then shrugged. "Hey, you're pulling it off. It's the fresh-off-the-ferry look."

Sirisha hugged her again. "I'll take it."

Chapter Fifty-Eight

Rani

It had been months since the four sisters had all been in the same place at the same time, but now their day of wild, windswept wishes culminated at the most elegant restaurant in the islands. A place with high gilt ceilings, intricate crown molding, and numerous crystal chandeliers. Round-back gold chairs with tufted gray cushions were arranged around tables draped with cool gray linen. A large film screen hung on one wall, waiting to share new stories spun from youthful dreams.

The reunion with Nidhi was like a rampaging windstorm, too: ephemeral and intense and damp with joyous tears. Blustering with possibilities and the scent of something familiar, something that the Singh sisters couldn't quite identify but knew was a part of them, like the tempestuous sea and the boundless sky. They'd scatter to the winds again in another year, all four of them. But on this November night, the moon glittering above, they were together.

Rani felt her heart swell as they pushed together three tables to fit her family, the cast and crew, and the people they'd found something of themselves in. The day's emotional rollercoaster left her a bit breathless and anxious, and also . . . amazed. They were here for her, supporting her—despite all her mistakes and flaws. And she was grateful.

Dinner was a joyous blur, and then it was time for everyone to turn their chairs toward the screen. Rani had never thought of herself as an artist. She'd always found the term kind of pretentious, but here she was. Hoping that her short film meant something to someone, whether or not it won the award. (Though she would obviously take the award!)

"I can't wait!" Dad said. "So proud of you, honey."

"Ugh. I'm worried because the film is so rough!" Rani said, covering her eyes.

"You said that they expected a rough cut," JJ reminded her dryly. "Besides, didn't you know? I fixed everything in post."

Everyone laughed at that, even Rani.

"Also," Fernando added, "you've got a Cloud Grifters song in the background, so obviously it will be amazing!"

Avani chuckled fondly. "Of course, *you* would think so."

"Actually," JJ cut in, "the right music can really make a film memorable. Thanks for getting us permission!"

Fernando looked pleased, and Rani was glad her twin and Fernando had found their way through all the twisty gray turns on the road. She'd known they would, somehow, but perhaps that was the optimist in her. After all, she'd thought she and Raj would, too.

Endings and beginnings, she reminded herself.

The restaurant lights dimmed, and the place became quiet, the kind of quiet that thrummed with anticipation. It was a relief that *Endings and Beginnings* wasn't the first film to be screened, but Rani had trouble focusing because she was so nervous. At least this one, like hers, was also very roughly edited; the transitions weren't super smooth, and there was wind noise in the background. Still, she enjoyed the five-minute story about a backpack that passes from hand to hand before winding up with the person it should be with.

Remeet-Cute had mainly been inspired by feature-length rom-coms, and it had been so tough to cram everything she wanted to say into such a short piece. But as Rani watched the multitude of films created just today, she realized that maybe Ed had a point; there was so much you could do with this medium in particular.

When Ed's film came on, she watched him just as much as she watched it. It was dark in the restaurant, but she could see his clammed up—and yes, somewhat snooty—look. But now that she knew him a little better, she understood it was just a facade, the face he showed the world to hide the fact that he too had insecurities. That he too was nervous.

Ed Yi, nervous. What a revelation.

Plus, strangely, the crack in the sidewalk, the falling leaf—it all really did come together. And she realized that it was about the cracks in our society, how ignorance and racism and selfishness could lead to the end of civilization as everyone knew it. But the film wasn't without hope. It was also about noticing the things nobody else noticed. Letting yourself be in the moment even as you cared about the world as a whole.

And suddenly she was noticing things she'd never noticed

before, too. Like how chiseled Ed's face was. His profile was actually very . . . handsome?

Where had that thought come from?

But she didn't have time to dig into it because . . .

"It's *Endings and Beginnings*!" Sirisha whispered excitedly.

Everyone at their table sat up a little bit straighter as they watched. After the whirlwind of filming and last-minute changes, Rani had no perspective on whether it was good or bad. Still, it was fun to see her family and friends intercut in the short vignettes. Relationships came and went on the screen. They changed and grew, and some didn't last. The vignettes sped up toward the end, shorter cuts. The song by the Cloud Grifters that Fernando had managed to license reached a crescendo.

The very last shot was of her and Ed's hands in the dark of a café. There weren't words, just two hands reaching through the shadows and clasping. And then, JJ had added the letters *Fin.*

(Which Rani wanted to snort at, but whatever. JJ liked it.)

The Dads yelled and hollered, everyone at the table stood up to applaud. Rani stood, too, clapping for her cast and crew. This time, she spotted Ed watching her, and she beamed at him.

INT. SOMEWHERE FANCY - EVENING

RANI is making her way down the red carpet in a stunning dress.

REPORTER #1

Rani, here!

(flashbulbs as reporter takes multiple photos)

REPORTER #2

Rani, your new film is a sensation! What do you have to
say to your fans?

RANI

I'm so honored that it has resonated with viewers across
the globe. I've always wanted to portray love in its many
forms, and I hope I've done it justice.

After posing a bit longer, RANI spots fellow famous director ED YI making his way.

ED

Congratulations, Rani. Your latest was a triumph.

RANI

Thank you, Ed. Yours wasn't bad, either. How many
Academy Awards are you up to?

ED

Just three. But why do I have a feeling you're going to
outdo me this year?

RANI

(chuckles)

I guess we'll see.

Of course, Rani's moment of triumph was over far too soon. The next contest entry was already on-screen. But Rani was still back on the red carpet in her imagination.

A girl had to have dreams, after all.

Endings and Beginnings didn't win the grand prize, but Olivia did call it out as an excellent "ode to relationships." She had kind words about each of the films.

"You were robbed," Amir said vehemently after the winners were announced.

Rani smiled. "Thanks for the support. But I'm okay with not winning. The one that did really was fantastic. It gave me some ideas actually."

Avani raised an eyebrow. *Wow, you weren't kidding about growing.*

Rani beamed. *Obviously, I'm incredibly wizened and mature.*

People were getting up, circulating the room. Rani made the rounds, complimenting the groups she recognized, shakings lots of hands. (She was so ready for actual Hollywood meetings.)

"*Endings and Beginnings*, huh?" Ed said, coming up to her. "Pretty clever. I can't believe you pulled that off in just the last few hours we had."

"Oh my gosh, I know," Rani said. "It was definitely hectic. But JJ was a champ, editing it so fast. Yours came out so good, too! I think maybe . . . I respect the scene with the falling leaf? You had a vision and you went for it. And it actually worked as the centerpiece of the whole freaking film!"

"Thanks. I thought it turned out decently." Ed grinned at her. And for once, there were no holds barred. He looked good that way, happy and open.

Rani was about to say something else, something about how he too was robbed of the prize (even though the winning film had been really cool). But then she spotted Olivia Lee. Coming toward her.

She was going to die. Her idol. The most amazing rom-com director ever.

"Don't faint," Ed whispered.

Rani playfully elbowed him just as Olivia said, "Hi!"

And then the director was reaching out her hand. Rani shook it, unable to believe that she was actually touching *the* Olivia Lee. (Internal screaming!)

"I really liked both of your films," Olivia said. "Ed, your attention to detail and your cinematography are to die for. The falling-leaf metaphor was so cleverly done. Are you interested in a little bit of feedback?"

"Yes, definitely!" Ed said.

Olivia gave him a few pointers, and Ed looked like his mind was completely blown. Rani would have teased him about it, but now Olivia turned to Rani.

"And you—what a clever idea to use all those little vignettes. I'm a fan of the HEA myself, as you must know, but I think sometimes we get a little too enraptured with the Hollywood version of it. Your message—that breakups happen, and that we will find love again—was just wonderful. Are you interested in a little bit of feedback?"

And that was how Rani—future auteur extraordinaire—got her very first film advice from a real-life Hollywood director.

Chapter Fifty-Nine

Avani

As Avani watched her twin's brilliant short film, she couldn't help but squeeze Fernando's hand tightly. Endings and beginnings were great and all . . . but she wasn't ready for an ending with Fernando. Not even close.

They'd been through too much together.

She wanted to do something for him. Not because it would make their fighting go away. Not to cover for some insecurity. She just wanted to do it to make him happy. But what?

Should she sneak out with him to the Cloud Grifters concert?

She pulled out her phone, under the table so as not to disrupt anyone's viewing. It was so cool that the band had responded to Fernando's email, giving permission for Rani to include their song. She emailed them quickly.

Would you be able to do a shout-out for my boyfriend Fernando at the show tonight? We'll be there.

But then, oh wait—she noticed that the time for the concert had actually changed. Now it wouldn't even start till 10:00 p.m. They'd have time to make it after the film awards, actually.

Convenient, but so much for her plan to romantically sneak out!

She poked Fernando's knee and showed him the updated time. His face glowed in reaction. Avani knew that colleges and careers were important

but so were moments
    where everything was so perfect
        the moments
    encased in crystal
        the moments
           you decorated your life with
when your boyfriend's
    moth-brown eyes glowed golden
in the light
    and your body turned
        warm like molten lava
the moments when you danced
    the moments when you kissed

even the moments
    when you were trapped
      or waiting
the moments when you were stressed
    but together
that was life
    and she wanted
      every
        bit
          of
            it

Chapter Sixty

Nidhi

As she watched *Endings and Beginnings,* Nidhi couldn't have been prouder of Rani. She whistled and cheered along with everyone else as the word *Fin* swept across the screen. At times everyone underestimated Rani; she was so earnest about her love for romance that it was easy to roll your eyes and dismiss her. Nidhi herself had been guilty of that before. Yet there was something so endearing and actually very brave about the way Rani lived her life, how she was full of grand ideas and great expectations, how she did everything she could to make them happen.

There are a few moments in your life when something that should have been obvious suddenly comes into startling clarity. This was one of those moments for Nidhi: *Endings were natural, perhaps even inevitable, but you couldn't let that stop you from beginnings. You had to put yourself out there, to let love loom large in your life.*

After the films were over, the awards announced, people began milling about. The restaurant was cozy and elegant at once, with plenty of lights and candles, keeping the November darkness at bay. Nidhi couldn't believe she was actually here, back on the islands with her family. Now there was so much she wanted to do and say:

- to congratulate Rani, and let her know how meaningful she'd found *Endings and Beginnings*

- to find out what Avani had wanted to discuss

- to ask Sirisha more about Lavi

- to hug Dad again and just bask in that warmth he always brought to every conversation

Rani was surrounded by her cast at the moment, but Dad and Amir each enveloped her in big hugs (again), and as she looked into Dad's warm brown eyes, she knew that he'd never tell her what to do with her life. He'd always tell her to follow her heart, just as he had. It had led him to the Songbird Inn and to Amir. What more proof did she need that the future would fall into place if you let it?

Surprisingly, Sirisha wasn't clicking away on her camera. In fact, she didn't even have it with her. Instead, she was laughing with Lavi.

"So you two just met today?" Nidhi asked. It was honestly hard to believe. She'd never seen Sirisha open up to someone so quickly. But her younger sis was obviously blossoming. Again, Nidhi felt that ache for all she'd missed. But she was here now.

Sirisha smiled. "Yes, but it feels like we've known each other longer. Maybe that happens when you save someone's life."

"Are you going to keep bringing that up?" Lavi asked.

"What happened?" Nidhi asked, bemused.

"There was wind and a crashing tree . . . Well, you know the drill."

"That sounds really scary."

"Trees can be a real menace," Lavi agreed.

Sirisha and Lavi giggled, a familiar look passing between them. Nidhi almost expected to see cartoon hearts bubbling up in the air. And she felt grateful to be here to see these little things, things that couldn't really be relayed over a zoom call.

Nidhi chatted with them for a bit, and then it was time to check on Avani. The younger twin (by seven minutes) was still seated, giving Fernando googly eyes as if they'd only just gotten together. Nidhi had a hunch that maybe things were okay with them, too, but she tapped Avani's shoulder anyway.

"How are things?" she asked. *Should I be concerned about all those texts you sent?*

Avani turned to Fernando. "Hey, can you give us a minute?"

Fernando nodded. "Totally. I think they're serving dessert anyway. Want me to grab you something chocolatey and delicious?"

"We had all that ice cream before . . . but yes," Avani said. "Obviously."

As he left to let them catch up, Avani leapt up and hugged her.

"I missed you!" Avani said, and she looked a little teary.

"You did?" Nidhi hugged her back, but she was honestly surprised by the fervency in Avani's voice.

Avani chuckled. "I know, it surprised me, too."

The two of them had often butted heads when Nidhi had still lived in the Songbird. Whether it was about the kitchen inventory or coordinating an event, Nidhi was an excessive planner while Avani was more of a carefree spirit. Which Nidhi now tried to respect, even if she didn't fully understand.

"I guess senior year has been a lot more pressure than I expected," Avani continued. "And I was sort of afraid that Fernando and I were having the same issues that you and Matt were, and that we were doomed to break up. . . ."

Nidhi pressed her forehead against her sister's. "Well, if we'd ever gotten a chance to talk, I would have told you that your relationship is its own thing. Matt and I weren't right for each other, but that has nothing to do with you and Fernando."

Avani took a deep breath. "Yeah, I see that now. Apparently, you can have a lot of epiphanies while being trapped in an elevator."

"Good to know!" Nidhi said with a smile.

Avani squeezed her again. "But I guess maybe if you'd been around, I wouldn't have signed up for so many clubs and then gotten totally overwhelmed. The Dads and Rani *kind of* warned me that I was taking on too much, but I just have this feeling that you would have been a little more . . . how can I put it?"

"Condescending and bossy?"

"Well, I was trying to find a nicer description. . . ."

They both laughed.

"It's funny," Nidhi said. "But I've been trying to take a page from your book. Trying lots of things. Being open to possibilities. But even if you don't know what to do with your life, it feels like you've known you wanted to stay with Fernando."

"He has been a constant for me these past months," Avani agreed. "Someone I can always depend on."

Nidhi nodded. "I've finally realized that I want Grayson to be a constant in mine."

Avani gave her a knowing look. "Finally! You two are great together."

Nidhi heard Grayson's laugh from across the room. She felt like she'd always be able to pick it out, no matter how many people were around. "Yeah, I guess we really are."

"I'm happy for you." Avani rested her chin on Nidhi's shoulder. "You know, I can't believe we're all four potentially going to be in different places next year."

"I know." Nidhi sighed, still excited about the vast, unknowable future but also a little anxious. "Everything's changing. Too quickly sometimes."

"I hate change," Avani said. "And I love it. And everything in between."

Nidhi nodded ruefully. "Same."

Chapter Sixty-One

Sirisha

The Cloud Grifters were playing in a cute little venue that fit in with Friday Harbor's coastal charm, a sea shack with a shingled roof and windows emulating a ship's portholes. It wasn't the kind of place with bouncers and disco balls, just a quaint little stage that looked at odds with the Cloud Grifters' bulky rock equipment. Still, there was enough of a crowd to make it standing room only.

The entire Singh family had decided to come to the concert, though the Dads were joking about their backs and the lack of seating. Fernando offered to find them chairs, but they waved him off. With a significant look, Avani dragged her boyfriend into the crowd.

Lavi leaned in close to Sirisha, her breath warm in her ear. "This place is so adorable."

Sirisha nodded, and a tingle went through her as she savored the night. Lavi's hair tickling her cheek, Lavi's breath, sweet from pear cider at the dinner. Lavi's eyes—big and brown and shining with whorls of light.

Would this last? Sirisha knew it was just a beginning, but doubts crept in. "It's no Chicago."

She was guessing, of course—she had never been.

Lavi chuckled. "It's a little different. But I can get used to it. Also, I like your family."

What Sirisha wanted to say: "Don't go back to Chicago and leave me!!!"

What she actually said: "Thanks. They mean a lot to me."

Usually, she would chide herself for not saying what she wanted to—but in this case, it was probably a sound choice. Her heart was still tender, and perhaps it would be for a while, but she knew she couldn't put all that neediness on Lavi. Instead, she let the moment just be, smiling a secret smile, one that had a bit of Scarlett in it.

And Lavi smiled back, with maybe a little bit of Lola's flirty smirk.

The Cloud Grifters came on, their fans screaming. As they weaved a tune like mist over the sea, Sirisha and Lavi ended up getting swallowed by the crowd, separated from the others. The soft lyrics were like the whispering of pines, the scent of island air. Enveloped in it, Sirisha danced with Lavi, as they had danced earlier that day.

She wasn't Scarlett anymore, and Lavi wasn't Lola, but something unique and vibrant still bloomed between them. Beauty, and not danger, exactly—but the tang of summer cherries, the crisp of autumn air. The glint of winter frost. And perhaps a glimmer of spring buds.

Chapter Sixty-Two

Avani

Avani took Fernando's hand, and they shouldered their way to get a better view. As the first song came to an end, the lead singer leaned into his microphone. "And now I want to tell you a true story. We received two requests for the same song. Fernando, this is for you from Avani. Avani, this is also for you from Fernando. You two must really be a special couple to have come up with the same song request for each other!"

Avani grinned at Fernando.

He grinned back.

"For real?" she whispered.

"Great minds think alike." Fernando chuckled.

And then they weren't talking any more as
the song enveloped them
   and a heat returned
      the embers of a flame
   lit from twigs
      gathered over so many years
   thirsty
      for a chance to
         ignite
      to burn
         to rage
      like a W.I.L.D.F.I.R.E.

"We have got to find some alone time," a girl whispered in a boy's ear.
"I'm free tomorrow evening," he returned.
"Me too," she said.

Chapter Sixty-Three

Rani

Rani was in a daze. She'd made her very first short film. She'd met her idol, Olivia Lee. And now she was dancing with Ed Yi. Okay, maybe just next to Ed Yi.

Nope, he'd caught her eye and offered his hand. She hadn't danced with any boy besides Raj in months, but now she shook her hips with snooty Ed Yi whose short film had been centered on a falling leaf. Who knew?

"This song is familiar!" he shouted over the music.

"It's the one Fernando got permission to put in *Endings and Beginnings*!" she shouted back.

"It was a good touch!"

"Thanks!"

Her words were drowned out by the hollering of the crowd as the

Cloud Grifters switched to what was apparently a fan favorite. The notes were catchy, the kind that made you want to dance, and Rani and Ed let loose. He actually had some moves, too. Some fancy footwork. Even if it was in loafers.

"Did you study dance when you were younger?" she guessed when the song came to an end.

He looked bashful. "Yeah, my mom put me in hip-hop classes."

Okay, that was kind of adorable.

"I need to see more," she said.

Ed laughed. "No."

"Come on, please?"

He showed off a little more impressive footwork, too quick to really follow, but it looked good. Her heart ached for a moment, remembering the wedding last July. When it came to dance moves, Raj was the opposite of Ed, not smooth at all, but he'd made her laugh and she'd loved the way he'd looked in a tux.

She shook all those memories away. Dancing the next dance was the only way to move on.

"Wow. I bet you can breakdance, too," she said to Ed.

"I'm not showing you," he said.

"Come on!"

"No!"

"Yes, you have to."

"No way."

"This is a trust exercise," she said. "If you don't do it, I'll never be comfortable enough to co-direct a film with you."

"Um, I didn't realize we were planning to do that?"

"Well, it just occurred to me." She flipped her hair, pretending to be totally blasé about the idea, even though a tingle traveled down her spine. Suddenly, she really wanted it. "My dialogue and your flair for cinematography could be an award-winning combination."

He nodded. "I could get into this idea. Tell me more."

"Just as soon as you show me your moves," Rani said.

Ed squinted at her, then obliged, twirling on his hands and knees with a flourish. He managed to look elegant and handsome and very *Ed* all at once, his lips pursed in concentration, his hair a little mussed. She suddenly had the urge to mess it up more.

And so she did.

Chapter Sixty-Four

Nidhi

The Cloud Grifters' lyrics were tinged with bittersweet edges and silver linings. Nidhi danced cheek to cheek with Grayson at the back of the club where there was more space. It felt so good to breathe in his scent, to feel his body against hers, to clasp his neck and lean in for a kiss.

She wanted *more*. She was ready for more. She let the song and the warmth of him take her across fantastical, uncharted waters. Because with Grayson, every moment was smoke and dragons and night whispers. With Grayson, magic was real.

Chapter Sixty-Five

The Singh Sisters

Avani:

Where are you guys? We need to catch the last ferry!

Rani:

Chill, twin. We've got time!

Avani:

We've got fifteen minutes.

Rani:

Since when are you the one who is on top of it?

Avani:

I'm on top of plenty of things, thank you.

Sirisha:

Avani's right, we need to go. Let's meet out front.

Dad:

Leave already? I thought this party was just getting started.

Amir:

Nice try. I saw you falling asleep while standing up!

Dad:

I was just resting my eyes.

Nidhi:

I think the club is closing soon anyway. But Grayson has offered to take us home on his boat!

Dad:

Ooh, moonlight cruise after-party!

Amir:

Now you're talking.

The Singh sisters sailed into a fantastical starry night, mist curling around the boat and cocooning it. Hot cocoa was passed around, as well as a few dad jokes and ham and cheese sandwiches on crusty baguettes.

The crescent moon glittered through the clouds, and the tamed wind nudged them gently back to the cozy inn atop a jagged edge. The air was no longer damp with unsaid wishes, but instead glimmered with promises of wild and wondrous things.

Acknowledgments

My wildest wish has come true: to publish joyful books featuring Indian American teens. None of this would be possible without two amazing women of color who believe in the power of representation: my agent, Penny Moore, and my editor, Christine Collins.

Kieran Viola, thank you for acquiring this series with such enthusiasm. I'm also grateful to all the wonderful folks at Hyperion who have worked on getting this book into the hands of readers. Marketing: Dina Sherman, Holly Nagel, Danielle DiMartino, Matt Schweitzer, Bekka Mills, and Maddie Hughes. Production: Anne Peters and Marybeth Tregarthen. Publicity: Crystal McCoy and Ann Day. Sales: Jess Brigman, Michael Freeman, Vicki Korlishin, Monique Diman, Kim Knueppel, Meredith Lisbin, Loren Godfrey, and Mili Nguyen. Managing editorial: Sara Liebling. Copyediting: Guy Cunningham, Jody Corbett, and Lisa Geller.

Chaaya Prabhat and Marci Senders, this cover was even more gorgeous than the first! Your talent amazes me. Thank you also Trisha Tobias, Lynn Weingarten, Blair Thornburgh, Chelsea Eberly, and the teams at Working Partners and Aevitas Creative Management for all your hard work.

Writing a sophomore book on deadline was a Herculean effort I'd gladly face again with the support of my writing communities. Thank you for taking a look at my messy early drafts: George Jreije, J. C. Peterson, Keely Parrack, and Michele Bacon. I have the world's best critique group:

Flor Salcedo, S. Isabelle, Linda Cheng, and Candace Buford. Thank you, Judy Lin and Brian D. Kennedy, for the sprints that helped me get the first draft across the finish line. I never felt lonely as I laughed, commiserated, and schemed with the '22 Debuts, Class of 2K22, and the Desi KidLit Community. Shout out to the folks who helped me promote my debut, especially Martha Brockenbrough, Jake Maia Arlow, Joy McCullough, Susan Azim Boyer, Priyanka Taslim, Jen Ferguson, and Gayatri Sethi. To the passionate booksellers, librarians, teachers, and parents: Diverse books thrive because of you. I deeply appreciate everyone who has supported my journey by coming to an event, leaving a review, or telling a friend about my books.

I come from a family that celebrates stories, and I'm so proud to be a part of it. Thanks for all the love. Cleo, thanks for taking me on lots of walks to brainstorm plot problems. I couldn't pursue this dream without my husband, who analyzes every movie with me and reads whatever I write. Commander B, my hype director and #1 fan: You always lift my spirits.

Finally, to the reader: You make it all worth it. May the force of your wildest wishes take you where you need to go.